November 3–7, 2014
Shanghai, China

I0028879

Association for Computing Machinery

Advancing Computing as a Science & Profession

CIKM'14

Proceedings of the 2014 ACM International
Conference on Information and Knowledge Management

Sponsored by:
ACM SIGIR and ACM SIGWEB

In-cooperation with:
CCF

Supported by:
SAP, Baibu, Google, EMC, Yahoo! Labs, Yandex, & Fudan University

**Association for
Computing Machinery**

Advancing Computing as a Science & Profession

The Association for Computing Machinery
2 Penn Plaza, Suite 701
New York, New York 10121-0701

ISBN: 978-1-4503-2598-1 (Digital)

ISBN: 978-1-4503-3424-2 (Print)

Additional copies may be ordered prepaid from:

ACM Order Department
PO Box 30777
New York, NY 10087-0777, USA

Phone: 1-800-342-6626 (USA and Canada)
+1-212-626-0500 (Global)
Fax: +1-212-944-1318
E-mail: acmhelp@acm.org
Hours of Operation: 8:30 am – 4:30 pm ET

Printed in the USA

Message from the General Chairs

On behalf of the conference organizing committee, it is our great pleasure to welcome you to the 23rd ACM International Conference on Information and Knowledge Management (CIKM 2014).

CIKM is a top-tier ACM conference in Databases, Information Retrieval, and Knowledge Management. The purpose of the conference is to identify challenging problems facing the development of future knowledge and information systems, and to shape future research directions through the publication of high quality, applied and theoretical research findings. The 23rd edition of CIKM continues the tradition of promoting collaboration among multiple areas.

The conference this year has attracted 838 valid full paper submissions, 260 valid poster submissions, 73 valid demonstration submissions, and 15 valid workshop proposals. Among them, we accepted 175 full papers, 57 posters, 29 demonstrations, and 9 workshops. On top of the regular track, the conference has an outstanding keynote program, an exciting industry event, and six tutorials of contemporary topics. This time again, the conference is standing out among the many of its peers in its ability to attract researchers to exchange ideas and to interact, and the sheer numbers are a testament of the vitality of the three research areas and their interactions.

We are honored to present three distinguished keynote speakers: Jeff Dean of Google, Qi Lu of Microsoft, and Gerhard Weikum of Max-Planck Institute for Informatics. We are also honored to present six industry event invitees to share their deep knowledge and insights: Soumen Chakrabarti, Chih Jen Lin, Wei-Ying Ma, Alex J. Smola, Limsoon Wong, and Tong Zhang.

At CIKM 2014, we inaugurate a programming competition, sponsored by Baidu Inc. The competition has attracted 571 teams to sign up from around the world, with top-ranked teams achieving significant results on the task given.

We thank all the authors who submitted their work to CIKM for making the conference happen, and the diligent and careful review work of the Program Committee led by its four PC chairs: Minos Garofalakis, Ian Soboroff, Torsten Suel, and Min Wang. We also thank all the other chairs in the CIKM 2014 organization team, whose effective, collegial teamwork made this complex task of conference organization spark with delight. We would also like to thank the local organization team and the student volunteers from Fudan University, who worked silently but efficiently and effectively behind the scene to make the conference run smoothly. We also thank the CIKM Steering Committee for its guidance, and Microsoft CMT team and the relevant ACM teams for their assistance.

We gratefully acknowledge the financial support of our sponsors: SAP as the Platinum Sponsor, Baidu and Google as the Gold Sponsors, EMC as the Silver Sponsor, and Yahoo Labs and Yandex as the Bronze Sponsors.

Finally, we thank all the authors, presenters, and participants of the conference. We hope that all of you enjoy the conference!

Jianzhong Li   **X. Sean Wang**

CIKM 2014 General Chair   *CIKM 2014 General Chair*

Harbin Inst. of Tech., China   *Fudan University, China*

Program Committee Chairs' Welcome

We are delighted to welcome you to the 23rd ACM International Conference on Information and Knowledge Management (CIKM 2014), held in Shanghai on November 3-7, 2014. CIKM has clearly established itself over the last two decades as the leading venue for bringing together researchers from across the Database, Information Retrieval, and Knowledge Management communities. Continuing the trend from recent years, we received a large number of high-quality submissions in all three tracks, with a significant increase in submissions to the Knowledge Management track. Altogether, we are very confident that CIKM 2014 has succeeded in creating a very high-quality technical program of plenary talks, paper session, and poster presentations.

In total, we received 838 full paper submissions and 260 4-page poster submissions, which were reviewed and discussed by 47 area chairs and about 450 program committee members, plus a number of expert external reviewers. We accepted 175 full papers (20.9%) and 57 posters (21.9%). The acceptance statistics per track were as follows: Databases 25/123 full papers and 8/27 posters, Information Retrieval 55/257 full papers and 28/110 posters, and Knowledge Management 95/458 papers and 21/123 posters.

We would like to thank all the many contributors that helped in putting this program together. We thank the General Chairs, Profs. Jianzhong Li and X. Sean Wang, along with their collaborators in the organization team, for putting the overall conference together, and the Proceedings Chairs, Profs. Hui Fang and Guoliang Li, for helping the publication of the conference proceedings. We would in particular like to recognize the tireless efforts of the area chairs, program committee members, and external reviewers, who performed the bulk of the work needed to select the program. Last but not least, thanks to everyone who submitted contributions for consideration.

We hope that participants as well as readers of the proceedings will find the technical program to be interesting and thought provoking.

Minos Garofalakis
CIKM'14 KM Track Chair
Technical University of Crete, Greece

Ian Soboroff
CIKM'14 IR Track Chair
National Institute of Standards, USA

Torsten Suel
CIKM'14 IR Track Chair
New York University, USA

Min Wang
CIKM'14 DB Track Chair
Google Research, USA

Table of Contents

DB Session 1 - Query Processing
November 4, Tuesday, Morning • Time: 10:00am - 12:00noon

IR Session 1 - IR Evaluation
November 4, Tuesday, Morning • Time: 10:00am - 12:00noon

R Session 2 - Models
November 4, Tuesday, Morning • Time: 10:00am - 12:00noon

KM Session 1: Social Networks & Social Media I
November 4, Tuesday, Morning • Time: 10:00am - 12:00noon

KM Session 2 - Classification I
November 4, Tuesday, Morning • Time: 10:00am - 12:00noon

DB Session 2 - Knowledge Base & Data Semantics
November 4, Tuesday, Afternoon • Time: 3:30pm - 5:00pm

IR Session 5 - Users
November 4, Tuesday, Afternoon • Time: 3:30pm - 5:30pm

IR Session 6 - Query Intent
November 4, Tuesday, Afternoon • Time: 3:30pm - 5:00pm

KM Session 7 - Social Networks & Social Media III
November 4, Tuesday, Afternoon • Time: 3:30pm - 5:30pm

KM Session 8 - Clustering and Ranking
November 4, Tuesday, Afternoon • Time: 3:30pm - 5:30pm

KM Session 9 - Recommenders & Collaborative Filtering II
November 4, Tuesday, Afternoon • Time: 3:30pm - 5:30pm (),

DB Session 3 - Social and Graph Data
November 5, Wednesday, Afternoon • Time: 1:30pm - 3:00pm

DB Session 4 - Data Integration and Big Data
November 5, Wednesday, Afternoon • Time: 3:30pm - 5:00pm

IR Session 8: Social Media
November 5, Wednesday, Afternoon • Time: 3:30pm - 5:00pm

IR Session 9: Machine Learning
November 5, Wednesday, Afternoon • Time: 3:30pm - 5:00pm

KM Session 12: Text Data Mining II
November 5, Wednesday, Afternoon • Time: 3:30pm - 5:00pm

Raymond K. Wong *(University of New South Wales & National ICT Australia)*,
Fang Chen *(National ICT Australia)*, Chi-Hung Chi *(CSIRO)*

KM Session 13: Mining Data Streams
November 5, Wednesday, Afternoon • Time: 3:30pm - 5:00pm

KM Session 14: Data Mining Theory & Methods
November 6, Thursday, Morning • Time: 10:00am - 12:00noon

KM Session 15: Knowledge Representation & Reasoning II
November 6, Thursday, Morning • Time: 10:00am - 12:00noon

KM Session 16: Large- Scale Machine Learning
November 6, Thursday, Morning • Time: 10:00am - 12:00noon

KM Session 17: Web Data Mining
November 6, Thursday, Morning • Time: 10:00am - 12:00noon

KM Session 18: Data Mining Applications & Bioinformatics
November 6, Thursday, Morning • Time: 10:00am - 12:00noon

DB Session 5 - Systems and Applications
November 6, Thursday, Afternoon • Time: 1:30pm - 3:00pm

IR Session 10: Engagement, Social, Crowdsourcing
November 6, Thursday, Afternoon • Time: 1:30pm - 3:00pm

IR Session 11: Semantics
November 6, Thursday, Afternoon • Time: 1:30pm - 3:00pm

KM Session 19: Graph Data Mining I
November 6, Thursday, Afternoon • Time: 1:30pm - 3:00pm

DB Session 6 - Privacy and Streams
November 6, Thursday, Afternoon • Time: 3:30pm - 5:00pm

IR Session 12: Efficiency
November 6, Thursday, Afternoon • Time: 3:30pm - 5:00pm

IR Session 13: Domain, Semistructured, Mobile
November 6, Thursday, Afternoon • Time: 3:30pm - 5:00pm

KM Session 20: Entity and Feature Extraction
November 6, Thursday, Afternoon • Time: 3:30pm - 5:00pm

KM Session 21: Graph Data Mining II
November 6, Thursday, Afternoon • Time: 3:30pm - 5:00pm

Vol. 2 Author Index

DB Track Posters

IR Track Posters

KM Track Posters

Demo Session 1

Demo Session 2

Workshop Summaries

CIKM 2014 Conference Organization

General Chairs: Jianzhong Li *(Harbin Inst. of Technology)*
X. Sean Wang *(Fudan University)*

Program Chairs: **DB Track**: Min Wang *(Google)*
IR Track: Ian Soboroff *(NIST)* & Torsten Suel *(NYU)*
KM Track: Minos Garofalakis *(TU Crete)*

Industrial Program Chairs: Hang Li *(Huawei)*
Rajeev Rastogi *(Amazon)*

Tutorial Chair: Zhi-Hua Zhou *(Nanjing University)*

Workshop Chairs: Xiaofeng Meng *(Renmin University)*
Huan Liu *(Arizona State University)*

Panels Chairs: Jun Yang *(Duke University)*
Ge Yu *(Northeastern University, China)*

Demo Chairs: Neoklis Polyzotis *(UC Santa Cruz)*
Xiaohui Yu *(Shandong University)*

Proceedings Chairs: Hui Fang *(University of Delaware)*
Guoliang Li *(Tsinghua University)*

Sponsorship Chairs: Lei Chen *(HKUST)*
Feifei Li *(University of Utah)*

Publicity Chair: Shimin Chen *(Chinese Academy of Science)*
Antonios Deligiannakis *(TU Crete)*
Anastasios Kementsietsidis *(IBM Research)*

Finance Chair: E.K. Park *(CSU Chico)*

Local Organization Chair: Xiangdong Zhou *(Fudan University)*

Competition Chair: Xuanjing Huang *(Fudan University)*

**Program Committee
(Program Area Chairs)
Knowledge Management
Track:**

Deepak Agarwal, LinkedIn *(Information Filtering and Recommender Systems)*

Diego Calvanese, Free University of Bozen-Bolzano *(Knowledge Representation, Reasoning, and Visualization)*

Soumen Chakrabarti, Indian Institute of Technology Bombay *(Text and Web Data Mining)*

Graham Cormode, University of Warwick *(Mining Big Data and Streams)*

Rainer Gemulla, Max-Planck-Institut fur Informatik *(Large-Scale Machine Learning and Statistical Techniques)*

Aristides Gioni, Aalto University *(Data Mining Theory, Methods, and Applications)*

Vanja Josifovski, Google *(Personalization, Advertising, and Search)*

Murat Kantarcioglu, University of Texas at Dallas *(Secure and Privacy-Preserving Data Mining)*

Eamonn Keogh, University of California Riverside *(Time-Series and Pattern Mining)*

Nikos Mamoulis, University of Hong Kong *(Spatial, Temporal, and Graph Data Mining)*

Joerg Sander, University of Alberta *(Clustering, Classification, and Ranking)*

Evimaria Terzi, Boston University *(Social Networks and Social Media)*

Mohammed J. Zaki, Rensselaer Polytechnic Institute *(Data Mining and Knowledge Management for Bioinformatics)*

Database Track Program Committee Members

Ashraf Aboulnaga, University of Waterloo

Nitin Agarwal, UALR

Periklis Andritsos, Univ. of Toronto

Walid Aref, Purdue University

Marcelo Arenas, Univ. of Chile

Spiros Bakiras, City University of New York

Klaus Berberich, Max-Planck-Institut für Informatik

Spyros Blanas, Ohio State University

Alexe Bogdan, IBM Research

Panagiotis Bouros, HU-Berlin

Erik Cambria, NSU

Zhao Cao, IBM China Research Lab

Bogdan Cautis, University of Paris-Sud

James Caverlee, Texas A&M

Muhammad Cheema, Monash University

Jinchuan Chen, Renmin University

Lei Chen, HKUST

Yi Chen, NJIT

James Cheney, Univ. of Edinburgh

Hong Cheng, CUHK

Gao Cong, Nanyang Technological University

Josep Domingo-Ferrer, Universitat Rovira i Virgili

Aaron Elmore, MIT

Wei Fan Huawei Research Lab

Csilla Farkas, University of South Carolina

Hongliang Fei, IBM T. J. Watson Research Center

Ariel Fuxman, Microsoft Research

Floris Geerts, Univ. of Antwerp

Dimitrios Gunopulos, National and Kapodistrian University of Athens

Yeye He, Microsoft Research

Seung-won Hwang, PosTech, Korea

Stratos Idreos, Harvard University

Mizuho Iwaihara, Waseda University

Arun Jagatheesan, Samsung R&D Center

Lili Jiang, Max-Planck-Institut für Informatik, Germany

Tim Kaldewey, IBM Research

Grigoris Karvounarakis, LogicBlox

Hideaki Kimura, HP Labs

Yannis Kotidis, Athens University of Economics and Business

Julien Leblay, U. Oxford

Justin Levandoski, Microsoft Research

Chengkai Li, University of Texas at Arlington

Guoliang Li, Tsinghua University

Mengchi Liu, Carleton University

Hua Lu, Aalborg University

Jiebo Luo, University of Rochester

Barzan Mozafari, University of Michigan

Stavros Papadopoulos, Intel and MIT

Olga Papaemmanouil, Brandeis University

Dino Pedreschi, University of Pisa, Italy

Wen-Chih Peng, National Chiao Tung University

Guenther Pernul, Universitat Regensburg

Ravi Ramamurthy, Microsoft

Vijayshankar Raman, IBM Almaden

Matthias Renz, University of Munich

Senjuti Roy, University of Washington Tacoma

Pierangela Samarati, University of Milan

Andreas Schaad, SAP

Rusty Sears, Pure Storage

Pierre Senellart, Telecom Paristech

Cyrus Shahabi, USC

Mohamed Sharaf, University of Queensland

Yangqiu Song, UIUC

Wei Shen, Nankai University, China

Fabian Suchanek, Telecom ParisTech University in Paris

Yannis Theodoridis, University of Piraeus

Pinar Tozun, EPFL

Goce Trajcevski , Northwestern University

Dimitris Tsirogiannis, Cloudera

Yannis Velegrakis, Univ. of Trento

Stratis Viglas, University of Edinburgh

Chi Wang, University of Illinois Urbana Champaign

Min Wang, Google

Wei Wang, Fudan University

Information Retrieval Track Program Committee Members

Jae-wook Ahn, Drexel University

Omar Alonso, Microsoft

Robin Aly, University of Twente

Linda Andersson, Vienna University of Technology

Jaime Arguello, University of North Carolina, USA

Diego Arroyuelo, Universidad Tecnica Federico Santa Maria

Javed Aslam, Northeastern University

Leif Azzopardi, University of Glasgow

Michele Banko, Microsoft

Hannah Bast, University of Freiburg

Andras Benczur, Hungarian Academy of Sciences

Pushpak Bhattacharya, IIT Bombay

Bodo Billerbeck, Bing, Microsoft

Pavel Braslavski, Ural Federal University

Georg Buscher, Microsoft

Liangliang Cao, IBM Research

Robert Capra, University of North Carolina

David Carmel, Yahoo! Labs

Carlos Castillo, QCRI

Michele Catasta, EPF Lausanne

Suleyman Cetintas, Yahoo! Labs

Praveen Chandar, University of Delaware

Raman Chandrasekar, ProQuest

Lin Chen, University of Illinois at Chidago

Wen-Huang Cheng, Academia Sinica, Taiwan

Ed Chi, Google

Philipp Cimiano, Bielefeld University

Francisco Claude, University of Chile

Paul Clough, University of Sheffield

Michael Cole, Rutgers University

John Conroy, IDA Center for Computing Sciences

Fabio Crestani, University of Lugano

Philippe Cudré-Mauroux, University of Fribourg

Peng Cui, Tsinghua University

Shane Culpepper, RMIT University

Na Dai, Yahoo! Labs

Mahashweta Das, HP Labs

Maarten de Rijke, University of Amsterdam

Gianluca Demartini, University of Fribourg

Thomas Demeester, University of Ghent

Fernando Diaz, Microsoft

Thanh Tran Duc, San Jose State University

Miles Efron, University of Illinois Urbana-Champagne

Carsten Eickhoff, ETH Zurich

Marcus Fontoura, Microsoft

Shlomo Geva, Queensland University of Technology

Lorraine Goeuriot, Dublin City University

Julio Gonzalo, UNED

Fan Guo, CMU

Manish Gupta, Microsoft

Martin Halvey, Glasgow Caledonian University

Allan Hanbury, Vienna University of Technology

Preben Hansen, Stockholm University

Claudia Hauff, University of Delft

Bruce Hedin, H5

Tomi Heimonen, University of Tampere

Daniel Herzig, SearchHaus GmbH

Yu Hong, RPI

Katja Hofmann, Microsoft

Steven Hoi, Nanyang Technological University

Liangjie Hong, Yahoo! Labs

inston Hsu, National Taiwan University

Vivian Hu, York University

Benoit Huet, Eurecom

Ichiro Ide, Nagoya University

Adam Jatowt, Kyoto University

Jiepu Jiang, University of Massachussetts

Yu-Gang Jiang, Fudan University

Roger Jie Luo, Yahoo! Labs

Hideo Joho, University of Tsukuba

Gareth Jones, Dublin City University

Joemon Jose, University of Glasgow

Flavio Junqueira, Microsoft Research

Jaap Kamps, University of Amsterdam

Evangelos Kanoulas, Google

Liadh Kelly, Dublin City University

Knowledge Management Track Program Committee Members

Knowledge Management Track

Gail-Joon Ahn, Arizona State University

Mohammad AlHassan, IUPUI

Mohammad Alrifai, L3S Research Center

Aris Anagnostopoulos, Sapienza University of Rome

Alexander Artikis, NCSR Demokritos

Bahman Bahmani, Stanford University

Krisztian Balog, University of Stavanger

Gustavo Batista, University of Sao Paulo

Srikanta Bedathur, IIIT, New Delhi

Ron Bekkerman, University of Haifa

Kedar Bellare, Facebook

Jonathan Berant, Stanford University

Arnab Bhattacharyya, IIT, Kanpur

Danny Bickson, Carnegie Mellon University

Albert Bifet, University of Waikato

Petkov Bogdanov, UC Santa Barbara

Mario Boley, University of Bonn/Fraunhofer IAIS

Christos Boutsidis, Yahoo! Labs

Andrea Cali, Birkbeck College, London

Ricardo Campello, University of Sao Paolo

Huiping Cao, New Mexico State University

Jeffrey Chan, University of Melbourne

Varun Chandola, University at Buffalo

Michael Chau, University of Hong Kong

Sanjay Chawla, University of Sydney

Ye Chen, Microsoft

Zhiyuan Chen, UIC

Vassilis Christophides, University of Crete

Brian Cooper, Google

Bernardo Cuenca-Grau, University of Oxford

Alfredo Cuzzocrea, University of Calabria

Theodore Dalamagas, Athena RC

Anirban Dasgupta, IIT Gandhinagar

Atish Das Sarma, eBay Research

Gianmarco De Francisci Morales, Yahoo! Research

Antonios Deligiannakis, Technical University of Crete

Christos Doulkeridis, University of Piraeus

Magdalini Eirinaki, San Jose State University

Eva Erdos, Boston University

Elena Ferrari, University of Insubria

Avrilia Floratou, IBM Almaden

Esther Galbrun, Boston University

Dinesh Garg, IBM India Research Lab

Chiara Ghidini, FBK Trento

Gabriel Ghinita, University of Massachusetts - Boston

Nikos Giatrakos, Technical University of Crete

Kasneci Gjergji, Hasso-Plattner-Institut fur Softwaresystemtechnik

Aris Gkoulalas-Divanis, IBM

Sreenivas Gollapudi, Microsoft Research

Manuel Gomez Rodriguez, MPI

Amit Goyal, Yahoo! Labs

Mihajlo Grbovic, Yahoo! Labs

Francesco Gullo, Yahoo! Research

Stephan Gunnemann, Carnegie Mellon University

Claudio Gutierrez, Universidad De Chile

Maria Halkidi, University of Piraeus

Raquel Hill, Indiana University

Thanh Lam Hoang, IBM Dublin Research Lab

Bing Hu, Samsung

Luke Huan, University of Kansas

Ekaterini Ioannou, Technical University of Crete

James Joshi, University of Pittsburg

Panos Kalnis, KAUST

Shivaram Kalyanakrishnan, Yahoo! Labs Bangalore

Bhargav Kanagal, Google

Anitha Kannan, Microsoft Research

Ben Kao, University of Hong Kong

Panagiotis Karras, Rutgers University

Asterios Katsifodimos, TU Berlin

Yiping Ke, Chinese University of Hong Kong

Daniel Keren, University of Haifa

Kristian Kersting, University of Bonn

Latifur Khan, University of Texas-Dallas

Ioannis Konstantinou, NTUA

Roman Kontchakov, Birkbeck College, London

Georgia Koutrika, HP Labs

Tim Kraska, Brown U

Markus Kroetzsch, Technical University of Dresden

Ashish Kundu, IBM Research

Ni Lao, Google Research

Theodoros Lappas, Stevens Institute of Technology

Silvio Lattanzi, Google

Hady Lauw, Singapore Management University

Mong Li Lee, National University of Singapore

Wolfgang Lehner, University of Dresden

Domenico Lembo, Sapienza University of Rome

Tao Li, Florida International University

Zhenhui Li, Pennsylvania State University

Claudio Lucchese, ISTI-CNR

Yoelle Maarek, Yahoo

Michael Mathioudakis, HIIT

Sebastian Michel, Saarland University

Pauli Miettinen, MPI

Iris Miliaraki, Yahoo Labs, Barcelona

Vahab Mirrokni, Google

Marco Montali, Free Universtiy of Bozen-Bolzano

Abdullah Mueen, UMN

Emmanuel Müller, Karlsruhe Institute of Technology, KIT

TM Murali, Virginia Tech

Ndapa Nakashole, Carnegie Mellon University

Raymond Ng, UBC

Maximilian Nickel, MIT

Eirini Ntoutsi, LMU

Werner Nutt, Free University of Bozen-Bolzano

Gaurav Pandey, Mount Sinai School of Medicine

Spiros Papadimitriou, Rutgers University

Apostolos Papadopoulos, Aristotle Univ of Thessaloniki

Evangelos Papalexakis, Carnegie Mellon University

Panagiotis Papapetrou, Stockholm University

Odysseas Papapetrou, Technical University of Crete

Stott Parker, UCLA

Konstantinos Pelechrinis, University of Pittsburgh

Peter Pietzuch, Imperial College

Ali Pinar, Sandia National Labs

Dimitris Plexousakis, University of Crete

Yinian Qi, Oracle

Lizhen Qu, MPI

Davood Rafiei, University of Alberta

Huzefa Rangwala, George Mason University

Chotirat Ann Ratanamahatana, Chulalongkorn University

Chandan Reddy, Wayne State University

Chiara Renso, CNR

Matteo Riondato, Brown University

Dimitris Sacharidis, Athena Research Center

Barna Saha, ATT Labs

Vasilis Samoladas, Technical University of Crete

Mohamed Sarwat, University of Minnesota

Marco Schaerf, Sapienza University of Rome

Ralf Schenkel, University of Passau

Erich Schubert, LMU Munich

Matthias Schubert, LMU Munich

Thomas Seidl, RWTH Aachen University

Izchak Sharfman, Technion

Entong Shen, Pivotal Inc.

Nisheeth Shrivastava, Amazon

Alkis Simitsis, HP Labs

Mantas Simkus, Technical University of Vienna

Sameer Singh, University of Washington

Yannis Sismanis, Google

Anna Squicciarini, The Pennsylvania State University

Yannis Stavrakas, Athena RC

Kostas Stefanidis, ICS-FORTH

Umberto Straccia, ISTI-CNR

Jimeng Sun, Georgia Tech

Shirish Tatikonda, IBM Almaden

Manolis Terrovitis, IMIS, Athena

Martin Theobald, University of Antwerp

Brian Thompson, Telcordia

Srikanta Tirthapura, Iowa State University

Hanghang Tong, CUNY

Demo Track Program Committee Members

CIKM 2014 External Reviewers

DB Track

Bin Yang
Hars Vardhan, Samsung Research America
Krishnamurthy Viswanathan, HP Labs
Marian-Andrei Rizoiu
Sabrina De Capitani di Vimercati, Universita` degli
  Studi di Milano

Stan Park, HP Labs
Umar Farooq Minhas, IBM Research
Vasilis Spyropoulos, Athens University
  of Economics and Business
Xike Xie

IR Track

Abhay Kashyap, WalmartLabs
Abon Chaudhuri, Intel
Alberto Tonon, University of Fribourg
Amit Gupta, EPFL
Antonio Fariña, Universidade da Coruña
Artem Lutov, University of Fribourg
Blaz Fortuna, Ghent University
Bo Hu, Linkedin
Bo Liu, National University of Singapore
Chen Chen, University of Texas at Dallas
Chris Develder, Ghent University
Claudiu Cobarzan, Klagenfurt University
Dayong Wang, Nanyang Technological University
Debasis Ganguly, Dublin City University
Dmitry Ustalov, Ural Branch of the Russian
  Academy of Sciences
Eamonn Newman, Dublin City University
Eric Tellez, Universidad de Chile
Farhana Murtaza Choudhury, RMIT University
Galina Lezina, Ural Federal University
Gaya Jayasinghe, RMIT University
Haishan Liu, Linkedin
Hao Li, National University of Singapore
Hua Ouyang, Yahoo!
Huiji Gao, Arizona State University
Idan Szpektor, Yahoo!
Javier Artiles, Rakuten
Jingyuan Zhang, University of Illinois at Chicago
Jouni Sirén, Universidad de Chile
Julia Greissl, WalmartLabs
Keiji Shinzato, Rakuten

Koji Murakami, Rakuten
Liang Tang, Florida International University
Liqiang Nie, National University of Singapore
Manfred del Fabro, Klagenfurt University
Manisha Verma, University College London
Masato Hagiwara, Rakuten
Masaya Murata, NTT Group
Mauricio Marin, Universidad de Santiago de Chile
Meenchul Kim, Drexel University
Min Xie, WalmartLabs
Ming Yan, Chinese Academy of Sciences
PeiFeng Yin, Pennsylvania State University
Quoc Viet Hung Nguyen, EPFL
Roberto Konow, Universidad de Chile
Roman Prokofyev, University of Fribourg
Rui Li, Yahoo!
Ruslan Mavlyutov, University of Fribourg
Sebastian Blohm, Microsoft
Senen González, Universidad de Chile
Simon Puglisi, Universidad of Helsinki
Soyoung Yu, Drexel University
Stefano Mizzaro, Università di Udine
Swanand Wakankar, WalmartLabs
Timothy Jones, RMIT University
Xiangjun Wang, Netflix
Xueliang Liu, National University of Singapore
Yingfei Wang, Princeton University
Yoshihiko Suhara, NTT Group
Zhengyu Deng, Chinese Academy of Sciences
Zofia Stankiewicz, Rakuten
Zoheb Vacheri, WalmartLabs

KM Track

Andreas Kunft, Technical University of Berlin

Alexander Alexandrov, Technical University of Berlin

Tobias Herb, Technical University of Berlin

Johannes Kirschnick, Technical University of Berlin

Christoph Boden, Technical University of Berlin

Reem Atassi, Sapienza University of Rome

Adriano Fazzone, Sapienza University of Rome

Mara Sorella, Sapienza University of Rome

Elias Alevizos, NCSR Demokritos, Greece

Nikos Katzouris, NCSR Demokritos, Greece

Anastasios Skarlatidis, NCSR Demokritos, Greece

Julia Kiseleva, Eindhoven University of Technology

Luca Pulina, University of Sassari, Italy

Zhiqiang Xu, Nanyang Technological University, Singapore

Reinhard Pichler, Vienna University of Technology

Dao Tran Minh, Vienna University of Technology

David Garcia Soriano, Yahoo Labs Barcelona

Nicolas Kourtellis, Yahoo Labs Barcelona

Jiangwei Yu, University of Alberta

Muhammad Waqar, University of Alberta

Cuneyt Akcora, University of Insubria

William Lucia, University of Insubria.

Efrat Egozi-Levi, HP

Noam Koenigstein, Microsoft

Zhuolan Bao, The University of Hong Kong

Fabian Keller, Karlsruhe Institute of Technology, Germany

Hoang Vu Nguyen, Karlsruhe Institute of Technology, Germany

Thomas Van Brussel, University of Antwerp, Belgium

Daniel Borchmann, TU Dresden

Yue Ma, TU Dresden

Tomas Masopust, TU Dresden

Panagis Magdalinos, Intracom Telecom Solutions S.A.

Maria Karanasou, University of Piraeus, Department of Digital Systems

Tuan M. V. Le, Singapore Management University

Loc Do, Singapore Management University

Maksim Tkachenko, Saint Petersburg State University

Diego Furtado Silva, Universidade de São Paulo

Vinícius Mourão Alves de Souza, Universidade de São Paulo

Celso André Rodrigues de Sousa, Universidade de São Paulo

Rafael Giusti, Universidade de São Paulo

Lifei Chen : Fujian Normal University, China

Mohamed Bouguessa, Universite du Quebec a Montreal (UQAM), Canada

Belkacem Chikhaoui, University of Toronto, Canada

Tengke Xiong, University of Sherbrooke, Canada

Jianfei Zhang, University of Sherbrooke, Canada

Jean-Pierre Glouzon, University of Sherbrooke, Canada

Sylvain Goulet, University of Sherbrooke

Mauricio Chiazzaro, University of Sherbrooke

Bhanukiran Vinzamuri

Yan Li

Rajiur Rahman

Geli Fei

Abhishek Kumar, IBM T J Watson Research Center

Siddharth Patwardhan, IBM T J Watson Research Center

Ahsanur Rahman

Anna Ritz

Evgeny Kharlamov, University of Oxford

Chuan Hu, New Mexico State University

Nikos Bikakis, "Athena" Research Center

Ilias Kanellos, "Athena" Research Center

Giorgos Giannopoulos, "Athena" Research Center

Dimitris Skoutas, "Athena" Research Center

Anveshi Charuvaka, George Mason University

Nikhil Muralidhar, George Mason University

Azad Naik, George Mason Univesriy

Deb Misra, George Mason University

Tanwistha Saha, George Mason University

Rongjing Xiang, Google

Michelle Chen, San Jose State University

Wenbo Shen, North Carolina State University

Ling Chen, North Carolina State University

Zhongxian Gu, Pivotal Inc.

Yuhong Li, University of Macau

Ngai Meng Kou, University of Macau

Jian Wang, University of Macau

Junjie Zhang, University of Macau

Yan Li, University of Macau

Gugan Thoppe, TIFR, Mumbai, India

CIKM 2014 Sponsors & Supporters

Sponsors:

SIGIR
Special Interest Group
on Information Retrieval

sig web

In cooperation with:

中国计算机学会
CCF

Platinum Sponsor:

SAP®

Gold Sponsors:

Bai du 百度

Google™

Silver Sponsor:

EMC²

Bronze Sponsors:

YAHOO! LABS

Yandex

Institutional supporter:

FUDAN UNIVERSITY 1905

Hashcube: A Data Structure for Space- and Query-Efficient Skycube Compression

Kenneth S. Bøgh, Sean Chester, Darius Šidlauskas, and Ira Assent
Aarhus University, Åbogade 34, Aarhus N, Denmark 8200
{ksb,schester,dariuss,ira}@cs.au.dk

ABSTRACT

The skyline operator returns records in a dataset that provide optimal trade-offs of multiple dimensions. It is an expensive operator whose query performance can greatly benefit from materialization. However, a skyline can be executed over any subspace of dimensions, and the materialization of all subspace skylines, called the skycube, dramatically multiplies data size. Existing methods for skycube compression sacrifice too much query performance; so, we present a novel hashing- and bitstring-based compressed data structure that supports orders of magnitude faster query performance.

Categories and Subject Descriptors

H.2.4 [**Database Management**]: Systems—*query processing*

Keywords

skycube;compression;hashmap;data structure

1. INTRODUCTION

The *skyline* operator [1] selects from a database *all* tuples that are not clearly less interesting than *any* others. For example, Table 1 lists some top movies from IMDB. Whether one is interested in movies that are newer, higher-rated, or higher-grossing, or any combination of these attributes, *Titanic* is still less interesting than *Avatar*: the latter has higher values on every attribute than the former. By contrast, *The Shawshank Redemption* is older and lower-grossing than *Avatar*, but still interesting for its high rating.

The skyline includes all data points that are strictly higher on at least one attribute or equal on every attribute, when compared to all other points (like *The Shawshank Redemption* but not *Titanic*). These are the most interesting points.

Subspace skylines Often, it is advantageous for a user to pose a skyline query on only the few attributes that are relevant to him/her: a typical moviegoer is unconcerned with

Movie Title	Year	Rating	Sales ($\times 10^6$)
Avatar	2009	7.9	2784 USD
The Avengers	2012	8.2	1514 USD
The Godfather	1972	9.2	245 USD
The Shawshank Redemption	1994	9.2	59 USD
Skyfall	2012	7.8	1108 USD
Titanic	1997	7.6	2186 USD

Table 1: Some top movies, courtesy IMDB.com.

a movie's sales figures, so is better served by the skyline on just the *year* and *rating* attributes. On the other hand, a studio accountant may have a very different perspective.

A subspace skyline query [6,9,10] returns the skyline computed over a subset of attributes specified by the user, personalizing the result. However, it is nearly as expensive to compute skylines in arbitrary subspaces as the full dimensionality, a cost amplified when users pose a series of queries in different subspaces (such as in exploratory scenarios [2]).

Skycube To offer the *best possible* response time for a subspace skyline query, one solution is to precompute the answer. To do so for every possible subspace skyline is to construct the *skycube* [6,11], a set of $2^d - 1$ subspace skylines. However, storage of the skycube is quite large. Although compressed skycube data structures exist [8,10], query performance on the state-of-the-art structure is inadequate.

Therefore, we introduce Hashcube to compress a skycube with bitstrings and hash maps. It achieves an order of magnitude compression over the default structure, while providing query performance 1000× faster than state-of-the-art.

2. BACKGROUND AND RELATED WORK

We assume a table P of n records, each described by d ordinal attributes. We denote the i'th record by p_i and the j'th attribute of p_i by $p_i[j]$. Our approach is based on bitstrings (fixed-length sequences of binary values).[1] We denote the j'th bit of a bitstring B_i by $B_i[j]$ and the substring of B_i from bit j to k, inclusive, by $B_i[j,k]$. Additionally, a subspace s is represented by a bitstring of length d, where $s[i] = 1$ iff the subspace includes the i'th dimension.

In this paper, we propose a compact data structure to rapidly answer skyline queries [1] over arbitrary subsets of attributes, which relies on a notion called *dominance* [1]:

Definition 1 (subspace dominance (p, q, s)). Given points $p, q \in P$ and a bitstring s of length d, let EQ, GT also be

CIKM'14, November 3–7, 2014, Shanghai, China.
Copyright 2014 ACM 978-1-4503-2598-1/14/11 ...$15.00.
http://dx.doi.org/10.1145/2661829.2661891 .

---

[1] Bitstrings and integers here mean both an integer value and the bitstring representing that value (e.g., 7 and 1110).

id	Movie Title	DOM$_i$ binary	DOM$_i$ integer
0	Avatar	1110 000	7 0
1	The Avengers	0101 000	10 0
2	The Godfather	1011 100	13 1
3	The Shawshank Redemption	1001 110	9 3
4	Skyfall	0111 111	14 7

Table 2: Table 1 movies and their domspaces vector (using subspace order $\langle$Y,R,YR,S,YS,RS,YRS$\rangle$ and big-endian).

bitstrings of length d, where:

$$EQ[i] = 1 \text{ iff } p[i] = q[i]$$
$$GT[i] = 1 \text{ iff } p[i] > q[i].$$

Then, p dominates q in subspace s, denoted $p \succ_s q$, iff:

$$((EQ \ \& \ s) \neq s) \wedge (((EQ \mid GT) \ \& \ s) = s).$$

If all data values are unique, known as *Distinct Value Condition* [7], EQ fades from Definition 1. A *subspace skyline* [6] is the subset of points not dominated in the subspace:

Definition 2 (subspace skyline (P, s)). Given set of records P and a bitstring s of length d, the *subspace skyline* of P is:

$$SKY(P, s) = \{p_i \in P : \nexists p_j \in P, p_j \succ_s p_i\}.$$

If $s = 2^d - 1$, Definition 2 produces the *full skyline*. The *skycube* [6,11] is the set of subspace skylines (each called a cuboid [11]) for all non-zero bitstrings of length d.

Finally, we define for our data structure a mapping between points and subspace skylines (examples in Table 2):

Definition 3 (domspaces vector of p_i). Point p_i's *domspaces vector*, denoted DOM$_i$, is a bitstring of length $2^d - 1$ where:

$$DOM_i[j] = 1 \text{ iff } p[i] \notin SKY(P, j).$$

In other words, a domspaces vector records the subspaces in which point p_i is dominated (*not* in the skyline).

The objective in this paper is to store a compact representation of all cuboids that can support more efficient subspace skyline queries than state-of-the-art algorithms.

Skycube algorithms Börzsönyi et al. [1] introduced the skyline with external-memory algorithms *block-nested-loops* (BNL) and *divide-and-conquer* (DC). Then, *Sort-First Skyline* (SFS) [3] improves BNL, pre-sorting the data so points will first be compared to those more likely to dominate them. *Object-based Space Partitioning* (OSP) [12] improves DC by recursively partitioning points based on existing skyline points, rather than a grid. BSkyTree [4] improves OSP by optimally choosing the points with which to partition P.

The skycube was introduced independently by Yuan et al. [11] and Pei et al. [6], with adaptations of the DC [1] and SFS [3] skyline algorithms, respectively. More recently, QSkyCube [5] adapted the BSkyTree algorithm [4]. These algorithms compute cuboids one-by-one, using the corresponding skyline algorithm. Based on results reported in [4,5], BSkyTree and QSkyCube are state-of-the-art.

Skycube data structures The default skycube structure is the *lattice*, used in QSkyCube [5]. It is an array of $2^d - 1$ vectors, and the i'th vector contains all points in the i'th cuboid. Naturally, this has optimal performance: one retrieves the proper vector from the array and then reports all points lying therein. However, it is *maximal* in terms of

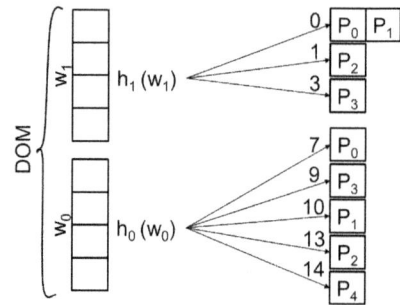

Figure 1: The Hashcube, built from Table 2 with $|w_i| = 4$.

space: each point is duplicated for every cuboid it is in, $\frac{1}{2} 2^d$ times for points with maximal values on some attribute.

Two smaller data structures have been proposed. The *closed skycube* [8] defines equivalence classes over subspaces and avoids duplicating points within an equivalence class.

The more recent *compressed skycube* [10] defines *minimal subspaces* skyline points and constructs a bipartite membership graph between points and minimum subspaces. Thus a point is not duplicated for any subspaces between its minimal subspaces and the full skyline. In the absence of Distinct Value Condition, it introduces overhead to rederive any particular cuboid, because false positives must be verified with dominance tests in all subspaces of the query subspace.

3. THE Hashcube DATA STRUCTURE

Here, we introduce the Hashcube, obtaining up to $|w|$-fold compression (for $|w|$, the number of bits in each logical word) and state-of-the-art query performance.

3.1 Layout of the Hashcube

We illustrate a Hashcube in Figure 1, using the data from Tables 1 and 2. The high-level idea is to split the domspaces vectors for each point into words of length $|w|$ (4 in examples, 32 in experiments), and to index the points by their resultant substrings using hash maps. Since the domspaces vector has length 2^d, each point will be indexed $\leq 2^{d - \lg|w|}$ times. The substrings are the keys for the hash maps. More precisely, if $\Sigma = \{0, 1\}^{|w|} \setminus \{1\}^{|w|}$ denotes the set of length $|w|$ bitstrings containing at least one zero, and $k = \max(1, 2^{d - \lg|w|})$:

Definition 4 (Hashcube (P)). A *Hashcube* on P is a set of k hash maps, $h_0, \ldots, h_{k-1}$, each mapping from valid bitstrings in Σ to subsets of P, $h_j : \Sigma \to \mathcal{P}(P)$, where:

$$p_i \in h_j(B) \text{ iff } DOM_i[|w|j, |w|(j+1) - 1] = B.$$

That is, each hash map corresponds to a group of $|w|$ cuboids. Points are binned according to the combination of those cuboids in which they appear. For example, in Figure 1, w_1 corresponds to subspaces {Year,Sales}, {Year, Rating}, and {Year,Rating,Sales}, respectively. Both *Avatar* and *The Avengers* are binned to 0, since they appear in all three cuboids. Although *The Godfather* appears in the last two cuboids, it does not appear in {Year,Sales}: it has a different combination, namely 1, and maps to that bin instead.

Compression for a Hashcube depends on the number of clear bits in the substring of a domspaces vector, up to $|w|$. Note, first, that a point is only ever indexed by a hash map if it has a zero bit, i.e., if it appears it at least one of the

Algorithm 1 Querying the Hashcube

Input: Hashcube; query subspace, B; word length, $|w|$
Output: The skyline of subspace B
1: Let $j = B/|w|$
2: Let $mask = (1 \ll (B\%|w|))$
3: **for all** active hash keys k_i of h_j **do**
4:     **if** $(k_i \& mask) == 0$ **then**
5:         Output all pid in $h_j(k_i)$

corresponding $|w|$ cuboids. If so, it must also be indexed for that cuboid by the lattice. Conversely, a point is only indexed once by each hash map, no matter how many of the $|w|$ cuboids in which it appears; the lattice may index the point $|w|$ times. Further compression comes by not storing unused hash keys and by points mapping to identical bins.

3.2 Querying the Hashcube

Notice from Definition 3 that the j'th cuboid consists of all points p_i for which $\text{DOM}_i[j] = 0$. So, for the Hashcube, the query operation is to concatenate all vectors of point ids for which that bit is not set. Because Definition 4 treats each group of $|w|$ bits/cuboids independently of the rest, the query can be resolved with just one of the $2^{d-\lg|w|}$ hash maps. Algorithm 1 describes the query operation: first the relevant hash map is determined, and then all $\leq 2^{|w|}$ *active* hash keys for that hash map are iterated. For those that have the relevant bit clear, the entire vector of point ids is output. No point will be output twice, because each point id is stored at most once per hash map. The iteration of active hash keys is the primary source of overhead relative to the lattice, a cost of at most $2 * 2^{|w|}$ binary/logical operations.[2]

The cost of querying the data structure is also very low. Lines $1-2$ require constant computations. We then read up to $2^{|w|}$ active hash keys, perform two operations, and (possibly) output some unique point ids (if the condition on Line 4 evaluates true). So, if there are m point ids to output, then the cost of querying the Hashcube is $\mathcal{O}(2^{|w|} + m)$.

4. EXPERIMENTAL EVALUATION

We compare Hashcube ($|w| = 32$) to the compressed skycube (CSC) [10], the lattice, and computation from scratch using the BSkyTree [4] skyline algorithm. (Note that larger $|w|$ improves compression; smaller $|w|$ improves query time.) We implement (code available[3]) the data structures and query algorithms in C++.[4] The lattice is built as an array of vectors of point ids. CSC is strongly implemented, evidenced by the faster performance than reported in [10] (albeit on newer hardware). The implementation of BSkyTree was provided by the authors, but adapted to handle subspace queries. We use an Intel Core i7-2700 machine with four 3.4 GHz cores and 16 GB of memory, running Linux (kernel version 3.5.0).

We evaluate the data structures in terms of space and query time. We measure space by counting 32-bit point ids and hash keys used, a more robust measure than physical disk space because of external libraries (e.g., std::map).

[2]The Hashcube also requires outputting up to $2^{|w|-1}$ separate lists, rather than one, long contiguous one.
[3]source at: http://cs.au.dk/research/research-areas/data-intensive-systems/repository/.
[4]compiled using g++ (4.7.2) with the -O3 optimization flag

We measure query time by dividing the total time to sequentially query every subspace by $2^d - 1$. In contrast to uniformly sampling subspaces with replacement as in [10], this better estimates expected performance: the worst cases ((d-1)-dimensional subspaces) are otherwise unlikely included. Output to an array in memory, but not init time, is included.

We evaluate how the structures scale with respect to both d and $|P|$ on anti/correlated data, generated as in [1]. We adopt default values, $d = 12$ and $|P| = 500$K, from [4].

Experiment Results Overall, CSC achieves the most compression. Figure 2 shows that all data structures scale well with $|P|$ in terms of size, since the size of each cuboid grows sub-linearly with $|P|$. That the CSC has a worse compression rate on anti-correlated data is intuitive, because the minimum subspaces for each point are larger. In Figure 3, see that CSC's compression relative to the lattice increases with d, because there are longer paths between minimum subspaces and the full skyline. Hashcube is generally closer to CSC than to the lattice. Relative to the lattice, it obtains $\approx 10\times$ compression and permits storing in the same amount of space 2–4 more dimensions (4–16$\times$ more cuboids).

The same trends exist for physical space (not shown). We use standard libraries, rather than more space-efficient, custom-built containers. Still, for $d = 12$ and $|P| = 500$K, HashCube achieves a compression ratio (in bytes) of 7.9$\times$ (compared to 13.8$\times$). The same ratios apply for CSC.

Figures 4 and 5 report average query performance. The Hashcube performs very strongly, closely following the optimal performance of the lattice, typically $1000 - 10000\times$ faster than CSC. The iteration of all hash keys only takes $5 - 10\times$ as long as the direct lookup in the lattice. Further, on anticorrelated data, Hashcube converges towards the lattice with increasing $|P|$ (Figure 4). By contrast, CSC is rather slow, beaten in most instances by simply computing the skyline from scratch with BSkyTree. CSC outperforms BSkyTree only on small, correlated instances of $< 200\mu s$.

The poor query performance of CSC results from dominance tests required to reconstruct each cuboid. As d increases, exponentially more subspaces of a query space must be examined for false positives. With respect to $|P|$, trends match the size plots. The correlation is expected: for each subspace, the number of dominance tests is quadratic in the number of points for which that is the minimum subspace. It should also be noted that the variance of query times for HashCube is small, i.e., never exceeds 1ms, while CSC typically spends minutes on high-dimensional queries. This is a result of the split into several bitstrings of size $|w|$, which limits the number of hash keys for each query, while CSC needs to iterate the data points in all subspaces of the chosen dimensions and needs to perform dominance checks.

Hashcube is efficient to query, typically $1000 - 10000\times$ faster than CSC and computing from scratch with BSkyTree. The iteration of all hash keys only slows Hashcube $5 - 10\times$ relative to the lattice. Further, on anticorrelated data, Hashcube converges towards the lattice with increasing $|P|$. The cost of outputting longer contiguous vectors is neglible; so, the increased input size only slows the data structure if new points associate with as-yet-unused hash keys. With respect to d, the curve follows that of the lattice quite closely.

We call particular attention to Figure 5, because it expresses very well the balance that Hashcube obtains. We are unable to finish the plot for both the lattice and CSC, but for opposite reasons. The lattice does not fit in 16 GB

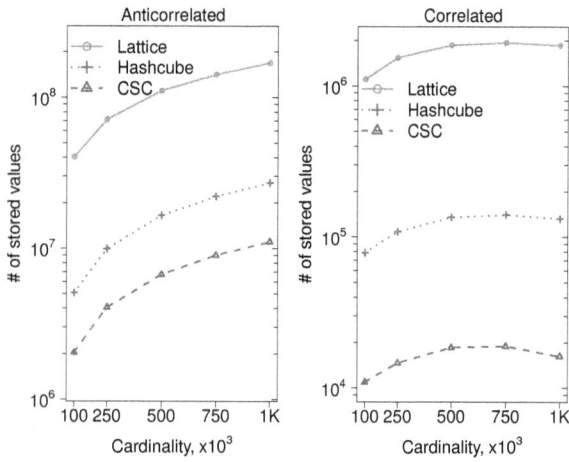

Figure 2: Size of the data structures w.r.t. to n (d=12).

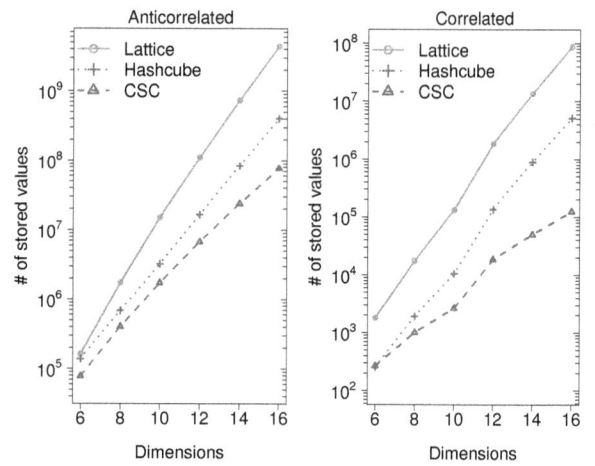

Figure 3: Size of the data structures w.r.t. to d (n=500K).

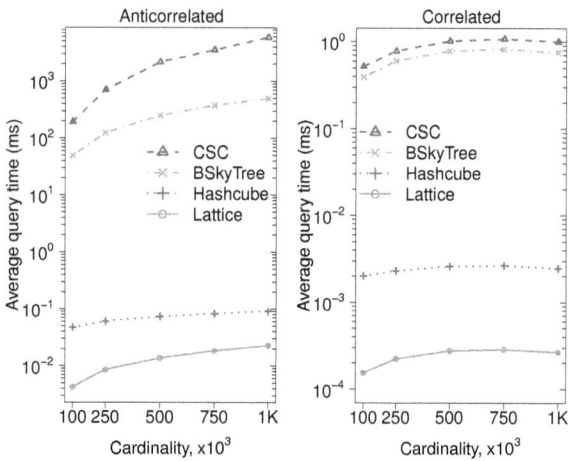

Figure 4: Data structure query time w.r.t. to n (d=12).

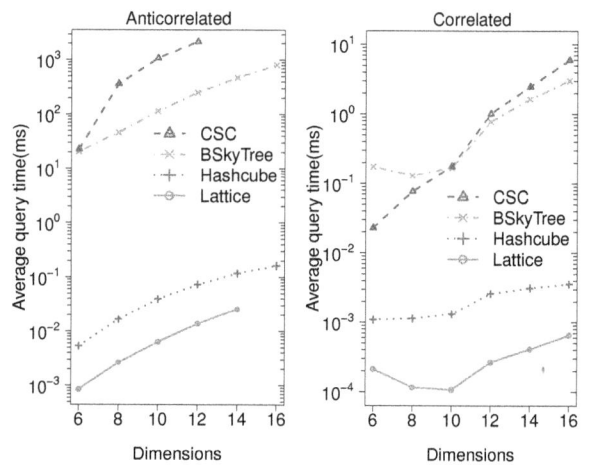

Figure 5: Data structure query time w.r.t. to d (n=500K).

of memory; so, we cannot query it fairly. On the other hand, CSC achieves good compression, but has prohibitive query time (> 48 hrs total). Hashcube is very efficient in both respects and supports this 16-dimensional, anticorrelated case. It compresses well and still, across all tested combinations of $|P|$ and d, can be queried on average in less than $200\mu s$.

5. CONCLUSION AND OUTLOOK

We introduced a compressed skycube based on bitstrings, the Hashcube. Relative to the lattice, it achieves $\approx 10\times$ compression. Relative to the state-of-the-art compressed skycube, queries are $\approx 1000\times$ faster. Further, we showed that, while the compressed skycube is updatable, it is outperformed by skyline computation from scratch. Thus, updating skycubes is still a challenging open problem. For future work, we believe equivalence class ideas from [8] and/or more sophisticated cuboid grouping choices can be integrated into the Hashcube to further improve compression. Small, auxilliary structures may help handle some update types.

6. ACKNOWLEDGMENTS

This research was supported in part by the Danish Council for Strategic Research, grant 10-092316. We thank the BSkyTree authors [4] for their skyline implementation.

7. REFERENCES

[1] S. Börzsönyi et al. The skyline operator. In *Proc. ICDE*, pages 421–430, 2001.
[2] S. Chester et al. On the suitability of skyline queries for data exploration. In *Proc. ExploreDB*, pages 6:1–6, 2014.
[3] J. Chomicki et al. Skyline with presorting. In *Proc. ICDE*, pages 717–719, 2003.
[4] J. Lee and S.-w. Hwang. Scalable skyline computation using a balanced pivot selection technique. *Inf. Syst.*, 39:1–24, 2014.
[5] J. Lee and S.-w. Hwang. Toward efficient multidimensional subspace skyline computation. *VLDB J*, 23(1):129–145, 2014.
[6] J. Pei et al. Catching the best views of the skyline: a semantic approach based on decisive subspaces. In *Proc. VLDB*, pages 253–264, 2005.
[7] J. Pei et al. Towards multidimensional subspace skyline analysis. *TODS*, 31(4):1335–1381, 2006.
[8] C. Raïssi et al. Computing closed skycubes. *PVLDB*, 3(1):838–847, 2010.
[9] A. Vlachou et al. Skypeer: Efficient subspace skyline computation over distributed data. In *Proc. ICDE*, pages 416–425, 2007.
[10] T. Xia et al. Online subspace skyline query processing using the compressed skycube. *TODS*, 37(2), 2012.
[11] Y. Yuan et al. Efficient computation of the skyline cube. In *Proc. VLDB*, pages 241–252, 2005.
[12] S. Zhang et al. Scalable skyline computation using object-based space partitioning. In *Proc. SIGMOD*, pages 483–494, 2009.

Distance or Coverage? Retrieving Knowledge-Rich Documents from Enterprise Text Collections

Vinay Deolalikar
Hewlett-Packard Research
Sunnyvale, CA
deolalikar.academic@gmail.com

ABSTRACT

We formulate a problem that arises in unstructured enterprise information management, and has high commercial impact: retrieve knowledge-rich documents in a large textual collection of technical documents. We call such documents *principal documents*.

We exploit the properties of large sparse text collections in order to address this problem. It is known that the centroids of document clusters on such collections form so-called "concept vectors" for the collection. However, typically these centroids do not correspond to documents in the collection. How then should they be used for retrieving documents? An immediate approach is to collect documents that are *closest* to the centroid, which we call CTC. We also propose an algorithm called PrinDocs. The key insight behind PrinDocs is the following: replace distance functions by coverage. In other words, instead of finding the "closest" documents to a concept vector, find those that "cover" the concept vector. PrinDocs employs greedy weighted set covering and uses the concept decomposition offered by centroids, but does not use the cosine distance on documents.

We compare CTC and PrinDocs for retrieving knowledge-rich documents in enterprise unstructured technical collections. We demonstrate that PrinDocs comprehensively outperforms CTC. Our work suggests that coverage based approaches might be preferable to distance based ones for similar retrieval tasks.

Keywords

Principal Documents; Knowledge-Rich Documents; Enterprise Unstructured Information

1. INTRODUCTION

Over 70% of all information in an enterprise exists in unstructured textual formats [5]. In light of this, the retrieval of definitive, knowledge-rich pieces of information from enterprise technical corpora has emerged as a major problem in diverse applications including eDiscovery, knowledge gathering and project discovery, salesforce support, etc. We call the definitive, knowledge-rich documents in an enterprise technical corpus its **principal documents**. Standing in the way of retrieving such documents are other documents that are not comprehensive and may represent previous stages in the development of the technology. Frequently, these have

already been culled into making the "final" definitive knowledge-rich versions that we seek.

Can we use known structural properties of large textual collections [4] in order to address this problem? It is known that clustering performs a "concept decomposition" of the major concepts in the collection. Furthermore, the centroids of the resulting clusters emerge as "concept vectors" in that their most significant coordinates correspond to significant concepts.

However, these concept vectors (or centroids) do not correspond to actual documents in the collection. Not only that, they typically do not lie very close to actual documents either. How then do we use the aforementioned structural properties in order to retrieve documents from the collection?

The immediate approach is simply to use the distance function of the collection, and retrieve the closest documents to the centroid. These could, conceivably, contain the knowledge-rich documents that we seek. We formalize this approach using an algorithm we call CTC, for "closest to centroid"—a known paradigm in retrieval.

We propose an alternative: retrieve documents that "cover" the concept vectors. In other words, ignore the standard distance function, and use a metric that relies on how well a document "covers" the concept vector. We formalize this approach using an algorithm we call PrinDocs. PrinDocs addresses several nuances: do we require a document to cover all of the concept vector, or parts of it? How do we then collect documents that cover different parts of the concept vector? How much coverage do we need?

We compare CTC and PrinDocs in detail in this paper. Our results are clear: PrinDocs outperforms CTC consistently, and by a widening margin as the number of clusters k increases. Our results suggest that coverage based approaches offer promise in enterprise retrieval tasks.

2. THE PrinDocs ALGORITHM

We now describe the stages of PrinDocs: our algorithm to discover principal documents in an enterprise corpus.

1. We cluster the corpus into k clusters denoted by $\{C_1, \ldots, C_k\}$. The value of k is usually dictated by the enterprise application. For cluster C_i, the concept vector truncated to its most significant ℓ terms will be denoted by

$$\mathfrak{C}_i = \sum_{j=1}^{\ell} w_{i_j} \mathbf{t}_{i_j},$$

where $\mathbf{t}_*$ denotes the unit vector in the corresponding direction.

2. We begin by representing each document D in C_i as a vector on the same ℓ-basis as $\mathfrak{C}_i$. Namely, we restrict the term frequency vector of D to the ℓ terms that occur in $\mathfrak{C}_i$, and drop all the remaining terms. Denote this vector by $\langle D \rangle = \sum_{j=1}^{\ell} n_{i_j}(D)\mathbf{t}_{i_j}$, where $n_*(\cdot)$ is the corresponding term frequency. We also form the binary representation of D, which is obtained by replacing each non-zero coordinate $n_{i_j}(D)$ in $\langle D \rangle$ by the Boolean 1. We denote this binary representation of D by $\langle \overline{D} \rangle = \sum_{j=1}^{\ell} b_{i_j}(D)\mathbf{t}_{i_j}$.

3. We weight the documents in C_i using the list $\mathfrak{C}_i$ and the representations constructed above. The weight of D is simply the sum of the concept weights of all its non-zero terms. Namely,

$$w(D) = \sum_{j=1}^{\ell} w_{i_j} b_{i_j}(D).$$

This step along with the next are called ClusterRankDocs.

4. The weighting above induces a ranking on the documents in C_i. We will denote this ranking by subscript, so that D_1 represents the document with the highest weight, and so on. In general, there will be ties in this ranking, which we break using the following rule: in the case of a tie, we traverse the list $\mathfrak{C}_i$ in decreasing order of concept weight until we reach a concept where the frequencies of the tied documents differ. We then rank the document whose frequency is higher above the other. We may need to iterate this in case of a tie between more than two documents. This choice also allows the user to control the number of principal documents.

5. We construct, on the set of concepts in $\mathfrak{C}_i$ a "coverage-profile" vector $T_i = \sum_{j=1}^{\ell} T_{i_j} \mathbf{t}_{i_j}$. Here, T_{i_j} denotes the desired coverage for the concept $\mathbf{t}_{i_j}$ in the cluster. We wish to set a higher coverage-level for terms that are more important for this cluster. We achieve this by setting the desired coverage for a concept to be the natural log of its concept weight plus one. Namely, $T_{i_j} = \ln(w_{i_j} + 1)$. This is the "logarithmic coverage" profile. Based on the needs of the application, other profiles may also be considered (for example, scaled logarithmic, linear, etc.).

6. We initialize an empty list $\mathcal{P}_i$. We will populate $\mathcal{P}_i$ with principal documents from C_i during the course of the algorithm.

7. Next, we cover each concept in the cluster to its desired coverage in the coverage-profile T_i, using our ranked list of documents and a greedy algorithm. We call this subroutine (encompassing Stage 8 as well) ClusterPrinDocs. We begin by examining the top ranked document from our ranked list, and identify concepts that are already covered to the desired coverage-level. Namely, whether $n_{i_j}(D_1) > T_{i_j}$ for any j. If the top-ranked document does not cover any concept to the desired level, we go to the second-ranked document, sum its coverages with the top-ranked, and inspect the coverage levels again. Namely, we check whether $n_{i_j}(D_1) + n_{i_j}(D_2) > T_{i_j}$ for any j. We proceed in this manner until at least one concept is covered.

8. Now, we remove the concepts thus covered from the set of concepts $\mathfrak{C}_i$, giving us a smaller concept list that we call $\mathfrak{C}_i^-$. We also remove the top-ranked document from the ranked list of documents, and insert it into $\mathcal{P}_i$. This gives us a smaller (by one) set of vectors of lower dimension than what we had before this stage. We now recompute the ranking of documents on this reduced dimensionality space and reiterate the steps outlined earlier. We iterate this process until either all concepts are covered or a maximum number of M documents have been added to $\mathcal{P}_i$. This maximum number M is pre-determined: we have experimented with values of $M = [2, 3, 5, 10]$ extensively, and recommend such low values in practice.

9. Finally, for each cluster C_i, we return $\mathcal{P}_i$ as a set of principal documents that is complete with respect to the concepts in $\mathfrak{C}_i$. Namely, PrinDocs returns $\mathcal{P} = \mathcal{P}_1 \cup \ldots \cup \mathcal{P}_k$.

What if the coverage-level for a particular concept is not met by the time the algorithm terminates? In that case, we settle for the maximum coverage afforded to it until M documents have been removed. In practice, we found that all concepts are usually covered by fewer than 10 principal documents, and the algorithm terminates after meeting the full desired coverage-profile.

PrinDocs converges in time $O(f)$ where f is the time complexity of the clustering algorithm. After clustering, the algorithm has to rank each document in each cluster, inspect the top ranked documents in each cluster, and iterate until all concepts are covered. Each of these tasks has time complexity dominated by $O(f)$.

Data: C_i, $\mathfrak{C}_i$, coverage-profile T_i, M
Result: Set of principal documents for C_i complete for concepts in $\mathfrak{C}_i$
Initialize: $\mathcal{P}_i \leftarrow \emptyset$; $\mathfrak{C}_i^- \leftarrow \mathfrak{C}_i$; $n \leftarrow 1$;
repeat
  Call ClusterRankDocs $(C_i, \mathfrak{C}_i^-)$;
  Traverse ranked list, summing over term frequencies, until at least one concept in $\mathfrak{C}_i^-$ is covered to level desired by T_i; Let set of concepts covered be V ;
  Move top-ranked document D_1 in list into $\mathcal{P}_i$: $C_i \leftarrow C_i \setminus D$;
  Remove covered concepts from concept list: $\mathfrak{C}_i^- \leftarrow \mathfrak{C}_i^- \setminus V$;
  $n += 1$;
until *(All concepts in $\mathfrak{C}_i$ covered) OR ($n > M$)*;
Return $\mathcal{P}_i$;

Algorithm 1: ClusterPrinDocs: Subroutine for identifying principal documents for a given cluster. Details in §2, 7-8.

3. RELATED WORK

The problem of clustering in retrieval has received much attention, starting from when information retrieval was in its infancy. Various schemes were proposed earlier on for increasing the effectiveness of search. These schemes used a static clustering of the entire corpus; see [12] for an excellent review of the main ideas in these early works.

The application of clustering to browsing, as opposed to search, was initiated by [3], who proposed scatter-gather—a browsing scheme for large file collections. [7] provide the first discussion of scatter-gather on the results of a query; namely, they cluster the documents returned by a search engine as the results of a query, and then perform scatter-gather on it. The paper provides anecdotal evidence of the efficacy of scatter-gather using a few examples. [8] and [11] also consider the problem of using clustering on top-ranked search results to improve retrieval.

The CTC baseline algorithm that we compare to is related to these cluster based browsing techniques. The use of the cluster centroid for search (as opposed to browsing) was one of the early ideas in clustering in information retrieval. For example, [2] proposed a strategy in which a document that was representative of the query (using similarity metrics) would be used for the comparison to the cluster centroids in order to determine relevant clusters.

We should stress that the work on clustering in information retrieval, though extensive, is not directly related to our work for the following two important reasons. Firstly, we address the problem of retrieving knowledge-rich documents from an enterprise corpus, which has not been addressed before. Secondly, our algorithm uses clustering in a very different manner than previous approaches: we do not use a cluster as a unit of retrieval, but rather use clustering and concept profiles within clusters as an intermediate technique to feed into our coverage algorithm. In particular, the coverage aspects of our approach are novel, and do not appear in information retrieval literature.

Three works that do not fall under the rubric of clustering in retrieval, but are related to ours are now described. [4] introduce "concept decompositions" of a corpus based on cluster centroids. Our work also uses a similar technique to create digests, which are then used later by the coverage part of our algorithm. [6] consider the choice of representatives from document clusters. The representatives they pick as "typical" are those that are closest to the centroid. This is the CTC algorithm that is our baseline. [1] consider a maximally diverse set of documents to represent clusters. The diversity is defined either in terms of distances, or categories. It would be interesting to apply their technique to diversity in terms of coverage. Since our work does not assume the notion of query, it is only peripherally related to the work on search diversification.

We also mention that [9] is related to our work because of the technique that they use: namely, centroid based summarization. Our baseline comparison algorithm CTC uses a closest to centroid criterion for choosing documents. Furthermore, the set of complete principal documents may be seen as a 'document-level summary" of the collection. Indeed, the algorithm is being considered for use in an enterprise-class leading retrieval platform in such a capacity.

4. EXPERIMENTAL VALIDATION

In order to validate our approach, we constructed a dataset starting from a real-world corpus of enterprise origins. We then performed a series of processes on this corpus in order to recreate the "mixed" nature of enterprise technical corpora. Now we describe this dataset.

4.1 The Corp-A-TR-Mixed Dataset

We began with the set of 301 technical reports generated by a Fortune-10 IT company 'Corp-A' in the years 2000 and 2005 that are publicly available. We spaced the two apart by five years to preclude significant concept overlaps. This yielded 301 finished documents, representing a roughly equal number of projects. This is called the Corp-A-TR dataset.

We then split each of these files between 0 (namely, no split) and 6 ways (namely, into 7 pieces), at random, into equal length components. These splits would then represent less knowledge-rich documents in the collection[1].

We concatenated each of the components produced earlier with itself the same number of times as the split that caused it. For example, if file F was split into 3 files F_A, F_B, and F_C, then each of the three F_A, F_B, F_C would be concatenated three times, leading to $F_A F_A F_A$, $F_B F_B F_B$, and $F_C F_C F_C$. This was done for length normalization, so that the original file F and the files $F_A F_A F_A$, $F_B F_B F_B$, and $F_C F_C F_C$ would be comparable in length. Notice that this length normalization makes it strictly harder for PrinDocs to identify principal documents. This is because this normalization does not affect the ranking of the documents (§2, Step 3) since that ranking only takes into account the binary representation of a document. However, it makes it more likely that if a concatenated document is at the top of the ranking, then it will cause concepts it contains to be removed from the list $\mathfrak{C}_i$ of concepts. This reduces the advantage that true principal documents have due to their coverage properties[2].

Finally, we added all the split-concatenated files to the original text files to create our dataset, which we call Corp-A-TR-Mixed.

The principal documents in the Corp-A-TR-Mixed dataset are naturally the original finished documents that came from the Corp-A-TR dataset. Therefore, our retrieval target was these originals.

We used bisecting k-means to produce our clusters, since the quality of clusters produced by it are among the best of any clustering algorithm [10].

4.2 Protocol

We ran PrinDocs on the Corp-A-TR-Mixed dataset. We ran four versions of PrinDocs. In the first, we allowed PrinDocs to identify its full set of principal documents from each cluster, no matter how high that number may be. In other words, we set M to be higher than the size of the corpus. We denote this regime by $M = \infty$.

To compare to a benchmark, we used the closest to cluster centroid (CTC) algorithm. The document(s) closest to centroid is frequently used in literature as the best "representative" of the cluster. We allowed the CTC algorithm to match ClusterPrinDocs for number of documents picked. Namely, if, say in cluster C_i, the

---

[1]These could come, for example, from portions of the original document, being worked on separately by different members of a project; from smaller, less informative versions of the final document, and so on

[2]We recognized this obstacle to PrinDocs during our extensive internal validation on real-world enterprise corpora.

ClusterPrinDocs subroutine identified m_i principal documents, then the CTC algorithm was also allowed to take the m_i documents whose cosine similarity to the centroid of cluster C_i was the highest. These would be the documents chosen by the CTC algorithm, and would be compared to the m_i principal documents identified by ClusterPrinDocs. By taking the union over all clusters, we obtained a full set of principal documents for the Corp-A-TR-Mixed dataset, as well as an equal number of documents chosen by the CTC algorithm.

Precision was computed as follows: it was the proportion of the documents retrieved by each algorithm that was from the Corp-A-TR dataset. Namely, the precision was the proportion of original finished technical reports that each algorithm was able to retrieve.

Each experiment was run three times, and averages are reported. We did not observe significant variations between runs.

Finally, the design above was repeated, but with the parameter M set to 5, 3, and 2 in turn.

On an AMD opteron 2GHz processor, at $k = 10$, the time taken to cluster our dataset was 1.98 sec, and the time taken to compute principal documents following it was 0.69 sec.

4.3 Results

Our results are enumerated below. Each result is shown for k in $[5, 10, 15, 20, 25, 30]$. M is varied in $[\infty, 5, 3, 2]$ for each k.

1. Fig. 1 shows the actual number of principal documents retrieved, and the number of these that were definitive documents from the Corp-A-TR dataset for PrinDocs and CTC.
2. Fig. 2 shows the precision of PrinDocs versus CTC.

Recall is immediately known once precision is, since the size of the Corp-A-TR dataset is known; therefore it is not reported separately.

4.4 Discussion

We may draw the following observations from the results of §4.3. The principal documents algorithm PrinDocs comprehensively outperforms the baseline CTC algorithm in identifying definitive documents in an enterprise corpus.

1. The improvement in precision demonstrated by PrinDocs over CTC is significant. The recall of the principal documents algorithm is often two orders of magnitude higher than the CTC algorithm, with an average over all k and M of 9.7 times higher recall.
2. PrinDocs *consistently* outperforms CTC. In cases where both algorithms have significant precision, as, say defined by the case where both have precision of over 0.05, the principal documents algorithm *always* performs (far) better than CTC once $k \geq 10$.
3. As k is increased, the gap between the precisions produced by PrinDocs and the CTC algorithms widens considerably.

5. CONCLUSIONS

We formulate the problem of retrieving knowledge-rich documents from enterprise technical corpora: a problem of high commercial impact. We compare two approaches to this problem: retrieving documents that lie closest to the centroids of a clustering of the corpus, and retrieving documents that "cover" the concepts represented in the centroids. We find that the coverage-based approach is significantly and consistently better than the closest to centroid approach. Distance based algorithms (such as CTC) may not give best results for the following reason. The space around a centroid in a cluster may be largely empty [4]. Thus, even though the centroid gives us a good concept decomposition of the cluster, it is *not necessarily* a good "geometric representative" in the sense that it may lie in a largely empty area in the cluster. PrinDocs, on the other hand, does not use any geometric assumptions. It merely says "concept vectors provide good concept decompositions. Let us find documents only using these decompositions."

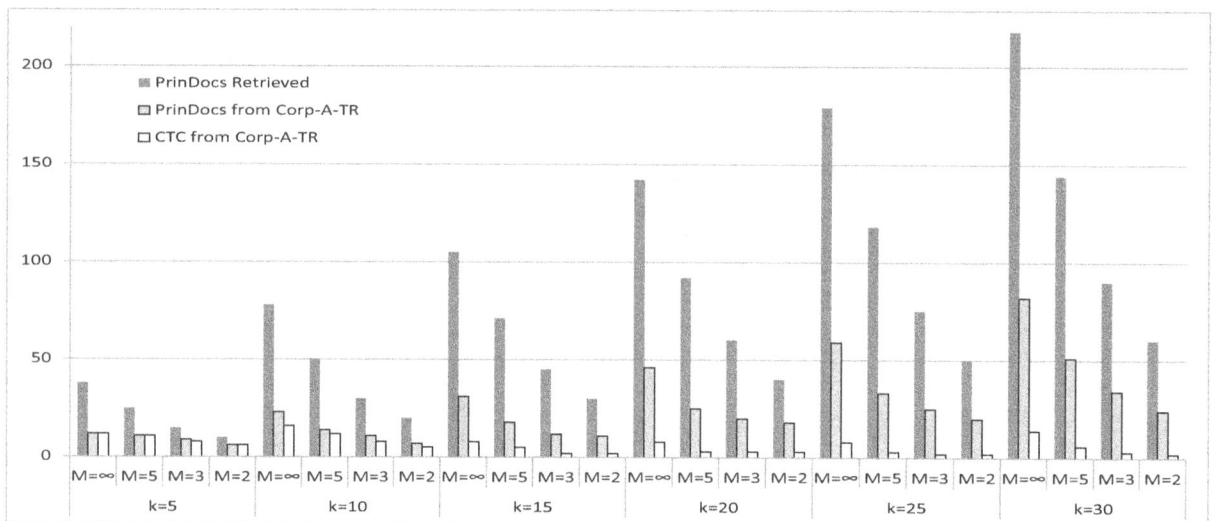

Figure 1: The Y-axis shows the actual numbers of principal documents retrieved by PrinDocs and the number of these that were from the Corp-A-TR corpus. The gap between the two approaches widens as k is increased. The X-axis shows the choice of parameters for PrinDocs.

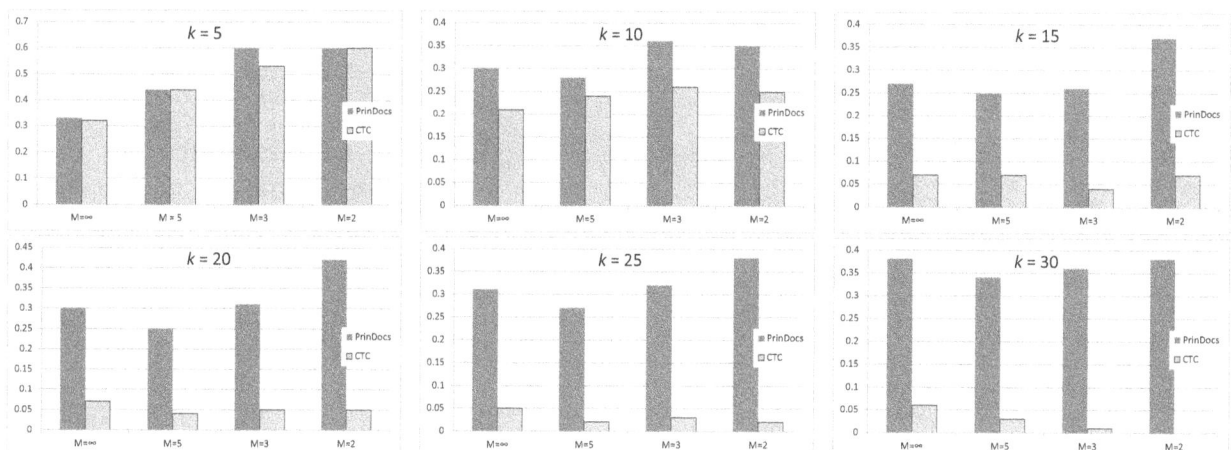

Figure 2: Precision (on Y-axis) of the principal documents algorithm versus that of baseline CTC algorithm for 5, 10, 15, 20, 25, and 30 clusters. M varied between $[\infty, 5, 3, 2]$.

Our results suggest that it might be advantageous to consider the coverage approach in other retrieval tasks, especially for the enterprise domain, where "mixed" corpora are the norm. PrinDocs adds an order or magnitude smaller time overhead on top of clustering, which makes it attractive for addition to existing clustering platforms. PrinDocs is currently being tested for deployment on a market leading enterprise unstructured information management platform from a Fortune-10 IT company.

Acknowledgements. Some of the data in this paper was gathered using scripts written by Hernan Laffitte.

References

[1] Z. Abbassi, V. S. Mirrokni, and M. Thakur. Diversity maximization under matroid constraints. In *Proc. 19th SIGKDD*, pages 32–40. ACM, 2013.

[2] W. Croft. A model of cluster searching based on classification. *Information Systems*, 5(3):189–195, 1980.

[3] D. R. Cutting, J. O. Pedersen, D. Karger, and J. W. Tukey. Scatter/gather: A cluster-based approach to browsing large document collections. In *Proc. 15th SIGIR*, pages 318–329. ACM, 1992.

[4] I. S. Dhillon and D. S. Modha. Concept decompositions for large sparse text data using clustering. *Machine learning*, 42(1-2):143–175, 2001.

[5] Gartner. The top 10 strategic technology trends for 2012. 2012.

[6] A. F. Gelbukh, M. Alexandrov, A. Bourek, and P. Makagonov. Selection of representative documents for clusters in a document collection. In *NLDB*, volume 29 of *LNI*, pages 120–126, 2003.

[7] M. A. Hearst and J. O. Pedersen. Reexamining the cluster hypothesis: Scatter/gather on retrieval results. In *Proc. 19th SIGIR*, pages 76–84, New York, 1996. ACM.

[8] A. Leuski. Evaluating document clustering for interactive information retrieval. In *Proc. 10th CIKM*, pages 33–40, New York, NY, USA, 2001. ACM.

[9] D. R. Radev, H. Jing, M. Styś, and D. Tam. Centroid-based summarization of multiple documents. *Information Processing Management*, 40(6):919 – 938, 2004.

[10] M. Steinbach, G. Karypis, and V. Kumar. A comparison of document clustering techniques. In *KDD Workshop on Text Mining*, volume 400, pages 525–526. Boston, 2000.

[11] A. Tombros, R. Villa, and C. J. Van Rijsbergen. The effectiveness of query-specific hierarchic clustering in information retrieval. *Information Processing & Management*, 38(4):559–582, July 2002.

[12] P. Willett. Recent trends in hierarchic document clustering: a critical review. *Information Processing & Management*, 24(5):577–597, 1988.

Indexing Linked Data in a Wireless Broadcast System with 3D Hilbert Space-Filling Curves

Yongrui Qin*, Quan Z. Sheng*, Nickolas J.G. Falkner*, Wei Emma Zhang*, Hua Wang†

*School of Computer Science
The University of Adelaide, Australia
{yongrui.qin,michael.sheng,nickolas.falkner,wei.zhang01}
@adelaide.edu.au

†Centre for Applied Informatics
College of Engineering & Science
Victoria University, Australia
hua.wang@vu.edu.au

ABSTRACT

Semantic technologies aim to facilitate machine-to-machine communication and are attracting more and more interest from both academia and industry, especially in the emerging Internet of Things (IoT). In this paper, we consider large-scale information sharing scenarios among mobile objects in IoT by leveraging semantic techniques. We propose to broadcast Linked Data on-air using RDF format to allow simultaneous access to the information and to achieve better scalability. We introduce a novel air indexing method to reduce the information access latency and energy consumption. To build air indexes, we firstly map RDF triples in the Linked Data into points in a 3D space and build B^+-trees based on 3D Hilbert curve mappings for all of the 3D points. We then convert these trees into linear sequences so that they can be broadcast over a wireless channel. A novel search algorithm is also designed to efficiently evaluate queries against the air indexes. Experiments show that our indexing method outperforms the air indexing method based on traditional 3D R-trees.

Categories and Subject Descriptors

H.3.5 [**Information Storage and Retrieval**]: Online Information Services—*Data sharing*

Keywords

Linked Data, wireless broadcast, air indexing

1. INTRODUCTION

In the era of the Internet of Things [8], due to a large amount of information produced by all kinds of things, one of the significant challenges is how to efficiently consume the large amount of information that is generated. In this context, semantic technologies such as Linked Data, which aim at facilitating machine-to-machine communications, play an increasingly important role [1]. Linked Data is taking an ac-

tive role in a trend towards highly distributed systems, with potentially millions of independent sources providing small amounts of structured data [9]. Event detection and entity discovery requires an effective way of information sharing. Compared with the *point-to-point* communication paradigm, *broadcast* (or *point-to-multipoint*) allows simultaneous access by an arbitrary number of listeners (or clients) without causing contention of server resources [7]. Considering information sharing among a large number of mobile and smart objects in the Internet of Things, broadcast is an attractive mechanism of information dissemination.

To further illustrate the motivation, let us consider the scenario of a future smart city, where intelligent objects will be acting as data collectors in different places of the city. They will be able to sense their vicinities (e.g., for air pollution information) and produce related Linked Data that is understandable by machines. These objects send such data to a nearby base station for further processing. The base station can then integrate and process all the data from various data collectors and broadcast to a much wider audience such as smart objects, which are not direct data collectors but are interested in such data. Since a smart object is normally only interested in a small part of the broadcast data, blindly checking every triple on air would lead to very long access latency and unnecessary energy consumption. As the batteries of smart objects are often limited, an efficient way to reduce energy consumption and lower access latency is imperative. Our work focuses on solving this challenge by designing effective and efficient air indexes for broadcasting Linked Data on air.

Inspired by recent work on data summaries on Linked Data using RDF format [5, 9], we adopt a similar technique to index Linked Data. This is mainly because it can be used to construct very concise indexes, which is critical in saving mobile clients' energy consumption. On the server side, we firstly map the RDF triples contained in Linked Data streams into points in a 3D space and then build indexes on these 3D points. A straightforward indexing solution is to use traditional spatial indexes, such as R-tree [4], which recursively index spatial points/objects in sub-regions. However, it is shown that the performance of R-tree degrades in higher dimension space [2]. Moreover, R-tree is designed for random access while, in a wireless broadcast system, indexes can only be accessed sequentially. Therefore, the R-tree approach is not suitable for indexing Linked Data on air. Motivated by this, we introduce a novel method by adopting 3D Hilbert curve mappings [6] for all the points converted from RDF triples. These mappings transform the 3D points into a sequence of one-dimensional points, which are suitable for efficient sequential access on air. We also build B^+-trees [3] for the one-dimensional points to facilitate point access on air. Finally, we convert these trees into linear sequences so that they can be broadcast on a wireless channel. On the client side, a novel search algorithm is designed to efficiently evaluate queries against the air indexes. The experimental results show that our indexing method outperforms the 3D R-tree based methods.

2. AIR INDEXING FOR LINKED DATA

2.1 Wireless Broadcast Model

In a wireless data broadcast system, generally there is a base station that pre-processes data before it broadcasts the data on the wireless channel. If mobile clients have registered an interest in some data on the server, they can listen to the wireless channel and download the data. The wireless channel can be shared by all mobile clients. In this way, the broadcast system could be able to serve an arbitrary number of mobile clients simultaneously.

In order for clients to efficiently locate data of interest, air indexing techniques are used to facilitate the searching of data on air. Air indexes are normally lightweight and concise summaries of the data to be broadcast. Based on air indexes, mobile clients within the communication range of the base station can evaluate their queries directly and then locate requested data on the wireless channel.

Similar to the existing work in data broadcast, we use *access latency* and *tuning time* as the primary performance metrics [7]. *Access latency* refers to the time elapsed between the moment when a query is formed and the client starts listening to the server to the moment when all requested data has been received. *Tuning time* refers to the period of time that a client has to stay active in order to complete a query.

2.2 Mapping between Triples and 3D Points

Existing light weight data summaries (e.g., [5, 9]) have been proven to be effective to index Linked Data. However, they are not suitable in a wireless broadcast system. In order to develop a new index structure for broadcasting Linked Data, similar to data summaries, we choose to use hash functions[1] to map RDF triples into numerical values. These numerical values can be regarded as *coordinates* in a 3D space. Specifically, given a hash function f, a triple (s, p, o) can be mapped into a 3D point $(f(s), f(p), f(o))$. We call such a point mapped from a triple a *data point* in order to differ it from other points in the 3D space. Using this approach, a set of RDF triples can be mapped into a set of 3D data points.

Basic Graph Patterns (BGPs) [9] are adopted as queries in our system. Similar to RDF triple mappings, a single BGP containing only one RDF triple pattern can be mapped into a point, a line, or a plane in a 3D space, or even the whole 3D space, depending on the number of variables in the triple pattern. The possible triple patterns in a BGP are: 1) (#s, #p, #o), 2) (?s, #p, #o), 3) (#s, ?p, #o), 4) (#s, #p, ?o), 5) (?s, ?p, #o), 6) (?s, #p, ?o), 7) (#s, ?p, ?o), and 8) (?s, ?p, ?o). Here, ? denotes a variable while #

<hr>

[1] There are many options of hash functions. For more details, please refer to [5, 9].

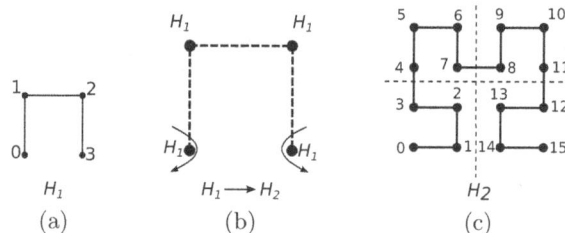

Figure 1: 2D Hilbert Curves of order 1 and 2. (a) H_1, (b) H_1 to H_2, (c) H_2

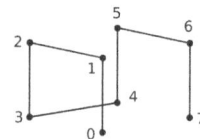

Figure 2: 3D Hilbert Curve of order 1

denotes a constant. Clearly, pattern 1 can be mapped into a 3D data point. Patterns 2 to 4 can be mapped into lines in the 3D space and patterns 5 to 7 can be mapped into planes. It should be noted that we do not consider pattern 8 in our work, as it will be mapped into the whole 3D space and require a traversal of all the data points in the whole 3D space, where air indexing is not required.

2.3 3D Hilbert Curve Index

A space-filling curve in d dimensions is a continuous, surjective mapping between one-dimensional space and d-dimensional space. A Hilbert curve is an example of a space-filling curve. It generally has good locality properties [6] and can efficiently support matching against BGPs with variables that can be mapped into lines or planes. Hence, the Hilbert curve is adopted as the foundation of our indexing method.

Mapping 3D points to one-dimensional points: To simplify our discussion, we use a 2D Hilbert curve to illustrate our ideas, which can then be generalized to 3D Hilbert curves. Figure 1 shows 2D Hilbert curves for order 1 and 2, i.e., H_1 and H_2, respectively. Note that, a k order Hilbert curve, denoted as H_k, passes all center points of 2^{kd} subdividing squares (or hypercubes) in a d-dimensional space. In Figure 1(a), each center point of a subdividing square in 2D space is assigned a *Hilbert value*, which can be regarded as a one-dimensional point. Note that, the mapping between center points and Hilbert values are bijective, which means for a given Hilbert curve, we can freely convert between center points and Hilbert values in constant time.

From Figure 1(b), we can see that high order Hilbert curves can be easily derived using transformation from low order Hilbert curves similar to the one shown in Figure 1(b). In order to derive H_2 from H_1, in Figure 1(b), the 2D space is divided into 2^d ($d = 2$ in this case) sub-regions, where each sub-region contains an H_1. After rotating the lower two H_1 curves, an H_2 Hilbert curve is derived (see Figure 1(c)). Since H_1 has 2^2 subdividing squares, H_2 has totally $2^{2 \times 2}$ subdividing squares.

Figure 2 presents an example of a 3D Hilbert curve of order 1. Higher order 3D Hilbert curves can be derived using a similar process described above. In order to accommodate a larger 3D data space, i.e., the hashing space for RDF triples, we need to utilize higher order 3D Hilbert curves. We can easily check that a k order 3D Hilbert curve can have up to $2^{3 \times k}$ data points. In other words, when mapping to a k order 3D Hilbert curve, all RDF triples will be mapped into at most $2^{3 \times k}$ data points (also center points of hypercubes) in a 3D space.

Indexing one-dimensional points on air: After mapping 3D points into one-dimensional points using 3D Hilbert curves, we can utilize B^+-trees to index one-dimensional points on a 3D Hilbert curve. An example is depicted in Figure 3. Each one-dimensional point in the leaf nodes contains a pointer to a real triple that will be broadcast on the wireless channel. Such B^+-trees can be serialized and broadcast on the linear wireless channel as air indexes for the Linked Data on air in the form of data packets. We adjust the fan-out of a B^+-tree according to the packet capacity of the wireless channel so that a complete node of a B^+-tree can fit in a packet. After downloading a part (e.g., a few packets) of an air index, mobile clients can then evaluate their queries (i.e., BGPs) against the partial index, determine which remaining index packets should be further retrieved, and finally compute the broadcast time of matched triples after all necessary index information has been acquired.

Evaluating queries against an air index: In the query evaluation process, one challenging issue is how to match a one-dimensional point against BGPs. As mentioned previously, BGPs could be mapped into a point, a line or a plane in a 3D space. In order to match BGPs with data points in the 3D space, we need to transform one-dimensional points in B^+-tree based air indexes into 3D points. We then examine whether such 3D points fall into the subspace defined by a BGP. If yes, RDF triples pointed to by these points match the BGP. Otherwise, they do not match.

Query evaluation example: We give an example of the query evaluation process in the following. Suppose a triple `(a, b, c)` can be hashed as `(112, 31, 92)` in a 3D space and its Hilbert value is 1137. Also suppose a mobile client issues a BGP `(a, b, ?o)`. This BGP can be converted into a 3D line `(112, 31, ?)`. After receiving Hilbert value 1137 from the air index, the mobile client firstly converts it back into a 3D point `(112, 31, 92)` and then it finds that this point falls on the 3D line defined by its BGP. Then the client knows the triple pointed to by Hilbert value 1137 is of its interest. As mentioned earlier, the conversion between a Hilbert value and a 3D point can be calculated in constant time given a Hilbert curve of order k (here, k is a constant).

Reducing search space: One issue needs to be addressed in the above query evaluation process: how to reduce the search space of Hilbert values indexed by B^+-trees, thereby leading to fewer index packets required to download for a query evaluation. Given an air index like the one shown in Figure 3, the root node has three child nodes. Based on the Hilbert values in the root node, we need to determine which child node would contain triples that may match a given BGP. We observe that each child node contains multiple Hilbert values and the range of these values can be easily computed from the root node. For example, the value ranges of the three child nodes are $[0, 8)$, $[8, 12)$ and $[12, h_{max}]$ (here h_{max} refers to the maximum Hilbert value of a Hilbert curve). For each value range, we have two bounding Hilbert values.

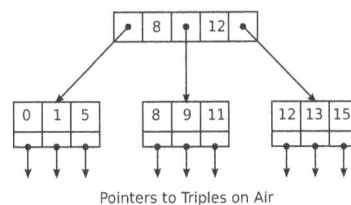

Figure 3: B^+-tree for some Points on Hilbert Curve

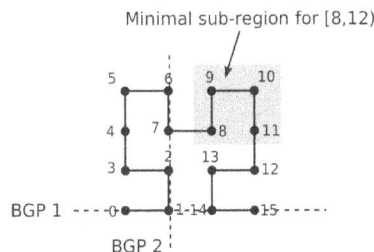

Figure 4: Minimal sub-region

To reduce the search space, we compute the minimal sub-region defined by a lower order Hilbert curve that covers the range defined by both bounding Hilbert values (see Figure 4, where two dash lines represent two BGPs). If such minimal sub-region intersects with sub-space (i.e., a line) defined by a BGP, the child node with the value range may contain triples that match that BGP. Otherwise, no triples in the child node will match that BGP. The example shown in Figure 4 illustrates a minimal sub-region for the value range $[8, 12)$. We can see that two BGPs that are represented as two dash lines have no intersections with it. So we can infer that no triples pointed to by the second child node (triples whose Hilbert values are 8, 9, and 11) in Figure 3 will match the two BGPs shown as two dash lines in Figure 4.

3. EXPERIMENTS

3.1 Experimental Setup

The data set used in our experiment is a subset of the current version of the English DBpedia[2]. It contains resources of type `dbpedia-owl:Event`. Each event is a triple of the form `<eventURI, rdf:type, dbpedia-owl:Event>`. An example of an event URI is `<http://dbpedia.org/resource/Battle_of_Brentford_(1642)>`. There are approximately 400,100 triples in the dataset.

As an initial work, we used simple BGPs as queries in the experiment and we leave extending our system to support complex BGPs or join queries as our future work. We randomly generated BGPs using the seven patterns mentioned in Section 2 based on our dataset. We generated 100,000 queries and reported the average experimental results.

We compared our B^+-tree HC (Hilbert Curve) indexes with traditional R-tree indexes which can be used to index 3D points directly. In the experiment, we varied the packet capacity of the wireless broadcast channel from 128 bytes to 2048 bytes. For each packet capacity setting, we assigned appropriate fan out and leaf order parameters for R-trees and B^+-trees to ensure that each packet was able to accommodate a complete node of a tree.

---

[2]`http://downloads.dbpedia.org/3.8/en/`

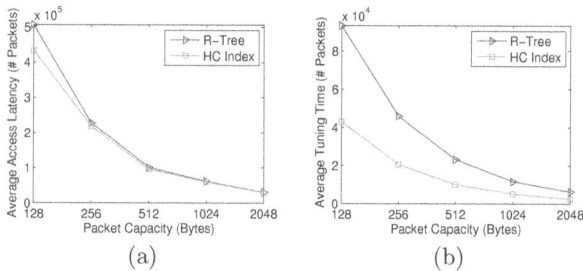

Figure 5: Access Latency and Tuning Time

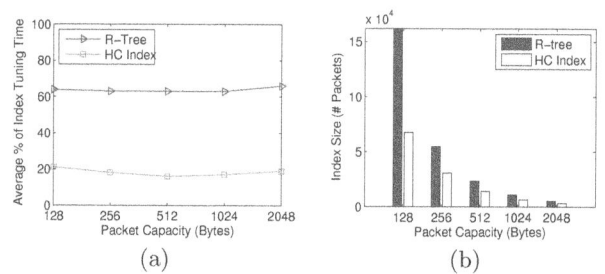

Figure 6: Index Tuning Time and Index Size

3.2 Performance Analysis

Figure 5 shows the results of average access latency and tuning time under different packet capacities. From Figure 5(a), we can see that the access latency for our Hilbert Curve (HC) based method is slightly better than the R-tree based method. The reason is that the index size is much smaller than the content (Linked Data stream) on air and hence the dominant factor of access latency is the content but not the index. Nevertheless, the size of HC based index is smaller (see also Figure 6(b)) than R-tree based method, resulting in lower access latency.

Figure 5(b) shows the comparisons of the tuning time. From the figure, we can clearly identify that HC based index outperforms R-tree based index. The reason for this is two-fold: firstly, by using our novel search algorithm, the searching space of the HC based index is smaller than the R-tree based index; secondly, the size of each index entry for the HC based index is smaller than the R-tree based index. This result confirms the effectiveness and efficiency of our search algorithm and HC based indexing technique.

The percentage of index tuning time is presented in Figure 6(a). Here, we define the *percentage of index tuning time* as the ratio between the index tuning time (caused by downloading necessary parts of the index on air) and the total tuning time (the sum of index tuning time and content tuning time). This metric is a good indicator for the effectiveness and efficiency of an index. The lower percentage we get, the better effectiveness we can achieve. Figure 6(a) shows that the HC-based index has a much lower percentage of index tuning time when compared with the R-tree based index. To be specific, the percentage of index tuning time of the HC-based index is below 20% under different packet capacities while that of the R-tree based index is above 60%.

The index sizes are compared in Figure 6(b). We can see that the number of packets required to accommodate the whole index for HC based index is only about half of that for R-tree based index. The main reason is that R-tree index has to store 3D points in its nodes while the HC based index only stores one-dimensional points.

4. CONCLUSIONS

In this paper, we have proposed an effective and efficient air indexing method for broadcasting Linked Data on air, which can be used in data sharing among a large number of mobile and smart objects in the era of Internet of Things. Our method is based on 3D Hilbert curve mappings. Firstly we map RDF triples into points in a 3D space and then adopt 3D Hilbert curve mappings to convert all the 3D points into one-dimensional points. We build B^+-trees upon these one-dimensional points and serialize these trees in order to accommodate them on the linear wireless channels. An efficient search algorithm has also been devised to facilitate query processing over the Linked Data on air. We have conducted experiments and compared our method with the traditional R-tree based spatial indexing method. Our method has shown better performance over the R-tree based method in various aspects, including access latency, tuning time, and index size.

In the future, we are going to extend our work to support join queries and to investigate the scalability of our method in terms of real-time construction of air indexes for broadcasting Linked Data streams with high stream rates, which we believe would be a challenging issue in the context of Internet of Things.

5. REFERENCES

[1] P. M. Barnaghi, W. Wang, C. A. Henson, and K. Taylor. Semantics for the Internet of Things: Early Progress and Back to the Future. *International Journal on Semantic Web Information Systems*, 8(1):1–21, 2012.

[2] S. Berchtold, D. A. Keim, and H.-P. Kriegel. The X-tree: An Index Structure for High-Dimensional Data. In *VLDB*, pages 28–39, Mumbai (Bombay), India, September 1996.

[3] D. Comer. The Ubiquitous B-Tree. *ACM Computing Surveys*, 11(2):121–137, 1979.

[4] A. Guttman. R-Trees: A Dynamic Index Structure for Spatial Searching. In *SIGMOD*, pages 47–57, Boston, USA, June 1984.

[5] A. Harth, K. Hose, M. Karnstedt, A. Polleres, K.-U. Sattler, and J. Umbrich. Data Summaries for On-Demand Queries over Linked Data. In *WWW*, pages 411–420, 2010.

[6] H. J. Haverkort. An Inventory of Three-dimensional Hilbert Space-filling Curves. *Computing Research Repository*, abs/1109.2323, 2011.

[7] T. Imielinski, S. Viswanathan, and B. R. Badrinath. Data on Air: Organization and Access. *IEEE Transactions on Knowledge and Data Engineering*, 9(3):353–372, 1997.

[8] Y. Qin, Q. Z. Sheng, N. J. G. Falkner, S. Dustdar, H. Wang, and A. V. Vasilakos. When Things Matter: A Data-Centric View of the Internet of Things. *CoRR*, abs/1407.2704, 2014.

[9] J. Umbrich, K. Hose, M. Karnstedt, A. Harth, and A. Polleres. Comparing Data Summaries for Processing Live Queries over Linked Data. *World Wide Web*, 14(5-6):495–544, 2011.

Towards Efficient Dissemination of Linked Data in the Internet of Things

Yongrui Qin*, Quan Z. Sheng*, Nickolas J.G. Falkner*, Ali Shemshadi*, Edward Curry†

*School of Computer Science
The University of Adelaide, Australia
{yongrui.qin,michael.sheng,nickolas.falkner,ali.shemshadi}
@adelaide.edu.au

†Insight
NUI Galway, Ireland
ed.curry@insight-centre.org

ABSTRACT

The Internet of Things (IoT) envisions smart objects collecting and sharing data at a global scale via the Internet. One challenging issue is how to disseminate data to relevant data consumers efficiently. In this paper, we leverage semantic technologies which can facilitate machine-to-machine communications, such as Linked Data, to build an efficient information dissemination system for semantic IoT. The system integrates Linked Data streams generated from various data collectors and disseminates matched data to relevant data consumers based on Basic Graph Patterns (BGPs) registered in the system by those consumers. To efficiently match BGPs against Linked Data streams, we introduce two types of matching, namely *semantic matching* and *pattern matching*, by considering whether the matching process supports semantic relatedness computation. Two new data structures, namely MVR-tree and TP-automata, are introduced to suit these types of matching respectively. Experiments show that an MVR-tree designed for semantic matching can achieve a twofold increase in throughput compared with the naive R-tree based method. TP-automata, as the first approach designed for pattern matching over Linked Data streams, also provides two to three orders of magnitude improvements on throughput compared with semantic matching approaches.

Categories and Subject Descriptors

H.3.4 [**Information Storage and Retrieval**]: Systems and Software—*Selective dissemination of information*

Keywords

Linked data, information dissemination, query index

1. INTRODUCTION

In the era of the Internet of Things (IoT) [9], it is envisioned that smart objects collect and share data at a global

scale via the Internet. In this context, semantic technologies such as Linked Data, which aim to facilitate machine-to-machine communications, play an increasingly important role [2]. Due to the large amount of data produced by various kinds of things, one challenging issue is how to efficiently disseminate data to relevant data consumers.

In this paper, we propose an efficient information dissemination system for semantic IoT by leveraging semantic technologies, such as Linked Data. Our system integrates Linked Data streams (in RDF format) generated from various data collectors. Data consumers can register their interest in the form of Basic Graph Patterns (BGPs) in the system. Based on these BGPs, the system disseminates matched Linked Data to relevant users. This work focuses on how to efficiently match a large number of BGPs against Linked Data streams.

Before introducing motivation, we identify three types of matching between Linked Data and BGPs as follows:

- *Match estimation* is typically used in source selection systems. It provides an estimation on how well a Linked Data source would match a given BGP. *Match estimation* may provide false negative and false positive match results. Recent work on data summaries on Linked Data [6] is an example of *match estimation*.

- *Semantic matching* aims to match semantically related RDF triples against BGPs. It may provide false positive match results but not false negative. Approximate event matching [7] applies *semantic matching*.

- *Pattern matching* means individual component matching between RDF triples and BGPs. It does not consider semantic relatedness between an RDF triple and a BGP. Similar to *semantic matching*, it may return false positive match results but not false negative. An example of *pattern matching* is recent work on stream reasoning [1].

In our Linked Data dissemination system, in order to disseminate high-quality information to data consumers (or subscribers), we only consider *semantic matching* and *pattern matching* as they will not return false negative match results. Or in other words, no matched triples will be missed.

Motivation. Recent work on data summaries on Linked Data [6] transforms RDF triples into numerical space. Then data summaries are built upon numerical data instead of strings as summarizing numbers is more efficient than summarizing strings. In order to transform triples into numbers, hash functions are applied on the individual components (s, p, o) of triples. Thus a derived triple of numbers can be considered as a 3D point. In this way, a set of RDF triples can be mapped into a set of points in 3D space. To facilitate query processing over data summaries, a spatial index named QTree [6], which is evolved from standard R-tree [5], is adopted as the basic index. Data summaries are designed mainly for indexing various Linked Data sources and used for identifying relevant sources for a given query.

However, data summaries are not suitable for our Linked Data dissemination system. Firstly, data summaries techniques, such as QTree, do not consider variables in the BGPs but only RDF triples with concrete strings. QTree only indexes points in a 3D space while our system is required to index points, lines or even planes in a 3D space, depending on the number of variables in BGPs. Further, since data summaries are concise and imprecise representations of data sources [6], they just provide *match estimation*. Hence, query evaluation on them would return false negative results, which is not allowed in our system.

Moreover, existing work on *pattern matching*, such as stream reasoning [1], does not support large scale query evaluation but focuses on evaluation of a single query over the streaming Linked Data. Therefore, the issue of supporting *pattern matching* over a large number of BGPs against Linked Data streams remains open.

In this paper, we introduce two techniques, namely Multi-Version R-tree (MVR-tree) and Triple Pattern automata (TP-automata), to index a large collection of BGPs, which can support *semantic matching* and *pattern matching* respectively. Experiments show that MVR-tree can achieve a twofold increase in throughput for *semantic matching* compared with the naive R-tree based method. Moreover, TP-automata, as the first approach designed for *pattern matching* between a large number of queries and Linked Data streams, can achieve up to three orders of magnitude improvements on throughput compared with *semantic matching* approaches.

2. LINKED DATA DISSEMINATION SYSTEM

System Overview. In our Linked Data dissemination system, when the user queries (BGPs) are registered, all queries will be transformed into spatial objects in a 3D space. Then a suitable index will be constructed for efficient evaluation between Linked Data streams and user queries. Before matching starts, RDF triples in the data streams will be mapped into data points in the same 3D space first. Then, these data points will be matched with BGPs represented as spatial objects in the constructed indexes. Finally, matched triples will be forwarded to their subscribers.

User Queries. Basic Graph Patterns (BGPs) [6] are adopted as user queries in our system. The possible triple patterns in a BGP are: 1) (#s, #p, #o), 2) (?s, #p, #o), 3) (#s, ?p, #o), 4) (#s, #p, ?o), 5) (?s, ?p, #o), 6) (?s, #p, ?o), 7) (#s, ?p, ?o), and 8) (?s, ?p, ?o). Note that, ? denotes a variable while # denotes a constant.

Similar to data summaries, we apply hash functions[1] to map these patterns into numerical values. These numerical values can be regarded as *coordinates* in a 3D space.

----

[1] There are many different hash functions. For more details, please refer to [6].

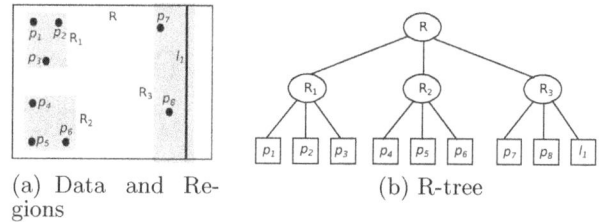

(a) Data and Regions
(b) R-tree

Figure 1: Two-dimensional R-tree example

Specifically, given a hash function f, a triple pattern (#s, #p, #o) can be mapped into a 3D point $(f(\#s), f(\#p), f(\#o))$. We call such a point mapped from a triple pattern a *data point* in order to differ it from other points in the 3D space. Using this approach, a set of triples or triple patterns without variables can be mapped into a set of 3D data points. To map triples with variables, the hash function f works in the following way: f will map a variable to the whole range of a coordinate axis. For example, pattern 2 (?s, #p, #o) will be mapped into $(x, f(\#p), f(\#o))$, which is a line in the 3D space. Triple patterns with more variables can be mapped in a similar way.

Clearly, pattern 1 can be mapped into a 3D data point. In order to match pattern 1 with a triple in the data stream, three coordinates of pattern 1's data point must match with those of the triple's data point altogether. Patterns 2 to 4 can be mapped into lines in the 3D space. To match a triple with patterns 2 to 4, only two coordinates have to be matched. Patterns 5 to 7 can be mapped into planes. Similarly, to match a triple with patterns 5 to 7, only one coordinate has to be matched. It should be noted that we do not consider to index pattern 8 in our work, as it will match all the triples in the Linked Data stream directly.

2.1 MVR-tree for Semantic Matching

Locality Sensitive Hashing (LSH) has been used to place similar documents into the same bucket of a hash table [8]. Similar technique can be used to hash RDF triples in our semantic matching.

Inspired by QTree [6], a naive solution to support semantic matching is to use R-Tree [5]. R-tree is a hierarchical structure and is used to index spatial objects. It consists of nodes representing regions in the data space. The region of a node always covers all the regions of its child nodes. The region of a node is also a Minimum Bounding Box (MBB). Leaf nodes store actual spatial objects. An 2D R-tree example is depicted in Figure 1. There are seven points and one line in Figure 1(a). These spatial objects are bounded by three regions, namely R_1, R_2 and R_3. These three regions are further bounded by region R. Figure 1(b) shows the R-tree structure for spatial objects in Figure 1(a). R-tree can support Nearest Neighbor (NN) searches efficiently [5] which in turn can support *semantic matching* efficiently after mapping BGPs into spatial objects in a 3D space.

Figure 1(a) shows that the region which contains a line usually occupies large space, such as region R_3 in the figure. Since regions that contain lines will occupy large space, if there are many lines in the space, the regions bounding these lines would overlap each other with high probability. If there are many overlapped regions in an R-tree, MBBs would overlap with each other with high probability and the R-tree performance would degrade greatly [5]. What is worse, there may be planes to bound, which further magnifies this problem. As a result, if we use R-tree to directly index spatial objects mapped from a set of BGPs with variables, the performance of R-tree would become an issue.

Based on this observation, we introduce Multi-Version R-tree (MVR-tree) to alleviate performance deterioration on R-tree. MVR-tree is an R-tree variant. As mentioned, BGPs can be mapped as points, lines, or planes in a 3D space, depending on the number variables they have. In MVR-tree, for BGPs mapped as points, we still use a 3D R-tree to index them because all three coordinates of them require to be matched. For BGPs mapped as lines, we use 2D R-trees to index them because only two coordinates require to be matched. Since there are three types of lines (in parallel with x coordinate, with y coordinate, or with z coordinate in the 3D space), we need to use three 2D-trees to index these three types of lines. For BGPs mapped as planes, we use one-dimensional R-trees to index them, which are B-trees, by definition [3]. Similar to indexing lines, we also need to use three B-trees to index the three types of planes.

To be more specific, in a MVR-tree, a 3D R-tree is used to index BGPs without variables (pattern (#s, #p, #o)), three 2D R-trees are used to index BGPs with only one variable (pattern (?s, #p, #o), (#s, ?p, #o), and (#s, #p, ?o)), and three B-trees are used to index BGPs with two variables (pattern (?s, ?p, #o), (?s, #p, ?o), and (#s, ?p, ?o)). We call describe these trees as versioned trees, which together form an MVR-tree index.

To evaluate an RDF triple with an MVR-tree, the system will need to check whether the data point mapped from the triple matches any points in at least one versioned tree of the MVR-tree. Since there only points in each versioned tree of the MVR-tree, the match process should be quite efficient.

Since R-tree can support NN queries efficiently, we can adapt its variant MVR-tree to support semantic matching where the most similar triples should be returned. Taking advantage of the LSH techniques, we can return NN query results as the most similar triples for a BGP query.

2.2 TP-automata for Pattern Matching

Automata techniques have been adopted to process XML data streams [4] They are mainly based on languages with SQL-like syntaxes, and relational database execution models adapted to process streaming data. In our system, to support *pattern matching*, we also apply automata to match each individual component of a triple with its counterparts of a BGP efficiently, which we call Triple Pattern automata (TP-automata).

Firstly, as mentioned, operating on numbers is more efficient than operating on strings. Similar to MVR-tree, we also map BGPs into spatial objects in 3D space. However, the difference is that we treat variables in a BGP as a universal match indicator, e.g. represented by "?". This indicator will be mapped into a fixed and unique numerical value but not the whole range of a specific coordinate axis. Such unique numerical values will be treated differently as well later in the triple evaluation process.

Figure 2 depicts the construction process of TP-automata. Firstly, user queries will be transformed into triple pattern state machines as shown in the middle of Figure 2. As can be seen from the figure, each triple state machine contains an initial state, two internal states, one final state and three

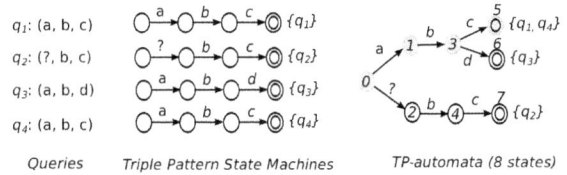

Figure 2: TP-automata

transitions. In the figure, the first circle of a state machine represents the initial state, the next two circles represent the two internal states and the doubled circle represents the final state. The three arrows associated with conditions are three transitions between different states. Similar to [4], these state machines can be combined into one machine by exploiting shared common states with same transitions. The combined machine, TP-automata, is shown on the right of Figure 2. The shaded circles represent combined states.

To perform *pattern matching* over TP-automata, triples in the Linked Data stream will be firstly mapped into 3D points. For example, suppose a triple (s, p, o) is mapped into a 3D point (a, b, c). The system will match it against TP-automata in the following process. It firstly checks the initial state of TP-automata and looks for state transitions with condition a or condition ?. Following the state transitions, state 1 and state 2 become the current active states at the same time. It then looks for state transitions with condition b or ? from state 1 and state 2. Following the transitions, state 3 and state 4 become active states. Finally, following transitions with condition c or ? from state 3 and state 4, two final states, state 5 and state 7, are reached. By checking both final states, the system returns $\{q_1, q_2, q_4\}$ as the matching results. The match process stops if and only all current active states are final states or states with no satisfied transition.

3. EXPERIMENTS

3.1 Experimental Setup

The data set used in our experiment is a subset of the current version of the English DBpedia[2]. It contains resources of type dbpedia-owl:Event. Each event is a triple in the form <eventURI, rdf:type, dbpedia-owl:Event>. An example of an event URI is <http://dbpedia.org/resource/Battle_of_Brentford_(1642)>. There are approximately 400,100 triples in the dataset.

As an initial work, we used simple BGPs as queries in the experiment and we leave extending our system to support complex BGPs or join queries as our future work. We randomly generated BGPs using the seven patterns mentioned in Section 2 based on our dataset.

We evaluated the performance of our methods in terms of Average Construction Time (in milliseconds) of the indexes and Average Throughput (in number of triples per second). We performed experiments in two scenarios. One was for *semantic matching* by comparing MVR-tree and R-tree methods, and the other was for *pattern matching* by comparing TP-automata and MVR-tree methods because TP-automata is the first method to evaluate Linked Data streams over a large number of user queries simultaneously.

[2]http://downloads.dbpedia.org/3.8/en/

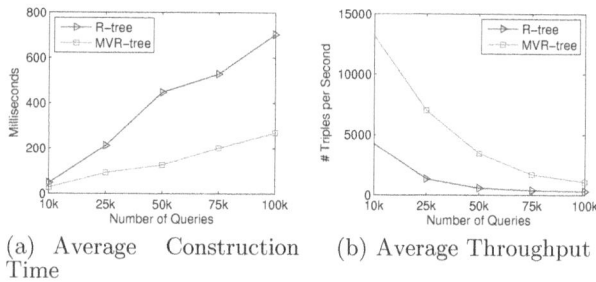

(a) Average Construction Time (b) Average Throughput

Figure 3: Performance on Semantic Matching

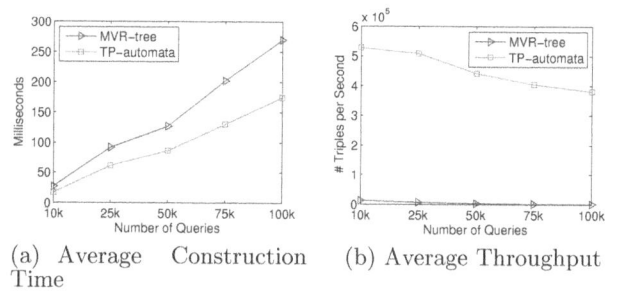

(a) Average Construction Time (b) Average Throughput

Figure 4: Performance on Pattern Matching

3.2 Experimental Results

3.2.1 Semantic Matching

Figure 3 presents performance on *semantic matching* by comparing R-tree and MVR-tree. Average construction time is depicted in Figure 3(a). We can see that construction time of both indexes increases linearly as the number of queries grows. Constructing MVR-tree indexes takes less time than R-tree. The reason for this is that there are multiple versioned trees in an MVR-tree index and each versioned tree is smaller than R-tree. When a new BGP is inserted into MVR-tree, only one versioned tree will be updated. Since versioned trees are smaller compared with R-tree, the update process in MVR-tree is more efficient.

Figure 3(b) shows the throughput results of R-tree and MVR-tree. It is evident that MVR-tree at least three times of R-tree's throughput under all query number settings. The root cause is that BGPs with variables are large spatial objects in R-tree leading to deteriorative throughput performance on R-tree. On the other hand, as described in Section 2, MVR-tree only has points as spatial objects in all its versioned trees. Hence NN searches on each versioned tree are quite efficient.

3.2.2 Pattern Matching

The performance of *pattern matching* on MVR-tree and TP-automata is presented in Figure 4. Firstly, average construction time is compared in Figure 4(a). TP-automata can be constructed faster than MVR-tree because TP-automata does not need to split nodes while MVR-tree would need to split some big nodes and adjust node levels and relationships during the construction process.

Throughput performance of *pattern matching* is presented in Figure 4(b). It shows very large differences between MVR-tree and TP-automata. TP-automata shows two to three orders of magnitude better throughput performance compared with MVR-tree. The root cause is that MVR-tree is designed for *semantic matching* in a hashing space (e.g., handling NN queries) while TP-automata is designed for *pattern matching*. To perform a *pattern matching* on MVR-tree is actually equivalent to processing an NN query while TP-automata just performs $O(1)$ lookups at each state transition. Hence, the TP-automata approach shows superior performance over the MVR-tree approach.

4. CONCLUSIONS

In this paper, we have leveraged semantic technologies, such as Linked Data, to build an efficient information dis-semination system for semantic IoT. We have identified three types of match, which are *match estimation, semantic matching*, and *pattern matching*, to establish the basic requirements for building a Linked Data dissemination system. In order to efficiently match a large number of BGPs against Linked Data streams, we have proposed two index schemes, namely MVR-tree and TP-automata. MVR-tree is a Multi-Version R-tree designed for efficiently processing *semantic matching* while TP-automata is an automata based method designed for efficient *pattern matching*. Experiments show that our methods outperform existing indexing methods that are derived from R-tree. Specifically, in *semantic matching*, MVR-tree achieves a twofold increase in throughput compared with the traditional R-tree. In *pattern matching* the TP-automata approach outperforms the MVR-tree approach by up to three orders of magnitude in terms of throughput.

5. REFERENCES

[1] D. Anicic, P. Fodor, S. Rudolph, and N. Stojanovic. EP-SPARQL: A Unified Language for Event Processing and Stream Reasoning. In *WWW*, pages 635–644, 2011.

[2] P. M. Barnaghi, W. Wang, C. A. Henson, and K. Taylor. Semantics for the Internet of Things: Early Progress and Back to the Future. *Int. J. Semantic Web Inf. Syst.*, 8(1):1–21, 2012.

[3] D. Comer. The ubiquitous b-tree. *ACM Comput. Surv.*, 11(2):121–137, 1979.

[4] Y. Diao, M. Altinel, M. J. Franklin, H. Zhang, and P. M. Fischer. Path Sharing and Predicate Evaluation for High-Performance XML Filtering. *ACM Trans. Database Syst.*, 28(4):467–516, 2003.

[5] A. Guttman. R-Trees: A Dynamic Index Structure for Spatial Searching. In *SIGMOD*, pages 47–57, 1984.

[6] A. Harth, K. Hose, M. Karnstedt, A. Polleres, K.-U. Sattler, and J. Umbrich. Data Summaries for On-Demand Queries over Linked Data. In *WWW*, pages 411–420, 2010.

[7] S. Hasan and E. Curry. Approximate Semantic Matching of Events for the Internet of Things. *ACM Trans. Internet Techn.*, 14(1):2, 2014.

[8] S. Petrovic, M. Osborne, and V. Lavrenko. Streaming First Story Detection with application to Twitter. In *HLT-NAACL*, pages 181–189, 2010.

[9] Y. Qin, Q. Z. Sheng, N. J. G. Falkner, S. Dustdar, H. Wang, and A. V. Vasilakos. When Things Matter: A Data-Centric View of the Internet of Things. *CoRR*, abs/1407.2704, 2014.

Tell Me What You Want and I Will Tell Others Where You Have Been

Anthony Quattrone, Elham Naghizade, Lars Kulik, Egemen Tanin
The University of Melbourne
{anthony.quattrone,enaghi,lkulik,etanin}@unimelb.edu.au

ABSTRACT

Trajectory data does not only show the location of users over a period of time, but also reveals a high level of detail regarding their lifestyle, preferences and habits. Hence, it is highly susceptible to privacy concerns. Trajectory privacy has become a key research topic when sharing/exchanging trajectory datasets. Most existing studies focus on protecting trajectory data through obfuscating, anonymising or perturbing the data with the aim to maximize user privacy. Although such approaches appear plausible, our work suggests that precise trajectory information can be inferred even from other sources of data. We consider the case in which a location service provider only shares POI query results of users with third parties instead of exchanging users' raw trajectory data to preserve privacy. We develop an inference algorithm and show that it can effectively approximate original trajectories using solely the POI query results.

Categories and Subject Descriptors

I.5 [**Pattern Recognition**]: Models; H.2.8 [**Database Applications**]: Data Mining

Keywords

Trajectory privacy; inference attacks

1. INTRODUCTION

As smartphones become ubiquitous tools of our everyday life, the growth of mobile applications has led to the generation and storage of massive amounts of location data. This data may be shared in social networks or exchanged among companies. Many applications, e.g., traffic management, urban management and geomarketing, gain substantial benefit through mining such sources of trajectory data. However, sharing this data in a raw format with third parties may incur serious privacy threats. Particularly, if inappropriately protected, such data may turn into powerful means of privacy invasions [3, 13, 19] such as location-based spams, physical threats, or inference attacks [7]. Findings of a recent study indicates that a large number of Location Based Service (LBS) users

are concerned about their privacy, which places a great impediment to sharing trajectory data and the growth of LBSs in general.

Various approaches in the literature focus on preserving privacy prior to publishing/sharing trajectory data [4, 6, 9, 17, 18]. The authors in [1, 15] propose publishing a *k-anonymous* trajectory dataset to make a user indistinguishable from $k-1$ other users [16]. Other studies adopt cloaking/obfuscation techniques to coarsen the spatial and/or temporal features of a trajectory [8] before publishing it. The authors in [11] propose an approach that adds dummy trajectories to keep the data private.

To motivate our work we consider the case of an LBS provider who sanitises a dataset by omitting all sensitive attributes from the dataset [5]. In other words, instead of anonymizing or obfuscating trajectory data, the LBS provider removes all GPS tracks of its users along with their identity, presuming this will provide maximum privacy. This means that only the *results* of user issued queries, which is generated and *owned* by the Location Service Provider (LSP), remain in the database when sharing it.

To identify the risks of such a plausibly bullet-proof practice, we consider a scenario where users continuously request the closest POIs to their position. For instance, a user issues a query like "Where is the nearest gas station to my path?" or "Send me the closest Italian restaurant?". If detailed GPS tracks are removed from the database, the LBS provider may lead others to believe that it is safe to exchange the POI query results – a set of POIs ordered based on querying time.

In order to demonstrate the vulnerability of sharing LSP query results with a third party, we develop an algorithm to perform an indirect inference attack on query results. The algorithm infers individuals' trajectories using the response of LSP to the requested POIs. The trajectory reconstruction is performed without using GPS tracks captured by the LSP but instead, the requested POIs sequence. As background knowledge we assume the availability of road types, and either their *edge centrality* or *edge frequency*, and *maximum velocity bound*, and basic transportation information about the area.

To the best of our knowledge, our work is the first to attack trajectory privacy without directly using trajectory information (either fine-grained or coarse-grained). The accuracy of our approach suggests that indirectly inferred paths are sufficiently precise to raise serious privacy concerns. By demonstrating what indirect trajectory inference attacks can achieve, we show that there is an urgent need to address the privacy implications of LBSs when exchanging trajectory datasets even when the provider omits the sensitive location data.

2. RELATED WORK

Generally, analysing data in order to gain knowledge about a subject in an adversarial manner is known as an "inference attack" [12]. A key work to highlight the potential of location data in predicting users' movement behavior was given in [2]. Ashbrook et al. have used GPS data of mobile users to determine significant places being visited by them [2]. To underline the risks of leaked location data [12] used real GPS data of 172 subjects and found each person's home location with a median error of about 60 meters. Finally, [12] identified people based on their pseudonymous location tracks using simple algorithms and a free Web service. In contrast, our algorithm can estimate a user's trajectory without using the GPS tracks stored by the LSP.

In another study, [10] succeeded at reconstructing an unknown trajectory using its distance to a few fixed trajectories. In order to achieve this, the authors have introduced speed limit and known trajectories as a background knowledge used by an adversary. Similarly, assuming it is possible to observe a user's movement behaviour in public places, or even inferring a couple of her visited spots using social networks, weblogs and etc. [14] used some snapshots of a user's trajectory as adversary's background knowledge. [14] proves that this "general world knowledge" can breach user's privacy with a high probability regardless of how much attempt is being taken to anonymize or cloak her location data. These two works clearly show the potential risks stemming from combining the available background knowledge along with the mutual distances released for analytical purposes.

3. PROBLEM DEFINITION

3.1 Closest POIs Database

POI queries are a common applications of LBSs. An LBS user sends her current location accompanied with a query asking for her closest points of interest, e.g., the closest gas station, Italian restaurant, etc., and the LSP returns a set of points as query result. The query database records are in the form of $(ID, \mathscr{P}_{\mathscr{T}})$, where ID determines a user. $\mathscr{P}_{\mathscr{T}}$ is the result of successive POI queries along the user's trip. In other words, $\mathscr{P}_{\mathscr{T}} = \{p_1, p_2, ..., p_n\}$ where each p_i represents a the closest point of interest for the i_{th} query. Note that ID is not necessarily a user's actual identity, but rather a unique identifier such as a pseudonym.

3.2 Adversary Model

An LSP may remove both user identity and location information as the sensitive attributes from the query database, presuming this would guarantee the user's privacy. This supposedly anonymised database is then shared with third parties. We suppose that an adversary is any third party with whom this query database is shared. In addition to the closest POIs database, we assume that the adversary has one of the following two types of background knowledge about a transportation network:

Edge Centrality: The adversary may consider each street as an edge in a graph and assume that the more central an edge is, i.e., how frequent an edge occurs in a set of candidate paths, the more likely it is that a user travels along it. Hence, edge centrality can be modelled introducing a weighting function. Generally, main roads are more likely to receive higher weights.

Edge Frequency: The adversary may have access to the trips users have taken in the past. In this model, we assume that the adversary assigns a higher weight to more frequently travelled edges. The count for a specific edge is incremented for every trip that it could be part of to account for the GPS error. In addition, we assume that an attacker also has the following information:

Maximum Velocity Bound: The adversary may also assume that there is a maximum velocity with which a user can travel between two subsequent time stamps. The velocity of a user at a given time can be estimated based on the maximum speed limit of a road.

3.3 Attack Success

GPS points do not uniquely identify the roads a user has taken, so the actual trip is generally not known. Thus, conventional trajectory similarity measures such as the Hausdorrf distance and DTW are not suitable to assess the success of our algorithm. Take Figure 1a as an example, where the GPS logs do not overlap with the actual path due to the measurement error. Using linear interpolation between GPS points (the dashed line connecting points) does not provide a robust means of inferring the original path, and as can be seen in Figure 1a, this interpolation may barely overlap with the underlying road network. Even map matching cannot resolve such a situation because a GPS point cannot be uniquely mapped to a single edge.

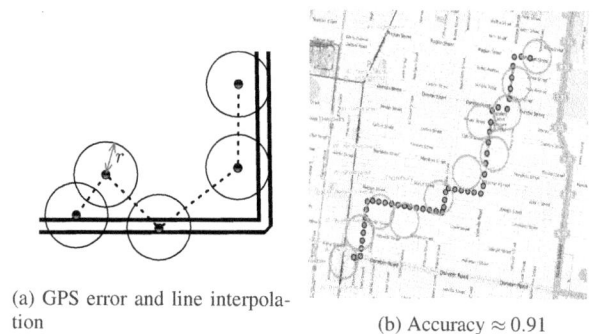

(a) GPS error and line interpolation

(b) Accuracy ≈ 0.91

Figure 1: Proximity circles.

To address this issue, we determine the closeness of an inferred path to the original one through proximity circles. We draw circles with r radius around the location of each GPS point (Figure 1a) and estimate the attack success based on the circles. More specifically, the overlapping percentage of the inferred path within r meters to the original path determines the success of the inference attack. This is measured by the number of proximity circles that are *visited* by the inferred path segments divided by the total number of circles.

Figure 1b shows the example of an inferred path as well as the proximity circles representing the original GPS logs. The inference accuracy is measured using the above equation and is 0.91. This metric is useful in evaluating how well the algorithm works in identifying the band a user is travelling along.

4. INDIRECT TRAJECTORY INFERENCE ALGORITHM

Our proposed inference algorithm utilizes the location of query results to generate a Voronoi diagram, which for a given set of points, $p_i \in \mathscr{P}$, divides the space into a number of cells (regions) such that all the points in any cell, c_i, are closer to the corresponding p_i than to any other p. Voronoi diagrams are widely applied in nearest POIs problems. For the set $\mathscr{P}_T$, we generate a Voronoi diagram V, and retrieve a set of *candidate paths* that travel from one Voronoi region to the next. However, since Voronoi cells can be quite large in many areas, the number of these candidate paths is not restrictive enough to reconstruct a unique trajectory and needs to be further reduced. Therefore, maximum velocity bound and edge centrality have been employed in this work to infer the most likely path that was taken by the users.

4.1 Indirect Path Generation

To generate our initial paths, we propose an incremental search algorithm that iterates through each pair of points. On the first iteration, the Voronoi edge between the first and second point is determined and every path segment that intersects with the Voronoi edge is retrieved. This is illustrated on the left of Figure 2. All streets that intersect the Voronoi edge between $p1$ and $p2$ are retrieved. The initial retrieved path segments are considered as the starting path segments for the candidate path(s). The initial segments are

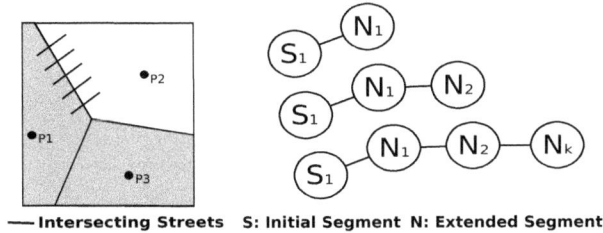

—Intersecting Streets   S: Initial Segment   N: Extended Segment

Figure 2: Generation and extension of initial segments.

then passed to a function which retrieves all the connected path segments to the initial one and add them to the respective candidate path (Figure 2). Once a set of paths is generated, the last path segment of each path is checked to ensure that it is in the destination Voronoi cell, otherwise the entire candidate path is discarded.

In addition, assuming a maximum velocity bound, max_v, we can compute the maximum distance, d, that a user could have travelled between two consecutive timestamps. Therefore, the length of the path is checked and only if its difference with d is less than a threshold, δ, it is added to the set of candidate paths. Since the beginning of a path segment is not necessarily the start point of the trajectory, we assume the generated path may be slightly longer than d, i.e., δ longer.

4.2 Candidate Path Selection

To select a single path from the set of generated candidate paths we derived a weighting function to rank the paths based on edge centrality, and then select the top ranked candidate path as the path representing the user's trajectory.

The weighting function counts the frequency of path segment occurrence in each candidate path and stores this value in a hashtable. The weight for each candidate path is calculated by the summation of each path segment length divided by the length of the whole candidate path which is then multiplied by the frequency value of each path segment stored in the hashtable divided by the total number of candidate paths.

$$w_{path} = \sum_{i=0}^{n} \frac{pathSegmentFreq_i}{n} \times \frac{pathSegmentLength_i}{totalLength_i} \quad (1)$$

The weighting function returns the path that contains the greatest overlap with other paths in the candidate path set. Therefore, edges that are more commonly used in a set of candidate paths are favoured over edges that are not. Provided users take fairly direct routes to their destination, this weighting function works well.

5. EXPERIMENTS

5.1 Dataset

In our work we employ the GeoLife trajectory dataset[1] to evaluate the performance, i.e., accuracy, of our inference approach. The

GeoLife dataset consists of more than 17,000 trajectories that have been collected by 182 individuals over three years. We focused on a smaller part of the city of Beijing and retrieved those trajectories that fully reside inside this part. In total we ran our inference algorithm on 279 routes.

5.2 Implementation

We generate random POIs in the city of Beijing and stored them in a database as our $\mathscr{P}_T$. These POIs are generated uniformly inside the boundary of Beijing and they are then mapped to their closest road segment. In order to evaluate the performance of our inference algorithm for different scenarios, we create four POI batches of 400, 800, 1600 and 3200 points to reflect sparse and dense areas. For example, 1600 POIs equate to 4 POIs per square kilometer.

In the road network, there are many path combinations a user can travel along to get to a destination. This leads to a large search space and an inefficient search process. To reduce the search complexity, we employ a pruning method that discards any combinations that terminates at the same road while expanding paths between Voronoi cells. Moreover, due to the geometric nature of Voronoi diagrams, individual Voronoi cells can become quite small and may create a case where some paths overshoot the cell and lead to zero candidate paths. In order to compensate for this case, the algorithm allows paths to continue to expand even if they did not terminate in the current Voronoi cell. However a path is finally removed if it does not end in the next Voronoi cell in the next iteration. In our

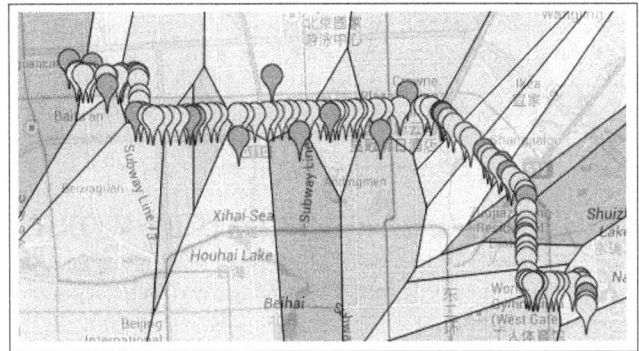

Figure 3: A sample Voronoi diagram.

implementation we use the OpenStreetMap[2] data to generate the road network graph. A web interface is also constructed to visually view the data using PHP, Javascript and the Google Maps API. Javascript is used to implement the trajectory inference algorithm and an OpenStack cloud computing environment is utilised to run the inference algorithm. Moreover, the Bower-Watson algorithm is employed to compute the Voronoi diagrams. An example GeoLife path is also illustrated in Figure 3, where the purple (darker) flags illustrate POIs along the path and their respective Voronoi cells. The green (lighter) flags show the original GPS logs.

5.3 Experimental Results

We measure the accuracy of our inference algorithm as the number of proximity circles that are visited by the inferred path divided by the total number of circles (Section 3.3). To estimate the inference accuracy of our approach, we consider varying radii, r, in meter to generate proximity circles, where $r \in \{10, 50, 100, 250, 500\}$. Table 2 shows the performance of our inference algorithm for varying POI densities. Although the overall accuracy is low for very

---

[1] www.research.microsoft.com/en-us/projects/geolife

[2] www.openstreetmap.org

POI	$r = 50$m	$r = 100$m	$r = 250$m	$r = 500$m
400	27.73	39.10	51.83	64.74
800	35.10	47.97	61.31	73.76
1600	39.00	53.90	69.63	80.84
3200	36.32	49.74	64.38	75.37

Table 1: Experimental results using edge centrality.

POI	$r = 50$m	$r = 100$m	$r = 250$m	$r = 500$m
400	32.15	44.52	58.09	71.31
800	38.03	51.93	65.85	77.79
1600	41.07	56.44	71.62	81.40
3200	37.97	52.45	67.70	77.97

Table 2: Experimental results using edge frequency.

small radius of 10 meters, our results show that for more realistic buffers and higher densities our approach is successful in accurately estimating a user trajectory and can achieve an average accuracy level beyond 80%. This shows with an increase in POI density and for urban areas with higher POI densities such as city centers, the inferred paths get closer to the original paths incurring higher privacy risks for a user.

In order to understand if access to the trip patterns of users can increase an attacker's ability to infer a user's original path, we ran experiments using edge frequency instead of edge centrality. The edge frequency (see Section 3.2) is computed on the basis of actually travelled trips. Our experiments show small gains in terms of accuracy but also demonstrate that this additional knowledge does not significantly improve an attacker's ability to infer a user's path. Our findings show that in either case the ability of an attacker to infer a user's path based on POI information is high.

6. CONCLUSIONS AND FUTURE WORK

In this paper, we presented an algorithm that only employs a set of POIs to indirectly infer a user's trajectory. Our results suggest that even coarse location information allows us to approximate a user's trajectory within dense urban areas with high accuracy. Therefore, exchanging query results of LBS users instead of their tracks does not offer adequate privacy protection.

While our inference attacks are effective in areas with high POI densities, there are still a number of directions that are likely to make the overall inference strategy more effective. We assume in our work that for every request there is only the closest POI available, however, an LSP usually provides users with several POIs for a single request. This information could be encoded as a higher-order Voronoi diagram that leads to smaller cells and thus should enable a more refined attack strategy.

In our work we have used positive information, i.e., information directly shared by a location service provider. However, another location service provider (or adversary) could also have the information about all the POIs that were not revealed because they were not among the closest POIs. Since the overall number of POIs is much larger than the number of POIs returned as a query result, the underlying Voronoi diagram may result in smaller cells, which in turn should improve the accuracy of an inference attack algorithm. We are currently investigating these strategies.

7. REFERENCES

[1] O. Abul, F. Bonchi, and M. Nanni. Never walk alone: Uncertainty for anonymity in moving objects databases. In *ICDE*, pages 376–385, 2008.

[2] D. Ashbrook and T. Starner. Using GPS to learn significant locations and predict movement across multiple users. *PerComp*, 7(5):275–286, 2003.

[3] R. Becker, R. Cáceres, K. Hanson, S. Isaacman, J. M. Loh, M. Martonosi, J. Rowland, S. Urbanek, A. Varshavsky, and C. Volinsky. Human mobility characterization from cellular network data. *Communications of the ACM*, 56(1):74–82, 2013.

[4] A. Beresford and F. Stajano. Location privacy in pervasive computing. *IEEE Pervasive Computing*, 2(1):46–55, 2003.

[5] J. Brickell and V. Shmatikov. The cost of privacy: Destruction of data-mining utility in anonymized data publishing. In *SIGKDD*, pages 70–78, New York, NY, USA, 2008.

[6] M. L. Damiani, E. Bertino, and C. Silvestri. Protecting location privacy against spatial inferences: the probe approach. In *ACM SPRINGL*, pages 32 – 41, 2009.

[7] M. Duckham and L. Kulik. A formal model of obfuscation and negotiation for location privacy. In H.-W. Gellersen, R. Want, and A. Schmidt, editors, *PerComp*, volume 3468, pages 152–170. 2005.

[8] M. Gruteser and D. Grunwald. Anonymous usage of location-based services through spatial and temporal cloaking. In *MobiSys*, pages 31 – 42, 2003.

[9] T. Hashem and L. Kulik. Don't trust anyone: Privacy protection for location-based services. *Pervasive and Mobile Computing*, 7(1):44 – 59, 2011.

[10] E. Kaplan, T. B. Pedersen, E. Savas, and Y. Saygin. Discovering private trajectories using background information. *Data and Knowledge Engineering*, 69(7):723 – 736, 2010.

[11] H. Kido, Y. Yanagisawa, and T. Satoh. An anonymous communication technique using dummies for location-based services. In *ICPS*, pages 88–97, 2005.

[12] J. Krumm. Inference attacks on location tracks. In *PerComp*, pages 127–143. 2007.

[13] M. Lin, W.-J. Hsu, and Z. Q. Lee. Predictability of individuals' mobility with high-resolution positioning data. In *UbiComp*, pages 381–390, 2012.

[14] C. Y. Ma, D. K. Yau, N. K. Yip, and N. S. Rao. Privacy vulnerability of published anonymous mobility traces. In *MobiCom*, pages 185 – 196, 2010.

[15] M. E. Nergiz, M. Atzori, and Y. Saygin. Towards trajectory anonymization: a generalization-based approach. In *ACM SPRINGL*, pages 52 – 61, 2008.

[16] L. Sweeney. K-anonymity: A model for protecting privacy. *International Journal of Uncertainty, Fuzziness and Knowledge-Based Systems*, 10(05):557–570, 2002.

[17] M. Terrovitis and N. Mamoulis. Privacy preservation in the publication of trajectories. In *MDM*, pages 65 – 72, 2008.

[18] M. Wernke, F. Durr, and K. Rothermel. Pshare: Position sharing for location privacy based on multi-secret sharing. In *PerCom*, pages 153–161, 2012.

[19] H. Zang and J. Bolot. Anonymization of location data does not work: A large-scale measurement study. In *MobiCom*, pages 145–156, 2011.

Forest-Based Dynamic Sorted Neighborhood Indexing for Real-Time Entity Resolution *

Banda Ramadan and Peter Christen
Research School of Computer Science, College of Engineering and Computer Science,
The Australian National University, Canberra ACT 0200, Australia
{banda.ramadan, peter.christen}@anu.edu.au

ABSTRACT

Real-time entity resolution (ER) is the process of matching a query record in sub-second time with records in a database that represent the same real-world entity. To facilitate real-time matching on large databases, appropriate indexing approaches are required to reduce the search space. Most available indexing techniques are based on batch algorithms that work only with static databases and are not suitable for real-time ER. In this paper, we propose a forest-based sorted neighborhood index that uses multiple index trees with different sorting keys to facilitate real-time ER for read-most databases. Our technique aims to reduce the effect of errors and variations in attribute values on matching quality by building several distinct index trees. We conduct an experimental evaluation on two large real-world data sets, and multiple synthetic data sets with various data corruption rates. The results show that our approach is scalable to large databases and that using multiple trees gives a noticeable improvement on matching quality with only a small increase in query time. Our approach also achieves over one order of magnitude faster indexing and querying times, as well as higher matching accuracy, compared to another recently proposed real-time ER technique.

Categories and Subject Descriptors

H.2.8 [**Database management**]: Database Applications—*Data mining*; H.2.4 [**Database management**]: Systems—*Textual databases*

General Terms

Algorithms, Experimentation

Keywords

Dynamic indexing; braided tree; real-time matching; record linkage; data matching.

*Funded by the Australian Research Council, Veda, and Funnelback Pty. Ltd., under Linkage Project LP100200079.

1. INTRODUCTION

Massive amounts of data are being collected by many business and government organizations. Given that many of these organizations rely on up-to-date information for their decision making processes, the quality of the collected data has a direct impact on the quality of the produced outcomes [2]. Data cleaning is generally employed to improve data quality. One important practice in data cleaning is entity resolution (ER), the task of matching all records that refer to the same real-world entity. An entity can be a person, a consumer product, or a business. ER is challenging because databases usually do not contain unique entity identifiers. Therefore, identifying attribute values (such as names and addresses) need to be used for matching, which requires approximate string matching techniques [2].

As services are being moved online, organizations increasingly require to perform real-time ER (with sub-second response times) on query records that need to be matched with existing entity databases [4]. However, most current ER techniques are batch algorithms that compare and resolve all records in one or more database(s) rather than resolving those relating to a single query record. There is a need for new techniques that support ER for large read-most databases that can resolve streams of query records in real-time. A major aspect of achieving this goal is to develop indexing techniques that allow updates and facilitate real-time matching by generating a small number of high-quality candidate records. In the context of our work, we define *read-most* as the situation where queries are inserted into the index and database, and where the majority of queries only requires a minor update of the index data structure, as will be described in Section 3.

Contributions: We propose an index that uses multiple trees with different sorting keys (described below) that can be used for real-time ER for read-most databases. We then conduct an experimental evaluation on several large data sets and we compare our approach with an alternative real-time ER indexing approach recently proposed [8]. We investigate the scalability of our approach, and the effect of using different numbers of trees with different sorting keys on both matching quality and query time.

2. RELATED WORK

The ER process consists of several steps [2]: data preprocessing, indexing, record pair comparison, record pair classification (into matches and non-matches), and evaluation with regard to matching accuracy and completeness. This paper is mostly concerned with the indexing step.

ID	FName	SName	Postcode
r1	percy	smith	10007
r2	paul	smith	02120
r3	robin	stevens	80202
r4	pedro	smith	90005
r5	abby	bond	10001
r6	sally	taylor	90002
r7	peter	smith	90012
r8	sally	taylor	98168
r9	pedro	smith	02121
r10	peter	smith	90002

The sorting key values (SKV) are a concatenation of FName and SName values.

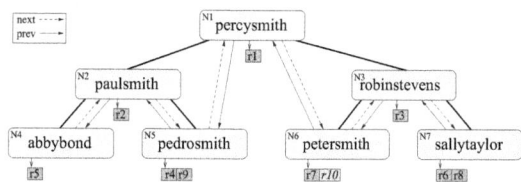

Figure 1: The table shows a small example data set, with record $r10$ being a query record. The figure represents one tree in the F-DySNI built from this data set after inserting the query record.

Standard blocking and the sorted neighborhood method (SNM) indexing techniques are commonly used in the ER process. Standard blocking [2] is based on inserting records into blocks according to a *blocking key* criterion and only comparing records that are in the same block. The SNM [5] arranges all records in the database(s) to be matched into a sorted array using a *sorting key* criterion. Then a fixed-size window is moved over the sorted records, comparing only those records that are within the sliding window at any one time. Both blocking and sorting keys are usually based on one or a concatenation of attribute values.

Other indexing techniques developed for ER include q-gram indexing, suffix array indexing, canopy clustering, and mapping-based indexing [2]. However, all these techniques are aimed at batch processing of static databases and not suitable for real-time ER.

Only limited research has so far concentrated on real-time ER. A first query-time ER approach was proposed based on collective clustering [1]. An average query time of 31.28 sec was reported, which makes this approach not suitable for real-time ER. Ioannou et al. [6] proposed an approach based on using links between the entities in a probabilistic database to resolve these entities. This approach works with dynamic databases and can be used for real-time ER.

Christen et al. [3] proposed a similarity-aware indexing technique where similarities between attribute values are pre-calculated when the index is built. Although this index facilitates real-time ER it is only applicable for static databases. Ramadan et al. [8] extended this index to work with dynamic data. The authors stated that the growing size of the index does not affect the average record insertion and query times, which were around 0.1 ms and 10 ms, respectively, on a data set of 2.5 million records. While this indexing technique is based on the idea of standard blocking [2], we propose a novel dynamic real-time indexing approach that is based on the SNM [5, 11].

3. FOREST-BASED DYNAMIC SORTED NEIGHBORHOOD INDEXING

The forest-based dynamic sorted neighborhood index (F-DySNI) is an index that facilitates real-time ER and that can be used with read-most databases. The index consists of multiple tree data structures where each tree is built using a different sorting key (SK). Using several trees with different SKs can help improve the quality of results in cases where errors and variations occur at the beginning of attribute values. For example, 'christine' and 'kristine' will not be inserted into the same tree node if a first name attribute is used as a SK, but they might be inserted into the same node in another tree where another SK is used. The F-DySNI has two phases: (1) a *build phase* where trees are built using records from an existing entity database, and (2) a *query phase* where the built index is queried by retrieving candidate records for a query record from all index trees, and the index is updated. We next describe the data structure of the tree, and then the build and query phases.

Tree Data Structure: Trees in the index are braided AVL trees which combine the properties of both a height balanced binary tree and a double-linked list [9]. Each node in the tree has a link to its alphabetically sorted predecessor node ('prev') and its successor node ('next'), and a list of identifiers of all records that have that node's key value as their sorting key value (SKV) [7]. Figure 1 illustrates an example tree built for the shown example data set.

Nodes in the tree are sorted alphabetically based on SKV. A SKV is generated for each record in the database, and a record's identifier is inserted into the tree based on its SKV. Identifiers of records that have the same SKV will be appended to the same tree node as a list (as shown in Figure 1). Assuming there are k different SKVs (nodes) in a tree, and n records in the database to be indexed (with $k < n$, potentially $k \ll n$), searching for a SKV will be reduced from $O(log(n))$ to $O(log(k))$ compared to the static array-based SNM [5].

Build Phase: During the build phase, multiple trees are built using different SKs where a record is inserted into every tree. To build one tree, records are loaded from a database, their SKVs are generated and inserted into the tree, with each unique SKV becoming a node in the tree. For example, node $N1$ in Figure 1 was generated when record $r1$ with SKV 'percysmith' was inserted into the empty index, while node $N3$ was generated when record $r3$ with SKV 'robinstevens' was inserted. If the SKV for a certain record already exists in the tree as a node key, then only the identifier of this record needs to be added to the corresponding list. The complete records with full attribute values are also inserted into an inverted index or disk-based database table **R** to be used later in the matching process.

The steps described above for building one tree are repeated to build all trees in the forest using different SKs.

Query Phase: In the query phase, a query record **q** is inserted into the F-DySNI and then it is matched in real-time against all trees that were constructed in the build phase. A new unique identifier is created for **q** and the different SKVs that are associated with the different trees are generated. **q** is then inserted into all trees using these SKVs and its record identifier is added in the same way records were inserted during the build phase. The full attribute values of **q** are also added to **R**.

To retrieve candidate records from a single tree, a window of size **w** of nodes neighboring the node containing the query record **q** is generated. All record identifiers that are stored in the nodes in the window are added to the candidate record set **C**. We implemented both a fixed and an

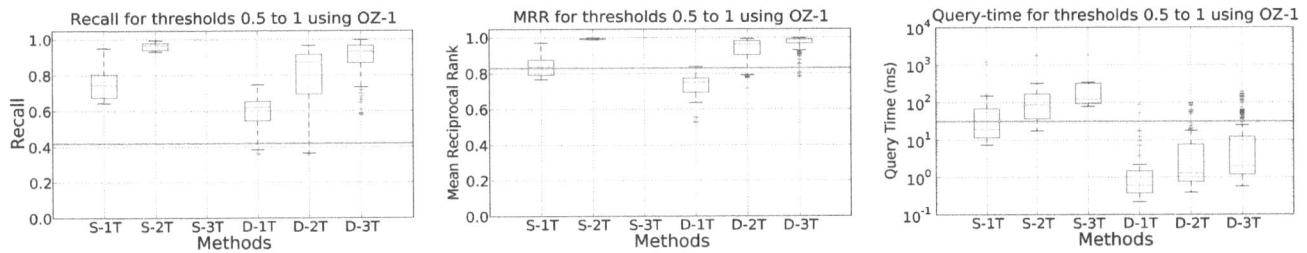

Figure 2: Results for running the F-DySNI on the OZ-1 data set (one corrupted attribute) using different numbers of trees. 'S' refers to using all single attributes as SK, while 'D' refers to using all SKs generated from the concatenation of two attributes. 'xT' refers to the number of trees. An adaptive window approach was used with a similarity threshold between 0.5 and 1.0. The horizontal line represents the DSAI approach [8].

adaptive window approach. In the fixed-size approach [5], a pre-defined window size is used to include neighboring nodes, while in the adaptive window approach [11] the window expands based on the similarities between the SKV of the node that has the query record and its neighboring nodes (calculated using an approximating string similarity function [2]). The window expands until the similarity between SKVs is below a specific threshold.

The steps described above are repeated for each tree, each adding candidate records into the overall candidate record set **C**. Then the query record **q** is compared in detail with all records in **C** using similarity comparison functions [2]. The actual attribute values are retrieved from **R**. The compared candidate records are returned as a list **M** sorted according to their overall similarities with **q**, where only candidates with similarities above a specific threshold are added to **M**.

4. EXPERIMENTAL EVALUATION

We implemented the F-DySNI approach, as well as the dynamic similarity-aware inverted index (DSAI) [8] which we used as a baseline, using Python (version 2.7.3). We ran experiments with memory-fitting data sets on a server with 128 GB of main memory and a 2.4 GHz Intel Xeon CPU. The results in Figure 3 (d) on the CCA data set (described below) were measured on a server with 64 GB of main memory and a 2.0 GHz Intel Xeon CPU. To facilitate repeatability of our experiments, the prototype codes and the synthetic data sets are available from the authors. Due to space limitations we only include results using an adaptive window size as it showed better results than using a fixed window size.

4.1 Data Sets and Evaluation Metrics

We evaluated our approach on the following data sets.

NC: this is a real voter registration data set from North Carolina. The data set was downloaded [1] every two months since October 2011 to build a temporal data set that contains the names, addresses, and registration numbers of voters. The data set contains 7,997,234 records (905 MB as CSV file). This data set contains realistic temporal information about a large number of people. We identified 142,673 individuals with two records, 3,566 with three, 92 with four, and two with five records in this data set.

CCA: this is a confidential commercial database which contains names and addresses of tens of millions of individuals, as well as a log file of query records against this database.

[1] Available from: ftp://www.att.ncste.gov/data

To evaluate the scalability of our indexing approach, we generated four subsets of different sizes by randomly selecting records from the full CCA data set. The first subset, CCA-1, contains 689,928 database records and 50,190 query records, CCA-3 contains 2,064,823 database records and 151,343 query records, CCA-10 contains 6,900,163 database records and 504,226 query records, and CCA-30 contains 20,708,303 records and 1,513,233 query records. The number of records in the larger subsets relative to CCA-1 is 3 times, 10 times, and 30 times, respectively.

OZ-x: We generated four synthetic data sets with various corruption ratios using the GeCo data generator and corrupter [10], for the purpose of investigating the effect of having different levels of data quality in attribute values on matching quality. The four data sets each contain 345,876 records (14.5 MB as CSV files) of personal details (such as names and addresses) selected randomly from a clean Australian telephone directory, and modified by adding duplicate records that had randomly corrupted attribute values based on typing, scanning and OCR errors, or phonetic variations. A single record in each synthetic data set has an average of five corrupted duplicates.

With a real-time ER technique, the aim is to match a query record with all records in the index that represent the same entity in the shortest possible time. Thus, we measure the quality of the obtained results, and query time of the approach. The evaluation metrics we use are:
- **Recall:** which is the fraction of true matching index records correctly included in the retrieved candidate set **C**.
- **Mean reciprocal rank (MRR):** which is the average of the reciprocal of the rank of the first true matching record in the returned result set **C** for a set of queries.
- **Time:** we measure the time to insert a single record into the index, and the time to query and match a single record.

4.2 Experimental Results and Discussion

In our first set of experiments, we evaluated the effect of using multiple trees and different SK combinations (using all possible single attributes and concatenated pairs of attributes) on recall, MRR, and average query time. The OZ-x data sets (with different data corruption ratios) were used for this set of experiments. Figure 2 illustrates the results for the OZ-1 data set (where one attribute in each record is corrupted). From the figure, plot (a) shows that when using three trees recall can increase significantly compared to when using a single tree. The MRR values (in plot (b)) also improve when using several trees. As for average query

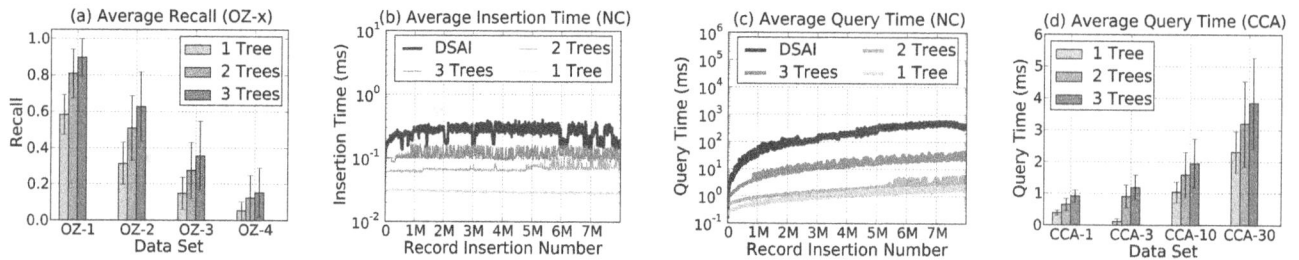

Figure 3: Plot (a) shows the average recall values for the OZ-x data sets with different corruption rates using all possible SKs generated from the concatenation of two attributes. Plots (b) and (c) show the average insertion and query times for the NC data set compared with the DSAI baseline [8]. Plot (d) shows the average query time for the different CCA subsets. For (b) and (c) 'FName+SName' was used as the SK.

time, plot (c) shows that using more trees in general leads to longer query times. However, SKVs that are generated from a concatenation of two attribute values achieve fast average query times while still attaining high recall values (which makes them suitable for use in real-time ER). We obtained similar results with the other OZ-x data sets where 2, 3, or 4 attribute values have been corrupted (see Figure 3 (a)).

In our second set of experiments, we evaluated the efficiency of F-DySNI using an adaptive window approach [11] with a similarity threshold of 0.8 to investigate the scalability of the approach to large databases, and we compared the results with the baseline DSAI approach [8]. We measured the average time required to insert a single record into the index, and the average time required to match a single query record across the growing size of the index. These experiments were conducted using the full NC data set using different numbers of trees and different SK based on two concatenated attributes. The results illustrated in Figure 3 (b) show that the average insertion times using the various numbers of trees is not affected by the growing size of the index data structure, while plot (c) shows that the average query time only increases slightly as the index becomes larger. As expected, the results show that using more trees increases the average insertion and query times, but the achieved times are still very fast (around 1 ms and 15 ms insertion and query times, respectively) for three trees. Our approach also achieves over one order of magnitude faster query times compared to the DSAI approach. The memory required for the index of one, two, and three trees for the NC data set was 1.8, 3.6, and 4.3 GBs, respectively.

In the last set of experiments we investigate how the F-DySNI approach scales to large real-world data sets with tens of millions of records. We used subsets of the CCA data set and measured the average query time using one, two, and three trees. An adaptive window approach [11] was used with similarity thresholds ranging from 0.7 to 0.9 The results in Figure 3 (d) show that for the increasing size of the data set the average query time increased sub-linearly yet was still very fast with an average query time of 4 ms for a data set with over 20 million records.

5. CONCLUSIONS AND FUTURE WORK

We proposed a dynamic forest-based index for real-time ER. The index uses multiple trees with different sorting keys to reduce the effects of errors and variations at the beginning of attribute values on the quality of matching results. Our evaluation shows that our approach is scalable with

respect to database size and that using multiple trees has a noticeable improvement on matching quality with only a small increase in query time when using sorting keys based on several concatenated attribute values. For future work, we plan to compare our approach with the static SNM and investigate the effect of using a disk-based index data structure on the approach. We also plan to investigate techniques to learn optimal sorting keys for building trees in the index and optimal tree selection for query records. We intent to parallelize our multiple-tree index to improve performance.

6. REFERENCES

[1] I. Bhattacharya and L. Getoor. Query-time entity resolution. *JAIR*, 30:621–657, 2007.

[2] P. Christen. *Data Matching - Concepts and Techniques for Record Linkage, Entity Resolution, and Duplicate Detection.* Springer, Berlin, 2012.

[3] P. Christen, R. Gayler, and D. Hawking. Similarity-aware indexing for real-time entity resolution. In *ACM CIKM*, Hong Kong, 2009.

[4] X. L. Dong and D. Srivastava. Big data integration. In *IEEE ICDE*, Brisbane, 2013.

[5] M. A. Hernandez and S. J. Stolfo. The merge/purge problem for large databases. In *ACM SIGMOD*, San Jose, 1995.

[6] E. Ioannou, W. Nejdl, C. Niederée, and Y. Velegrakis. On-the-fly entity-aware query processing in the presence of linkage. *VLDB Endowment*, 3(1), 2010.

[7] B. Ramadan, P. Christen, and H. Liang. Dynamic sorted neighborhood indexing for real-time entity resolution. In *ADC*, Brisbane, 2014. Springer LNCS 8506.

[8] B. Ramadan, P. Christen, H. Liang, R. Gayler, and D. Hawking. Dynamic similarity-aware inverted indexing for real-time entity resolution. In *PAKDD workshops*, Gold Coast, 2013. Springer LNCS 7867.

[9] S. V. Rice. Braided AVL trees for efficient event sets and ranked sets in the SIMSCRIPT III simulation programming language. In *Western Multiconference on Computer Simulation*, San Diego, 2007.

[10] K.-N. Tran, D. Vatsalan, and P. Christen. GeCo: an online personal data generator and corruptor. In *ACM CIKM*, San Fransisco, 2013.

[11] S. Yan, D. Lee, M. Y. Kan, and L. C. Giles. Adaptive sorted neighborhood methods for efficient record linkage. In *ACM/IEEE-CS JCDL*, Vancouver, 2007.

Travel Distance versus Navigation Complexity: A Study on Different Spatial Queries on Road Networks

Jie Shao[†]   Lars Kulik[‡]   Egemen Tanin[‡]   Long Guo[§]

[†]School of Computer Science & Engineering, University of Electronic Science and Technology of China
[‡]Department of Computing and Information Systems, The University of Melbourne, Australia
[§]School of Computing, National University of Singapore

shaojie@uestc.edu.cn {lkulik, etanin}@unimelb.edu.au guolong@comp.nus.edu.sg

ABSTRACT

Research on cognitive science indicates that humans often use different criteria for route selection. An alternative type of spatial proximity search on road networks recently has been proposed to find the easiest-to-reach neighboring object with the smallest navigation complexity. This paper presents an evaluation to compare the effectiveness of easiest-to-reach neighbor query against a classic nearest neighbor query in a real-world setting. Our user study demonstrates usability of the new spatial query type and suggests people may not always care about travel distance most. To provide flexibility to accommodate different requirements, we also show how to achieve tradeoff between navigation complexity and travel distance for advanced navigational assistance.

Categories and Subject Descriptors: H.2.8 [Database Applications]: Spatial databases and GIS

General Terms: Experimentation, Human Factors

Keywords: Navigation complexity; easiest-to-reach

1. INTRODUCTION

Modern navigation systems often rely on the criterion of shortest travel distance or time on a road network for path planning. However, many studies in spatial cognition [8, 2, 13, 14] have shown that people use more than distance or time as the optimization mechanism. Other criteria, such as the least number of turns and smallest chance of getting lost, can play an important role in the process of route selection. For a given pair of source and destination, traditionally Dijkstra's algorithm (or one of its variants) can be applied on a graph representation of the road network to find a shortest path. Node distances are used as travel costs (it is also possible to substitute distance with time). However, an optimal solution can also be found according to some cost function that minimizes cognitive effort [1, 3, 10, 5].

Recently, a new concept of *easiest-to-reach neighbor* [12] has been proposed in view of the fact that when travellers

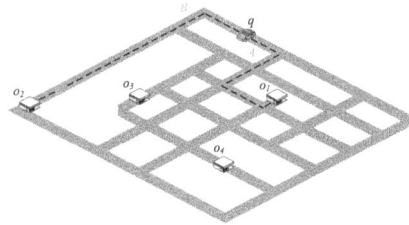

Figure 1: Nearest neighbor o_1 and easiest-to-reach neighbor o_2 of a query location q in a network.

choose from possible navigation destinations (multiple instances of a same facility type, such as different gas stations, are available nearby), often not the nearest one but the one which is easiest to get to is preferred, especially in an unfamiliar or complex urban environment. An example of such a neighboring object selection problem is given in Figure 1. q represents the query location, with four objects o_1, o_2, o_3 and o_4 of the requested facility type in the area. Nearest neighbor query algorithms developed in spatial databases [9, 7, 4, 11] can be applied to find that o_1 has the shortest travel distance from q. However, since a smaller number of turning instructions reduce cognitive effort as well as possible wayfinding errors, in this situation o_2 could be a better choice compared to o_1.

In our previous work [12], a spatial query that finds the easiest-to-reach neighbor with the smallest navigation complexity on a road network is formulated for the first time. The key idea is to adopt a weighting scheme based on a cognitive model to reflect the amount of information needed to successfully negotiate different types of road intersections [1]. The cognitive model in [12] further incorporates spatial chunking and landmark information, which are both important in human spatial cognition. With a set of chunking rules [6] applied to route direction elements (turn left, turn right, and go straight, etc.), navigation complexity can be measured from a cognitive perspective.

From database research point of view, when the number of possible destinations is large, sequential scan (i.e., to measure navigation complexity of each individual object and then compare them one-by-one) is usually inefficient and thus, indexing and pruning techniques are needed. Therefore, a computationally efficient query processing algorithm which is similar to Incremental Network Expansion (INE) for nearest neighbor query [9] is developed in [12]. Essentially, the algorithm is a single-source algorithm that performs node expansion starting from query location, and inspects objects in the order they are encountered. The most fundamental distinction of the algorithm from the conventional INE is that it works on a transformed graph that models turning instruction complexity. On the transformed graph, the nodes are dynamically labelled by several cognitive principles rather than geometric distance information, in order to evaluate navigation complexity. The proposed network expansion algorithm strictly expands the node with the smallest navigation complexity before any other node, so that it guarantees to visit the minimum number of nodes. Thus, it provides an optimal solution in terms of efficiency.

Nevertheless, the work of [12] focused on computational aspect of algorithm design, and its experiments only evaluated the *efficiency* of the query processing. In this paper, our work is on verifying the *effectiveness* of easiest-to-reach neighbor query, by comparing its usability with the traditional nearest neighbor query on a real road system through a user study. In particular, we examine two factors, travel distance and navigation complexity, of the easiest-to-reach neighbor and the nearest neighbor, to understand how they influence human navigation preference (Section 2). In addition, we show how to make the cost function used in the network expansion algorithm adapt to different user requirements. In this way, a spatial proximity search with flexibility can be customized to balance between travel distance and navigation complexity on demand (Section 3).

2. COMPARISON OF NEAREST NEIGHBOR AND EASIEST-TO-REACH NEIGHBOR

In this section, we first present the following study to verify the usability of easiest-to-reach neighbor query in a real-world setting. This is a fundamental task as if shown preferable, the classic understanding of nearest neighbor may require a rethink. Assume the task is to look for a gas station near the University of Melbourne (Barry Street, where the authors' previous department building was located), Google Maps™ service can list a few gas stations nearby (by typing 'The University of Melbourne, Barry Street, Carlton, Victoria' as the start address and 'gas station' as the end address). Figure 2 shows the actual nearest neighbor (①, which is Burmah Fuels Australia on Victoria Street) and the easiest-to-reach neighbor (②, which is BP on Elgin Street), and their suggested routes by Google Maps[1], with the corresponding Google Maps turning instructions.

We invited a group of 30 students and staff members (16 male and 14 female, aged 20~50) from the University of Queensland in Brisbane, Australia to participate in a user study (none of them had prior knowledge about the environment near the University of Melbourne). They were given the above realistic scenario and we supplied them with a map and turning instructions in Figure 2. We asked all the participants of the study to answer the question 'which gas station (① or ②) is a preferred one to navigate to' with a reason for their choice. None of the subjects had any background information about the research nor did they know about its intention. The outcome of the questionnaire shows that in total twenty-five participants chose ② as the preferred destination to navigate to. This group of people noted that the route to ② has fewer turns and is more straight. Three participants stated that they preferred ①: two gave the reason that ① has a shorter distance while another observed that arterial roads are used to go to ② so that route could be busy. The two remaining participants responded that they had no preference. This shows in summary that although ② has a slightly longer travel distance than ① (1.4 km versus 1.3 km), the route to ② is preferred by a large majority of the participants (25/30=83.3%, with confidence interval 13.35% at confidence level 95%) as this route is considered to be easier to follow.

We further run a simulation with a network dataset of 39800 nodes representing roads in and around Melbourne city area (objects representing facility instances are synthetically generated and distributed uniformly over the network with 5% density). For each of 50 random query locations, we compare the values of travel distance and navigation complexity of the easiest-to-reach neighbor with the nearest neighbor. The results of this simulation evaluation reveal that on average, network distance to travel to an easiest-to-reach neighbor has an increase of 16.2% compared to that of a nearest neighbor, but at the same time, navigation complexity is only 42.3% compared to that of the nearest neighbor. Conversely, network distance to travel to a nearest neighbor is 86.1% compared to that of the easiest-to-reach neighbor, but navigation complexity is 2.36 times.

We can see that, in return for slightly longer travel distances, easiest-to-reach neighbors offer considerable advantages over nearest neighbors in terms of their ease of navigation. This is particularly important for travellers unfamiliar with a foreign city (the directions to get to easiest-to-reach neighbors will be easier to understand, to remember and to follow). While for short trips with few segments and turns the exercise may be simple, but as a journey increases in navigation complexity, it could become more difficult for travellers to successfully reach a destination. Therefore, the new spatial query type of finding easiest-to-reach neighbor could be used as an alternative to the existing nearest neighbor query, to benefit users by reporting best choices in terms of navigation complexity.

3. BALANCE OF TRAVEL DISTANCE AND NAVIGATION COMPLEXITY

Given our observation with the study above, customization to user preferences is a desirable feature of navigation services. In addition, the algorithm to process easiest-to-reach neighbor query introduced in [12] tends to be reluctant to choose a turn in the network expansion process (since its cost is always larger than the cost of going straight), so in some extreme cases it could eventually lead to choose a route of considerable length. When there are multiple choices for the destination available, travellers being guided in unfamiliar geographic environments may have certain requirements in mind, such as achieving some tradeoff between nearest and easiest-to-reach neighbors. With the original network expansion algorithm in [12] as a basis, in this section we show an extension to support a more sophisticated and realistic behavior.

For destination choice, if a traveller would like to achieve some balance between travel distance and navigation complexity, we can introduce a parameter λ to assign the cost used in the network expansion process of graph representa-

---

[1]According to the cognitive model in [12], the navigation complexity to gas station ① and ② can be measured as 51 and 42 respectively.

The University of Melbourne
131 Barry Street, Carlton VIC 3053 - (03) 8344 9995

1. Head **south** on **Barry St** towards **Pelham St** About 4 mins	go **350 m** total 350 m	
2. Turn right onto **Leicester St**	go **36 m** total 400 m	
3. Turn left onto **Queensberry St** About 8 mins	go **550 m** total 950 m	
4. Turn right onto **Lygon St** About 3 mins	go **230 m** total 1.2 km	
5. Turn left onto **Victoria St** Destination will be on the right About 2 mins	go **100 m** total 1.3 km	

Burmah Fuels Australia
23-29 Victoria Street, East Melbourne VIC 3002

The University of Melbourne
131 Barry Street, Carlton VIC 3053 - (03) 8344 9995

1. Head **north** on **Barry St** towards **Grattan St** About 2 mins	go **99 m** total 99 m
2. Turn right onto **Grattan St** About 12 mins	go **900 m** total 1.0 km
3. Turn left onto **Rathdowne St** About 5 mins	go **400 m** total 1.4 km
4. Turn right onto **Elgin St** Destination will be on the right	go **21 m** total 1.4 km

BP
117 Elgin Street, Carlton VIC 3053 - (03) 9347 5193

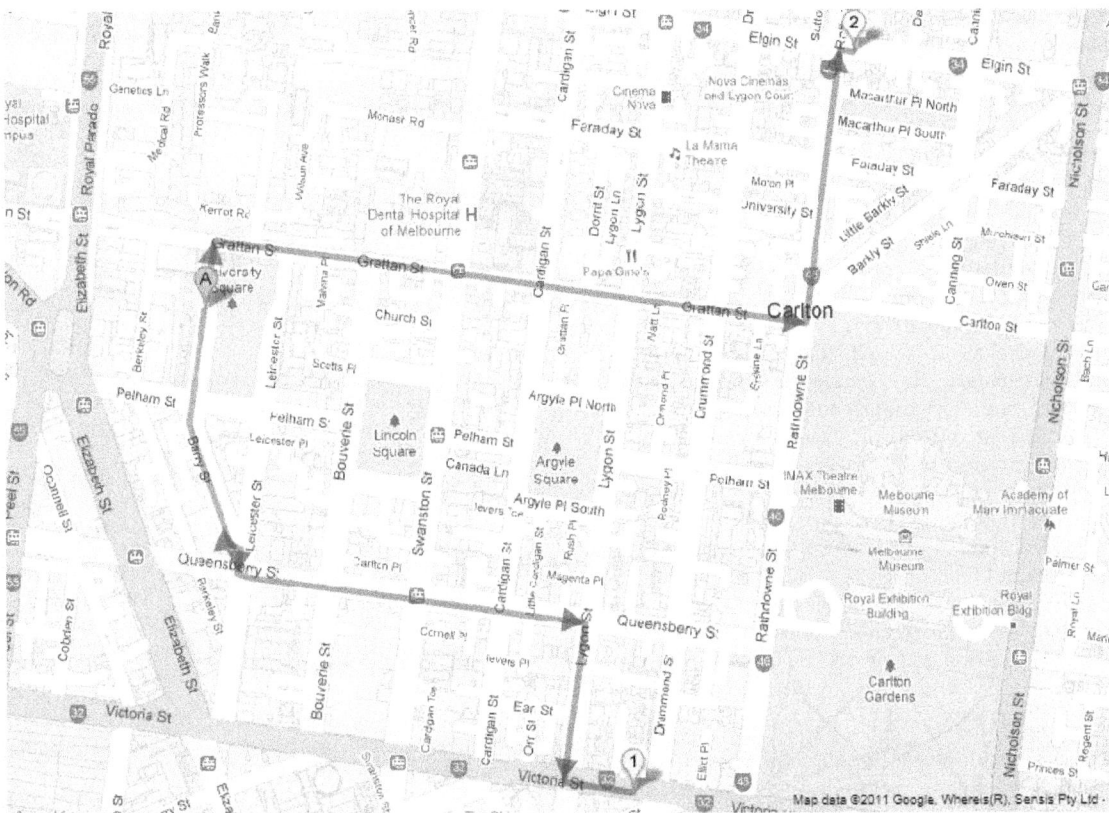

Figure 2: Google Maps routes from the University of Melbourne (A on the map) to two gas stations (① and ②) (map data ©Google, Whereis(R) Sensis Pty Ltd). ② has a slightly longer distance than ① but it has a smaller number of turning instructions.

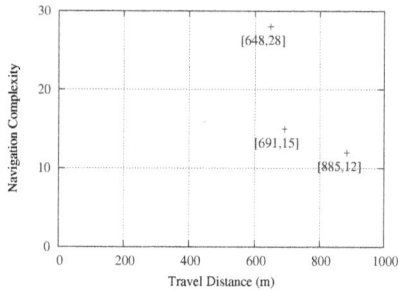

Figure 3: Travel distance and navigation complexity.

tion. The hybrid of these two criteria can be reflected by a modification of the cost function as

$$\lambda \cdot Cost_{distance} + (1 - \lambda) \cdot Cost_{instruction}$$

where $Cost_{distance}$ is derived from the cost function regarding network distance of traversing the edges, $Cost_{instruction}$ is derived from the cost function modelling instruction complexity of turning onto the edges, and $\lambda \in [0,1]$ is a heuristic parameter used for a weighted sum[2]. In this way, in the graph representation of the network, a node shared by a pair of adjacent edges can be labelled with some new cost value augmented with information about both travel distance and navigation complexity, and these costs can be computed on-the-fly from geometry and topology.

To study the effect of λ, an example of balancing between travel distance and navigation complexity is given in Figure 3. It shows that for one of the query locations in the Melbourne road network, the travel distance and navigation complexity of the easiest-to-reach neighbor are 885 and 12 respectively, while those of the nearest neighbor are 648 and 28. When the parameter $\lambda \in [0.11, 1]$, the network expansion algorithm returns the nearest neighbor as the answer. When $\lambda \in [0, 0.06]$, the network expansion algorithm returns the easiest-to-reach neighbor as the answer. If we set $\lambda \in (0.06, 0.11)$, another neighboring object with a moderate travel distance (691) and a moderate navigation complexity (15) will be returned as the answer.

With different choices of λ used, different objects could be returned. Particularly, by comparing the result pairs of travel distance and navigation complexity [648,28] and [691,15] of the different returned answers, we can see that a marginal increase of travel distance sometimes leads to a significant reduction of navigation complexity. This example also suggests that the pair [691,15] provides a compromise in terms of travel distance versus navigation complexity. In summary, this example motivates why it is highly beneficial to introduce a parameter λ. A simple slider can be used in an interface to allow the user to choose between travel distance versus navigation complexity.

4. CONCLUSIONS

Navigation services for people in unfamiliar geographic environments should be able to choose destinations with route directions which are easy to follow, even if their travel distances are not the shortest ones. The main contribution

of this work is a user study to validate the effectiveness of easiest-to-reach neighbor query so that the classic understanding on nearest neighbors may be flawed, and our extension of the query processing algorithm with the capacity of being tailored to user preferences is given. The influence of the complexity of alternative paths on human route selection and navigation behavior could be studied in future work.

5. REFERENCES

[1] M. Duckham and L. Kulik. "Simplest" paths: Automated route selection for navigation. In *Spatial Information Theory. Foundations of Geographic Information Science, International Conference, COSIT 2003, Ittingen, Switzerland, September 24-28, 2003, Proceedings*, pages 169–185, 2003.

[2] R. G. Golledge. Path selection and route preference in human navigation: A progress report. In *Spatial Information Theory: A Theoretical Basis for GIS, International Conference COSIT '95, Semmering, Austria, September 21-23, 1995, Proceedings*, pages 207–222, 1995.

[3] S. Haque, L. Kulik, and A. Klippel. Algorithms for reliable navigation and wayfinding. In *Spatial Cognition V: Reasoning, Action, Interaction, International Conference Spatial Cognition 2006, Bremen, Germany, September 24-28, 2006, Revised Selected Papers*, pages 308–326, 2006.

[4] X. Huang, C. S. Jensen, H. Lu, and S. Saltenis. S-grid: A versatile approach to efficient query processing in spatial networks. In *Advances in Spatial and Temporal Databases, 10th International Symposium, SSTD 2007, Boston, MA, USA, July 16-18, 2007, Proceedings*, pages 93–111, 2007.

[5] B. Jiang and X. Liu. Computing the fewest-turn map directions based on the connectivity of natural roads. *International Journal of Geographical Information Science*, 25(7):1069–1082, 2011.

[6] A. Klippel, H. Tappe, and C. Habel. Pictorial representations of routes: Chunking route segments during comprehension. In *Spatial Cognition III, Routes and Navigation, Human Memory and Learning, Spatial Representation and Spatial Learning*, pages 11–33, 2003.

[7] M. R. Kolahdouzan and C. Shahabi. Voronoi-based k nearest neighbor search for spatial network databases. In *Proceedings of the 2004 International Conference on Very Large Data Bases*, pages 840–851, 2004.

[8] D. M. Mark. Automated route selection for navigation. *IEEE Aerospace and Electronic Systems Magazine*, 1(9):2–5, 1986.

[9] D. Papadias, J. Zhang, N. Mamoulis, and Y. Tao. Query processing in spatial network databases. In *Proceedings of the 2003 International Conference on Very Large Data Bases*, pages 802–813, 2003.

[10] K.-F. Richter and M. Duckham. Simplest instructions: Finding easy-to-describe routes for navigation. In *Geographic Information Science, 5th International Conference, GIScience 2008, Park City, UT, USA, September 23-26, 2008. Proceedings*, pages 274–289, 2008.

[11] H. Samet, J. Sankaranarayanan, and H. Alborzi. Scalable network distance browsing in spatial databases. In *Proceedings of the 2008 ACM International Conference on Management of Data*, pages 43–54, 2008.

[12] J. Shao, L. Kulik, and E. Tanin. Easiest-to-reach neighbor search. In *Proceedings of the 2010 ACM International Conference on Advances in Geographic Information Systems*, pages 360–369, 2010.

[13] S. Winter. Weighting the path continuation in route planning. In *Proceedings of the 2001 ACM International Symposium on Advances in Geographic Information Systems*, pages 173–176, 2001.

[14] S. Winter. Modeling costs of turns in route planning. *GeoInformatica*, 6(4):363–380, 2002.

---

[2]In order to produce dimensional similitude, λ should be calibrated for road networks to scale $Cost_{distance}$ and $Cost_{instruction}$ to be in the same units.

Scalable Privacy-Preserving Record Linkage for Multiple Databases *

Dinusha Vatsalan and Peter Christen

Research School of Computer Science, College of Engineering and Computer Science,
The Australian National University, Canberra ACT 0200, Australia
{dinusha.vatsalan, peter.christen}@anu.edu.au

ABSTRACT

Privacy-preserving record linkage (PPRL) is the process of identifying records that correspond to the same real-world entities across several databases without revealing any sensitive information about these entities. Various techniques have been developed to tackle the problem of PPRL, with the majority of them only considering linking two databases. However, in many real-world applications data from more than two sources need to be linked. In this paper we consider the problem of linking data from three or more sources in an efficient and secure way. We propose a protocol that combines the use of Bloom filters, secure summation, and Dice coefficient similarity calculation with the aim to identify all records held by the different data sources that have a similarity above a certain threshold. Our protocol is secure in that no party learns any sensitive information about the other parties' data, but all parties learn which of their records have a high similarity with records held by the other parties. We evaluate our protocol on a large dataset showing the scalability, linkage quality, and privacy of our protocol.

Categories and Subject Descriptors

H2.7 [**Database Management**]: Database Administration-*Security, integrity, and protection*

General Terms

Algorithms, Experimentation, Security

Keywords

Record linkage; privacy; security; Bloom filter; multi-party.

1. INTRODUCTION

Linking records from different databases with the aim to improve data quality or enrich data for further analysis and mining is occurring in an increasing number of application areas including healthcare, government services, crime and fraud detection, and business applications [1]. The analysis of data linked across organizations can, for example, facilitate the detection of infectious diseases early before they spread widely around a country or worldwide, or enable the accurate identification of fraud, crime, or terrorism suspects [13]. These applications require data from several organizations, such as human health data, consumed drug data, and animal health data for the first of the above examples [3]; while the second above example requires data from law enforcement agencies, Internet service providers, the police, as well as financial institutions.

Today, record linkage not only faces computational challenges due to the increasing size of datasets and quality challenges due to the presence of real-world data errors, but also privacy and confidentiality challenges due to growing privacy concerns by the public. In the absence of unique entity identifiers in the databases that are linked, personal identifying attributes (such as names, addresses, gender, and dates of birth) need to be used for the linkage. Known as quasi-identifiers (QIDs) [12], values in such attributes are in general sufficiently well correlated with entities to allow accurate linkage. Using such personal information however often leads to privacy and confidentiality concerns.

The privacy challenges posed in the record linkage process led to the development of techniques that facilitate 'privacy-preserving record linkage' (PPRL) [13]. PPRL tackles the problem of how to identify records that refer to the same entities in different databases such that only masked (encoded) QIDs have to be revealed. Generally, the original data are transformed (using some encoding function) such that a specific functional relationship exists between the original and the masked data [12], without compromising the privacy and confidentiality of the entities represented by these data.

Many different approaches have been proposed for PPRL [13], but most of these are limited to linking data from two sources. As the example applications described above have shown, linking data from several sources is however commonly required. We propose an efficient solution for PPRL across multiple parties. While existing multi-party PPRL techniques [5, 7, 8, 9, 10] either perform only exact matching or use computationally expensive privacy techniques, the novelty of our solution is that it supports approximate matching based on two efficient privacy techniques: Bloom filters [11] and secure summation [6]. We conduct an empirical study on a large real dataset to validate the scalability, linkage quality, and privacy of our solution.

*Funded by the Australian Research Council under Discovery Project DP130101801.

2. RELATED WORK

Various techniques have been developed to address the PPRL research problem [13], but few among these have considered PPRL on multiple databases. The first approach to PPRL [10] links multiple databases by comparing the hash-encoded values (using one-way secure hash algorithms) from all data sources by using a third party. However, this approach only performs exact matching (i.e. a single variation in a QID results in a completely different hash-encoded value). A secure equi-join protocol for multiple database tables was proposed in [5] for exact matching, and a secure multi-party computation based approach using an oblivious transfer protocol was presented in [9] for PPRL on multiple databases. While provably secure, the approach is computationally expensive compared to perturbation-based privacy techniques. Recently, a multi-party PPRL approach for approximate matching of categorical values based on k-anonymity and game-theoretic concepts was proposed [8].

An efficient multi-party PPRL approach for exact matching using Bloom filters was introduced by Lai et al. [7]. In this approach, database values are first converted into a Bloom filter bit array. Each party then partitions its Bloom filter into segments according to the number of parties involved in the linkage, and sends these segments to the corresponding other parties. The segments received by a party are combined using a conjunction (logical AND) operation. The resulting combined Bloom filter segments are then exchanged between the parties. Each party checks its own full Bloom filter with the final result, and if the membership test is successful then the value is considered to be a match. Though the cost of this approach is low since the computation is completely distributed between the parties and the processing of Bloom filters is very fast, the approach can only perform exact matching. As we describe next, we use Lai et al.'s [7] multi-party Bloom filter based approach as a building block for our approximate matching solution.

3. MULTI-PARTY LINKAGE PROTOCOL

We now describe our approach to securely and efficiently link databases from three or more parties. We use the following notation: P is the number of parties involved in our protocol, where each party p_i holds a database D_i containing sensitive or confidential identifying information. Database D_i contains $N_i = |D_i|$ records. We assume a set of QID attributes A, which will be used for the linkage, is common to all these databases. Our protocol will calculate the similarity between sets of records using the values in A. We next describe the building blocks of our protocol, then explain each of the steps in our protocol, and finally analyze the complexity and privacy characteristics of our protocol.

3.1 Protocol Building Blocks

Bloom filter encoding: A Bloom filter b_i is a bit array data structure of length l bits where all bits are initially set to 0. k independent hash functions, $h_1, h_2, \ldots, h_k$, each with range $1, \ldots l$, are used to map each of the elements in a set S into the Bloom filter by setting k corresponding bit positions to 1. Bloom filters are one efficient perturbation-based privacy technique that has successfully been used in several privacy-preserving solutions [4, 11, 12].

Schnell et al. [11] were the first to propose a method for approximate matching in PPRL of two databases using Bloom

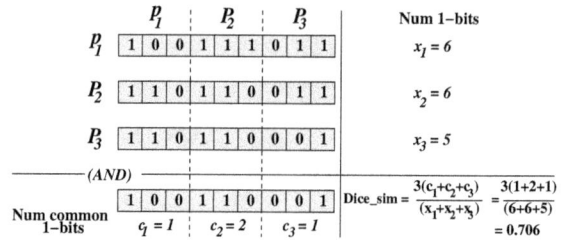

Figure 1: Dice similarity calculation of three Bloom filters (BFs) across three parties. Rows illustrate the BFs generated by the three parties, while columns show which party holds which BF segments.

filters. In their work, as in our protocol, the q-grams (substrings of length q) of attribute values in A of each record in the databases to be linked are hash-mapped into Bloom filters using k independent hash functions. The Bloom filters are then sent to a third party that calculates the Dice coefficient [1] similarity of pairs of Bloom filters.

Dice coefficient: Any set-based similarity function can be used to calculate the similarity of pairs or sets of Bloom filters. The Dice coefficient has been used for matching of Bloom filters, since it is insensitive to many matching zeros in long Bloom filters [11]. We calculate the Dice coefficient similarity of P Bloom filters $b_1, \cdots, b_P$ as:

$$Dice\_sim(b_1, \cdots, b_P) = \frac{P \times c}{\sum_{i=1}^{P} x_i} \quad (1)$$

where c is the number of common bit positions that are set to 1 in all P Bloom filters (common 1-bits), and x_i is the number of bit positions set to 1 in b_i (1-bits), $1 \leq i \leq P$.

Multi-party Bloom filter matching: In our protocol the calculation of the number of common 1-bits (c) is distributed among the parties, such that $c = \sum_{i=1}^{P} c_i$. Bloom filters are split into P segments and each party sends its segments to the corresponding other parties. The parties then individually calculate the number of common 1-bits c_i in their respective segments of the Bloom filters they receive from the other parties for all sets of records. As example, the distributed Dice coefficient calculation of three Bloom filters from three parties is illustrated in Figure 1.

Secure summation: Once each of the P parties has calculated its c_i and x_i values for each set of Bloom filters, a secure summation protocol [6] can be applied to calculate $c = \sum_{i=1}^{P} c_i$ and $x = \sum_{i=1}^{P} x_i$ in a secure way (in order to calculate the Dice similarity of a set of Bloom filters). This protocol uses two vectors R_c and R_x (of length equal to the number of sets) of large random numbers (values larger than l) to hide the actual sensitive values c_i and x_i, and employs a ring-based communication pattern over all parties which allows each party to learn the final values (c and x) but no party to learn the sensitive values of the other parties.

3.2 Protocol Steps

We divide the steps of our protocol into three phases: (1) data preparation, (2) distributed matching, and (3) similarity calculation. In the initial data preparation phase,

1. the parties agree upon a bit array length l; k hashing functions $h_1, \ldots, h_k$; the length (in characters) of grams q; a minimum Dice similarity threshold value,

s_t, above which a set of records is classified as a match; and a set of blocking keys [1] and QID attributes A;

2. each party p_i individually applies a private blocking function [13] to reduce the number of candidate sets of records (from $\prod_i^P N_i$); and

3. each party p_i hash-maps the q-gram values of A of each of its N_i records into N_i Bloom filters of length l using the hash functions $h_1, \ldots, h_k$.

In the distributed matching phase, for all records and their Bloom filters in each block, each party p_i:

4. segments its Bloom filters into P equal sized segments and sends the jth segment to party p_j, with $1 \leq j \leq P$ and $j \neq i$;

5. receives the ith segment of Bloom filters from all other parties p_j, with $1 \leq j \leq P$ and $j \neq i$;

6. applies a logical conjunction (AND) on each set of Bloom filter segments ($b_1^i \wedge b_2^i \wedge \cdots \wedge b_P^i$) for each record set combination within the block; and

7. calculates the number of common 1-bits (c_i) and the total number of 1-bits in its own Bloom filter (x_i) for each set of Bloom filter segments.

Finally, in the similarity calculation phase, the parties:

8. use the secure summation protocol to exchange the values of c_i and x_i for each set of Bloom filters for the calculation of the sums c and x, respectively; and

9. calculate the Dice coefficient similarity of each set of Bloom filters using c and x following Equation 1 to classify the compared sets of records into matches and non-matches based on the similarity threshold s_t.

3.3 Complexity and Privacy Analysis

We assume P parties participate in the protocol, each having a database of N records, and we assume $B \leq N$ blocks are being formed by each party [1]. In the first phase, agreement of parameters has a constant communication complexity, and blocking the databases has $O(N)$ computation complexity. Finding the intersection of blocks from all parties has a communication complexity of $O(P\,B)$ and a computation complexity of $O(B\,log\,B)$ at each party. The creation of Bloom filters using k hash functions for N records is $O(kN)$.

In the distributed matching phase, each party sends its Bloom filter segments (each of length l/P) to the other parties. If we assume direct communication, $P(P-1)$ messages are required in this step, each of these of size $N \times l/P$ ($O(N\,l\,P)$ total communication). With the simplified assumption that all blocks are of equal size (N/B), then in each block $(N/B)^P$ sets of Bloom filters (i.e. all candidate sets of records in a block) have to be generated and their logical conjunctions calculated, leading to a total of $O(B(N/B)^P)$ calculations. This combinatorial complexity currently limits our protocol to a small number of parties, or a large number of small blocks (i.e. N/B is small). Our main future research focus is to improve this step of our protocol by efficiently filtering non-matching record sets.

The similarity calculation phase consists of the secure summation of the calculated number of common 1-bits (c_i) and total 1-bits (x_i). This requires for each Bloom filter set two integer numbers to be sent in a ring communication (P messages) over all parties with a total communication of $O(P\,B(N/B)^P)$, followed by the distribution of the final results which is again $O(P\,B(N/B)^P)$.

To assess the privacy of our protocol, we assume all parties follow the honest-but-curious adversary model [13], in that they are curious and try to find out as much as possible about the other parties' data while following the protocol. Since calculations are distributed among the parties, each party only learns l/P bits of each other party's Bloom filters, which reduces with increasing P (and thus privacy improves with increasing P).

The values for the number of hash functions used (k) and the length of the Bloom filter (l) provide a trade-off between the linkage quality and privacy [11]. The higher the value for k/l, the higher the privacy and the lower the quality of linkage, because the number of q-grams mapped to a single bit increases, which leads to lower linkage quality but makes it more difficult for an adversary to learn the possible q-gram combinations. Hash-mapping several attribute values from each record into one compound Bloom filter [4] makes it even more difficult for an adversary to learn individual attribute values that correspond to a revealed bit pattern.

4. EXPERIMENTS AND DISCUSSION

We have implemented our proposed approach in Python (version 2.7.3), and ran all experiments on a server with 2.4 GHz CPUs, 128 GBytes of main memory and running Ubuntu 12.04. The programs and test datasets are available from the authors. Following other work in PPRL [4, 11], we set the parameters as $l = 1,000$, $k = 30$, $s_t = [0.8, 0.9]$, and $P = [3, 5, 7, 10]$. We apply a Soundex based phonetic blocking [1] to improve the scalability of our protocol.

We evaluate the scalability of our protocol measured by runtime, and the quality of the achieved linkage measured by precision and recall [1]. In line with other work in PPRL [12], we evaluate privacy using disclosure risk (DR) measures based on the probability of suspicion, i.e. the likelihood a masked database record can be matched with one or several (masked) record(s) in a publicly available global database. We show mean DR values, as well as marketeer DR values calculated as the proportion of records that match to exactly one record in the global database.

For all experiments we used the large real-world North Carolina Voter Registration database (named 'NC') as available from ftp://alt.ncsbe.gov/data/. We have downloaded this database every second month since October 2011 and built a compound temporal dataset that contains over 8 million records of voter's names and addresses.

To allow evaluation of our protocol with data of different sizes, different quality, and for different number of parties, we used a recently proposed data corruptor [2] to create a variety of datasets with different characteristics. From the full NC dataset we extracted sub-sets of 5,000, 10,000, 50,000, 100,000, 500,000, and 1,000,00 records for each party where the number of matching records is set to 50% (i.e. half of all selected records occur in the datasets of all parties).

To investigate how our protocol deals with dirty data (where attribute values contain errors and variations), we generated several series of datasets with one, two, or three modifications (corruptions) applied to randomly selected attribute values. These corruptions consisted of character edit operations (insert, delete, substitute, or transposition), as well as optical character recognition and phonetic modifications based on look-up tables and rules [2]. Because we generated our different datasets we know the true matching records which allows us to calculate linkage accuracy.

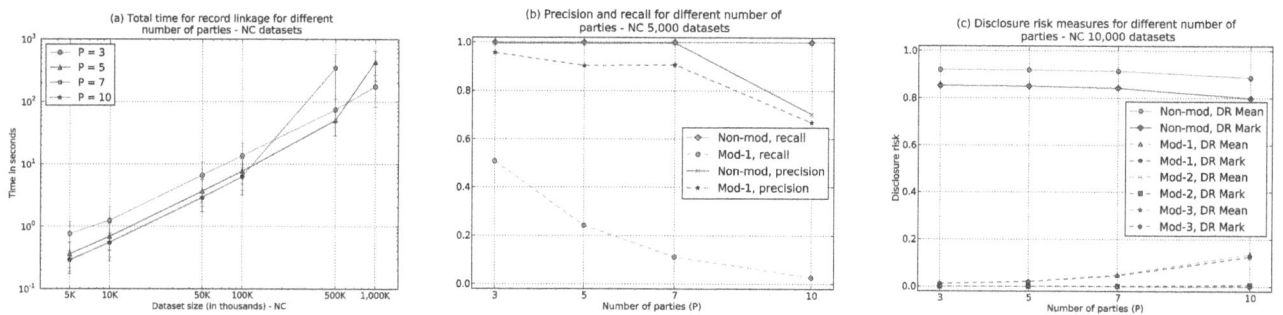

Figure 2: (a) Total time required for linkage (for one party, averaged over all parties), (b) precision and recall of the linkage of datasets with no and one modification, and (c) disclosure risk (DR) measures of privacy [12].

Figure 2 (a) shows the scalability of our approach, measured by runtime as averaged over all parties and over all variations of each dataset. Interestingly, runtime decreases with larger number of parties (P) because the Bloom filter segments at each party become shorter (l/P) and the similarity calculations are distributed among the parties.

The quality of linkage measured by precision and recall is presented in Figure 2 (b) on the NC 5,000 modified and non-modified datasets. As can be seen, precision and recall are high on the non-modified datasets. On the modified datasets the recall drops quite drastically with the number of parties. This is because when records are modified in each dataset the number of missed true matching record sets increases. In future work we will investigate similarity techniques that allow for matching records in sub-sets of parties only.

Finally, the privacy of our protocol, as measured by disclosure risk (DR) [12] of an exact matching attack using the full NC dataset as the global dataset, is shown in Figure 2 (c). As discussed in Section 3.3, DR decreases (i.e. privacy increases) with an increasing number of parties for the non-modified datasets as the Bloom filter segments become shorter and are therefore matched to more global records. Since all the records in these datasets are non-modified (an unlikely real-world situation) there exist exact matchings of records in the global datasets which leads to higher DR values. For the modified datasets (more likely in real applications), the DR values are lower and most Bloom filter segments match to no global record at all, but as these segments become shorter with more parties an increasing number of segments do match, leading to a slight increase in DR.

5. CONCLUSIONS AND FUTURE WORK

We have presented a secure protocol for PPRL across multiple parties based on Bloom filters. Our protocol identifies sets of records that have a high Dice similarity across all parties. The protocol has a communication complexity that is linear in the number of parties and the size of the databases that are linked, making the protocol scalable to applications where data from multiple parties need to be linked.

In future work, we plan to improve the scalability of our protocol by using improved private blocking or filtering approaches, and by investigating different communication patterns. A second avenue of future work will be to study linkage attacks with approximation of error bounds for privacy evaluation of our protocol. Finally, we plan to investigate improved classification techniques including relational clustering and graph-based approaches [1] which are successfully

used in non-PPRL applications. Our ultimate aim is to develop techniques that allow for large databases to be linked in secure, accurate, and scalable ways across many parties, thereby facilitating data analysis and mining that currently are not feasible due to privacy and confidentiality concerns.

6. REFERENCES

[1] P. Christen. *Data Matching*. Springer, 2012.
[2] P. Christen and D. Vatsalan. Flexible and extensible generation and corruption of personal data. In *ACM CIKM*, San Francisco, 2013.
[3] C. Clifton, M. Kantarcioglu, A. Doan, G. Schadow, J. Vaidya, A. Elmagarmid, and D. Suciu. Privacy-preserving data integration and sharing. In *ACM SIGMOD Workshop DMKD*, Paris, 2004.
[4] E. A. Durham, C. Toth, M. Kuzu, M. Kantarcioglu, Y. Xue, and B. Malin. Composite Bloom filters for secure record linkage. *TKDE*, 99(PrePrints), 2013.
[5] M. Kantarcioglu, W. Jiang, and B. Malin. A privacy-preserving framework for integrating person-specific databases. In *PSD*, Istanbul, 2008.
[6] A. F. Karr, X. Lin, A. P. Sanil, and J. P. Reiter. Analysis of integrated data without data integration. *Chance*, 17(3):26–29, 2004.
[7] P. Lai, S. Yiu, K. Chow, C. Chong, and L. Hui. An Efficient Bloom filter based Solution for Multiparty Private Matching. In *SAM*, Las Vegas, 2006.
[8] N. Mohammed, B. Fung, and M. Debbabi. Anonymity meets game theory: secure data integration with malicious participants. *VLDB*, 20(4):567–588, 2011.
[9] C. M. O'Keefe, M. Yung, L. Gu, and R. Baxter. Privacy-preserving data linkage protocols. In *ACM WPES*, Washington DC, 2004.
[10] C. Quantin, H. Bouzelat, F. Allaert, and et al. How to ensure data security of an epidemiological follow-up: quality assessment of an anonymous record linkage procedure. *IJMI*, 49(1):117–122, 1998.
[11] R. Schnell, T. Bachteler, and J. Reiher. Privacy-preserving record linkage using Bloom filters. *BMC Med Inform Decis Mak*, 9(1), 2009.
[12] D. Vatsalan, P. Christen, C. M. O'Keefe, and V. S. Verykios. An evaluation framework for privacy-preserving record linkage. *JPC*, 6(1), 2014.
[13] D. Vatsalan, P. Christen, and V. S. Verykios. A taxonomy of privacy-preserving record linkage techniques. *JIS*, 38(6):946–969, 2013.

Exploring Tag-free RFID-based Passive Localization and Tracking via Learning-based Probabilistic Approaches

Lina Yao
The University of Adelaide
Adelaide, Australia
lina.yao@adelaide.edu.au

Wenjie Ruan
The University of Adelaide
Adelaide, Australia
wenjie.ruan@adelaide.edu.au

Quan Z. Sheng
The University of Adelaide
Adelaide, Australia
qsheng@cs.adelaide.edu.au

Xue Li
The University of Queensland
Brisbane, Australia
xueli@itee.uq.edu.au

Nicholas J.G. Falkner
The University of Adelaide
Adelaide, Australia
nickolas.falkner@adelaide.edu.au

ABSTRACT

RFID-based localization and tracking has some promising potentials. By combining localization with its identification capability, existing applications can be enhanced and new applications can be developed. In this paper, we investigate a tag-free indoor localizing and tracking problem (e.g., people tracking) without requiring subjects to carry any tags or devices in a pure passive environment. We formulate localization as a classification task. In particular, we model the received signal strength indicator (RSSI) of passive tags using multivariate Gaussian Mixture Model (GMM), and use the Expectation Maximization (EM) to learn the maximum likelihood estimates of the model parameters. Several other learning-based probabilistic approaches are also explored in the localization problem. To track a moving subject, we propose GMM based Hidden Markov Model (HMM) and k Nearest Neighbor (kNN) based HMM approaches. We conduct extensive experiments in a testbed formed by passive RFID tags, and the experimental results demonstrate the effectiveness and accuracy of our approach.

Categories and Subject Descriptors

H.4.0 [**Information Systems Applications**]: General; H.2.8 [**Database Management**]: Database Applications

Keywords

Localization; RFID; Hidden Markov Model; Gaussian Mixture Model; Kernel-based; Nearest Neighbour

1. INTRODUCTION

Ambient intelligence has been drawing growing attention recently since it enables a smart environment which can respond to people's locations and behaviors using various wireless signal, sensors and Radio Frequency Identification (RFID) [7]. Under such smart environments, many promising applications can be realized such as

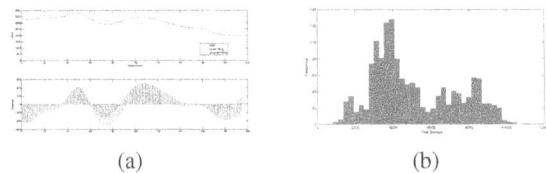

(a)   (b)

Figure 1: (a) RSSI variation along with distance (b) RSSI distribution when a person shows up at a certain location

aged care, surveillance, and indoor navigation [10]. A key prerequisite of enabling this intelligence is to localize and track people in the indoor environments.

RFID-based localization has gained much interest due to its low-cost and many RFID-based techniques for localization have been proposed [3, 4, 5, 8]. Most of these techniques, however, require the subjects to be attached with tags. This requirement has several inherent impractical issues (e.g., the tags may be lost or damaged by people accidentally or on purpose). As a result, a tag-free RFID-based localization applications is highly desirable.

It is well known that RSSI is quite complicated in real environments due to variability caused by multipath effects and ambient noise interference as well as physical antenna orientation, and fluctuations in the power source. The signal attenuates while increasing the distance. Figure 1(a) shows the relation of a certain tag' RSSI and its distance with antennas. Figure 1(b) shows the RSSI distribution at a particular location from a fixed access point. To sum up, RSSI is highly nonlinear and uncertain in a complex environment, which may be further corrupted when introducing people's presence or mobility. However, some underlying distinguishable patterns can be observed (e.g., how people disturb the pattern of received signal strength). In particular, two general intuitions are used in this paper. The first one is that when a subject appears in the testing area, the RSSI will change compared with a static environment. Secondly, when a subject appears at different locations, the RSSI of the same tag will embody various fluctuation patterns. Figure 2 shows the RSSI variations when people present in different locations. Based on these two intuitions, it is possible to develop an approach decoding the changes and learn people's locations.

Recently, some works have been proposed to target the tag-free RFID-based localization. For instance, Zhang et.al [11] and Liu et.al [1] propose to set up RFID tags (mix of passive and active tags) into an array, which captures the Received Signal Strength Indicator (RSSI) sequences for all tags. The trajectories information can then be recovered by exploring variation of RSSI series. Inspired by their work, we set up a *pure passive* tag arrays to make

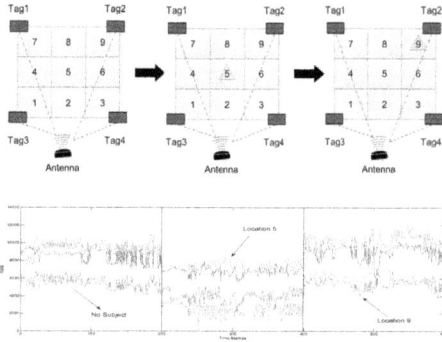

Figure 2: RSSI changes are different due to the presence of people in different locations

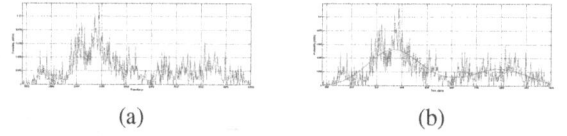

Figure 3: (a) Distribution pattern of RSSI (b) Fitted GMM with learned two components

an economical sensing environment and treat the location estimation as a machine learning problem. In particular, a sequence of RSSI of anchoring tags are collected from various known locations along with corresponding correct location label are used to train a model, which is then used to estimate the subject's location given a new RSSI. Our main contributions are summarized as follows:

- We treat the localization as a multi-class classification problem by learning the RSSI changes. We explore a series of probabilistic approaches to study the feasibility of localization in a pure passive tag array. We propose a Gaussian Mixture Model based Hidden Markov Model to track a moving subject. To the best of our knowledge, our work is first few to conduct such research in a pure passive-tag environment.

- We set up a a testbed and conduct extensive experiments. The initial results demonstrate the feasibility of our approach. Good estimation accuracy is achieved when locating and tracking a moving subject.

The remainder of the paper is organized as follows. Section 2 presents the solutions to targeting problems of localization and tracking. The experimental results and analysis are reported in Section 3. Finally, Section 4 concludes our work.

2. PROPOSED SOLUTIONS

We describe our approaches for dealing with i) localization problem (i.e., given a sequence of RSSI values, localizing a stationary subject) and ii) tracking a moving subject (i.e., given a continuous sequence of RSSI values, tracking the subject's movement).

2.1 Localizing Stationary Subjects

This problem can be formulated as to find the optimal posterior distribution $p(l_j|\mathbf{o}_i)$ given a new sequence of observed RSSI vectors:

$$j^* = \arg\max_j Pr(l_j|\mathbf{o}_i) \qquad (1)$$

2.1.1 Gaussian Mixture Model

As stated in Equation 1, our goal is to maximize $Pr(l_j|\mathbf{o}_i)$. It is noted that we will drop the subscripts i and j for sake of simplicity and clarity in the following.

$$\arg\max_{l\in\mathbb{I}} Pr(l|\mathbf{o}) = \arg\max_{l\in\mathbb{I}} \frac{Pr(\mathbf{o}|l)Pr(l)}{Pr(\mathbf{o})}$$
$$\propto \arg\max_{l\in\mathbb{I}} Pr(\mathbf{o}|l) \cdot Pr(l) \qquad (2)$$

where $Pr(l)$ is the probability of finding the subject at location l, and it is set as a uniform distribution $Pr(l) \sim 1/J$. In this work, we assume that this distribution of RSSI values x at each grid l follows a multivariate Gaussian Mixture Model. Figure 3 (a) shows an example of GMM distribution of RSSI values in our dataset.

$$f_l(x) = Pr(x|l) = \sum_{m=1}^{M} q_{l,m}\mathcal{N}(x|\mu_{l,m}, \boldsymbol{\Sigma}_{l,m})$$
$$= \sum_{m=1}^{M} \frac{q_{l,m}}{\sqrt{(2\pi)^{\mathcal{D}}|\boldsymbol{\Sigma}_{l,m}|}} \exp(-\frac{1}{2}(x-\mu_{l,m})^T \boldsymbol{\Sigma}_{l,m}^{-1}(x-\mu_{l,m}))$$
$$(3)$$

Here $q_{l,m}, \mu_{l,m}$, and $\Sigma_{l,m}$ form the model parameter set $\boldsymbol{\Phi}_l$ at grid l. q_m is the mixture weighted factor that describes the prior probability of the mth mixture component. $\mu_{l,m}$ and $\boldsymbol{\Sigma}_{l,m}$ are the mean and covariance of the mth Gaussian distribution. For each grid, the maximum likelihood estimation $\hat{\boldsymbol{\Phi}}_l$ of $\boldsymbol{\Phi}_l$ is expressed as:

$$\hat{\boldsymbol{\Phi}}_l = \arg\max_{\boldsymbol{\Phi}_l} Pr(x|l, \boldsymbol{\Phi}_l) = \arg\max_{\boldsymbol{\Phi}_l} \prod_{i=1}^{N} Pr(\mathbf{s}_i|l, \boldsymbol{\Phi}_l) \qquad (4)$$

where $\mathbf{s} = \{\mathbf{s}_1, \mathbf{s}_2, ..., \mathbf{s}_N\}$ is the training set.

We use the Expectation Maximization (EM) to solve Equation 4. The EM algorithm is an iterative process consisting of two steps: the expectation step (E-step) and the maximization step (M-step). During the iterations, a sequence of model parameters $\boldsymbol{\Phi}_l^0, \boldsymbol{\Phi}_l^1..., \boldsymbol{\Phi}_l^*$, where $\boldsymbol{\Phi}_l^0$ is the initial parameter and $\boldsymbol{\Phi}^*$ is the converged parameter when algorithm converges and terminates with satisfying predefined conditions. The sequence of model parameters can guarantee monotonic improvement of the likelihood function and can converge to a local maximum-likelihood estimation. The E-step is to find the posterior probability $Pr(l|\mathbf{s})$ given training RSSI set $\mathbf{s}$. The M-step is to maximize the expected log-likelihood of the observed data. This leads us to re-estimating the parameters for the next iteration based on the posterior probabilities calculated.

After learning the model parameters with EM, given the new RSSI signals $\mathbf{o}$ collected from tag arrays, the probability that the subject may present at certain grids is calculated according to the GMM parameters $\boldsymbol{\Phi}_l$ on each grid, then taking the location with maximal probability as the predicted location in Equation 2. In our approach, we adopt the AIC as the model selection criterion to select the best number of components for each GMM [2]. Figure 3 (b) shows the fitted GMM of RSSI with two components.

2.2 Tracking Moving Subjects

We propose the multivariate Gaussian mixture models based Hidden Markov models (GMM+HMM) and k nearest neighbor based Hidden Markov Models (kNN+HMM) to improve the performance of our approach on tracking a moving subject based on *continuous* sequence of RSSI, as shown in Figure 4. HMM has shown tremendous success in spatio-temporal features recognition and it defines a distribution over a sequence of observable RSSI $O_{1:T}$ and corre-

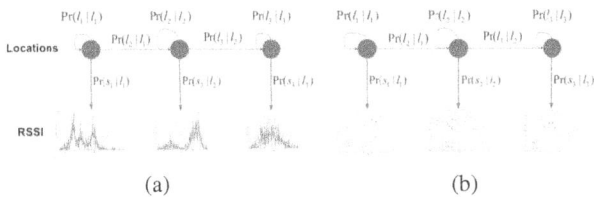

Figure 4: (a) GMM + HMM; (b)kNN + HMM

sponding locations $l_{1:T}$:

$$Pr(\mathbf{o}_{1:T}, l_{1:T}) = Pr(l_1)Pr(\mathbf{o}_1|l_1) \prod_{t=2}^{T} \underbrace{Pr(\mathbf{o}_t|l_t)}_{B} \underbrace{Pr(l_t|l_{t-1})}_{A} \tag{5}$$

Our HMM recognition approach is divided in three main steps, namely *emission matrix*, *state matrix*, and *viterbi searching*.

Emission Matrix. The emission matrix $B_{ij} = Pr(b_t = \mathbf{o}_i|b_t = l_j)$ in our case infers to the current state based on the observation RSSI vector $\mathbf{o}$ at each time stamp, which is generated by a grid map of corresponding $\mathbf{o}$. We aim at maximizing the likelihood $Pr(l_j|\mathbf{o}_i)$ when grid i is occupied. For GMM based HMM, its emission matrix can be obtained from Equation 3 in Section 2.1.1. For kNN+HMM, assuming for each observation $\mathbf{o}_j$, we find its k nearest neighbors from the training set $\mathbf{s}$, denoted as $N(\mathbf{o}_j)$, and $N^i(\mathbf{o}_j) = \{\mathbf{s}_k|\mathbf{s}_k \in \mathcal{N}(\mathbf{o}_j) \cap \mathbf{s}_k \in l_i\}$, $|N^i(\mathbf{o}_j)|$ denotes the total number of elements in $N^i(\mathbf{o}_j)$, the emission matrix is:

$$Pr(\mathbf{o}_j|l_i) = \frac{\sum_{\mathbf{s}_k \in \mathcal{N}^i(\mathbf{o}_j)}^{|\mathcal{N}^i(\mathbf{o}_j)|} \frac{1}{dis(\mathbf{o}_j, \mathbf{s}_k)}}{\sum_{\mathbf{s}_{k'} \in \mathcal{N}(\mathbf{o}_j)}^{|\mathcal{N}(\mathbf{o}_j)|} \frac{1}{dis(\mathbf{o}_j, \mathbf{s}_{k'})}} \tag{6}$$

State Matrix. For the state transition matrix, the subject can transit to next location at each time t. The transition is a Markov process where each state is conditionally independent of all other states given the previous state. The transition model can be defined as $A_{ij} = Pr(a_t = l_i|a_{t-1} = l_j)$. We adopt two strategies to calculate the next state for each given current state. The first one is 0 order, where we assume subject can move to any other locations in this testing area. The second strategy is 1-order move, where we consider subject only move to the locations which are immediate adjacent to his current location.

Viterbi Searching. The Viterbi algorithm defines $V_j(t)$, the highest probability of a single path of length t which accounts for the first t observations and ends in state l_j:

$$V_j(t) = \arg\max_{l_1, l_2, \ldots, l_{t-1}} Pr(l_1 l_2 \ldots l_t = j, \mathbf{o}_1 \mathbf{o}_2 \ldots, \mathbf{o}_t|A, B) \tag{7}$$

by induction

$$\begin{aligned} V_j(1) &= B_j(\mathbf{o}_1) \\ V_j(t+1) &= \arg\max_i V_i(t)A_{ij}B_i(\mathbf{o}_{t+1}) \end{aligned} \tag{8}$$

3. EXPERIMENTS

3.1 Data Collection and Metrics

We used one Alien ALR 9900 reader, two Circular Antennas and squiggle Higgs-4 passive tags in our experiments. We virtually divided the testing area into 9 grids, and each roughly $0.6m \times 0.6m$ in size. The RFID reader monitored and collected RSSI measurement at sampling rate of 0.5s. We collected training RSSI measurement from tags for each grid based on two strategies [9]. In the first case,

the subject stood at the center of each grid and spun around so that the resulting training data would focus on the gird center but involve different orientations. In the second case, the subject walked randomly within the cell. We mixed two RSSI collections together as the final training dataset.

We used two metrics, *accuracy* and *error distance*, to measure our proposed approaches in terms of localizing and tracking respectively. Accuracy is defined by:

$$Acc. = \frac{\sum_i^N \mathbb{I}(\hat{l}_i, l_i)}{N} \tag{9}$$

where $\mathbb{I}(a, b)$ is an indicator, 1 if a is equal to b, 0 otherwise. $\hat{l}_i$ is the predicted grid and l_i is the actual number of grids. N is the total number of observation RSSI vectors.

The error distance denotes the average accumulated deviation of error distance for each grid in each continuous trajectory:

$$Dis_{err.} = \frac{\sum_i^{|T|} dis(\hat{c}_i, c_i)}{|T|} \tag{10}$$

where c_i is the coordinates of the center of grid i, $dis(\hat{c}_i, c_i)$ is the distance between predicted grid and actual grid regarding their coordinates, $|T|$ is the total number of grids passed through by a subject in a trajectory, and t_i is the centroid distance between predicted grid and actual grid.

3.2 Results on Stationary Subject

As shown in Figure 1, RSSI collected from passive RFID tags is not free from noise, so we did some operations using sliding windows for better accuracy. We performed a moving average smoothing on the raw RSSI data, the sliding window size is set as 5.

When k is set as 2, kNN method gets the best performance in our case. The linear kernel is the best setting in SVM, and the number of weak classifiers is $1,000$ in boosting method. We adopted AIC for selecting the best number of components for each GMM. Table 1 shows the results of localizing a static subject with four different methods on varying training ratios (from 10% to 90%). Our proposed approach performs very well, and the accuracy can reach as high as 98.91%. The accuracy of all four methods are improved after preprocessing the raw data with smoothing, which reduces the effect of random fluctuations and improves the overall performance.

3.3 Results on Tracking Moving Subject

Before evaluating our approach in tracking a moving subject, two main issues closely related to dynamic tracking scenario need to be considered. One is experimental setting, e.g., what is the optimal grid size, and the other is how to deal with delay issue we found during the experiments.

Determining the Grid Size. In the experiment, we found that when the grid size is big ($0.9m \times 0.9m$), the 1-order strategy is better than the 0-order. When the grid size is small (e.g., $0.5m \times 0.5m$), the 0-order is better than the 1-order. The possible reason may lie in subject's step would become smaller under the smaller grid situations, in which the RSSI will not be distinguishable due to the increase of RSSI quick disturbance. We therefore determined each grid size as $0.6m$ based on our empirical study.

Coping with Impact of Latency. When we applied our proposed approach on tracking, we found that the latency of detecting a subject in the corresponding grid number is ≈ 1.5 seconds, which is mainly caused during the RSSI collection process. The RSSI collector is programmed with a timer to poll the RSSI with a predefined order of transmission, and needs to take around 1 second to

Table 1: Results Comparison on Localizing a Subject with Different Training Ratios

Train%	10		20		30		40		50		60		70		80		90	
	Raw	Smooth	Raw	Smooth	Raw	Smooth	Raw	Smooth	Raw	Smooth	Raw	Smooth	Raw	Smooth	Raw	Smooth	Raw	Smooth
kNN	0.863	**0.892**	0.916	**0.950**	0.943	**0.945**	0.963	**0.964**	0.962	**0.964**	0.963	**0.967**	0.970	**0.977**	0.976	**0.982**	0.987	**0.989**
SVM	0.851	**0.856**	0.888	**0.907**	0.893	**0.911**	0.908	**0.927**	0.930	**0.938**	0.933	**0.952**	0.933	**0.959**	0.878	**0.967**	0.953	**0.971**
GMM	0.752	**0.778**	0.855	**0.863**	0.909	**0.911**	0.930	**0.941**	0.936	**0.943**	0.946	**0.947**	0.967	**0.974**	0.974	**0.976**	0.979	**0.984**
AB	0.671	**0.735**	0.691	**0.779**	0.760	**0.799**	0.777	**0.810**	0.804	**0.862**	0.834	**0.881**	0.849	**0.910**	0.860	**0.927**	0.859	**0.966**

Table 2: Error Distance on Tracking Moving Subjects (m)

Methods	0-order	1-order
GMMHMM+Raw data	0.61	0.60
GMMHMM+Calibration	0.48	0.39
GMMHMM+Smooth	0.69	0.63
GMMHMM+Smooth+Calibration	0.60	0.50
kNNHMM+Raw data	0.63	0.53
kNNHMM+Calibration	0.42	0.35
kNNHMM+Smooth	0.59	0.53
kNNHMM+Smooth+Calibration	0.49	0.43

complete a new measurement with no workarounds. To cope with the impact of this latency, we adopted a forward calibration mechanism to calibrate the estimated location sequences [6]. We used a sliding time averaging window to smooth the location estimates. The technique obtains the location estimate by averaging the last few location estimates obtained by either the discrete space estimator or the spatial averaging estimator. The estimated location l_t at time t can be calculated as:

$$\hat{c}'_t = \frac{\sum_{i=t}^{t+|w|-1} \hat{c}_i}{|w|} \quad (11)$$

where $|w|$ is the window length, set as $|w| = 8$ based on our empirical study in this work. $\hat{c}_i$ is uncalibrated coordinates of the center of predicted grids at time t by Equation 7.

Table 2 shows the results on tracking a moving subject using GMM-based HMM and kNN-based HMM with the 0-order and 1-order strategies respectively. It is noted that the performance becomes worse compared with the one without smoothing the raw RSSI. This is different from the result of localizing a static subject. The possible reason may lie in that we still use the fixed length sliding window to smooth the raw RSSI in the dynamic tracking case. For example, an incorrect length may break the consistency of RSSI samples from one single grid, specially, when the window overlaps the end RSSI generated from one grid and the beginning of the next one. Or, the window length may be too short to provide the best information for the tracking process especially when the subject's walk velocity is not consistent. In our future work, we will explore a dynamic sliding window method to perform an adaptive varying length sliding window smoothing.

4. CONCLUSION

In this paper, we present the design, implementation, and evaluation of a tag-free RFID-based localization method based on probabilistic classification, in a pure passive RFID tag array. We propose to model RSSI distribution at each grid as a multivariate Gaussian Mixture Model, and Expectation Maximization (EM) is used to learn the maximum likelihood estimates of the model parameters. This approach enables us to localize a single subject based on the maximum a posteriori estimation. Furthermore, we present multivariate Gaussian mixture models (GMM) based HMM and k nearest neighbor (kNN) based HMM to track a moving subject based on continuous sequence of RSSI. We validate and evaluate our proposed approaches using a testbed consisting of pure passive RFID

tags. The results demonstrate the feasibility and effectiveness of our proposed approaches.

The experimental results show that the performance of tracking a moving subject is relatively worse than localizing a stationary subject in our current work. We will investigate how to improve the accuracy in real-time tracking in terms of reducing RSSI noise to more informative and stable features. We will also explore how to enhance our approach to enable multi-subjects localization and tracking.

5. REFERENCES

[1] Y. Liu, L. Chen, J. Pei, Q. Chen, and Y. Zhao. Mining frequent trajectory patterns for activity monitoring using radio frequency tag arrays. In *Pervasive Computing and Communications, 2007. PerCom'07. Fifth Annual IEEE International Conference on*, pages 37–46. IEEE, 2007.

[2] G. McLachlan and D. Peel. *Finite mixture models*. John Wiley & Sons, 2004.

[3] L. M. Ni, Y. Liu, Y. C. Lau, and A. P. Patil. Landmarc: indoor location sensing using active rfid. *Wireless networks*, 10(6):701–710, 2004.

[4] L. M. Ni, D. Zhang, and M. R. Souryal. Rfid-based localization and tracking technologies. *Wireless Communications, IEEE*, 18(2):45–51, 2011.

[5] C. Qian, H. Ngan, Y. Liu, and L. M. Ni. Cardinality estimation for large-scale rfid systems. *Parallel and Distributed Systems, IEEE Transactions on*, 22(9):1441–1454, 2011.

[6] M. Seifeldin and M. Youssef. A deterministic large-scale device-free passive localization system for wireless environments. In *Proceedings of the 3rd International Conference on PErvasive Technologies Related to Assistive Environments*, page 51. ACM, 2010.

[7] Q. Z. Sheng, X. Li, and S. Zeadally. Enabling next-generation rfid applications: Solutions and challenges. *IEEE Computer*, 41(9):21–28, 2008.

[8] P. Wilson, D. Prashanth, and H. Aghajan. Utilizing rfid signaling scheme for localization of stationary objects and speed estimation of mobile objects. In *RFID, 2007. IEEE International Conference on*, pages 94–99. IEEE, 2007.

[9] C. Xu, B. Firner, Y. Zhang, R. Howard, J. Li, and X. Lin. Improving rf-based device-free passive localization in cluttered indoor environments through probabilistic classification methods. In *Proceedings of the 11th international conference on Information Processing in Sensor Networks*, pages 209–220. ACM, 2012.

[10] L. Yao, Q. Z. Sheng, A. H. H. Ngu, and B. Gao. Keeping you in the loop: Enabling web-based things management in the internet of things. In *Proceedings of the 23rd ACM International Conference on Information and Knowledge Management*. ACM, 2014.

[11] D. Zhang, J. Zhou, M. Guo, J. Cao, and T. Li. Tasa: Tag-free activity sensing using rfid tag arrays. *Parallel and Distributed Systems, IEEE Transactions on*, 22(4):558–570, 2011.

Simple Arabic Stemmer

Mohammed Algarni[1]*, Brent Martin[2], Tim Bell[1], and Kourosh Neshatian[1]
[1]Computer Science and Software Engineering
University of Canterbury
Christchurch, New Zealand
[2]Enviro-Mark Solutions Ltd
Lincoln, New Zealand

ABSTRACT

We propose a root stemmer for the Modern Standard Arabic (MSA) language in an attempt to enhance the performance of Arabic Information Retrieval (AIR). The new Simple Arabic Stemmer (SAS) is based on the Quran morphology, since the Quran was a key source for the derivation of Arabic morphological rules. The stemmer is developed by decomposing all of the Quran words and studying their internal morphological structure including the roots, the patterns, and the affixes employed in the generation process. We were able to construct a relatively small lexicon capable of finding the root for most of the MSA vocabulary. Using the TREC corpus and queries, we test our approach against two well-known root stemmers, Khoja and Sebawai. The results show that SAS gives an improvement in terms of precision.

Categories and Subject Descriptors

H.3.1 [**Information Storage and Retrieval**]: Content Analysis and Indexing–Indexing methods, Linguistic processing; H.3.3 [**Information Storage and Retrieval**]: Information Search and Retrieval–Clustering, Information filtering

Keywords

Quran, Arabic, Root, Stemmer, Information Retrieval

1. INTRODUCTION

The Arabic language presents one of the most challenging morphologies in NLP. It descends from the Semitic family with many inflectional and derivational operations. What distinguishes the Semitic from the other languages is the mechanism by which surface words are generated. They follow a systematic derivational process that consists of the root (the smallest unit that can bear a meaning), vowels, and derivational affixes arranged in a precise sequence known as

the *pattern* [11]. The goal is to produce the surface word before the addition of any inflectional affixes, or as it will be referred to hereafter, the *stem*. Consider Fig. 1, where the root is "slm" ("having to do with submissiveness and safety") [5]. The Cs here represent the alphabet letters including the three long vowels (A, w, y), whereas the Vs represent the short vowels (a, u, i). There are two operations performed in this example: the first is the derivational which results in a stem with a new meaning produced by inserting the root's radicals and the short vowels into their respective slots in the pattern template. The second is inflectional which is used merely to mark the number, gender and case endings for that particular stem, or give it its surface form without altering its meaning. There are many more stems that can be generated using the same root with different patterns. For instance, the stem "silm" ("peace") with the pattern CVCC and an i as a vowel [5]. Strictly speaking, for this partic-

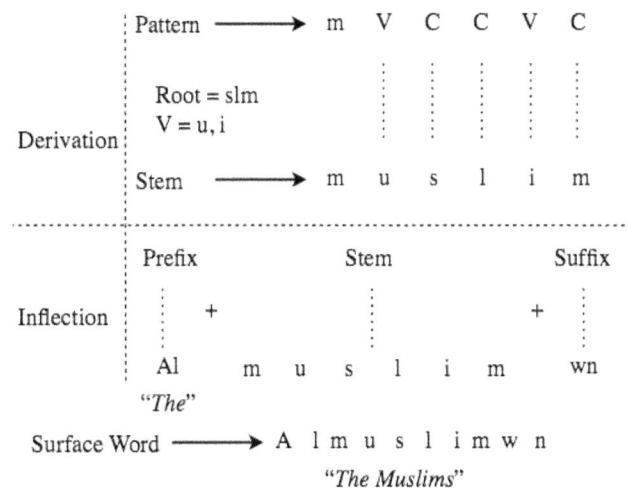

Figure 1: Arabic Word Generation Process.

ular root, and according to the author's best knowledge of the Arabic Morphology, there are 8 verbal and 34 nominal stems that can be generated using patterns found in Wright's Grammar Book [15].

The next section reviews the state-of-the-art root stemmers, and we present our approach in section 3. In section 4 we show the evaluation results of the three stemmers based on tests run on the TREC corpus, we shed light on our Simple Arabic Stemmer (SAS) future challenges and conclude in section 5.

*Corresponding Author: mafgarni@gmail.com

2. PREVIOUS RESEARCH

During the past two decades, the Arabic language has received more attention from the scientific community, and two root stemmers have emerged as a result: Khoja and Sebawai [9, 6]. Although there are several recorded attempts to find the root of an Arabic word in the past, Khoja and Sebawai are popular because they have been made available and deployed in Arabic Information Retrieval (AIR) research [1, 2, 10]. Table 1 gives a numerical comparison of the lexical contents for the two stemmers, along with the new SAS method proposed here.

The Khoja stemmer is a rule-based morphological analyser that attempts to find the root by matching the word against a list of 46 patterns. The stemmer keeps stripping off prefixes and suffixes until the remaining part matches either a pattern or a root from the lexicon. If a pattern is found, the root is produced by extracting the letters in the stem corresponding to the root's radicals in the pattern template. As a final step, the root is checked to ensure its correctness. Khoja's lexicon is composed of 4,748 roots, 46 patterns, 16 prefixes and 28 suffixes. The number of patterns is considered small compared to the actual number of patterns in the Arabic language [15]. Sebawai on the other hand is a statis-

Table 1: Lexicon Numerical Comparison

Stemmer	Root	Pattern	Prefix	Suffix
Khoja	4,748	46	16	28
Sebawai	10,405	245	215	290
SAS	2,520	110	84	183

tical morphological analyser which was trained on a list of 279,606 Arabic words in order to learn the prefix-stem-suffix combinations. The training list contained 270,000 words from the TREC Arabic corpus and 9,606 words from a classical Arabic collection called ZAD [6, 8]. The words were then segmented using the Xerox Morphological Analyser into the prefix-stem-suffix templates [4]. Another module was then developed which takes in an Arabic word and returns its root and stem based on the probability that the morphological units (prefix-stemTemplate-suffix) of this word have occurred in the training data.

3. PROPOSED SAS METHOD

The morphological content of the Quran is our focus since we are mainly concerned with the impact of morphology on AIR. The Quran is considered the first Arabic book ever written, and it has also provided linguists with the Arabic morphological rules, which were documented and taught as part of the Arabic Language Studies since then [3]. Therefore the decision was made to study this corpus more thoroughly and try to develop an Arabic morphological analyser to enhance AIR performance. The resulting stemmer uses a relatively concise lexicon; that is, because it has more general rules, the lexicon can be smaller than those used by other systems, and yet covers the language well. Fig. 2 shows the methodology we employed in developing SAS. We had to decompose all of the Quran words into their morphological units: the roots, the patterns, the prefixes and the suffixes.

For the prefixes and the suffixes, we utilised the SEQUITUR algorithm, which recognises repeated symbols in strings and substitute them to form what is called a rule [12]. We

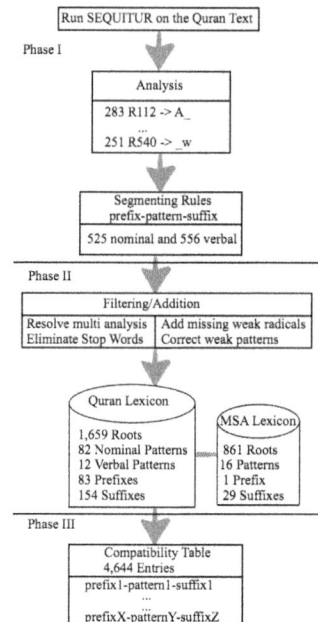

Figure 2: SAS Development Methodology.

analysed the rules with the highest frequencies to learn the most repeated affixes. Table 2 gives a sample from running SEQUITUR on the Quran. Rows 1 and 2 represent the definiteness marker "Al" ("The"), where we have rule R139 which itself consists of another rule R2294 and the letter "L". Rule2294 is just the letter "A" as a prefix, so we have "Al" which is the definiteness marker. Row 3 represents the suffix "wn" (plural.masculine.nominative), which can be used with both nouns and verbs. We leveraged an Arabic lexicon to learn the Quran's roots and patterns [14]. As there are words

Table 2: SEQUITUR Output Sample

Frequency	Rule	Symbol	Comment
57	R2294	A	
164	R139	R2294L	prefix AL
94	R399	wn	suffix wn

that could be represented with multiple analyses, each word was then manually checked to make certain it represented solely one valid morphological combination, and any extra analyses would be eliminated hence. We were able to create 7,091 nominal and 6,846 verbal surface forms, each of which is represented by a record containing its root, pattern, stem, prefix, suffix, and Part-Of-Speech (POS).

The lexicon we constructed from the Quran contained 1,659 roots, 94 patterns, 83 prefixes and 154 suffixes. Since the Modern Standard Arabic might include words that have no mention in the Quran, we extended our lexicon by stemming 6,000 more words from the Saudi newspaper Alriyadh and the Lebanese newspaper Alnahar web archives. From this corpus, we were able to add to our initial lexicon 861 roots, 16 patterns, 1 prefix and 29 suffixes. From both of the lexicons we created a compatibility table whose 4,644 entries correspond to the legal prefix-pattern-suffix combinations. It is through those compatibility tables that we determine if a root can be found. Since finding the correct pattern is a prerequisite step to finding the root, a pattern has to have an entry in the prefix-pattern-suffix table. In Arabic Broken Plurals (BPs) Morphology, it is a rule that case-marking suffixes (An, At, wn, yn) cannot be attached to them, and only possessive pronouns (k, y, hm, etc.) are allowed to be appended to them on the surface. Furthermore, when the definiteness marker "Al" ("the") appears with a stem of this type, there should be no suffix of any type attached. Fig. 3 depicts how this can be enforced using the compatibility table. The words "qwAfl" ("caravans") and "fwAkh" ("fruits")

pattern : CwACiC (Broken Plural)
root : qfl   fkh
stem : qwAfl   fwAkh
        "Caravans"   *"fruits"*

pre	stem		suf	Allowed surface forms
∅	qwAfl fwAkh	...	k	qwAflk *"your caravans"* fwAkhk *"your fruits"*
b	qwAfl fwAkh	...	nA	bqwAflnA *"by our caravans"* bfwAkhnA *"by our fruits"*
...	...	...	...	...
wl	qwAfl fwAkh	...	y	wlqwAfly *"and for my caravans"* wlfwAkhy *"and for my fruits"*

Al	qwAfl fwAkh	...	∅	AlqwAfl *"the caravans"* AlfwAkh *"the fruits"*
bAl	qwAfl fwAkh	...	∅	bAlqwAfl *"by the caravans"* bAlfwAkh *"by the fruits"*
...	...	...	...	...
wll	qwAfl fwAkh	...	∅	wllqwAfl *"and for the caravans"* wllfwAkh *"and for the fruits"*

Figure 3: Prefix-Pattern-Suffix Table Example.

share the same pattern CwACiC, but with different roots, "qfl" and "fkh" respectively. The allowed surface forms are those that either have possessive pronouns with no definiteness marker, or words with the definiteness marker, and its derivatives (bAl, fAl, kAl, wAl, ll, fbAl, fkAl, fll, wbAl, wkAl, wll), but with no suffixes.

SAS undertakes three main steps before producing the root of the word, as illustrated in Fig. 4. Consider the word llmuslimyn (plural.masculine.genitive) meaning ("for the Muslims"). SAS first attempts to decompose the word

	prefix		stem				suffix		
segment	l	l	m	s	l	m	y	n	possible template
analyze				Pattern					
	l	l	m	C	C	C	y	n	valid template
extract				s	l	m			

Figure 4: SAS Main Steps.

into all possible prefix-stem-suffix combinations and ll–muslim–yn is one of them. It then analyses those templates to val-

idate their composition by checking the compatibility table for the prefix-pattern-suffix existence. If the template is valid, it then passes the stem and the pattern to the root extraction module. As a final step, the root is checked to validate its existence. It is worth mentioning that SAS treats borrowed words with inflectional markers by simply stripping prefixes and suffixes off, therefore it does not attempt to produce the root for that particular word unless it has a pattern that exists in the compatibility table. The same approach is followed with stop words.

4. EVALUATION

Our experiments were conducted on the TREC collection containing 383,872 Arabic news articles from the Agence France Press covering the period from 1994 to 2000 [8]. There are 75 topics or queries with corresponding relevance

```
<DOC>
<DOCNO>20001208_AFP_ARB.
0003</DOCNO>
<HEADER>/ قبر 7200 ش 2 ارا 71100
84اهخ-افب / <HEADER>
<BODY>
<HEADLINE>الى السادة المشتركين</>
HEADLINE>
<TEXT>
<P>
نيقوسيا 21-8 (اف ب) - تعتذر وكالة فرانس
برس عن انقطاع البث لاسباب فنية طارئة
خارجة عن ارادتها وتستأنف الارسال.
</P>
</TEXT>
<FOOTER> افب ر غ ————— /<
FOOTER>
</BODY>
<TRAILER>جمت ديس 00 406080</
TRAILER>
</DOC>
```

```
<top>
<num> Number: AR7</
num>
<title> النقد والشعر السياسي
في العالم العربي<title/>
<desc>
كيف يعبر النقاد العرب عن
مواقفهم تجاه الشعر السياسي
سواء كان مع او ضد النظام
السياسي في بلدهم
</desc>
<narr>
يمكن ارفاق الاخبار المتعلقة
بالمهرجانات الشعرية في العالم
العربي بالموضوع ولكن الاخبار
السياسية والاخبار الفنية
الخارجة عن ميدان النقد الادبي
لا علاقة لها بالموضوع
</narr>
</top>
```

Figure 5: TREC-11 Document and Topic Sample.

judgments. Fig. 5 shows a sample of the TREC Article and Topic documents. In this example, the document consists of one paragraph conveying an apology for the AFP subscribers about the interruption of its broadcasting services. The queries were created in a collaboration effort between NIST and TREC participants [7, 13]. Using the procedure followed by the TREC participants, the results reported here were carried out using the title and the description fields of the topics as the queries. The search engine we used was the Lucene engine from Apache.

We randomly selected a sample of 100 words to measure the accuracy of the stemmers. Table 3 shows the percentage of correct roots for each stemmer. The errors fall into one of the following categories:

- Over-Stemming (OS): This occurs when a root's radical is deemed an affix and is stripped off as a result.

- Under-Stemming (US): When an extra letter that is supposed to be stemmed is left as a root's radical.

- Out-of-Lexicon (OOL): When a word contains a morphological unit that is not in the lexicon.

Table 3 shows that over-stemming appears to have the highest percentage of errors for Khoja and Sebawai. This is expected since prefixes and suffixes are stripped off blindly. SAS checks first for the legality of the prefixes and suffixes

Table 3: Correct Solution and Error Types

Stemmer	Correct	OS	US	OOL
Khoja	80%	14%	5%	1%
Sebawai	79%	15%	2%	4%
SAS	84%	4%	10%	2%

for a particular pattern before stemming them, which is why it has fewer over-stemming errors. SAS obviously needs a lexicon expansion to include more legal prefix-pattern-suffix combinations in order to overcome the under-stemming problem. Out-of-lexicon errors for SAS indicate that the lexicon does not contain the roots because there was no case found where the pattern was not recognised. For Khoja, out-of-lexicon errors point to the fact there are patterns that are missing and need to be added to the lexicon. Because the nominal pattern CACwC does not exist in the lexicon, the word "qAnwn" ("law") is not stemmed correctly to produce the root "qnn". Sebawai also needs the addition of more patterns and prefix-suffix combinations to its lexicon.

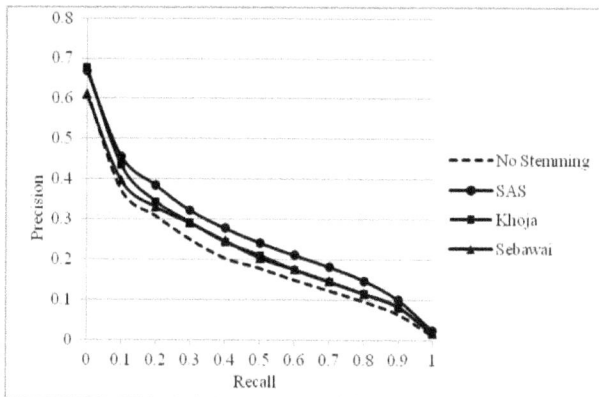

Figure 6: Average Precision and Recall.

Fig. 6 shows the 11-point average precision for the four indices: no stemming, and the roots generated using SAS, Khoja, and Sebawai respectively. SAS performs better than

Table 4: Mean Average Precision

Index	MAP
No Stemming	0.1949
Sebawai	0.2206
Khoja	0.2245
SAS	0.2538

the other two stemmers, giving higher precision at all recall points except for the 0% recall. Also, above 20% recall, Sebawai is essentially the same as Khoja while SAS produces better precisions for the remaining recall points. Table 4 shows the mean average precisions for the three stemmers compared to no stemming.

5. CONCLUSION

We presented a new approach in finding the root of any Arabic word by segmenting it into all possible prefix-pattern-suffix combinations, checking the validity of each combination and extracting the root's radicals. Further enhancements include expanding the lexicon to cover all legal prefix-pattern-suffix combinations. Moreover, the area of weak roots still needs a much deeper investigation.

6. REFERENCES

[1] R. Al-Shalabi. *Design and Implementation of an Arabic Morphological System to Support Natural Language Processing.* PhD thesis, IIT, Chicago, Illinois, 1996.

[2] M. Aljlayl, S. Beitzel, E. Jensen, A. Chowdhury, D. Holmes, M. Lee, D. Grossman, and O. Frieder. IIT at TREC-10. In *TREC-10*, Gaithersburg, Maryland, 2001.

[3] M. Alzrkshy. *AlburhAn fy Elwm AlqurAn.* Dar AlturAth, Cairo, Egypt, 1984.

[4] K. Beesley, T. Buckwalter, and S. Newton. Two-level Finite-State Analysis of Arabic Morphology. In *The Seminar on Bilingual Computing in Arabic and English*, University of Cambridge, Cambridge, England, 1989.

[5] M. Brame. *Arabic Phonology: Implications for Theory and Historical Semitic.* PhD thesis, MIT, Cambridge, Massachusetts, 1970.

[6] K. Darwish. *Probabilistic Methods for Searching OCR-Degraded Arabic Text.* PhD thesis, University of Maryland, College Park, Maryland, 2003.

[7] F. Gey and D. Oard. The TREC-2001 Cross-Language Information Retrieval Track: Searching Arabic using English, French or Arabic Queries. In *TREC-10*, Gaithersburg, Maryland, 2001.

[8] D. Graff and K. Walker. Arabic Newswire Part 1, 2001.

[9] S. Khoja and R. Garside. Stemming Arabic Text. *Computing Department, Lancaster University*, 1999.

[10] L. Larkey and M. Connel. Arabic Information Retrieval at UMASS. In *TREC-10*, Gaithersburg, Maryland, 2001.

[11] J. McCarthy. *Formal Problems in Semitic Phonology and Morphology.* PhD thesis, MIT, Cambridge, Massachusetts, 1979.

[12] C. Nevill-Manning and I. Witten. Identifying hierarchical structure in sequences: A linear-time algorithm. *Journal of Artificial Intelligence Research*, 7:67–82, 1997.

[13] D. Oard and F. Gey. The TREC-2002 Arabic/English CLIR Track. In *TREC-11*, Gaithersburg, Maryland, 2002.

[14] A. Omar. *The Comprehensive Lexicon of the Quran Words.* sTwr AlmErfh, Riyadh, Saudi Arabia, 2002.

[15] W. Wright. *A Grammar of the Arabic Language.* Cambridge University Press., Cambridge, England, 1971.

Phrase Query Optimization on Inverted Indexes

Avishek Anand*, Ida Mele†, Srikanta Bedathur‡, Klaus Berberich†

†Max Planck Institut für Informatik   ‡IIIT-Delhi   *L3S Research Center
Saarbrücken, Germany   New Delhi, India   Hannover, Germany
{imele,kberberi}@mpi-inf.mpg.de, bedathur@iiitd.ac.in, anand@l3s.de

ABSTRACT

Phrase queries are a key functionality of modern search engines. Beyond that, they increasingly serve as an important building block for applications such as entity-oriented search, text analytics, and plagiarism detection. Processing phrase queries is costly, though, since positional information has to be kept in the index and all words, including stopwords, need to be considered.

We consider an augmented inverted index that indexes selected variable-length multi-word sequences in addition to single words. We study how arbitrary phrase queries can be processed efficiently on such an augmented inverted index. We show that the underlying optimization problem is $\mathcal{NP}$-hard in the general case and describe an exact exponential algorithm and an approximation algorithm to its solution. Experiments on ClueWeb09 and The New York Times with different real-world query workloads examine the practical performance of our methods.

Categories and Subject Descriptors

H.3.3 [**Information Search & Retrieval**]: Search process

Keywords

Phrase Queries; Query Optimization; Multi-Word Indexing

1. INTRODUCTION

Phrase queries are supported by all modern search engines and one of their advanced features most popular with human users, accounting for up to 5% of query volume [10]. Even when unknown to users, phrase queries can still be implicitly invoked, for instance, by means of query-segmentation methods [6]. Beyond their use in search engines, phrase queries increasingly serve as a building block for other applications such as (a) *entity-oriented search and analytics* (e.g., to identify documents that refer to a specific entity using one of its known labels), (b) *plagiarism detection* (e.g., to identify documents that contain a highly discriminative fragment from the suspicious document), (c) *culturomics* (e.g., to identify documents that contain a specific n-gram and compute a time-series from their timestamps). Our focus in this work is on supporting phrase queries more efficiently.

Positional information about where words occur in documents has to be maintained to support phrase queries, which leads to indexes that are larger (e.g., [3] report a factor of about $4\times$ for the inverted index) than those required for keyword queries. Also, all words need to be considered in the case of phrase queries, as opposed to keyword queries for which stopwords can be ignored. Consequently, phrase queries are substantially more expensive to process, since more data has to be obtained from the index.

The problem of substring matching, which is at the core of phrase queries, has been studied extensively by the String Processing community. However, the solutions developed (e.g., suffix arrays [8] and permuterm indexes [5]) are designed for main memory and cannot cope with large-scale document collections. Solutions developed by the Information Retrieval community [11, 13] build on the inverted index, extending it to index selected multi-word sequences, so-called *phrases*, in addition to single words.

In this work, we follow the general approach of augmenting the inverted index with selected multi-word phrases. Given such an index, we focus on the problem of *phrase-query optimization*, that is, determining for a given phrase query an optimal set of terms to process it. Consider, as a concrete example, the phrase query "we are the champions" and assume that all bigrams have been indexed alongside single words. Here, the space of possible solutions includes among others {we, are, the, champions} and {we are, are the, champions}. Identifying a cost-minimal set of indexed terms is the problem addressed in this work. Existing work [13] has addressed this problem only using heuristics. In contrast, we study its hardness and devise an exact exponential algorithm and an approximation algorithm to its solution.

Contributions that we make in this work thus include (1) we study the problem of *phrase-query optimization*, establish its $\mathcal{NP}$-hardness, and describe an exact exponential algorithm as well as an $\mathcal{O}(\log n)$-approximation algorithm to its solution; (2) an *experimental evaluation* on ClueWeb09 and a corpus from The New York Times, as two real-world document collections and different workloads denoting the three kinds of tasks where phrase queries are applicable, comparing our approach against state-of-the-art competitor and establishing its efficiency and effectiveness.

Organization. The rest of this paper is organized as follows. Section 2 introduces our formal model and our augmented-index framework. Section 3 deals with optimizing phrase queries. Section 4 describes our experimental evaluation. Finally, we relate our work to existing prior work in Section 5.

2. MODEL AND FRAMEWORK

We let $\mathcal{V}$ denote the *vocabulary* of all words. The *set of all non-empty sequences of words* from this vocabulary is denoted $\mathcal{V}^+$. Given a word sequence $\mathbf{s} = \langle s_1, \ldots, s_n \rangle \in \mathcal{V}^+$, we let $|\mathbf{s}| = n$ denote its length. We use $\mathbf{s}[i]$ to refer to the word s_i at the i-

th position of **s**, and $\mathbf{s}[i..j]$ $(i \leq j)$ to refer to the word subsequence $\langle s_i, \ldots, s_j \rangle$. Given two word sequences **r** and **s**, we let $pos(\mathbf{r}, \mathbf{s})$ denote the set of positions at which **r** occurs in **s**, formally

$$pos(\mathbf{r}, \mathbf{s}) = \{\, 1 \leq i \leq |\mathbf{s}| \mid \forall 1 \leq j \leq |\mathbf{r}| : \mathbf{s}[i+j-1] = \mathbf{r}[j] \,\} \ .$$

For $\mathbf{r} = \langle ab \rangle$ and $\mathbf{s} = \langle cabcab \rangle$, as a concrete example, we have $pos(\mathbf{r}, \mathbf{s}) = \{\, 2, 5 \,\}$. We say that **s** *contains* **r** if $pos(\mathbf{r}, \mathbf{s}) \neq \emptyset$. To ease notation, we treat single words from $\mathcal{V}$ also as word sequences when convenient. This allows us, for instance, to write $pos(w, \mathbf{s})$ to refer to the positions at which w occurs in **s**.

We let the bag of word sequences $\mathcal{C}$ denote our *document collection*. Each document $\mathbf{d} \in \mathcal{C}$ is a word sequence from $\mathcal{V}^+$. Using our notation, we now define *document frequency* as common in Information Retrieval. Let $\mathcal{S}$ be a bag of word sequences (e.g., the document collection), we define the document frequency of the word sequence **r**, as the total number of word sequences from $\mathcal{S}$ containing it $df(\mathbf{r}, \mathcal{S}) = |\, \{\, \mathbf{s} \in \mathcal{S} \mid pos(\mathbf{r}, \mathbf{s}) \neq \emptyset \,\} \,|$.

Framework We build on the popular *inverted index* for our phrase query processing task. To support arbitrary phrase queries, an inverted index has to contain all words from the vocabulary in its dictionary (i.e., $\mathcal{V} \subseteq \mathcal{D}$) and record positional information in its posting lists. We denote each posting as $(id(\mathbf{d}), pos(w, \mathbf{d}))$ for word w and document **d** and the positions $pos(w, \mathbf{d})$ at which the word occurs. We augment the inverted index by adding multi-word sequences, so-called *phrases*, to the set of terms. The dictionary $\mathcal{D}$ of such an *augmented inverted index* thus consists of *individual words* alongside *phrases* (i.e., $\mathcal{D} \subseteq \mathcal{V}^+$) as terms. To process a given phrase query **q**, a set of terms is selected from the dictionary $\mathcal{D}$, and the corresponding posting lists are intersected to identify documents that contain the phrase.

Several authors [4, 11, 13] have exploited the high selectivity of word sequences and proposed phrase-augmented indexes. However, the approaches for *query-optimization problem*, determining the set of terms that should be used to process a given phrase query, are based on heuristics. We take a principled approach to address the problem, including its formalization and a study of its hardness as described in Section 3.

3. QUERY OPTIMIZATION

We now describe how a phrase query **q** can be processed using a given augmented inverted index with a concrete dictionary $\mathcal{D}$. Our objective is thus to determine, *at query-processing time*, a subset $\mathcal{P} \subseteq \mathcal{D}$ of terms, further referred to as *query plan*, that can be used to process **q**.

To formulate the problem, we first need to capture when a query plan $\mathcal{P}$ can be used to process a phrase query **q**. Intuitively, each word must be covered by at least one term from $\mathcal{P}$. We capture whether $\mathcal{P}$ *covers* **q** using the predicate

$$
\begin{aligned}
covers(\mathcal{P}, \mathbf{q}) \ = \ & \forall 1 \leq i \leq |\mathbf{q}| : \exists \mathbf{t} \in \mathcal{P} : \exists j \in pos(\mathbf{q}[i], \mathbf{t}) : \\
& \forall 1 \leq k \leq |\mathbf{t}| : \mathbf{q}[i-j+k] = \mathbf{t}[k]
\end{aligned}
$$

The phrase query $\mathbf{q} = \langle abc \rangle$, as a concrete example, can thus be processed using $\{\, \langle ab \rangle, \langle bc \rangle \,\}$ but not $\{\, \langle ab \rangle, \langle cd \rangle \,\}$. Second, we need to quantify the cost of processing a phrase query using a specific query plan.

Intersecting of posting lists can be done using *term-at-a-time* (TAAT) or *document-at-a-time query processing* (DAAT).

For both, in the worst case the cost of processing a phrase query depends on the sizes of posting lists read and thus the set of terms selected to process the query.

We model the cost of a query plan $\mathcal{P}$ as the total number of postings that has to be read $c(\mathcal{P}) = \sum_{t \in \mathcal{P}} df(t, \mathcal{C})$. While sizes of positional postings are not uniform (e.g., due to varying numbers of contained positions), suggesting collection frequency as a possibly more accurate cost measure, we found little difference in practice. The sum of document frequencies closely correlates with the response times of our system.

Assembling the above definitions of coverage and cost, we now formally define the problem of finding a cost-minimal query plan $\mathcal{P}$ for a phrase query **q** and dictionary $\mathcal{D}$ as the following $\mathcal{NP}$-hard optimization problem

DEFINITION 1. PHRASE-QUERY OPTIMIZATION

$$\arg\min_{\mathcal{P} \subseteq \mathcal{D}} \ c(\mathcal{P}) \quad s.t. \quad covers(\mathcal{P}, \mathbf{q}) \ .$$

THEOREM 1. PHRASE-QUERY OPTIMIZATION *is* $\mathcal{NP}$-*hard.*

Proofs of all theorems and corollaries are omitted but are available accompanying technical report [1].

3.1 Optimal Solution

If an optimal query plan $\mathcal{P}^*$ exists, so that every term therein occurs exactly once in the query, we can determine an optimal query plan using dynamic programming based on the recurrence

$$
\text{OPT}(i) =
\begin{cases}
df(\mathbf{q}[1..i], \mathcal{C}) & : \mathbf{q}[1..i] \in \mathcal{D} \\
\min\limits_{j < i} \left(\text{OPT}(j) + \min\limits_{\substack{k \leq j+1 \wedge \\ \mathbf{q}[k..i] \in \mathcal{D}}} df(\mathbf{q}[k..i], \mathcal{C}) \right) & : \text{otherwise}
\end{cases}
$$

in time $\mathcal{O}(n^2)$ and space $\mathcal{O}(n)$ where $|\mathbf{q}| = n$. $\text{OPT}(i)$ denotes the cost of an optimal solution to the prefix subproblem $\mathbf{q}[1..i]$ – once the dynamic-programming table has been populated, an optimal query plan can be constructed by means of backtracking. In the first case, the prefix subproblem can be covered using a single term. In the second case, the optimal solution combines an optimal solution to a smaller prefix subproblem, which is the optimal substructure inherent to dynamic programming, with a single term that covers the remaining suffix.

THEOREM 2. *If an optimal query plan* $\mathcal{P}^*$ *for a phrase query* **q** *exists such that* $\forall \mathbf{t} \in \mathcal{P}^* \ : \ |pos(\mathbf{t}, \mathbf{q})| = 1$ *, then* $c(\mathcal{P}^*) = \text{OPT}(|\mathbf{q}|)$*, that is, an optimal solution can be determined using the recurrence* OPT.

It entails that we can efficiently determine optimal query plans for phrase queries with no repeated words.

COROLLARY 1. *We can compute an optimal query plan for a phrase query* **q** *in polynomial time and space, if* $\forall 1 \leq i \leq |\mathbf{q}| \ : |pos(\mathbf{q}[i], \mathbf{q})| = 1$ *.*

In practice this special case is important, since a large fraction of phrases queries in typical workloads do not contain repeated words.

Otherwise, when there is no optimal query plan $\mathcal{P}^*$ according to Theorem 2, dynamic programming can not be directly applied, since there is no optimal substructure. Consider, as a concrete problem instance, the phrase query $\mathbf{q} = \langle abxayb \rangle$ with dictionary $\mathcal{D} = \{\, \langle a \rangle, \langle b \rangle, \langle x \rangle, \langle y \rangle, \langle ab \rangle \,\}$ and assume $df(\mathbf{t}, \mathcal{C}) > 1$ for $\mathbf{t} \in \{\, \langle a \rangle, \langle b \rangle, \langle x \rangle, \langle y \rangle \,\}$ and $df(\langle ab \rangle, \mathcal{C}) = 1$. Here, the optimal solution $\mathcal{P}^* = \{\, \langle a \rangle, \langle b \rangle, \langle x \rangle, \langle y \rangle \,\}$ does not contain an optimal solution to any prefix subproblem $\mathbf{q}[1..i]$ $(1 < i < |\mathbf{q}|)$, which all contain the term $\langle ab \rangle$.

However, as we describe next, an optimal query plan can be computed, in the general case, using a combination of exhaustive search over sets of repeated terms and a variant of our above recurrence.

For a phrase query **q** let the set of repeated terms be formally defined as $\mathcal{R} = \{\, \mathbf{t} \in \mathcal{D} \mid |pos(\mathbf{t}, \mathbf{q})| > 1 \,\}$. Let further $\mathcal{F} \subseteq$

Algorithm 1: PHRASE-QUERY OPTIMIZATION

Input: Phrase query $\mathbf{q}$, dictionary $\mathcal{D}$
Output: Cost $optCost$ of optimal query plan
1   $\mathcal{R} = \{\, \mathbf{t} \in \mathcal{D} \ : \ |\,pos(\mathbf{t}, \mathbf{q})\,| > 1 \,\}$
2   $optCost = \infty$
3   **for** $\mathcal{F} \in 2^{\mathcal{R}}$ **do**
4     $cost = c(\mathcal{F}) + \text{OPT}'(|\mathbf{q}|)$
5   **if** $cost < optCost$ **then**
6       $optCost = cost$

7   **return** $optCost$

$\mathcal{R}$ denote a subset of repeated terms. We now define a modified document frequency that is zero for terms from $\mathcal{F}$, formally

$$df'(\mathbf{t}, \mathcal{C}) = \begin{cases} 0 & : \quad \mathbf{t} \in \mathcal{F} \\ df(\mathbf{t}, \mathcal{C}) & : \quad \text{otherwise} \end{cases}$$

and denote by OPT$'$ the variant of our above recurrence that uses this modified document frequency.

Algorithm 1 considers all subsets of repeated terms and, for each of them, extends it into a query plan for $\mathbf{q}$ by means of the recurrence OPT$'$. The algorithm keeps track of the best solution seen and eventually returns it. Its correctness directly follows from the following theorem.

THEOREM 3. *Let $\mathcal{P}^*$ denote an optimal query plan for the phrase query $\mathbf{q}$ and $\mathcal{F} = \{\, \mathbf{t} \in \mathcal{P}^* \ | \ |\,pos(\mathbf{t}, \mathbf{q})\,| > 1 \,\}$ be the set of repeated terms therein, then $c(\mathcal{F}) + \text{OPT}'(|\mathbf{q}|) \leq c(\mathcal{P}^*)$.*

The cost of Algorithm 1 depends on the number of repeated terms $|\mathcal{R}|$, which is small in practice and can be bounded in terms of the number of positions in $\mathbf{q}$ occupied by a repeated word $r = |\{\, 0 \leq i \leq |\mathbf{q}| \ | \ |\,pos(\mathbf{q}[i], \mathbf{q})\,| > 1 \,\}|$. For our above example phrase query $\mathbf{q} = \langle abxayb \rangle$ we obtain $r = 4$. Note that $|R| \leq \frac{r \cdot (r+1)}{2}$ holds. Algorithm 1 thus has time complexity $\mathcal{O}(2^{\frac{r \cdot (r+1)}{2}} n^2)$ and space complexity $\mathcal{O}(n^2)$ where $|\mathbf{q}| = n$.

3.2 Approximation Guarantee

Computing an optimal query plan can be computationally expensive in the worst case, as just shown. It turns out, however, that we can efficiently compute an $\mathcal{O}(\log n)$-approximation, reusing results for SET COVER [12].

To this end, we convert an instance of our problem, consisting of a phrase query $\mathbf{q}$ and a dictionary $\mathcal{D}$ with associated costs, into a SET COVER instance. Let the universe of items $\mathcal{U} = \{\, 1, \ldots, |\mathbf{q}| \,\}$ correspond to positions in the phrase query. For each term $\mathbf{t} \in \mathcal{D}$, we define a subset $S_\mathbf{t} \subseteq \mathcal{U}$ of covered positions as

$$S_\mathbf{t} = \{\, 1 \leq i \leq |\mathbf{q}| \ | \ \exists j \in pos(\mathbf{t}, \mathbf{q}) \ : \ j \leq i < j + |\mathbf{t}| \,\} \ .$$

The collection of subsets of $\mathcal{U}$ is then defined as $\mathcal{S} = \{\, S_\mathbf{t} \ | \ \mathbf{t} \in \mathcal{D} \,\}$ and we define $cost(S_\mathbf{t}) = df(\mathbf{t}, \mathcal{C})$ as a cost function. For our concrete problem instance from above, we obtain the instance $\mathcal{U} = \{\, 1, \ldots, 6 \,\}$ and $\mathcal{S} = \{\, \{\, 1, 4 \,\}, \{\, 2, 6 \,\}, \{\, 3 \,\}, \{\, 5 \,\}, \{\, 1 \,\} \,\}$.

We can now use the greedy algorithm that selects sets from $\mathcal{S}$ based on their benefit-cost ratio, which is known to be a $\mathcal{O}(\log n)$-approximation algorithm [12]. This can be implemented in $\mathcal{O}(n^2)$ time and $\mathcal{O}(n^2)$ space where $|q| = n$.

Note that, as a key difference to the greedy algorithm described in [13], which to the best of our knowledge does not give an approximation guarantee, our greedy algorithm selects subsets (corresponding to terms from the dictionary) taking into account the number of additional items covered and the coverage already achieved by selected subsets.

4. EXPERIMENTAL EVALUATION

We now describe our experimental evaluation. We begin with the description of the datasets, followed by a comparison of the query-optimization methods from Section 3.

4.1 Setup

Document Collections. We use two real-world document collections: (1) *ClueWeb09-B* (CW) with more than 50 million English web documents crawled in 2009; and (2) *The New York Times Annotated Corpus* (NYT) with more than 1.8 million articles published by The New York Times between 1987 and 2007.

Workloads. To reflect different use cases including web search, entity-oriented search, and plagiarism detection, we consider four different workloads for our experimental evaluation: (1) **MSN** is a query workload made available for research by a commercial web search engine in 2009. It contains queries routed to the U.S. Microsoft search site and sampled during May 2006. (2) **MSNP** as the subset of explicit phrase queries from the aforementioned query workload, i.e., queries enclosed in quotes (e.g., "national pandemic influenza response plan"). (3) **YAGO** is a workload of entity labels from the YAGO2 knowledge base [7]. In its `rdfs:label` relation, it collects strings that may refer to a specific entity, which are mined from anchor texts in Wikipedia. For the entity `Bob_Dylan`, as a concrete example, it includes among others the entity labels "bob dylan," "bob allen zimmerman," and "robert allen zimmerman." (4) **NYTS/CWS** as workloads consisting of 1,000,000 sentences randomly sampled from the NYT and CW document collection, respectively.

Note that we excluded single-word queries from all workloads. Interestingly, queries are on average shorter in the YAGO workload (2.45 words) than in the web search query workloads. By design, the NYTS and CWS workloads consist of substantially longer phrase queries. We use document frequency as a cost measure for all our experiments. As mentioned earlier, one could use collection frequency instead. In practice, though, the two measures are highly correlated and we did not observe big differences. Also, as a one-time pre-processing performed using Hadoop and made available to all methods, we compute n-gram statistics for the workload and document collection using the method described in [2].

4.2 Experimental Results

The experiment examines the effect that the choice of query-optimization method can have on query-processing performance. We consider three query-optimization methods for this experiment: the greedy algorithm (GRD) from [13], our greedy algorithm (APX) that comes with an approximation guarantee, and our exponential exact algorithm (OPT). GRD considers terms in increasing order of their document frequency, thus based on their selectivity, and chooses a term if it covers any yet-uncovered portion of the phrase query. Originally designed to deal with bigrams only, we extend GRD to break ties based on term length, and thus favor the longer term, if two terms have the same document frequency.

To compare the query-optimization methods, we built augmented inverted indexes whose dictionaries include all phrases up to a specific maximum length $l \in \{\, 2, 3, 4, 5 \,\}$. Thus, for $l = 5$, all phrases of length five or less are indexed. This allows us to study the behavior of the methods as more terms to choose from become available.

Table 1 reports average query-processing costs, corresponding to the number of postings read, for all sensible combinations of our document collections and workloads for different choices of l. When studying the behavior of the different query-optimization methods on an augmented inverted index obtained for a specific choice of l, we exclude queries from all workloads that consist of

NYT												
	GRD				APX				OPT			
	$l=2$	$l=3$	$l=4$	$l=5$	$l=2$	$l=3$	$l=4$	$l=5$	$l=2$	$l=3$	$l=4$	$l=5$
YAGO	23,070	18,793	16,978	15,693	22,997	18,775	16,970	15,682	22,854	18,707	16,961	15,674
MSNP	32,466	21,415	19,866	19,734	32,177	21,392	19,857	19,726	31,796	21,333	19,844	19,714
MSN	29,755	22,635	21,596	21,442	29,596	22,621	21,590	21,436	29,300	22,590	21,582	21,427
NYTS	238,270	10,466	1,035	203	228,117	9,833	955	182	217,068	9,135	895	170

CW												
	GRD				APX				OPT			
	$l=2$	$l=3$	$l=4$	$l=5$	$l=2$	$l=3$	$l=4$	$l=5$	$l=2$	$l=3$	$l=4$	$l=5$
YAGO	142,451	67,046	58,463	55,651	140,659	66,398	58,374	55,572	138,889	65,938	58,327	55,537
MSNP	281,427	87,705	77,695	95,180	275,841	86,986	77,634	95,145	268,994	86,413	77,552	95,103
MSN	285,823	150,526	163,286	209,294	282,217	150,130	163,257	209,278	277,676	149,829	163,219	209,250
CWS	2,846,711	221,089	83,170	53,795	2,692,296	195,132	43,256	33,167	2,576,273	186,095	41,874	32,252

Table 1: Query optimization results

fewer than l words. This is reasonable, since those queries can simply be processed by looking up the corresponding n-gram and there is nothing to optimize.

As we can see from the table, the approximate solutions (GRD and APX) work well, and their costs are close to the ones obtained with the optimal algorithm (OPT). As expected, the performance of APX, our approximation algorithm, is closer to optimal than the performance of the heuristic GRD. This difference is more pronounced on the NYTS and CWS workloads consisting, by construction, of verbose queries.

Also, as expected, we observe that with increasing l, the number of posting read per query decreases for all query optimizers. The improvements are drastic when considering sentence workloads for all optimizers. For shorter queries there is less room for query optimization, as observed in the YAGO and MSNP workloads. For longer queries, in contrast, there is more room for query optimization and thus an opportunity for OPT and APX to make better choices, as observed on the NYTS/CWS workloads consisting of verbose queries. This is even more noticeable for larger choices of l, as can be seen from the results obtained for $l=4$ on CWS where OPT processes less than 50% of postings than GRD.

We also observe that a majority of queries does not contain repeated words. Even otherwise the number of repetitions is typically small. This has a favorable impact on the execution time of OPT. We observe that all query-optimization methods perform similarly in terms of execution time. Our optimization methods are thus robust and achieve superior performance to GRD.

5. RELATED WORK

Williams et al. [13] put forward the *combined index* to support phrase queries efficiently. It assembles three levels of indexing: (i) a *first-word index* as a positional inverted index, (ii) a *next-word index* that indexes all bigrams containing a stopword, and (iii) a *phrase index* with popular phrases from a query log. Its in-memory dictionary is kept compact by exploiting common first words between bigrams. Query processing escalates through these indexes – first it consults the phrase index and, if the phrase query is not found therein, processes it using bigrams and unigrams from the other indexes. Transier and Sanders [11] select bigrams to index based only on characteristics of the document collection. Selecting bigrams makes sense in settings where phrase queries are issued by human users and tend to be short – as observed for web

search by Spink et al. [10]. Variable-length multi-word sequences have previously been considered by Chang and Poon [4] in their *common phrase index*, which builds on [13], but indexes variable-length phrases common in the workload.

6. CONCLUSION

In this work, we studied the problem of phrase-query optimization on augmented inverted indexes. We established its $\mathcal{NP}$-hardness and put forward an exact exponential algorithm as well as an $\mathcal{O}(\log n)$-approximation algorithm to its solution. Our experiments on different document collections and workloads established that real-world instances are well-behaved, so that the approximate algorithms almost always get close to the optimum.

7. REFERENCES

[1] A. Anand, I. Mele, S. Bedathur, and K. Berberich. Phrase Query Optimization on Inverted Indexes. Technical Report MPI-I-2014-5-002, MPII, 2014.
[2] K. Berberich and S. Bedathur. Computing n-Gram Statistics in MapReduce *EDBT* 2013.
[3] S. Büttcher and C. Clarke. *Information Retrieval.* 2010.
[4] M. Chang and C. K. Poon. Efficient phrase querying with common phrase index. *IPM*, 44(2):756–769, 2008.
[5] P. Ferragina and R. Venturini. The compressed permuterm index. *ACM TALG*, 7(1):10, 2010.
[6] M. Hagen, M. Potthast, A. Beyer, and B. Stein. Towards optimum query segmentation: in doubt without. *CIKM* 2012
[7] J. Hoffart, F. Suchanek, K. Berberich, and G. Weikum. Yago2: A spatially and temporally enhanced knowledge base from wikipedia. *Artif. Intell.*, 2013.
[8] U. Manber and E. W. Myers. Suffix arrays: A new method for on-line string searches. *SIAM J. Comput.*, 22(5), 1993.
[9] J. Neraud. Elementariness of a finite set of words is co-np-complete. *ITA*, 24:459–470, 1990.
[10] A. Spink, D. Wolfram, B. J. Jansen, and T. Saracevic. Searching the web: The public and their queries. *JASIST*, 52(3):226–234, 2001.
[11] F. Transier and P. Sanders. Out of the box phrase indexing. *SPIRE* 2008.
[12] V. V. Vazirani. *Approximation algorithms.* 2001.
[13] H. E. Williams, J. Zobel, and D. Bahle. Fast phrase querying with combined indexes. *ACM TOIS*, 22(4):573–594, 2004.

CLIR for Informal Content in Arabic Forum Posts

Mossaab Bagdouri
Dep. of Computer Science
University of Maryland
College Park, MD, USA
mossaab@umd.edu

Douglas W. Oard
iSchool and UMIACS
University of Maryland
College Park, MD, USA
oard@umd.edu

Vittorio Castelli
T.J. Watson Research Center
IBM
Yorktown Heights, NY, USA
vittorio@us.ibm.com

ABSTRACT

The field of Cross-Language Information Retrieval (CLIR) addresses the problem of finding documents in some language that are relevant to a question posed in a different language. Retrieving answers to questions written using formal vocabulary from collections of informal documents, as with many types of social media, is a largely unexplored subfield of CLIR. Because formal and informal content are often intermingled, CLIR systems that excel at finding formal content may tend to select formal over informal content. To measure this effect, a test collection annotated for both relevance and informality is needed. This paper describes the development of a small test collection for this task, with questions posed in formal English and the documents consisting of intermixed formal and informal Arabic. Experiments with this collection show that dialect classification can help to recognize informal content, thus improving precision. At the same time, the results indicate that neither dialect-tuned morphological analysis nor a lightweight CLIR approach that minimizes propagation of translation errors yet yield a reliable improvement in recall for informal content when compared to a straightforward document translation architecture.

Categories and Subject Descriptors

H.3.3 [**Information Storage and Retrieval**]: Information Search and Retrieval

Keywords: CLIR; Informality; Social Media; Evaluation

1. INTRODUCTION

The history of information retrieval research has been strongly dominated by a focus on retrieval of what we might call "formal" content, content written with dissemination in mind. Such content potentially has high value, but constitutes only a tiny fraction of the words produced by our planet's 7 billion people. Recently, activities such as the TREC Blog and Microblog tracks have begun to explore

how retrieval systems might be tailored to the unique characteristics of informal content. Perhaps unsurprisingly, it turns out that informal content poses unique challenges for Cross-Language Information Retrieval (CLIR) as well. In this paper, we begin to explore those challenges.

For our experiments, we use what we believe to be the first test collection to focus on CLIR from informal content. We focus on a part of the collection developed initially for the DARPA Broad Operational Language Translation (BOLT) program that includes 11 English questions and 12.6 million Arabic Web forum posts. The questions are well-formed requests, written in formal English. We focus in this paper on retrieval of entire posts using post-scale annotations by independent annotators for relevance and informal language.

The remainder of this paper is organized as follows. Sections 2 and 3 address the consequences of translating documents with a state-of-the-art translation system. We describe a pilot study that shows how this approach results in an adverse selection bias. Section 4 then explores the use of an alternative CLIR architecture based on Probabilistic Structured Queries (PSQ) for recall enhancement, coupled with automatic detection of informal content for precision enhancement. Section 5 summarizes the process of building a collection to test our methods and reports results. We conclude in Section 6 with a discussion of the implications of our results for future work on CLIR from informal content.

2. THE BOLT IR TEST COLLECTION

The collection to be searched consists of Arabic Internet forums, which are Web sites in which users submit *posts* that either originate or extend *threads*; these form tree-like discussions. We used the BOLT Phase 2 IR test collection. This collection was crawled by the Linguistic Data Consortium (LDC) from public Web forums in Egypt with material written between 12 Dec 2001 and 19 May 2012[1] and consists of 12,612,144 posts from 773,861 threads distributed across 272 forums found on 32 Egyptian websites. Our retrieval task is to find relevant *posts* in which useful answers to well formed English questions can be found. For the experiments in this paper, we treat posts as isolated documents, making no use of the thread structure of the forums.

A crucial characteristic of Web forums is that authors will sometimes copy text from various sources (e.g., a news article) into their posts, and that copied text may be written in

---

---

[1]The collection, LDC2013E08, also contains English and Chinese, but we focus only on Arabic in our experiments. We will make our annotations available to the LDC for inclusion in their public release.

وقال إن ذلك سيؤدي إلي ارتفاع تكلفة الأنتاج للعصائر في مصر بنسبة في حدود20% تقريبا وأوضح
أن هذه الزيادة ستسري علي الإنتاج الجديد الذي سيستخدم المركزات بالأسعار المرتفعة (...)

He said that this would lead to a rise in the cost of production for juices in Egypt at a rate of approximately 20 borders and explained that this increase will apply to the new production, which will be used concentrates on high prices (...)

كلامها صحيح فعلا السياحة باى باى لسه خطفيين اتنين سياح فى سيناء
ذى ما قال الأخ توفيق عكاشة مصر هتشوف ايام ما شفتهاش قبل كده

Its really true words tourism <u>any any</u> <u>Khatfin</u> just two tourists in Sinai like <u>what</u> brother Tawfiq Okasha said Egypt will see days I don't see it before

Figure 1: Two Arabic passages with their machine translations. The translation of the MSA passage on the left is better than that of the Egyptian one on the right. The MT confused the Arabic transliteration of the English word "Bye" (i.e. باى) with the Arabic word بأي meaning "with any". Also, the word خطفيين, meaning kidnappers, was simply transliterated as "Khatfin".

formal language, even when the author otherwise uses informal language. This is different from the behavior observed on short messaging services such as Twitter, where strict limits on the number of characters make the use of Web links to refer to existing content more common. To determine the prevalence of posts containing at least some informal content, we randomly selected 1,000 posts from the collection and the first author of this paper manually annotated them as informal or formal. We found that 819 of the sampled posts contained one or more Egyptian Arabic terms and thus clearly contained some informal content, 50 contained only Modern Standard Arabic (MSA) terms but clearly contained some informal usage, 72 contained only MSA terms but were of debatable formality (i.e., they might be considered formal or informal by different annotators), and 59 contained only MSA terms and were clearly formal. In this paper we consistently treat posts that contain content of debatable formality to be formal. We conclude that approximately 87% (869 of 1000) of the posts in the collection contain some informal content, and that 94% (819/869) of these could be recognized by simply detecting the presence of one or more terms from some Arabic dialect.

The questions for our test collection are drawn from the BOLT Phase 2 IR Evaluation Questions, created also by the LDC (LDC2013E136). In addition to the 17 questions that explicitly targeted Egyptian Arabic, we included 7 questions that do not target any specific language, but that in our judgment are expected to return results from Arabic content. As spelling correction is not a focus of our current work, we removed one question for which a focal term was, in our opinion, incorrectly transliterated. The BOLT program reserved the odd-numbered questions for progress testing, so we used in our study only the 11 even-numbered questions.[2] Of these, we used three for exploratory analysis and eight for the experiments reported in Section 5.

3. EXPLORATORY ANALYSIS

For our exploratory analysis, we selected the three English questions for which the teams were instructed to retrieve answers from the Arabic portion of the test collection alone, and for which both participating systems in the 2013 BOLT IR evaluation returned answer passages that together spanned 25 or more different Arabic posts.[3] The first author of this paper, a native speaker of Arabic who is familiar with Egyptian Arabic, examined every post returned by either system that contained at least one passage marked as

relevant by the LDC to identify posts containing informal use of Arabic. For these annotations, and throughout this paper, we defined a post as containing informal use of Arabic if (a) it contains at least one lexical item that is not present in properly written MSA, or (b) if any of the expressions would not be used in a formal MSA document, in the annotator's opinion, even if each individual term is in MSA. We found only about one-third of the posts (32 of 90) in which a relevant passage had been found were annotated as containing any informal use of Arabic. This finding is surprising, as the test collection and the questions had been developed specifically to evaluate CLIR on informal content.

We proffer two possible explanations. Either (1) the small fraction of the collection that contains only formal content is particularly rich in relevant posts, or (2) the participating systems were much better at finding relevant content among the formal posts than among the informal ones. Given the nature of the questions, the first explanation seems unlikely. To understand whether the second one is plausible, we need to look under the hood to see how the two participating systems actually worked. These were complex systems for fully automatic question answering that were still at the time in the midst of development. One notable commonality was that both used a document translation architecture in which statistical Machine Translation (MT) was first used to translate the entire Arabic collection into English, with the question answering process then run on the resulting English translations. Figure 1 shows English translations of two Arabic passages, one of which was written in MSA, the other in Egyptian Arabic. Two effects are evident. First, limitations of the translation model result in transliterations being generated for some words. Second, the MT language model seems to make poor decisions in the vicinity of the transliterated words. The combination of these two effects is substantially more severe when translating Egyptian Arabic than MSA, despite the fact that the translation models were specifically tuned using Egyptian Arabic examples.

4. FINDING RELEVANT INFORMALITY

In this section we describe a three-step process for enhancing our ability to find relevant informal content. First, we clarify our goal. BOLT question answering systems were optimized for finding *relevant* content, with no specific requirement for informality. If it is informal content that we seek, we need evaluation measures that reward success at that task. Second, we need ways of enhancing recall on relevant informal content, even at some cost in precision; we describe two such techniques. Third, we then need to enhance precision on informal content by suppressing retrieval of posts that contain only formal content.

---

[2]Questions BIR_200052, BIR_200056, BIR_200058, BIR_200060, BIR_200062, BIR_200064, BIR_200066, BIR_200130, BIR_200134, BIR_200138, BIR_200144.
[3]BIR_200056, BIR_200060, BIR_200066.

4.1 Rethinking Evaluation Measures

Our goal is to optimize retrieval of informal content. Two parameters control this measure: Relevance and Informality. For a question $q \in \mathcal{Q}$ and a document $d \in \mathcal{D}$, we want an evaluation function $s : (\mathcal{Q}, \mathcal{D}) \to [\ ,1]$ that, for every pair of documents d_1 and d_2, satisfies:

- If d is not relevant to q, then $s(q, d)$

- If d is formal then $s(q, d)$

- If d_1 and d_2 are of equal relevance, but d_1 is more informal, then $s(q, d_1) \geq s(q, d_2)$

- If d_1 and d_2 are of equal informality, but d_1 is more relevant than d_2, then $s(q, d_1) \geq s(q, d_2)$

When relevance and informality are binary valued functions $r : (\mathcal{Q}, \mathcal{D}) \to\ , 1$ and $i : \mathcal{D} \to\ , 1$, this simplifies to:

$$s(q, d) \quad \begin{cases} 1 & \text{if } d \text{ is relevant to } q \text{ and informal} \\ & \text{otherwise} \end{cases}$$

4.2 Enhancing Recall on Informal Arabic

As the examples above illustrate, the translation model and the language model are both potential sources of error. Translation model errors on informal content are difficult to address. They originate from the greater variability of informal language compared to that of formal language, and from the lack of correspondingly larger training corpora. Presently available sentence-aligned informal-language parallel corpora are comparatively small and thus best used to tune or adapt translation models originally trained on the far larger amount of MSA for which parallel text is available. This approach yields MT results somewhere between that which could be achieved with MSA alone and that which we would expect if large quantities of dialectal Arabic were available as parallel text. One component we can control, however, is the language model. CLIR techniques that lack a word n-gram language model have been shown to yield retrieval results that are about as good as those achieved using an "MT First" document translation architecture. We therefore tried one such CLIR technique, Probabilistic Structured Queries [3], which is known to make good use of translation probabilities. We refer to this approach as "IR First."

Because of lexical and morphological differences between Egyptian Arabic and MSA, we want a form of morphological analysis or stemming that can process either. To this end, we use a combination of the Standard Arabic Morphological Analyzer (SAMA) [7] and the large-scale morphological analyzer for Egyptian Arabic (CALIMA) [4]. Habash et al. reported such a combination results in an analysis coverage of 92.1% [4]. The output for an input word is an unordered list of plausible stems. Inspired by the work of Darwish [2], we disambiguate these candidate stems by returning the one with the highest frequency within the BOLT IR collection.

4.3 Enhancing Precision on Informal Arabic

We are not aware of prior work on classification of informal Arabic, but there has been prior work on the closely related problem of Arabic dialect detection. In particular, Cotterell and Callison-Burch have released a total of 1.25 million words for five Arabic dialects [1]. This training data was originally collected from comments posted on newspaper Web sites and from Arabic Twitter posts. We merged the training examples for all dialects and removed those with fewer than 50 or more than 500 characters, yielding 46,174 positive training examples for the Arabic Dialect condition. As training data for the MSA condition we randomly sampled 59,437 news articles from the Egyptian newspaper Al-Youm Al-Sabe' [10], subject to the same length constraints. We evaluate the accuracy of this classifier on the 1000 random posts from Section 2, of which 869 are informal and the debatable 72 are considered to be formal; and on a balanced set of 118 posts with no debatable content. The accuracy was 88.0% for the former, and 83.1% for the latter. When we apply this classifier to the posts in the the BOLT collection, we find that the prevalence of informal content is estimated to be 93.7%. We also applied the same classifier to individual lines from the posts in this collection, finding that 89.7% of the lines are classified as informal.

5. EXPERIMENTS

We evaluate our methods with independent annotations of pools drawn from specific systems on eight held out topics.

5.1 Systems

In our experiments, we had access to a proprietary system, System **A**, with the MT First architecture. In this system, a question q is analyzed to automatically generate an Indri query, which is issued against the translations of all of the Arabic posts. The retrieved posts are then segmented and each segment is assigned a probability of containing a relevant answer to q by an ensemble of classifiers; the N relevant passages with highest scores are returned. Our system, System **B**, implements the IR First model, and the output is the top N posts. In a third architecture, System **C**, these posts are fed to the segment-scale relevance detection stage of System **A** to return the top N passages. Each of the systems **B** and **C** is controlled by two parameters, each taking two values. The first corresponds to the application of the informality classifier (Section 4.3). We use the subscript i when we prefilter for informal posts and a when we do not. The second parameter is related to the choice made for stemming. c indicates the use of CALIMA (Section 4.2) and l the use of the Lucene's Arabic light stemmer [5].

5.2 Annotations

We hired two annotators: a native speaker of Egyptian Arabic and a native speaker of Arabic who is fluent in Egyptian Arabic. We gave them two independent tasks, each on a 3-point scale. For relevance, a post had to be assessed as relevant, possibly relevant, or not relevant. For informality, a post could be formal MSA, possibly informal, or informal. We trained them independently using one of our exploratory analysis questions (BIR_200060), and we instructed them to discuss the task only with the authors of this paper and not with each other. The annotators then assessed the eight held out topics (four each) for which we report results. They also annotated one training topic (BIR_200056) to measure their agreement. To convert the 3-point scale into a binary judgment, we consider possibly relevant to be not relevant, and possibly informal to be formal. Table 1 shows Cohen's Kappa for this topic. The informality task exhibits a high agreement, with Kappa ranging from 0.794 to 0.867. The relevance task exhibits a high agreement between the first author and Annotator 1 (0.806), but both exhibit more modest agreement (0.502 and 0.459) with Annotator 2.

Table 1: Cohen's Kappa coefficient for topic BIR_200056. Top right triangle: relevance. Bottom left: informality.

Inform \\ Rel	First Author	Annotator 1	Annotator 2
First Author		0.502	0.806
Annotator 1	0.794		0.459
Annotator 2	0.863	0.867	

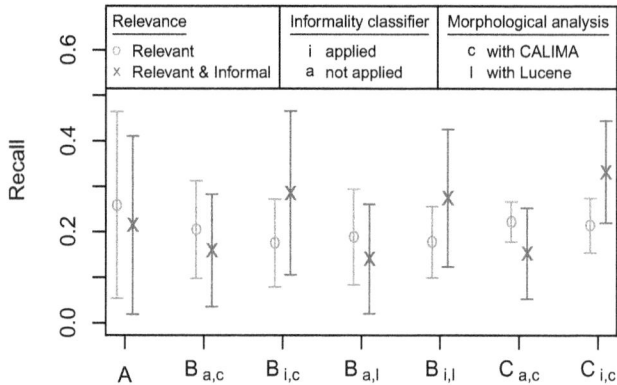

Relevance	Informality classifier	Morphological analysis
o Relevant	i applied	c with CALIMA
x Relevant & Informal	a not applied	l with Lucene

Figure 2: Mean and standard deviation of recall@25 across eight topics assessed by two independent annotators.

5.3 Results

Figure 2 shows the mean and standard deviation for recall at a fixed cutoff of 25 computed over eight topics. We first observe that the traditional recall measure that ignores informality substantially favors systems that are not tuned to retrieve informal content. In fact, the **o** of systems **A**, $\mathbf{B}_{a,c}$, $\mathbf{B}_{a,l}$ and $\mathbf{C}_{a,c}$ are higher than their **x** counterparts, that is, their performance is lower than what a traditional measure indicates. In contrast, the **o** of systems that are tuned to retrieve informal content—namely $\mathbf{B}_{i,c}$, $\mathbf{B}_{i,l}$ and $\mathbf{C}_{i,c}$—are lower than their **x** homologues, that is, their actual performance is higher than what a traditional measure states. Second, when the task is to retrieve relevant posts that are informal, the classifier trained to distinguish between MSA and Arabic Dialects improves precision (and thus recall at a fixed cutoff) substantially. These improvements are: 79% (from 0.1594 to 0.2855) for $\mathbf{B}_{\_,c}$, 95% (from 0.1407 to 0.2744) for $\mathbf{B}_{\_,l}$, and 118% (from 0.1526 to 0.3320) for $\mathbf{C}_{\_,c}$. All of these are statistically significant, at $p<0.05$, using a two-sided paired t-test. Third, no statistically significant difference is seen from CALIMA in the relevant and informal task, with the average recall of 0.2854 for System $\mathbf{B}_{i,c}$ being statistically indistinguishable from the 0.2744 for System $\mathbf{B}_{i,l}$. In contradiction to our expectations, we also find no statistically significant difference between the MT First approach and the IR First approach regardless of the inclusion of the informality condition with relevance; indeed if any undetected recall effect is present between System $\mathbf{C}_{a,c}$ and System **A** it would be a loss, not a gain, in recall.

6. CONCLUSIONS AND FUTURE WORK

We introduced the problem of retrieving informal content from Arabic forums in a CLIR setting. We have shown that traditional evaluation measures like recall that do not consider informality sometimes disadvantage systems that are tuned to retrieve relevant informal content. Our experi-

ments over eleven topics demonstrate that such systems can have their precision enhanced by applying an informality classifier that is actually trained to detect dialectal Arabic. We tested two techniques that might have improved recall at a fixed cutoff on this task, namely Probabilistic Structured Queries, and a morphological analyzer for Egyptian Arabic. Our results do not support that hypothesis.

Other techniques could augment the improvements we have obtained in other ways. Pseudo-Relevance Feedback has recently been shown to enhance the retrieval of informal content [6]. A dialect to MSA MT system such as Elissa [9] could be applied on posts that were identified to be informal, and we might leverage domain adaptation to better tune the morphology of specific dialects [8]. Our annotations should be a resource for exploring such possibilities, although similar annotations for a larger set of questions will ultimately be needed if we are to draw strong conclusions about small differences. Importantly, we have focused only on questions that use formal vocabulary; informal query vocabulary also merits study. We have also compared only to a document translation baseline; query translation and bidirectional translations baselines would also be useful points of comparison. While much remains to be done, we believe our results offer useful insights to help focus this future work.

Acknowledgments

This research was supported in part by DARPA Contract HR0011-12-C-0015. We thank LDC and NIST for making the BOLT IR collection available to us.

7. REFERENCES

[1] R. Cotterell and C. Callison-Burch. A multi-dialect, multi-genre corpus of informal written Arabic. In *LREC*, pages 241–245, 2014.

[2] K. Darwish. Building a shallow Arabic morphological analyzer in one day. In *ACL SEMITIC*, 2002.

[3] K. Darwish and D. Oard. Probabilistic structured query methods. In *SIGIR*, 2003.

[4] N. Habash, R. Eskander, and A. Hawwari. A morphological analyzer for Egyptian Arabic. In *SIGMORPHON*, 2012.

[5] L. Larkey, L. Ballesteros, and M. Connell. Light stemming for Arabic information retrieval. In *Arabic Computational Morphology*. Springer, 2007.

[6] C.-J. Lee and W. B. Croft. Cross-language pseudo-relevance feedback techniques for informal text. In *ECIR*, pages 260–272, 2014.

[7] M. Maamouri, D. Graff, B. Bouziri, S. Krouna, A. Bies, and S. Kulick. Standard Arabic morphological analyzer (SAMA) version 3.1 LDC2010L01. LDC, 2010.

[8] W. Monroe, S. Green, and C. D. Manning. Word segmentation of informal Arabic with domain adaptation. In *ACL*, pages 206–211, 2014.

[9] W. Salloum and N. Habash. Elissa: A dialectal to standard Arabic machine translation system. In *COLING (Demos)*, pages 385–392, 2012.

[10] O. F. Zaidan and C. Callison-Burch. The Arabic online commentary dataset: An annotated dataset of informal Arabic with high dialectal content. In *ACL*, 2011.

Head First: Living Labs for Ad-hoc Search Evaluation

Krisztian Balog
University of Stavanger
Norway
krisztian.balog@uis.no

Liadh Kelly
CNGL, School of Computing
Dublin City University
Ireland
lkelly@computing.dcu.ie

Anne Schuth
University of Amsterdam
The Netherlands
anne.schuth@uva.nl

ABSTRACT

The information retrieval (IR) community strives to make evaluation more centered on real users and their needs. The living labs evaluation paradigm, i.e., observing users in their natural task environments, offers great promise in this regard. Yet, progress in an academic setting has been limited. This paper presents the first living labs for the IR community benchmarking campaign initiative, taking as test two use-cases: local domain search on a university website and product search on an e-commerce site. There are many challenges associated with this setting, including incorporating results from experimental search systems into live production systems, and obtaining sufficiently many impressions from relatively low traffic sites. We propose that head queries can be used to generate result lists offline, which are then interleaved with results of the production system for live evaluation. An API is developed to orchestrate the communication between commercial parties and benchmark participants. This campaign acts to progress the living labs for IR evaluation methodology, and offers important insight into the role of living labs in this space.

Categories and Subject Descriptors

H.3 [**Information Storage and Retrieval**]: H.3.3 Information Search and Retrieval

Keywords

Evaluation; living labs

1. INTRODUCTION

The Cranfield methodology [9] introduced a way to enable cross-comparable evaluation of information retrieval (IR) systems, using a document collection, queries, and relevance assessments. Since then researchers have strived to make IR evaluations more "realistic," i.e., centered on real users, their needs, and behaviors. Living labs have been proposed as a way for researchers to perform *in situ* evaluations, with real users performing real tasks using real-world applications [13]. This concept has already been used for a number of years as an important instrument for technology development

in industrial settings; for example, A/B testing procedures are employed heavily by major web search providers [15]. This form of evaluation, however, is currently only available to those working at the said organizations.

"The basic idea of living labs for IR is that rather than individual research groups independently developing experimental search infrastructures and gathering their own groups of test searchers for IR evaluations, a central and shared experimental environment is developed to facilitate the sharing of resources" [5]. The potential benefits of living labs to the IR community are profound, including the availability of interaction and usage data for researchers and greater knowledge transfer between industry and academia [6]. Progress towards realizing actual living labs, in an academic setting, has nevertheless been limited. Azzopardi and Balog [5] discuss a number of search and recommendation tasks in an online shopping environment and present an idealized architecture based on web services. There are many challenges associated with operationalizing these ideas, including architecture, hosting, maintenance, security, privacy, participant recruiting, and scenarios and tasks for use development [5]. A recent development in this space was the Living Labs for IR Evaluation workshop at CIKM 2013 [6]. A key outcome of this workshop was the need to work towards community-driven living labs benchmarking initiatives.

In this paper we present a living labs for IR evaluation benchmarking platform. We propose that mid-sized organizations that lack their own R&D department are good potential collaborators, as they have the opportunity to gain much improved retrieval approaches. We present two specific use-cases for ad-hoc search: local domain search on a university website and product search on an e-commerce site. These use-cases represent a setting with at least two major challenges: (i) relatively low search volume (especially compared to major web search providers) and (ii) means to facilitate experimentation by "third parties" in live, production systems. We postulate that focusing on *head queries* (i.e., queries most frequently issued) can help overcome these challenges. The choice of head queries is critical because it removes a harsh requirement of providing rankings in real-time for query requests. Instead, experimental search systems (developed by benchmark participants) can generate ranked results lists for these queries offline. These participant rankings can then be used by the live system when head queries are next issued. Finally, feedback is made available to experimental search systems to facilitate improved offline ranking generation. Data exchange between live systems and participants is facilitated by a web-based API.

In summary, the main contributions of this work include the development of evaluation methodology, architecture, specific use-cases, as well as the implementation of the Living Labs API, made available as open source software.[1] An open challenge, with agreements with the use-case organizations in place, is currently being organized.[2] The outcomes of this benchmarking initiative will lead to answers to the following two important research questions: (RQ1) Are system rankings different when using historical clicks from those using online experiments? (RQ2) Are system rankings different when using manual relevance assessments ("expert judgments") from those using online experiments? These answers will provide the research community with concrete insight into the need, or lack thereof, of living labs as an additional tool for IR evaluation.

The remainder of the paper is organized as follows. In §2 we briefly discuss related work. Next, in §3, we introduce our evaluation platform and methodology. We present two particular use-cases in §4. Limitations and directions for future research are discussed in §5. Finally, we conclude in §6.

2. RELATED WORK

The need for more realistic evaluation, involving real users, was reiterated at recent IR workshops [1, 6, 12]. Approaches that attempt to incorporate user behavior into batch-style evaluations can be divided into two main categories. One is to create effectiveness measures that better model user behavior, e.g., [7, 10]. Another approach is to simulate user behavior and then validate these models against actual usage data, e.g., [3, 4]. These ideas have been implemented in a number of community benchmarking efforts, including the TREC Interactive, HARD, and Session tracks, and the INEX Interactive track. While user simulation is a great instrument for fine-tuning systems, it cannot substitute the user. Crowdsourcing, using e.g., Mechanical Turk, enables the sourcing of individuals in the online community to perform various relevance assessment and annotation tasks [2]. However, these individuals do not constitute *real* users performing *real* tasks driven by a *real* information need. Living labs offer this potential.

The living labs notion was first proposed in the information-seeking support space (ISSS) by Kelly et al. [13]: "Such a lab might contain resources and tools for evaluation as well as infrastructure for collaborative studies. It might also function as a point of contact with those interested in participating in ISSS studies." Azzopardi and Balog [5] provided greater insight into what this might be in the IR space: "A living lab would provide a common data repository and evaluation environment giving researchers (in particular from academia) the data required to undertake meaningful and applicable research." Kelly et al. [14] then showed a practical interpretation of this for personal desktop search. However, to date, there have been no attempts at operationalizing a living labs benchmark in the IR space. The nearest to this has been the 2014 CLEF NEWSREEL lab[3] and the Plista contest,[4] addressing the problem of news recommendation. Participants are expected to implement their recommender system as a service that can handle a large number of (recommendation) requests. Their response to a request is shown to a user and resulting clicks are then made available to participants so that they can update their system. One major difference between this and our proposal is the task itself: we are focusing on retrieval as opposed to recommendation. There are also important architectural differences stemming from the nature of our experimental environment; in our setup participants do not get full control over the results shown to the user, they are always interleaved with that of the production system.

[1] http://git.living-labs.net
[2] http://living-labs.net/challenge
[3] http://www.clef-newsreel.org
[4] http://contest.plista.com

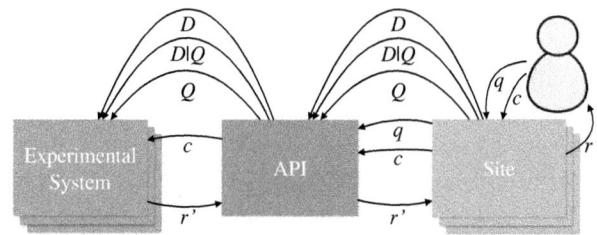

Figure 1: Schematic representation of the Living Labs API.

3. EVALUATION PLATFORM AND METHODOLOGY

The overall objective of our work is to design, implement, and operate an evaluation platform that allows researchers to test retrieval methods in live search environments with real users. A further important desideratum is the availability of usage and interaction data for model training and development. We are particularly interested in developing a solution that caters for medium-sized organizations as participating partners—those with a fair (but not excessive) amount of search volume on their websites, and without their own R&D department. To keep focus, we concentrate on one specific retrieval task: ad-hoc search.

There are certain restrictions to this setting that need to be addressed. First, search volume poses limitations on how much room there is for experimentation. For a fair comparison, systems should be evaluated on the same set of queries and ensured a minimum number of impressions. One of the key design decisions in our approach is to focus exclusively on head queries; this not only makes it easier to plan with and have control over the capacity of experimental resources, but also offers the availability of considerable amounts of historical log data. Moreover, it allows for rapid response time requirements, as rankings can be computed offline, before an actual instance of the query is issued (see §3.2). Second, experimentation takes place in production environments, where it is vital to maintain a certain level of quality of service, both in terms of efficiency (response time) and effectiveness (search relevancy). Organizations are unlikely to give up control of the whole search result page (SERP) and to blindly take ranked lists from experimental search systems. That is why the common online evaluation approach, A/B testing, cannot be used here. Also, given the traffic volume of these websites, it would take a long time to get reliable evaluation results using A/B testing. To overcome this, we propose interleaving experimental search results with those of the production system (see §3.3). Efficiency considerations are addressed head-on by the proposed architecture (see §3.1).

3.1 Architecture

The normal flow of information in a search system is as follows: the end user issues query q on the site, which responds with a ranking r; the clicks c made by the user are recorded by the site. A living lab for IR requires a means of transferring this information (queries, rankings, and feedback) between end users of the site and *experimental search systems*. We propose an architecture in the form of an API for this purpose that encapsulates data storage and access via HTTP calls. All communication between sites and experimental search systems is done via this API (i.e., experimental systems can not directly interact with sites); see Figure 1.

The set of (frequent) queries that are subject to experimentation (see §3.2) is denoted as Q. For each query q in Q, the site makes available (i) a set of candidate documents, (ii) the contents of these documents, and (iii) historical interaction data to the API. Additionally, sites can also provide collection-level statistics (such as document and collection frequencies of terms). Benchmark participants can obtain this information from the API. Then, for each query q in the fixed set of queries Q, the experimental search system generates a ranking r' that is submitted to the API. When a user issues a query q to the site that is in Q, the site requests a ranking r' from an experimental system through the API. This ranking r' is interleaved (see §3.3) with the production system and presented to the user. The user interactions with the interleaved list are sent back to the API and made available to the participant that contributed r'. Subsequently, this interaction data c can be used to update the ranking r', for one or all queries in Q.

3.2 Queries

The distribution of search queries in web search typically follows a power law [17], where a relatively small set of head queries are frequently posed by many users and there is a long tail of queries that appear in the logs only a few times (often only once). Here, we focus exclusively on head queries for a number of reasons: (i) this allows us to evaluate experimental search systems on the same set of queries, (ii) these queries have a stable volume level, even for mid-sized sites (cf. §4), and (iii) historical click and usage data is available in meaningful quantities. We take a simple measure to filter out "uninteresting" queries: queries for which virtually all historical clicks are associated with a single document are removed.

3.3 Interleaving

Prior work has shown that *interleaving* [8] can produce very reliable comparisons of rankers in online evaluation [16] using much less data than A/B testing. Such interleaved comparison methods take as input two rankings for the same query, and produce as output a combined result list to be shown to the user. The resulting clicks from this user are then interpreted by the interleaving method to decide on a winning ranker. There are several interleaving methods available. *Balanced interleave* (BI) [11] randomly selects a ranker to contribute the first document. Then, alternating, each ranker contributes its next document. A document is added to the interleaving only if it is not yet present there. BI, however, can produce biased results: when two very similar rankers are compared, it can favor one ranker regardless of actual user preferences expressed in clicks. This bias was removed in *team draft* (TD) [16], which makes it the most commonly used interleaving method in industry and, therefore, also our interleaving method of choice.

3.4 Evaluation metrics

We use two forms of online metrics, relative and absolute. The fraction of wins of interleaved comparisons for an experimental system against the production system is a *relative* metric and this is used as our overall evaluation criteria [15]. As shown in [16], relevance can also be inferred from user actions and used to compute *absolute click metrics*. We propose using several standard IR metrics (i.e., nDCG@10, ERR, MAP) as absolute click metrics. These are computed on raw clicks, but also on more reliable (but inherently more sparse) subsets of the clicks: clicks with long dwell times, last clicks, and deepest clicks. Additionally, we compute traditional metrics (again, nDCG@10, ERR, MAP) on assessments from professional human assessors. We refer to these as *offline evaluation metrics*. These offline metrics are merely used for analysis, such that we can answer research question RQ2 (cf. §1).

3.5 Benchmark organization

Evaluation is split into training and test phases. For each of the two use cases described in §4, sets of 50 training and 50 test queries

(following the TREC best practice), along with a set of candidate documents to be ranked for each query are provided.

Participants are allowed to partake in the benchmark with a single system. The challenge is to optimally rank the set of candidate documents provided for each query. Participants submit their current ranking to the benchmark API, which makes these rankings available to sites when requested. Note that experimental rankings from the participant are interleaved with the production ranking before presenting results to user (see §3.1). The benchmark operates by giving participants equal number of impressions for queries over both the training and test phases. During the training phases, participants can receive feedback on their own system (such as dwell time, click throughs, and the actual interleaved result list presented to the user), which they can use to refine their system. For the test phase, participants are provided with a two week window in which they can download the training queries and document collections. Once downloaded, participants must submit their rankings for the test queries within 24 hours of downloading the dataset.

We provide a dashboard for monitoring progress of participants. A "leaderboard" is also present with both the relative and absolute online metrics, as described in §3.4. During the training phase, the dashboard will not display offline relevance metrics (metrics that were computed on relevance assessments from human assessors). This is to avoid participants optimizing for this metric instead of learning from user feedback.

4. USE-CASES

We consider ad-hoc search in two different flavors, taking place on the websites of medium-sized organizations: (A) local domain search on the website of the University of Amsterdam[5] and (B) product search in the webshop of a toy retailer operating in Hungary.[6] These organizations have agreed to partake in our challenge and allow for experimentation with head queries.

Queries. Figure 2 shows the historical query counts for head (top 100) queries, for the period 2014-01-01 to 2014-08-20, on a daily basis. The absolute count is the total number of times head queries are issued. Relative click count refers to the fraction of the total query volume that falls on the head queries. There are interesting differences in the characteristics of the two sites; head queries constitute on average 63% of the overall search volume for local domain search, while it is only 25% for product search. There is an order of magnitude difference in absolute terms: 14, 500 vs. 1, 500 queries per day on average for use-cases (A) and (B), respectively. Importantly for us, the plots clearly show that there is a stable volume level on the head queries to experiment with (9, 600 per day for use-case (A) and 380 per day for use-case (B), on average).

Content. Both sites make available (i) the contents of candidate documents, (ii) relative historical click counts for these documents, and (iii) collection-level term statistics (document and collection frequencies). Use-case (A) represents a rather straightforward document search task; for each (HTML) document, the title and the (cleansed) body are made available. Documents in use-case (B) correspond to products. For each product a fielded representation is provided, including the product's name, description, brand, price (and bonus price, if applicable), product categories, (URLs of) product photos, and date of addition. The product categorization system (a 2-levels deep hierarchy) is also offered.

---

[5] http://uva.nl
[6] http://regiojatek.hu

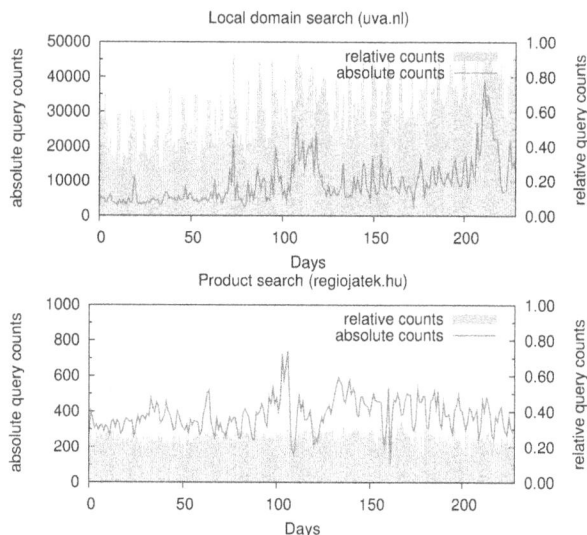

Figure 2: Historical query counts for the challenge use-cases. (Top): local domain search, (Bottom): product search.

Feedback. Feedback includes (i) click throughs, (ii) dwell time, and (iii) the actual interleaved result list presented to the user. Further, for use-case (B), feedback information also includes basket operations and actual purchases made.

5. LIMITATIONS AND FUTURE CONSIDERATIONS

Our proposal is a first of its kind and represents an important step towards making the living labs evaluation paradigm accessible to the wider IR research community. Nevertheless, it is not without limitations. Next, we briefly consider some of these limitations and look at ways in which they could be addressed.

L1) *Head queries only.* While head queries constitute a considerable portion of a site's traffic, they are representative of only one type of request, that is, popular information needs.

L2) *Lack of context.* The search algorithm has no knowledge of the searcher's context, such as location, previous searches, etc. This means that currently there is no room for personalization of results.

L3) *No real-time feedback.* While the proposed API does provide detailed feedback, it is not immediate. Thus, it cannot directly be used in the given search session.

L4) *Limited control.* Experimentation is limited to single searches, where results are interleaved with those of the production system. I.e., there is no control over the entire result list.

L5) *Ultimate measure of success.* Having better search facilities is usually only a means to an end—it is not the ultimate goal. E.g., in the e-commerce case the ultimate measure of success (from the company's perspective) is the profit made on purchases. Evaluation metrics should reflect this overall goal.

L1–L4 could be overcome by a live architecture, in which control is given to benchmark participants over entire sessions, with real-time access to context and feedback. However, it is still a very much open question how to ensure availability, response time, and quality of the experimental methods in production environments. Safety mechanisms are needed for "experiment shutdown" in which case methods can default back to the production system. L5 could be addressed by providing an "utility" score for documents (products); this could already be done with the existing architecture.

6. CONCLUSIONS

Living labs offer the IR community great potential to evaluate their approaches in *live* settings with *real* users. In this paper we presented the first practical methodology and implementation of a living labs for IR benchmarking campaign that is currently being organized, with local domain search and product search as use-cases. Efforts are underway to recruit additional organizations to join our initiative. While significant, this is just the beginning of the practical living labs for IR evaluation story. The results of our research questions, to be answered by this campaign, will yield further light on the living labs for IR paradigm. We expect that this work will pave the way for further progress in this exciting direction for IR evaluation.

Acknowledgments. This research was partially supported by the Evaluating Information Access Systems (ELIAS) ESF Research Networking Programme and the European Community's Seventh Framework Programme (FP7/ 2007-2013) under grant agreement nr 288024 (LiMoSINe project).

References

[1] J. Allan, B. Croft, A. Moffat, and M. Sanderson. Frontiers, challenges, and opportunities for information retrieval: Report from SWIRL 2012 the second strategic workshop on information retrieval in lorne. *SIGIR Forum*, 46(1):2–32, 2012.

[2] O. Alonso, D. E. Rose, and B. Stewart. Crowdsourcing for relevance evaluation. *SIGIR Forum*, 42(2):9–15, 2008.

[3] P. Arvola, J. Kekäläinen, and M. Junkkari. Expected reading effort in focused retrieval evaluation. *Inf. Retr.*, 13(5):460–484, 2010.

[4] L. Azzopardi. The economics in interactive information retrieval. In *Proc. of SIGIR '11*, 2011.

[5] L. Azzopardi and K. Balog. Towards a living lab for information retrieval research and development. A proposal for a living lab for product search tasks. In *Proc. of CLEF '11*, 2011.

[6] K. Balog, D. Elsweiler, E. Kanoulas, L. Kelly, and M. D. Smucker. Report on the CIKM workshop on living labs for information retrieval evaluation. *SIGIR Forum*, 48(1), 2014.

[7] B. Carterette. System effectiveness, user models, and user utility: A conceptual framework for investigation. In *Proc. of SIGIR '11*, 2011.

[8] O. Chapelle, T. Joachims, F. Radlinski, and Y. Yue. Large-scale validation and analysis of interleaved search evaluation. *ACM Trans. Inf. Syst.*, 30(1), 2012.

[9] C. Cleverdon and K. E. Factors Determining the Performance of Indexing Systems (Volume 1: Design; Volume 2: Results). Technical report, Cranfield, UK, 1966.

[10] K. Järvelin and J. Kekäläinen. Cumulated gain-based evaluation of IR techniques. *ACM Trans. Inf. Syst.*, 20(4):422–446, 2002.

[11] T. Joachims, L. A. Granka, B. Pan, H. Hembrooke, F. Radlinski, and G. Gay. Evaluating the accuracy of implicit feedback from clicks and query reformulations in Web search. *ACM Trans. Inf. Syst.*, 25(2), 2007.

[12] J. Kamps, S. Geva, C. Peters, T. Sakai, A. Trotman, and E. Voorhees. Report on the SIGIR 2009 workshop on the future of IR evaluation. *SIGIR Forum*, 43(2):13–23, 2009.

[13] D. Kelly, S. Dumais, and J. O. Pedersen. Evaluation challenges and directions for information-seeking support systems. *Computer*, 42 (3):60–66, 2009.

[14] L. Kelly, P. Bunbury, and G. J. F. Jones. Evaluating personal information retrieval. In *Proc. of ECIR '12*, 2012.

[15] R. Kohavi, R. Longbotham, D. Sommerfield, and R. M. Henne. Controlled experiments on the web: survey and practical guide. *Data Mining and Knowledge Discovery*, 18(1):140–181, 2009.

[16] F. Radlinski, M. Kurup, and T. Joachims. How does clickthrough data reflect retrieval quality? In *Proc. of CIKM '08*, 2008.

[17] A. Spink, D. Wolfram, M. B. J. Jansen, and T. Saracevic. Searching the web: The public and their queries. *J. Am. Soc. Inf. Sci. Technol.*, 52(3):226–234, 2001.

Medical Semantic Similarity with a Neural Language Model

Lance De Vine[1], Guido Zuccon[2], Bevan Koopman[3,2], Laurianne Sitbon[1], Peter Bruza[2]

[1]Electrical Engineering & Computer Science, Queensland University of Technology, Brisbane, Australia
[2]Information Systems, Queensland University of Technology, Brisbane, Australia
[3]Australian e-Health Research Centre, CSIRO, Brisbane, Australia
l.devine@student.qut.edu.au, g.zuccon@qut.edu.au, bevan.koopman@csiro.au,
laurianne.sitbon@qut.edu.au, p.bruza@qut.edu.au

ABSTRACT

Advances in neural network language models have demonstrated that these models can effectively learn representations of words meaning. In this paper, we explore a variation of neural language models that can learn on concepts taken from structured ontologies and extracted from free-text, rather than directly from terms in free-text.

This model is employed for the task of measuring semantic similarity between medical concepts, a task that is central to a number of techniques in medical informatics and information retrieval. The model is built with two medical corpora (journal abstracts and patient records) and empirically validated on two ground-truth datasets of human-judged concept pairs assessed by medical professionals. Empirically, our approach correlates closely with expert human assessors (≈ 0.9) and outperforms a number of state-of-the-art benchmarks for medical semantic similarity.

The demonstrated superiority of this model for providing an effective semantic similarity measure is promising in that this may translate into effectiveness gains for techniques in medical information retrieval and medical informatics (e.g., query expansion and literature-based discovery).

Categories and Subject Descriptors: H.3.3 [Information Storage and Retrieval]

General Terms: Theory, Experimentation, Measurement

Keywords: Neural Language Model; Skip-gram; Distributed Representations; Word2Vec; Semantic Similarity; Medical Information Retrieval.

1. INTRODUCTION

A variety of neural network-based methods have emerged as effective approaches for generating representations of words [4, 16, 12]; these are referred to as neural language models. These methods learn word embeddings based on the optimisation of an objective function. The term "word embeddings" generally refers to representations for words occupying a real valued vector space where the similarity between

words is measured by cosine similarity. An objective function that is often used for training word embeddings is to learn a vector for a target word which predicts the vectors for words occurring near to it (Skip-gram).

Recent research has demonstrated that neural language models (NLM) based on the continuous Skip-gram model proposed by Mikolov et al. [11] are highly effective in determining semantic relationships between words [13]. It is still not clear, however, whether these neurally inspired models are better than traditional distributional semantic methods. For example, Lebret et. al. [10] report results that suggest that computing a Hellinger PCA of a word co-ocurrence matrix provides similar results to neural network models on natural language processing tasks. On the other hand, Baroni et. al [3] report on comparisons between standard distributional semantic models and neural network models and conclude that neural network models do indeed provide superior word representations. They note however that not all neural network word models are equal.

Semantic similarity measures are central to several techniques used in health informatics and medical information retrieval, e.g., query expansion [6] and literature-based discovery [1]. A number of previous corpus-based approaches have been employed for semantic similarity measurements and have been evaluated by how well they correlate with human-judged similarity [15, 9]. These approaches were applied to medical concepts taken from the UMLS medical thesaurus and extracted from medical free-text. The results from these studies show that although corpus-based measures of similarity do correlate with human judgments, there is considerable room for improvement. Motivated by this and the recent findings in neural language models, we explore a variation to the original continuous Skip-gram NLM of Mikolov et al. [11], where instead of learning a distributed vector representation over sequences of terms, we train the model over sequences of UMLS medical concepts. This approach is evaluated over two human-judged semantic similarity datasets and is trained using two corpora: a collection of clinical records and a large set of MEDLINE medical journal abstracts. The empirical results of this study demonstrate that the proposed neural language models outperform a number of benchmark corpus-based approaches, strongly correlating with semantic similarity judgements provided by medical, expert judges.

2. SKIP-GRAM NEURAL LANGUAGE MODEL

The effectiveness of corpus-driven approaches relies on the distributional hypothesis [8, 14], which states that the degree of semantic similarity between two terms (or some other linguistic units) can be modelled as a function of the degree of overlap of their linguistic contexts. In practice, the counts of contextual features are generally accumulated into a term-context matrix and a transformation is then applied which re-weights the accumulated counts.

Neural language models also construct representations for terms based on linguistic contexts; however, they do so by optimising an objective function involving the target term and its linguistic context. The representations produced are often called "word embeddings". Word embeddings were first developed in the context of language modelling to overcome some of the well known problems relating to data sparsity that existed with n-gram based language models [4]. While NLMs were originally developed to model sequential term dependencies departing from the n-gram approach, a by-product of these models is that the constructed word representations were found to have useful semantic properties [11]. NLMs have more recently been employed for a large variety of natural language processing tasks, such as semantic role labelling, part-of-speech tagging, chunking, sentiment analysis and named entity recognition [7, 13]; they were found to be as good as, or better than, other state-of-the-art methods.

A particular instance of a NLM is the continuous Skip-gram model of Mikolov et al. [11]. The Skip-gram model constructs term representations by optimising their ability to predict the representations of surrounding terms. In this paper, we evaluate the continuous Skip-gram model on the task of predicting the semantic similarity of concept pairs. We employ the Skip-gram model in a way not previously seen in the literature; specifically, we use it to learn embedding vectors for concepts taken from structured ontologies rather than for terms. While previous work has considered the use of compound terms (e.g., named entities) in NLMs [13], these compound terms are not actually used as features; in addition, ontology concepts have not been used (to our knowledge).

Given a sequence $\mathcal{W} = \{w_1, \ldots, w_t, \ldots, w_n\}$ of training words, the objective of the Skip-gram model is to maximise the following average log probability

$$\frac{1}{2r} \sum_{i=1}^{2r} \sum_{-r \leq j \leq r, j \neq 0} \log p(w_{t+j}|w_t) \tag{1}$$

where r is the context window radius. The context window radius determines which words surrounding the target term w_t are considered for the computation of the log probability; the window is centred around the target term. The probability of an output word is computed according to

$$p(w_O|w_I) = \frac{\exp(v_{w_O}^\top v_{w_I})}{\sum_{w=1}^{W} \exp(v_w^\top, v_{w_I})} \tag{2}$$

where the v_{w_I} and v_{w_O} are the vector representations of the input and output vectors, respectively, and $\sum_{w=1}^{W} \exp(v_w^\top, v_{w_I})$ is the normalisation factor, whose role is to normalise the inner product results across all vocabulary words (W is the vocabulary size). In practice, a hierarchical approximation to this probability is used to reduce computational complexity [11]. At initialisation, the vector representations of the words are assigned random values; these vector representations are then optimised using gradient descent with decaying learning rate by iterating through sentences observed in the training corpus.

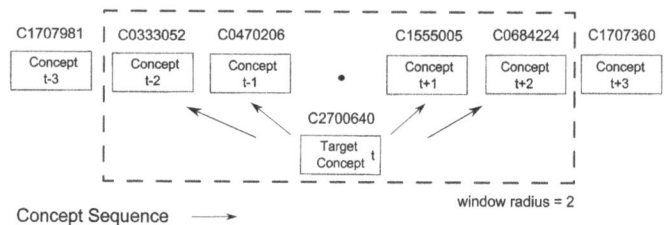

Figure 1: Skip-gram Neural Language Model applied to sequences of UMLS concept identifiers. In this example, the context radius r is set to 2.

In this paper, we explore a variation of the described Skip-gram NLM, where sequences of terms are substituted with sequences of UMLS concept identifiers. Thus, in practice, training is performed by iterating through sequences of concepts as shown in Figure 1. This method builds representations of concepts that are predictive of nearby concepts. It is this feature that, we hypothesise, would enhance semantic similarity measurements between medical concepts.

3. EXPERIMENT SETTINGS

3.1 Corpora and Human-judged Datasets

In this paper we adopted the evaluation framework setup by Koopman et al. [9], who empirically evaluated a number of different corpus-driven measures of semantic similarities for medical concepts. We refer to that work for details about the evaluation framework that are not reported in this paper. The evaluation framework comprised of two datasets:

- Ped: 29 UMLS medical concept pairs developed by Pedersen et al. [15]. Semantic similarity judgements were provided by 3 physician and 9 clinical terminologists, with an inter-coder correlation of 0.85.
- Cav: 45 MeSH/UMLS concept pairs developed by Cavides and Cimino [5]. Similarity between concept pairs was judged by 3 physicians, with no exact consensus value reported by Cavides and Cimino.

In addition, two corpora were used in the evaluation framework for learning concept representations:

- MedTrack: a collection of 17,198 clinical patient records used in the TREC 2011 and 2012 Medical Records Track [17]. Average document length was 932 tokens (words).
- OHSUMED: a collection of 348,566 MEDLINE medical journal abstracts used in TREC 2000 Filtering Track. Average document length was 100 tokens (words).

We specifically focus on two corpora because previous work has found that the effectiveness of corpus-based measures is influenced by corpus characteristics [9]. In particular, previous work has found that measures suited to the characteristics of one corpus are often not suited to those of another corpus, yielding significant differences in performance across corpora.

In accordance with [9], documents in both corpora where pre-processed using MetaMap v11.2, a state-of-the-art biomedical concept identification system [2], which converted the free-text into sequences of UMLS concept identifiers. Converting the test corpora to concepts allowed for direct comparison of the concept pairs contained in both the Ped and

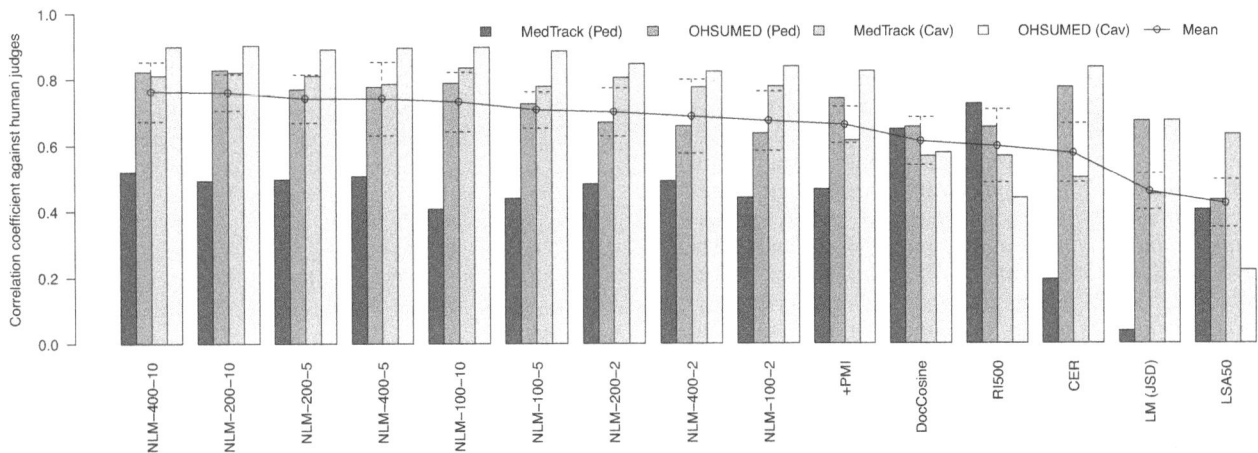

Figure 2: Pearson correlation coefficient against expert judged semantic similarity for the NLM and benchmark comparison methods. Correlations are computed for two gold standard datasets (**Ped** & **Cav**) using two corpora (MedTrack & OHSUMED). Methods are ordered from left to right by decreasing correlation averaged across all datasets/corpora, which is summarised by the trendline. Error bars for points in the trendline signify confidence intervals at 95% for the mean correlation value.

Cav datasets. Three concepts appearing in the Ped dataset were not found in the translated corpora (two in Medtrack and one in OHSUMED) and were, therefore, removed.[1]

3.2 Benchmark Comparison Methods

A number of other corpus-based measures of semantic similarity were included as benchmarks for comparison against the neural language model approach:

1. Random Indexing (RI)

2. Latent Semantic Analysis (LSA)

3. Document Vector Cosine Similarity (DocCosine)

4. Positive Pointwise Mutual Information (+PMI)

5. Cross Entropy Reduction (CER)

6. Language Model + Jensen-Shannon divergence (LM JSD)

A previous evaluation of the above models on the same task found that these were the most effective in terms of correlations with human judges [9]. We refer the reader to [9] for a description of each method.

3.3 Parameters Settings

For the benchmark comparison methods (e.g., RI and LSA) we selected the parameter settings, e.g., latent space dimensionality, that produced the highest correlations with human experts as reported in previous work [9][2].

For the Skip-gram NLM, we adopted the `word2vec` implementation provided by Mikolov et al. [11][3]. We used the hierarchical soft-max classification layer and set the "mincount" parameter to 1, thus effectively not excluding any concept occurrence from the computation of statistics. Each corpora was processed using only one thread so that processing was purely sequential. We studied the effect of window

radius and embedding dimensionality (i.e. the dimensionality of the reduced space) on semantic similarity by considering 2, 5 and 10 as window radius and 100, 200 and 400 as latent dimensions; these are values typical of the range generally reported in the NLM literature [7, 11, 13].

4. RESULTS & DISCUSSION

Results showing the Pearson correlation coefficient against human judges for each semantic similarity method are reported in Figure 2. The methods on the x-axis are ordered from left to right in decreasing correlation averaged across all datasets/corpora: the leftmost method exhibited the highest overall correlation with human experts. Significance intervals are also reported for the mean correlation values.

According to the empirical results reported in Figure 2, the mean correlation between different settings of the Skip-gram neural language model provides overall higher correlations with human assessed semantic similarity than the other benchmark methods. In particular, the NLM approach is found to consistently outperform the benchmarks for all but one datasets-corpora combinations, with DocCosine and RI providing stronger correlations with human experts in the Ped dataset when trained with the Medtrack corpus.

When MedTrack is used to train the methods, the correlation between NLM semantic similarity estimations and the expert assessments for the Ped dataset is less strong than that obtained by the DocCosine and RI benchmarks. This may suggest that NLM does not appropriately use evidence encoded in the Medtrack corpus to construct effective concept representations. However, this is not confirmed when analysing the results on the Cav dataset: in the latter case NLM is found to strongly correlate with expert assessments when using MedTrack. Previous work has found that there is no single method that does consistently outperform any other method across all datasets-corpora combinations considered in this evaluation framework: it was the choice of corpora used to prime the measures that affected their performance [9]. While NLM does not provide strong correlations on Ped when using Medtrack, the use of this corpus

---

[1]Removed concepts were C0702166, C0224701, C0029456.
[2]Tested dimensionalities: 50, 150, 300 and 500.
[3]http://word2vec.googlecode.com/.

does not seem to detriment NLM's performance when considering the Cav dataset.

We now consider how window radius and embedding dimensionality affect performance of the studied NLM. We found that the best performing model was the Skip-gram model with the largest dimensionality and window radius. Overall we found that increasing both the embedding dimensionality and the window radius helped to improve performance, with larger window radius contributing more than larger dimensionalities. While not true in every case, the overall trend suggests as a guideline for building NLM models for this tasks, that vectors with larger window radius and larger embedding dimensionality should be used.

The empirical results highlight that the investigated Skip-gram NLM constructs representations for concepts that, when used as a measure of semantic relations, strongly correlate with semantic similarity judgements provided by medical experts. We conjecture that the predictive nature of the objective function used by the considered Skip-gram NLM is the core feature that produces such strong performance. The validation of this intriguing conjecture would require further investigation; this is left for future work.

5. CONCLUSIONS

Neural network language models (NLM) have recently attracted attention because of promising results obtained in a number of natural language processing tasks, e.g., semantic role labelling and sentiment analysis, among others. The intuition behind these models is that effective representations that synthesise word meaning can be learnt by iteratively observing word occurrences in the close surroundings of target words along with the optimisation of a task-specific function.

In this paper, we have explored a variation of a specific NLM approach, the Skip-gram model, applied to the task of measuring the semantic similarity between medical concepts. While the traditional Skip-gram model creates distributed vector representations of words, the model in this study leverages distributed representations of UMLS concepts extracted from medical corpora, including clinical records and medical journal abstracts.

Empirical findings demonstrate that the concept-based Skip-gram NLM correlates more strongly to expert judgement of semantic similarity than established benchmark approaches. Window radius *in primis*, along with embedding dimensionality, are factors that influence performance, with representations learnt with larger radius and dimensionalities more strongly correlating with expert judgements.

This work opens up a number of avenues for future research. One important research question is *why* the predictive nature of the objective function used by the Skip-gram NLM is conducive of such strong performance. We also conjecture that the use of "mixed" features, e.g., learning representations from both term and concept corpora, may result in further improvements. Another factor that may influence performance is the ordering of the training data, considering that the importance of data samples varies according to the learning rate parameter included in the gradient descent procedure.

6. REFERENCES

[1] P. Agarwal and D. B. Searls. Can literature analysis identify innovation drivers in drug discovery? *Nature reviews. Drug discovery*, 8(11):865–78, Nov. 2009.

[2] A. R. Aronson and F.-M. Lang. An overview of MetaMap: historical perspective and recent advances. *JAMIA*, 17(3):229–236, 2010.

[3] M. Baroni, G. Dinu, and G. Kruszewski. Don't count, predict! a systematic comparison of context-counting vs. context-predicting semantic vectors. In *Proceedings of the 52nd Annual Meeting of the Association for Computational Linguistics*, 2014.

[4] Y. Bengio, R. Ducharme, P. Vincent, and C. Jauvin. A neural probabilistic language model. *Journal of Machine Learning Research*, 3:1137–1155, 2003.

[5] J. E. Caviedes and J. J. Cimino. Towards the development of a conceptual distance metric for the UMLS. *Journal of biomedical informatics*, 37(2):77–85, Apr. 2004.

[6] T. Cohen and D. Widdows. Empirical distributional semantics: Methods and biomedical applications. *Journal of Biomedical Informatics*, 42(2):390–405, 2009.

[7] R. Collobert and J. Weston. A unified architecture for natural language processing: Deep neural networks with multitask learning. In *Proceedings of the 25th international conference on Machine learning*, pages 160–167. ACM, 2008.

[8] Z. S. Harris. Distributional structure. *Word*, 1954.

[9] B. Koopman, G. Zuccon, P. Bruza, L. Sitbon, and M. Lawley. An evaluation of corpus-driven measures of medical concept similarity for information retrieval. In *Proceedings of the 21st ACM international conference on Information and knowledge management*, pages 2439–2442. ACM, 2012.

[10] R. Lebret, J. Legrand, and R. Collobert. Is deep learning really necessary for word embeddings? In *NIPS Workshop on Deep Learning*, 2013.

[11] T. Mikolov, K. Chen, G. Corrado, and J. Dean. Efficient estimation of word representations in vector space. *arXiv preprint arXiv:1301.3781*, 2013.

[12] T. Mikolov, M. Karafiát, L. Burget, J. Cernockỳ, and S. Khudanpur. Recurrent neural network based language model. In *INTERSPEECH*, pages 1045–1048, 2010.

[13] T. Mikolov, I. Sutskever, K. Chen, G. S. Corrado, and J. Dean. Distributed representations of words and phrases and their compositionality. In *Advances in Neural Information Processing Systems*, pages 3111–3119, 2013.

[14] G. A. Miller and W. G. Charles. Contextual correlates of semantic similarity. *Language and cognitive processes*, 6(1):1–28, 1991.

[15] T. Pedersen, S. Pakhomov, S. Patwardhan, and C. Chute. Measures of semantic similarity and relatedness in the biomedical domain. *Journal of Biomedical Informatics*, 40(3):288–299, 2007.

[16] H. Schwenk and J.-L. Gauvain. Training neural network language models on very large corpora. In *Proceedings of the conference on Human Language Technology and Empirical Methods in Natural Language Processing*, pages 201–208. Association for Computational Linguistics, 2005.

[17] E. Voorhees and R. Tong. Overview of the TREC Medical Records Track. In *Twentieth Text REtrieval Conference (TREC 2011)*, MD, USA, 2011.

Parameter Tuning with User Models: Influencing Aggregate User Behavior in Cluster Based Retrieval Systems

Vinay Deolalikar
Hewlett-Packard Research
Sunnyvale, CA
deolalikar.academic@gmail.com

ABSTRACT

Can we effectively influence aggregate user behavior in a cluster based retrieval (CBR) system by tuning its parameters? This question combines parameter tuning with models of user behavior. To address this question, we propose an approach based on three components: user model, criterion metric, and sensitivity analysis. We then demonstrate this approach on one of the most frequently asked questions to designers and operators of CBR systems in enterprises: namely, "suggest a value for k." Both the users and the system desire a value that is likely to maximize user satisfaction, and sway them towards a cluster based examination of their retrieved result set (rather than prefer the original ranked retrieved list). Based on observed user behavior in CBR systems, we posit a two-stage user model. We isolate its core element, which is a "query coverage metric." We then perform an empirical sensitivity analysis of this metric. Our analysis reveals that this metric is, surprisingly, robust to changes in k (i.e., insensitive to k) in a wide range around its de-facto value. We conclude that in cases where our model approximates user behavior, the system cannot substantially increase the chances of the user resorting to CBR by tuning k. This has practical implications on the design and day-to-day operation of CBR systems. Similar analyses can be carried out for other parameters.

Keywords

Cluster Based Retrieval; Parameter Tuning; User Models

1. INTRODUCTION

Consider an enterprise system offering a cluster based retrieval (CBR) interface. The user poses a query to the system. The system first retrieves a ranked list of results. It then also produces a clustered and reranked version of this retrieved list. Once the user begins interaction with the CBR system, they make choices at multiple stages. The first choice is, of course, whether to proceed on their information gathering by inspecting the clustered list, or simply return to the original ranked list. More choices await the user at later stages of the inspection.

This leads us to the following problem statement:

At each stage of the user experience, can we "tune" the

parameters of the CBR system so as to maximize user satisfaction with the clustered list?

The motivation for this question comes from the immense commercial potential[1] for such technologies. Designers and operators would like to know whether such systems can be "tuned" to yield more user satisfaction[2].

Questions of parameter tuning arise at various stages, and with respect to various parameters, in the working of an interactive CBR system. Yet to our knowledge, they have not received research attention. This is in contrast to the enormous amount of literature on parameter tuning questions in other areas of IR such as document representation, classification, language modeling, etc. The fundamental difference between these two types of questions is that the first *incorporates a user model*. Understanding the interaction of the user model with the CBR parameters is key to answering such a question.

In this work, we propose a broad framework for tackling such questions of parameter tuning for influencing user interactive behavior. Our framework uses three components: an abstract user model for the choice between CBR and ranked list, a criterion metric that captures roughly what the user bases his decision upon, and a sensitivity analysis of the *distribution* of the criterion metric to the parameter in question. We then demonstrate our framework for a central question: the choice of the number of clusters k in the CBR system. We posit a two-stage model for observed user behavior in enterprise CBR. We analyze the sensitivity of the distribution of the criterion metric to k in a wide range around its rule of thumb value of $\approx \sqrt{n/2}$ [7]. Our sensitivity analysis shows a surprising result: that the system is unlikely to be able to tune k to sway more users towards cluster based inspection of retrieved lists.

The contributions of this work are twofold. We (i) introduce the question of tuning of parameters to influence aggregate user behavior in CBR systems, and formulate a broad framework to tackle them, and (ii) instantiate this framework on a central question for CBR systems: the choice of k to maximize user satisfaction at the initial inspection of CBR list.

2. RELATED WORK

To our knowledge, there is no work that squarely focuses on the influence of CBR parameters on user behavior. However, our question is related to a vast body of work on users interacting with CBR. We first survey the work on clustering in search—that being our setting—and then clustering in browsing.

Earlier systems that used clustering for information retrieval did so to augment (nearest-neighbor) *search* in response to a query. These systems typically resorted to a static one-time clustering of

---

[1]CBR is part of ECM, projected to grow to $8B by 2017 (Ford and Sullivan).

[2]More so, since, in our experience, deployment of such systems is relatively meager compared to their potential.

the entire corpus. The actual clustering could be either flat or hierarchical. The results were mixed, and in some cases, studies showed that strategies such as those described above actually reduced the performance of the search on standard metrics such as precision and recall. See [13] for a survey of early work on clustering on search.

Search can also be carried out in an interactive setting: [4] shows that a user can quickly navigate to a set of relevant documents in this setting.

The use of clustering in information retrieval as a form of *browsing*, as opposed to search, was investigated by [2]. They called their method of browsing "scatter-gather." [10] discuss scatter-gather on a large text corpus. They conclude that scatter-gather is capable of providing a coherent conceptual image of such large corpora.

We now return to the context of search. [3] provide the first discussion of scatter-gather on the results of a query; namely, they cluster the documents returned by a search engine as the results of a query, and then perform scatter-gather on it. The paper provides anecdotal evidence of the efficacy of scatter-gather using a few examples. They also demonstrate that the distribution of relevant documents indeed tends to form clusters rather than follow a uniform distribution, thereby providing empirical evidence for the cluster hypothesis. See [11] for recent work on evaluating the cluster hypothesis on web documents.

Recently, CBR using language models [5] has gained much attention since it seems to affirm the benefits of CBR over document-based retrieval. This provides an avenue for extension of this work.

Lastly, we mention that cluster labelling itself is a vibrant research area: recent works in this field include [1, 9].

There is a vast body of *statistical* work on determining the number of clusters for a dataset: this does not involve the user, and is not therefore, directly related to this work. A comprehensive survey that captures the diverse methods is [8]. As stated in §1, there is an abundance of work on parameter tuning on other issues of relevance to IR. This is peripherally related to our work, but cannot be surveyed here due to space constraints.

3. BROAD APPROACH

Our approach to the question of parameter tuning to influence aggregate user behavior is as follows. A user interacts with the CBR system at various stages in the IR process. Fix a stage of interaction that is of interest. For this stage, we go through two steps.

First step. We study the user interaction with the CBR system, and extract out two components.

1. A *user model* of the interaction.

2. A (quantitative) *criterion metric* upon which the user bases their decision-making in accordance with the user model. This metric will serve as a proxy for user satisfaction during the stage of the interaction under study.

Second step. Here, we perform a *sensitivity analysis* of the metric with respect to the parameter in question. The goal of this sensitivity analysis is to inform us whether varying the value of the parameter is likely to increase or decrease the metric, and therefore the user satisfaction.

In §4 and §5 we describe the user model and criterion metrics for our task. In §6, we conduct an empirical sensitivity analysis.

4. CBR IN ENTERPRISES: USER MODEL

The impetus for our work came from observations of how users interact with a CBR system in some commercially important applications of clustering in IR, including eDiscovery, IT management, records management, compliance, and others. The majority of users of such systems are not technical experts in data mining or IR. They are generally application experts.

Now consider the situation where a user has posed a query to the CBR system. The system first retrieves a list of documents

ranked using some standard ranking function. It also performs a clustering of this set of documents, and prepares a presentation of this clustering for the user. Clusters are frequently presented to the user by means of a *digest* of terms. The digest serves as a proxy for the topics that the cluster speaks about. They give the user a high-level view of the contents of the cluster, from which they may determine importance and relevance of the cluster to their query.

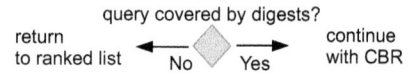

Figure 1: User model for preliminary inspection of the clustering.

The user now has to decide whether to proceed by inspecting the original ranked list, or the cluster based presentation.

We observed that users, faced with the choice of whether to proceed with CBR, or return to their original ranked retrieval list, frequently perform a "preliminary inspection" of the clustering. This inspection itself can be roughly broken into two stages.

1. The user inspects the cluster digests and tries to understand the contents of the cluster through them.

2. The user then evaluates a criterion of the form "are the terms of my query adequately represented in the cluster digests to warrant detailed examination of this clustering?"

If the clustering passes the criterion, the user proceeds along CBR. They may then open each cluster (either by the ranking the system has assigned to the clusters, or a heuristic ranking they may have given based on query coverage of each cluster). On the other hand, if the clustering fails the criterion, the user returns to the ranked list, and proceeds with standard (non-clustered) retrieval. See Fig. 1.

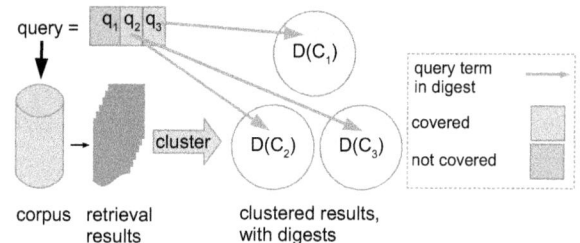

Figure 2: The coverage of a query by digests. In this toy example, the coverage of this particular query is $2/3$.

At this stage, we may state our research question more formally. Please also see Fig. 2.

Research Question. Let $\mathcal{Q}$ be a set of queries. For each query $Q \in \mathcal{Q}$ (where $Q = (q_1, \ldots, q_{|Q|})$), let the following be done. Let Q be issued to an IR system. Let the set of results $R(Q)$ be subjected to a k-way clustering $\mathcal{C} = (C_1, \ldots, C_k)$. Compute digests $\mathrm{D}^\ell(C)$ of length ℓ for each cluster by taking the top-ℓ terms, ranked by information gain with respect to cluster membership[3]. Let $\mathscr{P}_k^\ell$ be a criterion metric that models the second stage of the preliminary inspection described previously. How does the distribution of $\mathscr{P}_k^\ell$ vary as we vary k in a range around its "rule of thumb" value of $\approx \sqrt{n/2}$?

In addition to modeling user behavior, the above seems to be an interesting structural question. Note that k is a parameter in this question. Therefore, we would expect the answer to this question to depend (perhaps strongly) upon the value of k.

---

[3]We compute cluster digests in the standard manner as described in [6]. Namely, rank the terms in the cluster with respect to their information gain with respect to cluster membership, and present the user with the top-ℓ terms as a digest.

5. CRITERION METRICS

In order to address our research question, we need to specify the criterion metric(s) $\mathscr{P}_k^\ell$. We do so now. The setting and notation will be as in the research question in §4. In this section, we define two measures of the coverage of query terms in a clustering of the retrieved results of a query. The first measures what proportion of query terms occur in digests. The second measures how many times query terms occur in digests.

5.1 Query Term Coverage

Our user model posits that the *coverage* of the query by the cluster digests combined is a criterion metric.

Definition 1. $N_k^\ell(Q)$ is defined as the number of terms in Q that appear in at least one of the digests $\{\mathsf{D}^\ell(C_i) : 1 \le i \le k\}$.

Definition 2. We define the *query term coverage* of Q, denoted by $P_k^\ell(Q)$, as $P_k^\ell(Q) := \frac{N_k^\ell(Q)}{|Q|}$.

$P_k^\ell(Q)$ measures how much of a query is covered by the digests of its clustered results. Clearly, $0 \le P_k^\ell(Q) \le 1$.

Next, we need to ascertain the distribution of $P_k^\ell(Q)$ as Q ranges over the entire query set $\mathscr{Q}$.

Definition 3. The *query term coverage profile* of $\mathscr{Q}$, denoted by $\mathscr{P}_k^\ell$, is defined as the distribution $\mathscr{P}_k^\ell := \{P_k^\ell(Q) : Q \in \mathscr{Q}\}$.

We will also examine the effect of query size on the distribution $\mathscr{P}_k^\ell$. To this end, let us define the average coverage for a specific query size.

$$\mathrm{avg}_{|Q|=t}[\mathscr{P}_k^\ell] := \mathrm{avg}\{P_k^\ell(Q) : Q \in \mathscr{Q} \text{ and } |Q| = t\}.$$

5.2 Query Term Multiplicity

The measure $P_k^\ell(Q)$ did not take into account the multiplicities of the occurrences of query terms in cluster digests. We now define a measure that does so.

Definition 4. We define $M_k^\ell(Q)$ as the total number of times a term in Q appears in any of the digests $\mathsf{D}^\ell(C_i)$. Namely,

$$M_k^\ell(Q) := \sum_{q \in Q} \sum_{i=1}^{k} I[q \in \mathsf{D}^\ell(C_i)],$$

where $I[\cdot]$ is the indicator function.

Once more, we are interested in the distribution of $M_k^\ell(Q)$ as Q ranges through $\mathscr{Q}$.

Definition 5. The *query term multiplicity profile* of $\mathscr{Q}$, denoted by $\mathscr{M}_k^\ell$, is defined as $\mathscr{M}_k^\ell := \mathrm{avg}\{M_k^\ell(Q) : Q \in \mathscr{Q}\}$.

Note that $P_k^\ell(Q)$ and $M_k^\ell(Q)$ are independent. For example, if only one query term in a query having many terms appears in multiple digests, and no other term appears in any digest, then the query would score relatively high on $M_k^\ell(Q)$ but relatively low on $P_k^\ell(Q)$.

6. EMPIRICAL SENSITIVITY ANALYSIS

We now conduct an empirical sensitivity analysis of the two coverage metrics $\mathscr{P}_k^\ell$ and $\mathscr{M}_k^\ell$ to the number of clusters k.

Datasets. For our study, we used datasets obtained from the topic distillation category of TREC 2003 and 2004. We used 125 queries—50 queries from TREC 2003 (TD2003), and 75 from TREC 2004 (TD2004). The number of terms in these queries range from one to four. There were 21 queries with one term, 76 with two terms, 20 with three terms, and 8 with four terms. Thus, they broadly reflect query sizes in KDDCUP 2005[4] on query classification, where roughly 80% of the queries had size four or less. Corresponding to these 125 queries, there were 110,229 documents total

---

[4]http://www.sigkdd.org/kddcup

(about 1.85G) in the top-1000 *BM*25 lists. The top-1000 lists include all the documents deemed relevant to the queries by experts, except in a few cases, where more documents are retrieved. This scale is fairly representative of the real-world enterprise information management applications that we work on.

Design. For each query Q in the set of queries $\mathscr{Q}$ defined in the datasets above, we clustered $R(Q)$ into k clusters using the bisecting k-means algorithm. We chose this algorithm since it is known to produce among the highest quality of clusters of any document clustering algorithm [12]. The "rule of thumb" value ($\approx \sqrt{n/2}$ [7]) for the number of clusters for such list lengths would be approximately $k = 20$, and so we experimented with $k = 10$ to $k = 30$; larger values would yield clusters that were too small for typical enterprise applications. We also chose the upper value of ℓ to reflect real-world cluster digest sizes in enterprise-class CBR interfaces[5]. Therefore our parameter ranges were

$$k \in [5, 10, 15, 20, 30] \text{ and } \ell \in [10, 5, 3, 2, 1].$$

We computed $P_k^\ell(Q)$ and $M_k^\ell(Q)$, averaging over three runs of each experiment. As Q ranges through $\mathscr{Q}$, we get a clear picture of the resulting distribution of the coverage metrics over the range of the parameters above.

6.1 Metrics

6.1.1 Frequency Distribution of Query Term Coverage

Fig. 3 shows the query term informativeness profiles. For space considerations, $k = 5$ and $\ell = 5$ are not shown.

We have represented the distribution $\mathscr{P}_k^\ell$ using histograms. The number of queries sums to 125 in each histogram. We have chosen five equal-width bins for our histogram, and the queries have terms varying from one to four. Therefore, we have:

1. The size of the $[0, 0.2]$ bar is equal to the number of queries *none* of whose terms appear in $\{\mathsf{D}^\ell(C_i) : 1 \le i \le k\}$.
2. The size of the $[0.4, 1]$ bar is equal to the number of queries *all* of whose terms appear in $\{\mathsf{D}^\ell(C_i) : 1 \le i \le k\}$.

Let us first understand how the distribution $\mathscr{P}_k^\ell$ varies with ℓ using Fig. 3. Notice that, for all values of k, the size of the rightmost bar (which indicates that all the query terms are in the digest) falls monotonically with increasing ℓ. Let us now focus on $k = 10$. We find that roughly half the queries have all their terms in digests of $\ell = 10$. Naturally, this is also the most filled bin in the histogram. As we raise the bar to $\ell = 3$, we find that the most filled bin shifts to $[0.4, 0.6]$, which has about 40% of the queries. This means that a majority of queries now no longer have all their terms appearing in digests. Finally, at $\ell = 1$, the largest bin consists of queries none of whose terms is the most informative term of a digest. Namely, with such short digests, most queries have no coverage at all.

We should note here that in most enterprise applications that we have encountered, $\ell = 10$ is a good baseline for the size of digests.

6.1.2 Average Coverage for Query Size

Table 1 shows $\mathrm{avg}_{|Q|=t}[\mathscr{P}_k^\ell]$ for various values of k and ℓ.

6.1.3 Query Term Multiplicity Profiles

Fig. 4 shows the behavior of $\mathscr{M}_k^\ell$ as a function of k and ℓ.

6.2 Sensitivity to k

Now we come to our sensitivity analysis of the distribution to the parameter in question—the number of clusters k. Once again, we draw the reader's attention to Fig. 3. This time, we inspect differences in the sets of four profiles (for four values of ℓ) taken

---

[5]We work on a market leading enterprise CBR platform supporting a variety of enterprise applications from a Fortune-10 IT company.

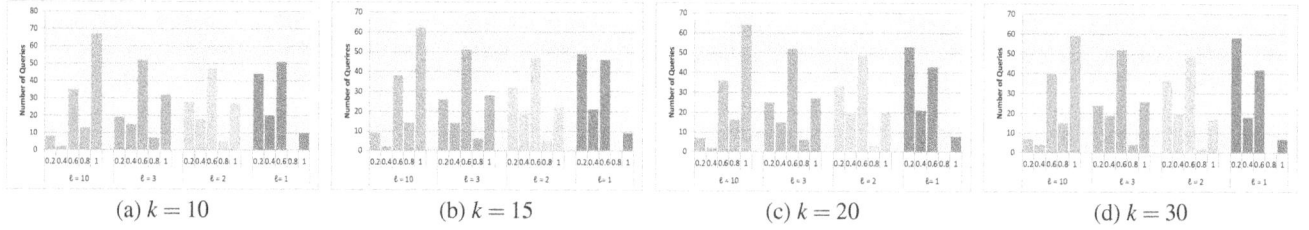

(a) $k = 10$	(b) $k = 15$	(c) $k = 20$	(d) $k = 30$

Figure 3: Query term coverage profiles, $\mathscr{P}_k^\ell$ as a function of k.

Table 1: Effect of query size on the coverage profile. Values of $\mathrm{avg}_{|Q|=t}[\mathscr{P}_k^\ell]$ are shown.

ℓ	k	$t = 1$	$t = 2$	$t = 3$	$t = 4$
10	10	0.76	0.86	0.85	0.72
	30	0.71	0.84	0.8	0.72
3	10	0.57	0.57	0.47	0.31
	30	0.48	0.51	0.37	0.25
1	10	0.48	0.34	0.25	0.15
	30	0.33	0.24	0.18	0.19

Figure 4: Query term multiplicity profiles $\mathscr{M}_k^\ell$ as a function of the number of clusters k and ℓ. Note that the profiles for $\ell = 1, 2, 3, 5$ are almost flat.

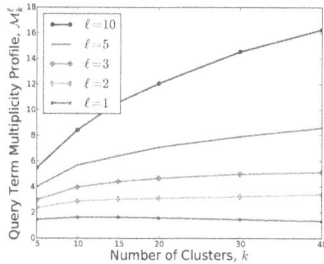

together, as k is varied from $k = 10$ to $k = 30$. We find a stable pattern. The query term coverage profiles (for each value of ℓ) are almost unaffected by the parameter k. The distribution of query term coverages does not display sensitivity to variations in k.

Next, we investigate the sensitivity of the query term coverage profile to k, for either of the four specific values of query size. Namely, we investigate whether $\mathrm{avg}_{|Q|=t}[\mathscr{P}_k^\ell]$ is sensitive to k for $t = 1, 2, 3, 4$ separately. We see that the insensitivity to k in Table 1 is independent of query size. For each query size, we see stability for higher values of ℓ, and small variations between $k = 10$ and $k = 30$ only at $\ell = 1$. However, this last feature must take noise into account, since the actual numbers at $\ell = 1$ are small.

Finally, we inspect Fig. 4. We find that, surprisingly, the multiplicity profiles for lower values of $\ell = 1, 2, 3, 5$ are almost flat. Note that lower values of ℓ correspond to the most significant and informative terms in the cluster digests. This tells us that as we increase the number of clusters k, the query terms do not occur more often in the most significant and informative terms in the digests.

Summary. We analyze three different views into query coverage: frequency view using histograms, averages for query sizes, and multiplicities. With the empirical evidence at our disposal, we may now answer our research question of §4. We observe a stability (i.e., lack of sensitivity) to variations in k displayed by the various criterion metrics $\mathscr{P}_k^\ell$ that model user behavior. This stability also holds for each specific query size, and for multiplicities at significant positions in cluster digests.

7. CONCLUSIONS AND FUTURE WORK

We have initiated research on tuning parameters using user models in a CBR system in order to influence aggregate user behavior. We formulated a generic method for tackling such questions. We then demonstrated a specific important and frequent instantiation of our research question: namely, how can we vary k so that more

users, after a preliminary inspection, choose cluster based inspection of a retrieved list. Our analysis leads to the conclusion that the system may not be able to satisfy more users/queries and compel them to resort to CBR over a simple retrieval ranked list only by varying k. This answers a question that is important to designers and operators of CBR systems.

Our work focuses on a first-stage examination of a CBR list. Another tuning question relates to a multi-stage scatter-gather workflow: what should be the number of clusters chosen at each stage? Note that our work ties in to this question too, since we can remove from consideration the variation to query coverage caused by different choices of k at each stage. However, the challenge will be to model the user's behavior across multiple stages.

References

[1] David Carmel, Haggai Roitman, and Naama Zwerdling. Enhancing cluster labeling using wikipedia. In *Proc. 32nd SIGIR*, pages 139–146, New York, NY, USA, 2009. ACM.

[2] Douglass Cutting, Jan Pedersen, David Karger, and John Tukey. Scatter/gather: A cluster-based approach to browsing large document collections. In *Proc. 15th SIGIR*, pages 318–329. ACM, 1992.

[3] Marti A. Hearst and Jan O. Pedersen. Reexamining the cluster hypothesis: Scatter/gather on retrieval results. In *Proc. 19th SIGIR*, pages 76–84. ACM, 1996.

[4] Anton Leuski. Evaluating document clustering for interactive information retrieval. In *Proc. 10th CIKM*, pages 33–40. ACM, 2001.

[5] Xiaoyong Liu and Bruce W. Croft. Cluster-based retrieval using language models. In *Proc. 27th SIGIR*, pages 186–193. ACM, 2004.

[6] Christopher D. Manning, Prabhakar Raghavan, and Hinrich Schtze. *Introduction to Information Retrieval*. Cambridge University Press, New York, NY, USA, 2008.

[7] K. V. Mardia, J. T. Kent, and J. M. Bibby. *Multivariate Analysis*. Academic Press, 1979.

[8] Glenn W Milligan and Martha C Cooper. An examination of procedures for determining the number of clusters in a data set. *Psychometrika*, 50(2):159–179, 1985.

[9] Markus Muhr, Roman Kern, and Michael Granitzer. Analysis of structural relationships for hierarchical cluster labeling. In *Proc. 33rd SIGIR*, pages 178–185. ACM, 2010.

[10] Peter Pirolli, Patricia Schank, Marti Hearst, and Christine Diehl. Scatter/gather browsing communicates the topic structure of a very large text collection. In *Proc. CHI 96 (Human Factors in Computing Systems)*, volume 1 of *PAPERS: Interactive Information Retrieval*, pages 213–220, 1996.

[11] Fiana Raiber and Oren Kurland. Exploring the cluster hypothesis, and cluster-based retrieval, over the web. In *Proc. CIKM*, pages 2507–2510. ACM, 2012.

[12] M. Steinbach, G. Karypis, and V. Kumar. A comparison of document clustering techniques. In *KDD Workshop on Text Mining*, volume 400, pages 525–526. Boston, 2000.

[13] P. Willett. Recent trends in hierarchic document clustering: a critical review. *Information Processing & Management*, 24(5):577–597, 1988.

On the Importance of Venue-Dependent Features for Learning to Rank Contextual Suggestions

Romain Deveaud   M-Dyaa Albakour   Craig Macdonald   Iadh Ounis

University of Glasgow, UK

firstame.lastname@glasgow.ac.uk

ABSTRACT

Suggesting venues to a user in a given geographic context is an emerging task that is currently attracting a lot of attention. Existing studies in the literature consist of approaches that rank candidate venues based on different features of the venues and the user, which either focus on modelling the preferences of the user or the quality of the venue. However, while providing insightful results and conclusions, none of these studies have explored the relative effectiveness of these different features. In this paper, we explore a variety of user-dependent and venue-dependent features and apply state-of-the-art learning to rank approaches to the problem of contextual suggestion in order to find what makes a venue relevant for a given context. Using the test collection of the TREC 2013 Contextual Suggestion track, we perform a number of experiments to evaluate our approach. Our results suggest that a learning to rank technique can significantly outperform a Language Modelling baseline that models the positive and negative preferences of the user. Moreover, despite the fact that the contextual suggestion task is a personalisation task (i.e. providing the user with personalised suggestions of venues), we surprisingly find that user-dependent features are less effective than venue-dependent features for estimating the relevance of a suggestion.

Categories and Subject Descriptors: H.3.3 [Information Storage & Retrieval]: Information Search & Retrieval

Keywords: venue recommendation; contextual suggestion; learning to rank; personalisation

1. INTRODUCTION

The ever increasing popularity of mobile devices, coupled with ubiquitous Internet access, allows people to search for information in almost every situation and at every hour of the day. As a consequence, search is becoming increasingly local, where people issue queries that are related to their surroundings, mainly for entertainment purposes [8] (e.g. finding a restaurant or activities for the afternoon). Di-

rectly suggesting informational content to the users without requiring them to issue a query (i.e. zero-query retrieval) has recently been identified as one of the major Information Retrieval (IR) research directions, according to the report of the SWIRL 2012 workshop [2].

The TREC Contextual Suggestion track [5] explores such a task and provides a common evaluation framework, allowing researchers to propose solutions aimed at tackling the wide range of challenges associated recommending venues in a city [6]. The aim of the task is to return a ranked list of suggestions (venues) that are relevant given the geographical context (a location in a city) of the users and their preferences. Successful TREC participants [7, 13, 14, 18] relied on the public API of travel sites (such as Foursquare, Yelp, or Google Places) to identify popular and interesting venues, and to filter out suggestions that do not satisfy these geographical constraints. Hence, one of the key challenges of the TREC track is to model the interests of the users, by making use of the preferences they indicated in their profile, and thereby provide them with a ranked list of personalised suggestions. This problem has been mainly tackled using content-based recommendation approaches, considering either the categories of the venues [7], the descriptions of example venues provided by the track organisers [13, 14], or the reviews entered by users on various travel sites for these venues [18].

However, while all of these preceding approaches have deployed useful ranking features, none has tried to combine them together into a single ranking model. In this paper, we propose to learn models that can take all these different features into account, and to explore their effectiveness with the aim of discovering what makes a contextual suggestion relevant. To this end, we define 64 different features before applying learning to rank techniques [10], and perform a thorough evaluation using the test collection of the TREC 2013 Contextual Suggestion track. The contributions of this paper are two-fold. Firstly, we experiment with several state-of-the-art learning to rank techniques for contextual suggestion and show that, while the models learned with the complete set of features can outperform a Language Modelling baseline [14] by up to 77% in terms of P@5, user-dependent features are surprisingly not as important as venue-dependent features for estimating the relevance of a venue. Secondly, we conduct an investigation of the importance of each of the venue-dependent features and find that the probability that a venue is "liked" or "tipped"[1], given a city, is the most prominent indicator of relevance.

---

[1]"Tips" are the equivalent of user reviews in Foursquare.

2. LEARNING TO RANK CONTEXTUAL SUGGESTIONS

The goal of the following experiments is to learn robust and effective models for ranking contextual suggestions. The problem investigated by the TREC 2013 Contextual Suggestion track [5] is to return a list of ranked suggestions, given a context and the profile of a user. The context can be one of the 50 American cities considered in the 2013 dataset, and the user's profile is built by asking the user to provide their preferences, through 5-point numerical ratings (0 to 4), for 50 example venues in Philadelphia, PA. In the Contextual Suggestion track, suggestions are represented by the Web pages of venues that can be extracted from the open Web. To remove the confounding variable of geographically irrelevant venues, we filter out the suggestions that are not relevant to any of the contexts. Most of the TREC participants followed the same approach when they used the API of travel sites to filter geographically irrelevant venues [7, 14, 18]. Using the Terrier IR platform [12], we then build an index containing the Web pages of these venues. For each *query* (i.e. a pair of user & context) from a total of 223 pairs in the dataset, we produce an initial *sample* of candidate Web pages that we will further re-rank through our learning to rank approach. This sample is composed of 216 venues on average and is generated using a Language Modelling (LM) baseline, which favours venues that are similar to the highly rated venues in the user's profile (rated with 3 or 4) and that are dissimilar to the poorly rated venues (rated with 0 or 1). We specifically use the technique detailed in [1], without the diversification step. This technique was found to be effective in previous work [14], and similar statistics were used in other successful approaches [18].

We adopt a learning to rank approach in this paper, hence we compute several features for each suggestion retrieved in the LM sample. Previous work has showed that the popularity of a venue [9] – represented by its all-time number of visitors, or *check-ins* – is a strong indicator of relevance, but such an attribute cannot be obtained directly from the venues' Web pages. However, travel sites or Location-Based Social Networks (LBSNs) such as Foursquare or Yelp allow to obtain such information about the venues. We automatically map Web pages to Foursquare venues by combining and intersecting the results of the Google and Foursquare search APIs when issuing a query formed by the title of the Web page (which always contains the name of the venue) and the name of its city. This method allows us to retrieve all the information and attributes provided by Foursquare, and to link them to the suggestion Web pages of our index. By performing a manual evaluation on a random subset of 100 suggestions, we observed that 87% of them were correctly mapped to their entry in Foursquare. However, we also noticed that only 57% of the relevant suggestions (according to the relevance judgments) have been associated with a Foursquare venue. Tackling this problem is out of the scope of this paper, but we plan to address it in future work by integrating several other LBSNs and Linked Open Data sources.

We then calculate a set of 64 features using the information obtained from Foursquare for the Web pages of the LM sample. These features can be divided into four different groups: 25 city-dependent (CITY), 20 category-dependent (CAT), 10 venue-dependent (VENUE), and 9 user-dependent (USER) features.

CITY: These features describe the context and they include the number of venues, and the total number of check-ins, likes, tips, and photos in the city. We also consider the minimum, maximum, average, median, and standard deviation of these four last attributes across the venues of the city.

CAT: The category-dependent features consist of the counts of the 10 highest level Foursquare categories of the venue[2], as well as the same counts using only the venues that the user labelled as relevant in her/his profile (rated with 3 or 4).

VENUE: Venue-dependent features are mostly related to the popularity of the venue, including its number of checkins, likes, tips, and photos entered by Foursquare users. Since explore the importance of each of these features in our experiments, we provide further details and a complete description of the features in Table 1.

Table 1: Description of the venue-dependent Foursquare features (VENUE) used in this work.

Feature name	Description
NbCheckins	Total number of check-ins in the venue.
NbLikes	Total number of "likes" for the venue.
NbTips	Total number of "tips" for the venue.
NbPhotos	Total number of photos that have been taken in the venue.
Rating	Average of all the ratings given by the users for the venue.
CheckinRatio	$\frac{NbCheckins}{NbCheckinsInCity}$
LikeRatio	$\frac{NbLikes}{NbLikesInCity}$
TipRatio	$\frac{NbTips}{NbTipsInCity}$
PhotoRatio	$\frac{NbPhotos}{NbPhotosInCity}$
Distance	Distance of the venue from the center of the city.

USER: The selected user-dependent features reproduce approaches that several studies and TREC participants have proposed for personalising the suggestions. Firstly, we consider the matches between the categories of the venue and the categories of the user [7] by computing the cosine similarity between the two vectors of category counts computed for the CAT features. We also compute another cosine similarity which considers the categories of the venues that the user did not like. Secondly, we consider the text description of the example venues, as well as the "tip" reviews entered by the Foursquare users, to build two textual user profiles [14]: a positive one generated from the example venues that the user rated highly (either 3 or 4), and a negative one (constructed from the example venues rated by either 0 or 1). Both these profiles are represented as term vectors. Using these profiles, we compute the cosine similarity between the term vector of the venue (generated from its tip reviews) and the positive and negative user profiles respectively. Furthermore, we consider the polarity of the tip reviews to generate four more features. Using the SentiStrength [15] sentiment analysis tool, we classify all of the tip reviews of the venues into three different classes: positive, negative, and neutral. Following this, we construct another positive user profile using the positive reviews of the example venues they rated highly. Likewise, the other negative profile is constructed from the negative reviews of the example venues the user rated poorly. As a result, four features of cosine similarity are generated from the combinations of the user profiles

---

[2]https://developer.foursquare.com/categorytree

Table 2: Contextual suggestion effectiveness results for the different learning to rank models, as well as for the ablated groups of features. All the models learned with the set of 64 features exhibit statistically significant improvements over the initial ranking (LM baseline) according to a paired t-test ($p < 0.01$). Significant decreases induced by features ablations are indicated by ▼, also according to a paired t-test ($p < 0.01$).

	P@5		P@10		MRR	
Initial ranking [1] (LM)	0.2099		0.1910		0.3660	
AFS [11] (All)	**0.3148**		0.2874		**0.5446**	
- CITY	0.3058	(-2.85%)	0.2848	(-0.94%)	0.5418	(-0.51%)
- CAT	0.3058	(-2.85%)	**0.2888**	(+0.47%)	0.5346	(-1.83%)
- USER	0.3031	(-3.70%)	0.2794	(-2.81%)	0.5308	(-2.53%)
- VENUE	0.3058	(-2.85%)	0.2744	(-4.52%)	0.5332	(-2.08%)
Adarank [17] (All)	**0.2735**		0.2565		0.4794	
- CITY	0.2709	(-0.98%)	0.2623	(+2.27%)	**0.4857**	(+1.31%)
- CAT	0.2610	(-4.59%)	**0.2713**	(+5.77%)	0.4717	(-1.61%)
- USER	0.2556	(-6.56%)	0.2435	(-5.07%)	0.4450	(-7.18%)
- VENUE	0.2458	(-10.13%)	0.2401	(-6.38%)	0.4423	(-7.74%)
RankNet [3] (All)	**0.2816**		0.2610		0.4648	
- CITY	0.2726	(-3.18%)	**0.2673**	(+2.41%)	**0.4665**	(+0.37%)
- CAT	0.2547▼	(-9.55%)	0.2502	(-4.12%)	0.4623	(-0.52%)
- USER	0.2559▼	(-9.15%)	0.2484	(-4.81%)	0.4401	(-5.31%)
- VENUE	0.2574▼	(-8.60%)	0.2507	(-3.95%)	0.4487	(-3.45%)
LambdaMART [16] (All)	0.3713		0.3211		0.6093	
- CITY	0.3668	(-1.21%)	0.3256	(+1.40%)	0.5874	(-3.59%)
- CAT	0.3570	(-3.86%)	0.3233	(+0.70%)	0.5918	(-2.87%)
- USER	**0.4009**	(+7.97%)	**0.3386**	(+5.45%)	**0.6584**	(+8.06%)
- VENUE	0.2960▼	(-20.29%)	0.2691▼	(-16.20%)	0.5348▼	(-12.22%)

and the venue's positive or negative reviews. The intuition behind these features, which showed good performances on the 2012 Contextual Suggestion dataset [18], is that people with similar opinions about why would they like or dislike a venue would have similar tastes, and vice versa. Our last USER feature estimates the variation in the diversity of interests between users and is estimated using the entropy of category probability distribution for a given user, from the top level categories in Foursquare of the venues they like. A low-entropy user is then likely to be interested in a few types of venues (e.g. only museums), while a high-entropy user is likely to be open to a wide range of suggestions.

We re-rank the venues of the LM sample and explore the effectiveness of four different learning to rank techniques: Automatic Feature Selection (AFS) [11], Adarank [17], RankNet [3], and LambdaMART [16][3]. So as to ascertain the effect of each group of features, all of these models are first learned using the aforementioned 64 features, then learned again after ablating one group of features at a time. Our experiments are conducted using a 5-fold cross validation across the 223 pairs of user/context of the TREC 2013 Contextual Suggestion track for which contextual suggestions have been judged. Each fold has separate training, validation, and test sets. We report the results of our learning to rank experiments in the following section.

3. EXPERIMENTAL RESULTS

For each group of feature (CITY, CAT, USER, or VENUE), we remove it from the set of 64 features and learn a ranking model. By performing such an ablation, we can explore the importance of each group of features and derive some in-

sights on their impact on the ranking of suggestions. We remove the groups of features independently from each other: no more than one group of features is removed at the same time. We show the effectiveness results of all of the learned models (AFS, Adarank, RankNet, and LambdaMART) and the results obtained for all feature group ablations in Table 2. Rows with (All) correspond to models that have been learned using the full set of 64 features. On analysing this table, we see that RankNet and AFS are similarly degraded by the removal of feature groups. On the other hand, Adarank and LambdaMART in particular (which is actually the best performing model in our experiments) exhibit their largest decreases in performance when removing the venue-dependent features from the features set. This suggests that, for these models, popular venues constitute relevant suggestions, even for a personalised task such as the TREC Contextual Suggestion track.

In particular, we observe that the best overall results are achieved by the LambdaMART technique, which already showed strong performance for Web search by winning the 2011 Yahoo! Learning to Rank Challenge [4]. For LambdaMART, ablating the user-dependent features leads to an ≈8% increase in P@5 (0.3713 → 0.4009) and MRR (0.6093 → 0.6584), and a 5.45% increase in P@10 (0.3211 → 0.3386), which shows that these features can confuse this model. On the other hand, ablating the venue-dependent features causes a statistically significant (t-test, $p < 0.01$) decrease of performance by up to 20.29% in terms of P@5 (0.3713 → 0.2960), showing the great importance of these features for learning an effective ranking model.

While all groups of features seem to play an important role in learning an effective model, venue-dependent features appear to be more important, especially when used with the

[3] http://code.google.com/p/jforests

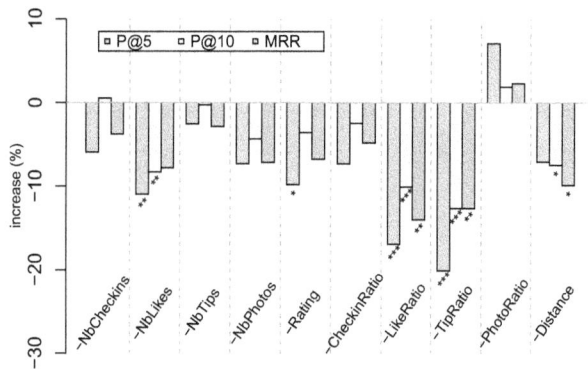

Figure 1: Percentage of improvement obtained when independently removing single venue-dependent features, with respect to a LambdaMART baseline that uses all 64 features. Improvements are expressed in terms of P@5, P@10, and MRR. Statistical significance is stated according to a paired t-test (*: $p < 0.05$, **: $p < 0.01$, ***: $p < 0.001$).

best performing learned model. Hence, we conduct another feature ablation experiment to explore the individual effectiveness of these venue-dependent features, in order to determine which single features are the most effective when suggesting venues to users. In this experiment, we consider the LambdaMART ranking model – learned using all the 64 features – as a baseline, and we compare its performances to other LambdaMART models that have been learned after removing each of the venue-dependent features individually.

Similarly to the previous experiment, a decrease in performance implies that the feature is deemed useful. We report the results in Figure 1. The first observation we make is that PhotoRatio appears to be harmful. When Foursquare venues do not have any photo, the value of this feature is equal to zero, which seems to confuse the learner. Likes and tips, which are more abundant and hence do not suffer from this problem, appear to be very strong indicators of relevance. It is important to note that the raw numbers (i.e. NbLikes and NbTips) are not enough, and that using the city context greatly improves the importance of these features (see LikeRatio and TipRatio). The rating of the venue (which is an average of all the ratings provided by Foursquare users) is also a good indicator of relevance, but to a less extent than LikeRatio and TipRatio. Finally, the distance between the venue and the center of the city also seems to play an important role. Since city centres usually are the most vibrant parts, using this distance as a feature allows the learned model to implicitly separate potentially relevant and attractive venues from unpopular ones.

4. CONCLUDING DISCUSSION

While we expected the learned models to take advantage of all groups of features, we observed surprising results, especially concerning LambdaMART (the best performing model) and Adarank, where venue-dependent features were found to be the most important. These results however raise several questions: are users really interested in personalised venue suggestions? If yes, does personalisation depend on other uncontrolled parameters (e.g. tourists vs. residents)? Do these observations result from a bias in the judging pro-

cess of the Contextual Suggestion track? We can also safely hypothesise that users, who are complex by nature, are more difficult to model than venues that are only described by a handful of attributes from location-based social networks. Nevertheless, the results of this paper open a wide range of research questions that might be interesting to answer in future work.

Acknowledgments

This work has been carried out in the scope of the EC co-funded project SMART (FP7-287583).

5. REFERENCES

[1] M.-D. Albakour, R. Deveaud, C. Macdonald, and I. Ounis. Diversifying Contextual Suggestions from Location-based Social Networks. In *Proc. of IIiX*, 2014.

[2] J. Allan, B. Croft, A. Moffat, and M. Sanderson. Frontiers, Challenges, and Opportunities for Information Retrieval: Report from SWIRL 2012 the Second Strategic Workshop on Information Retrieval in Lorne. *SIGIR Forum*, 46(1):2–32, May 2012.

[3] C. Burges, T. Shaked, E. Renshaw, A. Lazier, M. Deeds, N. Hamilton, and G. Hullender. Learning to Rank Using Gradient Descent. In *Proc. of ICML*, 2005.

[4] O. Chapelle and Y. Chang. Yahoo! Learning to Rank Challenge Overview. In *Yahoo! Learning to Rank Challenge at ICML 2010*, 2011.

[5] A. Dean-Hall, C. Clarke, J. Kamps, P. Thomas, N. Simone, and E. Vorhees. Overview of the TREC 2013 contextual suggestion track. In *Proc. of TREC*, 2013.

[6] R. Deveaud, M.-D. Albakour, C. Macdonald, and I. Ounis. Challenges in Recommending Venues within Smart Cities. In *Proc. of i-ASC at ECIR*, 2014.

[7] G. Hubert, G. Cabanac, K. Pinel-Sauvagnat, D. Palacio, and C. Sallaberry. IRIT, GeoComp, and LIUPPA at the TREC 2013 Contextual Suggestion Track. In *Proc. of TREC*, 2013.

[8] H. Kukka, V. Kostakos, T. Ojala, J. Ylipulli, T. Suopajärvi, M. Jurmu, and S. Hosio. This is Not Classified: Everyday Information Seeking and Encountering in Smart Urban Spaces. *Personal Ubiquitous Comput.*, 17(1), 2013.

[9] Y. Li, M. Steiner, L. Wang, Z.-L. Zhang, and J. Bao. Exploring venue popularity in Foursquare. In *Proc. of INFOCOM*, 2013.

[10] T.-Y. Liu. Learning to Rank for Information Retrieval. *Foundations and Trends in Information Retrieval*, 3(3):225–331, 2009.

[11] D. Metzler. Automatic Feature Selection in the Markov Random Field Model for Information Retrieval. In *Proc. of CIKM*, 2007.

[12] I. Ounis, G. Amati, V. Plachouras, B. He, C. Macdonald, and C. Lioma. Terrier: A High Performance and Scalable Information Retrieval Platform. In *Proc. of OSIR at SIGIR*, 2006.

[13] A. Rikitianskiy, M. Harvey, and F. Crestani. University of Lugano at the TREC 2013 Contextual Suggestion Track. In *Proc. of TREC*, 2013.

[14] M. Sappelli, S. Verberne, and W. Kraaij. Recommending Personalized Touristic Sights Using Google Places. In *Proc. of SIGIR*, 2013.

[15] M. Thelwall, K. Buckley, and G. Paltoglou. Sentiment Strength Detection for the Social Web. *Journal of the American Society for Information Science and Technology*, 63(1), 2012.

[16] Q. Wu, C. J. C. Burges, K. M. Svore, and J. Gao. Ranking, Boosting, and Model Adaptation. Technical Report MSR-TR-2008-109, Microsoft, 2008.

[17] J. Xu and H. Li. AdaRank: A Boosting Algorithm for Information Retrieval. In *Proc. of SIGIR*, 2007.

[18] P. Yang and H. Fang. Opinion-based User Profile Modeling for Contextual Suggestions. In *Proc. of ICTIR*, 2013.

Modelling Complex Relevance Spaces with Copulas

Carsten Eickhoff
Dept. of Computer Science
ETH Zurich, Switzerland
ecarsten@inf.ethz.ch

Arjen P. de Vries
CWI Amsterdam
Amsterdam, The Netherlands
arjen@acm.org

ABSTRACT

Modern relevance models consider a wide range of criteria in order to identify those documents that are expected to satisfy the user's information need. With growing dimensionality of the underlying relevance spaces the need for sophisticated score combination and estimation schemes arises. In this paper, we investigate the use of copulas, a model family from the domain of robust statistics, for the formal estimation of the probability of relevance in high-dimensional spaces. Our experiments are based on the *MSLR-WEB10K* and *WEB30K* datasets, two annotated, publicly available samples of hundreds of thousands of real Web search impressions, and suggest that copulas can significantly outperform linear combination models for high-dimensional problems. Our models achieved a performance on par with that of state-of-the-art machine learning approaches.

Categories and Subject Descriptors

Information Systems [**Information Retrieval**]:
Retrieval models

Keywords

Relevance models; Multivariate relevance; Ranking; Probabilistic framework.

1. INTRODUCTION

To address users' information needs, modern retrieval systems return result lists ordered by decreasing values in estimated *relevance*. Considering only topicality, relevance has been successfully estimated by term overlap between queries and documents [9]. There is, however, a wide range of theoretical relevance frameworks according to which relevance goes beyond mere topicality and is a composite notion comprised of dimensions such as document recency, credibility or monetary cost. There are several examples of applications focusing on non-topical factors such as textual complexity [2] or suitability for children [4]. Depending on the context of

the search session, such factors can have a strong influence on result lists. A topically highly relevant document that is not understandable due its complex syntactic structure or its excessive use of jargon should be considered of lower effective relevance. With respect to these developments, the traditional task shifts from a univariate ranking problem to a multivariate one with many, potentially independent, dimensions.

The state of the art in multidimensional relevance modelling is dominated by two popular approaches. On the one hand, linear score combinations deliver intuitively interpretable, yet simplistic results. On the other hand, sophisticated learning-to-rank models often show superior performance that can come at the cost of offering less direct insight to human investigators. The recently presented copula framework for information retrieval [3] tries to overcome these inherent limitations by presenting a model that is formally grounded in probability theory while at the same time enabling flexible fitting to complex real-world distributions of relevance. The model's ability to account for co-movements in extreme regions of the relevance scale, so-called *tail dependencies* makes it an especially powerful framework that exceeds the capabilities of strictly linear functions. The initial copula approach concentrated on rather simple, two-dimensional, models. In this paper, we expand the original work by investigating modifications to the framework, especially geared towards use in high dimensional settings.

The research presented in this paper is guided by two fundamental research questions: (**1**) How does the retrieval performance of copulas compare to that of established IR models in high-dimensional relevance spaces? (**2**) More specifically, can nested copulas provide better approximations of the true underlying distribution of relevance in high-dimensional settings?

This paper goes beyond the current state of IR literature by investigating the use of model families from the domain of robust statistics to information retrieval settings. Expanding on the recently proposed copula-based relevance models, we present a number of experiments in high-dimensional relevance spaces, motivating the use of formal, yet data-driven models even in complex settings that traditionally are reserved for machine-learned approaches.

2. RELATED WORK

"*Relevance*" is a central notion in IR theory and applications. Many theoretical relevance frameworks have been proposed, including for example, [10], or [8]. Despite different definitions of the concrete composition of relevance, most of these frameworks agree on the fact that relevance is a more complex notion than could be expressed in the form of a single criterion. Applied retrieval model implementations, for a long time, tended to rely on weighted linear combinations of individual relevance scores, for example in the popular BM25F scheme [9]. Gerani *et al.* [6] applied non-linear transformations prior to the linear combination step. Their positive results motivate the need for models whose capabilities go beyond strictly linear dependency structures. Kraaij *et al.* [7] investigated the formal combination of independent relevance dimensions in the form of prior probabilities injected into n-gram language models. As an alternative to the previously presented formal approaches, industrial solutions often rely on machine learning techniques in order to infer optimal rankings based on a wide range of features [1].

In order to combine the strengths of theoretically grounded models and machine-learned rankers, we applied copulas [3], a model family from the domain of robust statistics for the task of relevance modelling. Traditionally, copulas have been used in domains such as the analysis of stock portfolio risk, or meteorology, in which multitudes of variables interact in potentially non-linear fashion. While the original paper exclusively investigates two-dimensional relevance spaces, this paper studies high-dimensional relevance settings with more than one hundred individual features. Additionally, we further refine the previous approach by using nested copulas, an expansion to the copula framework that aims especially at high-dimensional settings.

3. METHODOLOGY

In the following, we will begin with a necessarily brief overview of the copula framework and its key properties. For a more comprehensive overview of this powerful model family, please refer to adjunct resources such as the survey by Embrechts *et al.* [5].

3.1 Copulas

Each copula is a multivariate *cumulative distribution function* (*cdf*). Given

$$X = (x_1, x_2, \ldots, x_k)$$

a k-dimensional random vector with continuous margins

$$F_i(x_i) = \mathbb{P}[X_i \leq x_i]$$

observations can be mapped to the unit cube $[0,1]^k$ as

$$U = (u_1, u_2, \ldots u_k) = (F_1(x_1), F_2(x_2), \ldots F_k(x_k)).$$

A k-dimensional copula $\mathcal{C}$ describes the joint cumulative distribution function of the normalized random vector U.

$$\mathcal{C} : [0,1]^k \to [0,1]$$

There are three particularly interesting properties that motivate the use of copulas for settings such as relevance modelling: (1) Since observations u and dependency structures $\mathcal{C}(.)$ are separated, each component is more straightforward to estimate. (2) The explicit dependency model operates on the unit cube which makes the method inherently scale invariant. (3) The ability to represent tail dependencies allows for accurate models of non-linear interdependence between relevance dimensions.

Different copula families have individual properties, strengths and limitations. Please refer to Embrechts *et al.* [5] for more

detail. In this paper, for reasons of brevity and scope, we focus on using Gumbel copulas. This choice is motivated theoretically by their ability to account for tail dependencies in both the upper and lower extremes of the scale, that other models lack. A dedicated set of experiments empirically supports our preference by showing Gumbel-family copulas to consistently and significantly outperform the competing methods in the candidate pool. The comparison was conducted on the training portion of the *MSLR-WEB10K* dataset and further considered Gaussian, Joe, Clayton and Frank copulas. Gumbel copulas are formally given by:

$$\mathcal{C}_{Gumbel}(U) = \exp(-(\sum_{i=1}^{k}(-\log(u_i))^\theta)^{\frac{1}{\theta}})$$

The model involves a single degree of freedom, the parameter $\theta \in [1, \infty]$, expressing the strength of dependency across dimensions k. In order to model the probability of document relevance via copulas, we propose a modification of the method presented in [3]. Based on the training portion of our dataset, we build individual copulas C_r and C_n (with parameters θ_r and θ_n) for modelling relevant and non-relevant documents, respectively. The probabilities of relevance and non-relevance are estimated by the respective copula densities given observation vector U. The final ranking criterion is given by $OR(rel|U)$, the odds ratio of relevance according to the two copulas.

$$
\begin{aligned}
OR(rel|U) &= \frac{P(rel|U)}{P(non|U)} \\
&= \frac{\mathcal{C}_r(U) \prod u_i}{\mathcal{C}_n(U) \prod u_i} \\
&= \frac{\mathcal{C}_r(U)}{\mathcal{C}_n(U)}
\end{aligned}
$$

3.2 Nested Copulas

Previous work [3] modelled low-dimensional document relevance spaces with a single copula with k components, where k equalled the cardinality of the entire relevance space. While this is possible in high-dimensional spaces as well, alternative options offer additional degrees of freedom. The use of so-called *nested* copulas is one such method. Instead of combining all dimensions in a single step as described earlier, they allow for a nested hierarchy of copulas that estimate joint distributions for sub sets of the full relevance space and subsequently combine scores until one global model is obtained. Formally, fully nested copulas with k dimensions are given by

$$\mathcal{C}(U) = \mathcal{C}_0(u_1, \mathcal{C}_1(u_2, \mathcal{C}_2(\ldots, \mathcal{C}_{k-2}(u_{k-1}, u_k))))$$

By means of the structure of the nesting "*tree*", nested copulas can explicitly model which dimensions depend on each other directly. The respective θ_i parameters determine the strengths of these (per-dimension) dependencies. This mechanism gives nested copulas a theoretical advantage in flexibility over their non-nested counterparts. As an alternative approach to full nesting, partially nested copulas hierarchically combine subsets of dimensions. Figure 1 shows a fully nested copula with $k-1$ copula modelling steps (left) and a conceptual example of a partially nested copula (right).

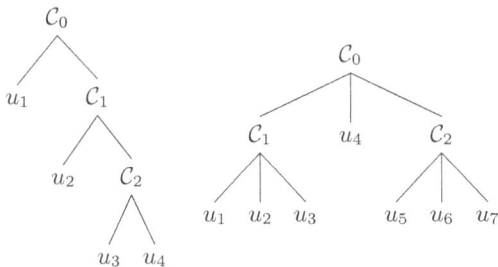

Figure 1: Examples of fully nested (left) and partially nested (right) copulas.

3.3 Data Set

In order to evaluate the use of copulas for high-dimensional relevance spaces, we use the *MSLR-WEB10K* and *WEB30K* datasets, two publicly available collections of 10,000 (30,000, respectively) real Web search queries and an annotated sample of hundreds of thousands of related impressions. For each query-url pair, a set of 136 features are available. The majority of the feature space considers dimensions related to topicality such as tf/idf scores or query term frequencies in different sections of the page. There are, however, several features that capture alternative relevance criteria such as general page authority, quality or textual complexity. For an overview of the full list of features, please consult the data set Web page (http://research.microsoft.com/en-us/projects/mslr/feature.aspx). The corpora are pre-partitioned into 5 equally sized folds to allow for cross validation in a 3-1-1 split of training, validation and test sets.

4. EXPERIMENTS

This section discusses our experimental set-up and findings. All experimental results were obtained by means of 5-fold cross validation on the *MSLR-WEB10K* and *MSLR-WEB10K* datasets. In order to set the performance of the various copula models into perspective, we include a common weighted linear combination scheme l as a baseline. Concrete settings of the mixture parameters λ_i are determined based on a greedy parameter sweep (ranging from $0 \ldots 1$ in steps of 0.005) on the training set of each CV fold.

$$l(U) = \sum_{i=1}^{k} \lambda_i u_i$$

Additionally, we compare to LambdaMART [11], a competitive learning-to-rank baseline. The relevant model parameters are tuned on the validation set. We rely on the implementation of the GBM package for R (http://cran.r-project.org/web/packages/gbm/).

We investigate three types of copula models. The "flattest" nesting hierarchy is given by copulas without any subnesting. All 136 dimensions are included in a single model, describing all inter-dimensional dependencies by a single parameter θ. This strategy is equivalent to the method presented in [3]. To study some simple, yet indicative examples of nested copulas, we include a fully nested approach in which the nesting order is determined randomly and the average results across 50 randomizations are reported. Note that the concrete nesting structure is an additional degree of freedom that holds significant modelling power. We leave

Table 1: Performance comparison of copula and L2R models.

Method	$nDCG_{10K}$	$nDCG_{30K}$	MAP_{10K}	MAP_{30K}
Linear Comb.	0.49	0.46	0.30	0.28
LambdaMart	0.56*	0.55*	0.37*	0.37*
Copula	0.51	0.50*	0.32	0.32*
Nested	0.53*	0.54*	0.33*	0.33*
Fully Nested	0.54*	0.54*	0.36*	0.35*

this aspect out of the scope of this paper. Finally, as an example of partially nested copulas, we rely on the existing semantic grouping of dimensions in the dataset (e.g., all *tf/idf* features, or all *query term coverage* features) and estimate individual copulas $\mathcal{C}_{d_i}$ for each group d_i. All of these group copulas are then combined in an overall copula $C_{partial}(U)$. Groups that comprise only a single dimension are directly included into $\mathcal{C}_{partial}(U)$. This will become especially relevant for the experiments presented later in Figure 2. For the extreme case of exclusively single-dimensional groups, this model becomes equivalent to non-nested copulas. All copula experiments presented in this paper are based on the publicly available implementation for R [12].

For model comparison, we use two well known metrics: normalized Discounted Cumulative Gain (nDCG) and Mean Average Precision (MAP). Table 1 shows the resulting cross-validation performance of the respective methods on the full 136-dimensional datasets. Statistically significant performance improvements with respect to the linear combination baseline are denoted by the * character. We used a Wilcoxon signed rank test with $\alpha < 0.05$ confidence level.

We can note a clear ordering of approaches in which linear combinations achieve the lowest overall performance and the LambdaMART method delivers the best results. The various copula-based models lie between these extremes. Global copulas show slightly better performance than a linear feature combination, these differences were, however, not found to be significant. For both forms of nested copulas, we can note significantly higher scores in terms of nDCG and MAP. With respect to our research questions, we note that copula-based models, especially nested ones, show strong ranking performance for high-dimensional settings. Fully nested copulas, especially, approximate the performance of the learning-to-rank model to the degree, that we could not note any statistically significant differences between the two methods.

In order to further investigate the individual performances of the various methods as the dimensionality of the relevance space increases, we modify the setting by varying the number of dimensions k between 1 and 136. Figure 2 shows the results of this experiment in terms of nDCG and MAP on the *MSLR-WEB10K* dataset. The figures for the *WEB30K* dataset are omitted to save space, as they display identical tendencies. For each choice of k, we randomly sample $n = 100$ feature subsets, train the respective models on each set and average the resulting retrieval performance. For all methods, we note steep performance gains with each dimension that is added early on. These improvements slowly level out and reach a largely stable performance for relevance spaces of size $75 \leq k \leq 136$. An especially noteworthy observation can be made in the comparison of global copulas and linear combination models. While early on, linear models show higher scores in both metrics, this tendency re-

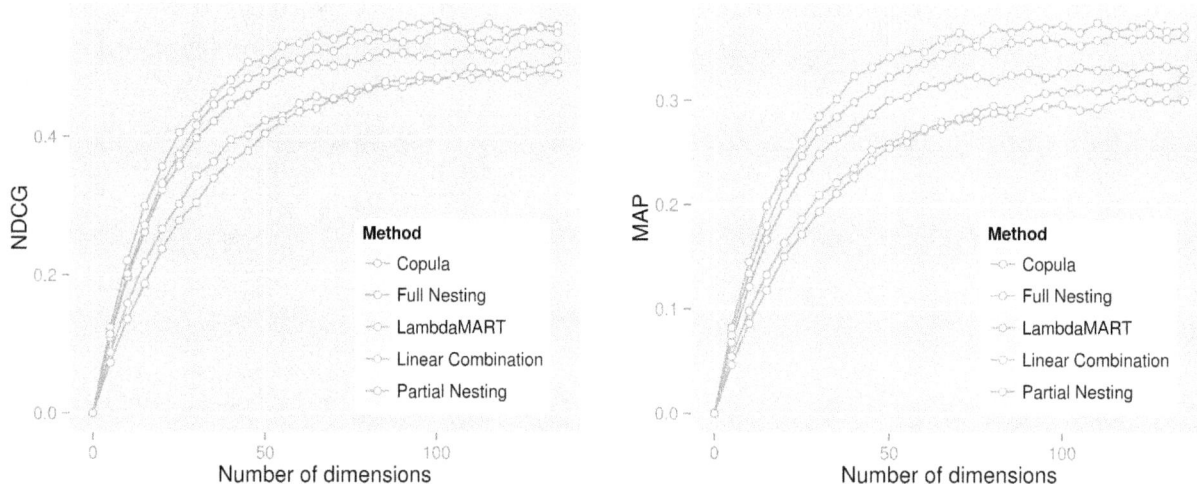

Figure 2: NDCG and MAP as functions of the dimensionality of the underlying *MSLR-WEB10K* relevance space.

verses for high-dimensional spaces ($60 \leq k \leq 80$). Previous work [3] noted competitive ranking performance of linear combination models for most of their experimental corpora. The authors concluded that the individual score distributions inherent to the respective domains may favour either of the approaches. Their study was, however, limited to two-dimensional relevance estimates. As we can see from the current example, even in domains that are seemingly well represented by linear models, copulas can achieve performance gains as the problem scales up in dimensionality.

5. CONCLUSION

This paper presents a piece of ongoing work, investigating the performance of copula-based relevance models for application in information retrieval. In particular, we looked at high-dimensional relevance spaces and used the *MSLR-WEB10K* and *WEB30K* datasets, two established learning-to-rank resources, as our experimental domain.

Our experiments suggest that for high-dimensional settings, copulas show significantly greater retrieval performance than linear combination models. When iteratively increasing the dimensionality of the relevance space, we note a widening gap between copula and linear fusion performance. Additionally, we found nested copulas to perform especially well when the number of dimensions increases.

We foresee several promising directions for future expansions of this work. In this paper, we gave an initial performance comparison of standard and nested copulas. Nested Archimedean copulas come with a high number of degrees of freedom, the tuning of which, however, exceeded the scope of this work. Here, we investigated fully nested copulas (of arbitrary nesting order) as well as partially nested ones of depth 2 with individual sub copulas per feature family. In the future, a careful investigation of nesting strategies should be conducted to find optimal order and nesting depth. In this regard, we are especially interested in applying machine learning techniques in order to construct copulas more effectively. During our investigation of relevance spaces of different dimensionality, we noted that optimal performance can be achieved long before the full pool of dimensions was

included. In this paper, we randomly sampled dimensions in order to investigate the effect of dimensionality on the performance based ranking of approaches. In the future, it would be interesting to investigate active learning techniques to efficiently construct relevance spaces for copulas using the minimal subset of dimensions that results in optimal ranking performance. In this way, a significant overhead in feature extraction and model training can be made redundant.

6. REFERENCES

[1] Chris Burges, Tal Shaked, Erin Renshaw, Ari Lazier, Matt Deeds, Nicole Hamilton, and Greg Hullender. Learning to rank using gradient descent. In *ICML 2005*. ACM.

[2] Kevyn Collins-Thompson, Paul N Bennett, Ryen W White, Sebastian de la Chica, and David Sontag. Personalizing web search results by reading level. In *CIKM 2011*. ACM.

[3] Carsten Eickhoff, Arjen P. de Vries, and Kevyn Collins-Thompson. Copulas for Information Retrieval. In *SIGIR 2013*. ACM.

[4] Carsten Eickhoff, Pavel Serdyukov, and Arjen P De Vries. A combined topical/non-topical approach to identifying web sites for children. In *WSDM 2011*. ACM.

[5] Paul Embrechts, Filip Lindskog, and Alexander McNeil. Modelling dependence with copulas and applications to risk management. *Handbook of heavy tailed distributions in finance*, 2003.

[6] Shima Gerani, ChengXiang Zhai, and Fabio Crestani. Score transformation in linear combination for multi-criteria relevance ranking. In *Advances in Information Retrieval*. Springer, 2012.

[7] Wessel Kraaij, Thijs Westerveld, and Djoerd Hiemstra. The importance of prior probabilities for entry page search. In *SIGIR 2002*. ACM.

[8] Stefano Mizzaro. Relevance: The whole history. *JASIS*, 48(9), 1997.

[9] Stephen Robertson, Hugo Zaragoza, and Michael Taylor. Simple bm25 extension to multiple weighted fields. In *CIKM 2004*. ACM.

[10] Tefko Saracevic. Relevance reconsidered. In *CoLIS*. ACM Press, 1996.

[11] Qiang Wu, Chris J. C. Burges, Krysta M. Svore, and Jianfeng Gao. Ranking, boosting, and model adaptation. *Tecnical Report, MSR-TR-2008-109*, 2008.

[12] Jun Yan. Enjoy the joy of copulas: with a package copula. *Journal of Statistical Software*, 21(4), 2007.

Identifying Time Intervals of Interest to Queries

Dhruv Gupta[†][*]   Klaus Berberich[†]

[†]Max Planck Institute for Informatics   [*]IIT Patna
Saarbrücken, Germany   Patna, India
{dhgupta,kberberi}@mpi-inf.mpg.de   dhruv.mc12@iitp.ac.in

ABSTRACT

We investigate how time intervals of interest to a query can be identified automatically based on pseudo-relevant documents, taking into account both their publication dates and temporal expressions from their contents. Our approach is based on a generative model and is able to determine time intervals at different temporal granularities (e.g., day, month, or year). We evaluate our approach on twenty years' worth of newspaper articles from The New York Times using two novel testbeds consisting of temporally unambiguous and temporally ambiguous queries, respectively.

Categories and Subject Descriptors

H.3.3 [**Information Search and Retrieval**]

Keywords

Temporal Information Retrieval

1. INTRODUCTION

Time has been recognized as an important dimension in Information Retrieval [2], and recent years have seen an increased interest in making use of temporal information associated with documents or information needs. Tasks that have been tackled include retrieving recent relevant documents [10] as well as documents relevant to implicitly [11] or explicitly [3, 4] temporal queries. Beyond that, also web search engines have meanwhile deployed features to keep up with the changing Web, indexing recently published documents, and filter results based on their publication dates.

In this work, we address the problem of automatically identifying time intervals of interest to a given keyword query. For instance, when presented with the keyword query bill clinton presidency, a good time interval to determine would be [1993, 2001], which covers the years of Clinton's presidency. This is a useful building block in temporal information retrieval with applications such as (i) temporal query reformulation and expansion – by adding time intervals of interest to the query, (ii) temporal diversification of search results – by making sure that the result covers diverse time intervals of interest to the query, and (iii) providing more structured query results to users – organized by important time intervals they refer to.

While ours is not the first effort in this direction, it differs from previous ones [4, 9] in several important aspects. First, our focus is on time intervals (e.g., [1993, 2001]) as opposed to time points at a fixed temporal granularity (e.g., the years 1993 and 2001). Second, we make use of both documents' publication dates, as part of their meta data, as well as temporal expressions from their contents. Third, our approach is not restricted to a fixed temporal granularity but can determine time intervals of interest at different temporal granularities (e.g., day, month, and year). Finally, we also consider temporally ambiguous queries for which more than one time interval is of interest – say george bush presidency or san francisco earthquake.

This work builds on prior research [3], which aims at improving retrieval effectiveness for explicitly temporal queries such as summer olympics 2004. Borrowing their formal model for representing temporal expressions contained in documents (e.g., in the summer of 2004) and capturing their inherent uncertainty, we put forward a generative model for identifying time intervals of interest to a given keyword query. Our model is based on the intuition that a time interval of interest should be often referred to in relevant documents. More specifically, it considers the top-k documents retrieved by a unigram language model, treating them as pseudo-relevant, and analyzes their contents, specifically the temporal expressions therein, for often referred to time intervals. We describe the design space and consider different concrete instantiations of our model. To evaluate their performance, we compile two novel testbeds, consisting of temporally unambiguous and temporally ambiguous queries obtained from high-quality web sources.

Contributions made in this work are: (i) a novel approach to identify time intervals of interest to a given keyword query, (ii) two testbeds consisting of temporally (un) ambiguous queries which are made publicly available, (iii) an experimental evaluation of our approach on The New York Times Corpus [1], as a publicly-available document collection, on the aforementioned query testbeds.

Organization. The rest of this paper is organized as follows. We put our work in context with prior research in Section 2. Section 3 then describes our approach, including a discussion of the design space and details on our concrete instantiation. Following that, we describe our experimental evaluation in Section 4, before concluding in Section 5.

CIKM'14, November 3–7, 2014, Shanghai, China.
Copyright 2014 ACM 978-1-4503-2598-1/14/11 ...$15.00.
http://dx.doi.org/10.1145/2661829.2661927

2. RELATED WORK

In this section, we put our work in context with existing prior work. Kanhabua et al. [9] is the work closest to ours. In contrast to the approach put forward in this work, their method focuses on identifying years of interest to a keyword query and does so only based on documents' publication dates. Their method is thus restricted to time points at year granularity and cannot identify time intervals at other granularities. Dakka et al. [4] as well as Diaz and Jones [7], as one building block in their respective research, describe methods that identify time points of interest to a query. Their methods, though, are solely based on the publication dates associated with documents and do not consider temporal expressions from their contents. Again, no time intervals are considered and the granularity is limited to that of documents' publication dates. Strötgen et al. [13] look into the related problem of identifying salient temporal expressions from a document. Other work has looked into improving the result quality of implicitly or explicitly temporal queries. For the former, this includes Metzler et al. [11], who identify implicitly temporal queries within the query log of a web search engine, and Dakka et al. [4], who analyze the distribution of publication dates to identify implicitly temporal queries. Peetz et al. [12] is a recent related work that leverages bursts in the temporal distribution of publication dates to improve retrieval effectiveness. Berberich et al. [3], as the work mentioned in the introduction, targets explicitly temporal queries and leverages both documents' publication dates and temporal expressions. Our work is orthogonal and the time intervals that we identify can be used to augment the query and obtain better results with one of the aforementioned approaches. Finally, there has been work on attaching a time point or time interval to an entire document. Thus, de Jong et al. [5] determine the likely publication time of a document based on its language; Kanhabua et al. [8] make use of temporal expressions from documents' contents to the same end. Jatowt et al. [6], even in the absence of any temporal expressions, determine a so-called focus time for a document, which delimits the time period the document predominantly refers to. For all of these approaches, the focus is on identifying a single time point or time interval (as opposed to possibly more than one) for a given document (as opposed to a query in our case).

3. IDENTIFYING INTERESTING TIME INTERVALS

In this section, we describe our approach for identifying interesting time intervals for a given keyword query.

3.1 Document Model

We largely adopt the formal model and notation introduced by [3]. Our document collection is denoted $\mathcal{D}$. A document $d \in \mathcal{D}$ consists of a multiset of keywords d_{text} and a multiset of temporal expressions d_{time}. We let $tf(v, d)$ and $tf(T, d)$ denote the term frequency of the keyword v and the temporal expression T in document d, respectively. We use $|d_{text}|$ and $|d_{time}|$ to denote the multiset cardinalities of the textual and temporal part, respectively. In the remainder, when it is clear from the context, we simply write d to refer to either of them. Keywords are drawn from a vocabulary $\mathcal{V}$. A temporal expression is a four-tuple

$$T = \langle tb_l, tb_u, te_l, te_u \rangle$$

with components from a time domain $\mathcal{T}$ (usually $\mathbb{N}$). Such a temporal expression can refer to any time interval $[tb, te] \in \mathcal{T} \times \mathcal{T}$ with $tb_l \leq tb \leq tb_u$ and $te_l \leq te \leq te_u$, i.e., tb_l (te_l) and tb_u (te_u) mark the earliest and latest begin (end) of such times intervals. This representation treats time intervals as having a precise meaning and captures the uncertainty inherent to temporal expressions such as in the 1990s, which at year-granularity would be mapped to $\langle$ 1990, 1999, 1990, 1999 $\rangle$, thus potentially referring to any time interval completely within the decade. Alternatively, a temporal expression T can be regarded as a set of time intervals, namely all of the time intervals that it can refer to. We will use this interchangeably and, for instance, use $|T|$ as the number of time intervals the temporal expression refers to.

3.2 Retrieval Model

As mentioned above, our approach determines time intervals of interest to a query based on pseudo-relevant documents. To determine those, we use a unigram language model with Dirichlet smoothing and thus estimate the query likelihood of a given keyword query q as

$$P(q \mid d) = \prod_{v \in q} \frac{tf(v, d) + \mu \cdot \frac{tf(v, D)}{|D|}}{|d| + \mu} . \qquad (1)$$

Here, D is the document collection, treated as a single document, for the purpose of smoothing probability estimates.

3.3 Time Intervals of Interest

Having identified documents believed to be relevant to the keyword query q, our approach analyzes their contents to determine time intervals of interest. We next describe the high-level components of our approach, before discussing possible instantiations.

Intuitively, a time interval $[tb, te]$ is considered interesting for a keyword query q, if it is frequently referred to by highly relevant documents. We cast this intuition into the following generative model:

$$P([tb, te] \mid q) = \sum_{d \in top(q,k)} P([tb, te] \mid d) P(d \mid q) \qquad (2)$$

According to this model, first a document d is selected from $top(q, k)$ as the set of k documents having highest likelihood of generating the keyword query q. Second, a time interval $[tb, te]$ is generated from the temporal expressions contained in document d. For each of the two steps, we consider different design alternatives.

Generating Documents

In the simplest case, in the first step, a document is selected at uniform random among the top-k results, yielding

$$P(d \mid q) = 1/k . \qquad (3)$$

Here, the query likelihood $P(q \mid d)$ is thus not taken into account. While this may not be a problem for small choices of k, we expect it to deteriorate performance for larger choices of k. As an alternative, we consider

$$P(d \mid q) = \frac{P(q \mid d)}{\sum_{d' \in top(q,k)} P(q \mid d')} , \qquad (4)$$

which estimates the probability of selecting a document in the first step as proportional to its query likelihood estimated according to Equation 1.

Generating Time Intervals

For the second step, we can estimate the probability of generating the time interval $[tb, te]$ from document d as

$$P([tb, te] \mid d) = \frac{1}{|d_{time}|} \sum_{T \in d_{time}} \mathbb{1}([tb, tb, te, te] = T) . \quad (5)$$

The time interval $[tb, te]$ can thus only be generated from documents containing temporal expressions that exactly map to it. To illustrate this, the time interval [1992, 1998] can only be generated from documents that contain from 1992 until 1998 but not from documents containing only in the 1990s. As a more relaxed advanced alternative, building on the generative model introduced in [3], we also consider

$$P([tb, te] \mid d) = \frac{1}{|d_{time}|} \sum_{T \in d_{time}} \frac{\mathbb{1}([tb, te] \in T)}{|T|} , \quad (6)$$

which takes into account the uncertainty inherent to temporal expressions. With this model, also a document containing in the 1990s, formally represented as $\langle 1990, 1999, 1990, 1999 \rangle$, could generate the time interval [1992, 1998].

Query Processing

At query time, our method first determines the set $top(q, k)$ of documents having highest query likelihoods. It then analyzes the temporal expressions therein, determining t_{min} and t_{max} corresponding, respectively, to the earliest and latest time mentioned in any of the result documents. Following that, it enumerates all valid time intervals $[tb, te] \subseteq [t_{min}, t_{max}]$ and determines their probability $P([tb, te] \mid d)$. For this last step, combining the two design alternatives for each of the two steps of our generative model, we obtain four possible instantiations, which we experimentally evaluate in the following section. We will use **N** and **A** to refer to the *naïve* and *advanced* design alternative for each of the two steps. The method combining Equation 4 and Equation 5, for example, will be referred to as **AN**.

4. EXPERIMENTAL EVALUATION

We now describe our experimental evaluation of the approach put forward in this work.

4.1 Setup & Datasets

Document Collection. As a document collection, we use The New York Times Annotated Corpus [1], which consists of about 2 million news articles published between 1987 and 2007. Publication dates are readily available. Temporal expressions are obtained from the data provided by [3] – they used TARSQI [14] to annotate temporal expressions augmented by a handful of handcrafted regular expressions to go after range expressions (e.g., from 1980 until 1984). Publication dates of documents are taken into account as additional temporal expressions – thus a document published on March 13, 1988 virtually contains the temporal expression on March 13, 1988.

Queries. We use two sets of test cases: (i) *temporally unambiguous queries* obtained from the "On this Day" website of The New York Times[1]. For each day of the year, this website lists an event of historic significance, including a concise description. For example, for July 1st, the event is described as *"In 1997, Hong Kong reverted to Chinese rule*

[1] http://learning.blogs.nytimes.com/on-this-day/

Sports	commonwealth games (21) | asian games (18) | summer olympics (34) | winter olympics (26) | super bowl winners (48)
Music	u2 album (13) | nirvana album (4) | beatles album (52) | red hot chilli peppers album (11) | michael jackson album (11)
Movies	harry potter movie (6) | oscar academy awards (88) | lord of the rings movie (3)
Politics	german federal elections (19) | us presidential elections (58) | australia federal elections (45)
History	iraq war (2) | world trade center bombing (2) | madrid bombing (9) | earthquake united states of america (73)

Table 3: Temporally ambiguous queries

after 156 years as a British colony.". We extract the indicated year (here: 1997) for each date to obtain a precise date at day granularity and keep the rest of the description as a query. This leaves us with a total of 366 temporally unambiguous queries; **(ii)** *temporally ambiguous queries* from the domains of Sports, Music, Movies, Politics, and History, which we compiled manually. For each of them, we consult Wikipedia to find out the associated time intervals at day granularity. The obtained set of 20 queries is given in Table 3. Here, the number of associated time intervals is given in parentheses, indicating the degree of ambiguity of each query. In the interest of repeatability, both query sets, including associated time intervals are made available at:

http://www.mpi-inf.mpg.de/~kberberi/data/cikm2014

Methods under comparison are the four combinations of the naïve and advanced models delineated in Section 3, referred to as **NN**, **AN**, **NA**, and **AA**. We can not sensibly compare against [9] as a baseline, since their method is based on publication dates and year granularity. For each of the methods under comparison, we set the smoothing parameter of the unigram language model as $\mu = 1000$ and vary the number of pseudo-relevant documents retrieved as $k = \{25, 50, 100\}$. We consider three different temporal granularities (day, month, year) in our experiments. When going for a coarser granularity (e.g., year), temporal expressions, which are natively stored at day granularity, are systematically coarsened. As a concrete example, the temporal expression $\langle 19980101, 19981231, 19980101, 19981231 \rangle$ would be converted into $\langle 1998, 1998, 1998, 1998 \rangle$ at year granularity. The same procedure is applied to the ground-truth time intervals of our query test cases.

Measures. We use Precision@k (P@k) as a measure of retrieval effectiveness. For the sake of comparability, we report P@1 and P@5 for both the unambiguous and ambiguous queries – instead of using mean reciprocal rank (MRR) for the unambiguous case.

4.2 Experimental Results

Table 1 shows values of P@1 and P@5 obtained for unambiguous queries. We observe relatively higher precision values for **NA** and **AA**, which rely on the advanced approach to estimate $P([tb, te] \mid d)$. Both achieve similar performance, indicating that our advanced method to estimate $P(d \mid q)$, taking into account query likelihoods, is not effective. This is substantiated by the performance of **NN** and **AN** – while the latter uses the advanced method to estimate

	Day						Month						Year					
	P@1			P@5			P@1			P@5			P@1			P@5		
k	25	50	100	25	50	100	25	50	100	25	50	100	25	50	100	25	50	100
NN	0.03	0.04	0.04	0.02	0.03	0.03	0.06	0.06	0.03	0.06	0.08	0.01	0.03	0.04	0.04	0.02	0.03	0.03
AN	0.03	0.03	0.04	0.02	0.03	0.03	0.06	0.05	0.03	0.06	0.08	0.01	0.02	0.01	0.01	0.01	0.01	0.01
NA	0.07	0.06	0.09	0.04	0.04	0.04	0.18	0.18	0.18	0.10	0.10	0.05	0.14	0.17	0.10	0.11	0.11	0.08
AA	0.06	0.06	0.09	0.04	0.04	0.04	0.19	0.17	0.20	0.09	0.10	0.07	0.14	0.17	0.10	0.11	0.11	0.08

Table 1: Temporally unambiguous queries

	Day						Month						Year					
	P@1			P@5			P@1			P@5			P@1			P@5		
k	25	50	100	25	50	100	25	50	100	25	50	100	25	50	100	25	50	100
NN	0.05	0.00	0.00	0.01	0.01	0.01	0.10	0.10	0.16	0.05	0.04	0.05	0.55	0.55	0.26	0.31	0.36	0.33
AN	0.05	0.05	0.05	0.01	0.01	0.02	0.10	0.15	0.16	0.05	0.05	0.05	0.60	0.60	0.32	0.35	0.34	0.34
NA	0.10	0.10	0.16	0.05	0.10	0.10	0.35	0.50	0.42	0.25	0.26	0.31	0.75	0.75	0.74	0.59	0.58	0.54
AA	0.10	0.10	0.16	0.04	0.10	0.10	0.35	0.50	0.42	0.25	0.26	0.31	0.75	0.75	0.74	0.59	0.58	0.54

Table 2: Temporally ambiguous queries

$P(d \mid q)$, its precision values are as low as those obtained by the completely naïve **NN**. It can also be seen that methods' performance varies with temporal granularity, peeking at month granularity. Finally, we observe that considering more pseudo-relevant documents only pays off to a point – for none of the methods performance increases consistently as we go beyond $k = 50$.

Results for ambiguous queries are shown in Table 2. All four methods consistently achieve higher values of P@1 and P@5 than for the unambiguous case. Comparing **NN** and **AN**, we again observe that the advanced method of estimating $P(d \mid q)$ is not very effective. In contrast, we see good improvements for **NA** and **AA**, indicating that the more advanced handling of temporal expressions pays off. For ambiguous queries, as a difference from the unambiguous case, we observe that all methods achieve their best performance for year granularity. However, again we do not see consistent improvements as more pseudo-relevant documents are considered for larger choices of k.

Summary

Our experiments, using temporally unambiguous and temporally ambiguous queries as test cases, have shown that **NA** and **AA** perform similarly and are ahead of the other two configurations. Thus, the advanced method to handle temporal expressions and estimate $P([tb, te] \mid d)$ is effective; the advanced method to estimate $P(d \mid q)$, on the other hand, has no effect.

5. CONCLUSION

We have proposed a novel approach to identify time intervals of interest for a given keyword query. Our approach is based on a generative model and we considered four possible instantiations of it. Experiments on temporally unambiguous queries and temporally ambiguous queries as test cases showed that there are effective instantiations of our approach – considering temporal expressions and their inherent uncertainty pays off; factoring in query likelihoods does not. As part of our future research, we plan to investigate (i) how users perceive the interestingness of the determined time intervals and (ii) how retrieval effectiveness is affected when using the determined time intervals in query expansion.

6. REFERENCES

[1] The New York Times Annotated Corpus http://corpus.nytimes.com.

[2] O. Alonso, M. Gertz, and R. A. Baeza-Yates. On the value of temporal information in information retrieval. SIGIR Forum, 41(2):35–41, 2007.

[3] K. Berberich, S. Bedathur, O. Alonso, and G. Weikum. A language modeling approach for temporal information needs. In ECIR, 2010

[4] W. Dakka, L. Gravano, and P. G. Ipeirotis. Answering general time-sensitive queries. IEEE Trans. Knowl. Data Eng., 24(2):220–235, 2012.

[5] F. M. G. de Jong, H. Rode, and D. Hiemstra. Temporal language models for the disclosure of historical text. In AHC, 2005

[6] A. Jatowt, C. Man Au Yeung, and K. Tanaka. Estimating document focus time. In CIKM, 2013.

[7] R. Jones and F. Diaz. Temporal profiles of queries. ACM Trans. Inf. Syst., 25, 2007.

[8] N. Kanhabua and K. Nørvåg. Using temporal language models for document dating. In ECML/PKDD, 2009.

[9] N. Kanhabua and K. Nørvåg. Determining time of queries for re-ranking search results. In ECDL, 2010.

[10] X. Li and W. B. Croft. Time-based language models. In CIKM, 2003.

[11] D. Metzler, R. Jones, F. Peng, and R. Zhang. Improving search relevance for implicitly temporal queries. In SIGIR, 2009.

[12] M.-H. Peetz, E. Meij, and M. de Rijke. Using temporal bursts for query modeling. Inf. Retr., 17(1):74–108, 2014.

[13] J. Strötgen, O. Alonso, and M. Gertz. Identification of top relevant temporal expressions in documents In TempWeb 2012.

[14] M. Verhagen, I. Mani, R. Sauri, J. Littman, R. Knippen, S. B. Jang, A. Rumshisky, J. Phillips, and J. Pustejovsky. Automating temporal annotation with tarsqi. In ACL, 2005.

Identification of Answer-Seeking Questions in Arabic Microblogs

Maram Hasanain[1]
maram.hasanain@qu.edu.qa

Tamer Elsayed[1]
telsayed@qu.edu.qa

Walid Magdy[2]
wmagdy@qf.org.qa

[1]Department of Computer Science and Engineering, Qatar University
[2]Qatar Computing Research Institute, Qatar Foundation
Doha, Qatar

ABSTRACT

Over the past years, Twitter has earned a growing reputation as a hub for communication, and events advertisement and tracking. However, several recent research studies have shown that Twitter users (and microblogging platforms' users in general) are increasingly posting microblogs containing questions seeking answers from their readers. To help those users answer or route their questions, the problem of question identification in tweets has been studied over English tweets; up to our knowledge, no study has attempted it over Arabic (not to mention dialectal Arabic) tweets.

In this paper, we tackle the problem of identifying answer-seeking questions in different dialects over a large collection of Arabic tweets. Our approach is 2-stage. We first used a rule-based filter to extract tweets with interrogative questions. We then leverage a binary classifier (trained using a carefully-developed set of features) to detect tweets with answer-seeking questions. In evaluating the classifier, we used a set of randomly-sampled dialectal Arabic tweets that were labeled using crowdsourcing. Our approach achieved a relatively-good performance as a first study of that problem on the Arabic domain, exhibiting 64% recall with 80% precision in identifying tweets with answer-seeking questions.

Categories and Subject Descriptors

H.3.3 [**Information Search and Retrieval**]: Text Mining

Keywords

Question Identification; Arabic; Twitter; Crowdsourcing

1. INTRODUCTION

With the increasing popularity and the wide spread of microblogging platforms such as Twitter, more patterns of usage tend to emerge. Among those patterns is posing questions, where users post questions to their followers or even to other users who might have common interests [11, 14,

12]. In an earlier study, Efron and Winget [8] reported that about 13% of a random sample of 2-million tweets were questions. This constitutes a large portion of the tweets and thus indicates a strong need for studying such behavior. Other studies suggested that about 50% of those questions seek answers [16]. Identifying this type of questions would help at several fronts such as understanding the information needs of such questions as well as building systems that either automatically answer them by finding existing answers or even route them to users who might be able to answer.

While the problem of automatic identification of questions in Twitter is not novel [10, 16], the focus of earlier studies was only on English tweets. In this paper, we present a first study that tackles the problem in the domain of dialectal Arabic tweets. Besides having different linguistic structure than English, the Arabic language imposes more challenges as the tweets are posted in several dialects [6].

We define the problem as follows. We first aim to automatically identify tweets that contain questions, i.e., *interrogative* tweets, denoted by *i*tweets. There are many different types of *i*tweets, such as tweets with rhetorical questions, quoted questions, or questions that are followed by answers in the same tweet [8]. Among those types of *i*tweets, we are interested in identifying those tweets with questions that are seeking answers, denoted by *qweets* [10]. Qweets are tweets whose authors expect answers from other Twitter users, or more formally, tweets that convey real information needs. In this study, our research question is simply: can we automatically identify qweets from Arabic tweets?

To tackle the problem, we formulated it as a two-stage classification problem. We first identify Arabic *i*tweets using a rule-based classifier enriched with a large collection of question words and phrases in different Arabic dialects. We then identify qweets from *i*tweets using a binary classifier that leverages a large set of features including lexical, structural, question-specific, tweet-specific, and (in)formality aspects of the tweets. We trained our classifier using manually-annotated tweets collected through crowdsourcing.

We summarize our contributions in this work as follows:

- A *first* study on question identification in *Arabic* microblogs is presented. A large dataset of about **865 millions** Arabic tweets spanning **9 months** was used in the study.
- A comprehensive list of question phrases in different Arabic dialects, with mapping to corresponding Mod-

ern Standard Arabic (MSA) question phrases, was constructed. List is made available online[1].

- Two labeled sets of Arabic tweets were developed and made available online[1]: one includes 5000 tweets labeled for *itweet* identification, and the other contains 3954 tweets labeled for qweet identification.

- Three new categories of features for question identification in Twitter were proposed and evaluated.

The remainder of the paper is organized as follows. We first introduce related work in Section 2. A detailed description of our approach is presented in Section 3. Experimental setup and results are discussed in Section 4, followed by the conclusion and some guidelines for future work in Section 5.

2. RELATED WORK

Question identification in text has been explored in different domains including community question answering platforms [15] and online forums [3]. In Twitter, understanding question-asking behavior of Twitter users has grabbed much attention in the past few years [11, 13, 14, 16]. Some studies on question-asking in Twitter focused on analyzing types and topics of questions asked by users [11, 14]. Others focused on establishing a taxonomy of questions in tweets [8].

Identifying tweets with questions is another problem investigated in literature. One of the approaches used to detect questions (not necessarily answer-seeking ones) is based on applying a set of rules to tweets [8, 14, 2]. This approach showed good recall, yet it introduced many false positives (i.e. tweets that did not have questions) [2]. Dent and Paul [7] applied natural language processing techniques adapted to handle challenges in language used in Twitter to identify questions in tweets. This approach managed to successfully identify tweets matching the syntactic form of a question, but it introduced noise since many filtered tweets did not have answer-seeking questions [7].

Other recent studies focused on using automatic classification to identify qweets specifically [10, 16]. Both of these studies started with a rule-based approach to filter candidate *itweets*. A set of features was used in a learning approach for qweet identification. Li et al. [10] have utilized question-specific, context-specific and metadata features in classification achieving 77.5% accuracy. Zhao and Mei [16] focused more on lexical features including unigrams, bigrams and trigrams in tweets. They have also attempted to add more semantics to tweets by using WordNet synonyms and part of speech tagging (POS). Their approach achieved a classification accuracy of 86.6%.

Almost all of the previously mentioned studies have focused on English tweets. Up to our knowledge, no studies on *itweets*/qweet identification in Arabic tweets exist.

3. QWEET IDENTIFICATION

Tweets are very short in length (maximum of 140 characters), usually informal, and naturally conversational. This implies that automatically-detecting qweets is not a trivial task due to the lack of context in tweets. The problem is indeed more challenging with dialectal Arabic. In our study, we focused on dialects of Arab countries with the highest tweeting rate over the past two years, according to a recently-conducted study [1]. We "grouped" those dialects

into three groups: Levantine, Egyptian, and Gulf, which was similarly adopted by Cotterell and Callison-Burch [5]. The Gulf group also covered the dialect of Iraq as it shares multiple question phrases with Gulf dialects. We also added MSA to the groups we cover.

In this section, we discuss our 2-stage approach of qweet identification. We first describe *itweet* identification as a pre-filtering step which provides a list of potential *itweets*. That list is then classified by a binary classifier to detect qweets. The process of manual annotatation of tweets needed for training the classifier is outlined next. Finally, we present the features developed for qweet classification[2].

3.1 Pre-Filtering

One of the approaches that showed reasonable effectiveness in detecting interrogative tweets uses a set of rules designed to capture questions in tweets [8, 10]. We follow a similar approach to pre-filter tweets in order to get candidate *itweets*. A tweet is considered an *itweet* if it contains a question mark (considering both ? or ؟) or a *question phrase*. A *question phrase* in Arabic (such as: إلى أين، ماذا) is a consecutive sequence of (one or more) words that is anlaogous to one of the 5W1H question keywords in English.

Since we are handling dialectal tweets, we could not find a comprehensive list of *dialectal question phrases* covering all dialect groups of interest in this work. Moreover, we wanted to obtain a rich set of dialectal question phrases to maximize the recall of detecting *itweets*. To overcome this problem, we developed such list using an online survey. We asked participants speaking Arabic in different dialects to provide a list of dialectal question phrases they use in their native dialect. The survey was answered by 105 participants resulting in a list of 348 unique phrases covering 6 dialect groups: Levantine, Gulf, Iraqi, Egyptian, Sudanese, and Maghrebi.

As pointed out earlier, we focus on 3 dialect groups: Egyptian, Levantine, and Gulf. We excluded phrases in other dialects from our initial list to get 264 unique phrases. We further extended this list by (a) augmenting it with question phrases manually-collected by searching online forum posts and Wikipedia pages listing dialectal question phrases, and (b) MSA equivalents of the dialectal phrases, where a dialectal phrase was manually-translated to one or more MSA phrases. Eventually, the list used in pre-filtering had 488 unique phrases, including both MSA and dialectal phrases. We consider any tweet with either a question mark or any of the collected question phrases as an *itweet*.

3.2 Human Annotations

The pre-filtering step produces a list of identified *itweets* that are next classified into qweets and non-qweets. To build such classifier, we need a set of manually-labeled *itweets* for training. Since the *itweet* identification was automatic, we also need to judge the accuracy of the pre-filtering step by manually-labeling them as true *itweets* or not.

To do both labeling tasks, we recruited annotators from CrowdFlower[3]. In the first task, workers were asked to label whether an Arabic tweet contains *at least one question* (i.e., is the tweet an *itweet* or not?). All tweets labeled as tweets containing a question were passed to the second la-

[1]http://faculty.qu.edu.qa/telsayed/datasets.aspx

[2]We thank Linah Lotfi and Nada Aboueata for their valuable help in earlier versions of the question phrases and feature set.

[3]http://www.crowdflower.com/

beling task, in which workers were asked whether a tweet contains an *answer-seeking question* (i.e., is the tweet is a qweet or not?). In each task, workers were provided with labeling guidelines in addition to example tweets on the labeling classes.

To ensure that our annotators understood the labeling tasks and the language of tweets (especially that a tweet can be in dialectal Arabic), only annotators residing in Arab countries were allowed to label tweets. Moreover, annotators were required to pass a qualification test on *golden tweets* (tweets we manually labeled based on our labeling guidelines) to be allowed to annotate tweets. Within each of the tasks, *golden tweets* were also employed to ensure the quality of labeling during the task. If an annotator failed to maintain a labeling accuracy above 70% over the golden tweets, her judgments were not considered. In both tasks, each tweet was labeled by 3 annotators. A final label was chosen for a tweet based on a labeling *confidence* level computed by the CrowdFlower platform. The confidence score is a measure of the annotators agreement weighted by their accuracy over the golden set.

3.3 Feature Extraction

To develop features, we reviewed the literature and analyzed a sample of Arabic tweets we manually labeled as *i*tweets or not and qweets or not. We identified a set of 29 features that can help filtering qweets, in addition to two sets of standard word features. We grouped the features into 6 groups: tweet-specific, structural, formality, question-specific, lexical, and question phrases.

Tweet-specific: In addition to text, tweets have other content elements that have been widely used in different learning problems on tweets. We used 6 features specific to these elements: a feature to indicate whether the tweet has a URL [10, 16], count of *question* hashtags (hashtags Twitter users sometimes use to tag tweets with questions such as: سؤال# equivalent to #question), mentions count, hashtags count, and similarity between the tweet and the title of a webpage posted in tweet [10]. Similarity is calculated using Jaccard coefficient.

Structural: Based on observing tweets, we realized that the structure of the tweet can be a good indicator for qweet classification. For example, we noticed that a tweet having a question and a quoted string is usually not seeking an answer. Features under this category include: length of the tweet in characters and words, and a feature to indicate if the tweet has a quoted string or not.

Formality: Features in this category are used to measure the level of formality of a tweet. Based on our analysis of tweets, we noticed that many tweets with answer-seeking questions are written in a more formal way than expected in tweets. The 5 features under this category are: count of emojis and emoticons (such as: :-)), a feature to indicate if signs of jokes appear in text, e.g., "هههههههه" (equivalent to "hhhhh" in English), count of diacritics on Arabic letters, and count of special characters such as: {}*(), etc.

Question-specific: We noticed that earlier studies [10, 16] on this problem on English tweets have not developed many features that are specific enough to describe questions in Tweets. Thus, we worked extensively on developing such features given the collected question phrases. Examples on such features include: count of single question marks, count of blobs of question and exclamation marks indicating strong

feeling e.g., "!!؟", number of characters and words following the last question mark in tweet, and a feature to indicate if question phrase(s) in a tweet is in MSA. We also developed some features related to the *question sentence* in tweet. We consider a sentence in a tweet as a question sentence if it has a question mark or one of the question phrases in our list. Examples on features related to question sentences include: length of the sentence in characters and words, length of text before and after the question sentence, and count of question sentences found in the tweet.

Lexical: A recent study [16] has showed that using words in tweets as lexical features has good effectiveness in classifying qweets. We used the set of unigrams and bigrams in the tweets as the lexical feature set.

Question Phrases: In addition to the above lexical features, we also used the question phrases extracted from the tweets as a separate feature set.

4. EXPERIMENTAL EVALUATION

4.1 Experimental Setup

In this study, we used a large set of Arabic tweets, collected through Twitter search API over a period of more than 9 months (from May 9th, 2012 to February 21st, 2013), resulting in about 865 million tweets. A tweet in the dataset can be in MSA, dialectal Arabic or a mix of both. We applied pre-filtering to this dataset resulting in about 69 million tweets (8%) marked as candidate *i*tweets. 5% of tweets in the dataset contained question mark(s) (both ? and ؟ are considered), which is about half of the ratio reported in [16] on a billion English tweets collection.

5000 tweets were randomly sampled out of the 69M tweets to be used in our experiments. In the first labeling task, annotators labeled the 5000 tweets as *i*tweets or not; only 3954 tweets of them were labeled as *i*tweets with a confidence level ≥ 0.5, showing a precision of about 79% in detecting *i*tweets. In the second labeling task, 1001 tweets out of the 3954 *i*tweets (25.3%) were labeled as qweets with a confidence level $\geq .5$.

Our main focus is on extracting qweets from a collection of candidate *i*tweets. We used Support Vector Machines (SVM) [4] classifier, and specifically SVM-light [9], to train and test our binary qweet classifier. The classifier is evaluated using Leave-one-out cross-validation over the labeled tweets produced during the second labeling task in addition to all non-*i*tweets found during the first labeling. We chose to only use the tweets labeled with labeling confidence level ≥ 0.7 out of the original sets, resulting in 3342 tweets.

4.2 Results and Discussion

We followed the classification approach described above using each of the feature groups individually. In evaluation, we mainly focus on the F1-measure. Results in Table 1 show that the structural group had the best performance compared to each of the other individual groups. We then attempted to find the best combination of feature groups (maximizing F1) by gradually adding a group at a time to the structural group. Adding all groups together except for the question phrases group had the best performance. Table 1 summarizes the performance of different combinations of feature groups in addition to the full set. Note that with some feature groups, all tweets were classified as non-qweets

Groups	Precision	Recall	F1
Tweet-specific(TS)	–	0	–
Structural(S)	0.7857	0.4310	**0.5566**
Formality(F)	–	0	–
Question-specific(QS)	–	0	–
Question phrases(QP)	0.4565	0.0392	0.0722
Lexical(L)	0.6944	0.0466	0.08734
S+TS	0.8114	0.5299	0.6411
S+TS+L	0.796	0.5896	0.6774
S+TS+L+QS	0.8119	0.6362	0.7134
S+TS+L+QS+F	0.8061	0.6437	**0.7158**
All	0.7968	0.6437	0.7121

Table 1: Results of classification using each of the feature groups in addition to the best performing combinations.

(getting a zero recall) and thus we marked the precision and F1 in these cases by dashes.

The structural features (the best performing group) mainly focused on length of tweet (including URLs, mentions and hashtags) and length of text in tweet, in addition to detecting existence of quoted strings. Further analysis is needed on a feature-level to determine which individual feature is the best contributor to these results. The performance improvement resulting by adding simple tweet-specific features to structural features increased F1 by 15%. We believe that tweet-specific features added more context to the tweet allowing for more distinctive representation which improved classification.

Enhancement resulting from adding the lexical features was 5.7% which might indicate that they are not as strong as expected in characterizing qweets. It is interesting to observe that adding lexical features resulted in a slight drop in precision (implying that it introduced noise), yet it enhanced recall by 11%. This enhancement in recall is probably due to the fact that lexical features were able to cover common question phrases used in asking questions.

Adding the Question-specific features enhanced performance by 5.3% over the combination S+TS+L indicating that this group might have captured aspects of qweets that were not fully covered yet. We emphasize here the fact that many features within this group were related to the question structure relevant to the tweet, indicating the importance of the structural aspects. Formality features had minimal improvement on F1 when furtherly added. Adding question phrases features did not enhance performance; a possible explanation is that many of them were already covered by the lexical features and thus were redundant.

5. CONCLUSION AND FUTURE WORK

In this work, we presented a first study on the problem of identifying answer-seeking questions in Arabic tweets. The reported preliminary results were encouraging as our approach achieved about 80% precision with 64% recall, which constitutes a strong reference point for future work.

Further result analysis is required especially on a feature-level. Since this is a work in progress, we will be experimenting using feature selection methods to reduce the feature space. Furthermore, as the results reported here are based on using one classifier (SVM), we will be exploring other types of classifiers as well. Moreover, more analysis

of the identified qweets is needed to better-understand the information needs of Arabic users of Twitter.

6. ACKNOWLEDGMENTS

This work was made possible by NPRP grant# NPRP 6-1377-1-257 from the Qatar National Research Fund (a member of Qatar Foundation). The statements made herein are solely the responsibility of the authors.

7. REFERENCES

[1] Arab Social Media Report. Technical report, Dubai School of Government, June 2013.

[2] A crowd-powered socially embedded search engine. In ICWSM, 2013.

[3] G. Cong, L. Wang, C.-Y. Lin, Y.-I. Song, and Y. Sun. Finding question-answer pairs from online forums. SIGIR '08, 2008.

[4] C. Cortes and V. Vapnik. Support-vector networks. Machine learning, 20(3):273–297, 1995.

[5] R. Cotterell and C. Callison-Burch. A multi-dialect, multi-genre corpus of informal written arabic. In LREC '14, 2014.

[6] K. Darwish and W. Magdy. Arabic information retrieval. Foundations and Trends in Information Retrieval, 7(4):239–342, 2014.

[7] K. D. Dent and S. A. Paul. Through the twitter glass: Detecting questions in micro-text. In Analyzing Microtext, 2011.

[8] M. Efron and M. Winget. Questions are content: A taxonomy of questions in a microblogging environment. ASIS&T '10, 2010.

[9] T. Joachims. Making large-scale svm learning practical. advances in kernel methods-support vector learning. schölkopf b. and burges c. and smola a, 1999.

[10] B. Li, X. Si, M. R. Lyu, I. King, and E. Y. Chang. Question identification on twitter. CIKM '11, 2011.

[11] M. R. Morris, J. Teevan, and K. Panovich. What do people ask their social networks, and why?: A survey study of status message q&a behavior. CHI '10, 2010.

[12] A. Oeldorf-Hirsch, B. Hecht, M. R. Morris, J. Teevan, and D. Gergle. To search or to ask: The routing of information needs between traditional search engines and social networks. CSCW'14, 2014.

[13] S. A. Paul, L. Hong, and E. Chi. What is a question? crowdsourcing tweet categorization. CHI'11, 2011.

[14] L. H. S.A. Paul and E. Chi. Is twitter a good place for asking questions? a characterization study. ICWSM'11, 2011.

[15] K. Wang and T.-S. Chua. Exploiting salient patterns for question detection and question retrieval in community-based question answering. COLING '10, 2010.

[16] Z. Zhao and Q. Mei. Questions about questions: An empirical analysis of information needs on twitter. WWW '13, 2013.

Size and Source Matter: Understanding Inconsistencies in Test Collection-Based Evaluation

Timothy Jones
RMIT University
timothy.jones@rmit.edu.au

Andrew Turpin
University of Melbourne
aturpin@unimelb.edu.au

Stefano Mizzaro
University of Udine
mizzaro@uniud.it

Falk Scholer
RMIT University
falk.scholer@rmit.edu.au

Mark Sanderson
RMIT University
mark.sanderson@rmit.edu.au

ABSTRACT

Past work showed that significant inconsistencies between retrieval results occurred on different test collections, even when one of the test collections contained only a subset of the documents in the other. However, the experimental methodologies in that paper made it hard to determine the cause of the inconsistencies. Using a novel methodology that eliminates the problems with uneven distribution of relevant documents, we confirm that observing a statistically significant improvement between two IR systems can be strongly influenced by the choice of documents in the test collection. We investigate two possible causes of this problem of test collections. Our results show that collection size and document source have a strong influence in the way that a test collection will rank one retrieval system relative to another. This is of particular interest when constructing test collections, as we show that using different subsets of a collection produces differing evaluation results.

Categories and Subject Descriptors

H.3.4 [**Information Storage and Retrieval**]: Systems and Software—*Performance evaluation*

General Terms

Measurement; Reliability

Keywords

Information retrieval; evaluation; subcollections; TREC

1. INTRODUCTION

If a significant difference is measured between two IR systems using a test collection, is the difference real or an artifact of the collection? This question has been asked ever since test collections were first described [2]. While the reliability of relevance assessors [3], evaluation measures [4], and topics [9, 10] has been inves-

CIKM '14 November 03 - 07 2014, Shanghai, China
Copyright 2014 ACM 978-1-4503-2598-1/14/11
http://dx.doi.org/10.1145/2661829.2661945 ...$15.00.

tigated, there has been little examination on whether the properties of a particular collection of documents influences search results.

While there is a general feeling in the IR community that it is preferable to demonstrate the superiority of one algorithm over another using multiple test collections, and this is often instantiated as using multiple metrics, topic sets, and relevance judgments, it is not uncommon to see published work that uses just one collection. Is this a safe experimental practice or not? There is little or no empirical evidence to show how many test collections are needed, what different types of collections are required, how one might measure the difference between collections, or indeed if it is necessary to test widely in the first place.

Sanderson et al. [6] presented evidence that the relative difference in effectiveness between retrieval systems varies across subsets (i.e. *subcollections*) of a single document collection, a result that had not been shown before. However, in that work, there were multiple differences between the subcollections being compared, making it difficult to know what the cause of this effect was. The work was also tested on relatively old retrieval systems.

In this paper, the experiments of Sanderson et al. are expanded using stricter controls on the differences between the subcollections, and a state-of-the-art retrieval system. The paper asks the following research questions:

1. What are the causes of the measured differences between subcollections described in past papers?
2. Do the measured differences still occur when relevant documents are contolled, and a state-of-the-art retrieval system is used?

2. PREVIOUS WORK

The work described here follows on from Sanderson et al. [6] who described a series of experiments examining TREC run data ranked using standard effectiveness measures based on different subcollections of a TREC test collection. They found that the ordering of the runs was substantially different between the subcollections and that these differences were much greater than would be expected by random chance.

Different ways of forming subcollections were investigated, such as splitting by document source (e.g. Financial Times, Congressional Record, etc.) or topical similarity (using k-means clustering). However, when the subcollections were formed based on any of the tested criteria, other factors also varied, which may have affected the comparisons. The most important of these factors were that the subcollections varied in size, sometimes substantially, and the number of relevant documents in each subcollection was different. In this paper, we mitigate these factors, in order to better understand what properties of subcollections may play a role in leading to inconsistent retrieval results.

Additionally Sanderson et al. used IR systems that were $10-20$ years old: their experiments may have identified old problems that were resolved in newer ranking algorithms. In this paper, we use a state-of-the-art retrieval system. Finally, their method for comparing run ordering was Kendall's τ. This measure quantifies the degree of correlation between the rank ordering of two lists. However, τ may be affected by statistically insignificant swaps between systems. Here, we investigate a new agreement-based approach, which focuses only on statistically significant differences.

There is little past work on the impact of collection choice when measuring retrieval effectiveness. A recent tutorial on test collection construction [8] did not mention collection choice or the properties of the documents that should make up a collection. There has perhaps been an assumption, that an IR system will be tested on a representative sample of the documents the system will be deployed on. However, if advances in IR systems are to generalize to any document collection, rigourous evaluation is necessary.

Apart from the work of Sanderson et al., Azzopardi and colleagues have investigated bias in ranking functions. They showed evidence that ranking algorithms appeared to be influenced by the length of the documents they retrieved (most recently in Wilkie and Azzopardi [11]). Further, they showed that different algorithms were affected by length in different ways. Although work in the past has attempted to eliminate such biases [7], it would appear, they are still present.

3. DATA AND METHODOLOGY

Here, we describe the collections, system and measures used to investigate Sanderson et al's "subcollection effect".

3.1 Collections

The TREC 4–8 ad hoc collections are used for our experiments, in-keeping with the analysis of Sanderson et al. These collections suit splitting by document source, as all five collections are composed of texts from multiple sources.

3.2 Avoiding a relevant document effect

When Sanderson et al. split subcollections by source, the number of judged relevant documents available in each subcollection varied substantially. To address this potential problem, we used the following methodology. We separated each test collection into two subsets: one containing all documents that were judged as relevant (*all-rel*); the other containing all the other documents in the collection, including documents judged as irrelevant (*not-rel*). All subcollection splits were then carried out by partitioning the *not-rel* subset of the collection based on document source. All the documents from *all-rel* were then added to each subcollection.

By forming subcollections in this way, we ask the question: is the ability of an IR system to retrieve the same relevant documents affected by distinct sets of non-relevant documents? Further, if there is an effect, are different IR systems affected in different ways?

3.3 Measuring collection agreement

Evaluating the effectiveness of a new ranking approach using a test collection typically compares two variants of an IR system—a new configuration of the system, and the previous configuration (the baseline)—over a fixed set of queries, documents, and relevance judgements. The outcome of such an experiment is typically quantified by reporting the mean effectiveness of each system accompanied by a statistical significance test. Having run such an experiment on one collection, one might ask whether the same out-come would be observed when comparing the same systems on another collection. To investigate this, we adapted an approach used by Moffat et al. [4] to investigate the agreement on IR experimental results when using different effectiveness metrics. However, here we examine the agreement on significance when using different collections. Consider the process of comparing systems, S1 and S2, on two subcollections, C1 and C2. There are a number of possible outcomes as follows.

- SS_a: Active agreement, S1 is significantly better than system S2 on both C1 and C2.
- SN: Passive disagreement, S1 is significantly better than S2 (or vice versa) on C1, but on C2, there is no significant difference between the systems.
- NS: Passive disagreement, S1 is significantly better than S2 (or vice versa) on C2, but on C1, there is no significant difference between the systems.
- SS_d: Active disagreement, S1 is significantly better than S2 on C1, but S2 is significantly better than S1 on C2.

As per Moffat et al. [4], for a given collection pair, the proportion of significant differences between systems observed for which both collections agree on which is the better system is given by

$$agree\text{-}SS_a = \frac{2 \cdot SS_a}{2 \cdot SS_a + 2 \cdot SS_d + SN + NS}.$$

3.4 State of the art IR system

In order to simulate multiple research experiments of IR systems, we used the Terrier search engine [5] configured to use sixteen different ranking models: BB2, BM25, DFR_BM25, DFRee, DLH13, DLH, DPH, Hiemstra_LM, IFB2, In_expB2, In_expC2, InL2, Lemur TF_IDF, LGD, PL2, and TF_IDF. The search engine was in default TREC mode. The models were run on each subcollection, and evaluated using MAP, producing 120 pairs of system comparisons for each subcollection.

4. RESULTS

The results of the experiments to test potential confounding factors in Sanderson et al's methodology are described here.

4.1 Investigating source-based splits

The first seven columns of Table 1 shows *agree-SS_a* for each source-based subcollection for the TREC 4–8 ad hoc collections, with the mean (μ) and standard error (s.e.) for each subcollection reported in columns eight and nine. Recall that the original collections are split by document source, but the number of relevant documents is held constant in each subcollection. Comparisons also included comparing the whole TREC collection with each subcollection. The minimum, median, and maximum of μ are 8%, 62%, and 74% respectively. The central 50% of the data are in the range from 40% to 67%. Broadly speaking, running experiments on different subcollections may lead to inconsistent conclusions about system superiority a substantial proportion of the time.

Kendall's Tau (τ) is shown to facilitate comparison to Sanderson et al. [6], and the values are in the same range as those obtained by Sanderson et al., and rather low. The τ values generally correlate with *agree-SS_a*, although differences exist.

For further context, the *agree-SS_a* values obtained when measuring agreement when comparing each subcollection against itself using two different effectiveness metrics—MAP and NDCG—are shown in the final column of Table 1. Both measures were calculated over the top-1000 retrieved documents. In all but three cases,

Collection	agree-SS_a						μ	s.e.	map ndcg	τ
	2	3	4	5	6	7				
TREC-4										
1. patents	81	63	61	54	50	56	61	2.1	92	0.39
2. fr		67	61	51	54	57	62	1.9	95	0.40
3. wsj			82	73	82	73	73	1.7	93	0.65
4. sjm				87	74	79	74	1.7	67	0.64
5. ap					69	64	66	1.9	88	0.57
6. ziff						70	66	1.8	96	0.65
7. trec4							66	2.0	80	0.62
TREC-5										
1. cr	48	64	50	48	50	61	53	2.2	85	0.62
2. ziff		48	46	37	38	48	44	2.1	94	0.36
3. wsj			82	82	84	83	74	1.6	87	0.67
4. fr				72	76	85	69	1.9	89	0.64
5. ap					87	74	67	1.8	93	0.60
6. ft						78	69	1.7	84	0.63
7. trec5							72	1.8	86	0.57
TREC-6										
1. cr	15	8	6	4	7	–	8	2.8	71	-0.00
2. fr		34	27	14	34	–	25	3.2	79	0.23
3. fbis			28	8	30	–	21	4.1	14	0.10
4. latimes				53	82	–	39	3.6	56	0.31
5. ft					41	–	24	2.9	85	0.28
6. trec6						–	39	3.9	67	0.31
TREC-7										
1. fr	48	34	39	32	–	–	38	3.0	86	0.57
2. fbis		68	77	63	–	–	64	3.2	58	0.64
3. latimes			70	68	–	–	60	3.4	72	0.67
4. ft				79	–	–	66	3.0	78	0.47
5. trec7					–	–	60	3.3	83	0.61
TREC-8										
1. fr	50	40	29	37	–	–	39	3.4	80	0.12
2. fbis		71	57	70	–	–	62	3.2	82	0.56
3. latimes			76	82	–	–	67	2.7	93	0.58
4. ft				81	–	–	61	2.7	80	0.55
5. trec8					–	–	67	2.7	75	0.43

Table 1: *agree-SS_a* **values (as percentages) for TRECs 4-8, when comparing systems across subcollections (labelled in the rows of each section and ranked by increasing size). Means (μ) are across all pairings for each subcollection, and the standard error of μ (s.e.) was derived using bootstrapping. For comparison, *agree-SS_a* when comparing systems using NDCG and MAP is shown, and mean τ is in the last column.**

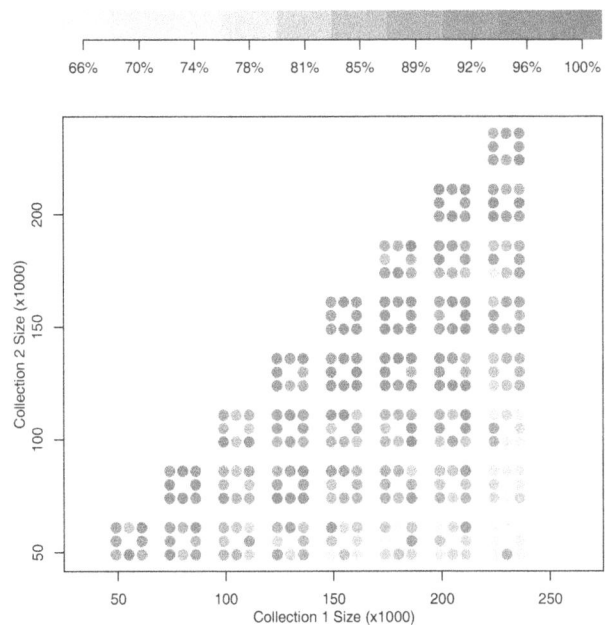

Figure 1: Agreement between collections as a function of collection size. Note the gradient of lighter points (less agreement) towards the bottom right of the figure. Eight distinct pairs of random subcollections were tested for each comparison, plotted as a square centered on the actual sizes.

the *agree-SS_a* on different evaluation measures was higher than the mean subcollection *agree-SS_a*.

Subcollections containing identical sets of relevant documents appear to inconsistently identify many significant differences in variations of the same retrieval system.

4.2 Investigating subcollection size

While relevant documents were kept constant across subcollections in the previous experiment, each compared collection was a different size, ranging from 12,994 to 223,751 documents. It is therefore plausible that size—which represents the number of non-relevant documents in a subcollection—affected the *agree-SS_a* rate. To further investigate the effect of size on the results, a simulation experiment was run measuring *agree-SS_a* across subcollections of different size. We created several new subcollections of similar sizes to the TREC subcollections, but using documents selected at random from the whole TREC-8 collection rather than split by source.

Figure 1 shows the inter-size agreements. The points on the diag-

onal compare random subcollections of the same size, and *agree-SS_a* between these collections is high. Towards the bottom right of the figure, where subcollection sizes differ by up to a factor of four, *agree-SS_a* reduces.

However, the low *agree-SS_a* values in Figure 1—even when subcollections were substantially different in size—are generally higher than those recorded in Table 1. While this result indicates that the relative size of subcollections could impact on *agree-SS_a*, it appears that this is not the main cause of the results shown in Table 1. Additionally, it was noted that two subcollections, fbis and latimes, were of similar size, but across TRECs-6,7,8 the *agree-SS_a* was low (28%, 68%, 71%), which we further examine.

4.3 Comparing fbis and latimes

To investigate why fbis and latimes had such a low *agree-SS_a*, but similar sizes, a series of comparisons were made between the subcollections by varying the amount of random documents that were added to each subcollection. To facilitate exposition, we label the new subcollections fbis-20, fbis-40, fbis-60 and fbis-80, where fbis-N is the same size as fbis, but contains N% documents pulled at random from the fbis subcollection, and 100-N% of documents pulled from the rest of the TREC-8 collection. As in the other collections used in this paper, these collections all follow the construction methodology described in Section 3.2. For example, an instance of the fbis-20 collection includes a portion the same size as the non-relevant documents from fbis, but that portion is instead comprised of 20% documents selected randomly from the non-relevant documents in fbis, and 80% documents from the non-relevant documents that are not in fbis. Then, the *all-rel* collection is added, for a total size equal to the non-relevant portion of fbis, plus the size of the *all-rel* collection. Using this methodology, we also constructed latimes-20, latimes-40, latimes-60 and latimes-80.

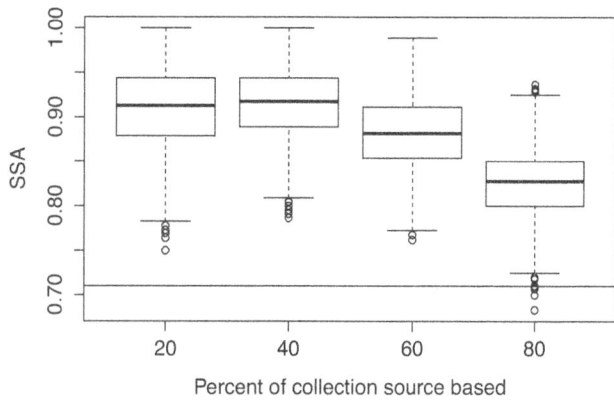

Figure 2: Agreement between collections for various percentages of source restricted splits using fbis and latimes from TREC8. The horizontal line indicates the agreement for a fully source based split.

For each value of $N \in \{20, 40, 60, 80\}$, 50 fbis and 50 latimes subcollections were formed and $agree\text{-}SS_a$ was measured (Figure 2). As collections become more source-based, there is a corresponding decrease in agreement, indicating that the source-based split is indeed contributing to the disagreement observed above.

5. DISCUSSION AND CONCLUSION

This paper addresses the following two research questions. What are the causes of the measured differences between subcollections described in past papers? Do the measured differences still occur when assessing a state-of-the-art retrieval system?

Using a novel methodology, this work has confirmed what Sanderson et al. reported in an earlier paper [6]. There is good evidence that the choice of collection impacts on whether one retrieval system will be measured to be significantly better than another retrieval system. Note also, this effect is visible even when a subset of a larger collection is used. The focus of work here has been to eliminate confounding factors introduced in Sanderson et al's methodology, and to begin to understand the causes of the effect.

To that end, the work here has established that the measured inconsistency in evaluation across subcollections is not an effect of the number of relevant documents in that collection or the relative difference in collection size. Additionally, the measured differences between subcollections also appear to still be occurring when using a state-of-the-art retrieval system and comparing between variants of the same collection.

While it has long been understood that one should test on multiple collections in order to cover for unknown variations in test collections, there has been little or no work understanding what those variations are. Such an understanding could reduce the number of collections one needs to test on.

We contend, as Sanderson et al did, that the results here are quite striking. Many of the subcollections in the early years of TREC were on the surface, quite similar to each other. In TREC-7 for example, three of the four subcollections, fbis, latimes, and ft, are collections of news, just from different sources. We view this work as a starting point: the most important issue to address now is what is causing the inconsistency in measurement of effectiveness?

In addition, this work has implications when creating collections, since test collections are typically subcollections of the available documents appropriate for the collection. It is important to create test collections that agree with the real world of all documents, and therefore it is important to understand the factors that cause evaluations on subcollections to disagree with the original collection.

Towards understanding the inconsistency in evaluation, this work has demonstrated that both collection size and source of documents contribute to the reliability of experiments. Although document source is a meta-feature that does not describe specifically how the document is different, and is not typically used as a feature by ranking algorithms, document source has been used at collection creation time, such as in the UK web spam collections—where only URLs ending in .uk were included [1].

Although the collection size and document source both strongly affect the consistency of evaluation, these features do not explain the whole effect. Some further underlying cause(s) must be affecting the results measured. Finding these will be our next focus.

Once we understand the effect well enough to predict whether particular subcollections will agree with each other (and with the whole collection that they are sampled from), many interesting applications are possible. For example, these results will allow the creations of test collections that are confidently generalizable, i.e., subcollections that agree with the larger set of available documents. Additionally, by splitting existing collections into subcollections where different retrieval approaches perform best, increases in retrieval performance may be possible.

Acknowledgements

This work was supported in part by the Australian Research Council (DP130104007) and also by a Google Faculty Research Award.

6. REFERENCES

[1] C. Castillo, D. Donato, L. Becchetti, P. Boldi, S. Leonardi, M. Santini, and S. Vigna. A reference collection for web spam. *SIGIR Forum*, 40(2):11–24, Dec. 2006.

[2] C. W. Cleverdon. *Report on the Testing and Analysis of an Investigation Into the Comparative Efficiency of Indexing Systems*. ASLIB Cranfield Research Project. 1962.

[3] C. W. Cleverdon. *The effect of variations in relevance assessments in comparative experimental tests of index languages*. Number 3 in Cranfield Library Report. 1970.

[4] A. Moffat, F. Scholer, and P. Thomas. Models and metrics: IR evaluation as a user process. In *Proc. ADCS*, pages 47–54. ACM, 2012.

[5] I. Ounis, G. Amati, V. Plachouras, B. He, C. Macdonald, and C. Lioma. Terrier: A high performance and scalable information retrieval platform. In *Proc. OSIR Workshop*, pages 18–25. Citeseer, 2006.

[6] M. Sanderson, A. Turpin, Y. Zhang, and F. Scholer. Differences in effectiveness across sub-collections. In *CIKM'12*, pages 1965–1969. ACM, 2012.

[7] A. Singhal, C. Buckley, and M. Mitra. Pivoted document length normalization. In *Proc. SIGIR*, pages 21–29. ACM, 1996.

[8] I. Soboroff. Test collection diagnosis and treatment. *Proc. EVIA 2010*, pages 34–41, 2010.

[9] J. Urbano, M. Marrero, and D. Martín. On the measurement of test collection reliability. In *Proc. SIGIR*, SIGIR '13, pages 393–402, New York, NY, USA, 2013. ACM.

[10] E. M. Voorhees. Topic set size redux. In *Proc. SIGIR*, SIGIR '09, pages 806–807, New York, NY, USA, 2009. ACM.

[11] C. Wilkie and L. Azzopardi. Best and fairest: An empirical analysis of retrieval system bias. In *Advances in Information Retrieval*, pages 13–25. Springer, Apr 2014.

Exploiting Knowledge Structure for Proximity-aware Movie Retrieval Model

Sansung Kim
KAIST
335, Gwahakro
Yuseong-gu, Daejeon
Republic of Korea
sansung@kaist.ac.kr

Keejun Han
KAIST
335, Gwahakro
Yuseong-gu, Daejeon
Republic of Korea
keejun.han@kaist.ac.kr

Mun Y. Yi *
KAIST
335, Gwahakro
Yuseong-gu, Daejeon
Republic of Korea
munyi@kaist.ac.kr

Sinhee Cho
KAIST
335, Gwahakro
Yuseong-gu, Daejeon
Republic of Korea
chosinhee@kaist.ac.kr

Seongchan Kim
KAIST
335, Gwahakro
Yuseong-gu, Daejeon
Republic of Korea
sckim@kaist.ac.kr

ABSTRACT

Current movie title retrieval models, such as IMDB, mainly focus on utilizing structured or semi-structured data. However, user queries for searching a movie title are often based on the movie plot, rather than its metadata. As a solution to this problem, our movie title retrieval model proposes a new way of elaborately utilizing associative relations between multiple key terms that exist in the movie plot, in order to improve search performance when users enter more than one keyword. More specifically, the proposed model exploits associative networks of key terms, called knowledge structures, derived from movie plots. Using the search query terms entered by Amazon Mechanical Turk users as the golden standard, experiments were conducted to compare the proposed retrieval model with the extant state-of-the-art retrieval models. The experiment results show that the proposed retrieval model consistently outperforms the baseline models. The findings have practical implications for semantic search of movie titles in particular, and of online entertainment contents in general.

Categories and Subject Descriptors

H.3.3 [**Information Search and Retrieval**]: Retrieval models

General Terms

Algorithms

Keywords

Movie search; knowledge structure; proximity

1. INTRODUCTION

Considering and incorporating query term proximity has been shown to be an effective probabilistic retrieval model in multiple studies [2, 11, 13, 14]. A key underlying assumption for proximity is that the more compact the query terms, the more likely that they are closely related; thereby, the more potentially relevant the documents will be to the topic represented in that particular set of user queries. For movie contents in particular, users often use scenic queries. For example, consider the following actual question that was observed on a commercial Q&A website (Naver Knowledge-iN[1]) in Korea: "Please tell me the title of the movie, in which a car is transformed into a robot. I want to watch it, but don't remember it's title" (translated). This example supports the idea that users tend to recall movies by describing the scenes or impressive moments from the movies, indicating that the query terms are related to each other, rather than being independent. In general, the term 'car' is not associated with 'robot'; however, those terms become closely linked in the context of the movie 'Transformers', in which a 'car' is transformed into a 'robot.'

To verify our assumption that the query terms entered to find a movie title are closely related, we analyzed the query sets of approximately 1,000 movies collected via Amazon Mechanical Turk.[2] We asked users to type queries for movies that they had seen once, but did not remember the titles clearly. The analysis results showed that a significant number of user queries were formulated from the movie plot, meaning that those terms have considerable associative relations.

Although our analysis demands the full utilization of the query term proximity information for movie retrieval, probabilistic proximity measures suggested in previous studies [2, 11, 13, 14] do not fully reflect the genuine relationships between the terms. For instance, the current best proximity measure is MinDist, reported in [13], which is the smallest positional distance of all pairs of unique matched query terms. Consider the following two

---

* Mun Y. Yi is the corresponding author
[1] http://kin.naver.com
[2] https://www.mturk.com

terms as an example: one that occurs at the end of a paragraph, and the other that occurs at the beginning of the next paragraph. The MinDist of the two terms is 1 and they are considered to have a significant relationship, but because a paragraph is a semantically separated segment, there is a high probability that the two terms are not semantically associated. More specifically, continuing from a previous example, given the actual query set Q = {giant, robot, car}, MinDist model located the target movie *Transformers* at the third position while located a non-target movie (i.e., *Monsters vs. Aliens,* designated *MvA*) at the first. This unsatisfying retrieval result is due to the minimum distance scores, which were 1 for both *Transformers* and *MvA*, thereby failing to provoke the re-ranking process.

To counteract the aforementioned limitation, in this paper we suggest a new proximity measure for exploiting knowledge structure, which was originally conceptualized in the field of educational psychology [5]. Unlike the probabilistic proximity measures, knowledge structures depict the various concepts and their associative relationships that exist in people's minds with regard to a specific domain. The knowledge structures of domain experts regarding a specific domain are known to be similar [5] and can be reliably extracted from a document [7]. By representing each movie as a knowledge structure that preserves the proximity semantics among the terms, the movies can be more reachable using descriptive sets of queries. Thus, we present a new movie title retrieval model that effectively searches for movie titles by leveraging the knowledge structures extracted from movie plots. Furthermore, the experiment results reveal that the proposed model outperforms other state-of-the-art retrieval models.

2. RELATED WORK
In this section, we review some of previous studies that are related to our movie retrieval model.

Proximity-aware retrieval model. Numerous studies have applied proximity measures to retrieval models. The early works discussed in [11] calculates a proximity score by considering the co-occurrence of a pair of queries in a document. In [2], the proximity computation process was then tuned to be faster for large text collection. In [13], a systematic approach was provided to heuristically combine proximity measures with the existing models of BM25 [12] and Language Model [9]. A probabilistic model [8] and enumerating sub-tree model [4] were proposed for multi-field documents such as XML. Furthermore, in [14], proximity factor was integrated into the unigram language model to weight the parameters of the multinomial document language models. In movie search, collaborative filtering method was used to generate personalized item authorities which were combined with item proximities for better search ranking [10].

Knowledge structure. A person is said to be knowledgeable if he or she knows the concepts present in a domain, and the relations between those concepts, all of which are captured in a knowledge structure [5]. Knowledge structures have mainly been used to understand cognitive behaviors during the learning process in the field of education [3]. Based on the co-occurrence of terms and the Pathfinder algorithm [6], a knowledge structure can be automatically created from a document. It was proven that the knowledge structure produced from a series of automated processes was similar to that produced by domain experts [7], meaning that the relations between terms were adequately represented in the generated knowledge structure.

To the best of our knowledge, knowledge structure has never been applied to information retrieval, though it can potentially be effective in developing probabilistic retrieval models. In this paper, we propose an automatic method of generating knowledge structures for movies, and exploit the use of knowledge structures on proximity-aware movie retrieval models.

3. PROPOSED MODEL
In this section, we first introduce an automated method for generating knowledge structures from movie plots, then moving on to explain how to utilize it in a movie retrieval model.

3.1 Knowledge Structure Creation
The proposed method that automatically generates a knowledge structure from a movie plot requires two specific information of the source: A set of keywords and distance scores of the keywords. These pieces of information are then processed with a number of refining steps to remove weak relations for noise deduction. As a first step, the keywords of the movie m need to be extracted to form the basis of a knowledge structure. To capture concepts, we only extracted nouns from a synopsis document D_m that contains a movie plot about movie m and added those nouns to concept list l_m. The distance between each pair of the keywords in the list l_m then can be measured by sentence co-occurrences similarity (SS). For SS, co-occurrence between two terms is defined only if those two terms appear in the same sentence. The distance score for SS between two terms w_i and w_j ($w_i, w_j \in l_m$) are defined as follows:

$$C_s(w_i, w_j) = \sum_1^{N_s} n(w_i \cap w_j) \qquad (1)$$

$$distance_{SS}(w_i, w_j) = \frac{C_s}{max(C_s)} \qquad (2)$$

where N_s is the number of sentences, $n(w_i \cap w_j)$ is the co-occurrences of two terms w_i and w_j, $max(C_s)$ indicates the maximum C_s between any terms in l_m for normalization. Similar to SS, we define paragraph co-occurrences similarity (PS) as the co-occurrence of two terms in the same paragraph.

Table 1. Example of co-occurrence matrix.

	S_1	S_2	S_1	...	S_N
w_i	3	0	1	...	1
w_j	2	1	0	...	2

On the other hand, we also can measure the distance score between two terms w_i and w_j in a different way by adapting cosine similarity of the co-occurrence matrices as shown in Table 1 as follows:

$$distance_{SCS}(w_i, w_j) = \frac{SV_i \cdot SV_j}{|SV_i| \times |SV_j|} \qquad (3)$$

where SV_i and SV_j are vectors based on the frequencies of w_i and w_j occurring in each sentence. Paragraph co-occurrence cosine similarity (PCS), can be defined similar to equation (3) but only to consider co-occurrence per paragraph.

As the manual knowledge structure creation in [3] measured the distance between two terms by involving human judges, for automatic knowledge structure creation, we also convert our initial distance score into a 7-point Likert Scale (1: strongly related, 7: not related at all) as follows:

$$distance_f(w_i, w_j) = 7 - distance(w_i, w_j) \times 6 \qquad (4)$$

Finally, the knowledge structure goes through the pathfinder algorithm [6] to eliminate data noise by removing redundant nodes.

3.2 Proximity-aware Retrieval Model

To combine the word associative relations into a new retrieval model, we obtained the original ranking scores using the existing retrieval model, Okapi BM25 [12] at first, and then re-ranked the result based on the proximity distance in a knowledge structure.

Once the original ranking was retrieved, proximity scores between the terms in a query were calculated in each movie plot. Because the query can have more than two words, average distance scores are calculated to integrate all associative relations. Given a query set Q and synopsis document D_m, the formula to determine the proximity score (PS) between Q and D_m is as follows:

$$PS(Q, D_m) = average \left(\frac{distance_f(q_i, q_j)}{maxDistance(D_m)} \right) \times n$$
$$= \frac{2}{n-1} \frac{\sum_{q_i, q_j \in Q \cap D_m, q_i \neq q_j} distance_f(q_i, q_j)}{maxDistance(D_m)} \quad (5)$$

where t_i and t_j are terms in a query, $distance_f(q_i, q_j)$ is the distance score between the two terms q_i and q_j in the knowledge structure of document D_m, n is the number of queries in the query set Q, and $maxDistance(D_m)$ is the longest distance between any two terms in the knowledge structure. For normalization, the formula is divided by $maxDistance(D_m)$ because the average distance between two terms and the plot length have a positive correlation ($\rho = 0.5638$). Furthermore n is multiplied to differentiate the score based on the length of queries. In the case that either of two terms does not occur in a movie plot, the distance between the terms is defined as $maxDistance(D_m)$.

To reflect proximity characteristic that a distance score drops fast when the distance between two terms is small while it does not change much as the distance becomes larger [13], we used a convex curve of which the first derivative is negative, and the second one is positive as follows:

$$PS_f(Q, D_m) = \exp(-PS(Q, D_m) \times \alpha) \quad (6)$$

We used an exponential function to put the range of the proximity score in the [0, 1] range, and to introduce α as a parameter for variation. As α becomes smaller, the proximity function becomes linear. Finally, we combined this function with the existing retrieval model, BM25, as follows:

$$R(Q, D_m) = BM25(Q, D_m) \cdot PS_f(Q, D_m) \quad (7)$$

where $BM25(Q, D_m) = \sum IDF(q_i) \cdot \frac{f(q_i, D_m) \cdot (k_1+1)}{f(q_i, D_m) + k_1 \cdot \left(1 - b + b \cdot \frac{|D_m|}{avgdl}\right)}$

where k_1 and b are two parameters often set to the standard values of 2 and 0.75, $f(q_i, D_m)$ is the term frequency of q_i in document D_m, $|D_m|$ is the length of the document vector, and $avgdl$ is the average length of all synopsis document vectors.

4. EXPERIMENTS

In this section, we describe our evaluation methodology and the evaluations we performed.

4.1 Experimental Setup

To evaluate our re-ranking model, we have crawled top 1,000 movies (based on box office sales) from IMDB,[3] one of the most popular movie portals. Among several sources for movie profiles, we chose to exploit synopsis offered by IMDB as it contains

abundant amount of movie plot information. The average number of words, sentences, and paragraphs in a synopsis is 904.613, 94.316, and 18.158 respectively, indicating that synopsis is substantial enough to create a representative knowledge structure for individual movies.

We also collected 10 queries[4] for each movie via Amazon Mechanical Turk, which has been used in information retrieval research for relevance assessment [1]. To control the quality of the input, we restricted users whose HIT approval rate was greater than or equal to 90%. The participants were asked to formulate a search query consisting of multiple keywords for a given movie and received $0.02 per query. In the end, 355 users participated, with an average time to formulate each query of 40.051 seconds, and an average number of words in each query of 3.749.

As our algorithm considers semantics of the words, we compared our algorithm with the proximity retrieval model (PRM) [13], which calculates proximity between words by measuring the minimum pair distance between the query terms. It was also reported to perform best among other state-of-the art models. Given a query Q= $(q_1, ..., q_m)$, the PRM score is tuned to show a consistent performance in our dataset as follows:

$$S_{prm}(Q, D_m) = BM25(Q, D_m) \cdot S_\pi(Q, D_m) \quad (8)$$
$$S_\pi(Q, D_m) = \log(\alpha + \exp(-\delta(Q, D_m))) \quad (9)$$

where α is a constant, and $\delta(Q, D_m)$ is a proximity-distance measure defined as the smallest positional distance of all pairs of uniquely matched-query terms. In the experiment, we set $\alpha = 0.3$, which is known to work best in a prior study [13]. This parameter value is also shown to perform best in our dataset.

For evaluation metrics, we use the Mean Reciprocal Rank (MRR) metric that assigns a value of performance for a target resource of $1/r$, where r is the position of the relevant document 'd' in the result list. We also provide the P@N (Precision at position N) metric, which has a value of 1 iff $r \leq N$.

4.2 Experiment Results

In this section, we analyze the performance of the proximity approaches while our approach adopts the different distance measures: SS, PS, SCS, and PCS. Table 2 shows MRR and P@N values of the different proximity approaches. An asterisk indicates that the value is statistically significantly higher than the BM 25 counterpart (Wilcoxon test, p < 0.01). A † indicate that the value is statistically significantly higher than the PRM counterpart (Wilcoxon test, p < 0.01), on top of the significant difference in relation to the BM25 approach.

Table 2. Proximity-aware model performances

	BM25	PRM	SCS	PCS	PS	SS
MRR	0.6222	0.6410*	0.6550*	0.6596*	0.6742†	**0.6749†**
P@1	0.5046	0.5254*	0.5445*	0.5525*	0.5679†	**0.5704†**
P@2	0.6222	0.6407*	0.6552*	0.6596*	0.6793†	**0.6798†**
P@5	0.7646	0.7816*	0.7885*	0.7898*	0.7999†	**0.8036†**
P@10	0.8515	0.8691*	0.8691*	0.8698*	0.8797†	**0.8813†**

Our approach shows higher performance (statistically significant) than the existing state-of-the-art algorithms in all metrics, regardless of the distance metric used, indicating that consideration of semantics of words through knowledge structure

---

[3] http://www.imdb.com

[4] The data are available at http://courseshare.kaist.ac.kr/movie/

positively affects search performance consistently. In particular, our algorithm with SS presents the best performance. This combination outperformed BM25 and PRM by 8.47% and 5.30% on MRR, 13.02% and 8.56% on P@1, 9.27% and 6.10% on P@2, respectively. Especially, P@1 result for SS implies that users are more likely to find their target movie in the top of the search result compared to PRM, indicating that our model can be more effective in the case that users would like to find a specific movie.

To understand why the performance of our approach increases compared to the other state-of-the-art methods, we re-visited our motivating example and analyzed the results. Given the query set Q = {giant, robot, car}, Table 3 shows that the distance for each pair of Q produced different results depending on the distance metric used. Note again that PRM adopts the minimum distance (MinDist), and thus does not provoke the re-ranking process. On the other hand, we can see that three queries are closer to each other in the knowledge structure[5] for *Transformers*, rather than in the knowledge structure for *MvA*. This implies that our model can discover that semantics among the three terms are stronger for *Transformers*, relative to *MvA*.

Furthermore, we investigated the effect of varying α for overall search performance. Enlarging the constant α in Equation 6 forms convex relations between two terms in a document. Figure 1 shows the MRR and P@N values when the constant α varies from 0 to 2. We can see that the best performance is achieved when α is between 0.6 and 0.8 in PS, PCS, and SCS, while the overall performance gradually reduces as α increases. However, SS shows the most stable performance regardless of the value of α, suggesting that our algorithm, in combination with the SS distance metric, has promise as an effective, parameter-free method.

Table 3. Comparison of distance measures

	PRM		SS	
	Transformers	MvA	Transformers	MvA
d(giant, robot)	1	1	0.2097	0.4700
d(giant, car)	12	256	0.2097	0.5112
d(robot, car)	13	23	0.4194	0.4706

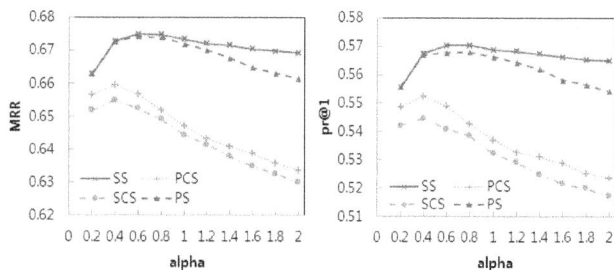

Figure 1. Performance depending on varying α

5. CONCLUSION

In this paper, we have observed that user queries are more descriptive and associative in searching movies because users tend to recall the scenes, or impressive moments of the movies, mainly in relation to the movie plot. We then presented a new movie-retrieval model that effectively searches movies by exploiting knowledge structures extracted from movie plots and measuring the proximity of terms in a query. Our algorithm outperformed

---

[5] Sample knowledge structures for those two movies are shown at http://courseshare.kaist.ac.kr/movie/

other state-of-the-art proximity algorithms as it effectively utilizes the semantics of terms from the movie plots.

Our study needs further work. First, we should expand knowledge structure incorporating other information about movies, not only movie plots. Second, we expect that other multimedia content is also likely to have similar associative queries, thus we should test our algorithm on other types of multimedia content, such as music and books. Despite the need for further work, the proposed algorithm already shows promise for utilizing the potential of knowledge structure to enhance proximity-probabilistic retrieval of multimedia content.

6. ACKNWLEDGMENTS

This research was supported by the BK21 Plus Program of Research and Talent Management on Intelligent Knowledge Service for Innovating Human-Machine Communication and Cooperation hosted at the Department of Knowledge Service Engineering, KAIST.

7. REFERENCES

[1] R. Blanco, H. Halpin, D. M. Herzig, P. Mika, J. Pound, H. S. Thompson, and T. T. Duc. Repeatable and reliable search system evaluation using crowdsourcing. In *SIGIR '11*, pages 923-932, 2011.

[2] S. Büttcher, C. L. Clarke, and B. Lushman. Term proximity scoring for ad-hoc retrieval on very large text collections. In *SIGIR'06*, pages 621-622, 2006.

[3] F. D. Davis, M. Y. Yi. Improving computer skill training: behavior modeling, symbolic mental rehearsal, and the role of knowledge structure. *Journal of applied psychology*, 89(3), 2004.

[4] K. Goldenberg, B. Kimelfeld, and Y. Sagiv, Keyword proximity search in complex data graphs, In *SIGMOD'08*, pages 927-940, 2008.

[5] T. E. Goldsmith, P. J. Johnson, and W. H. Acton. Assessing structural knowledge. *Journal of educational psychology*, 83(1), pages 88-96, 1991.

[6] S. Hauguel, C. Zhai, and J. Han. Parallel PathFinder algorithms for mining structures from graphs. In *ICDM'09*, pages 812-817, 2009.

[7] H. W. Kim, and M. Y. Yi. Empirical validation of an automated method of knowledge structure creation from single documents. In *IEEE ICT-KE'12*, pages 161-165, 2012.

[8] J. Y. Kim, X. Xue, W. Bruce Croft, A probabilistic model for semistructured data, In *ECIR'09*, pages 228-239, 2009.

[9] J. Lafferty, and C. Zhai. Document language models, query models, and risk minimization for information retrieval. In *SIGIR'01*, pages 111-119, 2001.

[10] S. T. Park, D. M. Pennock, Applying collaborative filtering techniques to movie search for better ranking and browsing, In *KDD'07*, pages 550-559, 2007.

[11] Y. Rasolofo and J. Savoy. Term Proximity Scoring for Keyword-Based Retrieval Systems. In *ECIR '03*, pages 207–218, 2003.

[12] S. E. Robertson, S. Walker, S. Jones, M. Hancock-Beaulieu, and M. Gatford. Okapi at TREC-3. In *TREC-3*, 1994.

[13] T. Tao, and C. Zhai. An exploration of proximity measures in information retrieval. In *SIGIR'07*, pages 295-302, 2007.

[14] J. Zhao, and Y. Yun. A proximity language model for information retrieval. In *SIGIR'09*, pages 291-298, 2009.

Supervised Hashing with Soft Constraints

Cong Leng, Jian Cheng, Jiaxiang Wu, Xi Zhang, Hanqing Lu
National Laboratory of Pattern Recognition
Institute of Automation, Chinese Academy of Sciences
Beijing, China
{cong.leng, jcheng, jiaxiang.wu, zhangxi, luhq}@nlpr.ia.ac.cn

ABSTRACT

Due to the ability to preserve semantic similarity in Hamming space, supervised hashing has been extensively studied recently. Most existing approaches encourage two dissimilar samples to have maximum Hamming distance. This may lead to an unexpected consequence that two unnecessarily similar samples would have the same code if they are both dissimilar with another sample. Besides, in existing methods, all labeled pairs are treated with equal importance without considering the semantic gap, which is not conducive to thoroughly leverage the supervised information. We present a general framework for supervised hashing to address the above two limitations. We do not toughly require a dissimilar pair to have maximum Hamming distance. Instead, a soft constraint which can be viewed as a regularization to avoid over-fitting is utilized. Moreover, we impose different weights to different training pairs, and these weights can be automatically adjusted in the learning process. Experiments on two benchmarks show that the proposed method can easily outperform other state-of-the-art methods.

Categories and Subject Descriptors

H.3.3 [**Information Systems**]: Information Search and Retrieval

Keywords

Supervised Hashing; Soft Constraints; Weights; Boosting

1. INTRODUCTION

Hashing based approximate nearest neighbor (ANN) search methods have attracted much attention recently. Hashing methods map the two nearby points in the original space to close binary codes in a compact Hamming space. This enables very fast searching since Hamming distance can be efficiently calculated with XOR operation in modern CPU. According to whether supervised information is utilized or not in the training process, hashing methods can be divided

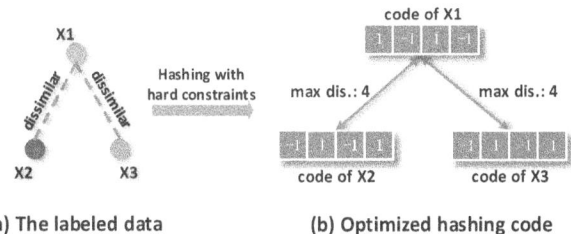

(a) The labeled data   (b) Optimized hashing code

Figure 1: Paradox in traditional supervised Hashing methods. Two unnecessarily similar data x_2 and x_3 will have the same code.

into unsupervised and supervised categories. In the unsupervised setting, hashing methods such as Locality Sensitive Hashing (LSH) [1] and Iterative Quantization (ITQ) [2] attempt to preserve the data similarity defined in Euclidean space, e.g., l_2 distance. However, this is not sufficient for various practical applications such as image retrieval, where semantically similar neighbors are preferred.

In order to construct efficient hash functions that preserve the semantic similarity, supervised hashing methods [3, 6, 5, 4, 7] have been extensively studied. The supervised information here is typically based on some pairwise constraints, i.e., "A and B is similar" or "A and B is dissimilar", which is analogous to the "must link" and "cannot link" constraints in metric learning [8]. Some representative supervised hashing methods include Binary Reconstruction Embedding (BRE) [3], Kernel Supervised Hashing (KSH) [5] and Two Step Hashing (TSH) [4]. These supervised methods can be formally formulated with following objective [4]:

$$\min_{\Phi} \sum_{(x_i, x_j) \in \mathcal{L}} L\left(\Phi(x_i), \Phi(x_j); y_{ij}\right) \qquad (1)$$

where $\Phi(x) \in \{-1, 1\}^r$ is the r bits code of x. $L(\cdot)$ is a loss function that measures how well the codes match the ground truth y_{ij}. Different algorithms corresponds to different loss functions, for example, l_2 loss for BRE and KSH. Although promising performance has been shown from these methods, some limitations exist in them.

Inspired by metric learning, all these supervised methods attempt to learn codes whose Hamming distances are minimized on similar pairs and simultaneously maximized on dissimilar pairs. This principle is widely used in metric learning and proved to be effective. However, metric learning executes in continuous real number space while hashing executes in discrete Hamming space. Importantly, although it makes sense in metric learning, we argue that maximiz-

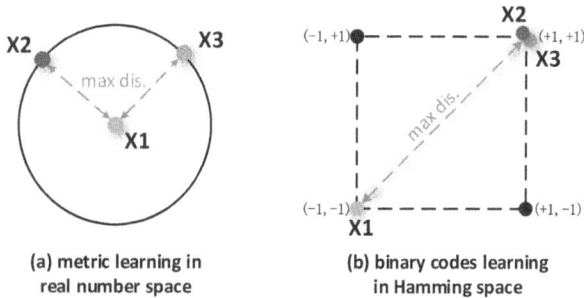

(a) metric learning in real number space

(b) binary codes learning in Hamming space

Figure 2: Difference between real space and Hamming space. (a) The circle is the "boundary" of a continuous real space. Maximizing the distance to x_1, point x_2 and x_3 can be anywhere on this circle. (b) However, in $2d$ discrete Hamming space, x_2 and x_3 will collide in one corner.

ing Hamming distance on dissimilar pairs, namely hard constraints, will lead to over-fitting in hashing. Fig.1 gives an illustration about our observation. In this example, point x_1 is labeled to be dissimilar with x_2 and x_3 separately, while the relationship between x_2 and x_3 is unknown. Under the hard constraints, both x_2 and x_3 would have optimized code that is completely opposite with x_1. As a result, x_2 and x_3 will have the same code. This is apparently unreasonable because x_2 and x_3 are not necessarily similar. This paradox derives from the difference between the continuous space and discrete space (Fig.2). In fact, all the supervised hashing methods with hard constraints contain an implicit assumption, namely, if both 'B' and 'C' are dissimilar with 'A', then 'B' and 'C' are similar. However, this assumption typically does not hold and leads to over-fitting.

In addition, existing methods treat all labeled pairs equally. If each labeled pair is taken as one constraint in hashing, some of them are easy to satisfy while some others not. This is because the gap between the feature space and semantic space. Sometimes two semantically similar points are also close in the feature space. These two points are easy to be embedded to similar codes even without supervised information. Meanwhile, other labeled pairs may be with larger semantic gap, and need more attention in the learning process. Therefore, treating different pairs with different importance is necessary.

In this paper, a general framework is presented to address the above two limitations. We propose to apply soft constraints to the dissimilar pairs. Specifically, instead of toughly requiring a dissimilar pair to have maximum Hamming distance in the objective, we just request them to be far enough in the Hamming space. This can be viewed as a regularization to avoid over-fitting in supervised hashing. Furthermore, we impose different weights to different training pairs, and these weights can be automatically adjusted with boosting technique in a batch-wise learning process. Experiments on two benchmarks show that the proposed method can significantly outperform other state-of-the-art supervised hashing methods.

2. THE PROPOSED APPROACH

First of all, some notations are defined as follows: Let $X = [x_1, x_2, \cdots, x_n]$ denote a set of n data points, where $x_i \in \mathbb{R}^d$ is the i-th data point. For each x_i, its binary hashing code is denoted as $\Phi(x_i) = [h_1(x_i), h_2(x_i), \cdots, h_r(x_i)] \in \{-1, 1\}^r$,

where r is the code length and $\Phi = [h_1(\cdot), h_2(\cdot), \cdots, h_r(\cdot)]$ is a set of r hash functions. $\mathcal{L}$ denotes the set of labeled data pairs. Two categories of label information, $\mathcal{S}$ and $\mathcal{D}$, are available. $(x_i, x_j) \in \mathcal{S}$ represents a similar-pair in which x_i and x_j are similar in semantic space, e.g., share the same labels. Similarly, $(x_i, x_j) \in \mathcal{D}$ is called a dissimilar-pair if two samples are far away in semantic space.

Without loss of generality, we establish our model based on Hamming affinity [5] in this paper. Specifically, Hamming affinity is defined as:

$$S_{ij} = \frac{\Phi(x_i)^T \Phi(x_j)}{r} \qquad (2)$$

Obviously, $\Phi(x_i)^T \Phi(x_j) \in [-r, r]$ and $S_{ij} \in [-1, 1]$. In this case, the ground truth affinity in Eq.(1) is defined as:

$$y_{ij} = \begin{cases} 1, & \text{if } (x_i, x_j) \in \mathcal{S} \\ -1, & \text{if } (x_i, x_j) \in \mathcal{D} \end{cases}$$

Following [5], by adopting Euclidean loss function, the objective function in Eq.(1) can be written as:

$$\min_{\Phi} \sum_{(x_i, x_j) \in \mathcal{L}} \left(\frac{\Phi(x_i)^T \Phi(x_j)}{r} - y_{ij} \right)^2 \qquad (3)$$

2.1 Soft Constraint and Weighted Loss

In Eq.(3) and the objectives of other supervised methods [3, 5], two dissimilar points are encouraged to have completely different codes so that the corresponding Hamming affinity will be -1 (i.e. maximal Hamming distance). This idea comes from metric learning and works very well in continuous real space [8]. However, as illustrated in Fig.1 and Fig.2, hashing executes in discrete Hamming space and the hard constraints will result in entirely opposite codes of a dissimilar pair, which brings over-fitting, e.g. two unnecessarily similar samples would have the same code.

With the target of hashing based ANN search, we only need to require the codes of a dissimilar pair to be far away enough but not necessarily entirely opposite. Considering an example that, if the difference between two data points in a pair $(x_i, x_j) \in \mathcal{D}$ is 90% of the total bits, their Hamming distance will be $0.9 \times r$ and the corresponding Hamming affinity will be -0.8, and this is typically enough to separate the two samples in Hamming space. That is to say, there is no need to restrict the Hamming affinity of a dissimilar pair to be -1. To this end, we modify the objective function in Eq.(3) to be:

$$\min_{\Phi} \sum_{(x_i, x_j) \in \mathcal{L}} \left(\frac{\Phi(x_i)^T \Phi(x_j)}{r} - \lambda_{ij} y_{ij} \right)^2 \qquad (4)$$

and λ_{ij} is defined as:

$$\lambda_{ij} = \begin{cases} 1, & \text{if } (x_i, x_j) \in \mathcal{S} \\ 0 < p < 1, & \text{if } (x_i, x_j) \in \mathcal{D} \end{cases} \qquad (5)$$

where $p \in (0, 1)$ is a parameter in our method.

For any dissimilar pair $(x_i, x_j) \in \mathcal{D}$, $\lambda_{ij} y_{ij} = -p \in (-1, 0)$. In other words, we relax the original hard labels into a soft range for the dissimilar pairs. Hence, the optimized codes will have $\frac{1+p}{2} \times r$ bits to be different. In this paper, we call this kind of constraint as soft constraint. Obviously, under such soft constraints, the codes of x_2 and x_3 are not necessarily identical like in Fig.1. It is worth noting that for a similar pair $(x_i, x_j) \in \mathcal{S}$, $\lambda_{ij} = 1$, we do not change the constraints on similar pairs, and keep to encourage similar samples in semantic space to have the same codes in Hamming space. Multiplying y_{ij} with λ_{ij} can be viewed as a kind of regularization to avoid over-fitting in supervised hashing. As we will find in the following experiments, this little change can greatly improve the quality of learned codes.

Eq.(4) treats each labeled pair as equally important, which fails to take the semantic gap into account. Regarding each labeled pair in $\mathcal{L}$ as a constraint, some of them are easy to satisfy while some others not. For the sake of maximally leveraging the supervised information, we need to treat different pairs with different importance. This can be implemented by giving a different weight w_{ij} to each pair $(x_i, x_j) \in \mathcal{L}$, and we arrive at:

$$\min_{\Phi} \sum_{(x_i,x_j)\in\mathcal{L}} w_{ij} \left(\frac{\Phi(x_i)^T \Phi(x_j)}{r} - \lambda_{ij} y_{ij} \right)^2 \quad (6)$$

While it can be intuitively understood, an important question arises: how to determine the weight of each labeled pair? In the next section, we present a batch-wise learning approach to automatically determine the adaptive weights for different labeled pairs in the learning process.

2.2 Learn one batch at a time

Most of methods solve the optimized code by a single-shot optimization to the objective, i.e., learn all bits in a single run of the algorithm. However, for any a piece of binary code, it can be regarded as a concatenation of many pieces of shorter codes. As an example, one piece of 32-bits code can be considered as the result of concatenating two pieces of 16-bits codes, or four pieces of 8-bits codes. The Hamming affinity evaluated with the long code is the mean of those evaluated with the short ones. From this point of view, hashing can be understood as an ensemble learning process if we repeatedly generate short codes and then concatenate them. The weight of each labeled pair can be adjusted automatically with boosting trick in this process.

Specifically, in the first run, all labeled pairs are treated with equal importance, and we only generate a piece of short code Φ_1 of t bits (e.g. 4 bits) for each sample. In the second and following runs, the weight of each pair will be updated by considering the deviation of the Hamming affinity evaluated with the previous code to the ground truth. Higher weights will be imposed to the pairs with bigger deviation. In detail, in the k-th run, the weight can be defined as:

$$w_{ij}^{(k)} = \begin{cases} 1 - \frac{\Phi(x_i)^T \Phi(x_j)}{(k-1) \times t}, & \text{if } (x_i, x_j) \in \mathcal{S} \\ max(\frac{\Phi(x_i)^T \Phi(x_j)}{(k-1) \times t} + p, 0), & \text{if } (x_i, x_j) \in \mathcal{D} \end{cases} \quad (7)$$

where $\Phi(x) = [\Phi_1(x); \Phi_2(x); \cdots ; \Phi_{k-1}(x)]$ is the $(k-1) \times t$ bits code of x by concatenating the previous $k-1$ pieces of short codes $\Phi_i(x)|_{i=1}^{k-1}$.

Obviously, $\frac{\Phi(x_i)^T \Phi(x_j)}{(k-1) \times t}$ is the Hamming affinity evaluated with the previous code. For the similar pairs, $1 - \frac{\Phi(x_i)^T \Phi(x_j)}{(k-1) \times t}$ is the deviation to the ground truth affinity. The pairs with bigger deviation are associated with higher weights in the next iteration. Note that for the dissimilar pairs, a hinge-like function is used to measure the bias. This is to be consistent with the soft constraints we have used. For any

dissimilar pair whose Hamming affinity is smaller than $-p$, the deviation is set to be zero. After K iterations, we can get a piece of $K \times t$ bits code for each training data.

2.3 Optimization

A remaining problem is optimizing Eq.(6) to learn one piece of t bits code for each training data. Here we follow the block coordinate descent (BCD) method which was also used in [5, 4]. In particular, BCD picks one bit to be optimized every time with other $t-1$ bits fixed. The optimization for the m-th bit can be written as:

$$\min_{\mathbf{z}_{(m)} \in \{-1,1\}^n} \sum_{(x_i,x_j)\in\mathcal{L}} w_{ij} l_m(z_{i,m}, z_{j,m}) \quad (8)$$

where $\mathbf{z}_{(m)}$ is the binary codes of the m-th bit. l_m is the loss function defined on the m-th bit, i.e.

$$l_m(z_{i,m}, z_{j,m}) = L(z_{i,m}, z_{j,m}, \bar{\mathbf{z}}_i, \bar{\mathbf{z}}_j; \lambda_{ij} y_{ij}) \quad (9)$$

Here L is the loss function defined in Eq.(4). $z_{i,m}$ is the binary code of the i-th sample and the m-th bit. $\bar{\mathbf{z}}_i$ is the binary codes of the i-th sample excluding the m-th bit.

When optimizing the m-th bit, as indicated in TSH [4], there are only two possible cases for the code of any pair, namely, same or different. We denote the loss of appointing the same code to x_i and x_j as $l_{m,i,j}^{(+)}$, and $l_{m,i,j}^{(-)}$ for appointing different code. By taking advantage of the Proposition 1 in [4], the optimization of Eq.(8) can be rewritten as:

$$\min_{\mathbf{z}_{(m)} \in \{-1,1\}^n} \sum_{(x_i,x_j)\in\mathcal{L}} w_{ij}(l_{m,i,j}^{(+)} - l_{m,i,j}^{(-)}) z_{i,m} z_{j,m} \quad (10)$$

Because w_{ij}, $l_{m,i,j}^{(+)}$ and $l_{m,i,j}^{(-)}$ are constants, the optimization can be written in a matrix form:

$$\min_{\mathbf{z}_{(m)} \in \{-1,1\}^n} \mathbf{z}_{(m)}^T \mathbf{A} \mathbf{z}_{(m)} \quad (11)$$

where the element of matrix $\mathbf{A}$ is $a_{ij} = w_{ij}(l_{m,i,j}^{(+)} - l_{m,i,j}^{(-)})$. The optimization of Eq. (11) have been well studied. To be specific, by dropping the binary constraints, the optimization becomes:

$$\min_{\mathbf{z}_{(m)}} \mathbf{z}_{(m)}^T \mathbf{A} \mathbf{z}_{(m)} \quad s.t. \ ||\mathbf{z}_{(m)}||_2^2 = n \quad (12)$$

The optimum solution is the eigenvector corresponding to the minimum eigenvalue of $\mathbf{A}$. Subsequently, the obtained solution will be quantized to $\{-1, 1\}^t$ with the sign function.

Until now, we have only optimized the binary codes for training data, which is not enough because hashing has to handle the out-of-sample extension problem, i.e., generating codes for new samples that are unseen before. Inspired by TSH [4], for every bit we regard the binary value $z_{i,m}$ as the pseudo label of training data x_i. Therefore the given training set has already been "labelled" by the above learning process, and we can learn a binary classifier $f^{(m)}$ based on it for every bit. The resulting binary classifiers $f^{(m)}|_{m=1}^t$ are taken as the hash function. In the experiments, we choose SVM with Gaussian kernel as classifier, which is widely used and of good performance.

3. EXPERIMENTS

We compare our method with several state-of-the-art approaches, including four supervised methods: BRE [3], MLH [6], KSH [5], TSH [4], and two representative unsupervised methods: LSH [1], ITQ [2]. Comparison experiments

Table 1: Hamming ranking performance of different algorithms with different code lengthes on MNSIT and CIFAR-10. Mean Average Precision (MAP) is reported. The best results are highlighted in bold.

Methods	MNIST				CIFAR-10			
	16-bits	24-bits	32-bits	64-bits	16-bits	24-bits	32-bits	64-bits
LSH	0.2343	0.2319	0.2536	0.3335	0.1282	0.1382	0.1398	0.1532
ITQ	0.4188	0.4375	0.4444	0.4629	0.1670	0.1707	0.1756	0.1798
BRE	0.5350	0.5592	0.5914	0.6010	0.1588	0.1637	0.1668	0.1760
MLH	0.7062	0.7433	0.7672	0.8011	0.1911	0.2072	0.2174	0.2462
KSH	0.7776	0.8008	0.8180	0.8268	0.2202	0.2379	0.2492	0.2683
TSH	0.5870	0.7978	0.8533	0.8793	0.2377	0.2685	0.2874	0.3117
SCH_uw	0.7314	0.8445	0.8650	0.8808	0.2666	0.2958	0.3102	0.3286
SCH	**0.8532**	**0.8663**	**0.8733**	**0.8875**	**0.2885**	**0.3154**	**0.3193**	**0.3385**

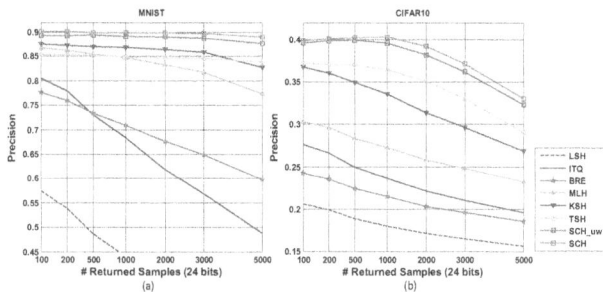

Figure 3: Precision curves of different methods with 24 bits on MNIST and CIFAR-10

are conducted on two widely used benchmarks: MNIST[1] and CIFAR-10[2]. MNIST consists of 784 dimensional 70,000 samples associated with digits from '0' to '9'. CIFAR-10 is a labeled subset of the Tiny Images dataset. 512 dimensional GIST descriptor is extracted to represent each image. For both datasets, we randomly select 1,000 samples to be the query set and the remainders as database. 1,000 samples in the database are used to randomly generate training pairs. Specifically, we suppose that for each sample in the training set, only the relationship to 500 other samples in this set are known. Thus, about 500,000 training pairs are available. We adopt the Hamming Ranking commonly used in the literature. All points in the database are ranked according to their Hamming distance to the query. The ground truth is defined as semantic neighbors based on label agreement.

To give a comprehensive validation of the proposed approach, we present two versions of our method. In the first version, denoted as SCH_uw, we only apply soft constraints to the learning process and ignore the weights of different pairs. The second version, denoted as SCH, considers both the soft constraints and weighted loss. In this version, the learning process optimizes 4 bits at each run and then adjusts the weight of each pair. We empirically set the parameter p in Eq.(5) as $p = 0.6$.

MAP scores: The MAP scores of SCH, SCH_uw and other baselines are shown in Table 1. By leveraging side-information, the supervised methods like KSH and TSH can achieve significant improvement on the unsupervised methods like ITQ. The proposed SCH achieves the highest search accuracy on both two datasets. The optimization of our method is similar to that in TSH and KSH, but it is easy to find that SCH outperforms them with a large margin, especially on the CIFAR-10 dataset. More notably, even

ignoring the weights of pairs, SCH_uw achieves the best results except SCH in most of settings. This confirms that the proposed soft constraints can effectively avoid over-fitting in the supervised hashing. By considering the weights of different pairs, SCH achieves further improvement on SCH_uw, which demonstrates that treating different pairs with different importance is beneficial to take full advantage of the supervised information.

Precision Curves: Fig.3 shows the precision curves of different methods with 24 bits on two datasets. Similar to the trends in Table 1, SCH works better than SCH_uw, which is the second best in all competitors. In Fig.3(a), the precision decreases in all hashing methods as the number of retrieved points increases, but our methods decrease more slowly and achieve a very high precision on MNIST even when 5,000 samples are returned. These results clearly show the superiority of the proposed methods over other state-of-the-art methods.

4. CONCLUSION

In this paper, we proposed a general framework for supervised hashing with soft constraints and weighted loss. Experiments on two benchmarks demonstrated the effectiveness of the proposed method.

Acknowledgements

This work was supported in part by National Natural Science Foundation of China (Grant No. 61332016), 863 program (Grant No. 2014AA015104 and 2014AA015105).

5. REFERENCES

[1] M. Charikar. Similarity estimation techniques from rounding algorithm. In *STOC*, 2002.
[2] Y. Gong and S. Lazebnik. Iterative quantization: A procrustean approach to learning binary codes. In *CVPR*, 2011.
[3] B. Kulis and T. Darrell. Learning to hash with binary reconstructive embeddings. In *NIPS*, 2009.
[4] G. Lin, C. Shen, D. Suter, and A. van den Hengel. A general two-step approach to learning-based hashing. In *ICCV*, 2013.
[5] W. Liu, J. Wang, R. Ji, Y. Jiang, and S. Chang. Supervised hashing with kernels. In *CVPR*, 2012.
[6] M. Norouzi and D. J. Fleet. Minimal loss hashing for compact binary codes. In *ICML*, 2011.
[7] M. Ou, P. Cui, F. Wang, J. Wang, W. Zhu, and S. Yang. Comparing apples to oranges: A scalable solution with heterogeneous hashing. In *KDD*, 2013.
[8] E. P. Xing, A. Y. Ng, M. I. Jordan, and S. Russell. Distance metric learning with application to clustering with side-information. In *NIPS*, 2003.

---

[1] http://yann.lecun.com/exdb/mnist/

[2] http://www.cs.toronto.edu/~kriz/cifar.html

Probabilistic Classifier Chain Inference via Gibbs Sampling

Li Li
Key Laboratory of
Computational Linguistics,
Ministry of Education,
Peking University, China
li.l@pku.edu.cn

Longkai Zhang
Key Laboratory of
Computational Linguistics,
Ministry of Education,
Peking University, China
zhlongk@qq.com

Guangyi Li
Key Laboratory of
Computational Linguistics,
Ministry of Education,
Peking University, China
liguangyi@pku.edu.cn

Houfeng Wang *
Key Laboratory of Computational Linguistics,
Ministry of Education,
Peking University, China
wanghf@pku.edu.cn

ABSTRACT

Multi-label classification is supervised learning, where an instance may be assigned with multiple categories (labels) simultaneously. Recently, a method called *Probabilistic Classifier Chain* (PCC) was proposed with numerous appealing properties, such as conceptual simplicity, flexibility, and theoretical justification. Nevertheless, PCC suffers from high inference complexity. To address this problem, we propose a novel inference method with *gibbs sampling*. An acceleration scheme is proposed to accelerate this method further. Our proposed method is based on our claim that PCC is a special case of Bayesian network. This claim may inspire more inference algorithms for PCC. Experiments with real-world data sets show effectiveness of our proposed method.

Categories and Subject Descriptors

I.5.1 [**Pattern Recognition**]: Models—*statistical,structural*

General Terms

Algorithms, Experimentation

Keywords

Multi-label Classification, Probabilistic Classifier Chain, Gibbs Sampling

1. INTRODUCTION

Multi-label classification is supervised learning, where an instances is usually assigned with *multiple* labels simultaneously. In recent years, the multi-label classification attracts increasing attentions from various domains, such as text

*corresponding author

CIKM'14, November 3–7, 2014, Shanghai, China.
Copyright 2014 ACM 978-1-4503-2598-1/14/11 ...$15.00.
http://dx.doi.org/10.1145/2661829.2661917 .

classification [4, 8], media categorization [9] and genomics [6]. In multi-label classification setting, $\mathcal{X} = R^d$ denotes the instance space, and $\mathcal{Y} = \{0,1\}^m$ denotes label space with m labels. An instance $\boldsymbol{x} \in \mathcal{X}$ is associated with a label vector $\boldsymbol{y} = (y_1, y_2, ..., y_m)$ (i.e., a label combination), where $y_j = 1$ denotes the instance has the j-th label and 0 otherwise.

Recent *Probabilistic Classifier Chain* (PCC) [1] is an attractive solution for multi-label classification. PCC trains a probabilistic classifier with respect to each label. The classifier corresponding to the j-th label takes $\boldsymbol{x}$ plus $y_1, ..., y_{j-1}$ as features. Hence the classifier is trained to estimate the distribution $p(y_j|\boldsymbol{x}, y_1, ..., y_{j-1})$. PCC obtains the joint conditional probabilities $p(\boldsymbol{y}|\boldsymbol{x})$ by multiplying probabilities by all classifiers, formulated as Eq.(1).

$$p(\boldsymbol{y}|\boldsymbol{x}) = p(y_1|\boldsymbol{x}) \prod_{j=1}^{m} p(y_j|\boldsymbol{x}, y_1, ..., y_{j-1})$$

(1)

During inference, PCC calculates the probabilities of all possible label combinations, and chooses the label combination with the highest probability, formulated as Eq.(2).

$$\boldsymbol{y}^* = \underset{\boldsymbol{y}}{\operatorname{argmin}}\, p(\boldsymbol{y}|\boldsymbol{x})$$

(2)

PCC is attractive for several reasons. First, it converts multi-label classification to some binary classification problems, which allows us to leverage existing researches. Second, it is a principled probabilistic model, and there is a theoretical guarantee that PCC produces Bayes optimal predictions. Third, it is computationally inexpensive to train. However, during inference, PCC calculates the probabilities of all possible label combinations (totally 2^m), resulting in high inference complexity. To reduce the inference complexity of PCC, we propose a novel inference method *Probabilistic Classifier Chain via Gibbs sampling* (P2CG). An acceleration scheme is proposed to further reduce the inference complexity. Actually, we propose our method inspired by that PCC is a special case of Bayesian network. Our experiments with real-world data sets show our proposed method dramatically extends the practical viability of PCC.

The remainder of this paper is organized as follows. P2CG is introduced in section 2. we claim PCC is a special case of Bayesian network in section 3. Experiments are conducted in section 4. Section 5 concludes this paper.

2. INFERENCE WITH GIBBS SAMPLING

2.1 Probabilistic Classifier Chain with Gibbs Sampling

P2CG employs gibbs sampling to PCC inference. Gibbs sampling algorithm samples each label variable successively or randomly from the conditional distributions $p(y_j|\boldsymbol{x}, \boldsymbol{y}_{\neg j})$. The conditional distribution $p(y_j|\boldsymbol{x}, \boldsymbol{y}_{\neg j})$ is derivated as Eq.(3).

$$
\begin{aligned}
&p(y_j = 1|\boldsymbol{x}, \boldsymbol{y}_{\neg j}) \\
&= \frac{p(y_j = 1, \boldsymbol{y}_{\neg j}|\boldsymbol{x})}{\sum_{y_j \in \{0,1\}} p(y_j, \boldsymbol{y}_{\neg j}|\boldsymbol{x})} \\
&= \frac{p(y_j = 1|\boldsymbol{x}, y_1, ..., y_{j-1}) \prod_{i=j+1}^{m} p(y_i|\boldsymbol{x}, y_1, ..., y_j = 1, ..., y_{i-1})}{\sum_{y_j = 0,1} p(y_j|\boldsymbol{x}, y_1, ..., y_{j-1}) \prod_{i=j+1}^{m} p(y_i|\boldsymbol{x}, y_1, ..., y_j, ..., y_{i-1})}
\end{aligned}
\tag{3}
$$

where y_j denotes the target label, $\boldsymbol{y}_{\neg j}$ denotes all label variables but the sample target label and $\boldsymbol{x}$ denotes the instance feature. With the formula of joint conditional distribution, the procedure of P2CG is shown in Algorithm 1.

Algorithm 1 P2CG

Initialize $\boldsymbol{y}$
for all $i \in 1, 2, .., nIter$ do
  for all $j \in 1, 2, .., m$ do
    $\boldsymbol{y}_j \sim p(y_j|\boldsymbol{x}, \boldsymbol{y}_{\neg j})$
  end for
end for
return $\boldsymbol{y}$

The label combinations generated by gibbs sampling algorithm obey the joint distribution $p(\boldsymbol{y}|\boldsymbol{x})$. Consequently, the label combination with higher joint probability is more likely to appear in the sample set. Hence, it is reasonable to choose the label combination with the highest joint probability in the sample set as output.

$$
\boldsymbol{y}^* = \underset{\boldsymbol{y} \in \mathsf{S}}{\arg\max}\, p(\boldsymbol{y}|\boldsymbol{x})
\tag{4}
$$

where S denotes the sample set generated by gibbs sampling algorithm.

How to choose the number of iterations is important in P2CG. Since large number of iteration will causes high inference time, we suggest to choose small number. In experiments of this paper, we will see P2CG achieves satisfactory performance even when small number of iterations.

2.2 Acceleration Scheme

We introduce the acceleration scheme when generalized linear model [5] is utilized as base classifier, and show the acceleration scheme works for other types of base classifier. Generalized linear model (linear regression, logistic regression, poisson regression, etc) produces probabilistic prediction with the dot product of the feature vector and the weight vector. Hence, the j-th classifier in the PCC model

produces probabilistic prediction with Eq.(5).

$$
\begin{aligned}
&p(y_j = 1|\boldsymbol{x}, y_1, ..., y_{j-1}) \\
&= f(\boldsymbol{w}_j^T[\boldsymbol{x}, y_1, ..., y_{j-1}])
\end{aligned}
\tag{5}
$$

where $\boldsymbol{w}_j$ and b_j are the j-th model's parameters. f is non-linear function of converting the dot product to probability. For example, when the general linear model is logistic regression, f is the logistic function, $f(s) = \frac{1}{1+exp(-s)}$. Let $\mathbf{s}$ denote the dot product vector, we have

$$
\boldsymbol{s} = [s_1, s_2, .., s_m]
\tag{6}
$$
$$
s_j = \boldsymbol{w}_j^T[\boldsymbol{x}, y_1, ..., y_{j-1}]
\tag{7}
$$

If we can maintain $\boldsymbol{s}$ and update it fastly, the classifiers in the PCC model will take less time to produce predictions and thus we will speed up the inference. Since P2CG changes only one label every time, we can update $\boldsymbol{s}$ fastly. When we change the k-th label, the dot products for latter labels $(s_j, j > k)$ will change according to Eq.(8).

$$
s_j^{new} = s_j^{old} + w_{j,k}(y_k^{new} - y_k^{old})
\tag{8}
$$

where w_{jk} is the j-th classifier's weight w.r.t the k-th label (When $j > k$, the k-th label is a feature of the j-th classifier. $w_{j,k}$ is the weight with respect to this feature).

By maintaining and updating $\boldsymbol{s}$, we develop a acceleration scheme, as shown in Algorithm 2. The inference complexity will be reduced with this acceleration scheme further. Without the acceleration scheme, as Algorithm 1 shows, each iteration of P2CG inference samples $O(m)$ labels successively, each sampling needs $O(m)$ predictions by classifiers, the time complexity of producing probabilistic prediction is $O(d + m)$. Hence, the inference complexity per iteration is $O(dm^2 + m^3)$. With $\boldsymbol{s}$, the time complexity of producing prediction is reduced from $O(d + m)$ to $O(1)$. Hence, the inference complexity per iteration is reduced from $O(dm^2 + m^3)$ to $O(m^2)$.

Algorithm 2 P2CG with the acceleration scheme

Initialize $\boldsymbol{y}$
Calculate $\boldsymbol{s}$ with Eq.(6).
for all $i \in 1, 2, .., nIter$ do
  for all $j \in 1, 2, .., m$ do
    $\boldsymbol{y}_j \sim p(y_j|\boldsymbol{x}, \boldsymbol{y}_{\neg j}^{old})$ // compute $p(y_j|\boldsymbol{x}, \boldsymbol{y}_{\neg j}^{old})$ with $\boldsymbol{s}$
    Update $\boldsymbol{s}$ with Eq.(8)
  end for
end for
return $\boldsymbol{y}$

It is obvious that this acceleration method still works when Naive Bayes and Maximum Entropy utilized. Generalized linear models, Naive Bayes and Maximum Entropy are the most popular models for probabilistic outputs. Hence, this acceleration method works for most cases.

3. PROBABILISTIC CLASSIFIER CHAIN AS BAYESIAN NETWORK

In this section, we claim that PCC is a special case of Bayesian network. The claim is made based on the following three reasons. First, PCC and Bayesian network can have the same structure. Figure 1 shows a special structure of Bayesian network. In this Bayesian network structure, all label variables have common cause $\boldsymbol{x}$ and the former label variables depend the latter label variables. This structure is exactly the structure of PCC. Second, their learning processes are equivalent. In the above Bayesian network, maximum likelihood estimation is to learn the parameters by estimating $p(y_1|\boldsymbol{x}),...,p(y_m|\boldsymbol{x}, y_1,...,y_{m-1})$. The classifiers in PCC are trained to estimate $p(y_1|\boldsymbol{x}),...,p(y_m|\boldsymbol{x}, y_1,...,y_{m-1})$. Therefore, they are equivalent. Third, both of them are to find the instantiation (label combination) with the highest joint probability during inference.

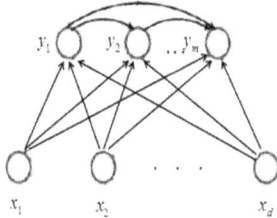

Figure 1: Bayesian network with a special structure

We propose to use gibbs sampling to reduce the inference complexity in this paper. Actually, this method is inspired by that gibbs sampling is an efficient inference algorithms for Bayesian network. The claim, that PCC is a special case of Bayesian network, may inspire more inference algorithms. There exist numerous inference algorithms for Bayesian network, such as stochastic MCMC simulation [2], variational methods [3] and so on. All of them can be employed to PCC inference. Since we have developed P2CG as the example, details of these extensions are omitted in this paper.

4. EXPERIMENTS

4.1 Setups and Datasets

We compare P2CG to the following methods: *Binary Relevance* (BR), *Classifier Chains* (CC) [7], *Probabilistic Classifier Chain* (PCC). BR learns a binary classifier with respect to each label, which suffers from ignoring label dependencies. CC [7] organizes the classifiers along a chain, and takes predictions produced by the former classifiers as the latter classifiers' additional features. CC exploits the label dependencies however CC usually plunges into local optima [1]. In our experiments, we use CC's result as initialization label combination of P2CG. Experiments are done in *ten-fold cross validation* (CV). We choose logistic regression as the base classifier for all algorithms in our experiments, since logistic regression is an effective probabilistic classification model. .

We perform experiments on four real-world data sets[1]. The statistics of these data sets are shown in Table 1, where n denotes the size of the dataset, d denotes the dimension of instance, and m denotes the number of labels.

[1]Available at http://mulan.sourceforge.net/datasets.html

dataset	n	d	m
Scene	2407	294	6
Slashdot	3782	1079	22
Enron	1702	1001	53
Corel5k	5000	499	374

Table 1: Data sets and associated statistics

4.2 Performance Comparison

We compare P2CG to BR, CC and PCC. We choose small number of iterations and set it to 20. Evaluation is done in terms of th evaluation metrics. The first one is 0/1 loss. The 0/1 loss is ratio of exact match of predicted label set $\boldsymbol{p}$ and true label set $\boldsymbol{y}$.

$$0/1loss = \frac{1}{n}\sum_{i=1}^{n} I(\boldsymbol{p}_i \neq \boldsymbol{y}_i) \qquad (9)$$

where $I(true) = 1$ and $I(false) = 0$. n denotes the size of dataset. The lower 0/1 loss, the better. The second metrics is hamming loss, which is defined as follows.

$$Hammingloss = \frac{1}{n}\sum_{i=1}^{n} \frac{1}{m}|\boldsymbol{p}_i \Delta \boldsymbol{y}_i| \qquad (10)$$

where Δ denotes the symmetric difference of two sets. The lower hamming loss, the better.

	BR	CC	PCC	P2CG
Scene	.485±.012	.441±.013	.386±.021	.386±.021
Slashdot	.789±.015	.628±.027	.557±.028	.557±.028
Enron	.854±.029	.847±.027	INF	.833±.023
Corel5k	.997±.002	.996±.003	INF	.986±.003

Table 2: Performance (mean ± std) of each algorithm in terms of 0/1 loss.

	BR	CC	PCC	P2CG
Scene	.107±.005	.105±.006	.096±.007	.096±.007
Slashdot	.056±.002	.047±.027	.041±.002	.041±.002
Enron	.045±.002	.048±.002	INF	.048±.002
Corel5k	.014±.000	.013±.000	INF	.010±.000

Table 3: Performance (mean ± std) of each algorithm in terms of hamming loss.

Table 3 shows the detailed results (*INF* means the algorithm is not suitable for the corresponding data set). The P2CG as well as PCC show clear superiorities to BR and CC. It shows the advantages of PCC and P2CG. When PCC is suitable (the *Scene* and *Slashdot* data set), P2CG has similar performance to PCC. The reasonable explanation for these experiment results is that P2CG (almost) reaches the global optimum. When the number of labels exceeds 30, it is hard to apply PCC (the inference complexity of PCC exceeds 2^{30}). But this isn't a problem with P2CG. Even the number of labels is 374 (the *corel5k* data set), P2CG is still applicable, which shows P2CG can reduce the inference complexity dramatically.

4.3 Efficiency Comparision

To compare P2CG with PCC in term of efficiency, we record test time of PC2G and PCC in the above experiments, which are reported in Table 4. The test times are similar when the number of labels is small (the label number of the scene is 6). As the number of labels grows, the test time of PCC grows rapidly. The label number of the slashdot is 22, the test time of PCC is 2.8h! However the test time of PC2G is still small (9.2s). The number of labels exceeds 30, PCC isn't applicable, but P2CG works. For the enron and corel5k, the number of labels are 53 and 374, PCC isn't able to complete the test procedure in a week, P2CG completes the test procedure in 40.3s and 150.4s respectively.

	PCC	P2CG
Scene	1.3s	1.8s
Slashdot	2.8h	9.2s
Enron	*INF*	40.3s
Corel5k	*INF*	150.4s

Table 4: Test time comparison

4.4 Convergence Rate

Convergence rate is an important property of P2CG. To examine the convergence rate of P2CG, we keep track of the probabilities $p(y|x)$ of the label combinations per iteration. Due to the page limit, we only report the results on the *Scene* and *Corel5k* data set.

Figure 2 shows the average value of probabilities of the result label combinations when performing experiments on the *Scene* data set. In figure (2), P2CG converges after around iteration 7. Figure (3) shows the average value of probabilities of the result label combinations when performing experiments on the *Corel5k* data set. In figure 3, P2CG converges after around iteration 70. The experiment results show convergence rate of P2CG is influenced by the number of labels. This is because convergence rate of gibbs sampling is influenced by the number of nodes. But even when the number of labels reaches 374, P2CG still converges fastly (after around iteration 70).

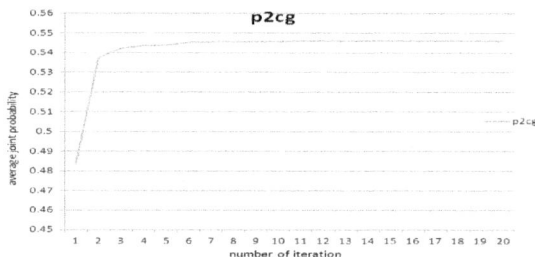

Figure 2: The average value of $p(y|x)$ as a function of iterations number, when applying P2CG on the *Scene* dataset

5. CONCLUSION

PCC achieves a good performance in multi-label classification. Nevertheless, PCC suffers from high inference complexity. In this paper, we are inspired by that PCC is a

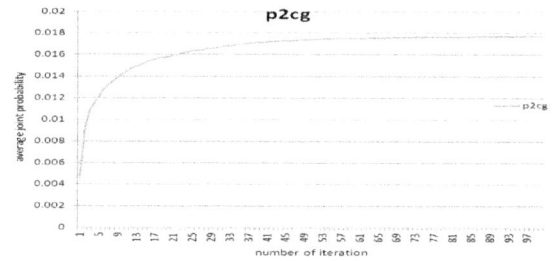

Figure 3: The average value of $p(y|x)$ as a function of iterations number, when applying P2CG on the *Corel5k* dataset

special case of Bayesian network, and propose P2CG to reduce the inference complexity. Experiments with real-world data sets show effectiveness of P2CG.

6. ACKNOWLEDGE

This research was partly supported by National High Technology Research and Development Program of China (863 Program) (No.2012AA011101), National Natural Science Foundation of China (No.91024009), Major National Social Science Fund of China (No. 12&ZD227).

7. REFERENCES

[1] K. Dembczynski, W. Cheng, and E. Hüllermeier. Bayes optimal multilabel classification via probabilistic classifier chains. In *Proceedings of the 27th international conference on machine learning (ICML-10)*, pages 279–286, 2010.

[2] D. Gamerman and H. F. Lopes. *Markov chain Monte Carlo: stochastic simulation for Bayesian inference*, volume 68. CRC Press, 2006.

[3] T. S. Jaakkola and M. I. Jordan. Bayesian parameter estimation via variational methods. *Statistics and Computing*, 10(1):25–37, 2000.

[4] I. Katakis, G. Tsoumakas, and I. Vlahavas. Multilabel text classification for automated tag suggestion. In *Proceedings of the ECML/PKDD*, 2008.

[5] J. A. Nelder and R. W. Wedderburn. Generalized linear models. *Journal of the Royal Statistical Society. Series A (General)*, pages 370–384, 1972.

[6] Y. Peng, G. Kou, Y. Shi, and Z. Chen. A multi-criteria convex quadratic programming model for credit data analysis. *Decision Support Systems*, 44(4):1016–1030, 2008.

[7] J. Read, B. Pfahringer, G. Holmes, and E. Frank. Classifier chains for multi-label classification. *Machine learning*, 85(3):333–359, 2011.

[8] A. N. Srivastava and B. Zane-Ulman. Discovering recurring anomalies in text reports regarding complex space systems. In *Aerospace Conference, 2005 IEEE*, pages 3853–3862. IEEE, 2005.

[9] K. T. G. Tsoumakas, G. Kalliris, and I. Vlahavas. Multi-label classification of music into emotions. In *ISMIR 2008: Proceedings of the 9th International Conference of Music Information Retrieval*, page 325. Lulu. com, 2008.

GPQ: Directly Optimizing Q-measure based on Genetic Programming

Yuan Lin, Hongfei Lin, Ping Zhang, Bo Xu
Information Retrieval Laboratory of DLUT
School of Computer Science and Technology, Dalian University of Technology
No. 2 LingGong Road GanJingZi District DaLian, China
zhlin@dlut.edu.cn, hflin@dlut.edu.cn, {pingzhang, xubo2011}@mail.dlut.edu.cn

ABSTRACT

Ranking plays an important role in information retrieval system. In recent years, a kind of research named 'learning to rank' becomes more and more popular, which applies machine learning technology to solve ranking problems. Lots of ranking models belonged to learning to rank have been proposed, such as Regression, RankNet, and ListNet. Inspired by this, we proposed a novel learning to rank algorithm named GPQ in this paper, in which genetic programming was employed to directly optimize Q-measure evaluation metric. Experimental results on OHSUMED benchmark dataset indicated that our method GPQ could be competitive with Ranking SVM, SVMMAP and ListNet, and improve the ranking accuracies.

Categories and Subject Descriptors

H.3.3 [**Information Search and Retrieval**]: Retrieval Models

General Terms

Algorithms, Experimentation, Theory

Keywords

Information Retrieval; Learning to Rank; Q-measure; Genetic Programming

1. INTRODUCTION

Learning to rank became a more popular research area in this decade, which employs machine learning technology to solve ranking problems in information retrieval. Many learning to rank algorithms are proposed in recent years. These methods could be graded into three categories: the Pointwise approach, the Pairwise approach and the Listwise approach. The experimental results on Letor3.0 indicates that listwise approach generally performs better than pointwise approach and pairwise approach[1]. The input space of the Listwise approach is an entire group of a query and is more similar with the real ranking. It could be divided into two categories. The first category measures the difference between the

CIKM '14, November 3-7, 2014, Shanghai, China.
Copyright © 2014 ACM 978-1-4503-2598-1/14/11...$15.00.
http://dx.doi.org/10.1145/2661829.2661932

permutation by the ranking model and the ground truth permutation, the representative algorithms are ListNet [2], ListMLE [3]. The output space of the second category contains the relevance degrees of all the document for a query, and the loss function of which is defined based on the bound of information evaluation measures. An example algorithm is SVMMAP [4]. Besides, RankGP [5] utilizes genetic programming to optimize Mean Average Precision metric. Similar to RankGP, we propose a novel ranking algorithm GPQ, in which genetic programming is employed to directly optimize the Q-measure [6] evaluation metric. In our method, we regard the objective ranking function as an individual in Genetic Programming process. Then a group of evolution operations will be executed iteratively. A population will be initialization at first. During each iteration, three operations will be applied to the population to generate new individuals, selection, crossover and mutation immediately. We use the Q-measure evaluation metric to evaluate the fitness of each individual, based on which excellent individuals are kept and weak individuals are discarded. We eventually obtain an individual that owned the best fitness. Unlike the RankGP, we employ the Artificial Neural Network to save the ranking model and take the encoded weights as the individual. Besides, we use the genetic programming to optimize a novel evaluation measure Q-measure which is a graded version of Average Precision.

The rest of this paper is organized as follows. Section 2 gives a detail introduction to the evaluation metric Q-measure which will be optimized in our GPQ method. Section 3 describes our proposed learning to rank method GPQ. Experimental results and analysis are presented in Section 4. Section 5 concludes this paper and presents avenues for future work.

2. Evaluation Measures

2.1 Q-measure

The evaluation metric Q-measure [6] is a graded version of Average Precision, inherits both the reliability of Average Precision (AP) and the multigrade relevance capability of Average Weighted Precision (AWP) [7]. Therefore, so as to introduce the Q-measure evaluation metric, we will firstly introduce the evaluation metrics Average Precision and AWP. The definition of Average Precision is well known. We then describe the definition of the AWP below, which was intended for evaluation based on multigrade relevance.

The AWP evaluation measure is intended for evaluation based on multigrade relevance. Let $J(r)$ denotes the relevance degree of the document at position r (If there are three relevant levels, we use digit 2 denotes relevant, 1 denotes partial relevant and 0 denotes irrelevant). If the document at position r is relevant, then a gain is generated which is denoted by $g(r) = $ gain $(J(r))$, else 0.

The cumulative gain at position r in the search result list is denoted as follows:

$$cg(r) = g(r) + cg(r-1) \quad r > 1$$
$$cg(1) = g(1) \quad r = 1 \tag{1}$$

Let $cg^*(r)$ denotes the cumulative gain at position r in an ideal ranked list, and then AWP is defined as follows:

$$\text{AWP} = \frac{1}{R} \sum_{1 \leq r \leq l} J(r) \frac{cg(r)}{cg^*(r)} \tag{2}$$

The AWP evaluation metric seems like an extension of Average Precision, but it suffers from a serious problem. After Rank R (the number of relevant documents), the cumulative gain $cg^*(r)$ in an ideal list becomes a constant. This leads to a problem that AWP could not distinguish between system A that has a relevant document at position r ($r<R$) and system B that has a relevant document at position r' ($r'>R$). In fact, system A is better than system B in terms of ranking performance. However, according to equation (2), the evaluation metric AWP could not tell the difference between the two systems. To tackle this problem, Sakai [6] proposed an evaluation measure Q-measure, which introduced the notion of bonused gain at position r: $bg(r)=g(r)+1$ if $g(r)>0$, else $bg(r)=0$. Then the cumulative bonused gain at position r is denoted as:

$$cbg(r) = bg(r) + cbg(r-1) \quad r > 1$$
$$cbg(1) = bg(1) \quad r = 1 \tag{3}$$

Hence the $cbg(r) = cg(r) + C(r)$. The expression $C(r)$ is the number of relevant documents from position 1 to r in the ranked list which could be denoted as follows.

$$C(r) = \sum_{k=1}^{r} *J(r) \tag{4}$$

Then, the value of Q-measure evaluation metric at cutoff l is:

$$Q@l = \frac{1}{\min(l,R)} \sum_{r=1}^{l} J(r) \frac{C(r) + \beta cg(r)}{r + \beta cg^*(r)} \tag{5}$$

The value of Q-measure is equal to 1 when the ranked list is ideal. The parameter β is a persistence parameter for Q-measure. If β is set to zero, then Q-measure is reduced to Average Precision. Here we set β to 1. Since the Q-measure evaluation metric has these excellent properties, we employ genetic programming to optimize Q-measure. In the next Section, we will give the detail description of our method GPQ.

3. Learning Method: GPQ

The Genetic Programming (GP) is an evolutionary algorithm-based methodology inspired by biological evolution to find computer programs that perform a user-defined task. In Genetic Programming, a population will be initialized at first which consists of a group of individuals. Then the whole evolution process is a series of iterative operations. At each iteration, three genetic operations will be applied to individuals in the population, named selection, crossover and mutation. The fitness is evaluated by a user-defined metric and is used to measure whether the potential solution is good or not. The genetic programming will eventually produce an individual with the best fitness. The Genetic Programming has been applied to many areas, such as Combinatorial Optimization, Machine Learning, and Image Processing. In this paper, we proposed a novel ranking algorithm GPQ in which Genetic Programming was employed to directly

optimize Q-measure evaluation metric. Figure 1 summarizes the procedure of GPQ.

From Figure 1 we could understand the key steps are population initialization, fitness calculation, crossover, mutation and selection. We will report them in the following parts.

3.1 Population Initialization

The training set S and the validation set V are standard learning to rank dataset, both of which contain a set of queries. There are a group of documents with respect to each query as well as their relevance judgments. In our GPQ method, a potential ranking model (individual) is corresponding to an artificial neural network (ANN). In order to calculate conveniently, an individual is denoted as an array list, each factor in which is a weight (real number) in ANN. Hence we need encoding and decoding process between the two implementations. In this paper we use three layers ANN and the length of an individual is defined by the input number and the hidden number of ANN, *length (Individual)* = (*InputNum*HidNum+HidNum*) immediately.

GPQ: Employing **G**enetic **P**rogramming to directly optimize **Q**-measure

Input 1: Training set **S**, Validation set **V**

Input2: Artificial Neural Network parameters: *InputNum*, *HidNum*, *Ihthreshold*, *Hothreshold*

Input3: Genetic Programming parameters: *Generations*, *Psize*, *Pcrossover*, *Pmutation*

(1) Initialize population P with a set of randomly generated individuals (*Psize*), calculate fitness of each individual

(2) Execute crossover with probability *Pcrossover* and mutation with probability *Pmutation*, calculate the fitness of new individuals

(3) Sort the individuals with the fitness in descending order, keep the first *Psize* individuals to population P and remove others

(4) Repeat steps (2)-(3) until the iterations is equal to *Generations*

(5) Calculate the fitness of each individual on validation set V, calculate the final fitness(fitness on S and V) of each individual

(6) Sort the individuals in descending order and return the first individual (the individual with the best fitness)

Output: The ranking model (an artificial neural network) owned the best fitness.

Fig. 1. The workflow of GPQ

In GPQ, we first randomly initialize a set of individuals. For each individual generation, what we actually do is initialize an artificial neural network. The weights between input layer and hidden layer are randomly set with threshold (-*Ihthreshold to Ihthreshold*). Similarly, the weights between hidden layer and output layer are randomly set with threshold (-*Hothreshold* to + *Hothreshold*). Then we encode each ANN to an individual and ensure the number of population P is *Psize*.

3.2 Fitness Calculation

The fitness of an individual is based on user-defined metric and used to evaluate the ranking performance of a ranking model. The Q-measure evaluation metric inherits both the reliability of

Average Precision and the multigrade relevance capability of Average Weighted Precision and could be used to multi-level relevant degrees evaluation. In the rest of this paper, we use letter 'Q' to denote the evaluation metric Q-measure. Hence, we take it as the fitness function in our GPQ method. When a fitness calculation process begins, we first decode the individual to the weights of ANN. Then training data (validation data) are inputted to the ANN and ANN gives the score of each document. Finally the value of Q-measure is calculated as the fitness over the whole queries.

3.3 Evolution Operations

In this section, there are three kinds of evolution operations, namely crossover, mutation and selection. In crossover process, for every two individual, we execute crossover with probability *Pcrossover*. We utilize arithmetic crossover to generate new individuals. For original individuals A and B, new individuals C and D, the crossover process is denoted as follows:

$$C = \alpha \cdot A + (1-\alpha) \cdot B$$
$$D = (1-\alpha) \cdot A + \alpha \cdot B \qquad (6)$$

The parameter α is a real number between 0.0 and 1.0. The new individuals generated by crossover will be added to the original population. In mutation process, for each original individual, we execute mutation with probability *Pmutation*. If an individual meets the mutation condition, a new weight will be set to a random position of the individual. By contrast, the selection operation is very simple. The first *Psize* individuals will be kept.

When select the best individual over training set S and validation set V, besides calculate the fitness of all individuals on S, we also calculate them on V. This paper uses simple sum of the value of Q-measure on S and V:

$$FinalScore(I) = Q - measure(S) + Q - measure(V) \qquad (7)$$

4. Experiments

4.1 Experiments Settings

We perform the GPQ method on the benchmark learning to rank dataset OHSUMED in LETOR3.0 released by MSLR [8]. The OHSUMED is a subset of MEDLINE, a database on medical publications, which consists of 348,566 records from 270 medical journals during the years of 1987-1991. A query set with 106 queries is used on the OHSUMED dataset, which contains 11303 irrelevant documents, 4837 relevant documents and 45 dimensions of features. The relevance degrees of the documents with respect to each query fall into three levels: definitely relevant, partially relevant or irrelevant.

Table 1 described the parameters of GPQ which are set empirically in the experiments. The experimental results are compared with the state-of-the-art learning to rank algorithms, such as Ranking SVM, ListNet, and SVMMAP. The experimental results are listed as follows.

Table 1. The parameters for the proposed algorithm GPQ

Name	Value	Name	Value
InputNum	45	Ihthreshold	0.01
HidNum	1/5*(InputNum)	Hothreshold	0.5
Generations	100	Pcrossover	0.95
Psize	300	Pmutation	0.05

4.2 Experimental Results

We performed 10 times GPQ on the OHSUMED dataset and get two groups of results. The first group of result is denoted as GPQ-Avg, which are the average results over the 10 times results. The other group is denoted as GPQ-Bst, which are the average results of the best run in the 10 times results. The initialization of the population in GPQ is a random process; we perform 10 times GPQ in order to reduce the influence of experimental results by the random process.

Table 2. Comparison with other methods by MAP

Algorithms	Ranking SVM	ListNet	SVMMAP	GPQ-Avg	GPQ-Bst
Fold1	0.3038	0.3464	0.3423	0.3415	**0.3516**
Fold2	0.4468	0.4499	0.4543	0.4579	**0.4797**
Fold3	**0.4648**	0.4606	0.4618	0.4579	0.4619
Fold4	0.4990	0.5106	**0.5179**	0.5100	0.5138
Fold5	0.4528	0.4611	0.4500	0.4609	**0.4642**
AvgMAP	0.4334	0.4457	0.4453	0.4456	**0.4542**

Table 2 presented the MAP values compared with baseline algorithms. From table 2, we could observe that GPQ-Avg outperformed baseline algorithms and achieved the best MAP value 0.4579 in Fold2. GPQ-Bst achieved the best ranking performance in terms of Fold1, Fold2 and Fold5. On the level of Average MAP value, GPQ-Avg performed better than Rank SVM, SVMMAP and has similar ranking performance to ListNet. Besides, GPQ-Bst achieved the best MAP value over all the algorithms listed in table 2. These experimental results indicated that the proposed algorithm GPQ could improve ranking accuracy.

Figure 2 showed the results of P@K values. From Figure 2, we could observe that GPQ-Bst almost obtained the best Precision over all of the positions. Besides, GPQ-Avg obtained similar ranking performance to ListNet in terms of Precision evaluation metric, and performed better than SVMMAP and Ranking SVM.

Figure 3 presented the evaluation results of NDCG@K over baseline algorithms, from which we observed similar results with respect to Figure 2. GPQ-Bst outperformed others and obtained the best NDCG values from position 1 to position 10. In addition, GPQ-Avg also performed better than all the baseline algorithms, especially at NDCG@3, NDCG@4, NDCG@5 and NDCG@6.

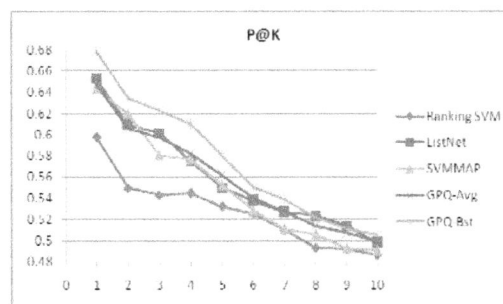

Fig. 2. The Average P@k Curve on OHSUMED dataset

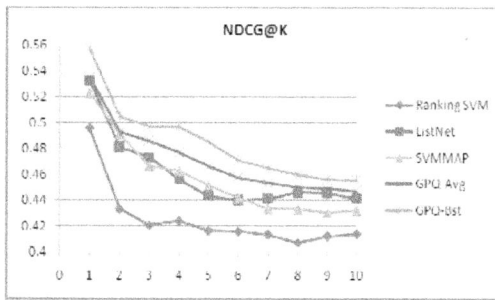

Fig. 3. The Average NDCG@k Curve on OHSUMED dataset

Table 3. The t-test results on OHSUMED in terms of P@K (P@1-P@10)

p-value	Ranking SVM	ListNet	SVMMAP
GPQ-Avg	0. 0002	-0.3978	0.0096
GPQ-Bst	0.0002	0.0016	0.00001

From Table 3, we observed that both of GPQ-Avg and GPQ-Bst significantly improve the ranking performance when compared to Ranking SVM. In terms of compared to ListNet, GPQ-Bst get a significant improvement, however GPQ-Avg didn't perform well. In addition, GPQ-Avg obtained improvements over SVMMAP (p-value=0.0096) and GPQ-Bst also made a significant improvement compared to SVMMAP. Table 4 also gives the similar observation. For the evaluation measure NDCG, both of GPQ-Avg and GPQ-Bst significantly improve the ranking performance when compared to the baseline algorithms.

Table 4. The t-test results on OHSUMED in terms of NDCG@K (NDCG@1-NDCG@10)

p-value	Ranking SVM	ListNet	SVMMAP
GPQ-Avg	<0.00001	0.0005	<0.00001
GPQ-Bst	<0.00001	0.00002	<0.00001

4.3 Experimental Analysis

The experimental results presented in Section 4.2 indicated that the proposed algorithms GPQ could improve the ranking performance, the reasons of this phenomenon contains two aspects at least. One hand is owed to the excellent properties of Genetic Programming. Genetic Programming is a random global search and optimization algorithm. GP algorithm takes the encoded parameters of a ranking model as the operated object, and could break through the limitation of traditional constraints, such as continuity and monotonicity. Besides, GP algorithm only uses objective function to search without other auxiliary information. Another good property is GP algorithm could directly optimize any evaluation measure. On the other hand, the GPQ ranking algorithm employs the novel evaluation metric Q-measure to measure the individual (ranking model). The Q-measure is a graded version of Average Precision which inherits the reliability of Average Precision and the multigrade relevance capability of Average Weighted Precision. Hence employing Genetic Programming to directly optimize Q-measure improved the ranking performance. In addition, the time cost of ranking algorithm GPQ in each iteration mainly comes from the evolution operations and the calculation of fitness. Besides, the population size and the generations are also related to time cost. More individuals and generations generally produce better ranking model. The real search system should consider the relationship between effectiveness and efficiency.

5. Conclusion

In this paper, we proposed a novel ranking algorithm GPQ, in which genetic programming is employed to directly optimize the Q-measure evaluation measure. In GPQ the potential ranking model is corresponded to an individual in GP algorithm and Artificial Neural Network is used to save the ranking model. The evolution operations are performed iteratively. Finally, GPQ generated an individual with the best fitness (the best Q-measure value), and then an excellent ranking model is generated through decoding the individual to the ANN. Experimental results on the OHSUMED dataset indicated that the proposed algorithm GPQ could improve the ranking performance compared to the state-of-the-art ranking algorithms, such as Ranking SVM, ListNet and SVMMAP. Our future work will focus on directly optimizing multiple evaluation metrics using Genetic Programming.

6. ACKNOWLEDGMENTS

This work is partially supported by grant from the Natural Science Foundation of China (No.61277370,61402075), Natural Science Foundation of Liaoning Province, China (No.201202031), State Education Ministry and The Research Fund for the Doctoral Program of Higher Education (No.20090041110002, 201100041110034), and the Fundamental Research Funds for the Central Universities.

7. REFERENCES

[1] Liu, T. Y.: Learning to Rank for Information Retrieval. Foundations and Trends in Information Retrieval. 3(3), 225-331(2009)

[2] Cao, Z., Qin, T., Liu, T., Y.: Learning to rank: from pairwise approach to listwise approach. In: Proceedings of ICML'2007, 129-136, Corvalis, Oregon, USA(2007)

[3] Xia, F., Liu, T., Y., Wang, J.: Listwise approach to learning to rank: theory and algorithm. In: Proceedings of ICML'2008, 1192-1199, Helsinki, Finland,(2008)

[4] Yue, Y., S., Finley, T., Radlinski, F.: A support vector method for optimizing average precision. In: Proceedings of SIGIR'2007, 271-278, Amsterdam, The Netherlands,(2007)

[5] Jen-Yuan, Y., Jung-Yi, L., Hao-Ren, K., Wei-Pang, Y.: Learning to Rank for Information Retrieval Using Genetic Programming. In: SIGIR 2007 workshop: Learning to Rank for Information Retrieval (2007)

[6] Sakai, T.: New Performance Metrics based on Multigrade Relevance: Their Application to Question Answering. In NTCIR-4: (2004)

[7] Sakai, T.: Ranking the NTCIR Systems based on multigrade Relevance. In: Proceedings of ARIS2004, 170-177 (2004)

[8] Qin, T., Liu, T., Y., Xu, J.: LETOR: Benchmark Collection for Research on Learning to Rank for Information Retrieval. In: SIGIR 2007 Workshop on Learning to Rank for Information Retrieval(LR4IR2007), 3-10, Amsterdam, The Netherlands (2007)

Revisiting the Divergence Minimization Feedback Model

Yuanhua Lv
Microsoft Research
Mountain View, CA 94043
yuanhual@microsoft.com

ChengXiang Zhai
University of Illinois at Urbana-Champaign
Urbana, IL 61801
czhai@illinois.edu

ABSTRACT

Pseudo-relevance feedback (PRF) has proven to be an effective strategy for improving retrieval accuracy. In this paper, we revisit a PRF method based on statistical language models, namely the divergence minimization model (DMM). DMM not only has apparently sound theoretical foundation, but also has been shown to satisfy most of the retrieval constraints. However, it turns out to perform surprisingly poorly in many previous experiments. We investigate the cause, and reveal that DMM inappropriately tackles the entropy of the feedback model, which generates highly skewed feedback model. To address this problem, we propose a maximum-entropy divergence minimization model (MEDMM) by introducing an entropy term to regularize DMM. Our experiments on various TREC collections demonstrate that MEDMM not only works much better than DMM, but also outperforms several other state of the art PRF methods, especially on web collections. Moreover, unlike existing PRF models that have to be combined with the original query to perform well, MEDMM can work effectively even without being combined with the original query.

Categories and Subject Descriptors

H.3.3 [**Information Search and Retrieval**]: Relevance feedback; Retrieval models

General Terms

Algorithms, Theory

Keywords

Divergence minimization; maximum entropy; additive smoothing; query language model

1. INTRODUCTION

Pseudo-relevance feedback (PRF) is an important general technique for improving retrieval accuracy in all retrieval models [13, 12, 2, 7, 15, 1, 14, 11, 9, 4, 5, 10, 3]. The basic idea of PRF is to assume that a small number of top-ranked

CIKM'14, November 03 - 07 2014, Shanghai, China.
Copyright 2014 ACM 978-1-4503-2598-1/14/11 ...$15.00.
http://dx.doi.org/10.1145/2661829.2661900.

documents in the initial retrieval results are relevant, and select from these documents related terms to estimate a more accurate query model, which generally leads to improvement of retrieval performance.

In this paper, we revisit an interesting PRF method based on statistical language models, namely the divergence minimization model (DMM) [15]. DMM uses an idea similar to the Rocchio algorithm in the vector space model [13]: it assumes that the feedback model is a language model that is very close to the language model of every document in the pseudo-relevant document set, but far away from the collection language model which can be regarded as an approximation of the non-relevant language model, and then casts the estimation of the feedback model as an optimization problem. DMM is not only apparently theoretically well-justified [15], but also has been shown to successfully satisfy most of the retrieval constraints [3]. However, DMM turns out to perform surprisingly poorly in many experiments (e.g., [9]), as compared with other feedback methods (e.g., the relevance model [7] and the mixture model [15, 14]) that do not satisfy the retrieval heuristics well [3]. In order to understand the cause, we revisit and investigate DMM analytically, and reveal that the major cause is that the objective function of DMM *inappropriately tackles the entropy of the feedback language model*, which generates highly skewed feedback model.

To address this problem, we propose a maximum-entropy divergence minimization model (MEDMM) by introducing an entropy term to regularize DMM. Our experiments on various TREC collections show that MEDMM not only works much better than DMM, but also outperforms other baseline PRF methods, especially on web collections that are noisier. Moreover, unlike existing PRF methods that have to be combined with the original query to perform well, MEDMM alone, without being interpolated with the original query, can already lead to consistently effective performance.

2. DIVERGENCE MINIMIZATION MODEL

Retrieval using language models is often based on the KL-divergence retrieval function [6], where a document language model and a query language model are estimated respectively, and the document is scored based on the negative KL-divergence between the document language model and the query language model. The query language model θ_Q intuitively captures what the user is interested in, and thus would affect retrieval accuracy significantly. Without feedback information, query language models are often estimated by using the MLE method on the original query text:

$p(w|\theta_Q) = \frac{c(w,Q)}{|Q|}$, where $c(w,Q)$ is the count of term w in query Q, and $|Q|$ is the total number of terms in the query.

In the scenario of pseudo-relevance feedback, we assume the top-ranked documents $F = \{d_1 \ldots d_{|F|}\}$ from the initial retrieval are relevant, based on which we can estimate a feedback language model θ_F. It has been widely accepted that the feedback model θ_F has to be interpolated with the original query model θ_Q to perform well [15, 1, 9].

$$p(w|\theta'_Q) = (1 - \alpha) \cdot p(w|\theta_Q) + \alpha \cdot p(w|\theta_F) \quad (1)$$

where α is the interpolation coefficient to control the amount of feedback.

The divergence minimization model (DMM) [15] was proposed for estimating θ_F. DMM uses an idea similar to the Rocchio algorithm in the vector space model [13]: it assumes that the feedback model θ_F is a language model that is very close to the language model of every document in the pseudo-relevant document set F, but far away from the collection language model θ_C which can be regarded as an approximation of the non-relevant language model. Specifically, KL-divergence is used to measure the distance between language models, and the problem of computing θ_F is cast as solving the following optimization problem:

$$\hat{\theta}_F = \arg\min_{\theta_F} \left(\sum_{d \in F} \alpha_d D(\theta_F || \theta_d) - \lambda D(\theta_F || \theta_C) \right) \quad (2)$$

where θ_d is the smoothed language model of feedback document d, $\alpha_d = \frac{1}{|F|}$ assumes uniform contribution of each document d to the feedback model, and λ is a non-negative parameter to force θ_F to be different from the background language model θ_C.

To diagnose the problem of DMM, we re-write the above optimization function (Formula 2) as follows:

$$\arg\min_{\theta_F} \left(\sum_{d \in F} \alpha_d H(\theta_F, \theta_d) - \lambda H(\theta_F, \theta_C) - (1 - \lambda) H(\theta_F) \right) \quad (3)$$

where $H(\theta_F) = -\sum_w p(w|\theta_F) \log p(w|\theta_F)$ is the entropy of θ_F; $H(\theta_F, \theta_d)$ and $H(\theta_F, \theta_C)$ are the cross entropy between θ_F and θ_d and between θ_F and θ_C, respectively.

We can see a term "$-(1 - \lambda)H(\theta_F)$" that captures the entropy of feedback model θ_F in Formula 3, and another term "$-\lambda H(\theta_F, \theta_C)$" that penalizes non-discriminative words:

On the one hand, we should ensure the impact of the entropy term to prevent θ_F from being too skewed as a distribution over words. Previous work has also shown the entropy heuristic is useful to improve the robustness of PRF [5].

On the other hand, we should generally choose a non-negative λ to force θ_F to be different from the background model, and thus penalize non-discriminative words, an IDF-like effect. The effectiveness of the IDF heuristic has also been demonstrated in the literature of PRF [15, 9].

Although DMM naturally incorporates both the entropy term and the IDF term, there is a dilemma: the penalization of non-discriminative words (i.e., increasing λ) will reduce the impact of the entropy term (i.e., decreasing $(1 - \lambda)$), and vice versa. This dilemma appears to be inevitable in DMM because the same parameter λ is shared by the two terms. We hypothesize that it is this dilemma that causes the poor performance of DMM.

3. DIVERGENCE MINIMIZATION MODEL WITH MAXIMUM ENTROPY

One possible way to relax this problem in DMM is to reduce the value of λ without dampening the IDF effect. Note that in the DMM optimization function (Formula 3), θ_d needs to be smoothed to avoid the zero-probability problem. DMM employs the standard smoothing methods using a collection language model θ_C [16]. We argue that, although the smoothing methods using a collection language model, such as the Dirichlet prior smoothing, have been shown to be effective for smoothing document language models in retrieval [16], they may be inappropriate for the estimation of query language models because they tend to introduce too many non-discriminative terms into θ_F. As a result, if we use such smoothing methods, we have to increase the value of λ to remove those non-discriminative terms, and this will further reduce the impact of the entropy term.

To prevent using a large λ, we evaluate smoothing methods that do not rely on the collection language model, and find that the additive smoothing method [8] works effectively. Formally, $p(w|\theta_d) = \frac{c(w,d)+\delta}{|d|+\delta \cdot |V_F|}$, where $c(w,d)$ is the term frequency of w in d, $|d|$ is the length of d, $|V_F|$ is the total number of distinct terms in the feedback document set F, and δ is a parameter that is set to 0.1 which works well in our experiments. As far as we know, our work is the first to study smoothing methods for query language models.

Although the above method may relax the dilemma, it does not solve the dilemma completely, because the weight of the entropy term "$-(1 - \lambda)$" still has a lower bound -1. In order to find a way out of the dilemma, we introduce an additional entropy component "$(1 - \lambda - \beta)H(\theta_F)$" into Formula 3 to further emphasize the entropy term, leading to the following optimization problem:

$$\arg\min_{\theta_F} \left(\sum_{d \in F} \alpha_d H(\theta_F, \theta_d) - \lambda H(\theta_F, \theta_C) - \beta H(\theta_F) \right) \quad (4)$$

Now, we can see that the dilemma is solved: the IDF term $H(\theta_F, \theta_C)$ and the entropy term $H(\theta_F)$ have independent parameters λ and β.

In addition, we propose another extension to further improve DMM by weighting feedback documents appropriately. DMM treats each feedback document equally by setting $\alpha = \frac{1}{|F|}$, which may be non-optimal. In fact, appropriately weighting feedback documents has been shown to be useful in PRF [9, 3]. Following the relevance model [7], we set a weight for d based on the posterior of document language model: $\alpha_d = p(\theta_d|Q) = \frac{p(Q|\theta_d)}{\sum_{d' \in F} p(Q|\theta_{d'})}$.

Finally, observing the constraint $\sum_{w \in V} p(w|\theta_F) = 1$, we can use the Lagrange Multiplier approach to solve this optimization problem and the following solution is obtained:

$$p(w|\hat{\theta_{\mathcal{F}}}) \propto \exp\left(\frac{1}{\beta} \sum_{d \in \mathcal{F}} \alpha_d \log p(w|\theta_d) - \frac{\lambda}{\beta} \log p(w|\mathcal{C}) \right) \quad (5)$$

This new feedback model is labeled as **MEDMM**. There are two free parameters:

- λ controls the IDF effect.

- β controls the entropy of the feedback language model.

Method	WT10G		WT2G		Robust04		AP	
	MAP	P@10	MAP	P@10	MAP	P@10	MAP	P@10
MLE	.2058	.3031	.3065	.4560	.2502	.4233	.2539	.4242
DMM	.2025	.2979	.3010	.4580	.2538	.4076	.3025	.4414
RMM	.2111	.3196	.3227	.4800	.2753	**.4426**	.3081	.4414
RM3	.2068	.2979	.2900	.4720	.2633	.4096	.3045	.4576
MEDMM	**.2313**[13]	**.3258**	**.3245**[13]	**.4900**	**.2842**[0123]	.4378	**.3200**[0123]	**.4737**

Table 2: Comparison of "pure" feedback language models without interpolation with the original query (i.e. $\alpha = 1$). Superscripts 0/1/2/3 indicate that the MAP improvement over MLE/DMM/RMM/RM3 is significant at the 0.05 level using the Wilcoxon non-directional test.

	AP	WT10G	Robust04	WT2G
queries	51-150	451-550	301-450 601-700	401-450
#qry(with qrel)	99	97	249	50
#total_qrel	10906	5,931	17,412	2,279
#documents	$165k$	$1692k$	$528k$	$247k$

Table 1: Document set characteristic

4. EXPERIMENTS

4.1 Experiment Setup

We use four TREC collections: WT2G, WT10G, Robust04 and AP, which represent different sizes and genre of text collections. The queries are taken from the title field of the TREC topics. We use the Lemur toolkit to carry out our experiments. For all the datasets, the preprocessing of documents and queries involve Porter's stemming and stopword removal using a standard InQuery stopword list. An overview of the involved query topics, the total number of relevance judgments and the total number of documents in each collection are shown in Table 1.

Following previous work [15, 9], we fix the document language model, and focus on the evaluation of query language models. Specifically, we use a Dirichlet smoothing method [16] to estimate the document language models in all the experiments, where we set the Dirichlet prior to $1,000$. We also fix the two basic parameters of PRF [15, 9], i.e., the number of feedback documents and the number of expansion terms, to their typical values 10 and 50, respectively.

Although there are two free parameters, i.e., λ and β, in MEDMM, our experiments show that their optimal settings appear to be stable across collections (see Figure 1). Therefore, we empirically set $\lambda = 0.1$ and $\beta = 1.2$ for MEDMM in all the following experiments, which works well.

Our baseline methods include (1) the basic MLE query language model without feedback (MLE), as well as 3 standard PRF based query language models: (2) the original divergence minimization model (DMM); (3) the regularized mixture model (RMM) [14], which works robustly and does not need to be interpolated with the original query; and (4) a state-of-the-art PRF query language model, the relevance model 3 (RM3) [1, 9].

Some existing works have also attempted to further extend PRF in language models by incorporating additional evidences (e.g., term proximity [10]), or by using a feature-based method (e.g., [11, 4]) on top of standard PRF methods. Generally, they either depend on the standard PRF methods, or take the standard PRF methods as features. And these methods mainly focus on different feedback evidences that are orthogonal to our work. In this regard, these methods are not involved in our experiments to avoid unnecessary apples-to-oranges comparison.

Method	WT10G			Robust04		
	MAP	P@10	RI	MAP	P@10	RI
MLE	.2058	.3031	-	.2502	.4233	-
DMM	.2186	.3093	.18	.2693	.4357	.21
RM3	.2366	.3247	.01	.2925	.4486	.36
DMM^{ent}	.2350	.3196	.19	.2806	.4369	.39
MEDMM	**.2429**[012]	**.3433**	**.24**	**.2944**[012]	**.4598**	**.43**

Table 3: Comparison of different feedback models. Superscripts 0/1/2 indicate that the MAP improvement over MLE/DMM/RM3 is significant at the 0.05 level using the Wilcoxon non-directional test.

The top-ranked 1000 documents for each run are compared in terms of their mean average precisions (MAP), which also serves as the objective function for parameter training. In addition, we also consider the precision at top-10 documents (P@10), as well as the robustness index (RI) [1].

4.2 Performance Comparison

Above all, we compare the performance of "pure" feedback models without being interpolated with the original query model. The goal is to investigate whether a feedback model is able to capture the "essence" of feedback documents while not drifting away from the query topic; we believe that an ideal feedback model should not rely on the interpolation with the original query to perform well. The comparison is summarized in Table 2, where we set the feedback coefficient $\alpha = 1.0$ (see Formula 1) for all methods (Note that we give priority to DMM by also optimizing its parameter λ), except RMM that does not require α. We first compare MEDMM with RMM, since RMM was purposely designed to work well without being interpolated with the original query. We can see that, MEDMM and RMM both consistently outperform other PRF methods and the MLE baseline, but MEDMM is clearly more effective which outperforms RMM in all except one case. In contrast to MEDMM and RMM, RM3 and DMM often do not improve over MLE, especially on Web collections WT10G and WT2G that are noisier. In summary, we demonstrate that MEDMM can be used to estimate a more accurate and robust feedback language model, relaxing the constraint that a feedback language model has to be interpolated with the original query.

Next, we allow DMM, RM3 and MEDMM to be interpolated with the original query, and the interpolation coefficient is tuned using 2-fold cross-validation, where the query topics are split into even and odd number topics to form the two folds. The performance comparison is reported in Table 3. We can see that MEDMM outperforms not only DMM but also the widely-accepted RM3. We also observe that the improvements of MEDMM over DMM and

---

[1] Given a set of N queries, $RI = \frac{N_p - N_n}{N}$, where N_p / N_n is the number of queries improved/decreased by the feedback method [4].

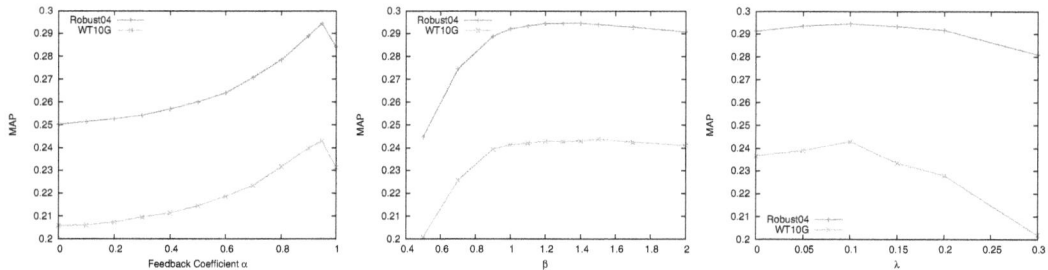

Figure 1: MAP Sensitivity to parameters α (left), β (middle) and λ (right) on Robust04 and WT10.

RM3 are larger on the heterogeneous Web collections (i.e., WT10G and WT2G) than on the homogeneous news collections (i.e., Robust04 and AP) [2], suggesting that MEDMM is more noise-tolerant. Moreover, we find that MEDMM is not only more effective but also more robust across queries than existing methods in terms of RI.

Both Table 2 and 3 show that MEDMM outperforms its original version DMM by 6%-15% in terms of MAP on all collections, confirming empirically that fixing the revealed deficiencies of DMM indeed leads to better PRF models.

One may be interested in how much the newly introduced entropy term contributes to the improvement. To answer this question, we only apply the entropy term to DMM, while excluding other extensions (i.e., additive smoothing and document weighting), which leads to another run, labeled as DMM^{ent}. We also do a similar cross-validation evaluation on DMM^{ent}, and report its performance in Table 3. We can see that DMM^{ent} outperforms DMM clearly in both effectiveness and robustness, suggesting that ensuring the feedback model to have relatively high entropy is desirable, though MEDMM is still more effective than DMM^{ent} thanks to the additive smoothing and document weighting.

Finally, we examine the sensitivity of retrieval performance with respect to different parameters in MEDMM, including α, β and λ (see Formulas 1 and 5). We first fix $\alpha = 0.95$, $\beta = 1.2$ and $\lambda = 0.1$. And when we look into one parameter, we only free that parameter while still fixing the other two. We plot the curves of MAP against each parameter in Figure 1. It demonstrates that all these parameters work stably across collections. The optimal α value is usually close to 1.0, say 0.95, suggesting again that MEFB works well without even being combined with the original query. The optimal β value is usually larger than 1.0, suggesting the additional entropy term is necessary; and the performance decreases quickly when we reduce β to be less than 1.0, confirming empirically that the entropy term in DMM, i.e., $\beta = 1 - \lambda < 1.0$, does not work well. λ works well in a small range around 0.1 for MEDMM, while the optimal λ value in DMM is around 0.3 [15], mainly because that the additive smoothing method does not introduce as much noise as the Dirichlet prior smoothing method in DMM.

5. CONCLUSIONS

We revisited the divergence minimization feedback model, and suggested the hypothesis that the reason why this apparently theoretically well-justified model does not perform well empirically is because it generates highly skewed feedback model. We then proposed to improve it by using an

entropy term, leading to the Maximum Entropy Divergence Minimization Model (MEDMM). Evaluation results on multiple collections show that MEDMM outperforms not only the original divergence minimization model but also several other state of the art feedback models, and that MEDMM can even perform effectively without being combined with the original query, which relaxes the widely-accepted constraint that any feedback model has to be interpolated with the original query. Our work suggests that ensuring a feedback model to have relatively high entropy may be an interesting new constraint applicable to all feedback methods. Further exploration of this new hypothesis would be an interesting future research direction.

6. REFERENCES

[1] N. Abdul-Jaleel, J. Allan, W. B. Croft, F. Diaz, L. Larkey, X. Li, D. Metzler, M. D. Smucker, T. Strohman, H. Turtle, and C. Wade. Umass at trec 2004: Novelty and hard. In *TREC '04*, 2004.

[2] C. Buckley, G. Salton, J. Allan, and A. Singhal. Automatic query expansion using smart: Trec 3. In *TREC '94*, pages 69–80, 1994.

[3] S. Clinchant and E. Gaussier. A theoretical analysis of pseudo-relevance feedback models. In *ICTIR '13*, pages 6–13, 2013.

[4] K. Collins-Thompson. Reducing the risk of query expansion via robust constrained optimization. In *CIKM '09*, pages 837–846, 2009.

[5] J. V. Dillon and K. Collins-Thompson. A unified optimization framework for robust pseudo-relevance feedback algorithms. In *CIKM '10*, pages 1069–1078, 2010.

[6] J. D. Lafferty and C. Zhai. Document language models, query models, and risk minimization for information retrieval. In *SIGIR '01*, pages 111–119, 2001.

[7] V. Lavrenko and W. B. Croft. Relevance-based language models. In *SIGIR '01*, pages 120–127, 2001.

[8] G. J. Lidstone. Note on the general case of the bayes-laplace formula for inductive or a posteriori probabilities. *Transactions of the Faculty of Actuaries*, 8:182–192, 1920.

[9] Y. Lv and C. Zhai. A comparative study of methods for estimating query language models with pseudo feedback. In *CIKM '09*, pages 1895–1898, 2009.

[10] Y. Lv and C. Zhai. Positional relevance model for pseudo-relevance feedback. In *SIGIR '10*, pages 579–586, 2010.

[11] D. Metzler and W. B. Croft. Latent concept expansion using markov random fields. In *SIGIR '07*, pages 311–318, 2007.

[12] S. E. Robertson and K. S. Jones. Relevance weighting of search terms. *JASIS*, 27(3):129–146, 1976.

[13] J. J. Rocchio. Relevance feedback in information retrieval. In *In The SMART Retrieval System: Experiments in Automatic Document Processing*, pages 313–323. Prentice-Hall Inc., 1971.

[14] T. Tao and C. Zhai. Regularized estimation of mixture models for robust pseudo-relevance feedback. In *SIGIR '06*, pages 162–169, 2006.

[15] C. Zhai and J. D. Lafferty. Model-based feedback in the language modeling approach to information retrieval. In *CIKM '01*, pages 403–410, 2001.

[16] C. Zhai and J. D. Lafferty. A study of smoothing methods for language models applied to ad hoc information retrieval. In *SIGIR '01*, pages 334–342, 2001.

---

[2] We do not report the results on two small collections, WT2G and AP, for the space reason.

Vertical-Aware Click Model-Based Effectiveness Metrics

Ilya Markov*[†]
i.markov@uva.nl

Eugene Kharitonov[‡]
kharitonov@yandex-team.ru

Vadim Nikulin[‡]
vnik@yandex-team.ru

Pavel Serdyukov[‡]
pavser@yandex-team.ru

Maarten de Rijke[†]
derijke@uva.nl

Fabio Crestani[§]
fabio.crestani@usi.ch

[†]University of Amsterdam, Amsterdam, The Netherlands
[‡]Yandex, Moscow, Russia
[§]University of Lugano (USI), Lugano, Switzerland

ABSTRACT

Today's web search systems present users with heterogeneous information coming from sources of different types, also known as verticals. Evaluating such systems is an important but complex task, which is still far from being solved. In this paper we examine the hypothesis that the use of models that capture user search behavior on heterogeneous result pages helps to improve the quality of offline metrics. We propose two vertical-aware metrics based on user click models for federated search and evaluate them using query logs of the Yandex search engine. We show that depending on the type of vertical, the proposed metrics have higher correlation with online user behavior than other state-of-the-art techniques.

Categories and Subject Descriptors

H.3.3 [**Information Storage and Retrieval**]: Information Search and Retrieval

Keywords

Click models; evaluation; aggregated search

1. INTRODUCTION

When evaluating a web search system, it is commonly assumed that users are presented with ten result snippets, known as "ten blues links," and that these snippets are examined by users from top to bottom. However, current web search systems go beyond the "ten blue links" paradigm and present users with heterogeneous information coming from multiple search engines, also known as *verticals* (e.g., images, news, maps, etc.). In this case user search behavior deviates significantly from that observed in standard web search [3, 10]. Although the changes in user behavior should be taken into account when evaluating heterogeneous search systems, still little is done in this direction [12].

The quality of web search results can be evaluated in two ways: online or offline. Online evaluation, such as A/B-testing or inter-

---

*Research mainly carried out while at Yandex, Moscow.

leaving, gathers feedback directly from users. The feedback usually includes clicks, page dwell times, mouse movements, etc. The quality of a system is then inferred from these signals. Alternatively, web search can be evaluated offline by gathering manual assessments of the quality of a whole search engine result page (SERP) and/or its parts. These assessments may be used directly or within offline effectiveness metrics. Recently, a mixed evaluation approach was proposed, where offline metrics are built based on models of user search behavior and their parameters are learned from query logs [4]. This way evaluation is done offline, producing instant results. Still, it uses direct user feedback (in the form of clicks), thus considering the preferences of actual users.

In this paper we approach the problem of evaluating heterogeneous web search systems by following the above idea. In particular, we develop click model-based effectiveness metrics that account for the presence of a vertical result on a SERP. The research question we address is the following: *is it possible to improve the quality of offline effectiveness metrics for web search by considering user behavior in the presence of a vertical result?*

The contributions of this paper are twofold. First, we develop two vertical-aware effectiveness metrics based on click models for federated search [3, 10]. Second, we evaluate the proposed metrics using a large query log, considering search sessions with different types of vertical results, namely images, video, locations and news.

2. CLICK MODEL-BASED METRICS

Effectiveness metrics in web search are intended to reflect the way users perceive the quality of search results. Increasingly, metrics tend to rely on models of user behavior. Traditional metrics, such as Precision at k or Average Precision, assume that users are interested in relevant documents and, therefore, focus on topical relevance. In addition to relevance, more advanced metrics, e.g., nDCG [7] and RBP [8], assume that users scan results from top to bottom and so discount the relevance of a document by its rank.

Recently, a number of effectiveness metrics were proposed based on user click models. Such models estimate the probability of a click for each document presented to a user. Model-based effectiveness metrics, in turn, use these estimated probabilities to measure the quality of search results. The Expected Reciprocal Rank metric (ERR) [2] uses a simplified version of the DBN click model [1], where a user scans search results from top to bottom until she finds a relevant document or abandons the search. The Expected Browsing Utility (EBU) [11] is also based on the simplified DBN model but, as opposed to ERR, which uses predefined parameter values, EBU estimates parameters directly from click logs.

Chuklin et al. [4] proposed a general way of converting click models into model-based effectiveness metrics and applied this idea to existing models for web search, such as DBN [1], DCM [6] and UBM [5]. As a result, a set of utility- and effort-based metrics were proposed, all of which showed higher correlation with online experiments than the baseline metrics that are not model-based.

3. VERTICAL-AWARE METRICS

The above metrics were shown to be effective in the standard web search scenario. However, existing offline metrics for web search do not consider the presence of vertical results on a SERP. Recent studies showed that user behavior changes considerably in this case [3, 10]. Several click models capturing these changes were proposed—the Federated Click Model (FCM) [3] and the Vertical-aware Click Model (VCM) [10]—showing higher likelihood and lower perplexity compared to click models for standard web search. However, no corresponding effectiveness metrics were developed. We fill this gap by converting the FCM and VCM models into corresponding model-based offline effectiveness metrics. We hypothesize that these metrics correlate better with online experiments than existing offline metrics when a vertical result is present on a SERP.

Both FCM and VCM extend the Utility Browsing Model (UBM) for web search [5] (although DCM- and DBN-based implementations are also possible). Following [4], UBM can be converted into a utility-based metric, so we focus on such metrics in this paper.

A utility-based metric is defined a follows:

$$uMetric = \sum_{k=1}^{N} P(C_k = 1) \cdot r_k \qquad (1)$$

where N is the number of documents on a result page, $P(C_k = 1)$ is the probability of the k-th document being clicked and r_k is the relevance of the k-th document.

In Eq. (1) the relevance r_k is derived from relevance judgements created offline, while the click probability $P(C_k = 1)$ is calculated based on a user click model. We follow the work on ERR [2] and define the relevance r based on a relevance grade R as follows: $r = (2^R - 1)/2^{R_{max}}$.

According to the UBM click model, a document is clicked if and only if it is examined and attractive:

$$P(C = 1) = P(E = 1)P(A = 1) = \gamma_{kd}\alpha_{uq},$$

where E and A are random variables denoting examination and attractiveness events. In UBM, attractiveness depends on a document u and query q and the examination probability depends on the position of the document and the distance from the last click.

During offline evaluation of web search, clicks are not available, so the distance d from the last-clicked document is not observed. Therefore, this distance has to be marginalized out in order to calculate the final click probabilities. Following [4], $P_{UBM}(C = 1)$ can be defined recursively as follows:

$$P(C_0 = 1) = 1 \qquad (2)$$
$$P(C_k = 1) = \sum_{i=0}^{k-1} P(C_i = 1) \left(\prod_{j=i+1}^{k-1} (1 - \gamma_j(i)\alpha_j) \right) \gamma_k(i)\alpha_k$$

where, for simplicity, $\alpha_k = \alpha_{u_k q}$ and $\gamma_{k(k-i)} = \gamma_k(i)$.

FCM-based Metric.

Studies on user behavior in federated search show that the presence of a vertical result affects examination probabilities of other documents on a SERP [3, 10]. To model this bias, FCM introduces an additional hidden variable F, which indicates whether user behavior changes due to the presence of a vertical result. We will call

it *vertical attractiveness* in this paper. The examination probability in FCM is then modeled as follows:

$$
\begin{aligned}
P(F = 1) &= \phi_{tv} \\
P(E = 1 | F = 0) &= \gamma_{kd} \\
P(E = 1 | F = 1) &= \gamma_{kd} + (1 - \gamma_{kd})\beta_l,
\end{aligned}
$$

where t is a type of a vertical result, v is its position and l is the distance between a vertical and other documents on a SERP, which can be both positive and negative. The total examination probability of the FCM model can be calculated as follows:

$$P_{FCM}(E = 1) = \gamma_{kd} + (1 - \gamma_{kd})\phi_{tv}\beta_l.$$

In order to obtain the click probability $P_{FCM}(C = 1)$, the examination probability $P_{FCM}(E = 1)$ should be plugged into Eq. (2) instead of $P_{UBM}(E = 1) = \gamma_{kd}$. Then, the *uFCM metric* can be constructed by plugging $P_{FCM}(C = 1)$ into Eq. (1).

VCM-based Metric.

Similarly to FCM, VCM assumes that examination probabilities change when an attractive vertical result is present on a SERP ($F = 1$). Additionally, VCM assumes that in this case a user examines the vertical result first and then continues examining other results in either a bottom-up or top-down direction. This is controlled by a hidden variable B. Overall, VCM models the examination probability as follows:

$$
\begin{aligned}
P(F = 1) &= \phi_{tv} \\
P(B = 1 | F = 0) &= 0 \\
P(B = 1 | F = 1) &= \sigma_{tv} \\
P(E = 1 | F = 0) &= \gamma_{kd} \\
P(E = 1 | F = 1) &= \gamma'_{kd}.
\end{aligned}
$$

These equations define three possible examination trails for a SERP: (i) starting from the top document down to the bottom ($F = 0$), (ii) starting from a vertical and then back to the top ($F = 1, B = 1$), and (iii) starting from a vertical down to the bottom ($F = 1, B = 0$). The total examination probability in VCM is the weighted average of examination probabilities over these trails:

$$P_{VCM}(E = 1) = (1 - \phi_{tv})\gamma_{kd} + \phi_{tv}\sigma_{tv}\gamma'_{kd'} + \phi_{tv}(1 - \sigma_{tv})\gamma'_{kd''}$$

where d, d' and d'' are the distances from the last clicked document according to each trail.

The overall examination probability of the VCM model cannot be directly plugged into Eq. (2), because it uses different distances for different trails. Each distance should be marginalized separately by deriving a click probability for each trail. Then the overall click probability of the VCM model can be calculated as follows:

$$
\begin{aligned}
P_{VCM}(C = 1) = {}&(1 - \phi_{tv})P_1(C = 1) + \phi_{tv}\sigma_{tv}P_2(C = 1) \\
&+ \phi_{tv}(1 - \sigma_{tv})P_3(C = 1),
\end{aligned}
$$

where P_i is the click probability for i-th trail. The *uVCM metric* is obtained by plugging $P_{VCM}(C = 1)$ into Equation (1).

4. EVALUATION

4.1 Experimental Setup

In order to evaluate the proposed vertical-aware effectiveness metrics, we collected user search sessions from click logs of a large commercial search engine, namely Yandex. Similarly to [3, 10], we use vertical results of three different types: images and video represent multimedia verticals, news comprises a text-based vertical

Table 1: Summary of user search sessions in training and test sets for different verticals.

	Training sets		
vertical	# queries	# configurations	# sessions
images	21,432	211,717	313,138
video	6,989	70,697	111,417
locations	745	20,532	71,753
news	352	1,407	1,994

	Test sets		
vertical	# queries	# configurations	# sessions
images	21,316	210,622	311,384
video	7,062	60,352	95,489
locations	733	20,378	71,456
news	424	1,516	2,069

Table 2: Weighted correlation between offline and online metrics when a news vertical result is present on a SERP.

	MaxRR	MeanRR	MinRR	UCTR
DCG	0.2390	0.3082	0.3481	0.1794
ERR	0.2562	0.3306	0.3732	0.1864
EBU	0.2588	0.3324	0.3748	0.1967
uDCM	0.2569	0.3304	0.3728	0.1952
uDBN	0.2682	0.3429	0.3856	0.2034
uUBM	0.2669	0.3421	0.3851	0.2012
uFCM	**0.2703**	0.3456	0.3886	**0.2044**
uVCM	0.2702	**0.3459**	**0.3892**	0.2033

Table 3: Weighted correlation between offline and online metrics when an image vertical result is present on a SERP.

	MaxRR	MeanRR	MinRR	UCTR
DCG	0.1979	0.2394	0.2559	0.1526
ERR	0.2170	0.2634	0.2823	0.1554
EBU	0.2110	0.2581	0.2774	0.1551
uDCM	0.2090	0.2563	0.2759	0.1529
uDBN	0.2216	0.2704	0.2905	0.1599
uUBM	0.2184	0.2672	0.2875	0.1566
uFCM	**0.2495**	**0.2973**	**0.3144**	**0.1917**
uVCM	0.2222	0.2713	0.2914	0.1615

and locations represent a vertical with composite results, containing both textual and visual information. We sampled sessions, containing one of these vertical results, during November 2013. The top-10 documents in each session were judged by human assessors using the standard five-grade scale (perfect, excellent, good, fair, and poor). The collected sessions are split based on user ids into training and test sets of roughly the same size (see Table 1). The uneven distribution of the number of sessions between verticals is due to the difference in frequency with which vertical results were triggered in the sampled part of our click logs.

Following [2, 4], we evaluate the quality of the proposed metrics based on their correlation with online metrics, such as UCTR and Max/Mean/MinRR. UCTR is a binary variable showing if there was a click in a session or not (opposite to abandonment). MeanRR is the mean reciprocal rank of clicks in a session, MaxRR is the reciprocal rank of the first click and MinRR is the reciprocal rank of the last click. For the above online metrics only clicks on web results are considered.

Since for the same query a SERP may vary depending on a user, her location, etc., we focus on *configurations* [2], which is a query with a fixed SERP (see Table 1 for statistics). Offline metrics produce the same value for the same configurations, while the values of online metrics are averaged over all sessions with the same configuration. The weighted correlation between offline and online metrics is calculated over all configurations as in [2]:

$$Corr = \frac{\sum_{c=1}^{N} n_c (m_1(c) - \bar{m}_1)(m_2(c) - \bar{m}_2)}{\sqrt{\sum_{c=1}^{N} n_c (m_1(c) - \bar{m}_1)^2} \sqrt{\sum_{c=1}^{N} n_c (m_2(c) - \bar{m}_2)^2}},$$

where N is the total number of configurations, n_c is the number of occurrences of the configuration c, $m_i(c)$ is the value of the metric m_i for the configuration c and $\bar{m}_i$ is the mean value of m_i.

We compare our vertical-aware metrics against two types of baseline: (i) static offline metrics where parameters are fixed (DCG and ERR), and (ii) click model-based metrics for web search, where parameters are learned from click logs (EBU, uDCM, uDBN and uUBM). When learning model parameters, the attractiveness probability $P(A = 1)$ (and the satisfaction probability $P(S = 1)$ for DBN) is assumed to be dependent only on the relevance grade of a document given a query as in [4].

4.2 Results and Discussion

The weighted correlation between offline and online metrics for different types of vertical results is shown in Tables 2–5, the best

values are given in bold. Table 2 presents results for the news vertical. News snippets contain mainly text and are, therefore, similar to standard web snippets. Due to this, most offline metrics (apart from DCG) have similar correlation with online metrics. Still, the proposed vertical-aware metrics, uFCM and uVCM, are slightly superior to others.

Tables 3 and 4 present results for multimedia verticals, namely images and video. In both cases, uFCM achieves much higher correlation values with all online metrics than the baselines. This result is intuitive considering that user behavior was reported to change considerably when a visually attractive vertical result (e.g., an image) is present on a SERP [3, 10]. The FCM model captures such changes, which, in turn, results in higher correlation values between uFCM and online metrics.

The uVCM metric is the second best among model-based metrics in terms of correlation values with online experiments, but it does not correlate as well as uFCM. This can be explained as follows. The FCM and VCM click models both use the vertical attractiveness parameter ϕ_{tv}, which shows how much user behavior deviates from the standard web search scenario when a vertical result of type t is shown at rank v. The lower the value of ϕ_{tv}, the closer a vertical-aware model is to the underlying UBM model. After training FCM and VCM for the image and video verticals, we observed that FCM estimated ϕ_{tv} to be relatively high, which means that FCM deviates considerably from UBM; in contrast, VCM estimated ϕ_{tv} to be quite low, thus being close to UBM. Indeed, Tables 3 and 4 show that the correlation of uVCM with online metrics is somewhat close to that of uUBM.

Table 5 presents results for the location vertical, which consists of both textual and visual information. Interestingly, DCG has the highest correlation with RR-based online metrics, followed by uDCM (which has the highest correlation with UCTR) and EBU. In order to get insights into these results, we conducted an A/B-testing

Table 4: Weighted correlation between offline and online metrics when a video vertical result is present on a SERP.

	MaxRR	MeanRR	MinRR	UCTR
DCG	0.1850	0.1982	0.1960	0.1538
ERR	0.2709	0.2876	0.2849	0.2424
EBU	0.2050	0.2185	0.2157	0.1681
uDCM	0.2037	0.2168	0.2137	0.1668
uDBN	0.2518	0.2663	0.2624	0.2171
uUBM	0.2465	0.2608	0.2568	0.2111
uFCM	**0.3034**	**0.3155**	**0.3074**	**0.2704**
uVCM	0.2611	0.2753	0.2708	0.2259

Table 5: Weighted correlation between offline and online metrics when a location vertical result is present on a SERP.

	MaxRR	MeanRR	MinRR	UCTR
DCG	**0.2107**	**0.2288**	**0.2380**	0.1321
ERR	0.1606	0.1772	0.1858	0.0872
EBU	0.1957	0.2093	0.2147	0.1372
uDCM	0.1966	0.2103	0.2158	**0.1379**
uDBN	0.1887	0.2046	0.2122	0.1175
uUBM	0.1887	0.2052	0.2134	0.1163
uFCM	0.1804	0.1949	0.2014	0.1156
uVCM	0.1816	0.1983	0.2067	0.1105

experiment on real users of the considered search engine, where the location vertical was suppressed for a period of one week. The experiment showed that the abandonment rate of the control (the vertical result is displayed) was significantly higher than for the treatment (the vertical result is suppressed). There might be two reasons for this: (i) users are satisfied with the information presented on a SERP (address, phone number, working hours, etc.) and leave the search without any click, which is known as good abandonment, or (ii) some users consider web results above the location vertical as a banner (especially for high positions of the vertical) and skip them, which is known as banner blindness. For navigational queries this results in no clicks on a SERP. In both cases, online metrics, like MeanRR and UCTR, do not fully capture the underlying user behavior. Thus, the low correlation of offline metrics in Table 5 cannot be interpreted as a failure. Instead, other means of evaluating the quality of offline metrics must be used (e.g., classifying abandonments into "good" and "bad" as in [9] and calculating correlation only for the latter), which we plan to do as future work.

Overall, our results show several important trends. First, they confirm the findings of previous studies on user behavior in federated search, that is, user behavior depends on the type of a vertical result present on a SERP, where visually attractive verticals, e.g., video, affect this behavior more than text-based ones such as news. Mixed-content verticals, such as the location vertical, trigger more complex user behavior, which requires further investigation.

Second, in answer to the research question posed in Section 1, we showed that, depending on the type of vertical, the proposed vertical-aware click model-based metrics have higher correlation values with online user behavior than other offline metrics for web search. In particular, uFCM has the highest correlation when a visualy attractive vertical, i.e. image or video, is present on a SERP. The uVCM metric, on the other hand, is more conservative, being closer to the underlying UBM model.

5. CONCLUSIONS AND FUTURE WORK

In this paper we approached the problem of offline evaluation for heterogeneous web search environments, where standard web results are augmented with results from vertical search engines. We investigated whether considering user behavior on such federated SERPs helps to improve the quality of offline metrics. To this end, we considered existing click models for federated search, namely FCM and VCM, and converted them into click model-based effectiveness metrics. Experimental results showed that, depending on the type of vertical, the proposed metrics have higher correlation values with online metrics, and especially so when visually attractive vertical results, such as images or video, are present on a SERP.

As future work, we plan to extend the proposed metrics to evaluate not only web results, but a SERP as a whole, including vertical results, sponsored search and other components. We also plan to investigate user behavior when a location vertical result is present on a SERP in more detail. We first need to understand the cause of the high abandonment rate observed in this case and then we plan to learn to distinguish between good and bad abandonments for a more precise evaluation of the quality of offline metrics.

Acknowledgments. The authors would like to thank Eugene Krokhalev and Sergey Protasov for inspiring discussions and technical support. This research was partially funded by grant P2T1P2_152269 of the Swiss National Science Foundation, the European Community's Seventh Framework Programme (FP7/2007-2013) under grant agreements nr 288024 (LiMoSINe) and nr 312827 (VOX-Pol), the Netherlands Organisation for Scientific Research (NWO) under project nrs 727.011.005, 612.001.116, HOR-11-10, 640.006.013, the Center for Creation, Content and Technology (CCCT), the Dutch national program COMMIT, the ESF Research Network Program ELIAS, the Elite Network Shifts project funded by the Royal Dutch Academy of Sciences (KNAW), the Netherlands eScience Center under project number 027.012.105, the Yahoo! Faculty Research and Engagement Program, the Microsoft Research PhD program, and the HPC Fund.

6. REFERENCES

[1] O. Chapelle and Y. Zhang. A dynamic bayesian network click model for web search ranking. In *WWW '09*, pages 1–10, 2009.

[2] O. Chapelle, D. Metzler, Y. Zhang, and P. Grinspan. Expected reciprocal rank for graded relevance. In *CIKM '09*, pages 621–630, 2009.

[3] D. Chen, W. Chen, H. Wang, Z. Chen, and Q. Yang. Beyond ten blue links: enabling user click modeling in federated web search. In *WSDM '12*, pages 463–472, 2012.

[4] A. Chuklin, P. Serdyukov, and M. de Rijke. Click model-based information retrieval metrics. In *SIGIR '13*, pages 493–502, 2013.

[5] G. E. Dupret and B. Piwowarski. A user browsing model to predict search engine click data from past observations. In *SIGIR '08*, pages 331–338, 2008.

[6] F. Guo, C. Liu, and Y. M. Wang. Efficient multiple-click models in web search. In *WSDM '09*, pages 124–131, 2009.

[7] K. Järvelin and J. Kekäläinen. Cumulated gain-based evaluation of IR techniques. *ACM Trans. Information Systems*, 20(4):422–446, 2002.

[8] A. Moffat and J. Zobel. Rank-biased precision for measurement of retrieval effectiveness. *ACM Trans. Information Systems*, 27(1):2:1–2:27, 2008.

[9] Y. Song, X. Shi, R. W. White, and A. Hassan. Context-aware web search abandonment prediction. In *SIGIR '14*, 2014.

[10] C. Wang, Y. Liu, M. Zhang, S. Ma, M. Zheng, J. Qian, and K. Zhang. Incorporating vertical results into search click models. In *SIGIR '13*, pages 503–512, 2013.

[11] E. Yilmaz, M. Shokouhi, N. Craswell, and S. Robertson. Expected browsing utility for web search evaluation. In *CIKM '10*, pages 1561–1564, 2010.

[12] K. Zhou, T. Sakai, M. Lalmas, Z. Dou, and J. M. Jose. Evaluating heterogeneous information access. In *Proc. MUBE workshop*, 2013.

Query Performance Prediction for Aspect Weighting in Search Result Diversification

Ahmet Murat Ozdemiray
Middle East Technical University
Ankara, Turkey
murat.ozdemiray@tubitak.gov.tr

Ismail Sengor Altingovde
Middle East Technical University
Ankara, Turkey
altingovde@ceng.metu.edu.tr

ABSTRACT

Accurate estimation of query aspect weights is an important issue to improve the performance of explicit search result diversification algorithms. For the first time in the literature, we propose using post-retrieval query performance predictors (QPPs) to estimate, for each aspect, the retrieval effectiveness on the candidate document set, and leverage these estimations to set the aspect weights. In addition to utilizing well-known QPPs from the literature, we also introduce three new QPPs that are based on score distributions and hence, can be employed for online query processing in real-life search engines. Our exhaustive experiments reveal that using QPPs for aspect weighting improves almost all state-of-the-art diversification algorithms in comparison to using a uniform weight estimator. Furthermore, the proposed QPPs are comparable or superior to the existing predictors in the context of aspect weighting.

1. INTRODUCTION

A major challenge for search engines is satisfying its users with a few top-ranked query results in a setting where users' search intents are inherently ambiguous or underspecified. To address this problem, a promising solution is diversifying the top-ranked results so that they are both relevant to a given query, but, at the same time, can cover its different aspects.

Approaches for search result diversification are typically categorized as either *implicit* or *explicit* [11]. Given a set of candidate documents initially retrieved for a query, implicit methods aim to discover the possible different query aspects by utilizing the content of these documents. In contrast, explicit diversification methods directly model the query aspects, exploiting manually or automatically assigned query labels in a taxonomy [1], or query reformulations in a search log [11]. In the latter case, aspects weights that can represent the importance [11], popularity [2] or likelihood [1] of each aspect for a given query is of utmost importance to optimize the quality of the final result.

In this paper, we put a new perspective on aspect weighting to improve the performance of explicit search result diversification. The weight to be assigned to an aspect in a diversification method should not only depend on the aspects' intrinsic properties (such as those exemplified above), but it should better reflect the expected retrieval effectiveness of the top-ranked results (in the candidate set) that match to this aspect. We explain the underlying intuition as follows. In a typical explicit diversification framework, the relevance score of candidate documents for each explicit aspect is computed (using some retrieval model); and each aspect contributes *its* highest scoring documents to the final query result, which is typically of size 10 or 20. Thus, given an aspect (regardless of how important or likely it is for a given query), if the candidate documents with the highest matching scores to this aspect are indeed irrelevant, such an aspect cannot help improving the final result quality, and may even degrade it.

In this light, we propose leveraging query performance predictors (QPPs) to estimate the retrieval effectiveness of the query aspects over the candidate documents. To this end, we employ post-retrieval QPPs that are based on score distribution analysis, namely, weighted information gain (WIG) [14], normalized query commitment (NQC) [12] and their variants presented in [8]. The choice of these QPPs is intentional, to satisfy the demanding efficiency requirements of online query processing. As mentioned above, all state-of-the-art explicit diversification algorithms [1, 5, 11, 9] compute the relevance of aspects to candidate documents, and hence, the input to these predictors will be created for free, without any additional cost or effort. To the best of our knowledge, no previous work employs QPPs for weighting query aspects in the context of search result diversification.

As our second contribution, we introduce three new predictors that are again based on the score distribution analysis and hence, directly applicable in aspect weighting scenario. The first one is a simple yet effective QPP that is based on the score ratios. The other two predictors are novel in that their performance estimations are based on a virtual document that yields the best possible relevance score for a given query aspect (in a similar manner to the score normalization technique presented in [9]).

We evaluate the existing and proposed QPPs in the context of aspect weighting using the standard TREC Diversity Task framework. Our experiments include a wide range of explicit diversification methods, namely, IA-Select [1], xQuAD [11] (and its variants proposed in [9]), PM2 [5], and CombSUM, a well known score-based aggregation strategy adapted to diversification problem [9]. Our findings show that, performance based weighting of query aspects consistently improves the result quality for these algorithms. Furthermore, the proposed predictors are superior to the existing QPPs when applied in the context of aspect weighting.

2. QPPs FOR ASPECT WEIGHTING

Let's assume that a given query q retrieves an initial set of N documents, i.e., so-called the candidate set D_q, over a corpus C. The goal of result diversification is constructing a ranking D_q^k of k documents that maximizes both relevance and diversity. In case of the explicit result diversification, it is assumed that there is a set of explicitly identified query aspects (a.k.a., sub-topics, interpretations, sub-queries) denoted as $T = \{q_1, ..., q_m\}$ associated with the original query q. These aspects are usually obtained from external resources, such as a taxonomy or query log.

In most explicit diversification methods (as discussed in the next section), there is an aspect weight component, which may represent the likelihood, popularity or importance of a given aspect q_i for the query q. This aspect weight can be assigned in various ways. For instance, Agrawal et al. employ a classifier trained on the ODP taxonomy to associate categories (as aspects) to the queries along with the class likelihood scores (as weights) [1]. Santos et al. apply three different methods to compute aspect weights, the simplest being the uniform probability assigned as a weight to each aspect [11]. They also suggest weighting methods based on the number of results retrieved by the query aspects from an external collection (e.g., using a search engine) and the local corpora C (in a similar manner to resource selection methods employed in distributed retrieval systems). In their work, the simple uniform estimator is reported to yield the best performing aspect weights, and hence, it is also adopted in the succeeding works by others (like [5, 9]).

In this paper, we propose a novel perspective for aspect weighting that is different from all the aforementioned approaches. Our proposal is based on the observation that the most successful explicit diversification methods (such as [5, 11]) compute and exploit the relevance $rel(d, q_i)$ of each candidate document $d \in D_q$ to each aspect q_i during the diversification process. Furthermore, since the ultimate goal is coming up with a final ranking D_q^k and there may be several aspects of a query, only the highest scoring documents for an aspect can have a chance to be selected into this final ranking. Subsequently, an aspect q_i can improve the quality of the final result only if its top-p documents over the candidate set, $D_{q_i}^p$, is highly relevant to q_i. This suggests that the effectiveness of $D_{q_i}^p$ for the aspect q_i is a natural indicator of the weight that should be assigned to q_i during diversification. Hence, in this paper, we propose using QPPs to assign weights to query aspects in result diversification algorithms.

Since the rankings $D_{q_i}^p$ per aspect are typically computed by the state-of-the-art diversification methods, it is a natural choice to employ post-retrieval QPPs that rely on the score distribution analysis for aspect weighting task. By doing so, we avoid additional costs that may be incurred by the predictors and can satisfy the demanding requirements of online query processing in large-scale search engines. In what follows, we describe these baseline QPPs (in addition to simple uniform estimator) adopted for query aspect weighting. Next, in Section 2.2, we introduce our own QPPs that are again based on score distributions.

2.1 Baseline QPPs for Aspect Weighting

Uniform predictor. This is the straightforward approach employed in several earlier works [5, 11, 9]. For a query with the set of aspects $T = \{q_1, ..., q_m\}$, the aspect weights are computed as $W(q_i) = 1/m$.

Weighted Information Gain (WIG). This predictor is originally proposed to capture the divergence between the mean retrieval score of top ranked documents and that of the entire corpus [14]. To compute WIG, we use Eq. 1 presented in [3]. Note that, $rel(C, q_i)$ represents the relevance score of the corpus C to the aspect q_i, and it further helps to make different aspect weights comparable, i.e., serves as a normalization factor.

$$W(q_i) = \frac{1}{p\sqrt{|q_i|}} \left(avg_{d \in D_{q_i}^p} (rel(d, q_i)) - rel(C, q_i) \right) \quad (1)$$

Normalized Query Commitment (NQC). Shtok et al. propose that the mean retrieval score for the top-ranked results of a query represents the score of a possible misleader (as the result list would include some irrelevant documents besides the relevant ones) [12]. Therefore, NQC computes the standard deviation of the relevance scores over the list $D_{q_i}^p$ and again normalizes the result value by the relevance score of the corpus (Eq. 2).

$$W(q_i) = \frac{\sqrt{\frac{1}{p}\sum_{d \in D_{q_i}^p} (rel(d, q_i) - avg_{d \in D_{q_i}^p}(rel(d, q_i)))^2}}{|rel(C, q_i)|}$$
$$(2)$$

ScoreAvg. Markovits et al. employ a simpler variant of WIG in a data fusion setting [8]. In this variant, called here ScoreAvg, instead of using $rel(C, q_i)$ for normalization as in WIG, the relevance scores $rel(d, q_i)$ are sum normalized to $[0, 1]$ before computing their average.

ScoreDev. This method [8] is a variant of NQC, and applies Eq. 2 without the normalization factor $rel(C, q_i)$. Note that, there are other works [10, 4, 12] that again make use of the standard deviation of the document scores in various ways, and not considered here for the sake of space.

2.2 Proposed QPPs for Aspect Weighting

ScoreRatio. This predictor is motivated by the intuition that as the gap between the scores of the documents in a ranking widens, the likelihood of seeing irrelevant documents also increases. Thus, the ScoreRatio predictor computes the ratio of the scores of the first and last documents in $D_{q_i}^p$.

VScoreAvg. In a recent work, we have shown that explicit diversification algorithms are quite sensitive to techniques that are employed for normalizing the relevance scores between documents and query aspects [9]. Furthermore, we have proposed an effective score normalization technique, so-called Virtual, which we adapt here for the purposes of query performance prediction.

Our virtual-score based predictors differ from the previously described QPPs in the following way. Instead of considering the score of the entire corpus (as a huge single document) for normalization (as in WIG or NQC), we consider a virtual document that can yield the highest possible relevance score for a query aspect q_i on a given corpus. More specifically, for a given aspect q_i, we assume a virtual document d^V that includes each term in the aspect with the frequency of the document length and no other terms, i.e., as if the document is only composed of the query terms. The length of the virtual document is set to the average document length in the corpus. Then, we compute the relevance score of this virtual document d^V to q_i as an upper-bound value, i.e., the score of an imaginary perfect match for this aspect. Assume that for a given q_i, the virtual(-normalized) scores for each d in $D_{q_i}^p$ are defined as follows:

$$rel_{Virtual}(d, q_i) = \frac{rel(d, q_i)}{rel(d^V, q_i)} \quad (3)$$

Then, VScoreAvg predictor computes the weight of an aspect q_i as shown in Eq. 4

$$W(q_i) = \frac{1}{k} \sum_{d \in D_q^k} rel_{Virtual}(d, q_i) \quad (4)$$

VScoreFirst. Inspired from the earlier approaches that use highest retrieval score as an indicator of the query performance [13], for each aspect q_i, we use the virtual score of the top-ranked document in $D_{q_i}^p$.

3. EXPERIMENTAL EVALUATION

3.1 Dataset, query topics and initial retrieval

Dataset. We use the standard framework of TREC Diversity Task. In particular, we employ ClueWeb09 collection Part-B that includes around 50 million English web documents. We report our results for TREC 2010 topic set that includes 48 query topics. For each topic, a number of aspects (up to 8) are described and the relevance judgments are provided at the aspect (sub-topic) level. In the experiments, following the common practice in previous works [5, 11], we use the "query" field of the topic as the initial query and generate aspects using the official sub-topic descriptions.

Initial retrieval model. For each query, we first retrieve top-N candidate documents, D_q, and then run the diversification methods to obtain the final top-k results, D_q^k. For the initial retrieval, we use our homemade IR system with the well-known Okapi BM25 metric. In our experiments, we set $N = 100$ and $k = 20$.

We also apply spam filtering by utilizing the publicly available Waterloo Spam Rankings[1] that assigns a spam percentile score to each document in the ClueWeb09 collection. During the initial retrieval, the documents with a spam score less than 60 are eliminated from the candidate set.

3.2 Explicit diversification methods

In this paper, we employ various explicit diversification methods that can be broadly categorized as greedy approaches and aggregation-based approaches. While outlining these methods we conform to their original descriptions that are typically based on a probabilistic mixture model, where $P(d|q)$ ($P(d|q_i)$) represents the likelihood of a document for a given query (aspect), respectively; and $P(q_i|q)$ corresponds to the aspect weight. In our experiments, for the former probability, we employ $rel(d, q)$ and $rel(d, q_i)$ scores that are computed by BM25 retrieval model, after normalizing them with one of the techniques discussed later in this section. For the latter probability, aspect weight, we use the baseline and proposed QPP strategies described in the previous section. While doing so, the weights computed for the aspects of a query are sum normalized to [0, 1] so that they can replace $P(q_i|q)$ in the following methods.

[1] http://plg.uwaterloo.ca/~gvcormac/clueweb09spam/

Greedy methods. These methods run in rounds. In each iteration, they score the documents in D_q and select the document d with the highest score into D_q^k. They differ in the scoring function used in the latter stage.

Intent Aware (IA)-select. This method aims to choose the document with the highest probability of satisfying the user given that all previously selected ones fail to do so [1]. The scoring function of IA-Select is as follows:

$$s(d, q) = \sum_{q_i \in T} P(q_i|q)V(d|q, q_i) \prod_{d_j \in D_q^k} (1 - V(d_j|q, q_i)).$$

where $V(d|q, q_i)$ is the likelihood of d satisfying q for the underlying aspect q_i. As in [11], we replace the latter by $P(d|q_i)$, and subsequently, by $rel(d, q_i)$, as discussed above.

xQuAD. The original xQuAD algorithm proposed in [11] has the following scoring function:

$$s(d, q) = (1 - \lambda)P(d|q) + \lambda \sum_{q_i \in T} \left[P(q_i|q)P(d|q_i)P(\bar{D}_q^k|q_i) \right].$$

where λ is the trade-off parameter between the relevance and diversity, and $P(\bar{D}_q^k|q_i)$ denotes the probability of q_i not being satisfied by the documents that are already in D_q^k. Actually, this latter probability captures the novelty and it can be represented as the product of the probabilities of each document in D_q^k for not satisfying q_i:

$$P(\bar{D}_q^k|q_i) = \prod_{d_j \in D_q^k} (1 - P(d_j|q_i)). \quad (5)$$

art_xQuAD and geo_xQuAD. In a recent work, we have identified that the computation shown in Eq. 5 can lead to a problem, i.e., very small numeric values for the novelty part, due to the nature of the multiplication operation [9]. As a remedy, two variants of xQuAD with superior diversification effectiveness have been introduced, namely, art_xQuAD and geo_xQuAD. These variants replace the product operation in Eq. 5 with arithmetic and geometric means of the probability values $(1 - P(d_j|q_i))$, where $d_j \in D_q^k$.

PM2. In PM2 method [5], at a given iteration, first the *winner* aspect q_{i*} is determined by the popularity of the aspect in D_q and number of positions in D_q^k that are allocated to this aspect up to this iteration (i.e., referred to as *quotient score*). Next, for this winner aspect q_{i*}, PM2 selects the document d that maximizes the following score function:

$$s(d, q) = \lambda \times qt[i^*] \times P(d|q_{i*}) + (1 - \lambda) \sum_{i \neq i^*} qt[i]P(d|q_i)$$

where $qt[i]$ is the quotient score. Note that, we incorporate the aspect weights assigned by the QPPs into PM2 by modifying the way $qt[i]$ is computed after each iteration.

Aggregation-based methods. We have recently adapted score and rank(-based) aggregation methods to the diversification problem [9], and found that the most promising method is based on the well-known **CombSUM** [6, 7] approach. This method computes the scores of all candidate documents in a single round as follows:

$$s(d, q) = (1 - \lambda)P(d|q) + \lambda \sum_{q_i \in T} P(q_i|q)P(d|q_i)$$

In our experiments, for all the diversification strategies that employ the trade-off parameter λ, we test all values in [0,1] range with a step size of 0.01, and report the results for the λ values that maximize the α-NDCG@20 scores.

Table 1: Diversification performance (α-NDCG@20) of the algorithms using the aspect weights assigned by the baseline and proposed QPPs. The highest score in each group is bold, the overall winner is underlined.

Diversification method	Relevance norm.	Uniform	Baseline QPPs				Proposed QPPs		
			WIG	NQC	ScoreAvg	ScoreDev	VScoreFirst	VScoreAvg	ScoreRatio
IA-Select	MinMax	0.3386	0.3291	0.3430	0.3452	**0.3543**	0.3400	0.3385	**0.3442**
	Sum	0.3568	**0.3490**	0.3350	0.3447	0.3488	0.3574	0.3565	**0.3682**
	Virtual	**0.3660**	0.3568	0.3464	0.3555	0.3485	0.3633	0.3632	**0.3636**
xQuAD	MinMax	0.3386	0.3308	0.3430	0.3452	**0.3543**	0.3400	0.3385	**0.3442**
	Sum	0.3664	**0.3681**	0.3440	0.3546	0.3586	0.3655	0.3711	**0.3804**
	Virtual	**0.3660**	0.3568	0.3464	0.3555	0.3485	0.3633	0.3632	**0.3636**
art_xQuAD	MinMax	0.3751	0.3755	0.3717	0.3671	**0.3810**	**0.3818**	0.3777	0.3716
	Sum	0.3612	**0.3622**	0.3417	0.3519	0.3525	0.3579	0.3645	**0.3758**
	Virtual	**0.3892**	0.3802	0.3670	0.3753	0.3808	0.3858	**0.3878**	0.3805
geo_xQuAD	MinMax	0.3581	0.3602	0.3523	0.3539	**0.3646**	0.3637	0.3602	0.3594
	Sum	0.3612	**0.3622**	0.3417	0.3519	0.3525	0.3579	0.3645	**0.3758**
	Virtual	**0.3890**	0.3796	0.3671	0.3746	0.3802	0.3863	**0.3886**	0.3798
PM2	MinMax	0.3705	0.3707	0.3645	0.3664	**0.3754**	0.3728	0.3691	0.3664
	Sum	0.3669	**0.3657**	0.3524	0.3578	0.3591	0.3722	0.3732	**0.3755**
	Virtual	0.3756	0.3666	0.3593	0.3588	**0.3726**	0.3776	0.3732	**0.3778**
CombSUM	MinMax	0.3662	0.3674	0.3658	0.3635	**0.3813**	0.3758	0.3728	0.3632
	Sum	0.3613	**0.3610**	0.3410	0.3516	0.3531	0.3580	0.3621	**0.3720**
	Virtual	**0.3811**	0.3747	0.3634	0.3702	**0.3806**	0.3761	**0.3788**	0.3742

Normalization techniques. We employ three alternative techniques, namely MinMax, Sum and Virtual [9], to normalize the relevance scores as generated by BM25, so that these scores can replace the corresponding probabilities in the diversification methods. Our results are reported for all three techniques, as diversification algorithms are shown to be sensitive to the applied normalization [9].

3.3 Experimental Results

We evaluate the baseline and proposed QPPs by incorporating the predicted aspect weights into each of the six diversification algorithms. Note that, for all QPPs, we set the parameter p as 10, i.e., we obtain top-10 documents (out of a candidate set of 100 documents) for each aspect and provide their scores to the performance predictors. Since every query in TREC topic set has more than one aspect and the final ranking has size 20, we believe setting p as 10 would be adequate (as will be justified by the results). We report α-NDCG@20 scores computed with `ndeval` software.

From our results shown in Table 1, we draw the following conclusions: (i) We see that using QPPs for aspect weighting improves almost all the diversification methods (13 out of 18 cases) in comparison to assigning uniform weights to each aspect. The absolute improvements in α-NDCG scores reach up to 1.5%, whereas the relative improvements are up to 4% (e.g., for the **xQuAD** method with Sum normalization). (ii) Considering the baseline predictors, WIG and ScoreDev are the most effective ones. Among the proposed QPPs, the ScoreRatio predictor outperforms the other two. (iii) Comparing baseline predictors to the proposed ones, we observe that the latter are more effective as the ScoreRatio (VScoreAvg) predictor yields higher α-NDCG scores than all the baseline estimators in 10 (11) out of 18 cases, respectively. Overall, the proposed predictors yield the highest α-NDCG scores in 8 cases (covering all algorithms and most normalization techniques), whereas the baseline estimators yield the best effectiveness for a total of 5 cases.

4. CONCLUSION

For the first time in the literature, we used post-retrieval QPPs in the context of aspect weighting in explicit search result diversification. To this end, we introduced three new QPPs that are based on score distributions, as well as using several others from the literature. Through extensive experiments, we showed that predicting the retrieval effectiveness of each individual aspect on the candidate document set is a good indicator of an aspect's contribution to the quality of the final result. As a future work, we plan to combine and utilize multiple QPPs for aspect weighting.

5. REFERENCES

[1] R. Agrawal, S. Gollapudi, A. Halverson, and S. Ieong. Diversifying search results. In *WSDM*, pages 5–14, 2009.
[2] G. Capannini, F. M. Nardini, R. Perego, and F. Silvestri. Efficient diversification of web search results. *PVLDB*, 4(7):451–459, 2011.
[3] D. Carmel and O. Kurland. Query performance prediction for ir. In *SIGIR*, pages 1196–1197, 2012.
[4] R. Cummins, J. M. Jose, and C. O'Riordan. Improved query performance prediction using standard deviation. In *SIGIR*, pages 1089–1090, 2011.
[5] V. Dang and W. B. Croft. Diversity by proportionality: an election-based approach to search result diversification. In *SIGIR*, pages 65–74, 2012.
[6] J. A. Fox and E. Shaw. Combination of multiple sources: The trec-2 interactive track matrix experiment. In *SIGIR*, 1994.
[7] J. H. Lee. Analyses of multiple evidence combination. In *SIGIR*, pages 267–276, 1997.
[8] G. Markovits, A. Shtok, O. Kurland, and D. Carmel. Predicting query performance for fusion-based retrieval. In *CIKM*, pages 813–822, 2012.
[9] A. M. Ozdemiray and I. S. Altingovde. Explicit search result diversification using score and rank aggregation methods. *JASIST*. In press. Extended technical report is available at www.ceng.metu.edu.tr/~altingovde/pubs
[10] J. Pérez-Iglesias and L. Araujo. Standard deviation as a query hardness estimator. In *SPIRE*, pages 207–212, 2010.
[11] R. L. T. Santos, C. Macdonald, and I. Ounis. Exploiting query reformulations for web search result diversification. In *WWW*, pages 881–890, 2010.
[12] A. Shtok, O. Kurland, D. Carmel, F. Raiber, and G. Markovits. Predicting query performance by query-drift estimation. *ACM Trans. Inf. Syst.*, 30(2):11, 2012.
[13] S. Tomlinson. Robust, web and terabyte retrieval with hummingbird searchserver at trec 2004. In *TREC-13*, 2004.
[14] Y. Zhou and W. B. Croft. Query performance prediction in web search environments. In *SIGIR*, pages 543–550, 2007.

Axiomatic Analysis of Cross-Language Information Retrieval

Razieh Rahimi
School of Electrical and
Computer Engineering,
College of Engineering
University of Tehran
Tehran, Iran
r.rahimi@ece.ut.ac.ir

Azadeh Shakery
School of Electrical and
Computer Engineering,
College of Engineering
University of Tehran
Tehran, Iran
shakery@ut.ac.ir

Irwin King
Department of Computer
Science and Engineering
The Chinese University of
Hong Kong
Shatin, N.T., Hong Kong
king@cse.cuhk.edu.hk

ABSTRACT

A major challenge in Cross-Language Information Retrieval (CLIR) is the adoption of translation knowledge in retrieval models, as it affects the term weighting which is known to highly impact the retrieval performance. In this paper, we present an analytical study of using translation knowledge in CLIR. In particular, by adopting axiomatic analysis framework, we formulate the impacts of translation knowledge on document ranking as constraints that any cross-language retrieval model should satisfy. We then consider the state-of-the-art CLIR methods and check whether they satisfy these constraints. Finally, we show through empirical evaluation that violating one of the constraints harms the retrieval performance significantly which calls for further investigation.

Categories and Subject Descriptors

H.3.3 [**Information Search and Retrieval**]: Retrieval Models

Keywords

Cross-Language information retrieval; axiomatic analysis; language modeling framework; structured query

1. INTRODUCTION

Cross-Language Information Retrieval (CLIR) allows users to formulate queries in one language, usually their native language, in order to seek information in another language. Therefore, some sort of translation is needed to cross the language barrier between the query and the documents. Machine-readable bilingual dictionaries do not provide sufficient coverage for CLIR due to out of vocabulary words and neologisms. To compensate this deficiency, CLIR approaches tend to use learned translation probabilities from other translation resources, such as bilingual corpora, to

achieve acceptable performance. Thus, employing word translation probabilities, referred to as a *translation model*, are essential to improve the CLIR performance.

Using translation models in retrieval approaches is one of the major challenges of doing CLIR [14]. This is because translation models impact retrieval heuristics, e.g. *Term Frequency* (TF) and *Document Frequency* (DF), which, in turn, substantially affect the retrieval performance. The impacts of retrieval heuristics on the performance of monolingual retrieval models are studied in [5], where it is referred to as *axiomatic analysis* of retrieval models. In this analysis, the desirable impacts of retrieval heuristics are formulated as constraints that any reasonable retrieval model should satisfy. However, to the best of our knowledge, the impact of translation models on retrieval heuristics in cross-language environments has not been studied yet.

Following the axiomatic analysis, we define specific constraints to regulate the utilization of translation models into cross-language retrieval models. More specifically, we aim to address three questions: **i)** How do constraints on usage of retrieval heuristics in monolingual retrieval models extend to cross-language ones? **ii)** Are there any additional constraints specific to cross-language retrieval models? **iii)** Can we further improve the state-of-the-art CLIR models based on analytical evaluation? We investigate these questions through following contributions:

1. We propose three constraints that a reasonable CLIR model should satisfy. The constraints reveal new issues regarding the adoption of the translation model for weighting terms in CLIR (see Section 3).

2. We investigate the validity of these constraints on the state-of-the-art CLIR models which shows their deficiency when query terms have different numbers of synonymous translations in the language of the documents (see Section 4).

2. BACKGROUND AND RELATED WORK

Background. The goal of CLIR is to score a document D in a collection C with respect to a query Q in another language than that of D. Here, we discuss two CLIR models which seek to optimize the retrieval effectiveness when reliable translation probabilities are available.

PSQ method. The first method is *Probabilistic Structured Queries* (PSQ) [4] in which translation probabilities

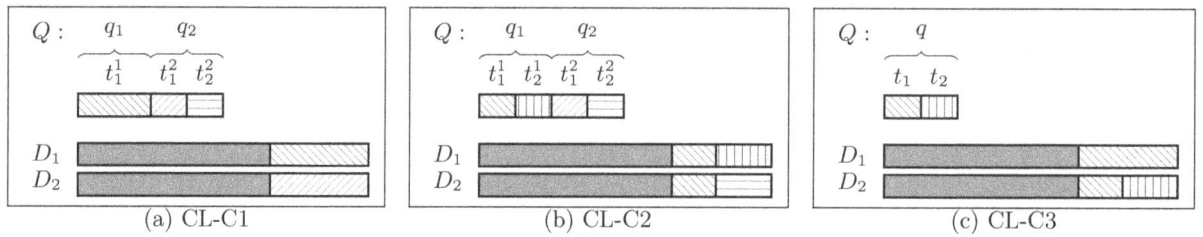

Figure 1: Examples for CLIR constraints.

are considered in TF and DF computations as follows:

$$\text{TF}(q_i, D) = \sum_{w_t \in V_t} p(w_t|q_i)\text{TF}(w_t, D), \quad (1)$$

$$\text{DF}(q_i) = \sum_{w_t \in V_t} p(w_t|q_i)\text{DF}(w_t), \quad (2)$$

where $w_t \in V_t$ is a term belonging to the vocabulary set of the target language (the language of documents), $q_i \in Q$ is a query term, and $p(w_t|q_i)$ is the probability of translating word q_i into word w_t. These TF and DF estimations are then used in BM25 retrieval model to score document D w.r.t. query Q.

LM-based. In this method, the translation model can be integrated into either the query or the document language model [13]. Here, we only mention the *Query Translation* approach because it has been the dominant approach due to its efficiency. In query translation approach, a new language model is built for the query and documents are ranked using:

$$S(Q, D) = \sum_{w_t \in V_t} p(w_t|\theta'_Q) \log p(w_t|\theta_D), \quad (3)$$

$$p(w_t|\theta'_Q) = \sum_{w_s \in V_s} p(w_t|w_s) p(w_s|\theta_Q), \quad (4)$$

where $S(Q, D)$ is the similarity score between query Q and document D, w_s and w_t are source and target words respectively, and $p(w_t|w_s)$ indicates the probability of translating the source word w_s to the target word w_t.

Related work. Axiomatic analysis, introduced by Fang et al. [5, 7], is based on formal constraints that any reasonable retrieval model should satisfy. Several constraints are defined for different factors impacting the retrieval performance, such as term frequency, document frequency, document length [5, 7, 12, 11], semantically related terms [8, 9], feedback information [3], term proximity [16], and evaluation metrics [1, 2]. All these studies focus on investigating monolingual retrieval models.

Although there is a substantial body of research on analytical study of monolingual retrieval models, the corresponding literature on cross-language retrieval models is very thin. Indeed, to the best of our knowledge, the only relevant studies are [10, 7]. But, none of these studies fulfills our goal in this article, which is to define formal constraints specific to any reasonable CLIR model. In particular, [10] adopted the corrected BM25 retrieval model, proposed in [7] for monolingual retrieval through axiomatic analysis, for document ranking in CLIR. The proposed constraints in [9] are to regulate the estimation of relations between words in one language.

3. CONSTRAINTS ON CLIR MODELS

We start our analytic evaluation of CLIR models by defining basic constraints on the use of translation models. Before proceeding to formal constraints, let us define some notations. For a document D and a term x, $|D|$ is the length of D, $c(x, D)$ is the count of x in D, and $\text{DV}(x)$ is the discrimination value of x which can be estimated by a measure like the *inverse document frequency*.

3.1 Constraint on Synonymous Translations

The first constraint targets queries in which query terms have different numbers of translation alternatives in the target language, in particular when query terms are not ambiguous and translation alternatives are synonyms. Figure 1(a) illustrates this constraint, where the goal is to figure out the reasonable relative scores for documents in language l_1 w.r.t. query $Q = \{q_1 q_2\}$ in l_2. Two documents D_1 and D_2 in the figure have equal occurrences of translations of query terms, t_1^1 and t_1^2 respectively. Assume that these translations have the same discrimination value. Considering translation probabilities, $p(t_1^1|q_1) > p(t_1^2|q_2)$, D_1 seems a better match to the query, because it contains t_1^1. However, the lower probability for t_1^2 compared to t_1^1 may be due to the presence of two synonymous translations for q_2 compared to only one translation for q_1. In this case, weighting based on translation probabilities will artificially enhance query terms with fewer synonym translations, which the following constraint intends to avoid.

CL-C1: Let $Q = \{q_1 q_2\}$ be a two-term query. Assume that $p(t_1^1|q_1) = \alpha$, $p(t_1^2|q_2) = \beta$, $p(t_2^2|q_2) = \gamma$, $\alpha > \beta$, $\beta + \gamma > \alpha$, and $\text{DV}(t_1^1) = \text{DV}(t_1^2)$. Also, suppose $|D_1| = |D_2|$, $c(t_1^1, D_1) = c(t_1^2, D_2)$, and other translations of query terms do not occur in these documents. If q_2 is not ambiguous and its translations, t_1^2 and t_2^2, are synonyms or related words, then $S(Q, D_2) > S(Q, D_1)$.

Considering that t_1^2 and t_2^2 are synonyms, we can say that $p(t_1^2|q_2) = \beta + \gamma$ which is greater than $p(t_1^1|q_1)$. Therefore, CL-C1 assigns a higher score to D_2 compared to D_1. The constraint states that $p(t_1^1|q_1) > p(t_1^2|q_2)$ does not necessarily imply that t_1^1 is a more important word than t_1^2 in the translated query. This can happen because q_2 has more synonymous translations in the target language compared to q_1. In this case, it is necessary to consider synonym or related translations of a term.

3.2 Constraints on Translation Coverage

The *TFC3* constraint for monolingual retrieval models implies that "if two documents have the same total occurrences of all query terms and all the query terms have the same term discrimination value, a higher score will be given to the document covering more distinct query terms" [6]. Our goal is to extend this constraint to CLIR models where occurrences of query terms are determined using a translation model.

The second CLIR constraint is about the coverage of translations of distinct query terms. For illustration, con-

Table 1: Performance of CLIR models on selected queries from Ham'08 & Ham'09 CLEF topics.

Method	RUN	MAP (% All)	P@10	R@1000
LM-Based	Mono	0.4548	0.7074	0.8886
	All	0.2292	0.4704	0.6489
	Syn	0.2959* (29.1%)	0.5333	0.7226
PSQ	Mono	0.4422	0.6741	0.8851
	All	0.2513	0.4148	0.6814
	Syn	0.2815 (12.0%)	0.4444	0.7069

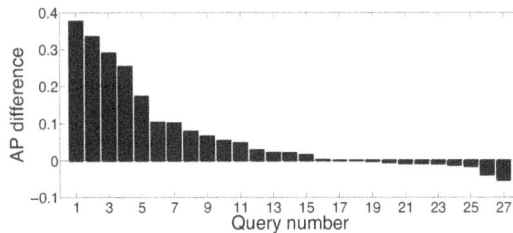

Figure 2: Per query AP difference.

sider the example in Figure 1(b), where t_1^1 and t_2^1 occur in document D_1 with the same total number as the occurrences of t_1^1 and t_2^2 in document D_2. But, D_1 covers only the translations of one query term q_1 while D_2 covers the translations of both query terms q_1 and q_2. Assuming t_1^1 and t_2^2 have the same discrimination value, D_2 should get a higher score since it covers translations of more distinct original query terms.

CL-C2: Let $Q = \{q_1 q_2\}$ be a two-term query. Assume two translations of query terms have the same translation probability and discrimination value, i.e. $p(t_i^1|q_1) = p(t_j^2|q_2)$ and $DV(t_i^1) = DV(t_j^2)$. Also, suppose $|D_1| = |D_2|$. If $c(t_k^1, D_1) = c(t_k^1, D_2)$ where t_k^1 is a translation of q_1 and $k \neq i$, $c(t_i^1, D_1) = c(t_j^2, D_2)$, and other translations of query terms do not occur in these documents, then $S(Q, D_2) > S(Q, D_1)$.

Consider two documents that have the same total occurrences of translations of query terms and the same coverage of different translation alternatives of all query terms. According to CL-C2, the document that covers translations of more distinct original query terms should get a higher score.

The third constraint is about the coverage of different translation alternatives of a query term. As an illustration, consider the example in Figure 1(c). Two documents D_1 and D_2 have the same total occurrences of t_1 and t_2, which are translations of q with equal probabilities. But, D_2 covers two distinct translations of query term q, while D_1 covers only one translation of q. Assuming that t_1 and t_2 have the same discrimination value, D_2 should get a higher score w.r.t. query Q.

CL-C3: Let $Q = \{q\}$ be a query. Assume that two translations of q have the same translation probability, $p(t_1|q) = p(t_2|q)$, and the same discrimination value, $DV(t_1) = DV(t_2)$. Also, suppose $|D_1| = |D_2|$. If $c(t_1, D_1) = c(t_1, D_2) + c(t_2, D_2)$, $c(t_2, D_1) = 0$, $c(t_1, D_2) > 0$, $c(t_2, D_2) > 0$ and other translations of query terms do not occur in these documents, then $S(Q, D_2) > S(Q, D_1)$.

This constraint can be derived based on the concavity of scoring functions (see constraint TFC2 in [6]). CL-C3 is merely a tiebreaker rule when t_1 and t_2 are synonyms. On the other hand, the "one sense per discourse" heuristic suggests that having translations of both meanings of a homonomous query term in the same document would be rare. Therefore, the previous two constraints are more important to be satisfied by a retrieval model compared to this constraint.

4. CONSTRAINT ANALYSIS ON CLIR MODELS

4.1 Constraint on Synonymous Translations

Neither the PSQ nor the LM-based method satisfies CL-C1, because these methods do not consider the effect of different numbers of translation alternatives. In the sequel, we show that not satisfying CL-C1 constraint harms the CLIR performance.

Data sets and experimental setup. Experiments are done using Hamshahri collection consisting of 166,774 documents in Persian with two sets of CLEF topics, 551-600 and 601-650 in Persian and English. Translation model is trained using the GIZA++ toolkit on *TEP*, a sentence-aligned English-Persian parallel corpus extracted from movie subtitles [15]. In both Hamshahri and TEP collections, stopwords are removed, Persian words are normalized by replacing all orthographic variations of letters by one form, and English terms are stemmed using Porter stemmer. We use the title of topics for the evaluation. All experiments are done using the Lemur toolkit. Mean Average Precision (MAP), Precision at top 10 documents (P@10), and Recall at 1000 documents (R@1000) are reported.

Parameter setting. For CLIR using LM-based model, we smooth document language models using *Dirichlet Prior* smoothing and do not tune the smoothing parameter μ which is set to the default value of 1000. For retrieval using the PSQ method, we use parameter values as $k_1 = 1.2$, $b = 0.75$, and $k_3 = 7$ [17].

Impact of synonymous translations. The goal here is to show the importance of how to use word translation probabilities when query terms have different numbers of synonymous translations in the target language. After training using the parallel corpus, we impose a probability threshold of 0.1 to build a translation model. We then ask two volunteers, who are not involved in this work, to manually separate queries in which the query terms have different numbers of synonymous translations in the devised translation model. Twenty seven topics are selected out of 100 CLEF topics. In the following experiments, we want to use these selected topics to study the effectiveness of using all translation alternatives for each query term, where:

1. each translation is weighted according to the devised translation model.

2. we consider the most probable translation with probability one and consider all other translations as instances of the most probable translation.

In item 1, the importance of each translation is determined according to its translation probability in the translation model. This usual strategy of using translation models in CLIR is referred to as *"All"* in the experiments. On the other hand, in item 2, all translations of all query terms are considered as equally important. Runs using this strategy are denoted by *"Syn"*.

Table 1 shows the performance of PSQ and LM-based retrieval models on the selected queries. Also, in Table 1, we report the performance of monolingual retrieval for these queries as a baseline. We achieve substantial improvements in the performance using both CLIR models with the second strategy. Statistical significant differences at the 0.01 level using a two-tailed paired t-test are marked with "*". Figure 2 provides a complete comparison between the effectiveness of using the "Syn" and the "All" strategies by presenting the Average Precision (AP) difference between results obtained using the two strategies for each query in LM-based method. As the figure illustrates, for most queries, the run using the "Syn" strategy outperforms the one using the other strategy.

In the above experiment, our aim is not to show that the second strategy can be a substitution of the first one. Instead, we have shown that when query terms have different numbers of synonymous translations, the usual adoption of the first strategy harms the CLIR performance. We show this by adopting the second strategy in which having different numbers of translation alternatives does not impact the retrieval performance. In conclusion, this experiment shows that we need a systematic way to handle the situation where there are different numbers of synonymous translations.

4.2 Constraint on Translation Coverage

PSQ method. This method scores documents using the BM25 model for monolingual retrieval given new estimations of TF and DF statistics. Thus, we validate the constraints on PSQ method according to the behavior of BM25 model given TF and DF estimated using Eq. (1) and Eq. (2) respectively.

Applying the assumptions of CL-C2 into Eq. (1), one has $\text{TF}(q_1, D_1) + \text{TF}(q_2, D_1) = \text{TF}(q_1, D_2) + \text{TF}(q_2, D_2)$, i.e., two documents have the same total frequencies of query terms. But, document D_2 covers q_1 and q_2 while D_1 covers only q_1. Hence, D_2 covers more distinct query terms. $DF(q_1)$ and $DF(q_2)$ are estimated using Eq. (2) which depends on all translation alternatives for query terms. Therefore, according to the assumptions of CL-C2, we cannot compare $DF(q_1)$ and $DF(q_2)$. But, if $DF(q_1) = DF(q_2)$, then the PSQ method satisfies CL-C2, because the BM25 retrieval model prefers a document covering more distinct query terms in the conditions above [6].

According to the assumptions of CL-C3, one has $\text{TF}(q, D_1) = \text{TF}(q, D_2)$. Thus, D_1 and D_2 get the same score using this method which means that the PSQ method does not satisfy CL-C3.

LM-based method. To score documents using this method, a new language model is built for the query. The similarity score of a document with respect to the new query language model is then calculated similar to monolingual retrieval using the language modeling framework. Therefore, we first estimate the new query language model using Eq. (4). We then validate the constraints on LM-based method. This validation is done according to the behavior of the language modeling framework given the new estimated language model for the query.

Applying the assumptions of CL-C2 into Eq. (4), one has $p(t_i^1|\theta'_Q) = p(t_j^2|\theta'_Q)$. Also, according to the assumptions of CL-C2, $p(t_k^1|\theta_{D_1}) = p(t_k^1|\theta_{D_2})$ and $p(t_i^1|\theta_{D_1}) = p(t_j^2|\theta_{D_2})$. Therefore, the scores of these documents, which are calculated using Eq. (3) as: $S(Q, D_1) = p(t_k^1|\theta'_Q)p(t_k^1|\theta_{D_1}) + p(t_i^1|\theta'_Q)p(t_i^1|\theta_{D_1})$ and $S(Q, D_2) = p(t_k^1|\theta'_Q)p(t_k^1|\theta_{D_2}) + p(t_j^2|\theta'_Q)p(t_j^2|\theta_{D_2})$, are equal. Thus, LM-based model does not satisfy CL-C2.

Applying the assumptions of CL-C3 into Eq. (4), one has $p(t_1|\theta'_Q) = p(t_2|\theta'_Q) > 0$. Also, two documents cover different numbers of terms that have non-zero probabilities in the new query language model, while both documents have the same total occurrences of these terms. Therefore, the language modeling framework prefers document D_2 (according to TFC3 in [6]) and consequently, LM-based model satisfies CL-C3.

5. CONCLUSION AND FUTURE WORK

In this paper, we provide formal representations of the impacts of translation knowledge on retrieval heuristics and, consequently, on the ranking of documents in CLIR. The main motivation of the proposed formalism is the deficiency of existing CLIR models when one can detect and select the appropriate number of translation alternatives for each source word. Our proposed constraints and their empirical effects stimulate further research. A promising direction is to study the effects that violating constraints on translation coverage has on the CLIR performance and to improve the existing CLIR models to satisfy all of the constraints. Indeed, the proposed constraints are focused on basic retrieval heuristics and there are several aspects affecting document ranking that can also be formalized through constraints.

6. ACKNOWLEDGMENTS

The authors would like to thank Dr. Bahman Angoshtari for his helpful comments. The work described in this paper was partially supported by the National Grand Fundamental Research 973 Program of China (No. 2014CB340405), the Research Grants Council of the Hong Kong Special Administrative Region, China (Project No. CUHK 413213), and Microsoft Research Asia Regional Seed Fund in Big Data Research (Grant No. FY13-RES-SPONSOR-036).

7. REFERENCES

[1] E. Amigó, J. Gonzalo, and F. Verdejo. A general evaluation measure for document organization tasks. In *SIGIR*, 2013.

[2] L. Busin and S. Mizzaro. Axiometrics: An axiomatic approach to information retrieval effectiveness metrics. In *ICTIR*, 2013.

[3] S. Clinchant and E. Gaussier. A theoretical analysis of pseudo-relevance feedback models. In *ICTIR*, 2013.

[4] K. Darwish and D. W. Oard. Probabilistic structured query methods. In *SIGIR*, pages 338–344. ACM, 2003.

[5] H. Fang, T. Tao, and C. Zhai. A formal study of information retrieval heuristics. In *SIGIR*, pages 49–56. ACM, 2004.

[6] H. Fang, T. Tao, and C. Zhai. Diagnostic evaluation of information retrieval models. *ACM Trans. Inf. Syst.*, 2011.

[7] H. Fang and C. Zhai. An exploration of axiomatic approaches to information retrieval. In *SIGIR*, pages 480–487. ACM, 2005.

[8] H. Fang and C. Zhai. Semantic term matching in axiomatic approaches to information retrieval. In *SIGIR*, 2006.

[9] M. Karimzadehgan and C. Zhai. Axiomatic analysis of translation language model for information retrieval. In *ECIR*, pages 268–280. Springer-Verlag, 2012.

[10] R. Kern, A. Juffinger, and M. Granitzer. Evaluation of axiomatic approaches to crosslanguage retrieval. In *CLEF*, pages 142–149. Springer-Verlag, 2009.

[11] Y. Lv and C. Zhai. Lower-bounding term frequency normalization. In *CIKM*, pages 7–16. ACM, 2011.

[12] S.-H. Na, I.-S. Kang, and J.-H. Lee. Improving term frequency normalization for multi-topical documents and application to language modeling approaches. In *ECIR*, 2008.

[13] J. Y. Nie. *Cross-Language Information Retrieval*. Synthesis Lectures on Human Language Technologies. Morgan & Claypool Publishers, 2010.

[14] D. W. Oard and A. R. Diekema. Cross-language information retrieval. *Annual Review of Information Science*, 33(2):223–256, June 1998.

[15] M. T. Pilevar, H. Faili, and A. H. Pilevar. TEP: Tehran English-Persian parallel corpus. In *CICLing*, 2011.

[16] T. Tao and C. Zhai. An exploration of proximity measures in information retrieval. In *SIGIR*, pages 295–302. ACM, 2007.

[17] J. Wang and D. W. Oard. Matching meaning for cross-language information retrieval. *Inf. Process. Manage.*, 2012.

How People Use the Web in Large Indoor Spaces

Yongli Ren[1], Martin Tomko[2], Kevin Ong[1], Mark Sanderson[1]
[1]School of Computer Science and Information Technology, RMIT University, Melbourne, Australia
[2]Department of Computing and Information Systems, the University of Melbourne, Melbourne, Australia
yongli.ren@rmit.edu.au, tomkom@unimelb.edu.au, kevin.ong@rmit.edu.au,
mark.sanderson@rmit.edu.au

ABSTRACT

We report a preliminary study of mobile Web behaviour in a large indoor retail space. By analysing a Web log collected over a 1 year period at an inner city shopping mall in Sydney, Australia, we found that 1) around 60% of registered Wi-Fi users actively browse the Internet, and the rest 40% do not, with around 10% of these users using Web search engines. Around 70% of this Web activity in the investigated mall come from frequent visitors; 2) the content that indoor users search for is different from the content they consume while browsing; 3) the popularity of future indoor search queries can be predicted with a simple theoretical model based on past queries treated as a weighted directed graph. The work described in this paper underpins applications such as the prediction of users' information needs, retail recommendation systems, and improving the mobile Web search experience.

Categories and Subject Descriptors

H.3.3 [**Information Search and Retrieval**]: Search process; H.1.2 [**User/Machine Systems**]: [Human factors]

General Terms

Experimentation

Keywords

Indoor mobile Web behaviour, query popularity propagation

1. INTRODUCTION

Large-scale indoor spaces are increasingly equipped with free Internet via Wi-Fi, the use of which can be logged and studied. With such infrastructure in place, it is possible to collect a variety of parameters about user behaviour. These environments are visited on a regular basis by a large number of visitors. For instance, The Mall in Dubai attracted 75 million visitors in 2013 [2]. Tracking the location of users in

time and space along with their Web activity allows for the study of their needs, establishing whether these are appropriately supported by the environments, and exploring how the indoor spaces cope with the presence of diverse visitors; an important consideration in, for example, hospitals [11].

An indoor space imposes a range of social, technical, and physical constraints. While Web query logs have been widely studied, both on desktop machines [9, 5] and on mobile devices [12, 7, 4, 8], there are few published studies that analyse Web search in large-scale indoor spaces. By analysing a log of Web activities of more than 120,000 users in over 1 year period, we study how people behave on the Web in indoor spaces and whether information access trends can be predicted. Such predictions have practical applications, e.g. for predicting consumer behaviour.

In this paper, we address the following questions:

- How do people behave on the Web in large indoor retail spaces? (Section 3)

- What is the indoor Web search behaviour? (Section 4)

- Can the popularity of indoor Web search queries be predicted? (Section 5)

2. DATA ACQUISITION

We study an anonymized dataset of internet accesses taken from a free Wi-Fi network operated by a large inner-city shopping mall. The mall is covered by around 70 Wi-Fi Access Points (AP). The dataset includes three kinds of logs: a Wi-Fi Access-point association Log (AL), a Web Browsing Log (BL) and a Web Query Log (QL), collected between September 2012 and October 2013. Table 1 shows summary statistics of the three logs. For this research, all user identifiable information was replaced by a hash key in an non-invertible way.

Only devices connected to the free Wi-Fi provided by the mall are logged. The logs do not track users but rather mobile devices through the device's Wi-Fi MAC address, which was replaced by a hash key. Thus, there is no ground truth about the identities of the users (e.g. shoppers or mall employees). The term *Users* is used to refer to unique devices appearing in AL, a subset of such users are *browsers* who appear in the BL, and *searchers* are those users who appear in the QL. The BL includes traffic to the Web originating from the mobile Web browser, as well as from other apps. Traffic from apps currently cannot be easily filtered out. The QL was extracted from the BL (it is a subset of BL), by isolating searches pointing to search engines, including Google(110148, 92.4% of QL), Yahoo (6915, 5.8%

Table 1: Summary statistics of the AL, BL and QL.

Wi-Fi Access point Log (AL)			
Number of users:	120,548		
Number of AP association:	907,084		
Number of User Visits:	261,369		
(hour)	Mean	(Max, Min)	SD
Mean duration per visit:	2.77	(21.67, 0.08)	1.52
Duration per visit:	#	%	
(0, <1h)	43,680	16.71%	
(1h, <2h)	14,119	5.4%	
(2h, <3h)	10,589	4.1%	
(3h, <4h)	172,149	65.86%	
(4h, max)	20,832	7.97%	
Web Browsing Log (BL)			
	#	%(AL)	
Number of browsers:	70,196	58.23%	
Number of Web accesses:	18,088,018		
Number of User Visits:	139,004		
	Mean	(Max, Min)	SD
Web accesses per visit:	135	(5393, 1)	209
	#	%	
(0, <50)	58,629	42.18%	
(50, <100)	26,068	18.75%	
(100, <150)	15,956	11.48%	
(150, max)	38,351	27.59%	
Query Log (QL)			
	#	%(AL)	%(BL)
Number of searchers :	11,169	9.27%	15.91%
Number of queries:	119,196		
Number of query sessions:	20,637		
	Mean	(Max, Min)	SD
Mean queries per session:	5.78	(622, 1)	11.00
Queries per session:			
1	6,333	28.3%	
2	4,787	21.4%	
3+	11,255	50.3%	

of QL), Bing (954, 0.8% of QL), Baidu (1086, 0.9% of QL), AOL (43, 0.04% of QL) and ASK (50, 0.04% of QL).

The AL captures information about user physical behaviour through the following parameters: (1) users' location in the mall defined by the location of the Wi-Fi access point associated with the user's mobile device; (2) timestamp and duration of users' association with the access point. The BL includes the users' information behaviour, characterised by: (1) the timestamp of the Web request; (2) the Uniform Resource Locator (URL) of the requested Web page.

The QL was processed as follows: (1) search queries were treated as case insensitive; (2) a query term was defined as any unbroken string of characters in a query delimited by the whitespace symbol (U+0020); (3) Following [7, 4], sessions were defined as "a series of queries by a single user made within a small range of time". Following a recent study in Mobile Web search [12], we also use 30 minutes as the threshold for maximum session duration; (4) session length was defined as the number of queries in a session; (5) query length was defined as the number of terms in a query.

3. PHYSICAL BEHAVIOUR AND WEB INFORMATION BEHAVIOUR

In this study, we analyse the physical behaviour and Web information behaviour for indoor users by dividing them into four groups (number of unique users in brackets): (1) *Open (112,322)* denotes the users who appear during the mall's business hours (when shops are open); (2) *Closed (8,226)* denotes the users who appear when the mall is closed (there

are some restaurants which are still open to the public after the retail part of the mall is closed); (3) *Once (80,900)* denotes the users who appear only once in the collected period when the mall is open; (4) *Many (31,422)* denotes the users who appear more than once in the collected period when the mall is open. We observe that the majority of users come from the *Open* group, and there are more *Once* users than *Many* users. The *Closed* group was not split due to its small size. The majority of this group visited only once. Table 2 shows the comparison of the physical, browsing, and query activities among these user groups.

From AL, we can observe that (Table 1 and Table 2): (1) around 66% of users stay in the mall between three and four hours per visit, with 26% staying less than two hours and 8% exceeding three hours; (2) while *Once* users outnumber *Many* users, *Many* users tend to contribute more to the AL logs than *Once* users, due to their repeated visits to the mall (56.99% of *Many* visited twice, 16.13% of them visited 3 times, and 26.88% visited 4 times or more); (3) *Many* stay in average longer than *Once* users (2.9 hour vs 2.4 hour), while *Closed* users stay longest (3.2 hour). Overall, mall users are most likely to stay in the mall for around 3 hours on average across different user groups.

From the BL, we observe that: (1) around 60% of Wi-Fi users in the AL actively browsed the Web, while the rest visited the mall but did not use the Web; (2) around 60% of these users accessed fewer than 100 URLs; (3) *Many* is the most Web-active user group (around 144 URLs per visit, significantly more than values for groups *Once* and *Closed*); (4) the number of BL logs from *Closed* is fairly low, with users only averaging 13 URLs per visit. Table 3 shows a breakdown of the content these users browse for on the Web. The top-10 popular Web categories of indoor browsing[1]. While some of the top categories are related with retail activities (e.g. *Business and Economy* and *Web Advertisements*), many are related to social networking, infotainment and Personal information management (PIM). These results indicate that frequent visitors tend to be the most active on the Web, where they use diverse, and not only retail related content.

Consequently, we explore what indoor users search for on the Web. Is this content similar to their general search? From the QL, we find that: (1) around 10% of overall users in the AL (16% of browsers in BL) are searchers; (2) there is no big difference for indoor searching among different user groups in terms of the number of queries per session. (3) around 50% of the searchers issued three or more queries per session, which is different from general Web searchers [13]: most general Web searchers issue only one query per session. Potential explanations for these differences include: (a) people search differently in indoor retail spaces; (b) mobile search behaviours have changed since the publication of earlier studies; or (c) the behaviour of the modern interfaces has altered the patterns detectable in the logs (e.g., query suggestion by Google); (4) the top 10 indoor search categories (query-click) (Table 3, right column) are dominated by retail-related activities, e.g. *Travel*, *Shopping*,

---

[1]The Web page categories were generated through the public Webroot Content Classification Service *bcws.brightcloud. com*. Although DMOZ has higher accuracy, its coverage is to limited for our study. E.g. *www.gumtree.com.au* is not categorized in DMOZ but correctly categorized as *shopping* by *BrightCloud*.

Table 2: Physical and Web activities by user group

| Log | statistics | Open | | Closed |
		Once	Many	
AL	No. of AP association	257,444	530,028	119,612
	% of AP association	28.4%	58.4%	13.2%
	mean duration (hour)	2.4	2.9	3.2
BL	No. of Web accesses	4,202,073	12,738,140	1,147,805
	% of Web accesses	23.2%	70.4%	6.3%
	mean Web access	47.4	143.7	13.0
QL	No. of Queries	29,802	83,997	5,397
	% of Queries	25%	70.5%	4.5%
	mean queries per session	5.50	5.87	5.85

Table 3: Top 10 Categories of Browsing and Query-Click

Browsing	Query-Click
Social Networking (20%)	Travel (12%)
Content Delivery Networks (13%)	Entertainment and Arts (9%)
Computer and Internet Info (12%)	Society (8%)
Search Engines (11%)	News and Media (8%)
Business and Economy (10%)	Shopping (8%)
Personal Storage (5%)	Reference and Research (7%)
Web based email (3%)	Social Networking (6%)
Web Advertisements (3%)	Business and Economy (6%)
News and Media (3%)	Personal Sites and Blogs (4%)
Internet Portals (2%)	Computer and Internet Info (4%)

Reference and Research and *Business and Economy*; (5) the search patterns of indoor users are different from their browsing activity, e.g. while *Social Networking* is the most popular browsing category (consistently with mobile Internet usage [3]); *Travel* is the most popular query-click category. Specifically, *Travel* makes 1.4% of browsing but 12% of searching and *Social Networking* takes 20% in browsing but only 6% in searching.

These differences imply that indoor browsing and searching should be treated differently to improve users' Web experience, because users are likely to satisfy different information needs via browsing and searching, respectively. For example, top browsing activities tend to be retail irrelevant, and may be accessed to satisfy common information needs not directly linked to the retail environment; while top search activities tend to be linked to retail, which may indicate tighter dependence on the spatial context of the retail environment. The role of specialised apps is also likely contributing to the difference in browsing vs. query traffic – users are more likely to use pre-installed specialised apps (e.g., Facebook) for social interaction rather than using the mobile version of the sites, and in any case the related Websites represent known target that need not be searched for. Moreover, while adult-related search was popular in general mobile search [12, 7, 4], it is not popular in both indoor browsing and searching. We suspect one main reason is because the data were collected in a public indoor retail space.

Overall, we conclude that indoor users of the *Many* category tend to be much more active in the Web browsing. What indoor users browse for is different from what they search for. The Web categories of the searching activity are more related with the retail environment. Moreover, while the user groups differ in the number of URLs per visit in their Web browsing patterns (for a deeper analysis of BL, see [10].), the difference is small in the average number of search queries per session. We focus on the analysis of QL in the following Section 4.

Table 4: The session length l, $mean(l)$ and $|q|$ of indoor Web queries, general mobile Web queries and general Web queries. "-" means that the value was not listed in the corresponding paper.

| l | Indoor | General Mobile | | | General Web Search | |
		Bing	Google	Euro	Dogpile06	Dogpile05
1	**28.3%**	-	68.0%	45.0%	52.8%	53.9%
2	21.4%	-	19.0%	17.0%	17.2%	16.6%
3+	50.3%	-	13.0%	38.0%	30.0%	29.4%
$mean(l)$	5.78	1.48	1.6	5.78	-	2.85
$|q|$	2.79	3.05	2.3	2.06	2.83	2.79

4. INDOOR WEB SEARCH BEHAVIOUR

In this section, we investigate Web search session length l and query length $|q|$, which are two of the fundamental characterics in Web search [1]. Table 4 shows the comparison of l, $mean(l)$ and $|q|$ among indoor queries, general mobile Web queries and general Web queries. We compare to past work on: Bing [12], Google Mobile [7], Euro Mobile [4], Dogpile '06 & '05 [5, 9]. These studies are selected because they study general mobile Web search or they define sessions in a similar way to our study. We observe that users tend to issue more queries than general mobile searchers and general Web searchers, but type queries in a similar way. The difference in query numbers again points to our hypothesis above, pointing to the recent introduction of query suggestion mechanisms in search engine interfaces. Overall, these statistics differ significantly for indoor queries from general mobile Web queries and general Web queries. Specifically, in the distribution of l amongst indoor searchers, this user group has the lowest percentage of single query sessions, with the majority of indoor searchers submitting more than one query per session. We further focus on the regular patterns of the session length l for indoor searchers in Section 5.

5. INDOOR WEB SEARCH PATTERNS

We investigate the predictability of popular queries in indoor retail spaces, which has practical implications for the prediction of consumer behaviour.

5.1 Search Patterns

We first determine if the number of queries per session follows a two-parameter Inverse Gaussian (IG) distribution:

$$p(l) = IG(l; \mu, \lambda) = \left[\frac{\lambda}{2\pi l^3}\right]^{\frac{1}{2}} \exp \frac{-\lambda(l-\mu)^2}{2\mu^2 l}, \quad (1)$$

where $\mu = E(l) = \frac{1}{m}\sum_{i=1}^{m} l^i$ denotes the mean (m is the total number of sessions in the log and l^i is the length of i-th session), $\lambda = \frac{\mu^3}{var(l)}$ is the shape parameter, and $var(l)$ denotes the variance of l.

There are two theoretical underpinnings in IG distribution, which makes itself a good model of l: 1) the indoor searching has a longer tail distribution (around half of the searchers submit more than two query per session). Thus, the consequent μ and λ in IG can form a large and long tail; 2) the relatively larger head of the l distribution can be fitted by the asymmetry feature of the IG distribution.

As Aijferuke et. al. [1] pointed out, when the sample size is large, the data can not be satisfactorily fitted using goodness-of-fit techniques, including chi-square χ^2 test and Kolmogorov-

Table 5: PCC r Values (Google and Yahoo are investigated here, because they are the two most popular search engines on mobile devices in 2012 and 2013 *netmarketshare.com* and they are also the top two search engines in our QL)

methods	All	Closed	Open	Google	Yahoo
$C(q_i)$	0.9280	0.7560	0.9269	0.9211	0.9364

Smirnov test. Following [6], we apply the coefficient of variation R^2 as an indication of the closeness of the fit.

To make a precise measurement of the quality of the theoretical fit, we perform a quantile-quantile analysis and observe that the R^2 value is 0.9597 ($P < 0.001$), which means that the theoretical fit describes almost all of the observed l's variance.

5.2 Predicting Query Behaviour

Here, we apply Eq. 1 to model and predict the popularity of queries in terms of query counts. We treat the collection of queries as a weighted directed graph $G = (Q, E)$, where the nodes $Q = \{q_1, \cdots, q_n\}$ denote the set of queries and weighted, directed arcs $E = \{e_{ij}, \cdots, e_{hk}\}$ connect consecutive queries. If query q_j is issued by a user immediately after query q_i, e_{ij} is defined as $e_{ij} = (q_i, q_j)$. The weight w_{ij} on e_{ij} is defined as the fraction of users who search q_i and then continue to q_j: $w_{ij} = \frac{o_{ij}}{\deg^-(q_i)}$, where o_{ij} is the number of sequential co-occurrences from q_i to q_j, and $\deg^-(q_i)$ is the in-degree of query q_i.

The prediction of the query popularity can then be modelled as the propagation process of query searching on the given graph G. Let N_{l-1}^j denote the number of users who reach q_j after searching $l-1$ queries, then the number of users who reach q_i after searching l queries is defined as: $N_l^i = \delta_l \sum_{j=1}^n w_{ji} N_{l-1}^j$, where $\delta_l = \frac{\int_l^{l+1} IG(\mu, \lambda)}{\int_{l-1}^l IG(\mu, \lambda)}$ and $IG(\mu, \lambda)$ is defined in Eq. 1. δ_l is interpreted as the fraction of users who search more than l queries over users who search more than $l-1$ queries. This propagation process stops when the majority of modelled users stops searching.

The query log was chronologically split $80\% - 20\%$ into continuous *training* and *test* sets, respectively. The *training* set is used to build the graph G, to estimate μ and λ for the Inverse Gaussian distribution, and to initialize N_1^i for all queries. The popularities of queries in the *test* are predicted by the method described above in terms of query counts, and the prediction of the query counts $C(q_i)$ for query q_i is defined as: $C(q_i) = \sum_{k=1}^l N_k^i$. To measure the accuracy of prediction, we apply the Pearson Correlation Coefficient (PCC). As shown in Table 5, the predicted counts fit 4 out of 5 datasets with a r value over 0.90. The fit for the *Closed* subset is relatively low, a possible reason is that the search behaviour of the *Closed* group is less conditioned by the indoor environment (since shops are closed) and their Web search behaviour is therefore more varied and less predictable.

6. CONCLUSION & FUTURE WORK

In this paper, we report the key characteristics of users' physical and Web behaviours in large indoor spaces. This shows an initial understanding of how mall visitors behave on the Web, and provides a chance to improve their Web and shopping experience. We have established that the indoor query behaviour is predictable in terms of query popularity, which has a practical application for the detection of search trends and recommendation services. In future work, we will further characterize and model location-based indoor search behaviour in order to better suggest contextualised results.

Acknowledgement

This research is supported by a Linkage Project grant of the Australian Research Council (LP120200413). We would like to thank Stefano Mizzaro for helpful discussions, and the anonymous reviewers and CIKM shepherd for valuable suggestions.

7. REFERENCES

[1] I. Ajiferuke, D. Wolfram, and F. Famoye. Sample size and informetric model goodness-of-fit outcomes: a search engine log case study. *Journal of Information Science*, 32(3):212–222, June 2006.

[2] S. Algethami. Dubai Mall welcomes more than 200,000 shoppers a day. *Gulfnews*, 2014.

[3] K. Church and N. Oliver. Understanding Mobile Web and Mobile Search Use in Today's Dynamic Mobile Landscape. In *MobileHCI'11*, pages 67–76, 2011.

[4] K. Church, B. Smyth, P. Cotter, and K. Bradley. Mobile information access: A study of emerging search behavior on the mobile Internet. *ACM TWEB*, 1(1), May 2007.

[5] B. J. Jansen, C. C. Ciamacca, and A. Spink. An Analysis of Travel Information Searching on the Web. *Information Technology & Tourism*, 10(2):101–118, June 2008.

[6] S. Joo, D. Wolfram, and S. Song. Nonparametric estimation of search query patterns. In *iConference 2013 Proceedings*, pages 919–924, 2013.

[7] M. Kamvar and S. Baluja. A large scale study of wireless search behavior: Google mobile search. In *CHI*, pages 701–709, 2006.

[8] M. Kamvar, M. Kellar, R. Patel, and Y. Xu. Computers and iphones and mobile phones, oh my!: a logs-based comparison of search users on different devices. In *WWW*, pages 801–810, 2009.

[9] A. Kathuria, B. J. Jansen, C. Hafernik, and A. Spink. Classifying the user intent of web queries using k-means clustering. *Internet Research*, 20(5):563–581, 2010.

[10] Y. Ren, M. Tomko, K. Ong, Y. B. Bai, and M. Sanderson. The Influence of Indoor Spatial Context on User Information Behaviours. In *i-ASC Workshop in conjunction with ECIR 2014*, 2014.

[11] A. J. Ruiz Ruiz, H. Blunck, T. S. Prentow, A. Stisen, and M. B. Kjærgaard. Analysis Methods for Extracting Knowledge from Large-Scale WiFi Monitoring to Inform Building Facility Planning. In *PerCom*, pages 130–138. IEEE, 2014.

[12] Y. Song, H. Ma, H. Wang, and K. Wang. Exploring and Exploiting User Search Behavior on Mobile. In *WWW*, pages 1201–1212, 2013.

[13] A. Spink, D. Wolfram, M. B. Jansen, and T. Saracevic. Searching the Web: The Public and Their Queries. *JASIST*, 53(3):226–234, 2001.

Succinct Queries for
Linking and Tracking News in Social Media

Luchen Tan
School of Computer Science
University of Waterloo, Canada
l8tan@uwaterloo.ca

Charles L. A. Clarke
School of Computer Science
University of Waterloo, Canada
claclark@plg.uwaterloo.ca

ABSTRACT

Given a current news article, we wish to create a succinct query reflecting its content, which may be used to follow the news story over a period of days, or even weeks. In part, the need for succinct queries is occasioned by limitations of commercial social media search engines, which can perform poorly with longer queries. We start by applying established key phrase extraction methods to the article, creating an initial set of candidate query terms. We then generate a series of probe queries, each a subset of these candidate terms, which we apply to search current social media streams. By analyzing the results of these probes, we rank and trim the candidate set to create a succinct query. We present an experimental study of this method based on a collection of news articles taken from March-April 2014, with the resulting succinct queries used to re-query social media one week later.

Categories and Subject Descriptors

H.3.3 [**Information Storage and Retrieval**]: Information Search and Retrieval—*Query formulation*

General Terms

Algorithms, Experimentation

Keywords

Search; News; Social media; Microblogs

1. INTRODUCTION

Starting with a news article, or a similar source document, we wish to find related material in social media, or in a similar target resource. Prior research has approached this *query by document* problem [18] in a variety of ways. As one approach, we might extract key words and phrases from the source document, forming queries from these extracted terms. For example, given the news article "More than 100

CIKM'14, November 3–7, 2014, Shanghai, China.
Copyright 2014 ACM 978-1-4503-2598-1/14/11 ...$15.00.
http://dx.doi.org/10.1145/2661829.2661963 .

Congolese refugees killed in boat accident, Uganda says[1]" we might extract the query "Lake Albert boat accident", which may produce higher precision results than querying with more general terms, such as "Uganda" or "Congo".

To query by document across blogs and other media, Yang et al. [18] employ a part-of-speech tagger to identify candidate terms in the source document. They rank these terms using TF-IDF and mutual information, supplementing them with associated terms from Wikipedia. Similarly, Tsagkias et al. [15] explore query-by-document methods for linking news with social media. They employ multiple methods for extracting query terms from the source document, supplementing them with terms extracted from social media posts that explicitly reference the news article. They then separately execute the queries from each method, generating multiple ranked lists and merging them through late fusion.

Unfortunately, this approach can produce large and complex queries. For example, one method employed by Tsagkias et al. simply uses the full document as the query. Perhaps unsurprisingly, using full documents as queries produces the best results of any single method they explore, and it also provides a challenging baseline for evaluating late fusion.

The execution and fusion of multiple large and complex queries may not be feasible to support casual queries to find related material. Even if this process can be justified, re-querying to follow updates to an evolving news story requires the process to be repeated. Moreover, from a practical standpoint, commercial social media search engines may provide poor external support for long queries, requiring this approach to be built into the engine itself.

As an alternative, we present an approach for generating *succinct queries* from a candidate set of extracted terms. These succinct queries (comprising perhaps four or five terms in total) provide a lightweight way to follow the story over hours, days, or even weeks. Starting with the candidate terms, we execute a series of *probe queries* over a sample of contemporaneous social media. By analyzing the results of the probes, and comparing them to the language of the source document, we rank the terms according to their ability to retrieve related material, when used in combination with other terms. While we define our succinct query generation algorithm in general terms, in this short paper we concentrate on implementing each step using straightforward techniques, aiming to demonstrate the viability of probe queries as a method for ranking and trimming extracted terms.

---

[1] http://www.cnn.com/2014/03/24/world/africa/uganda-boat-capsizes-death-toll

```
Input:     Primary source document A
           Secondary source collection β = {B₁, B₂, ...}
Output:    Ranked list of terms Q = {q₁, ..., qₙ}

1) Extract initial candidate term set from A.
        T = {t₁, ..., tₘ}

2) Select subsets of T as probe queries.
        P₁, P₂, ..., where each Pᵢ ⊆ T

3) Apply each probe query to rank documents in β; producing a probe ranking βᵢ corresponding to each Pᵢ.

4) Compute similarities between the source document A and each probe ranking βᵢ.
        sᵢ = similarity(A, βᵢ)

5) Estimate the term ranking that best explains the similarity values.
        Q = {q₁, ..., qₙ}
```

Figure 1: Generating succinct queries. Any prefix of Q may be used as a succinct query.

2. RELATED WORK

The problem of finding additional documents related to a given source document has been a longstanding research topic within the information retrieval community [7,13,16]. Generally these methods assume that the search engine will directly support a "find similar" feature, although Dandan et al. [5] consider the generation of queries for identifying near-duplicate documents by querying against a search engine. In this paper, rather than finding similar documents within a given collection, we create succinct queries to efficiently search across collections and across time.

Other research considers the problem of trimming and re-weighting verbose queries, although without probe queries. Bendersky and Croft [2] train a classifier to recognize key words and phrases in queries consisting of a few sentences, as is typically seen in the topic descriptions from older TREC topics. Bendersky et al. [3] extended this approach to incorporate pseudo-relevance feedback and information derived from external sources. Lease et al. [11] re-weight these terms using simple term features in a learning to rank framework. Xue et al. [17] use conditional random fields to model query subset distributions and select the terms to keep.

Closer to our work, Kumaran and Carvalho [10] analyze term subsets from TREC topic descriptions. They use various query quality features to rank subsets, with some features based on the execution of subsets as probe queries. While we start with full documents and introduce a post-probe analysis step, we intend to expand our work with their ideas, extending them to social media.

Balasubramanian et al. [1] build on the work of Kumaran and Carvalho to improve the performance of longer Web queries, i.e., those with five terms or more. They employ query quality features to predict which term, if any, could be removed to improve the performance of these longer queries. Datta and Varma [6] further extend this work by probing with randomly selected subsets.

Other related work includes methods for term select in pseudo-relevance feedback [4]. Jiang and Allan introduce the notion of necessary and frequent terms [8]. Kumaran and Allan [9] examine interactive query reduction.

3. GENERATING SUCCINCT QUERIES

Figure 1 presents our succinct query generation algorithm. While we express the algorithm in general terms, within this paper the primary source document is a news article taken from a mainstream news source, while the secondary source collection is sample of tweets from a three-day window starting at the date of the news article. This secondary source collection is used to execute probe queries. Tweets for the secondary source collection were gathered through the Twitter Streaming API, which produces a maximum yield of 1% of the total tweet stream. Twitter's search engine cannot be used to execute probe queries, since it restricts the speed at which it accepts queries from a particular user.

Output from the algorithm is a ranked list of query terms intended to find social media content related to the news story. The term ranking is intended to reflect the expected value of the terms for this purpose. For the experiments reported in this paper, we form a succinct query from the top five terms of Q, which are then executed on the main Twitter search service.

Each step of this algorithm could be implemented in numerous ways. In this paper, we explore simple implementations of these steps, with suggestions for future work provided in our concluding discussion. Details appear below.

The algorithm could be further generalized by repeating steps 2-5 multiple times, with the results of each iteration applied to suggest new subsets for probing in the next iteration, and with each iteration improving the estimated ranking. New terms might be extracted from the probe rankings through pseudo-relevance feedback and added to the candidate set. We leave the exploration of these ideas to future work.

3.1 Extracting candidate terms

To extract an initial candidate term set (step 1) we apply standard key phrase extraction methods to the news article. We first use pointwise K-L divergence [12,14]

$$p_t \log(p_t/q_t), \qquad (1)$$

to rank terms appearing in the article's full contents, where p_t is the relative frequency of term t in the article and q_t is the relative frequency of term t in the secondary collection. We take the top-20 terms from this ranking to form a set L, with the choice of 20 terms based on preliminary experiments over a set of pilot news articles. In later steps, we also use L as a simple language model for the news story.

As suggested by the results of Tsagkias et al. [15], the non-stopword terms in the headline H provide a solid baseline query for linking news to social media. For our initial candidate term set we use

$$T = L \cup H. \tag{2}$$

In our experiments, we also use terms from H as a baseline for evaluating our succinct query generation algorithm.

3.2 Selecting probe queries

Given that $|T| \geq 20$, we do not probe with all $2^{|T|}$ subsets. Instead, we probe all pairs from T, which provided reasonable performance in our preliminary experiments. Probing all subsets of size three, four or five terms [10] might also be feasible, especially given that probes queries are executed over a subset of tweets. Random selection of subsets is another possibility [6].

3.3 Executing probes

We execute each probe query P_i over the secondary source collection to produce a ranking β_i corresponding to each probe (step 3). We use the Terrier IR Platform[2] for this purpose. We rank tweets using the PL2 divergence from randomness formula, with the restriction that all probe terms are required to appear in all the retrieved tweets.

Each β_i consists of up to the top-50 documents returned by Terrier, with the choice of 50 documents based on our preliminary experiments. Since retrieved tweets are required to contain all probe terms, some probes produce less than 50 documents. Since we seek material related to the news article, rather than re-tweets and re-postings of the article, we apply near-duplicate detection before computing similarities in the next step. We also assume that tweets containing all terms from the headline merely repeat the original story, and these tweets are removed from the β_i rankings.

3.4 Computing similarities

We analyze the probes by computing the similarity between the source document A and each β_i (step 4):

$$s_i = similarity(A, \beta_i) \tag{3}$$

The computation of this similarity is critical to the performance of the algorithm, and we are actively working on improvements in our ongoing research. For this paper, we compute similarity from two simple matching functions, both based on the un-weighted language model provided by L.

The first of these matching functions $f_1(L - P_i, \beta_i)$ counts matches between terms in $L - P_i$ (i.e., L with the probe terms excluded) and the tweets in β_i taken as a group. It returns the proportion of terms in $L - P_i$ appearing in β_i. The second matching function $f_2(L - P_i, \beta_i)$ compares each individual tweet in β_i to $L - P_i$. The number of matching terms is used to estimate a probability of relevance for each tweet. To compute these probabilities, we derived a

http://terrier.org

	P@5	P@10	P@25	NDCG	ERR
Headline	0.391	0.334	0.287	0.321	0.353
Succinct query	0.594	0.542	0.455	0.495	0.480

Figure 2: Experimental results. All improvements over the baseline are significant (two-sided paired t-test, $p < .01$).

mapping between the number of matching terms and the estimated probability of relevance from the results of our preliminary experiments. These estimates are then summed and divided by $|\beta_i|$ to return an overall precision estimate for β_i. To compute similarity, we take an unweighted linear combination of these two functions:

$$s_i = f_1(L - P_i, \beta_i) + f_2(L - P_i, \beta_i). \tag{4}$$

3.5 Ranking candidate terms

The similarity values $(s_1, s_2, ...)$ essentially represent a system of equations, each parameterized by a pair of probe terms. If we imagine a latent variable associated with each term, our goal is to estimate values for these variables, ranking T according to these values to produce Q. We explored several approaches, which often produced similar rankings.

For this paper, we adopt a pagerank-like algorithm, allowing terms that produce high similarity value across many pairs to be properly recognized. We create a Markov chain with each term in T represented by a state. Transition probabilities are derived from the similarity values associated with each term pair. Let $S(t_x, t_y)$ be the similarity value associated with a term pair $\{t_x, t_y\}$. We set the transition probability to

$$trans(t_x, t_y) = \frac{\delta}{|T|} + \frac{(1 - \delta)S(t_x, t_y)}{\sum_{t \in T} S(t_x, t)}. \tag{5}$$

Following the example of pagerank, δ is a jump or teleportation probability, which we set to 0.01. We then apply the power method to determine the stationary distribution, which ranks the terms in T.

4. EXPERIMENTS

We evaluated our approach using a collection of news articles taken from March and April 2014, with the resulting succinct queries used to re-query social media one week later. As mentioned above, we worked with a set of pilot news articles to conduct preliminary experiments during the development of our succinct query generation algorithm. These articles were not re-used for the experiments reported in this section.

We developed a fresh test set based on news articles linked from Wikipedia's news pages for March-April 2014. We use Wikipedia as a method for selecting articles to provide breadth and to prevent our personal news preferences from unduly influencing the selection. For simplicity, we restrict the selection to articles from six high-quality mainstream news sources: BBC, CNN, Reuters, the Washington Post, the Guardian, and CBC. Together, these sources provide coverage from a variety of perspectives across much of the English-speaking world. For some major events (e.g., MH370 and Crimea) we removed all but one related article to avoid having these events dominate the test set. A few other articles were removed for technical issues (e.g., parsing problems). This process produced a test set of 66 articles.

1885

We applied our succinct query generation algorithm to each of these articles, taking the top-5 terms from Q as our succinct query. As a baseline for comparison, we ranked the terms from article's headline (H) according to their IDF values in β, again taking the top-5 terms. Tsagkias et al. [15] identify the headline terms as providing a solid baseline for our task, outperformed only by a small number of their methods, which were either based on full articles or on substantial external resources. We executed the queries on Twitter's commercial search service, restricted to English-language tweets. If a query produced less than 25 tweets, we removed the lowest ranking term and re-issued the query, ranking new tweets below existing tweets and repeating until 25 tweets were returned.

For each article, the tweets returned from both methods were merged and placed in random order for relevance assessment. The assessor first read the associated article and formulated a brief statement describing material that could be considered relevant up to one week later. The tweets were then judged in terms of this statement. Judgments were binary, relevant or not. Tweets considered to be borderline were judged as not relevant. For this short paper, a single assessor performed all assessments.

Results are shown in Figure 2, which gives average values for several standard effectiveness measures. Although ERR and NDCG are designed for graded relevance values, they adapt naturally to binary values (i.e., two relevance grades). NDCG is computed down to depth 25 and normalized by assuming the collection contains an unlimited number of relevant tweets. All improvements over the baseline are statistically significant ($p < 0.01$) under a two-sided paired t-test. Beyond statistical significance, we would expect these improvements, e.g., more than 50% in precision@5, to be practically significant, i.e., noticeable at the user level.

For the news article used as an example in the introduction ("More than 100 Congolese refugees killed in boat accident, Uganda says") the algorithm produced the ranked query $Q = \{$"albert","boat","lake","accident","capsized"$\}$. As with any query re-weighting method, there were misses as well as hits. For an article on President Obama's new health secretary the query over-emphasizes the departing secretary $Q = \{$"kathleen","sebelius","secretary","obama","obamacare"$\}$, although many tweets were still relevant. In some cases, the generated query merely copied terms from the headline. And, of course, in others the headline outperformed it.

5. CONCLUDING DISCUSSION

In this short paper, we explore probe queries as a method for extracting succinct queries from full documents. We apply our algorithm to the problem of linking mainstream news articles to social media. Our evaluation shows statistically and practically significant improvements over baseline queries derived from the headlines of the news articles.

Our ongoing efforts focus on improvements to the similarity function in Equation 3, which must recognize related material while avoiding near-duplicate material, We are currently adapting ideas from Kumaran and Carvalho [10]. Other directions for future work include dynamic probing and improved methods for subset selection. The integration of pseudo-relevance feedback would allow hashtags to be added to the succinct query, which may be important in a microblogging context. We also plan to extend our evaluation with a broader range of assessments through crowdsourcing.

6. REFERENCES

[1] Niranjan Balasubramanian, Giridhar Kumaran, and Vitor R. Carvalho. Exploring reductions for long Web queries. In *33rd ACM SIGIR*, pages 571–578, 2010.

[2] Michael Bendersky and W. Bruce Croft. Discovering key concepts in verbose queries. In *31st ACM SIGIR*, pages 491–498, 2008.

[3] Michael Bendersky, Donald Metzler, and W. Bruce Croft. Parameterized concept weighting in verbose queries. In *34th ACM SIGIR*, pages 605–614, 2011.

[4] Guihong Cao, Jian-Yun Nie, Jianfeng Gao, and Stephen Robertson. Selecting good expansion terms for pseudo-relevance feedback. In *31st ACM SIGIR*, pages 243–250, 2008.

[5] Ali Dasdan, Paolo D'Alberto, Santanu Kolay, and Chris Drome. Automatic retrieval of similar content using search engine query interface. In *18th ACM CIKM*, pages 701–710, 2009.

[6] Sudip Datta and Vasudeva Varma. Tossing coins to trim long queries. In *34th ACM SIGIR*, pages 1255–1256, 2011.

[7] Jeffrey Dean and Monika R. Henzinger. Finding related pages in the World Wide Web. *Computer Networks*, 31(11–16):1467–1479, May 1999.

[8] Jiepu Jiang and James Allan. Necessary and frequent terms in queries. In *37th ACM SIGIR*, 2014.

[9] Giridhar Kumaran and James Allan. A case for shorter queries, and helping users create them. In *Human Language Technology Conference of the North American Chapter of the Association of Computational Linguistics*, pages 220–227, 2007.

[10] Giridhar Kumaran and Vitor R. Carvalho. Reducing long queries using query quality predictors. In *32nd ACM SIGIR*, pages 564–571, 2009.

[11] Matthew Lease, James Allan, and W. Bruce Croft. Regression rank: Learning to meet the opportunity of descriptive queries. In *31st ECIR*, pages 90–101, 2009.

[12] Juan Martinez-Romo and Lourdes Araujo. Updating broken Web links: An automatic recommendation system. *Information Processing & Management*, 48(2), March 2012.

[13] Mark D. Smucker and James Allan. Find-similar: Similarity browsing as a search tool. In *29th ACM SIGIR*, pages 461–468, 2006.

[14] Takashi Tomokiyo and Matthew Hurst. A language model approach to keyphrase extraction. In *ACL 2003 Workshop on Multiword Expressions: Analysis, Acquisition and Treatment*, pages 33–40, 2003.

[15] Manos Tsagkias, Maarten de Rijke, and Wouter Weerkamp. Linking online news and social media. In *4th ACM WSDM*, pages 565–574, 2011.

[16] W.John Wilbur and Leona Coffee. The effectiveness of document neighboring in search enhancement. *Information Processing & Management*, 30(2), March–April 1994.

[17] Xiaobing Xue, Samuel Huston, and W. Bruce Croft. Improving verbose queries using subset distribution. In *19th ACM CIKM*, pages 1059–1068, 2010.

[18] Yin Yang, Nilesh Bansal, Wisam Dakka, Panagiotis Ipeirotis, Nick Koudas, and Dimitris Papadias. Query by document. In *2nd ACM WSDM*, pages 34–43, 2009.

Exploring Shared Subspace and Joint Sparsity for Canonical Correlation Analysis

Liang Tao[1,2], Horace H. S. Ip[1], Yinglin Wang[3,2] and Xin Shu[4]
[1]Department of Computer Science, City University of Hong Kong
[2]Department of Computer Science and Engineering, Shanghai Jiao Tong University
[3]Department of Computer Science and Technology, Shanghai University of Finance and Economics
[4]College of Information Science and Technology, Nanjing Agricultural University
liang.tao@my.cityu.edu.hk, cship@cityu.edu.hk, wang-yl@cs.sjtu.edu.cn, xinshu@njau.edu.cn

ABSTRACT

Canonical correlation analysis (CCA) has been extensively employed in various real-world applications of multi-label annotation. However, two major challenges are raised by the classical CCA. First, CCA frequently fails to remove noisy and irrelevant features. Second, CCA cannot effectively capture correlations between multiple labels, which are especially beneficial for multi-label learning. In this paper, we propose a novel framework that integrates joint sparsity and low-rank shared subspace into the least-squares formulation of CCA. Under this framework, multiple label interactions can be uncovered by the shared structure of the input features and a few highly discriminative features can be decided via structured sparsity inducing norm. Owing to the inclusion of the non-smooth row sparsity, a new efficient iterative algorithm is derived with proved convergence. The empirical studies on several popular web image and movie data collections consistently deliver the effectiveness of our new formulation in comparison with competing algorithms.

Categories and Subject Descriptors

H.3.3 [**Information Storage and Retrieval**]: Content Analysis and Indexing

General Terms

Algorithms, Experimentation, Performance

Keywords

Canonical correlation, Multi-label, Subspace, Sparsity

1. INTRODUCTION

Multi-label dimensionality reduction (MLDR), manipulating data associated with multiple labels, has gained increasing interest in many potential multimedia applications [3]. One of the promising MLDR methods is the canonical correlation analysis (CCA) [2, 8] that is widely leveraged to maximally measure the similarity between a pair of data sets, i.e., the high dimensional input feature space and the dimensionality-reduced label space. However, there are several inherent limitations of the standard CCA. From the perspective of feature learning [2, 7, 6, 5], there are typically a small number of informative features in the high dimensional original features, but CCA cannot yield the attractive sparse representation. On the other hand, CCA does not effectively take into account the intrinsic interactions [1, 4, 5, 10] among multiple pre-given labels that are quite helpful for multi-label annotations.

Inspired by the equivalence relationship [8, 2] between the least-squares and the generalized eigenvalue problem, we propose a new CCA model by simultaneously incorporating the shared common structure and row sparsity-inducing $\ell_{2,p}$-norm into a unified objective, dubbed shared S̲ubspace and structural S̲parsity CCA (SSCCA$_{2,p}$). Specifically, we employ a row-wise structured sparsity regularizer, shrinking some rows of projection functions to zeros, to identify the essential discriminative features and eliminate the redundant and noisy dimensions for predictive functions; meanwhile, we exploit the shared common structure to encourage the interactions among different labels so as to compensate for the CCA's lack of the label correlation capture in the embedded space. Further, owing to the involvement of the non-smooth row-sparsity term in this unified formulation, we derive an iterative alternating learning paradigm with guaranteed convergence. With the learned predictive classifiers, empirical evaluations are conducted on four public Internet data sets with hundreds of thousands of samples to showcase the competitive advantages of our model for efficient multi-label annotation.

2. THE SSCCA$_{2,p}$ FRAMEWORK

We formulate the problem of the least-squares CCA under a new framework by introducing the structural sparsity-inducing norm and the common subspace shared by different labels. We first briefly review the shared structures that greatly assist the multi-label prediction, then present our new model solved by the efficient alternating iterative optimization in this section. Additionally, we use $X = \{x_1, \cdots, x_n\} \in \mathbb{R}^{d \times n}$ denoting the n data points of dimension d and $L \in \{0,1\}^{n \times c}$ designating the label space such that $L_i^j = 1$ if x_i is grouped into j-th label, and 0 otherwise, where c is the number of labels. Without any loss of generality, we consider both the input data space X and the label space L are normalized to have zero mean.

CIKM'14, November 3–7, 2014, Shanghai, China.
Copyright 2014 ACM 978-1-4503-2598-1/14/11...$15.00.
http://dx.doi.org/10.1145/2661829.2661970.

2.1 Shared subspace and joint sparsity for CCA

Following the supervised learning framework, we aim to learn the projection functions $\{f_Q^j(x)\}_{j=1}^c$ and the low rank discriminative subspace Q from the input training data X by minimizing the below regularized empirical risk:

$$\min_{Q, f_Q^j} \sum_{j=1}^c \Big(\sum_{i=1}^n \mathcal{F}(f_Q^j(x_i), y_i^j) + \lambda \mathcal{G}(f_Q^j) \Big), \quad (1)$$

where y_i^j is a well-defined response variable, $\mathcal{F}(\cdot)$ is a prescribed loss function over the labeled data, the regularizer $\mathcal{G}(\cdot)$ measures the complexity of f_Q^j and the tradeoff regularization parameter λ controls the fitness of predictive functions. In order to capture the common subspace [1, 4] shared among different labels, we can define the predictive classifier

$$f_Q^j(x) = w_j^{\mathrm{T}} x = p_j^{\mathrm{T}} x + r_j^{\mathrm{T}} Q^{\mathrm{T}} x, \quad j = 1, \ldots, c, \quad (2)$$

in which $w_j \in \mathbb{R}^d$ is the weight vector for the predictor, $p_j \in \mathbb{R}^d$ denotes the weight vector minimizing the fitting residue $w_j - Q r_j$, $Q \in \mathbb{R}^{d \times r}$ is a shared subspace matrix for the c predictors and $r_j \in \mathbb{R}^r$ is the weight vector for the low-dimensional embedded shared structure $Q^{\mathrm{T}} x$ that can better elucidate the label dependency [5, 1, 4]. Note that the shared dimensionality r is much smaller than the input space dimensionality d, i.e., $r \ll d$. Importantly, the column orthogonality constraint is subtly imposed on the shared projection operator Q, $Q^{\mathrm{T}} Q = I$, which can be thought of as looking for the principle component of these c predictive functions. To be specific, there are several major advantages of the column orthogonality constraint: first, to preserve as much discriminative information as possible; second, to avoid the arbitrary rotation and to reduce the burden of computation (see Section 2.2 in detail).

Although the shared structure can properly exploit such label dependency, it fully lacks the characteristic of sparsity for the learned classifiers from the viewpoint of sparse feature learning. The sparseness has shown the prominent performance in multimedia understanding [6, 7, 5], especially for the input data with noisy and redundant features. As a result, we investigate the joint structred sparsity-inducing norm $\|\cdot\|_{2,p}$, designating the $\ell_{2,p}$-norm of a matrix, i.e.,

$$\|W\|_{2,p} = \Big(\sum_{i=1}^d (\|W_{i\cdot}\|_2^p) \Big)^{\frac{1}{p}}, \quad (3)$$

in which $p \in (0, 2)$ and $W_{i\cdot}$ represents the ith row of the matrix W. Unlike the ℓ_p regularizer resulting in the entry sparsity, $\ell_{2,p}$-norm (3) is designed to first compute the ℓ_2-norm distance for each decision classifier and then perform ℓ_p-norm over dimensions of c classifiers. Hence the $\ell_{2,p}$-norm shrinks the rows of predictive functions to zero, leading to the row sparsity, and also $\ell_{2,p}$-norm can be interpreted as flexibly select those highly discriminative features associated with those nonzero rows in the predictors $W = [w_1, \cdots, w_c]$. We emphasize that the smaller the value of p, the sparser the predictive classifiers, and so the different degree of sparsity between features can be tuned by the value of p. Typically, $p = 1$ or 0.5 has demonstrated the efficacy in multimedia feature learning [6]. Further, it is worth noting that $\ell_{2,p}$ ($1 > p > 0$) matrix norm is nonconvex and so it should be regarded as pseudo-norm of a matrix, whereas $\ell_{2,1}$-norm is convex. When the value of p increases to 2, the $\ell_{2,p}$-norm

apparently becomes the Frobenius norm of a matrix which does not impose any sparsity in predictors.

We now direct our attention to the design of the empirical loss $\mathcal{F}(\cdot)$ in (1) on the labeled data. We propose to take advantage of CCA as the loss function that substantially differs from the conventional linear regression for the loss function because CCA can maximally leverage the correlation between the instance space and the label space. Nonetheless, the aforementioned two promising constraints: the shared subspace and row sparsity, cannot be straightforwardly introduced into the standard CCA formulation

$$\max_{W_X} \quad W_X^{\mathrm{T}} X L (L^{\mathrm{T}} L)^{-1} L^{\mathrm{T}} X^{\mathrm{T}} W_X \quad (4)$$
$$\text{s.t.} \quad W_X^{\mathrm{T}} X X^{\mathrm{T}} W_X = I_c,$$

where W_X is the projection matrix of CCA with the dimension of $d \times c$ and I_c is a $c \times c$ identity matrix. Owing to the inherent connection [8] between the generalized eigenvalue problem and the least-squares, the optimization (4) can be derived as a least-squares formulation

$$\min_W \|X^{\mathrm{T}} W - Y\|_F^2, \quad (5)$$

where W is the regression coefficients with size of $d \times c$ and the response Y can be computed as follows. Let $\tilde{L} = L(L^{\mathrm{T}} L)^{-\frac{1}{2}}$ and its QR-decompostion of $\tilde{L}$ be $\tilde{L} = \tilde{Q} \tilde{R}$. Next, let the SVD of $\tilde{R}$ be $\tilde{R} = U \Sigma V^{\mathrm{T}}$, and thus the target Y is given by $Y = \tilde{Q} U$. Note that $\tilde{L}$ is well-defined because it is reasonable to assume that the number of data samples is significantly larger than the number of labels ($n \gg c$).

Proceeding as above, we arrive at our proposed objective $\mathcal{Q}$ by integrating the shared structure (2) and the structured sparsity-inducing norm (3) into the least-squares CCA (5):

$$\min_{W, Q, R} \quad \mathcal{Q} = \|X^{\mathrm{T}} W - Y\|_F^2 + \alpha \|W - QR\|_F^2 + \beta \|W\|_{2,p}^p \quad (6)$$
$$\text{s.t.} \quad Q^{\mathrm{T}} Q = I_r,$$

where $R = [r_1, \cdots, r_c] \in \mathbb{R}^{r \times c}$, I_r is an identity matrix with size of r, and both $\alpha, \beta > 0$ are the penalty parameters.

2.2 Optimization Algorithm

As the objective (6) compromises the column orthogonality constraint and the non-smooth regularization term $\ell_{2,p}$-norm, it is generally not easy to be solved and so we derive an efficient iterative algorithm to optimize (6). To begin with, we denote a diagonal matrix

$$D = \mathrm{diag}\{\frac{p}{2\|W_{1\cdot}\|_2^{2-p}}, \cdots, \frac{p}{2\|W_{i\cdot}\|_2^{2-p}}, \cdots \frac{p}{2\|w_{d\cdot}\|_2^{2-p}}\}. \quad (7)$$

Then the objective (6) can be equivalently rewritten as:

$$\min_{W, Q, R} \|X^{\mathrm{T}} W - Y\|_F^2 + \alpha \|W - QR\|_F^2 + \beta \mathrm{Tr}(W^{\mathrm{T}} DW) \quad (8)$$
$$\text{s.t.} \quad Q^{\mathrm{T}} Q = I_r,$$

where Tr designates the trace operator of a matrix. Zeroing the derivative of (8) with respect to R and ignoring those terms independent of R, we gain $Q^{\mathrm{T}}(W - QR) = 0$ and then

$$R^* = Q^{\mathrm{T}} W. \quad (9)$$

From (9) it follows that the objective in (8) can be rewritten as follows by regrouping the terms dependent on W

$$\min_W \|X^{\mathrm{T}} W - Y\|_F^2 + \mathrm{Tr}(W^{\mathrm{T}}(\alpha(I - QQ^{\mathrm{T}}) + \beta D)W). \quad (10)$$

Setting the derivative of (10) equal to zero gives the solution for W

$$W^* = (XX^{\mathrm{T}} + \alpha(I - QQ^{\mathrm{T}}) + \beta D)^{-1}XY. \quad (11)$$

By removing the terms independent of the W, we note that (10) can be alternatively seen as

$$\min_W \mathrm{Tr}(W^{\mathrm{T}}(XX^{\mathrm{T}} + \alpha(I - QQ^{\mathrm{T}}) + \beta D)W) - 2\mathrm{Tr}(W^{\mathrm{T}}XY). \,(12)$$

By plugging the solution to W (11) back into (12), we arrive at the optimization of Q:

$$\max_Q \quad \mathrm{Tr}(Y^{\mathrm{T}}X^{\mathrm{T}}(XX^{\mathrm{T}} + \alpha(I - QQ^{\mathrm{T}}) + \beta D)^{-1}XY) \quad (13)$$

$$\text{s.t.} \qquad Q^{\mathrm{T}}Q = I_r.$$

On the basis of Woodbury formula, by rearranging the terms dependent on Q we get

$$(XX^{\mathrm{T}} + \alpha(I - QQ^{\mathrm{T}}) + \beta D)^{-1} \triangleq (A - \alpha QQ^{\mathrm{T}})^{-1}$$
$$= A^{-1} + \alpha A^{-1}Q(I - \alpha Q^{\mathrm{T}}A^{-1}Q)^{-1}Q^{\mathrm{T}}A^{-1}, \quad (14)$$

in which $A \triangleq XX^{\mathrm{T}} + \alpha I + \beta D$. By substituting (14) back into (13) and dropping the terms independent of Q, we obtain the below generarlized eigenvalue problem to solve Q:

$$\max_Q \quad \mathrm{Tr}\frac{Q^{\mathrm{T}}(A^{-1}XYY^{\mathrm{T}}X^{\mathrm{T}}A^{-1})Q}{Q^{\mathrm{T}}(I - \alpha A^{-1})Q} \quad (15)$$

$$\text{s.t.} \qquad Q^{\mathrm{T}}Q = I_r.$$

Hence the solution to Q can be derived analytically via the eigen-decomposition of $(I - \alpha A^{-1})^{-1}(A^{-1}XYY^{\mathrm{T}}X^{\mathrm{T}}A^{-1})$. However, we emphasise that A is also an unknown variable due to the dependence upon in D (7). Consequently, we resort to an iterative procedure to tackle our presented model (6) outlined in Algo.1. The computational cost of our model is primarily dominated by the eigen-decompostion for Q and several inverse operations for A and W, leading to an overall time complexity $O(d^3)$, but all these computations are offline and we may further employ the first order Taylor expansion to approximate $(I - \alpha A^{-1})^{-1}$ because of the small α. Besides, the convergence proof is omitted due to the page limits. However, following the proof in [7], we can prove that the objective value of (1) monotonically decreases w.r.t. each iteration until convergence using Algo. 1.

3. EVALUATIONS AND ANALYSES

Three well-noted image data corpora and one movie data collection are used in the experiment to verify the effectiveness of our $\text{SSCCA}_{2,p}$ model in comparison with the following state-of-the-art multi-label learning methods: (1) MLDA [9]: Multi-label linear discriminant analysis is an extension of the classical LDA for dealing with multi-label classification; (2) MDDM [10]: Multi-label Dimensionality reduction via Dependence Maximization is designed to maximize the dependence between the input space and the label space by virtue of the Hilbert-Schmidt independence criterion; (3) MDSS [4]: Multi-label DR via the Shared Subspace directly combines the common shared structure with the square loss function; (4) CCA [8]: Canonical Correlation Analysis maximizes the correlations between variables in the embedded space and the corresponding regularized CCA (regCCA) [8] is to avoid singularity and overfitting. As for MLDA, MDDM, CCA and regCCA, after obtaining the low dimensional projected space, we apply the ridge regression with the

---

Algorithm 1: <u>S</u>ubspace and structural <u>S</u>parsity <u>CCA</u>

Input: • The input data features X and its corresponding label matrix L;
• Parameters: $\alpha, \beta > 0$; $p = \{0.5, 1\}$;
• The shared dimensionality: $r = 2c/3$;
• Convergence tolerance: $\tau = 1e - 6$;
• Random initialization: $W^{(0)}$.
repeat
 Update the diagonal matrix
$$D_t = \begin{bmatrix} \frac{p}{2\|W_{1\cdot}^{(t)}\|_2^{2-P}+\varepsilon} & & \\ & \ddots & \\ & & \frac{p}{2\|W_{d\cdot}^{(t)}\|_2^{2-P}+\varepsilon} \end{bmatrix}$$
 Compute $Q^{(t+1)}$ by (15) ;
 Compute $W^{(t+1)}$ by (11);
 $t \leftarrow t + 1$;
until Convergence: $\|\mathcal{Q}^{(t)} - \mathcal{Q}^{(t+1)}\| \leq \tau \|\mathcal{Q}^{(t)}\|$;
Output: Projection vectors $W \in \mathbb{R}^{d \times c}$.

---

regularization parameter tuned in $\{10^i\}_{i=-3}^3$ rather than the SVM to achieve the fast speed of multi-label annotations in the embedded space. In terms of the performance measures, we adopt the widely used AUC, Macro and Micro F1 [5, 10, 4] whose higher values indicate better performance.

For all the data sets, we can directly access their descriptions and features by searching for their titles, so we simply list their important statistics in Table 1. We note that three types of visual descriptors, including 100-D DenseHue, 300-D DenseHueV3H1 and 1000-D DenseSift, are concatenated to represent the images in the MIRFlickr08. Moreover, we remove the samples without any pre-given labels and also discard those labels without any training samples. On top of that, we select the most popular 40 labels among all 374 labels in the Corel5k in order to better illustrate the results of different learning models.

Concerning the NUS-WIDE and IMDB Updated data sets, because of the several hundreds of thousands of data points, we pick 1 out of 10 random partitions as the training data whereas the remaining partition as the testing data. For the Corel5K, 1 out of 3 random partitions is taken as the training set while the rest as the test set. For the MIRFlickr08, we use the original partitioned training data with one half size and the other half as the test data.

We highlight that in the objective (6), there are two parameters α and β, both of which are tuned in the range $\{\{10^i\}\bigcup\{5*10^i\}\}_{i=-3}^3$ as well as the parameter $p = \{0.5, 1\}$ in the sparsity inducing $\ell_{2,p}$-norm. In light of the other compared algorithms, we also tune their corresponding parameters and then the best results are reported.

3.1 Results and Discussions

We offer the following observations in Table 1: (1) Compared with CCA based algorithms like CCA and regCCA, our proposed $\text{SSCCA}_{2,p}$ significantly outperforms these baselines over all benchmark data sets, which provide strong support for our interpretation of integrating the shared common subspace and joint sparsity into the standard CCA. (2) In contrast with MLDA, MDDM and MDSS, our SSCCA simultaneously considers the mechanism of the shared common structure and the advantage of CCA that finds the max-

Table 1: Performance Comparison over four data corpora. The components in $(n, d, c, Card, Den)$ respectively denote the number of samples, the dimension of samples, the number of targeted labels, the label cardinality and density.

Data sets $(n, d, c, Card, Den)$	Metrics	MLDA	MDDM	MDSS	CCA	regCCA	$\mathbf{SSCCA_{2,1}}$	$\mathbf{SSCCA_{2,1/2}}$
NUS-WIDE	AUC	0.6384	0.6363	0.6375	0.6028	0.6368	*0.6889*	**0.6918**
$(133441, 500, 81,$	Macro F1	0.0752	0.0766	0.0768	0.0648	0.0765	*0.0858*	**0.0872**
$1.7610, 0.0217)$	Micro F1	0.1672	0.1648	0.1640	0.0954	0.1652	*0.1657*	**0.1672**
Corel5K	AUC	0.6350	0.6806	0.6965	0.6374	0.6832	**0.7237**	*0.6997*
$(4758, 499, 40,$	Macro F1	0.1712	0.1993	0.2096	0.1762	0.2038	**0.2179**	*0.2142*
$2.2404, 0.0560)$	Micro F1	0.2067	0.2357	0.2559	0.2091	0.2525	**0.2635**	*0.2559*
IMDB Updated	AUC	0.5963	0.5975	0.6001	0.5968	0.5991	**0.6469**	*0.6385*
$(120919, 1001, 28,$	Macro F1	0.1441	0.1446	0.1448	0.1440	0.1447	**0.1673**	*0.1637*
$1.9997, 0.0714)$	Micro F1	0.3022	0.2949	0.2966	0.2939	0.2959	**0.3192**	*0.3105*
MIRFlickr08	AUC	0.7718	0.7867	0.7761	0.7752	0.7794	**0.8130**	*0.8115*
$(24581, 1400, 38,$	Macro F1	0.3685	0.3764	0.3706	0.3687	0.3715	**0.3903**	*0.3874*
$4.7966, 0.1262)$	Micro F1	0.5144	0.5215	0.5159	0.5165	0.5189	**0.5337**	*0.5320*

imal similarity between the transformed space and the label space. (3) Although the smaller value p in the $\ell_{2,p}$-norm implies row sparser predictor, the quality of the sparsity-induced norm $SSCCA_{2,1/2}$ does not often exceed those of $SSCCA_{2,1}$, which means that the best results of $SSCCA_{2,p}$ varies according to the unique domain.

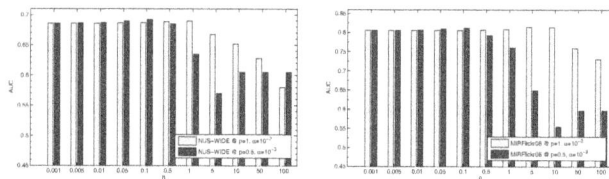

(a) $SSCCA_{2,p}$@ NUS-WIDE   (b) $SSCCA_{2,p}$@ MIRFlickr08

Figure 1: Perf. variation w.r.t. β and fixed $\alpha = 10^{-3}$.

In what follows, we meticulously carry out experiments on the NUS-WIDE and MIRFlickr08 to exemplify how the parameters affect the performance. For simplicity, we fix $\alpha = 10^{-3}$ because in contrast with α, the parameter β is more sensitivity to the quality of $SSCCA_{2,p}$, largely dependent on the row sparsity for the predictive functions. As seen in Figure 1, it is clear that the DR accuracy decreases when the value of β goes up. However, we may generally achieve good quality due to relatively wide ranges of β that are smaller than 10^{-1}.

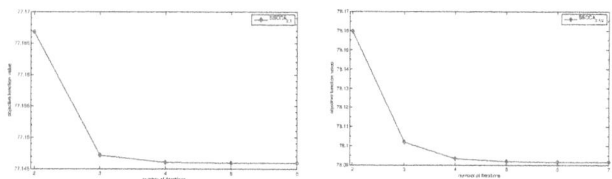

(a) $SSCCA_{2,1}$@ NUS-WIDE with $\alpha = 10^{-3}$ and $\beta = 10^{0}$ (b) $SSCCA_{2,1/2}$@ NUS-WIDE with $\alpha = 10^{-3}$ and $\beta = 10^{-1}$

Figure 2: Convergence curves of obj. values of (6) via Algo. 1.

Even though the convergence behavior of Algo. 1 can be mathematically proved, in practice how fast our proposed algorithm converges is also crucial. As a result, Fig. 2 depicts the convergence curves over NUS-WIDE under the two fixed parameters that generate the best results listed in Table 1.

Practically, our proposed alternating scheme can speedily converges within about dozens of iterations shown in Fig. 2.

4. CONCLUSIONS

We have studied the problem of new least-squares CCA oriented feature learning by taking into consideration of the shared common subspace and structured sparsity patterns. Under this scheme, not only can we elucidate the multiple label dependence unveiled by the shared common subspace, but also maximally characterize the similarity between the input feature space and the label space via CCA. Owing to the row sparsity-inducing $\ell_{2,p}$-norm regularizer, a new alternating algorithm is derived to handle the formulated objective. Experimental studies on a collection of four web data sets have shown the effectiveness and efficiency of our new model. In the future, we will perform the diagonalization technique to further expedite the offline computation of the proposed $SSCCA_{2,p}$.

Acknowledgments The third author was partially supported by the Research Funds of Shanghai Municipal Science and Technology Commission Grant 12511502902 and the National Natural Science Foundation of China Grant 61375053.

5. REFERENCES

[1] B. Chen, W. Lam, I. W. Tsang, and T.-L. Wong. Discovering low-rank shared concept space for adapting text mining models. *TPAMI*, 35(6):1284–1297, June 2013.

[2] D. Chu, L.-Z. Liao, M. K. Ng, and X. Zhang. Sparse canonical correlation analysis: New formulation and algorithm. *TPAMI*, 35(12):3050–3065, 2013.

[3] Y. Gong, Q. Ke, M. Isard, and S. Lazebnik. A multi-view embedding space for modeling internet images, tags, and their semantics. *IJCV*, 106(2):210–233, 2014.

[4] S. Ji, L. Tang, S. Yu, and J. Ye. A shared-subspace learning framework for multi-label classification. *TKDD*, May 2010.

[5] Z. Ma, F. Nie, Y. Yang, J. R. R. Uijlings, and N. Sebe. Web image annotation via subspace-sparsity collaborated feature selection. *TMM*, 14(4):1021–1030, 2012.

[6] Z. Ma, Y. Yang, N. Sebe, and A. Hauptmann. Knowledge adaptation with partially shared features for event detection using few exemplars. *TPAMI*, 36(9):1789–1802, 2014.

[7] F. Nie, H. Huang, X. Cai, and C. Ding. Efficient and robust feature selection via joint $\ell_{2,1}$-norms minimization. In *NIPS*, 2010.

[8] L. Sun, S. Ji, and J. Ye. Canonical correlation analysis for multilabel classification: A least-squares formulation, extensions, and analysis. *TPAMI*, 33(1):194–200, 2011.

[9] H. Wang, C. Ding, and H. Huang. Multi-label linear discriminant analysis. In *ECCV*, 2010.

[10] Y. Zhang and Z.-H. Zhou. Multilabel dimensionality reduction via dependence maximization. *TKDD*, Oct. 2010.

Query Performance Prediction By Considering Score Magnitude and Variance Together

Yongquan Tao[1] Shengli Wu[1,2]
[1]School of Computer Science and Telecommunication Engineering, Jiangsu University, Zhenjiang, China
[2]School of Computing and Mathematics, Ulster University, Newtownabbey, UK
taoyongquan77@126.com,swu@ujs.edu.cn

ABSTRACT

Query Performance prediction aims to evaluate the effectiveness of the results returned by a search system in response to a query without any relevance information. In this paper, we propose a method that considers both magnitude and variance of scores of the ranked list of results to measure the performance of a query. Using six different TREC test sets, we compare our predictor with three of the state-of-the-art techniques. The experimental results show that our method is very competitive. Pairwise comparisons with each of the three other methods show that our predictor performs better in more data sets.

Categories and Subject Descriptors

H.3.3 [**Information Search and Retrieval**]: Information Search and Retrieval

General Terms

Algorithms

Keywords

query difficulty; query performance prediction; score distribution

1. INTRODUCTION

Query difficulty prediction aims to predict whether a query will return a high quality result list ("easy" queries), or low quality result list ("hard" queries), when no relevance information is given by a human operator. Query difficulty prediction is also referred to as query performance prediction. It has many potential applications in a variety of IR tasks such as improving retrieval consistency, query refinement, and distributed IR. This is why the problem has received considerable attention in the IR community in recent years.

Accurate performance predictions can help a user decide if the results are acceptable. If more relevant results are needed, then the user may decide to reformulate the query so as to obtain some different results from the same search engine as before or use other search services available.

Query performance prediction can be roughly categorized into two types: pre-retrieval prediction and post-retrieval prediction. Pre-retrieval methods evaluate the query before the search takes place, thus they must rely on the statistics of the query terms in the collection [8]. The advantage of such methods is that they can be computed quickly, using available statistics of the query terms gathered at indexing time. However, a disadvantage of such predictors is that they do not take into account the specific retrieval algorithms, so the predictions may not be as accurate as the post-retrieval prediction methods [3].

Post-retrieval prediction methods are usually more complex and expensive as the search results need to be analyzed after retrieval. Post-retrieval prediction algorithms can be further divided into clarity score based methods [10], ranking robustness based methods [14], and score analysis based methods [12, 13].

Prior research on score analysis demonstrates that magnitude and variance of scores are two factors that are correlated with query performance. The score-based performance prediction methods proposed previously consider either magnitude or variance of scores [13, 2, 9] but not both. In this paper, we propose a method that takes both magnitude and variance of scores into consideration at the same time. Experiments with 6 groups of TREC data are very promising..

The rest of this paper is organized as follows: related prior work is discussed in section 2. Section 3 describes our method for creating an estimator for query performance in detail. Section 4 presents the experiments we conducted on TREC data. Section 5 concludes the paper.

2. PRIOR WORK

In this section, we review some prior work on post-retrieval query prediction which category our proposed method falls into.

Cronen-Townsend et al.[10] proposed a method of computing the relative entropy between the models of the query and the collection. Afterwards, a few more clarity-based predictors have been proposed by other researchers [5, 6, 7].

Zhou et al.[14] built a novel framework called ranking robustness to predict query performance. Robustness based approaches evaluate how robust the results are to perturbations in the query, the result list and the retrieval method.

CIKM'14, November 3–7, 2014, Shanghai, China.
Copyright 2014 ACM 978-1-4503-2598-1/14/11 ...$15.00.
http://dx.doi.org/10.1145/2661829.2661906.

Related research by others may be found, for example, in [1, 4, 11].

A main branch of the post-retrieval prediction methods is score analysis. Zhou et al. proposed a predictor, Weighted Information Gain (WIG) [13], which measures the divergence between the mean retrieval score of some top-ranked documents and that of a typical document in the entire corpus. Shtok et al. proposed another predictor called Normalized Query Commitment (NQC) [2] to estimate query drift in the list of top-ranked and/or bottom-ranked documents. More recently, Pérez-Iglesias et al. also focused on the variance aspect of scores. Some experiments are conducted by using standard deviation and some of its variants to capture the differences between "hard" and "easy" queries. [9].

In this paper, we investigate the problem of query performance prediction by analyzing score distribution. Those methods based on score analysis focused on either the magnitude [13] or the variance [2, 9] of the scores, yet none are able to utilize both. Therefore, we propose a query performance prediction method that takes both factors into consideration at the same time. As we can see later, such a combination is not trivial. Experiments with TREC data are conducted to evaluate the effectiveness of our method.

3. METHODOLOGY

Let us begin by setting out the notation. Let q, $\mathcal{D}$, and $\mathcal{M}$ denote a query, a corpus, and a retrieval method, respectively. We use $L(q, \mathcal{M})$ and $\mathcal{D}_q^{[k]}$ to denote the result list returned in response to query q by $\mathcal{M}$ over $\mathcal{D}$ and the top-k documents ranked highly in the result list $L(q, \mathcal{M})$, respectively. k is a free parameter, set to an arbitrary natural number prior to the search. Our goal is to establish a predictor for evaluating the quality of the ranking list returned by $\mathcal{M}$ over $\mathcal{D}$ for a given query q without relevance judgment information.

Previous work on query performance prediction observes that there is a certain relationship between score distribution and query performance [2, 9, 13]. In particular, two factors, namely the magnitude and deviation of scores may be used to predict query performance.

WIG [13] uses Equation 1

$$WIG(q, M) = \frac{1}{k} \sum_{d \in \mathcal{D}_q^{[k]}} \frac{1}{\sqrt{|q|}} (Score(d) - Score(\mathcal{D})) \quad (1)$$

to calculate scores for a given query q. [1] Here $Score(d)$ is the score that document d is awarded by $\mathcal{M}$, $Score(\mathcal{D})$ is the score that an average document in $\mathcal{D}$ would be given by $\mathcal{M}$, and $|q|$ is the number of terms in q. In Figure 1, we can see that WIG mainly considers the magnitude of scores that those retrieved documents obtain. $\sqrt{|q|}$ serves as an scale factor to make WIG scores comparable over different queries.

NQC uses Equation 2

$$NQC(q, \mathcal{M}) = \frac{1}{Score(\mathcal{D})} \sqrt{\frac{1}{k} \sum_{d \in \mathcal{D}_q^{[k]}} (Score(d) - \hat{\mu})^2} \quad (2)$$

---

[1]This is a simplified version of WIG, which only uses score information of the results. According to [12], it is a very effective method.

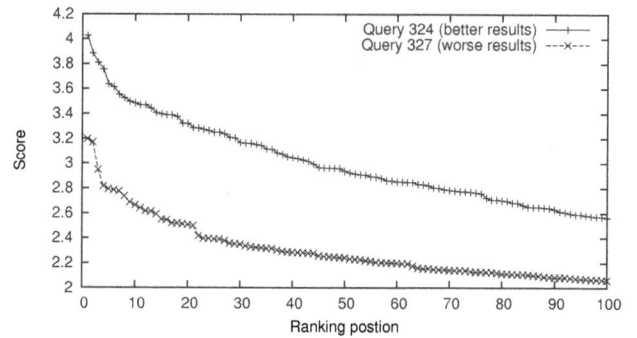

Figure 1: Topic 324 "Argentine/British Relations", average precision is 0.6670; topic 327 "Modern Slavery", average precision is 0.1773. Data is taken from *pircRB04t3*, a run submitted to the Robust Track in 2004.

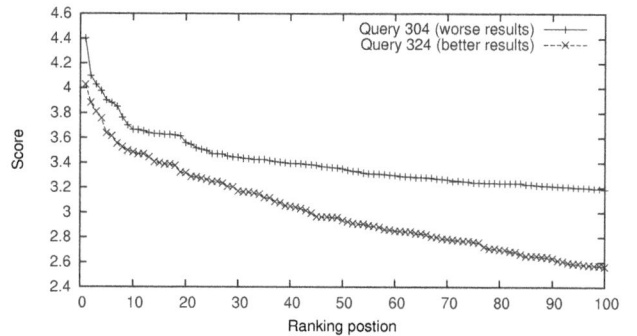

Figure 2: Topic 324 "Argentine/British Relations", average precision is 0.6670; topic 304 "Endangered Species (Mammals)", average precision is 0.1049. Data is taken from *pircRB04t3*, a run submitted to the Robust Track in 2004.

to calculate scores for a given query q. Here $\hat{\mu}$ is the average of the scores of all k results in $\mathcal{D}_q^{[k]}$. NQC [2] can be regarded as a variation of standard deviation (referred to as SD), which is investigated in [9].

Let us consider two examples to illustrate why WIG and NQC work in some situations, but fail in others. All the data is taken from *pircRB04t3*, which is the best (measured by MAP) among all those submitted to TREC Robust 2004. Figure 1 shows the results for queries 324 and 327. The results for query 324 obtain higher scores than that for query 327, and the variance of both score distributions are similar. MAP(324)>MAP(327). These conditions are ideal for performance prediction methods such as WIG. On the other hand, methods such as SD and NQC may not work well since the curves for both queries have very similar shape. As a matter of fact, we have

$$NQC(324, pircRB04t3) = 0.202$$

and

$$NQC(327, pircRB04t3) = 0.210$$

so NQC would make a wrong decision about performance comparison of these two queries.

The second example is to compare 324 "Argentine/British Relations"and query 304 "Endangered Species (Mammals)".

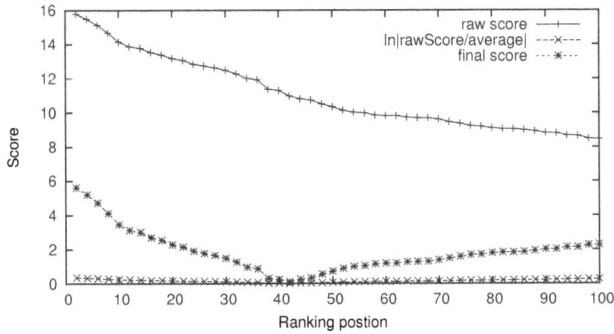

Figure 3: Topic 561. Data is taken from *pircRB04t3*, a run submitted to the Robust Track in 2004.

MAP(324) >MAP(304). Figure 2 shows the score curves for both results. The results for query 304 obtain higher scores than that for query 327, but the latter has a greater variance than the former. These conditions are ideal for performance prediction methods such as NQC and SD, but they are not good for methods such as WIG.

From the above two examples we can see that considering either score magnitude or deviation may work in some situations but not the others. It would be an advantage if we can consider both of them together. We use the following Equation 3

$$SMV(q, \mathcal{M}) = \frac{\frac{1}{k}\sum_{d \in \mathcal{D}_q^{[k]}}(Score(d)|\ln\frac{Score(d)}{\hat{\mu}}|)}{Score(\mathcal{D})} \quad (3)$$

to calculate scores for a given query q. Here SMV stands for our method, which considers both Score Magnitude and Variance. $\hat{\mu}$ is the average of the scores of all k results in $\mathcal{D}_q^{[k]}$. Inside the summation of Equation 3, there are two components. One is $Score(d)$ and the other is $|\ln\frac{Score(d)}{\hat{\mu}}|$. The former is used to represent score magnitude and the latter is used to represent a form of score variance. We combine the two by multiplication.

In order to understand the contribution that results at different ranks can make, let us consider an example, the results for query 561 from *thutd5*. At each rank, the value of raw score $Score(d)$, the value of $w(d) = |\ln\frac{Score(d)}{\hat{\mu}}|$, and the final score (product of $w(d) * Score(d)$) are shown in Figure 3. We can see that each result makes some contribution to the final score. Results at the very top and bottom make more contribution than those in the middle. This is reasonable because results at both ends are more informative than those in the middle. Let us recall the two aforementioned examples. WIG works in the first example, but not the second; NQC works in the second example, but not the first. SMV works in both examples.

In its current form, Equation 3 works with positive scores but not negative scores. If there are negative scores, then Equation 3 can be modified to support that. Let us define *low_s* to be the lowest score from the results for a group of queries. $Score(d)$ can be replaced by $Score(d) - low\_s$, thus all negative scores transform to positive scores and Equation 3 can be used without any problems.

---

[2]Topic 672 is removed because of no relevant results identified.

Table 1: Summary of test collections

Collection	Size	TREC Task	Topics
Disks 2&3	567,529	Ad hoc 4	50
Disks 2&4	524,929	Ad hoc 5	50
Disks 4&5-CR	528,155	Robust 2004	249 [2]
WT10G	1.69 m	Web 2001	50
GOV	1.25 m	Web 2002	50
GOV2	25.2 m	Terabyte 2004	50

Table 2: *Pearson's* correlation coefficients for correlation with actual retrieval performance. Bold cases mean the most accurate prediction per collection.

TREC TASK	SD	WIG	NQC	SMV
TREC 4	0.418	**0.505**	0.414	0.442
TREC 5	0.296	0.474	0.573	**0.586**
ROBUST 2004	**0.646**	0.575	0.597	0.591
WebTrack 2001	0.359	0.312	0.329	**0.397**
WebTrack 2002	0.330	0.295	0.444	**0.452**
Terabyte 2004	0.373	0.307	0.493	**0.521**

4. EVALUATION

In this section, we evaluate SMV. Experiments are conducted on 6 different TREC collections. Table 1 summarizes the information of these test collections. They are used in different tasks including ad hoc, web, terabyte, and robust. Their sizes vary from 0.5 million (disks 2&3, disks2&4, disks 4&5-CR) to 25 million (GOV2). We compare the prediction quality of SMV with that of the three state-of-the-art predictors: Standard Deviation (SD) [9],Weighted Information Gain (WIG) [13] and NQC [2].

As described in previous section, we need to set a value for the parameter k in all the predictors. As recommended in [12], k is set to 5 for WIG. For the three other methods NQC, SD and SMV, k is set to the same value. It is set to 1000 for the GOV2 collection and 100 for all other collections, as in [2]. Special treatment is given to GOV2 because in the TREC 2004 Terabyte task, 10000 results were retrieved for each query, whereas only 1000 results were retrieved for all other cases. We use the average score of all the retrieved results (1000 or 10000) to estimate $Score(D)$.

For each collection, we select the best run (measured by MAP) that is submitted to TREC to carry out the experiment. They are *CnQst2* (TREC 4), *ETHme1* (TREC 5), *fub01be2* (TREC 2001), *thutd5* (TREC 2002), *pircRB04t3* (TREC 2004 Robust), *uogTBQEL* (TREC 2004 Terabyte).

The prediction quality of a method is evaluated by measuring both *Pearson's* and *Kendall's* $-\tau$ correlation between the ranking of queries by their actual performance (measured by MAP) and the ranking of queries by a performance predictor. In statistics, *Pearson's* correlation is a measure of the linear correlation between two variables. Its range is [-1,1], where 1 presents total positive correlation, 0 no correlation and -1 total negative correlation. *Kendall's* $-\tau$ coefficient is used to measure the association between two measured quantities. Its range is also [-1,1], where 1 denotes that the two rankings are the same, and -1 denotes that one ranking is the reverse of the other.

The experimental results are shown in Tables 2 and 3 for *Pearson's* correlation and *Kendall's* $-\tau$ rank coefficient

Table 3: $Kendall's-\tau$ **rank coefficients for correlation with actual retrieval performance. Bold cases mean the most accurate prediction per collection.**

TREC TASK	SD	WIG	NQC	SMV
TREC 4	0.333	**0.352**	0.269	0.299
TREC 5	0.229	0.350	**0.427**	0.425
ROBUST 2004	**0.444**	0.404	0.394	0.396
WebTrack 2001	0.279	0.230	0.273	**0.301**
WebTrack 2002	0.139	0.158	0.177	**0.194**
Terabyte 2004	0.243	0.185	0.340	**0.364**

Table 4: **Average of** $Pearson's$ **correlation (P) and** $Kendall's-\tau$ **rank coefficients (K) for correlation with actual retrieval performance. 6 collections are divided into two types: clean (including Disks 2&3, Disks 2&4 and Disks 4&5-CR) and noisy (including WT10g, GOV and GOV2).**

Collections	SD	WIG	NQC	SMV
Clean	0.453(P)	0.518(P)	0.528(P)	0.540(P)
	0.336(K)	0.369(K)	0.363(K)	0.373(K)
Noisy	0.354(P)	0.305(P)	0.422(P)	0.457(P)
	0.220(K)	0.191(K)	0.263(K)	0.286(K)

respectively. Generally speaking, SMV predicts query performance better in more collections when either of the two measures is used. More specifically and compared in pairwise fashion with any of the three other methods, SMV outperforms each of the three methods in 5 out of 6 collections with respect to $Pearson's$ correlation; the figures are 4 (SD), 4 (WIG), and 5 (NQC) out of 6 if considering $Kendall's - \tau$ rank coefficient. Apart from the best run in each task, we also randomly select and evaluate a few more runs. The experimental results are similar to those reported in the paper. Therefore, SMV performs very well compared to other state-of-the-art techniques under the same conditions.

In all 6 collections, WT10G, GOV and GOV2 are collections whose documents are crawled from the web. Unlike the three other collections, these web collections are noisy because there are many duplicates or near-duplicates, spam, documents written in foreign languages, binary data documents, etc. Some researchers (e.g., in [9]) observe that for such collections, query performance prediction is less accurate. In our experiment, we divide the 6 collections into 2 types: clean and noisy. Thus 3 web collections are classified as noisy whilst the rest are clean. For these collections, too, SMV performs better on average than each of the other methods. Table 4 gives more detailed information. We can see that on average, all performance prediction methods do better with clean collections than with noisy collections.

5. SUMMARY AND FUTURE WORK

We have presented a performance prediction method SMV by considering both score magnitude and variance at the same time. Evaluated with 6 different collections used in TREC, we find that our predictor performs better than any of the three other predictors in more data sets. Thus, we can conclude that the proposed method is very competitive.

In terms of future work, we shall focus on a few specific retrieval systems and models such as Terrier, Indri, BM25, Kullback-Leibler Divergence Language Model to further investigate the performance prediction problem. If we can treat those results from different systems/models in different ways then more accurate prediction is possible since the distribution of scores may differ from one system to another.

In a different vein, we can take more information such as certain statistics of the collection, query terms, and so on into consideration. Thus the method proposed in this paper can be used together with others for more accurate performance prediction.

6. REFERENCES

[1] J. A. Aslam and V. Pavlu. Query hardness estimation using Jensen-Shannon divergence among multiple scoring functions. In *Proceedings of ECIR*, pages 198–209, 2007.

[2] O. A. Shtok and D. Carmel. Predicting query performance by query-drift estimation. In *Proceedings of ICTIR*, pages 305–312, 2009.

[3] C. Hauff, D. Hiemstra and F. de Jong. A survey of pre-retrieval query performance predictors. In *Proceedings of CIKM*, pages 1419–1420, 2008.

[4] E. Yom-Tov, S. Fine, D. Carmel and A. Darlow. Learning to estimate query difficulty: including applications to missing content detection and distributed information retrieval. In *Proceedings of SIGIR*, pages 512–519, 2005.

[5] F. Diaz and R. Jones. Using temporal profiles of queries for precision prediction. In *Proceedings of SIGIR*, pages 18–24, 2004.

[6] G. Amati, C. Carpineto and G. Romano. Query difficulty ,robustness, and selective application of query expansion. In *Proceedings of ECIR*, pages 127–137, 2004.

[7] B. He and I. Ounis. Inferring query performance using preretrieval predictors. In *Proceedings of SPIRE*, pages 43–54, 2004.

[8] B. He and I. Ounis. Query performance prediction. *Information System*, 31(7):585–594, 2006.

[9] J. Pérez-Iglesias and L. Araujo. Standard deviation as a query hardness estimator. In *Proceedings of SPIRE*, pages 207–212, 2010.

[10] S. Cronen-Townsend, Y Zhou and W. Bruce Croft. Predicting query performance. In *Proceedings of SIGIR*, pages 299–306, 2002.

[11] V. Vinay, I. J. Cox, N. Millic-Frayling and K. R. Wood. On ranking the effectiveness of searches. In *Proceedings of SIGIR*, pages 398–404, 2006.

[12] Y. Zhou. Retrieval performance prediction and document quality. *PhD thesis, University of Massachusetts*, September 2007.

[13] Y. Zhou and W. Bruce Croft. Query performance prediction in web search environments. In *Proceedings of SIGIR*, pages 543–550, 2007.

[14] Y. Zhou and W. Croft. Ranking robustness: a novel framework to predict query performance. In *Proceedings of CIKM*, pages 567–574, 2006.

Log-Bilinear Document Language Model for Ad-hoc Information Retrieval

Xinhui Tu[1], Jing Luo[2], Bo Li[1], Tingting He[1]

[1]School of Computer Science, Central China Normal University, Wuhan, China

[2]School of Computer Science, Wuhan University, Wuhan, China

tuxinhui@gmail.com, luoluocat@gmail.com, liboccnu@126.com, tthe@mail.ccnu.edu.cn

ABSTRACT

Incorporating semantic information into document representation is effective and potentially significant to improve retrieval performance. Recently, log-bilinear language model (LBL), as a form of neural language model, has been proved to be an effective way to learn semantic word representations, but its feasibility and effectiveness in information retrieval is mostly unknown. In this paper, we study how to efficiently use LBL to improve as-hoc retrieval. We propose a log-bilinear document language model (LB-DM) within the language modeling framework. The key idea is to learn semantically oriented representations for words, and estimate document language models based on these representations. Noise-constrictive estimation is employed to perform fast training on large document collections. Experiment results on standard TREC collections show that LB-DM performs better than translation language model and LDA-based retrieval model.

Categories and Subject Descriptors

H.3.3 [Information Search and Retrieval]: Retrieval Models

General Terms

Algorithms, Theory.

Keywords

Information Retrieval; Document Model; Log-Bilinear Language Model

1. INTRODUCTION

Language modeling (LM) for Information Retrieval (IR) has been a promising area of research over the past decade and a half. It provides an elegant mathematical model for ad-hoc text retrieval with excellent empirical results reported in the literature [10][14]. The basic language modeling approach is primarily based on exact matching of words between documents and queries. Since queries are short and relevant documents might use different vocabulary, such an approach suffers from vocabulary gap which is common for all retrieval models.

To address this problem, two main directions are investigated. The first one is based on the use of semantic relationships between words. A typical approach is translation language model (TLM) [2]. Although retrieval based on TLM performed consistently well across several TREC collections, TLM is not effective to incorporate the underlying topical information of a document. In reality, a document contains both the content-carrying (topical) words as well as background (non-topical) words. Furthermore, many words in natural language have different meanings when used in different contexts. Word-level translation may introduce much noise and result in topic drift. The second one considers the use of topic model. A recent work is LDA-based retrieval model [12]. A major drawback of LDA model is that it can never make predictions for words that are sharper than the distributions predicted by any of the individual topics [11].

Recently, neural language models have been successfully applied in various natural language processing tasks [1][7][8]. One key idea of neural language models is to learn distributed representations for words. In distributed representations, the distributions predicted by individual active features get multiplied together to give the distribution predicted by a whole set of active features. For example, distributed representations allow the topics government, mafia and playboy to combine to give very high probability to a word "Berlusconi" that is not predicted nearly as strongly by each topic alone [11]. Log-bilinear language model (LBL), as a form of neural language model, has been proved to be an effective way to encode semantic term-document information [7][8]. LBL has been successfully applied in several NLP tasks such as text classification, but its feasibility and effectiveness in information retrieval is mostly unknown.

Given the potential advantages of LBL as a form of a neural language model, and the encouraging results with LBL in previous work, we makes a systematically study on how to efficiently use LBL to improve ad-hoc retrieval. In this paper, we propose a log-bilinear document language model for IR and evaluate it on TREC collections. In Section 2, we discuss related work in language model-based retrieval and neural language models. We present the log-bilinear document language model in section 3. Then, we describe the data sets and experimental methods in section 4. Finally, section 5 concludes and discusses possible directions for future work.

2. RELATED WORKS

The key challenge in language model-based information retrieval is the estimation of document model [14]. The simplest way is the maximum likelihood estimator. However, it is very difficult to estimate an accurate document model due to the sparsity of training data. When a term does not occur in a document, the maximum likelihood estimator would give it a zero probability.

Therefore, some effective smoothing approaches, which combine the document model with the background collection model, have been proposed [14]. Jelinek-Mercer (JM) and Dirichlet are two commonly used smoothing methods.

Since queries are short and relevant documents might use different vocabulary, it will be more effective if the semantic relationship between words can be incorporated into the estimation of document models. Berger and Lafferty firstly adopt statistical translation model for information retrieval [2]. The basic idea of translation language models (TLM) is to estimate the probabilities of translating a word in a document into query words. Since a word in a document could be translated into its semantically related words, TLM can avoid exact matching of words between documents and queries. The key issue for TLM is the estimation of word-level translation probabilities. The quality of the translation probabilities can directly affect the performance of TLM. The original paper proposes to use synthetically generated query-document pairs to estimate translation probabilities. This method is inefficient and do not have good coverage of query words. In order to overcome these limitations, recent works have relied on document-level word co-occurrences to estimate word-level translation probabilities [5][6]. Retrieval based on TLMs performed consistently well across several TREC collections, and significant improvements over the basic language models were reported.

Another way to address the problem of vocabulary gap is to incorporate some form of topic model into retrieval model. Wei et al. [12] propose to use the Latent Dirichlet Allocation (LDA) to smooth document language models. With this model (referred as LDA-DM), we assume that there exist multiple topics in the collection, each being characterized by a unigram language model. In effect, this allows a document to be in multiple topics with some probabilities. Thus, smoothing of a document can involve an interpolation of potentially many topic clusters.

Recently, significant progress in statistical language modeling has been made by using models that rely on such distributed representations. Neural network language models have been both the most popular and most successful models of this type. Log-bilinear language model (LBL), as a simplest type of neural language models, is first proposed by Mnih et al [8]. Experiments have proven that LBL is more effective than standard n-gram models. However, learning word vectors via LBL produces representations with a syntactic focus, where word similarity is based upon how words are used in sentences. Maas et al. [7] introduce a model which learns semantically focused word vectors using a probabilistic model of documents. The model's word vectors are successfully used in several NLP tasks such as sentiment analysis and text classification [7].

3. PROPOSED WORK

In this section, we introduce a probabilistic model to learn distributed representations for words and then use these representations for document model estimation.

3.1 Learning distributed representations for words

We build a probabilistic model with log-bilinear energy function (referred as log-bilinear model) to learn distributed representations for words. In this model, similarities between words are encoded as distance or angle between word vectors in a multi-dimensional space.

First, we construct a probabilistic model for a document by using a continuous mixture distribution over words indexed by a multi-dimensional random variable x. The words in a document are assumed conditionally independent given the random variable x. The probability of d is determined using a joint distribution over d and x. The probability of a document d is as follows

$$P(d) = \int P(d, x)dx = \int P(x) \prod_{i=1}^{N} P(w_i|x)\, dx \qquad (1)$$

where N is the number of words in d and w_i is the ith word.

Then define the conditional distribution $P(w_i|x)$ using a log-bilinear model with parameters R and b. R is virtually a word representation matrix $R \in \mathbb{R}^{\beta \times |V|}$ where the β-dimensional vector representation of each word w in vocabulary V corresponds to that word's column in R, i.e., $\phi_w = R_w$. The random variable x is also a β-dimensional vector ($x \in \mathbb{R}^{\beta}$), indicating the weights of the β dimensions of word's representation vectors. In addition, a bias b_w is introduced for each word to capture differences in overall word frequencies. The energy assigned to a word w, given these model parameters, is

$$E(w, x; \theta) = -x^T \phi_w - b_w \qquad (2)$$

To obtain the distribution $p(w|x; \theta)$, we use a softmax,

$$P(w|x; \theta) = \frac{\exp(-E(w, x; \theta))}{\sum_{w' \in V} \exp(-E(w', x; \theta))} \qquad (3)$$
$$= \frac{\exp(x^T \phi_w + b_w)}{\sum_{w' \in V} \exp(x^T \phi_{w'} + b_{w'})}$$

For a given x, a word w's occurrence probability is related to how closely its representation vector ϕ_w matches the scaling direction of x.

In order to learn the parameters in the distributed representations, we propose to train the log-bilinear model using noise-contrastive estimation (NCE) [3]. NCE has been recently introduced for training unnormalized probabilistic models, and is shown to be less expensive than maximum likelihood learning and more stable than importance sampling for training neural probabilistic language models [9].

Assume that we have a data distribution $P(w|x)$, which are the distributions of words appearing in document d. We propose to distinguish the observed data from artificially generated noise samples. We assume that observed samples appear k times less frequently than noise samples, and data samples come from the mixture distribution. We denote the context-independent noise distribution as $P_n(w)$. We would like to fit the context dependent parameter model $P(w|x; \theta)$ to $P(w|x)$. Then given a document d, the posterior probabilities that a sample word w comes from the observed source data distribution and the observed target data distribution are

$$P(D = 1|w, x; \theta) = \frac{P(w|x; \theta)}{kP_n(w) + P(w|x; \theta)} \qquad (4)$$

In practice, given an observation word w in document d, we generate k noise samples $u_1, u_2, ..., u_k$ from the unigram noise distribution $P_n(w)$, and consider an approximate objective $J(w, x; \theta)$ such that

$$J(w, x; \theta) = \log P(D = 1 | w, x; \theta) \qquad (5)$$

$$+ \sum_{i=1}^{k} \log(1 - P(D = 1 | u_i, x; \theta))$$

In order to avoid over-fitting, we add regularization terms for the parameters R and $\{x_i\}$. Given a document collection Col, the final optimization problem can be defined as,

$$\max_{\theta} \sum_{d_k \in \text{Col}} \sum_{j=1}^{N_k} J(w_j, \hat{x}_k; \theta) - \sum_{d_k \in \text{Col}} \gamma ||\hat{x}_k||_2^2 - \alpha ||R||_F^2 \quad (6)$$

where $\hat{x}_k$ denote the MAP estimate of x_k for d_k, γ and α are trade-off parameters, $||.||_F^2$ denote the Frobenius norm and $||.||_2^2$ denote the Euclidean norm.

The final objective function is not jointly convex in all model parameters. The learning process can be divided into two steps. First, we optimize the word representations (R and b) while leaving the MAP estimates ($\hat{x}$) fixed. Then we find the new MAP estimate for each document while leaving the word representations fixed, and continue this process until convergence. The optimization algorithm quickly finds a global solution for each $\hat{x}_k$ because we have a low-dimensional, convex problem in each $\hat{x}_k$. The MAP estimation problems for different documents are independent, thus we provide a parallel implementation to handle large document collections.

3.2 Estimating document language models

The estimation of document model is a critical part of language model-based retrieval. In section 3.1, we provide a new way to model document. However, estimating document model using solely their representations has also its own deficiency: We may overestimate the generative probabilities of the words whose representation vectors closely match the scaling direction of a document, and underestimate the generative probabilities of the words which occur in a document.

Similar to other topic models, the log-bilinear model described in section 3.1 may not be as precise a representation as word in bag-of-word model. Therefore, the log-bilinear model itself may be not effective to be used as the only representation for retrieval. In our preliminary experiments, it is proved that the log-bilinear model hurt retrieval performance.

Intuitively, such a combination allows us to both benefit from the latent semantic representation in matching semantically related words and retain the needed discrimination from the word-level representation.

So, we instead combine the unigram document model with the log-bilinear model and construct a new log-bilinear document language model (LB-DM). There are three ways to combine the different parts: (a) linearly combining the original document model and the log-bilinear model, which is illustrated in (7). (b) additively combining the log-bilinear model with the maximum likelihood estimate of word w in the document d, and (c) combining the log-bilinear model with the Dirichlet smoothing part, i.e. the maximum likelihood estimate of word w in the entire collection. In this paper, we adopt the first combination strategy, which is reported performs slightly better than others in [12]. Therefore, we can estimate the probability of word w in document d can as following,

$$P(w|d) = \lambda \left(\frac{|d|}{|d| + \mu} P(w|d) + \frac{\mu}{|d| + \mu} P(w|\text{Coll}) \right) \qquad (7)$$

$$+ (1 - \lambda)P(w|x; \theta)$$

where $P(w|x; \theta)$ can be calculated by the method mentioned in section 3.1.

Compared to translation language model, LB-DM uses the underlying topical information of a document to predict the generative probabilities of semantically related words; thus LB-DM overcomes the limitation of word-level translation.

Compared to LDA-based model, which can never make predictions for words that are sharper than the distributions predicted by any of the individual topics, LB-DM can make predictions use the topic distribution of a document.

4. EXPERIMENTS
4.1 Data Set

The experiments in this section use six main document collections: (1) the Associated Press Newswire (AP) 1988-90 with TREC topics 51-150 (2) San Jose Mercury News (SJMN) 1991 with TREC topics 51-150 (3) LA Times (LA) with TREC topics 301-400 (4) ad hoc data in TREC7 with TREC topics 351-400 and 528,155 articles (5) WSJ news articles with TREC topics 51-100 and (6) technical reports in DOE abstracts with TREC topics 51-100. Each document is processed in a standard way for indexing. Words are stemmed (using porter-stemmer), and stop words are removed. In the experiments, we only use title of the queries because semantic word matching is necessary for such short queries. In order to evaluate our model and compare it to other models, we use the MAP measure, which is widely accepted measure for evaluating effectiveness of ranked retrieval systems. The methods used for the experiments in the following sections are:

QL: baseline, i.e., basic query likelihood method with Dirichlet prior smoothing [13].
TLM-CCON: translation language model with conditional context analysis [6].
LDA-DM: LDA-based document language model [12].
LB-DM: log-bilinear document language model.

4.2 Parameters

In the experiments, there are several controlling parameters to tune. We use the AP collection as our training collection to estimate the parameters. The other collections are used for testing whether the parameters optimized on AP can be used consistently on other collections. At the current stage of our work, the parameters are selected through grid search. All parameter values are tuned based on average precision since retrieval is our final task.

Selecting the right size of word-embedding is an important problem in distributed representations. A range of 50 to 600 is typically used in the literature [9]. The IR collections are much larger than the collections used in previous studies. It is well known that larger data sets may need larger dimension in general, and it is confirmed here by our experiments with different values of β (20, 50, ...) on the AP collection. As shown in Table 1, large β gives better MAP. However, the running time of learning with larger β can be expensive. 500 is a good tradeoff between accuracy and running time.

Table 1. Retrieval result (MAP) on AP with different size of word-embedding

β	20	50	100	200	300
MAP	0.2489	0.2515	0.2567	0.2652	0.2693
β	400	500	600	700	800
MAP	0.2708	0.2715	0.2716	0.2716	0.2717

Another important issue that may affect the robustness of our model is the sensitivity of the parameter λ (in Equation 7). In order to select a suitable value of λ , we use a similar procedure as above on the AP collection and find 0.7 to be the best value in our search. From the experiments on the testing collections, we also find that λ =0.7 is the best value or almost the best value for other collections.

We set the Dirichlet prior μ =1000 for all data sets since the best results are consistently obtained with this setting.

4.3 Comparing with existing works

With the parameter setting β = 500, λ =0.7 and μ =1000, we run experiments on other collections. Table 2 and 3 present the retrieval results of the LB-DM with the TLM-CCON and the LDA-DM respectively. The results of TLM-CCON and LDA-DM are directly from [6] and [12].The results indicate that LB-DM is more effective than the other two models. Considering that TLM-CCON and LDA-DM have already obtained significant improvements over the query likelihood model on all of these collections, and is therefore a high baseline, the significant performance improvements from LB-DM are very encouraging. The results confirm that LBL can be used to improve ad-hoc retrieval.

*(In table 2 and 3, * mean improvements over LDA-DM or TM-CCON are statistically significant with Wilcoxon signed-rank test)*

Table 2. Comparison of QL, LDA-DM and LB-DM.

Collection	QL	LDA-DM	LB-DM
AP	0.2179	0.2651	0.2715*
SJMN	0.2032	0.2307	0.2396*
LA	0.2468	0.2666	0.2743*

Table 3. Comparison of QL, TLM-CCON and LB-DM.

Collection	QL	TLM-CCON	LB-DM
TREC7	0.1852	0.1854	0.1962*
WSJ	0.2600	0.2658	0.2803*
DOE	0.1740	0.1750	0.1964*

5. CONCLUSION

In this paper, we propose a log-bilinear document language model for ad-hoc retrieval, and evaluate it using several TREC collections. Experimental results have demonstrated that the proposed model consistently outperforms translation language model and LDA-based document model. In summary, log-bilinear document language model is a promising method for IR, although more work needs to be done with even larger collections, such as Web TREC collections.

6. ACKNOWLEDGMENTS

This work was partially supported by the Key Projects of National Social Science Foundation of China under grant number 12&ZD223, the National Science Foundation of China under grants number 61300144, and the self-determined research funds of CCNU under grants number CCNU14A05015.

7. REFERENCES

[1] Bengio, Y., Ducharme, R., Vincent, P., and Janvin,C. 2003. A neural probabilistic language model. *The Journal of Machine Learning Research*, 3 (March 2003), 1137–1155.

[2] Berger, A., and Lafferty, J. 1999. Information retrieval as statistical translation. In *Proceedings of the 22nd annual international ACM SIGIR conference on research and development in information retrieval* .SIGIR '99. ACM, New York, NY, USA, 222-229.

[3] Gutmann, M. U., and Hyvärinen, A. 2012. Noise-contrastive estimation of unnormalized statistical models, with applications to natural image statistics. *The Journal of Machine Learning Research*, 13 (February 2012), 307-361.

[4] Jin, R., Hauptmann, A. G., and Zhai, C. X. 2002. Title language model for information retrieval. In *Proceedings of the 25th annual international ACM SIGIR conference on research and development in information retrieval*. SIGIR '02. ACM, New York, NY, USA, 42-48.

[5] Karimzadehgan, M. and Zhai, C. X. 2010. Estimation of statistical translation models based on mutual information for ad hoc information retrieval. In *Proceedings of the 33rd international ACM SIGIR conference on research and development in information retrieval* .SIGIR '10. ACM, New York, NY, USA, 323-330.

[6] Karimzadehgan, M., and Zhai, C. X. 2012. Axiomatic analysis of translation language model for information retrieval. In *Proceedings of the 34th European conference on Advances in Information Retrieval*. ECIR'12. Springer-Verlag, Berlin, Heidelberg, 268-280.

[7] Maas, A. L., and Ng, A. Y. 2010. A probabilistic model for semantic word vectors. In *NIPS Workshop on Deep Learning and Unsupervised Feature Learning*.

[8] Mnih, A., and Hinton, G. (2007). Three new graphical models for statistical language modeling. In Proceedings of the 24th international conference on Machine learning. ACM. (ICML '07), ACM, New York, NY, USA, 641-648.

[9] Mnih, A., and Kavukcuoglu, K. 2013. Learning word embeddings efficiently with noise-contrastive estimation. *Advances in Neural Information Processing Systems*, 26, 2265-2273.

[10] Ponte, J. M., and Croft, W. B. 1998. A language modeling approach to information retrieval. In *Proceedings of the 21st annual international ACM SIGIR conference on Research and development in information retrieval*. SIGIR '98. ACM, New York, NY, USA, 275-281.

[11] Salakhutdinov, R., and Hinton, G. E. (2009). Replicated Softmax: an Undirected Topic Model. *Advances in Neural Information Processing Systems*, 22, 1607-1614.

[12] Wei, X., and Croft, W. B. 2006. LDA-based document models for ad-hoc retrieval. In *Proceedings of the 29th annual international ACM SIGIR conference on Research and development in information retrieval*. SIGIR'06. ACM, New York, NY, USA, 178-185.

[13] Zhai, C.X., and Lafferty, J. 2001. A study of smoothing methods for language models applied to Ad Hoc information retrieval. In *Proceedings of the 24th annual international ACM SIGIR conference on research and development in information retrieval*. SIGIR '01. ACM, New York, NY, USA, 334-342.

[14] Zhai, C.X. 2008. Statistical Language Models for Information Retrieval A Critical Review. *Foundations and Trends in Information Retrieval*. 2, 3 (March 2008), 137-213.

Sparse Semantic Hashing for Efficient Large Scale Similarity Search

Qifan Wang, Bin Shen, Zhiwei Zhang and Luo Si
Department of Computer Science
Purdue University
West Lafayette, IN 47907, US
{wang868, bshen, zhan1187, lsi}@purdue.edu

ABSTRACT

Similarity search, or finding approximate nearest neighbors, is an important technique in various large scale information retrieval applications such as document retrieval. Many recent research demonstrate that hashing methods can achieve promising results for large scale similarity search due to its computational and memory efficiency. However, most existing hashing methods ignore the hidden semantic structure of documents but only use the keyword features (e.g., tf-idf) in hashing codes learning. This paper proposes a novel sparse semantic hashing (SpSH) approach that explores the hidden semantic representation of documents in learning their corresponding hashing codes. In particular, a unified framework is designed for ensuring the hidden semantic structure among the documents by a sparse coding model, while at the same time preserving the document similarity via graph Laplacian. An iterative coordinate descent procedure is then proposed for solving the optimization problem. Extensive experiments on two large scale datasets demonstrate the superior performance of the proposed research over several state-of-the-art hashing methods.

Categories and Subject Descriptors

H.3.1 [**Information Storage and Retrieval**]: Content Analysis and Indexing

Keywords

Hashing; Similarity Search; Sparse Coding

1. INTRODUCTION

Similarity search, also known as approximate nearest neighbor search, is a key problem in many information retrieval applications including document and image retrieval [5], similar content reuse detection [11] and collaborative filtering [12]. The purpose of similarity search is to identify similar data examples given a query example. With the

explosive growth of the internet, a huge amount of data have been generated, which indicates that efficient similarity search with large scale data becomes more important. Traditional similarity search methods are difficult to be used directly for large scale data since computing the similarity using the original features (i.e., often in high dimensional space) exhaustively between the query example and every candidate example is impractical for large applications. Recently, hashing methods [6, 7, 8, 9, 10] have been successfully used for large scale similarity search due to its fast query speed and low storage cost. These hashing methods design compact binary code in a low-dimensional space for each document so that similar documents are mapped to similar binary codes. In the retrieval process, these hashing methods first transform each query example into its corresponding binary code. Then similarity search can be simply conducted by calculating the Hamming distances between the codes of available data examples and the query and selecting data examples within small Hamming distances, which can be calculated using efficient bitwise operator XOR.

Locality-Sensitive Hashing (LSH) [1] is one of the most commonly used data-independent hashing methods. It utilizes random linear projections, which are independent of training data, to map data points from a high-dimensional feature space to a low-dimensional binary space. Another class of hashing methods are called data-dependent methods, whose projection functions are learned from training data. These data-dependent methods include spectral hashing (SH) [9], principal component analysis based hashing (PCAH) [4], self-taught hashing (STH) [10] and iterative quantization (ITQ) [3]. SH learns the hashing codes based on spectral graph partitioning and forcing the balanced and uncorrelated constraints into the learned codes. PCAH utilizes principal component analysis (PCA) to learn the projection functions. STH combines an unsupervised learning step with a supervised learning step to learn effective hashing codes. ITQ learns an orthogonal rotation matrix to refine the initial projection matrix learned by PCA so that the quantization error of mapping the data to binary codes is minimized. Compared with the data-independent methods, these data-dependent methods generally provide more effective hashing codes.

Hashing methods generate promising results by successfully addressing the storage and search efficiency challenges. However, most existing hashing methods ignore the hidden semantic structure of documents but only learns hashing codes using original features (i.e., tf-idf). In document retrieval, the hidden semantics usually reflect the true meanings/categories of a document. It is more desirable to find those documents that share same semantics instead of keywords to a query. In other words, the semantic captures the hidden information contained in a document and thus can better represent documents than original keyword features. Therefore, it is important to design hashing method that preserve the semantic structure among documents in the learned Hamming space.

This paper proposes a novel Sparse Semantic Hashing (SpSH) approach that explores the hidden semantic representation of documents in learning their corresponding hashing codes. In particular, a unified framework is designed for ensuring the hidden semantic structure among the documents by a sparse coding model, while at the same time preserving the document similarity using graph Laplacian. An iterative coordinate descent procedure is then proposed for solving the optimization problem. Extensive experiments on two large scale datasets demonstrate the superior performance of the proposed research over several state-of-the-art hashing methods.

2. SPARSE SEMANTIC HASHING

This section first states the problem setting of SpSH. Assume there are total n training data examples, denoted as: $X = \{x_1, x_2, \ldots, x_n\} \in R^{d \times n}$, where d is the dimensionality of the feature. The main purpose of SpSH is to map these training examples to the optimal binary hashing codes $Y = \{y_1, y_2, \ldots, y_n\} \in \{0,1\}^{k \times n}$ through a hashing function $f : R^d \rightarrow \{0,1\}^k$, such that the similarities among data examples in original feature space are preserved in the hashing codes . Here k is the number of hashing bits and $y_j = f(x_j)$.

2.1 Problem Formulation

The proposed SpSH approach is a general learning framework that consists of two stages. In the first stage, the hashing codes are learned in a unified framework by simultaneously learning the hidden semantic representation of documents and preserving the document similarity. In particular, the objective function of SpSH is composed of two components: (1) Semantic representation component, which ensures that the hashing codes are consistent with hidden semantics via a sparse coding model [2]; (2) Similarity preservation component, which aims at preserving the document similarity in the learned hashing codes. An iterative algorithm is then derived based on the objective function using a coordinate descent optimization procedure. In the second stage, the hashing function is learned with respect to the hashing codes for training documents.

2.1.1 Sparse Semantic Reconstruction

The goal of semantic reconstruction of documents is to learn a basis $B \in R^{d \times k}$ and corresponding sparse codes such that input data can be well approximated/represented. Here we assume there are k hidden semantics, each represented by a column of basis B. For the k hashing bits of each document, if the document contains the j-th semantic, then its corresponding j-th bit should be 1, otherwise 0. In this way, the hashing code essentially represents the hidden semantics of the document. Since a document usually related to a small number of semantics, we impose a sparse constraint to ensure that there are few 1's in the hashing

code. Then the sparse semantic reconstruction term can be written as:

$$\|X - BY\|_F^2 + \alpha\|B\|_F^2 + \gamma\|Y\|_1 \quad (1)$$

here $\|\|_F$ is the matrix Frobenius norm. $\|B\|_F^2$ is introduced to avoid overfitting. $\|Y\|_1$ is the sparsity constraint. α and γ are the weight parameters. Intuitively, we reconstruct each document in the corpus X using a small number of basis in B indicated by the hashing code, where a 1 in the code means the corresponding semantic is related to the document and a 0 means irrelevant semantic. By minimizing this term, the hidden semantic structure among the documents are preserved in the learned hashing codes.

2.1.2 Similarity Preservation

One of the key problems in hashing algorithms is similarity preserving, which indicates that similar documents should be mapped to similar hashing codes within a short Hamming distance. The Hamming distance between two binary codes y_i and y_j can be calculated as $\frac{1}{4}\|y_i - y_j\|^2$. To measure the similarity between documents represented by the binary hashing codes, one natural way is to minimize the weighted average Hamming distance as follows:

$$\sum_{i,j} S_{ij}\|y_i - y_j\|^2 \quad (2)$$

Here, S is the similarity matrix which is calculated based on the document features. To meet the similarity preservation criterion, we seek to minimize this quantity, because it incurs a heavy penalty if two similar documents are mapped far away. There are many different ways to define the similarity matrix S. In this paper, we adopt the local similarity due to its nice property in many information retrieval applications [7, 10]. In particular, the corresponding similarities are computed by Gaussian functions, i.e., $S_{ij} = e^{-\|x_i - x_j\|^2/\sigma_{ij}^2}$, where σ_{ij} is a scaling parameter.

By introducing a diagonal $n \times n$ matrix D, whose entries are given by $D_{ii} = \sum_{j=1}^{n} S_{ij}$, Eqn.1 can be rewritten as:

$$tr(Y(D - S)Y^T) = tr(YLY^T) \quad (3)$$

where L is the graph *Laplacian* and $tr()$ is the matrix trace. By minimizing this term, the similarity between different documents can be preserved in the learned hashing codes.

2.2 Optimization Algorithm

The entire objective function of the proposed SpSH combines the above two components as follows:

$$\min_{B,Y} \|X - BY\|_F^2 + \alpha\|B\|_F^2 + \beta tr(YLY^T) + \gamma\|Y\|_1$$
$$s.t. \ Y \in \{0,1\}^{k \times n} \quad (4)$$

2.2.1 Relaxation

Directly minimizing the objective function in Eqn.4 is intractable because of the discrete constraint. Therefore, we propose to relax this constraint to $0 \leq Y \leq 1$. However, even after the relaxation, the objective function is still difficult to optimize since Y and B are coupled together and it is non-convex with respect to Y and B jointly. We propose to use a coordinate descent algorithm for solving this relaxed optimization problem by iteratively optimizing the objective with respect to Y and B. In particular, after initializing B, the relaxed problem can be solved by doing the following two steps iteratively until convergence.

Step 1: Fix B, optimize w.r.t. Y:

$$\min_{Y} \|X - BY\|_F^2 + \beta tr(YLY^T) + \gamma\|Y\|_1 \quad (5)$$

The objective function is differentiable with respect to Y and the partial derivative of Eqn.5 can be calculated as:

$$\partial\frac{Eqn(5)}{Y} = -2B^T X + 2B^T BY + 2\beta YL + \gamma\mathbf{1} \quad (6)$$

With this obtained gradient, L-BFGS Quasi-Newton method is applied to solve this optimization problem.

Step 2: Fix Y, solve for B:

$$\min_{B} \|X - BY\|_F^2 + \alpha\|B\|_F^2 \quad (7)$$

We can obtain the close form solution of B as:

$$B = XY^T(YY^T + \alpha I)^{-1} \quad (8)$$

By solving Eqns.5 and 7 iteratively, the optimal values of Y and B can be obtained.

2.2.2 Binarization

After obtaining the optimal solution for the relaxed problem, we need to binarize them to obtain binary hashing codes that satisfy the relaxed constraints. The binary hashing codes for the training set can be obtained by thresholding Y. It was pointed out in [4] and [7] that desired hashing codes should also maximize the entropy to ensure efficiency. Following the maximum entropy principle, a binary bit that gives balanced partitioning of the whole dataset should provides maximum information. Therefore, we set the threshold for binarizing the *p-th* bit to be the median of y^p. In particular, if *p-th* bit of y_j is larger than median value, y_j^p is set to 1, otherwise y_j^p is set to 0. In this way, the binary code achieves the best balance.

2.2.3 Hashing Function

A linear hashing function is utilized to map documents to the binary hashing codes as:

$$y_j = f(x_j) = Hx_j \quad (9)$$

where H is a $k \times d$ parameter matrix representing the hashing function. Then the optimal hashing function can be obtained by minimizing $\|Y - HX\|^2$.

3. EXPERIMENTS

3.1 Datasets and Implementation

Two text datasets are used in our experiments. $ReutersV1$[1] dataset contains over 800,000 manually categorized newswire stories. A subset of 365001 documents of ReutersV1 is used in our experiment. 328501 documents are randomly selected as the training data, while the remaining 36500 documents are used as testing queries. $20Newsgroups$[2] corpus is collected and originally used for document categorization. We use the popular '18828' version which contains 18828 documents. 16946 documents are randomly chosen for training and the rest 1882

[1]http://www.daviddlewis.com/resources/text/rcv1/
[2]http://people.csail.mit.edu/jrennie/20Newsgroups/

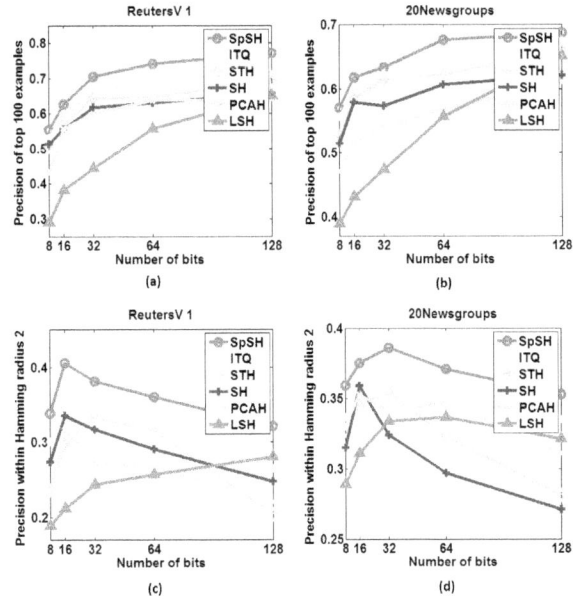

Figure 1: Precision results on two datasets with different hashing bits. (a)-(b): Precision of the top 100 retrieved examples using *Hamming Ranking*. (c)-(d): Precision within Hamming radius 2 using *Hash Lookup*.

documents are used for testing. *tf-idf* features are used to represent the documents.

The parameters α, β and γ are tuned by cross validation on the training set. The number of nearest neighbors is fixed to be 7 when constructing the graph *Laplacian* for all experiments. The source codes of LSH, PCAH, SH, STH and ITQ provided by the authors are used in our experiments.

3.2 Evaluation Method

The search results are evaluated based on the ground-truth labels. We use several metrics to measure the performance of different methods. For evaluation with *Hamming Ranking*, we calculate the precision at top k that is the percentage of relevant neighbors among the top k returned examples, where we set k to be 100 in the experiments. For evaluation with *Hash Lookup*, all the examples within a fixed Hamming distance, r, of the query are evaluated. In particular, following [5] and [9], a Hamming distance $r = 2$ is used to retrieve the neighbors in the case of *Hash Lookup*. The precision of the returned examples falling within Hamming distance 2 is reported.

3.3 Results and Discussion

The proposed SpSH approach is compared with five different methods, *i.e.*, Spectral Hashing (SH) [9], PCA Hashing (PCAH) [4], Latent Semantic Hashing (LSH) [1], Self Taught Hashing (STH) [10] and Iterative Quantization (ITQ) [3]. We evaluate the performance of different methods by varying the number of hashing bits in the range of $\{8, 16, 32, 64, 128\}$.

Three sets of experiments are conducted on both datasets to evaluate the performance of SpSH. In the first set of experiments, we report the precision values for the top 100

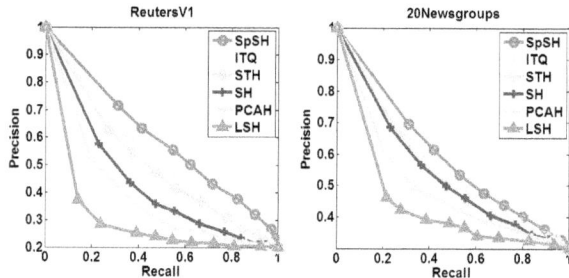

Figure 2: Precision-Recall behavior on two datasets with 32 hashing bits.

Methods	ReutersV1		20Newsgroups	
	training	testing	training	testing
SpSH	123.86	0.4×10^{-4}	74.84	0.5×10^{-4}
ITQ [3]	45.34	0.4×10^{-4}	11.19	0.5×10^{-4}
STH [10]	76.39	0.4×10^{-4}	48.77	0.5×10^{-4}
SH [9]	58.37	3.6×10^{-4}	16.23	3.9×10^{-4}
PCAH [4]	23.17	0.4×10^{-4}	8.18	0.5×10^{-4}
LSH [1]	2.24	0.4×10^{-4}	2.21	0.5×10^{-4}

Table 1: Training and testing time (in second) on two datasets with 32 hashing bits.

retrieved examples in Fig.1(a)-(b). The precision values for retrieved examples with Hamming distance 2 are reported in Fig.1(c)-(d). From these comparison results, we can see that SpSH achieves the best performance among all compared hashing methods on both datasets. We also observe from Fig.1(c)-(d) that the precisions of *Hash Lookup* decrease significantly with the increasing number of hashing bits. This is because when using longer hashing bits, the Hamming space becomes increasingly sparse and very few data points fall within the Hamming ball with radius 2, resulting in many 0 precision queries. However, the precision values of SpSH are still consistently higher than other methods.

In the second set of experiments, the precision-recall curves with 32 hashing bits on both datasets are reported in Fig.2. It is clear that among all of these comparison methods, SpSH shows the best performance. From the reported figures, we can see that LSH does not perform well in most cases. This is because the LSH method is data-independent and may lead to inefficient codes in practice. For SH and STH, although these methods try to preserve the similarity between data examples in their learned hashing codes, they do not model the hidden semantic structure among the documents while our SpSH learns a better sparse semantic representations for document corpus. ITQ achieves better performance than SH and STH since it somehow tries to minimize the quantization errors. However, different from these methods, the proposed SpSH learns the optimal hashing codes and hidden semantic basis jointly to better represent the documents and thus achieves better hashing performance.

The third set of experiments study the training cost for learning hashing function and testing cost for encoding each query. The results on both datasets with 32 bits is reported in Table 1. We can see from this table that the training cost of SpSH is around one hundred seconds, which is comparable with most of the other hashing methods and it is not slow in practice considering the complexity of training. The test time for SpSH is sufficiently fast especially when compared to the nonlinear hashing method SH. The reason is that it only needs linear projection and binarization to generate the hashing codes for queries.

4. CONCLUSION

This paper proposes a novel sparse semantic hashing approach that explores the hidden semantic representation of documents in learning their corresponding hashing codes.

A unified framework is designed for ensuring the hidden semantic structure among the documents by a sparse coding model, while at the same time preserving the document similarity using graph Laplacian. Extensive experiments on two datasets demonstrate the superior performance of the proposed research over several state-of-the-art hashing methods.

5. ACKNOWLEDGMENTS

This work is partially supported by NSF research grants IIS-0746830, DRL-0822296, CNS-1012208, IIS-1017837, CNS-1314688 and a research grant from Office of Naval Research (ONR-11627465). This work is also partially supported by the Center for Science of Information (CSoI), an NSF Science and Technology Center, under grant agreement CCF-0939370.

6. REFERENCES

[1] M. Datar, N. Immorlica, P. Indyk, and V. S. Mirrokni. Locality-sensitive hashing scheme based on p-stable distributions. In *Symposium on Computational Geometry*, pages 253–262, 2004.

[2] S. Gao, I. W.-H. Tsang, L.-T. Chia, and P. Zhao. Local features are not lonely - laplacian sparse coding for image classification. In *CVPR*, pages 3555–3561, 2010.

[3] Y. Gong, S. Lazebnik, A. Gordo, and F. Perronnin. Iterative quantization: A procrustean approach to learning binary codes for large-scale image retrieval. *TPAMI*, 2012.

[4] R.-S. Lin, D. A. Ross, and J. Yagnik. Spec hashing: Similarity preserving algorithm for entropy-based coding. In *CVPR*, pages 848–854, 2010.

[5] J. Wang, S. Kumar, and S.-F. Chang. Semi-supervised hashing for large-scale search. *IEEE TPAMI*, 34(12):2393–2406, 2012.

[6] Q. Wang, L. Si, Z. Zhang, and N. Zhang. Active hashing with joint data example and tag selection. In *SIGIR*, 2014.

[7] Q. Wang, D. Zhang, and L. Si. Semantic hashing using tags and topic modeling. In *SIGIR*, pages 213–222, 2013.

[8] Q. Wang, D. Zhang, and L. Si. Weighted hashing for fast large scale similarity search. In *CIKM*, pages 1185–1188, 2013.

[9] Y. Weiss, A. Torralba, and R. Fergus. Spectral hashing. In *NIPS*, pages 1753–1760, 2008.

[10] D. Zhang, J. Wang, D. Cai, and J. Lu. Self-taught hashing for fast similarity search. In *SIGIR*, pages 18–25, 2010.

[11] Q. Zhang, Y. Wu, Z. Ding, and X. Huang. Learning hash codes for efficient content reuse detection. In *SIGIR*, pages 405–414, 2012.

[12] Z. Zhang, Q. Wang, L. Ruan, and L. Si. Preference preserving hashing for efficient recommendation. In *SIGIR*, 2014.

Spatial Verification for Scalable Mobile Image Retrieval

Xiyu Yang and Xueming Qian*

SMILES LAB, Xi'an Jiaotong University, Xi'an China, 710049

yangxiyu@stu.xjtu.edu.cn; qianxm@mail.xjtu.edu.cn

ABSTRACT

Owing to the portable and excellent phone camera, people now prefer to take photos and upload them by mobile phone. Content based image retrieval is effective for users to obtain relevant information about a photo. Taking the limited bandwidth and instability into account, we propose an effective scalable mobile image retrieval approach in this paper. The proposed mobile image retrieval algorithm first determines the relevant photos according to visual similarity in mobile end, then mines salient visual words by exploring saliency from multiple relevant images, and finally we determine the contribution order of salient visual words for scalable retrieval. In server terminal, spatial verification is performed to re-rank the results. Compared to the existing approaches of mobile image retrieval, our approach transmits less data and reduces the computational cost of spatial verification. Most importantly, when the bandwidth is limited, we can transmit a part of features according their contributions to retrieval. Experimental results show the effectiveness of the proposed approach.

Categories and Subject Descriptors

I.2.10 [**Vision and Scene Understanding**]: VISION

General Terms

Algorithms, Measurement, Performance, Experimentation, Verification

Keywords

Mobile Image Retrieval; Scalable Retrieval; Salient Visual Word (SVW); Multiple Relevant Photos; Spatial Verification

1. INTRODUCTION

Recent years, the research on content based image retrieval flourished owing to the BoW [1] model and local features, such as SIFT [2]. And Chum et al. [10] proposed to update the query by combining it with retrieval results every time to learn better representation of query and improve the retrieval performance. Usually single visual word is not distinctive and stable enough. To improve the BoW model, co-occurrence pattern and spatial verification are introduced. Co-occurrence pattern constructs visual phrase or group and represents image as bag of visual groups [3]. Spatial verification enforces geometric consistent constraint on common words that query and dataset image share, such as RANSAC [4] and spatial coding [5]. Spatial coding

*Corresponding author.

CIKM'14, November 3–7, 2014, Shanghai, China.
Copyright © 2014 ACM 978-1-4503-2598-1/14/11…$15.00.
http://dx.doi.org/10.1145/2661829.2661971

performs well in partial duplicate image retrieval. Due to the rapid development of digital camera, photos usually have high definition, which results in that too many local features are extracted from one photo. Thus spatial coding will be time-consuming.

Smartphone is experiencing booming development recently. It has been an indispensable part of people's lives. With the pervasiveness of digital image-capture devices such as mobile phone, it is likely that user take many photos about same object or scene. Hence, it is rational to acquire salient visual words from multiple relevant photos. These salient visual words should be stable and significant, which capture the repeated crucial content from multiple photos.

In this paper, a novel spatial verification algorithm is proposed based on salient visual word. Our approach consists of 3 steps: 1) mining multiple relevant photos. Once user inputs a query, our approach automatically mines some relevant photos; 2) extracting salient visual words (SVWs) and ranking them for scalable image retrieval. With the relevant photos, we extract the stable, robust and distinctive visual words from them for image retrieval; 3) re-ranking the retrieval results based on spatial verification to improve the performance. Figure1 shows the flowchart.

query   Mining multi-photos

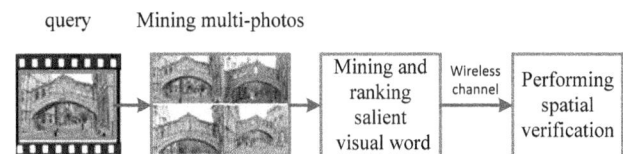

Figure 1. The system flowchart.

The main contributions of this paper are summarized as following: 1) we extract salient visual words, which eliminates the effect of noisy, unstable and irrelevant features; 2) the small number of robust salient visual words reduces the computational complexity of spatial verification and is suitable for mobile retrieval; 3) we change the restrict spatial consistent constraint into a soft type of accumulating consistent score, which makes spatial coding applicable to universal image retrieval task besides duplicate image retrieval and achieves notable performance; 4) considering the instability of invariance of wireless channel, we propose selection scheme for salient visual words, which achieves scalable retrieval.

The remainder of this paper is organized as follows. Section 2 overviews the system. Section 3 describes the method of mining multiple relevant photos. Section 4 details the strategy of extracting salient visual word from multiple relevant photos and the re-ranking scheme. In section 5, we introduce the spatial verification model. Experimental results and discussion are represented in Section 6.

2. SYSTEM OVERVIEW

As shown in Fig. 1, the proposed mobile image retrieval approach consists of three steps: 1) multiple relevant photos mining; 2) salient visual words mining and re-ranking; 3) performing spatial verification to re-rank the initial retrieval results. Once the user inputs a query image, our system mines multiple most relevant photos automatically in mobile end. Then, with the multi-photos, we extract salient visual word from them to eliminate noise, improve precision and reduce computational complexity. To make our algorithm adaptive to labile wireless channel, we rank the SVWs according to their stability in multiple relevant images. Thus in the circumstance than bandwidth is narrow, we transmit part of the salient visual words to server terminal. In the server end, we perform spatial verification to re-rank the initial results that are retrieved by SVWs. For the noisy feature in matched dataset image may assigned to same visual word with salient visual word, spatial verification can judge whether the matched feature in truly matched.

3. MINING MULTIPLE PHOTOS

It is possible that, there are many relevant photos to the image that user submitted to retrieval. Our aim is to find visually similar images in the user's mobile end, and to extract salient visual words from them for retrieval.

We describe each image with a set of local features. An image represented through local features can be more powerful than global features [6]. SIFT (scale invariant feature transform) feature is robust against illumination, affine change, scale and other local distortions [2]. A SIFT feature consists of a 128-D descriptor vector and a 4-dimensional DoG key-point detector vector (x, y, scale, and orientation). Each of the 128-dimension SIFT descriptors of an image is quantized to a bag-of-words (BOW) visual vocabulary with W codebooks by hierarchical quantization [7].

To mine the most relevant multiple photos, we measure the similarity between the query and other images in mobile end. Assuming that the normalized BoW histograms of the input image and the images in mobile end are respectively denoted as hq and $hm(k)$, the similarity score of k-th image in smart phone to query, $D(k)$, can be calculated using the city block distance as following:

$$D(k) = \exp(-|h_q - h_m(k)|) \qquad (1)$$

where $|\cdot|$ denotes L1 norm, and $k=1,\cdots,P$, P is the number of images in mobile end, which are primarily from user's photo album.

We sort the similarity scores in descending order. The top ranked M-1 results along with the original query form candidate multiple photos. Although the candidate multiple photos are the most relevant to the input, there still exist noisy images among them. As the noisy images degenerate the performance and the number of multiple photos is tightly related to the calculating cost, it is necessary to remove the noisy. If the similarity score of one candidate photo is too small, we eliminate it. The remnant X candidates are final multiple relevant photos which are used for exploring saliency.

4. MINING AND RANKING SVW

After finding multiple relevant photos for the query image at user's mobile end, we mine the robust and distinctive salient visual words from these relevant photos. Generally, the crucial content occurs more frequently than disturbance in these photos, i.e. the frequency of visual words occurring in crucial content is higher than that in background. As shown in Fig. 2, the house is the crucial content, which occurs more frequently than the trees and pedestrians. Our purpose is to pick out these high-frequency salient visual words for retrieval. Then, to achieve scalable mobile image retrieval, we rank the salient visual words.

4.1 Detecting Identical Semantic Point

We mine salient visual word based on identical semantic point (ISP) detection in our previous work [8]. As in [8], detecting ISP needs to match SIFT features between every two images. For one local feature in an image, it is matched with all the features in other images to detect the optimal matched pair. To speed up the process of mining salient visual word, we perform feature matching on features that are assigned to same visual word. Thus the scope of features that one sift is matched with is shrunk tremendously.

Firstly, we find common words that at least two of the mined multiple relevant photos share. Given that w is a visual word that occurs in i-th and j-th image, we denote the local features that are assigned to w in the two images as S^i and S^j respectively.

Figure 2. The comparison between raw SIFT features and extracted ISPs.

Following [8], then we perform optimal matching pair determination between every two images in multi-images to capture repeated content. During each image-image match, we record all the optimal matched SIFT points pairs (u,q) and their matching scores MS(u,q). The similarity score of two optimal matched SIFT points (u,q) are measured as follows:

$$MS(u,q) = \left(u \times q^T\right) / \left(|u| \times |q|\right) \qquad (2)$$

where u denotes 128-D SIFT descriptor vector from S^i, and q is from S^j. |x| denotes the norm of vector x.

Identical Salient Points (ISP) is determined based on the matching score. An ISP is a set of matched SIFT points, denoted as:

$$ISP_l = \{d_l^1,...,d_l^i,...,d_l^X\} \qquad (3)$$

where ISP_l denotes the l-th ISP, X denotes the number of multiple images, d_l^i is the SIFT ID of l-th ISP in i-th image, which implies the occurrence of l-th ISP in i-th image. d_l^i =0, if no feature in the i-th image matches with other features in ISP_l.

The corresponding visual word of the ISP is defined as salient visual word (SVW). SVWs are pertinent to the crucial content, and the number of SVWs is very small. As shown in Fig.2, the average SIFT point number of the three images is 5418, the average ISP number is only 263, which is about 5% of raw SIFT feature. And the ISP rarely occurs in pedestrian and trees, which manifest that extracting SVW eliminates the noise effectively.

4.2 Ranking the Salient Visual Word

Wireless channel is vulnerable to interference. There exists serious latency when mobile devices suffer from weak signal. To adapt to the variant wireless channel, we propose scalable retrieval. We rank the salient visual words according to their contribution to retrieval, so that we can adjust the data volume to the channel condition. We rank the SVWs in two levels: frequency of occurrence of SVW to rank them on the whole and stability in the multi-photos to rank them in detail.

We denote occurrence of an ISP in multiple relevant images as C:

$$C_l = \{c_l^1, ..., c_l^i, ..., c_l^X\} \qquad (4)$$

where, c_l^i stands for the occurrence of l-th ISP in i-th image. $c_l^i=1$, if $d_l^i \neq 0$, otherwise $c_l^i=0$.

The significance of the l-th ISP is measured based on its consistency score (CS) as following:

$$CS_l = \sum_{i=1}^{X} c_l^i \qquad (5)$$

Thus by ranking the consistency score CS for all the identical salient points, we rank the SVWs on the whole.

Then we rank the SVWs in detail. We accumulate the matched score of the descriptors in an ISP to measure the stability of this ISP. For the SVWs that occur in same number of multiple photos, they are ranked according to the total matched score of the corresponding ISP.

5. SPATIAL VERIFICATION ON SVW

The salient visual words along with their coordinate information in the query image are sent to server end. In server end, we first search the candidate similar images which should contain at least one of the salient visual words transmitted from the mobile end. For the candidate similar images, we perform spatial verification to re-rank them. Spatial coding [5] is adopted to describe the relative position among SVWs. It is possible that the mined multiple images are all eliminated and only the input is remained. In this case, we refine the features extracted from the query image as in [9].

Firstly, SIFT feature assigned to the same visual word will be considered as valid match when its orientation difference with the query feature is less than π/t.

Spatial coding encodes the spatial relationship among visual words in an image into two binary maps: X-map and Y-map. The two maps describe the relative position of each valid feature pairs.

Each element in X-map and Y-map is defined as following:

$$Xmap_{i,j} = \begin{cases} 1 & if \ x_i < x_j \\ 0 & if \ x_i > x_j \end{cases} \qquad (6)$$

$$Ymap_{i,j} = \begin{cases} 1 & if \ y_i < y_j \\ 0 & if \ y_i > y_j \end{cases} \qquad (7)$$

where x_i and x_j denote the horizontal coordinates of i-th feature and j-th feature, and y_i and y_j denote the vertical coordinates.

For query image Iq and matched image Im, X-map and Y-map are generated for each, denoted as (Xq, Yq) and (Xm, Ym), which encode the spatial relationship among the salient visual words which occur in database image. Hence, to verify the spatial layout of common visual words is to compare the X-map and Y-map. Logical Exclusive OR (XOR) operation $\oplus$ is performed on the spatial maps as following:

$$SV_X = X_q \oplus X_m \qquad (8)$$

$$SV_Y = Y_q \oplus Y_m \qquad (9)$$

where SV_X and SV_Y denote the difference in X-map and Y-map.

Thus the spatial consistency of matched feature in two images can be denoted as:

$$SP_X(i) = \sum_{j=1}^{N} SV_X(i,j) \qquad (10)$$

$$SP_Y(i) = \sum_{j=1}^{N} SV_Y(i,j) \qquad (11)$$

where N denotes the number of common visual words. $SP_X(i)$ and $SP_Y(i)$ denote the spatial consistency of i-th common visual word.

For partial duplicate image retrieval, $SP_X(i)$ and $SP_Y(i)$ are required to be zero strictly if i-th common visual word is truly matched in Zhou's paper [5]. However, for universal image retrieval, too rigorous spatial constraint may regards the true matched features as false. To address this problem, we change the absolute way of judgment into a soft way, i.e. calculating the consistency score as following:

$$Score = \sum_{i=1}^{N} \left(SP_X(i) + SP_Y(i) \right) / N \times R(i) \qquad (12)$$

where Score denotes the spatial consistency score of two images. $R(i)$ is a binary function. $R(i)=1$, if $\left(SP_X(i) + SP_Y(i) \right) / N < thr$, otherwise $R(i)=0$. thr is the threshold.

After computing the spatial consistency score for each initial retrieved image, the initial results are re-ranked according to their spatial consistency with query image.

6. EXPERIMENTATION

We conduct our experiments on the Oxford Buildings Dataset. The scalable vocabulary tree (SVT) is learned on the dataset. It includes 61724 leaf nodes in total. To show the effectiveness of our approach, we compare our method with BoW model [1], Query Expansion [10]. Some main factors that influence the performance are discussed as well.

6.1 Dataset

The Oxford Buildings Dataset consists of 5062 images collected from Flickr by searching for particular Oxford landmarks, 11 landmarks in total. For each landmark, 5 possible queries are given. Our test set consists of the given 55 query images. The first step of our approach, obtaining multiple relevant photos, is run on Oxford Buildings set. If the system is applied in reality, the first step should be conducted on photos stored in mobile end.

6.2 Evaluation Criterion

Mean precision at top K (P@K) is the evaluation criterion measuring the mean percent of relevant images in the top N retrieved results. It is defined as:

$$P@K = (1/T) \times \sum_{i=1}^{T} \left(R_i / K \right) \qquad (13)$$

where T is the size of test set, $T=55$ in this paper. R_i denotes the number of retrieved relevant images up to K for i-th query image.

6.3 Performance Comparison

We compare our approach with the BoW model and query expansion. In BoW model, the retrieval results are ranked based on their similarity of BoW histogram to the query. In query expansion, a query region is given as input. To be fair with our method, we carry out retrieval with the whole image instead of query region. In addition, our approach is also compared with the original spatial coding proposed in [5], denoted as SP, in which all the local features extracted from the query image are used for spatial coding. The results shown in Fig. 3 demonstrate the effectiveness of our approach. SSV denotes our method. Owing to the too strict requirement in spatial consistency, SP performs inferior in universal image retrieval to in duplicate retrieval. When the object is not clear or occupies a small region of query, QE cannot perform well, whereas our approach can mine the salient visual word that is relevant to the object.

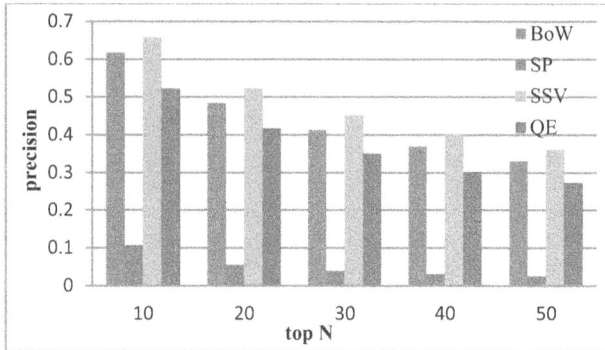

Figure 3. The mean precision of three different methods.

In addition, to show the less necessary data volume of our approach, we estimate the data size of different methods. In our approach, the salient visual words along with their corresponding horizontal and vertical coordinates are transmitted. Considering the sparse distribution of SVWs, their coordinates are rounded to short integer. Supposing that 50 SVWs are transmitted, 300 bytes are needed. Table 1 show the data size of different methods.

Table 1. The comparison of necessary data size

Approaches	SSV	SP	BoW	JPEG
Data(bytes)	300	18K	60.3K	385.8K

6.4 Discussion

The performance of our approach is influence by two main factors: *thr* and the number of SVWs that are transmitted to server end. We discuss their impact in this subsection.

6.4.1 The impact of thr

The parameter *thr* determines whether a matched feature pair is regarded as truly matched. Figure 4 shows the performance with different *thr* value. The results show that the performance is best when *thr* is around 0.8. Bigger *thr* will not lead better performance, because some actually false matching will be taken for right matching.

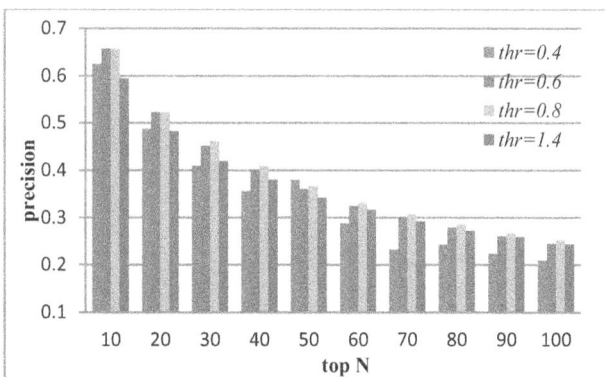

Figure 4. The performance for different *thr* value.

6.4.2 The impact of data volume transmitted

Another main factor that influences the retrieval performance is the number of salient visual words that are sent to server terminal. We use 20, 50,100, and 200 SVWs for retrieval respectively. Figure 5 shows that more SVWs result in better performance. However, when the data volume reaches 100 SVWs, the improvement in precision decelerates. And we find that 20 SVWs are enough for retrieval, for SVWs are pertinent to the crucial content of the query image.

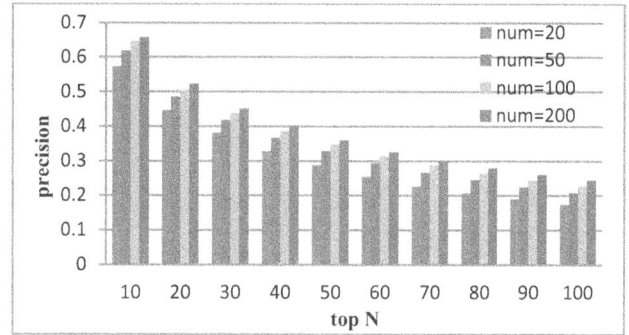

Figure 5. The comparison for different data volume.

7. CONCLUSION

In this paper, we propose a novel mobile image retrieval scheme based on mining salient visual words from multiple relevant photos. Our approach achieves better performance with less data. Our future work will focus on mining salient visual words from single query image to make our method available in the case that multiple relevant images cannot be mined in mobile end.

8. ACKNOWLEDGMENTS

Our thanks to ACM SIGGHI for allowing us to modify the templates. This work is supported by NSFC No. 60903121, No. 61332018, No. 61173109, Microsoft Research Asia.

9. REFERENCES

[1] J. Sivic, A. Zisserman. Video google: a text retrieval approach to object matching in videos. ICCV, 2003.

[2] D. G. Lowe. Distinctive image features from scale-invariant keypoints. IJCV, 60(2): 91-110, Nov. 2004

[3] S. Zhang, Q. Tian, G. Hua, Q. Huang and S. Li. Descriptive visual words and visual phrases for image. ACM MM, 2009.

[4] M. A. Fischler and R. C. Bolles. Random sample consensus. Comm. ACM, 24(6):381–395, 1981.

[5] W. Zhou, Y. Lu, H. Li, Y. Song and Q. Tian. Spatial coding for large scale partial-duplicate web image search. ACM MM, 2010.

[6] A. Qamra and E. Chang. Scalable landmark recognition using EXTENT. Multimedia tools and Applications, 2008.

[7] D. Nistér and H. Stewénius. Scalable Recognition with a Vocabulary Tree. CVPR, 2006.

[8] Y. Xue and X. Qian. Visual summarization of landmarks via viewpoint modeling. ICIP, 2012.

[9] S. Zhang, Q. Huang, G. Hua, S. Jiang, W. Gao and Q. Tian. Building contextual Visual Vocabulary for large-scale image application. ACM MM, Oct. 2010

[10] O. Chum, J. Philbin, J. Sivic, M. Isard, and A. Zisserman. Total recall: automatic query expansion with a generative feature model for object retrieval. ICCV, 2007.

A Generative Model for Generating Relevance Labels from Human Judgments and Click-Logs

Xugang Ye, Jingjing Li, Zijie Qi, Bingyue Peng, Dan Massey

Microsoft

Bellevue, WA, USA

{xugangye, jingjing.li, zijieqi, bpeng, danmass}@microsoft.com

ABSTRACT

Lack of high quality relevance labels is a common challenge in the early stage of search engine development. In media search, due to the high recruiting and training cost, the labeling process is usually conducted by a small number of human judges. Consequently, the generated labels are often limited and biased. On the contrary, the click data that is extracted from a large population of real users is massive and less biased. However, the click data also contains considerable noise. Therefore, more and more researchers have begun to focus on combining those two resources to generate a better ground-truth approximation. In this paper, we present a novel method of generating the relevance labels for media search. The method is based on a generative model that considers human judgment, position, and click status as observations generated from a hidden relevance with multinomial prior. The model considers the position bias with a requirement that the click status depends on both the hidden relevance and the position. We infer the model parameters by using a Gibbs sampling procedure with hyper-parameter optimization. From experiments on the Xbox's data, the newly inferred relevance labels significantly increase the data volume for ranker training and have demonstrated superior performance compared to using the limited human labels only, the click-through-rates only, and the heuristic combination of the two.

Categories and Subject Descriptors

H.3.3 [Information Storage and Retrieval]: Information Search and Retrieval; I.2.6 [Artificial Intelligence]: Learning

General Terms

Algorithms, Experimentation

Keywords

Search; relevance; labeling; generative model

1. INTRODUCTION

To generate the relevance labels in search problems is essentially to approximate the ground truth, which can only be revealed from the information of many users. To be able to train a good ranker, the most important thing is to have enough labeled query-document pairs that truly reflect the users' preference. However,

in reality, it's very difficult to obtain a large number of high quality labels directly from users especially when a search engine is in its early phase. Therefore a common approach is to employ a small number of human judges to do the labeling work under limited budget. One problem is that it's hard to generate enough labeled data for ranker training. Another problem is that the labels provided by a small number of judges are biased toward a small group of users. Compared with the human labels, the click-logs are cheap, scalable, and much less biased. For these reasons, mining the click-logs for relevance information has been an appealing topic in information retrieval and tremendous research efforts have been put into modeling click data during the past decade.

Although the click-logs are very informative, they are also noisy. Chen et al. [3] presented an interesting statistical summary of a combined web-search data that contains 474,185 human-judged query-document pairs and 16.18 million clicks on these query-document pairs. The judgments have five levels: *Perfect*, *Excellent*, *Good*, *Fair*, and *Bad*. Among all the clicks the portion under *Excellent* is less than 35% and the portion under *Bad* or *Fair* is more than 28%. This indicates that the reasons for a click event are much more than just the relevance. Probably one of the mostly discussed click factors is the position bias, which was first noticed by Granka et al. [7] and many researchers such as Richardson et al. [12] and Craswell et al. [5] quickly proposed methods to correct it. Later on more complicated models [6][8][9][2] were proposed to address the position bias in various forms. While those models intensively consider the position factor, they don't handle other potential reasons for clicks. In our search practices in the media domain, we found that a noticeable number of clicks are not based on relevance but on the popularity of the returned content, especially when the irrelevant content is returned due to the poor quality of the search engine. We also found that some users are more likely to click than others and a lot of clicks seem to be very random. For a very relevant result, a user might not click simply because it has been read before and the user doesn't want to get into it this time. Since there are too many reasons for click/nonclick, it may not be enough to depend solely on the click-logs for relevance retrial when it's hard to distinguish the high-quality clicks that lead to user consumption and the low-quality clicks that look like random browsing. A solution is to utilize the limited human judgments and find a way to combine them with the click-logs. The recent noise-aware click model [3] is such an attempt. There can be many noise-aware models, as the generalizations of previous click models.

Based on the literature and our practice in media searches, we also made an effort to combine the usage of human judgments and click-logs. Just like the peer reports, we also found that the human labels are of higher quality than the clicks. However, due to the fact that there are only a very limited number of human judges, it has been found that even if a result is judged at the highest relevance level at the beginning, it can still be confirmed to be irrelevant later on, and vice versa. In the case that bias or errors are easily identified, the human judgments should not be treated as the ground truth, rather it may be treated as observations in addition to the click-logs. In practice we observed that the human judgment and the click-through-rate (CTR) can correct each other. For example, if a result is very relevant, then the chance that both the human rating and the CTR are low is less than the chance that at least one of them is high. If one is observed as high and the other is observed as low, then probably the higher one shouldn't be that high and the lower one shouldn't be that low. Starting from here, we explored the idea of adding the human judgment as less noisy observation and imagining there is a true relevance behind. We formulated the idea into a new generative model that views the observable human judgment, position, and click status as being generated from the hidden relevance. The rest of the paper is organized as follows: we first formulate our generative model; we then present our Gibbs sampling method with hyper-parameter optimization for inference; after introducing the evaluation metrics, we present some experimental test results of applying our inferred relevance to the Xbox's ranker training; finally we conclude by highlighting our model and pointing out the directions of future work.

2. FORMULATION

The basic idea is that for a query-document pair in a query session, the human judgment of the relevance, the position of the document, and the click-status of the document are all generated by the hidden true relevance. We require that the click-status of the document also depends on its position in the session. In addition, the hidden true relevance is a multinomial sample. In our notations, we let (h_t, i_t, c_t) denote the triplet of the document d under the t-th (out of T) session of the query q, where $h_t \in \{1, ..., H\}$, $i_t \in \{1, ..., M\}$, and $c_t \in \{1, 0\}$ respectively are the human judgment, the position, and the click status. H is number of human judgment categories including the missing judgment and M is the position truncation level. We let $r_t \in \{1, ..., K\}$ denote the hidden true relevance level that has the multinomial prior parameterized by $\vec{\theta} = (\theta_1, ..., \theta_K)$, where K is number of the true relevance levels and level k represents the k-th highest level. The following Figure 1 illustrates the structure of the model.

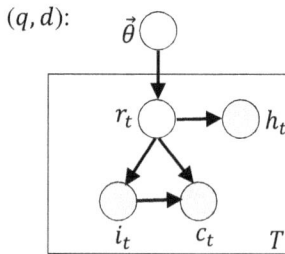

Figure 1: The graphical model representation of the (human judgment, position, click)-generation

In practice, the human judgments are very sparse. Hence it's commonly observed that a lot of h_t are empty. Also in most sessions, there might be just one single rating as *Excellent*, *Good*,

or *Bad* etc. However, the data of (i_t, c_t) is abundant. Our goal is to infer the parameters $\vec{\theta}$ from the observations $\vec{h} = (h_1, h_2, ...)$, $\vec{\iota} = (i_1, i_2, ...)$, and $\vec{c} = (c_1, c_2, ...)$. This can be achieved through the maximum likelihood estimation method.

Under the structure of our model, the joint likelihood of observing $(\vec{h}, \vec{\iota}, \vec{c})$ can be computed via conditioning on the latent relevance sequence $\vec{r} = (r_1, r_2, ...)$. That is

$$P(\vec{h}, \vec{\iota}, \vec{c} | \vec{\theta})$$
$$= \sum_{\vec{r}} P(\vec{h}, \vec{\iota}, \vec{c} | \vec{r}) P(\vec{r} | \vec{\theta})$$
$$= \sum_{\vec{r}} \prod_t P(h_t | r_t) \prod_t P(i_t, c_t | r_t) \prod_t P(r_t | \vec{\theta})$$
$$= \sum_{\vec{r}} \prod_t [P(h_t | r_t) P(i_t, c_t | r_t) P(r_t | \vec{\theta})]$$
$$= \prod_t \sum_{r=1}^{K} P(h_t | r) P(i_t, c_t | r) \theta_r. \quad (1)$$

Hence the joint likelihood is determined by several basic probabilities. They include $P(h|r)$: the probability of observing human judgment h given the relevance level r, $P(i, c|r)$: the probability of observing position i and click status c given the relevance level r, and θ_r: the probability of the relevance level r. Note that $P(h|r)$ measures the quality of the human judgment, $P(i, c|r)$ can be factorized into the product of $P(c|i, r)$ and $P(i|r)$, which respectively measures the position bias and the search engine's quality.

3. INFERENCE

To maximize the joint likelihood (1), our strategy is a Gibbs sampling procedure that is similar to the one used in [11][13], but without using the Dirichlet prior for the purpose of simplicity. According to our model, the full conditional posterior for sampling r_t given $\vec{r} \backslash r_t, \vec{h}, \vec{\iota}, \vec{c}$, and $\vec{\theta}$ is

$$P(r_t = r | \vec{r} \backslash r_t, \vec{h}, \vec{\iota}, \vec{c}, \vec{\theta})$$
$$= \frac{P(r_t = r, \vec{r} \backslash r_t, \vec{h}, \vec{\iota}, \vec{c} | \vec{\theta})}{P(\vec{r} \backslash r_t, \vec{h}, \vec{\iota}, \vec{c} | \vec{\theta})}$$
$$\propto P(r_t = r, \vec{r} \backslash r_t, \vec{h}, \vec{\iota}, \vec{c} | \vec{\theta})$$
$$= P(\vec{h}, \vec{\iota}, \vec{c} | r_t = r, \vec{r} \backslash r_t) P(r_t = r, \vec{r} \backslash r_t | \vec{\theta})$$
$$\propto P(h_t | r) P(i_t, c_t | r) \theta_r. \quad (2)$$

We start from initial guesses of $P(h|r)$, $P(i, c|r)$, and $\vec{\theta}$ and sample $\vec{r}$ using the full conditional posterior (2). Given $\vec{r}$, we can re-estimate $P(h|r)$, $P(i, c|r)$, and $\vec{\theta}$ via smoothed counting. The smoothing is based on the pre-counts that are the results of aggregating over all the qd-pairs. After a certain number of sweepings, we perform a hyper-parameter optimization step for $\vec{\theta}$. The optimization is to minimize a loss function of $\theta_1, ..., \theta_{K-1}$ under the constraints: $0 \leq \theta_r \leq 1$ for $r = 1, ..., K-1$ and $\sum_{r=1}^{K-1} \theta_r \leq 1$. By substituting the estimates $\hat{P}(h_t | r)$ and $\hat{P}(i_t, c_t | r)$ into (1) and taking the negative of the natural logarithm, we obtain the loss function of $\theta_1, ..., \theta_{K-1}$ as

$$L^{\vec{\theta}}(\theta_1, ..., \theta_{K-1}) =$$
$$-\sum_t \ln[\sum_{r=1}^{K-1} \hat{P}(h_t | r) \hat{P}(i_t, c_t | r) \theta_r + \hat{P}(h_t | K) \hat{P}(i_t, c_t | K)(1 - \sum_{r=1}^{K-1} \theta_r)].$$
$$(3)$$

A nice property of this loss function is that it's convex. Hence we can apply the gradient descent method. Let $\eta > 0$ denote the learning rate (usually 0.01). We start from a feasible $\vec{\theta}$. If $0 \leq \theta_r' = \theta_r - \eta \cdot \frac{\partial L^{\vec{\theta}}}{\partial \theta_r} / ||\nabla L^{\vec{\theta}}||_2 \leq 1$ for all $r = 1, ..., K-1$ and $\sum_{r=1}^{K-1} \theta_r' \leq 1$ we then perform the update: $\theta_r \leftarrow \theta_r'$ for all $r =$

$1, \dots, K-1$. Since there could be hundreds of thousands of qd-pairs, a practical implementation is to use the map-reduce [4] for parallelization.

4. EVALUATION METRICS

Practically the quality of the labels is tested by training a ranker and evaluating its performance on the test data sets. We consider the future performance by click-metrics and NDCG (normalized discounted cumulative gain) [10] measurements. Ideally, a good ranker should have good test performance under both the click-metrics and NDCG measurements if the click-signals are consistent with the human judgments. We use the click-happening-rate (CHR) and the last-click-rate (LCR) of the top i positions for $i = 1,2,4$ as our click-metrics. We also use the NDCG of the top i positions for $i = 1,2,4$ as our NDCG measurements. The CHR of the top i positions is calculated as

$$\text{CHR}_i = \frac{\text{Number of sessions having} \geq 1 \text{ click in first } i \text{ positions}}{\text{Number of sessions}}. \quad (4)$$

The LCR of the top i positions is calculated as

$$\text{LCR}_i = \frac{\text{Number of sessions having the last click in first } i \text{ positions}}{\text{Number of sessions}}. \quad (5)$$

The NDCG of the top i positions is calculated as

$$\text{NDCG}_i = \frac{1}{N} \sum_q \left(\sum_{j=1}^{i} \frac{rel_j^q}{\log_2(1+j)} \right) / \left(\sum_{j=1}^{i} \frac{\overline{rel}_j^q}{\log_2(1+j)} \right), \quad (6)$$

where $\overline{rel}_1^q \geq \overline{rel}_2^q \geq \cdots$ represent the descending order of $rel_1^q, rel_2^q, \dots$, which respectively are the relevance gains of the documents at positions $1,2,\dots$ under the query q that does not have all zero-gain results, and N is total number of such queries.

5. EXPERIMENTAL RESULTS

In this section, we present some experimental results of comparing the relevance labels generated by our method with several other types of relevance labels. We used an Xbox's data set that contains the human judgments and click-logs from February 2013 to May 2013 to generate the training data for deriving rankers. Among 260,126 unique query-document pairs that appeared in no less than 30 sessions, about 16.9% were judged with three levels of judgments: *Excellent, Good, Bad*. We built six training data sets with each of them having the same feature set but different label type. They are named and explained as the follows:

i. HJ: Training data with human judgment labels. The labels have three unique values of gain: 15 for *Excellent*, 7 for *Good*, and 0 for *Bad*.

ii. lCTR: Training data with lCTR labels. The lCTR is calculated under the assumption that in a session, the returned results before the last click are viewed and those after the last click are not viewed. The label gain is calculated as lCTR $\cdot$ 15 and rounded.

iii. tCTR: Training data with tCTR labels. The tCTR is calculated under the assumption that in a session, the returned results before a pre-defined truncated position are viewed and those after the truncated position are not viewed. The label gain is calculated as tCTR $\cdot$ 15 and rounded.

iv. tCTR∪HJ: Training data with tCTR∪HJ labels. The query-document pairs in the training data are the union of those with tCTR-labels and those with HJ-labels. For each with both the tCTR-label and the HJ-label, the final label gain is calculated as the rounded average.

v. GM2: Training data with GM2 labels. The labels are inferred from our generative model in binary case $K = 2$. The label gain is calculated as $15 \cdot \theta_1$ and rounded.

vi. GM3: Training data with GM3 labels. The labels are inferred from our generative model in trinary case $K = 3$. The label gain is calculated as $15 \cdot \theta_1 + 7 \cdot \theta_2$ and rounded.

For the training data with the HJ labels, there are 6838 unique queries and 43961 unique query-document pairs; for each of the other five sets of training data, there are 31,075 unique queries and 260,126 unique query-document pairs. For calculating the tCTR, we truncate at position 50. For inferring $\vec{\theta}$, we also truncate at position 50 so that our generative model can fit the same range of positions. For ranker training, we used the same learning algorithm as LambdaRank [1].

After the six rankers were trained, we used the click-logs in June 2013 to test the future click-performance and used a set of human judgments that contains 6654 unique queries and 36,000 unique query-document pairs in movie and TV domains to test the future NDCG-performance. Those query-document pairs were judged from June 2013 to August 2013. For each ranker, to calculate both the click-metrics and the NDCG values, the documents under each query are ordered by the corresponding ranker-scores. To score each query-document pair in the test sets, the same feature set in the training data was used. The test results are summarized in the following Tables 1, 2, where the performance of HJ at the top 1 position is treated as baseline represented by value 1 and all the other values are the relative ones.

Table 1: The relative click-performance

Label	CHR_1	CHR_2	CHR_4	LCR_1	LCR_2	LCR_4
HJ	1.0000	1.2668	1.5313	1.0000	1.3157	1.6571
lCTR	0.9523	1.2455	1.5193	0.9457	1.2894	1.6459
tCTR	1.0290	1.2801	1.5365	1.0241	1.3310	1.6669
tCTR∪HJ	1.0244	1.2779	**1.5381**	1.0239	1.3316	1.6676
GM2	1.0344	**1.2819**	1.5370	1.0318	**1.3345**	**1.6692**
GM3	**1.0434**	**1.2819**	1.5351	**1.0465**	1.3343	1.6655

Table 2: The relative NDCG-performance

Label	Movie			TV		
	NDCG_1	NDCG_2	NDCG_4	NDCG_1	NDCG_2	NDCG_4
HJ	1.0000	1.0099	1.0216	1.0000	0.9920	1.0001
lCTR	0.9362	0.9308	0.9516	0.9376	0.9170	0.9258
tCTR	0.9421	0.9263	0.9455	0.9145	0.9094	0.9150
tCTR∪HJ	0.9912	0.9870	1.0029	0.9819	0.9777	0.9879
GM2	0.9925	0.9847	1.0041	0.9814	0.9753	0.9833
GM3	**1.0254**	**1.0148**	**1.0251**	**1.0034**	**0.9970**	**1.0010**

An observation is that our model in trinary case ($K = 3$) has the superior performance at the top 1 position under both the click metrics and the NDCG measures. This is very encouraging since the top 1 position is very important. For the binary case ($K = 2$), the NDCG values drop a lot possibly because for any query-document pair, the *Excellent* with gain = 15 and the *Good* with gain = 7 in human labels are grouped together as relevant so that the gain 15 and the gain 7 are not differentiated. However, it still has the second best click performance at the top 1 position and its values of the click-metrics are very good at the top 2 and top 4 positions compared to the other label types. The lCTR in overall has the worst performance that indicates certain effect of noise. The tCTR has much better click-performance, but its NDCG-performance is relatively poor. This implies that there exists some discrepancy between the human judgments and the click signals. The tCTR∪HJ has better-balanced results in that the click-performance is very similar to that of the tCTR, but the NDCG-performance is much better. The benefit of combining human judgments and click signals was confirmed again by our generative model under $K = 2$ and $K = 3$. The purpose of the tCTR∪HJ is the same as the goal of our generative model, but it's more like an ad hoc heuristic. On the other hand, our generative model is based on a solid foundation of Bayesian statistics.

6. CONCLUSION

In this paper, we introduce a novel method of generating relevance labels from human judgments and click-logs. The method is based on a generative model that views the human judgment, the position, and the click status as the observations generated from the hidden relevance. Additionally, the latent relevance level is assumed to have the multinomial prior. Hence the model is Bayesian and can be inferred using the Gibbs sampling procedure with the hyper-parameter optimization steps. The model considers the relevance, the quality of the human judgment, the position bias, and the quality of the search engine behind. We performed experiments on the Xbox's data and generated relevance labels to construct the training data that was significantly larger than the training data with only human labels. We also derived a superior ranker measured by the future click-performance and NDCG metrics. Our ranker comparison is fair in the sense that in the ranker training, we kept the same feature set and the same learning algorithm as LambdaRank and in the ranker testing, we used the same future click data and the same future human judgment data under the same feature set. We found superior performance of our method at the top 1 position, which is very important in Xbox's search. Compared with the ad hoc heuristics of combining human judgments and click information, our method is built on a solid statistical foundation and can be generalized to incorporate more click factors. Our suggestion for immediate next work is to add the popularity and recentness of the returned content as observable factors that affect both the human judgments and the clicks into the probabilistic graphical model.

7. ACKNOWLEDGMENTS

We thank Microsoft's Aeather team and Cosmos team for providing powerful computing tools and resources. We also thank those colleagues in Microsoft's IPE media discovery team for their helps in preparing the data.

8. REFERENCES

[1] Burges, C. J. 2010. From ranknet to lambdarank to lambdamart: An overview. *Learning*, *11*, 23-581.

[2] Chapelle, O., & Zhang, Y. (2009, April). A dynamic bayesian network click model for web search ranking. In *Proceedings of the 18th international conference on World wide web* (pp. 1-10). ACM.

[3] Chen, W., Wang, D., Zhang, Y., Chen, Z., Singla, A., & Yang, Q. (2012, February). A noise-aware click model for web search. In *Proceedings of the fifth ACM international conference on Web search and data mining* (pp. 313-322). ACM.

[4] Chu, C. T., Kim, S. K., Lin, Y. A., Yu, Y., Bradski, G., Ng, A. Y., & Olukotun, K. (2006, December). Map-reduce for machine learning on multicore. In *NIPS* (Vol. 6, pp. 281-288).

[5] Craswell, N., Zoeter, O., Taylor, M., & Ramsey, B. (2008, February). An experimental comparison of click position-bias models. In *Proceedings of the 2008 International Conference on Web Search and Data Mining* (pp. 87-94). ACM.

[6] Dupret, G. E., & Piwowarski, B. (2008, July). A user browsing model to predict search engine click data from past observations. In *Proceedings of the 31st annual international ACM SIGIR conference on Research and development in information retrieval* (pp. 331-338). ACM.

[7] Granka, L. A., Joachims, T., & Gay, G. (2004, July). Eye-tracking analysis of user behavior in WWW search. In *Proceedings of the 27th annual international ACM SIGIR conference on Research and development in information retrieval* (pp. 478-479). ACM.

[8] Guo, F., Liu, C., & Wang, Y. M. (2009, February). Efficient multiple-click models in web search. In *Proceedings of the Second ACM International Conference on Web Search and Data Mining* (pp. 124-131). ACM.

[9] Guo, F., Liu, C., Kannan, A., Minka, T., Taylor, M., Wang, Y. M., & Faloutsos, C. (2009, April). Click chain model in web search. In *Proceedings of the 18th international conference on World wide web* (pp. 11-20). ACM.

[10] Järvelin, K., & Kekäläinen, J. 2002. Cumulated gain-based evaluation of IR techniques. *ACM Transactions on Information Systems (TOIS)*, *20*(4), 422-446.

[11] McCallum, A., & Kachites, A. 2002. "MALLET: A Machine Learning for Language Toolkit." *http://mallet.cs.umass.edu*.

[12] Richardson, M., Dominowska, E., & Ragno, R. (2007, May). Predicting clicks: estimating the click-through rate for new ads. In *Proceedings of the 16th international conference on World Wide Web* (pp. 521-530). ACM.

[13] Yao, L., Mimno, D., & McCallum, A. 2009. Efficient methods for topic model inference on streaming document collections. In *KDD 2009*.

Generalized Bias-Variance Evaluation of TREC Participated Systems

Peng Zhang[1], Linxue Hao[1], Dawei Song[1,2], Jun Wang[3], Yuexian Hou[1], Bin Hu[4]

[1]Tianjin Key Laboratory of Cognitive Computing and Application, Tianjin University, China
[2]The Computing Department, The Open University, United Kingdom
[3]Department of Computer Science, University College London, United Kingdom
[4]Ubiquitous Awareness and Intelligent Solutions Lab, Lanzhou University, China
{darcyzzj, haolinxue, dawei.song2010}@gmail.com,
jun_wang@acm.org, yxhou@tju.edu.cn, bh@lzu.edu.cn

ABSTRACT

Recent research has shown that the improvement of mean retrieval effectiveness (e.g., MAP) may sacrifice the retrieval stability across queries, implying a tradeoff between effectiveness and stability. The evaluation of both effectiveness and stability are often based on a baseline model, which could be weak or biased. In addition, the effectiveness-stability tradeoff has not been systematically or quantitatively evaluated over TREC participated systems. The above two problems, to some extent, limit our awareness of such tradeoff and its impact on developing future IR models. In this paper, motivated by a recently proposed bias-variance based evaluation, we adopt a strong and unbiased "baseline", which is a virtual target model constructed by the best performance (for each query) among all the participated systems in a retrieval task. We also propose generalized bias-variance metrics, based on which a systematic and quantitative evaluation of the effectiveness-stability tradeoff is carried out over the participated systems in the TREC Ad-hoc Track (1993-1999) and Web Track (2010-2012). We observe a clear effectiveness-stability tradeoff, with a trend of becoming more obvious in more recent years. This implies that when we pursue more effective IR systems over years, the stability has become problematic and could have been largely overlooked.

Category and Subject Descriptors: H.3.3 [Information Search and Retrieval]

General Terms: Theory, Measurement, Performance

Keywords: Evaluation, Effectiveness-stability tradeoff, Bias-variance tradeoff, Virtual target model

1. INTRODUCTION

While IR research is often focused on improving the retrieval effectiveness (e.g., mean average precision), the performance could become instable across queries. Such an

effectiveness-stability tradeoff has been evidenced by some recent experiments [1, 3, 8, 9], but the tradeoff has not been systematically and quantitatively evaluated over the systems participated in TREC tasks.

The effectiveness evaluation has a long history in IR. One of the most commonly used effectiveness metrics is the mean average precision (MAP). The evaluation often involves the comparison with a baseline. Armstrong et al. [2] argued that the effectiveness evaluation based on a weak baseline is not sufficient to prove the effectiveness of a test method. On the other hand, the retrieval stability issue is an emerging topic. To address this issue, some risk metrics (e.g., RI(reliability of improvement) and U_{risk}) [7, 4] have been proposed. These risk metrics usually rely on the performance comparison against a single baseline method. However, Dincer et al. [5] described that the evaluation based on a single baseline system is biased since different baselines can yield different risk values. It is suggested that a less biased approach is to construct the baseline from a set of different systems/runs [5]. To sum up, we need a strong and unbiased baseline to evaluate the effectiveness-stability tradeoff.

In this paper, our "baseline" is a virtual target model made from the best performance (for each query) among all the IR systems in a TREC task. The concept of the virtual target model was mentioned in [8]. Indeed, to evaluate the retrieval effectiveness and stability in an integrated manner, the bias-variance metrics of average precision (AP) were proposed in [8]. However, the experiments in [8] are limited to query expansion using a single target model, and have nothing to do with the systems that participated in a real TREC task.

We will propose a generalized formulation of the bias-variance analysis with respect to IR performance metrics (such as MAP and ERR) and construct a systematic evaluation of TREC participated systems. Specifically, we generalize the original bias-variance framework by 1) making the bias-variance definition more consistent with the definition in estimation theory, 2) extending from the bias-variance of AP to MAP and any other mean effectiveness metrics, and 3) explicitly formulate the target model in the evaluation metrics. We extend AP to MAP for avoiding the adverse influence of some too big/small AP values in the computation of variance. In addition, we propose to quantify the tradeoff degree by two standard correlation coefficient measures. Furthermore, we carry out systematic evaluation of the systems that participated in the TREC Ad-hoc Track (1993-1999) and Web Track (2010-2012).

2. GENERALIZED BIAS-VARIANCE EVAL-UATION

2.1 Bias-Variance of AP

In [8], the performance difference between a current model under evaluation and the target model is viewed as a kind of error. By assuming the target AP is 1, which is AP's maximal value, this error can be formulated as $E(AP-1)^2$. It can be decomposed into bias and variance:

$$
\begin{aligned}
&E(AP-1)^2 \\
&= E(AP-E(AP))^2 + [E(AP)-1]^2 \\
&= Var(AP) + Bias^2(AP)
\end{aligned}
\tag{1}
$$

where the expectation $E(\cdot)$ is computed over all queries and $E(AP)$ computes the mean of AP, i.e., the MAP of the current model. A smaller $E(AP-1)^2$ means that the current model is closer to the target model. Since $E(AP)$ computes MAP, the smaller bias (i.e., $[E(AP)-1]^2$) can reflect the better retrieval effectiveness. The smaller variance of AP suggests that the current model is more stable.

Since the maximal AP (i.e., 1) is an ideal case, a practical version of $Bias^2(AP)$ is also defined in [8] as $[E(AP) - MAP_T]^2$, where MAP_T is the upper-bound MAP that is achieved by a single model in the reported case study [8]. In [8], it states that this practical bias has the similar trend as the original bias in Eq. 1. Using the practical bias, the sum of bias and variance can be:

$$
\begin{aligned}
&Bias^2(AP) + Var(AP) \\
&= [E(AP) - MAP_T]^2 + E(AP - E(AP))^2 \\
&= E(AP - MAP_T)^2
\end{aligned}
\tag{2}
$$

In [8], the retrieval effectiveness-stability tradeoff has been observed based on the above bias-variance in a case study.

2.2 Generalized Bias-variance Formulation

Now, we introduce a generalized bias-variance formulation. Our motivation is that in the estimation theory [6], bias and variance are defined to evaluate the estimation quality of the distribution parameter (i.e., mean) of a variable. If AP is treated as a variable like in [8], it is more general to define bias-variance on the mean of AP's distribution across queries, i.e., Mean of Average Precision (MAP).

2.2.1 Bias-Variance Decomposition on MAP's Squared Error

We first introduce an expected squared error based on MAP as:

$$
\int_{Q_S} [MAP(f, Q_S) - MAP(f_T, Q)]^2 p(Q_S) dQ_S
\tag{3}
$$

where f is a current model under evaluation, and f_T is the target model which has the best performance for each query; Q_S is a query sample of the query population Q which contains all the possible queries. This expected squared error considers the MAP's difference between the current model f on the query samples Q_S and the target model f_T on the query population Q.

To facilitate the bias-variance decomposition, we can rewrite Eq. 3 and decompose it as:

$$
\begin{aligned}
&E[MAP(f, Q_S) - MAP(f_T, Q)]^2 \\
&= E[MAP(f, Q_S) - E(MAP(f, Q_S))]^2 \\
&\quad + [E(MAP(f, Q_S)) - MAP(f_T, Q)]^2 \\
&= Var(MAP(f, Q_S)) + Bias^2(MAP(f, Q_S))
\end{aligned}
\tag{4}
$$

where the expectation $E(\cdot)$ is computed over all query samples. If we consider each query as a query sample, the bias-variance of MAP in Eq. 4 is equivalent to the bias-variance of AP in Eq. 2. Therefore, the bias-variance of AP can be considered as a *special case* of the bias-variance of MAP.

In addition to the single query sampling, we can partition all the queries (denoted as Q) in a test collection into several subsets Q_S, and treat each query subset as a query sample. In the experiments, we adopt two partition methods: one is random partitioning and the other is based on query difficulty (detailed in Section 3.2.2).

Under the above query sample configurations, the term of bias in Eq. 4 can be derived as:

$$
\begin{aligned}
&Bias^2(MAP(f, Q_S)) \\
&= [E(MAP(f, Q_S)) - MAP(f_T, Q)]^2 \\
&= [MAP(f, Q) - MAP(f_T, Q)]^2
\end{aligned}
\tag{5}
$$

It computes the derivation of $MAP(f, Q)$ w.r.t. $MAP(f_T, Q)$ which explicitly formulates a virtual target model f_T. f_T is constructed by assigning the best performance (for each query among all the considered systems/runs in a retrieval task) to it. Dincer et al. [5] described that the evaluation based on a single baseline system is biased since different baselines can yield different risk values. The virtual target model f_T designed in this paper is unbiased, since it is constructed by all various considered systems.

From the formulation of the bias in Eq. 5, we can know that the better the retrieval effectiveness (measured by MAP of the current model f) is, the smaller the bias will be. However, the better retrieval effectiveness does not guarantee a better retrieval stability, which will be measured by the variance term (i.e., $Var(MAP(f, Q_S))$ in Eq. 4).

2.2.2 Bias-Variance Decomposition on Normalized MAP

In Eq. 4, the variance term is a direct way to measure the variance of MAP of the current model. However, in this manner, even the target model may have a big variance value because of the variability of the query difficulty across different query subsets. Therefore, we normalize $MAP(f, Q_S)$ as:

$$
MAP^c(f, Q_S) = MAP(f, Q_S)) / MAP(f_T, Q_S).
$$

The target MAP, i.e., $MAP(f_T, Q_S)$ will be 1 for all the query samples after the normalization. Then, the bias-variance formulation on the normalized MAP can be

$$
\begin{aligned}
&E[MAP^c(f, Q_S) - MAP^c(f_T, Q)]^2 \\
&= E[MAP^c(f, Q_S) - 1]^2 \\
&= E[MAP^c(f, Q_S) - E(MAP^c(f, Q_S))]^2 \\
&\quad + [E(MAP^c(f, Q_S)) - 1]^2 \\
&= Var(MAP^c(f, Q_S)) + Bias^2(MAP^c(f, Q_S))
\end{aligned}
\tag{6}
$$

Table 1: Datasets and topics used for Ad-hoc Track.

	Datasets	Topics
1993(TREC-2)	disk1&2	101-150
1994(TREC-3)	disk1&2	151-200
1995(TREC-4)	disk2&3	201-250
1996(TREC-5)	disk2&4	251-300
1997(TREC-6)	disk4&5	301-350
1998(TREC-7)	disk4&5	351-400
1999(TREC-8)	disk4&5	401-450

where the variance considers the variance of the normalized MAP. We refer this variance as the normalized variance. In this manner, the normalized variance of the target model becomes zero. Now, we can focus on the performance variability caused by the model/system rather than the query difficulty across different query samples. Note that if we use the normalized MAP, the smaller normalized bias can still imply a better retrieval effectiveness.

2.2.3 *A General Expected Squared Error and its Bias-Variance Decomposition*

In addition to MAP, we can use other metrics (e.g., ERR or NDCG) in Eq. 3. Denoting a mean performance metric as M, we have a more general expected squared error:

$$\int_{Q_S} [M(f, Q_S) - M(f_T, Q)]^2 p(Q_S) dQ_S \qquad (7)$$

Correspondingly, we can have the bias-variance decomposition as we did for MAP and the normalized MAP. The retrieval effectiveness-stability tradeoff reflected by the bias-variance formulation of the metric ERR will also evaluated in our experiments.

3. EXPERIMENTS

3.1 Evaluation Set-up

We carry out bias-variance evaluation on Ad-hoc Track and Web Track. For each task, we evaluated all the submitted systems/runs for several years. Table 1 shows the document collections and query topics used for Ad-hoc Track. For Web Track from 2010 to 2012, ClueWeb09 dataset and the query topics (provided by organizers) are used, based on one task (i.e., adhoc task) on Web Track. The Web Track 2013 data are not available to us.

MAP is the effectiveness measure for Ad-hoc Track, and the main effectiveness measure for Web Track is expected reciprocal rank at 20 documents (denoted as ERR@20). For a better distinguishability, we adopt (M)ERR@20 to represent the mean value of ERR@20 on all test queries.

3.2 Evaluation Results

3.2.1 *Results of Bias-variance of AP and ERR@20*

We analyze the tradeoff between the squared bias and variance of AP on Ad-hoc Track from 1993 to 1999 and ERR@20 on Web Track from 2010 to 2012. In Table 2(a), we quantify the tradeoff by the Pearson and Spearman correlation coefficient of $Bias^2$ and Var. It shows that the correlation coefficients are often strongly negative (i.e., $r < -0.7$) on Ad-hoc Track and Web Track, indicating quite significant tradeoff between effectiveness and stability of runs/systems.

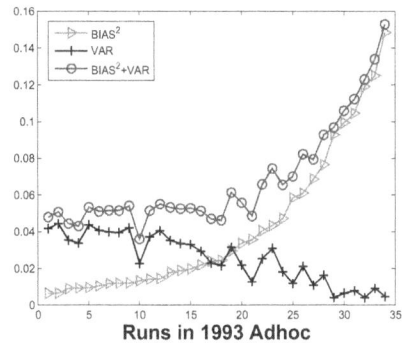

(a) Adhoc1993

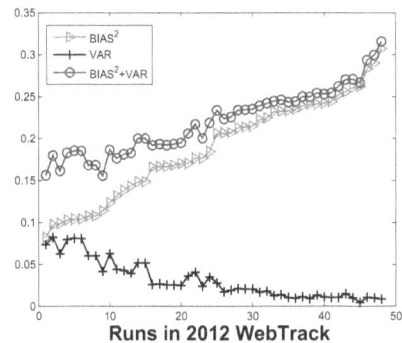

(b) WebTrack2012

Figure 1: Results of $Bias^2$, Var and $Bias^2 + Var$ of MAP and (M)ERR@20 based on query difficulty partition, where x-axis represents the runs participated in Ad hoc 1993 and Web Track 2012.

3.2.2 *Results of Bias-variance of MAP and (M)ERR@20*

The partition strategy of Q can affect the bias-variance results. We first randomly partition the whole query set and each partitioned subset includes 10 queries. The process is repeated for ten times, based on which the average value of these bias and variance is computed.

We can obsrve $Bias^2$ and Var of MAP and (M)ERR@20 in Table 2(b). On both tracks, it shows a clear bias-variance tradeoff, evidenced by the strongly negative correlation coefficients. The absolute values of correlation coefficients of MAP and (M)ERR@20 are often smaller than those of AP. This indicates that the variance is more smooth which is consistent with our motivation in designing the variance of MAP (see the last paragraph in Introduction).

There is a problem of random partition: the bias-variance results are different for different random partitioning processes. Therefore, we partition all the queries into several subsets on the basis of query difficulty. The query difficulty is measured by the best performance (i.e., the best AP) of a given query. The lower the best AP is, the more difficult the corresponding query is. We rank all the queries based on the query difficulty degree and group them into several subsets based on the rank, with each subset including 10 queries. Note that we have similar results when we set each subset as different sizes, or measure the query difficulty based on the average performance (among systems) of a query.

Table 2(c) shows bias-variance results based on the query difficulty partition. We still see a clear bias-variance trade-

Table 2: Correlation between $Bias^2$ and Var on four configurations: (a)AP/ERR@20, (b)MAP/(M)ERR@20 based on random partition, (c)MAP/(M)ERR@20 based on query difficulty partition, (d)Normalized MAP/(M)ERR@20 based on query difficulty partition.

	(a)		(b)		(c)		(d)	
	Pearson	Spearman	Pearson	Spearman	Pearson	Spearman	Pearson	Spearman
Adhoc1993	0.87	0.8686	0.8611	0.9016	0.8761	0.9	-0.3433	-0.1878
Adhoc1994	0.86 0	0.7	0.7 8	-0.5824	0.8	0.88 7	-0.3830	-0.2616
Adhoc1995	0.9 76	0.89 7	0.90 8	0.878	0.88	0.9 88	0.80 1	-0.6775
Adhoc1996	0.89 9	0.81	0.8 10	0.7 16	0.8 1	0.867	-0.4553	-0.4079
Adhoc1997	0.91 9	0.88	0.8008	0.70 7	0.817	0.880	-0.6005	-0.5983
Adhoc1998	0.8981	0.8 6	0.8 1	0.8187	0.81 8	0.9091	-0.6330	-0.6592
Adhoc1999	0.9109	0.7 01	0.881	0.7	0.860	0.787	-0.6859	-0.5622
WebTrack2010	0.7981	0.7 77	0.8 6	0.87	0.71 8	0.8690	-0.4498	-0.4372
WebTrack2011	0.7687	0.7 19	-0.6556	-0.5912	0.8 9	0.8098	-0.3890	-0.3586
WebTrack2012	0.9 09	0.97 8	0.91	0.9 6	0.9 99	0.96 7	0.7719	0.7 66

off. Figure 1 visualizes the tradeoff on the Ad-hoc 1993 and Web track 2012. In Figure 1, all the systems are sorted in an ascending order of $Bias^2$. In addition to bias and variance, it also plots the sum of them ($Bias^2 + Var$). We can observe that the Var of most systems/runs increases along with the decrease of $Bias^2$. This stresses a research question: how to get a better retrieval stability (a lower variance) when we pursue a high effectiveness (a lower bias).

In [8], it is stated that the smaller $Bias^2 + Var$ reflects the better overall retrieval performance (considering both effectiveness and variance). In Figure 1, we observe that the lowest $Bias^2 + Var$ is not corresponding to the lowest squared bias. This verifies that the best overall performance is not only determined by the best effectiveness.

3.2.3 Results of Normalized Bias-Variance of MAP and (M)ERR@20

We now report the evaluation results when the bias and variance are all obtained by a normalization process imposed on $MAP(f, Q_S)$. As discussed in Section 2.2.2, the normalization is expected to help us focus more on the performance variability caused by the model/system rather than the variability of the query difficulty.

In Table 2(d), there still exists a tradeoff between $Bias^2$ and Var of regularization MAP and (M)ERR@20 (because of the negative correlation coefficients), but it is less serious compared with the former results. This is because that we have normalized the performance variability caused by the variability of query difficulty.

One interesting point is that if we look at the correlation coefficients along the TREC years, we can observe that the coefficients often become closer to -1 (a more obvious bias-variance tradeoff) along with the increasing "recentness" of years. This indicates a more obvious effectiveness-stability tradeoff, in more recent years.

4. CONCLUSIONS AND FUTURE WORK

In this paper, we have proposed a generalized bias-variance evaluation strategy and evaluated the IR systems which participated in Ad-hoc track(1993-1999) and Web track (2010-2012). The bias-variance evaluation results can show the effectiveness-stability trends with respect to different systems, tasks, and years. We observe clear bias-variance tradeoff, which indicates retrieval effectiveness-stability tradeoff of the participated systems. In addition, the experimental results (in Figure 1) show that the improvement of effectiveness does not always mean the improvement of the overall retrieval performance (considering both effectiveness and stability). Moreover, the effectiveness-stability tradeoff could become more obvious in more recent TREC years (see Table 2(d)). Since participated systems (especially before 2013) are mainly designed to achieve better performance based on traditional effectiveness metrics, we can speculate that the stability of IR may become more problematic yet could have been overlooked in TREC contests over years.

Currently, we do not know the detailed algorithms/methods behind those tested systems, so our evaluation has a limitation that we do not fully understand why some systems have good effectiveness but bad stability, or are both effective and stable. In the future we will carry out a systematical evaluation of a large number of typical IR models, and analyze such questions in depth, for more insights in how to improve both retrieval effectiveness and stability.

5. ACKNOWLEDGMENTS

The authors would like to thank Mr. Qian Yu for the help on the experiments. This work is supported in part by the Chinese National Program on Key Basic Research Project (973 Program, grant No.2013CB329304, 2014CB744604), and the Natural Science Foundation of China(grant No. 61402324, 61272265, 61105072).

6. REFERENCES

[1] G. Amati, C. Carpineto, and G. Romano. Query difficulty, robustness, and selective application of query expansion. In *ECIR*, pages 127–137. Springer, 2004.

[2] T. G. Armstrong, A. Moffat, W. Webber, and J. Zobel. Improvements that don't add up: ad-hoc retrieval results since 1998. In *CIKM*, pages 601–610. ACM, 2009.

[3] K. Collins-Thompson. Reducing the risk of query expansion via robust constrained optimization. In *CIKM*, pages 837–846. ACM, 2009.

[4] K. Collins-Thompson, P. N.Bennett, F. Diaz, and C. Clarke. Trec 2013 web track guidelines.

[5] B. T. Dinçer, I. Ounis, and C. Macdonald. Tackling biased baselines in the risk-sensitive evaluation of retrieval systems. In *ECIR*, pages 26–38. Springer, 2014.

[6] G. Lebanon. Bias, variance, and mse of estimators, 2010.

[7] T. Sakai, T. Manabe, and M. Koyama. Flexible pseudo-relevance feedback via selective sampling. *TALIP*, 4(2):111–135, 2005.

[8] P. Zhang, D. Song, J. Wang, and Y. Hou. Bias-variance decomposition of ir evaluation. In *SIGIR*, pages 1021–1024. ACM, 2013.

[9] P. Zhang, D. Song, J. Wang, and Y. Hou. Bias–variance analysis in estimating true query model for information retrieval. *IP&M*, 50(1):199–217, 2014.

Aligning Vertical Collection Relevance with User Intent

Ke Zhou
Yahoo Labs
London, U.K.
zhouke.nlp@gmail.com

Thomas Demeester
Ghent University
Ghent, Belgium
tdmeeste@intec.ugent.be

Dong Nguyen
University of Twente
Enschede, Netherlands
d.nguyen@utwente.nl

Djoerd Hiemstra
University of Twente
Enschede, Netherlands
d.hiemstra@utwente.nl

Dolf Trieschnigg
University of Twente
Enschede, Netherlands
d.trieschnigg@utwente.nl

ABSTRACT

Selecting and aggregating different types of content from multiple vertical search engines is becoming popular in web search. The *user vertical intent*, the verticals the user expects to be relevant for a particular information need, might not correspond to the *vertical collection relevance*, the verticals containing the most relevant content. In this work we propose different approaches to define the set of relevant verticals based on document judgments. We correlate the collection-based relevant verticals obtained from these approaches to the real user vertical intent, and show that they can be aligned relatively well. The set of relevant verticals defined by those approaches could therefore serve as an approximate but reliable ground-truth for evaluating vertical selection, avoiding the need for collecting explicit user vertical intent, and vice versa.

Categories and Subject Descriptors: H.3.3 [Information Search and Retrieval]

Keywords: aggregated search, federated search, vertical relevance, evaluation, user intent

1. INTRODUCTION

Due to the increasing diversity of data on the web, most of the current search engines aggregate search results from a set of vertical search engines (e.g. News, Images). This search paradigm is called aggregated search [1]. The verticals are associated with content dedicated to either a topic (e.g. "sports"), a media type (e.g. "images"), or a genre (e.g. "news"). For a given user information need, only a subset of verticals will potentially provide the most relevant results to satisfy it. For example, relevant verticals for a query such as "flowers" might include "image" and "encyclopedia" verticals. Vertical selection (VS), a subtask, deals with selecting a subset of the most relevant verticals to a given user information need and improves the search effectiveness while reducing the load of querying a large set of multiple verticals.

The relevance of a vertical could depend on the relevance of the documents within the vertical collection [3, 7] and on the user's intent (orientation) to the vertical [9]. For evaluation purposes, from the *collection* perspective, Gravano et al. [3] assumed that any collection (vertical) with at least one relevant document for a query is relevant. Powell et al. [7] refined and formalized this notion by assuming that the relevance level of the collection (vertical) depends on the number or relevant documents within. In this work, we call this the *collection-based vertical relevance*. On the other hand, from the *user intent* perspective, researchers [6, 9] found that user orientation (intent), or how oriented each vertical is to a user's information need (i.e., expectation), also plays an important role in user preference of the aggregated search page. We refer to this as the *user vertical intent*. Most of the previous work either assumes that the relevance of the vertical solely depends on the collection (i.e., its recall of relevant documents) or the user intent (the user's orientation to issue the query to the given vertical).

Although previous work [9] has shown that *user vertical intent* and *result relevance* are both correlated for influencing user experience, it fails to connect both criteria within the context of evaluation in this area. The key question is whether we could align the collection-based vertical relevance with the user vertical intent for evaluation purposes. This can be further split up into two sub-questions:

- Can the vertical relevance be derived from document relevance judgments and therefore ranked similarly to the user vertical intent (orientation)?

- Can we appropriately threshold the derived vertical rankings and ultimately align them with the binary vertical selection decision made by the users?

In this paper, we propose and test different approaches to derive the collection-based vertical relevance based on document relevance judgments as are widely used in the IR evaluation community (e.g., TREC). The approaches differ in how they quantify the relevance of a vertical and how the ultimate set of relevant verticals is derived. By conducting user studies to collect the user vertical intent, we compare those approaches on deriving collection-based vertical relevance and investigate which approach best aligns with the actual user intent.

The contributions of this paper are twofold: **(i)**. We extensively study different approaches to derive collection-based vertical relevance in the context of over a hundred heterogeneous resources (search engines). The scale and diversity

Table 1: Summary of this work.

Tasks	ranking of verticals		set of relevant verticals	
Variants	(1). Resource Relevance	(2). Aggregation	(3). Vertical Dependency	(4). Thresholding Criterion
Collection	a. **K** (Key relevant doc recall) b. **G** (Graded precision of docs)	a. **MR** (Maximal Resource) b. **AR** (Average of Resource)	a. **D** (Dependent) b. **I** (Independent)	a. **I** (Individual vertical utility) b. **O** (Overall vertical set utility)
User Study	Fraction of majority user preference of each vertical over "General Web"		User type: 1. risk-seeking (diversity); 2. risk-medium; 3. risk-averse (relevance)	
Evaluation	Spearman Correlation		Precision, Recall and F-measure	

of the resources used has not been studied previously for our task. **(ii)**. We conduct a user study to verify that the collection-based vertical relevance derived from document judgments can be aligned with the user vertical intent. This is novel to verify that the Cranfield evaluation paradigm used in TREC could also be useful to line up with user experience [5] for evaluation in the *heterogeneous environment*.

The main elements of this paper are summarized in Table 1. We first describe different approaches to obtain both the vertical ranking and a set of relevant verticals using the collection-based document judgments (Sec. 2). We then conduct a user study (Sec. 3) to obtain the vertical ranking and relevant vertical sets from the user (as the ground-truths). Finally, we evaluate different approaches proposed in Sec. 2 and study how well they can be aligned with the user intent (Sec. 4), after which the paper is concluded (Sec. 5).

2. VERTICAL COLLECTION RELEVANCE

Formally, given a set of verticals $V = \{v_1, v_2, ...v_n\}$, the collection-based vertical relevance I_t^C derived from the collection C for topic t is represented by a weighted vector $I_t^C = \{i_1, i_2, ...i_n\}$, where each value i_k indicates the relevance of the given vertical v_k to topic t. A vertical could contain multiple resources (search engines). For example, an "image" vertical could contain resources such as Flickr and Picasa. Therefore, each vertical v_i consists of a set of resources $v_i = \{r_1, r_2, ...r_m\}$ while each resource r_j consists of a set of documents $r_j = \{d_1, d_2, ...d_k\}$. Given all the relevance judgments $rel(d_l, t)$ between any document d_l and a topic t, we aim to derive I_t^C.

Ultimately, given the collection-based vertical relevance I_t^C, we aim to threshold it in order to obtain the final binary verticle relevance vector $S_t^C = \{s_1, s_2, ...s_n\}$ where each value s_k is either 1 (indicating corresponding vertical v_k is relevant and should be selected in VS) or 0 (indicating irrelevant and should not be selected).

2.1 Approaches

We describe approaches to derive the vertical ranking, followed by methods to infer the set of relevant verticals.

2.1.1 Vertical Ranking

The strategies to derive the collection-based vertical relevance I_t^C (i.e., the vertical score) from the document relevance judgments $rel(d_l, t)$ vary in two aspects: (1). (**Resource Relevance**) the way to estimate the relevance of each resource within a given vertical; and (2). (**Vertical Relevance Aggregation**) the way to aggregate scores of the resources within the vertical to derive the vertical score.

Following previous work [2, 3], we propose two approaches to estimate **resource relevance**: (a). **K** (Key): using the recall of "key" (most relevant) documents in the resource and (b). **G** (Graded precision): the graded precision of documents in the resource [4]. The **K** approach is similar to

the assumption made in Gravano et al [3] and using "key" is to reflect the relevance of the resource to return the most rel- evant results that maintain high impacts on user search experience [5]. The **G** approach is following the evaluation setup [2] made in the TREC FedWeb track 2013[1] and the essential idea is to characterize the effectiveness of each resource to "recall" relevant documents in a similar fashion as in previous work [7] when graded relevance judgments are available. Then given the estimated resource relevance scores, we test two ways to **aggregate** those scores in order to obtain the vertical scores (rankings) I_t^C: (a). (**MR**) Maximal Resource score and (b). (**AR**) Average Resource score. The **MR** approach reflects most of current web search setting that one vertical solely contains one best performing resource while the **AR** approach represents the averaged vertical performance.

By combining the different *resource relevance* and *aggregation* methods, we obtain four approaches to quantify I_t^C: **KMR**, **KAR**, **GMR**, **GAR**. Since we could also apply the same technique to the whole vertical (rather than resource), we propose another approach **GV** by using graded precision on all the documents within the entire vertical[2].

2.1.2 Relevant Vertical Set

To infer the set of relevant verticals S_t^C from the obtained collection-based vertical relevance I_t^C, we argue that the strategies could vary in two aspects: (3). (**Vertical Dependency**): assumption of whether vertical relevance is dependent on each other; and (4). (**Thresholding Criterion**): assumption of which is the criterion of thresholding. For **vertical dependency**, we tested both assumptions. By assuming (a). (**D**) Dependent, we normalize the vertical scores across all verticals following previous work [1]. By assuming (b). (**I**) Independent, we simply use the original vertical scores I_t^C.

For **thresholding criterion**, we tested two different approaches. The differences between them are the criterion that the thresholding is based on: (a). (**I**) Individual vertical score: the individual vertical relevance scores; (b). (**O**) Overall relevance of the vertical set. The **I** approach basically assumes that the individual vertical requires a certain relevance to remain in the relevant vertical set while the **O** approach assumes that the relevant vertical set is required to maintain a certain percentage of relevance of the whole vertical set. By combining *vertical dependency* and *thresholding criterion*, we obtain four different approaches to infer S_t^C from I_t^C: **DI**, **DO**, **II**, **IO**.

2.2 FedWeb'13 Data

In this study, we use the TREC 2013 FedWeb track data [2]. The dataset contains 50 test topics and 157 crawled

---

[1]https://sites.google.com/site/trecfedweb/2013-track.
[2]We do not propose **KV** approach since practically, it outputs the same vertical ranking to **KAR** approach.

| Query: calculate inertia sphere | | | | | | | | | | | | |
| **Description:** You want to know how to calculate the inertia of a sphere. | | | | | | | | | | | | |

	Entertain	Travel	Sports	Health	Jobs	Games	Recipes	Kids	Jokes	Tech	Software	General Web
Narrative: You know how the inertia is defined, but you don't feel like deriving the formula for a sphere all the way from the start, so you are quickly trying to find it online.												✓

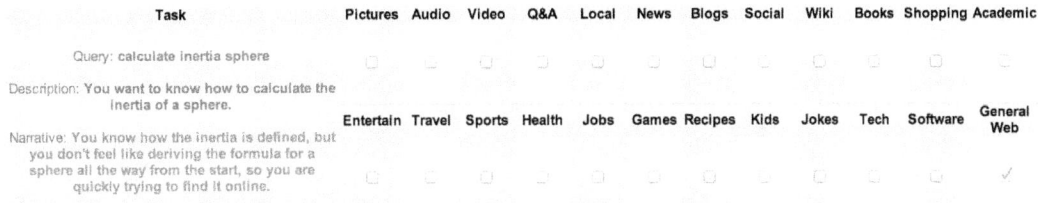

Figure 1: An examplar task of the user intent study.

resources. It also categorizes the resources into different verticals and provides a set of 24 verticals, as shown in Table 2. Each vertical consists of a set of resources (search engines). For each resource, the top 10 retrieved document results are returned. The relevance judgments are made on each document with five graded relevance levels.

The 50 test topics were chosen in such a way to avoid a strong bias towards general web search engines. For the most important verticals (in terms of number or size of resources, e.g. Video, Blogs), many topics provide a significant number of relevant results. In addition, at least a few topics targeting smaller verticals (e.g., Recipes) are also selected.

Table 2: 24 verticals used in FedWeb'13: a vertical consists of a set of resources (search engines), each retrieving one unique type of documents.

Vertical	Document	Resource Count	Type
Pictures	online pictures	13	
Audio	online audios	6	media
Video	online videos	14	
Q&A	answers to questions	7	
Local	local information pages	1	
News	news articles	15	
Blogs	blog articles	4	
Social	social network pages	3	genre
Encyclopedia	encyclopedic entries	5	
Books	book review page	5	
Shopping	product shopping page	9	
Academic	research technical report	18	
Entertainment	entertainment pages	4	
Travel	travel pages	2	
Sports	sports pages	9	
Health	health related pages	12	
Jobs	job posts	5	
Games	electronic game pages	6	topic
Recipes	recipe page	5	
Kids	cartoon pages	10	
Jokes	joke threads	2	
Tech	technology pages	8	
Software	software downloading pages	3	
General Web	standard web pages	6	

3. VERTICAL USER INTENT STUDY

Given a set of verticals $V = \{v_1, v_2, ...v_n\}$, the vertical user intent I_t^U for topic t is represented by a weighted vector $I_t^U = \{i_1, i_2, ...i_n\}$, where each value i_k indicates the relevance of the given vertical v_k to topic t. To obtain I_t^U, we conducted a user study, asking assessors $U = \{u_1, u_2, ..., u_m\}$ to make binary decisions over all verticals V: $A = \{a_1, a_2, ..., a_n\}$. Therefore, we have a $m \times n$ matrix M_t for topic t. We aim to derive I_t^U by aggregating M_t and ultimately obtain a binary vector indicating the set of relevant verticals $S_t^U = \{s_1, s_2, ...s_n\}$ where each value s_k is either 1 or 0.

We conducted this user study following previous work on gathering user vertical intent [9]. Basically, two assumptions were made in guiding the assessment. Firstly, instead of asking assessors to associate an absolute score to each vertical, we asked them to make *pairwise preference assessments*, comparing each vertical in turn to the reference "general web" vertical (i.e. "is adding results from this vertical likely to improve the quality of the *ten blue links*?"). Secondly, instead of providing actual vertical results to the assessors, we only provided the *vertical names* (with a description of their characteristics presented before their assessments). Although this may not be ideal from an end-user perspective (as different assessors might have different views on the perceived usefulness of a vertical, especially as the vertical items are hidden), this assumption helped to lower the assessment burden, and yet reflects the perceived vertical user intent (orientation). We used the same FedWeb'13 data as described in Sec. 2.2. Most of the assessors are university students who were recruited to participate via a web interface. To eliminate order bias, we randomized all topics into a set of pages (with five topics per page) and provided each assessor the option to assess as many pages as he/she wished. A screenshot of one examplar task is presented in Figure 1.

In total, we collected 20 assessment sessions (i.e., assessors) with a total of 845 assessments[3]. The average number of relevant verticals per topic and per session is 2.64, with a standard deviation of 1.28. Similar to previous findings [9], the mean of inter-annotator Fleiss' Kappa is *moderate* (0.48), showing that assessors might have different preferences over the relevance of verticals, despite the clearly described query information need (as seen from the description and narrative shown in Figure 1).

To derive I_t^U, we use the fraction of majority user preferences for each vertical v_k over "General Web" as the vertical score i_k. To further obtain S_t^U, we threshold the majority user preference for each vertical i_k in I_t^U. It has been shown in our data (moderate inter-annotator Fleiss' Kappa agreement) and previous work [8] that the user's preferred number of verticals varies significantly and different users tend to have different risk-levels. By thresholding 30%, 60% and 90% of majority user preference, we obtain three different types of S_t^U, representing three types of users respectively: *risk-seeking*, *risk-medium* and *risk-averse*. The *risk-seeking* users prefer *diversity* of verticals presented (with a mean of 3.08 relevant verticals) while the *risk-averse* users are more careful when selecting verticals (with a mean of 0.52 relevant verticals): they only select verticals (as relevant) when highly confident (large fraction of user's preferences). The *risk-medium* is an average user, with a mean of 1.68 relevant verticals (following a similar distribution as shown in [1]).

4. EVALUATION

We evaluate the alignment between collection and user, on both vertical rankings and ultimate relevant vertical sets.

---

[3]We have made this publicly available at http://bit.ly/VJQ53B.

Table 4: Precision, Recall and F-measure of the set of relevant verticals using collection-based vertical relevance I^C from GMR approach against user vertical intent I^U with different risk-level.

User Intent	Risk-seeking (diversity)				Risk-medium				Risk-averse (relevance)			
Approaches	DI	DO	II	IO	DI	DO	II	IO	DI	DO	II	IO
Precision	0.264	0.289	**0.338**	0.271	0.303	0.330	**0.391**	0.327	0.339	0.377	**0.421**	0.381
Recall	**0.829**	0.803	0.796	0.782	**0.552**	0.523	0.516	0.520	**0.426**	0.398	0.401	0.394
F-measure	0.380	0.406	**0.446**	0.384	0.367	0.387	**0.413**	0.383	0.357	0.374	**0.379**	0.373

4.1 Vertical Ranking

Given the collection-based vertical relevance I_t^C derived from document relevance judgments and user vertical intent I_t^U obtained from user preference judgments, we evaluate whether they align with each other. We aim to evaluate five different approaches of utilizing relevance judgments for ranking verticals, as described in Sec 2.1.1. Specifically, we utilize the nonparametric Spearman Rank Correlation Coefficient as our main metric to measure the correlation between a collection-based vertical ranking and a user-based one. Since we are more concerned with highly ranked verticals (potentially relevant), we also investigate whether there are overlaps between the top-3 and top-5 ranked verticals in the collection-based and user-based rankings. The evaluation results of different approaches are shown in Table 3.

Several trends can be observed. Firstly, all the collection-based approaches have a moderate correlation (0.6-0.7) with the user-based vertical ranking. We also study whether this correlation is statistically significant (against random) by performing a permutation test. We found that the correlation for all the five approaches are statistically significant (with $p < 0.05$). Note that the performance difference between different approaches is marginal while the approaches using the graded precision metric outperforms the others. Secondly, we observed that there tends to be some overlap between the top ranked verticals from both collection-based and user-based vertical rankings, albeit moderate (0.4-0.5). However, it is interesting to see that when using simple metrics on document-based relevance judgements, around half of the top-ranked verticals are aligned with the user intent.

In summary, our experiments suggest that collection-based vertical relevance can be utilized as an approximate surrogate for measuring user's vertical intent, and vice versa.

4.2 Vertical Relevant Set

We study whether the obtained set of relevant verticals after thresholding is aligned with the ones derived from the user perspectives. For simplicity, we only present results on thresholding with one collection-based vertical ranking approach **GMR** (Graded precision of Maximal Resource) since we found similar results across all those different approaches.

As we have mentioned, we defined three types of ground-truths, representing three different types of users: risk-seeking users prefer a large set of diverse verticals, while the risk-averse users prefer selecting verticals only when they are

most relevant, and risk-medium are in between. We test different thresholding approaches for these user settings.

For each thresholding approach, its numerical threshold was determined based on iterative data analysis, such that the maximum number of relevant verticals for any test topic could not exceed five. In addition, since almost all the FedWeb'13 test topics target verticals, we also make sure that at least 80% of the topics have at least one relevant vertical using the selected threshold.

The results are shown in Table 4. We observe similar performance trends for different thresholding approaches under different user settings (risk-level). **II** (Independent Individual) thresholding approach performs best in terms of precision and F-measure while **DI** (Dependent Individual) thresholding approach generally would achieve better recall. Generally, an F-measure of around 0.4 could be achieved by mapping the estimated collection-based relevant vertical set with the users' relevant (intended) vertical set. Although not particularly high, this still shows that vertical collection relevance could be aligned relatively well with users' vertical intent and therefore this could serve as a surrogate of ground-truths for evaluating vertical selection.

5. CONCLUSIONS

In this paper, we propose a set of different approaches to utilize document judgments to derive the set of relevant verticals. We evaluate the effectiveness of those approaches by correlating with the user vertical intent obtained from a user study. We found that collection-based vertical relevance can be aligned relatively well with users' vertical intent. This implies that we could reliably use document relevance judgments to evaluate vertical selection for capturing user intent in heterogeneous federated web search, and vice versa.

6. REFERENCES

[1] J. Arguello, F. Diaz, J. Callan, and J.-F. Crespo. Sources of evidence for vertical selection. In *SIGIR '09*.
[2] T. Demeester, D. Trieschnigg, D. Nguyen, D. Hiemstra. Overview of the TREC 2013 Federated Web Search Track. In *TREC'13*.
[3] L. Gravano, H. Garcia-Molina and A. Tomasic. Precision and recall of GlOSS estimators for database discovery. In IEEE Parallel and Distributed Information Systems, 1994.
[4] J. Kekalainen and J. Kalervo. Using graded relevance assessments in IR evaluation. In *JASIST'02*.
[5] M. Sanderson, M. L. Paramita, P. Clough, and E. Kanoulas. Do user preferences and evaluation measures line up? In *SIGIR'10*.
[6] S. Sushmita, H. Joho, M. Lalmas, and R. Villa. Factors affecting click-through behavior in aggregated search interfaces. In *CIKM '10*.
[7] A. Powell and J. French. Comparing the performance of collection selection algorithms. In *ACM TOIS'03*.
[8] K. Zhou, R. Cummins, M. Lalmas, and J. M. Jose. Evaluating reward and risk for vertical selection. In *CIKM'12*.
[9] K. Zhou, R. Cummins, M. Lalmas and J.M. Jose. Which Vertical Search Engines are Relevant? In *WWW'13*.

Table 3: Spearman correlation and overlap of top-k verticals between vertical rankings from collection-based vertical relevance I^C and user intent I^U.

Approaches	KMR	KAR	GMR	GAR	GV
Correlation	0.656	0.659	0.664	0.689	0.671
Overlap (5)	0.496	0.492	0.516	0.532	0.508
Overlap (3)	0.340	0.340	0.327	0.400	0.353

Multi-document Hyperedge-based Ranking for Text Summarization

Abdelghani Bellaachia
Department of Computer Science
The George Washington University
Washington, DC 20052, USA
bell@gwu.edu

Mohammed Al-Dhelaan[*]
Department of Computer Science
The George Washington University
Washington, DC 20052, USA
mdhelaan@gwu.edu

ABSTRACT

In a multi-document settings, graph-based extractive summarization approaches build a similarity graph out of sentences in each cluster of documents then use graph centrality approaches to measure the importance of sentences. The similarity is computed between each pair of sentences. However, it is not clear if such approach captures high-order relations among more than two sentences or can differentiate between descriptive sentences of the cluster in comparison with other clusters. In this paper, we propose to model sentences as hyperedges and words as vertices using a hypergraph and combine it with topic signatures to differentiate between descriptive sentences and non-descriptive sentences. To rank sentences, we propose a new random walk over hyperedges that will prefer descriptive sentences of the cluster when measuring their centrality scores. Our approach outperform a number of baseline in the DUC 2001 dataset using the ROUGE metric.

Categories and Subject Descriptors

I.2.7 [**ARTIFICIAL INTELLIGENCE**]: Natural Language Processing—*Text analysis*

Keywords

Text summarization; Text hypergraph; Multi-document summarization; Topic signatures

1. INTRODUCTION

Automatic text summarization of a document is the process of automatically creating a succinct version of the document. The need for accurate text summarizers is evident for a number of areas as in information retrieval and information visualization. For instance, search engines need to create snippets of the retrieved documents to be displayed

---

[*]This author is sponsored by King Saud University, Saudi Arabia

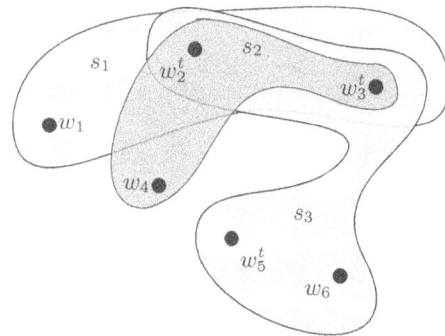

Figure 1: **Hypergraph example:** s **represents sentences,** w **represents words, and** w^t **represents topical words**

in the search result. Additionally, short summaries are important for visualizing information as in news headlines.

Text summarization is generally categorized into either *generic summarization* where we summarize a document to cover all the important information or *query-focused summarization* where the goal is to summarize an answer to a specific question called a query. Additionally, it can be classified as either single-document summarization where we generate the summary from a single document or multi-document summarization with the summary being for multiple documents. In this paper, we focus on multi-document generic summarization.

A common approach to multi-document generic summarization is to extract a small number of sentences that cover all topic information discussed in a group of related documents. One of the well-known approaches is modeling sentences in a similarity graph, then choosing sentences that are central in the graph to be included in the summary, as in LexRank[5] and TextRank[8]. These approaches have shown remarkable success in summarization. However, graph-based approaches only model the similarity between pairs of sentences with no clear representation of word relations either. Therefore, it is not clear if they adequately *cover* all topical information. For example, whether a sentence contains a large number of informative words or only common words is not clear in standard graph-based approaches. To overcome such limitations, we propose to model both words and sentences in a hypergraph that clearly captures the high-order relations between both sentences and words. For instance, if

$n > 2$ sentences share the same group of informative words as in phrases or proper nouns, they won't be the same as if each pair of the n sentences shared different words.

In this paper, we propose to model words as vertices and sentences as hyperedges in a hypergraph and approach the problem as a random walk over hyperedges. A hypergraph is a generalization of graphs that relaxed the condition of edges being pair-wise and makes high-order relation explicitly represented. We rank hyperedges by assessing how much time the random walker spends in each hyperedge traveling from one to another through words. Naturally, such approach will prefer hyperedges that cover more words. Additionally, we use topic signatures[6] as a hyperedge weight to make the random walk favors sentences that are descriptive of the cluster of documents. For instance in Figure 1, words as $\{w_2^t, w_3^t, w_5^t\}$ are topic words that should effect the random walk. Our approach shows interesting improvements on the multi-documents summarization task compared to other standard graph-based methods when tested on the Document Understanding Conference DUC 2001 datasets.

2. DEFINITIONS & PRELIMINARIES

Let $HG(V, \mathcal{E}, w)$ be a weighted undirected hypergraph with the vertex set V and the hyperedge set $\mathcal{E}$. A hyperedge e is a subset of V where $\cup_{e \in \mathcal{E}} e = V$ and $w : \mathcal{E} \to \mathbb{R}_+^{|\mathcal{E}|}$ is the hyperedge weight. A hyperedge e is said to be incident to v when $v \in e$. A hypergraph has an incidence matrix $H \in \mathbb{R}^{|V| \times |E|}$ as follows:

$$h(v, e) = \begin{cases} 1 & \text{if } v \in e \\ 0 & \text{if } v \notin e \end{cases} \quad (1)$$

The vertex and hyperedge degree are defined as follows:

$$d(v) = \sum_{e \in E} w(e) h(v, e) \quad (2)$$

$$\delta(e) = \sum_{v \in V} h(v, e) = |e| \quad (3)$$

D_e and D_v are the diagonal matrices representing the degrees of hyperedges and vertices, respectively. W_e is the diagonal matrix with the hyperedge weights.

3. PROPOSED APPROACH

We propose a new approach for graph-based extractive summarization that models the high-order relation between words and sentences. The high-order relations found on text is modeled using a hypergraph where words are represented as distinct vertices, and sentences are represented as hyperedges. We formulate the problem of ranking sentences as a random walk between hyperedges (sentences) and the transition is performed over vertices (distinct words). By ranking hyperedges, we can find the most salient sentences that describe the text and use them as a summary. However, simply using random walks will naturally be biased towards longer sentences. Therefore, we define hyperedge weights by measuring the constituent words' informativeness using topic signatures[6]. First, we will describe the calculation of hyperedge weights using topic signatures, second, we will describe the hyperedge ranking model over hypergraphs to measure the saliency score of sentences.

3.1 Hyperedge Weights Using Topic Signatures

We design our hypergraph-based random walk approach to be drawn to descriptive sentences. Descriptive sentences are not necessarily longer sentences. They are sentences that contain a large number of descriptive words. To find out which words are descriptive and which are not, we use the log likelihood ratio known as topic signatures[6] in the summarization literature. The log likelihood ratio λ of a given word $\lambda(w)$ is calculated as the ratio between observing the occurrence probability $P(w)$, using a binomial distribution, in both the input document D_I, which is the document to be summarized, and the background corpus D_B. The ratio is calculated between two hypothesis: H_1 being $P(w|D_I) = P(w|D_B)$ which is the null hypothesis, and H_2 observing the occurrence probability of the word in D_I being greater than its probability in D_B, $P(w|D_I) > P(w|D_B)$ which indicates that the word is descriptive of document D_I. We use $-2log\lambda$ for statistical significance testing of words' descriptiveness which is asymptotically approximated to the χ^2 distribution. We classify words to be descriptive if their $R(w) = 1$ iff$(-2log\lambda(w) > 10.83), 0$ which is equal to confidence level of 0.001. This makes it possible to set a cutoff threshold for descriptive words unlike other frequency-based weighting measures as in tf or tf-idf. Words with higher $-2log\lambda$ values indicate a higher chance of being descriptive of the document. The hyperedge (sentence) weight could be calculated as the density of topic signatures over total words in the sentence[4]. However, such approach does not penalize long sentence effectively since longer sentences have a higher chance of containing larger number of topic signatures than shorter sentences. Therefore, we calculate the hyperedge weights as the following:

$$w(e_i) = \frac{1 + \sum_{w \in e_i} R(w)}{\delta(e_i)^2} \quad (4)$$

Where $\sum_{w \in e_i} R(w)$ is the number of topic signatures words in the sentence e_i, and $\delta(e_i)^2$ is the square of the length of the sentence to penalize longer sentences more effectively. Now that we define the descriptiveness score of a sentence as a hyperedge's weight, we move on to describe the random walk model over hyperedges in the next section.

3.2 Ranking Hyperedges with Random Walks

Traditionally, random walks are defined over vertices while transitioning is done over edges. Similarly, we can define the random walk over edges and the transitioning over vertices. In this paper, we are interested in ranking hyperedges instead of vertices found in a hypergraph. To rank hyperedges, we define a new random walk that transitions from a hyperedge to another. A random walk over hyperedges is the process of transitioning between hyperedges by starting at a given hyperedge and moving to a neighboring hyperedge through shared vertices every discrete time unit t. We define a Markov chain $\mathcal{M}$ with different states being hyperedges. The chain is represented as a transition matrix $P \in \mathbb{R}^{|\mathcal{E}| \times |\mathcal{E}|}$ which captures all transitions between any pair of hyperedges.

The random walk over hypergraphs is a generalization of random walks over graphs. In graphs, a random walk over edges is described as choosing a connecting vertex and transitioning to another edge incident with that vertex. In a hypergraph, hyperedges can be connected through more than a single vertex. Therefore, the need for generalizing the random walk to be suitable for a hypergraph structure is clear. The random walk over hyperedges is formed as two steps. First, the surfer chooses a vertex v uniformly at random from the current hyperedge e_i. Second, the surfer chooses a hyperedge e_j proportional to the hyperedge weight $w(e_j)$ satisfying $v \in e_i \cap e_j$. The probability of transitioning between two hyperedges e_i and e_j is defined as follows:

$$P(e_i, e_j) = \sum_{v \in V} \frac{h(v, e_i)}{\delta(e_i)} \frac{w(e_j)h(v, e_j)}{\sum_{\hat{e} \in \mathcal{E}(v)} w(\hat{e})} \quad (5)$$

$$= \frac{1}{\delta(e_i)} \sum_{v \in e_i \cap e_j} \frac{w(e_j)}{\sum_{\hat{e} \in \mathcal{E}(v)} w(\hat{e})} \quad (6)$$

Or in matrix notation:

$$P = D_e^{-1} H^T D_v^{-1} H W_e$$

Where D_e is the diagonal matrix of the hyperedge degree in Equation 3. H^T is the hypergraph incident matrix where rows are hyperedges and columns are vertices. D_v is the diagonal matrix of the weighted vertex degrees as in Equation 2. W_e is a diagonal matrix with the hyperedge weights. Note that the transition matrix P is *stochastic* where we have every row sums to 1.

To get the stationary distribution of the hypergraph from the transition matrix P, we use the power method until convergence. To ensure convergence, we need to guarantee that the Markov chain is *irreducible*, for any two states $s_i, s_j \in \mathcal{M}$ they must satisfy $P(s_i, s_j) > 0$. Also, 2) the chain is *aperiodic*, where the greatest common divisor of every state $\{t : P_t(s_i, s_i) > 0\}$ is 1. To guarantee irreducibility and aperiodicity, we use the PageRank algorithm [2]. The algorithm uses the idea of *teleporting* which will restart the random walk process making it useful for the previous conditions. The teleporting is depicted with a small probability called the *damping factor* α. Let $\vec{v}$ be a vector of all hyperedges to be ranked. The ranking is calculated as follows:

$$\vec{v}_{(i+1)} = \alpha P^T \vec{v}_{(i)} + (1 - \alpha)\vec{e}/n \quad (7)$$

The damping factor α is set to 0.85. n is the number of hyperedges in the hypergraph. $\vec{e} \in \mathbb{R}^{n \times 1}$ is a vector of all elements being 1. $\alpha P^T \vec{v}$ means that the random walker will choose to go with one of the incident vertices. $(1 - \alpha)\vec{e}/n$ represents a vector of an introductory probabilities with each entry being $(1 - \alpha)/n$ to teleport the random walk to a new hyperedge.

The intuition of this approach for text summarization is that ranking hyperedges (sentences) by traversing their vertices (words) will explicitly represent information subsumption of sentences more than standard graph-based approaches. For instance, if we have many short sentences represented in smaller sets of words and a larger set that contains most of the small sentences the random walk will naturally prefer the more informative sentence that contain them all. Also, the hyperedge ranking approach takes into account the high-order relation of words and naturally ranks sentences that share them higher than sentences that are only pair-wise similar.

After ranking all sentences, we order them in a descending order and choose the most central sentences to be included in the summary. However, we need to ensure that sentences are of diverse nature and do not contain redundant information. To eliminate the redundancy in the summaries, we employ a reranking approach known as Maximal Marginal Relevance

(MMR)[3] similar to [11]. We start by having two lists $A = \emptyset, B = \{S_1, ..., S_n\}$ where list B contains ranked sentences in a descending order. Then, we move the highest ranked sentence S_1 from B to A, and penalize any sentence in B that shares a relation with S_1. Assume the rank of sentence S_1 is $R(S_1)$, the reranking of any other sentence connected to S_1 is recalculated as $R(S_i)' = R(S_i) - w_{S_i S_1} R(S_1)$ where $w_{S_i S_1}$ is the transition probability from sentence S_i to S_1. We stop when the list $B = \emptyset$.

4. EXPERIMENT

We used the common Task 1 of the Document Understanding Conference (DUC 2001) benchmark dataset to evaluate all the systems. The task was designed for generic summarization of English news articles. The dataset contains 308 news documents that are clustered manually to 30 clusters that represent topics. Each cluster roughly contains from 7 to 11 documents and comes with 3 human reference summaries to compare against. Since our task is a multi-document summarization, we build a summarization system to each cluster separately[1]. The length of the summaries for each cluster was set to a 100 words. For the preprocessing, we lowercased all characters, removed punctuations, and stem the text. For calculating the topic signatures, we used the cluster to be summarized as D_I and the rest of the clusters to be D_B.

To measure the performance of the summarization systems, we use the common recall metric ROUGE[7]. It measures the quality of the system produced summaries by the percentage of overlap with the human summaries. ROUGE produces different scores depending on the size of the textual elements used for comparison. The unigram measure, ROUGE-1, has been shown to agree with human judgment the most[7]. We also show ROUGE-2 for bigrams, ROUGE-3 for trigrams, ROUGE-4, and ROUGE-L which stand for the longest common subsequence of words.

To show the effectiveness of our proposed approach, we compare it with three different baselines. The baselines consist of graph-based and statistical approaches that are used for multi-document summarizations. The baselines are described as follows:

- **Log Likelihood** The sentences are ranked based on the density of topic signature words in a sentence. The ranking is based on equation 4. This method helps distinguishing the effectiveness of the hypergraph edge-ranking approach from the log likelihood measure by itself.

- **TextRank**[8] builds a graph of sentences where the edge weights are the number of overlapped words divided by the length of the sentences. This baseline helps in showing the difference between a graph with pairwise relations and a hypergraph with high-order relations.

- **NE-Rank**[1] combines nodes and edges weights to calculate the rank. Like TextRank, builds a graph of sentences where edges are weighted similar to TextRank and node weights are the sum of the tf-idf of constituent words.

---

[1]Cluster d31 has been excluded since the organizers made a mistake in its summaries making the collection 29 clusters

Table 1: Multi-document Summarization Results over DUC 2001

	ROUGE-1	ROUGE-2	ROUGE-3	ROUGE-4	ROUGE-L
Log Likelihood	0.47433 (95%-conf.int. 0.45634 - 0.49182)	0.31205	0.26083	0.22457	0.45782
TextRank + MMR	0.47545 (95%-conf.int. 0.44862 - 0.50071)	0.31768	0.26979	0.23362	0.45569
NE-Rank + MMR	0.48534 (95%-conf.int. 0.46260 - 0.50690)	0.33282	0.28661	0.24916	0.46753
Hypergraph + MMR	0.51612 (95%-conf.int. 0.48926 - 0.54228)	0.37431	0.32444	0.28285	0.50291

To help validate our hypergraph random walk approach, we compare it with ranking sentences by the topic signatures. The results in Table 1 show that combining the random walk with the topic signature ranking helps in selecting more succinct sentences and performs better than using the topic signature alone. Additionally, we compare our hypergraph-based approach with other graph-based approaches to test the effectiveness of modeling high-order relations compared to pairwise similarity. The results demonstrate that the hypergraph-based approach outperformed both the TextRank and the NE-Rank approaches.

The effectiveness of the hypergraph-based approach in text summarization is in its ability to represent subsumption of information in an explicit way. When a number of short sentences represented in small hyperedges are a subset of a larger hyperedge, the random walk will naturally prefer the larger hyperedge more. This helps in summarization because it will choose sentences that convey more information from shorter uninformative sentences. Therefore, when the random walk is defined over hyperedges as in our proposed approach, the coverage of information is clearer than if we model sentences as nodes which is standard in graphs-based methods. Another idea behind the hypergraph approach is that by modeling sentences as hyperedges and vertices as words, the random walk will be able to recognize high-order relation of both words and sentences. For instance, the approach is capable of recognizing subparts of a sentence that connects it to multiple sentences as in sets of shared words between more than two sentences. In standard graphs, the similarity is only measured between two sentences which makes the hypergraph perform better in ranking sentences.

5. RELATED WORK

Graph-based summarization is a well-researched area where the centrality of sentences is based on a similarity graph. Mihalcea and Tarau propose the TextRank algorithm which builds a graph of sentences when they share words between them. The pair-wise similarity of sentences is based on the edge weights being the number of overlapping words over the length of both sentences[8]. Similarly, Erkan and Radev propose LexRank which similarly builds a graph of sentences with the relation being the cosine similarity between the pair of sentences[5]. Both TextRank and LexRank use a random walk approach for ranking nodes based on eigenvector centrality as in PageRank [2]. Wan et al. propose to use a mutual ranking of words and sentences where the relations between words, relations between sentences, and inter-relations between both sides is used for more effective ranking[9].

Wang et al. propose a hypergraph-based model for query-focused summarization where their ranking uses a semi-supervised approach to rank sentences based on their relation to the labeled sentence which represent the query[10].

Similar sentences are joined in a hyperedge if they belong to the same cluster. Their approach uses the high-order relation between sentences effectively to measure the similarity to the query. However, the approach is tailored towards query-focused approaches and it is not clear how to use such approach for generic summarization.

6. CONCLUSION & FUTURE WORK

In this paper, we proposed a new hypergraph-based approach for multi-document summarization. By representing words as vertices and sentences as hyperedges, our approach showed an effective way of capturing high-order relations between both words and sentences. We showed a new random walk approach to rank hyperedges by transitioning through common words. Additionally, we combine hypergraphs with a statistical topic signatures approach to draw the random walk towards sentences that contain a lot of topical words. The approach showed interesting notion of combining both corpus level as in topic signatures and cluster level as in the hypergraph indicators for multi-document summarization.

For future work, we plan to test our approach in more DUC datasets to show its validity. We also plan to study the effect of topic signatures on the hypergraph in more detail. Additionally, we plan to compare our approach to other summarizer besides the graph-based approaches.

7. REFERENCES

[1] A. Bellaachia and M. Al-Dhelaan. Ne-rank: A novel graph-based keyphrase extraction in twitter. In *WI-IAT*, pages 372–379, 2012.

[2] S. Brin and L. Page. The anatomy of a large-scale hypertextual web search engine. In *WWW*, pages 107–117, 1998.

[3] J. Carbonell and J. Goldstein. The use of mmr, diversity-based reranking for reordering documents and producing summaries. In *SIGIR*, pages 335–336, 1998.

[4] J. M. Conroy, J. D. Schlesinger, and D. P. O'Leary. Topic-focused multi-document summarization using an approximate oracle score. In *COLING-ACL*, pages 152–159, 2006.

[5] G. Erkan and D. R. Radev. Lexrank: graph-based lexical centrality as salience in summarization. *Journal of Artificial Intelligence Research*, 22(1):457–479, Dec. 2004.

[6] C.-Y. Lin and E. Hovy. The automated acquisition of topic signatures for text summarization. In *COLING*, pages 495–501, 2000.

[7] C.-Y. Lin and E. Hovy. Automatic evaluation of summaries using n-gram co-occurrence statistics. In *NAACL*, pages 71–78, 2003.

[8] R. Mihalcea and P. Tarau. Textrank: Bringing order into texts. In D. Lin and D. Wu, editors, *EMNLP, 2004*, pages 404–411, Barcelona, Spain, July.

[9] X. Wan, J. Yang, and J. Xiao. Towards an iterative reinforcement approach for simultaneous document summarization and keyword extraction. In *ACL*, pages 552–559, Prague, Czech Republic, 2007.

[10] W. Wang, F. Wei, W. Li, and S. Li. Hypersum: hypergraph based semi-supervised sentence ranking for query-oriented summarization. In *CIKM*, pages 1855–1858, 2009.

[11] B. Zhang, H. Li, Y. Liu, L. Ji, W. Xi, W. Fan, Z. Chen, and W.-Y. Ma. Improving web search results using affinity graph. In *SIGIR*, pages 504–511, 2005.

Non-independent Cascade Formation: Temporal and Spatial Effects

Biru Cui
Computing and Information Science
Rochester Institute of Technology
bxc2868@rit.edu

Shanchieh Jay Yang
Department of Computer Engineering
Rochester Institute of Technology
jay.yang@rit.edu

Christopher Homan
Department of Computer Science
Rochester Institute of Technology
cmh@cs.rit.edu

ABSTRACT

Determining cascade size and the factors affecting cascade size are two fundamental research problems in social network analysis. The commonly considered independent cascade model, when applied to social networks such as Digg, produces a phase-transition phenomenon where the cascade is either very small or very large. This phenomenon can be explained based on the concept of Giant Propagation Component (GPC). The GPC is defined as a maximally connected component, such that, by applying the independent cascade model, once any node of the component is infected, most of the remaining nodes in the component will eventually become infected with a high probability. While GPC exists in social networks, the phase-transition phenomenon, is not observed in the actual cascade size distribution when the information propagation is due to actions such as "like" or "dig". This paper hypothesizes that the cascade process, *i.e.*, the likeliness of a node being infected changes over time and depends on how far away the node is from the seed. Furthermore, each node will not be exactly independently considered for infection from each of its infected friends, because the chance of information propagation through "like" or "dig" does not necessarily increase when there are more friends like/dig the information. To this end, we develop and simulate a new non-independent infection cascade process. The experiment results show that the proposed cascade process generates power-law like cascade size distribution without phase transition, which resembles much better the real-world cascade distribution observed in the Digg social network.

Categories and Subject Descriptors

H.3.1 [**Information Storage and Retrieval**]: Content Analysis and Indexing; J.4 [**Social and Behavioral Sciences**]: Sociology

Keywords

information cascade; cascade size

1. INTRODUCTION

Leskovec *et al.* [9] discussed the information cascades in blogs, where a cascade is defined as a DAG structure which has a single starting post called cascade seed. Each node of the cascade is a blog post and a child node is any post that contains the parent post's URL. A blog has a link pointing to another blog if its post refers (contains the URL) to the second blog's post. Each seed creates a cascade, and the information is propagated to other blogs by post referring. They found that most (97%) cascades were trivial (isolated posts); only a very small number of cascades contained multiple levels, and the distribution of cascade size follows a power law where the cascade size is the total number of nodes involved in the cascade. Similar observations were found in [6], [2], [1]. With these observations, existing works attempted to develop cascade generation models to explain the cascade process. Kermack *et al.* [7] proposed the SIR (Susceptible, Infected, and Removed) model to describe the disease infection process among populations and to estimate the likelihood of an epidemic. This *infection* concept was borrowed and applied to explain the information propagation. The infection is defined as the process where a person adopts the information after being exposed to the information from her friends. Granovetter *et al.* [5] proposed a threshold model where each node has a predefined threshold. The influence each node receives is the accumulated link weights from its infected friends. The node is infected once the received influence crosses the threshold. Goldenberg *et al.* [3] defined an independent cascade model that a node is infected by its friends independently with a probability. Leskovec *et al.* [9] also proposed a simple cascade generation model based on this independent cascade model. Besides modeling the cascade process, other studies attempted to predict the cascade size. Given the initial cascade size, Cheng *et al.* [2] predicted whether the cascade size could be doubled by including the temporal and spatial features. They solved the cascade size prediction as a classification problem, but ignored the step-by-step propagation dynamics. Also, few of the aforementioned studies noticed that the simulated cascade size distribution based on the conventional cascade generation models are very different from the actual cascade size distribution.

This paper attempts to fill the gap by investigating the cascade size and factors affecting the cascade size distribution. A phase-transition phenomenon is found in simulated cascades on the Digg social network using the independent cascade model where the size of a cascade is either very small or very large. Also the probability to have a large size cascade in the actual network is much smaller than the one in the simulated cases. The paper first developed the concept of GPC (Giant Propagation Component) to explain the phase-transition phenomenon. While the GPC exists in the social network, the phase transition is not observed in the actual cascades. To explain the difference, this work hypothesizes that the cascade size depends on the influence network structure and is also affected by temporal and spatial factors. Furthermore, a non-independent cascade model is proposed to explain the information propagation through "dig/like" actions, where a node is not infected independently by each of its infected friends, but makes the infection decision upon the aggregated effects of its friends and other temporal and spatial factors.

2. CONFLICTING OBSERVATIONS ON CASCADE SIZE DISTRIBUTION

This section first exhibits the difference between the simulated cascade size distribution and the actual cascade size distribution. For convenience, this paper defines *parent* and *child* to represent the friend's relationship as: *child* $\rightarrow$ *parent*, where *child* is watching *parent*'s activities, and *parent* can infect *child*. Table 1 shows the independent cascade generation process which is similar to the cascade generation model of [9].

Algorithm 1 Independent Cascade Generation Process

Initialize empty infected and susceptible list;
  randomly select a node s as seed;
  add each of s's uninfected children k into the susceptible list
    associated with a probability P_{sk};
Loop While susceptible list not empty:
    check the susceptible node j against its associated
      probability P_{ij};
    if infected:
      add j into the infected list;
      add each of j's uninfected children k' into
        the susceptible list
        associated with a probability $P_{jk'}$;
    remove j from the susceptible list;
End Loop

Table 1: Independent cascade generation process

In Table 1, i is the infected parent of j, P_{ij} is the probability of node i infecting node j. According to [4], P_{ij} can be extracted based on the number of same actions done by two nodes over the number of actions done by i. Each simulation run generates one cascade. The experiment considers the Digg network as the influence network. The simulated cascade size distribution is shown in Fig.1a by running the simulation 100,000 times. However, it is very different from the actual cascade size distribution[1] as shown in Fig.1b.

There are two differences. The first difference is that there is a phase transition in the simulation, but no such gap in the real cascade size distribution. Steeg *et al.* [6] observed similar phenomenon, where they assumed all link weights are the same in their experiment. The second difference is that the probability to reach a large cascade in the actual case is much lower, and the distribution is in a power-law shape. The simulation has much higher probability (about 0.0134, 1338 out of 100,000 cascades) to have a large cascade (size

---
[1]The cascades are generated using the cascades extraction method specified in [9] on Digg dataset [8].

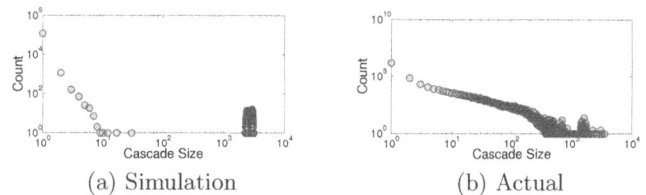

(a) Simulation   (b) Actual

Figure 1: Cascade size distribution

greater than 2500) than the actual cascades (about 0.000008, 15 out of 1780522 cascades).

3. PHASE-TRANSITION AND GPC

To explain the first difference, the phase-transition phenomenon, we introduce the concept of GPC (Giant Propagation Component). The key point of the phase transition is that the cascade is either very large or very small. Intuitively, to have a large size cascade, the propagation needs to keep on infecting new nodes at each iteration, *i.e.*, the probability of infecting at least one node must approach 1. Based on the independent cascade model, the probability P_i of a node i infecting at least one of its children is defined as:

$$P_i = 1 - \prod_{j \in N(i)} (1 - P_{ij}) \geq 1 - \epsilon \qquad (1)$$

where P_{ij} is the probability of node i infecting j; $N(i)$ is the set of children that could be infected by i; ϵ is a very small number. The GPC is the maximally connected component where all nodes of the component satisfy (1). If a node in the GPC is infected, it will infect at least one other node with a high probability; and this newly infected node will attempt to infect another new node. Thus, if any node of the GPC is infected, it will cause a number of other nodes of the GPC being infected with a high probability, and this number is proportional to the size of the GPC [2]. Therefore, the existence of the GPC causes the phase-transition scenario in that:

- If any node of the GPC is infected during the propagation process, the cascade will reach a large size which is proportional to the size of the GPC plus the number of nodes adjacent to the GPC in a high probability.

- If no node of the GPC is infected during the propagation process, the cascade will die quickly and end with a small size.

The algorithm to locate the GPC is by continuously pruning nodes that do not satisfy (1). In this way, the GPC found in the Digg network has 310 nodes with $\epsilon = 0.01$. By selecting any node of the GPC as seed, it will infect most nodes (about 290 out of 310) of GPC, and will eventually infect about 3000 nodes by counting the adjacent nodes of GPC with relevant link infection probability. This numerical estimation is close to the large cascade size of the simulation result shown in Fig.1a. By checking all cascades in Fig.1b with size large than 2500, the infected nodes include most nodes of the derived GPC. This also validates the statement that the

---
[2]It is possible that all children of infected nodes are already infected, which will cause the propagation to stop.

activation of the GPC is the necessary condition of a large cascade.

Since the GPC is related to the infection probability, we want to test whether changing the infection probability will remove the phase transition. The following experiment assumes all links weights having the same λ. Fig.2 shows the cascade size distribution as λ increases. By increasing the λ, each node has a higher chance to infect new nodes and the GPC size is larger, and thus, a larger cascade. The phase-transition phenomenon disappears when λ is too small to support a GPC. Though a low infection probability can eliminate the GPC and phase transitions, it also greatly constrain the size of a cascade, where no cascade can be large. This shows that changing λ does not provide a solution to remove the phase transition.

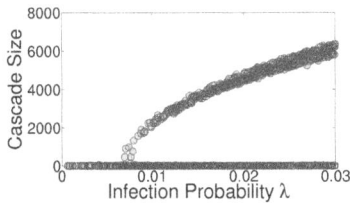

Figure 2: Cascade size distribution with different uniform infection probability λ

The primary issue that causes the GPC is the "independent" infection process. This motivates us to investigate a non-independent cascade model to explain the information propagation in the Digg network. This also accords to the "dig/like" user experience in the Digg social network and Facebook. Intuitively, people make the "dig/like" decision by reading the story and influenced by the aggregated result of the parents "dug/liked" the same story, but not being infected independently by each of their parents.

4. WHAT AFFECTS THE CASCADE SIZE?

Besides the phase transition, the other difference is that the probability to reach a large size cascade in the actual cascade size distribution is much lower than the simulation's based on the independent cascade model. In other words, a cascade can reach a large size with only a very small chance. So what prevents a cascade to grow large in the real world? To answer this question, we hypothesize that the infection probability, i.e., the likeliness of being infected, is affected by several temporal and spatial factors, and consequently affects the cascade size. The reason of selecting temporal and spatial factors is based on the intuition that the propagation of the information is dependent on whether the information is new (temporal) and whether it is widely (spatial) known.

4.1 Temporal Factor

Each story in the Digg network has its lifetime, even for the most popular news. A typical story in the Digg social network will not last for more than a week. This motivates us to think about the attractiveness of the information may constrain a cascade to propagate further. The attractiveness can be represented as the information's infection probability which will decay over time.

4.1.1 Information Attractiveness

The seeds are the nodes adopt the information without being influenced by other nodes but solely attracted by the

information. Thus, the number of seeds emerged along the time represents the attractiveness of the information. Imaging the "information" as a virtual node, the seeds are infected by the information itself. Fig.3 shows the $5\% \sim 95\%$ percentile of the number of the newly emerged seeds for different stories over time. The red square-marker curve is the mean value, and the green diamond-marker curve is the relevant exponential function fitting. These curves show that the infection probability from the information itself to the uninfected nodes decays exponentially over time.

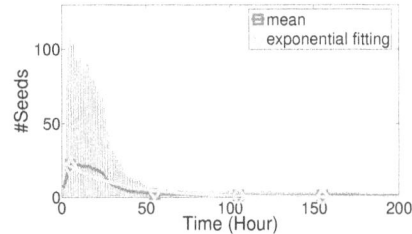

Figure 3: Number of seeds emerged over time

4.2 Spatial Factors

4.2.1 Infection at Different Locations

Location is defined as the number of hops a node is away from the seed where the information is originated. By monitoring the infection happened in the same time period, the dots in Fig.4 represents the normalized infection probability (defined as the number of infected nodes over the total number of children could be infected) at different locations. The infection probability is smaller if the infection happens farther away from the seed, and the probability decays exponentially. The curve shows the fitted exponential function.

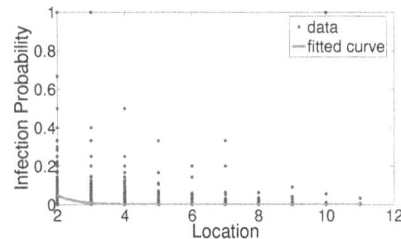

Figure 4: Exponential fitting of the decay of the infection probability at different locations

4.2.2 Number of Infected Friends(Parents)

Besides the location where the infection happens, another possible factor is the infected parents. According to the independent cascade model [3], the conditional infection probability increases exponentially with the number of infected parents. However, Steeg et al. [6] observed that it is not true; the infection probability almost keeps consistent regardless of the number of infected parents in the Digg network. We repeated their experiment and verified the result. This also implies that neither the independent cascade model nor the linear threshold model may be applicable in the information propagation of "dig/like" actions.

5. AGGREGATE CASCADE MODEL

Sections 3 and 4 discussed the reasons causing the two differences observed in Fig.1. To overcome the limitation of the current independent cascade model, we propose an "aggregate cascade model" by considering the following factors.

- The probability a node is infected depends on the time passed since the information is originated.

- The probability a node is infected depends on the distance the node is away from the seed where the information is originated.

- The infection is not triggered independently by each infected parent, but every node assesses its situation to make infection decision only once; the time when the node will assess the infection is defined by an infection waiting time model.

The infection waiting time model comes from the distribution of the infection time difference between the parent node and its child. Fig.5 shows the waiting time distribution extracted from the actual cascades of the Digg network.

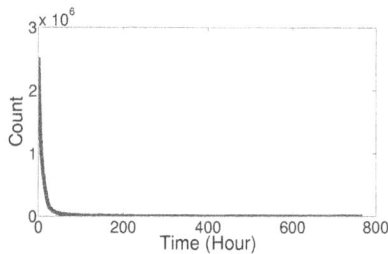

Figure 5: Distribution of the infection waiting time in the Digg network dataset

The waiting time distribution follows an exponential distribution $\frac{1}{\mu}\exp(-\frac{x}{\mu})$ with $\mu = 9$ (Kolmogorov-Smirnov goodness-of-fit test, sample size 243483, critical value 0.0033, p-value < 2.2e-16). Let δ_l represent the infection waiting time at location l and drawn from this distribution. Table 2 shows the aggregate cascade generation model: In Table

---

Algorithm 2 Aggregate Cascade Generation Process

Initialize empty infected, accessed and susceptible list;
randomly select a node s as seed;
add each uninfected child into the susceptible list
with a timer t and its location L;
Loop While susceptible list not empty:
    if any timer of a susceptible node j expires:
        assess node j's infection against the probability
        $P_j = (\frac{1}{|K(j)|}\sum_{i \in K(j)} P_{ij}) * exp(a * t + b * L)$;
        if infected:
            add node j into the infected list;
            for each of j's uninfected child k:
                if k not in accessed list, add k into the
                    susceptible list with a timer t
                    and its location L;
        remove node j from the susceptible list
        and add j into the accessed list;
End Loop

Table 2: Aggregate cascade generation process

2, $K(j)$ is the set of infected parents which can infect j and $|K(j)|$ is the size of the set; $a = -0.03, b = -0.2$ are derived from Sections 4.1.1 and 4.2.1 accordingly; t is the elapsed time since the moment information is originated estimated by $\sum_{l=1}^{L} \delta_l$; L is the shortest distance of node i to the seed through the infected parents. Fig.6 is the simulated cascade

size distribution based on the aggregate cascade algorithm. The distribution is in a power-low like shape without phase transitions, similar to the distribution in Fig.1b.

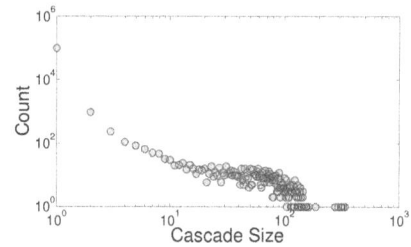

Figure 6: Cascade size distribution with the aggregate cascade generation algorithm

6. CONCLUSION

This paper analyzed the difference of simulated cascade size distribution based on the independent cascade model from the actual cascade size distribution. GPC is introduced to explain the phase-transition phenomenon; and temporal and spatial factors are investigated to adjust the infection probability. Furthermore, a non-independent cascade model is proposed to better reflect the essence of the information propagation of "dig/like" actions, where people make information adoption decision based on the aggregated effects of its parents and other temporal spatial factors.

Acknowledgments

Funding for this research was provided by NSF Award #SBE-1111016.

7. REFERENCES

[1] A.-L. Barabasi. The origin of bursts and heavy tails in human dynamics. *Nature*, 435(7039):207–211, 2005.

[2] J. Cheng, L. Adamic, P. A. Dow, J. M. Kleinberg, and J. Leskovec. Can cascades be predicted? In *Proceedings of WWW*, pages 925–936, 2014.

[3] J. Goldenberg, B. Libai, and E. Muller. Talk of the network: A complex systems look at the underlying process of word-of-mouth. *Marketing letters*, 12(3):211–223, 2001.

[4] A. Goyal, F. Bonchi, and L. V. Lakshmanan. Learning influence probabilities in social networks. In *Proceedings of WSDM*, pages 241–250, 2010.

[5] M. Granovetter. Threshold models of collective behavior. *American journal of sociology*, 83(6):1420, 1978.

[6] Greg Ver Steeg, R. Ghosh, and K. Lerman. What stops social epidemics? In *Proceedings of ICWSM*, 2011.

[7] W. Kermack and A. McKendrick. Contributions to the mathematical theory of epidemics. ii. the problem of endemicity. *Bulletin of Mathematical Biology*, 53(1-2):57–87, 1991.

[8] K. Lerman and R. Ghosh. Information contagion: An empirical study of the spread of news on digg and twitter social networks. *ICWSM*, 10:90–97, 2010.

[9] J. Leskovec, M. McGlohon, C. Faloutsos, N. S. Glance, and M. Hurst. Patterns of cascading behavior in large blog graphs. In *Proceedings of SDM*, pages 551–556, 2007.

What is the Shape of a Cluster?
Structural Comparisons of Document Clusters

Vinay Deolalikar
Hewlett-Packard Research
Sunnyvale, CA
deolalikar.academic@gmail.com

ABSTRACT

Even today, most interfaces to document clustering present clusters to users and applications as a "bag of descriptive terms"—a technique that was proposed two decades ago. Consequently, users and applications are not able to obtain sophisticated structural knowledge that is indeed lying hidden in document clusters. In particular, the structural information about interaction of concepts that the cluster speaks about is completely missing from the bag of terms presentation. As the needs of unstructured information management increase, this shortcoming is coming into sharper focus.

To address this shortcoming, we propose a rich representation of document clusters that surfaces the concept interactions within a cluster into the representation. We show that these interactions give a "shape" to the cluster. This "shape" is conveniently captured using a *directed, colored, vertex-weighted graph*, called the *shape graph* or, simply, the *shape of the cluster*. We show that shapes convey important structural information about document clusters, and can be computed efficiently.

Keywords

Cluster Shape; Shape Graphs, Concept Interactions

1. INTRODUCTION

Document clustering can be used in several applications in unstructured information management (UIM). However, how do you present a cluster to a user or an application? And how does the user or application gather the information they need from the clustering?

As UIM applications of clustering become more sophisticated, they will require sophisticated *presentations* of clusters so that they may extract the information they need from these presentations. However, in spite of the enormous research attention given to clustering algorithms, there is meager attention being given to the problem of cluster presentation and information that can be extracted from them.

Today, clusters are usually presented to a user or application by means of a *digest*, which is a bag of important terms in the cluster, possibly along with a weight that indicates importance [10]. A standard means to compute a digest for a cluster is to rank the terms in the cluster with respect to their frequency of occurrence, and then present the user with the top-ℓ terms and their weights as

a digest. Terms in the digest serve as a proxy for the topics in the cluster.

The above technology was proposed at least two decades ago [4] and is not rich enough for today's applications. To see this, consider the following two cluster digests from a 20-way clustering of the 20 Newsgroups dataset.

game	team	player	play	baseball	hockey	win	season
9.6	7.6	4.8	2.9	2.3	2.2	2.1	1.8

israel	armenian	arab	jew	turkish	armenia	palestinian
10.8	9.1	4.4	3.9	3.2	1.4	1.2

Carefully examining both digests indicates that the respective clusters might be speaking of two topics each. The first about baseball and hockey and the second about two middle eastern conflicts. But are documents in these clusters comparing these two, or are they mostly disjoint discussions centered around these two? This is impossible to tell from the digest.

The obvious shortcomings of the current digest representation of clusters include the following.

1. It is not visual. A significant proportion of users understand information far better if it is presented visually. Inspecting a list of terms is not appealing to such users.

2. It does not indicate to the user which sets of concepts (important terms) tend to co-occur within documents in the cluster. The user has no way to know what the natural sub-groups in the cluster are. For example, the first of our three example digests does not tell a user whether the documents in the cluster (a) compare two sports and their seasons, or (b) whether there is a dichotomy in the cluster, with one group of documents speaking of hockey, and another speaking of baseball. In the example digest of (5), without further knowledge of which concepts co-occur, there is no hope of interpreting the contents of the cluster.

3. It does not permit easy structural comparison between clusters. There is no way to pose, or answer the question "Is cluster A structurally similar to cluster B?" For example, each of the two clusters speaks about two topics. Are they structurally similar?

4. The inspections done above are tedious and do not scale.

5. Most cluster digests do not admit an easy interpretation. For example, the following digest, which is typical, does not admit an easy interpretation.

moral	islam	object	keith	atheist	religion	science	livesey
12.7	6.2	4.6	3.2	2.9	1.4	1.4	1.3

Our Approach. We propose a richer cluster presentation that rectifies these shortcomings. At first, it may seem that since a cluster is collection of documents, we may not be able to do better than display it using important terms in these documents, and/or titles of a subset of these documents. However, we may view a cluster as an *interaction of concepts*. Further, this concept interaction structure can be unearthed from each cluser using a framework that carefully records frequent itemsets in a cluster and the overlaps between them.[1]

Our framework yields, for each cluster, a *directed, colored, vertex-weighted graph* that translates the rich, concept interaction structure of the cluster into the language of the graph. This is the *shape graph* of the cluster. The shape graph conveys structural information that is not visible in a "bag of terms" digest.

Our contributions are as follows. We provide a pictorial and structurally rich presentation of individual clusters in a document clustering. Our framework enables structural comparison between clusters. Finally, we demonstrate our framework on benchmark text corpora.

2. RELATED WORK

Our work is related to two streams of research.

2.1 Clustering Interfaces

As noted, there is relatively scant research devoted specifically to clustering interfaces. [4] introduce scatter/gather, a workflow that uses clustering to navigate document corpora. The clustering interface consists of frequent and discriminative terms taken from clusters. This interface has been, more or less, retained by subsequent work. [3, 11] develop scatter/gather further, but retain the original interface. [5] compare interfaces for organizing query search results by categorization and clustering. Their clustering interface uses descriptive terms taken from each cluster's centroid, along with titles of a few documents from the cluster. Grouper [14] uses six phrases taken from documents in the cluster, with redundancy removed, as its interface. In addition to the above, various commerical vendors provide their custom interfaces to clustering. All of these that we are aware of use a combination of terms, phrases, document titles, and representative documents to present a cluster.

2.2 Cluster Based Visualization

Due to the pictorial nature of our interface, it may also be seen as a form of visualization.
Visualizing Corpus Structure. The goal of this work is to visualize a *dataset* using clustering. [2] study unexpected relationships arising in document similarity graphs that use latent Dirichlet allocation. [8] propose a topic model for visualizing documents in a dataset using probabilistic latent semantic indexing. There is no clustering of the dataset. [12] present CLUSION, which is a relationship centric view of document clustering, as opposed to an object centric view that represents clusters as a set of terms. Our presentation is also relationship centric, but it is relationship centric at a lower-level: at the level of terms within a cluster, whereas CLUSION presents relationships between clusters. [13] propose a visualization called "Galaxies" where documents and clusters are represented as a 2-D scatterplot that resembles stars in a night sky. The clusters themselves are represented by terms from a digest. DICON [1] represents clusters by means of icons that encode their high-level statistical information.

Visualization to Assist Navigation. [7] propose a topological version of probabilistic latent semantic analysis, which allows a user to navigate large text corpora by choosing a set of topics, expanding upon them, and iterating the above using a multi-resolution visualization using grid maps. [9] present iVisClustering: an interactive visual clustering tool that uses topic modeling. iVisClustering offers the user control over how to cluster, using various devices such as the ability to control the weights of terms in a clustering. The visualization of a cluster is, however, a set of terms and their weights.

We use frequent itemsets in order to unearth concept interactions for our representation. Frequent itemsets first arose in association

---

[1]We may think of this structure as a form of conceptual *skeleton* of the cluster.

mining [6], and the literature on them is too vast to be recounted here. However, to our knowledge, they have not been used before to construct pictorial representations of document clusters.

3. PRELIMINARIES

In this section, we clarify the setting and describe some of the techniques that we will use later.

Corpus and Processing. Our data $\mathcal{D}$ will be comprised of a document collection (or corpus) $\mathcal{D} = \{D_1, \ldots, D_n\}$. A *K-clustering* $\mathcal{C} = \{C_1, \ldots, C_K\}$ of $\mathcal{D}$ is a partition of $\mathcal{D}$ into K disjoint nonempty subsets whose union is $\mathcal{D}$. We assume a standard preprocessing of documents for clustering: tokenization of words, stemming, removal of stoplists, and removal of words occurring very infrequently (say, less than thrice) in the corpus. The resulting set of tokens will be called *terms*. The *vocabulary* of $\mathcal{D}$ is the set of all terms in the documents of $\mathcal{D}$. Sets of terms will be referred to as *itemsets*. Itemsets will be denoted by F, with subscripts when necessary. The *support* of an itemset F in $\mathcal{D}$, denoted by $supp(F, \mathcal{D})$, is the set of all documents in $\mathcal{D}$ in which all the terms of F co-occur. Likewise, $supp(F, C)$ is the set of all documents in the cluster C that contain all the terms of F.

Frequent Itemsets. For the definitions below, C is a generic cluster in $\mathcal{C}$. First we define notions of frequent, and frequent relative to C.

Definition 1. 1. Let α be a positive integer that is called *minimum support*. F is said to be *frequent* (w.r.t. α) if the size of the support of F exceeds α.

2. A frequent itemset F is said to be *frequent relative to C* if $supp(F, C) > \zeta \times supp(F, \mathcal{D})$, where ζ is a threshold and $0 < \zeta < 1$.

3. Then F is said to be *maximal frequent relative to C* if it is the maximal (w.r.t. set inclusion) itemset with the preceding property.

By "frequent", we henceforth mean "maximal frequent relative to a cluster C": namely, maximally large sets of co-frequent terms are considered.

Norms for Terms. Next, we need a norm for terms in clusters that takes into account the clustering structure. Let $N(t, C)$ denote the number of times a term t appears, in total, in all the documents of cluster C.

Definition 2. Let t be a term that occurs in C. The *proportional L_1 norm* of t with respect to C, denoted $\pi(t)$, is defined as

$$\pi(t) = \frac{N(t, C)}{\sum_{u \in C} N(u, C)}.$$

Namely, it is the proportion of the number of times t appears in C to the total number of term occurrences in C.

We denote by $C^{[\ell]}$ the ℓ most frequent terms in C. Equivalently, these are the ℓ terms having the highest proportional L_1 norm in C.

We denote the maximal frequent itemsets of our generic cluster C by $\mathscr{F}(C) = \{F_1, \ldots, F_q\}$. However, we will use a more manageable set of frequent itemsets—those whose terms are all taken from $C^{[\ell]}$.

Definition 3. We define $\mathscr{F}(C^{[\ell]})$ as the set of frequent itemsets for C such that for all $F \in \mathscr{F}(C^{[\ell]})$, each term in F is from $C^{[\ell]}$.

This technique is not only justified because it computes frequent itemsets using only significant terms, but it also allows for a computationally inexpensive implementation. This is because the $C^{[\ell]}$ are just the top-ℓ terms in the cluster centroid, which is usually computed during clustering.

4. THE SHAPE OF A CLUSTER

In this section, we describe how we associate a "shape" to each cluster. We describe this process in stages, providing an intuitive justification for each stage.

4.1 Cluster Information

First, we explain the information needed to produce a shape for each cluster. This information is described below.

Definition 4. The *cluster information* for a cluster C, denoted $\mathcal{I}(C)$, is comprised of the following data:

1. The terms in $C^{[\ell]}$, along with their proportional L_1 norms.
2. The maximal frequent itemsets $\mathscr{F}(C^{[\ell]})$.

We have experimented extensively with various values of ℓ and recommend $\ell = 10$ or 15 since the weights of the terms after that are too low in comparison to the higher weights.

4.2 The Shape Graph of a Cluster

Next, we use the information about the cluster gathered thus far to construct a coherent "shape" for the cluster. As mentioned earlier, the shape is a vertex weighted colored directed graph that captures the interactions between various concepts and topics in the cluster. We denote the shape graph of cluster C_k, where $1 \leq k \leq K$, by $\mathcal{G}_k$. We specify $\mathcal{G}_k$ in three steps.

Step I: Constructing Subgraphs for Each Concept-Class

First, for each of the concept-classes F_j (represented by the frequent itemset) in C_k, we construct the subgraph $\mathcal{G}_k^j$ of $\mathcal{G}_k$ corresponding to the concept-class. This construction is described below.

1. The vertices of $\mathcal{G}_k^j$ are the set of concepts in F_j. The color of each vertex is the corresponding color of the concept.
2. Now we need to specify the edges.
   (a) We first order the concepts in F_j in descending order of their concept weights.
   (b) We add a directed edge between each adjacent pair of concepts in this ordering, from the concept that is ranked higher to the one that is ranked lower. There is no edge incident upon the highest ranked concept.

Step II: Joining the Subgraphs, Associating Degrees to Vertices

Next we "join" the various subgraphs $\mathcal{G}_k^j$, for the index j running through the concept-classes of C_k. In order to do this, we simply aggregate all the incoming and outgoing edges for each concept over all the subgraphs $\{\mathcal{G}_k^j\}$. Therefore, in general, there will be vertices that have multiple edges emanating from them, as well as incident upon them.

Finally, for each $1 \leq i \leq \ell$, we attach a weight ν_i that measures concept overlaps to the ith vertex: this is the number of concept-classes the concept-classes the concept represented by the vertex occurs in. Note that this weight is not the same as the concept weight of the vertex. In order to emphasize this difference, we shall call ν the *degree* of the vertex.

Step III: Coloring Vertices by Concept Weight

The mapping of concepts to weights by importance is too fine for our purposes. We would like to transform the range of this mapping to a small discrete set of "colors," with each color coding a relative level of importance. The natural way to do this is to place the weights of the concepts into a small number of buckets.

Definition 5. Let $C^{[\ell]}$ be the ℓ most frequent terms in C. Let ξ be the number of colors that are desired. Let the individual colors be denoted by $c_1, c_2, \ldots c_\xi$. Then we assign the colors to the terms as follows. We approximate the distribution of norms of the most frequent terms to be log-linear. In this way, the curve of their logs is a straight line. We then simply equally divide this line between the start and end values into ξ segments.

$\mathcal{G}_k$ is the "shape graph," or simply the shape of the cluster.
Note: We emphasize that once the graph has been colored, the concept weights are no longer used (except for laying out the graph as described in §4.3). The vertex weight (called the degree) ν is *not* the concept weight of the vertex.

t	israel	isra	armenian	arab	jew	turkish	armenia	palestinian	turk	kill
$\pi(t)$	10.8	10.8	9.1	4.4	3.9	3.2	1.4	1.2	1.1	1

(a) The table of norms for $C^{[10]}$. We see the top three terms having roughly twice the frequency of the next three. These, in turn, have 3-4 times the frequency of the last four.

F_1	armenian turkish armenia turk kill
F_2	israel isra arab jew palestinian kill

(b) The frequently co-occurring sets of terms in this cluster (namely, $\mathscr{F}(C^{[10]})$). The first co-occurrence represents the Armenian-Turkish issue, and the second the Israel-Palestine issue.

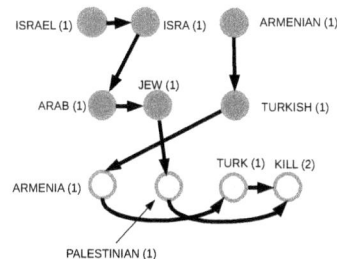

(c) The shape of the cluster clearly shows two themes. These two themes represent two long-standing conflict issues in the middle east. The two themes are joined at one common node, which is at the lowest level. This is unlike the following shape graphs, where themes are joined at various levels. Therefore, this cluster is essentially a union of two smaller clusters which would have occurred separately had we increased K.

Figure 1: The shape graph of a cluster in N20 at $K = 10$ having size 505 documents.

4.3 Laying out the Shape

In order to lay out (or draw) $\mathcal{G}_k$, we proceed in two steps.
1. The vertices are laid out by color, in levels from top to bottom, in order of decreasing (concept weight) color. Namely, all vertices of the same color are at the same level.
2. Within a single level (equivalently, among vertices having the same color), vertices are laid out from left to right in order of decreasing concept weight.

5. EMPIRICAL WORK

We demonstrate our cluster shapes on two standard research benchmark datasets: N20[2] comprising of articles posted to 20 newsgroups; and REU, comprising documents that appeared on the Reuters newswire in 1987. For a manageable set of clusters for our examples, we clustered at $K = 10$ and $K = 20$ using the repeat-bisect method [?] to generate clusters. We used $(\alpha, \zeta) = (15, 0.3)$. For the purposes of pedagogy in the examples of this paper, we adopt the following reasonable approximation of Def. 5. In many clusters, the highest weighted term has a weight of around 10. Therefore, we let $\xi = 4$ and the colors be red, green, blue, and yellow. Then, weights above 7 will be given the red color, between 7 and 4 the green color, between 4 and 2 the blue color, and below 2 the yellow color.

For lack of space, we show three cluster shapes from $K = 10$ and 20 of N20 in Figs 1 to 3, move their discussion to their captions, and provide a qualitative summary of the other shapes observed.
Summary. The set of shapes observed showed a rich variety. We observed line graphs, disconnected graphs, graphs with peculiar connected components, and so on. This represents the richness in variety of concept interactions that are possible in document clustering. We emphasize that all of this richness is lost when the clus-

[2] http://qwone.com/~jason/20Newsgroups/

t	game	team	player	play	baseball	hockey	win	season	fan	score
$\pi(t)$	9.6	7.6	4.8	2.9	2.3	2.2	2.1	1.8	1.6	1.5

(a) The norms of terms in $C^{[10]}$.

F_1	game team player play hockey win season fan score
F_2	game team player play baseball win season fan score

(b) The frequently co-occurring terms in the cluster (namely, $\mathcal{F}(C^{[10]})$). One represents the cluster theme in the context of hockey, while the other does so in the context of baseball.

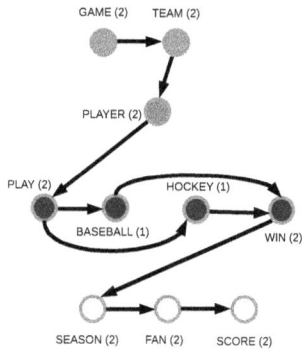

(c) The shape of the cluster. The shape indicates a single theme. Within that theme, there are two sub-contexts, namely, baseball and hockey. The connectivity of this shape graph is high, since all the terms in the theme are common, except for baseball and hockey. In particular, here the two components coincide at the red, green, and yellow levels; they only differ at the blue level. In contrast, in Fig. 1 the two components do not coincide at all, except at the least significant node of the yellow level.

Figure 2: The shape graph of a cluster in N20 at $K = 10$ having 1,196 documents.

t	moral	islam	object	keith	atheist	religion	scienc	livesei	sandvik	muslim
$\pi(t)$	12.7	6.2	4.6	3.2	2.9	1.4	1.4	1.3	1.3	1

(a) The norms of terms in $C^{[10]}$.

F_1	livesei muslim	F_5	islam sandvik muslim
F_2	religion scienc	F_6	islam religion muslim
F_3	atheist religion	F_7	moral object sandvik
F_4	object scienc	F_8	moral object keith atheist livesei

(b) The frequently co-occurring terms in the cluster (namely, $\mathcal{F}(C^{[10]})$). Note the high number of such frequently co-occurring terms.

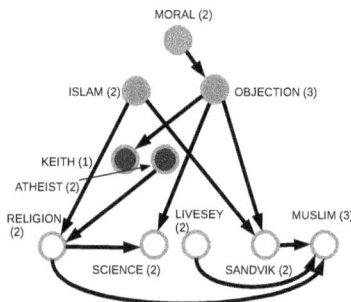

(c) The shape graph. Due to the large number of frequently co-occurring sets of terms, and the number of terms in common between these sets, the shape acquires a "spaghetti" like nature. Even so, the connectivity is low, since two sets of frequently co-occurring terms can be separated easily.

Figure 3: The shape graph of a cluster in N20 at $K = 20$ with 444 documents.

ter is represented by a digest. We are currently building an enterprise prototype that uses this rich information for data analysis.

6. CONCLUSIONS AND FUTURE WORK

Rich shape-based presentations of clusters provide structural information that is increasingly demanded by todays UIM applications. The shape of a cluster readily reveals several important characteristics of the cluster, notably the interaction structure of the concepts that are discussed in the cluster. The shape readily answers the questions posed in §1. The shape is widely deployable: it can replace other cluster presentations (for example, digests) in any application where richer interfaces are desired.

This work suggests the following two avenues (among others) for further research: retrieval of clusters by shapes and comparison of clusters based on their graphs (by using graph isomorphism). If an UIM application could specify a shape that it was interested in, could it be retrieved from a collection by means of isomorphism?

References

[1] N. Cao, D. Gotz, J. Sun, and H. Qu. Dicon: Interactive visual analysis of multidimensional clusters. *IEEE Trans. Vis. Comput. Graph.*, 17(12):2581–2590, 2011.

[2] P. Crossno, A. T. Wilson, T. M. Shead, and D. M. Dunlavy. Topicview: Visually comparing topic models of text collections. In *Proc. ICTAI*, pages 936–943. IEEE, 2011.

[3] D. Cutting, D. Karger, and J. Pedersen. Constant interaction-time scatter/gather browsing of very large document collections. In *Proc. 16th SIGIR*, pages 126–134. ACM, 1993.

[4] D. Cutting, J. Pedersen, D. Karger, and J. Tukey. Scatter/gather: A cluster-based approach to browsing large document collections. In *Proc. 15th SIGIR*, pages 318–329. ACM, 1992.

[5] M. A. Hearst. The use of categories and clusters for organizing retrieval results. In *Natural Language Information Retrieval*, pages 333–374. Springer, 1999.

[6] J. Hipp, U. Güntzer, and G. Nakhaeizadeh. Algorithms for association rule mining—a general survey and comparison. *SIGKDD Explorations Newsletter*, 2(1):58–64, June 2000.

[7] T. Hofmann. Probabilistic topic maps: Navigating through large text collections. *Advances in Intelligent Data Analysis*, pages 161–172, 1999.

[8] T. Iwata, T. Yamada, and N. Ueda. Probabilistic latent semantic visualization: topic model for visualizing documents. In *Proc. 14th SIGKDD*, KDD '08, pages 363–371, New York, NY, USA, 2008. ACM.

[9] H. Lee, J. Kihm, J. Choo, J. T. Stasko, and H. Park. iVisClustering: An interactive visual document clustering via topic modeling. *Comput. Graph. Forum*, 31(3):1155–1164, 2012.

[10] C. D. Manning, P. Raghavan, and H. Schtze. *Introduction to Information Retrieval*. Cambridge University Press, New York, NY, USA, 2008.

[11] P. Pirolli, P. Schank, M. Hearst, and C. Diehl. Scatter/gather browsing communicates the topic structure of a very large text collection. In *Proc. CHI 96 (Human Factors in Computing Systems)*, volume 1 of *PAPERS: Interactive Information Retrieval*, pages 213–220. ACM, 1996.

[12] A. Strehl and J. Ghosh. Relationship-based clustering and visualization for high-dimensional data mining. *INFORMS Journal on Computing*, 15(2):208–230, 2003.

[13] J. A. Wise, J. J. Thomas, K. Pennock, D. Lantrip, M. Pottier, A. Schur, and V. Crow. Visualizing the non-visual: Spatial analysis and interaction with information from text documents. In *Proc. INFOVIS*, pages 51–58, Washington, DC, USA, 1995. IEEE Computer Society.

[14] O. Zamir and O. Etzioni. Grouper: a dynamic clustering interface to web search results. *Computer Networks*, 31(11):1361–1374, 1999.

Ranking Sentiment Explanations for Review Summarization Using Dual Decomposition

Lei Fang, Qiao Qian, Minlie Huang and Xiaoyan Zhu
State Key Laboratory of Intelligent Technology and Systems
Tsinghua National Laboratory for Information Science and Technology
Department of Computer Science and Technology
Tsinghua University, Beijing 100084, PR China
fang-l10@mails.tsinghua.edu.cn, qianqiaodecember29@126.com,
aihuang@tsinghua.edu.cn, zxy-dcs@tsinghua.edu.cn

ABSTRACT

For online reviews, sentiment explanations refer to the sentences that may suggest detailed reasons of sentiment, which are very important for applications in review mining like opinion summarization. In this paper, we address the problem of ranking sentiment explanations by formulating the process as two subproblems: sentence informativeness ranking and structural sentiment analysis. Tractable inference in joint prediction is performed through dual decomposition. Preliminary experiments on publicly available data demonstrate that our approach obtains promising performance.

Categories and Subject Descriptors

H.3.3 [**Information Storage and Retrieval**]: Information Search and Retrieval—*Information filtering*; I.2.7 [**Artificial Intelligence**]: Natural language processing—*Text Analysis*

General Terms

Algorithms, Experimentation

Keywords

Opinion Mining; Sentiment Explanation; Dual Decomposition

1. INTRODUCTION

With the ongoing increasing amount of user-generated reviews on the web, many people consider online reviews as guidelines for decision making. However, few websites provide brief summaries, which makes it difficult for users to find what they focus on, particularly when the size of reviews is very large. On the other hand, for a single review, not every part is equally informative. It would be important to highlight the informative part of each review before review summarization. We term the informative part as "sentiment explanations".

From our point of view, "sentiment explanations" may be several sentences that suggest the detailed reasons of sentiment. Sentiment

explanations are valuable for abstracting a single review, which would also benefit the performance of summarizing a collection of reviews. We propose that good sentiment explanations of a single review should have the following properties:

1) from the summarization perspective, they best represent the content of original review.
2) from the sentiment perspective, they best represent the key opinion of original review.

The second property ensures that sentiment explanations should represent original reviews in terms of sentiment polarity, because a review might consist of various opinions. It is an advanced property compared with traditional single or multi document summarization.

In this paper, we propose to rank the sentences of a single review such that sentiment explanations rank higher. We formulate the ranking process as two subproblems: sentence informativeness ranking and multi-level sentiment analysis, which also echo the two properties for sentiment explanations. For sentence informativeness ranking, we train a simple ranking model from unlabeled data with several heuristic rules; for multi-level sentiment analysis, we employ the approach proposed by Yessenalina *et al.*[16] which aims to select sentences that best represent the original review in terms of polarity. Tractable inference in joint models is performed through dual decomposition [14]. Preliminary experiments on publicly available data set demonstrate that our approach of joint modeling obtains promising performance.

2. RELATED WORK

Recent years, there has been many studies focused on sentiment analysis [12]. Pang and Lee [11] and Yessenalina *et al.*[16] shown that not every part of the review was equally informative, they obtained improved sentiment classification performance as they considered that subjective part was more important for inferring the review rating.

For review summarization, generally it is considered as a sentence or review selection problem [1, 7]. Other studies performed review summarization in cascade approaches[3, 4, 10, 18] with first opinion extraction and then document summarization. However, these approaches don't highlight on sentiment explanations.

One similar work with this paper is [6], they scored the explanatoriness for each sentence, and then ranked explanatory sentences for opinion summarization. Though their approach was unsupervised, their formulation was based on the assumption that exiting technique can be used to classify the aspect and sentiment of each review. Our setting is more fundamental and our approach is closer to pragmatic needs.

Symbol	Description
x	a review document
$|x|$	number of sentences in x
y	sentiment polarity
x^j	a review sentence
A	a set of aspect seeds
a	a aspect label
V	vocabulary

Table 1: Basic Notations

3. JOINT SENTENCE RANKING AND SENTIMENT ANALYSIS

We first propose two subproblems for each property of sentiment explanation: sentence informativeness ranking and multi-level sentiment analysis. After that, joint inference of two subproblems will benefit the sentence informativeness ranking model such that sentiment explanations rank higher. For our task here, tractable inference in joint prediction is performed through dual decomposition [14].

Dual decomposition is a general approach for combinatorial optimization, with each sub-problem can be solved separately. With the help of dual decomposition, it makes the task of sentiment explanation ranking much more easier. We first present the setting for sentence informativeness ranking and multi-level sentiment analysis, respectively; then we give details for joint inference on a new review using dual decomposition. Table 1 presents notations we will use throughout this paper.

3.1 Sentence Informativeness Ranking

We propose the following heuristic rules for sentence informativeness ranking:

- the sentence would rank higher if it contains more opinion words[1];
- the sentence would rank higher if it contains more aspect words.

Aspects can be considered as certain properties of a product or service. For example, the aspects are "story", "music", "acting", "picture" and "director" for movie reviews; "taste", "ambience", "service", "price" and "location" for restaurant reviews. We extract aspect terms using a bootstrapping algorithm based on Chi-Square (χ^2) statistics shown in Algorithm 1, which is similar with[15].

The χ^2 statistic to compute the dependencies between word v and aspect a_j is

$$\chi^2(v, a_j) = \frac{C \times (C_1 C_4 - C_2 C_3)}{(C_1 + C_3) \times (C_2 + C_4) \times (C_1 + C_2) \times (C_3 + C_4)};$$

where C_1 is the number of times v occurs in sentences with aspect label a_j, C_2 is the number of times v occurs in sentences not labeled with a_j, C_3 is the number of sentences with aspect a_j but do not contain v, C_4 is the number of sentences that neither belong to aspect a_j nor contain word v, and C is the total number of word occurrences.

After extraction of aspect words, we generate the rank of each sentence for a collection of unlabeled sentences based on the aforementioned two rules. Then, we are able to train a ranking model using some learning to rank [8] techniques. In this work, we choose a pairwise ranking approach: SVM^{rank}[5], and use bag-of-words features to train the ranking model.

---

[1]We use the sentiment lexicon from http://www.cs.uic.edu/~liub/FBS/sentiment-analysis.html

---

Algorithm 1 Bootstrapping Framework.

Input:
 A collection of review sentences, $X = \{x^1, x^2, \ldots\}$;
 A collection of aspect seeds sets $A_1, A_2, \ldots$;
 Selection threshold n, iteration step limit l;
Output:
 Extended aspect word sets $T_1, T_2, \ldots$;
1: Initialize $T_i = A_i$ for all aspects
2: **repeat**
3: **for all** sentence $x^i \in X$ **do**
4:   Match aspect words for x^i, and record the matching hits for aspect a_j in $Count(j)$
5:   Assign aspect label a_j to x^i if $a_j = \underset{j}{\operatorname{argmax}} Count(j)$
6: **end for**
7: **for all** aspect a_j **do**
8:   **for all** word $v \in V$ **do**
9:    Calculate $\chi^2(v, a_j)$
10:   **end for**
11:   $T_j = T_j \bigcup \{$ Top ranked n words $\}$
12: **end for**
13: **until** No new aspect words are identified or iteration exceeds l
14: **return** $T_1, T_2, \ldots$;

Suppose $\mathcal{G}$ is the learnt ranking model parameterized by $\vec{w}_r$, for a new sentence x^i, $\psi(x^i)$ denotes the corresponding bag-of-words features vector, we calculate the ranking score as

$$score_r(x^i) = \mathcal{G}(x^i; \vec{w}_r) = \vec{w}_r \cdot \psi(x^i).$$

Then for all the reviews, our model outputs a ranking score for each sentences.

3.2 Multi-level Sentiment Analysis

For sentiment analysis, we adopt the approach for multi-level sentiment analysis proposed by Yessenalina et al.[16]. A benefit of this approach is that it extracts a set of sentences that best represent the polarity of original review only with the supervision of document-level review polarity, which can be easily obtained since many online review websites provide semi-structural reviews with overall ratings. Here, we give a brief description of this approach. A review document is represented by x with corresponding polarity $y \in \{+1, -1\}$. The quality of a sentence with polarity y is computed as

$$q(x^j, y) = \underbrace{y \cdot \vec{w}_{pol} \psi_{pol}(x^j)}_{polarity\ part} + \underbrace{\vec{w}_{subj} \psi_{subj}(x^j)}_{subjective\ part};$$

where $\psi_{pol}(x^j)$ and $\psi_{subj}(x^j)$ denote the polarity and subjectivity features of sentence x^j, $\vec{w}_{pol}$ and $\vec{w}_{subj}$ are learnt weights for polarity and subjectivity features, respectively. It can be seen that the polarity part captures the quality of sentence x^j with polarity y, and the subjective part captures the quality of x^j as a subjective sentence.

Suppose s is a set of sentences that best represents the key opinion of original review x. We define $\mathcal{F}$ parameterized by $\vec{w}_s$ as the function that jointly predicts the document polarity y^* and extracts sentence set s^*, we have

$$(y^*, s^*) = \underset{y \in \{+1, -1\}, s \in \mathcal{P}(x)}{\operatorname{argmax}} \mathcal{F}(x, (y, s); \vec{w}_s); \qquad (1)$$

where $\mathcal{P}(x)$ is the power set of all the sentences in x. Clearly, $\mathcal{F}$ has the form

$$\mathcal{F}(x,(y,s);\vec{w}_s) = \frac{1}{N(x)} \sum_{x^j \in s} q(x^j, y)$$

$$= \frac{1}{N(x)} \sum_{x^j \in s} y \cdot \vec{w}_{pol} \psi_{pol}(x^j) + \vec{w}_{subj} \psi_{subj}(x^j) \, ;$$

where $N(x)$ is a normalizing factor. As $\psi_{pol}(x^j)$ and $\psi_{subj}(x^j)$ are disjoint by construction, we have

$$\vec{w}_s = [\vec{w}_{pol}, \vec{w}_{subj}];$$

For simplicity, let $\Psi(x,(y,s))$ denote the joint feature map, $\mathcal{F}$ can be written as $\mathcal{F} = \vec{w}_s \Psi(x,(y,s))$. The training process is to optimize the following problem using latent variable structural SVMs [17]:

Optimization Problem 1:

$$\min_{\vec{w}, \xi \geq 0} \frac{1}{2} ||w||^2 + \frac{C}{N} \sum_{i=1}^{N} \xi_i$$

$$s.t. \forall i :$$

$$\max_{s_i \in \mathcal{P}(x)} \vec{w}_s \Psi(x_i, (y_i, s_i)) \geq \max_{s_i' \in \mathcal{P}(x)} \vec{w}_s \Psi(x_i, (-y_i, s_i'))$$

$$+ \Delta(y_i, -y_i, s_i') - \xi_i$$

where C is the regularization parameter, N is the number of training instances. Then we employ the model to jointly predict sentiment and extract a set of sentences that best represent the key polarity of original review using Equation 1.

3.3 Dual Decomposition

Dual decomposition is a general approach for combinatorial optimization, and has been successfully applied to many tasks in natural language processing [13]. For our task here, we expect that sentences in s modeled by multi-level sentiment analysis rank higher in informativeness ranking, i.e., suppose h is the top $|s|$ ranked sentences by the sentence ranking model, our goal is to make an alignment between h and s such that there are as many sentences in common as possible. The joint inference problem is

Joint Inference Problem 1:

$$\underset{(y,s),h}{\mathrm{argmax}} \mathcal{F}(x,(y,s);\vec{w}_s) + \sum_{x^i \in h} \mathcal{G}(x^i; \vec{w}_r)$$

$$s.t. \qquad f(s) = g(h)$$

where f and g are linear functions that map the output s and h to two vectors of length $|x|$, with 1 for the chosen sentences and 0 elsewhere. To solve the joint inference problem, we introduce a vector of Lagrange multipliers, $\vec{u} \in \mathbb{R}^{|x|}$ to obtain the Lagrangian

$$L((y,s),h,\vec{u}) = \mathcal{F}(x,(y,s);\vec{w}_s) + \sum_{x^i \in h} \mathcal{G}(x^i; \vec{w}_r)$$

$$+ \vec{u} \cdot (f(s) - g(h))$$

with the dual objective

$$L(\vec{u}) = \max_{(y,s),h} L((y,s),h,\vec{u}).$$

The optimization can be solved using subgradient algorithm. We initialize the Lagrange multipliers to $\vec{u}^{(0)} = \mathbf{0}$. For $k = 1, 2, \dots,$ and perform the following steps:

$$((y,s)^{(k)}, h^{(k)}) = \max_{(y,s),h} L((y,s),h,\vec{u}^{(k-1)}) \qquad (2)$$

followed by

$$\vec{u}^{(k)} = \vec{u}^{(k-1)} - \delta(f(s^{(k)}) - g(h^{(k)}));$$

where δ is the step size. It can be verified that Equation 2 can be solved easily using dual decomposition.

For each review x, we obtain a new ranking model $\mathcal{G}'$ with updated parameters that encoding sentiment information benefitted from dual decomposition. Then we apply the ranking function $\mathcal{G}'$ to rank all the sentences in x, which will naturally make the "sentiment explanations" rank higher.

4. EXPERIMENTS

4.1 Data Preparation

We use the data for explanatory sentence extraction[2][6], which is based on a collection of Amazon product reviews[3] used in[2] and [4]. Kim *et al.*[6] asked 4 labelers to make explanatoriness labels for each sentence with 0 for "no explanation", 1 for "weak explanation" and 2 for "strong explanation". Further, for sentences that are labeled as sentiment explanation, an additional label is introduced with 1 for "less than/equal to half of the text provides good explanation" and 2 for "most of the text provides good explanation". We employ the results of all the labelers, therefore, each sentence has a score ranging from 0 to 16.

Since the test input of our approach is a review, to make evaluations, we ensure that at least one sentence of the review for testing is labeled as sentiment explanation, filtering out those reviews with no sentence labeled as sentiment explanation. Our approach needs training data for the subproblem of multi-level sentiment analysis, we then sample training reviews published from 2004 to 2008 from Amazon product reviews used in [9][4]. For each product domain, we sample 2000 positive (rating greater than or equal to 4) and 2000 negative (rating less than or equal to 2) reviews for training, 500 positive and 500 negative reviews for development. Table 2 presents the statistics of evaluation data[5] where "#." means number of.

domain	camera	cellphone	mp3
#.testing reviews	88	71	137
#.sentiment explanations	87	203	377
#.testing sentences	1,067	814	2,775

Table 2: Data Statistics

4.2 Baselines

To make comparisons, we use the Normalized Discounted Cumulative Gain (nDCG) as the measure to calculate the score of each review, and we choose the following baselines:

- the expected performance of a random ranking, denoted by "*random*";
- SVM^{rank} with only aspect terms, denoted by "*rank(asp)*";
- SVM^{rank} with only sentiment lexicon, denoted by "*rank(op)*";

---

[2] http://sifaka.cs.uiuc.edu/~hkim277/expSum/
[3] http://www.cs.uic.edu/~liub/FBS/sentiment-analysis.html
[4] http://snap.stanford.edu/data/web-Amazon.html
[5] We only use the following product reviews: Canon G3, Nikon coolpix4300, Canon S100, Nokia 6600, Nokia 6600, Creative Labs Nomad Jukebox Zen Xtra 40GB and MicroMP3. For other products, either the reviews are in forms of sentences or the corresponding category can not be easily recognized by product names.

- SVM^{rank} with aspect terms and sentiment lexicon, denoted by "*rank(asp+op)*";
  - rule based approach consider aspect terms, sentiment lexicon and sentence length, denoted by "*rule(asp+op)*";

Our approach can be considered as joint inference with *rank(asp+op)* and multi-level sentiment analysis, and we then employ the ranking model with updated parameters of the last iteration in dual decomposition to rank the sentences for a given review.

4.3 Results

Table 3 presents the averaged nDCG score of all the reviews for each product domain. It can be seen that *rank(asp+op)* has a slightly better performance over purely rule based approach *rule (asp+op)*, and our approach achieves a relative high performance compared with baselines.

Domain	camera	cellphone	mp3
random	0.497	0.526	0.484
rank(asp)	0.558	0.662	0.561
rank(op)	0.585	0.609	0.594
rank(asp+op)	0.599	0.669	0.605
rule(asp+op)	0.599	0.644	0.600
Ours	**0.615**	**0.680**	**0.667**

Table 3: Comparison with baselines

5. CONCLUSION AND FUTURE WORK

In this paper, we address the problem of ranking sentiment explanations by formulating the process as two subproblems: sentence informativeness ranking and structural sentiment analysis. Tractable inference is performed through dual decomposition. Preliminary experiments on publicly available data-set demonstrate that our approach is effective and obtains promising performance. For future work, we plan to encode aspect information for fine granular opinion summarization using dual decomposition.

Acknowledgments

This work was partly supported by the following grants from: the National Basic Research Program (973 Program) under grant No. 2012CB316301 & 2013CB329403, the National Science Foundation of China project under grant No. 61332007 and No. 61272227, and the Beijing Higher Education Young Elite Teacher Project.

6. REFERENCES

[1] M. Bonzanini, M. Martinez-Alvarez, and T. Roelleke. Extractive summarisation via sentence removal: Condensing relevant sentences into a short summary. In *Proceedings of the 36th International ACM SIGIR Conference on Research and Development in Information Retrieval*, SIGIR '13, pages 893–896, 2013.

[2] X. Ding, B. Liu, and P. S. Yu. A holistic lexicon-based approach to opinion mining. In *Proceedings of the 2008 International Conference on Web Search and Data Mining*, WSDM '08, pages 231–240, 2008.

[3] A. Glaser and H. Schütze. Automatic generation of short informative sentiment summaries. In *Proceedings of the 13th Conference of the European Chapter of the Association for Computational Linguistics*, EACL '12, pages 276–285, 2012.

[4] M. Hu and B. Liu. Mining and summarizing customer reviews. In *Proceedings of the tenth ACM SIGKDD international conference on Knowledge discovery and data mining*, KDD '04, pages 168–177, 2004.

[5] T. Joachims. Optimizing search engines using clickthrough data. In *Proceedings of the Eighth ACM SIGKDD International Conference on Knowledge Discovery and Data Mining*, KDD '02, pages 133–142, 2002.

[6] H. D. Kim, M. G. Castellanos, M. Hsu, C. Zhai, U. Dayal, and R. Ghosh. Ranking explanatory sentences for opinion summarization. In *Proceedings of the 36th International ACM SIGIR Conference on Research and Development in Information Retrieval*, SIGIR '13, pages 1069–1072, 2013.

[7] T. Lappas, M. Crovella, and E. Terzi. Selecting a characteristic set of reviews. In *Proceedings of the 18th ACM SIGKDD International Conference on Knowledge Discovery and Data Mining*, KDD '12, pages 832–840, 2012.

[8] T.-Y. Liu. Learning to rank for information retrieval. *Foundations and Trends in Information Retrieval*, 3(3):225–331, 2009.

[9] J. McAuley and J. Leskovec. Hidden factors and hidden topics: Understanding rating dimensions with review text. In *Proceedings of the 7th ACM Conference on Recommender Systems*, RecSys '13, pages 165–172, 2013.

[10] X. Meng and H. Wang. Mining user reviews: From specification to summarization. In *Proceedings of the ACL-IJCNLP 2009 Conference Short Papers*, ACLShort '09, pages 177–180, 2009.

[11] B. Pang and L. Lee. A sentimental education: Sentiment analysis using subjectivity summarization based on minimum cuts. In *Proceedings of the 42Nd Annual Meeting on Association for Computational Linguistics*, ACL '04, 2004.

[12] B. Pang, L. Lee, and S. Vaithyanathan. Thumbs up? sentiment classification using machine learning techniques. In *Proceedings of Empirical methods in natural language processing*, EMNLP '02, pages 79–86, 2002.

[13] A. M. Rush and M. Collins. A tutorial on dual decomposition and lagrangian relaxation for inference in natural language processing. *J. Artif. Int. Res.*, 45(1):305–362, Sept. 2012.

[14] A. M. Rush, D. Sontag, M. Collins, and T. Jaakkola. On dual decomposition and linear programming relaxations for natural language processing. In *Proceedings of the 2010 Conference on Empirical Methods in Natural Language Processing*, EMNLP '10, pages 1–11, 2010.

[15] H. Wang, Y. Lu, and C. Zhai. Latent aspect rating analysis on review text data: a rating regression approach. In *Proceedings of the 16th ACM SIGKDD international conference on Knowledge discovery and data mining*, KDD '10, pages 783–792, 2010.

[16] A. Yessenalina, Y. Yue, and C. Cardie. Multi-level structured models for document-level sentiment classification. In *Proceedings of the 2010 Conference on Empirical Methods in Natural Language Processing*, EMNLP '10, pages 1046–1056, 2010.

[17] C.-N. J. Yu and T. Joachims. Learning structural svms with latent variables. In *Proceedings of the 26th Annual International Conference on Machine Learning*, ICML '09, pages 1169–1176, 2009.

[18] L. Zhuang, F. Jing, and X.-Y. Zhu. Movie review mining and summarization. In *Proceedings of the 15th ACM International Conference on Information and Knowledge Management*, CIKM '06, pages 43–50, 2006.

A Meta-reasoner to Rule Them All

Automated Selection of OWL Reasoners Based on Efficiency

Yong-Bin Kang
Faculty of Information
Technology
Monash University
Australia
yongbin.kang@monash.edu

Shonali Krishnaswamy
Institute for Infocomm
Research
Singapore
spkrishna@i2r.a-
star.edu.sg

Yuan-Fang Li
Faculty of Information
Technology
Monash University
Australia
yuanfang.li@monash.edu

ABSTRACT

It has been shown, both theoretically and empirically, that reasoning about large and expressive ontologies is computationally hard. Moreover, due to the different reasoning algorithms and optimisation techniques employed, each reasoner may be efficient for ontologies with different characteristics. Based on recently-developed prediction models for various reasoners for reasoning performance, we present our work in developing a meta-reasoner that automatically selects from a number of state-of-the-art OWL reasoners to achieve optimal efficiency. Our preliminary evaluation shows that the meta-reasoner significantly and consistently outperforms 6 state-of-the-art reasoners and it achieves a performance close to the hypothetical gold standard reasoner.

Categories and Subject Descriptors

I.2.4 [**Computing methodologies**]: Artificial Intelligence—
Knowledge representation and reasoning

Keywords

Meta-reasoner, OWL reasoner, Ontology, Prediction models, The Semantic Web

1. INTRODUCTION

Core reasoning services such as consistency checking and classification are at the heart of ontology-based applications. For ontologies in expressive logics, such reasoning services have a very high worst-case complexity [2, 8]. For instance, satisfiability checking for logic $\mathcal{SROIQ}$ has worst-case complexity of 2NExpTime-complete [2]. Recent works have also demonstrated empirically [3, 6, 9] that large and complex ontologies indeed pose a real computational challenge even for the state-of-the-art reasoners.

Ontology reasoners such as FaCT++, HermiT and Pellet implement different reasoning algorithms and employ different sets of preprocessing and optimisation techniques. As

a result, they are optimised for certain, but not all ontologies. For some ontologies, dramatic performance disparity among reasoners has been observed [6]. Moreover, for different versions of the same ontology, considerable performance differences for the same reasoner have also been observed [5]. Such disparity can cause significant and unnecessary loss in productivity for developers and users of ontologies.

The *robustness* of ontology reasoners was recently investigated [5], with a particular focus on reasoning efficiency. It was observed that given a corpus of ontologies and a number of state-of-the-art reasoners, it is highly likely that one of the reasoners performs sufficiently well on any given ontology in the corpus. However, no further research was conducted on how such a best reasoner can be selected automatically, given an ontology.

We recently studied the predictability of reasoning performance [9]. In this work, a *prediction model* is trained for a given reasoner to make predictions on (discretized) reasoning performance of a given ontology. High accuracy of over 80% is achieved for 4 state-of-the-art reasoners. The prediction model makes it possible to efficiently and accurately estimate a reasoner's performance on an ontology. However, it was not discussed how such prediction models can be used in a real-world scenario.

Inspired by portfolio-based algorithm selection work in SAT [12], the above works motivate and enable us to propose a *meta-reasoner* that is based on the prediction models. The meta-reasoner combines prediction models and their respective reasoners, and aims at determining the most efficient reasoner for a given ontology. It achieves this by (1) training *prediction models* for reasoning performance for all reasoners, and (2) by learning a *ranking model* that automatically and efficiently ranks the reasoners according to their predicted reasoning performance.

Our main contribution is the proposal of a novel meta-reasoner that automatically and efficiently combines and ranks reasoners with the aim to achieve optimal efficiency. We note that once the meta-reasoner is trained, which is an offline task that only needs to be carried out once, making both reasoning performance predictions and ranking predictions is straightforward and fast. Therefore, the meta-reasoner only imposes a small performance overhead. A preliminary evaluation shows that our meta-reasoner significantly and consistently outperforms 6 state-of-the-art reasoners and it achieves a performance close to the hypothetical gold standard reasoner.

2. BUILDING THE META-REASONER

The basic premise of the meta-reasoner lies in the automatic ranking of a number of reasoners and selection of one reasoner that is most likely to be the most efficient. The key components in building the meta-reasoner include the training of *prediction models* for individual reasoners and the training of *ranking models* (simply *rankers*) to generate rankings of the reasoners, based on their reasoning efficiency as predicted by those models. The learning of such rankers follows the same idea under the realm of *preference learning* [4] whose goal is to learn total orders (i.e. rankings) of all possible labels (i.e. prediction models) from a training example and predict an order to an unseen instance.

The ranking performance of the rankers is analyzed, and the best ranker that leads to the best ranking performance is selected. Then, given an unseen ontology, the selected ranker predicts the most efficient reasoner, which the meta-reasoner eventually invokes to perform reasoning on the ontology. In the following, we elaborate on the above steps to train our meta-reasoner.

Let $R = \{r_1, ..., r_n\}$ be a set of n reasoners, $O = \{o_1, ..., o_p\}$ be a set of p ontologies and $OM = \{om_1, ..., om_q\}$ be the set of q *ontology metrics*. Ontology metrics represent different aspects of an ontology's size and structural characteristics [9]. The ontology set O is divided into three disjoint subsets: O_p, O_r and O_t, for training of the prediction models, training of the ranking models and testing of the meta-reasoner, respectively.

2.1 Training Prediction Models of Reasoners

As the first phase, for each reasoner $r_{i[1,n]} \in R$, we train a prediction model M_i in the spirit of [9], with the aim to estimate the *discretized* reasoning time. We employ a discretization method similar to those used in [5, 9]: reasoning time is discretized into one of 4 bins of increasing difficulty: 0s < 'A' ≤ 0.1s, 0.1s < 'B' ≤ 10s, 10s < 'C' ≤ 100s, and 'D' > 100s, with a 20,000-second timeout.

For each reasoner, we only train a single prediction model based on *random forest* (RF), since it leads to overall best prediction models for all reasoners as suggested in [9]. Instead of using feature selection algorithms to select a subset of features to train the model [9], we use all the 27 metrics used in [9] as features, as we find the full metrics set leads to more accurate prediction models in the experiments of this work.

The performance of each prediction model M_i for reasoner r_i is measured, based on 10-fold cross validation [7], using the micro-averaged F-measure [10] as the performance measure, since it takes the sizes of the bins into account.

The prediction models are trained using the entire dataset Q_p. They are used to estimate the reasoning time of reasoners for a given ontology. Such predictions will be used in generating a ranking matrix to train the rankers.

2.2 Generating a Ranking Matrix

As the second phase, for the purpose of training the ranking models, we generate a *ranking matrix* that is the key matrix for building a meta-reasoner. Let $O_r \subset O = \{o'_1, ..., o'_m\}$ be the set of m ontologies. Initially, we build an $m \times (q + n)$ data matrix $\mathbf{M}_d$ (recall that $m = |O_r|$, $q = |OM|$, $n = |R|$),

where row i represents $o'_i \in O_r$ and is constructed as:

$$\underbrace{(om_{i,1}, \ldots, om_{i,q})}_{\text{ontology metrics}}, \underbrace{(c_{i,1}, \ldots, c_{i,n})}_{\text{predicted labels}} \quad (1)$$

where $om_{i,j}$ is the value of the jth ontology metric value of ontology o'_i, and $c_{i,k}$ denotes a discretized label (i.e. 'A', 'B', 'C' or 'D') predicted by the prediction model M_k of the reasoner r_k.

Based on $\mathbf{M}_d$, we build the corresponding $m \times (q + n)$ ranking matrix $\mathbf{M}_r$, where row i is represented as:

$$\underbrace{(om_{i,1}, \ldots, om_{i,q})}_{\text{ontology metrics}}, \underbrace{(\pi(c_{i,1}), \ldots, \pi(c_{i,n}))}_{\text{ranking of predicted labels}} \quad (2)$$

where $\pi(c_{i,k})$ denotes the *rank* of the reasoner r_k on ontology o_i, ranked by the discretized reasoning time $c_{i,k}$ (i.e., the bin labels) predicted by the prediction model M_k. The ranking principle is that the more efficient a predicted time is the higher its rank is (lower number). For example, suppose the predicted bin labels are 'C', 'B', 'A' for 3 reasoners r_1, r_2 and r_3 on an ontology o_j, i.e., $(c_{j,1}, c_{j,2}, c_{j,3}) = $ ('C', 'B', 'A'), then the ranking of the reasoners is $(\pi(c_{j,1}), \pi(c_{j,2}), \pi(c_{j,3})) = (3, 2, 1)$, as 'A' is faster than 'B', which is faster than 'C'. If such labels are ('A', 'A', 'B') instead, the ranking is $(1, 1, 2)$.

2.3 Building the Meta-reasoner

As the last phase, the meta-reasoner is built using the following 3 steps. The key idea is to train a number of rankers aiming to produce a ranked list of reasoners for unseen ontologies in a way similar to rankings in $\mathbf{M}_r$. We train a number of rankers to learn how all instances, represented as vectors of ontology metrics in $\mathbf{M}_r$, are associated with the reasoners in R ranked by their predicted reasoning performance. We then select the best one in terms of 'precision at 1' (P@1) to rank the reasoners for an unknown ontology instance.

1. **Ranker training:** A number of rankers are trained on $\mathbf{M}_r$. Their goal is to learn the rankings of reasoners in the ranking matrix.

2. **Best ranker selection:** We then select the best ranker Ω from the trained rankers. We employ 10-fold cross validation to assess the ranking performance of the rankers using $\mathbf{M}_r$ in terms of P@1. We use P@1 as we are only interested in finding the ranker whose estimation of the *highest ranked* reasoner is the closest to the most efficient reasoner (i.e. prediction model).

3. **Reasoner Invocation:** Given an unseen ontology, the meta-reasoner first uses Ω to determine the prediction model whose corresponding reasoner is most likely to be the most efficient for the ontology. If more than 2 prediction models are ranked the highest by Ω, we use a *default ranking* of those reasoners to break the tie. The default ranking takes into consideration the *prediction confidence* (in terms of F-measure) of the prediction models and a measure of the *average reasoning performance* of the prediction models. Tie-breaking that finds the best possible prediction model M_{best} is achieved from the following formula:

$$M_{best} = \arg \min_{M_i \in \mathcal{M}'} tb(M_i), \quad (3)$$

where $\mathcal{M}'$ denotes the set of the prediction models ranked the highest, and we choose M_i that minimizes $tb(M_i)$ for all models in $\mathcal{M}'$. The function $tb(M_i)$ is defined as:

$$tb(M_i) = (1 - fm(M_i)) * ar(M_i), \qquad (4)$$

where $fm(M_i)$ is the F-measure score of M_i (the higher the better) and $ar(M_i)$ is the average ranking of M_i (the lower the better). Note that the above formula is only calculated once and can be calculated efficiently offline. Finally, the meta-reasoner determines the best prediction model M_k using Eq. 3, and then invokes $r_k \in R$ to perform reasoning for the unseen ontology.

3. EVALUATION

For this work, we used 798 real-world ontologies collected from the Tones Ontology Repository and the BioOntology repository.[1] To build our meta-reasoner, 6 state-of-the art OWL 2 DL reasoners are included: FaCT++ (version 1.5.3),[2] HermiT (version 1.3.6),[3] JFact (version 0.9),[4] MORe (version 0.1.6, with HermiT as the underlying OWL 2 DL reasoner),[5] Pellet (version 2.2.0),[6] and TrOWL (version 1.4).[7]

We first measured the reasoning time (consistency checking and classification) of each reasoner for the 798 ontologies on a high-performance server running OS Linux 2.6.18 and Java 1.6 on an Intel Xeon X7560 CPU at 2.27GHz, with a maximum of 32GB memory allocated to the reasoner.

Of the 798 ontologies, 535 ontologies were successfully reasoned by all the 6 reasoners, while the others encountered processing problems by at least one reasoner. These 535 ontologies constitute our dataset O. In O, 90% of the 535 ontologies (482) were randomly chosen to build our prediction models and meta-reasoner, where 60% (290 ontologies) are randomly chosen as O_p for building the 6 prediction models of the 6 reasoners, and 40% (192 ontologies) as O_r for generating the ranking matrix to build the rankers. The remaining 10%, O_t, were used to assess the effectiveness of the meta-reasoner. We repeated this experiment procedure 3 times to alleviate the effect of randomness.

For each of the 3 experiments, we built the 6 prediction models, $\mathcal{M} = \{M_{\text{FaCT++}}, M_{\text{HermiT}}, M_{\text{JFact}}, M_{\text{MORe}}, M_{\text{Pellet}}, M_{\text{TrOWL}}\}$, on O_p using the RF classifier with the 27 ontology metrics (i.e. features) used in [9]. Table 1 shows the effectiveness of $\mathcal{M}$ in terms of the micro-average F-measure (simply F-measure) scores obtained from 10-fold cross validation using O_p in all the 3 experiments. As observed, although there are slight differences in the F-measure scores between prediction models, all the models are shown to be highly effective, achieving over 80% F-measure.

Using the predicted reasoning time of the ontologies in O_r obtained from prediction models in $\mathcal{M}$, we trained 6 rankers [11]: kNN (based on a k-NN algorithm), BinaryPCT (based on predictive clustering trees), PairwiseComparison (based on binary pairwise classification models), BinaryART

[1] http://owl.cs.manchester.ac.uk/repository/, http://www.bioontology.org/.

[2] https://code.google.com/p/factplusplus

[3] http://hermit-reasoner.com

[4] http://jfact.sourceforge.net

[5] http://www.cs.ox.ac.uk/isg/tools/MORe

[6] http://clarkparsia.com/pellet

[7] http://trowl.eu

Table 1: F-measure scores of the prediction models.

Prediction Model	Experiment		
	1	2	3
$M_{\text{FaCT++}}$	0.89	0.88	0.88
M_{HermiT}	0.88	0.88	0.86
M_{JFact}	0.78	0.81	0.82
M_{MORe}	0.87	0.86	0.87
M_{Pellet}	0.84	0.84	0.86
M_{TrOWL}	0.92	0.91	0.88

(approximate ranking trees), ARTForests (approximate ranking tree forests), and Regression (multiple single-target regression).

The performance of each ranker evaluated using 10-fold cross validation in terms of P@1 is presented in Table 2. As can be seen, in most cases, all rankers show high performance, achieving P@1 of around 0.9. For each experiment, the highest P@1 value is highlighted in bold. As can be observed, in all the 3 experiments, 'BinaryART' is the best ranker with P@1 value over 0.95.

Table 2: The P@1 values of the 6 rankers in training.

Ranker	Experiment		
	1	2	3
kNN	0.964	0.865	0.843
BinaryPCT	0.969	0.989	0.964
PairwiseComparison	0.807	0.942	0.918
BinaryART	**0.974**	**0.990**	**0.963**
ARTForests	0.948	0.906	0.932
Regression	0.917	0.839	0.750

We now examine the evaluation result of our meta-reasoner, incorporating BinaryART as the best ranker, on O_t. Table 3 shows a performance comparison between our meta-reasoner and the 6 reasoners in terms of P@1. In each of the 3 experiments, for the meta-reasoner, its P@1 value is calculated with BinaryART as the ranker and tie-breaking using Eq. 3. For each of the other 6 reasoners, its P@1 value is calculated by its proportion of *actually* being the most efficient reasoner among the 6 reasoners over all ontologies in O_t. As can be seen, our meta-reasoner highly outperforms all the 6 reasoners across the 3 experiments.

Table 3: The P@1 values of the meta-reasoner and the 6 reasoners in testing.

Reasoner	Experiment		
	1	2	3
Meta-reasoner	**0.943**	**0.943**	**0.906**
FaCT++	0.925	0.924	0.887
HermiT	0.679	0.679	0.792
JFact	0.792	0.792	0.754
MORe	0.887	0.849	0.887
Pellet	0.773	0.736	0.717
TrOWL	0.811	0.792	0.830

Note that P@1 alone does not distinguish wrong highest ranked reasoners with different actual reasoning performance. For example, for a given ontology o, assume the most efficient reasoner r_{best} has reasoning performance 'A'. Suppose that the meta-reasoner selects a less efficient reasoner r_1 with actual reasoning performance 'B'. P@1 score does not distinguish r_1 with another wrong selection, say, r_2, with actual performance 'D'. However, clearly, r_2 is much more inefficient than r_1 for o. Therefore, we further evaluate the performance of the meta-reasoner and the other reasoners, taking into consideration their discretized reasoning time. As explained in Section 2.1, the reasoning time was discretized in a way that the *width* of the bins increase with their difficulty. Table 4 summarizes the reasoning time difference between bins, calculated using the difference between upper-bound of the time intervals of pairs of bins.

Table 4: Approximated time difference (in sec) between discretized reasoning time labels (bins).

		Most efficient reasoning time			
		A	B	C	D
Actual reasoning time	A	0	-	-	-
	B	10-0.1	0	-	-
	C	100-0.1	100-10	0	-
	D	20,000-0.1	20,000-10	20,000-100	0

Finally, Table 5 presents the *average reasoning performance difference* (μ_{rpd}, in seconds), on the basis of Table 4, between each reasoner and the gold standard r_{best}, the most efficient possible reasoner of the 6 reasoners. Hence, the smaller the value of μ_{rpd}, the more efficient the reasoner is. The smallest μ_{rpd} value of all reasoners in each experiment is highlighted in bold. As can be observed from Table 5, the meta-reasoner substantially outperforms all the other 6 reasoners in all the 3 experiments with performance improvement of up to 3 orders of magnitude. The meta-reasoner is also *near-optimal*, with a small subsecond average reasoning performance difference (μ_{rpd}) from the gold standard. Evaluation on P@1 and average reasoning performance difference shows that the meta-reasoner exhibits significant and consistent performance improvement over all of the 6 state-of-the-art reasoners.

Table 5: Average reasoning performance difference (μ_{rpd}, in seconds) on the testing ontologies.

Reasoner	Experiment		
	1	2	3
Meta-reasoner	**0.17**	**0.55**	**0.92**
FaCT++	2.25	5.26	381.11
HermiT	9.40	6.19	2.06
JFact	758.85	1,136.02	1,136.02
MORe	4.13	3.00	19.67
Pellet	8.28	7.13	1,136.77
TrOWL	378.66	2.04	1.68

4. CONCLUSIONS

In this paper, we present a novel meta-reasoning approach that combines reasoners in an efficient way, by automatically selecting the reasoner that is most probably the most efficient for any given ontology. A key feature of our approach

is the use of the state-of-the art prediction models of the 6 reasoners with ontology metrics for estimating reasoning time [9]. Another important feature is the training of a number of rankers to determine the best ranker, which is incorporated into our meta-reasoner. To train rankers, we make use of the prediction models to efficiently estimate reasoning time, instead of real reasoning time, which may be prohibitively expensive for hard/large ontologies.

Preliminary evaluation suggests the practicability of our meta-reasoner. We show that the meta-reasoner achieves significant efficiency improvements over 6 state-of-the-art reasoners. The meta-reasoner is also shown to be near-optimal, with only a subsecond performance difference from the gold standard (the best possible reasoner for a given ontology).

5. REFERENCES

[1] P. Cudré-Mauroux, et al, editors. *The Semantic Web - ISWC 2012 - 11th International Semantic Web Conference, Boston, MA, USA, November 11-15, 2012, Proceedings, Part I*, volume 7649 of *Lecture Notes in Computer Science*. Springer, 2012.

[2] B. Cuenca Grau, I. Horrocks, B. Motik, B. Parsia, P. Patel-Schneider, and U. Sattler. OWL 2: The next step for OWL. *Journal of Web Semantics*, 6:309–322, November 2008.

[3] K. Dentler, R. Cornet, A. ten Teije, and N. de Keizer. Comparison of reasoners for large ontologies in the OWL 2 EL profile. *Semantic Web Journal*, 2(2):71–87, 2011.

[4] J. Frnkranz and E. Hllermeier. *Preference Learning*. Springer-Verlag New York, Inc., New York, NY, USA, 1st edition, 2010.

[5] R. S. Gonçalves, N. Matentzoglu, B. Parsia, and U. Sattler. The empirical robustness of description logic classification. In T. Eiter, B. Glimm, Y. Kazakov, and M. Krötzsch, editors, *Description Logics*, volume 1014 of *CEUR Workshop Proceedings*, pages 197–208. CEUR-WS.org, 2013.

[6] R. S. Gonçalves, B. Parsia, and U. Sattler. Performance heterogeneity and approximate reasoning in description logic ontologies. In Cudré-Mauroux et al. [1], pages 82–98.

[7] T. Hastie, R. Tibshirani, and J. Friedman. *The elements of statistical learning: data mining, inference and prediction*. Springer, 2 edition, 2009.

[8] I. Horrocks, P. F. Patel-Schneider, and F. van Harmelen. From $\mathcal{SHIQ}$ and RDF to OWL: The Making of a Web Ontology Language. *Journal of Web Semantics*, 1(1):7–26, 2003.

[9] Y.-B. Kang, Y.-F. Li, and S. Krishnaswamy. Predicting reasoning performance using ontology metrics. In Cudré-Mauroux et al. [1], pages 198–214.

[10] F. Sebastiani. Machine learning in automated text categorization. *ACM Comput. Surv.*, 34(1):1–47, Mar. 2002.

[11] Q. Sun and B. Pfahringer. Pairwise meta-rules for better meta-learning-based algorithm ranking. *Machine Learning*, 93(1):141–161, 2013.

[12] L. Xu, F. Hutter, H. H. Hoos, and K. Leyton-Brown. Satzilla: Portfolio-based algorithm selection for SAT. *J. Artif. Int. Res.*, 32(1):565–606, June 2008.

Semantic Topology

Jussi Karlgren
Gabriel Isheden

Martin Bohman
Emelie Kullmann

Ariel Ekgren
David Nilsson

Gavagai
Stockholm, Sweden

KTH, Royal Institute of
Technology
Stockholm, Sweden

1. REQUIREMENTS FOR A PRACTICAL MODEL OF MEANING

A reasonable requirement (among many others) for a lexical or semantic component in an information system is that it should be able to learn incrementally from the linguistic data it is exposed to, that it can distinguish between the topical impact of various terms, and that it knows if it knows stuff or not.

We work with a specific representation framework – *semantic spaces* – which well accommodates the first requirement; we study the global qualities of semantic spaces by a topological procedure – *mapper* – which gives an indication of topical density of the space; we examine the local context of terms of interest in the semantic space using another topologically inspired approach which gives an indication of the neighbourhood of the terms of interest. Our aim is to be able to establish the qualities of the semantic space under consideration without resorting to inspection of the data used to build it.

2. DISTRIBUTIONAL MODELS

Distributional models, such as collocational analyses or probabilistic language models, are based on the analysis of observed item distribution and collocation in linguistic data and have a long history in linguistics. [3] Today, they provide a theoretical base and profitable results for tasks such as speech recognition, language modelling and information retrieval.

In general, distributional semantic models use the notion of *distance* between two words to describe relation in meaning. This combination of distributional data with a geometric interpretation is what defines *semantic spaces*. [15, 14] The geometric model is appealing: the notion of *closeness in meaning* speaks to our intuitions about how semantics work. This, however, would seem to be a somewhat false friend. Our geometric intuitions do not hold water for several thousand-dimensional spaces. Also, the metaphor of closeness does not deliver useful help if more complex se-

mantic relations are considered or larger distances in the space are queried: "What is the relation between *bell pepper* and *one-pass compiler*"?; "Is *cow* closer to *horse* than *coffee* is to *tea*"?; "Is a *bullfinch* closer to *bird* than LATEX is to *language*"? Arguably those questions are meaningless for human semantics, but are handily and uselessly answered with great exactitude by geometric semantic spaces. [7]

3. GEOMETRY AND TOPOLOGY

The insight that geometric models are overly specific and unwieldy, especially if built on realistic scale, is the motivation for e.g. dimensionality reduction approaches, various latent variable models [2, 12], graph-based models [11], and e.g. Laplacian transforms such as in self-taught hashing [18, 17, 5]. We propose here to use generalise some of those insights, and move from a semantic geometry to a semantic topology.

Semantic space models have no natural scale and no given base vectors. Topological models are resilient with respect to scale, rotational transformations, deformations, and coordinate choice, and can be constructed to focus on local structure and similarity in near relations. [1] A topological perspective of the data affords us an effective view of the structure of models, and is useful for the diagnosis and practical quality assessment of models which already have proven to be of value in real-world applications.

The basis for our experimentation are semantic spaces created using *random indexing*, [12] trained on various corpora of relevance for information processing tasks which require lexical semantics, e.g. ontology mapping, media monitoring, or topic tracking. We currently use such semantic spaces in practical large-scale industrial applications to find synonyms or near-synonyms of terms of interest, and to track associative concepts over time, as an up-to-date lexical resource. We frequently find we need to examine the models we have trained to ascertain their qualities with respect to some topic of interest. In these following experiments we will use models which are trained on traditional research corpora using the same procedure we would use on internet data for commercial purposes.

4. THE MAPPER PROCEDURE

Mapper, first introduced by Singh, Mémoli, and Carlsson [16], is an algorithm based on topological principles to visualize high dimensional data. The intuition behind Mapper is to analyze the structure of the data as a whole instead of analyzing the entire dataset in detail. Mapper is intended to capture such regularities of massive data sets which are obscured by focus on geometric coordinates, by transforming the data set to a *simplicial complex*, a combinatorial and discrete data structure. If the steps of this transformation is done well, the resulting structure can be inspected to understand the characteristics of the data set.

Given a dataset $D = d_i : d_i \in X$, the Mapper procedure can be given in 4 steps:

Filtering We analyze the data using a *filter function* $f : X \to \mathbb{R}$ which creates an image of the datapoints in $\mathbb{R}$. The filter function should capture some interesting or relevant aspect of the data. In this case, in an analysis of a semantic space, we can set f to be the distance in that space of each point from a target notion of interest.

Cover Given our dataset D, we structure it by applying a *covering* to its image $f(D)$ by a set C of subsets of $\mathbb{R}$: where $C = c_i : c_i \subset \mathbb{R}$. This covering can be given by an expert or through other means. In our case we use overlapping intervals of the filter function itself, essentially grouping data into overlapping bins of a histogram. The datapoints in each bin are given by the datapoints with their image in the specified interval of $\mathbb{R}$.

Clustering The points in each bin, meaning each subset of C (the elements in C are themselves subsets of $\mathbb{R}$) are then clustered individually. The clustering algorithm can be chosen to be whatever clustering algorithm is required. We use single-linkage clustering.

Graph A graph G is created with every individual cluster from the clustering of the points in the subsets of C as a node of G. When two clusters share a common datapoint in D, an edge is drawn between the two nodes that represent them.

We illustrate the procedure first using artificially generated point cloud data, as shown in Figure 1. The data consists of 5000 points randomly generated from a Gaussian distribution surrounding three centroids at $[x, y]$ coordinates: $[10, 20]$, $[-10, -10]$, $[17, -10]$ with a standard deviation of 9. The filter function f was chosen to be Gaussian kernel density estimation. The coloring of the points in the graph follow the density estimation. The covering was set to 7 intervals with an overlap of 10 percent. After Mapper processing those same data can be visualized as shown in Figure 2 using a similar colouring scheme. Here, the graph shows that if the points at high density are clustered, there are three clusters; the points at low density cluster into one. Overlapping density ranges show the expected correspondences from high to low.

This procedure, in our application of it to semantic spaces, serves to illuminate shared structure across different distance scales of the semantic space by showing if the cluster structure in one distance range correspond or differ from another distance range.

5. GLOBAL TOPOLOGICAL CHARACTER

One of the specific questions we wish to investigate is that of *expertise*. Given two semantic spaces, what is the extent of training in some topical domain? We will assume that expertise, in the sense of being trained on a set of texts, should

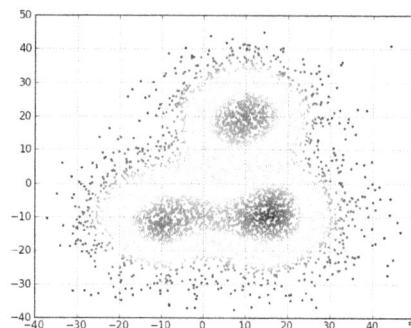

Figure 1: Artificially generated geometric data

Figure 2: Geometric data transformed by Mapper

have effects on the topological makeup of the semantic space. We trained two semantic spaces on general English-language text[1] and then added some selected topics to each of the spaces. One semantic space was trained by including entire Wikipedia articles related to the topics; another semantic space was only given the introductory paragraphs of those same articles. Thus both semantic spaces are familiar with the foundational vocabulary of the topics, but one of them would have a passing knowledge while the other would have a more in-depth understanding of the topic.

If we now apply a filter function to the points of the semantic space based on relation to T, the target concept of interest, our expectation would be that in the one semantic space, terms for probe concepts t_i known to be related to T should cluster relatively close to T; in the other they would be more or less randomly distributed over the scale intervals. This is borne out in experiments. Figure 3 shows the difference, as measured by a filter function defined by ten probe words relative to the target topic "Finland". The graph shows how the probe words cluster both better with respect to each other, and closer to the target.

6. LOCAL TOPOLOGICAL STRUCTURE

The second question we wish to address is that of differential qualities of terms we have observed. Some words are more topical than others, which has been observed in numerous different research traditions, but most notably in practically oriented text analysis. [9, 10, 6, 4, 13] We wish to examine

---

[1]Settings: 2000 random indexing dimensions, $2 + 2$ context, trained on the The British National Corpus. (Distributed by Oxford University Computing Services at url http://www.natcorp.ox.ac.uk/).

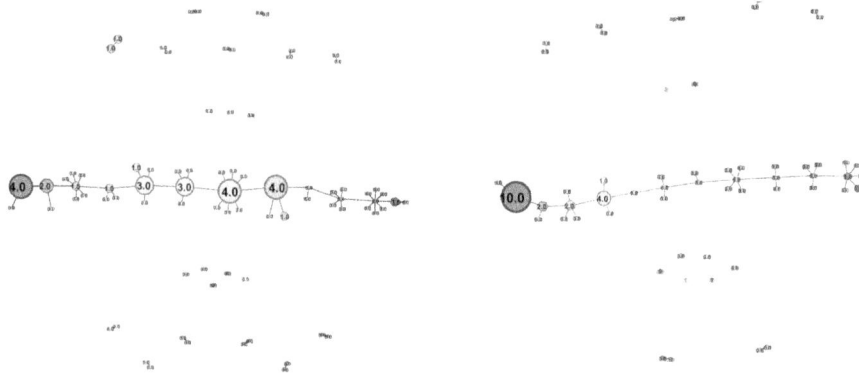

Figure 3: Data for passing knowledge vs expertise for "Finland"

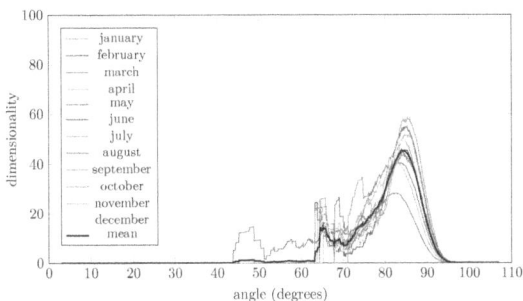

Figure 4: Local dimensionality at various angular separation for names of months

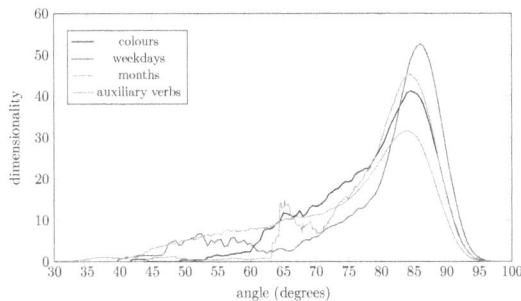

Figure 5: Local dimensionality at various angular separation for names of months, weekdays, colours and auxiliary verbs

the local structure of the semantic space around a term of interest.

We recently experimented using a topologically related approach to establish the density of a neighbourhood for terms in a semantic space and to thus infer the *intrinsic dimensionality* of the local space around the term. While we expand the radius around the spatial coordinates of a term of interest we record the rate of increase in number of neighbours within that radius. We begin by establishing how rapidly the number of neighbours of a term grows in relation to the growth of the radius of the neighbourhood. We define the rate of growth in the interval $r \in I = [r_1, r_2]$ to be

$$d = \frac{log(n_2/n_1)}{log(r_2/r_1)}, \qquad (1)$$

with n_i being the number of observed term neighbours within the radius r_i. We use d as an estimate of the local dimensionality around the probe term in r. Averaging the results of those computations over an entire semantic space we find that the local dimensionality was considerably lower than that of the representation itself. [8]

Here, we follow a similar approach, but instead study the particularities of individual terms, or specific categories of term.[2] In Figures 4, 5, 6, 7, we plot d at various radius

ranges on the surface of a unit hypersphere, with the radius here graphed as the angle of separation between the probe term vector and the neighbouring vectors.

As a first illustration, Figure 4 shows the rate of neighbourhood growth curves for names of months, with the angle as computed from the origin on the x-axis. Note that *May* behaves differently from the other months, due to the polysemy of the word. Figure 5 shows a comparison of results between names of months, weekdays, colours, and auxiliary verbs. The latter have a much more flattened distribution; the former three all have higher neighbourhood density at lower angular distances, and then the majority of neighbours at around ninety degrees, i.e. at maximum distance from the term, indicating no semantic relation. This is to be expected since months, weekdays, and colours all have fairly well delimited semantics and thus contexts of use, whereas auxiliaries can be expected to cooccur with numerous subjects and verbs and thus have a much more promiscuous context. This comparison would lead us to expect that content-heavy words are likely to have neighbours accrue earlier, at smaller angular distances.

A comparison between the figures in Figures 6 and 7 confirms this. One shows the neighbourhood growth curves for the 150 most frequent words found in the corpus: *the, be, to, of, and, ...*. The other shows the same curves for some 300 terms which are found in Wikipedia: topic headers *england,*

[2]Settings: 1000 random indexing dimensions, $2 + 2$ context, trained on the TASA corpus.

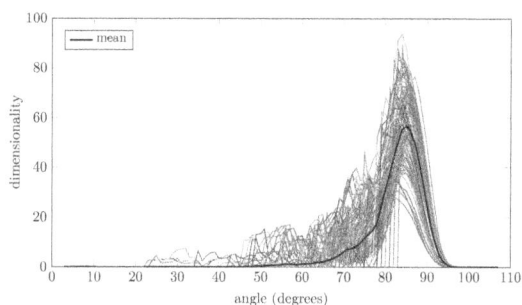

Figure 6: Local dimensionality at various angular separation for the most frequent words in the corpus

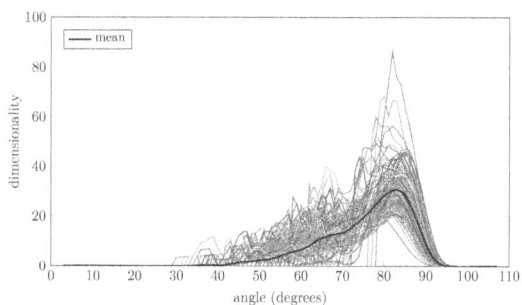

Figure 7: Local dimensionality at various angular separation for the most frequent words in the corpus

mississippi, instagram, socrates ... . The form of the curves are clearly different even at a cursory inspection.

To verify this observation, we performed several simple categorisation experiments, based on minimising square error to the dimensionality graprh, to distinguish parts of speech and term lists of various classes of word. Table 1 shows the result of categorising the classes given in Figure 5. Similarly useful results were found between other categories of term such as various semantic categories of verbs.

7. CONCLUSIONS

Semantic spaces, a useful learning framework for lexical resources, are typically treated as black boxes and applied using geometric and linear algebraic processing tools. We have found that topological methods are useful for exploring the makeup of a semantic space.

8. REFERENCES

[1] Gunnar Carlsson. Topology and data. *American Mathematical Society*, 46, 2009.

Inferred class → Actual class ↓	Colour	Month	Auxiliary verb	Weekday
Colour	56%	33%	11%	0%
Month	17%	67%	8%	8%
Auxiliary verbs	3%	13%	84%	0%
Weekday	0%	0%	0%	100%

Table 1: Confusion matrix for categorisation

[2] Scott Deerwester, Susan T. Dumais, George W. Furnas, Thomas K. Landauer, and Richard Harshman. Indexing by latent semantic analysis. *Journal of the American Society of Information Science*, 41(6), 1990.

[3] Zellig Harris. *Mathematical Structures of Language*. Interscience publishers, 1968.

[4] Stephen Harter. A probabilistic approach to automated keyword indexing. *Journal of the American Society for Information Science*, 26, 1975.

[5] Xiaofei He, Deng Cai, Haifeng Liu, , and Wei-Ying Ma. Locality preserving indexing for document representation. In *Proceedings of the 27th Annual International ACM SIGIR Conference on Research and Development in Information Retrieval*, 2004.

[6] Aurélie Herbelot and Mohan Ganesalingam. Measuring semantic content in distributional vectors. In *Proceedings of the 51st Annual Meeting of the Association for Computational Linguistics*, Sofia, Bulgaria, 2013.

[7] Jussi Karlgren. Meaningful models for information access systems. In Arppe, Carlson, Heinämäki, Lindén, Miestamo, Piitulainen, Tupakka, Westerlund, and Yli-Jyrä, editors, *A Finnish Computer Linguist: Kimmo Koskenniemi Festschrift on the 60th birthday*. CSLI Publications, 2005.

[8] Jussi Karlgren, Anders Holst, and Magnus Sahlgren. Filaments of meaning in word space. In *Proceedings of the 30th European Conference on Information Retrieval*, 2008.

[9] Slava Katz. Distribution of content words and phrases in text and language modelling. *Natural Language Engineering*, 2(1), 1996.

[10] Lillian Lee. Measures of distributional similarity. In *Proceedings of the 37th Annual Meeting of the Association for Computational Linguistics*, 1999.

[11] Irina Matveeva, Gael Dìaz, and Ahmed Hassan, editors. *TextGraphs-7 '12: Workshop Proceedings of TextGraphs-7 on Graph-based Methods for Natural Language Processing*, Stroudsburg, PA, USA, 2012. Association for Computational Linguistics.

[12] Gabriel Recchia, Michael Jones, Magnus Sahlgren, and Pentti Kanerva. Encoding sequential information in vector space models of semantics: Comparing holographic reduced representation and random permutation. In *Proceedings of the 32nd Annual Conference of the Cognitive Science Society*, 2010.

[13] Stephen Robertson, Cornelis J. van Rijsbergen, and Michael Porter. Probabilistic models of indexing and searching. In *Proceedings of the 3d Annual International ACM SIGIR Conference on Research and Development in Information Retrieval*, 1980.

[14] Magnus Sahlgren. *The Word-Space Model: Using distributional analysis to represent syntagmatic and paradigmatic relations between words in high-dimensional vector spaces*. PhD Dissertation, Department of Linguistics, Stockholm University, 2006.

[15] Hinrich Schütze. Word space. In *Advances in Neural Information Processing Systems 5*, San Francisco, CA, USA, 1993. Morgan Kaufmann.

[16] Gurjeet Singh, Facundo Mémoli, and Gunnar Carlsson. Topological methods for the analysis of high dimensional data sets and 3d object recognition. In M. Botsch and R. Pajarola, editors, *Eurographics Symposium on Point-Based Graphics*. The Eurographics Association, 2007.

[17] D. Zhang, J. Wang, D. Cai, and J. Lu. Laplacian co-hashing of terms and documents. In *Proceedings of the 32nd European Conference on Information Retrieval*, 2010.

[18] Dell Zhang, Jun Wang, Deng Cai, and Jinsong Lu. Self-taught hashing for fast similarity search. In *Proceedings of the 33rd international ACM SIGIR conference on Research and development in information retrieval*, 2010.

CONR: A Novel Method for Sentiment Word Identification

Jiguang Liang[1], Xiaofei Zhou[1], Yue Hu[1], Li Guo[1]*, Shuo Bai[1,2]

[1]National Engineering Laboratory for Information Security Technologies
Institute of Information Engineering, Chinese Academy of Sciences
Beijing 100190, China
[2]Shanghai Stock Exchange, Shanghai 200120, China
{liangjiguang, zhouxiaofei, huyue, guoli, baishuo}@iie.ac.cn

ABSTRACT

Sentiment word identification (SWI) is of high relevance to sentiment analysis technologies and applications. Currently most SWI methods heavily rely on sentiment seed words that have limited sentiment information. Even though there emerge non-seed approaches based on sentiment labels of documents, but in which the context information has not been fully considered. In this paper, based on matrix factorization with co-occurrence neighbor regularization which is derived from context, we propose a novel non-seed model called CONR for SWI. Instead of seed words, CONR exploits two important factors: sentiment matching and sentiment consistency for sentiment word identification. Experimental results on four publicly available datasets show that CONR can outperform the state of-the-art methods.

Categories and Subject Descriptors

I.2 [**Natural Language Processing**]: Text analysis

General Terms

Theory

Keywords

sentiment word identification; sentiment lexicon; sentiment analysis; matrix factorization

1. INTRODUCTION

In recent years, sentiment analysis has become a hot issue and has been used across a wide range of domains. The task is to predict the sentiment polarities (also known as semantic orientations) of opinions by analyzing sentiment words and expressions in sentences and documents [1]. Sentiment words are words that express a positive or negative sentiment polarity. Therefore, sentiment word identification (SWI) is a critical and necessary initial procedure with respect to the majority of tasks of sentiment analysis such as

subjectivity detection, appraisal expression recognition and sentiment polarity classification. So we focus on SWI in this paper.

The main existing approaches infer the polarities of sentiment words from the labels of seed words. The semantic orientation of a given word is calculated from the strength of its association with a set of positive words, minus the strength of its association with a set of negative words [1, 2, 3]. But the outstanding problem among these models is that they rely heavily on seed words with sentiment labels which are usually manually selected. These models are very sensitive to seed words. Any missing key word could lead to poor performance. In fact, subjective documents often provide additional information other than content information [4, 7, 8] as shown in Figure 1(a). Specifically, the polarities of subjective documents and their most component sentiment words are the same. This phenomenon is called sentiment matching which is represented via a document-word contribution matrix as shown in Figure 1(b). Motivated by this observation, Yu et al. first propose an optimization-based method for SWI [4]. It utilizes the sentiment labels of documents instead of seed words, but it ignores the semantic association in context.

Intuitively, two frequently co-occur sentiment words are more likely to have similar sentiment than those of two randomly selected words. In principle, a positive sentiment word occurs more frequently alongside positive words in positive documents, whereas negative sentiment words will occur most often in the vicinity of negative words in negative documents. We call the above semantic association phenomenons as sentiment consistency. Inspired by this observation, we explore the utilization of sentiment consistency information to facilitate SWI. In Figure 1(c), these information can be represented via a word-word influence matrix. Traditional methods do not utilize it.

In this paper, we propose a matrix factorization framework called CONR without seed words for SWI. In particular, we first construct the document-word contribution matrix and word-word influence matrix. Then we discuss how these relations could be modeled and utilized for SWI. Finally, we conduct extensive experiments on four publicly available datasets to verify the proposed model.

To the best of our knowledge, this paper is the first work that identifies sentiment words using matrix factorization without seed words.

2. PROBLEM STATEMENT

In this section, we present the notations and then formal-

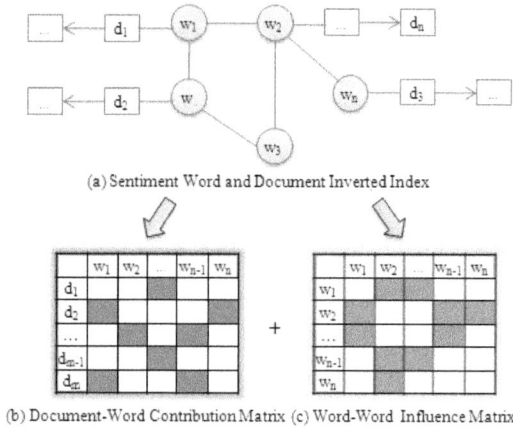

(a) Sentiment Word and Document Inverted Index

(b) Document-Word Contribution Matrix (c) Word-Word Influence Matrix

Figure 1: Subjective document Representation and Sentiment Word Influence Information

ly define the problem of sentiment words identification in the context of matrix factorization. We use $D = \{d_1, d_2, \cdots, d_m\}$ to denote a set of m subjective documents. $L = \{l_i\}_{i=1}^m$ is denoted as the corresponding sentiment label set. If d_i is a positive document, then $l_i = +1$; otherwise $l_i = -1$. The vocabulary index is denoted by $W = \{w_1, w_2, \cdots, w_n\}$. We define an $m \times n$ matrix I to indicate the associations between documents and words. I_{ij} is equal to 1 if $w_j \in d_i$ and equal to 0 otherwise. $R \in \mathbb{R}^{m,n}$ is defined as the document-word contribution matrix that describes n candidate words's numerical contributions on m documents in sentiment view. Influence matrix is denoted by $X \in \mathbb{R}^{n,n}$ which depicts the relations between words.

With the notations above, our task in this paper can be described as: given a corpus $G = \{D, W, L\}$, we aim to recognize and assign sentiment labels for candidate words based on R and X.

3. METHOD

In this section, we convert sentiment word identification problem to predict the unobserved entries in R based on the observed statistics with matrix factorization algorithm. We use the labeled documents to label candidate words with semantic association information.

Intuitively, words with high frequencies are more important than the ones with low frequencies in a subjective document; and if a word only occurs in positive or negative documents, it tends to hold a high sentiment strength and contributes a lot to subjective documents. Based on these intuitions, we define R as follows:

$$R_{ij} = \frac{\mathcal{F}^{(i)}(j)}{h_i} \cdot \left(\frac{\mathcal{F}^{(pos)}(j)}{\mathcal{F}^{(neg)}(j)} \right)^{l_i} \quad (1)$$

where $\mathcal{F}^{(i)}(j)$ is the word frequency of w_j in d_i, h_i is the length of d_i, $\mathcal{F}^{(pos)}(j)$ is the frequency of w_j in positive corpus and $\mathcal{F}^{(neg)}(j)$ is the frequency that w_j occurs in negative corpus.

A low-rank matrix factorization approach seeks to an ap-

proximate $\widehat{R}$ ($R \approx \widehat{R}$) by minimizing

$$\min_{U,V} \mathcal{J}(R, U, V) = \frac{1}{2} \sum_{i=1}^m \sum_{j=1}^n I_{ij}(R_{ij} - U_i^T V_j)^2$$
$$+ \frac{\beta}{2} \|U\|_F^2 + \frac{\gamma}{2} \|V\|_F^2 \quad (2)$$

where $\mathbf{U} \in \mathbb{R}^{k,m}$ is latent document feature matrix, $\mathbf{V} \in \mathbb{R}^{k,n}$ is latent candidate word feature matrix, $k < min(m,n)$ and $\beta, \gamma > 0$. Sigular value decomposition (SVD) [5] and non-negative matrix factorization (NMF) [6] are often used to find a local minimum.

As mentioned in Section 1, two frequently co-occur candidate sentiment words tend to hold the same polarity. Inspired by this observation, We define co-occurrence neighbor as follows.

Definition 1: *Co-Occurrence Neighbor*: Two words in a document are considered as co-occurrence neighbor. For w_i, $\mathcal{K}(i)$ is denoted to its neighbors.

By Definition 1, $X_{ij}=0$ indicates that w_i has never co-occurred with w_j in the corpus. A larger value corresponds to more frequent co-occurrence and stronger influence from w_i to w_j. So, we calculate X_{ij} by

$$X_{ij} = \mathcal{S}(i,j) / \sum_{k \in \mathcal{K}(j)} \mathcal{S}(k,j) \quad (3)$$

where $\mathcal{S}(i,j)$ is the similarity function to indicate the similarity between w_i and w_j. Obviously, the more similar w_i to w_j, the bigger influence on w_j. We use point mutual information to depict the similarity between w_i and w_j.

Next, we explore the utilization of co-occurrence neighborhood information to regularize the learned model. For computational convenience, we assume that all these neighbors are linear i.e. each candidate word can be optimally approximated using a linear combination of its neighbors. Then we change the optimization function to

$$\min_{U,V} \mathcal{J}(R, U, V) = \frac{1}{2} \sum_{i=1}^m \sum_{j=1}^n I_{ij}(R_{ij} - U_i^T V_j)^2$$
$$+ \frac{\alpha}{2} \sum_{j=1}^n \|V_j - \frac{1}{|\mathcal{K}(j)|} \sum_{k \in \mathcal{K}(j)} V_k\|_F^2 \quad (4)$$
$$+ \frac{\beta}{2} \|U\|_F^2 + \frac{\gamma}{2} \|V\|_F^2$$

where $\alpha > 0$ and the second term is a co-occurrence neighborhood regularization which is used to fit the influences from neighbors to V_j. Factually, V_j is more influenced by the neighbors with which frequently co-occur. So we can change this regularization term to

$$\frac{\alpha}{2} \sum_{j=1}^n \|V_j - \sum_{k \in \mathcal{K}(j)} X_{jk} V_k\|_F^2 \quad (5)$$

where X_{jk} allows the term to treat co-occurrence neighbors differently. Thus, our matrix factorization model with co-

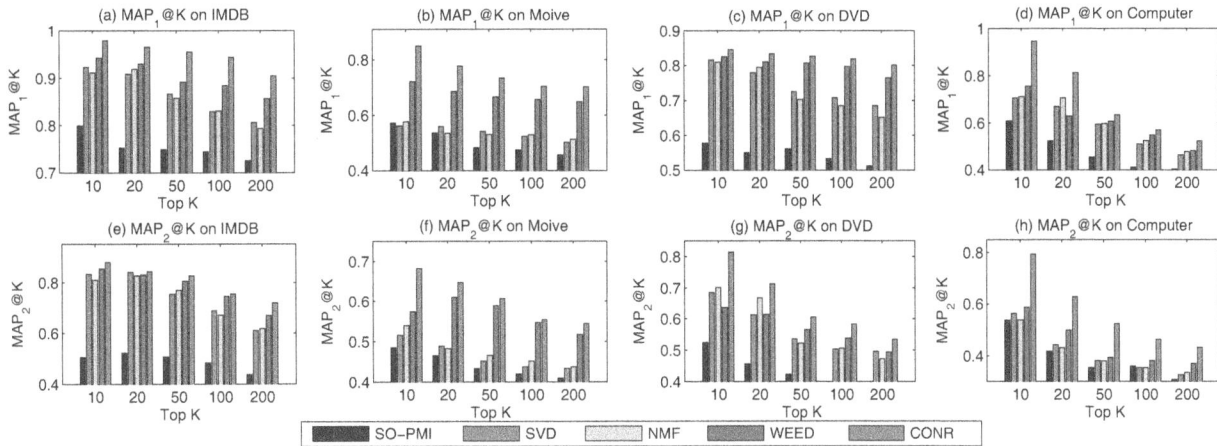

Figure 2: MAP@K Performance Comparisons (Dimensionality k = 10).

occurrence neighbor regularization can be formulated as:

$$\min_{U,V} \mathcal{J}(R,U,V) = \frac{1}{2}\sum_{i=1}^{m}\sum_{j=1}^{n} I_{ij}(R_{ij} - U_i^T V_j)^2$$

$$+ \frac{\alpha}{2}\sum_{j=1}^{n}\left\| V_j - \sum_{k \in \mathcal{K}(j)} X_{jk}V_k \right\|_F^2 \qquad (6)$$

$$+ \frac{\beta}{2}\|U\|_F^2 + \frac{\gamma}{2}\|V\|_F^2$$

We use gradient descent method to search the solution. After that, we can get the semantic orientation of w_j by

$$\omega_j = \frac{1}{|\mathcal{N}^{(+)}|}\sum_{i \in \mathcal{N}^{(+)}} \widehat{R}_{i,j} - \frac{1}{|\mathcal{N}^{(-)}|}\sum_{i \in \mathcal{N}^{(-)}} \widehat{R}_{i,j} \qquad (7)$$

Here, $\mathcal{N}^{(+)}$ represents the positive documents in the corpus while $\mathcal{N}^{(-)}$ represents the negative ones. w_j is classified as having a positive semantic orientation when $\omega_j > 0$ and a negative orientation when $\omega_j < 0$. The magnitude (absolute value) considers the strength of the semantic orientation. Larger values correspond to stronger semantic orientation.

4. EXPERIMENTS

4.1 Datasets

In this section, subsets of four publicly available datasets are employed. The first dataset is the Internet Movie Database (IMDB) [1]. The second dataset we employ for evaluation is the movie reviews [2]. The third one is DVD reviews from NLP&CC2013 [3]. And the last one is computer reviews [4] in Chinese. Sentiment words are generated based on MPQA subjective lexicon [5] and HowNet [6]. To increase the difficulty, a comparable amount of non-sentiment words are added for testing. So our first task is subjectivity detection which distinguishes sentiment words from

[1] http://ai.stanfor.edu/amaas/data/sentiment/
[2] http://www.cs.cornell.edu/people/pabo/movie-review-data/
[3] http://www.datatang.com/data/44115/
[4] http://www.searchforum.org.cn/tansongbo/
[5] http://mpqa.cs.pitt.edu/
[6] http://www.keenage.com/

non-sentiment ones and the second task is polarity classification that assigns a polarity label to each sentiment word. Detailed statistics of datasets are summarized in Table 1.

Table 1: Dataset statistics.

Dataset	Document	Polarity Word	Non	Total
IMDB	4000	1083	1000	2083
Moive	2000	1801	1800	3601
DVD	4000	1123	1100	2223
Computer	4000	617	600	1217

4.2 Evaluation Metrics

In face of the long lists of recommended polarity words, people are only concerned about the top-ranked words with the highest sentiment values [4]. So we consider the precision of the top K ranked sentiment words in our experiments:

$$P@K = \frac{\#right\ words\ in\ top\ K\ result}{K} \qquad (8)$$

For a ranked sequence of words, it is desirable to consider the order. For this purpose, we introduce mean average precision (MAP) which are commonly used in information retrieval to evaluate the results. Average precision (AP) is defined as:

$$AP@K = \frac{\sum_{k=1}^{K}(P@K * f(K))}{K} \qquad (9)$$

where f(k) is the indicator function that is equal to 1 if the kth word is a right word and equal to 0 otherwise. We average the AP@K values of the positive sequence and the negative sequence to get MAP@K.

We consider $P_1@K$ and $MAP_1@K$ as the measurements for subjectivity detection in which right words are the words that identified as sentiment words. And we use $P_2@K$ and $MAP_2@K$ for polarity classification where rights words are these assigned correct sentiment labels. For example, if the top 3 words for the positive sequence are {positive, non-sentiment, negative}, $P_1@3$, $P_2@3$, $AP_1@3$, $AP_2@3$ values are { 2/3, 1/3, (1/1+2/3)/3, (1/1)/3} respectively.

4.3 Experimental Results

In order to show the effectiveness of our proposed sentiment words identification model CONR, we compare the identification results with four baselines, SO-PMI[2], WEED[4],

Table 2: P@K Performance Comparisons (Dimensionality k= 10).

Datasets	Methods	$P_1@K$					$P_2@K$				
		Top10	Top20	Top50	Top100	Top200	Top10	Top20	Top50	Top100	Top200
IMDB	SO-PMI	0.8182	0.7803	0.7923	0.7935	0.7931	0.5121	0.5533	0.5083	0.5187	0.5267
	WEED	0.9801	0.9651	0.9576	0.9481	**0.9326**	0.8944	0.8613	0.8507	0.8288	0.7768
	SVD	0.9696	0.9754	0.9461	0.9375	0.9206	0.8848	0.8361	0.8147	0.7904	0.7342
	NMF	0.9761	0.9625	0.9483	0.9312	0.9175	0.8919	0.8704	0.8140	0.7950	0.7433
	CONR	**0.9839**	**0.9752**	**0.9757**	**0.9625**	0.9275	**0.9383**	**0.9171**	**0.8782**	**0.8466**	**0.7930**
Moive	SO-PMI	0.8182	0.7803	0.7929	0.7835	0.7637	0.5121	0.5537	0.5289	0.5187	0.4879
	WEED	0.9167	**0.8779**	**0.8267**	0.8084	0.8004	0.7448	0.6951	0.7083	0.6687	0.6475
	SVD	0.6861	0.7071	0.7376	0.7611	0.7905	0.6341	0.6511	0.6085	0.5937	0.6375
	NMF	0.6583	0.6221	0.6732	0.7512	0.7917	0.6814	0.5609	0.5833	0.5812	0.6113
	CONR	**0.9472**	0.8535	**0.8267**	**0.8208**	**0.8329**	**0.8333**	**0.7804**	**0.7625**	**0.7353**	**0.6694**
DVD	SO-PMI	0.6251	0.5952	0.6274	0.6089	0.6218	0.5625	0.5238	0.4901	0.4455	0.4404
	WEED	0.9091	0.9130	0.9019	0.8762	0.8955	0.8064	0.7380	0.7745	0.7326	0.6487
	SVD	0.8846	0.9047	0.8627	0.8415	0.8358	0.8489	0.7727	0.7843	0.7178	0.6959
	NMF	0.8928	0.8809	0.8725	0.8217	0.8159	0.8333	0.7857	**0.7884**	0.7128	0.6717
	CONR	**0.9316**	**0.9166**	**0.9285**	**0.9108**	**0.9029**	**0.9085**	**0.8809**	0.7841	**0.7623**	**0.7233**
Computer	SO-PMI	0.6672	0.5892	0.5306	0.5773	0.5105	0.5919	0.4771	0.4814	0.5427	0.4925
	WEED	0.8076	0.6904	0.6504	0.5793	0.5220	0.7307	0.6428	0.6078	0.5642	0.5347
	SVD	0.8458	0.7231	0.6514	0.5739	0.5445	0.7594	0.6127	0.5531	0.5262	0.5322
	NMF	0.7692	0.7119	0.6470	0.5890	0.5473	0.7513	0.6257	0.6116	0.5714	0.5425
	CONR	**0.9615**	**0.8657**	**0.6967**	**0.6098**	**0.5643**	**0.9090**	**0.7619**	**0.6862**	**0.5916**	**0.5612**

SVD[5] and NMF[6]. SO-PMI needs seed words, so we randomly select 20% seeds for it.

The $P_1@K$ and $P_2@K$ results are shown in Table 2, which are the average scores of the top ranked positive and negative words lists with k=10. By comparing the results of different methods, we can draw the following conclusions:

(1)Compared with the optimization-based method WEED, CONR achieves consistently better performances on all four datasets with different K. In particular, CONR is 2.65%-17.83% higher than the state-of-the-art method WEED on Computer dataset.

(2)The matrix factorization based methods SVD and N-MF outperform SO-PMI. This shows that the sentiment matching factor has positive impacts on the sentiment word identification. It is also noted that CONR outperforms SVD and NMF baselines. The highest improvement with respect to SVD and NMF are obtained on the Moive dataset when the K is 10. The experiment results demonstrate that, by exploiting co-occurrence neighbor information, CONR is able to achieve significant improvement.

(3) We also notice totally different characteristics of these four datasets. The results generated by all the methods on IMDB and DVD datasets are much higher than those on Moive and Computer dataset. This indicates that maybe any two sentiment words frequently occur together in the former two datasets.

Figure 2 shows the final results of $MAP_1@K$ and $MAP_2@K$. We can draw some similar conclusions as above. It should be also noted that $MAP@K$ values are lower than $P@K$. It is because that the order is considered in $MAP@K$.

In addition, as the size of K increases, $P@K$ and $MAP@K$ of all methods falls accordingly. It means that all methods can rank the the most probable sentiment words in the front of the word list.

5. CONCLUSIONS

In this paper, we introduce a matrix factorization model CONR for SWI. In CONR, we not only consider the document-word contribution matrix but also incorporate co-occurrence neighbor information of the sentiment words. To the best of our knowledge, this paper is the first work that identifies sentiment words using matrix factorization framework without seed words. Experimental results shows that CONR outperforms the state-of-the-art optimization-based model.

Acknowledgments

This work was supported by Strategic Priority Research Program of Chinese Academy of Sciences (XDA06030600) and National Nature Science Foundation of China (No. 61202226).

6. REFERENCES

[1] G. Qiu, B. Liu, J.J Bu, Ch. Chen. Expanding domain sentiment lexicon through double propagation. In *Proceedings of IJCAI,* pages 1199-1204,2009.

[2] P.D. Turney, M.L. Littman. Measuring praise and criticism: Inference of semantic orientation from association. ACM Transactions on Information Systems, 21(4): 315-346, 2003.

[3] A.L. Mass. R.E. Daly, et al.. Learning word vectors for sentiment analysis. In *Proceedings of ACL,*2011.

[4] H. Yu, Z. Deng, S. Li. Identifying sentiment words using an optimization-based model without seed words. In *Proceedings of ACL,*pages 855-859, 2013.

[5] G.H. Golub, C. Reinsch. Singular value decomposition and least squares solutions. Numerische Mathematik, 14(5): 403-420, 1970.

[6] D.D. Lee, H.S. Seung. Learning the parts of objects by non-negative matrix factorization. Nature, 401(6755): 788-791, 1999.

[7] J. Bross, H. Ehrig. Automatic construction of domain and aspect specific sentiment lexicons for customer review mining. In *Proceedings of CIKM,*pages 1077-1086, 2013.

[8] Y. Lu, M. Castellanos et al.. Automatic construction of a context-aware sentiment lexicon: An optimization approach. In *Proceedings of WWW,*pages 347-356, 2011.

Using Local Information to Significantly Improve Classification Performance

Wei Liu[†], Dong Lee[‡], and Kotagiri Rao[‡]
[†]The University of Technology, Sydney, Australia   [‡]The University of Melbourne, Australia
wei.liu@uts.edu.au, {dongl, kotagiri}@unimelb.edu.au

ABSTRACT

In this research we propose to derive new features based on data samples' local information with the aim of improving the performance of general supervised learning algorithms. The creation of new features is inspired by the measure of average precision which is known to be a robust measure that is insensitive to the number of retrieved items in information retrieval. We use the idea of average precision to weight the neighbours of an instance and show that this weighting strategy is insensitive to the number of neighbours in the locality. Information captured in the new features allows a general classifier to learn additional useful peripheral knowledge that are helpful in building effective classification models. We comprehensively evaluate our method on real datasets and the results show substantial improvements in the performance of classifiers including SVM, Bayesian networks, random forest, and C4.5.

Categories and Subject Descriptors

H.2.8 [**Database Applications**]: [Data mining]

Keywords

Local information; average precision; classification

1. INTRODUCTION.

As one fundamental assumption made in the paradigm of lazy learning methods, local information such as nearest neighbours provide insightful information on the characteristics of data instances. The use of such local information inspires us to design a new feature creation method for tackling supervised learning problems with the target of improving the performance of any general classifiers. Our method utilize local information of each training sample to create extra new feature space, which captures additional information that is helpful for training highly effective learners.

The values of new features of an instance i are derived from the class labels of training data instances that are

nearest neighbours of i. While distance-weighted nearest neighbours are one common way of making use of the local information, we employ *average precision* for deriving the new feature values, which we will show advantageous than pure distance-weighted methods. We show that by calculating average-precision-weighted difference between two (or more) class labels among neighbours of an input sample, we can obtain extra valuable information in association with the class label of this sample.

By using average precision to create new features for supervised learning tasks, our work targets to build on the connection between the community of information retrieval and that of knowledge management. Specifically, we make the following contributions in this research:

1. We propose to use data samples' local information to create new features that capture useful information about training label distributions in the locality;

2. We define the values of the new features by using average precision to weight the neighbours, which is more robust to the changes of the locality and is less sensitive to the number of neighbours compared to pure distance-based weighting methods.

3. We perform comprehensive experiments on 41 real data sets which testify the superiority of the new features in improving a large spectrum of existing popular classifiers.

The rest of the paper is structured as follows. In Section 2 we briefly review related work. In Section 3 we explain the average precision weighting algorithm, and provide our feature creation strategy. Section 4 reports experiments and Section 5 concludes this paper.

2. RELATED WORK

Many recent studies have made efforts to improve the performance on speed and accuracy for lazy learning methods such as k-nearest neighbour (kNN) classifiers. Novel methods including Neighbour Component Analysis [1], Large Margin Nearest Neighbour [2] and Weighted Distance Nearest Neighbour [3] have mainly focused on the transformation of data set or the selection of k value to improve the performance of k-nearest neighbour method in terms of computational speed and accuracy. Goldberger et. al. [1] proposed Neighbourhood Component Analysis (NCA) for learning a Mahalanobis distance measure. This method assumes that Euclidean distances in space transformed by Mahalanobis distance metrics can be used for calculating the probability with which a point will be correctly classified. Despite the simplicity of NCA objective function, it performs the same or slightly better than that of other distance measures (Euclidean distance, whitening, and RCA) for kNN. Tao Yang et al. [5] suggested Weighted Distance k-Nearest Neighbours(WDkNN) method which can improve kNN method rather than NN method. Liu and Chawla [4] proposed a new weighting method for kNN to improve performance of kNN classifier in imbalanced dataset. Their method employs the confidence of a data instance's attribute values given a class label. Zhang and Zhou [7] proposed the modified application of kNN for not single-label learning but multi-label learning. Their proposed system suggests the category vector to determine multi-label based on maximum a posterior principle. Galvan et al. [8] introduces the extended application of lazy learning strategy. This strategy can be used for pre-processing of eager learning methods such as decision tree. There has been applications that used kNN as data transforming method. But existing applications are for the additional function such as multilabel classification [7] or require repetitive computation for building a classifier [8].

Motivation for our methods: The above approaches are mostly based on pure distance weighting mechanism (e.g., additive inverse or multiplicative inverse of Euclidean distances), which is sensitivity to subtle changes on the ordering of neighbours as well as the selection of neighbour number k. This motivates us the design of a new weighting method that can overcome these shortcomings. Besides, we also study the application of local information for improving the information explicitly expressed in training data, which allows the performance improvements of an arbitrary general classifier.

3. WEIGHTING METHOD SELECTION

Before we elaborate on our neighbour-weighting method, we first review the weighting strategies used in a standard kNN classifier. Given a test instance D_t, the simplest kNN method employs a majority voting strategy which when under no weighting (NW) is computed as in the following:

$$l_t = \operatorname*{argmax}_{c \in C} \sum_{k \in \xi(D_t)} I(l_c(k)) \quad \text{where } I(x) = \begin{cases} 1 & x \text{ is labelled as } c \\ 0 & \text{otherwise} \end{cases} \quad (1)$$

where l_t is the expected label of D_t, C denotes all class labels, and $\xi(D_t)$ is a set of ordered k nearest neighbours $\{N_1, N_2, \ldots, N_k\}$ of D_t. N_i is nearer than N_j for $i < j$. $l_c(i)$ defines a function which tells whether the instance i is labelled as c. To incorporate distances, a weighting scheme gives more weights to the neighbour with closer distance [4]. For that reason, neighbours are weighted with the multiplicative inverse (MI)

$$\text{MI: } l_t = \operatorname*{argmax}_{c \in C} \sum_{k \in \xi(D_t)} I(l_c(k)) \cdot dist(k, D_t)^{-1}, \quad (2)$$

or the additive inverse (AI)

$$\text{AI: } l_t = \operatorname*{argmax}_{c \in C} \sum_{k \in \xi(D_t)} I(l_c(k)) \cdot (1 - \frac{dist(k, D_t)}{dist_{max}}), \quad (3)$$

where $dist_{max}$ denotes the largest distances between D_t and its neighbours.

3.1 The proposed weighting method

Our approach considers the precision of classes of k-nearest neighbours according to their distances to the test instance. In the domain of information retrieval, a precision is the fraction of relevant items in all searched items, and the average precision (AveP) is defined as

$$AveP(R) = \frac{\sum_{r=1}^{R} P(r) \times \text{rel}(r)}{\text{number of relevant items}} \quad (4)$$

where $P(r)$ is the precision at rth rank and $\text{rel}(r)$ indicates whether the item at rth rank is relevant (returning value 1) or not (returning 0).

In our approach, analogical to k ranked items, there are k neighbours found from the training data which are associated with specific classes. In other words, we compute the average precision for each neighbour's class label by taking its rank into consideration. In addition, in order to handle the possible influence of class imbalance (i.e., the scenarios where training data samples are dominated by a majority class), we use the expectation of each class in the overall training set to adjust the average precision values.

We define the average precision weight (APW) for the rth ($1 \leq r \leq k$) neighbour associated with class label c as:

$$APW(c) = \frac{\sum_{i=1}^{r} \frac{\Im(i, c, D_t)}{i} \cdot dist(N(D_t, r), D_t)^{-1}}{\text{number of instances for class c in training data}} \quad (5)$$

where $\Im(i, c, D_t)$ defines the total number of neighbours which have class c between the first neighbour and the ith neighbour of the data instance D_t:

$$\Im(i, c, D_t) = \sum_{j=1}^{i} I(l_c(N(D_t, j))) \quad (6)$$

This measure has the same meaning as the number of relevant items. $N(D_t, j)$ indicates the jth closest neighbour of test data instance D_t. The following example gives an illustration on how we compute average precision to weight the neighbours.

Example 1: In the synthetic example shown in Figure 1, sample A is the test data instance which has 2 neighbours of + class followed by 3 neighbours of – class. Notations d1, d2, d3, d4, and d5 represent distances from the 5 neighbours to A. Following Eq. 5, the APWs of the 5th neighbour are calculated in the following way (assuming that there are 10 instances for + class and 20 instances for – class in the training data).

$$APW(+) = \left(\frac{1}{1} \cdot \frac{1}{d1} + \frac{2}{2} \cdot \frac{1}{d2} + \frac{2}{3} \cdot 0 + \frac{2}{4} \cdot 0 + \frac{2}{5} \cdot 0 \right) \cdot \frac{1}{10} \quad (7)$$

$$APW(-) = \left(\frac{0}{1} \cdot 0 + \frac{0}{2} \cdot 0 + \frac{1}{3} \cdot \frac{1}{d3} + \frac{2}{4} \cdot \frac{1}{d4} + \frac{3}{5} \cdot \frac{1}{d5} \right) \cdot \frac{1}{20} \quad (8)$$

We define the values of the features as the difference between APW of positive class and that of negative class. Algorithm 1 explains our concrete method for creating the new features in training data, with a demonstration shown in Figure 1. Note that for both training and testing data, we use the original training data to find data samples' neighbours and to create new features. In our algorithm, the value of a new feature indicates how far the instance is to a specific class in k-nearest neighbour locality. The information about how large the value is plays an important role of indicating the class distribution in the locality.

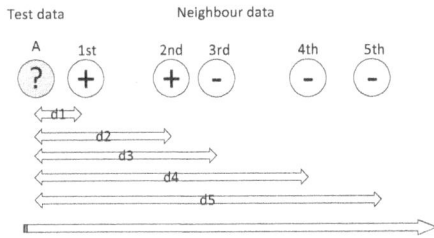

Figure 1: Abstraction of k-nearest neighbours on space

Algorithm 1 The feature creation algorithm

1: **procedure** FEATURECREATION(D, k)
2:     // D is training dataset, k is number of neighbours
3:     $D_{new} = \emptyset$
4:     **for** $i = 1$ to number of D **do**
5:         // D_i is one of data instances D
6:         $ND = kNN(D_i, k, D)$
7:         // ND contains k nearest neighbours of D_i found from D
8:         **for** $j = 1$ to k **do**
9:             $F_j = APW_j(+) - APW_j(-)$
10:            // $APW_j(C)$ is the average precision of class C at jth neighbour
11:            $D_i = D_i \cup F_j$
12:        **end for**
13:    **end for**
14:    return D
15: **end procedure**

Advantages of APW

When there are erratic changes in distances among data, existing distance weighting approaches (such as MI and AI as in Eq. 2 and 3) can be easily affected in the accuracy of deciding the class, especially when the value of k changes. This is one of the reasons that distance weighting scheme is not as popular as the standard equal weighting kNN method. However, when the precision over the class of each neighbour is employed for calculating the weight, each class will be weighted by its rank in the ordering in addition to the numerical value of its distance. The total number of instances for a class reflects the expectation of that specific class. As a result, the average precision combined with distance and expectation of class weighting will be less affected by dramatic discrepancy between distances among data. This is also the same observation on the insensitivity of average precision to the number of items retrieved in the information retrieval domain. Therefore, we expect that our approach will show more stable performance compared with distance-only weighting metrics, even when the data distribution is unstable in its original feature space with respect to the number of neighbours. As we will show empirically, we examine this hypothesis through practical experiments and the results show better performance than that of other methods such as majority voting and distance weighting.

4. EXPERIMENTS AND ANALYSIS

Our experiments are conducted with two objectives. Firstly, we measure how much our novel weighting method APW can enhance the performance compared with other weighting methods such as NW (No Weighting), MI (Multiplicative Inverse), and AI (Addictive Inverse), where we use kNN as the base classifier. Secondly, we evaluate the performance improvements brought by our new features for general classifiers such as Bayesian networks, C45 decision tree, random

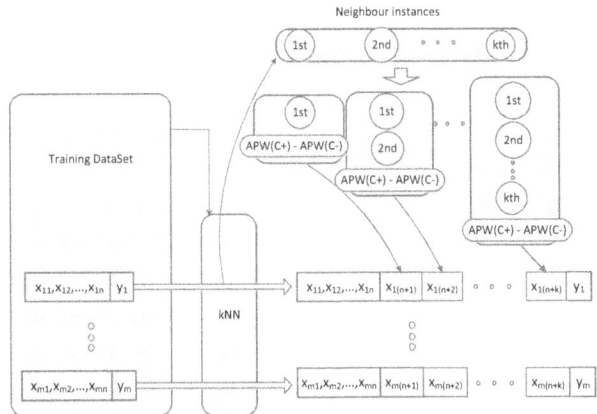

Figure 2: An illustration on the feature creation procedure using APW. Each data instance is associated with additional feature values which are based on the APW values calculated by its neighbours.

forests, and SVMs (with linear kernels). Our experiments are conducted using 41 datasets from UCI [10] shown in Table 1. For data sets that have more than two classes, we keep the majority class as the positive class and combine the other classes as the negative class. Our proposed method is implemented in Weka [9], which also contains the other classifiers that we use in the experiments (with their default parameter settings).

We compare and analyse our APW method against existing weighting methods such as NW, MI, and AI (as defined in Eq. 1 to 3 respectively) using kNN as the base learner. Figure 3 shows the performance in F-measure according to different settings of k values, where the x-axis is the number of neighbours used and the y-axis is the F-measure. Due to space limit, we only show results for 9 of the 41 data sets in experiments (the data sets not shown in the figure make the same conclusions as those shown). From the results, it is easy to see that our APW method gives more stable and robust performance compared with other methods, and is much less sensitive to changes of k.

4.1 Evaluations on New Features

We evaluate our feature creation strategy by examining the improvements on classification accuracy using the following different classifiers: Bayesian networks, C4.5, Random Forest, and SVM with linear kernels. We control the values of k from 1 to 15, and inspect the performance in terms of average accuracy on 5x2 cross-validation. The statistical significance test is conducted on the basis of paired t-tests.

Table 2 shows the comparisons between classifiers learned on data with new features and those learned from original data. In the table, 'W/D/L' indicates the total count of 'win', 'draw', and 'lose'. 'Win' means significant improvement with 95% confidence in paired t-tests, whereas 'lose' means worse performance with 95% confidence. Besides, we use two more measures to evaluate the classification improvements: "ARI" denoting average relative improvement, and "AAI" denoting average accuracy improvement, calculated in the following way:

Table 1: List of Datasets

Dataset	Instances	Features	Class	Dataset	Instances	Features	Class
ADA	4562	49	2	Eye	10936	28	3
Ionosphere	351	35	2	Landsat	4435	37	3
Lym11	96	4026	11	Colon	96	4026	9
Oil	937	50	2	Sensor	2212	13	3
Sonar	208	61	2	Zip	9298	257	10
Breast	699	10	2	Car	1728	7	2
CNAE-9	1080	857	2	Eighthr	2534	73	2
Eucalyptus	736	20	2	Fbis	1049	2001	2
Gas	13910	129	2	Hand	606	101	2
Hill_1	606	101	2	HRA	7352	562	2
kr-vs-kp	3196	37	2	Madelon	2000	501	2
Mfeat-pixel	2000	241	2	Nursery	12960	9	2
Onehr	2536	73	2	PlantM	1600	65	2
PlantS	1600	65	2	PlantT	1600	65	2
Re0	1504	2887	2	Seed	210	8	2
Segment	2310	20	2	Semeion	1593	257	2
Sensor_24	5456	25	2	Skin	36758	4	2
Soybean	683	36	2	Spambase	4601	58	2
Vowel	990	14	2	Waveform	5000	41	2
Red wine	1599	12	2	White wine	4898	12	2
Yeast	1484	10	2				

Table 2: Improvements of classification performance

	C4.5	Bayesian net	Rand Forest	SVM
k	W/D/L ARI(AAI)	W/D/L ARI(AAI)	W/D/L ARI(AAI)	W/D/L ARI(AAI)
1	17/24/0 25.8(5.8)	16/25/0 11.3(3)	14/27/0 16(2.5)	16/23/2 19.3(3.7)
2	17/24/0 23.9(5.7)	18/22/1 14.6(3.8)	15/25/1 13.9(2.6)	15/24/2 19.1(3.5)
3	18/22/1 22.4(5.6)	21/20/0 18.9(4.6)	15/25/1 14.6(2.5)	16/22/3 20.4(3.5)
4	17/23/1 22.4(5.8)	21/20/0 20.7(5)	14/26/1 14.8(2.5)	18/20/3 20.5(3.4)
5	17/23/1 23.9(5.8)	21/20/0 23(5.3)	14/26/1 13.3(2.5)	18/20/3 20.9(3.4)
6	17/23/1 23.9(5.8)	22/19/0 23.9(5.5)	14/26/1 13.5(2.5)	16/22/3 21.3(3.3)
7	17/23/1 23.8(5.8)	21/20/0 24.3(5.6)	14/26/1 11.2(2.2)	16/22/3 21.3(3.3)
8	17/23/1 22.3(5.8)	21/20/0 24.6(5.7)	14/26/1 10.8(2.1)	16/22/3 21(3.1)
9	16/24/1 21.1(5.8)	21/20/0 25(5.7)	14/25/2 9.8(2.2)	16/22/3 20.6(3.1)
10	16/24/1 21.8(5.8)	23/18/0 25(5.8)	13/27/1 8.4(2)	16/22/3 20.4(3.1)
11	18/22/1 21.7(5.9)	21/20/0 26.2(6)	10/29/2 7.9(1.9)	16/20/5 20.5(2.9)
12	17/23/1 22.4(5.8)	22/19/0 26.3(6.2)	9/31/1 5.8(1.7)	16/20/5 19.8(2.8)
13	17/22/2 20.9(5.8)	23/17/1 26.8(6.4)	8/29/4 2.9(1.3)	16/18/7 18.6(2.6)
14	18/21/2 20.1(5.8)	23/17/1 27(6.5)	9/29/3 2.7(1.1)	16/18/7 17.5(2.5)
15	18/21/3 19.9(5.7)	23/17/1 26.9(6.5)	9/27/5 2.8(0.7)	17/17/7 16.4(2.4)

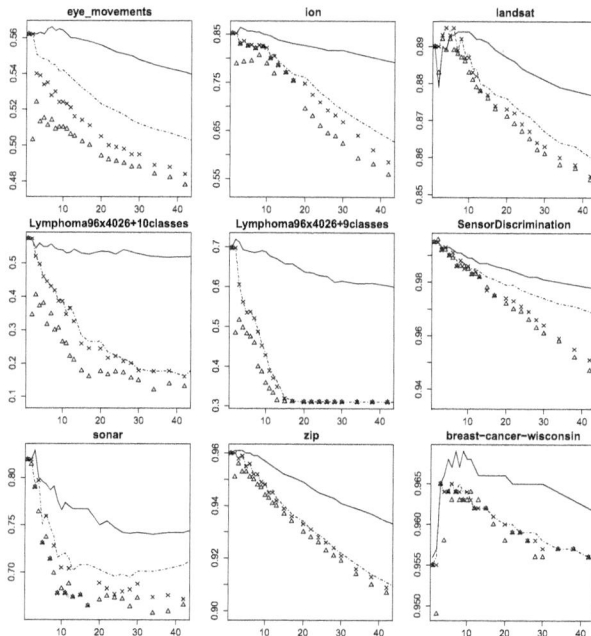

Figure 3: Comparisons of weighting methods. The x-axis represents the number of neighbours used, while the y-axis represents F-measure. The solid lines represent Average Precision Weighting, the dotted lines represent Multiplicative Inverse Distance Weighting, the cross marks represent Additive Inverse Distance Weighting, and the triangles are for No Weighting.

$$ARI = \frac{\sum_{i=1}^{n} \frac{A_i - AO_i}{100 - AO_i} * 100}{n}, \quad AAI = \frac{\sum_{i=1}^{n} A_i - AO_i}{n} \quad (9)$$

where AO_i is the accuracy of an original classifier and A_i is accuracy of the classifier learned with APW features.

4.2 Evaluation on APW

As shown in the Table 2, the classifiers trained on data with extra new features show better performance compared those on original features by clearly more 'wins' than 'loses'. In many case of the classifiers, more than half of datasets are associated with substantial improvements. We can observe that in many case the performance of the classifier doesn't

change dramatically, which suggests that APW is stale with respect to changes of k.

5. CONCLUSION

In this paper we have proposed the use of average precision as a highly effective weighting method to capture local information of data samples. This novel method has more stable and robust performance compared with conventional distance-based weighting methods. Importantly, we use this weighting method to create new features so that any general classifier can benefit from training on them. Experiments on real datasets illustrate that our method is less sensitive to changes of the number of neighbours, and at the same time brings forward substantially improved performance in existing popular classifiers. In future, we plan to experiment the use of our method in multi-label classification problems.

6. REFERENCES

[1] Goldberger, J. and Roweis, S. and Hinton, G. and Salakhutdinov, R., *Neighbourhood components analysis*, (2004).

[2] Weinberger, K. Q and Saul, L. K, *A Distance metric learning for large margin nearest neighbor classification*, The Journal of Machine Learning Research, 10 (2009), pp. 207–244.

[3] Jahromi, M. Z. and Parvinnia, E. and John, R. , *A method of learning weighted similarity function to improve the performance of nearest neighbor*, Information Sciences, 179 (2009), pp. 2964–2973.

[4] Liu, W. and Chawla, S., *Class confidence weighted kNN algorithms for imbalanced data sets*, In Proceedings of PAKDD 2011, pp. 345–356.

[5] Yang, T. and Cao, L. and Zhang, C., *A novel prototype reduction method for the k-nearest neighbor algorithm*, In Proceedings of PAKDD 2010, pp. 89–100.

[6] Dudani, S. A, *The distance-weighted k-nearest-neighbor rule*, IEEE Transactions on Systems, Man and Cybernetics, 4 (1976) pp. 325–327.

[7] Zhang, M. and Zhou, Z.H., *ML-kNN: A lazy learning approach to multi-label learning*, Pattern Recognition, Elsevier, 40 (2007), pp. 2038–2048.

[8] Galván, I. M. and Valls, J.M. and García, M. and Isasi, P., *A lazy learning approach for building classification models*, International Journal of Intelligent Systems, 26 (2011), pp. 773–786.

[9] Hall, M. and Frank, E. and Holmes, G. and Pfahringer, B. and Reutemann, P. and Witten, I. H. *The WEKA Data Mining Software: An Update*, SIGKDD Explorations, 11 (2009).

[10] Bache, K. and Lichman, M. (2013). UCI Machine Learning Repository [http://archive.ics.uci.edu/ml].

Improving Recommendation Accuracy by Combining Trust Communities and Collaborative Filtering

Xiao Ma,Hongwei Lu,Zaobin Gan✉
School of Computer Science and Technology
Huazhong University of Science and Technology
Wuhan China, 430074
{cindyma,luhw,zgan}@hust.edu.cn

ABSTRACT

With the booming of online social networks, social trust has been used to cluster users in recommender systems. It has been proven to improve the recommendation accuracy when trust communities are integrated into memory-based collaborative filtering algorithms. However, existing trust community mining methods only consider the trust relationships, regardless of the distrust information. In this paper, considering both the trust and distrust relationships, a SVD signs based community mining method is proposed to process the trust relationship matrix in order to discover the trust communities. A modified trust metric which considers a given user's expertise level in a community is presented to obtain the indirect trust values between users. Then some missing ratings of the given user are complemented by the weighted average preference of his/her trusted neighbors selected in the same community during the random walk procedures. Finally, the prediction for a given item is generated by the conventional collaborative filtering. The comparison experiments on Epinions data set demonstrate that our approach outperforms other state-of-the-art methods in terms of RMSE and RC.

Categories and Subject Descriptors

H.3.3 [**Information Search Retrieval**]: Information Filtering; J.4 [**Computer Applications**]: Social and Behavioral Sciences

Keywords

trust communities;clustering;trust and distrust;collaborative filtering

1. INTRODUCTION

With the explosion of information on the Internet, Recommender Systems(RSs) as an indispensable type of Information Filtering technique have attracted lots of attention in the past decades. Typically, recommender systems are based on Collaborative Filtering (CF), which is a technique that automatically predicts the interests of an active user by collecting rating information from other similar users or items[1]. CF based RSs can be classified into memory-based and model-based approaches. In this paper, we focus on the memory-based method.

In order to alleviate the inherent problems of traditional CF based RSs, such as data sparsity, cold start and scalability, some clustering based CF[11] and trust based CF methods[6, 7] have been proposed, which have improved the quality of RSs. Recently, some works are exploring the benefits of combining clustering and social trust information to further enhance the Recommender Systems[4, 8, 9]. However, as far as we know, these works only consider the clustering of trust relationships, regardless of the distrust information.

Motivated by the research of signed network mining, which believes that a signed network is often composed of communities, entities within the same community are all positive relationships and negative relationships exist between different communities[2]. We argue that trust network, as a special type of signed network will also follow the so-called 'balanced' patterns[2, 12]. That is to say, users in the same community trust each other and users between different communities have distrust relationships with each other.

Therefore, we focus on mining trust communities based on the trust and distrust relationships in order to make the densely connected users into the same trust community. Empirical study shows a correlation between trust and user similarity[4], in our work we assume that users share more similarity in the same community than users in different communities. By combining with the collaborative filtering method, the prediction of missing ratings will be generated within each community. The main contributions of this paper are summarized as follows:

1)A trust community mining method is proposed by clustering the trust relationship matrix based on the Singular Value Decomposition signs algorithm[3]. 2) A modified trust metric which considers a given user's expertise level in a community is proposed to obtain the indirect trust values between users. 3) Some missing ratings of a given user are complemented by the weighted average preference of his/her trusted neighbors selected in the same community during the random walk procedures. 4) We conduct experiments on the Epinions data set. Experiment results show better performance of our method in terms of RMSE and RC.

The rest of the paper is organized as follows: the notations are defined in Section 2. Section 3 introduced the proposed recommendation method. The experiment results and anal-

CIKM'14, November 3–7, 2014, Shanghai, China.
Copyright 2014 ACM 978-1-4503-2598-1/14/11 ...$15.00.
http://dx.doi.org/10.1145/2661829.2662085.

ysis are presented in Section 4. Finally, Section 5 concludes this study with future work.

2. PRELIMINARY

We denote the sets of all users, all items, all ratings and all communities as U,I,R and C,respectively. We keep the symbols u,v for two different users, i,j for two different items and c for a community. Then $r_{u,i} \in \{1, 2, 3, 4, 5\}$ represents a rating given by user u on item i. I_u is the set of items rated by user u. The trust network can be defined as a directed graph $G = \langle U, E \rangle$, where E represents the set of trust relationships. Binary trust relationships (i.e. trust and distrust relationships) are considered in this paper. $\forall e_{u,v} \in E, \exists |s_{e_{u,v}} \in \{1, -1\}$ and $u,v \in U$. Here $s_{e_{u,v}}$ is the sign of the trust relationship,$s_{e_{u,v}} = 1$ means u trusts v,$s_{e_{u,v}} = -1$ means u distrusts v. TN_u represents the set of neighbors user u trust in the trust network. TEN_u represents the set of users who trust user u.

3. THE APPROACH

3.1 Trust Communities Mining

Inspired by the research of signed network mining, which believes that a signed network is often composed of communities. Users share positive relationships within the same community and negative relationships exist between different communities[2]. In this paper, we choose to use the SVD signs proposed by[3] to cluster users into different communities according to how they are trusted and distrusted by others. The trust relationships can be represented by a square matrix $T_{|U| \times |U|} = (t_{u,v})$ and $t_{u,v} = s_{e_{u,v}}$. Note that matrix T is different from the adjacency matrix, it describes both the connection and the trust or distrust relationships between each other. By decomposing the matrix with truncated SVD, we can cluster the users by how they trust and distrust others and how they are trusted and distrusted by others with less dimensions. The decomposed trust relationship matrix with rank k can be represented by:

$$\tilde{T}_{|U| \times |U|} = P_{|U| \times k} S_{k \times k} Q^{\mathrm{T}}_{|U| \times k} \qquad (1)$$

Where matrix $\tilde{T}$ is the best possible rank k approximation to matrix T, $k \ll rank(T)$. The singular values can be plotted on a line graph in descending order, and the turning point of the line can be chosen as the best k. Therefore, the elements of matrix S are the k dominant singular values and the rows of matrix P and Q can be regarded as the coordinates of the participants in the k dimensional spaces.

Since the matrix T is asymmetric, clustering methods by rows of P and Q have different meanings. If the rows of P have the same sign patterns on the k dimensions are classified into one cluster, this may lead to up to 2^k clusters (actually may fewer than it). It clusters the users by how they trust and distrust others. Similarly, the sign patterns of the rows of Q are also applicable and this clusters the users by how they are trusted and distrusted by others.

Figure 1 is a toy example of the SVD signs based trust community mining result by using sign patterns of the first two left singular vectors. In the instance, the user number is 10, the rank k is set to be 2. According to the sign patterns of $\{(+,+),(+,-),(-,-)\}$ the rows of $P_{10 \times 2}$(on the right side of Fig.1), the original trust network are clustered into three parts as circled by the different colors of dotted line.

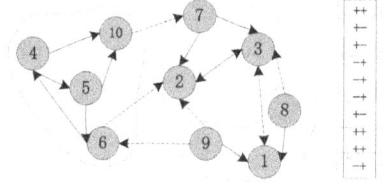

Figure 1: SVD signs based trust community mining

From the result we can see that each user belongs to a unique cluster, users in a same cluster trust each other while distrust each other between different clusters.

3.2 Rating Complement

In this section, we first apply the random walk approach to explore the trust communities to collect the top-K trusted neighbors for users, then fill in some missing ratings of users by the weighted average ratings of their trusted neighbors.

Basically, user u first finds a set of direct trust neighbors in the trust community u belongs to. As we know that, direct trust relationships in trust networks are few. Therefore, we also consider the indirect trust relationships in order to collect enough trusted neighbors. The MoleTrust[7] algorithm which performs depth-first search to propagate and infer trust in the trust networks is adopted to infer the trust value of indirectly connected users. As the MoleTrust approach can just produce binary inferred trust values with the binary data set, i.e., 0 or 1, where 0 means no direct trust connections whereas 1 indicates a direct trust value between users. We modify the inferred result as follows:

$$t^c_{u,v} = t'_{u,v} \times dis^c_{u,v}, dis^c_{u,v} = \begin{cases} 1, & E^c_v > \bar{E}^c \\ \frac{1}{d}, & E^c_v \leq \bar{E}^c \end{cases} \qquad (2)$$

where $\forall u,v \in c$, $E^c_v = \frac{N_v}{N^c} + \frac{TEN_v}{TEN^c}$, $\bar{E}^c = \frac{N^c}{n^c} + \frac{TEN^c}{n^c}$. $t'_{u,v}$ is the inferred trust value by the MoleTrust algorithm. $dis^c_{u,v}$ represents the shortest distance between user u and user v determined by a breath first search algorithm. N_v is the rating number of user v. N^c is the total rating number of community c. TEN_v is the number of users who trust user v. TEN^c is the number of trust relationships in community c. n^c is the number of users in community c.

The idea of Equation 2 can be explained as: when calculating the indirect trust between the source user u and the target user v, if the target user v's expertise level E^c_v is greater than the average expertise level $\bar{E}^c$, we believe that the target user is an expert in that community(Actually, no more than 10% users are experts.). Then the distance factor will not affect the final results. According to the six degrees theory, we set the propagation step $d = 6$.

If the number of directly connected neighbors cannot reach the predefined trust neighbor selection threshold K, then starting from one of the direct neighbors of u to explore the second step neighbors to collect more trusted neighbors. Note that the probability for choosing each friend to be further explored is equal to his/her trust score. Obviously, the more trustworthy a neighbor is, this neighbor's neighbors are more likely to be trustworthy to u, and hence these neighbors will be explored with a higher probability.

The exploration is terminated if one of the two conditions is met: (1) the size of trusted neighbors reaches the predefined threshold K; (2) the distance between user u and the neighbor to be explored exceeds the propagation step 6. Note that the step $t+1$ start to be processed only after all step t users have been processed.

It is worth mentioning that some cold users who have few ratings may also have few trusted neighbors. Most existing trust based recommendation approaches will fail to work when facing such situation. In order to address this issue, we select some experts from the communities the cold users belong to, and regard these experts as the trusted neighbors of the cold users. We leave as a future work a more detailed discussion on selection of the expert.

Then the missing rating of the given user u to item i can be computed by Equation 3. The idea is that user u's missing ratings of item i can be estimated by the weighted average ratings of his/her trusted neighbors who have rated item i in community c.

$$\hat{r}_{u,i} = \frac{\sum_{v \in TN_u} t_{u,v}^c \cdot r_{v,i}}{\sum_{v \in TN_u} t_{u,v}^c} \qquad (3)$$

Therefore, user u's sparse rating profile can be complemented by his trusted neighbors to some extent, which is helpful to perform the standard CF recommendation in Section 3.3. We denote the new items set rated by user u as $\tilde{I}_u$, which contains the set of items rated by user u and the set of items aggregated by his trusted neighbors.

3.3 Incorporating with collaborative f ltering

With the new rating profiles of all users, we follow the classical CF technique to predict the rating of a target item i that has not been rated by user u. The first step is to find similar neighbors of the given user u in the community he/she belongs to. We use the pearson correlation coefficient(PCC)[1]to measure the similarity between two users according to their ratings on the items that they rated in common(we set the overlap threshold to be 5). Therefore, a set of similar neighbors of the given user u can be denoted as $SN_u = \{v/s_{u,v} > \theta_s, v \in U^c\}$, where U^c is the user set in community c. θ_s is a predefined similarity threshold which will be discussed in Section 4.3.

The classical last step of memory based CF methods is aggregating ratings for a given user u from the correlated neighbors SN_u obtained in the first step for missing ratings. Hence, the predicted rating of item $i(i \in I \backslash \tilde{I}_u)$ for the given user u is the weighted average of the ratings given to item i by the neighbors of u as shown in Equation 4. $\hat{r}_{u,i}$ represents the predicted value on item i for user u. $sim_{u,v}$ is the similarity value generated by PCC.

$$\hat{r}_{u,i} = \frac{\sum_{v \in SN_u} sim_{u,v} \cdot r_{v,i}}{\sum_{v \in SN_u} |sim_{u,v}|} \qquad (4)$$

4. EXPERIMENTS AND ANALYSIS

In this section, we conduct series of experiments to evaluate the performance of the proposed recommendation method which combines the trust communities and collaborative filtering(TCCF), and compare with two existing approaches on Epinions data set. The compared approaches include a classical user based CF approach which only considered the similarity between users named as UBCF[10]and an efficient recommendation approach proposed by Pham et al.[8] which run a density-based clustering algorithm just on trust relationships to cluster users into communities.

4.1 Dataset Description

Epinions is a consumer reviews web site in which users can express their opinions about items by assigning numerical ratings and writing article reviews. The extended Epinions data set[1]generated by[7] describes the trust and distrust relationships among users and their ratings on other users' articles. In this paper, we use the sampling method proposed in [5] to scale down the original data set. Therefore, the sampled data set contains 33k users who issued 84k trust/distrust statements and 332k ratings.

4.2 Methodology and Metrics

In order to validate the performance of our TCCF method, we use a popular technique for evaluating recommender systems named as Leave-one-out with 1000 randomly chosen common users and 1000 cold users(users who have rated less than 5 items). Firstly, one rating from a given sampled user is masked. The predicted ratings generated by all the comparative recommendation approaches are then compared with the real rating and the difference in absolute value is the prediction error. The procedure is repeated for all the masked ratings and an average of all the errors is computed, that is, the Root Mean Square Error (RMSE):

$RMSE = \sqrt{\frac{1}{n} \sum_{r=1}^{n} (R - \hat{R})^2}$, where n denotes the number

of tested ratings. R is the real rating of an item and $\hat{R}$ is the corresponding predicted rating. Another evaluation metrics we are interested in is the RatingsCoverage(RC): $RC = \frac{M}{N}$, where M and N are the number of predictable and all the testing ratings, respectively. RC measures the degree to which the testing ratings can be predicted and covered relative to the whole testing ratings.

4.3 Effect of similarity threshold θ_s

In Section 3.3, we need to choose a proper similarity threshold θ_s to select the nearest neighbors of the tested users. As we are most interested in the effect of similarity threshold for cold users, we will not discuss the effect for common users. The threshold θ_s is varied from 0.0 to 0.9 with step 0.1. The result is illustrated in Figure 2.

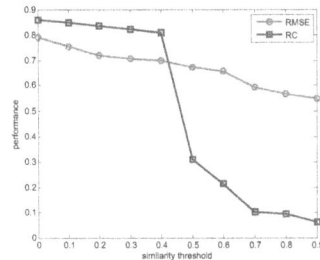

Figure 2: The effect of similarity threshold for cold users.

From Figure 2 we can observe that as the threshold θ_s increase, both the RMSE and RC decreases at the same time. Note that when θ_s reaches 0.4, the RC drops dramatically. Therefore, in our work, the similarity threshold is set to be 0.4 considering the tradeoff between the RMSE and RC.

---

[1]www.trustlet.org

4.4 Result and Analysis

In trust communities mining algorithm, we set rank k to be 4 which can achieve the best community structure(The method of choosing k is discussed in Section 3.1). The re-ordered trust relationship matrix is shown in Figure 3. The blue dots represent trust relationships and the red ones represent distrust relationships. From Figure 3, it is observed that there are clusters where the users mainly trust each other in the same cluster and overall distrust the users in some other clusters.

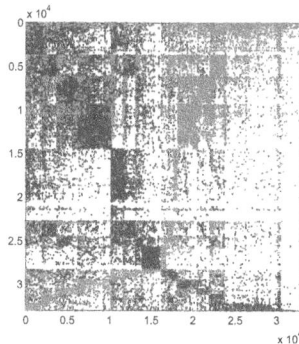

Figure 3: Reordered trust relationship matrix after clustering

In Section 3.2, we employed the random walk algorithm to select the top-K trusted users for a given user in the same community. In this paper, we set K as 100. Due to limited space, we will not discuss it further.

The sparsity of the sampled common users and cold users are 79.96% and 99.36%,respectively. Figure 4 is the comparison results for both the common users and cold users.

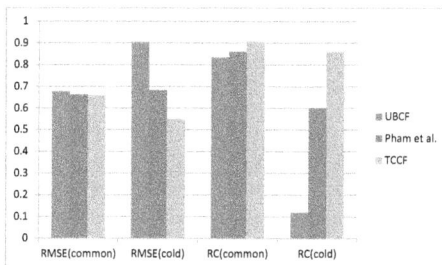

Figure 4: Performance Comparison

In the UBCF method, the similarity threshold is set to be 0.4 which leads to the best performance. In Figure 4, it is observed that UBCF performs worst for common users and cold users no matter in RMSE or RC due to its inherent problems. In Pham et al.'s method, the trust network is regarded as an undirected graph which can just represent the connection between users and may lower the accuracy of the clustering result. In addition, they didn't consider the distrust relationships.

TCCF considers both the trust and distrust relationships which may increase the accuracy of the clustering, then better neighbors will be generated which may further improve the recommendation accuracy; on the other hand, we complement the sparse rating profiles for all the users before performing the CF algorithm, which may improve the

recommendation coverage. From Figure 4 we can conclude that TCCF performs better than Pham et al's approach and gets the best result in all the metrics.

5. CONCLUSION

In this paper, we presented a new recommendation method by combining trust communities and collaborative filtering. We run the SVD signs algorithm on the trust relationship matrix to detect trust communities. Based on a random walk approach and a modified trust metric, a given user's sparse rating profile can be complemented by his/her trusted neighbors in the same community. Then the predictions can be generated by the traditional collaborative filtering based on the complemented user rating profiles. Real data set based experiments demonstrate that TCCF outperforms the comparison approaches both in RMSE and RC. In the future, we will explore some better trust metrics and validate our method on some other data sets.

6. REFERENCES

[1] G. Adomavicius and A. Tuzhilin. Toward the next generation of recommender systems: A survey of the state-of-the-art and possible extensions. *IEEE Trans. on Knowl. and Data Engg.*, 17(6):734–749, 2005.

[2] K.-Y. Chiang, J. J. Whang, and I. S. Dhillon. Scalable clustering of signed networks using balance normalized cut. In *CIKM'12*, pages 615–624, 2012.

[3] E. P. Douglas. *Clustering datasets with singular value decomposition*. PhD thesis, College of Charleston, 2009.

[4] T. DuBois, J. Golbeck, J. Kleint, and A. Srinivasan. Improving recommendation accuracy by clustering social networks with trust. In *RecSys workshop on Recommender Systems and the Social Web*, volume 532, 2009.

[5] J. Leskovec and C. Faloutsos. Sampling from large graphs. In *SIGKDD'06*, pages 631–636, 2006.

[6] Y.-M. Li, C.-T. Wu, and C.-Y. Lai. A social recommender mechanism for e-commerce: Combining similarity, trust, and relationship. *Decision Support Systems*, 55(3):740–752, 2013.

[7] P. Massa and P. Avesani. Trust-aware recommender systems. In *RecSys'09*, pages 17–24, 2007.

[8] M. C. Pham, Y. Cao, R. Klamma, and M. Jarke. A clustering approach for collaborative filtering recommendation using social network analysis. *J. UCS*, 17(4):583–604, 2011.

[9] G. Pitsilis, X. Zhang, and W. Wang. Clustering recommenders in collaborative filtering using explicit trust information. In *Trust Management V*, pages 82–97. Springer, 2011.

[10] P. Resnick, N. Iacovou, M. Suchak, P. Bergstrom, and J. Riedl. Grouplens: an open architecture for collaborative filtering of netnews. In *CSCW'94*, pages 175–186. ACM, 1994.

[11] L. H. Ungar and D. P. Foster. Clustering methods for collaborative filtering. In *AAAI Workshop on Recommendation Systems*, volume 1, 1998.

[12] B. Yang, W. K. Cheung, and J. Liu. Community mining from signed social networks. *IEEE Trans. on Knowl. and Data Engg.*, 19(10):1333–1348, 2007.

Nonlinear Classification via Linear SVMs and Multi-Task Learning

Xue Mao, Ou Wu, Weiming Hu
NLPR, Institute of Automation
Chinese Academy of Sciences, China
{xue.mao, wuou, wmhu}@nlpr.ia.ac.cn

Peter O'Donovan
Department of Computer Science
University of Toronto, Canada
odonovan@dgp.toronto.edu

ABSTRACT

Kernel SVM is prohibitively expensive when dealing with large nonlinear data. While ensembles of linear classifiers have been proposed to address this inefficiency, these methods are time-consuming or lack robustness. We propose an efficient classifier for nonlinear data using a new iterative learning algorithm, which partitions the data into clusters, and then trains a linear SVM for each cluster. These two steps are combined into a graphical model, with the parameters estimated efficiently using the EM algorithm. During training, clustered multi-task learning is used to capture the relatedness among the multiple linear SVMs and avoid overfitting. Experimental results on benchmark datasets show that our method outperforms state-of-the-art methods. During prediction, it also obtains comparable classification performance to kernel SVM, with much higher efficiency.

Categories and Subject Descriptors

G.3 [**Probability and Statistics**]: Statistical computing; I.2.6 [**Artificial Intelligence**]: Learning

General Terms

Algorithms, Performance, Experimentation

Keywords

Nonlinear Classification; Linear SVMs; Multi-Task Learning

1. INTRODUCTION

Kernel SVM often produces satisfactory classification results on nonlinear data. Unfortunately, the complexity of kernel SVM relies on the number of support vectors. Alternatively, while linear SVM is extremely efficient, it performs poorly on nonlinear data. Ensembles of linear SVMs can improve performance, though these methods either lack robustness, such as CSVM [5] which aligns the linear SVM weight vectors with a global weight vector, or are time-consuming, such as SVM-KNN [8] which uses a lazy learning strategy.

CIKM'14, November 3–7, 2014, Shanghai, China.
Copyright 2014 ACM 978-1-4503-2598-1/14/11 ...$15.00.
http://dx.doi.org/10.1145/2661829.2662068.

In this paper, an efficient classifier for nonlinear data is constructed by using Linear SVMs and Multi-Task Learning (LSVM-MTL). The method uses a divide-and-conquer strategy which partitions the data into clusters using a Gaussian mixture model (GMM), and then trains a linear SVM for each cluster. Instead of being treated independently, the two steps are combined into a generative model and alternatively performed in each iteration. To ensure the data points in each cluster are linearly separable, some clusters may have relatively few points, and can overfit. In this work, we consider training a linear SVM for a cluster as a single task, and the training of the classifier ensemble as a multi-task learning problem. Clustered multi-task learning is used to exploit the relatedness between tasks, and avoid overfitting. To our knowledge, multi-task learning has not previously been used to train multiple linear SVMs on nonlinear datasets. Experimental results on benchmark datasets demonstrate that the model outperforms state-of-the-art methods. For prediction, LSVM-MTL achieves much higher efficiency than kernel SVM, with comparable classification performance.

2. RELATED WORK

Methods for learning multiple linear SVMs for nonlinear data can be roughly divided into two categories. In lazy learning methods, such as SVM-KNN [8], the learning process is postponed until the testing phase, which is therefore expensive. By contrast, eager learning methods construct local classifiers during the training phase, usually employing a divide-and-conquer strategy. MLSVM [4] and CSVM [5] fall into this category. Other eager learning methods, such as LLSVM [6], use local coordinate coding. These methods either lack robustness, such as CSVM, or are time-consuming, such as SVM-KNN, MLSVM and LLSVM.

Multi-task learning (MTL) is a method where multiple related tasks are learned simultaneously to improve generalization [9]. It has been used in various areas, such as web mining [7].

3. LSVM-MTL MODEL

3.1 Model Formulation

At a high level, LSVM-MTL is an iterative divide-and-conquer approach which alternates between two steps: partitioning the data into clusters with a GMM and training a linear SVM in each cluster. Instead of being independent, the two steps promote each other: GMM clustering improves the SVM classification performance for each cluster, and vice versa. This idea is integrated into our LSVM-MTL model

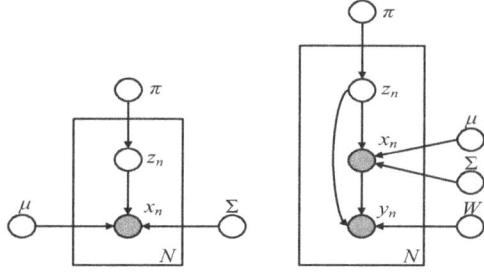

Figure 1: (a) GMM   (b) LSVM-MTL

as shown in Figure 1(b). The upper part of the model corresponds to the GMM in Figure 1(a), which is responsible for partitioning the data into clusters. The lower part of the model trains linear SVMs for each cluster.

We introduce the following notation: in Figure 1(b), there are N i.i.d. samples $X = \{x_n\}_{n=1,\cdots,N}$ and their corresponding labels $Y = \{y_n\}_{n=1,\cdots,N}$. The latent variables $Z = \{z_n\}_{n=1,\cdots,N}$ denote the assignments of samples to the K mixtures. The parameters $\mu = \{\mu_j\}_{j=1,\cdots,K}$ and $\Sigma = \{\Sigma_j\}_{j=1,\cdots,K}$ denote the centroids and covariance matrixes of Gaussian components respectively. $W = \{w_j\}_{j=1,\cdots,K}$ represents the weight vectors of the linear SVMs for the K clusters. $\pi = \{\pi_j\}_{j=1,\cdots,K}$ are the mixing coefficients of the GMM. Let $\Theta = \{\pi, \mu, \Sigma, W\}$ be the total set of model parameters. The joint distribution over X and Y is:

$$
\begin{aligned}
P(X, Y|\Theta) &= \prod_{n=1}^{N} P(x_n, y_n|\Theta) \\
&= \prod_{n=1}^{N} \sum_{z_n=1}^{K} \pi_{z_n} P(x_n|z_n, \mu, \Sigma) P(y_n|x_n, z_n, W) \\
&= \prod_{n=1}^{N} \sum_{j=1}^{K} \pi_j \mathcal{N}(x_n|z_n = j, \mu_j, \Sigma_j) P(y_n|x_n, w_j) \quad (1)
\end{aligned}
$$

which is obtained by summing the joint distribution of observed variables X, Y and latent variables Z over all possible states of Z, with z_n taking values in $\{1, \cdots, K\}$. The mixing coefficient π_j is the prior probability of picking the jth Gaussian component. $P(x_n|z_n = j, \mu, \Sigma) = \mathcal{N}(x_n|z_n = j, \mu_j, \Sigma_j)$ is a Gaussian component of the mixture, specifying the probability of x_n conditioned on the jth component. $P(y_n|x_n, w_j)$ is the posterior probability of the nth sample output by the jth linear SVM. We estimate the parameters by maximum likelihood. The regularized log-likelihood is:

$$
\begin{aligned}
\mathcal{L}(\Theta) &= \sum_{n=1}^{N} \log P(x_n, y_n|\Theta) + \Omega(W) \\
&= \sum_{n=1}^{N} \log \sum_{j=1}^{K} \pi_j \mathcal{N}(x_n|z_n = j, \mu_j, \Sigma_j) P(y_n|x_n, w_j) + \Omega(W) \quad (2)
\end{aligned}
$$

where $\Omega(W)$ is a regularization term on the linear SVM weight vectors. This term encodes prior knowledge about the K classifiers, and is defined shortly.

Unlike previous work, our model learns the multiple linear classifiers simultaneously rather than independently. More specifically, if training a linear SVM in a cluster is regarded as a task, training linear SVMs for all clusters corresponds to a multi-task learning problem. To ensure that the samples in each cluster are linearly separable, the samples available for each cluster may be limited, possibly leading to over-fitting. More importantly, since all the clusters are partitioned from the same dataset, they should be latently related. Multi-task learning can be employed to capture the intrinsic relatedness between tasks and avoid over-fitting in each task.

We use clustered multi-task learning [9], which clusters tasks into groups, with tasks in each group having similar weight vectors. This approach is motivated by the desire for the decision boundary to be smooth and have constrained curvature, since a decision boundary with arbitrary curvature will likely overfit the data [6]. Hence, tasks in adjacent regions on the decision boundary should have similar weight vectors and should be clustered into one group. We illustrate this issue with a synthetic dataset in the experimental section. In practice, we find this clustering is beneficial for using multiple linear SVMs to nonlinear datasets. Note that LSVM-MTL clusters based on task similarities and the cluster structure is unknown beforehand. Furthermore, note that this clustering of SVM weight vectors is distinct from the GMM data clustering described previously.

In order to incorporate multi-task learning and linear SVMs into the above maximum likelihood estimation framework (2), we recall that training a linear SVM usually leads to the following quadratic optimization problem:

$$
\min_w \frac{\|w\|^2}{2} + C \sum_n \ell(w; x_n, y_n) \quad (3)
$$

where the first term regularizes the SVM weight vector, and the second term measures the total loss. We next describe correspondence between minimization problem in (3) and maximization problem of the log-likelihood function in (2). The first term in (3) corresponds to the second term in (2), since they both regularize the weight vector. Finally, to incorporate multi-task learning, $\Omega(W)$ is formulated as:

$$
\Omega(W) = -\alpha \sum_{c=1}^{r} \sum_{j \in \mathcal{I}_c} \|w_j - \bar{w}_c\|_2^2 - \beta \sum_{j=1}^{K} \|w_j\|_2^2 \quad (4)
$$

where the first term on the right-hand side assumes that the total K tasks are clustered into r clusters, with the index set of the cth cluster defined as $\mathcal{I}_c = \{j | j \in \text{cluster } c\}$. The average weight vector of the cth cluster is $\bar{w}_c = \frac{1}{m_c} \sum_{j \in \mathcal{I}_c} w_j$, where there are m_c tasks in the cth cluster. The first term measures the within-cluster variance, which requires tasks from the same cluster to have similar weight vectors. The second term improves the generalization performance.

We next establish the relationship between the first term in (2) and the second term in (3) by defining:

$$
P(y_n|x_n, w_j) = \exp(-\ell(w_j; x_n, y_n)) \quad (5)
$$

The posterior probability $P(y_n|x_n, w_j)$ will be equal to 1 if the loss $\ell(w_j; x_n, y_n)$ is zero, otherwise $P(y_n|x_n, w_j)$ will be less than 1. To facilitate computation, $P(y_n|x_n, w_j)$ is not normalized. When we employ the EM algorithm to maximize (2) in the following section, the value of the log-likelihood function will increase in each iteration, regardless of whether $P(y_n|x_n, w_j)$ is a proper probability measure.

3.2 The EM Algorithm and Implementation

We now apply the EM algorithm to the above LSVM-MTL model. Let $\Theta^{(t)} = \{\pi_j^{(t)}, \mu_j^{(t)}, \Sigma_j^{(t)}, w_j^{(t)} | j = 1, \cdots, K\}$ denote the collection of parameters at the tth iteration.

In each E step, the posterior probability of assigning the nth sample to the jth linear SVM is evaluated as:

$$
q_{n,j}^{(t)} = \frac{\pi_j^{(t)} \mathcal{N}(x_n|z_n = j, \mu_j^{(t)}, \Sigma_j^{(t)}) P(y_n|x_n, w_j^{(t)})}{\sum_{j=1}^{K} \pi_j^{(t)} \mathcal{N}(x_n|z_n = j, \mu_j^{(t)}, \Sigma_j^{(t)}) P(y_n|x_n, w_j^{(t)})} \quad (6)
$$

Algorithm 1 LSVM-MTL

Input: Training data $\{(x_n, y_n)|n = 1, \cdots, N\} \subset \mathbb{R}^d \times \{-1, 1\}$ and the number of clusters K

Output: Parameter $\Theta = \{\pi_j, \mu_j, \Sigma_j, w_j | j = 1, \cdots, K\}$

Initialise Θ by K-means.

   repeat

      E step: Evaluate $q_{n,j}$ using Equation (6).

      M step: Re-estimate the GMM-related parameters π_j, μ_j and Σ_j by following the steps in [2].

         Re-estimate w_j for all j simultaneously as a multi-task learning problem using Equation (8).

   until convergence

This posterior probability is then utilized to derive the following lower bound on the log-likelihood function:

$$Q(\Theta^{(t+1)}; \Theta^{(t)}) = \sum_{n=1}^{N} \sum_{j=1}^{K} q_{n,j}^{(t)} \log \left[\pi_j^{(t+1)} \cdot \right.$$
$$\left. \mathcal{N}(x_n|z_n = j, \mu_j^{(t+1)}, \Sigma_j^{(t+1)}) P(y_n|x_n, w_j^{(t+1)}) \right] + \Omega(W^{(t+1)}) \quad (7)$$

where $\Omega(W^{(t+1)})$ is the regularization term given by (4). $\Theta^{(t)}$ is the parameter for the current iteration, which directly determines the posterior probability $q_{n,j}^{(t)}$ on the right-hand side through Equation (6).

In the M step, the parameter is updated to $\Theta^{(t+1)}$ by maximizing (7). Fortunately, updating the parameters of the GMM and the linear SVMs is decoupled in (7). For updating the GMM-related parameters $\{\pi, \mu, \Sigma\}$, we follow the steps in [2]. To update the weight vectors W of the linear SVMs, we solve the following optimization problem:

$$\max_W \sum_{n=1}^{N} \sum_{j=1}^{K} q_{n,j}^{(t)} \log P(y_n|x_n, w_j^{(t+1)})$$
$$- \alpha \sum_{c=1}^{r} \sum_{j \in \mathcal{I}_c} \|w_j^{(t+1)} - \bar{w}_c^{(t+1)}\|_2^2 - \beta \sum_{j=1}^{K} \|w_j^{(t+1)}\|_2^2 \quad (8)$$

where $\log P(y_n|x_n, w_j^{(t+1)}) = -\ell(w_j^{(t+1)}; x_n, y_n)$ using Equation (5). With the first term regarded as a weighted loss function, Equation (8) is equivalent to the clustered multi-task learning and is solved by the method of [9].

A sketch of our algorithm is presented in Algorithm 1. K-means is utilized to initialize the mixing coefficients π, centroids μ and covariance matrixes Σ. A linear SVM is then trained for each cluster, resulting in the initial weight vectors W. With the log-likelihood function in Equation (2) being increased in each iteration of EM, our algorithm is guaranteed to converge.

During testing, a new sample x is classified by the weighted average of the linear classifiers:

$$\sum_{j=1}^{K} \pi_j \mathcal{N}(x|z = j, \mu_j, \Sigma_j) \left(P(1|x, w_j) - P(-1|x, w_j) \right) \quad (9)$$

The sample is classified as positive if the weighted average is greater than 0, and negative otherwise. Obviously, the prediction complexity is linear in the number of tasks K. Prediction efficiency is particularly critical for large-scale or online applications.

4. EXPERIMENTS

4.1 Synthetic Dataset

The synthetic dataset in Figure 2 consists of two shifted sine signals, with 1000 points each, and each signal considered a separate class. K-means is used to partition the data into five clusters, denoted with different colors. Linear SVM is then applied to each cluster. This simple baseline is denoted as K-means+SVM, and is also the initial stage of LSVM-MTL. Figure 2(a) shows that the linear SVM does not accurately classify the data points in each cluster. Applying CSVM [5] gives similar results. The lack of improvement for CSVM here is because the method is not iterative, so its performance is directly determined by the initial K-means clustering. Additionally, CSVM aligns each SVM weight vector with a global weight vector, which is inappropriate here. In contrast to CSVM, LSVM-MTL is iterative; Figure 2(b) shows the result at the fifth iteration. The linear SVMs correctly classify the data in each cluster, which empirically shows that the two steps in LSVM-MTL mutually reinforce each other. When the number of clusters (tasks) is increased to ten, Figure 2(c) illustrates that the ten tasks are clustered into five groups, with each group containing two tasks in adjacent regions. This result occurs because the decision boundary is smooth and tasks in adjacent regions on the decision boundary are similar. Note that the decision boundaries in Figure 2(c) correctly classify all the data points, since each linear SVM is only applied to its corresponding cluster.

4.2 Real Datasets

We use six benchmark datasets: IJCNN1, SVMGUIDE1, SKIN segmentation, LETTER recognition, Pendigits and Landsat Satellite. The first two are available at the LibSVM website [3], and the others are taken from the UCI machine learning repository [1].

We compare LSVM-MTL with seven previously-mentioned methods: Linear SVM, Kernel SVM, SVM-KNN, K-means+SVM, MLSVM, LLSVM, and CSVM. The parameters of all the methods are set as in [5], with most parameters set by cross validation. For methods using K-means clustering, we calculate the average accuracy and the standard deviation on the test set over 10 random repetitions. The results are presented in Table 1. Here, we set the number of clusters K to 14 for K-means+SVM, CSVM and LSVM-MTL. As expected, linear and kernel SVM achieve the worst and best performance, respectively, over all datasets. Nevertheless, kernel SVM can be prohibitively expensive for large-scale datasets. Our proposed LSVM-MTL achieves not only comparable performance to kernel SVM, but also much higher efficiency for prediction. The reason is that the prediction complexity of LSVM-MTL is linear in the number of tasks K, while the complexity of kernel SVM scales with the number of support vectors. For example, with $K = 14$, the prediction time of LSVM-MTL on the IJCNN1 dataset is 0.62 seconds, whereas the time of kernel SVM is 34.71 seconds, with 7924 support vectors learned. Even though SVM-KNN and LLSVM also perform well in most cases, they are slow due to the nature of lazy learning and local coordinate coding respectively. LLSVM is sometimes slower than kernel SVM [5]. The relatively poor performance of K-means+SVM is likely due to its ignorance of the relatedness

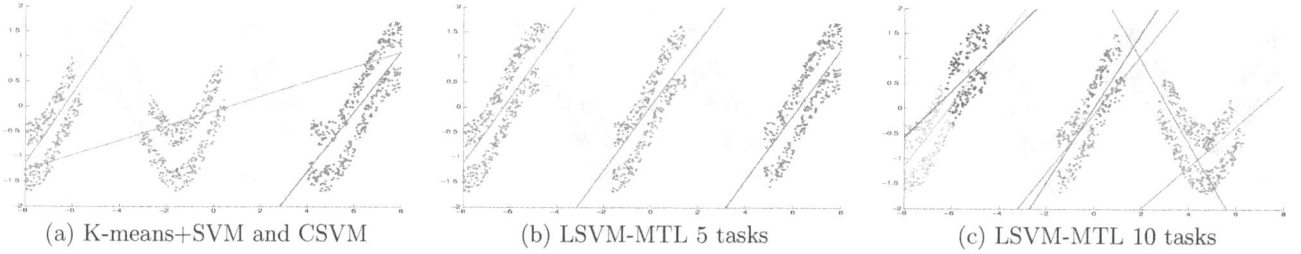

(a) K-means+SVM and CSVM   (b) LSVM-MTL 5 tasks   (c) LSVM-MTL 10 tasks

Figure 2: Learned classifiers on the synthetic sine dataset

Table 1: Comparison of different classifiers in terms of classification accuracy (%)

Datasets	IJCNN1	SVMGUIDE1	SKIN	LETTER	Pendigits	Landsat Satellite
Linear SVM	91.01	79.13	97.43	84.60	80.84	86.01
Kernel SVM	98.72	87.95	99.60	99.35	98.91	91.20
SVM-KNN	92.45	85.78	98.88	95.05	97.43	86.93
K-means+SVM	93.87±0.53	83.25±0.72	97.82±0.28	93.66±0.35	96.89±0.19	87.55±0.23
MLSVM	93.41±0.19	83.27±0.64	98.12±0.37	93.89±0.42	97.21±0.26	87.63±0.28
LLSVM	94.07±0.45	87.64±0.30	98.36±0.21	95.68±0.17	98.11±0.38	87.42±0.11
CSVM	95.41±0.34	86.32±0.47	98.72±0.15	94.37±0.26	97.14±0.18	88.98±0.21
LSVM-MTL	96.32±0.27	87.88±0.43	98.70±0.19	96.12±0.14	98.28±0.23	89.70±0.15

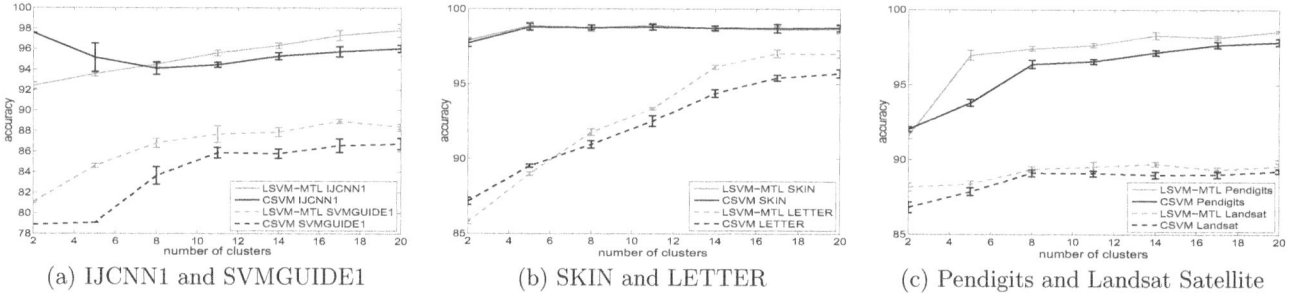

(a) IJCNN1 and SVMGUIDE1   (b) SKIN and LETTER   (c) Pendigits and Landsat Satellite

Figure 3: Classification accuracy of CSVM and LSVM-MTL with respect to the number of clusters K

among the multiple tasks. MLSVM only yields slightly better results than K-means+SVM, with increased complexity.

CSVM is state-of-the-art for this field, so we compare it with LSVM-MTL in detail. Figure 3 shows the classification accuracy of CSVM and LSVM-MTL with the number of clusters ranging from 2 to 20. LSVM-MTL outperforms CSVM on all the datasets except the SKIN dataset. However, the SKIN dataset is simple, so even linear SVM produces satisfactory results. The performance of LSVM-MTL generally improves with the number of clusters. Two factors may account for this improvement. First, when the number of clusters increases, the samples in each cluster become linearly separable, and the SVM can classify them well. Second, with more clusters (tasks), multi-task learning is better utilized to transfer knowledge between tasks and avoid overfitting. The performance of LSVM-MTL generally stabilizes as the number of clusters exceeds a certain threshold.

5. CONCLUSIONS

In this paper, we have proposed the LSVM-MTL model, which clusters the data with a GMM and trains a linear SVM for each cluster. These two steps are combined into a generative model and implemented with an EM algorithm. Furthermore, we consider the training of each linear SVM as a single task and use clustered multi-task learning to capture the relatedness between tasks. Experimental results on benchmark datasets demonstrate that LSVM-MTL outperforms state-of-the-art methods. In the prediction phase, it also achieves much higher efficiency than kernel SVM with comparable classification performance.

6. ACKNOWLEDGMENTS

This work is partly supported by NSFC (Grant No. 61379098, 61003115, 61103056) and Baidu research fund.

7. REFERENCES

[1] K. Bache and M. Lichman. UCI machine learning repository, 2013.

[2] C. M. Bishop. *Pattern Recognition and Machine Learning*. Springer, 2006.

[3] C.-C. Chang and C.-J. Lin. LIBSVM: a library for support vector machines. *ACM TIST*, 2(3):27, 2011.

[4] Z. Fu, A. Robles-Kelly, and J. Zhou. Mixing linear SVMs for nonlinear classification. *IEEE TNN*, 21(12):1963–1975, 2010.

[5] Q. Gu and J. Han. Clustered support vector machines. In *Proc. of AISTATS*, pages 307–315, 2013.

[6] L. Ladicky and P. Torr. Locally linear support vector machines. In *Proc. of ICML*, pages 985–992, 2011.

[7] O. Wu, R. Hu, X. Mao, and W. Hu. Quality-based learning for web data classification. In *Proc. of AAAI*, pages 194–200, 2014.

[8] H. Zhang, A. C. Berg, M. Maire, and J. Malik. SVM-KNN: Discriminative nearest neighbor classification for visual category recognition. In *Proc. of CVPR*, pages 2126–2136, 2006.

[9] J. Zhou, J. Chen, and J. Ye. Clustered multi-task learning via alternating structure optimization. In *Proc. of NIPS*, pages 702–710, 2011.

Dynamic Clustering of Contextual Multi-Armed Bandits

Trong T. Nguyen
School of Information Systems
Singapore Management University
ttnguyen.2014@smu.edu.sg

Hady W. Lauw
School of Information Systems
Singapore Management University
hadywlauw@smu.edu.sg

ABSTRACT

With the prevalence of the Web and social media, users increasingly express their preferences online. In learning these preferences, recommender systems need to balance the trade-off between *exploitation*, by providing users with more of the "same", and *exploration*, by providing users with something "new" so as to expand the systems' knowledge. Multi-armed bandit (MAB) is a framework to balance this trade-off. Most of the previous work in MAB either models a single bandit for the whole population, or one bandit for each user. We propose an algorithm to divide the population of users into multiple clusters, and to customize the bandits to each cluster. This clustering is dynamic, i.e., users can switch from one cluster to another, as their preferences change. We evaluate the proposed algorithm on two real-life datasets.

Categories and Subject Descriptors

H.4 [**Information Systems Applications**]: Miscellaneous; H.2.8 [**Database Applications**]: Data Mining

Keywords

multi-armed bandit; clustering; exploitation and exploration

1. INTRODUCTION

With the rapid growth of the Web and the social media, users have to navigate a huge number of options in their daily lives. To help users in making these choices, content providers rely on recommender systems [1, 10] that learn user preferences based on their historical activities. In a rapidly changing environment [2], where new items appear all the time, relying on historical data alone (*exploitation*) may not work as well. Instead, what is needed is another paradigm that can continually explore the space of user preferences (*exploration*) as new items appear, or as users change their preferences. The exploitation vs. exploration trade-off refers to balancing the short term interest of making the next recommendation as accurate as possible, with the long

term interest in learning about the users as much as possible (perhaps at the cost of lower accuracy in the short term).

One such paradigm is the multi-armed bandit [14]. A bandit (a recommender system) has multiple arms (items to recommend). Pulling an arm (recommending an item) generates some amount of reward (such as user liking the recommendation). This reward is not known in advance. Because the bandit has multiple chances, the main objective is to maximize the accumulated rewards (or to minimize the regret of not pulling the best arms) over time. For this, the bandit should not just pull the arms that produce the highest rewards in the past, but also explore other arms that could potentially generate even higher rewards in the future.

Multi-armed bandits have been shown to work well in various Web recommendation scenarios, such as advertisements [2], news articles [11], and comments [12]. In many cases, it is advantageous to contextualize the bandit, such that the reward of an arm also depends on the "context" of a recommendation, e.g., the content of a Web page (see Section 4).

In this paper, we study the research question of whether there is an appropriate number of bandits to serve a population of users. Most current approaches fall into two extremes. One option is to build a single bandit for all users, which has the advantage of scale, in learning from the observed rewards of many users. However, a global recommendation may not be appropriate for all users. Another option is to personalize it completely, by building one bandit for every user, which is fully customized to every individual, but may suffer from the sparsity of learning instances.

To address the above disadvantages of the two extremes, we advocate a *dynamic clustering* approach. In this approach, the population of users are partitioned into K clusters. The bandits of individual users in the same cluster can "collaborate" in estimating the expected reward of an arm for any one user in the same cluster. That way, we can keep a bandit customized to an individual user, and yet allow users to benefit from the collective set of learning instances in their cluster. Moreover, as a user changes preferences, or as we learn the user's preference better, the user may switch from one cluster to another more "suitable" cluster.

Contributions. *First*, we propose a clustering-based contextual bandit algorithm called DYNUCB in Section 2, building on the contextual bandit LinUCB [11]. Its novelty arises from dynamic clustering, which we relate to existing work in Section 4. *Second*, in Section 3, we verify the efficacy of this approach through experiments on two real-life datasets, studying the appropriate number of clusters for each dataset, and comparing against the baselines.

2. DYNAMIC CLUSTERING OF BANDITS

We first review the framework of contextual bandit, before introducing our proposed algorithm, which we call DynUCB.

Contextual Bandit. A contextual bandit algorithm proceeds in discrete iterations. At any iteration t, the bandit observes a particular user u_t. There are also a set of available arms $\mathcal{A}_t$ that the bandit may choose to pull for this user. For each arm $a \in \mathcal{A}_t$, the bandit observes its context, in the form of a d-dimensional feature vector $\mathbf{x}_{t,a} \in \mathbb{R}^d$. Based on the reward experience in previous iterations, the bandit may choose to pull an arm a_t. Upon pulling a_t, the bandit observes a reward r_{t,a_t}. There is no reward observation for $a \neq a_t$. The bandit therefore needs to learn from the observations of $\langle \mathbf{x}_{t,a_t}, a_t, r_{t,a_t} \rangle$ for ongoing iterations t's to improve its strategy for choosing arms in future iterations.

After T iterations, the bandit would observe a cumulative reward of $\sum_{t=1}^{T} r_{t,a_t}$. The objective is to design an intelligent way to choose arms so as to maximize this cumulative reward over time. Equivalently, we can express the objective in terms of minimizing total regret, where regret is defined as the difference between the observed reward r_{t,a_t} and the reward of the "optimal" arm in each iteration.

A popular framework for contextual bandit is LinUCB [11], which estimates the expected reward of each arm a as a linear regression on the context vector $\mathbf{w}^{\mathrm{T}} \mathbf{x}_{t,a}$, where $\mathbf{w} \in \mathbb{R}^d$ is the regression coefficient to be learned. However, maximizing the expected reward alone may result in a long term regret from not discovering a better arm through exploration. Therefore, it also considers the confidence bound $\alpha \sqrt{\mathbf{x}_{t,a}^{\mathrm{T}} \mathbf{M}^{-1} \mathbf{x}_{t,a}}$. Here, α is a parameter for the importance of exploration. It is expressed as $\alpha = 1 + \sqrt{\ln(2/\delta)/2}$, where $1 - \delta$ is the confidence interval. We set $\delta = 0.05$ for 0.95 confidence interval. $\mathbf{M}^{-1} \in \mathbb{R}^{d \times d}$ is the update weights, which can be interpreted as the covariance of the coefficient $\mathbf{w}$. The arm a_t selected is the one maximizing the upper confidence bound: $a_t = \arg\max_{a \in \mathcal{A}_t} \left(\mathbf{w}^{\mathrm{T}} \mathbf{x}_{t,a} + \alpha \sqrt{\mathbf{x}_{t,a}^{\mathrm{T}} \mathbf{M}^{-1} \mathbf{x}_{t,a}} \right)$.

Clustering of Contextual Bandits. To build a recommender system that serves N users, one option is to build a SINgle instance of LinUCB for all users, which we call LinUCB-SIN. Another option is to train a bandit for every INDividual user, which we call LinUCB-IND. The former benefits more from the wealth of training instances, while the latter benefits from a more customized bandit. However, we hypothesize that a large population of users are neither as monolithic as in LinUCB-SIN, nor as heavily splintered as in LinUCB-IND. Rather, there may be several communities or clusters in the population, where users within the same cluster may share preferences. By grouping together like-minded users, we can benefit from having a larger number of training instances, while still customizing the bandits.

We therefore propose an algorithm, called DynUCB, as described in Algorithm 1. Since the appropriate number of clusters may vary in different domains and populations, the algorithm takes as its input the desired number of clusters K. Initially, we start out with K random clusters, denoted C_k for $k = 1, \ldots, K$, and refine the clustering over iterations.

In a way, DynUCB still maintains N bandits for N users. For each user u, its coefficient $\mathbf{w}_u$ is learned from its own bandit parameters $\mathbf{b}_u$ and $\mathbf{M}_u$ (initialized to $\mathbf{0}$ and identity matrix I respectively). However, unlike LinUCB-IND's N independent bandits, in DynUCB the bandits in the same

---

Algorithm 1: DynUCB

Input: The number of clusters K.
Output: At iteration t, recommended arm a_t for u_t.

Set $\mathbf{b}_u = \mathbf{0} \in \mathbb{R}^d$, $\mathbf{M}_u = I \in \mathbb{R}^{d \times d}$ for all users $u = 1, \ldots, N$.
Randomly assign users to K clusters $\{C_k\}_{k=1}^K$.
Compute the coefficient $\bar{\mathbf{w}}_k$ for each cluster C_k:
$$\bar{\mathbf{M}}_k = I + \sum_{u' \in C_k} (\mathbf{M}_{u'} - I)$$
$$\bar{\mathbf{b}}_k = \sum_{u' \in C_k} \mathbf{b}_{u'}$$
$$\bar{\mathbf{w}}_k = \bar{\mathbf{M}}_k^{-1} \bar{\mathbf{b}}_k$$
for *iteration* $t = 1, \ldots, T$ **do**
  Select a user u_t, and its current cluster $C_k \ni u_t$.
  Observe the contexts of arms $\{\mathbf{x}_{t,a}\}, \forall a \in \mathcal{A}_t$.
  Find the arm a_t with the highest UCB, i.e.,
  $a_t =$
  $\arg\max_{a \in \mathcal{A}_t} \left(\bar{\mathbf{w}}_k^{\mathrm{T}} \mathbf{x}_{t,a} + \alpha \sqrt{\mathbf{x}_{t,a}^{\mathrm{T}} \bar{\mathbf{M}}_k^{-1} \mathbf{x}_{t,a} \log(t+1)} \right)$
  Observe the reward r_{t,a_t} from recommending a_t.
  Let $\tilde{\mathbf{x}}_t = \mathbf{x}_{t,a_t}$.
  Update the user u_t's parameters:
    $\mathbf{M}_{u_t} = \mathbf{M}_{u_t} + \tilde{\mathbf{x}}_t \tilde{\mathbf{x}}_t^{\mathrm{T}}$
    $\mathbf{b}_{u_t} = \mathbf{b}_{u_t} + r_{t,a_t} \tilde{\mathbf{x}}_t$
    $\mathbf{w}_{u_t} = \mathbf{M}_{u_t}^{-1} \mathbf{b}_{u_t}$
  Re-assign the user u_t to the closest cluster $C_{k'}$:
    $k' = \arg\min_{k'=1,\ldots,K} \|\mathbf{w}_{u_t} - \bar{\mathbf{w}}_{k'}\|$
    If $k' \neq k$, move u_t from C_k to C'_k.
    Re-compute coefficients $\bar{\mathbf{w}}_k$ and $\bar{\mathbf{w}}_{k'}$ as above.

---

cluster C_k "collaborate" with one another. For instance, at iteration t, when generating a recommendation for $u_t \in C_k$, the estimation of expected reward for each arm $a \in \mathcal{A}_t$, i.e., $\left(\bar{\mathbf{w}}_k^{\mathrm{T}} \mathbf{x}_{t,a} + \alpha \sqrt{\mathbf{x}_{t,a}^{\mathrm{T}} \bar{\mathbf{M}}_k^{-1} \mathbf{x}_{t,a} \log(t+1)} \right)$, is based on cluster-level coefficient $\bar{\mathbf{w}}_k$, learned from cluster-level parameters $\bar{\mathbf{b}}_k$ and $\bar{\mathbf{M}}_k$ derived from the bandit parameters $\mathbf{b}_u$ and $\mathbf{M}_u$ of each user $u \in C_k$. The confidence bound is a simplified version of the theoretical confidence bound shown in [8].

Consequently, each user benefits from the reward experiences of other users in the same cluster. The observed reward r_{t,a_t} from recommending the arm a_t to u_t is then used to update u_t's own coefficient $\mathbf{w}_{u_t}$, which reflects u_t's reward experience over iterations. Due to the clustering hypothesis, u_t benefits more from belonging to the "right" cluster of like-minded users that complement one another. Therefore, at each iteration, we re-assign u_t to the cluster $C_{k'}$ whose coefficient $\bar{\mathbf{w}}_{k'}$ is closest to $\mathbf{w}_{u_t}$, a practice reminiscent of the K-means clustering algorithm but conducted within the contextual bandit framework. This dynamic re-assignment of clusters is a key feature of DynUCB, allowing it to be adaptive to changing contexts and user preferences over time.

3. EXPERIMENTS

The objective of experiments is to investigate the effectiveness of our proposed method DynUCB. First, we describe the two real-life datasets for experiments. Then, we investigate the effects of different number of clusters, before presenting a comparison against state-of-the-art baselines.

3.1 Experimental Setup

Datasets. We use two publicly-available[1] datasets that have previously been used for contextual bandits evaluation [6]. The first dataset is on the social bookmarking site **Deli-**

---

[1]http://grouplens.org/datasets/hetrec-2011

	Delicious	LastFM
No. of unique users	1867	1892
No. of unique tags	11619	9643
No. of unique items	69226	17632
No. of unique <user, item> pairs	104220	71064

Table 1: Dataset Sizes

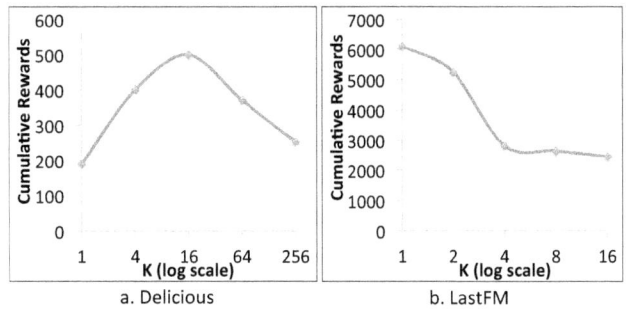

a. Delicious   b. LastFM

Figure 1: Vary Number of Clusters K

cious, where a set of users assign tags to a set of bookmarked URLs. The second dataset is on the online radio **LastFM**, where a set of users assign tags to a set of music artists. We follow similar processing steps as in [6]. The statistics for these datasets after processing are shown in Table 1.

The task of interest is to recommend a new item to a user, where an item refers to a bookmark URL for Delicious, and a music artist for LastFM. Importantly, for both datasets, the tags are used to generate the contexts for items, as follows. First, we treat each item as a "document" consisting of tags (and their frequencies) assigned by all users. Then, we compute a TFIDF vector for each item from the "document" representations. We further reduce this vector into a 25-dimensional context vector using PCA [9].

Metric. The prediction task is as follows. For every round t of the bandit algorithm, for the user u_t, we pick one of her items i randomly. We then present the context vector of the item i, together with 24 other randomly generated context vectors, to a bandit algorithm. If it makes the correct recommendation, i.e., it picks the item i out of the 25 options, the reward is 1. Otherwise, the reward is $-\frac{1}{24}$. Random guesses are expected to have a cumulative reward of 0. A better algorithm is expected to have a higher positive cumulative reward over iterations. We consider $T = 50000$ iterations, which is considered large. For all algorithms, we average the cumulative rewards across ten different runs.

3.2 Number of Clusters

Here, we study the relationship between the number of clusters in DynUCB with the cumulative rewards.

Delicious. First, we consider the case of Delicious. Figure 1(a) shows the cumulative rewards of DynUCB after 50000 iterations, for different number of clusters K's. As we increase K from 1 to 256, there is a trend whereby the rewards at first increase, reaching the peak at around $K = 16$, and then eventually begin to decrease. This trend helps to validate that the clustering hypothesis indeed applies to the Delicious dataset. We hypothesize that being a social bookmarking website, Delicious may support a number of user communities, e.g., technology, music, sports. By clustering the bandits, we can customize the bandits to cater to different communities, while still benefiting from the collection of training instances from users of that community. Having too few or too many clusters may be counter-productive, as we begin to clump unrelated users, or to split related users.

It is also interesting to look into the distribution of cluster sizes. For $K = 16$, we get one large cluster containing 58% of the users, and the other 15 small clusters are roughly even-sized, containing between 2% to 5% of the users. These numbers are based on one specific run, but we observe virtually similar distributions across all the runs. This suggests the presence of one main group, and several smaller communities that benefit from having more customized bandits.

LastFM. Figure 1(b) shows a very different picture for the LastFM dataset. It shows that cumulative reward of

DynUCB after 50000 iterations is highest for $K = 1$, and goes downhill for larger K's. This result is very revelatory, suggesting that there are populations, such as in LastFM, where most of the general users pretty much agree in their preferences. This potentially arises from the phenomenon where there are a few artists that practically everyone listens to, unlike social bookmarking (Delicious) where different users may have different bookmark preferences.

3.3 Comparison against Baselines

We now compare DynUCB (with the optimal number of clusters found in the previous section, i.e., $K = 16$ for Delicious, and $K = 1$ for LastFM) against baselines.

Baselines. Since we propose a dynamic clustering approach, we compare to two types of baselines. The first are the non-clustering baselines LinUCB-IND and LinUCB-SIN. The second is a clustering baseline CLUB [8], which is hierarchical and does not model dynamic movements between clusters (see Section 4). Because CLUB[2] assumes an input graph, we use a complete graph of users so as not to restrict the clustering that it could discover. We have also tried randomly-generated input graphs as described in [8], but find the results to be worse than a complete graph. We tune its parameter α_2 in the range 0 to 1, and use the best parameter at 5000 iterations ($\alpha_2 = 0.55$ for Delicious, $\alpha_2 = 0.9$ for LastFM) to obtain the rewards for 50000 iterations.

Delicious. For Delicious, Figure 2 shows the cumulative rewards over iterations up to $T = 50000$. Evidently, DynUCB at $K = 16$ has higher cumulative rewards than the baselines over the long run. In the short run (for $t < 20000$), LinUCB-SIN tends to have a higher cumulative reward, because it benefits from "faster" learning from the large number of training instances of all users. Since DynUCB partitions the users into different clusters, and begins with random clusters, it learns more slowly in the early stages as it figures out the clustering. In the long run, DynUCB more than catches up, benefiting from more customized bandits in each cluster. LinUCB-IND performs at a similar level, if slightly lower than LinUCB-SIN. Unexpectedly, the clustering baseline CLUB does not perform well. Upon further investigation, we observe that 90% of users belong to one cluster, while the other users are splintered into 6 clusters of 2 users each, and 175 independent users. It is unclear if this is an artefact of parameter tuning or the algorithm itself.

LastFM. Figure 3 shows the comparison for LastFM. As previously mentioned, LastFM is not conducive for cluster-

---

[2]We implement CLUB as there is no publicly available implementation at the point of writing.

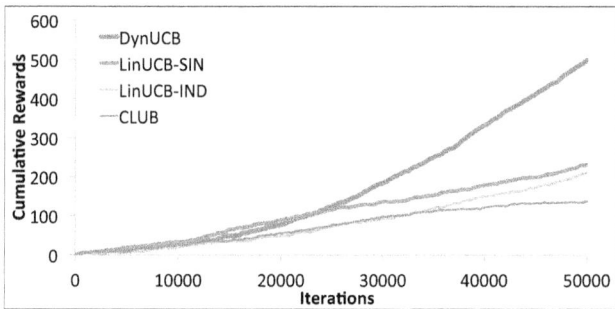

Figure 2: Delicious: Rewards over Iterations

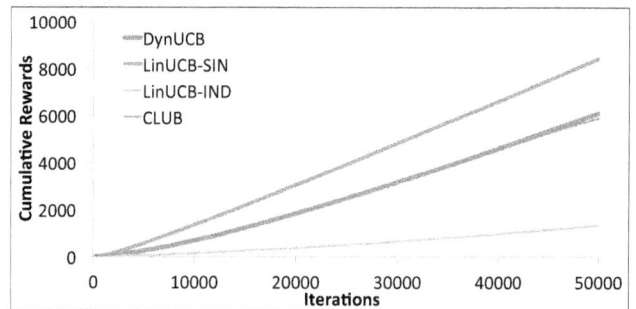

Figure 3: LastFM: Rewards over Iterations

ing, because of the bias for the most popular items. As expected, LinUCB-SIN has the highest reward, for the same reason why DYNUCB is optimal for $K = 1$. DYNUCB is second, followed by CLUB with a very similar performance. CLUB keeps virtually all the users (~96%) within a single cluster. LinUCB-IND is the worst, because of the lack of training instances for the independent bandits. Notably, even for a non-conducive dataset, DYNUCB does not degenerate completely (unlike LinUCB-IND), and still manages to get a reasonable performance. We interpret this as the need to fit the right algorithm for the right dataset, based on how well the underlying hypothesis holds for the dataset.

4. RELATED WORK

The principle behind bandits is to balance the trade-off between exploration and exploitation. For instance, ϵ-greedy [14] picks a random arm (exploration) with probability ϵ, and picks the arm with the highest expected reward (exploitation) with probability $(1 - \epsilon)$. Instead of a "random" exploration, the Upper Confidence Bound or UCB approach [3, 4] estimates not just the expected reward, but also the confidence interval, of every arm. It then picks the arm with the highest sum of reward and confidence interval, which is the upper confidence bound. Thompson Sampling [7] picks an arm that has the largest success probability.

Contextual bandits make bandit algorithms more adaptive to the changing "contexts". This context is usually expressed as a feature vector. Similar contexts would have correlated rewards. For instance, LinUCB [11], used as a foundation for our method, models the expected reward through a linear regression on context vectors. LogUCB [12] models it through logistic regression.

One related bandit clustering work is CLUB [8]. It models a cluster as a connected component in a graph of users. From the input graph, it slowly removes edges over iterations, splintering the graph into multiple clusters. CLUB and our method seek a partitioning of the user population. There are a couple of crucial differences between the two. Firstly, CLUB does hierarchical clustering, whereas we pursue a flat clustering. Secondly, and more importantly, our clustering is dynamic, allowing users to move between clusters, whereas CLUB only models the splintering of clusters, but not the movement of users across clusters. Other clustering works are based on standard bandits [13, 5]. Previously [11], contextual bandit (i.e., LinUCB) has been shown to outperform standard bandit (i.e., UCB). Social bandits [6] correlate bandits of different users based on a social network graph (which we do not consider).

5. CONCLUSION

We investigate the problem of dynamic clustering of contextual bandits, and propose an algorithm DYNUCB. In the case where the clustering hypothesis applies (Delicious), DYNUCB achieves a significant gain in rewards when compared to non-clustering bandit baselines. This result points to a promising direction of customizing bandits to specific segments of users who may have distinct preferences. As future work, we plan to investigate the clustering hypothesis further, to analysize the confidence bound the algorithm, and to consider extensions such as overlapping clusters.

Acknowledgments

This research is supported by the Singapore National Research Foundation under its International Research Centre @ Singapore Funding Initiative and administered by the IDM Programme Office, Media Development Authority (MDA).

6. REFERENCES

[1] G. Adomavicius and A. Tuzhilin. Toward the next generation of recommender systems: A survey of the state-of-the-art and possible extensions. *TKDE*, 2005.

[2] D. Agarwal, B.-C. Chen, and P. Elango. Explore/exploit schemes for web content optimization. In *ICDM*, 2009.

[3] P. Auer. Using confidence bounds for exploitation-exploration trade-offs. *JMLR*, 3, 2003.

[4] P. Auer, N. Cesa-Bianchi, and P. Fischer. Finite-time analysis of the multiarmed bandit problem. *Machine Learning*, 47(2-3), 2002.

[5] L. Bui, R. Johari, and S. Mannor. Clustered bandits. In *arXiv:1206.4169v1 [cs.LG]*, 2012.

[6] N. Cesa-Bianchi, C. Gentile, and G. Zappella. A gang of bandits. In *NIPS*, 2013.

[7] O. Chapelle and L. Li. An empirical evaluation of thompson sampling. In *NIPS*, 2011.

[8] C. Gentile, S. Li, and G. Zappella. Online clustering of bandits. In *ICML*, 2014.

[9] I. Jolliffe. *Principal component analysis*. Wiley Online Library, 2005.

[10] Y. Koren, R. Bell, and C. Volinsky. Matrix factorization techniques for recommender systems. *Computer*, 2009.

[11] L. Li, W. Chu, J. Langford, and R. E. Schapire. A contextual-bandit approach to personalized news article recommendation. In *WWW*, 2010.

[12] D. K. Mahajan, R. Rastogi, C. Tiwari, and A. Mitra. LogUCB: an explore-exploit algorithm for comments recommendation. In *CIKM*, 2012.

[13] O.-A. Maillard and S. Mannor. Latent bandits. In *ICML*, 2014.

[14] R. S. Sutton and A. G. Barto. *Introduction to Reinforcement Learning*. MIT Press, 1998.

Unsupervised Feature Selection for Multi-View Clustering on Text-Image Web News Data

Mingjie Qian
Department of Computer Science
University of Illinois at Urbana-Champaign
Urbana, IL, USA
mqian2@illinois.edu

Chengxiang Zhai
Department of Computer Science
University of Illinois at Urbana-Champaign
Urbana, IL, USA
czhai@illinois.edu

ABSTRACT

Unlabeled high-dimensional text-image web news data are produced every day, presenting new challenges to unsupervised feature selection on multi-view data. State-of-the-art multi-view unsupervised feature selection methods learn pseudo class labels by spectral analysis, which is sensitive to the choice of similarity metric for each view. For text-image data, the raw text itself contains more discriminative information than similarity graph which loses information during construction, and thus the text feature can be directly used for label learning, avoiding information loss as in spectral analysis. We propose a new multi-view unsupervised feature selection method in which image local learning regularized orthogonal nonnegative matrix factorization is used to learn pseudo labels and simultaneously robust joint $l_{2,1}$-norm minimization is performed to select discriminative features. Cross-view consensus on pseudo labels can be obtained as much as possible. We systematically evaluate the proposed method in multi-view text-image web news datasets. Our extensive experiments on web news datasets crawled from two major US media channels: CNN and FOXNews demonstrate the efficacy of the new method over state-of-the-art multi-view and single-view unsupervised feature selection methods.

Categories and Subject Descriptors

I.5.2 [**Pattern Recognition**]: Design Methodology—*Feature Evaluation and Selection*

Keywords

Multi-View Unsupervised Feature Selection

1. INTRODUCTION

Reading web news articles is an important part of people's daily life, especially in the current "big data" era that we are facing a large amount of information every day due to the advancement and development of information technology. One ideal way is to automatically group the web news per their content into multiple clusters, e.g., technology and health care, then one can choose to read the latest and the most representative news articles in a group of interest. This procedure can be done recursively so that one can explore the news in different resolution hierarchically. Clustering web news is also an effective way to organize, manage, and search news articles. Unlike traditional document clustering, images play an important role in web news articles as is evident from the fact that almost all news articles have one picture associated. How to effectively and efficiently group web news articles of multiple modality is challenging because different data types have different properties and different feature spaces and also because the dimensionality of feature spaces is usually very high. For example in text feature space, the vocabulary size can be over a million. Besides, there are a lot of unrelated and noisy features which often lead to low efficiency and poor performance.

Multi-view unsupervised feature selection is desirable to solve the problem mentioned above, since it can select most discriminative features while considering the consensus from data of multiple views in an unsupervised fashion. Feature size can be extremely reduced and feature quality can be greatly enhanced. As a result, not only computation can be more efficient but clustering performance can also be greatly improved. However, not much work have been done to be able to solve this problem well, especially for multi-view clustering on web news data. State-of-the-art unsupervised feature selection methods [2, 13] for multi-view data use spectral clustering across different views to learn the most consistent pseudo class labels and simultaneously use the learned labels to do feature selection. More specifically, Adaptive Unsupervised Multi-view Feature Selection (AUMFS) [2] uses spectral clustering on a combined data similarity graph from different views to learn the labels that have most consensus across different views, and then use $l_{2,1}$-norm regularized robust sparse regression to learn one weight matrix for all the features of different views to best approximate the cluster labels. [13] presents a new unsupervised multi-view feature selection method called Multi-View Feature Selection (MVFS). MVFS also uses spectral clustering on the combined data similarity graph from different views to learn the labels, but learn one weight matrix for each view to best fit the learned pseudo class labels by joint squared Frobenius norm (fitting term) and $l_{2,1}$-norm (rowise sparsity-inducing). Both [2] and [13] share the disadvantage that they're sensitive to the combined data similarity graph, especially when there are quite a number of unrelated and noisy features in the feature space, and there is information loss during graph construction.

We propose to directly utilize raw features in the main view (e.g., text for text-image web news data) to learn pseudo cluster labels which should also have the most consensus with other views (e.g., image), and meanwhile the discriminative features in the feature selection process will win out to contribute more on label learning process, and in return the improved cluster labels will help to select more discriminative features for each view. Technically, we propose a new method called Multi-View Unsupervised Feature Selection (MVUFS) to do unsupervised feature selection for multi-view clustering, especially focused on analyzing text-image web news data. We propose to minimize the sum of regularized data matrix factorization error and data fitting error in a unified optimization setting. We use local learning regularized orthogonal nonnegative matrix factorization to learn pseudo cluster labels and simultaneously learn rowise sparse weight matrices for each view by joint $l_{2,1}$-norm minimization guided by the learned pseudo cluster labels. The label learning process and feature selection process are mutually enhanced. For label learning, we factorize the data matrix in the main view (e.g. text) and ensure that the learned indicator matrix is as consistent as local learning predictors on other views (e.g. image). To objectively evaluate the new method, we build two text-image web news datasets from two major US news media web sites: CNN and FOXNews. Our extensive experiments show that MVUFS significantly outperforms state-of-the-art single-view and multi-view unsupervised feature selection methods.

2. NOTATIONS AND PRELIMINARIES

Throughout this paper, matrices are written as boldface capital letters and vectors are denoted as boldface lowercase letters. For matrix $\mathbf{M} = (m_{ij})$, its i-th row, j-th column are denoted by $\mathbf{m}^i, \mathbf{m}_j$ respectively. $\|\mathbf{M}\|_F$ is the Frobenius norm of $\mathbf{M}$. For any matrix $\mathbf{M} \in \mathcal{R}^{r \times t}$, its $l_{2,1}$-norm is defined as $\|\mathbf{M}\|_{2,1} = \sum_{i=1}^r \sqrt{\sum_{j=1}^p m_{ij}^2} = \sum_{i=1}^r \|\mathbf{m}^i\|_2$. Assume that we have n instances $\mathcal{X} = \{\mathbf{x}_i\}_{i=1}^n$. Let $\mathbf{X}_v \in \mathcal{R}^{n \times d_v}$ denote the data matrix in the v-th view where the i-th row $\mathbf{x}_v^i \in \mathcal{R}^{d_v}$ is the feature descriptor of the i-th instance in the v-th view. For text-image web news data, $\mathbf{X}_1$ is text view data matrix, and $\mathbf{X}_2$ is image view data matrix. Suppose these n instances are sampled from c classes and denote $\mathbf{Y} = [\mathbf{y}_1, \cdots, \mathbf{y}_n]^T \in \{0,1\}^{n \times c}$, where $\mathbf{y}_i \in \{0,1\}^{c \times 1}$ is the cluster indicator vector for $\mathbf{x}_i$. The scaled cluster indicator matrix $\mathbf{G}$ is defined as $\mathbf{G} = [\mathbf{g}_1, \cdots, \mathbf{g}_n]^T = \mathbf{Y}(\mathbf{Y}^T\mathbf{Y})^{-\frac{1}{2}}$, where $\mathbf{g}_i$ is the scaled cluster indicator of $\mathbf{x}_i$. It can be seen that $\mathbf{G}^T\mathbf{G} = \mathbf{I}_c$, where $\mathbf{I}_c \in \mathcal{R}^{c \times c}$ is an identity matrix.

2.1 Local learning regularization

It is often easier to produce good predictions on some local regions of the input space instead of searching a good global predictor f, because the function set $f(\mathbf{x})$ may not contain a good predictor for the entire input space. And it is usually more effective to minimize prediction cost for each local region. We adopt the local learning regularization proposed in [3]. Let $\mathcal{N}(\mathbf{x}_i)$ denote the neighborhood of $\mathbf{x}_i$, the local learning regularization aims to minimize the sum of prediction errors between the local prediction from $\mathcal{N}(\mathbf{x}_i)$

and the cluster assignment of $\mathbf{x}_i$:

$$
\begin{aligned}
&\sum_{k=1}^K \sum_{i=1}^n \left\| f_i^k(\mathbf{x}_i) - g_{ik} \right\| \\
&= \sum_{k=1}^K \sum_{i=1}^n \left\| \mathbf{k}_i^T(\mathbf{K}_i + n_i\lambda\mathbf{I})^{-1}\mathbf{g}_i^k - g_{ik} \right\| \\
&= \sum_{k=1}^K \sum_{i=1}^n \left\| \alpha_i^T\mathbf{g}_i^k - g_{ik} \right\| \\
&= \operatorname{Tr}\left[\mathbf{G}^T\mathbf{L}^{\mathbf{llr}}\mathbf{G} \right].
\end{aligned}
$$

where $f_i^k(\mathbf{x}_i)$ is the locally predicted label for k-th cluster from $\mathcal{N}(\mathbf{x}_i)$, λ is a positive parameter, $\mathbf{K}_i$ is the kernel matrix defined on the neighborhood of $\mathbf{x}_i$, i.e., $\mathcal{N}(\mathbf{x}_i)$, with size of n_i, $\mathbf{k}_i$ is the kernel vector defined between $\mathbf{x}_i$ and $\mathcal{N}(\mathbf{x}_i)$, $\mathbf{g}_i^k$ is the cluster assignments of $\mathcal{N}(\mathbf{x}_i)$, $\mathbf{L}^{\mathbf{llr}} = (\mathbf{A} - \mathbf{I})^{\mathbf{T}}(\mathbf{A} - \mathbf{I})$, $\mathbf{I} \in \mathcal{R}^{n \times n}$ is an identity matrix, and $\mathbf{A} \in \mathcal{R}^{n \times n}$ is defined by $\mathbf{A}_{ij} = \begin{cases} \alpha_{ij}, & \text{if } \mathbf{x}_j \in \mathcal{N}(\mathbf{x}_i) \\ 0, & \text{otherwise} \end{cases}$.

3. OPTIMIZATION PROBLEM

MVUFS solves the following optimization problem:

$$
\begin{aligned}
\min \quad & \|\mathbf{X}_1 - \mathbf{GF}\|_F^2 + \operatorname{Tr}\left[\mathbf{G}^T\mathbf{L}_2^{llr}\mathbf{G}\right] + \\
& \alpha \sum_{v=1}^2 \|\mathbf{G} - \mathbf{X}_v\mathbf{W}_v\|_{2,1} + \beta \sum_{v=1}^2 \|\mathbf{W}_v\|_{2,1} \\
\text{s.t.} \quad & \mathbf{G}^T\mathbf{G} = \mathbf{I}_c, \mathbf{G} \geq 0, \mathbf{F} \geq 0, \mathbf{W}_v \in \mathcal{R}^{d_v \times c} \quad (1)
\end{aligned}
$$

where α, β are nonnegative parameters. To learn the most consistent pseudo labels across different views, we use orthogonal nonnegative matrix factorization on the text view regularized by local learning prediction error on the image view. $\mathbf{F}$ is the basis matrix with each row being a cluster center. The fitting term $\sum_{v=1}^2 \|\mathbf{G} - \mathbf{X}_v\mathbf{W}_v\|_{2,1}$ will also push the pseudo labels to be close to the linear prediction by the feature weight matrices for each view, which gives the desirable mutual reinforcement between label learning and feature selection. Nonnegative and orthogonal constraints imposed on the cluster indicator matrix variable are desirable to give a single non-zero positive entry on each row of the label matrix. For feature selection, we adopt joint $l_{2,1}$-norm minimization [6] to learn rowise sparse weight matrices for each view. The sparsity-inducing property of l_2/l_1-norm pushes the feature selection matrix $\mathbf{W}_v$ to be sparse in rows. More specifically, $\mathbf{w}_v^j$ shrinks to zero if the j-th feature is less correlated to the pseudo labels $\mathbf{Y}$. We can thus filter out the features corresponding to zero rows of $\mathbf{W}_v$.

We apply alternating optimization to solve problem (1). To optimize $\mathbf{G}$ given $\mathbf{F}$, $\mathbf{W}_v$, $v = 1, 2$, and $\mathbf{G}^t$ in the last iteration, we solve the following subproblem:

$$
\begin{aligned}
\min \quad & \|\mathbf{X}_1 - \mathbf{GF}\|_F^2 + \operatorname{Tr}\left[\mathbf{G}^T\mathbf{L}_2^{llr}\mathbf{G}\right] + \alpha \sum_{v=1}^2 \|\mathbf{D}_v\mathbf{G} - \mathbf{D}_v\mathbf{X}_v\mathbf{W}_v\|_F^2 \\
\text{s.t.} \quad & \mathbf{G}^T\mathbf{G} = \mathbf{I}_c, \mathbf{G} \geq 0, \quad (2)
\end{aligned}
$$

where $\mathbf{D}_v$ is a diagonal matrix: $D_{ii}^v = \frac{1}{2^{0.5}}\left\|\mathbf{g}_i^t - \mathbf{x}_v^i\mathbf{W}_v\right\|_2^{-0.5}$. It can be proved (due to space limit, we omit the proof) that if $\mathbf{G}^{t+1}$ is the solution of problem (2), $\mathbf{G}^{t+1}$ will monotonically decrease the objective function of problem (1). Denote the objective function in problem (2) by $J(\mathbf{G})$, the Lagrange function is given by $\mathcal{L}(\mathbf{G}, \mathbf{\Lambda}, \mathbf{\Sigma}) = J(\mathbf{G}) - \operatorname{Tr}\left[\mathbf{\Lambda}(\mathbf{G}^T\mathbf{G} - \mathbf{I})\right] - \operatorname{Tr}\left[\mathbf{\Sigma}^T\mathbf{G}\right]$. The optimal $\mathbf{G}$ must satisfy the KKT condis-

Table 1: Dataset Description.

Dataset	# Instances	# Words	# IMG-features	# Classes
CNN	2107	7989	996	7
FOX	1523	5477	996	4

tions: $\begin{cases} \nabla J\left(\mathbf{G}\right) - 2\mathbf{G}\mathbf{\Lambda} - \mathbf{\Sigma} = 0 \\ \mathbf{G}^T\mathbf{G} = \mathbf{I} \\ \mathbf{\Sigma}\odot\mathbf{G} = 0;\ \mathbf{\Sigma}\geq 0;\ \mathbf{G}\geq 0 \end{cases}$. Since the updated $\mathbf{G}$ is guaranteed to be nonnegative, we can ignore $\mathbf{\Sigma}$, we thus have $\frac{\partial J}{\partial \mathbf{G}} - 2\mathbf{G}\mathbf{\Lambda} = 0$, giving $\mathbf{\Lambda} = \frac{1}{2}\mathbf{G}^T\frac{\partial J}{\partial \mathbf{G}}$. We first decompose $\mathbf{W}_v = \mathbf{W}_v^+ - \mathbf{W}_v^-$ and $\mathbf{\Lambda} = \mathbf{\Lambda}^+ - \mathbf{\Lambda}^-$, where

$$\begin{aligned} \mathbf{\Lambda}^+ &= \mathbf{G}^T\mathbf{G}\mathbf{F}\mathbf{F}^T + \mathbf{G}^T\mathbf{L}_2^{llr+}\mathbf{G} + \alpha\mathbf{G}^T\left(\sum_{v=1}^{2}\mathbf{D}_v^2\right)\mathbf{G} \\ &\quad + \alpha\mathbf{G}^T\left(\sum_{v=1}^{2}\mathbf{D}_v^2\mathbf{X}_v\mathbf{W}_v^-\right) \\ \mathbf{\Lambda}^- &= \mathbf{G}^T\mathbf{X}_1\mathbf{F}^T + \mathbf{G}^T\mathbf{L}_2^{llr-}\mathbf{G} + \alpha\mathbf{G}^T\left(\sum_{v=1}^{2}\mathbf{D}_v^2\mathbf{X}_v\mathbf{W}_v^+\right). \end{aligned}$$

We then obtain the following update formula for $\mathbf{G}$ by applying the auxiliary function approach in [11]:

$$G_{ik} \leftarrow G_{ik}\frac{\left[\mathbf{X}_1\mathbf{F}^T + \mathbf{L}_2^-\mathbf{G} + \alpha\sum_{v=1}^{2}\mathbf{D}_v^2\mathbf{X}_v\mathbf{W}_v^+ + \mathbf{G}\mathbf{\Lambda}^+\right]_{ik}}{\left[\mathbf{G}\mathbf{F}\mathbf{F}^T + \mathbf{L}_2^+\mathbf{G} + \alpha\sum_{v=1}^{2}\mathbf{D}_v^2\mathbf{G} + \alpha\sum_{v=1}^{2}\mathbf{D}_v^2\mathbf{X}_v\mathbf{W}_v + \mathbf{G}\mathbf{\Lambda}^-\right]_{ik}}. \tag{3}$$

followed by column-wise normalization. When converges, we have $(\nabla J\left(\mathbf{G}\right) - 2\mathbf{G}\mathbf{\Lambda})\odot\mathbf{G} = 0$, which is exactly the KKT complementary slackness condition.

To optimize $\mathbf{F}$, we solve the subproblem: $\min_{\mathbf{F}\geq 0}\|\mathbf{X}_1 - \mathbf{G}\mathbf{F}\|_F^2$. Since the objective function is quadratic, and $\mathbf{F}$'s columns are mutually independent, we can use blockwise coordinate descent to update one row at a time in a cyclic order, and the objective function value is guaranteed to decrease. The updating formula for $\mathbf{F}$ is

$$\mathbf{F}_{i:} \leftarrow \max\left(\mathbf{0}, \mathbf{F}_{i:} - \frac{\left[\mathbf{G}^T\mathbf{G}\right]_{i:}\mathbf{F} - \left[\mathbf{G}^T\mathbf{X}_1\right]_{i:}}{\left[\mathbf{G}^T\mathbf{G}\right]_{ii}}\right). \tag{4}$$

To optimize $\mathbf{W}_v$, we need to solve the unconstrained problem $\min_{\mathbf{W}_v\in\mathcal{R}^{d_v\times c}}\alpha\|\mathbf{G} - \mathbf{X}_v\mathbf{W}_v\|_{2,1} + \beta\|\mathbf{W}_v\|_{2,1}$ for each view. There're several optimization strategies that can solve it. Here we adopt the simple algorithm given in [6].

Algorithm 1 MVUFS

Input: $\{\mathbf{X}_v, p_v\}_{v=1}^{2}, \mathbf{L}_2^{llr}, \alpha, \beta$
Output: p_v features for the v-th view, $v = 1, 2$
1: Initialize $\mathbf{G}^0$ s.t. $\mathbf{G}^{0T}\mathbf{G}^0 = \mathbf{I}$ (e.g., by K-means) and $\mathbf{F}^0 = \mathbf{G}^{0T}\mathbf{X}_1$, $t \leftarrow 0$
2: **while** Not convergent **do**
3:      Given $\mathbf{G}^t$ and $\mathbf{F}^t$, compute $\mathbf{W}_v^{t+1}$ as in [6]
4:      Given $\mathbf{W}_v^{t+1}$ and $\mathbf{F}^t$, compute $\mathbf{G}^{t+1}$ by Eq. (3)
5:      Given $\mathbf{W}_v^{t+1}$ and $\mathbf{G}^{t+1}$, compute $\mathbf{F}^{t+1}$ by Eq. (4)
6:      $t \leftarrow t + 1$
7: **end while**
8: **for** $v = 1$ to 2 **do**
9:      Sort all d_v features according to $\|\mathbf{w}_v^i\|_2$ in descending order and select the top p_v ranked features for the v-th view.
10: **end for**

---

4. EXPERIMENTS

4.1 Datasets

We crawled CNN and FOXNews web news from Jan. 1st, 2014 to Apr. 4th, 2014. The category information contained in the RSS feeds for each news article can be viewed as reliable ground truth. Titles, abstracts, and text body contents are extracted as the text view data, and the image associated with the article is stored as the image view data. Since the vocabulary has a very long tail word distribution, We filtered out those words that occur less than or equal to 5 times. All text content is stemmed by portStemmer [8], and we use l_2-normalized TFIDF as text. For image features, we use 7 groups of color features: Color features include RGB dominant color, HSV dominant color, RGB color moment, HSV color moment, RGB color histogram, HSV color histogram, color coherence vector [7], and 5 textural features: four Tamura textural features [12] (coarseness, contrast, directionality, line-likeness) and Gabor transform [4, 10].

4.2 Settings

Two widely used evaluation metrics for measuring clustering performance: accuracy (ACC) and Normalized Mutual Information (NMI) are used. We compare MVUFS with KMeans on text with all features (KM-TXT), KMeans on image with all features (KM-IMG), state-of-the-art single view unsupervised feature selection methods: NDFS [5] - Joint nonnegative spectral analysis and $l_{2,1}$-norm regularized regression and RUFS [9] - joint local learning regularized robust NMF and robust $l_{2,1}$-norm regression; multi-view spherical KMeans with all features (MVSKM) [1], state-of-the-art multi-view unsupervised feature selection: AUMFS [2] - spectral clustering and $l_{2,1}$-norm regularized robust sparse regression and MVFS [13] - spectral clustering and $l_{2,1}$-norm regression. For single-view unsupervised feature selection methods, KMeans is used to calculate the clustering performance. For multi-view unsupervised feature selection methods, multi-view spherical KMeans [1] is used for multi-view clustering. We set the neighborhood size to be 5. We use cosine similarity to build text graph and Gaussian kernel for image graph. All feature selection methods have two parameters: α for regression, and β for sparsity control. We do grid search for α in $\{10^{-2}, 10^{-1}, \ldots, 10^2\}$, and β in $\alpha \times \{10^{-2}, 10^{-1}, \ldots, 10^2\}$. We vary the number of selected text features as $\{100, 300, 500, 700, 900\}$. The number of selected image features is half of selected text features. Since K-means depends on initialization, we repeat clustering 10 times with random initialization.

4.3 Results

We need to answer several questions. First, is multi-view clustering always better than single view clustering? From Table 2, Table 3, and Figure 1, we can see that the answer is no. It depends on the feature quality of different views. Here the color and texture features we used for image view is not tightly tied with clustering measures, which does severely hurt the performance of multi-view clustering (MVSKM behaves much worse than KM-TXT). Fortunately, if discriminative features are selected by using multi-view feature selection methods, the multi-view clustering performance may be significantly improved and can be better than single-view performance. For example, MVUFS significantly outperforms all single-view methods. Second, is multi-view feature selection better than single-view feature selection? We see that AUMFS, MVFS, and MVUFS outperform standard single view features election methods such as NDFS and RUFS, which indicates that different views can mutually bootstrap each other. It's interesting to see that both NDFS and RUFS even behave worse than without doing feature selection. At last, it turns out that MVUFS

Table 2: Clustering Results (ACC% ± std), * means statistical significance at 5% level.

Dataset	KM-TXT	KM-IMG	NDFS	RUFS	MVSKM	AUMFS	MVFS	MVUFS
CNN	50.1 ± 7.2	23.2 ± 1.0	31.6 ± 6.1	31.3 ± 5.3	32.0 ± 2.8	54.2 ± 4.6	50.2 ± 4.8	$\mathbf{57.9 \pm 4.9^*}$
FOX	76.2 ± 7.7	43.0 ± 0.3	56.6 ± 9.3	61.2 ± 8.3	73.3 ± 2.1	83.7 ± 1.3	84.7 ± 0.6	$\mathbf{87.9 \pm 1.0^*}$

Table 3: Clustering Results (NMI% ± std), * means statistical significance at 5% level.

Dataset	KM-TXT	KM-IMG	NDFS	RUFS	MVSKM	AUMFS	MVFS	MVUFS
CNN	42.0 ± 4.3	3.7 ± 0.1	21.1 ± 5.5	22.8 ± 4.9	16.6 ± 1.1	36.4 ± 3.2	30.8 ± 2.5	$\mathbf{44.1 \pm 2.4^*}$
FOX	67.3 ± 6.1	7.6 ± 0.3	37.3 ± 8.5	42.6 ± 12.5	50.0 ± 1.8	64.4 ± 0.9	66.5 ± 0.6	$\mathbf{72.1 \pm 0.5^*}$

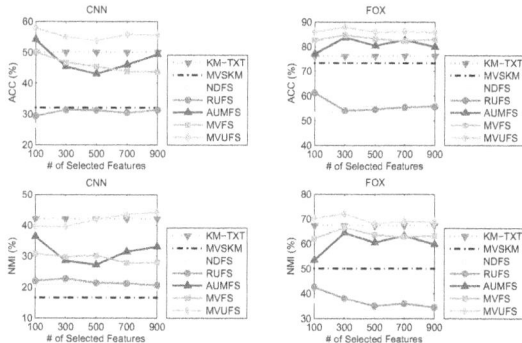

Figure 1: ACC and NMI with varying number of selected features.

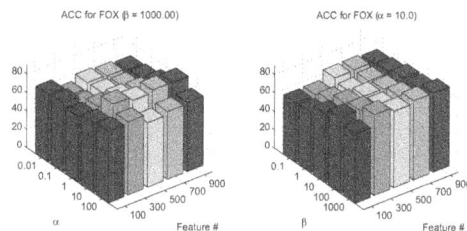

Figure 2: ACC v.s. different α, β, and number of selected features on FOX dataset for MVUFS.

outperforms both single-view clustering and feature selection methods and multi-view clustering and feature selection methods. Since the major difference between MVUFS and AUMFS, MVFS is label learning, we conclude that directly learning labels from raw features from one view while ensuring the most consensus with other views could select a more discriminative feature set for all views, and spectral clustering relies on the combined similarity graphs of all views which may result in loss of discriminative information and could undermine the performance.

4.4 Parameter Analysis

We plot ACC versus different α, β, and number of selected features on FOXNews for MVUFS in Figure 2 (similar figures for NMI and on CNN dataset) due to space limit. We see that an appropriate combination of these parameters is crucial. However, it is unknown to us theoretically how to choose the best parameter setting. It may depends on datasets and measures. In practice, like many other methods, one can build a validation set in a mild scale to tune parameters by e.g., grid search.

5. CONCLUSION

We propose a new unsupervised feature selection methods for multi-view clustering: MVUFS where local learning regularized orthogonal nonnegative matrix factorization is performed to learn pseudo class labels on raw features. We built two web news text-image datasets from CNN and FOXNews, and systematically evaluate MVUFS with state-of-the-art single-view and multi-view unsupervised feature selection methods. Experimental results validate the effectiveness of the proposed method.

Acknowledgments

This material is based upon work supported by the National Science Foundation under Grant Number CNS-1027965.

6. REFERENCES

[1] S. Bickel and T. Scheffer. Multi-view clustering. In *Proceedings of the Fourth IEEE International Conference on Data Mining*, pages 19–26. IEEE Computer Society, 2004.

[2] Y. Feng, J. Xiao, Y. Zhuang, and X. Liu. Adaptive unsupervised multi-view feature selection for visual concept recognition. In *Proceedings of the 11th Asian conference on Computer Vision-Volume Part I*, pages 343–357. Springer-Verlag, 2012.

[3] Q. Gu and J. Zhou. Local learning regularized nonnegative matrix factorization. In *Twenty-First International Joint Conference on Artificial Intelligence*, 2009.

[4] T. Lee. Image representation using 2d gabor wavelets. *Pattern Analysis and Machine Intelligence, IEEE Transactions on*, 18(10):959–971, 1996.

[5] Z. Li, Y. Yang, J. Liu, X. Zhou, and H. Lu. Unsupervised feature selection using nonnegative spectral analysis. In *26th AAAI Conference on Artificial Intelligence*, 2012.

[6] F. Nie, H. Huang, X. Cai, and C. Ding. Efficient and robust feature selection via joint l2, 1-norms minimization. *Advances in Neural Information Processing Systems*, 23:1813–1821, 2010.

[7] G. Pass, R. Zabih, and J. Miller. Comparing images using color coherence vectors. In *Proceedings of the fourth ACM international conference on Multimedia*. ACM, 1997.

[8] M. Porter. An algorithm for suffix stripping. *Program: electronic library and information systems*, 14(3):130–137, 1993.

[9] M. Qian and C. Zhai. Robust unsupervised feature selection. In *Proceedings of the Twenty-Third international joint conference on Artificial Intelligence*, pages 1621–1627. AAAI Press, 2013.

[10] Y. Ro, M. Kim, H. Kang, B. Manjunath, and J. Kim. Mpeg-7 homogeneous texture descriptor. *ETRI journal*, 23(2):41–51, 2001.

[11] D. Seung and L. Lee. Algorithms for non-negative matrix factorization. *Advances in neural information processing systems*, 13:556–562, 2001.

[12] H. Tamura, S. Mori, and T. Yamawaki. Textural features corresponding to visual perception. *Systems, Man and Cybernetics, IEEE Transactions on*, 8(6), 1978.

[13] J. Tang, X. Hu, H. Gao, and H. Liu. Unsupervised feature selection for multi-view data in social media. In *Proceedings of the 13th SIAM International Conference on Data Mining, 2013*. SIAM, 2013.

Enterprise Discussion Analysis

Sara Rosenthal
Department of Computer Science
Columbia University
New York, NY 10027, USA
sara@cs.columbia.edu

Ashish Jagmohan
IBM Research
Yorktown Heights, NY 10598, USA
ashishja@us.ibm.com

ABSTRACT

Recent business studies have shown that social technologies can significantly improve productivity within enterprises by improving access to information, ideas, and collaborators. A manifestation of the growing adoption of enterprise social technologies is the increasing use of enterprise virtual discussions to engage customers and employees. In this paper we present an enterprise discussion analysis system which seeks to enable rapid interactive inference of insights from virtual online enterprise discussions. Rapid understanding is facilitated by extracting a hierarchy of key concepts, which represent a multi-faceted thematic categorization of discussion content, and by identifying high-quality thematic exemplar comments. The concept hierarchy and exemplar comments are presented through an intuitive web user-interface which allows an analyst to quickly navigate through the main concepts and the most relevant comments extracted from the discussion. We present a preliminary validation of system efficacy through user surveys provided to test users.

Categories and Subject Descriptors

H.3.3 [**Information Search and Retrieval**]: Subjects—*information filtering, selection process*

Keywords

discussion analysis; enterprise discussions; comment selection; concept hierarchy; social enterprise; web interfaces

1. INTRODUCTION

The use of social technologies for collaboration has the potential to significantly improve productivity within enterprises. An analysis by the Mckinsey Global Institute ([Chui et al. 2012]) has estimated that such technologies can yield a 20-25% improvement in productivity, by improving access to information and collaborators. This, in turn, translates into a US$1.6-1.9T benefit across several sectors within four major economies. Not surprisingly, an IDC study ([Thompson

2012]) reports rapid growth in the social enterprise software market, projecting a compound annual revenue growth of 42%, reaching US$4.5B in 2016.

A specific manifestation of the adoption of enterprise social technologies is the increasing use of enterprise virtual discussions to collaboratively harness knowledge, opinion, and innovation, from employees and clients. In this context, an often encountered issue is how to effectively cull insight from the large quantities of discussion material typically generated by such an event. A completely manual analysis process can be costly and even infeasible, depending on discussion size.

In this paper, we present a novel discussion analysis system which aims at enabling rapid interactive analysis of enterprise virtual discussions. Rapid extraction of discussion insights is facilitated through a multi-faceted thematic categorization of discussion content, and identification of high-quality thematic examples. To this end, the proposed system uses a variety of natural language processing techniques to decompose a discussion, or a group of related discussions, into an automatically extracted thematic concept hierarchy. Individual comments serve as atomic content entities, and are associated with one or more elements in the concept hierarchy. The concept hierarchy and categorized comment exemplars are presented through an intuitive web user-interface, which allows an analyst to quickly navigate through the main discussion themes and most relevant comments exemplars, and form a rapid understanding of the discussion content. We present preliminary validation of the efficacy of the proposed approach through a user survey provided to test-users for a real-world enterprise discussion.

2. RELATED WORK

There has been a significant amount of work in building concept hierarchies from text. Earlier work [Sanderson and Lawrie 2000, Sanderson and Croft 1999] has been performed on a group of documents across several topics, such as web pages. More recent work has explored concept hierarchies in discussions such as spoken conversations [Rashid et al. 2012], e-mail [Yang and Callan 2008] and social media [Selcuk et al. 2008]. Using a hierarchy as a visualization method for browsing and search has been used in several genres, such as music and image search. For example, a hierarchical menu on the results of a web search is used in [Sanderson and Lawrie 2000]. To our knowledge, we are the first to leverage concept hierarchy and related comment extraction for analyzing virtual enterprise discussions, and the first to build a web interface using a concept hierarchy as the general technique for visualizing an online discussion. The proposed technique, while designed for virtual enterprise discussions, has general applicability; it is well-suited to analyzing discussions such as those found in web forums.

The prior work which is perhaps most similar to our system is [Rashid et al. 2012]. This work provides an ontology of concepts, a word cloud of the discussion, and summaries. However, their approach analyzes meeting conversations as opposed to online discussions. There are also significant differences in the underlying technology. For instance, the concepts represent speakers and dialog acts as opposed to concepts extracted from text. It is also built on the sentence level as opposed to the post (or speaker) level which can cause a loss of information. Further they generate summaries rather than the proposed exemplar comment extraction. In terms of visualization, the previous work is built as a Java GUI application while our interface is a webpage built with HTML and JavaScript, which allows it to easily be integrated into online discussions and provide real-time analysis. We also provide several filtering options, including ones exclusive to online discussions, such as likes and votes.

3. DISCUSSION ANALYSIS SYSTEM

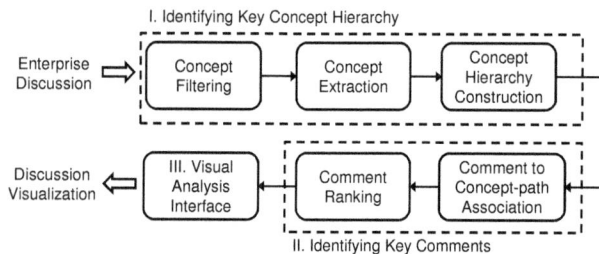

Figure 1: Overview of discussion analysis system.

Figure 1 shows an overview of the discussion analysis system. The input to the system is the content of a virtual discussion. A typical discussion can consist of one or more topics or "questions" around which collective intelligence is sought. For example, a discussion question may be "How can your company increase use of analytics technology?". The discussion around a single question consists of a group of threads, where each thread is a set of several posts constituting a mutual dialogue. These threads can span over any time-range and may be synchronous or asynchronous, but are all related to the single question or topic. Our focus is on discussions conducted within an enterprise environment where clear questions have been asked of the participants.

The discussion content is supplied to the system through connectors for supported discussion platforms, or through flat-file content dumps. The system has three components. The first is the automated construction of a concept hierarchy through extraction of individual concepts, filtering to identify 'meaningful' concepts, and organization of identified concepts in a hierarchy. The second component is the identification and ranking of exemplar comments related to each concept-path in the hierarchy. Finally, the third component is the visual interface which presents the concept hierarchy and exemplar comments to the analyst, and allows interactive browsing and filtering. Each component is described in further detail in the following sections.

Table 1: Concept Filters

Filter	Description	Example
Stop Words	Exclude Lucene stopword list, custom stopwords	the, it
Plural Words	Merge plural and singular forms using WordNet	tools, businesses
Part-of-Speech	Include Noun, Noun-Noun, Noun-Adjective phrases	big data, analytics
HTML	Exclude html tags, urls	www.web.com
Gutenberg filtering	Exclude words in top 5% of Gutenberg corpus	use, need
Names	Exclude author names	Gary, Anne

3.1 Concept Hierarchy Identification

Concept hierarchy identification consists of three main steps (Figure 1): filtering the discussion text to identify potentially meaningful concepts, extracting a subset of significant concepts, and constructing a concept hierarchy from the extracted concepts. All information retrieval performed by our system is done via the Lucene package.[1]

A concept is a term that is considered to be meaningful in the discussion. Potential concepts are identified through the use of multiple filters, shown in Table 1. Terms or phrases of type noun, noun-noun and noun-adjective are considered as potentially meaningful concepts. Pluralization is detected using metadata from the WordNet [Miller 1995] lexical database, and singular and plural forms are merged. Stop-words, HTML tags and participant names are excluded. Also used is a 'Gutenberg' filter which excludes words which are very frequently found in the Gutenberg corpus;[2] very common words generally do not constitute meaningful concepts in business discussions, and this filter helps exclude such terms.

The filtered concepts are then ranked using a variety of metrics. Denote t as a concept term, d as a discussion from a set of discussions D, and q as a discussion-question from the set of questions Q in discussion d. Then, the following metrics are used to quantify the potential importance of the term t in discussion d:

- **Term Frequency** $tf(t, d)$ **and Term-Question Frequency** $tqf(t, q)$, the normalized number of occurrences of the term t in discussion d, and question q, respectively. This finds the most used terms in the current discussion and discussion topic.
- **Term Frequency-Inverse Document Frequency** $tfidf(t, d) = tf(t, d) \times idf(t, D)$ to find terms that are important to this discussion in contrast to all discussions.
- **Question Term Frequency-Inverse Question Frequency** $qtfiqf(t, q) = tqf(t, q) \times iqf(t, Q)$ to find terms that are important for this question in contrast to other questions within the discussion
- **Bigram frequency** $bf(t, d)$ which is zero if t is not a bigram, and is the normalized frequency of t in d otherwise. This specifically finds significant word pairs (e.g. "big data" or "machine learning"), which may be under-ranked by generic term-frequency metrics.

We gather the top m terms (typically $150 - 200$) for each metric and remove overlapping terms.

---

[1] lucene.apache.org

[2] www.gutenberg.org

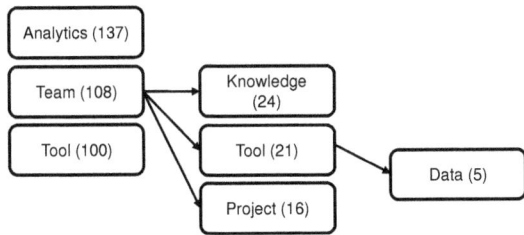

Figure 2: Example of hierarchical layout. Numbers in parenthesis indicate occurrence in query results of the current concept and its ancestor concepts (e.g. 'team + tool + data' occurs 5 times).

Finally, the gathered concept terms are organized into a hierarchy, for ease of exploration. Hierarchies have been found to be useful as a method for organizing information by the Library of Congress and the Dewey Decimal System. We automatically generate a hierarchy of concepts recursively in contrast to these manually created hierarchies. We initially order the filtered concepts based on the number of query results in Lucene. Each subsequent level of the hierarchy is constituted on the basis of the number of query results containing a given concept and all of its ancestors. In order to minimize the size of the hierarchical tree, we limit each level to show only the top n concepts (n can be configured by the analyst, typically, $n = 10$ or 15). Notably, we allow each concept to appear at several levels in the hierarchy. This is a parametric design choice (that can be disabled) which has been made to allow a user to explore complete alternate views of the concept hierarchy starting from any initial concept at the highest level of the hierarchy. Figure 2 shows an example hierarchy segment.

3.2 Identifying Exemplar Comments

The concept hierarchy represents a multi-faceted organization of the main thematic elements of the discussion. Next, we identify exemplar comments associated with each concept path, which, when presented to the end analyst, will allow the analyst to rapidly form an understanding of the discussion around that theme. We define a concept path as the list of concepts from the top level of the hierarchy to the current concept; a concept path thus identifies a fine-grained theme of discussion. An example is the concept path 'team -> tool -> data' shown in Figure 2. We find associated comments by querying the discussion for occurrence of the concept path terms in close proximity, using the SrndQuery class in Lucene. For example the query '(team) 10n (tool) 10n (data)' is used to find all comments with occurrences of the words team, tool, and data within a 10-word window (the window size is a configurable parameter), where the option 'n' indicates that the order of the words does not matter. Bigrams are queried using the 'w' option which constrains the words to be in order, e.g. '(big w data)'.

Ranking the comments for relevance at the most fine-grained level of the concept path is simple; we use the Lucene scores returned from running the SrndQuery for all concept path terms as described above. However, as we proceed up the concept path toward the root, the number of results increases and the SrndQuery scores become less meaningful from the perspective of relevance ranking. This is because the score is based off of number of occurrences, which may not translate into exemplar relevance. We hypothesize that

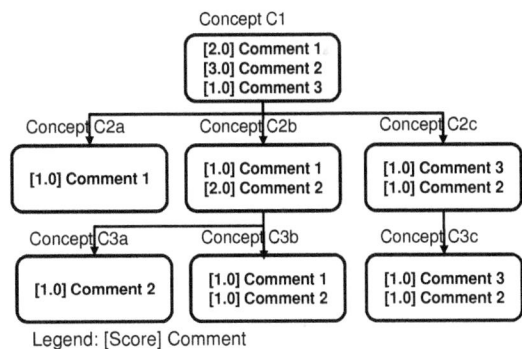

Figure 3: Combining comment scores for ranking.

comment relevance is related to how well the comment aligns with all fine-grained paths rooted at the current concept in the hierarchy. We quantitatively measure this heuristic for a comment by recursively summing the scores from each occurrence of the comment in lower levels of the hierarchy. Thus, for example, in Figure 3, comment 2 has the highest relevance score for concept C1, because it occurs most frequently on lower levels of the hierarchy tree rooted at C1. Ranking the comments in this manner ensures that comments which are well-aligned with multiple thematic facets associated with the current concept have higher rankings. The highest ranked comments are interactively displayed on the user interface.

4. USER INTERFACE

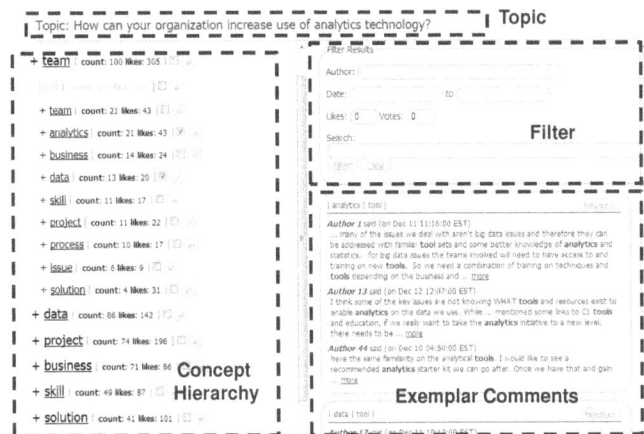

Figure 4: User interface layout and example.

The concept hierarchy and extracted comments are presented to the analyst through a web interface built using HTML, CSS, and JavaScript. Figure 4 shows an example discussion analysis produced by the tool, overlaid with a description of the interface layout. The user interface consists of two main parts; the concept hierarchy (on the left), and the comment snippets (right). In addition, the topic associated with the discussion is shown at the top. The hierarchy is initially displayed as an ordered list of the top concepts. Each concept can be expanded to show the key concepts that are connected to it. Each level in the hierarchy can be expanded until all concepts have been reached.

Table 2: Top exemplar comments corresponding to example concept-paths for topic "How can your organization increase use of analytics technology?"

Concept Path	Top exemplar snippet
tool - analytics	"... many of the issues we deal with aren't big data issues and therefore they can be addressed with familiar tool sets and some better knowledge of analytics and statistics.. for big data issues the teams involved will need to have access to and training on new tools. So we need a combination of training on techniques and tools depending on the business ..."
skill	"While many of our analysts have stronger system and tool skills I think it would be beneficial to team them with [other] analysts who tend to have more business experience and knowledge ..."

When a concept on the left hand side is selected, the exemplar comments associated with it appear on the right hand side in the comments section. Several concepts can be selected at once by clicking on the checkbox to the left of each concept. There is also the ability to view the comments for all of the concepts. This enables the end analyst to rapidly gain understanding of the main discussion themes in breadth-wise and/or depth-wise fashion, as desired.

The comments can be filtered by several criteria; date, author, number of likes or votes, and key concepts. Comments and comment sets, corresponding to concepts, can also be sorted using one of multiple criteria. By default, the tool uses the novel information-based metric to rank comments described in section 3.2. The tool also allows sorting of comments by various meta-data metrics, such as the number of comment responses, comment likes, votes, etc. The content around each comment can be expanded to view the entire thread, which enables the user to quickly gain insight into the context of the comment.

The current version of the interface uses static html that is built from the discussion in advance. The advantage to this approach is that the user does not have to wait for most content to load. We use AJAX (notably JQuery) to do filtering on the fly. The web.py framework is used to provide certain server-side functionalities, for complex types of filtering such as customized sorting.

5. EVALUATION

In our experience with business discussions analyzed using the proposed tool, it generally does well at extracting important high-level concept-paths, and high-quality associated exemplars. Table 2 shows two examples[3] of the top exemplar found for two example concept paths for a real-world discussion analyzed by the tool. In each case the exemplars constitute high-quality suggestions which are holistically relevant to the discussion at hand. Thus, the first exemplar corresponding to the 'tool-analytics' path points out how training in analytics and tooling needs to be combined in the context of big data. The second exemplar, for the top-level 'skills' concept contrasts the team's system and tooling skills with business skills, and suggests a relevant course of

---

[3]Identifiable personal and business information has been removed from exemplars.

action. The tool is less effective at identifying niche concepts which may occur infrequently, but may be important.

As a preliminary evaluation of the efficacy of the tool in aiding the user in understanding the discussion, we created a survey for analyst-users of our tool. The aims of the survey were to determine: 1. How useful is the tool in identifying important concepts and comments, and in providing an understanding of the discussion? 2. How easy is the tool to use for analysis? 3. How long did it take to use the tool to gain an understanding of the discussion? We asked detailed questions related to each of these aspects, on a Likert scale of 1-5. The questions dealt with the interface as a whole as well as specific aspects including understanding key concepts, finding comments, understanding the discussion, filtering the results, and tool design. The survey was filled out by 5 respondents who were each given the same discussion to analyze with the help of the tool. The majority of the respondents reported that they found the tool useful and easy to use; the overall usefulness of the tool and ease-of-use were each rated at the highest or second-highest level by four of the five users. In addition, the majority of respondents reported that the tool improved the speed at which they could understand the key concepts, find important comments, and understand the discussion.

6. CONCLUSION

We have described a discussion analysis system that can be used to gain insight into enterprise discussions. We have conducted surveys to determine its effectiveness, showing that users find the tool to be useful for rapidly gaining in-depth understanding of a discussion. The current interface is a strong foundation for understanding a conversation and there are many additions, such as opinion, that can be integrated to enhance user understanding of the conversation. We believe the system can also easily be adapted to include multiple discussions and other domains.

7. REFERENCES

[Chui et al. 2012] M. Chui and others. 2012. The social economy: Unlocking value ... *Mckinsey and Company, Insights and Publications* (2012).

[Miller 1995] G.A. Miller. 1995. WordNet: A Lexical Database for English. *Commun. ACM* 38 (Nov. 1995), 39–41.

[Rashid et al. 2012] S. Rashid, G. Carenini, and R.T. Ng. 2012. *A Visual Interface for Analyzing Text Conversations*. Springer. 93 – 108 pages.

[Sanderson and Croft 1999] M. Sanderson and B. Croft. 1999. Deriving concept hierarchies from text. In *ACM SIGIR*. 206 – 213.

[Sanderson and Lawrie 2000] M. Sanderson and D. Lawrie. 2000. *Building, Testing, and Applying Concept Hierarchies*. 235 – 266 pages.

[Selcuk et al. 2008] K.C. Selcuk, L.D. Caro, and M.L. Sapino. 2008. Creating tag hierarchies for effective navigation in social media. In *ACM SSM*. 75 – 82.

[Thompson 2012] V. Thompson. 2012. IDC Worldwide Ent. Soc. Software 2012-2016 Forecast Upd. (2012).

[Yang and Callan 2008] H. Yang and J. Callan. 2008. Ontology Generation for Large Email Collections. In *Int. Conf. Dig. Govt. Res.* 254 – 261.

A Problem-Action Relation Extraction Based on Causality Patterns of Clinical Events in Discharge Summaries

Jae-Wook Seol[1], Seung-Hyeon Jo[1], Wangjin Yi[2], Jinwook Choi[3*], Kyung-Soon Lee[1*]

[1] Dept. of Computer Science & Engineering, CAIIT, Chonbuk National University, Republic of Korea
[2] Interdisciplinary Program of Bioengineering, College of Engineering,
Seoul National University, Republic of Korea
[3] Dept. of Biomedical Engineering, College of Medicine, Seoul National University, Republic of Korea
{wodnr754, jackaa}@chonbuk.ac.kr, {jinsamdol, jinchoi}@snu.ac.kr, selfsolee@chonbuk.ac.kr

ABSTRACT

Medical knowledge extraction has great potential to improve the treatment quality of hospitals. In this paper, we propose a clinical problem-action relation extraction method. It is based on clinical semantic units and event causality patterns in order to present a chronological view of a patient's problem and a physician's action. Based on our observation, a clinical semantic unit is defined as a conceptual medical knowledge for a problem and/or action. Since a clinical event is a basic concept of the problem-action relation, events are detected from clinical texts based on conditional random fields. A clinical semantic unit is segmented from a sentence based on time expressions and inherent structure of events. Then, a clinical semantic unit is classified into a problem and/or action relation based on event causality features in support vector machines. The experimental result on Korean medical collection shows 78.8% in F-measure when given the answer of clinical events. This result shows that the proposed method is effective for extracting clinical problem-action relations.

Categories and Subject Descriptors

I.2.7 [**ARTIFICIAL INTELLIGENCE**] Natural Language Processing - *Text analysis*

Keywords

Relation extraction; Clinical semantic unit; problem-action relation; causal relationship

1. INTRODUCTION

As the digitalization of clinical information is one of the major trends in the healthcare domain, there is an increasing demand in utilization of the information. In digitalized healthcare environment the medical data mining and automatic summarization will be a key element for the improvement of care quality. Clinical narrative texts include information that relate to a

patient's medical history such as chronological progression of medical problems and clinical treatments. It would be extremely useful if relevant knowledge could be extracted from clinical texts and presented in structured form for physicians to identify effective treatments and for patients to receive better and more affordable services.

In recent years, a lot of research has been done on effectively analyzing clinical data due to i2b2 (Informatics for Integrating Biology and the Bedside) challenge [1, 2]. The challenges include extracting clinical events and relation classification, and identifying temporal relation between two events. Many research groups have participated and proposed technologies of natural language processing for medical texts [1, 2, 3, 4].

On the other hand, Park and Choi [5] introduced a V-Model to chronologically visualize narrative clinical texts by grouping clinical events and plotting on a timeline. The usability study on the timeline model by medical students showed very useful in effectively understanding a patient's history.

Based on our observation that a clinical text is described in chronological order of a patient's medical problems and a physician's treatments at a time, we define a problem and/or action relationship as a clinical semantic unit.

In this paper, we propose an extraction method of clinical problem-action relation in order to present the causal relationship of a problem and an action in clinical texts. Our research focuses on clinical semantic units and event causality patterns. A clinical semantic unit is segmented from each sentence by considering inherent structure among events and classified into problem and/or action relation based on Support Vector Machine (SVM) [6] and event causality patterns that consider a causal relationship between clinical events that occurred simultaneously in a point on a timeline. To see the effectiveness of the proposed method, experiments are conducted on the 150 discharge summaries from a division of Rheumatology/Nephrology of a general hospital in South Korea.

2. RELATED WORK

Recent technologies in natural language processing (NLP) and machine learning have enabled a variety of semantic components such as clinical events, temporal relations and time expressions to be extracted automatically from electronic medical texts.

Clinical narrative texts have various facets of relationship. Recent research on relation extraction proposed the relationship based on utilization. Savova et al. [7] proposed the temporal relationship between two clinical events as CONTINUE, INITIATE,

REINITIATE and TERMINATE using Aspectual Link. In the i2b2 2010 challenge [1] on concepts, assertions, and relations, relation classification aimed to classify relations of a pair of given concepts from a sentence such as problem-treatment, problem-test and problem-problem. In the 2012 i2b2 challenge [2], temporal relations such as BEFORE, AFTER and OVERLAP are extracted from medical text. The difference between our problem-action relation extraction and relation extraction of i2b2 is described in Table 1.

Table 1. Comparison of our task and i2b2 task

	Problem-Action relation	i2b2
Task	clinical semantic relation extraction	temporal relation extraction
Relation categories	problem-action, problem, action, time anchoring point (TAP)	i2b2 2012 (overlap, after, before) i2b2 2010 (problem-problem, problem-treatment, problem-test)
Relation unit	A clinical semantic unit	a sentence
Relationship partners	Causal relationship among three or more events	Binary relationship between two events
Information provided	causal-effect relation on a time among events	temporal relation between events
Event categories	*Problem*: Symptom, Finding, Purpose *Action*: Treatment, Drug, Test *TAP*: Visit, Time	Problem, Treatment, Test, Time

Most participants of the i2b2 temporal relation extraction used SVM with contextual features and/or rules to classify temporal relationship between two events [3, 4]. Our approach is based on SVM with event causality features and rules to classify a semantic unit into a causal relationship.

3. PROBLEM-ACTION RELATION EXTRATION

The overall system architecture for the problem-action relation extraction is shown in Figure 1.

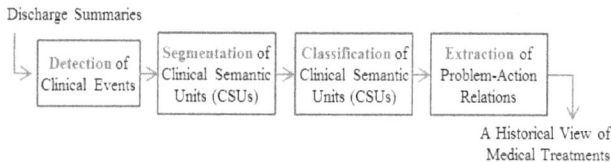

Figure 1. Overall system architecture

3.1 Clinical Event Detection

Since a clinical event is a basic concept consisting of a problem-action relation, a clinical event is detected from clinical texts based on conditional random fields (CRF) [8] with conventional features [9] and lexical patterns to consider properties of Korean clinical texts. The categories of clinical events include Symptom, Purpose, Finding, Diagnosis, Drug, Treatment, Test, Time, and Visit.

The discharge summaries in our experiments are described in a mix of English and Korean words. The primary tendency for language use was that most medical event terms are written in English and descriptions of an event are written in Korean.

Conventional features are used for CRF such as word features, symbol features, contexture features, and UMLS matching features [3] for English and Korean. To deal with the language properties, co-occurrence words and lexical patterns are used for the mixed Korean and English narratives. To improve the performance of event detection, we have used Wikipedia category features and Korean-to-English translation features for concept-level matching.

Based on our observation that some lexical clues are deterministic to classify events such as drug, diagnosis and symptom, the lexical patterns are used to correct event categories and to extract additional events as post processing after CRF results.

We have applied regular expressions to detect a time which could not be detected by CRF since expressions of a time in discharge summaries are diverse depending on clinicians.

3.2 Clinical Semantic Unit Segmentation

A basic semantic structure of a problem-action relationship between events is composed of a time and clinical events that occurred at a relevant time. We define this basic unit as a clinical semantic unit (CSU). A clinical semantic unit is segmented from each sentence based on time expressions and inherent structure of events.

Since a time anchoring point (TAP) represents temporal information when problems and actions took place, the range from a current time until to the next time can be a segment of a CSU. A CSU can contain one or more events and events appear in order of occurrence. For example, when TAP is an expression of a time and E is an event, a CSU can be several forms such as (TAP_1, E_1), (E_1, TAP_1), (E_1, E_2, TAP_1), and $(E_1, TAP_1, E_2, \ldots, E_n)$.

There are four cases according to the position of a TAP: 1) a time appears at the beginning position, 2) a time appears at the end position, 3) a time appears between events, and 4) a CSU contains no time. When a CSU contains only a TAP by case 2) and 3), it should be combined with the nearest CSU. The CSUs are detected from each sentence by the following straightforward algorithm.

1. Detect a sentence boundary using a punctuation mark.
2. Find time expressions (TAPs) from the sentence.
3. Segment a CSU, range from a current TAP until the next TAP.
4. Do for each CSU
   If the CSU contains one time event only, then combine it with the previous CSU.
   If the CSU contains one event which is not time and visit event, then combine it with the next CSU.
End.

Original text

Figure 2. Examples of segments of clinical semantic units

The example of the CSU segmentation is shown in Figure 2. The CSUs segments make it possible to recognize clinical situations by the component events.

3.3 Clinical Semantic Unit Classification

Clinical semantic units are classified using multiclass SVM [10] with event causality features as well as lexical and context features into four classes such as 'TAP,' 'Problem,' 'Action', and 'Problem-Action' relation.

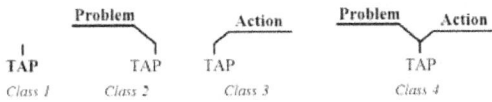

Figure 3. Classes of clinical semantic units

Figure 3 shows the four templates to be classified: *TAP* is a case when there is only a Time or Visit in the CSU. *Problem* is a case when an event in the CSU is a symptom, diagnosis or finding about a patient. *Action* is when an event in the CSU is a treatment, drug or test to treat a patient. Finally, *Problem-Action* is a case when an order of events in the CSU is a treatment for a symptom.

A CSU can be classified according to an order of event tags since a causal relationship is described by the inherent relation of semantics of events and a time. The following sets of features are used in our SVM classification: lexical, context, frequency and event causality features as shown in Table 2.

Table 2. SVM features for the CSU classification

Feature	Description
Lexical features	Occurrence of clues for TAP, Problem, and Action
Context features	Bag of events (window size 3)
	The first event tag (except Time, Visit)
	Occurrence of each event tag such as Time, Visit, and other Events
Frequency features	Frequency of each event tag
	The number of all event tags in a CSU
Event causality features	Event occurrence patterns for the problem and action relation, as shown in Table 3

Lexical features are binary features whether a clue word appears in each CSU template. For examples, clue words such as 'since', 'from', 'before', and 'after' are for TAP, words 'doubt', 'appeal', and 'opinion' are clues for Problem, and words 'take a dose', 'quantity', 'mg', and 'Bx' are used for Action.

Context features represent contextual information of a CSU. Three events are given as the context of a CSU. The first event tag can imply a medical situation for a CSU.

Frequency features are for the frequency information of events in a CSU. This feature includes the frequency number of each semantic tag, the total number of tags in a CSU and whether each tag is emerged or not.

Table 3. Event occurrence patterns for causality relationships

Causal Relationship	Event Occurrence Patterns
Drug-Effect	Drug -> Event_1+..+ Event_n
Treatment-Effect	Treatment -> Event_1+..+ Event_n
Symptom-Treatment	Symptom -> {Treatment | Drug | Test}
Symptom-Disease	Symptom -> Diagnosis
Finding-Treatment	Finding -> {Treatment | Drug | Test}
Finding-Disease	Finding -> Diagnosis
Disease-Treatment	Diagnosis -> {Treatment | Drug | Test}
Test-Treatment	Test -> Treatment
Test-Result	Test -> {Diagnosis | Finding|Symptom}

Event causality features are important clues to express the problem-action relation. We defined event occurrence patterns to detect the causal relation that exists among events such as the cause and the effect. Table 3 shows our event causality patterns used for the SVM features.

Since the causal relationships imply semantics of events as well as the implicit structure, they can be also used for the assignment of the problem and action part (in the next section).

3.4 Problem-Action Relation Extraction Based on Event Causality Patterns

The event causality patterns are used to determine the positions of events (problem side or action side) for the CSU classified.

The event occurrence patterns in discharge summaries imply causality relations with the cause event and the effect event such as Drug-Effect, Treatment-Effect, Symptom-Treatment, Symptom-Disease, Diagnosis-Treatment, and Test-Treatment.

The following Figure 4 shows the extraction examples for the original clinical text and CSUs of the Figure 2.

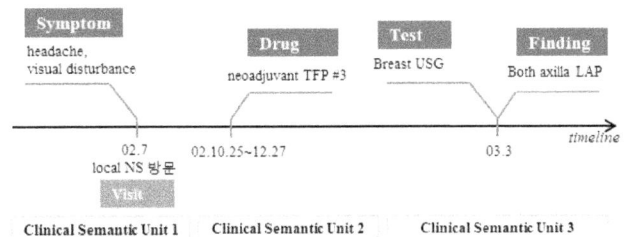

Figure 4. Examples of relation extraction

Based on the causality relationship, <Test> is assigned for the problem side, and <Treatment> is assigned for the action side.

The representation by the causal relation enables a reader to easily infer that a patient took the diagnosis due to the test even though the medical term may not be known.

4. EXPERIMENTS

4.1 Data Set

To see the effectiveness of the proposed method, we have experimented on a Korean clinical test collection. The collection contains 150 discharge summaries of patients diagnosed with systemic lupus erythematosus and discharged from the division of Rheumatology/Nephrology. As the answer set, clinical events, time expressions, CSU segments, and problem and/or relations are manually annotated by human experts. Table 4 shows the statistics of our test collection for 5-fold cross validation.

Table 4. A Korean clinical test collection

Collection			Training	Test
Documents	# of clinical texts		120	30
	avg. # of terms		80.9	86.6
Answers	avg. # of clinical events		9,316	2,598
	avg. # of CSUs		4,026	1,254
	avg. # of relations	TAP	661	214
		Problem	1,231	410
		Action	1,030	322
		Problem-Action	1,104	308

4.2 Experimental Results

The performance is measured in precision (P), recall (R), and F_1-measure (F). For the event detection, the performance is measured on a strict or lenient basis. Strict matching requires two annotations to have an identical span, where lenient matching accepts a partial match. Table 5 shows the performance of event detection based on CRF.

Table 5. Results of event extraction

Clinical Events	Strict matching			Lenient matching		
	R	P	F	R	P	F
Symptom	52.3	55.3	53.7	71.3	79.1	74.9
Diagnosis	68.9	68.1	68.4	79.6	78.2	78.8
Test	62.7	63.6	63.1	73.5	70.5	71.9
Drug	63.0	64.5	63.7	74.2	79.2	76.6
Treatment	43.2	59.7	50.1	48.7	67.0	56.4
Finding	60.4	63.1	61.7	78.1	79.1	78.5
Purpose	77.4	75.6	76.4	80.1	81.0	80.5
Time	79.0	77.4	78.1	83.2	86.4	84.7
Visit	66.3	72.6	69.3	73.4	76.7	75.0
Average	**63.6**	**66.6**	**65.1**	**73.5**	**77.4**	**75.4**

Table 6 shows results of the segmentation of CSUs. The comparisons are conducted when event tags are given with human answers. Our system is affected by the extraction of Time event.

Table 6. Results of CSU segmentation

Comparisons	R	P	F
Segmentation with Answers of event tags	93.3	91.4	92.3
Segmentation by the CRF system	79.7	76.5	78.1

Table 7 shows the effectiveness of each feature for the classification of CSUs. Here the events and CSUs are given as answers. The baseline is the result by the classification with the event causality patterns. When combining all features, the performance shows 87.8% in F-measure. The result shows that context, frequency and causality features are effective in classifying CSU templates.

Table 7. Results of classification of clinical semantic units

	Feature	R	P	F
Classification with Answers of event tags and CSUs	Baseline (causality patterns)	65.4	87.1	74.7
	Lexical Feature	66.5	69.6	68.0
	+ Context Feature	81.2	85.0	83.0
	+ Frequency Feature	83.0	87.4	85.1
	+ Event Causality Feature	86.0	89.7	87.8
Classification by CRF and SVM		69.1	73.6	71.3

Table 8 show results of the extraction of problem and/or action relations for each template.

Table 8. Results of extraction of Problem-Action relations

Relation	R	P	F
TAP	73.7	71.0	72.3
Problem	68.1	72.3	70.1
Action	58.4	52.9	55.5
Problem-Action	52.6	46.1	49.1
Average	**63.2**	**60.5**	**61.8**

Table 9. Upper bounds of the proposed method

Comparisons	R	P	F
Extraction with Answers of events and CSUs	90.5	88.9	89.7
Extraction with Answers of events	81.2	76.7	78.8

The upper bound analyses for the CSUs classification and relation extraction are shown in Table 9. The performance comparisons are conducted when event tags and CSUs are given with human answers. The result indicates that the classification of CSUs and relation extraction needs further research to improve performance.

5. CONCLUSION

In this paper, we proposed the event causality relations to classify clinical semantic units and extract the problem and/or action relation. The structured knowledge could be extracted from clinical texts and presented in chronological order for physicians to identify effective treatments. The experimental result on the Korean medical test collection showed 78.8% in F-measure when given the answer of clinical events. The upper bound analysis indicates that each procedure of our system is effective.

In the future work, similar patients can be detected by searching similar medical histories such as making a treatment for a patient, and/or making a diagnosis with problem-action relations.

6. ACKNOWLEDGEMENTS

This research was supported by Microsoft Research. This work was also supported in part by Basic Science Research Program through the National Research Foundation of Korea(NRF) funded by the Ministry of Education, Science and Technology (NRF-2012R1A1A2044811), and the Brain Korea 21 PLUS Project, National Research Foundation of Korea.

7. REFERENCES

[1] Uzuner, Ö., South, B. R., Shen, S., and DuVall, S. L. 2011. 2010 i2b2/VA challenge on concepts, assertions, and relations in clinical text. Journal of the American Medical Informatics Association. 18.5, 552-556.

[2] Sun, W., Rumshisky, A., and Uzuner, O. 2013. Evaluating temporal relations in clinical text: 2012 i2b2 Challenge. Journal of the American Medical Informatics Association. 20(5), 806-813.

[3] Xu, Y., Wang, Y., Liu, T., Tsujii, J., Eric, I., and Chang, C. 2013. An end-to-end system to identify temporal relation in discharge summaries: 2012 i2b2 challenge. *Journal of the American Medical Informatics Association.* 20(5), 849-858.

[4] Roberts, K., Rink, B., and Harabagiu, S.M. 2013. A flexible framework for recognizing events, temporal expressions, and temporal relations in clinical text. Journal of the American Medical Informatics Association, 20(5), 867-875.

[5] Park, H. and Choi, J. 2012. V-Model: A New Innovative Model to Chronologically Visualize Narrative Clinical Texts. In Proc. of the SIGCHI Conference on Human Factors in Computing Systems, 453-462.

[6] Cortes, C., and Vapnik, V. 1995. Support-vector networks. *Machine learning.* 20(3), 273-297.

[7] Savova, G., Bethard, S., Styler, W., Martin, J., Palmer, M., Masanz, J., and Ward, W. 2009. Towards temporal relation discovery from the clinical narrative. In AMIA annual symposium proceedings.

[8] Lafferty, J., McCallum, A., and Pereira, F. C. 2001. Conditional random fields: Probabilistic models for segmenting and labeling sequence data. In Proc. Of 18th International Conference on Machine Learning, 282–289.

[9] Xu, Y., Hong, K., Tsujii, J., and Chang, E. 2012. Feature engineering combined with machine learning and rule-based methods for structured information extraction from narrative clinical discharge summaries. Journal of the American Medical Informatics Association, 19(5), 824-832.

[10] McCallum, A.K. 2002. MALLET: A Machine Learning for Language Toolkit. http://mallet.cs.umass.edu.

Entity oriented Task Extraction from Query Logs

Manisha Verma
University College London
m.verma@cs.ucl.ac.uk

Emine Yilmaz
University College London
emine.yilmaz@ucl.ac.uk

ABSTRACT

Identifying user tasks from query logs has garnered considerable interest from the research community lately. Several approaches have been proposed to extract tasks from search sessions. Current approaches segment a user session into disjoint tasks using features extracted from query, session or clicked document text. However, user tasks most often than not are entity centric and text based features will not exploit entities directly for task extraction. In this work, we explore entity specific task extraction from search logs. We evaluate the quality of extracted tasks with Session track data. Empirical evaluation shows that terms associated with entity oriented tasks can not only be used to predict terms in user sessions but also improve retrieval when used for query expansion.

Categories and Subject Descriptors

H.3.3 [**Information Search and Retrieval**]: Information Search and Retrieval

Keywords

search tasks, query log analysis, task discovery

1. INTRODUCTION

Users constantly interact with search engines to accomplish some tasks such as '*buy a car*', '*plan a wedding*' etc. Such broad requirements prompts the use of multiple queries, sometimes spanning multiple sessions. Approximately 75% of user search sessions involve multi-tasking [5], which makes, task identification an important step towards understanding user goals. Recent approaches [3, 4, 5, 6] use either search query or clicked documents to identify tasks. Most of these approaches cluster queries from current or neighboring sessions into tasks based on lexical or semantic similarity.

Often, tasks are associated with some entity. Extracting and mining entity information from queries across users can provide insight into different tasks that can be accomplished

CIKM'14, November 3–7, 2014, Shanghai, China.
Copyright 2014 ACM 978-1-4503-2598-1/14/11 ...$15.00.
http://dx.doi.org/10.1145/2661829.2662076.

with a search engine. However, current approaches do not directly leverage entities for task extraction. They use entity or entity type information as features. They semantically represent a query using features extracted, either from Wikipedia [5] or from some knowledge base [3]. These representations do not concretely capture entity specific intents in user queries. For instance, two queries that share same or similar type of entities, may still have diverse concept representation. Such queries will not be classified as part of the same task. For example, above approaches may not consider '*buy wedding flowers*' and '*book wedding destinations*' to be part of the same task due to the topic drift that '*destination*' and '*flower*' induce in concept vectors, even though both queries represent the same task - '*wedding planning*'. Whereas the entities in these two queries - '*flower*', '*destination*' and '*wedding*' shall have high co-occurrence in search logs. Queries, such as these, can be easily mapped to the same task by leveraging their entities. By considering the entities and their associations one can extract better semantics from user queries. Existing work extracts tasks from independent sessions, thus providing information only about a single user. Such tasks have limited applications as they do not give a complete picture about tasks that exist globally. However, entity oriented tasks can be extracted from search sessions accross several users. Such a global set of tasks can benefit related search applications too. For instance, it can be used to find similar users by mining their task histories or for query suggestions.

With this motivation, in this work we explore entity based task extraction from search logs. Our system finds entity oriented tasks for each category by populating words that co-occur with entities from that category. We evaluate the quality of extracted tasks in two ways: 1) Query term prediction and 2) Query expansion. Given a session, we use task terms related to entities in the first query to predict terms of subsequent queries in the session. We further show that the proposed method can improve retrieval performance when used for query expansion. Experiments on Session track[1] data indicate that terms associated with entity oriented tasks can not only predict query terms in a session but can also improve retrieval when used for query expansion.

2. RELATED WORK

Recent work mainly explores task extraction from search sessions. The objective in [3, 4, 5] is to segment a search session into disjoint sets of queries where each set represents

---

[1] http://ir.cis.udel.edu/sessions/

Figure 1: Task dictionary construction example

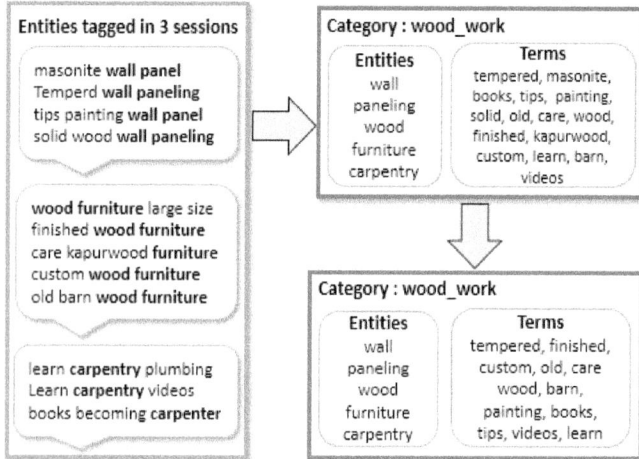

Figure 1: Task dictionary construction example

Table 2: Summary of Category Task Dictionaries

No of Categories	15510
Avg #entities per cat	20
Max #entities per cat	9356 (living people)
Avg #terms per cat	118
Max #terms per cat	11538 (states of US)

a different task. These approaches do not aggregate tasks across users, thus cannot combine or differentiate between tasks extracted from different sessions. Although, Lucchese *et al.* [6] attempt to cluster tasks across users to create a global representation, their approach uses only category information in Wikipedia to calculate semantic features. However, their approach cannot distinguish between tasks associated with different types of entities. Entity recognition with a knowledge base is used in [3], again, only to enrich concept vectors. Ji *et al.* [4] find global task representations using a similar approach, but they manually tag phrases with tasks. Our work differs from previous work as we identify tasks not by calculating semantic similarity, but by aggregating queries with its entities and their category information.

To find entities in text one can use entity linking techniques such as [2, 7]. These systems can link short texts such as queries to a knowledge base such as DBPedia[2]. Another work [8], closely related to ours, finds query reformulations using entity linking and Wikipedia. They extract expansion terms from Wikipedia and score them using anchor text information. However, we extract expansion terms from search logs and use only category information of an entity to score terms.

3. ENTITY BASED TASK EXTRACTION

Our goal is to use search queries to create a comprehensive list of tasks associated with an entity. Several factors have to be considered before building such a list. First consideration is the representation of task itself. What shall be used to represent a task? In earlier works, it was a sequence of queries. For simplicity, we use a dictionary of terms to represent a list of tasks. Alternatively, one can use a list of phrases, queries or more complicated representations. We chose terms as they can succinctly capture the task (e.g. buy, sell, design) associated with an entity (e.g. ticket) while providing the flexibility to build more complex representations (vectors, networks etc.) of tasks.

The second factor is the granularity of tasks associated with an entity. How specific or general will this list be? It depends on the source of entities. For instance, Freebase has more entities and entity types than DBPedia. Thus,

[2]http://www.dbpedia.org

tasks for more categories will be extracted from Freebase than DBPedia. However, since DBPedia is extracted from Wikipedia it is less prone to noise. In this work, we use DBPedia entities and categories to extract tasks.

Final consideration is the method of creating this task list. One can use several approaches like K-Means clustering or algorithms like Random Walk to build task list for an entity. We choose to group terms based on the entities and queries they appear with to build a list of task terms.

3.1 Entity Linking

Naturally, a system relying on entities needs a method to link query text with entities. We use Dexter [1] to link queries with entities. Dexter, in turn relies on DBPedia for entities and their type information. An entity may belong to different categories. For each query, Dexter returns the phrases that map to an entity (entity mentions), the entity and its categories.

3.2 Task Dictionary Construction

We represent tasks as a collection of diverse but conceptually related terms. We refer to these lists as task dictionaries. Constructing a dictionary for every entity will yield too many entities with only handful of words. The Zipfian distribution of queries will yield a skewed list of terms, since popular entities will contain more words than rare entities. However, aggregating these terms under entity category will yield a comprehensive list as terms from similar entities (popular or rare) will get grouped together. The process of creating these task dictionaries is as follows.

- We begin by tagging entities in a query. As mentioned before, we shall aggregate query terms on category level. For each entity in the query, we associate non entity terms with its categories. Non-entity terms are query terms other than the entity mentions. For example, in query *'flights between paris and London'*, *'London'* is an entity, *'City'* its category and *'flights'* and *'paris'* are non-entity terms.

- The previous step results in each category (or entity type) containing several terms. This list, even though exhaustive, will contain some noise. Filtering and scoring this list is important since we want a clean (even if small) task terms list. We rank these terms on the basis of category tf-Idf given by

$$tf\text{-}Idf(t_i, c_j) = tf(t_i, c_j) \times log(N_c/N_{t_i}) \quad (1)$$

where $tf(t_i, c_j)$ is the frequency of term t_i in category c_j, N_c is the total number of categories and N_{t_i} is the number of categories that contain the term t_i. We retain those words in the dictionary whose tf-Idf exceeds a certain threshold.

An example of aggregating and filtering query terms for the task dictionary of category *'wood_work'* is depicted in

Table 1: Comparison of Term Prediction Results [3]

	2011 Session Track					2012 Session Track				
		50 Tasks		100 Tasks			50 Tasks		100 Tasks	
Prec	Ent	HTC	QCC	HTC	QCC	Ent	HTC	QCC	HTC	QCC
1	**0.014**	0.012	0.004	0.005	0	0.001	0.012	0.012	0.004	**0.019**
5	0.04	0.021	0.019	0.02	**0.046**	0.022	0.019	0.031	**0.034**	0.026
10	0.046	0.035	0.037	0.038	**0.050**	0.041	0.045	0.049	**0.051**	0.049
15	0.051	0.052	0.059	0.061*	**0.064***	0.034	0.045	0.055	0.059	**0.062**
20	**0.072**	0.057	0.062	0.064	0.067	**0.073**	0.049	0.055	0.066	0.072
40	0.086*	0.062*	0.083*	0.084*	**0.089***	**0.096***	0.062	0.069	0.090*	0.092*
50	0.093*	0.066*	0.096*	0.089*	**0.106***	**0.113***	0.070	0.075	0.102*	0.092*

Figure 1. During Step 1, the system aggregates terms on a category node and in Step 2 it cleans this term set.

4. TASK DICTIONARY EVALUATION

Manual evaluation of dictionaries constructed above is infeasible. Since there is no labeled dataset for tasks evaluation, in this work, we evaluate them indirectly with query term prediction and query expansion. Query reformulations in a session are users' indication of possible terms that can be added or removed from the query to accomplish a certain task. The tasks associated with entities in current query can be used to predict terms of future queries. Similarly, the terms from these tasks can be used to enrich this query to improve retrieval. This is the underlying intuition of using both query term prediction and query expansion to evaluate the quality of generated task dictionaries.

Since a limited number of quality terms are required for evaluation, we need to score task dictionary terms with respect to the query. For instance, the query '*lake murray resort*' has one entity '*lake murray*' whose category is '*Reservoirs in South Carolina*'. Task dictionary of this category contains over 50 terms, and since all its terms may not be equally relevant (either for query term prediction or query expansion), its necessary to rank them with respect to the query. Thus, we propose the following scoring mechanism to find most suitable terms for a query given its entities and their types respectively.

- We begin by finding entities in the query. An entity may belong to several categories, for instance, entity '*apple*' may belong to two categories- '*company*' and '*fruit*'. Since all categories of an entity are not equally important, we need to find the one that aligns best with input query. For a given query q_k with entity mention e_i that maps to category c_j, we score categories with Eq 2.

$$mc_i = \underset{c_j}{\mathrm{argmax}} \frac{cos(Q_k, C_j) + jac(Q_k, C_j)}{2} \quad (2)$$

where $cos(Q_k, C_j)$ is Cosine similarity between query vector Q_k, built from terms in the query and category vector C_j, built from its task dictionary terms. $jac(Q_k, C_j)$ is the Jaccard similarity between C_j and Q_k. For this work, we only consider query terms for calculating the best category for an entity. Since, Jaccard and Cosine are computationally quick to compute, we use the average of both metrics to find most likely category for an entity.

- For queries with multiple entities, we shall get terms from different categories. We aggregate terms from the best category of each entity in a single set. We represent this set as T, where $T = \cup_{mc_i} S_i$, and S_i is the term dictionary of category mc_i. Since we need only a few terms, we score terms $t_m \in T$ with respect to the query using Eq 3.

$$score(t_m, q_k) = tf(t_m, mc_i) \frac{\sum_{w_k \in Q_k} PMI(t_m, w_k)}{|Q_k|} \quad (3)$$

where $PMI(t_m, w_k)$ represents the Pointwise Mutual Information between query word w_k, and task term t_m. $tf(t_m, mc_i)$ is the term frequency of term t_m in category mc_i. The objective of Eq 3 is to capture both the importance of a term given a certain category ($tf(t_m, mc_i)$) and the average likelihood (PMI) of that term occurring with the query terms. That is, a term should not only be important in the category but should also frequently co-occur with query terms.

We use the above method to rank terms both for term prediction and query expansion. To summarize, we adopt the following mechanism for evaluation:

Query Term Prediction: For each session, we use the first query to predict terms in subsequent queries of the session. We remove the overlapping terms between the base query and subsequent queries in the session to avoid scoring query terms twice during prediction. We also remove stop words from this list. We ignore those sessions where subsequent queries do not contain additional terms.

Query Expansion: For this work, we use the category task dictionaries to expand a user query. An input query is first tagged using Dexter, each entity is then mapped to a single category. The system ranks terms from these categories and uses the top scored terms for expansion. We choose top K terms to expand the query. Terms are ranked using the approach above.

We refer to our approach as **ENT** in the tables. To construct a dictionary of task phrases we use publicly available 2006 AOL query logs which consists of 20 mil search queries issued by over 657000 users within 3 months. We empirically determined the frequency thresholds to filter terms for tasks in each category. For each category, we retain terms with tf-Idf greater than 9. This was selected by manually sampling and inspecting term quality of some categories. Table 2 summarizes the resulting task phrase dictionaries. In the

---

[3]statistically significant values are marked with * and highest values are in bold

Table 3: Comparison of Retrieval results [3]

METHOD	2011 Session Track				2012 Session Track			
	MAP	P@5	NDCG	NDCG@10	MAP	P@5	NDCG	NDCG@10
No_Exp	0.1004	0.1759	0.3021	0.1662	0.1618	0.3247	0.3465	0.2402
HTC_50	0.103	0.1828	0.3071	0.1655	0.1624	0.3294	0.349	0.2453
HTC_100	0.1025	0.1862	0.3067	0.1674	0.163	0.3318	**0.3507**	0.2486
QCC_50	0.1048	0.1828	0.3068	0.1686	**0.1634**	**0.3341***	0.3483	**0.2502***
QCC_100	0.1036	**0.1897***	0.3069	0.1676	0.1631	0.3294	0.3495	0.2452
Ent	**0.1086***	0.1828	**0.3105***	**0.1709**	0.1609	0.3153	0.3464	0.2258

following section, we briefly explain the task extraction baselines used to compare our approach.

4.1 Task Extraction Baselines

As baselines, we use task identification approaches proposed in [5] to find tasks in a session. They refer to a set of (consecutive or otherwise) queries with same intent in a session as a single task. Lucchese *et al.* [5] explore several clustering methods to identify these tasks. We use QCC-wcc (**QCC**), query clustering based on weighted connected components, a graph based algorithm to identify tasks. It builds a graph $G = (V, E)$, whose nodes V are queries in a session and edges E are weighted by the similarity of the corresponding nodes. The aim is to drop edges with low similarity, and to build clusters on the basis of the strong edges which identify the related query pairs. We also compare our approach with QCC-htc (**HTC**), which clusters queries based on head-tail components, a variation of the connected components based algorithm, which does not need to compute the full similarity graph. We use the same similarity functions proposed in the paper for both the algorithms. We use similar parameter settings from [5] for both methods.

We use the following setup to compare our tasks with [5]. We begin by building a task index using tasks extracted by QCC and HTC on a large query log. This is done to improve real time task identification for a query. For an input query, we retrieve top K tasks. The system then extracts and ranks terms from these tasks based on their frequency in this set.

5. RESULTS AND DISCUSSION

The results of both query term prediction and query expansion are shown in Table 1 and Table 3 respectively.

Query Term Prediction: We use Session track 2011 and 2012 dataset with 145 sessions, with total of 456 terms, i.e. an average of 3 terms per session. The table shows precision values for term prediction at various cutoffs. For a given query, we retrieve top 50 and 100 tasks using QCC and HTC to extract terms. We follow the method in Section 4 to score terms from entity task dictionaries. Entity based task dictionaries (ENT) perform significantly better for 2012 sessions but do not outperform the baselines QCC and HTC for 2011 sessions.

Query expansion: We compare the both QCC and HTC with 50 and 100 tasks each to retrieve top terms. We also report results with no expansion- **No_Exp**. We varied the value of K and found K=25 to be ideal as addition of more terms did not affect the retrieval performance. The results indicate that task based query expansion is effective in improving performance. The results, however, indicate a mixed performance of our approach on 2011 and 2012 ses-

Table 4: Evaluation on 2012 Exploratory Queries[3]

	MAP	Ndcg@10	Ndcg
No_Exp	0.2108	0.3427	0.3873
HTC_{100}	0.2171	**0.3689***	0.3973*
QCC_{100}	0.2153	0.3593*	0.3949*
ENT	**0.2207***	0.3535*	**0.4025***

sion dataset. While, we outperform the baselines on 2011 queries, for 2012, retrieval performance does not improve with expansion.

On manually inspecting expansion terms, we observed that task based query expansion is effective for queries exploratory in nature. Exploratory queries are more ambiguous in nature, thus adding terms from different tasks related to the query would improve performance. On the other hand, for specific queries, adding terms from different tasks will only harm retrieval. Hence, task specific expansion does not do well on specific queries. In 2012 dataset, there are 19 exploratory queries, for which our method outperform the baseline. The results are shown in Table 4. We shall perform further experiments to confirm this hypothesis.

6. CONCLUSION

In this work, we explored entity specific task extraction from search logs. We evaluated the quality of extracted tasks with Session track data. Empirical evaluation indicates that terms associated with entity oriented tasks can improve query expansion, especially for queries that are exploratory in nature. It can also predict subsequent query terms in a session.

7. REFERENCES

[1] D. Ceccarelli, C. Lucchese, S. Orlando, R. Perego, and S. Trani. Dexter: An open source framework for entity linking. In *ESAIR*, 2013.

[2] P. Ferragina and U. Scaiella. Tagme: On-the-fly annotation of short text fragments (by wikipedia entities). In *CIKM*, 2010.

[3] W. Hua, Y. Song, H. Wang, and X. Zhou. Identifying users' topical tasks in web search. In *WSDM*, 2013.

[4] M. Ji, J. Yan, S. Gu, J. Han, X. He, W. V. Zhang, and Z. Chen. Learning search tasks in queries and web pages via graph regularization. In *SIGIR*, 2011.

[5] C. Lucchese, S. Orlando, R. Perego, F. Silvestri, and G. Tolomei. Identifying task-based sessions in search engine query logs. In *WSDM*, 2011.

[6] C. Lucchese, S. Orlando, R. Perego, F. Silvestri, and G. Tolomei. Discovering tasks from search engine query logs. *ACM Trans. Inf. Syst.*, 2013.

[7] D. Milne and I. H. Witten. Learning to link with wikipedia. In *CIKM*, 2008.

[8] Y. Xu, G. J. Jones, and B. Wang. Query dependent pseudo-relevance feedback based on wikipedia. In *SIGIR*, 2009.

Modeling Retail Transaction Data for Personalized Shopping Recommendation

Pengfei Wang,Jiangfeng Guo,Yanyan Lan,Xueqi Cheng
Key lab of Network Data Science and Technology in ICT
Beijing, China
wangpengfei@software.ict.ac.cn,{guojiafeng,lanyanyan},cxq@ict.ac.cn

ABSTRACT

Retail transaction data conveys rich preference information on brands and goods from customers. How to mine the transaction data to provide personalized recommendation to customers becomes a critical task for retailers. Previous recommendation methods either focus on the user-product matrix and ignore the transactions, or only use the partial information of transactions, leading to inferior performance in recommendation. Inspired by association rule mining, we introduce association pattern as a basic unit to capture the correlation between products from both intra- and inter-transactions. A *Probabilistic* model over the *Association Patterns* (PAP for short) is then employed to learn the potential shopping interests and also to provide personalized recommendations. Experimental results on two real world retail data sets show that our proposed method can outperform the state-of-the-art recommendation methods.

Categories and Subject Descriptors

H.2.8 [**Database Applications**]: Data mining

Keywords

recommendation, association pattern, probabilistic model

1. INTRODUCTION

Massive transaction data sets have been routinely recorded in offline retails, which convey rich preference information on brands and goods from customers. It becomes a critical task for retailers to mine these valuable transaction data to provide personalized recommendation to customers, so that they can stimulate consumption and compete with e-commerce business where recommender systems have already been widely employed. In fact, in the past decades data mining technologies, like association rule mining, have been applied on transaction data to discover interesting relations between products. For example, some useful rules are found in the sales data of a supermarket indicating that

if a customer buys onions and potatoes together, he or she is likely to also buy hamburger meat. The obtained rules can help retailers in promotional pricing or product placements, but usually lack personalization which is important to customers. Therefore, how to model the transaction data to provide personalized shopping recommendations becomes a key challenge.

Previous methods on recommender systems, like collaborative filtering methods [3], mainly focus on directly modeling the user-product matrix. In this way, the transaction information is usually ignored in these methods. However, transactions indicate the strong correlation between products and are very prominent in retail as compared with the correlation in e-commerce. For example, we compared the sales data from a large retailer BeiRen with data from the biggest e-commerce website Taobao in China. We found that in the retail data set there is 33.6% transactions containing more than two products, while in the e-commerce data set there is less than 12%. Some recent work on basket recommendation did take transactions into account . However, in their work, only partial transaction information: either patterns across transactions [4], or patterns within transactions [7] has been utilized.

In this paper, we present a novel approach on modeling retail transaction data for personalized shopping recommendation. Inspired by association rules, we introduce association patterns as basic units to capture the correlation between products and summarize the dataset. Here an association pattern is defined as a weighted pair of products from either intra- and inter- transactions of a user. The weight of a pattern describes correlations strength between the two products in the pattern, which is defined according to the time span between the two products. In this way, the original transaction data can been turned into a collection of association patterns, which preserves the important correlation information within and across transactions.

By assuming the association patterns are generated from some low-dimensional latent shopping interests, we propose a *Probabilistic* model over the *Association Patterns* (PAP for short) to model the generation process and learn the representation of shopping interests. With the learned model, we can then inference the shopping interests of each individual and provide personalized shopping recommendations. Experimental results on two real world retail datasets show that our proposed method can outperform the state-of-the-art recommendation methods.

The remainder of this paper is organized as follows. We first discuss related work in section 2. Section 3 introduce

CIKM'14, November 3–7, 2014, Shanghai, China.
Copyright 2014 ACM 978-1-4503-2598-1/14/11 ...$15.00.
http://dx.doi.org/10.1145/2661829.2662020 .

our model. We present our experiments and discussion in section 4, then make a conclusion in section 5.

2. RELATED WORK

In this section, we will briefly review the related work on general recommender systems, and the work on transaction data mining for recommendations.

The content-based method recommends products based on a comparison between contents of products [1]. However, content information may not always available in many cases, which limits the usage of this model. Collaborative filtering is a popular recommendation method, which tries to predict the utility of products for a particular user based on the products rated by other users [1, 5]. Algorithms of collaborative filtering essentially can be grouped into two general classes: memory-based methods, e.g. KNN, and model-based methods, e.g. matrix factorization model.

KNN makes prediction based on the entire collection of previous rated products [6]. The rate to an unknown product for a given user can be calculated as an aggregation of similar users' behaviors. However this kind of algorithm only concerns local information in choosing similar users, and it leads to a inferior performance in recommendation.

Matrix factorization models map both products and users into a low-dimensional latent space. For example, BPR (Bayesian Personalized Ranking) is a popular factorization model[5, 8]. The model tries to obtain the representation of users and products by optimizing a personalized ranking for all products.

Recently, some work in recommendation also take transaction information into account. For example, the rule-based models utilize data mining algorithms(i.e. Apriori and FP-growth)to recommend products by mining frequent itemsets from dataset. However the models tend to generate a large number of patterns once mining a large data set, most of which are spurious, not relevant to recommendations [4]. Rendle et al. [6] propose a factorization model by emphasizing correlations of products belonging to different transactions, while Xiang Wu et al. [7] utilize relations of products in the same transaction to recommendation songs for users.

3. OUR APPROACH

In this section we will describe our *Probabilistic model over Association Pattern* in detail. In the following, we first introduce the concept of association patterns, then describe the generative model (i.e. PAP) over the association patterns, we finally present how to infer customers' shopping interests with the learned model and provide personalized recommendations.

3.1 Association Pattern

Correlation between products is a basic factor in shopping behavior and critical for recommendation, which can be revealed by the co-occurrences between products. We introduce the concept of association patterns to describe the co-occurrences between products in user transaction data. According to different co-occurrence types, there are two kinds of association patterns, namely Intra Association Pattern and Inter Association Pattern, as shown in Figure 1.

DEFINITION 1. *Intra Association Pattern. Given the transaction set $T^u = \{t_1^u, t_2^u, \ldots, t_{|T|}^u\}$ of user u, where $|T|$*

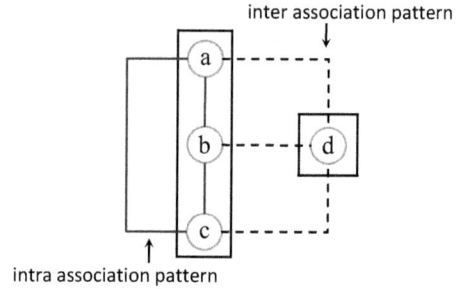

Figure 1: Association patterns between two transactions. The solid lines among product a, b, c stand for intra association patterns, and the dotted lines among a, b, c and d stand for inter association patterns.

is the count of transactions belonging to u, an intra association pattern is defined as a weighted pair of products $< I_i, I_j, w_{ij} >$, where $I_i, I_j \in t_m^u$ and w_{ij} denotes the weight of the pattern.

DEFINITION 2. *Inter Association Pattern. Given the transaction set $T^u = \{t_1^u, t_2^u, \ldots, t_{|T|}^u\}$ of user u, where $|T|$ is the count of transactions belonging to u, an inter association pattern is defined as a weighted pair of products $< I_i, I_j, w_{ij} >$, where $I_i \in t_m^u$, $I_j \in t_n^u$, $m \neq n$, and w_{ij} denotes the weight of the pattern.*

The weight of an association pattern represents the correlation strength between the pair of products. Obviously, the intra association pattern indicates strong correlations between products since customers prefer to buy them together, while the inter association pattern indicates weak correlation. To reflect this, here we define the weight based on the time-stamp of the transaction the products belong to. Let $I_i \in t_m^u$ and $I_j \in t_n^u$, the weight of an association pattern is defined in following unified form:

$$w_{ij} = \exp\{-\frac{|time(t_m^u) - time(t_n^u)|}{K}\} \quad (1)$$

where K is a normalization factor. As we can see, the weight of an intra association pattern is 1 by definition, while that of an inter association pattern is less than 1 and decayed with the time span between the two transactions.

Based on the definition of association patterns, the original transaction data set can be turned into a collection of association patterns. By this transformation, we can accumulate all the important co-occurrence information within and across transactions from different users.

3.2 The Generative Model

Although the association patterns reflect the correlations between products, they can be hardly directly utilized for recommendation due to the sparsity. To learn useful correlation information for recommendation, we assume that all the association patterns are generated from some latent low-dimension shopping interests. In this way, we introduce a generative model, namely PAP, to describe the generation of the association patterns and learn the latent shopping interests.

Specifically, PAP assumes that two products in an association pattern are drawn independently from a latent shopping interest. The key idea is that if two products co-occur more frequently, they are more likely to belong to the same interest.

Formally, let S denotes the whole collection of association patterns, S shares a n-dimensional latent shopping interests. Θ denotes a multinomial distribution of shopping interests, with $\Theta_k = p(z = k)$ standing for the proportion of the k-th shopping interest. Φ_k denotes a multinomial distribution of products, with $\Phi_{k,m}$ standing for the proportion of product I_m on the k-th shopping interest($\sum_m \Phi_{k,m} = 1$). The generative process of PAP is described as follows:

Algorithm 1 The generative process of PAP

1: sample a distribution of shopping interests $\Theta \sim$ Dirichlet(α)
2: for each shopping interest z
    draw a distribution $\Phi_z \sim$ Dirichlet(β)
3: for each pattern $< I_i, I_j > \in S$
    draw a latent shopping interest $z \sim$ Multinomial(Θ)
    draw a pattern $< I_i, I_j > \sim$ Multinomial(Φ_z)

---

where parameter α and β are Dirichlet priors. Figure 2 shows the probability graph of generative process.

Based on the generative process mentioned above, we can obtain the joint probability of pattern $< I_i, I_j >$:

$$P(< I_i, I_j > | \Theta, \Phi) = \sum_z P(z)P(I_i|z)P(I_j|z)$$
$$= \sum_k \theta_k \Phi_{k,i} \Phi_{k,j}$$

the marginal distribution of $< I_i, I_j >$ can be calculated through integrated Θ and Φ:

$$P(< I_i, I_j > | \alpha, \beta) = \iint \sum_k \theta_k \Phi_{k,i} \Phi_{k,j} d\Theta d\Phi$$

and the likelihood of the whole pattern-set S is:

$$P(S|\alpha, \beta) = \prod_{< I_i, I_j > \in S} \iint \sum_k \theta_k \Phi_{k,i} \Phi_{k,j} d\Theta d\Phi$$

We use Gibbs sampling to approximate inference. In our model there are three parameters need to be estimated: z, Θ, and Φ. Concerning that we can integrate out parameters Θ, Φ because of conjugate prior α, β. Given association pattern $< I_i, I_j >$, we just need to sample parameter z:

$$P(z = k|\mathbf{z}_{-<I_i,I_j>}, S, \alpha, \beta) \propto (n_k + \alpha)\frac{(n_{k,i} + \beta)(n_{k,j} + \beta)}{(\Sigma_m n_{k,m} + M\beta)^2}$$

where $\mathbf{z}_{-<I_i,I_j>}$ denotes the interest assignments for all patterns, except $< I_i, I_j >$. Θ_k, $\Phi_{k,m}$ can be calculated as:

$$\Theta_k = \frac{n_k + \alpha}{|S| + K\alpha}$$
$$\Phi_{k,m} = \frac{n_{k,m}}{\sum_m n_{k,m} + M\beta}$$

where n_k is the number of pattern $< I_i, I_j >$ assigned to the k-th interest, $n_{k,i}$ is the number of I_i assigned to the k-th interest, and $|S|$ is the number of patterns in pattern-set S.

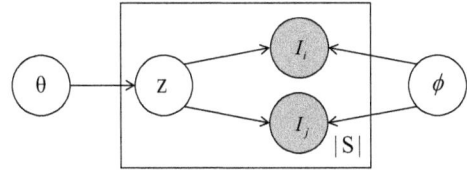

Figure 2: probabilistic model over association patterns

3.3 Inference of User Preference

With the learned shopping interests, we now aim to infer individual shopping interests for each user for recommendation. Through Bayesian theory, given association pattern $< I_i, I_j >$, we can get the probability of the k-th shopping interest:

$$P(z = k| < I_i, I_j >) = \frac{P(< I_i, I_j > |z = k)P(z = k)}{\sum_z P(< I_i, I_j > |z)P(z)}$$
$$= \frac{P(z = k)P(I_i|z = k)P(I_j|z = k)}{\sum_z P(I_i|z)P(I_j|z)P(z)}$$
$$= \frac{\theta_k \phi_{k,i} \phi_{k,j}}{\sum_k \theta_k \phi_{k,i} \phi_{k,j}}$$

Then the proportion on k-th shopping interest for user u can be calculated as:

$$\theta_k^u = P(z = k|u)$$
$$= \sum_{<I_i,I_j> \in S^u} P(z = k| < I_i, I_j >)P(< I_i, I_j > |u)$$

where S^u denotes the collection of association patterns mined from transaction set T^u, and $P(< I_i, I_j > |u)$ can be obtained as follows:

$$P(< I_i, I_j > |u) = \frac{w_{ij}}{\sum_{<I_i,I_j> \in S^u} w_{ij}}$$

To conduct personalized shopping recommendation to users, we calculate users' preference to products with respect to their shopping interests as follows:

$$P(I_i|u) = \sum_z P(I_i|z)P(z|u) = \sum_k \theta_k^u \phi_{k,i}$$

By sorting the products according to $P(I_i|u)$, we can recommend top-k products to uesrs.

4. EVALUATION

To demonstrate the effectiveness of our model, we choose two real retail data sets: BeiRen dateset and Tafeng dataset. BeiRen dataset is collected by a large retail department store in China, recording brands of merchandise products from 2011 to 2013. Tafeng dataset[1] is offered by RecSys, which covers products from food, office supplies to furniture. The detail is showed in Table 1.

First we preprocess two datasets before evaluation. We reserve products and brands in datasets bought at least 10 times. We hold out 50% of the data set for training, with the remaining for test, The time of transactions in two datasets is recorded by the day, thus we assign $K = 365$ in Equation 1. We evaluate our model against four state-of-the-art methods in product recommendation:TOP(the most

---
[1]http://recsyswiki.com/wiki/Grocery_shopping_datasets

Table 1: data set statistics

id	name	# users	# products	# transactions
1	*BeiRen*	18315	1442	242894
2	*Tafeng*	7141	6894	37269

popular products are recommended),KNN, NMF, and BPR method.

We compare the performance of different recommendation methods with the widely used *F*-measure [2, 6, 7] over top-5, top-10 products.

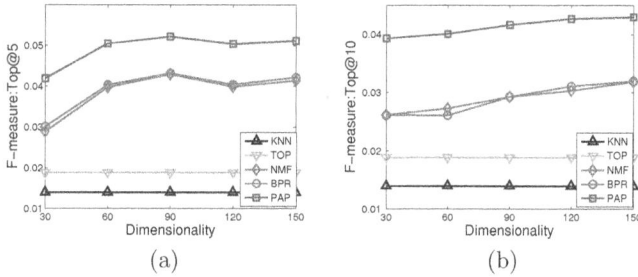

(a) (b)

Figure 3: Comparisons of TOP, KNN, NMF, BPR and our model PAP on BeiRen data set.

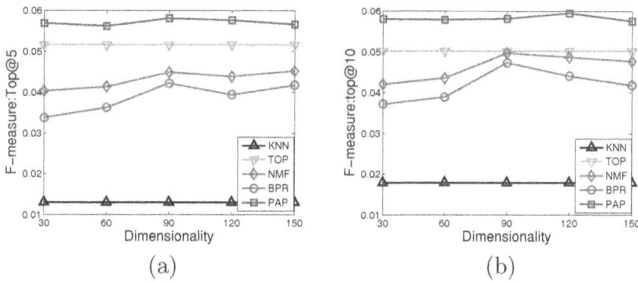

(a) (b)

Figure 4: Comparisons of TOP, KNN, NMF, BPR and our model PAP on Tafeng data set.

Figure 3 and Figure 4 show the results on BeiRen and Tafeng dataset. We can see that KNN performs worst in recommendation because it only utilizes local information. By simply recommending top popular products, Top method outperforms KNN slightly. Surprisingly, Top method performs the second best on Tafeng datset, indicating that the top method is very unstable. The BPR and NMF methods represent users and products into a low-dimensional latent space to avoid data sparsity, and the two methods show little difference in performance.

Comparing to other methods, our model outperforms all other methods, with *F*-score promoted at least 33% and 16% respectively. The improvement is statistically significant(*p-value* < 0.01)

5. CONCLUSIONS

In this paper we proposed a novel *P*robabilistic model over the *A*ssociation *P*attern for personalized recommendation.

With a generative process to reduce association patterns into a n-dimensional latent shopping interests, we recommend user top-k products by user's preference. In the future we will try to consider sequential patterns, and make dynamic personalized recommendation.

6. ACKNOWLEDGMENTS

This research work has funded by 973 Program of China under Grants No.2014CB340401, 863 Program of China under Grants No.2014AA015204, No.2012AA011003, Project supported by the State Key Program of National Natural Science of China under Grant No.61232010, Project supported by the National Science Foundation for Young Scientists of China under Grant No.61203298, and The National Key Technology *R&D* Program under Grants No.2012BAH39B04.We would like to thank the anonymous reviewers for their helpful comments.

7. REFERENCES

[1] G. Adomavicius and A. Tuzhilin. Toward the next generation of recommender systems: A survey of the state-of-the-art and possible extensions. *IEEE Trans. on Knowl. and Data Eng.*, 17(6):734–749, June 2005.

[2] K. Choi, D. Yoo, G. Kim, and Y. Suh. A hybrid online-product recommendation system: Combining implicit rating-based collaborative filtering and sequential pattern analysis. *Electron. Commer. Rec. Appl.*, 11(4):309–317, July 2012.

[3] Y. Koren, R. Bell, and C. Volinsky. Matrix factorization techniques for recommender systems. *Computer*, 42(8):30–37, Aug. 2009.

[4] B. Mobasher, H. Dai, T. Luo, and M. Nakagawa. Effective personalization based on association rule discovery from web usage data. In *Proceedings of the 3rd International Workshop on Web Information and Data Management*, WIDM '01, pages 9–15, New York, NY, USA, 2001. ACM.

[5] S. Rendle, C. Freudenthaler, Z. Gantner, and L. Schmidt-Thieme. Bpr: Bayesian personalized ranking from implicit feedback. In *Proceedings of the Twenty-Fifth Conference on Uncertainty in Artificial Intelligence*, UAI '09, pages 452–461, Arlington, Virginia, United States, 2009. AUAI Press.

[6] S. Rendle, C. Freudenthaler, and L. Schmidt-Thieme. Factorizing personalized markov chains for next-basket recommendation. In *Proceedings of the 19th International Conference on World Wide Web*, WWW '10, pages 811–820, New York, NY, USA, 2010. ACM.

[7] X. Wu, Q. Liu, E. Chen, L. He, J. Lv, C. Cao, and G. Hu. Personalized next-song recommendation in online karaokes. In *Proceedings of the 7th ACM Conference on Recommender Systems*, RecSys '13, pages 137–140, New York, NY, USA, 2013. ACM.

[8] X. Yu, X. Ren, Y. Sun, Q. Gu, B. Sturt, U. Khandelwal, B. Norick, and J. Han. Personalized entity recommendation: A heterogeneous information network approach. In *Proceedings of the 7th ACM International Conference on Web Search and Data Mining*, WSDM '14, pages 283–292, New York, NY, USA, 2014. ACM.

Identifying Latent Study Habits by Mining Learner Behavior Patterns in Massive Open Online Courses

Miaomiao Wen
Language Technologies Institute
Carnegie Mellon University
Pittsburgh, PA 15213
mwen@cs.cmu.edu

Carolyn Penstein Rosé
Language Technologies Institute
Carnegie Mellon University
Pittsburgh, PA 15213
cprose@cs.cmu.edu

ABSTRACT

MOOCs attract diverse users with varying habits. Identifying those patterns through clickstream analysis could enable more effective personalized support for student information seeking and learning in that online context. We propose a novel method to characterize types of sessions in MOOCs by mining the habitual behaviors of students within individual sessions. We model learning sessions as a distribution of activities and activity sequences with a topical N-gram model. The representation offers insights into what groupings of habitual student behaviors are associated with higher or lower success in the course. We also investigate how context information, such as time of day or a user's demographic information, is associated with the types of learning sessions.

Categories and Subject Descriptors

H.2.8 [**Database Management**]: Database Applications

Keywords

Massive Open Online Course; MOOCs; learning behavior patterns; sequence mining

1. INTRODUCTION

Massive Open Online Courses (MOOCs) have recently garnered widespread public attention for their potential to make high quality education accessible to everyone. Researchers, educators, and the general public have become interested in understanding learning experiences in MOOCs. A major component of the learning experience is navigation through course content. The MOOC literature so far has focused on a summative view of user participation over extended periods of time, such as over the whole course or over a whole week - trying to identify different groups of users based on aggregated statistics such as total number of lectures and assignments completed by the student [1]. We develop a more fine grained representation of MOOC clickstream data using topical N-gram models with single

MOOC	#Users	#Sessions	#Clicks
Virtual Instruction	20,372	76,770	2,112,857
Financial Planning	112,318	469,238	10,073,997

Table 1: Statistics of the two Coursera MOOCs.

sessions as the unit of analysis, with the goal of identifying habbits and strategies.

In a MOOC, each student's complete interaction with the course materials is recorded as a clickstream, similar to other online environments. However, the different nature of the interaction provides new challenges for the community of researchers developing techniques for clickstream analysis. Understanding how students interact with MOOCs is a crucial issue because it affects how MOOC engineers and instructors design future online courses. Effective analysis of clickstream data could enable dynamic interventions to improve success of students to achieve their information access goals. What makes the mining of learning behavior patterns hard is that learning sessions are typically composed of a range of loosely coordinated activities. The composition of a session is highly variable depending on factors such as learner engagement and time available. Previous behavior mining methods, such as those designed for search engine clicklog analysis, are not quite rich enough to capture these distinctions. We propose to leverage topical N-gram models to (1) capture the typical combination of learning activities and (2) identify frequent learning activity sequence which can suggest learning strategies. Thus we can characterize each session of MOOC interaction as a composition of such activities or activity sequence patterns. We find that there are typically a small number of latent session types across MOOCs we have studied. In this paper we present results that demonstrate that we can observe meaningful differences in student orientations towards course content. To understand how the learning sessions can be affected by context or individual user's engagement level, we mine the associations between user session type and context information captured by system trace logs.

2. DATASET AND PRE-PROCESSING

Our dataset consists of two Coursera[1] MOOCs, one is about virtual instruction(VI) and the other one is about personal financial planning(FP). They were both offered in 2013. Table 1 shows an overview of the data we extracted from the system trace logs.

---

[1] https://www.coursera.org/

MOOC	None $\leq 10\%$	Fail 10%-60%	Pass 60%-90%	Distinction $\geq 90\%$
VI	17,562	1,418	507	881
FP	71,522	8,768	1,025	2,918

Table 2: Number of students within each final grade level.

Pre-processing is the first part of Web Usage Mining which includes the domain dependent tasks such as data cleaning and session identification. In our case, a new session is considered to begin when the time interval between two successive inter-transaction clicks adds up to 60 minutes. The visited or submitted contents during each session are considered to be part of that session.

We extract 18 types of learning activities from the trace data. In particular, we distinguish between submitted quizzes, assignments, peer assessments and those that are attempted but not submitted. We also differentiate passive activities such as browsing and active activities such as publishing a post in the forums. Only the underlined activities are graded.

- Video lecture
  (1)Watch a video lecture (Lecture).

- Assignment
  (2)Browse an assignment (BrowseAssignment); (3)Submit an assignment (SubmitAssignment); (4)Start a peer-asse ssment[2] (BrowsePeerAssessment); (5)Submit a peer-assessment (SubmitPeerAssessment).

- Quiz
  (6)Submit an in-video quiz[3] (SubmitVideoQuiz); (7) Browse a weekly quiz (BrowseQuiz); (8)Submit a weekly quiz (SubmitQuiz). (9)Browse the final quiz (BrowseFinalQuiz); (10)Submit a final quiz (SubmitFinalQuiz).

- Survey
  (11)Browse a pre-course or post-course survey (BrowseSurvey); (12)Submit a survey (SubmitSurvey).

- Forum participation
  (13)Browse a thread in the course forums (BrowseForum); (14)Post a new post in the course forums (Post); (15)Comment on the other posts in the course forums (Comment); (16)Upvote a post(Upvote); (17)Downvote a post (Downvote).

- Browse the course material
  (18)Browse the course material without clicking on videos, quizzes, surveys, forums or assignments (BrowseCourse).

We extract information for each session and each user. The contextual information associated with each session includes: (1) Time information, including *Hour of the day*, *Day Period*, *Day of the week* and *Course week*. (2) *Device* used during the current session. The device can be Desktop, Tablet or Mobile. (3) *Length* of the session. A Short session is shorter than 5 minutes. A Long session is longer than 30 minutes. Otherwise the session length is Medium.

Information extracted for each user includes: *Gender*, *Age*, *Country of Origin* and *Final Grade*. *Gender* and *Age* are only known for the users who filled out the pre-course survey. *Country of Origin* is determined based on the IP address.

---

[2]Peer assessment is the practice of classmates evaluating each other's work.

[3]In-video quizzes are quizzes that pop up during the lectures.

As there are more than 100 different countries of origin, we group them into *US* and *NON-US*. As for achievement, we group the users into four groups according to their final grade. Students who successfully complete this class with a grade of around 60% - 70% will receive a Statement of Accomplishment. Students who complete this course with a grade of 90% or better will receive a Statement of Accomplishment with Distinction from Coursera. The statistics are shown in Table 2.

3. METHODS

In this section, we describe how we model each learning session with a topical N-gram model and how we extract the typical context associated with different types of learning sessions.

3.1 Characterizing Learning Sessions with the Topical N-gram Model

A learning session can be characterized as a probabilistic combination of interaction and interaction sequence patterns. To motivate our work with intuitive examples, an intense learning session may be one that includes an assignment submission. In the same session, the user may watch video lectures to prepare for the assignment or go to the discussion forums to find related discussions. Just as word order and phrases are often critical to capturing the meaning of text in many text mining tasks, the order of activities within sessions is important for capturing a user's learning strategies. For example, a sequence, "FinalQuizBrowse_Lecture_FinalQuizSubmit", implies the user tries to refer to the lecture during the final quiz. Activity sequences as the whole may carry more information than an unordered collection of its individual components.

A topical N-gram model is a topic model that discovers topics as well as topical phrases [10]. The probabilistic model generates words, or actions in our case, in their order of appearance. This is accomplished by iterating over words, and for each word, first sampling a topic, then sampling its status as a unigram or bigram, and then sampling the word from the selected topic-specific unigram or bigram distribution. Successive bigrams can form longer phrases. Thus the model can distinguish that "white house" has a special meaning as a phrase in the 'politics' topic, but not in the 'real estate' topic. We apply topical N-gram models to our learning session modeling task where we treat each learning activity defined during pre-processing (Section 2) as a word and each session as a document. Then we can characterize learning sessions with topic proportions.

3.2 Mining Learner Behavior Patterns

Intuitively, some learner behaviors are context-sensitive, that is, the occurrences of these behaviors are influenced by contextual factors like time and course schedule. For example, some users prefer to have an intense learning session, which involves doing assignments, on Sundays but only browse the course forums on weeknights. The associations between user interaction records and the corresponding contexts, which can be referred to as behavior patterns, can be used to characterize user habits[2]. We are especially interested in how students' study habits influence their success. This is important because it may enable context sensitive support to be generated for students. Instead of traditional association rule mining, we use classification rule mining to

Session Topic	Top Activities and Activity Sequences
Lecture and Peer-Assessment	Lecture_Lecture, Lecture_Lecture_Quiz, Lecture, Quiz, SubmitPeerAssessment
Browse Course	BrowseCourse
Assignment and Forum	BrowseAssignment, BrowseForum, BrowseForum_BrowseForum, Lecture_Lecture, Upvote, SubmitQuiz, SubmitAssignment
Final Quiz and Survey	Quiz, BrowseForum_BrowseForum, BrowseSurvey, BrowseFinalQuiz, SubmitSurvey, BrowseLecture_BrowseLecture_BrowseFinalQuiz, SubmitFinalQuiz
Lecture and Quiz	Quiz, Lecture, Lecture_Lecture, Lecture_Lecture_SubmitVideoQuiz, SubmitVideoQuiz, Lecture_SubmitVideoQuiz, SubmitQuiz

Table 3: Topics generated by topical N-grams for the Virtual Instruction MOOC. Lecture_Lecture represents watching two different videos consecutively. BrowseForum_BrowseForum represents browsing two different forum threads consecutively

discover a small set of rules in the context logs that predict session types generated by topic modeling[7].

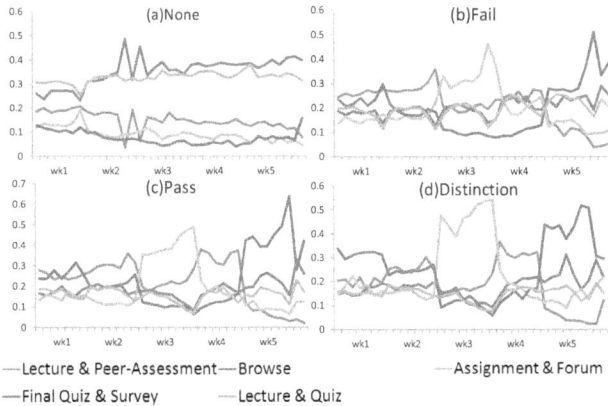

Figure 1: Daily average topic distributions for four final grade groups in the Virtual Instruction MOOC.

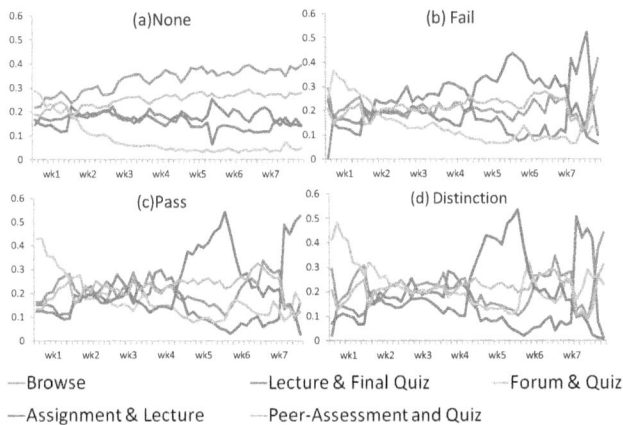

Figure 2: Daily average topic distributions for four final grade groups in the Financial Planning MOOC.

4. RESULTS

In this section, we first present the session topics generated from the topical N-gram model. The visualization of average topic distribution on each course day shows different engagement patterns of different final grade groups in our two MOOCs. Then we group each learning session

based on its topic distributions. Interesting learning behavior patterns are mined from the context-rich log dataset.

4.1 Pattern Analysis

We show the top ranking activities and activity sequences for each topic for the VI MOOC in Table 3[4]. The number of topics is set to five. The topics generated by topical N-gram models capture both the typical combination of interactions and typical sequences of learning activities, such as "BrowseLecture_BrowseLecture_BrowseFinalQuiz", which implies the user watches more than one video lectures before taking the final quiz.

Based on the topic distribution, we assign a session type to each session with the largest topic proportion. We set the session type as the variable to predict and use classification rule mining to mine learner behavior patters. Our definitions of Confidence and Support are similar to those in [2]. On a course level, all the behavior patterns with Confidence larger than 0.25 are mined. Then we select at most the top 20 behavior patterns for each session type instead of using all the mined behavior patterns. We manually check the mined behavior patterns. Table 4 shows some patterns mined from the VI course. These behavior patterns reflect some interesting learning habits of the students in this course. For example, on course week 3, students are likely to engage in an *Assignment and Forum* session.

4.2 Validation

We now investigate how a student's final grade is related to her learning session distribution. Final grade can indicate student knowledge and also engagement. Here we think of the final grade as an independent variable; our goal is not to predict a student's grade from her activity but rather to gain insight into how high-grade and low-grade students distribute their activities differently along the course weeks. On each course day, we compute the average session topic proportions over all the learning sessions that happened on that day. In Figures 1 and 2 we show trends for our two MOOCs. We find that the distribution patterns are qualitatively similar. For example in both MOOCs, The None achievement users(Figure 1(a) and Figure 2(a)) are characterized with a flat distribution across the five learning session topics, which means they are insensitive to course schedules and deadlines. Since MOOCs have created space for these less performance-oriented types of learning, such as auditing or exploring a course, they have more purely *Browsing* sessions. The other three achievement groups reflect the course

---

[4]The activities for the FP MOOC are very similar but slightly different. To save space, we do not show them here.

Behavior Pattern	Support	Confidence
Context:{*Final Grade* = None, *Device* = Desktop, *Country* = NON-US, *Length* = Short} ⇒ *Session* = BrowseCourse	8,787	0.78
Context:{ *Gender* = Male } ⇒ *Session* = BrowseCourse	3,888	0.49
Context:{ *Length* = Long } ⇒ *Session* = Lecture and Peer-Assessment	8,943	0.37
Context:{ *Course Week* = 3 } ⇒ *Session* = Assignment and Forum	4,048	0.34
Context:{ *Final Grade* = Distinction, *Device* = Desktop } ⇒ *Session* = Assignment and Forum	5,075	0.27
Context:{ *Final Grade* = Distinction, *Length* = Long } ⇒ *Session* = Final Quiz and Survey	5,521	0.26

Table 4: Top-ranking mined behavior patterns for the Virtual Instruction MOOC.

schedule in different levels. In the VI course (Figure 1), the assignment is released on Monday of course week 3, users have more *Assignment and Forum* sessions to check out or do the assignment. Towards the assignment deadline, which is the end of week 3, an even higher proportion of the sessions are *Assignment and Forum*. Similar trends (bumps in the curve) can also be observed for peer-assessment(released and due in course week 4) and final quiz(week 5). It is interesting to compare the trends between Fail and Pass(Figure 1(b) vs. Figure 1(c); Figure 2(b) vs. Figure 2(c)), they have similar trends except that Fail users mostly do not have the clear Peer-Assessment bump in week 4. This may largely be due to the fact that they did not finish their own assignments so they cannot do peer-assessment. If we compare Pass and Distinction users(Figure 1(c) vs. Figure 1(d); Figure 2(c) vs. Figure 2(d)), we can see that Pass users tend to "procrastinate" towards a deadline, as much more of their Assignment or Final Quiz related sessions are in the later part of the week (deadlines are on Sunday nights). We leave deeper analysis of these behavior patterns, such as procrastination, for future work.

5. RELATED WORK

Though there have been some quantitative, large-scale studies of student behavior in MOOCs to date, there is still much room for development of techniques that offer high resolution into student routines and habits at a fine grained level. Very few prior studies have utilized the full spectrum of rich information captured by activity trace data in an integrated way. Recently, Anderson et al.[1] have developed a taxonomy of individual learner behaviors related specifically to assignments, designed to examine the different behavior patterns aggregated across a student's entire experience in the course to distinguish high- and low-achieving students. Most commonly in prior studies, only one or two types or aspects of student interaction have been investigated at a time, for example, students navigating backwards [4], in-video dropouts[6], forum posting behaviors[11] and students' time on specific tasks [3].

Since late 1990, web usage mining has been widely studied. [9] surveyed the popular techniques in this field such as Association Rule Mining and Clustering. Sequential pattern discovery can characterize user episodes for the mining of traversal patterns on search engines, shopping sites, etc. A distinct property of the user interactions with MOOCs is that user navigation is less dependent on the linking structure in the website and more related to their course goals. Thus typical sequential pattern mining algorithms may be less suitable for our task. Inspired by [5], which uses topic models to discover patterns in a user's daily routine from sensor data, we adopt a form of topic model to extract leaning activity patterns.

6. CONCLUSION AND FUTURE WORK

In this paper, we propose a novel approach for characterizing learning behavior patterns. The experiments show that learning sessions can be modeled as combinations of several session topics, which provides insights into how high-grade and low-grade students distribute their activities differently along the course weeks. Based on context information associated with each learning session, we mine learning behavior patterns and then observe how these patterns play out over a course. In the future, we want to mine individual learning behavior patterns to discover latent learner types [8].

7. ACKNOWLEDGMENTS

This research was funded in part by NSF grants IIS-1320064 and OMA-0836012.

8. REFERENCES

[1] A. Anderson, D. Huttenlocher, J. Kleinberg, and J. Leskovec. Engaging with massive online courses. In *WWW'14*, pages 687–698, 2014.

[2] H. Cao, T. Bao, Q. Yang, E. Chen, and J. Tian. An effective approach for mining mobile user habits. In *CIKM'10*, 2010.

[3] J. Champaign, K. F. Colvin, A. Liu, C. Fredericks, D. Seaton, and D. E. Pritchard. Correlating skill and improvement in 2 moocs with a student's time on tasks. In *L@S'14*, pages 11–20, 2014.

[4] P. J. Guo and K. Reinecke. Demographic differences in how students navigate through moocs.

[5] T. Huynh, M. Fritz, and B. Schiele. Discovery of activity patterns using topic models. In *Ubicomp'08*, pages 10–19. ACM, 2008.

[6] J. Kim. Understanding in-video dropouts and interaction peaks inonline lecture videos. L@S '14, pages 31–40, 2014.

[7] B. Liu, W. Hsu, and Y. Ma. Integrating classification and association rule mining. In *KDD'98*, 1998.

[8] H. Ma, H. Cao, Q. Yang, E. Chen, and J. Tian. A habit mining approach for discovering similar mobile users. In *WWW'12*, pages 231–240. ACM, 2012.

[9] J. Srivastava, R. Cooley, M. Deshpande, and P.-N. Tan. Web usage mining: Discovery and applications of usage patterns from web data. *ACM SIGKDD Explorations Newsletter*, 1(2):12–23, 2000.

[10] X. Wang, A. McCallum, and X. Wei. Topical n-grams: Phrase and topic discovery, with an application to information retrieval. In *ICDM 2007*, pages 697–702, 2007.

[11] M. Wen, D. Yang, and C. Rosé. Linguistic reflections of student engagement in massive open online courses. *In ICWSM*, 2014.

Constrained Question Recommendation in MOOCs via Submodularity

Diyi Yang
Language Technologies
Institute
Carnegie Mellon University
Pittsburgh, PA, 15213
diyiy@cs.cmu.edu

Jingbo Shang
Computer Science
Department
Shanghai Jiaotong University
Shanghai, China, 200240
shangjingbo@gmail.com

Carolyn Penstein Rosé
Language Technologies
Institute
Carnegie Mellon University
Pittsburgh, PA, 15213
cprose@cs.cmu.edu

ABSTRACT

A recent area in which recommender systems have shown their value is in online discussion forums and question-answer sites. Earlier work in this space has focused on the problem of matching participants to opportunities but has not adequately addressed the problem that in these social contexts, multiple dimensions of constraints must be satisfied, including limitations on capacity and minimal requirements for expertise. In this work, we propose such a constrained question recommendation problem with load balance constraints in discussion forums and use flow based model to generate the optimal solution. In particular, to address the introduced computation complexity, we investigate the concept of submodularity of the objective function and propose a specific submodular method to give an approximated solution. We present experiments conducted on two Massive Open Online Course (MOOC) discussion forum datasets, and demonstrate the effectiveness and efficiency of our submodular method in solving constrained question recommendation tasks.

Categories and Subject Descriptors

H.3.3 [**Information Systems**]: Information Search and Retrieval—*Information Filtering*

Keywords

Constrained Question Recommendation; Max-cost Flow; Submodularity

1. INTRODUCTION

The past decade has witnessed an explosive growth of accessible information. Recommender systems provide one means for assisting users to find items and opportunities that are of interest, or to get other information needs met. In this paper, we focus specifically on a form of social recommendation where we direct participate in discussion forums to interesting discussions while increasing the likelihood that posted information requests will garner the necessary attention from qualified question answerers. In such scenarios, it is necessary to consider constraints in a more comprehensive manner than in the simplest case of product recommendation, where it is only necessary to consider the desires of the consumer. In the case of social recommendation where people are being matched, the match must be desirable on both sides. In the case of information seeking, the additional constraints of asymmetric expertise and limitations on the number of requests a single participant can be expected to address must also be considered [10]. A similar issue comes up in the context of peer review. In this context, each reviewer may be assigned a personalized budget specifying the maximum number of papers to review. At the same time, regardless of popularity in the bidding process, each paper should not be reviewed by too many people [9].

Max cost flow based techniques have been applied in order to achieve optimal satisfaction in this load balanced constrained question recommendation problem [10]. However, they are too computationally expensive to generalize and scale to massive datasets. Therefore, in this paper, we propose a constrained question recommendation problem built on earlier formulation and introduce a submodularity method to reduce the computational complexity and speed up the optimization. The contributions of this paper are highlighted as below.

- We build on the max cost flow approach to globally optimizing a multi-dimensional set of constraints on question recommendation.

- We investigate the submodularity of this problem, prove its submodularity, and propose a submodular method to provide acceptable recommendations efficiently (with orders of magnitude improvement in efficiency).

- We present experiments conducted on two discussion forum datasets to demonstrate the effectiveness and efficiency of this submodular method.

This paper is organized as follows. Section 2 introduces related work. The constrained question recommendation problem is formulated in Section 3 while solving methods are presented in Section 4. Section 5 shows the experimental results, and conclusion is presented in Section 6.

CIKM'14, November 3–7, 2014, Shanghai, China.
Copyright 2014 ACM 978-1-4503-2598-1/14/11 ...$15.00.
http://dx.doi.org/10.1145/2661829.2662089 .

Table 1: Notation

Notation	Meaning
U, I	User/question set
u, i	User/question
E	Candidate user-question pairs
$r_{u,i} \in [0,1]$	*Given* relevance score between u and i

2. RELATED WORK

Traditional recommender systems mainly focus on approximating the extent to which a recommended item will be desirable to users. Collaborative filtering (CF) has been demonstrated to be an effective technique for accomplishing this goal. Neighborhood based models [8] and latent factor models [6] are two classical approaches of CF. For example, Koren et al. [5] designed a framework to combine latent modeling and neighborhood modeling between users and movies in order to provide better movie recommendation performance. When it comes to question recommendation, i.e. recommending questions to potential answerers, most work also focuses on predicting the affinity between users and question content. For instance, Kabutoya et al. [4] generates a suitable user set to answer a given question based on question and user histories using CF techniques.

However, such question recommender systems have not addressed the possible constraints associated with users and questions. Especially in the Massive Open Online Courses (MOOCs), recommending questions to students should be based on not only the affinity of students for the topic of the questions, but also under the constraints of student time budget and ability to answer the question. For instance, Yang et al. [10] propose a constrained question recommendation problem with load balance and expertise matching constraints and develop a max cost flow model to optimally generate recommendations. Similar recommendation tasks with constraints also include recommending reviewers for papers. Tang et al. [9] propose a minimum cost flow based model to meet kinds of constraints associated with reviewers and papers. However, the disadvantage of such flow models is the expensive computational complexity. Therefore, we propose to further develop this approach by investigating the submodularity of the objective function [7].

3. CONSTRAINED RECOMMENDATION FORMULATION

We begin our discussion by listing some basic notations in Table 1 that we will use later. The constrained question recommendation (CQR) task is to recommend a set of questions to users under the simultaneous constraints of users and questions. These balancing constraints can be phrased in this way: each question i is associated with a question capacity M_i, meaning we should not guide more than M_i users to a question since it might be easy and does not require too many people to provide help; for each user u, we associate a user capacity R_u, representing the idea that the number of questions that are comfortable for u to work on should not be larger than R_u. We formulate this constrained question recommendation problem as follows, and maximize this objective function, with the extent to minimize the load given to each user:

$$OB = -\lambda \sum_{u \in U} \left(\sum_{i \in I} f_{u,i}\right)^2 + \sum_{u,i \in E} f_{u,i} r_{u,i}$$

subject to
$$\forall u \in U, \sum_{i \in I} f_{u,i} \leq R_u \qquad (1)$$
$$\forall i \in I, \sum_{u \in U} f_{u,i} \leq M_i$$

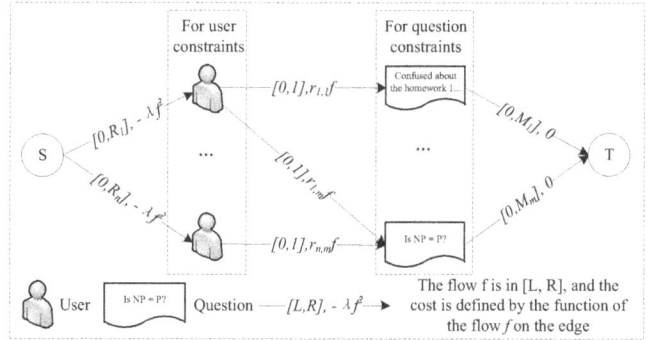

Figure 1: The Max-cost Flow Network Model

Here, $\lambda(\geq 0)$ is a non-negative coefficient for the load penalty and $f_{u,i}$ is a binary indicator of whether question i will be recommended to user u. Instead of working on approximating the preference scores $r_{u,i}$ of user u on item i, in this work, we assume $r_{u,i}$ is *given*, i.e. generated by some state-of-the-art algorithms as in our earlier work, and focus on solving the constrained question recommendation problem efficiently.

4. OPTIMIZATION METHODS

In this section, we present three methods to maximize the objective function in Equation 1, which we experimentally compare in our evaluation. The first top-K technique will be the baseline for our experimental comparisons. It is a greedy method that efficiently provides possible solutions. The two experimental approaches are the max-cost flow model, which is theoretically optimal, but suffers from high computational complexity; and the submodularity approach, which can approximate the optimal solution well with less expensive computation compared to the max-cost flow model.

4.1 Traditional Top-K Recommendation

The traditional top-K method recommends questions to users by selecting the top-K ranked items for each user individually and ignores the capacity constraints. To fit our setting, we develop a post-processing model that prunes the extraneous users with low relevance scores. That is, we first run the traditional top-K item selection to recommend R_u items to each user. Then, for each item, if the number of recommended users exceeds its limit, we prune the users in the increasing order of their relevance scores (beginning with the least relevant).

4.2 Max-cost Flow Model

To maximize the objective function in Equation 1, we construct a concave cost network as summarized in Figure 1. Then we conduct a max-cost flow optimization over this network to get an optimal solution under the constraints. We prove that conducting max-cost flow on this network can give an optimal solution to the problem defined in Equation 1.

THEOREM 1. *The cost network constructed in Figure 1 is equivalent to the problem defined in Equation 1 and provides an optimal solution.*

PROOF. First, the maximum concave cost flow (MCCF) problem can be formulated as the following optimization

Algorithm 1 Submodular Method for CQR

1: $A \leftarrow \emptyset$, $B \leftarrow E$.
2: **for** user item pair $< u,i > \in E$ **do**
3:     $v_+ \leftarrow \max(OB_{ext}(A \cup < u,i >) - OB_{ext}(A), 0)$
4:     $v_- \leftarrow \max(OB_{ext}(B \backslash < u,i >) - OB_{ext}(B), 0)$
5:     x $\sim$ Uniform$[0, 1]$
6:     **if** x $\leq v_+/(v_+ + v_-)$ **then**
7:         $A \leftarrow A \cup < u,i >$
8:     **else**
9:         $B \leftarrow B \backslash < u,i >$
10: **return** $A (= B)$
---

problem:

$$\max \sum_{(a \rightarrow b) \in E(G)} Cost_{a \rightarrow b}(Flow_{a \rightarrow b})$$

subject to

$$\forall a (\neq S,T) \in V(G), \sum_b Flow_{a \rightarrow b} = \sum_b Flow_{b \rightarrow a}$$

$$0 \leq Flow_{a \rightarrow b} \leq R_{a \rightarrow b} \tag{2}$$

where, S is the source node and T is the sink; $Flow_{a \rightarrow b}$ is the flow from node a to b; $Cost_{a \rightarrow b}$ is the concave cost function on the edge. In our network, there are only (negative) square functions, linear functions, and constant functions. If we set $f_{u,i}$ as the corresponding flow in the network $flow_{u \rightarrow i}$, the objective in MCCF is equal to Equation 1. After that, we consider the remaining constraints one by one.

- The user constraint is bounded by the capacity $[0, R_u]$ from the source S to the user nodes u.

- The question constraint is limited by the flow range $[0, M_i]$ from question nodes i to the sink T.

In summary, all constraints in CQR problem are satisfied in the max-cost flow model, and these constraints are the only limitations in the network. Thus, the MCCF problem defined here is equivalent to the CQR problem. Then we can formally build the network, solve the MCCF problem as shown in Figure 1, and get the final recommendation plan by examining flows between u and the corresponding i. $\square$

Based on the Theorem 1, we can transform the integer programming problem in Equation 1 to a max-cost flow model with $O(|U| + |I|)$ nodes and $O(|E| + |U| + |I|)$ edges. Using the basic max-cost flow algorithm implemented using the Bellman-ford algorithm [1], we can compute the optimal solution in $O((|U|+|I|)^2|E|)$ (the scale of flows is in $O(|U|+|I|)$ if we assume the R_u and M_i are both constants).

4.3 Submodular Method

Even though the constructed max cost flow model above can achieve an optimal solution, it suffers from the high computational complexity which prevents it from scaling to massive datasets. To overcome this issue, we introduce a submodular method to maximize Equation 1 here. First, we extend the objective function as described below,

$$OB_{ext} = \begin{cases} OB & \text{satisfied} \\ OB - C^{\sum_u \sum_i f_{u,i}} & \text{violated} \end{cases} \tag{3}$$

where C is a sufficiently large constant that it helps the negative term dominate the value of OB_{ext} when it is

violated. It is clear that the optimal solution of OB_{ext} is equal to the OB's optimal solution, because violating the constraints leads to an exponential extra penalty. In what follows, we show the submodulatity exhibited by OB_{ext}.

THEOREM 2. OB_{ext} is a submodular function. The submodular property is is defined as follows: $\forall A \subseteq B, < u,i > \notin B$, s.t. $OB_{ext}(A \cup < u,i >) - OB_{ext}(A) \geq OB_{ext}(B \cup < u,i >) - OB_{ext}(B)$.

PROOF. Recall that $f(a + \Delta) - f(a) \geq f(b + \Delta) - f(b)$ holds for any concave function $f(x)$ when $a \leq b$ and $\Delta \geq 0$. It is worth noting that concavity is a special case of submodularity. Adding a user-item pair $< u,i >$ is equal to setting $f_{u,i}$ to 1 from 0. Consider the following three cases:
Case 1, A and B both violate the constraints. In this case, since $-C^{\sum_u \sum_i f_{u,i}}$ dominates OB_{ext} which is concave, OB_{ext} is submodular.
Case 2, A satisfies the constraints but B violates the constraints. Here are two subcases: (1) $A \cup < u,i >$ satisfies the constraints. In this subcase, the value of $OB_{ext}(B \cup < u,i >) - OB_{ext}(B)$ is sufficiently large so that the inequality holds. (2) $A \cup < u,i >$ violates the constraints. In this subcase, because the term $\sum_u \sum_i f_{u,i}$ is the index of C and $|A| \leq |B|$, the inequality still holds. Thus OB_{ext} is submodular.
Case 3, A and B both satisfy the constraints. In this case, the relevant part ($r_{u,i}$) of the OB_{ext} difference (either $OB_{ext}(A \cup < u,i >) - OB_{ext}(A)$ or $OB_{ext}(B \cup < u,i >) - OB_{ext}(B)$) is the same and the penalty part ($-\lambda x^2$) is concave, thus OB_{ext} is submodular. $\square$

Based on Theorem 2, the extended objective function OB_{ext} is a submodular function. Thus, we can utilize the RandomizedUSM [2] algorithm as shown in Algorithm 1, which guarantees a $\frac{1}{2}$ approximation for maximizing nonnegative submodular functions. This algorithm has a time complexity $O(|E|)$.

5. EXPERIMENTS

In this section, we firstly present our datasets and experimental setup. Then we investigate whether the submodular method achieves the desired reduction in time complexity with minimal sacrifice of performance.

5.1 Dataset and Settings

Our experiments are conducted on two discussion forums of courses from Coursera[1], (1) 'Accountable Talk: Conversation that works', shortened to 'A', is a teacher professional development course with 1,148 users, 511 questions, and 582,945 edges ; (2) 'Fantasy and Science Fiction: the human mind, our modern world', shortened to 'F', is a course about literature appreciation, which has 770 users, 603 questions and 460,448 edges. In our datasets, most posts (around 82%) are about proposing and resolving problems.

Here, we assume that students have a certain time budget and cannot be directed to too many questions, thus R_u is defined as how many questions this student has participated so far in the forum; for questions, we empirically set M_i to 10. It is worth mentioning that one can simulate the use of different values of R_u and M_i based

---
[1]Permission to conduct research on Coursera datasets was provided by Coursera.

Table 2: Objective Function Comparison

Method	OB-A	OB-F
Top-K Method	1342.70	1120.43
Max-cost Flow	2898.17	2652.99
Submodular	2546.45	2238.58

Table 3: Time Complexity Comparison

Method	Theoretical	Time-A	Time-F
Top-K Method	$O(|E|log|E|)$	0.14s	0.17s
Max-cost Flow	$O((|U| + |I|)^2|E|)$	341.42s	269.90s
Submodular	$O(|E|)$	0.045s	0.048s

on specific problem needs. To get the relevance score $r_{u,i}$ of students' affinity over questions, we adopted the feature-based matrix factorization technique [3], which is a state-of-the-art method. Similarly, one can adopt other strategies to generate the relevance scores. In this work, we assume the relevance scores are all given and focus merely on the fast optimization of the constrained recommendation problem. The optimization performance is evaluated by the objective value (OB) of Equation 1. For comparison, we use the Top-K Method and Max-cost Flow as baselines; the λ is set as 0.001. The machine we used is equipped with Intel Xeon(R) CPU E5-2680 @2.70GHz and 128GB memory.

5.2 Performance Comparsion

We present the results of Top-K Method, Max-cost Flow and Submodular Method in Table 2. As we can see, Max-cost Flow performs the best on both datasets in terms of the objective function, because it gives the optimal solution; the runner-up is the Submodular Method, and there are no substantial difference between the OB values of the two models. The Submodular Method achieves 87.9% of the optimal solution on the Accountable Course and 84.4% of the optimal solution on the Fantasy Course. Top-K Method gives the lowest OB, because it does not take into account the possible constraints in its first step and many pairs are pruned to satisfy the load balance constraints in the second step. Furthermore, the Submodular method is even more efficient than the baseline Top-K approach.

Taking both the time complexity comparison presented in Table 3 and the objective function optimization comparison into account, we can have a better understanding of the advantage of the Submodular Method. For Table 3, $O(|E|)$ is the number of candidate user-question pairs and also the number of edges in the built max-cost flow network. $O(|U| + |I|)$ is the node number. Since R_u and M_i can be treated as constants, the flow is in $O(|U| + |I|)$. Therefore, the theoretical time complexity of Max-cost Flow is $O((|U| + |I|)^2|E|)$, about $O((|U| + |I|)^4)$. However, the theoretical complexity of Submodular Method is only $O(|E|)$, about $O((|U| + |I|)^2)$. The running times on the two datasets also validate the theoretical results. Based on the running time on the Accountable Course, Submodular Method costs 0.01% of the running time of the Max-cost Flow method; this is consistent on the Fantasy Course. Taking into account the objective function optimization and time complexity comparison results, we can conclude that, the Submodular Method can give an 80% approximation of the optimal solution with very large reduction of the time complexity.

6. CONCLUSION

In this work, we formulate a constrained question recommendation problem with load balancing constraints in online discussion forums. To address the high computational complexity introduced by the optimal flow model, we investigate the submodularity of the objective function and propose a submodular method to speed up the optimization, with little sacrifice in quality. In future work, we propose to investigate submodularity further and derive a theoretical approximation bound.

ACKNOWLEDGEMENT

This research was funded in part by NSF grants IIS-1320064 and OMA-0836012.

7. REFERENCES

[1] R. K. Ahuja, T. L. Magnanti, and J. B. Orlin. *Network Flows: Theory, Algorithms, and Applications.* Prentice-Hall, Inc., Upper Saddle River, NJ, USA, 1993.

[2] N. Buchbinder, M. Feldman, J. Naor, and R. Schwartz. A tight linear time (1/2)-approximation for unconstrained submodular maximization. In *Foundations of Computer Science (FOCS), 2012 IEEE 53rd Annual Symposium on*, pages 649–658. IEEE, 2012.

[3] T. Chen, W. Zhang, Q. Lu, K. Chen, Z. Zheng, and Y. Yu. SVDFeature: A toolkit for feature-based collaborative filtering. *Journal of Machine Learning Research*, 13:3619–3622, 2012.

[4] Y. Kabutoya, T. Iwata, H. Shiohara, and K. Fujimura. Effective question recommendation based on multiple features for question answering communities. In *ICWSM*, 2010.

[5] Y. Koren. Factorization meets the neighborhood: A multifaceted collaborative filtering model. In *Proceedings of the 14th ACM SIGKDD International Conference on Knowledge Discovery and Data Mining*, KDD '08, pages 426–434, 2008.

[6] Y. Koren, R. Bell, and C. Volinsky. Matrix factorization techniques for recommender systems. *Computer*, 42(8):30–37, Aug. 2009.

[7] G. L. Nemhauser, L. A. Wolsey, and M. L. Fisher. An analysis of approximations for maximizing submodular set functions. *Mathematical Programming*, 14(1):265–294, 1978.

[8] B. Sarwar, G. Karypis, J. Konstan, and J. Riedl. Item-based collaborative filtering recommendation algorithms. In *Proceedings of the 10th International Conference on World Wide Web*, WWW '01, pages 285–295, 2001.

[9] W. Tang, J. Tang, and C. Tan. Expertise matching via constraint-based optimization. In *Web Intelligence and Intelligent Agent Technology (WI-IAT), 2010 IEEE/WIC/ACM International Conference on*, volume 1, pages 34–41. IEEE, 2010.

[10] D. Yang, D. Adamson, and C. Rose. Question recommendation with constraints for massive open online courses. In *Proceedings of the Eighth ACM Conference on Recommender Systems*, RecSys '14, 2014.

Exploit Latent Dirichlet Allocation for One-Class Collaborative Filtering

Haijun Zhang, Zhoujun Li, Yan Chen, Xiaoming Zhang, Senzhang Wang

State Key Laboratory of Software Development Environment, Beihang University, Beijing 100191, China

haijun_cumtb@126.com, lizj@buaa.edu.cn, yanchensmile@gmail.com, yolixs@buaa.edu.cn, szwang@cse.buaa.edu.cn.

ABSTRACT

Previous work studied one-class collaborative filtering (OCCF) problems including pointwise methods, pairwise methods, and content-based methods. The fundamental assumptions made on these approaches are roughly the same. They regard all missing values as negative. However, this is unreasonable since the missing values actually are the mixture of negative and positive examples. A user does not give a positive feedback on an item probably only because she/he is unaware of the item, but in fact, she/he is fond of it. Furthermore, content-based methods, e.g. collaborative topic regression (CTR), usually require textual content information of items. This cannot be satisfied in some cases. In this paper, we exploit latent Dirichlet allocation (LDA) model on OCCF problem. It assumes missing values unknown and only models the observed data, and it also does not need content information of items. In our model items are regarded as words and users are considered as documents and the user-item feedback matrix denotes the corpus. Experimental results show that our proposed method outperforms the previous methods on various ranking–oriented evaluation metrics.

Categories and Subject Descriptors

H.3.3 [**Information Search and Retrieval**]: Information filtering- *Recommendation System.*

General Terms

Algorithms.

Keywords

One-class Collaborative Filtering; Latent Dirichlet Allocation; Topic Model

1. INTRODUCTION

The goal of recommendation system is to automatically suggest items to each user that she/he may find appealing. Traditional collaborative filtering approaches predict users' interests by mining user rating history data, and these rating data are multi-valued scores, which can be categorized as "multi-class" recommendation problem [1]. Many machine learning based algorithms are designed to predict user's interesting on these multi-valued data, among of which matrix factorization based algorithm achieved great success [2].

However, in many applications, the collected data of user behaviors are in "one-class" form rather than multi-class form, e.g., "like" in Facebook, "bought" in Amazon, "collect" in Taobao and "follow" in Sina weibo. Such data are usually called implicit [3] or one-class [1, 4, 5] feedback. The one-class collaborative filtering (OCCF) problem is different from that of multi-valued rating prediction problem, since the former only contains positive feedback rather than both positive feedback and negative feedback, and the goal is item ranking instead of rating prediction. Traditional machine learning based algorithms cannot directly be used to tackle OCCF because of imbalanced data [6].

The important difficulty to tackle OCCF problem is over fitting, because only positive feedbacks are observed. In order to avoid over fitting previous methods, including pointwise methods [4], pairwise methods [1, 3] and content-based methods [7, 8], all assume missing data negative. However they introduced newer over fitting problem caused by too many negative data.

A good learning method is that it fits the observed data well and as well as avoids over fitting. In this paper, similar to [7, 8], we introduce topic model, i.e., latent Dirichlet allocation [9, 10] (LDA) to deal with this problem. Our model is different from the methods proposed in [7, 8] in two aspects: (1) we only model the observed data, and the latter assume missing data negative and strive to fit all the data. (2) our model does not need contents information of items. Compared with the pointwise [4] and pairwise methods [1, 3], the parameters learned by our model are probability distributions, which have the inherent characteristics that the probability is a positive number and the summation of probabilities is equals to 1. These characteristics made our model have excellent ability to avoid over fitting. Experimental results show that our proposed method outperforms the previous methods on various ranking–oriented evaluation metrics.

The rest of the paper is organized as follows. In the next section, we review previous works related to the OCCF problems. In Section 3, we propose our approach for OCCF problems. In Section 4, we empirically compare our method to state-of-the-art methods on three real world data sets. Finally, we conclude the paper and give some future works.

2. RELATED WORKS

In this section, we review the literature of a few state-of-the-art approaches proposed for OCCF problems. There are mainly three types of approaches, (1) pointwise methods, (2) pairwise methods, and (3) content-based methods.

2.1 Pointwise Methods

Pointwise methods take implicit feedback as absolute preference scores. For example, an observed user-item pair is interpreted as a positive feedback and is assigned with a high absolute rating score, e.g., 1, and the unobserved user-item pair is seen as a negative feedback and is assigned with rating score 0. Then, machine learning based methods, e.g. weighted low-rank approximations (WLRA) [4], are designed to fit the rating score matrix. Because most of the data are negative, in order to correct the bias there are two kinds of techniques are adopted, (1) the weight of the negative data is assigned with a small value relative to it of the positive data, and (2) the negative data are sampled with a small probability. The limitation of these methods is that taking unobserved user-item pairs as negative feedback may introduce errors.

2.2 Pairwise Methods

Pairwise methods achieved great success in OCCF problems, which mainly include Bayesian personalized ranking based matrix factorization (BPR) [3] and group Bayesian personalized ranking (GBPR) [1]. BPR supposes that a user u prefer an item i to an item j if the user-item pair (u, i) is observed, and (u, j) is not observed, and then take pairs of items as basic units and maximize the likelihood of pairwise preferences over observed items and unobserved items. Different from BPR, GBPR proposes a stronger constraint which can be expressed by Eq.(1) and Eq. (2):

$$if \ u \in G_i \ and \ u \notin G_j \ then \ r_{G_i,i} > r_{u,j} \quad (1)$$

$$r_{G_i,i} = \frac{\sum_{u \in G_i} r_{u,i}}{|G_i|} \quad (2)$$

Where G_i is the group of users who give a positive feedback to item i, and $r_{u,j}$ denotes the preference value of user u on item j, and $r_{G_i,i}$ denotes the group preference value of group G_i on item i and it is the average preference value of all users in group G_i on item i which is expressed by Eq.(2).

GBPR use sigmoid function $f\left(r_{G_i,i} - r_{u,j}\right) = \frac{1}{1+\exp\left(-r_{G_i,i}+r_{u,j}\right)}$ to approximate the probability $\Pr\left(r_{G_i,i} > r_{u,j}\right)$, and $r_{u,j}$ is factorized by a product of two vectors which is expressed by Eq(3).

$$r_{u,j} = q_u \cdot s_j^T \quad (3)$$

Where q_u is the latent vector of user u and s_j is the latent vector of item j. These latent vectors are learned by maximize the likelihood of pairwise preferences.

Pairwise methods [1, 3] outperforms pointwise methods [4], but both of them have roughly the same fundamental assumptions that all missing data should be negative. Because according to their optimization goal, if a user-item pair (u, j) is unobserved, the smaller the preference of user u on item j is the easier the optimization goal can be realized. Matrix factorization technique is adopted in these methods to access to the optimization goal, and meanwhile it utilizes the interaction between latent vectors to bound the value of the preference.

2.3 Content-based Methods

In this OCCF scenario, items have textual contents. Topic model is used in this scenario to model the corpus and the user-item rating scores at the same time. Where an item is seen as a

document and all the items' contents constitute a corpus. Meanwhile, all missing data are assumed negative and are assigned with a small value, e.g. 0, and positive feedback are assigned with value 1 [7, 8]. The models proposed in [7] and [8] are called collaborative topic regression (CTR) and collaborative topic regression with social matrix factorization (CTR-SMF) respectively. Figure 1 shows the CTR model. CTR represents users with topic interests and assumes that items are generated by a topic model. CTR additionally includes a latent variable ε_j which offsets the topic proportions θ_j when modeling the user ratings. This offset variable can capture the item preference of a particular user based on their ratings. Assume there are K topics, and let $\beta = \beta_{1:K}$. The generative process of CTR is as follows.

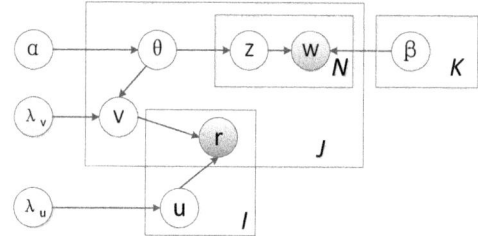

Figure 1. The graphical model for the CTR model.

1. For each user i, draw user latent vector $u_i \sim N\left(0, \lambda_u^{-1} I_K\right)$.

2. For each item j,

   (a) Draw topic proportions $\theta_j \sim Dirichlet\left(\alpha\right)$.

   (b) Draw item latent offset $\varepsilon_j \sim N\left(0, \lambda_v^{-1} I_K\right)$ and set the item latent vector as $v_j = \varepsilon_j + \theta_j$.

   (c) For each word w_{jn},

      i.   Draw topic assignment $z_{jn} \sim Mult\left(\theta_j\right)$.

      ii.   Draw word $w_{jn} \sim Mult\left(\beta_{zjn}\right)$.

3. For each user-item pair (i, j), draw the rating $r_{ij} \sim N\left(u_i^T v_j, c_{ij}^{-1}\right)$.

Where c_{ij} is the precision parameter for r_{ij} which need be determined in advance by cross validation, and it represents the confidence for rating r_{ij}. For positive examples (i.e. $r_{ij} = 1$), c_{ij} is set with a big value relative to negative examples (i.e. $r_{ij} = 0$).

CTR-SMF model extended CTR model, and it can be used to address the recommendation problem when item's content, rating records and social network information are all known. However, in recommendation scenario, items usually have no textual contents, and these two methods assume missing data negative, which may not hold water, so, these two methods have limitations.

3. OUR METHOD

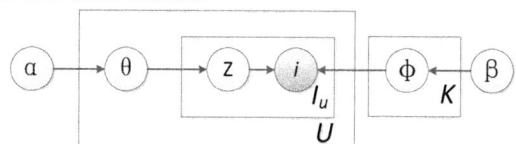

Figure 2. LDA model for OCCF.

In this paper, similar to the articles [7,8], we also use topic model to tackle OCCF problem, but in our model, a user is seen as a document, and an item is regarded as a word, and a positive feedback of user u for item i denotes an occurrence of word i in document u. We use latent Dirichlet allocation (LDA) [9] to model OCCF problem, which is represented by Figure 2.

Our method has two stages. **Step 1**, LDA model for OCCF was used to learn the matrices θ and ϕ, i.e., topic distributions of users and item distributions of topics respectively. The generative process is as follows.

1.   For each user u, Draw topic proportions $\theta_u \sim Dirichlet(\alpha)$.

2.   For each topic k, draw item proportions $\phi_k \sim Dirichlet(\beta)$.

3.   For each observed user-item pair (u, i),

   (a) Draw topic assignment $z_{ui} \sim Mult(\theta_u)$.

   (b) Draw item $i \sim Mult(\phi_{z_{ui}})$.

We use Gibbs sampling method to estimate the parameters θ and ϕ, for more information please refer to [11]. Here, the topic number K and the super parameters α and β need to be tuned.

Step 2, compute the preference of user u on item i by Eq. (4).

$$r_{ui} = \theta_{u_v} \cdot \phi_{.,i}^T = \sum_{k=1}^{K} \theta_{u,k}\phi_{k,i} \qquad (4)$$

Where $\theta_{u,k}$ is the distribution of user u on topic k, and $\phi_{k,i}$ is the distribution of topic k on item i, and they are all positive numbers. From Eq.(4), we can see that only $\theta_{u,k}$ and $\phi_{k,i}$ are all bigger numbers, r_{ui} becomes bigger. This conforms to actuality. For example, if user u very likes action movie, and movie i has many action scenes, we can concluded that user u has a bigger probability like this movie. Conversely, if user u hates to see action movie or movie i has no action scenes, he will not like this movie. Here, the genre of action denotes a topic. Thus, using Eq.(4) to measure the preference of user u on item i is reasonable other than the Euclidean distance between the two vectors. When a target user's preferences on all items are figured out, recommendation item list can be ranked.

We call this proposed method LDA-OCCF, which has three better characteristics than previous works: (1) Compared with the previous methods, in LDA-OCCF, missing ratings are assumed unknown other than negative; (2) Compared with CTR or CTR-SMF model, LDA-OCCF does not need contents information of items; (3) Compared with pointwise or pairwise methods, the parameters learned in LDA-OCCF are probability distributions, which are positive numbers and the summation of them is equal to 1. These strong constraints help LDA-OCCF avoid over fitting.

4. EXPERIMENTS
4.1 Datasets
We use three real-world datasets in our empirical studies, including MovieLens100K [1], MovieLens1M[1], and a subset of

Netflix[2]. MovieLens100K contains 100, 000 ratings assigned by 943 users on 1, 682 movies, MovieLens1M contains 1, 000, 209 ratings assigned by 6, 040 users on 3, 952 movies. Similar to [1], we sample 155,872 ratings larger than 3 as the observed positive feedbacks (to simulate the one-class feedback) from the Netflix dataset, and the ratings contain 5039 users and 5018 movies. We call this subset of Netflix dataset Netflix5K5K. We use "item" to denote movie. For MovieLens100K, MovieLens1M, we also take a pre-processing step, which only keeps the ratings larger than 3. Then, we randomly divide each dataset into 5 equal parts for five-fold cross validation, i.e., for each dataset, 4 parts of the data (i.e., 80%) is used to train the model and the rest data is used to test the model, and the reported result is the average value over 5 independent runs. The final datasets used in the experiments are shown in Table 1.

Table 1. Datasets used in the experiments

Datasets	Users	Items	Ratings
MovieLens100K	942	1447	55,375
MovieLens1M	6038	3533	575,281
Netflix5K5K	5039	5018	155,872

4.2 Evaluation Metrics
Because users usually only check a few top-ranked items, we use top-k evaluation metrics to study the recommendation performance, including top-k results of precision, recall, and MAP. For each evaluation metric, we first calculate the performance for each user from the test data, and then obtain the averaged performance over all users.

Precision is the proportion of top recommendation results that are relevant. Recall is the proportion of all relevant results included in the top results. They can be computed by Eq. (5) and (6) respectively.

$$Prec@N = \frac{r}{N} \qquad (5)$$

$$Rec@N = \frac{r}{|T|} \qquad (6)$$

Where r is the number of relevant items in top N recommendation list of a user u which means these r items are preferred by user u in test set, and $|T|$ is the number of items that user u preferred in test set.

MAP (Mean Average Precision) is widely used in information retrieval for evaluating the ranked documents over a set of queries. We use it in this paper to assess the overall performance based on precisions at different recall levels on a test set. It computes the mean of average precision (AP) over all users in the test set. AP for user u is computed at the point of each of the preferred items in the ranked list:

$$AP_u = \frac{\sum_{i=1}^{N} prec(i) \times pref(i)}{\# \text{ of preferred items}} \qquad (7)$$

where i is the position in the rank list, N is the number of recommended items which are the items that user u did not express positive feedback in training set, $prec(i)$ is the precision (fractions of recommended items that are preferred by user u in

---

[1] http://grouplens.org/datasets/movielens/

[2] http://www.netflixprize.com/

test set) of a cut-off rank list from 1 to i, and *pref(i)* is a binary indicator returning 1 if the *i-th* item is preferred by user u or 0 otherwise. The MAP is the mean of AP_u over all users.

4.3 Baselines and Parameter Settings

We use three popular baseline algorithms in our experiments, PopRank, BPR [3], and GBPR [1]. PopRank is a basic algorithm in one-class collaborative filtering, which ranks the items according to their popularity in the training data. BPR [3] is a seminal work for OCCF problem and is also a very strong baseline, which is shown to be much better than two well-known pointwise methods, i.e., iMF [12] and OCCF [4]. Note that the implementation of this baseline is done with the publicly available software MyMediaLite [13]. GBPR [1] is recently proposed method, which outperforms BPR.

The parameters in BPR and GBPR are tuned according to the papers [3] and [1] respectively. In our method LDA-OCCF, for all experiments, the topic number K is tried with {10, 20, 50}, the parameter α is set to 0.5 and β is set to 0.02, and Gibbs sampling times are chosen from {1000, 10000, 100000}.

4.4 Experimental Results

The recommendation performance of LDA-OCCF and other baselines are shown in Table 2, from which we can have the following observations.

1. Both BPR, GBPR and LDA-OCCF are much better than the PopRank algorithm, which means that personalized recommendation method is better than most popularity based recommendation method.

2. LDA-OCCF further outperforms BPR and GBPR on all evaluation metrics on all three datasets, which shows the effectiveness of our method, and validates its better characteristics described in section 3.

On the other hand, LDA-OCCF only samples observed data, so its computation complexity is lower than BPR and GBPR if all of them take the same sampling times.

Table 2. Compared Results with Baselines

Dataset	Algorithm	Prec@5	Rec@5	MAP
MovieLens 100K	PopRank	0.1418	0.0650	0.1081
	BPR	0.2135	0.1308	0.1798
	GBPR	0.2565	0.1412	0.2106
	LDA-OCCF	**0.2642**	**0.1481**	**0.2119**
MovieLens 1M	PopRank	0.1518	0.0485	0.0905
	BPR	0.2602	0.1034	0.1752
	GBPR	0.2696	0.1055	0.1815
	LDA-OCCF	**0.2897**	**0.1091**	**0.1877**
Netflix 5K5K	PopRank	0.0101	0.0507	0.0432
	BPR	0.1150	0.05968	0.1009
	GBPR	0.1213	0.05183	0.0987
	LDA-OCCF	**0.1451**	**0.0708**	**0.1170**

5. CONCLUSIONS

In this paper, we study the one-class collaborative filtering problem and design a topic model based algorithm LDA-OCCF. Different from previous proposed methods, it avoided the unreasonable assumption that missing data are negative. Due to the strong constraint that the learned probabilities are positive and their summation is equal to 1, LDA-OCCF alleviates the over fitting problem. Meanwhile, different from previous topic model based recommendation methods, it does not need content information of items. Experimental results show that, this proposed method outperforms the compared algorithms. In the future, we will further study how to integrate more information such as social structure into the algorithm to improve the performance further.

6. ACKNOWLEDGMENTS

We greatly appreciate Weike Pan, i.e., the author of paper [1], for his codes of algorithm GBPR, which makes us able to evaluate the algorithm more efficiently and more fairly. This work is supported by NSFC (Nos.61170189, 61370126, 61202239), the Research Fund for the Doctoral Program of Higher Education (No. 20111102130003), the Fund of the Stage Key Laboratory of Software Development Environment (No. SKLSDE-2013ZX-19), Microsoft Research Asia Fund (No. FY14-RES-OPP-105), the Fund of Beijing Social Science [No.14JGC103], and the Statistics Research Project of National Bureau [No. 2013LY055]. The third author thanks the Innovation Foundation of Beihang University for Ph.D. Graduates (YWF-13-T-YJSY- 024).

7. REFERENCES

[1] Pan W, Chen L. GBPR: group preference based Bayesian personalized ranking for one-class collaborative filtering[C]. AAAI 2013: 2691-2697.

[2] Koren Y, Bell R, Volinsky C. Matrix factorization techniques for recommender systems[J]. Computer, 2009, 42(8): 30-37.

[3] Rendle S, Freudenthaler C, Gantner Z, et al. BPR: Bayesian personalized ranking from implicit feedback[C]. AUAI 2009: 452-461.

[4] Pan R, Zhou Y, Cao B, et al. One-class collaborative filtering[C]. ICDM 2008, 502-511.

[5] Li Y, Hu J, Zhai C X, et al. Improving one-class collaborative filtering by incorporating rich user information[C].CIKM 2010: 959-968.

[6] He H, Garcia E A. Learning from imbalanced data[J]. TKDE 2009, 21(9): 1263-1284.

[7] Wang C, Blei D M. Collaborative topic modeling for recommending scientific articles[C]. KDD 2011: 448-456.

[8] Purushotham S, Liu Y, Kuo C C J. Collaborative topic regression with social matrix factorization for recommendation systems[J]. arXiv preprint arXiv:1206.4684, 2012.

[9] Blei D M, Ng A Y, Jordan M I. Latent dirichlet allocation[J]. the Journal of machine Learning research, 2003, 3: 993-1022.

[10] Chen Y, Yin X, Li Z, et al. A LDA-based approach to promoting ranking diversity for genomics information retrieval[J]. BMC genomics, 2012, 13(Suppl 3): S2.

[11] Heinrich G. Parameter estimation for text analysis[R]. Technical report, 2005.

[12] Hu Y, Koren Y, Volinsky C. Collaborative filtering for implicit feedback datasets[C]. ICDM'08: 263-272.

[13] Gantner Z, Rendle S, Freudenthaler C, et al. MyMediaLite: A free recommender system library[C]. RecSys 2011: 305-308.

A Bootstrapping Based Refinement Framework for Mining Opinion Words and Targets

Qiyun Zhao[1], Hao Wang[* 1,2], Pin Lv[1], Chen Zhang[1]

[1]Science and Technology on Integrated Information System Laboratory
[2]State Key Laboratory of Computer Science
Institute of Software Chinese Academy of Sciences
Beijing, 100190, China
{qiyun12, wanghao, lvpin, zhangchen}@iscas.ac.cn

ABSTRACT

This paper proposes a novel bootstrapping based framework jointed with automatic refinement to extract opinion words and targets. We employ a reasonable set of opinion seed words and pre-defined rules to start bootstrapping. We leverage statistical word co-occurrence and dependency patterns for propagation between opinion words and targets. A Sentiment Graph Model (SGM) is constructed to evaluate these opinion relations. Furthermore, we employ Automatic Rule Refinement (ARR) to refine the rules to extract false results. By using false results pruning and ARR process, we can efficiently alleviate the error propagation problem in traditional bootstrapping-based methods. Preliminary evaluation shows the effectiveness of our method.

Categories and Subject Descriptors

H.3.3 [**Information Search and Retrieval**]:Information Filtering; I.2.7 [**Artificial Intelligence**]: Natural Language Processing – *Text Analysis*

General Terms

Experimentation, Performance.

Keywords

Opinion mining; Sentiment analysis; Bootstrapping; Refinement.

1. INTRODUCTION

In this paper, we investigate the methods for opinion words and target extraction. In this task, identifying the relations between opinion words and targets plays an important role. Syntactic dependency structures are often used to understand grammatical modification relation between opinion words and their targets [1][2]. Recent researches on opinion targets extraction have shown the effectiveness of syntactic patterns for opinion words and targets extraction [3][4][5]. Similarly, in this paper, we utilize the dependency tree to discover the potential relations between opinion words and targets.

*Corresponding Author

Existing approaches on opinion words and targets extraction have two types of framework: one is pipeline framework; the other is propagation (or bootstrapping-based) framework. In the pipeline framework, candidates of opinion expressions and opinion targets are generated first, and then they filter false results with refinement methods [6]. In the refinement process, they took rule-based or machine learning approaches to identify potential relations between opinions and targets. The main challenge is the effectiveness of the refinement methods, because it decides the extraction result. In addition to the pipeline framework, researchers try to identify opinion words and targets iteratively in the propagation framework [3][4]. The extraction result extends with heuristic rules in the iterative propagation process, but it could be affected by the error propagation.

Based on previous researchers, we point out some major challenges in the opinion words and targets extraction:

- **False opinion targets pruning.** The problem of error propagation increases the probability to extract false results

- **Long-tail opinion targets discovery.** Pre-defined syntactic rules are difficult to cover all real-world cases because most of the reviews are informal and they contain a lot of grammatically incorrect sentences.

In this paper, we propose novel bootstrapping based refinement framework to extract opinion words and targets. The basic idea of our method is to adopt refinement methods jointed with propagation. Our contributions in this paper are summarized as follows:

(1) We propose a novel framework that combines the refinement process based on bootstrapping in a jointed framework. By using this method we can alleviate the problems of error propagation and long-tail results discovery in previous propagation or pipeline methods.

(2) We identify potential opinion relations to extract more latent opinion words and targets in the case of informal texts and error parsing in real world. Meanwhile, we employ Automatic Rule Refinement (ARR) to pruning false results and update rules of extraction iteratively to improve the extraction performance.

(3) We evaluate our method using real-world datasets, and experimental results show the effectiveness of our approach compared with the state-of-art methods.

2. FRAMEWORK

Our framework is based on bootstrapping. Figure 1 introduces the detailed process of our refinement framework. We take opinion seed words set, dependency patterns and review data as the system input. We scan all the sentences in the dataset, and we adopt a syntactic parsing method to capture the dependency structure on each sentence. At the beginning, we generate two candidate sets of opinion words and targets by employing the pre-defined rules. Then we iteratively extract opinion words and targets using predefined extraction rules and existing result set. There is a rule set containing several rules to identify the conditions for extraction. Most of the rules describe the latent relations between opinion words and targets, i.e. word co-occurrence or dependency patterns. The details of the rules will be described later in section 3.

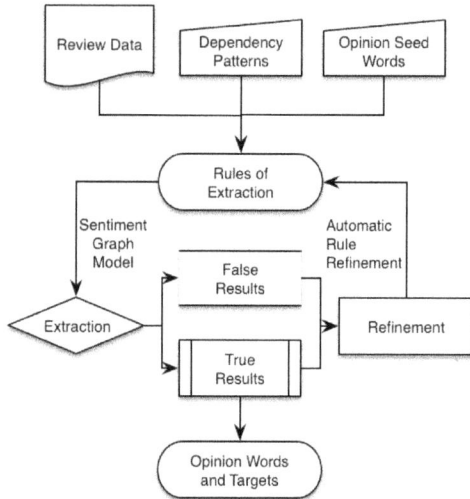

Figure 1: A Bootstrapping based Refinement Framework

In the propagation process, existing opinion words are used to find new opinion targets, which satisfy the rules of extraction. At the same time, the relations between opinion words and targets are identified during the extraction. We apply the structure of Sentiment Graph Model (SGM) to measure the relations between opinion words and targets, and quantize the relations by computing the weight on each edge on the graph. After the extraction, we employ several refinement methods to prune false results.

In the refinement process, we check the conditions of the rules to prune false opinion words and targets in the candidate sets $\{OC\}$ and $\{TC\}$. After pruning and refining, the remained extracted opinion words and targets are added to the refined result set $\{O\}$ and $\{T\}$, and pruned words generate a false result set $\{O_{false}\}$ and $\{T_{false}\}$. Then we apply these refined result set $\{O\}$ and $\{T\}$ to update SGM by adjusting the model parameters. We also take the rule refinement by the false result set $\{O_{false}\}$ and $\{T_{false}\}$ to update or remove rules of extraction. The refined opinion words and targets $\{O\}$ and $\{T\}$, updated SGM, as well as the refined rules of extraction are all applied for further opinion words and targets extraction. Repeat the propagation of extraction until no new opinion words and targets are identified.

The advantages of our refinement framework are listed below:

- Domain-independence. Our framework employ heuristic extraction rules and self-adapted learning strategy.

- Automatic rule refinement method. We update the rules after extraction to reduce error propagation.

- Potential dependency patterns discovery. Different types of opinion words and long-tail targets are identified by discovering potential patterns.

Therefore, we may draw the conclusion that our bootstrapping based refinement framework is domain-independent, scalable and high-performance for opinion words and targets extraction

3. SENTIMENT GRAPH MODEL

Sentiment Graph Model: is a weighted, directed graph. Opinion words, opinion targets and dependency patterns are represented as vertices in the graph model.

First, we need to generate two candidate sets of opinion words and targets. Then we connect pairs of co-occurrence candidates in these sets. As dependency patterns are useful to identify relations between opinions and targets, we add them as vertices to the SGM. Each dependency represents a syntactic relation between opinion words and targets. Though it is difficult to construct a comprehensive set of dependency relations between targets and opinions to cover all real-world cases, we discover potential dependency patterns and measure its confidence to discover new opinion words and targets. New edges that connect the patterns and opinion words or targets would be also added to the graph. The construction of the graph is shown in Figure 2.

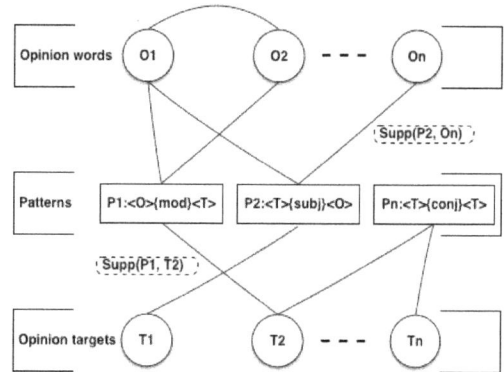

Figure 2: Sentiment Graph with dependency patterns

Now we introduce the estimation of the weight on the SGM. First, we calculate a frequency table of two terms i and j, which represent opinion word or target candidates. As shown in Table 1, $N_{i,j}$ is the number of reviews containing term i and j; $N_{i,\bar{j}}$ is the number of reviews containing term i but not j; $N_{\bar{i},j}$ is the number of reviews containing term j but not i; $N_{\bar{i},\bar{j}}$ is the number of reviews containing neither i nor j.

Frequency	j	$\bar{j}$
i	$N_{i,j}$	$N_{i,\bar{j}}$
$\bar{i}$	$N_{\bar{i},j}$	$N_{\bar{i},\bar{j}}$

Table 1: Frequency table of candidates.

Then we measure the association of pair-wise terms as the support level for each pair of candidates. Here is the function to calculate the support level:

$$Supp(i,j) = 2[log\ L\big(P(i|j), N_{i,j}, N_j\big)$$
$$+ log\ L\big(P(i|\bar{j}), N_{i,\bar{j}}, N_{\bar{j}}\big) - log\ L(P(i), N_i, N] \qquad (1)$$

where,

$$P(i|j) = \frac{N_{i,j}}{N_j} \qquad (2)$$

$$L(p,k,n) = p^k(1-p)^{n-k} \qquad (3)$$

N is the number of reviews. N_i is the frequency of term i in the corpus. $P(i|j)$ is the conditional probability of term i when term j occurs. We define $Supp(i,j)$ as the support level of term i to j. Then we use $Supp(o,t)$ as the weight of the edge $(e: v_o \rightarrow v_t)$ on the Sentiment Graph. Similarly, we use $Supp(t,o)$ and $Supp(t,t)$ as the weight of edges $(e: v_t \rightarrow v_o)$ and $(e: v_t \rightarrow v_t)$ representatively.

We compute the support level for each associated pattern and opinion word, or target, which are used to evaluate the confidence of the dependency pattern used to extract new opinion words and targets. We take the support level as the weights on the Sentiment Graph Model. We evaluate the confidence of each dependency pattern by employing the following function:

$$Conf(p) = \sum_{i=1}^{N_o} Supp(p,o_i) + \sum_{j=1}^{N_t} Supp\big(p,t_j\big) \qquad (4)$$

$Conf(p)$ is the sum of weights on all associated opinion words and targets with the pattern. Only with high confidence can the patterns be used to extract new opinion words and targets. The confidence score is used in rules of extraction. After refinement process, the confidence score need to be updated as some false results have been pruned.

4. REFINEMENT

In the propagation process, we define several rules of extraction to discover new opinion words and targets. The initial rule set is shown in the Table 2 below:

The first two rules are used to generate the initial candidate sets of opinion words and targets. We simply extract adjective as opinion words and nouns as opinion targets candidates. The rest of the rules contain different restriction to specify the conditions for extraction. In the propagation process, these rules are applied to filter the candidate set and identify opinion words and targets that satisfy the words co-occurrence threshold or match the dependency patterns with high confidence score.

No.	Rules of Extraction
R1	Extract adj. as opinion word.
R2	Extract noun. as opinion target.
R3	If o is in $\{O\}$ and $Supp(o, t)$ > threshold, extract t as target.
R4	If t is in $\{T\}$ and $Supp(t, o)$ > threshold, extract o as target.
R5	If t is in $\{T\}$ and $Supp(t, t)$ > threshold, extract t as target.
R6	If o is in $\{O\}$ and pattern "O-T" is in $\{P\}$ in dependency structure, extract t as target.
R7	If t is in $\{T\}$ and pattern "O-T" is in $\{P\}$ in dependency structure, extract o as target.
R8	If o is in $\{O\}$ and t is in $\{T\}$ in dependency structure, add p to $\{P\}$.

Table 2: Rules of extraction

We construct the SGM on the candidate result set before propagation. Then we apply the rules of extraction to filter the candidate set. Taking R3 as example to demonstrate the process of extraction, we find an opinion word o existing in the result set in a sentence. If there is a target candidate t in the same sentence, we check the support level of o and t on the SGM. Then we identify t as a target if the support level is higher then the threshold. After dependency parsing on one sentence, we check the rules with dependency patterns. If one pattern matches the dependency path on the sentence, we apply the corresponding rules to extract new opinion words or targets. We also discover potential dependency patterns with the help of extracted opinion words and targets.

In addition, we also update our rules of extraction by considering the pruned false results. This process is called automatic rule refinement. We collect the pruned candidates to a false result set. The false results are examples of incorrect extraction. Then we find out the rules used to extract these results, and adjust parameters in these rules, such as threshold, support level of opinion relation and confidence score of patterns. We expect to learn and update the rules with the help of the extraction results automatically, which is self-adaption in different domain and application. Modifying a rule to remove false result can simultaneously remove other false results. However, this action may also remove some correct results. Only when the false results are extracted by specific rule frequently, can the rule be refined seriously in order to reduce the side effect.

5. EXPERIMENTS

We select a real world dataset in Chinese to evaluate our method. The datasets contain reviews on different products, so we test the performance of our method on cross-domain data. The dataset published in COAE2008[1] has about 5000 sentences, which contains Chinese review data on camera (D1) and car (D2). Besides some pre-annotated opinion targets in the datasets, we manually annotate opinion words and targets in sentences.

Evaluation Metrics: We evaluate our method by precision (P), recall (R) and F-measure (F).

We evaluate our opinion words and targets extraction performance of the proposed framework against four state-of-art competitors listed below:

- **DP**: *Double Propagation* in [3].
- **DPHITS**: *DP* with hyperlink-induced topic search algorithm in [4].
- **LSTBOOT**: likelihood ratio tests for bootstrapping in [7].
- **TSF**: *Two-Stage Framework* in [5].

All of the above competitors are unsupervised methods. The first three methods are based on bootstrapping framework. DP extracts opinion words and targets using syntactic dependency relations. Some syntactic rules are manually defined for extraction. DPHITS uses hyperlink-induced topic search algorithm (HITS) to validate potential targets recognized by DP plus two additional syntactic patterns of "part-whole" and "no". The last competitor TSF is a typical pipeline framework. TSF first generates candidates of opinion words and targets, and then uses well-designed models to refine the result.

---

[1] http://ir-china.org.cn/coae2008.html

All of the above approaches use same five common opinion word seeds as {good, bad, nice, poor, perfect}. The choice of opinion seeds seems reasonable, as most people can easily use this opinion words to express their basic opinion and sentiment orientation.

We take the task of the opinion target extraction on these five methods. As DPHITS and LRTBOOT don't extract opinion words, we only show the performance of opinion words extraction on DP, TSF and our JPR method.

Table 3 shows the experimental results for opinion targets extraction and Table 4 shows the results for opinion words extraction. We have the following analysis from the results table:

Methods	D1			D2		
	P	R	F	P	R	F
DP	0.60	0.56	0.58	0.58	0.53	0.55
DPHITS	0.68	0.64	0.66	0.69	0.66	0.67
LRTBOOT	0.68	0.72	0.70	0.70	0.73	0.71
TSF	0.74	**0.76**	0.75	0.76	0.73	0.74
Ours	**0.80**	**0.76**	**0.80**	**0.80**	**0.75**	**0.77**

Table 3: Results for opinion targets extraction

Methods	D1			D2		
	P	R	F	P	R	F
DP	0.66	0.65	0.65	0.67	0.6	0.68
TSF	0.78	0.76	0.77	0.77	0.73	0.75
Ours	**0.80**	**0.78**	**0.79**	**0.82**	**0.78**	**0.80**

Table 4: Results for opinion words extraction

(1) Our method outperforms the four competitors in terms of F-measure on all domains, and it outperforms the method ranked only second to our method at 0.03-0.05 in two tasks. It indicates the effectiveness and domain-independence of our method.

(2) Our method achieves highest 0.22 improvement in F-measure compared with DP. Our method also outperforms the other two bootstrapping methods at 0.06-0.10 in F-measure. We believe the improvement on recall benefits from our pattern discovery, as new patterns can identify more opinion words and targets. The improvement in precision indicates the effectiveness of our iterative refinement process, which reduces the error propagation. In addition, the automatic rule refinement also makes contributions to extract more correct opinion words and targets compared with static and rules chosen manually.

(3) Our method outperforms pipeline methods in terms of precision at 0.06 and has comparable recall. It indicates that the process of refinement during the iterations plays an important role to reduce false extraction. The reason for the close score of recall is that some correct results are filtered in the refinement process. Therefore, the refinement process should be carried out carefully to reduce such side effect.

6. CONCLUSIONS

This paper proposes a novel bootstrapping based refinement framework for opinion words and targets extraction. Unlike the existing propagation framework or pipeline framework, our framework combines the refinement process based on bootstrapping. We employ a Sentiment Graph Model containing dependency patterns to evaluate the relations between opinion words and targets. We also adopt an automatic rule refinement to pruning the false results and update the rules for extraction to improve performance. The experimental results show that ours achieves higher performance over current state of the art unsupervised methods.

In the future, we plan to focus on improving the precision of opinion words and targets extraction by working on the refinement methods. We also plan to reduce the false drop to increase recall in the process of refinement, which is a side effect of rule refinement. Then we will also try to design new models to improve the Sentiment Graph Model to discover the potential relations between opinion words and targets.

7. ACKNOWLEDGMENT

This work is supported by National Natural Science Foundation of China (61303164), Beijing Natural Science Foundation (9144037), National Basic Research Program of China (973 Program) (2013CB329305) and National High Technology Research and Development Program of China (863 Program) (2012AA011206).

8. REFERENCES

[1] A. Popescu and O. Etzioni. 2005. Extracting product features and opinions from reviews. In *Proceedings of the conference on Human Language Technology and Empirical Methods in Natural Language Processing* (HLT '05). Association for Computational Linguistics, Stroudsburg, PA, USA, 339-346. DOI=10.3115/1220575.1220618 http://dx.doi.org/10.3115/1220575.1220618

[2] N. Kobayashi, K. Inui, and Y. Matsumoto. 2007. Opinion mining from web documents: Extraction and structurization. *Information and Media Technologies 2*, no. 1 2007, 326-337.

[3] G. Qiu, B. Liu, J. Bu, and C. Chen. 2009. Expanding domain sentiment lexicon through double propagation. In *Proceedings of the 21st international joint conference on Artificial intelligence* (IJCAI'09), Hiroaki Kitano (Ed.). Morgan Kaufmann Publishers Inc., San Francisco, CA, USA, 1199-1204.

[4] L. Zhang, B. Liu, S. H. Lim, and E. O'Brien-Strain. 2010. Extracting and ranking product features in opinion documents. In *Proceedings of the 23rd International Conference on Computational Linguistics: Posters* (COLING '10). Association for Computational Linguistics, Stroudsburg, PA, USA, 1462-1470.

[5] L. Xu, K. Liu, S. Lai, Y. Chen and J. Zhao. 2013. Mining Opinion Words and Opinion Targets in a Two-Stage Framework. In Proceedings of the 51st Annual Meeting of the Association for Computational Linguistics (ACL'13), pages 1764–1773, 2013.

[6] Y. Wu, Q. Zhang, X. Huang, and L. Wu. 2009. Phrase dependency parsing for opinion mining. In *Proceedings of the 2009 Conference on Empirical Methods in Natural Language Processing: Volume 3 - Volume 3* (EMNLP '09), Vol. 3. Association for Computational Linguistics, Stroudsburg, PA, USA, 1533-1541.

[7] Z. Hai, K. Chang, and G. Cong. 2012. One seed to find them all: mining opinion features via association. In *Proceedings of the 21st ACM international conference on Information and knowledge management* (CIKM '12). ACM, New York, NY, USA, 255-264. DOI=10.1145/2396761.2396797 http://doi.acm.org/10.1145/2396761.2396797

Adaptive Pairwise Preference Learning for Collaborative Recommendation with Implicit Feedbacks

Hao Zhong†, Weike Pan‡, Congfu Xu†*, Zhi Yin§ and Zhong Ming‡
†Institute of Artificial Intelligence, College of Computer Science, Zhejiang University
‡College of Computer Science and Software Engineering, Shenzhen University
§College of Science, Ningbo University of Technology
{haozhong,xucongfu}@zju.edu.cn, {panweike,mingz}@szu.edu.cn, yz@nbut.edu.cn
* Corresponding author

ABSTRACT

Learning users' preferences is critical to enable personalized recommendation services in various online applications such as e-commerce, entertainment and many others. In this paper, we study on how to learn users' preferences from abundant online activities, e.g., browsing and examination, which are usually called implicit feedbacks since they cannot be interpreted as users' *likes* or *dislikes* on the corresponding products directly. Pairwise preference learning algorithms are the state-of-the-art methods for this important problem, but they have two major limitations of *low accuracy* and *low efficiency* caused by noise in observed feedbacks and non-optimal learning steps in update rules. As a response, we propose a novel adaptive pairwise preference learning algorithm, which addresses the above two limitations in a single algorithm with a concise and general learning scheme. Specifically, in the proposed learning scheme, we design an *adaptive* utility function and an *adaptive* learning step for the aforementioned two problems, respectively. Empirical studies show that our algorithm achieves significantly better results than the state-of-the-art method on two real-world data sets.

Categories and Subject Descriptors

H.3.3 [**Information Search and Retrieval**]: Information Filtering

Keywords

Collaborative Recommendation; Implicit Feedbacks; Pairwise Preference Learning

1. INTRODUCTION

Recommendation and personalization technology has an extremely wide spectrum of online applications, including e-commerce, entertainment, professional networks, mobile ad-

CIKM'14, November 3–7, 2014, Shanghai, China.
Copyright 2014 ACM 978-1-4503-2598-1/14/11 ...$15.00.
http://dx.doi.org/10.1145/2661829.2661986.

vertisement, etc. Automatically mining and learning users' preferences from their online activities such as browsing and examination records is critical to provide qualified personalized services. Such activities are usually called users' implicit feedbacks, which is very different from explicit feedbacks like graded ratings in the contest of Netflix \$1 million prize because we cannot infer users' true preferences from implicit feedbacks directly. In this paper, we focus on this important problem of learning users' preferences from implicit feedbacks. Note that implicit feedbacks are usually represented as (user, item) pairs instead of (user, item, rating) triples for explicit feedbacks.

Previous works on preference learning with implicit feedbacks include algorithms based on preference regression [1] and preference paired comparison [5], where the latter usually performs better in empirical studies due to the more relaxed pairwise assumption as compared with that of the former. Specifically, paired comparison is defined on an observed (user, item) activity (u, i) and an unobserved (user, item) activity (u, j), where (u, i) can be interpreted that user u has implicitly expressed some preference on item i while (u, j) means that such activity is not observed. Paired comparison usually simplifies the hidden relationships and assumes that a user u has a higher preference score on item i than on item j, i.e., $(u, i) \succ (u, j)$ [5]. Note that such two (user, item) pairs or a triple (u, i, j) is usually randomly sampled from the database of users' feedbacks for preference learning. With the paired comparisons, different forms of loss functions can then be designed and optimized for different purposes.

However, previous works based on paired comparison usually have two major limitations. First, most algorithms adopt the pairwise relationship $(u, i) \succ (u, j)$ without considering the existence of some noisy triples that may not satisfy the pairwise relationships, and thus results in low accuracy. Second, most algorithms randomly sample triples from a huge set of (u, i, j)s as constructed from the observed implicit feedbacks, which is often of low efficiency due to the resulted non-optimal learning steps. Some works have realized the above two problems and relax the pairwise relationships via introducing a new preference score on a set of items [2] instead of on a single item [5], which introduces a more general loss function. Some other works design some advanced sampling strategies for the second issue such as [4].

In this paper, we aim to address the aforementioned two problems in one single algorithm. Specifically, we design a concise and general learning scheme, which is able to absorb different loss functions and sampling strategies as special cases. Furthermore, we design an *adaptive* utility function and learning step in a pairwise preference learning algorithm, which is thus called APPLE (adaptive pairwise preference learning).

2. OUR SOLUTION: ADAPTIVE PAIRWISE PREFERENCE LEARNING

2.1 Problem Definition

We use $\mathcal{R} = \{(u, i)\}$ to denote a set of implicit feedbacks or activities from n users and m items. Each (user, item) pair (u, i) means that user u has browsed or examined item i, which is usually called an implicit feedback of user u on item i due to the uncertainty of the user's true preference. Our goal is then to exploit the data $\mathcal{R}$ in order to generate a personalized ranked list of items from $\{j | (u, j) \notin \mathcal{R}\}$ for each user u.

2.2 A General Learning Scheme

A pairwise preference learning algorithm usually minimizes a tentative objective function $f(u, i, j)$ for a randomly sampled triple (u, i, j). A triple (u, i, j) means that the relationship between user u and item i is observed while the relationship between user u and item j is not observed. In order to encourage pairwise competition, the tentative objective function is usually defined on a pairwise preference difference, i.e., $f(u, i, j) = f(\hat{r}_{uij})$, where $\hat{r}_{uij} = \hat{r}_{ui} - \hat{r}_{uj}$ is the difference between user u's preferences on item i and item j. A user u's preference on an item i, i.e., $\hat{r}_{ui}$, is typically modeled by a set of parameters denoted by θ, which include user u's latent feature vector $U_{u\cdot} \in \mathbb{R}^{1 \times d}$, item i's latent feature vector $V_{i\cdot} \in \mathbb{R}^{1 \times d}$ and item i's bias $b_i \in \mathbb{R}$. With the model parameter θ, we can estimate a user's preference on a certain item via $\hat{r}_{ui} = U_{u\cdot} V_{i\cdot}^T + b_i$.

With a sampled triple (u, i, j) and a tentative objective function $f(\hat{r}_{uij})$, the model parameter θ can then be learned or updated accordingly. The update rule is usually represented as follows,

$$\theta = \theta - \gamma \left(\frac{\partial f(\hat{r}_{uij})}{\partial \hat{r}_{uij}} \frac{\partial \hat{r}_{uij}}{\partial \theta} + \alpha \theta \right). \quad (1)$$

where $f(\hat{r}_{uij})$ can be $-\ln 1/(1 + e^{-\hat{r}_{uij}})$ [5], $\max(0, 1 - \hat{r}_{uij})$ [6] or in other forms, in order to encourage different types of pairwise competitions between an observed pair (u, i) and an unobserved pair (u, j). Note that $\alpha \theta$ in Eq.(1) is from a regularization term $\frac{\alpha}{2} \|\theta\|^2$ used to avoid overfitting.

There are two fundamental questions associated with the update rule in Eq.(1), namely (i) how to choose a specific form of the tentative objective function $f(\hat{r}_{uij})$, and (ii) how to sample a triple (u, i, j). For the first question, different works usually incorporate different loss functions into $f(\hat{r}_{uij})$ with different goals, which will then result in different values of $\frac{\partial f(\hat{r}_{uij})}{\partial \hat{r}_{uij}}$. For the second question, most previous works sample a triple in a uniformly random manner [5, 6].

Mathematically, the above two questions can be represented by a concise and general learning scheme,

$$\textbf{Learning Scheme:} \ (\rho(u, i, j), \tau(u, i, j)) := (\rho, \tau) \quad (2)$$

where (i) the first term $\rho(u, i, j)$ denotes the utility of a randomly sampled triple (u, i, j), which answers the question of how to sample a triple, and (ii) the second term $\tau(u, i, j) =$

Input: Triples $\mathcal{T} = \{(u, i, j)\}_{1 \leq u \leq n, 1 \leq i \leq m}$, and learning scheme $(\rho(u, i, j), \tau(u, i, j))$.
Output: Model $\Theta = \{U_{u\cdot}, V_{i\cdot}, b_i\}_{1 \leq u \leq n, 1 \leq i \leq m}$.

1: **for** $t = 1, \ldots, T$ **do**
2:   **repeat**
3:     Randomly sample a triple (u, i, j) from $\mathcal{T}$.
4:     Generate a random variable $\rho_{rand} \in [0, 1]$.
5:     Calculate the utility $\rho(u, i, j)$.
6:   **until** $\rho_{rand} \leq \rho(u, i, j)$
7:   Update model via Eq.(3) with $\tau(u, i, j)$.
8:   **if** S-II & mod $(t, K) = 0$ **then**
9:     Update τ_2 via Eq.(7).

Figure 1: The algorithm of adaptive pairwise preference learning (APPLE).

$\frac{\partial f(\hat{r}_{uij})}{\partial \hat{r}_{uij}}$ is the gradient, which answers the question of how to choose a specific form of the tentative objective function. The update rule in Eq.(1) can then be equivalently written as follows,

$$\theta = \theta - \gamma \left(\tau(u, i, j) \frac{\partial \hat{r}_{uij}}{\partial \theta} + \alpha \theta \right). \quad (3)$$

The learning scheme $(\rho(u, i, j), \tau(u, i, j))$ in Eq.(2) for pairwise preference learning can also be described by an algorithm, which is shown in Figure 1, in particular of lines 5-7. In Figure 1, we can see that the chance of sampling a triple (u, i, j) is $\rho(u, i, j)/|\mathcal{T}|$, where $|\mathcal{T}|$ is the number of triples in $\mathcal{T}$ and $\rho(u, i, j)$ is the utility of the randomly sampled triple.

With the general learning scheme in Eq.(2), we can represent a typical pairwise preference learning algorithm in a concise way. For example, the seminal algorithm BPR (Bayesian personalized ranking) [5] can be represented as follows,

$$\textbf{S-BPR:} \ \left(1, -\frac{e^{-\hat{r}_{uij}}}{1 + e^{-\hat{r}_{uij}}} \right) := (\rho_{BPR}, \tau_{BPR}), \quad (4)$$

from which we can see that our learning scheme in Eq.(2) is quite powerful and is able to absorb other pairwise preference learning algorithms as special cases.

Based on the general learning scheme in Eq.(2), we propose one preliminary learning scheme and two specific learning schemes so as to learn users' true preferences in a more effective and efficient way.

2.3 Two Specific Learning Schemes

It is well known [4] that a large preference difference $\hat{r}_{uij}$ means that the pairwise competition between (u, i) and (u, j) of a typical triple (u, i, j) has been well encouraged, and thus may not be helpful to use this $\hat{r}_{uij}$ in the update rule in Eq.(1). This observation motivates us to sample triples with small preference differences. We thus propose a preliminary learning scheme with an adaptive utility function without changing the expectation of the learning step,

$$\textbf{S-0:} \ \left(\frac{e^{-\hat{r}_{uij}}}{1 + e^{-\hat{r}_{uij}}}, -1 \right) := (\rho_0, \tau_0). \quad (5)$$

It is easy to show that a smaller $\hat{r}_{uij}$ will result in a larger utility, and the expectation of the learning step $|\tau|$ for (u, i, j)

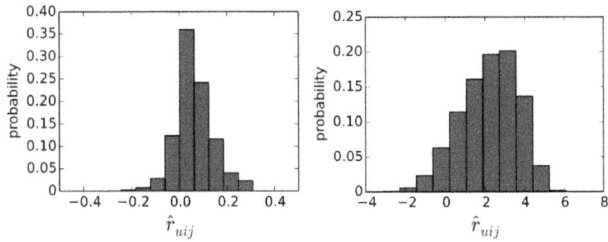

(a) In the beginning. (b) In the end.

Figure 2: The distribution of $\hat{r}_{uij}$ in different learning stages.

of S-0 and S-BPR are the same, $\frac{1}{|\mathcal{T}|} \times \rho_{BPR} \times |\tau_{BPR}| = \frac{1}{|\mathcal{T}|} \times \rho_0 \times |\tau_0|$. The advantages of the learning scheme S-0 as compared with S-BPR are, (i) a triple (u, i, j) with larger $\hat{r}_{uij}$ will have a lower chance to be sampled, and (ii) the learning step $|\tau_0|$ is larger than $|\tau_{BPR}|$, which is assumed to be helpful for the learning efficiency.

In the following sections, we will describe two specific learning schemes based on this preliminary learning scheme.

2.3.1 Scheme I

We assume that a triple (u, i, j) with a very small $\hat{r}_{uij}$ has a higher chance to be noise, especially when the learning process has been conducted for a cerntain time. Specifically, a small $\hat{r}_{uij}$ often denotes a high chance that user u *dislikes* item i or user u *likes* item j, and then we may not encourage the pairwise competition between (u, i) and (u, j) any more. Hence, such a triple (u, i, j) is considered noise for pairwise preference learning. As a response, we design a new utility function, $\rho(u, i, j) = \frac{1}{1+e^{-\hat{r}_{uij}}} \times \frac{e^{-\hat{r}_{uij}}}{1+e^{-\hat{r}_{uij}}} = \frac{e^{-\hat{r}_{uij}}}{(1+e^{-\hat{r}_{uij}})^2}$, in order to reduce the chance that a triple (u, i, j) with lower $\hat{r}_{uij}$ will be sampled. This new utility function reaches the peak value 0.25 when $\hat{r}_{uij} = 0$, and becomes smaller as $\hat{r}_{uij}$ increases or decreases. In order to constrain the value range to $[0, 1]$, we obtain our first learning scheme,

$$\textbf{S-I:} \left(\frac{4e^{-\hat{r}_{uij}}}{(1+e^{-\hat{r}_{uij}})^2}, -1 \right) := (\rho_1, \tau_1). \quad (6)$$

We can see that the difference between S-I and S-0 is the utility $\rho(u, i, j)$, i.e., ρ_1 and ρ_0, where ρ_1 is designed to reduce the impact of noisy triples (i.e., triples with small preference difference $\hat{r}_{uij}$ when the learning process has conducted for some time).

2.3.2 Scheme II

In order to improve the learning efficiency, we may set the learning step $|\tau|$ to be a larger value in the beginning, since most $\hat{r}_{uij}$ are very small. While in the middle or in the end of the learning process, we shall decrease the learning step $|\tau|$ so as to reach the optimal solution in a smooth manner and thus to achieve high recommendation accuracy. We then propose a more sophisticated learning scheme accordingly in order to benefit both learning efficiency with large $|\tau|$ and recommendation accuracy with small $|\tau|$.

We first show the distribution of preference difference $\hat{r}_{uij}$ of MovieLens1M data (see more information in the Section of Experimental Results) in different learning stages in Figure 2. We can see that the whole distribution will move from

the origin to the right, which means that the difference $\hat{r}_{uij}$ becomes larger in the learning process as expected by the competition encouragement. Based on this observation, we propose to use the average preference difference to update the value of $|\tau|$ in a certain monotonic decreasing function. Due to the complexity of ρ_1 and the fact that $\hat{r}_{uij} \geq 0$ in most cases, we use $\rho_1' = \frac{e^{-y(\hat{r}_{uij}-x)}}{1+e^{-y(\hat{r}_{uij}-x)}}$ to approximate ρ_1 when $\hat{r}_{uij} \in [0, \infty)$ in Eq.(6), and obtain an estimation $x = 2, y = 1.5$ via minimizing the KL-divergence between ρ_1' and ρ_1 with $\hat{r}_{uij} \geq 0$. We then have $\hat{r}_{uij} = \frac{\ln(1/\rho_1'-1)}{1.5} + 2$, and use $\bar{r}_{uij} = \frac{\ln\left(1/\frac{1}{|\mathcal{T}|}\sum_{(u,i,j) \in \mathcal{T}} \rho_1' - 1\right)}{1.5} + 2 \approx \frac{\ln(\bar{N}-1)}{1.5} + 2$ to represent the average preference difference, where $\bar{N} = \frac{1}{K}\sum_{k=t-K+1}^{t} N_k$ with N_k as the repeat number of lines 2-6 of the k's iteration in Figure 1. With $\bar{r}_{uij}$, we reach our second learning scheme,

$$\textbf{S-II:} \left(\frac{4e^{-\hat{r}_{uij}}}{(1+e^{-\hat{r}_{uij}})^2}, -\ln(g+1-\bar{r}_{uij})-1 \right) := (\rho_2, \tau_2), \quad (7)$$

where g is set as the maximal value of $\bar{r}_{uij}$ obtained when the learning process converges so as to ensure that $|\tau_2|$ is larger than 1 in the learning process and is roughly equal to 1 in the end. We can see that the major difference between S-II and S-I is the gradient τ, which is not static and fixed as -1 in Eq.(6), but is dynamic w.r.t. the preference difference. The new gradient τ aims to achieve better learning efficiency and recommendation accuracy, which is also supported by our empirical studies.

3. EXPERIMENTAL RESULTS

3.1 Data Sets

In our empirical studies, we use two data sets, including MovieLens1M[1] and Douban[2].

MovieLens1M MovieLens1M contains about 1 million triples in the form of (user, movie, rating) with $n = 6,040$ users and $m = 3,952$ movies. In our experiments, we randomly take about 50% triples as training data, about 10% triples as validation data, and the remaining about 40% triples as test data. For training data, we keep all triples and take the corresponding (user, movie) pairs as implicit feedbacks. For validation data and test data, we only keep triples with ratings equal to 4 or 5 and take the corresponding (user, movie) pairs as implicit feedbacks [3].

Douban We crawled a real implicit data of users' feedbacks on books from Douban.com in December 2013, which is one of the largest Chinese online social media websites. The Douban data contains about 3 million (user, book) reading records from 10,000 users and 10,000 books. Similarly, we randomly take about 50% records as training data, about 10% records as validation data and the remaining about 40% records as test data.

We conduct the above "50%, 10%, 40%" splitting procedure of each data for 5 times and thus get 5 copies of training data, validation data and test data.

3.2 Evaluation Metric

We adopt a commonly used top-k evaluation metric for implicit feedbacks [3], i.e., precision ($Pre@k$). We use $k = 5$

[1]http://grouplens.org/datasets/movielens/
[2]http://www.douban.com/

in our experiments since most people may only check a few recommended items.

3.3 Baselines and Parameter Settings

In our experiments, we study our proposed algorithm AP-PLE with two specific learning schemes in comparison with the state-of-the-art algorithm BPR (Bayesian personalized ranking) [5]. We implement both learning schemes in Eq.(6) and Eq.(7) and that of BPR in Eq.(4) in the same algorithmic framework in Figure 1 for fair comparison.

For all experiments, we use the validation data and $Pre@5$ to tune the hyperparameters. Specifically, we search the regularization parameter α in the range of $[0.001, 0.5]$. For the parameter g of our learning scheme S-II in Eq.(7), we have tried $g \in \{1, 2, 3, 4\}$ to find an approximation of the maximal value of $\bar{r}_{uij}$ in Eq.(7). For the learning rate γ in Eq.(3), we fix it as 0.01 [3]. The parameter K is set as 10^5, and the iteration number T is searched around 10^8 for sufficient convergence. The number of latent features for users and items is fixed as $d = 10$ for MovieLens1M and $d = 20$ for Douban.

3.4 Summary of Experimental Results

The recommendation performance of our two learning schemes and S-BPR are shown in Table 1, from which we can see that the overall recommendation performance ordering is S-II≈S-I>S-BPR. We also conduct significance test and find that S-I and S-II are significantly better than S-BPR on both data sets. The results in Table 1 clearly demonstrates the advantages of our proposed learning schemes in our algorithm AP-PLE, in particular of the learning scheme S-II with sophisticated utility $\rho(u, i, j)$ and dynamic learning step $|\tau(u, i, j)|$.

The learning efficiency of our two learning schemes and S-BPR are shown in Figure 3, from which we have a similar observation, i.e., the overall convergence performance ordering is S-II>S-I>S-BPR. It is interesting to see that this ordering is consistent with that of the learning step of the learning schemes, i.e., $|\tau_2| > |\tau_1| > |\tau_{BPR}|$, which means that increasing the learning step can indeed improve the convergence performance.

Table 1: Recommendation accuracy of our proposed algorithm APPLE with learning schemes S-I in Eq.(6) and S-II in Eq.(7), and the seminal algorithm BPR [5] with S-BPR in Eq.(4) on MovieLens1M and Douban data sets.

Algorithm \ Data	MovieLens1M	Douban
PopRank	$0.2322_{\pm 0.0037}$	$0.2845_{\pm 0.0017}$
BPR	$0.3403_{\pm 0.0030}$	$0.3821_{\pm 0.0032}$
APPLE(I)	$0.3483_{\pm 0.0020}$	$0.3976_{\pm 0.0023}$
APPLE(II)	$\mathbf{0.3497}_{\pm 0.0044}$	$\mathbf{0.3983}_{\pm 0.0013}$

4. CONCLUSIONS AND FUTURE WORK

In this paper, we propose a novel algorithm called adaptive pairwise preference learning (APPLE) for collaborative recommendation with implicit feedbacks. Our proposed algorithm improves the state-of-the-art pairwise preference

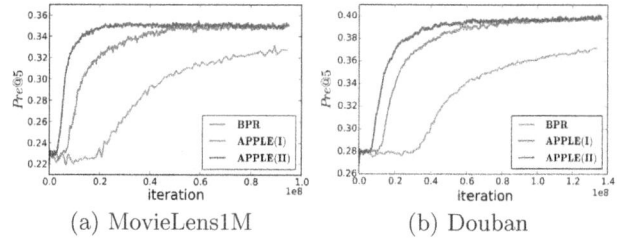

(a) MovieLens1M   (b) Douban

Figure 3: Learning efficiency of our proposed algorithm APPLE with learning schemes S-I in Eq.(6) and S-II in Eq.(7), and the seminal algorithm BPR [5] with S-BPR in Eq.(4) on MovieLens1M and Douban data sets.

learning algorithm, i.e., BPR [5], via a concise and general learning scheme with an adaptive utility function and an adaptive learning step. Empirical studies show that our algorithm performs significantly better than the BPR algorithm regarding both the recommendation accuracy and learning efficiency.

For future work, we are mainly interested in generalizing our learning scheme in APPLE to include heterogeneous user feedbacks and social context information.

5. ACKNOWLEDGMENT

We thank the support of National Natural Science Foundation of China (NSFC) No. 61272303, National Basic Research Program of China (973 Plan) No. 2010CB327903, Natural Science Foundation of SZU No. 201436, NSFC No. 61170077, NSF GD No. 10351806001000000, GD S&T No. 2012B091100198, S&T of SZ No. JCYJ20130326110956468 and No. JCYJ20120613102030248, Natural Science Foundation of Ningbo No. 2012A610029 and Department of Education of Zhejiang Province(Y201120179).

6. REFERENCES

[1] Rong Pan, Yunhong Zhou, Bin Cao, Nathan N. Liu, Rajan Lukose, Martin Scholz, and Qiang Yang. One-class collaborative filtering. In *Proceedings of the 8th IEEE International Conference on Data Mining*, ICDM '08, pages 502–511, 2008.

[2] Weike Pan and Li Chen. Cofiset: Collaborative filtering via learning pairwise preferences over item-sets. In *Proceedings of SIAM Data Mining*, SDM '13, pages 180–188, 2013.

[3] Weike Pan and Li Chen. Gbpr: group preference based bayesian personalized ranking for one-class collaborative filtering. In *Proceedings of the 23rd International Joint Conference on Artificial Intelligence*, IJCAI '13, pages 2691–2697, 2013.

[4] Steffen Rendle and Christoph Freudenthaler. Improving pairwise learning for item recommendation from implicit feedback. In *Proceedings of the 7th ACM International Conference on Web Search and Data Mining*, WSDM '14, pages 273–282, 2014.

[5] Steffen Rendle, Christoph Freudenthaler, Zeno Gantner, and Lars Schmidt-Thieme. Bpr: Bayesian personalized ranking from implicit feedback. In *Proceedings of the 25th Conference on Uncertainty in Artificial Intelligence*, UAI '09, pages 452–461, 2009.

[6] Shuang-Hong Yang, Bo Long, Alexander J. Smola, Hongyuan Zha, and Zhaohui Zheng. Collaborative competitive filtering: learning recommender using context of user choice. In *Proceedings of the 34th International ACM SIGIR Conference on Research and Development in Information Retrieval*, SIGIR '11, pages 295–304, 2011.

INK: A Cloud-Based System for Efficient Top-k Interval Keyword Search

Rui Li   Xiao Zhang [*]   Xin Zhou   Shan Wang

[1] Key Laboratory of Data Engineering and Knowledge Engineering of the Ministry of Education
(Renmin University of China), Beijing, China
[2] School of Information, Renmin University of China, Beijing, China
{lrbeckham, zhangxiao, zhouxin314159, swang}@ruc.edu.cn

ABSTRACT

It is insufficient to search temporal text by only focusing on either time attribute or keywords today as we pay close attention to the evolution of event with time. Both temporal and textual constraints need to be considered in one single query, called *Top-k Interval Keyword Query (TIKQ)*. In this paper, we presents a cloud-based system named INK that supports efficient execution of TIKQs with appropriate effectiveness on Hadoop and HBase. In INK, an *Adaptive Index Selector* (AIS) is devised to choose the better execution plan for various TIKQs adaptively based on the proposed cost model, and leverage two novel hybrid index modules (TriI and IS-Tree) to combine keyword and interval filtration seamlessly.

Categories and Subject Descriptors

H.3.4 [**Information Search and Retrieval**]: Search process; H.2.4 [**Database Management**]: System—*Query Processing*

General Terms

Experimentation, Algorithms, Performance

Keywords

Top-k Interval Keyword Query; Adaptive Index Selector; Interval Inverted Index; Inverted Segment Tree

1. INTRODUCTION

Given one *Top-k Interval Keyword Query* (a type of queries involving both textual and interval predicates), it is supposed to return a ranked set of temporal-textual objects in descending order of relevance scores, which are computed from two metrics: interval similarity and keyword relevance.

---

[*]Corresponding author.

CIKM'14, November 3–7, 2014, Shanghai, China.
ACM 978-1-4503-2598-1/14/11.
http://dx.doi.org/10.1145/2661829.2661830.

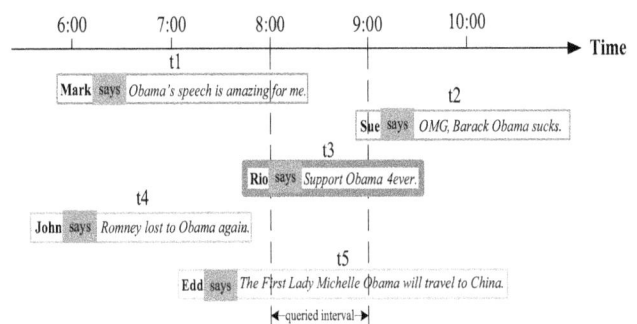

Figure 1: Example Top-k Interval Keyword Query. (Hot tweets' intervals depict the period when their hit rates exceed one given threshold)

Example 1. Fig. 1 plots five hot tweets marked with intervals and contents. Given one **top-1** *interval keyword query*: **the most relevant hot tweet that contains the keyword 'Obama' and exists** *during 8 o'clock*. According to the figure, the result should be *t3*. Because it contains the word *'Obama'* with a relatively large weight, and has the maximum intersection ratio with the query interval.

In this demonstration, we design and present one system named INK to handle interval keyword search over large-scale temporal text effectively and efficiently:

First, two hybrid index structures (TriI and IS-Tree) are employed to integrate content predicates and temporal constraint in a common data structure. TriI is highly suitable for queries with selective content predicates; while IS-Tree is good at processing queries with selective temporal constraint.

Second, the two index methods deal with different kinds of queries, the system can determine the better search path for a specific query. So Adaptive Index Selector (AIS) is introduced in INK to estimate respective cost with little overhead and further improve the overall efficiency stably.

In addition, the design of our system is based on the cloud environment. Specifically, we choose open source implementation Apache Hadoop [1] and HBase [2] to guarantee high concurrency and scalability.

The rest of the paper is organized as follows. An overview of the system architecture is provided in Section 2. The user interfaces of INK for two query scenarios are demonstrated in Section 3. Concluding remarks are presented in Section 4 in detail.

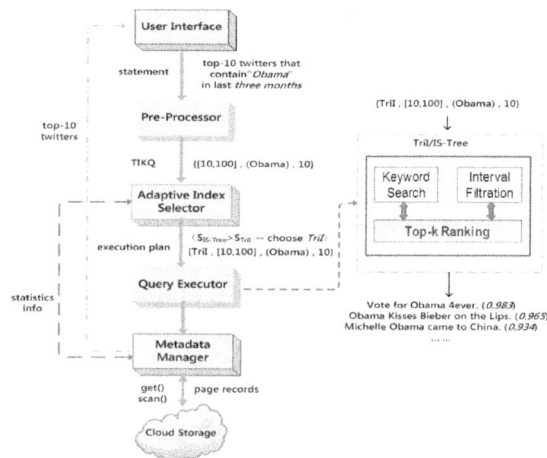

Figure 2: The Overview Architecture of INK.

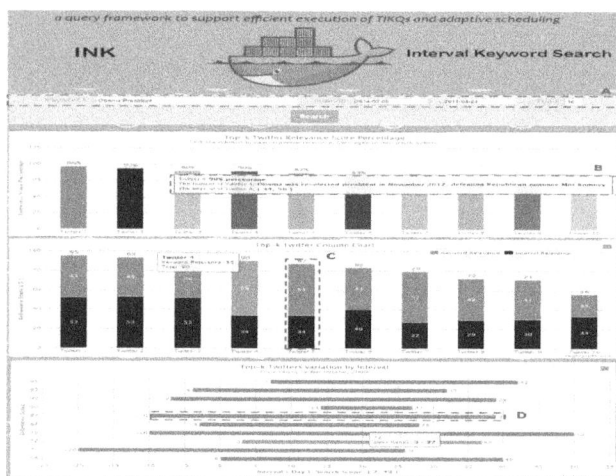

Figure 3: Webpage Interface for TIKQ.

2. INK IMPLEMENTATION

INK can support four kinds of top-k queries: (i) keyword query, (ii) interval query, (iii) single keyword and interval query and (iv) multiple keywords and interval query. In INK, query execution involves three stages, whose order is determined at runtime: **Keyword Search**, retrieving textually relevant pages with respect to query keywords; **Interval Filtration**, obtaining temporally relevant pages which interrelate with the given interval; **Top-k Ranking**, ranking the pages based on relevance scores to return top-k results. As shown in Fig. 2, INK is composed of six major components: *User Interface, Pre-Processor, Adaptive Index Selector, Executor, Metadata Manager* and *Cloud Storage.*

i. User Interface

Based on the B/S architecture, INK provides interactive and intuitive user interfaces. In addition, the graphical interface which includes several charts facilitates users to observe query results from many perspectives: top-k scores, respective textual content and valid intervals etc. INK also indicates the estimated costs of chosen index module (TriI or IS-Tree) and the actual finished time.

ii. Pre-Processor

INK supports ad-hoc TIKQs and batch request, which is stand-alone files comprised of statements. Given one user statement, for example, "top-10 pages that contain 'Obama' in last three months", using automatic IE techniques [3, 5], the Pre-Processor parses and transforms the statement into three parts: interval range I, query keywords Q and required number of results K, i.e., (I, Q, K). Then it determines the target internal scheme of TIKQ (e.g., {[10,100], (Obama), 10}).

iii. Adaptive Index Selector(AIS)

AIS works as a middleware to uniformly process these preprocessed queries. It has two important functionalities. **First**, it can retrieve, cache and process batch all queries. **Second**, AIS can dynamically choose TriI or IS-Tree modules to process a specific query according to cost model.

In detail, AIS relies on the statistics stored in the metadata cache of *Metadata Manager* to estimate respective costs. Based on statistics, AIS measures the selectivity of each module for various queries (S_{TriI} and $S_{IS-Tree}$), we could roughly compare their response time and make the right choice. That is, if $S_{TriI} > S_{IS-Tree}$, IS-Tree module is used to process the query. Otherwise, TriI would be exploited.

As in Fig. 2, AIS generates the final execution plan: {TriI, [10,100], (Obama), 10}. INK deploys the AIS on multiple nodes to process the incoming workload parallelly.

iv. Executor

The Executor checks the execution plan of one TIKQ and activates the corresponding index module to process query based on the early-termination top-k techniques [4]. INK provides two hybrid distributed index modules: **Interval Inverted Index** (TriI) that supports textually preferred queries and Inverted **Segment Tree** (IS-Tree) that supports temporally prior search.

Specifically, Fig. 2 shows that in the case of plan semantics as {TriI, [10,100], (Obama), 10}, TriI is chosen to complete the three stages of the query execution and delivers top-10 pages to users.

v. Metadata Manager

Ad-hoc measurement of selectivity for each query in AIS needs to take the statistics stored in the *Metadata Manager* into account; Meanwhile, metadata in this component serves for the final plan established in the *Executor* and facilitate the data access process. The goal of *Metadata Manager* is to improve the accuracy of the estimated costs for various queries dynamically and speed up the retrieval of the underlying data.

vi. Cloud Storage

We make use of the Hadoop DFS system (HDFS) and HBase for the implementation and validation in the *Cloud Storage* component. Essentially, we treat them as underlying raw byte devices, rely on their built-in capacities of fault tolerance and load balancing to achieve high data scalability and availability.

3. DEMONSTRATION SCENARIO

In the demonstration, we present the online processing of two scenarios to prove effective and efficient execution of queries over Twitter dataset[1]. Each tweet in this dataset contains three parts: tweet id, textual content and the creation time. In order to be compatible with subsequent queries, we add two synthetic attributes in all 2,000,000 tweets: an-

---

[1]http://snap.stanford.edu/data/twitter7.html

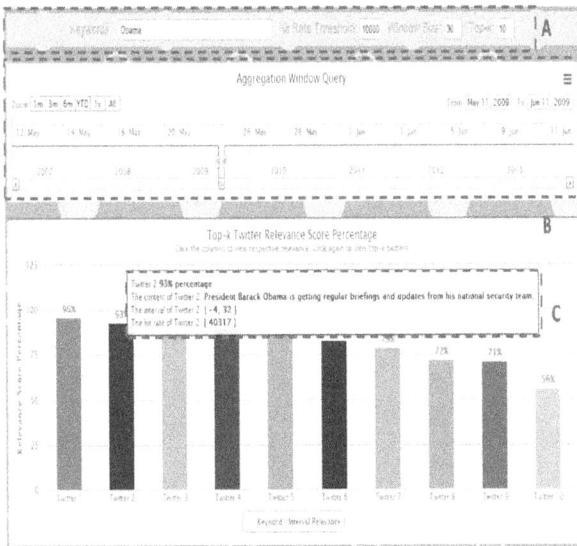

Figure 4: Webpage Interface for Aggregation Window Query.

Table 1: Dataset Details

Parameter	Values
Tot. # of tweets	2,000,000
Tot. # of words	236,572,157
Tot. # of unique words	3,384,477
Tot. # of unique intervals	107,358

other time point ($\mu = 21.58$ and $\sigma = 26.19$) which constitutes an interval with the creation time, the hit rate of the tweet ($\mu = 8931$ and $\sigma = 28.27$). Table 1 summarizes the properties of this dataset.

3.1 Processing TIKQ

Assume that one user wants to find the most relevant tweets which contain specified keywords and actively exist between certain interval. Based on the B/S architecture of INK, he or she can issue one TIKQ to get result feedbacks via the webpage interface.

Fig. 3 is the interface presenting the query result of one TIKQ from three perspectives: top-k tweets ranking, relevance scores constitution and respective intervals.

Part A provides the interface for users to submit TIKQs, namely query keywords, interval range and required number of results. When users submit all query parameters, internal representation of this query would be constructed prior to submitting. Part B displays one of the top-10 tweets, including the percentage of its relevance score, textual content and valid interval. Part C shows the proportion of keyword relevance and interval relevance in one score value. Take tweet 5 as example, the keyword relevance of 53 plus the interval relevance of 34 equals the score of 87, ranking the fifth. And Part D displays the distribution of all tweets' intervals. Hence we demonstrate that INK can address single TIKQ within a time period of millionseconds.

3.2 Processing Aggregation Window Query

Note that although TIKQ needs to specify two explicit interval endpoints, users may only confirm the interval size (i.e. window) and want to vary this window over the entire range of dataset. Here we introduce one novel query – aggregation window query. As users merely specify the window size, they can choose one particular interval with the same size at random. For instance, one user issues such aggregation window query: in one month (30 days), the top-10 tweets whose hit rate exceeds 10000 and textual content includes the keyword 'Obama'.

A snapshot of INK system for aggregation window query is shown in Fig. 4, which consists of three parts.

Part A shows the user-defined area. As described before, aggregation window query has 4 constraints on the Webpage Interface: keywords, hit rate threshold, the window size and the top-k number. Part B presents the entire interval range of the dataset. This part can facilitate user to assign specific interval with the same window size. After the explicit interval is chosen, it would trigger INK to start query process and get relevant results. Part C displays one exemplary tweet in results. It describes the details why it appears in top-k results. This part serves to show the results in a graphical way, and also help users to decide when to stop.

4. CONCLUSIONS

Efficient processing of interval keyword queries is critical for searching temporal-textual data. This demonstration presents a cloud-based system named INK to address the TIKQs. In INK, two index modules, TriI and IS-Tree, are utilized and an Adaptive Index Selector is used to identify the better query execution plan based on estimated costs for each particular query. Moreover, INK handles one kind of novel query – aggregation window query in an efficient and friendly manner.

5. ACKNOWLEDGMENTS

This research was partially supported by the Fundamental Research Funds for the Central Universities, the Research Funds of Renmin University of China(No. 14XN-H115), the National Key Basic Research Program (973 Program) of China(No. 2014CB340403), and the National 863 High Tech. Program of China(No. 2012AA011001).

6. REFERENCES

[1] "apache hadoop", http://hadoop.apache.org/.

[2] "apache hbase", http://hbase.apache.org/.

[3] O. Alonso, M. Gertz, and R. Baeza-Yates. On the value of temporal information in information retrieval. *SIGIR Forum*, 41(2):35–41, 2007.

[4] J. B. Rocha-Junior, A. Vlachou, C. Doulkeridis, and K. Nørvåg. Efficient processing of top-k spatial preference queries. *VLDB Journal*, 4(2):93–104, 2010.

[5] K. F. Wong, Y. Xia, W. Li, and C. Yuan. An overview of temporal information extraction. In *Int. J. Comput. Proc.*, volume 18, pages 137–152, 2005.

CoDEM: An Ingenious Tool of Insight into Community Detection in Social Networks *

Meng Wang, Chaokun Wang, Jun Chen
School of Software, Tsinghua University, Beijing 100084, China
{meng-wang12, chaokun, junchen12}@tsinghua.edu.cn

ABSTRACT

In recent years, community structure has attracted increasing attention in social network analysis. However, performances of multifarious approaches to community detection are seldom evaluated in a suite of systematic measurements. Furthermore, we can hardly find works which reveal diverse features based on the detected community structure. In this paper, we build a tool called **CoDEM** to make both quality evaluations of community detection and an in-depth mining for pivotal nodes inside communities. This tool integrates several effective approaches to community detection, establishes an overall evaluation system and gets the multi-dimensional ranking for the local importance of nodes. Moreover, the tool is built with a friendly user interface.

Categories and Subject Descriptors

H.3.3 [**Information Search and Retrieval**]: Clustering; D.2.8 [**Software Engineering**]: Metrics—*complexity measures, performance measures*

Keywords

Community Detection, Evaluation, CoDEM

1. OVERVIEW OF CODEM

Social networks usually possess inherent communities where members cluster together to form closely connected groups. Revealing latent community structure is a crucial problem in social network analysis. It also leads to advances in various social network services and applications. Considering the diversity of datasets and various perspectives to address this issue, it is a puzzle to choose a best-performed approach from the abundant candidates. Although a comparative study [8] has been proposed recently, up to now, we do not have a suite of systematic evaluation metrics to make a comprehensive comparison based on the quality of the community assignment. Moreover, to explore the formation and evolution of the

---

*Corresponding author: Chaokun Wang.

CIKM'14, November 3–7, 2014, Shanghai, China.
ACM 978-1-4503-2598-1/14/11.
http://dx.doi.org/10.1145/2661829.2661831.

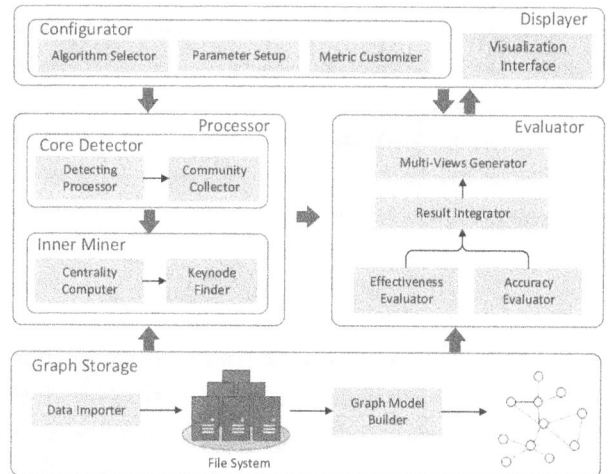

Figure 1: The System Architecture of CoDEM

massive groups, mining important features of them is also a significant work. Since members of a community usually play various roles, those high-impact or pivotal members are always the people we are interested in. Therefore, an ingenious tool of insight into community detection to solve these problems is worth expecting.

In this paper, we present a tool called **CoDEM** for **Co**mmunity **D**etection **E**valuating and **M**ining. Different from the existing tools, such as Gephi[1] and Graphviz[2], CoDEM aims at the evaluation of community detection, not only the ways of visualization. In addition, it does not focus on the global network analyses, but the insight into communities. More specifically, CoDEM has the following characteristics:

- Many well-performed community detection approaches of various categories are integrated in this tool, including *Newman-Clauset Fast Greedy* method [5, 2], *Label Propagation* method [7], *Top Leaders* method [4], and *Dense Subgraph Extract* method [1].

- It adopts a suite of objective metrics to make the evaluation, such as *modularity*, *strength*, *clustering coefficient* and *purity*. The employed metrics embody full structure characteristics of communities.

- A variety of centralities in social network analysis are used to indicate the local (intragroup) importance of nodes. Then, inside *keynodes* can be mined by some multi-dimensional ranking method, such as the Fagin algorithm [3].

---

[1] https://gephi.github.io/
[2] http://www.graphviz.org/

- Moreover, CoDEM provides a friendly user interface, including customizable setup and multiple novel views for display.

2. SYSTEM DESIGN AND WORKFLOW

The major functions of our CoDEM have been implemented in standard C++; the data-driven technique D3[3] is adopted for the visualization. According to the system function and workflow, CoDEM consists of four basic modules: Displayer, Processor, Evaluator and Graph Storage (as shown in Fig. 1) . They can be mapped to different system layers, and we will introduce them in further detail below.

User Access Layer. The included Configurator covers selections and requisite parameters of algorithms as well as the customized evaluation metrics. The overall setup will be sent out for both detection and evaluation. Displayer itself also accepts and presents the produced results from the evaluation layer in various views, such as table, diagram and multiple graph displays.

Core Processing Layer. The Core Detector is mainly responsible for the implementation of community detection approaches. Apart from that, the detector is extendible and any other method can be implemented in it easily. The Inner Miner aims at finding the pivotal nodes inside a community by a series of node centralities (*degree, betweenness, closeness* and *PageRank*). Considering the customized centralities, the ranking of nodes inside the community can be obtained by the Fagin algorithm as an example.

Core Evaluation Layer. With insight into community detection, the Evaluator covers both effectiveness and accuracy. In CoDEM, comparisons are made in this layer based on the customized metrics which are reasonable, recognized and comprehensive enough. Then, evaluation results upon different metrics of all approaches are integrated and ultimately organized from multiple views.

Data Storage Layer. Any network in a certain format can be imported from the browser; the same as the ground truth file if we have one. Datasets here consist of two parts. First, we use the well-known datasets which have the corresponding ground truth, such as Karate-Club, Strike and Football-NCAA. Moreover, we also use large-scale networks in the Stanford Large Network Dataset Collection[4]. The established graph model records attributes of nodes and edges in the whole detection and evaluation process.

3. SYSTEM FEATURES

CoDEM consists of two prime processes: 1) evaluating the detected communities; 2) mining the keynodes inside them.

3.1 Overall Evaluation of Communities

Many approaches are proposed along with the performance test by the only criterion. In addition, many former evaluations have overfull dependence on the ground truth. Actually, we have confronted two problems in this field: 1) In practice, we can hardly know what the exact community assignment is in the real world; 2) The single criterion cannot represent the performance of an approach objectively. Therefore, in CoDEM, metrics from multiple aspects are employed to make the evaluation of community detection.

Modularity [2] is the most widespread quality function for community detection. Essentially, modularity compares the result with a randomized one to indicate how reasonable the nodes are assigned

[3]http://d3js.org/
[4]http://snap.stanford.edu/data/

into different groups. The modularity Q of a community assignment is defined as $\sum_{i=1}^{k} \left[\frac{I_i}{m} - \left(\frac{2I_i + O_i}{2m} \right) \right]$ where I_i indicates the total number of internal relationships within the community C_i, O_i indicates the number of outgoing relationships between nodes in C_i and any node outside.

Strength of a community is more intuitive to show whether the internal linkages among its members are stronger than those outside. We inherit Radicchi's definitions [6] to classify communities by the intensity. Given a node v, k_v^{in} and k_v^{in} stand for degrees within and without the community C, respectively. Then, the community C is called *strong* if $k_v^{in} > k_v^{out}$ for $\forall v \in C$, and is called *weak* if $\sum_v k_v^{in} > \sum_v k_v^{out}$ for $\forall v \in C$. Any group which does not satisfy any of the two criteria above will be invalid. We attach labels to each discovered community. Besides that, we also present the corresponding proportions of the two categories.

Clustering Coefficient of a community focuses on the members' tendency to form a tightly intertwined group. In social networks, clustering coefficient may indicate the possibility that two friends of someone happen to be friends as well. The local computation for a community C_i is $CC_i = \sum_{v \in C_i} \frac{2|\{e_{ts}: v_t, v_s \in N(v) \cap C_i, e_{ts} \in E\}|}{k_v(k_v - 1)}$ where $N(v)$ is the neighbors of node v, k_v is the degree of v, and C_i is the ith community.

Purity shows the accuracy of the discovered communities versus the ground truth [4]. On this occasion, we can get the disparity between the result produced by the algorithm and that in the real world. Suppose R_d and R_r are two different results of the same graph with n nodes. R_d includes s subsets $\{C_{d1}', ..., C_{dk_1}'\}$, and R_r includes t similar subsets. The purity of the detected result R_d is defined as $P(R_d, R_r) = \frac{1}{n} \sum_j max_i |C_{dj}' \cap C_{ri}'|$.

3.2 Multi-Dimensional Keynode Mining

As mentioned before, CoDEM adopts four centralities to indicate the local importance of nodes. Using some multi-dimensional ranking method, such as the Fagin algorithm, local rankings of nodes can be produced according to the multi-dimensional scores. As shown in Fig. 2, the process of keynode mining can be personalized via the optional indicators below.

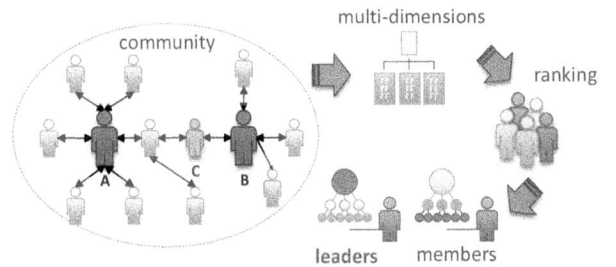

Figure 2: Keynode Mining

Degree. High-degree nodes, such as A and B, inside a community usually play as the cores.

Betweenness. Generally, the community structure is hierarchical. Nodes with high betweenness, such as C, can bridge the connections among different smaller groups.

Closeness. It simply shows the ability of transmission, that is how close a member is with all the other ones via indirect relations inside the community.

PageRank. Pivotal nodes are likely to receive high-quality links from others, therefore, the influence of a node can be obtained via its intragroup neighbours.

4. DEMONSTRATION

In this section, an example is given to demonstrate how CoDEM works.

Setup. First, on the setup page, we can upload a network file, e.g. Strike, as well as the available ground truth. Then the basic information will be shown in the right information bar. We can find that the network has 24 nodes and 76 relationships and it is an undirected network with weight=1 on each relationships. Then, we can make a personalized setup since approaches in the category lists, requisite parameters and evaluation metrics are all customizable for users. Note that some approaches assign each node to a certain community. However, in social network theory, the entire network always consists of grouped members and independent outliers. Therefore, based on the results by algorithms, we can set the global filter to 2 to eliminate tiny groups, making the evaluation more fair and reasonable.

Display for Evaluation. After clicking the button "Compare", the integrated evaluation results can be shown in the "Table" view (Fig. 3). We can get the overall results and find which approach stands out clearly w.r.t. the current dataset. Results, including modularity, strength (percentages of strong and weak communities), maximal clustering coefficient, purity and time cost, of different approaches from various perspectives are shown together. Therefore, we can make full use of the information to analyze the differences among various kinds of approaches. We can find that label propagation algorithms perform better on this dataset. Furthermore, histograms in the "Chart" view can intuitively rank the approaches according to a specific metric so that the variances in the aspect can be shown clearly.

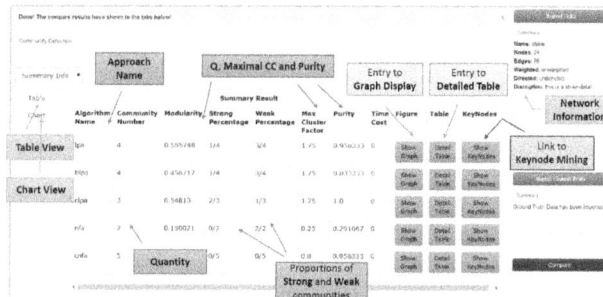

Figure 3: Evaluation Results

Entries for Details. If we want to find some more details about the results, we can utilize the entries for details. In Fig. 3, if we click the first yellow button "Show Graph", the detected communities in both the "Community" view (Fig. 4(b)) and the "Relation" view (Fig. 4(a)) will be shown. The former clearly presents the community structure and the latter shows the assignment in the relational graph by different colors. In Fig. 4, we can find that the result of the original label propagation algorithm is nearly consistent with the ground truth. If we click the next button "Detail Table", details about each community, including the size, members, strength (labeled as "strong", "weak" or "neither") and the clustering coefficient will be shown. Combined with the above results, we can make a comparison of these approaches intuitively. Suppose that an approach performs terribly in modularity, we may find that the color distribution is scattered in the relation view. If an approach reacts badly in most cases, we may think that it does not perform well enough.

Keynode Mining. The right-most button "Show KeyNodes" links to the other page to mine keynodes inside each community. After

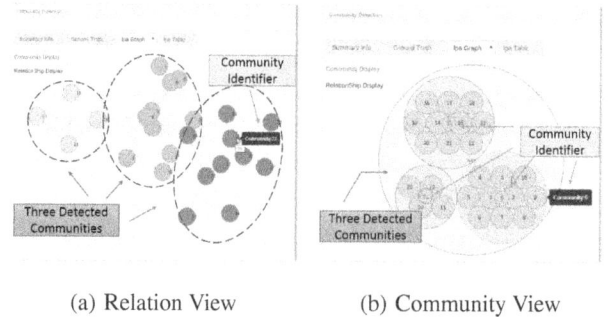

| (a) Relation View | (b) Community View |

Figure 4: Two Views of the Community Structure

selecting the criteria to measure the local importance of nodes as well as a given k (say 3), we can click the button "Find Key Nodes". Then, a relation view will be shown, where the top-k keynodes are highlighted by size based on the overall scores. Similarly, both table and chart view are provided so that we can make a comparison of different centralities, total scores and rankings of nodes.

All in all, CoDEM is extensible and modularized in the implementation for a lot of sound design. Besides the approaches already adopted in this tool, other community detection approaches can be appended easily.

5. CONCLUSIONS

CoDEM is designed for customizable evaluations on the communities detected by various approaches. It is quite helpful for users to analyze the results of diverse approaches on different datasets. Moreover, it provides the multi-dimensional in-depth mining of the inside keynodes. Either the optional quality metrics or the centralities are representative and all-around. The results are presented in a nice user interface as well as various novel views. As the future work, we will try to reveal other important features related to the community structure to enrich this tool.

6. ACKNOWLEDGMENTS

This work was supported by the National Natural Science Foundation of China (No. 61170064, No. 61373023) and the National High Technology Research and Development Program of China (No. 2013AA013204).

7. REFERENCES

[1] J. Chen and Y. Saad. Dense subgraph extraction with application to community detection. *IEEE TKDE*, 24(7):1216–1230, 2012.

[2] A. Clauset, M. E. Newman, and C. Moore. Finding community structure in very large networks. *Physical review E*, 70(6):066111, 2004.

[3] R. Fagin, A. Lotem, and M. Naor. Optimal aggregation algorithms for middleware. *JCSS*, 66(4):614–656, 2003.

[4] R. R. Khorasgani, J. Chen, and O. R. Zaïane. Top leaders community detection approach in information networks. In *SNMA*, 2010.

[5] M. E. Newman. Fast algorithm for detecting community structure in networks. *Physical review E*, 69(6):066133, 2004.

[6] F. Radicchi, C. Castellano, F. Cecconi, V. Loreto, and D. Parisi. Defining and identifying communities in networks. *PNAS*, 101(9):2658–2663, 2004.

[7] U. N. Raghavan, R. Albert, and S. Kumara. Near linear time algorithm to detect community structures in large-scale networks. *Physical Review E*, 76(3):036106, 2007.

[8] J. Xie, S. Kelley, and B. K. Szymanski. Overlapping community detection in networks: The state-of-the-art and comparative study. *ACM Computing Surveys (CSUR)*, 45(4):43, 2013.

Faceted Exploring for Domain Knowledge over Linked Open Data

Meng Wang[+], Jun Liu[+], Wenqiang Liu[+], Qinghua Zheng[+], Wei Zhang[++], Lingyun Song[+], Siyu Yao[+]

[+]MOEKLINNS Lab, Department of Computer Science, Xi'an Jiaotong University, 710049, China
[++]Amazon.com Inc, Seattle, WA 98109, USA

wangmengsd@stu.xjtu.edu.cn, liukeen@mail.xjtu.edu.cn, liuwenqiangcs@stu.xjtu.edu.cn, qhzheng@mail.xjtu.edu.cn,
wzhan@amazon.com, xjtuslysm@gmail.com, cheryl@stu.xjtu.edu.cn

ABSTRACT

The rapidly increasing RDF data in the Linked Open Data (LOD) community project is a valuable resource for obtaining domain knowledge. However, RDF data of specific topics also shows a trend of being more decentralized and fragmented, which makes it difficult and inefficient for the users to get an overview of a specific topic and retrieve the desired information. In this paper, we demonstrate a novel system called KFM, which can aggregate the distributed RDF data of a topic according to the facets of this topic. KFM provides a new way for users to obtain and explore domain knowledge in the LOD cloud.

Categories and Subject Descriptors

H.3.5 [**On-line Information Services**]: Web-based services; H.3.3 [**Information Search and Retrieval**]: Clustering;

General Terms

Algorithms, Management, Design

Keywords

RDF, linked open data, data fusion, domain knowledge

1. INTRODUCTION

As of September 2011, Linked Open Data (LOD) contains 295 datasets with more than 31 billion RDF triples from a variety of domains [1]. A plethora of valuable information regarding domain knowledge can be found within these data sets. But RDF data of specific topics also shows a steady trend of being more decentralized and fragmented. More specifically, when searching a specific topic via the traditional semantic search engine, the results usually distribute across a large number of datasets which are rather loosely connected. The RDF data in each dataset only covers a few facets (a facet in this study means an aspect or dimension) of the topic. We call this the RDF data fragmentation problem.

For instance, when searching *k-means* in Sindice[3], about 800 RDF documents, which contain about 63,000 RDF triples will be returned (as of June 23th, 2014). However, these RDF data are distributed in more than 30 datasets, and are blended into a long and daunting list. Furthermore, information about *k-means* in each result item includes different facets and is incomplete. For exam-

ple, some result items are about the *algorithm steps* of *k-means*, whereas some only contain the *references* about *k-means*.

RDF data fragmentation problem makes it difficult for the users to get an overview of a specific topic, or efficiently retrieve their desired information. To solve this RDF data fragmentation problem, we present a novel system called KFM (Knowledge Fusion Map) [2] in this demonstration. KFM fuses the distributed RDF data according to the topic's different facets, and provides an intuitive and visual presentation for users. This differs from the traditional semantic search engine and provides a new way for users to explore the domain knowledge over the LOD. Figure 2 shows the fusion result of *k-means*.

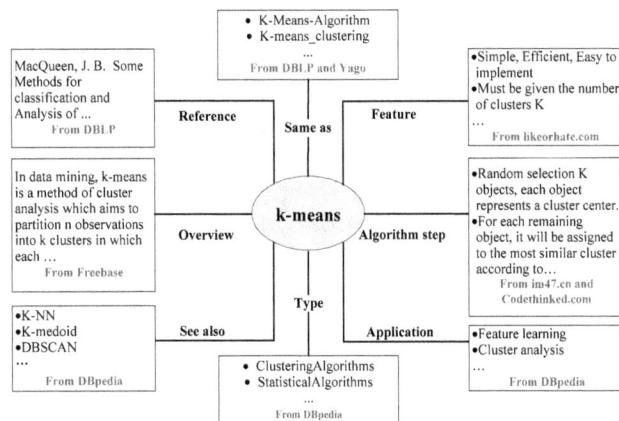

Figure 1. Fusion result of *k-means*

KFM tries to solve three problems:

● How to determine what facets a given topic has so that we can generate a complete fusion result?

● How to fuse the extracted RDF data to the topic's different facets?

● How to organize and visualize the fusion results to users?

The rest of this demonstration is organized as follows. Section 2 introduces several concepts about KFM. Section 3 shows the architecture of KFM and explains important technical issues. Section 4 demonstrates how KFM offers a new visual way for users to obtain domain knowledge and reports the preliminary results on three domains. Section 5 summarizes the conclusions of this demonstration.

2. PRELIMINARY

The important concepts in KFM include:

---

[1] The LOD cloud diagram: http://lod-cloud.net/
[2] http://kfm.skyclass.net

Topic-specific RDF Graph: The RDF data about a specific topic T is a collection of RDF triples Q_T. Each RDF triple consists of a subject, a predicate, and an object. Q_T can also be represented as a graph, called topic-specific RDF graph (TRG). TRG can be formally defined as $G_T=\{V,E,P\}$. V refers to the vertices in the graph, it is a set of subjects or objects; $E \subseteq V \times V$ represents a set of directed edges, with each edge corresponding to a triple in Q_T; P is a set of predicates and indicates the labels of edges.

Facet Template: The RDF data of a specific topic often contains diverse facets. Every facet has a facet label (such as the *Feature* of *k-means*) which summarizes the meaning of RDF data it represents. A facet template describes the facets of a topic T and can be formally defined as $FT_T=\{l_i\}_n$, where l_i denotes a label to represent a topic's facet. With an example shown in Figure 1, the facet template of *k-means* is {*Reference, Same as, Feature, Overview, Algorithm step, See also, Type, Application*}.

Knowledge Fusion Map: A knowledge fusion map is the fusion result for a given topic T, which can be formally defined as $KFM_T = \{l_i, F_i\}_n$, where $l_i \in FT_T$, $F_i \subseteq Q_T$. F_i corresponds to the related facet and satisfy $\forall x, y \in [1...n].x \neq y, F_x \cap F_y=\varnothing$.

3. The KFM SYSTEM

3.1 Architecture

For a certain domain, KFM generates knowledge fusion maps for specific topics by employing a three-module framework, as shown in Figure 2.

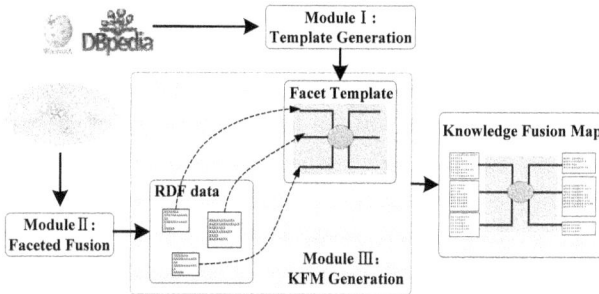

Figure 2. Architecture of KFM

Module I generates a facet template for a group of similar topics from DBpedia[3] and Wikpedia[4].

Module II crawls RDF data of a specific topic from LOD and fuses them based on two topological properties of TRG.

Module III assigns fused RDF data to corresponding facets and generates a knowledge fusion map.

3.2 Facet Template Generation

Similar topics usually have similar facets. For example, *k-means* and *k-medoid* are algorithms in *Data mining*. They have common facets such as *Algorithm step, Feature, Application*. So generating facet template can be divided into two subtasks: clustering topics and generating facet labels for every cluster.

To generate topic clusters, KFM uses DBpedia as the initial dataset because DBpedia encompasses numerous domains and almost any topic can be found there. Each topic corresponds to an

RDF entity in DBpedia (in this section, we use the term of *topic* and *entity* interchangeably). By analyzing the RDF entities, we find two features that can be used for clustering: *predicate similarity* and *category relatedness*.

Predicate Similarity: Similar RDF entities in DBpedia usually have similar predicates. KFM compresses the predicates of each entity into a bag of words and represents each entity with a word vector based on TF-IDF[1]. The predicate similarity $ps(e_i, e_j)$ of two entities e_i, e_j can be further defined as the cosine of the angle between the two vectors.

Category Relatedness: Each RDF entity usually links to an arbitrary number of categories. Categories in DBpedia are connected by *skos:broader* relations ("a-type-of" relationship)[5]. For example, *Array* is *skos:broader* of *Data structure*. Given two RDF entities e_i and e_j, KFM determines the category relatedness value $cr(e_i, e_j)$ by using the method proposed in [5], which is based on the topological properties of category graph.

With these two features, the similarity between RDF entity e_i and e_j can be defined as:

$$sim(e_i, e_j) = \lambda ps(e_i, e_j) + (1 - \lambda)cr(e_i, e_j), \qquad (1)$$

where λ is an empirical value. KFM uses the similarity to cluster the entities with an agglomerative hierarchical clustering algorithm. Preliminary result using 6 datasets shows that KFM achieves a best average clustering precision of 89.6% at a recall of 84.7% when λ is set to 0.3.

To generate facet labels, we find each DBpedia entity contains an RDF triple to link its article in Wikipedia. The *Contents table* and *Infobox* in a Wikipedia article provide a set of facet labels for the topic. These candidate labels have two problems, schema duplication and sparsity. As an example of schema duplication, *abstract* and *overview* are used to describe the same meaning of a facet. Sparsity means many labels are used very rarely. KFM currently uses a statistical method to extract representative labels for each template from Wikipedia articles.

3.3 Faceted Fusion

We find that two topological properties of TRG serve as the foundation in the module II, namely *homogeneity of adjacent vertices* and *homogeneity of similar predicate vertices*.

Homogeneity of adjacent vertices: By scrutinizing the degree distribution of the TRGs, we find that the average degree $< k >$ is between 2 and 3.5. Around 98% of the vertices in each TRG are isolated. This indicates that a TRG is a highly-sparse graph. We find that two connected vertices are very likely belonging to the same facet, by focusing on the vertices that are connected by links in a TRG.

Homogeneity of similar predicate vertices: We also find that the Jaccard similarity score between two vertices is associated with the facet of the topic. The similarity score s_{v_i, v_j} of vertices v_i and v_j, can be computed based on their shared predicates as follows.

$$s_{v_i, v_j} = \frac{|c(v_i, v_j)|}{|p(v_i)| + |p(v_j)| - |c(v_i, v_j)|}, \qquad (2)$$

[3] http://wiki.dbpedia.org/Datasets

[4] http://en.wikipedia.org/

[5] http://www.w3.org/2009/08/skos-reference/skos.html#broader

where $p(v_i)$ and $p(v_j)$ are the sets of predicates for vertices v_i and v_j. $c(v_i, v_j)$ represents the set of common predicates/objects shared by v_i and v_j. By analyzing the similarity of any two distinct vertices in each TRG from six different domains, we find that the probability of two vertices belonging to the same facet increases with their similarity. It indicates that the higher the similarity, the more likely the two vertices belong to the same facet.

For a specific topic, the procedure of fusing RDF data includes: (1)KFM uses LDSpider[2] to crawl its RDF data returned by Sindice; (2)KFM generates a set of fused facets by leveraging *the homogeneity of similar predicate vertices*; (3)KFM merges these facets based on *the homogeneity of adjacent vertices*, and outputs the final fused RDF data.

3.4 Knowledge Fusion Map Generation

The fused RDF data generated by Module II are not corresponding to the facet labels of the facet template. So KFM automatically assigns these fused results to the template items and generates a knowledge fusion map. This can be seen as a multi-class classification problem.

Inspired by [4], KFM automatically extracts the RDF data from DBpedia entity, their corresponding faceted labels from Wikipedia and heuristically labels the training sets. This makes KFM robust to domain changes. The predicate, the part of speech tags of the objects, and the labels of data source are utilized as features for classification. KFM employs a Maximum Entropy Model as the classifier, which is suitable for multi-class classification.

The data model of a knowledge fusion map is a hierarchical tree whose root is the topic and leaf nodes are RDF data. There exist edges with facet labels between the topic and corresponding RDF data. With this model, knowledge fusion maps can be easily presented by XML or Jason data on the Web.

4. DEMONSTRATION

4.1 Visualization

KFM is implemented as a Java Web application. It allows users to search their interested topics via a Web-based interface. To visualize the knowledge fusion map, JavaScript InfoVis Toolkit[6] (an open-source tool for creating interactive data visualizations on the Web) is incorporated into KFM. We also designed a new layout algorithm so that the knowledge fusion map looks more reasonable and intuitive.

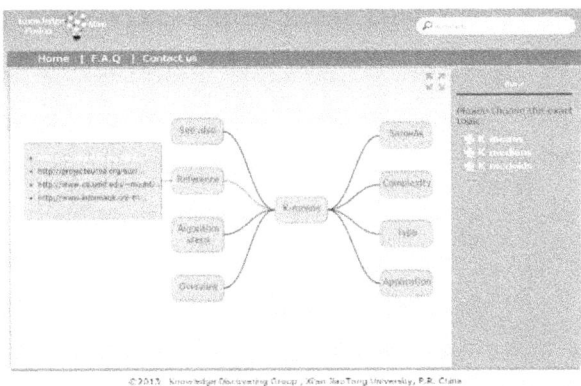

Figure 3. Screenshot of searching *k-means* in KFM

---

6 http://philogb.github.io/jit/

A screenshot of the UI is shown in Figure 3, when the search button is clicked, a knowledge fusion map will be shown in the left panel. The topic is represented by the central node. Its subnodes indicate the facets of the topic, and are represented as rounded rectangles. Rectangles following the rounded rectangles contain the corresponding knowledge. The right panel contains some related topics of the searching topic.

4.2 Preliminary Results

By experimenting in three domains, KFM has constructed 13 categories of facet templates, totally 1,708 topics and their knowledge fusion maps, as shown in Table 1. All RDF data about topics is crawled by LDspider. The knowledge fusion maps are updated dynamically.

Table 1. Three domains and their topics in KFM

Domain	Categories of facet templates	#Topics
Data structure	Graph, Tree, Array, List, Computer algorithm	519
Data mining	Data, Classification, Cluster algorithm, Artificial neural network	625
Computer network	Routing algorithm, Network architecture, Protocol, Networking standards	564

5. CONCLUSION AND FUTURE WORK

To solve the RDF data fragmentation problem, we have developed a novel system KFM, which automatically generates facet templates for domain topics and fuses RDF data by leveraging topological properties of TRG. KFM not only helps users get a thorough understanding about a specific topic, but it also provides an effective way of facet navigation for topics in LOD. In the future, we will improve the search model over knowledge fusion maps so that KFM can support more functions, such as facet searching and question answering.

6. ACKNOWLEDGMENTS

The research was supported in part by the National High-Tech R&D Program of China under Grant No. 2012AA011003, the National Science Foundation of China under Grant Nos. 61221063, 61173112, the National Key Technologies R&D Program of China under Grant No. 2013BAK09B01, the Doctoral Fund of Ministry of Education of China under Grant No. 20130201130002, the Ministry of Education Innovation Research Team under Grant No. IRT13035.

7. REFERENCES

[1] Blei, D.M., Ng, A.Y., and Jordan, M.I., 2003. Latent dirichlet allocation. *Journal of Machine Learning Research 3*, 993-1022.

[2] Isele, R., Umbrich, J., Bizer, C., and Harth, A., 2010. LDspider: An open-source crawling framework for the web of linked data. In *Proceedings of the 9th International Semantic Web Conference, Posters&Demos 658*.

[3] Tummarello, G., Delbru, R., and Oren, E., 2007. Sindice. com: Weaving the open linked data. *Semantic Web*, 552-565.

[4] Wu, F., Weld, D.S., 2007. Autonomously semantifying wikipedia. In *Proceedings of the 16th ACM International Conference on Information and Knowledge Management*, 41-50.

[5] Zesch, T., Gurevych, I., 2007. Analysis of the Wikipedia category graph for NLP applications. In *Proceedings of the TextGraphs-2 Workshop*,1-8.

Building and Exploring Dynamic Topic Models on the Web

Michael Derntl, Nikou Günnemann[†], Alexander Tillmann, Ralf Klamma, Matthias Jarke

RWTH Aachen University
Aachen, Germany
lastname@dbis.rwth-aachen.de

[†]Carnegie Mellon University
Pittsburgh, PA, USA
nguennem@cs.cmu.edu

ABSTRACT

Topic modeling is a machine learning technique that identifies latent topics in a text corpus. There are several existing tools that allow end-users to create and explore topic models using graphical user interfaces. In this paper, we present a visual analytics system for dynamic topic models that goes beyond the existing breed of tools. First, it decouples the Web-based user interface from the underlying data sets, enabling exploration of arbitrary text data sets in the Web browser. Second, it allows users to explore dynamic topic models, while existing tools are often limited to static topic models. Finally, it comes with a tool server in the backend that allows the design and execution of scientific workflows to build topic models from any data source. The system is demonstrated by building and exploring a dynamic topic model of CIKM proceedings published since 2001.

Categories and Subject Descriptors

H.4 [**Information Systems Applications**]: Miscellaneous

Keywords

topic models; text mining; visual analytics; web crawling

1. INTRODUCTION

The amount of available data and its rapid growth makes it difficult for humans to keep track of trends and topic shifts particularly in large document collections like scientific libraries or social media channels. This not only applies to data that is available on the Web; it equally applies to classified knowledge and information sources, e.g., for business intelligence or communication surveillance. Fortunately, there are machine learning techniques that alleviate the task of understanding the structure and evolution of latent topics in documents. One of these techniques is called dynamic topic modeling [1], which uses algorithms that are able to identify the latent topics "hidden" in a set of documents and how these have evolved over time. While topic models can

CIKM'14, November 3–7, 2014, Shanghai, China.
ACM 978-1-4503-2598-1/14/11.
http://dx.doi.org/10.1145/2661829.2661833

be great tools for information and knowledge management, e.g., for research information management [5], an obstacle is that each topic model is a set of numbers with little meaning for a person who is not familiar with the algorithms. There are tools for exploring topic models, yet these are mostly limited to topic models that reflect a particular point in time and/or come hardwired with a particular data set.

Tackling these shortcomings, this paper presents a Web app that empowers stakeholders to engage in visual analytics with topic models of data sets, without having to consult a topic modeling professional. The tool is called D-VITA (shorthand for Dynamic Visual Topic Analytics). While the first tool prototype was presented in [4], we present here a mature evolution of the system that allows building topic models from any data source with a few mouse clicks using flexibly arrangeable toolchains. We demonstrate this in Section 4 by building a dynamic topic model of proceedings indexed on DBLP by example of the CIKM proceedings.

2. DYNAMIC TOPIC MODELS

A topic model is a mathematical model about how a text corpus is generated by distributing words over documents. It can be used for finding the latent thematic structure in document collections. There are various methods to obtain a topic model, with the most prominent being Latent Dirichlet Allocation (LDA) [1], which is also used for computing topic models in D-VITA. LDA assumes that a document corpus exhibits latent topics from a set of topics. The number of topics is an input to LDA to be pre-set by the user. All documents share the same set of topics, but the proportion to which each topic is exhibited in the documents varies.

Topics are distributions over words from a shared vocabulary. Some words will be more relevant and some less relevant to a topic. For instance consider the present paper. Broadly speaking, it should be about information and knowledge management, since this is the thematic scope of CIKM. Yet, it uses words that is typical of a particular subset of CIKM topics, e.g., topic modeling, visual analytics, etc. It shall be noted that LDA does not produce labels for the topics; it simply outputs a set of discrete word distributions. This is why—in the absence of a human being that manually assigns labels to those distributions—topics are typically labeled as an n-tuple using the n most important words for the topic, e.g., "topic modeling" could be labeled `document text collection topics`.

To consider the evolution of the distributions of topics and words in a collection of documents, the concept of dynamic topic models was developed in [2]. It factors in the *epoch* in which a document was created. The time window of an epoch can be defined by the topic modeler; it can be a year, a day, or even a second, depending on the nature of the document collection. The dynamic topic model explains how the variables in the topic model change when transitioning to the subsequent epoch. The implementation of the model explained in [2] is offered as a C library called `dtm`.

3. SYSTEM OVERVIEW

D-VITA implements a classic three-tier system architecture on the Web using Google Web Toolkit (GWT) and Java. The **data tier** comprises arbitrary relational databases. The only required database is the D-VITA configuration database.

The data are accessed via a component on the **logic tier** called *DBAccess*, which offers an interface for all data operations. Other components on the logic tier are the server-side GWT components and the Tool Server, which acts as a simple design- and runtime environment for scientific workflows, represented as sequences of tools that can be chained one after the other, with the only restriction being that the output of a tool must be compatible with expected input of the next tool in the chain. Each toolchain can have an arbitrary number of input parameters, which are described using a simple XML dialect in a manifest file provided with each tool. For instance, a simple toolchain could consist of a web crawler that fetches data from a web archive, followed by a tool that filters the data according to certain user-defined criteria, and finally an LDA tool that builds the topic model.

On the **presentation tier** we have the client-side GWT components running in any Web browser, i.e., the topic explorer (Figure 2), which represents the main visual analytics interface; the document browser, which allows searching documents by words in their topic distributions; and the control panel, which allows configuring database connections and management of the Tool Server and toolchain designer.

4. DEMO: A TOPIC MODEL OF CIKM

This section presents how D-VITA was used to build a dynamic topic model of all papers published in CIKM proceedings between 2001 and 2013[1] (Section 4.1), and to perform visual analytics interactions with the topic model visualization to understand the development of topics in CIKM papers during that time window (Section 4.2).

4.1 Building the CIKM Topic Model

The CIKM topic model was obtained by executing a toolchain including the following tools (cf. Figure 1):

1. Abstracts Crawler. Implements the provision of raw data to the D-VITA analysis tools. It takes the URL of the DBLP page of any conference as an argument and crawls the proceedings of all events in the range of years given as an (optional) second argument. The output of this tool is a CSV file containing paper metadata (authors, title, abstract, year of publication) crawled from the publisher library. Currently the crawler supports the digital libraries of ACM, Springer, and IEEE. For our CIKM topic model the crawler fetched 2926 abstracts from the ACM digital library.

2. Raw Database Generator. Takes the CSV file produced by the Abstracts Crawler (or any other raw data

[1] We chose this timeframe because before 2001 many CIKM paper abstracts are missing in the ACM digital library.

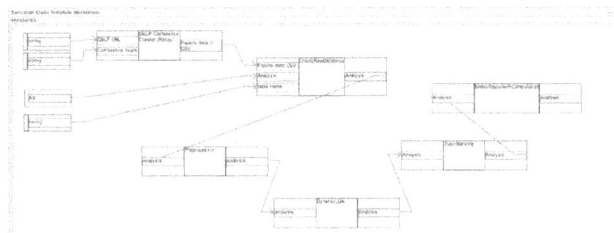

Figure 1: Toolchain designer (partial)

provider) and feeds the data into a relational database. Since data access is managed by the DBAccess component, any database system on any server can be used.

3. Preprocessor. Preprocesses the raw data by extracting the set of words from the documents and records for each word in which documents it occurs; this is needed for running LDA. Stop words are removed and word stemming is performed. For use in the Web GUI the most common full word of each stem is recorded. The CIKM topic model includes 3863 distinct word stems.

4. Dynamic LDA. The output of the preprocessor is fed into the dynamic topic mining program. We reuse the C library "`dtm`", an implementation of [2]. The tool fills several DB tables representing the topic model for use by GUI components. For CIKM we chose a model with 20 topics.

5. Topic Ranking. Computes the topic ranking lists for all available sorting options in the D-VITA Web GUI (explained in Section 4.2) and stores the results the DB.

6. Document Similarity Computation. Computes the similarity of documents based on their topic distributions and stores the results in the DB. Document similarities can be imagined as a $|D| \times |D| \times T$ array, with D being the set of documents and T being the number of epochs in the topic model. This data is used for browsing documents by similarity in the D-VITA Web GUI.

4.2 Exploring the CIKM Topic Model

We explain visual analytics in D-VITA using the CIKM topic model, which is accessible at `http://goo.gl/JSDrck`. The "Topic Explorer" is the main GUI widget for this purpose (see Figure 2). It consists of three panels:

Topic Evolution Panel. Shows a stacked area chart of the evolution of relevance of the selected topics. Clicking in the chart area triggers the display of detailed information on the clicked topic at the clicked time slice in the Document and Word Evolution Panel. The relevance value (vertical axis) is computed as follows. Let D_t be the set of documents at time $t \in 1 \dots T$, the complete corpus $D = \bigcup_{t=1}^{T} D_t$, and θ_d the topic distribution for document $d \in D$. Then the relevance of topic $k \in K$ at time t is $rel(k,t) := \frac{1}{|D_t|} \cdot \sum_{d \in D_t} \theta_d[k]$, obviously with $\forall t (\sum_{k \in K} rel(k,t) = 1)$.

Topic Selection Panel. Displays the list of topics in the topic model, which can be sorted by various criteria, e.g.:

- Recent rise in relevance $\delta_k := \sum_{t=1}^{T-1} \Delta_t \, e^{-\lambda \cdot (T-t)}$, with $\Delta_t = rel(k, t+1) - rel(k,t)$. This uses the idea of decay functions [3] to put emphasis on more recent time slices, thus identifying hot topics. The value of λ controls the "steepness" of the decay. In D-VITA $\lambda = 0.1$. This sorting method is applied in the screen-

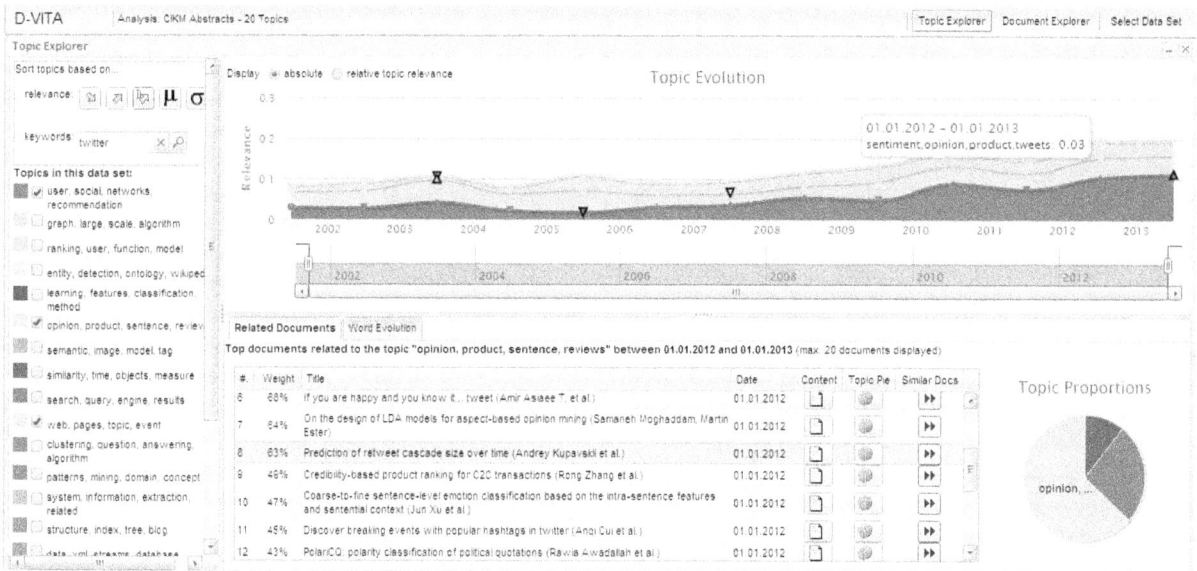

Figure 2: D-VITA Topic Model Explorer

shot in Figure 2. It shows the hottest topic currently is 'user social networks recommendation', followed by 'graph large scale algorithms'.

- Average relevance $\mu_k := \frac{1}{T}\sum_{t=1}^{T} rel(k,t)$. The topic with the highest average relevance for CIKM is about 'retrieval model terms relevance'. It used to account for about 12% of the topic distribution in 2003, with a current relevance at slightly below 5%.

- Variance in relevance $\sigma_k^2 := \frac{1}{T}\sum_{t=1}^{T}(rel(k,t)-\mu_k)^2$. The topic with the strongest swings in relevance is 'user social networks recommendation'. The most stable topic—i.e., the one with the lowest variance—is 'large scale graph algorithms', accounting quite steadily for about 4% of the distribution until 2011, when it started to rise in relevance to 7% in 2013.

The topics can be filtered using keywords; in the screenshot the keyword "twitter" is used as a filter. To match the user provided string with the word distributions, the string is first chopped up into keywords separated by whitespace. Each keyword is then reduced to its word stem and compared to the word stems of all words in the topic model. To be eligible for the result set the word must exceed a threshold relevance of 1% for the topic. The result sets are joined using the union operator and sorted by descending word relevance. Formally, let Q be the set of words in the query term, and β_k the word distribution in topic k, then $result := \bigcup_{q \in Q}\{k \in K : \exists w(stem(q) = w \wedge \beta_k[w] \geq .01)\}$.

In the CIKM topic model three topics (the checked ones in Figure 2) matched the "twitter" query. Not surprisingly the topics involving Twitter have been gaining relevance starting in 2006, the year when Twitter was launched.

Document and Word Evolution Panel. Lists the most relevant papers for the selected topic and point in time. For each paper one can view the distribution of topics as a pie chart. The user can also explore papers related to the selected one. This panel also offers a chart illustrating the "Word Evolution" showing the distribution of words in the selected topic over time. In the screenshot in Figure 2 the

user was interested in the topic 'opinion product sentence reviews' in the year 2013 (this is indicated by the popup in the topic evolution chart). In the related documents list the user has selected the paper "Prediction of retweet cascade size over time", for which this topic accounts for 63% of the topic distribution. The pie chart shows that the paper exhibits two other topics, with details being displayed when the user hovers over the pie slices.

Overall, the CIKM topic model showed that classic information and knowledge management topics like information retrieval or query processing have declined in attention lately; it appears that the CIKM community has put increasing emphasis on topics related to social networks, large graphs, recommendations, and user modeling.

5. CONCLUSION

This paper has presented D-VITA, a visual analytics toolkit for dynamic topic models that comes with a flexible topic modeling tool engine in the backend. A demo video is available at http://youtu.be/ozWf-knmzEI.

Acknowledgments

This work was supported in part by the European Commission through the FP7 project "TEL-Map", grant no. 257822.

6. REFERENCES

[1] D. M. Blei. Probabilistic topic models. *Commun. ACM*, 55(4):77–84, 2012.

[2] D. M. Blei and J. D. Lafferty. Dynamic topic models. In *Proc. ICML'06*, pages 113–120, 2006.

[3] E. Cohen. Decay models. In *Encyclopedia of Database Systems*, pages 757–761. 2009.

[4] N. Günnemann, M. Derntl, R. Klamma, and M. Jarke. Interactive system for visual analytics of dynamic topic models. *Datenbank-Spektrum*, 13(3):213–223, 2013.

[5] C. Quix and M. Jarke. Information Integration in Research Information Systems. In *Proc. CRIS'14*, pages 18–24, 2014.

A Demonstration of SearchonTS: An Efficient Pattern Search Framework for Time Series Data

Xiaomin Xu*, Sheng Huang*, Yaoliang Chen*, Chen Wang*,
Inge Halilovic△, Kevin Brown△, Mark (M.A.) Ashworth△

*IBM China Research Laboratory
{xuxxm,huangssh,
yaoliangc,wangcwc}
@cn.ibm.com

△IBM Informix Product Team
{kbrown3,ingeh}
@us.ibm.com
ashworth@ca.ibm.com

ABSTRACT

In recent years, time series data are everywhere across different industry, which creates a huge demand on time series data analysis, such as pattern search. Meanwhile, it is increasingly realized that only when pattern search results together with information from relational tables could be used in a programming-free way, can they perform analysis on time series conveniently. Hence, casual users highly demand that queries involving pattern search could be performed via SQLs. However, existing database products supporting time series data type lack the capability to perform pattern searches on time series data. This paper presents SearchonTS, an extendable framework for in-database pattern search on time series data. It provides a series of interfaces so that time series index and pattern search can be added and performed in a uniformed and query optimized manner. SearchonTS is implemented as an extension on Informix, which is a database product in IBM software product series. It targets a future release of IBM Informix. We have implemented index-based pattern search for Euclid Distance(ED) via SearhonTS to demonstrate its usability for developers. And real scenario is also provided to show SQL involving pattern search so that users can have a more clear experience of the convenience.

Keywords

pattern search; times series;

1. INTRODUCTION

The goal of time series pattern searching is to find the subsequence in a set of time series similar to a given query pattern. In many applications, users commonly require that time series analysis capability should be provided in such a way that they can combine pattern search results and other results retrieved from databases in a programming-free manner. For example, in the scenario of power meter management, users may want to find the meters that are located in the "East" district whose time series contain pattern sequences similar to a given pattern of an anomaly event in the last 5 days.

CIKM'14, November 3–7, 2014, Shanghai, China.
ACM 978-1-4503-2598-1/14/11.
http://dx.doi.org/10.1145/2661829.2661834.

Many database products, such as Oracle and Informix, have provided custom data types to support fast and scalable time series storage, but none of them supports pattern search directly. Moreover, some other application-oriented systems such as GridMW [7], a scalable time series data management for Smart Grid, and TempDB [3], a time series data storage service based on HBase [8] have been built to address the same issue. However, these systems are hard to support SQL directly access to time series pattern query, which makes it difficult for users to fuse search results with tables in databases easily. Hence, it is more promising for database products to address this issue.

The most dominating challenge prohibiting database products from supporting pattern search well mainly lies in that database products cannot register and manage pattern search techniques dynamically and no query optimization is designed specially for pattern search in this case now, because performance of pattern search is highly related to similarity measure and its associated index techniques adopted. Much effort have been made on accelerating pattern search on various measures in the past two decades. Considering pattern search on Euclid Distance (ED), there exists Discrete Fourier Transform (DFT) and its indexing technique ST-index [2], Piecewise Aggregate Approximation (PAA) [1] and other generalized index techniques, like [6, 5], which are very promising. For DTW, [4] has proposed an efficient search approach. Currently, customers could only perform pattern search at their side, which significantly suffers from high network I/O for data transferring and the inconvenience when the query requires join with other relational tables in Database.

In this paper, we present SearchonTS as the first full-ledged pattern search framework with native SQL support on time series data. It provides an uniform way to adopt state-of-the-art pattern searching techniques on time series data as a plugin to Informix. SearchonTS also supports SQL statements involving pattern searches for casual users. We envision that SearchonTS will act as a research vehicle for various researchers to contribute associated pattern search techniques, thus providing a rich system to be widely used by developers, casual users. As a demonstration, in section A, we illustrate how to implement and perform pattern searching on Informix Database Server(version 11.7).

2. ARCHITECTURE

Fig. 1 depicts the architecture of SearchonTS. It has three layers on Informix database server: the SQL parsing layer, the search access layer, and the query accelerating layer. The SQL parsing layer extends standard SQL to support pattern searching on time series data, which also supports join pattern search results with other

SQL clauses. The search access layer provides a group of interfaces called "searchclass" to support index-based and scan-based pattern search. Here, two pattern search types: *wholematch query* and *subsequence query* is considered. *Wholematch query* could discover time series, which is naturally aligned on time (i.e., one-day or one-week partition common in smart-meter-related scenarios) and contains some partitions similar to the given pattern (i.e., one-day or one-week profile). Meanwhile, *Subsequence query* can locate subsequences similar to given pattern in a long time series. Query optimization on pattern search is also addressed in this layer. The query accelerating layer provides the management of index data and access. It stores and update information between similarity measures, index types, and the storage of index data via a group of system tables.

There are two types of users who interact with SearchonTS: casual users and developers. Casual users are non-technical users who write SQL statements to perform pattern search queries on time series data. Developers can implement pattern search approaches for new similarity measures and then, register pattern search approaches into the database server.

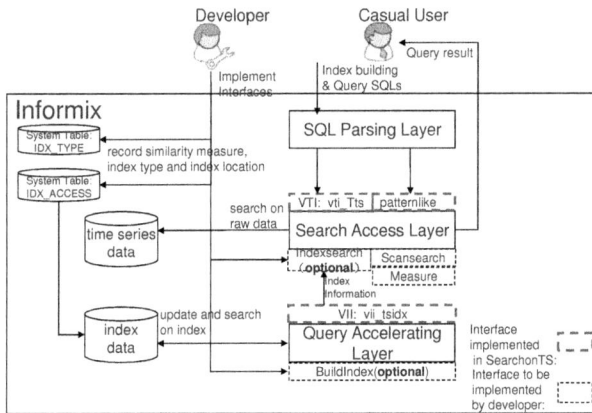

Figure 1: SearchonTS architecture

3. SQL PARSING LAYER

SearchonTS provides extended SQL to simplify the interaction with the system for non-technical users. This layer provides Informix s native time series data types, similarity measure specifications, and a virtual table "VT_SearchResult" that presents search result as a view to support SQL queries involving pattern searches and join.

SearchonTS supports pattern searching by adding new SQL clauses for index building and pattern searching. In terms of index building, we override the CREATE INDEX clause for a time series column and invoke user-defined routines (UDRs) to build the index. Fig. 3(a) is an example of building index on a time series whose attribute is "consumption".

For pattern search processing, when this table appears in an SQL FROM clause, a pattern search query is detected and handled by the "searchclass" as determined by the "measure" parameter in the "patternlike" function (see Fig. 3(b)).

4. SEARCH ACCESS LAYER

The search access layer is responsible for two tasks. The first mission is to optimize the query plan according to the input SQL statement. The second task is to execute pattern searching by invoking appropriate UDRs.

For the first mission, SearchonTS leverages the existing API from Informix to retrieve the original query plan and rebuild it according our query optimization strategy shown as follows. Our current optimization strategy considers two issues: how to optimize pattern search query involving join and how to choose an appropriate search method for the given time series data. For the first issue, we just push down the join conditions as a selection on relational tables so that unnecessary pattern search could be avoided. While in terms of the second one, the challenge mainly lies in that pattern search is both data sensitive(i.e., one search method may work for one data set, but is less efficient on others). To address this issue, we decide the search method according to the historical performance of each candidate method. During each pattern search on a time series table, the adopted search method and its search performance is recorded as Query Statistic Vector(QSV) and the performance metrics considered here includes Pruning Ratio(PR) and Tme Cost Per-Match(TCPM) which are stored in a system table and indexed by spatial index. When choosing search method on a given time series table, the aforementioned system table can tell us a search method with relatively high PR and low TCPM on the given table, which are expected to be more promising. If no QSV records are found for the time series table, we just randomly select an available search method and collect its performance record. For the second task, this layer provides a group of interfaces for developers to describe the similarity measure and the pattern search methods that can manipulate index in query accelerating layer. The similarity measure quantifies the degree of similarity between the given pair of time series sequences. There are two pattern search interfaces: one performs index-based pattern searches which is optional and the other performs scan-based pattern searches, which is mandatory.

Table 1: Interfaces and API Provided in SearchonTS

Name/Type	Input Para.	Output Para.	User
Measure/Interface	*P*:Sequence *S*:Sequence *Type*:'dist.' or 'sim.'	Dist, or Sim. Measure: Float	developer
ScanSearch/Interface	*S*:Time Series, *measure*: measure name	virtual table: vt_ts_searchresult	developer
IndexSearch/Interface	*S*:Time Series, *TR*: time range, *measure*: Dist/Sim, *idx_type*: index type	virtual table: vt_ts_searchresult	developer
BuildIndex/Interface	*S*:Time Series, *TR*: time range, *measure*: Dist/Sim	boolean	developer
RegSearchClass/API	*Measure, ScanSearch, searchclassname, IndexSearch, BuildIndex*	boolean	developer
patternlike/API	*P*:Sequence, *Measure, Threshold, mode*:'whole','subseq'	boolean	casual user

5. QUERY ACCELERATING LAYER

This layer provides developers a possible way to adopt additional support(i.e., index techniques) to accelerate the process of pattern search so that some state-of-art index techniques can be adopted in Informix in a uniformly and dynamically plugged-in manner.

For simplicity, SearchonTS provides an API called "RegSearchClass" (see table 1) for developers to declare the mapping between similarity measures, pattern search techniques (scan-based or index-based), and any related index techniques. An interface called "BuildIndex" for developers is also provided for index building. Moreover, SearchonTS also internally organizes the index data storage.

The relationship between similarity measures, index types, and information about index data is stored as two system tables. The table "IDX_TYPE" records the mapping relationship between the similarity measures and index types. The second table, "IDX_ACCESS" records the mapping relationship between the time series data and the related way to access the index data in the schema: *ts_id, t-*

s_attribute, *ts_table*, *time_range* and *idx_access*, in which *idx_access* is used to describe the location information (such as path or filename or the table name) of the related index data.

For developers, the query accelerating layer is extendable in such a way that developers can implement and register index building methods in Informix and hook them to the interface "BuildIndex" by declaring in *idx_access* to support various index building techniques.

For casual users, the "searchclassname" specified in the CREATE INDEX statement enables casual users to implicitly choose the index type that is associated with the specified "searchclass" on a specific time series.

APPENDIX

A. DEMONSTRATION SCENARIO

In this section, we provide a real usage scenario to demonstrate the flexibility and efficiency of the proposed framework. In section A.1, due to the lack of space, we just describe how to plugin pattern search method based on ST-index [2] designed for Euclid Distance. In section A.2, we demonstrate the way in which casual users can build indexes and perform pattern searches via SQL statements on a real data set from smart meters. Moreover, we show how to join search results with relational tables and verify the query plan optimization strategy, as discussed in Section 4.

A.1 Scenario of Developer

Developers can develop their own pattern search toolkits as a library and register the UDRs they implemented in Informix for the interfaces shown in Table 1. When interfaces related to a "searchclass" are registered, developers can give this "searchclass" a name and register it by running API "RegSearchClass" in Informix.

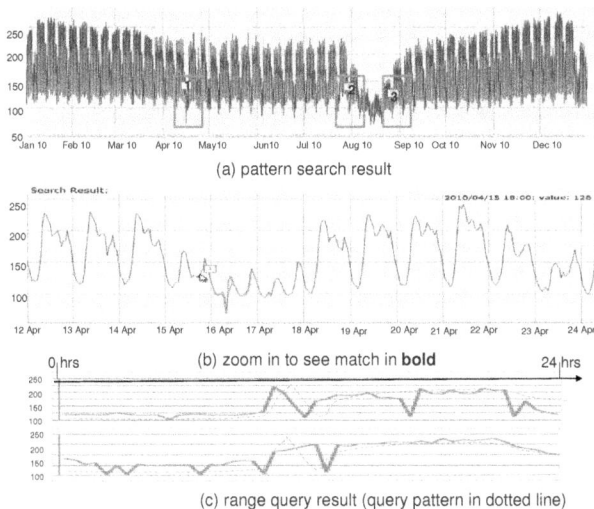

(a) pattern search result

(b) zoom in to see match in **bold**

(c) range query result (query pattern in dotted line)

Figure 2: Pattern search Results

A.2 Scenario of Casual User

Fig. 3 demonstrates SQL scripts for building an index and performing pattern searches. In this scenario, the time series table "smart_meter" stores 10,000 one-year-long time series (96 points per day) for smart meters. Users launch two SQL querys: pattern search query, and queries involving both pattern searches and relational table joins for subsequence queries and wholematch queries. Users are encouraged to modify the SQL statements shown in this

```
Create Index on
smart_meter (meter_data)
using vii_tsindex
{
tsid='*',
attribute='voltage',
startts='2013-12-19 ',
endts ='2014-01-01 ',
searchclass='ED_ST_IDX'
};
```
(a) Create Index in SQL

```
Select * from
VT_SearchResult
where where
patternlike('10,20...',
'ED',0.1) and
tstable=
'smart_meter' and
attribute='current'
and tsid=1 and
startts='2013-12-19'
and endts= '2014-01-
01';
```
Subsequence Query

```
Select tsid from
VT_SearchResult
where where
patternlike('10,20...',
'ED',0.1) and
tstable =
'smart_meter'
and attribute=
'current' and
startts='2013-12-19'
and
endts= '2014-01-01';
```
Wholematch query

(b) Pattern Search in SQL

```
Select tsid from
VT_SearchResult,Meter_location
where patternlike('10,20...',
'EuclidDistance',0.1) and
tstable = 'smart_meter' and
attribute='voltage' and
startts='2013-12-19' and
endts= '2014-01-01' and
VT_SearchResult.tsid
=Meter_location.tsid and
Meter_location.location
='East_District';
```
(c) Pattern Search join with tables

Figure 3: Demonstration of Casual User on SearchonTS

demo. Fig. 3(a) showed that SQL script to build ST-index for all *consumption* time series in table "smart_meter".

Case 1: Fig. 3(b) shows two queries. The first query is a *subsequence query* to find subsequences similar to a given outlier pattern on time series of a meter. The second query is a *wholematch query* to find all meters whose time series contain subsequences similar to an abnormal power usage pattern.

Fig. 2 shows a simple graphical interface to visualize time series. When users load a query pattern and issue the subsequence query shown in Fig. 3(b), the subsequences similar to the given pattern are marked with rectangles, as shown in Fig. 2(a). The user can also zoom in the view to see the curve in detail, as shown in Fig. 2(b). When users issue the *wholematch query* to find the time series from all meters in "East" district that contain one-day consumption profile similar to the given one-day pattern shown in Fig. 2(c) in the last month. Here, they find matches in two time series.

Case 2: Casual users can also write SQL involving both pattern searches and joins with relational tables. As an example, Fig. 3(c) shows how to find all meters locating in the "East" district of the city and also contain subsequences similar to the given query pattern. This query highlights the advantages of handling joins that involve pattern searches via SearchonTS. We found that the query performance of the the optimized query plan beats the original query plan as expected.

B. REFERENCES

[1] K. Chakrabarti, E. J. Keogh, S. Mehrotra, and M. J. Pazzani. Locally adaptive dimensionality reduction for indexing large time series databases. *ACM Trans. Database Syst.*, pages 188–228, 2002.

[2] C. Faloutsos, M. Ranganathan, and Y. Manolopoulos. Fast subsequence matching in time-series databases. In *SIGMOD Conference'94*, pages 419–429, 1994.

[3] TEMPDB. https://tempo-db.com/.

[4] A. M. Thanawin Rakthanmanon, Bilson Campana and G. Batista. Searching and mining trillions of time series subsequences under dynamic time warping. In *KDD'12*, pages 282–286, 2012.

[5] M. Vlachos, E. Keogh, and et al. Indexing multidimensional time-series. *The VLDB Journal*, 15(1):1–20, 2006.

[6] Y. Wang, P. Wang, and et al. A data-adaptive and dynamic segmentation index for whole matching on time series. *Proc. VLDB Endow.*, 6(10):793–804, 2013.

[7] J. Yin, A. Kulkarni, and et al. Scalable real time data management for smart grid. Middleware '11, pages 1:1–1:6. ACM, 2011.

[8] C. Zhang and H. D. Sterck. Cloudwf: A computational workflow system for clouds based on hadoop. In *CloudCom'09*, pages 393–404, 2009.

AESTHETICS: Analytics with Strings, Things, and Cats

Johannes Hoffart
Max Planck Institute for Informatics
jhoffart@mpi-inf.mpg.de

Dragan Milchevski
Max Planck Institute for Informatics
dmilchev@mpi-inf.mpg.de

Gerhard Weikum
Max Planck Institute for Informatics
weikum@mpi-inf.mpg.de

ABSTRACT

This paper describes an advanced news analytics and exploration system that allows users to visualize trends of entities like politicians, countries, and organizations in continuously updated news articles. Our system improves state-of-the-art text analytics by linking ambiguous names in news articles to entities in knowledge bases like Freebase, DBpedia or YAGO. This step enables indexing entities and interpreting the contents in terms of entities. This way, the analysis of trends and co-occurrences of entities gains accuracy, and by leveraging the taxonomic type hierarchy of knowledge bases, also in expressiveness and usability. In particular, we can analyze not only individual entities, but also categories of entities and their combinations, including co-occurrences with informative text phrases. Our Web-based system demonstrates the power of this approach by insightful anecdotic analysis of recent events in the news.

1. MOTIVATION AND INTRODUCTION

Proper analysis and understanding of large amounts of texts has become a major necessity, as the amount of natural-language contents keeps growing, especially in the context of social media and daily news, but also regarding scholarly publications and digitized books. A notable project in this line is the Culturomics [9] project, which supports an aggregated view of trends in the recent human history captured by the Google books corpus. Here, interesting conclusions are drawn about linguistic changes or cultural phenomena using string-level keywords, by comparing frequencies over time periods and across languages.

The system presented in this paper, called AESTHETICS (short for Analysis and Exploration with Strings, Things, and Categories), goes beyond mere string-based analysis, by supporting the analysis and exploration of entities ("things") and categories ("cats"). This semantic level is provided by linking text phrases to knowledge bases like Google's Knowledge Graph (freebase.com) or yago-knowledge.org. Knowledge bases contain a large number of persons, places, or-

ganizations, etc. providing a repository of unique entities in canonicalized form, with assignment to fine-grained semantic classes (categories). The AESTHETICS system automatically discovers and disambiguates these entities in news texts, linking the unstructured to the structured world. Instead of specifying words or phrases as the target of mining trends and patterns, we can now see and analyze entities directly. AESTHETICS supports the analysis of textual surface phrases ("strings") as well, but its full power comes from combining these with proper entities and categories.

To illustrate why this is a major step with strong benefits, consider the task of visualizing trends around the recent Ukrainian crisis, which originated from the Maidan, the square in Kiev where thousands of Ukrainians protested in early 2014. A search for "Maidan" quickly reveals that the name is highly ambiguous, as it means "square" not only in Ukrainian, but also in Hindi and Arabic. Thus, simply counting the string "Maidan" will result in a large number of false positives, leading to an imprecise analysis, as shown in Figure 1. By specifying the canonicalized entity `Maidan Nezalezhnosti`, not only do we get rid of spurious mentions of other Maidans, but also find articles where the square is mentioned only by its English name "Independence Square". Thus, entity-level analytics, as supported by AESTHETICS, is the only way to get accurate numbers.

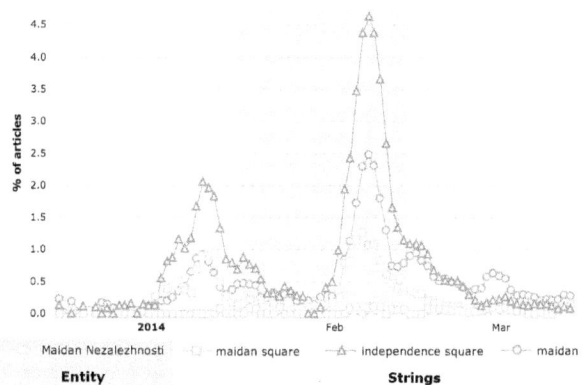

Figure 1: Accurate analytics for Maidan Square

Additionally, as we now have the full potential of a structured knowledge base in the background, further opportunities are opened up. In all semantic knowledge bases, entities are organized in a category hierarchy, e. g. `Greenpeace` is an `environmental organization`, which in turn is a subclass

CIKM'14, Nov 03–07, 2014, Shanghai, China.
ACM 978-1-4503-2598-1/14/11.
http://dx.doi.org/10.1145/2661829.2661835.

of a general `organization`. Using this category hierarchy, we can conduct analyses for entire groups of entities, for example, comparing the presence of `environmental organizations` and `power companies` in news of different parts of the world, deriving a picture of how their importance changes over time. The hierarchical organization of categories adds another dimension for aggregation to the usual temporal and spatial dimensions (where news can be aggregated by publishing times and originating regions).

2. RELATED WORK

There is ample work on text analytics for identifying (and visualizing) trends and patterns. Although this is of importance also for enterprise documents, most of the published research addresses social media (see, e.g., [8] and references there). The goals here are manifold: discovering events [3], connecting topics and users [1], and more.

Applications of such methods include culturomics [9] over the Google books corpus and computational journalism [5]. Although some of this work refers to "entities", the granularity of analyses really is noun phrases, disregarding the ambiguity of entity names. Also, there is no awareness of background knowledge bases. Two notable exceptions are the recent works by [10] and [7]. The former is a proof-of-concept project for annotating Web archive contents with entities. The latter applies shallow methods for entity markup to the French newspaper Le Monde, to support entity-aware culturomics. Our system uses much deeper methods for entity disambiguation and supports much richer analytics over both entities and categories. Other related work addresses the retrieval of entities in web or enterprise search (e.g., [2, 4]), as opposed to retrieving documents.

3. NEWS ANALYTICS ARCHITECTURE

The AESTHETICS engine for news analytics allows users to quickly spot trends of entities or groups of entities specified by a semantic category. The trend visualization is computed on daily occurrences of entities in articles of nearly 300 news sources. Continuously gathering news since June 2013, the AESTHETICS corpus now comprises more than 1.1 million articles. In each article, all entities are discovered and disambiguated using AIDA [6], which links all mentions in the article to entities in YAGO. YAGO contains ca. 500,000 semantic categories, comprising 4 million individual entities for which users can query. The entity index of AESTHETICS contains ca. 300,000 distinct YAGO entities which have been spotted in the news, and ca. 22 million entity occurrences.

One challenge is to support the user when specifying the entities and categories of interest for the actual analysis. The scale of YAGO renders the naive approach of letting a user choose from a list of everything infeasible. We solve this problem by providing automatic suggestions for entities and categories while the user is typing in the search field. When selected, a suggestion becomes a tag in the query field. The suggestion for entities and categories use a similar approach, first finding potential matching candidates based on a prefix matching, then ranking the candidates appropriately:

Entity Suggestions. All canonical entity names are stored in a trie for fast prefix lookup. Additionally, all token-wise suffixes are stored. For this, the name is split at whitespaces into tokens, and the complete string starting at each token is added as an additional label for the entity in the trie. This allows users to start typing a name in the middle; for example when typing "Obama", AESTHETICS still returns `Barack Obama` as a candidate. All matching candidates are then ranked based on the overall popularity in Wikipedia, which is estimated by the number of incoming links. Thus, typing "Obama" results in the suggestion `Barack Obama`, and `Michelle Obama`, in that order.

Category Suggestions. As with entities, all category names are stored in a trie. In contrast to entity names, category names can have an arbitrary order of words. For example, both `United States presidents` and `Presidents of the United States` are perfectly valid categories, and it is up to the Wikipedia edtiors' judgment which one to use. To cope with this diversity issue, we add all 3-token permutations as additional lookup keys, making sure that the real category shows for any permutation of {"united", "states", "president"}. The ranking is done based on the popularity of the contained entities, preferring categories with high average popularity. However, when typing "compan", the expected result should not be `American IT companies`, even though their average popularity might be very high; instead our method prioritizes more generic `IT companies` or just `companies`. Thus, the popularity-based ranking is balanced with a preference for categories that are closer to the root of the class hierarchy the categories are organized in.

A screenshot of the AESTHETICS Web interface is shown in Figure 2. In the search box at the top, entities, categories, and strings can be specified using the auto-completion method described above. On execution of the query, our system displays a chart showing the trend lines based on the daily occurrences of each item in the central area.

4. DEMO SCENARIOS

Our AESTHETICS system provides rich functionality for ad-hoc search and analytics over more than 1.1 million news articles. Conference participants will be able to flexibly explore the system's capabilities. The following are some of the conceivable use-cases.

Accurate entity counts. Entity-based analysis improves the accuracy over string-based analysis. The precision is improved as ambiguous names are resolved to the correct entity, removing unwanted occurrences. Better recall is achieved by also finding occurrences of the same entity under different names. Figure 1 shows a graph contrasting the various ways of specifying the target of the frequency analysis, using the example of the Maidan square in Kiev. Searching merely for "Maidan" overestimates the actual numbers by a factor of up to 2 (in February), while sometimes underestimating the true count (in late January). Searching for its English name "Independence Square" is not useful, either, as there are squares with this name all around the world.

Entity co-occurrence analysis. Comparing individual entity occurrences is already a powerful way of analyzing news and spotting trends or interesting topic shifts. A common scenario is that there is one main entity of interest, e.g. the `Ukraine`, and an analyst is interested in viewing and interpreting news in terms of other entities co-occurring with the main entity. Consider again the events around the Ukrainian crisis, analyzing the involvement of `Barack Obama` and `Vladimir Putin` over time, as depicted in Figure 3. AESTHETICS provides the advanced functionality of viewing occurrences for the three entities `Crimea`, `Obama`, and `Putin` given that `Ukraine` has to be mentioned in the

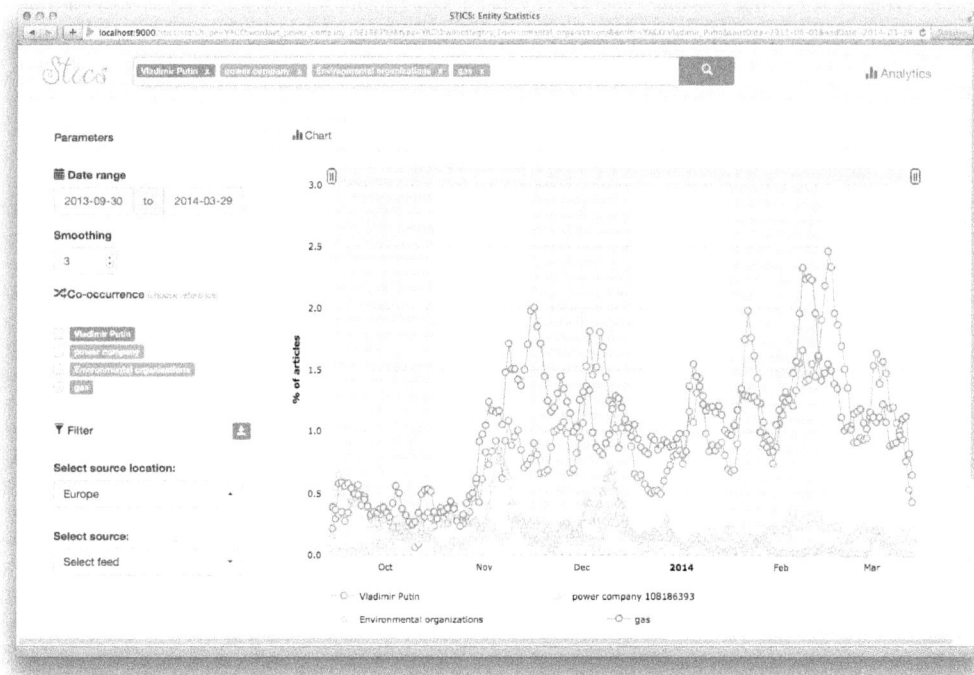

Figure 2: Analyzing the connection between Vladimir Putin and "gas" in the Aesthetics interface.

text. Without this constraint, analyzing the impact of the event on mentions of Obama is hard, as he is mentioned in a large number of totally unrelated contexts. Using the co-occurrence restriction, it becomes easy to spot that he became only involved once the Crimea situation escalated, and not in the initial protests in Ukraine.

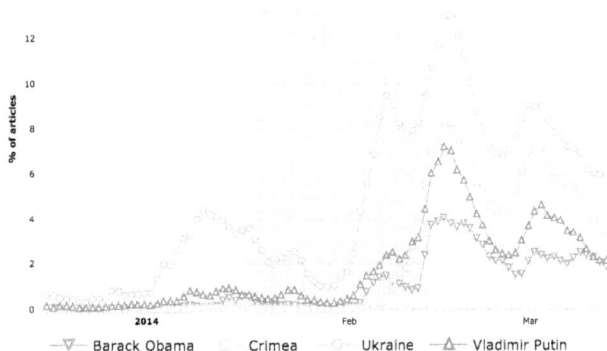

Figure 3: Entities in the context of the Ukraine crisis

Analyzing semantic groups of entities. Analyzing occurrences of all entities in a semantic group (e.g., Ukrainian politicians, female political activists, etc.) is impossible with just strings. With unstructured text linked to entities in a category hierarchy, it becomes a natural thing to do. The screenshot in in Figure 2 shows an example of an insightful analysis of this kind. The figure shows how often power companies or environmental organizations have been mentioned in news. This analysis reveals that the rise of the Crimea tensions in February had a remarkable effect on the frequency of mentions of power companies – driven by Europe's dependence on Russian gas, which is of-

ten transported through Ukraine. On the other hand, mentions of environmental organizations, opposing environmentally hazardous ways of getting gas by fracking, have gone down. This anecdotic evidence is strengthened by the observation that the effect is especially pronounced in European news, and harder to spot when removing the region filter.

Our demo is available online at
http://www.mpi-inf.mpg.de/yago-naga/stics/

5. REFERENCES

[1] S. Amer-Yahia et al.: MAQSA: A System for Social Analytics on News. SIGMOD 2012

[2] K. Balog, M. Bron, M. de Rijke: Query modeling for entity search based on terms, categories, and examples. TOIS 29(4), 2011

[3] A. Das Sarma, A. Jain, C. Yu: Dynamic relationship and event discovery. WSDM 2011

[4] H. Bast, B. Buchhold: An Index for Efficient Semantic Full-Text Search. CIKM 2013.

[5] A. Y. Halevy, S. McGregor: Data Management for Journalism. IEEE Data Eng. Bull. 35(3), 2012

[6] J. Hoffart et al.: Robust Disambiguation of Named Entities in Text. EMNLP 2011

[7] T. Huet, J. Biega, F. M. Suchanek: Mining History with Le Monde. AKBC 2013

[8] Sharad Mehrotra (Editor): IEEE-CS Data Engineering Bulletin 36(3), Special Issue on Social Media and Data Analysis, 2013.

[9] J.B. Michel et al. 2011. Quantitative Analysis of Culture Using Millions of Digitized Books. Science 331(6014), 2011

[10] M. Spaniol, G. Weikum: Tracking entities in web archives: the LAWA project. WWW 2012

Accelerometer-based Activity Recognition on Smartphone

Xing Su
City University of New York
New York, NY 10016
sunnyxing@gmail.com

Hanghang Tong
Arizona State University
Tempe, AZ 85281
Htong6@asu.edu

Ping Ji
City University of New York
New York, NY 10016
pj.ping@gmail.com

ABSTRACT

Smartphones are ubiquitous and becoming more and more sophisticated, with ever-growing computing, networking and sensing powers. How can we help the users form a healthy habit by sending a reminder if s/he is sitting too long? How can we localize where we are inside a building and/or find the reception desk? Recognizing the physical activities (e.g., sitting, walking, jogging, etc) is a core building block to answer these questions and many more.

We present AcRe, a human activity recognition application on smartphone. AcRe takes the motion data from different sensors on smartphones as inputs (e.g., accelerometer, compass, etc), and predicts a user's motion activities (e.g., walking upstairs, standing, sitting, etc) in real-time. It provides some additional functionalities, such as incorporating a user's feedback, daily activity summerization, etc. The application is built on iOS 7.0 and will be released soon in Apple's App Store. We will invite the audience to experiment with our AcRe in terms of its effectiveness, efficiency and applicability to various domains and the potential for further improvements.

1. INTRODUCTION

Smartphones are ubiquitous and becoming an important part of people's daily life. Moreover, they are becoming more and more sophisticated, with ever-growing computing, networking, and sensing powers. Many main stream smartphones are equipped with various sensors, including accelerometers, GPS, light sensors, temperature sensors, gyroscopes, barometers, etc. This has opened the door for many interesting data mining applications, ranging from health and fitness monitoring, personal biometric signature, urban computing, assistive technology and elderly-care, to indoor localization and navigation, etc.

A common, key building block (often as the very first step) behind these applications is to recognize a user's physical activities, such as walking, sitting, walking upstairs, jogging, etc. For example, in order to help the user form a

CIKM'14, November 3–7, 2014, Shanghai, China.
Copyright 2014 ACM 978-1-4503-2598-1/14/11
http://dx.doi.org/10.1145/2661829.2661836 .

healthy fitness habit, we can send a reminder if s/he has been sitting too long. Several recent popular fitness trackers are built upon wearable sensors and activity recognition techniques. They track people's steps taken, stairs climbed, calorie burned, distance travelled, quality of sleep, etc, and provide online services for living statistics.

We develop AcRe, a human activity recognition application on smartphones. AcRe takes the motion data from different sensors on smartphones as inputs (e.g., accelerometer, compass, etc) and predicts a user's motion activities (e.g., walking upstairs, standing, sitting, etc). Compared to other mobile activity detection applications, our work has the following key features. First (*Effectiveness and Efficiency*), by carefully designing the features and classification algorithms, AcRe is able to detect *more types* of activities, with a *higher detection accuracy* (up to 98.7%) in cross validation. Second (*Personalization*), AcRe provides the functionality to incorporate user-feedback so as to personalize the detection model to a specific user. Third (*Summarization*), AcRe provides a daily activity summerization, such as the statistics of each type of activities as well as the comparison of moving speed at different time ticks, etc. Fourth (*Deployment*), our application is built on iOS 7.0 combining the latest motion recognition API[1] and will soon be released in Apple's App Store (currently in the review process).

The rest of the paper is organized as follows. Section 2 demonstrates the main functionalities of AcRe. Section 3 presents the technical details. Section 4 reviews the related works and Section 5 concludes the paper.

2. APPLICATION DEMONSTRATION

In this section, we demonstrate the main functionalities of AcRe. Fig. 1 shows the three major parts of AcRe. Fig. 1(a) is the main screen is for *raw data reading*, including the line chart of accelerometion in X, Y and Z axis, followed by accelerometer data and the compass reading. The second part of the main screen is for *recognition*. The recognized activity will be shown with bigger and bold font, such as "Walking" in Fig. 1(a), a picture indicating current activity would appear on the left also. The *Turn* field is for turn detection. The button *View Activity* will lead to the second screen Fig. 1(b), the button *View Stats* will lead to the third screen Fig. 1(c), and the button *Send Data* will send current raw data to the server.

The second screen (Fig. 1(b)) is for activity recognition and personalization. AcRe displays the three most probable activities of a user at the current time tick. For each type of recognized activity, it also shows the confidence level. The

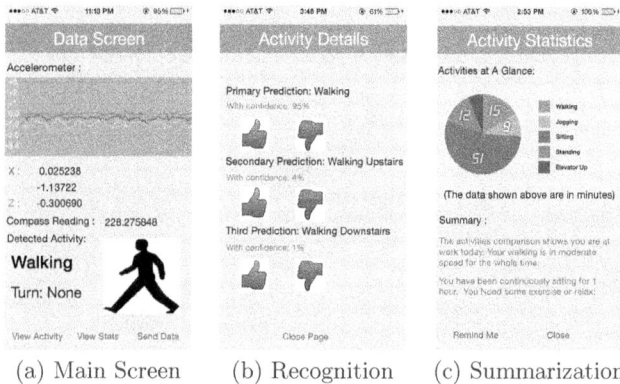

(a) Main Screen   (b) Recognition   (c) Summarization

Figure 1: Activity Recognition and Summarization

thumb up and thumb down buttons provide the functionality to collect a user's feedback. If there's a hit in the three most possible activities, user could click the *"Thumb Up"* button under the correct prediction. The user can always click the *"Thumb Down"* as a negative feedback for the wrong predictions. The feedback information will be sent to the backend server to refine the prediction model so that it fits better with the current user's specific moving patterns.

The third screen (Fig. 1(c)) in is for the daily activity summarization and comparison. It has two parts. The first part is a pie chart showing a comparison of the total durations of the different activities within a certain period (e.g., one day). The second part is a summary of the daily overview in terms of his motion status. This could help reveal the user's status of the day, e.g., s/he was busy rushing here and there in the morning, or s/he had a healthy day with lots of exercise, or it was just a long day of work with the dominant "sitting" activity for a long period.

Engaging the Audience. We expect that our demo will mainly attract two types of audience, including (1) the practitioners who are interested in developing novel mobile applications based on the activity recognition, and (2) database and data mining researchers who are interested in developing new algorithms and tools to address the unique challenges posed by human activity recognition.

3. TECHNICAL DETAILS

In this section, we present the algorithm details of our AcRe, followed by some implementation and evaluation details. Fig. 2 shows the overall flowchart of AcRe. It consists of two main parts. The *activity recognition* part shows the recognition process. AcRe will then collect data and train a general classification model in the backend. In the real-time recognition stage, by incoporating users' feedback, it refines the classification model to be tailored to the current individual. The applications module lists several potential web services based on activity recognition results. These services include (but are not limited to) building users' biometric database for individuals, displaying the user's daily activity statistics, providing a life style logger and activity recognition augmented indoor localization service.

3.1 Method Details

Data Description and Feature Extraction. We use two types of raw data as the inputs of our AcRe application,

including the acceleration and the compass data. For the accelerometer data, we record acceleration along the x, y and z axis respectively, together with the corresponding time stamps. A vector A is used to represent one such reading in the following format: $A_i = < accX_i, accY_i, accZ_i, t_i >$, where $-2.0 \leq accX_i, accY_i, accZ_i \leq 2.0$ in the unit of g-force and t_i is the time stamp. Sampling rate is set to 64Hz.

Based on the raw accelerometer reading data, we extract features in both time and frequency domains. For each of the three axis (x, y and z), we segment the data every four seconds. In the time domain, we compute the basic statistics of each axis (x, y and z), including the mean, the average, the maximum, the minimum and the standard deviation. In the frequency domain, we first perform Fast Fourier Transform (FFT) and compute an energy/magnitude array of the length 256 as $E_i = \sqrt{T\_real_i^2 + T\_image_i^2}, i = 0, 1, 2...255$, where T_real_i and T_image_i are the real and imaginary parts of the FFT of a time series T. Different activities have distinctive frequency domain features. We compute the offset, the maximum, the standard deviation of the energy array. We also generate a histogram for the energy array, and calculate the top four peak frequencies.

Another type of raw data is the compass reading. In the iOS platform, the compass data is represented as float numbers between 0 and 360 and indicates the angle between current smartphone's heading direction and the absolute north in the clockwise. We use a vector C to represent one compass reading: $C_i = < comp_i, t_i >$, where $0 \leq comp_i \leq 360$ is the smartphone's heading angle, and t_i is time stamp.

In our AcRe application, we use the compass reading for *turn detection*. To be specific, we created a direction dictionary: $Direction\_Dict = [N : (330, 30), NE : (30, 60), E : (60, 120), ES : (120, 150), S : (120, 210), SW : (210, 240), W : (240, 300), WN : (300, 330)]$. Each key value entry in this dictionary defines the range of a specific direction. A significant change in the compass reading indicates the potential turn. For example, if the last average reading is 317.88 and the current average reading is 42.34, we will detect a right turn as the direction changes from WN to NE.

Model Building and Refinement. The basic activity recognition model is trained off-line using the data recorded from different users at different time inside a building. If we treat the activity recognition at every time window (4 seconds) separately, it can be naturally casted as a classification task with the actual activity (e.g., walking, jogging, etc) as the class label. Many classic (supervised) data mining algorithms (e.g., logistic regression, decision tree, multi-player perception, etc) can be plugged into AcRe. In the current deployment of AcRe, we chose decision tree as the basic classification model.

In order to maximally boost the recognition performance, we further impose a *smoothing* phase. Here, our key observation is that the adjacent activities of a user often follow a specific pattern. For example, almost every other activity happens after the *walking* activity. In order to capture such a temporal dependency, we apply hidden Markov model (HMM) on top of the classification model.

Finally (*personalization*), the motion patterns might differ from user to user. In order to make the model more personalized to a special user, we provide the feedback functionality in AcRe. If the user gives a positive feedback on certain prediction, the application rewards the correspond-

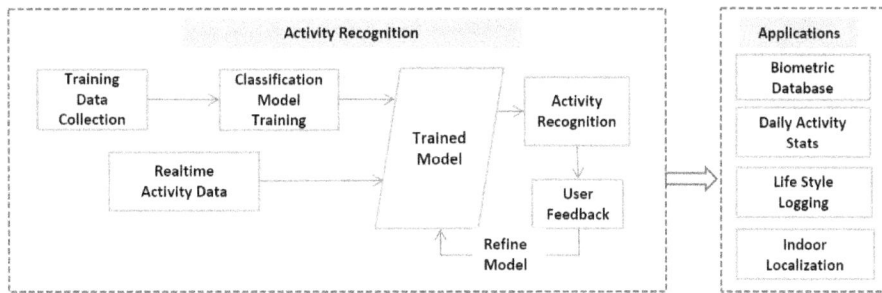

Figure 2: Application Work Flow Chart

ing learning parameter. In contrast, a penalty is imposed when a negative feedback is received.

3.2 Evaluation

We perform a systematic cross-validation evaluation on a benchmark data set [4]. The result is summarized in Fig. 3. Compared with the existing method in [4], our method is consistently better in terms of the recognition accuracy.

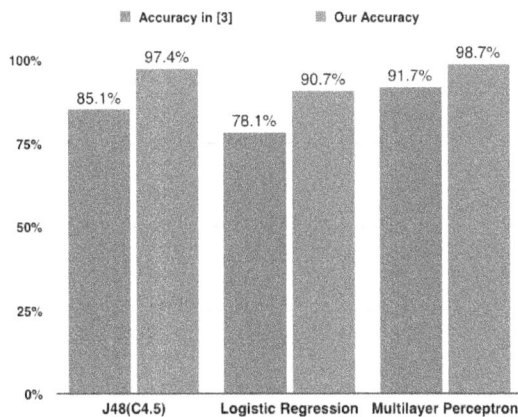

Figure 3: Cross Validation Result Comparison

4. RELATED WORK

Human activity recognition can be naturally casted as a (supervised) data mining problem. Kwapisz et al [4] used the standard *WEKA* tools for activity recognition with the accelerometer readings. Longstaff et al [5] leveraged active and semi-supervised learning to make the pre-trained recognition model adaptive to a specific user. Human activity recognition is a very powerful building block for many applications, including health and fitness monitoring [7], personal biometric signature [3], assistive technology [6], elderly-care [2], indoor localization and navigation[8], etc.

5. CONCLUSIONS

We present ACRE, a human activity recognition application on smartphone. ACRE takes the motion data from different sensors on smartphones as inputs and predicts a user's motion activities in real-time. It is able to recognize *eight* types of different activities in total with a much higher detection accuracy. It can be naturally personalized to a user's specific motion pattern by incorporating his/her feedback.

It also provides a daily activity summarization functionality. The application will be released soon in Apple's App Store. We will invite the audience to experiment with our ACRE in terms of its effectiveness, efficiency, applicability to various domains (e.g., smart-phone based navigation, traffic mode detection, etc) and the potential for further improvements (e.g., adaptive algorithms to accommodate different individuals as well as different body parts; multi-modality classification algorithm to incorporate other types of sensors, etc).

6. ACKNOWLEDGEMENT

This material is supported by the National Science Foundation under Grant No. IIS1017415, by the Army Research Laboratory under Cooperative Agreement Number W911NF-09-2-0053, by Defense Advanced Research Projects Agency (DARPA) under Contract Number W911NF-11-C-0200 and W911NF-12-C-0028, and by Region II University Transportation Center under the project number 49997-33 25.

7. REFERENCES

[1] Apple Document: https://developer.apple.com.
[2] C. N. Doukas and I. Maglogiannis. Emergency fall incidents detection in assisted living environments utilizing motion, sound, and visual perceptual components. *Information Technology in Biomedicine, IEEE Transactions on*, 2011
[3] J. R. Kwapisz, G. M. Weiss, and S. A. Moore. Cell phone-based biometric identification. In *BATS*, 2010.
[4] J. R. Kwapisz, G. M. Weiss, and S. A. Moore. Activity recognition using cell phone accelerometers. *ACM SIGKDD Explorations Newsletter*, 2011.
[5] B. Longstaff, S. Reddy, and D. Estrin. Improving activity classification for health applications on mobile devices using active and semi-supervised learning. In *4th PervasiveHealth*, 2010.
[6] D. Lymberopoulos, A. Bamis, and A. Savvides. Extracting spatiotemporal human activity patterns in assisted living using a home sensor network. *Universal Access in the Information Society*, 2011.
[7] C. Seeger, A. Buchmann, and K. Van Laerhoven. myhealthassistant: a phone-based body sensor network that captures the wearer's exercises throughout the day. In *ICST*, 2011.
[8] H. Ye, T. Gu, X. Zhu, J. Xu, X. Tao, J. Lu, and N. Jin. Ftrack: Infrastructure-free floor localization via mobile phone sensing. In *PerCom*, 2012.

Cleanix: A Big Data Cleaning Parfait

Hongzhi Wang
Harbin Institute of Technology
wangzh@hit.edu.cn

Mingda Li
Harbin Institute of Technology
limingda@hit.edu.cn

Yingyi Bu
University of California, Irvine
yingyib@ics.uci.edu

Jianzhong Li
Harbin Institute of Technology
lijzh@hit.edu.cn

Hong Gao
Harbin Institute of Technology
honggao@hit.edu.cn

Jiacheng Zhang
Harbin Institute of Technology
chinahitzjc@gmail.com

ABSTRACT

In this demo, we present Cleanix, a prototype system for cleaning relational Big Data. Cleanix takes data integrated from multiple data sources and cleans them on a shared-nothing machine cluster. The backend system is built on-top-of an extensible and flexible data-parallel substrate— the Hyracks framework. Cleanix supports various data cleaning tasks such as abnormal value detection and correction, incomplete data filling, de-duplication, and conflict resolution. We demonstrate that Cleanix is a practical tool that supports effective and efficient data cleaning at the large scale.

1. INTRODUCTION

Recent popular Big Data analytics applications are motivating both industry and academia to design and implement highly scalable data management tools. However, the value of data not only depends on the quantity but also relies on the quality. On one side, due of the high volume and the high variation, those Big Data applications suffer way more data quality issues than traditional applications. On the other side, efficiently cleaning a huge amount of data in a shared-nothing architecture has not been well studied yet. Therefore, to improve the data quality is an important yet challenging task

Many data cleaning tools [6] have been proposed to help users to detect and repair errors in the data. Although these systems could clean data effectively for many datasets, they are not suitable for cleaning Big Data due to the following three reasons. First, none of the existing systems can scale out to hundreds and thousands of machines in a shared-nothing manner. Second, various error types such as incompleteness, inconsistency, duplication, and value conflicting may co-exist in the Big Data while most existing systems are ad-hoc and only focus on a specific error type. As examples, CerFix [4] focus on inconsistency while AJAX [5] is for de-duplication and conflict resolution. The last but not least, the existing systems often require users to have specific data cleaning expertise. For example, CerFix [4] require users to understand the concept of conditional functional dependency (CFD), while AJAX [5] lets users express data cleaning tasks with a declarative language. However, many real-world users do not have a solid data cleaning background nor understand the semantics of a specific data cleaning language.

In order to address the fundamental issues in existing systems and support data cleaning at a very large scale, we design and implement a new system called Cleanix. We list the key features of Cleanix as follows.

- **Scalability**. Cleanix performs data quality reporting tasks and data cleaning tasks in parallel on a shared-nothing commidity machine cluster. The backend system is built on-top-of Hyracks [1], an extensible, flexible, scalable and general-purpose data parallel execution engine, with our user-defined data cleaning second-order operators and first-order functions.
- **Unification**. Cleanix unifies various automated data repairing tasks for errors by integrating them into a single parallel dataflow. New cleaning functionalities for newly discovered data quality issues could be easily added to the Cleanix dataflow as either user-defined second-order operators or first-order functions.
- **Usability**. Cleanix does not require users to be data cleaning experts. It provides a simple and friendly graphical user interface for users to select rules with intuitive meanings and high-level descriptions. Cleanix also provides a bunch of visualization utilities for users to better understand error statistics, easily locate the errors and fix them.

The main goal of this demonstration is to present the Cleanix system architecture and execution process by performing a series of data integration and cleaning tasks. We show how the data cleaning operators are used to clean the data integrated from multiple data sources.

2. SYSTEM OVERVIEW

We give a system overview in this section. First, we discuss the data cleaning tasks in Section 2.1. Then, Section 2.2 briefly introduces the Hyracks execution engine and illustrates why Hyracks is chosen as the Cleanix backend. Finally, we discuss the Cleanix architecture of the system in Section 2.3.

2.1 Data Cleaning Tasks

Cleanix aims to handle four types of data quality issues in a unified way:

- *Abnormal value detection and correcting* is to find the anomalies according to the users' options of rules and modify them to a near value that coincides with the rules.
- *Incomplete data filling* is to find the empty attributes in the data and fill them with proper values.
- *De-duplication* is to merge and remove duplicated data.

CIKM'14, November 3–7, 2014, Shanghai, China.
ACM 978-1-4503-2598-1/14/11.
http://dx.doi.org/10.1145/2661829.2661837.

- *Conflict resolution* is to find conflicting attributes in the tuples referring to the same real-world entity and find the true values for these attributes.

We believe that these four data cleaning tasks cover most data quality issues. Note that even though some data errors could not be processed directly such as non-concurrency and inconsistency, one can take care of them by dynamically deploying new first-order user-defined functions into our system. For example, non-concurrency can be processed as conflict resolutions among the data referring to the same real-world entity.

2.2 The Hyracks Execution Engine

We use Hyracks as the Cleanix backend to accomplish the above tasks efficiently at large scales Hyracks is a data-parallel execution engine for Big Data computations on shared-nothing commodity machine clusters. Compared to MapReduce [3], Hyracks has the following advantages:

- **Extensibility**. It allows users to add data processing operators and connectors, and orchestrate them into whatever DAGs. However, in the MapReduce world, we need to cast the data cleaning semantics into a scan (map)—group-by(reduce) framework.
- **Flexibility**. Hyracks supports a variety of materialization policies for repartitioning connectors, while MapReduce only has the local file system blocking-materialization policy and the HDFS materialization policy. This allows Hyracks to be elastic to different cluster configurations.
- **Efficiency**. The extensibility and flexibility together lead to significant efficiency potentials.

Several cloud computing vendors are developing non-MapReduce parallel SQL enginesto support fast Big Data analytics. However, these systems are like "onions" [2]—one cannot directly use their internal Hyracks-like engines under the SQL skin for data cleaning. However, the Hyracks software stack is like a layered "parfait" [2] and Cleanix is yet-another parfait layer on-top-of the core Hyracks layer.

2.3 Cleanix Architecture

Cleanix provides web interfaces for users to input the information of data sources, parameters and rule selections. Data from multiple data sources are preprocessed and loaded into a distributed file system—HDFS[1]. Then each slave machine reads part of the data to start the cleaning. The data cleaning dataflow containing second-order operators and connectors is executed on slaves according to the user specified parameters and rules (e.g., first-order functions). At the end of the dataflow, the cleaned data are written to HDFS. Finally, the cleaned data are extracted from HDFS and loaded into the desired target database.

3. THE SYSTEM INTERNALS

In this section, we discuss the details of the Cleanix data cleaning pipeline, the algorithmic operators and the profiling mechanism.

3.1 Data Processing Ordering

To make the discussion brief, we use A, I and D and C to represent the modules of the process of abnormal value detection and correcting, incomplete data filling, de-duplication and conflict resolution, respectively. The order of four tasks of data cleaning in Cleanix is determined with the consideration of effectiveness and efficiency. These four modules could be divided into two groups.

---

[1]http://en.wikipedia.org/wiki/Apache_Hadoop

Module A and I are in the same group (Group 1) sharing the same detection phase since the detection of abnormal values and empty attributes can be accomplished in a single scan of the data. Module D and C are in the same group (Group 2) since the identifications of entities with the entity resolution operator are required for both de-duplication and conflict resolution. De-duplication merges tuples with the same entity identification while conflict resolution is to find true values for conflicting attributes for the different tuples referring the same entity identification. The reason why Group 1 is executed before Group 2 is that the repairation of abnormal values and empty attributed will increase the accuracy of entity resolution. In Group 1, Module A is before I since abnormal values interfere the incomplete attribute filing and lead to incorrect fillings. In Group 2, Module D is before C since only when different tuples referring to the same entity are found and grouped, the true values of conflicting attributes could be found.

3.2 Dataflow Details

The dataflow graph is shown in Figure 1. The dataflow has 8 algorithmic operators and 4 stages, where the computation of each stage is "local" to each single machine and the data exchange (e.g., broadcast or hash repartitioning) happens at the stage boundaries. In the following part, we illustrate the algorithmic operators and the rules for each stage in the topological order in Figure 1.

Stage 1. This stage is performed on each slave machine.

- *DataRead*. It scans incoming file splits from the HDFS. The data are parsed and translated into the Cleanix internal format.
- *Correct*. This is blocking operator—data are checked according to the rules selected by users to detect the abnormal values and incomplete tuples. When an abnormal value is detected, it is corrected according to corresponding revision rules (first-order functions). When an incomplete tuple is encountered, it is identified for further processing.
- *BuildNullGram*. This operator builds an inverted list for all incomplete tuples for the imputation based on similar tuples. The inverted list is called the *gram table*. It is a hash table in which the k-gram is the key and the id set of tuples containing such a k-gram is the value.

Stage 2. The incoming broadcast connector to this stage broadcasts the gram tables such that all slaves share the same global gram table.

- *Fill*. For each tuple with incomplete attribute, similar tuples are found according to the gram table. The incomplete attribute is filled with the aggregated value of the corresponding attribute in similar tuples according to the imputation rules (first-order functions) selected by users such as average, max or the most frequent.
- *BuildGram*. A local gram table is built for the local data for the attributes potentially containing duplications or conflicts, which are chosen by users. Since a local gram table has been built with BuildNullGram operator, only the newly filled values of corresponding attributes are scanned in this step.

Stage 3. The local gram tables are broadcast to make all slaves share the same global gram table. Note that in this stage, only the updated values in local gram tables are broadcast.

- *ComputeSimilarity*. The similarities between each local tuple and other tuples are computed according to the global gram table. When the similarity between two tuples is larger than a threshold, they are added to the same group. After local data are scanned, many groups are obtained.

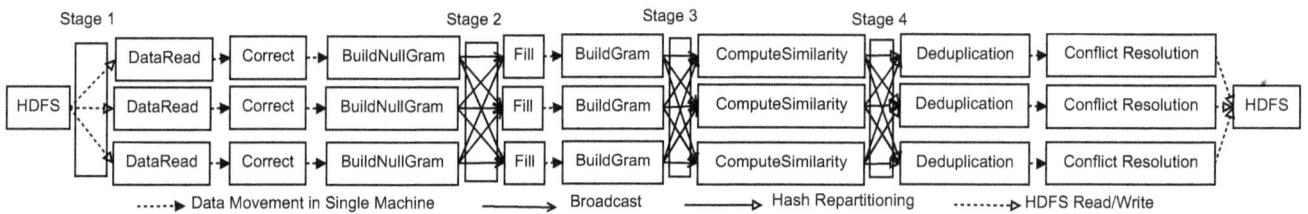

Figure 1: The Cleanix Dataflow Graph

Stage 4. The groups are partitioned according to the hashing value of bloom filter of the union of gram sets in this group.

- *De-duplication.* A weighted graph G is built to describe the similarity between tuples in each group. Similar vertices are merged iteratively in G until no pairs of vertices can be merged [7]. This step is executed iteratively until the ratio between the number of shared connected vertices and the number of the adjacent vertices of each vertex is smaller than a threshold. The tuples corresponding to all merged vertices are considered as duplications.
- *Conflict Resolution.* Tuples corresponding to the merged vertices are merged. During the merging, when an attribute with conflicting values is detected, it is resolved with voting according to the selected rules chosen by users. The options (first-order functions) include max, min, average and the most frequent.

3.3 Profiling

Each stage sends a corresponding profiling report back to the Hyracks master machine by using the Hyracks management events. When the master machine receives the profiling reports, it redirects them to the Cleanix graphical user interface such that users can see the error exploration report, the data quality report and the data cleaning result review.

4. DEMONSTRATIONS

In this section we describe the user interfaces of Cleanix in details and explain the aims of our demonstration.

Specifying Parameters. The first step in using Cleanix is to load data from data sources into the system. Users simply need to provide the name, port, username and password of the data sources. Our system also supports databases on the web with a reachable IP address.

The interface for user inputting parameters is generated according to the schema of databases. Our system requires users to input three kinds of required information for each attribute: (1) whether the attribute should be checked; (2) whether the attribute is allowed to be null; (3) the data type of an attribute.

Error Exploration. Our system shows the error in the data exploration interface for users to review data errors. In this demonstration we show the following features.

- How the users can explore the data with error identifications. The errors in data are distinguished with different colors in this interface. The user can then further select a tuple in a table. Then the details of the data errors are shown. In this way, users can identify the reasons why the tuple is marked as an error tuple.
- How the users explore the data by means of data errors. When the user selects an data error, its corresponding tuples will be displayed in a table. A user could further select a data error de-

tection or correction rule and the tuples with attributes violating the rules are shown with the desired attribute highlighted.

Data Quality Report. Statistics of data quality information are summarized and shown to users to check the data quality in high level. In the demonstration we show:

- The data quality problem in table and attribute level. In particular, this component computes various data quality problem in quantity by means of data sources, tuples and attributes shown in histogram. A similar categorization exists at both the attribute and tuple level.
- How the violations are distributed among the data. Cleanix computes various statistical measures and reports statistics regarding to the selected rules. The user can choose to retrieve this information at different levels.

Data Cleaning Results Review. In the final part of the demonstration, we illustrate the exploration of data cleaning results and interaction of user and the system. More specifically, we compare the repaired data with the original ones. The original and modified data are distinguished in different colors. When the user selects a modified value, the modifications are shown. Additionally, the user could modify the data. The modifications are merged when the cleaned data is transmitted from HDFS to the target database If the input value has some errors, they will be identified and suggested correct modifications close to the input value are shown for selection. In the interface, the revised tuples and the revision results are highlighted.

Acknowledgements. This paper was partially supported by NGFR 973 grant 2012CB316200 and NSFC grant 61472099.

5. REFERENCES

[1] Vinayak R. Borkar, Michael J. Carey, Raman Grover, Nicola Onose, and Rares Vernica. Hyracks: A flexible and extensible foundation for data-intensive computing. In *ICDE*, pages 1151–1162, 2011.

[2] Vinayak R. Borkar, Michael J. Carey, and Chen Li. Inside "Big Data management": ogres, onions, or parfaits? In *EDBT*, pages 3–14, 2012.

[3] Jeffrey Dean and Sanjay Ghemawat. MapReduce: Simplified data processing on large clusters. In *OSDI*, pages 137–150, 2004.

[4] Wenfei Fan, Jianzhong Li, Shuai Ma, Nan Tang, and Wenyuan Yu. CerFix: A system for cleaning data with certain fixes. *PVLDB*, 4(12):1375–1378, 2011.

[5] Helena Galhardas, Daniela Florescu, Dennis Shasha, Eric Simon, and Cristian-Augustin Saita. Declarative data cleaning: Language, model, and algorithms. In *VLDB*, pages 371–380, 2001.

[6] Thomas N. Herzog, Fritz J. Scheuren, and William E. Winkler. *Data quality and record linkage techniques*. Springer, 2007.

[7] Lingli Li, Hongzhi Wang, Hong Gao, and Jianzhong Li. EIF: A framework of effective entity identification. In *WAIM*, pages 717–728, 2010.

Keeping You in the Loop: Enabling Web-based Things Management in the Internet of Things

Lina Yao and Quan Z. Sheng
School of Computer Science
The University of Adelaide
Adelaide, SA 5005, Australia
{lina, qsheng}@cs.adelaide.edu.au

Anne H.H. Ngu and Byron Gao
Department of Computer Science
Texas State University
601 University Drive, San Marcos, USA
{angu, bgao}@txstate.edu

ABSTRACT

Internet of Things (IoT) is an emerging paradigm where physical objects are connected and communicated over the Web. Its capability in assimilating the virtual world and the physical one offers many exciting opportunities. However, how to realize a smooth, seamless integration of the two worlds remains an interesting and challenging topic. In this paper, we showcase an IoT prototype system that enables seamless integration of the virtual and the physical worlds and efficient management of things of interest (TOIs), where services and resources offered by things can be easily monitored, visualized, and aggregated for value-added services by users. This paper presents the motivation, system design, implementation, and demonstration scenario of the system.

Categories and Subject Descriptors

H.3.5 [**Information Storage and Retrieval**]: Online Information Services.; H.4.0 [**Information Systems Applications**]: General

Keywords

Internet of Things, RFID, RESTful Web Services

1. INTRODUCTION

As pointed out by Tim Berners-Lee, the inventor of the World Wide Web, it isn't the documents which are actually interesting, it is the things they are about[1]. The last level of abstraction for the Web is to connect physical things. With the recent advances in radio-frequency identification (RFID), wireless sensors network, and Web services, Internet of Things (IoT) offers the capability of integrating the information from both the physical world and the virtual one. With IoT, it becomes possible to infer the status of real-world entities with minimal delay using a standard Web browser [2].

---

[1]http://ercim-news.ercim.eu/en72/keynote/the-web-of-things

CIKM'14, November 3–7, 2014, Shanghai, China.
Copyright 2014 ACM 978-1-4503-2598-1/14/11 ...$15.00.
http://dx.doi.org/10.1145/2661829.2661838.

Motivation. IoT describes the evolution from systems linking digital documents to systems relating digital information to real world physical items. While it is well understood that IoT offers numerous opportunities and benefits, it also presents significant technical challenges. One of the main challenges is to provide a smooth and seamless integration of the virtual world and the physical one for effectively managing *things of interest* (TOIs) in IoT [4]. A crucial prerequisite is acknowledging the seamless information access, exchange and manipulation between the two worlds. However, in general, the communication and changes among things in IoT are implicit and invisible to humans, which leads to difficulties in representing and capturing them in formal models.

Our Approach. We explore a new direction in realizing information integration between the physical and the virtual worlds. We design and develop a prototype system that offers an integrated Web-based interface to manage (i.e., connect, monitor, control, mashup, and visualize) things in an IoT environment, which helps people to be aware of their surrounding world and make better decisions. The system provides a Web-based framework, where the information produced by physical things can be managed and socialized.

A central component of our system is the context-aware composition of things. In our system, contextual information includes environmental information (e.g., motion, temperature, light condition), activities (e.g., a person approaching the door of a house) and social events (e.g., tweet updates from people or socialized things). Since things are socialized, they can talk, respond to the context, and behave like humans. We particularly adopt a rule-based approach to aggregate individual things and build context-aware, personalized new value-added services. The context of a real, inhabituated home environment demonstrated in this paper by both virtual resources and physical things provides the basis for various other research in specific domains, such as independent living of the elderly, healthcare and smart homes. Our system can be considered as a step further to realizing the IoT vision. In the following sections, we will overview the design and implementation of the system, and sketch the proposed demonstration.

2. SYSTEM ARCHITECTURE

Figure 1 shows the architecture of our prototype system. The system has a layered architecture, and is developed using the Microsoft .NET framework and SQL Server 2012. Physical things and their related data and events are mapped to the corresponding virtual resources, which can be aggregated and visualized via a range of software components.

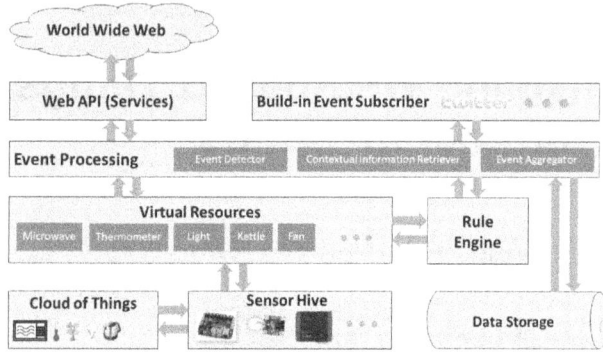

Figure 1: System architecture

The system has two ways to identify physical objects and connect them to the Web. The first one is to use RFID technology, where the physical objects are attached with RFID tags and interrogated by RFID readers. The second one is to attach sensors to objects for transferring the raw data to the network. The raw data captured by readers and sensors will be further processed. In the following, we describe the key modules of the system and their implementation details.

Sensor Hive. This module manages sensors and RFID tags, establishes connections, and queries sensor/RFID status, thus allowing physical things to be mapped to their corresponding virtual resources. It provides a universal API so that higher level programs can retrieve status of sensors with specified address without knowing where and how to find the physical sensors. This module works in a scalable, plug-and-play fashion, where new sensors can be added and old sensors can be easily removed.

Virtual Resources. This module maps a collection of classes to their corresponding physical devices. Each virtual device collects related sensor readings from Sensor Hive and uses the collected information to check the current status of the corresponding physical device. For example, the virtual device of a microwave oven can query its sensor values from the Sensor Hive, then use these readings to decide the current status (idle or busy) of the physical microwave oven. Virtual devices generate events based on the readings, which can be subscribed by high-level programs. Since each kind of device has a virtual resource, systems built with this architecture can be easily extended and maintained.

Event Processing. This module automatically extracts and aggregates things usage events based on data feeds from Virtual Resources in a pipelined fashion. The pipeline consists of three main phases: *event detection, contextual information retrieval*, and *event aggregation*.

The Event Detector captures and decides whether a physical thing is in-use. In our implementation, there are two ways to detect usage events of things: *sensor-based* for detecting state changes and *RFID-based* for detecting mobility [4]. In the sensor-based detection, the usage of an object is reflected by changes of the object's status, e.g., a microwave oven moved from an idle to an in-use state. In the RFID-based detection, the movement of an object indicates that the object is being used. For example, if a coffee mug is moving, it is likely that the mug is being used. In this situation, we adopt a generic method based on comparing descriptive statistics of the Received Signal Strength Indication (RSSI) values in consecutive sliding windows [1].

The statistics obtained from two consecutive windows are expected to differ significantly when an object is moved.

The Contextual Information Retriever fetches contextual information contained in things usage events. In our current implementation, we focus on three types of contextual information: *identity* (user), *temporal* (timestamp) and *spatial* (location) information [3, 4]. For the spatial information, we consider two situations. For *static* objects (e.g., refrigerator), the spatial information is a prior knowledge. For *mobile* objects (e.g., RFID-tagged coffee mug), we provide coarse-grain and fine-grain methods for localization. The coarse-grain method uses the RSSI signal received from a tagged object to approximate its proximity to an RFID antenna. Each zone is covered by a mutually exclusive set of RFID antennas. The zone scanned by an antenna with the maximum RSSI signal is regarded as the object's location. The fine-grain method compares the signal descriptors from an object at an unknown location to a previously constructed radio map or fingerprint. We use the Weighted k Nearest Neighbors algorithm (w-kNN) to find the most similar fingerprints and compute a weighted average of their 2D positions to estimate the unknown tag location [4].

The Event Aggregator indexes and stores all the events and services, together with their related information. The indexed events and services, as well as their corresponding contextual information are stored in a database, which can be mined for various purposes (e.g., finding hidden correlations among things, recommendation) [3, 4, 5]. A list of elements are constructed, storing the identifiers of objects, their types and values, as well as the calculated contextual information. In this way, applications can focus on the functionalities without worrying about operations such as connecting to the database, opening connections, querying with specified languages and handling the results.

Rule Engine. This module allows users to control a device automatically by setting up a series of basic rules. The Rule Engine includes three main components: the *Rule Builder*, the *Rule Interpreter*, and the *Rule Parser*. The Rule Builder is a Web-based application implementing a user-friendly GUI for rule creation and action setup, where a user only needs to drag the icon of a device to the editing area, then setup the details by several simple clicks. A string expression is generated for the rule. The Rule Interpreter analyzes and annotates the string statement based on a state machine. The string expression is then translated to a list of annotated objects. The outcome of the Rule Interpreter is a sequence of annotated inputs, which will be passed to the Rule Parser. The Rule Interpreter can also convert the string statement into a simple structure so that the Rule Builder can generate a corresponding GUI for rules. This is important for users who need to modify their existing rules. The Rule Parser is a compiler based on the *shunting-yard* algorithm. It first compiles each part of the input sequence into a .NET Expression object. Then, it combines all such objects together into a complex Expression Tree, which will be compiled into a Lambda Expression, which will be stored in memory when the system is running. It can be invoked when a device status changes or time elapses. If the Lambda expression returns true, a corresponding action will be called.

Web API/Services. This module converts events and data into corresponding services. By providing RESTful APIs for things, applications can easily access data associ-

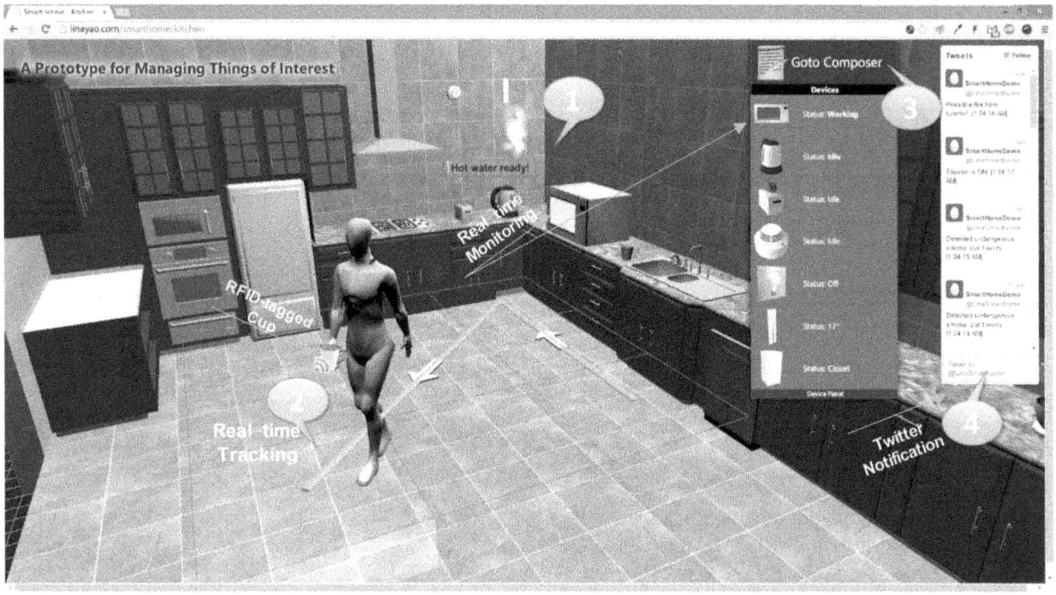

Figure 2: 3D Web-based interface

ated with a particular thing stored in the database, as well as manipulate the sensors (e.g., turning on or off a light). The APIs are represented using JavaScript Object Notation (JSON), which is developed from the JavaScript for representing simple data structures and associated objects. Our system also offers a 3D Web-based interface (see Figure 2). We particularly adopt WebGL in HTML 5 to enable 3D scene recreation. The 3D models are stored as Digital Asset Exchange (DAE) files, and imported and rendered by using three.js[2] with plug-ins.

3. DEMONSTRATION PLAN

Our system offers an integrated Web-based interface where a user can monitor and visualize status changes of things of interest in real-time. Users can monitor, track, and control the current status of physical things by directly observing the status of their corresponding icons (also called avatars) from a Web browser. In addition, our system augments the physical things with key social network functionality. We have developed a real-time notification of things' status by exploiting the Twitter public API. Real-time status changes are sent to the subscribers. Figure 2 shows the integrated Web-based user interface, and we will focus on demonstrating the following main functionalities.

- *Real-time visualizer and monitor:* This function offers access to, and control of, the physical things, allowing the real status of physical things to be visualized in real time. We render the icons with different effects to be consistent with real status of things. For example, if the microwave oven is being used, the microwave oven icon will change to a highlighted status (yellow), otherwise gray (Part 1 in Figure 2). The learned position information from the Event Processing module is used to visualize the locations and traces of things of interest at a coarse-grain level. For example, as shown in Part 2 of Figure 2, the trace of a tagged coffee mug held by a subject is displayed in the green lines.

- *Rules composer:* This function provides a complex graphical interface for users to control the devices by setting up a series of basic rules via Web browser without any programming efforts (Part 3 in Figure 2, please see the video clips for more details). It can create a composite service using the rule-based composition component provided by the system, which consists of a *Widget* panel and a *Rules Editor* panel. The Widget panel shows the virtualized objects (things and people) and each object has a set of actions (e.g., the light is associated with two actions: turn on and turn off). Users just drag any thing's widget to the Rules Editor panel and start to create a new rule or change the old rules by clicking the Edit button next to each rule.

Our demonstrative video clips can be accessed from the Youtube[3].

4. REFERENCES

[1] S. Parlak, I. Marsic, and R. S. Burd. Activity Recognition for Emergency Care Using RFID. In *Proc. of the 6th Intl. Conf. on Body Area Networks*, 2011.

[2] A. Pintus, D. Carboni, and A. Piras. Paraimpu: A Platform for a Social Web of Things. In *Proc. of the 21st Intl. World Wide Web Conf. (WWW)*, 2012.

[3] L. Yao and Q. Z. Sheng. Exploiting Latent Relevance for Relational Learning of Ubiquitous Things. In *Proc. of the 21st ACM Intl. Conf. on Information and Knowledge Management (CIKM)*, 2012.

[4] L. Yao, Q. Z. Sheng, B. Gao, A. Ngu, and X. Li. A Model for Discovering Correlations of Ubiquitous Things. In *Proc. of the 13th IEEE Intl. Conf. on Data Mining (ICDM)*, 2013.

[5] L. Yao, Q. Z. Sheng, A. H. Ngu, H. Ashman, and X. Li. Exploring Recommendations in Internet of Things. In *Proc. of the 37th ACM SIGIR Conf.*, 2014.

[2] http://threejs.org

[3] https://www.youtube.com/playlist?list=PL8nHiAwRrq8I4aYQBPdelwGXIaqMVtYni

Anything You Can Do, I Can Do Better: Finding Expert Teams by CrewScout*

Naeemul Hassan [1], Huadong Feng [1], Ramesh Venkataraman [1]
Gautam Das [1], Chengkai Li [1], Nan Zhang [2]
[1]University of Texas at Arlington, [2]George Washington University

ABSTRACT

CrewScout is an expert-team finding system based on the concept of *skyline teams* and efficient algorithms for finding such teams. Given a set of experts, CrewScout finds all k-expert skyline teams, which are not dominated by any other k-expert teams. The dominance between teams is governed by comparing their aggregated expertise vectors. The need for finding expert teams prevails in applications such as question answering, crowdsourcing, panel selection, and project team formation. The new contributions of this paper include an end-to-end system with an interactive user interface that assists users in choosing teams and an demonstration of its application domains.

Categories and Subject Descriptors

H.2 [**DATABASE MANAGEMENT**]: Database applications

Keywords

Skyline Queries; Team Recommendation

1. OVERVIEW

We introduce CrewScout (http://idir.uta.edu/crewscout), a system for finding expert teams in accomplishing tasks. The underpinning concept of the system is *skyline teams* (called *skyline groups* in [2, 3]). The new contributions made in this paper include an end-to-end system with an interactive user interface that assists users in choosing teams among potentially many skyline teams and an extension of application and demonstration scenarios into more general areas ([2, 3] mostly focused on the application of forming teams in fantasy sports games.)

Consider a set D of n experts $t_1, \ldots, t_n$, modeled by m numeric attributes $A_1, \ldots, A_m$ that represent their skills and expertise. Any subset of k experts form a k-*expert team*. CrewScout finds, for a given k, all k-expert skyline teams, i.e., k-expert teams that are

*Das is supported in part by NSF grant 1018865 and grants from Microsoft Research. Hassan and Li are partially supported by NSF grants 1018865, 1117369, 1408928, and the National Natural Science Foundation of China Grant 61370-019. Zhang is supported in part by NSF grants 0852674, 0915834, 1117297, and 1343976. Any opinions, findings, and conclusions or recommendations expressed in this publication are those of the authors and do not necessarily reflect the views of the funding agencies. The U.S. Government is authorized to reproduce and distribute reprints for Government purposes notwithstanding any copyright notice herein.

CIKM'14, November 3–7, 2014, Shanghai, China.
ACM 978-1-4503-2598-1/14/11.
http://dx.doi.org/10.1145/2661829.2661839.

	database	indexing
t_1	3	0
t_2	0	3
t_3	2	1
t_4	2	2
t_5	0	2

Table 1: Experts

team	AVG	MIN	MAX
$G_{1,2}$	$\langle 1.5, 1.5 \rangle$	$\langle 0, 0 \rangle$	$\langle \mathbf{3,3} \rangle$
$G_{1,3}$	$\langle 2.5, 0.5 \rangle$	$\langle 2, 0 \rangle$	$\langle 3, 1 \rangle$
$G_{1,4}$	$\langle \mathbf{2.5, 1.0} \rangle$	$\langle 2, 0 \rangle$	$\langle 3, 2 \rangle$
$G_{1,5}$	$\langle 1.5, 1.0 \rangle$	$\langle 0, 0 \rangle$	$\langle 3, 2 \rangle$
$G_{2,3}$	$\langle 1.0, 2.0 \rangle$	$\langle 0, 1 \rangle$	$\langle 2, 3 \rangle$
$G_{2,4}$	$\langle \mathbf{1.0, 2.5} \rangle$	$\langle \mathbf{0, 2} \rangle$	$\langle 2, 3 \rangle$
$G_{2,5}$	$\langle 0, 2.5 \rangle$	$\langle \mathbf{0, 2} \rangle$	$\langle 0, 3 \rangle$
$G_{3,4}$	$\langle \mathbf{2.0, 1.5} \rangle$	$\langle \mathbf{2, 1} \rangle$	$\langle 2, 2 \rangle$
$G_{3,5}$	$\langle 1.0, 1.5 \rangle$	$\langle 0, 1 \rangle$	$\langle 2, 2 \rangle$
$G_{4,5}$	$\langle 1.0, 2.0 \rangle$	$\langle \mathbf{0, 2} \rangle$	$\langle 2, 2 \rangle$

Table 2: All possible 2-expert teams

not *dominated* by any other k-expert teams. It further assists users in choosing among the skyline teams. The notion of dominance between teams is analogous to the dominance relation between tuples in skyline analysis [1]. CrewScout calculates for each team an aggregate vector of its experts' individual vectors. CrewScout provides efficient algorithms for four commonly used aggregate functions—AVG (i.e, SUM, since we only compare teams with equal size), MIN and MAX. [1] A team G_1 *dominates* another team G_2 (denoted $G_1 \succ G_2$), if and only if the aggregate value of G_1 on every attribute is better than or equal to the corresponding value of G_2 and G_1 has better value on at least one attribute.

The need for finding expert teams prevails in several application areas, including question answering, crowdsourcing, panel selection, project team formation, and so on. This is illustrated by the following motivating examples.

CrowdSourcing Consider forming a team of Wikipedia editors to write a new Wikipedia article related to "database" and "indexing". Table 1 shows all relevant editors $t_1, \ldots, t_5$ and their expertise on the two topics. We want to assign the task to a team of 2 editors. Table 2 shows the aggregate vectors under AVG, MIN and MAX, for all possible 2-expert teams where $G_{i,j}$ stands for a team of experts t_i and t_j. A simple scheme such as picking top editors on individual topics does not work. For example, $G_{1,2}$ consists of the top editor on each topic and has an aggregated vector $\langle 1.5, 1.5 \rangle$ with regard to AVG. $G_{3,4}$, with vector $\langle 2.0, 1.5 \rangle$, dominates $G_{1,2}$ (denoted $G_{3,4} \succ G_{1,2}$) under AVG. Hence, $G_{3,4}$ is a better team in terms of collective expertise. In fact, $G_{3,4}$ is a 2-expert skyline team, since no other team dominates it under AVG. Table 2 highlights all 2-expert skyline teams for every aggregate function.

Questing Answering Consider a question-answering platform such as Quora.com. A question is displayed to users who might answer it. The question asker can also explicitly solicit answers from certain users, oftentimes by offering rewards. To receive quality answers, it is necessary to intelligently post the question to users with proper expertise. More often than not, a question requires expertise on several aspects that cannot be fulfilled by any single user, needing attention from a diverse team of experts who collectively

---

[1]While the concept allows arbitrary aggregate functions, efficient algorithms for less common functions remain an open problem.

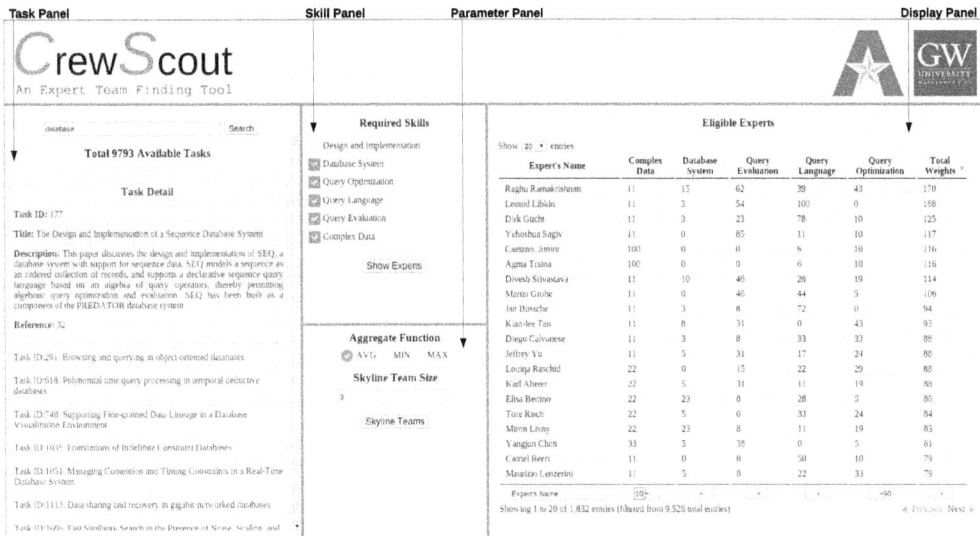

Figure 1: CrewScout Interface

excel. For instance, consider question "Is C or Python better for high-performance computing?" To get a comprehensive answer, we need experts in "high performance computing", "C", and so on.

Other Motivating Applications The need for finding expert teams arises in several other applications. **1)** Consider the task of choosing a panel of experts to evaluate a research paper or a grant proposal. An expert can be modeled as a tuple in the multi-dimensional space defined by the paper's topics, to reflect the expert's strength on these topics. The collective expertise of a panel is modeled as the aggregate vector of the corresponding tuples. **2)** Forming collaborative teams for a software development project can be viewed as finding programmers who are collectively strong in the multi-dimensional space of desired skills for the project. **3)** In a variety of applications we look for "teams" in more general sense, such as bundles of products, reviews, stocks, and so on. For instance, to summarize a product's many customer reviews, choosing a set of diverse reviews is forming a "team" of reviews, where the reviews are modeled by attributes such as "sentiment", "length", "quality", etc. Another example is online fantasy sports where gamers compete by forming and managing team rosters of real-world athletes, aiming at outperforming other gamers' teams. The teams are compared by aggregated statistics (e.g., "points", "rebounds", "assists" in basketball games) of the athletes in real games.

An attractive characteristic of a skyline team is that no other team of equal size can dominate it. In contrast, given a non-skyline team, there is always a better skyline team. This property distinguishes CrewScout from other team recommendation techniques. The skyline teams consist of the teams that are worth recommending. They become the input to further manual or automated post-processing that eventually finds one team. Admittedly, determining the "best" team is a complex task that may involve more factors than what skyline teams can capture—e.g., which experts are available for a task, whether they have good relationship to work together, and so on. The post-processing is thus crucial. Examples of such post-processing include eye-balling the skyline teams, filtering and ranking them by user preferences, and browsing and visualization of the skyline teams. Particularly, CrewScout provides an interactive tool to assist a human user in exploring and choosing skyline teams.

2. USER INTERFACE

Figure 1 shows the GUI of CrewScout, which is comprised of a *task panel*, a *skill panel*, a *parameter panel*, and a *display panel*.

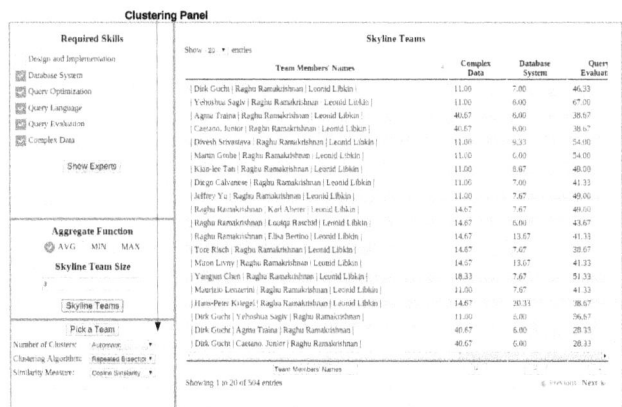

Figure 2: Display Panel Showing Skyline Teams

The task panel presents a list of available tasks. When a user clicks a task, CrewScout provides more details about it. CrewScout also provides a keyword search box at the top of this panel for searching available tasks. The skill panel presents the skills required for completing the selected task. It shows a checkbox for each skill. By default, all the checkboxes are checked. The user can check/uncheck some of them according to their preference. When the user clicks the "Show Experts" button, the display panel presents a paginated list of all experts who have expertise in at least one checked skill. If the user further checks/unchecks some skills, the expert list is automatically refreshed to reflect the change. Experts are ordered by summations of their expertise in all selected skills in the current implementation. In the expert list, a filter is provided for each skill. The user can filter the experts by setting the minimum and maximum expertise for one or more skills. The user can also filter the experts by their names through partial string matching.

The parameter panel allows the user to set parameters for skyline team computation. It includes a textbox for specifying the skyline team size and radio buttons for choosing an aggregate function (AVG, MIN, or MAX). Once the user clicks the "Skyline Teams" button, CrewScout calculates all skyline teams (considering all experts satisfying the aforementioned filters) and shows them in the display panel (Figure 2). Similar to the filters on experts, CrewScout also provides filters for the skyline team list, including filters on team members' names and minimum/maximum aggregated exper-

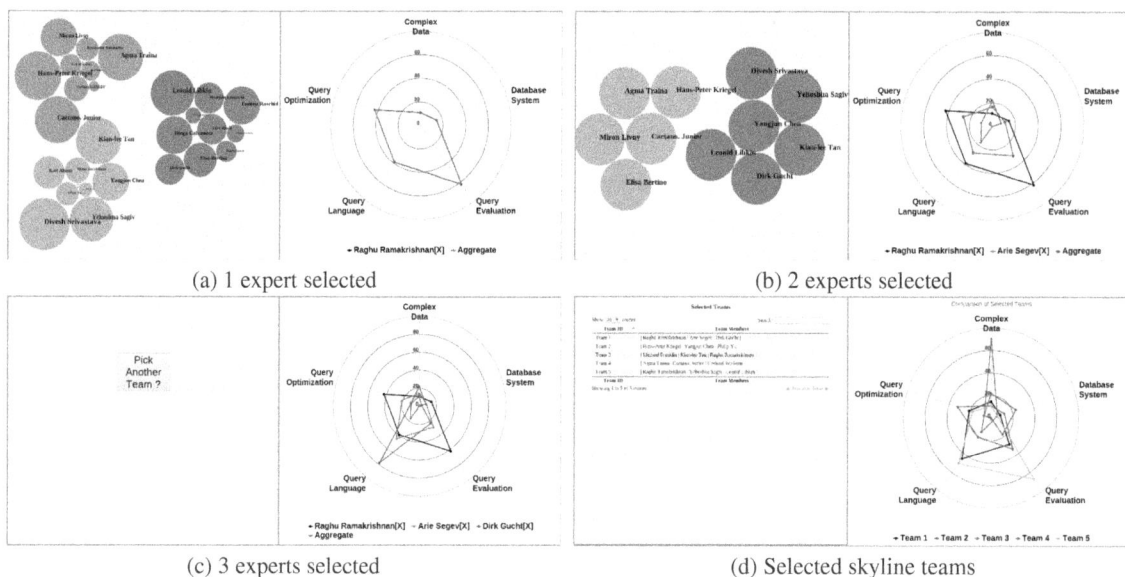

(a) 1 expert selected   (b) 2 experts selected

(c) 3 experts selected   (d) Selected skyline teams

Figure 3: Selecting and Comparing Teams

tise on individual skills. The teams satisfying the conditions are called the *qualifying skyline teams*. When the display panel exhibits the skyline teams, a *clustering panel* is added below the parameter panel. It provides a "Pick a Team" button and three drop-down lists that allow the user to choose a clustering algorithm (e.g., *K-means*), a similarity/distance function (e.g., Euclidean distance) for the clustering algorithm, and the number of clusters. When the user clicks the button, CrewScout will display below the current panels a visualization interface (Figure 3) that clusters the experts in the qualifying skyline teams and assists the user in exploring and choosing teams.

The visualization interface has two panels. The left panel visualizes the clusters. Each expert that belongs to at least one qualifying skyline team is represented as a circle. Circles in the same cluster are annotated with the same color. Their positions are automatically determined by the *multi-foci force layout* (https://github.com/mbostock/d3/wiki/Force-Layout). The size of a circle is proportional to the number of qualifying skyline teams containing the corresponding expert. At the beginning, only the labels of big circles (containing information of corresponding experts) are visible. When the user hovers the mouse over a circle, the expert's profile (including the name and the number of skyline teams containing the expert) is displayed in a small pop-up window. The user can gradually zoom in to see the labels of smaller circles. The user can iteratively select k experts. Whenever the user selects an expert, CrewScout removes those circles whose corresponding experts do not belong to any skyline teams with all selected experts so far. The remaining circles are re-clustered and resized, based on only qualifying skyline teams containing the selected experts. The right panel presents a polar-chart. Each polygon in the polar-chart represents a selected expert's expertise on the chosen skills. The aggregated expertise of the selected experts is also represented by a polygon. The selected experts are listed under the polar-chart. The user can remove any expert by clicking the cross sign beside it, and the clusters of circles are refreshed accordingly. Once k experts are selected, a skyline team is chosen. A "Pick Another Team?" button appears in the left panel. If the user clicks it, two more panels are added to the lower portion of the visualization interface—the left one lists all selected teams and the right one presents another polar-chart that compares them.

3. DEMONSTRATION PLAN

An online demonstration of CrewScout is hosted at http://idir.uta.edu/crewscout. Its front-end UI is developed in PHP+JavaScript. The system demonstrates three application scenarios, including paper reviewer selection, question answering, and team formation, on a 900K-publication dataset collected through Microsoft Academic Search API, a stackoverflow.com dataset and an NBA dataset from databasebasketball.com, respectively. It also supports user-uploaded datasets. Below we describe the demonstration steps for the reviewer selection scenario, with an imaginary user Amy.

(1) Amy searches for, say "database", and matching publications are displayed in the task panel. A default publication is highlighted.
(2) Amy clicks a publication to show or hide its abstract, depending on its status. When a publication is selected, the skill and display panels are refreshed with the corresponding required expertise and qualifying reviewers, respectively. Amy checks/unchecks one or more skills, the qualifying reviewers are automatically refreshed. Amy filters the reviewers by setting minimum and/or maximum thresholds on one or more skills. (Figure 1)
(3) Amy specifies an aggregate function and a skyline team size in the parameter panel. Once Amy clicks the "Skyline Teams" button, the display panel shows the skyline teams (Figure 2). Amy can filter them by reviewer name and thresholds on aggregated skills.
(4) After choosing clustering parameters, Amy clicks the "Pick a Team" button and the visualization interface presents the reviewer clusters (Figure 3).
(5) Amy moves the mouse over the circles to see the reviewers' profiles and she also zooms in and out. When Amy selects a reviewer, the corresponding expertise polygon is inserted into the polar-chart. Amy repeats this step multiple times until a k-reviewer team is formed.
(6) Amy clicks the "Pick Another Team?" button to select another team. In this way, Amy chooses multiple teams and compares them in a polar-chart.

4. REFERENCES

[1] S. Borzsony, D. Kossmann, and K. Stocker. The skyline operator. In *ICDE*, pages 421–430, 2001.
[2] C. Li, N. Zhang, N. Hassan, S. Rajasekaran, and G. Das. On skyline groups. In *CIKM*, pages 2119–2123, 2012.
[3] N. Zhang, C. Li, N. Hassan, S. Rajasekaran, and G. Das. On skyline groups. *TKDE*, 26(4):942–956, April 2014.

WiiCluster: a Platform for Wikipedia Infobox Generation

Kezun Zhang§, Yanghua Xiao§*, Hanghang Tong‡, Haixun Wang†, Wei Wang§
†School of Computer Science, Shanghai Key Laboratory of Data Science, Fudan University, Shanghai, China
§{kzhang12, shawyh, weiwang1}@fudan.edu.cn

‡ Arizona State University, USA   †Google Research, USA
‡hanghang.tong@asu.edu   †haixun@google.com

ABSTRACT

Wikipedia has become one of the best sources for creating and sharing a massive volume of human knowledge. Much effort has been devoted to generating and enriching the structured data by *automatic* information extraction from unstructured text in Wikipedia. Most, if not all, of the existing work share the same paradigm, that is, starting with information extraction over the unstructured text data, followed by supervised machine learning. Although remarkable progresses have been made, this paradigm has its own limitations in terms of effectiveness, scalability as well as the high labeling cost.

We present WIICLUSTER, a scalable platform for automatically generating infobox for articles in Wikipedia. The heart of our system is an effective *cluster-then-label* algorithm over a rich set of semi-structured data in Wikipedia articles: *linked entities*. It is totally unsupervised and thus does not require any human label. It is effective in generating semantically meaningful summarization for Wikipedia articles. We further propose a cluster-reuse algorithm to scale up our system. Overall, our WIICLUSTER is able to generate nearly 10 million new facts. We also develop a web-based platform to demonstrate WIICLUSTER, which enables the users to access and browse the generated knowledge.

Categories and Subject Descriptors

H.3.3 [**Information Search and Retrieval**]: Clustering; Information filtering

Keywords

Knowledge Extraction; Summarization; Cluster Visualization

---

*Correspondence author. This work was partially supported by the National NSFC(No.61472085, 61171132, 61033010), by National Key Basic Research Program of China under No.2015CB358800, by Shanghai STCF under No.13511505302, by NSF of Jiangsu Prov. under No. BK2010280, by the NSF under Grant No. IIS1017415, by the Army Research Laboratory under Cooperative Agreement No. W911NF-09-2-0053, by Defense Advanced Research Projects Agency (DARPA) under Contract No. W911NF-11-C-0200 and W911NF-12-C-0028, and by Region II University Transportation Center under the project No. 49997-33 25.

CIKM'14, November 3–7, 2014, Shanghai, China.
ACM 978-1-4503-2598-1/14/11.
http://dx.doi.org/10.1145/2661829.2661840 .

1. INTRODUCTION

Wikipedia[1] has become one of the best sources for creating and sharing a massive volume of human knowledge. Among others, an important reason that makes it extremely valuable is that part of its data is *structured*, and hence machine processible. Usually, a Wikipedia article is about an entity. Many Wikipedia articles contain structured information such as *table, text, hyper link*, etc., all of which are the targets of information extraction. More importantly, many entities are associated with an *infobox* which consists of a set of (*property, value*) pairs about the entities. Such structured information is the core building block behind many applications, including search engines, for answering user questions about these entities, etc. But the current infobox in Wikipedia is often *incomplete* [3].

In this paper, we present WIICLUSTER, a scalable platform for automatically generating structural information to supply knowledge for infobox in Wikipedia. Instead of performing information extraction over unstructured natural language text directly, we focus on a rich set of semi-structured data in Wikipedia articles: *linked entities*. A Wikipedia article typically consists of many links to other Wikipedia articles. Intuitively, the author of the article, in describing a Wikipedia entity, refers the reader to many other entities that are important or related to the entity. The key idea of this paper is the following: *If we can summarize the relationship between the entity and its linked entities, we immediately harvest some of the most important information about the entity.*

In order to convert such semi-structured data (i.e., linked entities) to the structure infobox, we propose an effective *cluster-then-label* algorithm to map the (*cluster-label, cluster*) to (*property, value*) pairs. For example, the article *"Shanghai"* in Wikipedia has the linked entity like *"The Bund"*,*"Oriental Pearl Tower"*,*"Fudan University"*,*"Shanghai Jiao Tong University"*. We group *"The Bund"*,*"Oriental Pearl Tower"* together by clustering and assign a label (such as *"Visitor Attractions in Shanghai"*) to the cluster. The cluster label explains how the entities in the cluster are related to *"Shanghai"* and can be considered as a property of *"Shanghai"*. Similarly we can group *"Fudan University"*,*"Shanghai Jiao Tong University"* together and generate a corresponding label *"Universities in Shanghai"*.

Recently, extensive effort has focused on expanding and enriching the structured data by *automatic* information extraction from unstructured text in Wikipedia [3, 2] to complete infobox. Although remarkable progresses have been made, its effectiveness and scalability are still somewhat limited (related work for detail).

Our approach outperforms above methods in scale and efficiency, because we harvest knowledge from all linked entities instead of limiting "property" in the infobox template (scale guaranteed), and knowledge are harvested by summarizing instead of pairwise relationship extracting (efficiency guaranteed). Even if the quality of our method might not be as good as those by dedicated human labeling, since our "cluster-label" is not constrained as "property" in infobox template, the infobox we generate could still represent knowledge in human sense and provide a starting point for further manual editing by human (which might save part of their labeling/editing cost).

---

[1] http://www.wikipedia.org

Our WIICLUSTER enjoys three key advantages. First, it is *effective* in generating semantically meaningful summarization for Wikipedia articles. Second, it is totally *unsupervised* and thus does not require any human label. Third, it is *scalable* by adopting an efficient cluster-reuse algorithm. Overall, our WIICLUSTER is able to generate nearly 10 million new facts. We also develop a web-based platform to demonstrate WIICLUSTER, which enables the users to access and browse the generated knowledge.

2. DEMONSTRATING WIICLUSTER

In this section, we demonstrate the main functionalities of WIICLUSTER. We implement the WIICLUSTER in Java. The knowledge is stored in MySql database and can be accessed on our web platform http://gdm.fudan.edu.cn/WiiCluster. The platform receives a user's search request and retrieves its infobox generated by WIICLUSTER from the database. It further supports the browsing and visualization of the intrinsic knowledge of a given infobox.

Scale of WiiCluster. We run the experiments on Wikipedia (released in January 1, 2013), which has 3.2 million English articles in total. After removing the noisy, unrelated linked entities and filtering the linked entities without feature for clustering, we have 1.95 million valid articles in total. Our WIICLUSTER finds 9.8M clusters for these 1.95M articles. On average, we find 5 clusters for each article; and 3.3 entities for each cluster. If we treat the *(article entity, property, an entity in a cluster)* as a single fact, WIICLUSTER generates 32M such facts in total.

Display Platform. Figure 1 shows the main interface of WIICLUSTER. It has a search box on the top. If the user types in an entity name (e.g., *Shanghai*), WIICLUSTER retrieves its infobox from the database and displays it in the main screen. There are three main parts/views to browse a given infobox. Let us use the example of *"Shanghai"* to illustrate these views. In Figure 1, part A lists the primary property index in the alphabetical order (e.g., *"airports"*, *"attractions"*). A user can be further navigated to browse the corresponding dependent clusters in part B. Part B shows all the primary properties and their dependent clusters, each of which is composed of a secondary property and one or more linked entities. For example, the two primary properties *"attractions"* and *"universities"*, each of which has a dependent cluster. Furthermore, secondary property of *"attractions"* is *"visitor attractions in Shanghai"* and it contains 18 entities such as *"The Bund"*, *"Oriental Pearl Tower"* etc. famous tourist attractions in *Shanghai*. The secondary property represents the label of a group of the linked entities in the same cluster. Each entity can be used to navigate the user to browse the information of the corresponding article. In part C, we use prefuse (an open source graph view package)[2] to visualize the intrinsic knowledge of a given infobox. For example, if the user clicks the primary property *"districts"*, its dependent cluster will be shown in an aggregated area.

We present two different models to visualize the clusters: (a) *aggregate graph model* and (b) *tree model*. For example, If the user clicks the entry *Graph* in part C, the aggregate graph viewer will show. This visualization model displays the properties and values in the form of a graph, where all the properties and entities are represented as nodes and their dependency are represented as the directed edges. The nodes in one cluster are wrapped within an aggregated area. In the display panel, the central node is the article (*"Shanghai"*), the red node represents the primary property of the article, the linked aggregated areas represent their inner clusters. Each aggregated area composes of a green node and a set of white nodes. The green node represents the secondary property, and it is dependent on the primary property by which it is linked. And the linked white nodes represent the linked entities, which depend on the secondary property. By default, we display the article and its primary properties in the panel only, and all the inner clusters are hidden. A user can click the primary property to display or hide its inner clusters.

The generated summarization WIICLUSTER is meaningful and sensible. In the *"Shanghai"* example, we generate a number of clusters of entities with the primary and secondary properties.

[2]http://prefuse.org

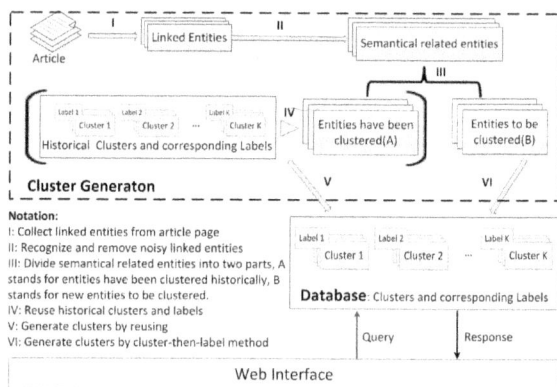

Figure 2: Flowchart of our platform

Each cluster and the corresponding properties are good supplement for the infobox of the article.

3. TECHNICAL DETAILS

In this section, we present the algorithmic details. Figure 2 shows the overall flowchart of WIICLUSTER. From algorithmic perspective, there are two challenges, including *C1. how to accurately summarize linked entities?*, and *C2. how to efficiently extract knowledge for all articles?*. Next, we describe an effective *cluster-then-label* algorithm and a *cluster reuse* strategy to address these two challenges, respectively. Details of the algorithms and quantitative comparison can be found in [4].

3.1 Cluster-then-Label

In order to convert the semi-structured linked entities into structured *(property, value)* pairs as infobox in Wikipedia, we need to group the similar linked entities (i.e., values) together as well as assign a label (i.e., property) for each group.

We thus propose a "cluster-then-label" approach: we cluster linked entities into different semantic groups, and then assign each group a semantic label (a property). More specifically, we use a G-means based clustering algorithm to cluster the linked entities into different semantic groups. And further propose a LCA (Least Common Ancestor) based label generating algorithm to assign a label for each group. Each labeled group is eventually a candidate *(property, value)* pair for the infobox.

A. Clustering. In Wikipedia, an entity is typically associated with one or more categories by editors. A category is widely used to characterize the concept of an entity. Hence, we use the categories to construct the feature vector for the entity.

However, the clustering performance is poor if we use the categories directly as the feature vector, mainly due to the following two limitations. First, some categories are not hypernyms of the corresponding entities, which may lead to mis-clustering. Second, direct categories of article are usually too specific, which leads to the small clusters with the limited number of linked entities. To address these two limitations, we propose a *feature expansion-and-weighting* procedure to construct the feature vectors for the entities. To be specific, for a given entity e, we recursively extend its feature set from its direct categories to the higher level categories. For each expanded category c, we define its weight $p(c|e)$ as the probability of category c being a hypernym of the entity e. The higher the weight $p(c|e)$ is, the more the clustering algorithm will reply on this expanded feature c. Once we have constructed the feature vectors for all the linked entities, many off-the-shelf clustering algorithms can be plugged in. In our current implementation, we use G-means [1] algorithm to cluster the linked entities with the cosine distance that is defined on the expanded and weighted feature vectors.

B. Labeling. Next, we assign a semantic label for each group/cluster. In this way, we could explain why the group of entities are linked by the article entity. The semantic label as well as the group of entities thus becomes a property of the article entity and its corresponding value. This information might provide a good supplement of the current infobox. In WIICLUSTER, we design the following two labeling methods, including *Category as Label* and *Word as Label*.

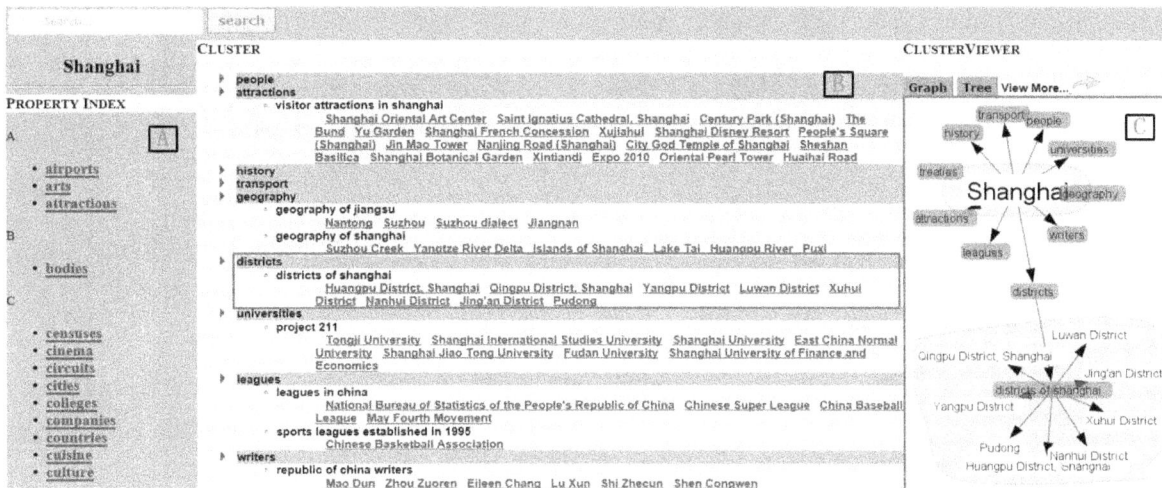

Figure 1: Screenshot of WiiCluster: searching entity *"Shanghai"* and clicking primary property *"districts"*.

Category as Label. Generally speaking, a good cluster label should capture the common theme of entities within each cluster *completeness* and in the meanwhile differentiate itself from other clusters *informativeness*. The completeness and the informativeness could be contradicting to each other. In general, the more abstract a label is, the more entities it can cover, but the less informative it might be.

Since we use the (directed and indirected) categories as the feature vectors of the entities, we can select an appropriate category as the cluster label. In order to carefully balance the completeness and informativeness, we propose a LCA (Least Common Ancestor) model. The LCA model is defined on the taxonomy graph G(Wikipedia category system). Given a cluster of entities, we search the LCA of these entities in the taxonomy G. The LCA is the nearest category which is reachable from all entities in the cluster via the hypernym edges in the taxonomy graph G. In this way, the label we get is specific enough (i.e., informativeness) yet still covers the entire cluster (i.e., completeness).

Word as Label. Using the above labeling strategy, we assign an appropriate category for each cluster. However, the categories in Wikipedia are manually edited, which are often represented as a phrase and organized in a specific Wiki style. Thus, some categories might be hard for the machine to understand (e.g., *"people by status"* instead of *"people"*). Therefore, our WIICLUSTER uses additional strategies to generate a more structural and machine processable label.

To distinguish these two labeling methods, we refer to the category label as the *secondary property*, and the word label as *primary property* since the word label might be upper concept of the category label.

3.2 Cluster Reuse

If we apply the above *cluster-then-label* procedure to each of the million of articles in wikipedia independently, the computation quickly becomes the bottleneck. In order to address the scalability issue, we propose a novel *cluster reuse* strategy to speedup the computation. Here, the key observation is that different articles might share many common linked entities. Thus, once the knowledge extraction for one article is done, the other article might reuse/inherit its summarization result instead of recomputing from scratch. For example, the two Wikipedia articles, *"Shanghai"* and *"Pudong"*, have some common linked entities such as *"Huangpu District"*, *"Yangpu District"* etc. district in Shanghai. When we process *"Shanghai"*, suppose that we have grouped *"Huangpu District"*, *"Yangpu District"* together with the label *"Districts of Shanghai"*. Thus, when we process *"Pudong"*, we might be able to directly inherit/reuse this result. Apparently, this strategy would be much more efficient in terms of computation. To do this, we construct a maximal spanning tree from the article graph (article as node, hyper link between articles as edge)

in Wikipedia, and serve weight of edge as percent of their common linked entities. It's obvious that the more common linked entities exist, the larger probability reuse working and the less time cost on direct clustering and labeling.

4. RELATED WORK

Extensive efforts have focused on extracting structural information from unstructural text from Wikipedia to supply knowledge for infobox, such as [3, 2]. Limitation for these methods are: First, these methods, such as [2], rely on several natural language understanding tasks (e.g., named entity recognition, dependency parsing, and relationship extraction), which themselves are extremely challenging and error prone. [2] can harvests knowledge only from the sentences that contain both the article or its variation and the linked entity, it's obvious time consuming and is not scale guaranteed. Second, many of the existing approaches are costly, such as [3], since they are essentially supervised learning methods, and hence require a large amount of labeled training examples. In our approach, we harvest structural information though summarizing linked entities instead of pairwise relationship extraction or template constrained extraction, then we will harvest more knowledge in an efficient manner.

5. CONCLUSION

Discovering and enriching structural information in online encyclopedia is a valuable yet challenging task. We present WIICLUSTER, a scalable platform for automatically generating infobox for articles in Wikipedia. Unlike the existing "Information Extraction+Supervised Learning" paradigm, WIICLUSTER offers a radically different, yet promising avenue for automatic infobox generation. The heart of our system is an effective *cluster-then-label* algorithm over a rich set of semi-structured data in Wikipedia articles: *linked entities*. It has three key features, including (a) requiring no human labels; (b) effective in generating meaningful knowledge and (c) scalable to millions of new facts. We demonstrate its main functionalities through web-based platform.

6. REFERENCES

[1] G. Hamerly and C. Elkan. Learning the k in k-means. In *Proc. of 17th NIPS*, 2003.

[2] D. P. Nguyen, Y. Matsuo, and M. Ishizuka. Exploiting syntactic and semantic information for relation extraction from wikipedia. *IJCAI07-TextLinkWS*, 2007.

[3] A. Sultana, Q. M. Hasan, A. K. Biswas, S. Das, H. Rahman, C. Ding, and C. Li. Infobox suggestion for wikipedia entities. In *Proc. of CIKM*, 2012.

[4] K. Zhang, Y. Xiao, H. Tong, H. Wang, and W. Wang. The links have it: Infobox generation by summarization over linked entities. arXiv:1406.6449, 2014.

Negative FaceBlurring: A privacy-by-design approach to visual lifelogging with Google Glass

TengQi Ye and Brian Moynagh and Rami Albatal and Cathal Gurrin
Insight Centre for Data Analytics
Dublin City University, Ireland
yetengqi@gmail.com

ABSTRACT

Wearable devices such as Google Glass are receiving increasing attention and look set to become part of our technical landscape over the next few years. At the same time, lifelogging is a topic that is growing in popularity with a host of new devices on the market that visually capture life experience in an automated manner. In this paper, we describe a visual lifelogging solution for Google Glass that is designed to capture life experience in rich visual detail, yet maintain the privacy of unknown bystanders.

We present the approach called negative face blurring and evaluate it on a collection of lifelogging data of around nine thousand pictures from Google Glass.

Categories and Subject Descriptors

H.4 [**Information Systems Applications**]: Miscellaneous

General Terms

Algorithms, Human Factors, Management

1. INTRODUCTION

Lifelogging is the process of digitally sensing life activities in detail and storing this in a digital archive for later referral [5]. There are many forms of lifelogging from the Quantified Self style personal analytics to the extreme lifelogging of MyLifeBits [4] or the visual lifelogging of Lee et al. [8]. Lifelogging relies in the main on the availability of wearable computing devices that can sense life activities in sufficiently high fidelity. The dominant lifelogging devices used to date are wearable cameras that passively capture user activities. Wearable cameras such as the OMG Autographer, the Narrative Clip, and even more flexible camera equipped wearable devices (e.g. Google Glass [1]) , all support the gen-

---

[1] Although Google Glass is not designed as a lifelogging device, it is a programmable platform, hence we have been able to develop lifelogging tools as Glassware

CIKM'14, November 3–7, 2014, Shanghai, China.
ACM 978-1-4503-2598-1/14/11.
http://dx.doi.org/10.1145/2661829.2661841

eration of rich lifelogs, with some of these devices capturing up to 4,000 images per day.

Lifelogging (unlike other forms of personal logging, such as diary keeping or quantified self analytics) therefore involves gathering data by observing the individual's activities as well as the environment around the individual. This typically means capturing the image of other people, many of whom will not have given the lifelogger permission to do so. In fact, most of the faces captured in a visual lifelog are of unknown bystanders. Naturally this creates a tension between data gathering on one hand and society's concerns about the impact on privacy of the individual. Consequently, wearable devices, especially Google Glass, are prohibited in some locations. However, looking forward, the benefits of lifelogging are likely to outweigh the long-term privacy risks [9], especially so if their lifelogging solutions can be developed with privacy-by-design employed. In many cases, privacy for these first generation lifelogs can be effectively protected by blurring faces. In this paper, we propose employing user privacy policies for regulating *dynamic views* over lifelog data. In this way, any person is free to choose which lifelogs their recognisable image can appear in, because the system assumes privacy as the default. Since we separate the *view* of the lifelog data from the actual stored data, then these policies can be updated in real-time so that an individual can retrospectively add or remove access rights to their identifiable image. We call this approach *real-time policy-driven negative face blurring* and this demonstration implements it in real-time for a Google Glass gathered lifelog of six months of curated lifelog data. Hence, this paper contributes the first version of a *privacy-aware lifelogging* solution, the first *Google Glass visual lifelogging* solution that we are aware of and introduces the concept of *policy-driven negative face blurring at access time* as a reasonable and flexible method of maintaining privacy for lifelogging, but also for any type of visual media.

2. RELATED WORK

Lifelogging represents a phenomenon whereby people can digitally record their own daily lives in varying amounts of detail, and for a variety of purposes. This means that lifelogging will often result in the capture of significant quantities of data about the lifelogger, but by necessity also, about the environment of the lifelogging, and the people/objects contained therein. Typically lifelogging has focused on utilising wearable cameras to capture the essence of the individual's activities in the real-world. The rationale behind lifelogging is that it can provide benefits to the user in terms of enhanced *reminiscence* or *reflection* about their past, the ability to search through past activities to answer specific questions (*retrieval*) or to *recollect* past experiences or even to remember *future intentions*. Many of the early uses of lifelogging have focused on deploying wearable cameras to provide memory assistance for memory impaired and conventional users, along with a new source of data for long-term user studies [6].

However, none of the previously developed lifelogging prototypes take a privacy-by-design [7] approach, which is a proposed framework for ubiquitous computing that integrates privacy and data protection as core considerations throughout the entire life cycle of a technology, from design, through use and eventual disposal. Privacy by design principles are based on seven foundations from [3]; proactive not reactive, privacy as the default configuration, privacy embedded into the design, privacy as additional (not reduced) functionality, end-to-end data security, visibility/transparency and respect for the privacy of the individual user. From these seven principles, we choose to make privacy the proactive default configuration, inherent in the design of the software, that separates the lifelogger from the data and which respects the privacy of unwilling subjects and bystanders.

We believe that the identifiability of an individuals face in lifelog imagery is the main factor currently in preserving or violating that individual's privacy. For this reason, the evaluation of our system is based on the effectiveness of face detection and face recognition in lifelogging images. Much previous research has been done on face detection and recognition, among the most widely used are Haar-like Feature-based Cascade Classifiers [11] for detection, and Eigenfaces [10], Fisherfaces [2] and Local Binary Patterns [1] for recognition.

3. IMPLEMENTATION

Our system is composed of two parts: a Google Glass glassware application and an independent online server (the lifelog), see Figure 1. The glassware acts as the data gathering tool and can either capture images automatically based on time triggers, or can capture images triggered by a user blink. The glassware uploads the image to the server post-capture and there the images are stored (along with metadata) in their original form. Faces in the images are identified (see below) and at query/request time, the current privacy policies are applied (using the privacy filter) before the data is shown to the lifelogger. The interaction interface is currently WWW-based.

Although the expectation is that any source of faces could be employed to train the system to identify recognisable faces (for example a social network photo list), in this implementation, the individual is required to provide sample face images to generate the policy profile for that user. A face is blurred if it is not recognized to be a known face from the policy store, hence the default configuration of this system is that a face is blurred by default, unless it is recognised as a known and allowed face.

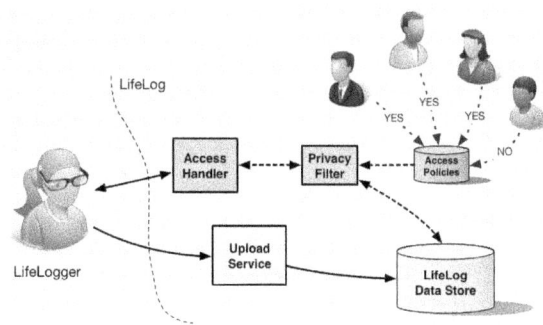

Figure 1: System Conceptual Diagram

3.1 Face detection and recognition

Haar-like Feature-based Cascade Classifiers are used in the face detection process[11]. To obtain Haar-like features, integral image is adopted to allow fast feature evaluation which can be extracted from an image with only a few operations per pixel. We incorporate three different face recognition techniques in this cascade:

1. **Eigenfaces**. Eigenfaces seek to find the principal components of the distribution of faces, or the eigenvectors of the covariance matrix of the set of face images [10]. The face space is defined by training on a set of face images and calculating the Eigenfaces from user's profile face photos.

2. **Fisherfaces**. The method is based on Fisher's Linear Discriminant and produces well separated classes in a low-dimensional subspace, even under severe condition like lighting and facial expressions [2]. The idea is same classes should cluster tightly together, while different classes are as far away as possible from each other in the lower-dimensional representation.

3. **Local Binary Patterns**. The method considers both shape and texture from face images. Local Binary Pattern histograms are extracted from small regions of face area and concatenated into a single, spatially enhanced feature histogram [1]. The recognition is performed based on a nearest neighbour classifier in the computed feature space as a dissimilarity measure.

Thresholds for each method are obtained by analysing the Euclidean distances of each face from other faces in the training dataset. These thresholds are necessary to distinguish friends' faces from bystanders and are optimised by cross-validation on the training dataset. The higher the value of the threshold the more likely bystanders' faces are to be predicted as friends. In our system, these three recognition methods are all employed and assigned the same weight for the final decision.

3.2 Lifelog Interface

From a HCI perspective Google Glass is at present somewhat under developed, offering users a limited view of, and minimal interaction with, any images that they have captured. Instead of implementing a card-based glassware viewing mechanism, we developed a WWW interface, as shown in Figure 2. The interface presents images captured by Glass to the user chronologically. It allows the user to view, download and delete their own images, add and remove nominated friends, as well as offering a simple breakdown of the number of images captured per day, month and year. At present, the friend/bystander relationship is reciprocal, meaning that the image of the lifelogger will not be subject to blurring in the lifelogs of any of their nominated friends.

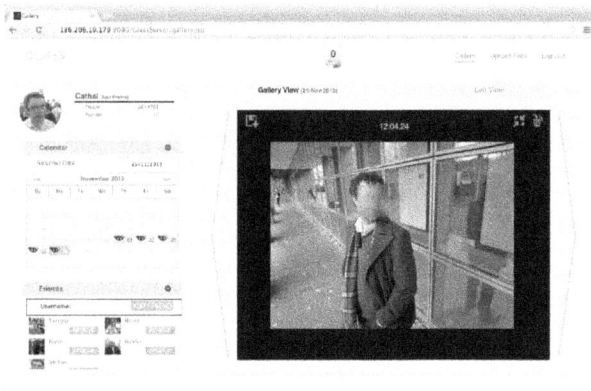

Figure 2: WWW Interface showing showing the blurred face of an unknown bystander.

4. DATA AND EXPERIMENT

Successful implementation of a user's privacy policy is dependant upon two factors, face detection and face recognition. To determine the effectiveness of our system, two evaluations were performed using 8,657 images collected from Google Glass by three users over 148 days.

For face detection, images containing faces, in which all faces were detected and images that contained no faces that were correctly identified as such, were considered a pass. Images containing faces in which any of the faces were not detected were considered a fail. Of the 8,657 images, the system produced 6,985 passes and 1,672 fails generating a pass face detection accuracy of 80.68%. Some faces fail to be detected because they are too small, heavily shadowed or are in some way occluded.

For the second part of our evaluation we concerned ourselves with implementing the privacy policy and blurring unknown faces (the negative face blurring). Taking the output of the face detection process, each detected face was extracted from the image and the number of faces that were correctly classified as friends, the number of false positives (i.e bystanders classified as friends) and false negatives (i.e. friends classified as bystanders) were identified. For this evaluation, 1,300 pictures with faces were randomly selected from the data set. Using the approach outlined above, 1,310 faces were detected. The false positive rate was 0.76% and the false negative rate was 29.01%. A total of 67.18% of the faces were correctly identified as bystanders.

5. CONCLUSION AND FUTURE WORK

In this paper, we presented a first implementation of a *privacy-aware lifelogging* solution and the first *Google Glass visual lifelogging* solution that actively blurs all faces except those

who explicitly allow their face to be logged (we call this negative face blurring). Since, the user is separated from their lifelog data, accessing the data is via the privacy policies, thereby helping to maintain privacy of all concerned and potentially protecting the lifelogger from unintended consequences of pervasive automatic capture. We have not explored in detail how the privacy policies are designed, rather we have assumed their presence in this work. Our future work will focus on extending the lifelogging tool to incorporate other sensors as well as detecting the relationship (and potential) between people.

6. REFERENCES

[1] T. Ahonen, A. Hadid, and M. Pietikäinen. Face recognition with local binary patterns. In *Computer vision-eccv 2004*, pages 469–481. Springer, 2004.

[2] P. N. Belhumeur, J. P. Hespanha, and D. Kriegman. Eigenfaces vs. fisherfaces: Recognition using class specific linear projection. *Pattern Analysis and Machine Intelligence, IEEE Transactions on*, 19(7):711–720, 1997.

[3] A. Cavoukian. Privacy by design. *Report of the Information & Privacy Commissioner Ontario, Canada*, 2012.

[4] J. Gemmell, G. Bell, and R. Lueder. Mylifebits: A personal database for everything. *Commun. ACM*, 49(1):88–95, Jan. 2006.

[5] C. Gurrin, A. F. Smeaton, D. Byrne, N. O'Hare, G. J. Jones, and N. O'Connor. An examination of a large visual lifelog. In *Information Retrieval Technology*, pages 537–542. Springer, 2008.

[6] C. Gurrin, A. F. Smeaton, and A. R. Doherty. Lifelogging: personal big data. *Foundations and Trends in Information Retrieval*, 8(1):1–125, 2014.

[7] M. Langheinrich. Privacy by design-principles of privacy-aware ubiquitous systems. In *Ubicomp 2001: Ubiquitous Computing*, pages 273–291. Springer, 2001.

[8] H. Lee, A. Smeaton, N. O'Connor, G. Jones, M. Blighe, D. Byrne, A. Doherty, and C. Gurrin. Constructing a sensecam visual diary as a media process. *Multimedia Systems*, 14(6):341–349, 2008.

[9] K. O'Hara, M. Tuffield, and N. Shadbolt. Lifelogging: Privacy and empowerment with memories for life. *Identity in the Information Society*, 1(1):155–172, 2008.

[10] M. A. Turk and A. P. Pentland. Face recognition using eigenfaces. In *Computer Vision and Pattern Recognition, 1991. Proceedings CVPR'91., IEEE Computer Society Conference on*, pages 586–591. IEEE, 1991.

[11] P. Viola and M. Jones. Rapid object detection using a boosted cascade of simple features. In *Computer Vision and Pattern Recognition, 2001. CVPR 2001. Proceedings of the 2001 IEEE Computer Society Conference on*, volume 1, pages I–511. IEEE, 2001.

7. ACKNOWLEDGEMENTS

This publication has emanated from research supported in part by research grants from Irish Research Council (IRCSET) under Grant Number GOIPG/2013/330 and Science Foundation Ireland (SFI) under Grant Number SFI/12/RC/2289.

TensorDB: In-Database Tensor Manipulation with Tensor-Relational Query Plans*

Mijung Kim
Arizona State University
Tempe, AZ 85287, USA
mijung.kim.1@asu.edu

K. Selçuk Candan
Arizona State University
Tempe, AZ 85287, USA
candan@asu.edu

ABSTRACT

Today's data management systems increasingly need to support both tensor-algebraic operations (for analysis) as well as relational-algebraic operations (for data manipulation and integration). Tensor decomposition techniques are commonly used for discovering underlying structures of multidimensional data sets. However, as the relevant data sets get large, existing in-memory schemes for tensor decomposition become increasingly ineffective and, instead, memory-independent solutions, such as in-database analytics, are necessitated. We introduce an in-database analytic system for efficient implementations of in-database tensor decompositions on chunk-based array data stores, so called, TensorDB. TensorDB includes *static* in-database tensor decomposition and *dynamic* in-database tensor decomposition operators. TensorDB extends an array database and leverages array operations for data manipulation and integration. TensorDB supports complex data processing plans where multiple relational algebraic and tensor algebraic operations are composed with each other.

Categories and Subject Descriptors

H.2.8 [**Database Management**]: Database Applications—*Data mining*

Keywords

Tensor Decomposition; In-Database Tensor Decomposition

1. INTRODUCTION

Multidimensional data have various representations. As well as the tensor model provides a natural representation in modeling multidimensional data, the availability of mathematical tools, such as tensor decomposition, that support multi-aspect analysis of multidimensional data promotes the use of tensors in many application domains including scientific data management, sensor data management, and social

---
*This work is partially funded by NSF grants 116394, "RanKloud: Data Partitioning and Resource Allocation Strategies for Scalable Multimedia and Social Media Analysis" and 1016921, "One Size Does Not Fit All: Empowering the User with User-Driven Integration"

CIKM'14, November 3–7, 2014, Shanghai, China.
ACM 978-1-4503-2598-1/14/11.
http://dx.doi.org/10.1145/2661829.2661842.

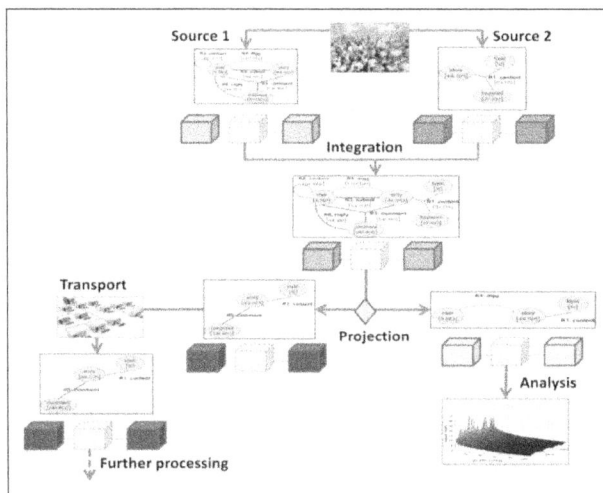

Figure 1: Sample lifecycle of data; this includes various operations, such as capture, integration, projection, decomposition, and data analysis

network data analysis. Relational model, on the other hand, enables semantic manipulation of data using relational operators, such as projection, selection, join, and set operators. Therefore, combining the tensor model and the relational model enables to support both data management and analysis operations, i.e., the relational algebraic operations support data manipulation and integration and the tensor algebraic operations support data analysis for the complete life cycle of data that involves consecutive steps of integration, manipulation, and data analysis (see Figure 1).

1.1 Tensors and Tensor Decomposition

Matrix data is often analyzed for its latent semantics and indexed for search using a matrix decomposition operation known as the singular value decomposition (SVD). This operation identifies a transformation which takes data, described in terms of an m dimensional vector space, and maps them into a vector space defined by $k \leq m$ orthogonal basis vectors (also known as latent semantics) each with a score denoting its contributions in the given data set. The more general analysis operation which applies to tensors with more than two modes is known as the *tensor decomposition*. CANDECOMP [4] and PARAFAC [6] decompositions (together known as the CP decomposition), for example, decompose a tensor into a sum of rank-1 tensors. Tucker decomposition [11] decomposes a given tensor into a core tensor multiplied by a matrix along each mode.

1.2 In-Memory Limitations of Tensor Decomposition Operations

To support a tensor model and tensor algorithms such as CP and Tucker decompositions for data analysis, MATLAB-based in-memory linear algebra operations are widely used. However, these implementations are limited with the amount of memory available to the MATLAB software. As the today's data sets get large, these in-memory based schemes for tensor decomposition become increasingly ineffective. Moreover tensor decomposition operations often result in large intermediary data that renders purely in-memory implementations of tensor-decomposition difficult. In-database tensor decomposition operation on disk-resident tensor data can be a solution to eliminate the challenge posed by the memory limitations.

2. TENSORDB

We introduce an in-database analytic system for efficient implementations of in-database tensor decompositions on chunk-based array data stores, so called, TensorDB.

TensorDB extends an open source software platform of data management and analytic system for array data, SciDB [1]. As an extension of SciDB, TensorDB shares the basic system architecture and the query languages of SciDB and performs all-in-one from the query interface to the query execution for tensor-relational operations.

TensorDB provides *static* and *dynamic* in-database tensor decomposition operators that address the constraints imposed by the main memory limitations when handling large and high-order tensor data.

TensorDB is based on a tensor-relational model (TRM) [7], which brings together relational algebraic operations (for data manipulation and integration) and tensor algebraic operations (for data analysis). Leveraging the SciDB engine and SciDB languages, TensorDB supports tensor-relational query plans of tensor decomposition operations, along with relational operations such as selection and join operations, which we will demonstrate.

Figure 2 illustrates the query processing workflow of TensorDB for tensor-relational query plans using tensor-algebraic and relational-algebraic operations.

2.1 Array Databases

The array model [1, 3] is a natural representation to store multidimensional data and facilitate multidimensional data analysis. How arrays are organized and stored depends largely on whether they are dense or sparse. Approaches to represent array based data can be broadly categorized into four types. (a) The first approach is to represent the array in the form of a table. (b) A second approach is to use blob type in a relational database as a storage layer for array data [3]. (c) Sparse matrices can also be represented using a graph-based abstraction [9]. (d) The last approach is to consider a native array model and an array-based storage scheme, such as a chunk-store, as in SciDB [1].

SciDB uses multidimensional arrays as its basic storage and processing unit. Arrays are partitioned into chunks and each chunk is processed in a parallel manner, whenever possible. SciDB also provides various chunk-based array manipulation operations, including linear algebra operators.

Most array databases provide limited built-in array operations and leave the responsibility of implementing complex operations through user-defined functions (UDF) and aggregates (UDA) [5] to the users. One critical limitation of

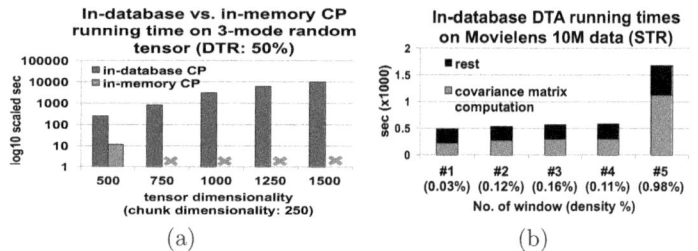

Figure 3: Running times of (a) in-database (vs. in-memory) CP decomposition on random dense tensors (DTR) with density 50% and (b) in-database DTA on sparse tensors (STR) of 5 windows of MovieLens 10M data

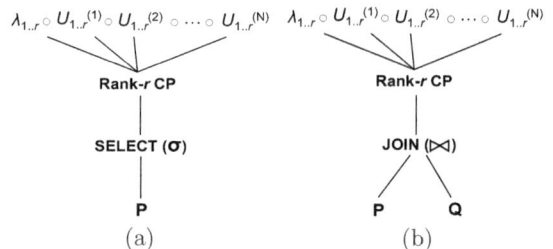

Figure 4: Tensor-relational query plans with (a) a selection operation of a tensor, $\mathcal{P}$ and (b) a join operation of two tensors, $\mathcal{P}$ and $\mathcal{Q}$, in which each operation is preceding a rank-r CP decomposition operation, respectively (r is the target rank)

UDF/UDA-based approaches is that the data should reside in the available memory [5] and this is not always the case in many tensor operations, such as tensor decomposition. This limitation necessitates in-database, chunk-based implementation of tensor decomposition operations.

2.2 TensorDB Operators

TensorDB deals with complex query plans where relational operations run along with tensor operations. SciDB supports array operations for data manipulation and integration and linear algebra operations. However it lacks the tensor-algebraic operations such as tensor decompositions. Therefore, as the main TensorDB operators, we build static and dynamic tensor decompositions.

For a static in-database tensor decomposition, we consider an alternating least squares (ALS) based implementation of CP decomposition [4, 6]. We provide chunk-based implementations of the various operations involved in the CP decomposition. Figure 3(a) shows sample running time results for CP on random tensors [8]. As expected, when the data fits into the memory, in-memory decomposition is faster than in-database operation; however, the proposed in-database decomposition is able to operate even in situations where the in-memory decomposition is infeasible.[1]

For a dynamic in-database tensor decomposition, we adapt the Dynamic Tensor Analysis (DTA) algorithm [10]. DTA incrementally maintains covariance matrices for each mode and computes factor matrices by taking the leading eigen-vectors of the covariance matrices. Figure 3(b) shows running time results of DTA for MovieLens rating data [2].

---

[1]Note that since in this experiment we focused on overcoming scalability issues imposed by memory, we did not consider pipelined execution plans. A disadvantage of this non-pipelined execution is the slowdown of in-database scheme compared against in-memory scheme we see in Figure 3(a).

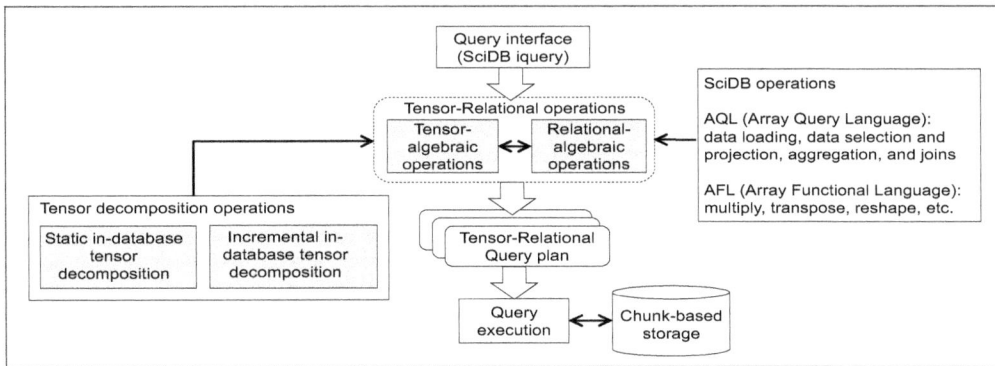

Figure 2: Query processing workflow of TensorDB for tensor-relational query plans using tensor-algebraic and relational-algebraic operations

2.3 Tensor-Relational Query Plans

TensorDB supports tensor-relational query plans needed for both data manipulation and integration, and data analysis. SciDB provides data manipulation operations such as `SELECT`, `subarray`, `slice`, etc. and data integration operations such as `JOIN`. For details of the SciDB operators, see the SciDB user guide [1]. TensorDB provides tensor decomposition operations for data analysis, e.g., `cp_als.py`, which is a python application for the CP decomposition.[2] Figure 4 shows examples for these query plans.

3. USER INTERACTION SCENARIOS

We describe a number of demonstration scenarios for tensor-relational query plans. We use tensors of different densities, different tensor representations: sparse tensor representation (shortly referred to as STR), where only non-zero entries are kept, and dense tensor representation (DTR), and different dimensionality and numbers of modes.

EXAMPLE 3.1. `slice` *and* `cp_als` *operations.*
- `iquery -nq "SELECT * into T_slice FROM slice(T, i, 1)"`
  - *Selects the 1st slice of mode* `i` *of a tensor* `T` *of size* $I_1 \times I_2 \times I_3 \times I_4$ *with chunk size* $J_1 \times J_2 \times J_3 \times J_4$ *and saves the result into* `T_slice`. `iquery` *is the SciDB query interface.*
- `cp_als.py T_slice` I_2, I_3, I_4 J_2, J_3, J_4 `rank`
  - *Runs* `cp_als` *on* `T_slice`.
  - *(Usage:* `cp_als.py` *<tensor_name> <tensor_size> <chunk_size> <target_rank>).*

EXAMPLE 3.2. `subarray` *and* `cp_als` *operations.*
- `iquery -nq "SELECT * into T_subarray FROM sub-array(T, 1, 1, 1,` I_1', I_2', I_3'`)"`
  - *Takes a sub-tensor of size* $I_1' \times I_2' \times I_3'$ *from a tensor* `T` *of size* $I_1 \times I_2 \times I_3$ *with chunk size* $J_1 \times J_2 \times J_3$ *and saves the result into* `T_subarray`.
- `cp_als.py T_subarray` I_1', I_2', I_3' J_1, J_2, J_3 `rank`
  - *Runs* `cp_als` *on* `T_subarray`.

EXAMPLE 3.3. `join` *and* `cp_als` *operations.*
- `iquery -nq "SELECT ratings.val * genre.val into ratings_genre FROM ratings JOIN genre ON ratings.movie_id = genre.movie_id"`
  - *Joins the two tensors,* `ratings` *of size* $I_1 \times I_2 \times I_3$ *with chunk size* $J_1 \times J_2 \times J_3$ *and* `genre` *of size* $I_1 \times I_4$ *with chunk size* $J_1 \times J_4$ *on the 1st mode of each tensor,* `movie_id` *and saves the result into* `ratings_genre`.

- `cp_als.py ratings_genre` I_1, I_2, I_3, I_4 J_1, J_2, J_3, J_4 `rank`
  - *Runs* `cp_als` *on* `ratings_genre`.

EXAMPLE 3.4. `dta` *operations.*
- `dta.py T1` I_1, I_2, I_3 J_1, J_2, J_3 r_1, r_2, r_3
  - *Takes a tensor* `T1` *of size* $I_1 \times I_2 \times I_3$ *with chunk size* $J_1 \times J_2 \times J_3$ *and decomposes the tensor with target ranks* $r_1 \times r_2 \times r_3$.
- `dta.py T2` I_1, I_2, I_3 J_1, J_2, J_3 r_1, r_2, r_3 `T1`
  - *Takes a tensor* `T2` *of size* $I_1 \times I_2 \times I_3$ *with chunk size* $J_1 \times J_2 \times J_3$ *and incrementally updates the tensor decomposition with target ranks* $r_1 \times r_2 \times r_3$ *of the old tensor* `T1` *with the new tensor* `T2`.

We also provide a video demonstration for these scenarios at one of the authors' home page.[3]

4. CONCLUSION

This demonstration introduces TensorDB, an in-database analytic system that supports both tensor-algebraic operations for data analysis and relational-algebraic operations for data manipulation and integration. Our demonstration includes in-database tensor decompositions of TensorDB along with relational operations for tensor-relational query plans.

5. REFERENCES

[1] http://www.scidb.org.
[2] Movielens dataset from grouplens research group. http://www.grouplens.org.
[3] Baumann et al. The multidimensional database system rasdaman. *SIGMOD*, 1998.
[4] J. Carroll and J.-J. Chang. Analysis of individual differences in multidimensional scaling via an n-way generalization of "eckart-young" decomposition. *Psychometrika*, 1970.
[5] Cohen et al. Mad skills: new analysis practices for big data. *Proc. VLDB Endow.*, 2(2):1481–1492, Aug. 2009.
[6] R. A. Harshman. Foundations of the PARAFAC procedure: Models and conditions for an "explanatory" multi-modal factor analysis. *UCLA Working Papers in Phonetics*, 16(1):84, 1970.
[7] M. Kim and K. S. Candan. Approximate tensor decomposition within a tensor-relational algebraic framework. *CIKM*, 2011.
[8] M. Kim and K. S. Candan. Efficient static and dynamic in-database tensor decompositions on chunk-based array stores. *CIKM*, 2014.
[9] Low et al. Distributed graphlab: a framework for machine learning and data mining in the cloud. *PVLDB* Apr. 2012.
[10] Sun et al. Incremental tensor analysis: Theory and applications. *ACM Trans. Knowl. Discov. Data*, 2(3):11:1–11:37, 2008.
[11] L. Tucker. Some mathematical notes on three-mode factor analysis. *Psychometrika*, 31(3):279–311, Sept. 1966.

[2] The source code and user guide of TensorDB are available at `https://github.com/mkim48/TensorDB`.

[3] `http://www.public.asu.edu/~candan/CIKM_demo_TensorDB.pptx`

TweetMogaz v2: Identifying News Stories in Social Media

Eslam Elsawy[1], Moamen Mokhtar[1], Walid Magdy[2]

[1]BadrIT inc., Alexandria, Egypt
{eslam.ashraf, moamen.mokhtar}@badrit.com
[2]Qatar Computing Research Institute, Qatar Foundation, Doha, Qatar
wmagdy@qf.org.qa

ABSTRACT

TweetMogaz is a news portal platform that generates news reports from social media content. It uses an adaptive information filtering technique for tracking tweets relevant to news topics, such as politics and sports in some regions. Relevant tweets for each topic are used to generate a comprehensive report about public reaction toward events happening. Showing a news report about an entire topic may be suboptimal for some users, since users prefer story-oriented presentation. In this demonstration, we present a technique for identifying stories within a stream of microblogs on a given topic. Detected tweets on a news story are used to generate a dynamic pseudo-article that gets its content updated in real-time based on trends on Twitter. Pseudo-article consists of a title, front-page image, set of tweets on the story, and links to external news articles. The platform is running live and tracks news on hot topics including Egyptian politics, Syrian conflict, and international sports.

Categories and Subject Descriptors

H.3.3 [**Information Search and Retrieval**]: Clustering, Information filtering

Keywords

TweetMogaz; Twitter; Story detection; Clustering; Arabic

1. INTRODUCTION

Interest in monitoring news from social media has increased in recent years. For example, Twitter was shown to be one of the fastest methods for spreading news [3]. Different methods and applications were developed for extracting useful information about events happening and discussions on news from social media [4, 5, 6, 8, 9]. TweetMogaz [6] is one of these platforms that offers users a news portal entirely generated from social media to follow ongoing news with no bias to a given opinion. The platform uses an adaptive method [8] for tracking tweets relevant to events hap-

CIKM'14, Nov 03-07 2014, Shanghai, China
ACM 978-1-4503-2598-1/14/11.
http://dx.doi.org/10.1145/2661829.2661843 .

pening in hot regions such as Syria and Egypt, and popular domains such as sports. It generates a comprehensive report on the top shared content on Twitter related to a given topic including most popular tweets, images, videos, and links.

In this demonstration, we present the second version of TweetMogaz [6], which applies a story identification approach for detecting individual stories discussed on Twitter within each topic to be displayed to users as a set of *pseudo-articles* instead of just one comprehensive report. Displaying news in this form allows users to maintain the experience of standard news websites, but with the advantage of unbiased and rich social-generated content. A hierarchical clustering algorithm is used to identify hot stories that have enough content on Twitter. Each cluster of tweets is used to generate a real-time pseudo-articles containing most popular tweets as the content, top shared video/image as the article front image, links in tweets as the links to external related articles, and an automatically generated title as news headline. Our story identification algorithm is applied each 15 minutes to either detect new stories or update existing ones with emerging new content. We also propose a mechanism to prevent the detection of duplicate stories.

The contributions in this demonstration can be listed as follows: 1) An online real-time story identification service is proposed; 2) A duplicate events detection mechanism is introduced to deliver only distinct events to users; 3) A novel method is presented for displaying tweets relevant to a news story in the form of automatically generated pseudo-article.

2. RELATED WORK

A related work to our story identification problem is event detection [4, 11]. Two main approaches have been studied for event detection: *document-pivot* and *feature-pivot*. The former cluster documents into clusters, each is related to a specific event and then tries to detect features related to the event from the cluster. The latter extracts high frequency terms in documents stream and groups them to events. We mainly focus on feature-pivot approach, since it fits our task better, where documents are of short length.

Weng et al. proposed a system named EDCoW [11], which builds wavelet signals for terms. Then it computes the cross correlation between signals to cluster associated signals together as events. Although this approach showed effectiveness and could be applied for our story identification task, it requires high computational cost, which may be not efficient for a real time application. Li et al. proposed a system named Twevent [4]. The system detects burst phrases based on frequencies. It performs KNN clustering to pro-

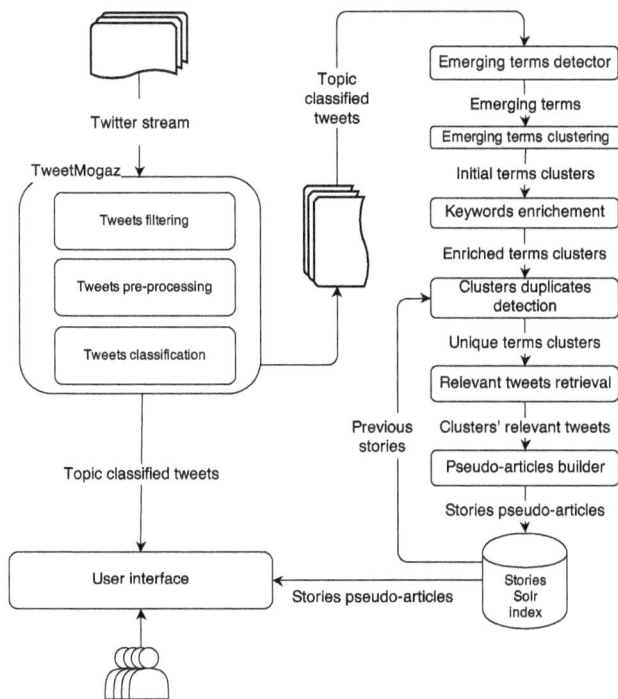

Figure 1: News stories detection architecture

duce disjoint clusters. This approach may not fit our application, where fuzzy clustering is required since terms in different clusters can overlap. Li et.al. [5] proposed an event detection system dedicated for Crime and Disaster related Events (CDE). They crawled Twitter by searching for specific keywords describing crimes and disasters. Tweets are then classified to CDE and non-CDE. Their algorithm depends mainly on spatial and temporal features of tweets.

3. SYSTEM ARCHITECTURE

The full system architecture of TweetMogaz v2 is shown in Figure 1. The left part of the architecture shows the main components of TweetMogaz v1, which is responsible for retrieving relevant tweets to the tracked news topics [6, 8]. The right part represents our main contribution to the old version, which is the story identification system.

3.1 TweetMogaz v1

As introduced earlier, TweetMogaz [6] is a platform for tweets filtering and search [7]. "Mogaz" (موجز) means in Arabic "summary" or "digest", which means that the platform presents a digest of tweets relevant to certain topics. An input of a predefined set of keywords representing a broad topic (e.g. *Syrian conflict*) is prepared, and an adaptive information filtering technique is used to identify relevant tweets from a stream of tweets [8]. Identified tweets are used to generate a comprehensive report (Mogaz) about what is discussed on the topic on Twitter. The platform applies state-of-the-art normalization techniques for Arabic social text [1, 2], and uses Solr [1] for indexing the full stream of tweets to enable effective and efficient search.

---
[1] http://lucene.apache.org/solr/

3.2 Story Identification System

Several components are integrated to produce an effective and efficient system for identifying emerging stories within a stream of tweets on a given topic. For a set of relevant tweets to topic x in a time-window w, denoted as $T_x(w)$, sets of tweets within $T_x(w)$ representing individual news stories are identified through the following steps:

1. Detecting emerging terms: Most frequent terms, after applying stopwords removal and stemming, appearing in $T_x(w)$ are extracted. This set of terms represents the main discussed stories in w and is referred to as $E_x(w)$.

2. Clustering emerging terms: Emerging terms $E_x(w)$ are clustered to group related terms representing a certain story together. Term co-occurrence probability is used as the distance measure for applying clustering using a fuzzy agglomerative hierarchical clustering technique [10]. For each term t_i in $E_x(w)$, distance to other terms are calculated as shown in equation 1. If mutual $distance(t_i, t_j)$ and $distance(t_j, t_i)$ are less than a given threshold (selected as 0.6), t_j is added to the same cluster with t_i. Remaining terms in $E_x(w)$ are compared to all terms of the cluster and a term gets added if distance between any of the cluster terms and this term is less than the threshold. This leads to the presence of fuzzy clusters, where a term can exist in multiple clusters. Any cluster contains less than three terms is discarded. Also clusters are limited to a number of 6 terms at most, where the closest 6 terms are kept and the remaining are discarded from the cluster. This clustering method does not require setting a predefined number of clusters, where the number of clusters depends on the selected distance threshold.

$$distance(t_i, t_j) = 1 - P(t_j | t_i) = 1 - \frac{count(t_i, t_j)}{count(t_i)} \quad (1)$$

3. Enriching small clusters by additional keywords: To improve the representation of clusters with less than 6 terms, we apply query expansion to enrich the cluster with additional keywords. We create an *AND* Boolean query with all keywords in the cluster to search the tweets set $T_x(w)$. Top terms achieving the highest TFIDF are selected from the result tweets and then added to the cluster making it containing a total of 6 terms. TFIDF is calculated as shown in equation 2.

$$TFIDF(t_i) = tf_{search}(t_i) \cdot log(\frac{N}{df(t_i)}) \quad (2)$$

where, $tf_{search}(t_i)$ is the term frequency of term t_i in the search results of the Boolean query. $df(t_i)$ and N are the number of tweets containing the term t_i and the total number of tweets in $T_x(w)$ respectively.

4. Detecting clusters that can lead to duplicate stories: Performing story identification periodically allows the detection of recent stories. However, sometimes duplicate stories are detected. To overcome this problem we apply the following steps: (1) Keywords of each cluster are used to search $T_x(w)$ with a BM25 retrieval model, and top 100 results are retrieved. (2) Vector representation of terms is constructed for each cluster using the terms appearing in results list more than 10 times. (3) Cosine similarity is computed between vectors of each two clusters, and if similarity is more than 0.5, clusters are merged into one. This threshold was selected based on experimenting different values.

Figure 2: Sample of pseudo-article (translated from Arabic to English)

The output from previous steps produces set of clusters that potentially map to different news stories. Terms in each cluster are then used to search the Solr index for relevant tweets in the past 48 hours. All tweets achieving a retrieval score higher than a predefined threshold are considered for the generation of the pseudo-article as described later.

The process of clustering is applied frequently to cope with emerging stories happening in news. Cluster duplication test is applied between new and old clusters to prevent the generation of duplicate pseudo-articles. Detected duplicate clusters with old ones, are used to update the content of the old article while maintaining the chronological order of the identified stories.

3.3 Pseudo-Articles Generation

The input of this component is a set of tweets relevant to a potential news story, and the objective is to generate an article-like document that can show users the news story and how people think about it. The typical components of an article are: a title, a front image, article body, and possibly links to related content. We use the relevant tweets to each cluster to generate these components as follows:

• **Article body:** We display tweets relevant to the story as the body. Tweets are sorted by normalized retweet count, which is the number of retweets divided by the age of the tweet in minutes. This ensures displaying the most popular and recent tweets on the top. A "see more" button is offered to allow users to read all retrieved tweets on the story.

• **Front image:** We have three options for selecting a front image to the article according to availability: 1) Top tweet with an image is used. 2) Top tweet with link to YouTube video is used by taking the video thumbnail as the front image. 3) Top tweet with link to a news article is used by extracting the front image of the article.

• **Links to related articles:** This is simply achieved by extracting all links to news articles embedded in relevant tweets and sorting them by the number of occurrences in the tweets. This offers the reader external content to read driven by the trend on Twitter.

• **Title of the article:** The title of the pseudo-article is generated using the top tweet text after pruning the name mentions and links from its text. If top tweet is linking to an external news article, then the title of the article is used, since it is expected to have well-formed sentence than normal tweets that tend to use colloquial language.

Figure 2 shows an example of a generated pseudo-article. As shown the article is talking about a story happened in the Egyptian politics topic. Some of the displayed tweets are

supporting and others are opposing the news. This feature is unique for TweetMogaz over standard news websites.

4. SYSTEM PERFORMANCE

The performance of our system depends a lot on the parameters and thresholds we use in our approach. These parameters can tune the performance of our system to be recall-based vs. precision-based. Since our platform is a public live service, we decided to select thresholds that would achieve high precision, as this is more acceptable by users. Based on manual evaluation of our platform over few months, the number of identified stories varies according to the events happening related to the topic on a given date. On average 10 stories per topic per day are identified. Around 80% of these stories map clearly to real-life events, while 20% may be seen as general tweets on the topic that do not relate to a specific story. Our duplicate stories detection approach proved to be effective as 95% of the events were unique.

5. DEMONSTRATION

TweetMogaz is a live news portal of tweets accessible for public at http://www.tweetmogaz.com. It collects Arabic tweets and generates comprehensive reports about news happening in different Arabic regions and international sports. A stream of up to 12 million Arabic tweets are collected daily, and processing is performed online for filtering information to different topics, generating comprehensive reports to each topic, and identifying hot stories in each one. The website is entirely in Arabic, since it is directed to the Arabic region. Information on the website is automatically updated every 15 minutes to cope with the trends on Twitter.

6. REFERENCES

[1] K. Darwish and W. Magdy. Arabic information retrieval. *Foundations and Trends® in Information Retrieval*, 7(4), 2014.

[2] K. Darwish, W. Magdy, and A. Mourad. Language processing for arabic microblog retrieval. In *CIKM*, 2012.

[3] H. Kwak, C. Lee, H. Park, and S. Moon. What is twitter, a social network or a news media? In *WWW*, 2010.

[4] C. Li, A. Sun, and A. Datta. Twevent: Segment-based event detection from tweets. In *CIKM*, 2012.

[5] R. Li, K. H. Lei, R. Khadiwala, and K.-C. Chang. Tedas: A twitter-based event detection and analysis system. In *ICDE*, 2012.

[6] W. Magdy. Tweetmogaz: a news portal of tweets. In *SIGIR*, 2013.

[7] W. Magdy, A. Ali, and K. Darwish. A summarization tool for time-sensitive social media. In *CIKM*, 2012.

[8] W. Magdy and T. Elsayed. Adaptive method for following dynamic topics on twitter. In *ICWSM*, 2014.

[9] T. Sakaki, M. Okazaki, and Y. Matsuo. Earthquake shakes twitter users: real-time event detection by social sensors. In *WWW*, 2010.

[10] R. Sibson. Slink: an optimally efficient algorithm for the single-link cluster method. *The Computer Journal*, 16(1), 1973.

[11] J. Weng and B.-S. Lee. Event detection in twitter. In *ICWSM*, 2011.

TWinChat: A Twitter and Web User Interactive Chat System

Yuanyuan Wang
Kyoto Sangyo University
603-8555 Japan
yuanw@cc.kyoto-su.ac.jp

Gouki Yasui
Kyoto Sangyo University
603-8555 Japan
i1458085@cse.kyoto-su.ac.jp

Yuji Hosokawa
Kyoto Sangyo University
603-8555 Japan
i1358103@cc.kyoto-su.ac.jp

Yukiko Kawai
Kyoto Sangyo University
603-8555 Japan
kawai@cc.kyoto-su.ac.jp

Toyokazu Akiyama
Kyoto Sangyo University
603-8555 Japan
akiyama@cse.kyoto-su.ac.jp

Kazutoshi Sumiya
University of Hyogo
670-0092 Japan
sumiya@shse.u-hyogo.ac.jp

ABSTRACT

This paper presents *TWinChat*, a Twitter and Web user interactive chat system to support simultaneous communication between microbloggers and Web users in real time through both the contents of microblogs and Web pages. *TWinChat* provides a question answering interface attached to Web pages, which allows Web users to chat with Twitter users in real time while presenting tweets that are associated with Web pages, i.e., simultaneous cross-media communication. In order to map heterogeneous media, the system extracts relationship between tweets and Web pages by generating queries based on location names. Thus, our system can effectively present messages from Web users to help Twitter users immediately obtain useful information or knowledge, and it also can effectively present tweets from the Twitter users to help the Web users easily grasp the current situation in real time.

Categories and Subject Descriptors

H.3.4 [**Systems and Software**]: Question-answering (fact retrieval) systems; H.3.5 [**Online Information Services**]: Web-based services

Keywords

location-based microblogs; cross-media user communication

1. INTRODUCTION

In recent years, microblogging services such as Twitter[1], Tumblr[2], and Plurk[3], are now one of the most frequently used tools for online communication. For instance, Twitter users can broadcast and share information about their activities, opinions, and statuses

---

[1] https://twitter.com

[2] https://www.tumblr.com/

[3] http://www.plurk.com/top/

CIKM '14 Nov 03-07 2014, Shanghai, China
ACM 978-1-4503-2598-1/14/11.
http://dx.doi.org/10.1145/2661829.2661844.

in short messages (tweets), up to 140 characters long, using smartphones at anytime and anywhere. Despite the useful information on Twitter, there still exists a lack of Twitter users' requirements. That is, tweet senders are difficult to obtain useful information (e.g., bus timetables, sightseeing maps, etc.) about their current location, since they are often posted on Web pages, the tweet senders will have to access each Web page using smartphones. Meanwhile, Twitter users can gain information about current scenarios from tweet senders; however, Web users cannot simultaneously obtain this information through tweets while they browse Web pages. Furthermore, Twitter supports only limited communication between its users (i.e., followees and followers). Web users cannot access the most recent information from Web pages of popular places (e.g., tourist spots, shopping centers, etc.) because the Web pages are not updated in real time. Therefore, it is important to focus on associating Twitter feed and Web pages to facilitate simultaneous communication for Twitter and Web users.

Although several techniques on social communication have been studied [4, 6, 3], these studies have focused on content-based communication between users who browse the similar Web pages, they do not solve the mentioned issues without microblogging. We have proposed *TWinChat*, a novel simultaneous commutation system between Twitter users and Web users in real time through both the contents of tweets and Web pages. To achieve this, we first acquired geo-tagged tweets based on content analysis and region selection. Therefore, our method can detect tweets if they are related to, or nearby, a target location, even though that they do not include the location names, or it can also detect tweets from Twitter users who are not in the target location. Furthermore, the proposed method can filter out tweets from the target location for which the content is not related to the target location. The system then maps the acquired tweets and Web pages by generating queries based on location names is explained in Section 3. As depicted in Figure 1, *TWinChat* has two features: 1) streaming tweets are associated with each Web page that are presented to Web users based on the common locations; 2) a chat box is attached to each Web page so that Web users can communicate with the Twitter users who follow an account of our system in real time.

2. SYSTEM OVERVIEW

To use *TWinChat*, which is on the basis of existing Web services, Twitter users first required to follow an account[4] of our system, as

---

[4] https://Twitter.com/@RtQAService

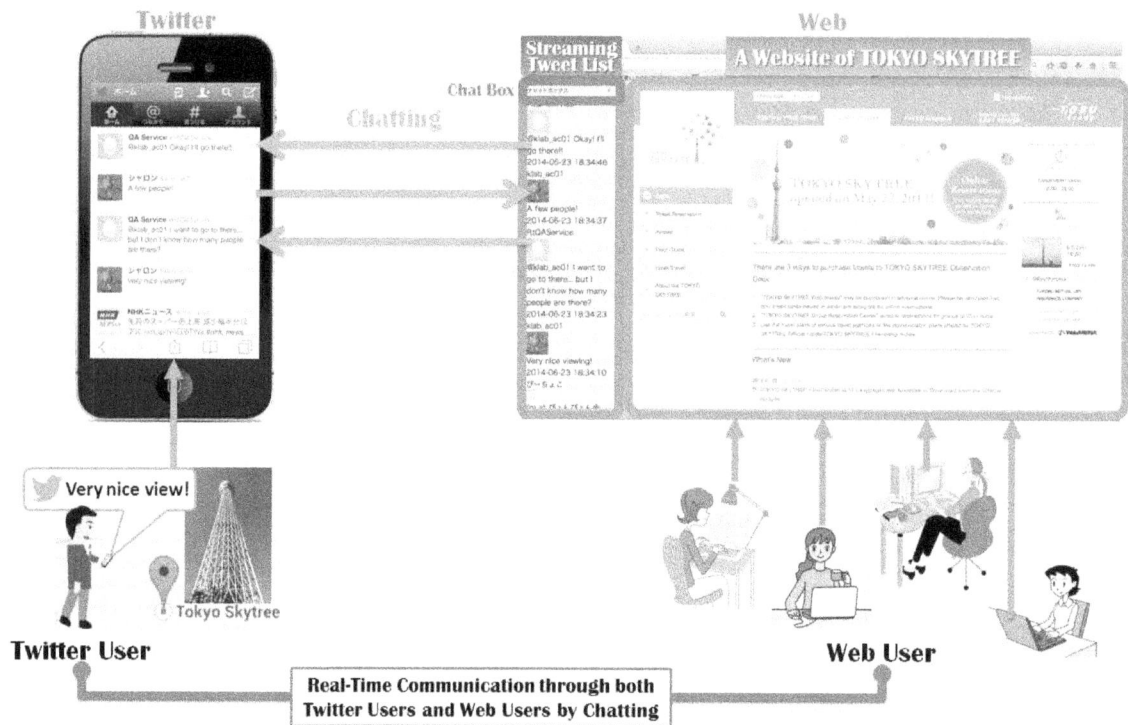

Figure 1: System snapshot of *TWinChat*

followers of our service, and Web users first required to simply install a toolbar (a Firefox add-on). Once a Web user browses a Web page, the system records the information into a server database, which is used for mapping tweets from Twitter users and the Web page, and he can chat with the Twitter users and other Web users. In our system, anonymous of all messages (tweets) can be maintained through a server.

The flow of *TWinChat* is described as follows:

1. A Web user selects a Web page to browse, the system then returns a streaming tweet list, in which tweets from Twitter users with respect to the Web page are presented in the Web browser in real time.

2. When the Web user submits a message in the chat box, the system presents the message in the streaming tweet list, all other users who browse the same Web page, or the Twitter users whose tweets are presented in the streaming tweet list, can receive the message.

3. When the Twitter user replies the message of the Web user through Twitter service and the server of the system; the system presents the reply that are related to the Web page in the streaming tweet list in real time.

An example is shown in Figure 1, which depicts a Web user browsing an official Website of Tokyo Skytree in the Web browser of our system. Streaming tweets, e.g., "Very nice view!" located in the Tokyo Skytree, are associated with the Web page by generating a query based on a common location name, "Tokyo Skytree," even though the tweets do not include the location name. This allows the Web user to gain insight into the congestion level or gain impressions of the Tokyo Skytree from the presented tweets in real time. On the other hand, this allows the Twitter user to obtain useful information or knowledge such as observation deck or tallest tower

rank of the Tokyo Skytree from the Web users by chatting through our system.

3. MAPPING FUNCTION

3.1 Acquisition of Streaming Tweets

A conventional method based on a content analysis of tweets and hashtag search [5], it can detect the tweets of Twitter users who are not in the locations in the real world. Also, tweets can be acquired by identifying the location information from geo-tagged tweets [2]. However, many detected tweets are still not related to the locations of them, it is difficult to report the current situation from the detect tweets. Therefore, we first obtain geo-tagged tweets except duplicates from a specified region by using Streaming APIs (left part of Figure 2), and we analyze the content of the tweets focusing on nouns by a morphological analysis. The specified region is determined by a northeast point and a southwest point, then, we can obtain streaming tweets in a rectangular region surrounding these two points. Next, we detect location names within a radius d of a region by using Google Places API v3[5], from the latitude and longitude information of the obtained streaming tweets, and we empirically set $d = 5$m by considering the movement of Twitter users. Then, our server database manages {Twitter user ID, icon URL, latitude, longitude, location name, tweet, word set, acquisition time} in a certain time (central part of Figure 2).

3.2 Mapping of Tweets and Web Pages

For selecting tweets related to the detected location names, we extract high frequency words from the tweets as feature terms of the locations. Then, we selected the tweets that contain many feature

---

[5]https://developers.google.com/place

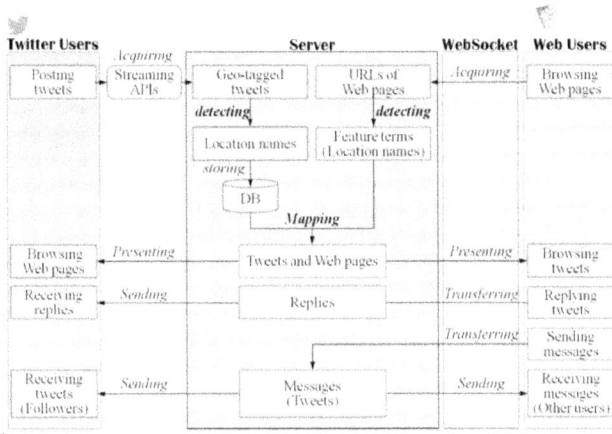

Figure 2: System configuration diagram

terms. For this, we obtain a total amount n of tweets in a certain time within a radius d of a region based on a given location of the acquired tweet t. The average of the frequency of each word i that appears in t is then calculated by the following equation:

$$\sum_{i=1}^{q} \frac{\#\text{tweets with } i}{n} \times \frac{1}{q} \tag{1}$$

Here, q denotes the total number of words that appear in tweet t. If a value of Eq. (1) is more than the empirical threshold value, t related to the location of it is selected.

To extract location names from Web pages, we acquire URLs of the Web pages that Web users are browsing (right part of Figure 2). Then, we extract high frequency words from snippets of the acquired URLs as feature terms of the Web pages and detect location names of the Web pages by using a morphological analyzer.

Based on the above, when Twitter users post tweets and a Web user browses a Web page, the system can obtain and present the tweets that are relevant based on a common location name from the Web page and the tweets. In this case, the server database of the system stores the obtained tweets, the obtained Web pages, and the detected common location names (central part of Figure 2).

4. COMMUNICATION FUNCTION

4.1 Server Side

The server side is built using Apache httpd 2.4, Java, PHP 5.5. The servlet can perform parallel processing for multiple requests, since it makes a "user thread" for each request. When the user thread receives the requests from the clients, it parses them, performs the corresponding action, returns information to the requesting user, and sends information to other users. The browsing, acquiring, and communication logs are stored in the server database using SQLite 3.8.5.

4.2 Client Side

The client side is implemented as a toolbar (browsing plug-in). The question answering interface is programmed using XUL (extensible user interface language) and the development is programmed using JavaScript. A Twitter user is connected to the server using Twitter service, and a Web user is connected to the server using an asynchronous communication program running in a WebSocket[6].

---

[6]http://gihyo.jp/dev/feature/01/websocket/0001

5. DEMONSTRATION

With *TWinChat*, Twitter users and Web users can communication with each other in real time by chatting (see Figure 1), and a demonstration video is shown in [1]. *TWinChat* could present tweets from the Twitter users and messages from the Web users within 2 seconds, respectively; and the Web users could reply the tweets to the Twitter users within 3 seconds.

5.1 Tweet Presentation into a Web Page

Web users can browse a Web page and simultaneously obtain a list of streaming tweets that with respect to the Web page in real time. The server database of our system stores the acquired tweets, the most recently viewed Web pages, and the detected common location names from them.

Since *TWinChat* presents tweets into a Web page that Web users are browsing, the Web users can gain the current situation in real time, not only through the presented tweets on the Web page but also through Twitter users of them.

5.2 Real-Time Cross-Media Communication

Twitter users and Web users can chat with each other in real time. *TWinChat* allows the Web users to send messages in the chat box to the Twitter users of the presented tweets or other Web users who browse the same Web page. If the Web user has a question about the current situation while browsing a Web page, he can immediately ask the Twitter users by entering the question in the chat box. The Twitter users, who follow the account of *TWinChat*, can receive the question and reply it to the Web user through Twitter service. The replies from the Twitter users can be simultaneously presented on Twitter and streaming tweet list of our system.

Meanwhile, if the Twitter user has a question about something on the Web page, he can immediately ask the Web users by posting the question on Twitter. The Web users can receive the question and send messages as tweets, reply to the Twitter user through the chat box. The messages from the Web users can be simultaneously presented on streaming tweet list of our system and Twitter.

6. ACKNOWLEDGMENTS

This work was partially supported by SCOPE (the Ministry of Internal Affairs and Communications of Japan), and a Grant-in-Aid for Scientific Research (B)(2) 26280042 (the Ministry of Education, Culture, Sports, Science, and Technology of Japan).

7. REFERENCES

[1] Demostration Video Page of Developed TWinChat. http://klab.kyoto-su.ac.jp/ȳasui/TWINChat.html.

[2] G. Ference, M. Ye, and W.-C. Lee. Location recommendation for out-of-town users in location-based social networks. In *Proc. of CIKM 2013*, pages 721–726, 2013.

[3] S. Fragoso, R. R. Rebs, and D. L. Barth. Interface affordances and social practices in online communication systems. In *Proc. of AVI 2012*, pages 50–57, 2012.

[4] Y. Shiraishi, J. Zhang, Y. Kawai, and T. Akiyama. Simultaneous realization of page-centric communication and search. In *Proc. of CIKM 2012*, pages 2719–2721, 2012.

[5] S. Tajima and T. Ushiama. A method for composing ad-hoc following networks on twitter for sharing information among event participants. *Journal of ADADA*, 17(4):119–124, 2013.

[6] B. Wang, C. Wang, J. Bu, C. Chen, W. V. Zhang, D. Cai, and X. He. Whom to mention: Expand the diffusion of tweets by @ recommendation on micro-blogging systems. In *Proc. of WWW 2013*, pages 1331–1340, 2013.

VFDS: An Application to Generate Fast Sample Databases

Teodora Sandra Buda #1, Thomas Cerqueus #2, John Murphy #3, Morten Kristiansen *4

#Lero, PEL, School of Computer Science and Informatics, University College Dublin
*IBM Collaboration Solutions, IBM Software Group, Dublin, Ireland
1 teodora.buda@ucdconnect.ie, 2 thomas.cerqueus@ucd.ie, 3 j.murphy@ucd.ie
4 morten_kristiansen@ie.ibm.com

ABSTRACT

Large amounts of data often require expensive and time-consuming analysis. Therefore, highly scalable and efficient techniques are necessary to process, analyze and discover useful information. Database sampling has proven to be a powerful method to surpass these limitations. Using only a sample of the original large database brings the benefit of obtaining useful information faster, at the potential expense of lower accuracy. In this paper, we demonstrate VFDS, a novel fast database sampling system that maintains the referential integrity of the data. The system is developed over the open-source database management system, MySQL. We present various scenarios to demonstrate the effectiveness of VFDS in approximate query answering, sample size, and execution time, on both real and synthetic databases.

Categories and Subject Descriptors

H.2 [**Database Management**]: Miscellaneous

Keywords

Database Sampling, Random, Relational Database.

1. INTRODUCTION

Nowadays, data is growing at an exponential rate and it becomes a difficult challenge not only to store large volumes of data, but most importantly to analyze it. For this purpose, techniques are constantly improved, and optimal solutions are being sought in order to process big volumes of data. However, database sampling applied on the existing original database provides a useful balance between the cost of the analysis to be performed on the original data, and the accuracy of the results determined.

Database sampling has proven to be a useful technique, starting with Olken's major contribution [9], and currently being used in a wide range of application areas in computer science (e.g. data mining [7], software testing [11]). Several closely related sampling techniques are described below:

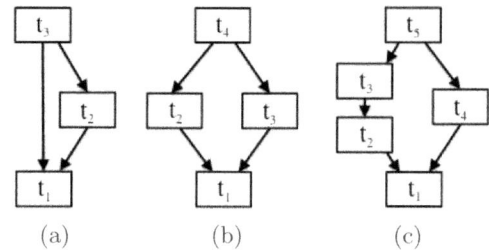

Figure 1: Diamond patterns.

General methods. Several methods for general purposes have been proposed in academia [2, 5]. Olken's major contribution to random sampling by randomly selecting tuples from each table from the original database is one of them [9]. Bisbal's sampling technique extends table-level sampling and targets relational databases, while preserving the integrity constraints of the original database [2]. However, current relational database sampling practices, that preserve the integrity of the data, are computationally costly [1, 6].

Software testing. There is a vast amount of research that propose to utilize the operational data available for testing the core functionality of the system under test [11, 13]. Such methods include studying the data characteristics and trying to reproduce them in the testing environment [12], or using random or simple constraint-based techniques to select the data to be included in the resulting database, as the production environment is generally very large [10].

Data mining. Single-table database sampling is a popular technique in the data mining community [8]. However, most of today's structured databases are composed of multiple tables. Recent work in the data mining community avoided this shortcoming [7]. The approaches devised in this community are generally oriented towards the data mining algorithm used on the sample data [4].

Approximate query answering. *Join Synopses* (JS) [1] represents a technique that aims to provide fast approximate query answers for queries that contain joins over multiple tables. Based on JS, the authors of [6] propose the *Linked Bernoulli Synopses* (LBS) sampling method that aims to improve the query answering accuracy of the sample. We compare our proposed system against the two methods in [3].

In this paper, we propose to demonstrate VFDS [3], a novel automated system that generates a random sample database, given an original **relational** database and a sampling rate. Its objective is to generate fast the sample database, while preserving the referential integrity intact. Its novelty

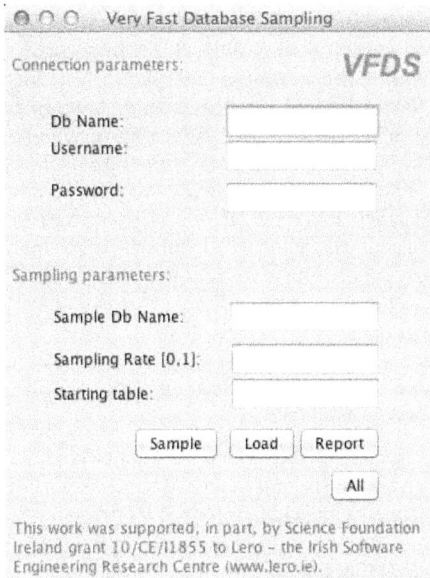

Figure 2: The VFDS interface.

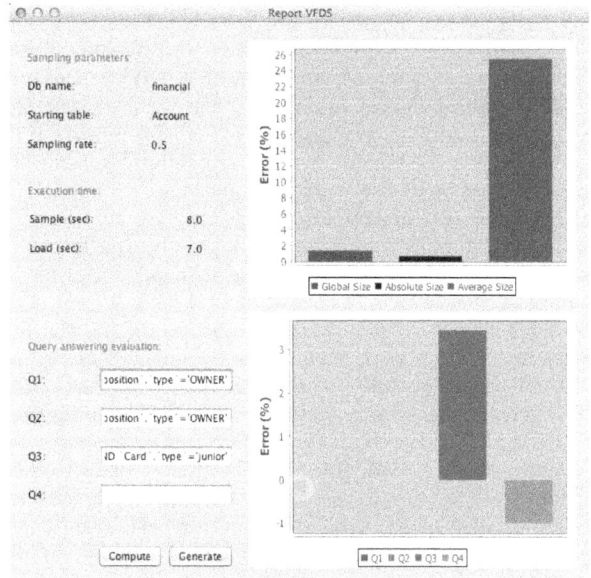

Figure 3: A VFDS sample report.

stands in the method for generating at high speed the sample, and in the way it handles diamond patterns, exemplified in Figure 1. Diamond patterns represent a difficult challenge for the sampling process due to potential space overhead. For instance, in Figure 1(c), populating the summit (i.e. the diamond's root), t_5, from a single child, t_3, will cause revisiting t_5 after populating its other child t_4 to add missing references. VFDS automatically handles diamond patterns such that the space overhead is minimum. The system is a generic one and can be applied to any relational database, regardless of it containing a diamond pattern. VFDS performs between 300 and 1000 times faster than the compared techniques [3]. The high performance of the method makes VFDS a suitable candidate for real-time systems that require to quickly analyze a database. With our demonstration, we intend to give an insight of the system and show its effectiveness in real-time, on both synthetic and real databases, from the following perspectives: (1) execution time, (2) sample size, and (3) approximate query answering.

2. BACKGROUND

The system proposed implemented the automated random sampling method VFDS [3]. Its objective is to maintain the referential integrity of the sampled data, while speeding up the sampling process. The method receives as input an original relational database O and a sampling rate α. It produces the sample database in a single pass over O, as follows:

1. Selecting a starting table $t_\star$: The method begins with the detection of $t_\star$. The starting table has a high impact on the sampling process, as only its associated tuples (i.e. referencing and referenced) are further sampled. Thus, $t_\star$ is selected as the table with the maximum number of related tuples (i.e. the number of tuples of $t_\star$ itself together with the number of distinct associated tuples).

2. Sampling tuples of $t_\star$: The method randomly selects a percentage of the tuples of $t_\star$ from the original database.

3. Sampling recursively tuples of $t_\star$'s referencing and referenced tables: The method propagates the population of the sample database using the hierarchy of children and parents. This continues until all the tables have been visited.

Experiments in [3] show that selecting the starting table with the most number of related tuples determines the lowest errors in terms of sample size and approximate query answering. [3] also presents the algorithm for selecting the starting table and for populating the sample database. In the case of diamond patterns, certain constraints are applied based on the table type (e.g. summit) in order to minimize the space overhead. For instance, one condition is that when the base of the diamond has already been visited, the summit is only populated once all its children are visited.

3. VFDS SYSTEM

In this section, we describe the features provided by the VFDS system. Before the sampling process occurs, the user should provide only the basic configuration inputs to the system. After the sampling process finishes and the data is loaded in the resulting database, the system produces a report with its performance in terms of execution time, database sample size, and approximate query answering. The interface of the system is presented in Figure 2. The user can choose between the following options: (i) *Sample*: runs the sampling process which creates the sample data files, (ii) *Load*: loads the files containing the sample data in the actual sample database, (iii) *Report*: creates a report that measures the execution time and evaluates the accuracy of the sample database in terms of expected size, and approximate query answering, and (iv) *All*: all of the previous actions. The VFDS system[1] was developed using Java 1.6, and applied on MySQL 5.5.35 Community Server.

Configuration The user should provide the following parameters to VFDS: (1) connection parameters, and (2) sam-

---

[1]https://github.com/tbuda/VFDS

pling parameters. These are illustrated in Figure 2. The following inputs are required by the system: (i) the DBMS credentials (i.e. username and password), (ii) the name of the database to be sampled, and (iii) the sample rate when running the sampling process or creating the report. The system extracts the schema of the original database and ensures the creation of the sample database accordingly. Furthermore, the system samples the original database according to the sampling rate given, α. Finally, the user can optionally provide the starting table manually in order to manipulate the sampling process.

Report The system generates a report containing the following information with regards to the metrics described in [3]: (i) execution time, (ii) size errors, and (iii) the query relative error. The system measures both the sampling time (i.e. the time it takes to create the files containing the sampled data) and the load time (i.e. the time it takes to load the data from the files in the sample database). The size errors are divided in: (i) absolute size error, which computes the difference between the expected and the actual sample size, (ii) the global size error, which is equal to the absolute size error relative to the expected sample size, and (iii) the average size error, which reflects the average between the global size error of each table. The query relative error measures the difference between the expected and the actual query result, relative to the expected query result. Other information included in the report are the input parameters (e.g. database name, username). The system generates four queries, Q_j, $j \in [1, 4]$, as follows: (1) A set of j tables, linked through foreign key constraints, are selected for the query, (2) A random aggregate operator (i.e. `avg`, `min`, `max`, `count`, `sum`) is selected and applied on a random field of the first table, (3) A random field is selected from the last table and is included in the `where` clause, (4) A random value is chosen for the random field previously selected and included in the `where` clause. If no query was found for the number of tables required in the join, then -1 is displayed for the query relative error (e.g. Q_4 in Fig. 3). The system also allows the user to input its own queries and it will regenerate the report by clicking the *Compute* button. Moreover, the user can regenerate new random queries using the *Generate* button. The report is exemplified in Figure 3, given as input the real database, *Financial*, and a sampling rate $\alpha = 0.5$. We observe that VFDS produces a sample with only 1% absolute, and 1.5% global size error. The sample shows higher average size error, 25.8% due to the diamond pattern contained in the *Financial* database which enforces the method to sample one of the tables entirely. Even though the table has only 77 tuples, this highly impacts the average size error metric. The compared techniques are more severely affected by this, with 29.3% for LBS, and 57.5% error for JS [3]. Moreover, we notice the query relative error of VFDS is below 5% for all queries generated, with a maximum error of 3.5%. In terms of query answering, the methods generally produce similar errors as they represent random techniques [3].

4. DEMONSTRATION SCENARIOS

This section discusses the four demonstration scenarios we plan to present at the conference. To demonstrate VFDS' effectiveness, we plan to apply the system on both real data from the *Financial* database[2] from the PKDD'99 Challenge

[2]http://lisp.vse.cz/pkdd99/Challenge/berka.htm

Discovery, and synthetic data produced by the TPC-H Benchmark[3]. The scenarios prepared exhibit how certain configurations influence the results of the system in terms of query answering, database size, and execution time. In particular, we plan to demonstrate how different sampling rates and databases impact the results of the evaluation (i.e. basic features and scalability). Moreover, we plan to demonstrate VFDS's accuracy in terms of query answering by interactively modifying the generated queries with manually inputted queries (i.e. approximate query evaluation). Finally, we plan to demonstrate the efficiency of the automated system in choosing the appropriate starting table. For this purpose, we plan to interactively show how selecting different starting tables impacts the accuracy of the sample database for all metrics considered.

Acknowledgments This work was supported, in part, by Science Foundation Ireland grant 10/CE/I1855 to Lero - the Irish Software Engineering Research Centre (www.lero.ie).

5. REFERENCES

[1] S. Acharya, P. B. Gibbons, V. Poosala, and S. Ramaswamy. Join synopses for approximate query answering. In *SIGMOD*, pages 275–286, 1999.

[2] J. Bisbal, J. Grimson, and D. Bell. A formal framework for database sampling. *Information and Software Technology*, 47(12):819–828, 2005.

[3] T. S. Buda, T. Cerqueus, J. Murphy, and M. Kristiansen. VFDS: Very fast database sampling system. In *IEEE IRI*, pages 153–160, 2013.

[4] V. T. Chakaravarthy, V. Pandit, and Y. Sabharwal. Analysis of sampling techniques for association rule mining. In *ICST*, pages 276–283, 2009.

[5] S. Chaudhuri, R. Motwani, and V. Narasayya. On random sampling over joins. In *SIGMOD*, pages 263–274, 1999.

[6] R. Gemulla, P. Rösch, and W. Lehner. Linked bernoulli synopses: Sampling along foreign keys. In *SSDBM*, pages 6–23, 2008.

[7] B. Goethals, W. Le Page, and M. Mampaey. Mining interesting sets and rules in relational databases. In *SAC*, pages 997–1001, 2010.

[8] G. John and P. Langley. Static versus dynamic sampling for data mining. In *KDD*, pages 367–370, 1996.

[9] F. Olken. *Random Sampling from Databases*. PhD thesis, University of California at Berkeley, 1993.

[10] C. Olston, S. Chopra, and U. Srivastava. Generating example data for dataflow programs. In *SIGMOD*, pages 245–256, 2009.

[11] K. Taneja, Y. Zhang, and T. Xie. MODA: Automated test generation for database applications via mock objects. In *ASE*, pages 289–292, 2010.

[12] X. Wu, Y. Wang, S. Guo, and Y. Zheng. Privacy preserving database generation for database application testing. *Fundamenta Informaticae*, 78(4):595–612, 2007.

[13] R. Yahalom, E. Shmueli, and T. Zrihen. Constrained anonymization of production data: a constraint satisfaction problem approach. In *SDM*, pages 41–53, 2010.

[3]http://www.tpc.org/tpch/

Knowledge Management for Keyword Search over Data Graphs[*]

Yosi Mass[†]
IBM Haifa Research Lab
Haifa 31905, Israel
yosimass@il.ibm.com

Yehoshua Sagiv
The Hebrew University
Jerusalem 91904, Israel
sagiv@cs.huji.ac.il

ABSTRACT

This demo presents exploratory keyword search over data graphs by means of semantic facets. The demo starts with a keyword search over data graphs. Answers are first ranked by an existing search engine that considers their textual relevance and semantic structure. The user can then explore the answers through facets of structural patterns (i.e., schemas) as well as through other features. A particular way of presenting answers in a compact form is also supported and is applicable when looking for a single entity that connects the keywords. The demo is based on a working prototype that users can try on their own. It includes five data graphs that are quite diversified. In particular, three of them were generated from relational databases and two—from RDF triples. The demo shows that the system enables users to easily and quickly perform various search tasks by means of exploration, filtering and summarization.

Keywords

Keyword search; data graph; semantic faceted search; exploratory search

1. INTRODUCTION

Keyword search over knowledge bases has been investigated quite extensively (cf. [2]). Current systems are based on two pillars, namely, information-retrieval and database techniques. In this paper, we describe a system that adds a third pillar of knowledge management that facilitates iterative query processing [8]. We demonstrate why it is needed and how it speeds up the search for particular answers that are of interest to the user.

In keyword search over data graphs, an answer consists of some relevant text as well as a semantic structure (i.e., a

---

[*]This work was partially supported by the Israel Science Foundation (Grant No. 1632/12).

[†]Work done as a PhD candidate at The Hebrew University of Jerusalem.

CIKM'14, November 3–7, 2014, Shanghai, China.
ACM 978-1-4503-2598-1/14/11.
http://dx.doi.org/10.1145/2661829.2661846.

tree or a graph) of entities and relationships among them. Current systems, however, are not effective in determining which semantic structures are relevant to the user. Typically, there could be a variety of semantic structures while only a few of them may meet the user needs. Therefore, a user may have to browse through many irrelevant answers before finding the ones she is looking for. Consequently, a knowledge-management component is needed so that a user can explore and filter semantic structures, and then find the most relevant answers for each desired structure. Another problem is that an answer usually involves several entities and their relationships while a user may only be interested in a tiny, succinct part thereof. Thus, result summarization and aggregation is needed.

Our knowledge-management component is based on *semantic faceted search*. Traditional faceted search [6] uses a variety of attributes (e.g., color, size, price, etc.) that serve as filters. In comparison, semantic facets are structured (i.e., tree patterns) and are not predefined (since there is no global schema).

A user starts with a keyword search. Answers are first ranked by an existing search engine and then aggregated to form the semantic facets, as well as other facets. The user can explore the various *schemas* (i.e., tree patterns) of answers and quickly zoom-in on the relevant results.

Our system also supports a single-entity mode, where an answer (which is a tree) can be reduced to a single entity, thereby applying a form of summarization and aggregation. A mixture of tree and single-entity answers can be explored by means of the semantic facets. This is more general than what can be done by systems that focus on entity search and exploration (e.g., [11]).

To summarize, our contributions are as follows.

- We introduce semantic facets for knowledge exploration in keyword search over data graphs. Thus, our system is a synergy of information-retrieval, database and knowledge-management techniques.

- We describe a single-entity mode of querying that further enables summarization and aggregation.

- We demonstrate the effectiveness of the system through use cases in a variety of knowledge bases and scenarios. In particular, we show how users can easily and quickly find answers even to complex queries that are hard to express precisely in keyword search.

Now, we briefly discuss related work on iteratively exploring results. In [8], they deal with search over data graphs (i.e., knowledge bases) and enunciate the principle of *iterative querying* that consists of exploration, filtering and aggregation. Our method is a concrete implementation of iterative querying by means of semantic faceted search. The works [3, 5, 10, 12] support result exploration and query refinement over knowledge bases. However, they either assume an underlying relational database schema that is preprocessed [3, 12] or they use some structured query language [5, 10]. Hence, those are not full-fledged systems for keyword search over data graphs. The method of [7] allows users to start with keyword search, and then it selects the best interpretation and presents the results to the user, whereas we let users explore the whole gamut of semantic connections among the keywords.

2. SYSTEM DESCRIPTION

In this section, we describe the semantic facets and the functionality they provide. We also give some highlights of the implementation and system architecture.

2.1 Preliminaries

A data graph represents entities and relationships. It can be derived from relational databases, RDF, XML, etc. In a data graph, nodes are either entities or relationships, while edges represent connections among them. When creating a data graph from a relational database, edges correspond to foreign-key references. If the source data is RDF, edges are the predicates that connect subjects and objects. And if the data graph is obtained from XML, edges correspond to IDREF(s) attributes.

Each node and edge in a data graph has a set of attribute-value pairs. Nodes and edges may also have free text, resulting in richer information. Two special attributes are *type* and *name*. The former exists in all nodes and edges. The latter exists in all the entity nodes, but not in relationship nodes or edges.

A *query* Q is a set of keywords. An *answer* A to Q is a subtree A of the data graph, such that A contains all the keywords of Q and is *non-redundant*, in the sense that no proper subtree of A also has all the keywords. The *schema* of an answer A is the same tree as A, but with only the type (and no other information) in each node and edge. Thus, a schema can have multiple corresponding answers. If the schema is not sufficiently informative, the system can show some specific answers (of the schema) in order to better understand its meaning.

2.2 Semantic Faceted Search

Figure 1 depicts how results are presented to the user . The UI consists of two panes. Answers appear, in ranked order, in the right pane. The left pane consists of facets. The figure is just a snippet of the UI created from the top-1000 answers to the query "Rhein Germany" on the Mondial data graph [2].

A node is depicted as a gray rectangle. An edge is shown with a red circle in the middle. The value of the attribute `type` is shown in purple and red fonts in nodes and edges, respectively. The value of the attribute `name` (of entity nodes) is shown in a blue font. For example, in the first answer (appearing in the right pane) of Figure 1, the top rectangle is an instance of the relationship `located` and the bottom one represents the entity `Germany`. The top of the left pane of Figure 1 comprises the schemas (i.e., tree patterns) of

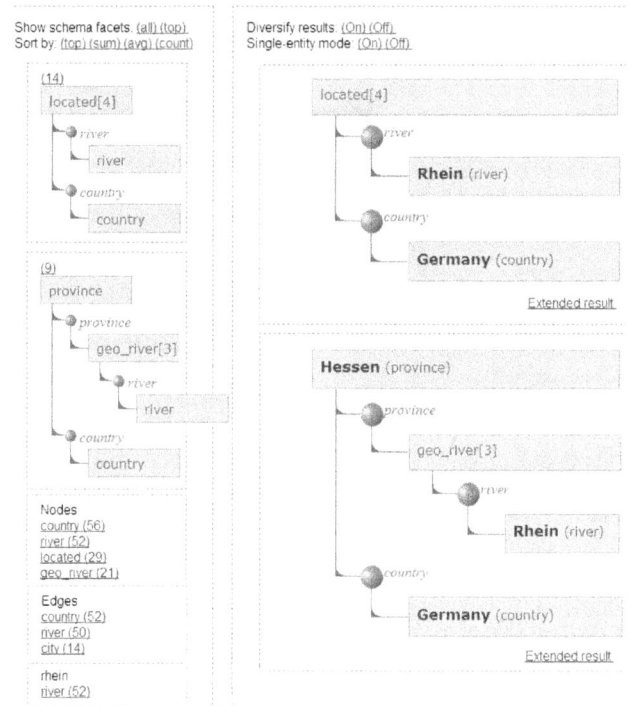

Figure 1: A snippet of the UI

the two answers shown in the right pane. For example, the first schema has two entities (of types `river` and `country`) that are connected through a relationship (of type `located`). The number in parentheses indicates that there are fourteen answers with that schema.

In a relationship node, the number of entities that it connects is shown inside square brackets following its type. For example, consider again the node of the relationship `located` in the top answer of Figure 1. In the whole data graph, it connects four entities, but only two of them are shown in Figure 1. Those two are the entities `Rhein` and `Germany` of types `river` and `country`, respectively.

The system creates the following groups of facets from the top-K answers. First, the left pane shows the *schemas* (which represent semantics) of the top-K answers. The number of the corresponding answers (among the top-K) is shown above each schema. Second, there is a list of the *nodes* and *edges* appearing in the top-K answers, where each one is represented by its type and count. Third, for each *query keyword*, there is a list of all the types of nodes and edges (and their count) where it appears.

After posing a query and getting the initial set of answers, the user can drill down by clicking on any facet. As a result, the system would display the matching answers and their facets. The user can continue recursively, by choosing another facet, or backtrack. In the next section we describe some scenarios that demonstrate the effectiveness of exploration through the semantic facets.

2.3 System Architecture

We use an underlying engine for keyword search over data graphs. We assume that the engine exposes some API that gets a keyword query and returns the top-K answers (usually, we choose $K = 1,000$). In the demo, we use [9]; however, other engines with a similar API can be used. We extended [9] to generate the semantic, as well as the other, facets and to support drilling down by means of filtering.

The UI of our system is based on [1]. They use a REST API with XSL (EXtensible Stylesheet Language) and CSS (Cascading Style Sheets) for the presentation of answers, and JavaScript for navigation. We extended those components to support the new facet pane and its operations.

Some rudimentary form or result exploration is available in [1] (e.g., by selecting an answer and choosing to either display only or exclude all answers with the same schema). In comparison, our system introduces a full-fledged facet pane that (among other things) features schemas and enables single-entity search.

3. DEMO SCENARIOS

We now describe the demo setup and some possible scenarios for knowledge exploration and result summarization. The demo uses five diversified data graphs. Three of them were generated from the relational databases of [2] that are based on the Mondial, Wikipedia and IMDB datasets. Two data graphs were created from the RDF triplets of [4] that are based on the IMDB and LibraryThing datasets.

In the demo, users will be able to pose their own queries or apply those of [2,4]. The latter illustrate that many queries have several plausible interpretations in addition to the intended one. The demo shows that semantic faceted search is essential when querying data graphs.

3.1 Exploration and Filtering

In Figure 1, where the query is "Rhein Germany" (taken from [2]), the top subtree in the answer pane shows that the Rhein river is located in Germany. Note that the two are connected through the `located` relationship. This is indeed the most relevant answer. More details can be obtained by clicking on `Extended_result`, thereby seeing the other entities of the `located` relationship (a city and a province).

The user can further explore other types of relationships between those two entities. For example, the second schema in the facet pane shows that in nine answers the connection is through a `geo_river` relationship and a `province`. Note that in the second answer, the province is Hessen. That answer shows that the Rhein river flows through Hessen, which is a province in Germany. The user can drill down on the second schema and see the provinces through which the Rhein river flows. The user can explore more types of connections (e.g., through cities and countries using schemas that are not shown in Figure 1).

It is also possible to change the ranking of the semantic facets by the following options: *top, sum, avg,* and *count.* Top means sorting by the highest score among all the answers of each schema. The other options are by the sum of scores, average score and count of all the answers of each schema. Since there may be a large number of schemas, the user can select whether to show all of them or only the top-n (by default, $n = 5$).

3.2 Single-Entity Mode

In [8], they discuss several types of aggregating answers, such as grouping, diversifying and summarizing. The facets presented earlier enable aggregation of answers according to various criteria (e.g., same schema). We now describe *aggregation by entity type.* It is applicable when (in an answer)

there is a single entity with no occurrences of the query's keywords. For example, consider again the query "Rhein Germany" for finding the various ways that the Rhein river and Germany are related. One of those ways is through a province . Showing the province itself without the whole subtree (of the answer) could satisfy the user and may even be preferable, because it is a more compact representation. The whole subtree is the evidence why the query's keywords are related through the province.

Next, we give some definitions related to when an answer can be represented by a single entity, rather than its complete subtree. The *structure field* of a node comprises the names of all the attributes as well as the value of the type attribute, but does not include the value of any other attribute. For example, the node named `Germany` in Figure 1 has `country` in its structure field. Intuitively, the structure field is the same for all nodes of a given type, so it captures the semantics of a node, but not its content.

An occurrence of a keyword is *ordinary* if it is not in the structure field. An entity node v is *free* if it has no ordinary occurrences of the query's keywords. An answer (i.e., nonredundant subtree) t can be *summarized* by a single node v if v is the only free entity in t.

As an example, the second answer in Figure 1 has three entity nodes, but only the one of type `province` is free. (Note that the answer also has a relationship node of type `geo_river`.) When our system operates in *single-entity* mode, only the `province` node would be returned as the answer. As another example, the `province` node is free also when the query is "Rhein Germany Province," because the occurrence of "Province" in that node is not ordinary.

The single-entity mode can display many answers and schemas compactly, so the user can find the desired ones more quickly. The user can still see the full subtree of an answer by clicking on `Extended_result`.

4. REFERENCES

[1] H. Achiezra, K. Golenberg, B. Kimelfeld, and Y. Sagiv. Exploratory keyword search on data graphs. In *SIGMOD*, pages 1163–1166, 2010.

[2] J. Coffman and A. C. Weaver. A framework for evaluating database keyword search strategies. In *CIKM*, 2010.

[3] E. Demidova, X. Zhou, and W. Nejdl. IQP: Incremental query construction, a probabilistic approach. In *ICDE*, 2010.

[4] S. Elbassuoni and R. Blanco. Keyword search over rdf graphs. In *CIKM*, 2011.

[5] S. Ferré, A. Hermann, and M. Ducassé. Semantic Faceted Search: Safe and Expressive Navigation in RDF Graphs. Technical report.

[6] M. A. Hearst. Design recommendations for hierarchical faceted search interfaces. In *Andrei Z. Broder and Yoelle S. Maarek, editors, Proc. SIGIR 2006 Workshop on Faceted Search*, pages 26–30, 2006.

[7] E. Kandogan, R. Krishnamurthy, S. Raghavan, S. Vaithyanathan, and H. Zhu. Avatar semantic search: a database approach to information retrieval. In *SIGMOD*, 2006.

[8] Y. Mass, M. Ramanath, Y. Sagiv, and G. Weikum. Iq: The case for iterative querying for knowledge. In *CIDR*, 2011.

[9] Y. Mass and Y. Sagiv. Language models for keyword search over data graphs. In *WSDM*, 2012.

[10] J. Pound, I. F. Ilyas, and G. Weddell. Expressive and flexible access to web-extracted data: A keyword-based structured query languag. In *SIGMOD*, 2010.

[11] S. Stamou and L. Kozanidis. Towards faceted search for named entity queries. In *APWeb/WAIM*, pages 100–112, 2009.

[12] G. Zenz, X. Zhou, E. Minack, W. Siberski, and W. Nejdl. From keywords to semantic queries incremental query construction on the semantic web. In *Journal of Web Semantics*, volume 7(3), pages 166–176, 2009.

Clairvoyant: An Early Prediction System For Video Hits

Hao Chen
Department of Computer
Science & Technology
East China Normal University
500, Dong Chuan Road
Shanghai, China
gameboyinfx@gmail.com

Qinmin Hu
Department of Computer
Science & Technology
East China Normal University
500, Dong Chuan Road
Shanghai, China
qmhu@cs.ecnu.edu.cn

Liang He
Department of Computer
Science & Technology
East China Normal University
500, Dong Chuan Road
Shanghai, China
lhe@cs.ecnu.edu.cn

ABSTRACT

Our slogan for the proposed Clairvoyant system is "with several clicks, the future is in your hand, the plan comes into your mind". Clairvoyant is to predict the future of new videos with only few data. The core function in the system is the novel shifted shape match prediction algorithm, based on a K-Nearest Neighbor model. Tons of experiments have been conducted on the open data sets. The experimental results confirm that the proposed SSMP algorithm is promising and outperforms the baselines with significant improvements on various evaluation methods. A demonstration video has been published at http://1drv.ms/1nyH3hD.

1. INTRODUCTION & MOTIVATION

Since people like video producers, the VOD (video on demand) service providers and advertisers desire to know the future of all their video programs, especially the new ones, we propose our Clairvoyant system to give an early prediction on video hits to support their decisions. A demonstration video about three minutes can be online reached at http://1drv.ms/1nyH3hD. We highly recommend the readers kindly download the demo for better quality.

Traditional time series prediction algorithms have the restrictions as (1) the parameters need to be learnt from a large amount of historical data in the series and (2) most algorithms are only suitable for stationary time series. Unfortunately, for the early prediction problems, these two restrictions are difficult to be satisfied, where the available series is not only short but also unstable.

In the Clairvoyant system, the core function is the novel shifted shape match prediction (SSMP) algorithm. SSMP can effectively and efficiently find the high quality neighbors and give out the video hits prediction in the early stage of a new video's lifetime, through the proposed *scaling*, *shifting* and *smoothing* techniques. Therefore, our target users can not only get the visualized prediction results, but also discover the underlying patterns behind different programs through the neighbor finding interface.

CIKM'14, November 3–7, 2014, Shanghai, China.
ACM 978-1-4503-2598-1/14/11.
http://dx.doi.org/10.1145/2661829.2661847.

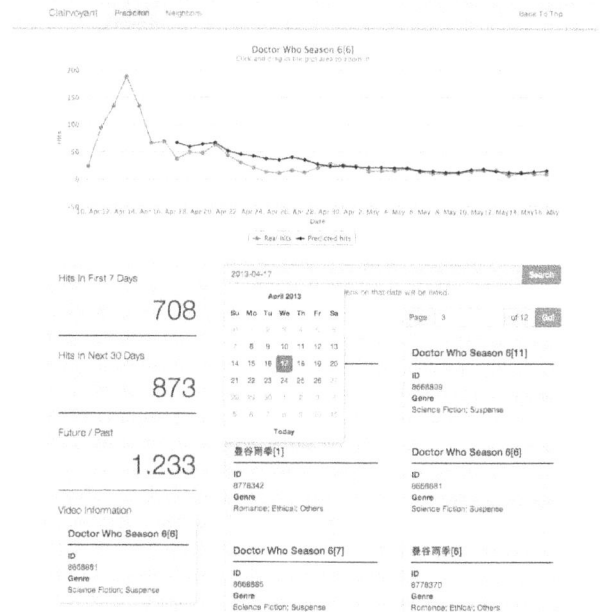

Figure 1: The hit prediction and its real value for "Doctor Who Season 6[6]".

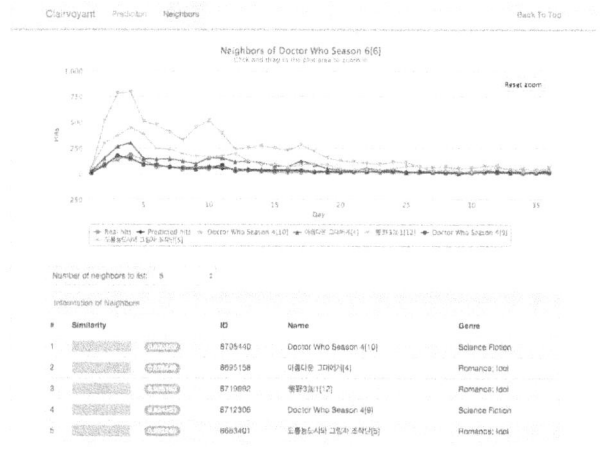

Figure 2: The selected neighbors for "Doctor Who Season 6[6]".

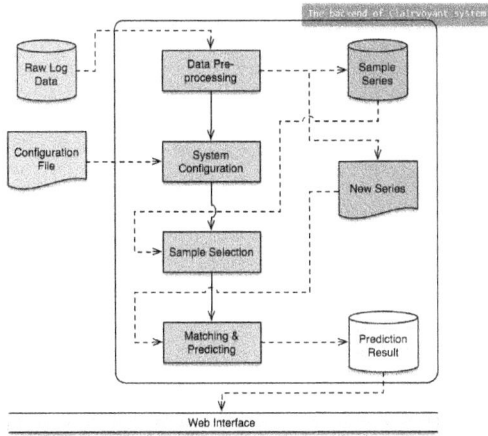

Figure 3: Architecture of the Clairvoyant system.

[ ] proved that there is a high correlation between total hits in the first K days and the following N days (N > K). Moreover, [ ] confirmed that different trends in the first K days also affect the future hits. We are then intuitively motivated that the video hits series can be predicted through finding their similar neighbors, such as adopting K-Nearest Neighbor regression (KNN). However, traditional Euclid distance can't find suitable neighbors.

Here is an example of Clairvoyant only given the data of the first 7 days. Figure 1 shows the day-to-day predictions for the following 30 days on "Doctor Who Season 6[6]". The real series is also plotted for evaluation. Figure 2 presents the found neighbors, using the scaling, shifting and smoothing techniques. The quality of neighbor is listed in details as well. It's interesting that the hit series of an English drama is quite similar to some Chinese and even Korean programs. Furthermore, our Clairvoyant system can fit multiple languages, multiple devices so that the users can visit Clairvoyant anytime and everywhere.

2. SYSTEM ARCHITECTURE

Clairvoyant runs automatically at the background everyday. As shown in Figure 3, the data of both the new videos and sample videos are extracted, transformed and loaded from the user's log system through the "data pre-processing" module. Following "system configuration", "matching & predicting" module matches the new series with the sample series selected by the "sample selection" module as well as gives out the final prediction result. All the prediction results are stored into the database. Our users can see the visualized result through the web interfaces.

In details, *"data pre-processing"* transforms the log data into time series data. New series, whose length is 7 according to our demo configuration, are stored into the "new series" file and waited for prediction. Other series are recorded in the "sample series" database.

"System configuration" loads the algorithm parameters including the input length (T_{train}), the output length (T_{pred}) and the number of neighbors (K) from the "configuration file". Meanwhile, the paths of the "new series" file, the selected samples and the prediction results are also loaded.

"Sample selection" chooses series whose length is larger than $2 * T_{train} + T_{pred} - 1$ from the "sample series" database

and smooths the first T_{train} elements with *moving average* algorithm.

"Matching & predicting" finds K best neighbors for each of the "new series" among the samples selected by the "Sample selection" module and finally produces the prediction result using the SSMP algorithm.

3. SSMP

The SSMP algorithm includes the basic KNN model and the scaling, shifting and smoothing techniques. Throughout the whole paper, the notations are all listed in Table 1.

3.1 KNN Regression

When using KNN to predict the future of a new series, K nearest neighbors are selected according to a distance metric, like Euclid distance. The prediction result is calculated according to Equation 1.

$$s_{new}^{predict} = \frac{1}{K} \sum_{i=0}^{K} s_i^{neighbor} \qquad (1)$$

The key of this prediction model is the distance/similarity metric, but Euclid distance is not good enough.

3.2 Scaling

To make the similarity measurement irrelevant to the magnitude, *scaling* technique mentioned in [ ] is adopted. We define a similarity measurement as shown in Equation 2:

$$sim(s_a, s_b) = 1 - \min_{\alpha} \frac{\|s_a - \alpha s_b\|}{\|s_a\|} \qquad (2)$$

where $\|.\|$ represents the Euclid distance, α is the scaling parameter applied on s_b. Note that α can be solved by set the gradient to zero $\frac{d(sim(s_a,s_b))}{d\alpha} = 0$, $\alpha = \frac{s_a^T s_b}{\|s_b\|}$.

Moreover, the scaling operation is also applied in the final calculation to improve equation 1. Neighbor series are scaled to fit $s_{new}[0 : T_{train}]$. $s_{new}^{predict}$ is also scaled to ensure that the distance between $s_{new}^{predict}[0 : T_{train}]$ and $s_{new}[0 : T_{train}]$ has reached the minimum point.

3.3 Shifting

Furthermore, besides the magnitude difference, we ignore the affect of different spike time when calculating similarity. Thus, Equation 2 can be rewritten with the *shift* operation as shown in Equation 3:

$$sim(s_a, s_b) = 1 - \min_{\alpha,\beta} \frac{\|s_a - \alpha * shift(s_b, \beta)\|}{\|s_a\|} \qquad (3)$$

If $\beta > 0$, s_b will be moved β steps forward and the first β elements will be filled with 0. Otherwise, s_b will be moved β steps backward and the last β elements will be filled with 0. Equation 3 is the similarity metric that is finally adopted in SSMP.

Table 1: Notations

Symbol	Meaning
T_{train}	Available length of a new series
T_{pred}	Prediction length
$s[m : n]$	The $(m + 1)$th to the nth elements in series s
s_{new}	The hit series of a new video.
$s_{new}^{predict}$	The predict result of s_{new}
$s_i^{neighbor}$	The i th neighbor of s_{new}
sim_i	The similarity between s_{new} and $s_i^{neighbor}$

3.4 Smoothing

Since the smoothing technique has been proved to be effective for noise reduction, s_{new} will be smoothed before the similarity calculation, so as to improve the effect of trend extracting. Similar to the "Sample Selection" module, the moving average with the same window size will be adopted.

All in all, combining these three ideas, the $s_{new}^{predict}$ can be calculated according to Equation 5.

$$s_{new}^{predict\_temp} = \sum_{i=1}^{K} \frac{sim_i * \alpha_i * s_i^{neighbor}}{\sum_{i=1}^{K} sim_i} \quad (4)$$

$$s_{new}^{predict} = \alpha_{total} * s_{new}^{predict\_temp} \quad (5)$$

where α_{total} is the final scaling parameter which minimizes the distance between $s_{new}^{predict\_temp}[0 : T_{train}]$ and $s_{new}[0 : T_{train}]$. α_is are the parameters that fit the neighbors to $s_{new}[0 : T_{train}]$'s magnitude.

Table 2: Experimental Results

	K	MAE	MAPE	R^2
K	5	1880	26.89%	-0.24
N	10	1860	26.09%	-0.18
N	15	1846	26.24%	-0.16
	20	1843	26.62%	-0.18
	30	1858	26.67%	-0.15
	40	1889	27.01%	-0.11
	Best	**1836@18**	**26.07%@11**	**-0.09@49**
S	5	1473	18.64%	0.38
S	10	1456	18.55%	0.40
M	15	1405	18.07%	0.42
P	20	1406	18.00%	0.42
	30	1410	18.06%	0.42
	40	1420	18.11%	0.42
	Best	**1400@23**	**18.00%@17**	**0.42@18**
S	5	1679	20.76%	0.30
S	10	1573	19.89%	0.36
M	15	1549	19.50%	0.39
P	20	1518	19.21%	0.39
N	30	1474	18.88%	0.41
S	40	1474	19.01%	0.41
	Best	**1470@42**	**18.88%@30**	**0.41@32**
RF	-	1480	19.70%	0.38

4. EXPERIMENTS

In the real application, we claw the up-to-date videos world widely, such as from IMDb, YouTube, China Bestv and Youku etc.

In order to validate the effect of our Clairvoyant system, we conduct the experiments on the following open data sets. The data sets contain 3854 TV-drama videos, in which 3126 videos from December 1st, 2012 to March 31st, 2013 are selected as the training data set, and 728 between April 1st, 2013 and May 31st, 2013 as the testing data set. T_{train} is set to 7 according to our Kendall's τ [ ] comparing experiments and the real needs. T_{pred} is set to 30.

We apply the mean absolute error (MAE) [ ], mean absolute percentage error (MAPE) [ ] and R squared [ ] as the evaluation metrics.

4.1 Results and Analysis

We present the experimental results in Table 2: (1) KNN is the baseline; (2) SSMP is the proposed algorithm with scaling, shifting and smoothing; (3) SSMPNS stands for SSMP without considering smoothing; (4) the Random Forest (RF) regression [ ], as a state-of-the-art regression algorithm, is adopted to be an outside comparison to the above

three methods; (5) we exhaustively test K in the experiments to get the local optimization value, here we only list $K = \{5, 10, 15, 20, 30, 40\}$ as the samples; (6) the best result is shown with the best K after @.

We draw the first conclusion as that *scaling* and *shifting* work very well, since the performance of SSMP without smoothing is much better than the performance of KNN. The second conclusion is that smoothing plays a very important role as well, because SSMP outperforms SSMP without smoothing. We dig into the experimental details and confirm that less is more. We observe that SSMP can find more accurate neighbors, but the number of neighbors is less than that of SSMP without smoothing.

For the tuning of parameter K, we conduct a 5-fold cross validation on the training data set, such that we get the best K of SSMP around 13 in terms of MAE, MAPE and R^2. However, in the testing data sets, the best K is around 20 in terms of all the evaluation methods. Therefore, we suggest tunning K dependently on the dataset when using SSMP.

5. CONCLUSIONS & FUTURE WORK

With the smoothing, scaling and shifting techniques, SSMP outperforms the traditional KNN regression and the state-of-the-art random forest regression. Furthermore, this early prediction system is flexible enough to fit all kinds of videos, since the only thing it needs is the data in the first 7 days. And the neighbor information can also help dig more from the data. The experiments have confirmed that the proposed SSMP algorithm is promising. The parameter K has also been discussed and suggested to be tuned according to the data sets. With the visualized result provided by Clairvoyant, the future can be seen, and the decisions are supported.

In the future, we will extend Clairvoyant to deal with the long-term prediction problems. This is also our ongoing work.

6. ACKNOWLEDGEMENTS

This research is funded by Ministry of Science and Technology of the People's Republic of China (2012BAH74F02) and Science and Technology Commission of Shanghai Municipality (No.13511507902). We also thank the anonymous reviewers for their comments on this work.

7. REFERENCES

[1] L. Breiman. Random forests. *Machine learning*, 45(1):5–32, 2001.
[2] R. Carpenter. Principles and procedures of statistics, with special reference to the biological sciences. *The Eugenics Review*, 52(3):172, 1960.
[3] K. K. W. Chu and M. H. Wong. Fast time-series searching with scaling and shifting. In *Proceedings of the eighteenth ACM SIGMOD-SIGACT-SIGART symposium on Principles of database systems*, pages 237–248. ACM, 1999.
[4] R. J. Hyndman and A. B. Koehler. Another look at measures of forecast accuracy. *International journal of forecasting*, 22(4):679–688, 2006.
[5] H. Pinto, J. M. Almeida, and M. A. Gonçalves. Using early view patterns to predict the popularity of youtube videos. In *Proceedings of the sixth ACM international conference on Web search and data mining*, pages 365–374. ACM, 2013.
[6] G. Szabo and B. A. Huberman. Predicting the popularity of online content. *Communications of the ACM*, 53(8):80–88, 2010.
[7] W. Webber, A. Moffat, and J. Zobel. A similarity measure for indefinite rankings. *ACM Transactions on Information Systems (TOIS)*, 28(4):20, 2010.

iMiner: Mining Inventory Data for Intelligent Management

Lei Li[†], Chao Shen[†], Long Wang[†], Li Zheng[†], Yexi Jiang[†], Liang Tang[†], Hongtai Li[†]
Longhui Zhang[†], Chunqiu Zeng[†], Tao Li[†], Jun Tang[‡], Dong Liu[‡]

[†]School of Computing and Information Sciences
Florida International University
Miami, FL 33199
{lli003,taoli}@cs.fiu.edu

[‡]ChangHong Hongxin Software Co., Ltd
35 East Mianxing High-Tech Park
Mianyang, Sichuan, China 621000
{tang.jun,liu.dong}@changhong.com

ABSTRACT

Inventory management refers to tracing inventory levels, orders and sales of a retailing business. In the current retailing market, a tremendous amount of data regarding stocked goods (items) in an inventory will be generated everyday. Due to the increasing volume of transaction data and the correlated relations of items, it is often a non-trivial task to efficiently and effectively manage stocked goods. In this demo, we present an intelligent system, called iMiner, to ease the management of enormous inventory data. We utilize distributed computing resources to process the huge volume of inventory data, and incorporate the latest advances of data mining technologies into the system to perform the tasks of inventory management, e.g., forecasting inventory, detecting abnormal items, and analyzing inventory aging. Since 2014, iMiner has been deployed as the major inventory management platform of ChangHong Electric Co., Ltd, one of the world's largest TV selling companies in China.

Categories and Subject Descriptors: H.2.8[Database Applications]: Data Mining

Keywords: Inventory Management; Inventory Forecasting; Anomaly Detection; Inventory Aging

1. INTRODUCTION

Inventory management is often an indispensable process for most retailing companies, as it has the functionalities to avoid product overstock and outages. It refers to the general process of monitoring the fluctuant flow of goods (items) into and out of an existing inventory. This process usually generates two types of time series data, representing the amount of stock in/out evolving over time. Complete inventory management also seeks to control the costs associated with inventory operations [10].

In current retailing businesses, a huge amount of items are often stored at different locations of a supply network to precede the planned course of sales. For example, in our demo case, the retailing vendor has 251,874 items in total, with 132,140 transactions daily on an average. The

CIKM'14, November 3–7, 2014, Shanghai, China.
ACM 978-1-4503-2598-1/14/11.
http://dx.doi.org/10.1145/2661829.2661848.

increasing volume of such data renders it difficult to manually manage the inventory, e.g., to specify the shape and percentage of stocked items. In addition, some items may have correlations with others. For example, when a customer is buying a TV, he/she may also choose multiple auxiliary products, e.g., TV mount or DVD players. Such correlations further increase the difficulty of efficient inventory management. Existing inventory management softwares, such as inFlow[1] and Inventoria[2], provide functionalities to facilitate businesses to manage the inventory. However, most of these systems only rely on statistical analysis of the existing inventory data, and have very limited capability of intelligent management, e.g., forecasting item demand and detecting abnormal patterns of item inventory transactions.

To address the limitations of existing systems, we design and develop iMiner to assist retailing businesses in efficiently performing inventory management. iMiner provides a set of key functionalities that help businesses conveniently and effectively manage huge volume of inventory data. Specifically, the system has the following merits:

- *Efficient support of large-scale inventory data analysis.* The analytical platform is built on a distributed system (FIU-Miner [9]) to support high-performance data analysis. The platform manages all the transaction data in a distributed environment, which is capable of configuring and executing data preprocessing and data analysis tasks in an automatic way.

- *Effective management of complex analysis tasks.* iMiner integrates appropriate data mining algorithms and adapts them to the problem of analyzing inventory data. In particular, the system 1) adopts various regression models and combines them with time series data analysis to fulfill the task of *inventory forecasting*; 2) employs context-aware anomaly detection algorithms to *identify abnormal items*; and 3) utilizes statistical regression models to perform *inventory aging analysis*.

2. SYSTEM OVERVIEW

iMiner has been designed and developed by a research team consisting of 12 members for one year. The system is designed under the following principles: 1) The methods used in the system should provide accurate, and more importantly, interpretable results; 2) The system should provide users with interactive functionalities; and 3) The system should be able to handle large-scale data analysis. A demo

---

[1]http://www.inflowinventory.com.
[2]http://www.nchsoftware.com/inventory.

can be found in http://matrix.cs.fiu.edu/iMiner. Figure 1 presents an overview of the system architecture of iMiner. The system is composed of four layers: *User Interface, Data Analysis Layer, Task and System Management Layer*, and *Physical Resource Layer*.

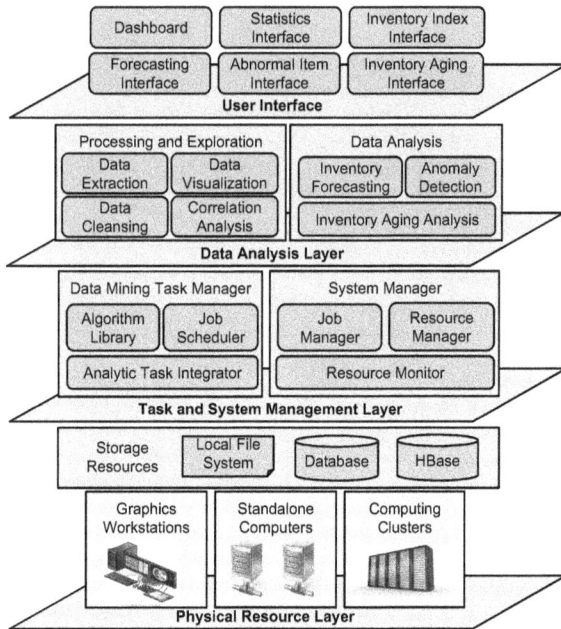

Figure 1: An overview of the system architecture.

Existing inventory management softwares have two limitations when applied to the practice: 1) They do not support handy algorithm plug-in; and 2) They do not support large scale analysis tasks running in parallel in heterogeneous environments. *Task and System Management Layer* provides a fast, integrated, and user-friendly system to address the aforementioned limitations, where all the data analysis tasks in *Data Analysis Layer* can be configured as workflows and automatically scheduled. This system is built on our previous large-scale data mining system, FIU-Miner. More details of this system can be found in [9].

Data Analysis Layer consists of appropriate data mining solutions to the corresponding tasks of inventory management, including *Inventory Forecasting, Anomaly Detection*, and *Inventory Aging Analysis*. In Section 3, more details are provided by presenting our data mining solutions customized for inventory management tasks. The system also provides basic data processing and exploration functionalities.

User Interface contains various interactive interfaces for inventory operations. Specifically, it provides *Dashboard* and *Statistics Interface* to allow users to have an overview of the current inventory status. In addition, several key indices of inventory, e.g., turnover rate and stock-to-use ratio, are presented in *Inventory Index Interface*, assisting users in promptly querying the status of a particular item.

3. FUNCTIONAL COMPONENTS

3.1 Inventory Forecasting

The primary goal of inventory forecasting is to minimize the inventory loading. Excess inventory is sub-optimal as it requires additional maintenance and cost. Hence, in inventory management, it is imperative to perform accurate

forecasting so as to reduce the inventory investment and risk of obsolescence. A common practice of inventory forecasting is to predict the demand of a specific item in the future, and reserve the amount of item based on the forecasting result. This often refers to as demand forecasting. In existing solutions to this problem, this is often achieved by calculating past averages. However, the demand of an item is determined by not only contemporary comparison, but also a list of factors, such as seasonality, trend, and special events. Hence, a much more accurate and optimal forecasting method is expected.

To this end, we design and implement a forecasting mechanism in iMiner based on the past inventory transaction data. It takes as input the past transaction data of an item (as a real-valued time series), and processes the data into a list of instances. In each instance i, the amount of stock out of the item in timestamp i is treated as the label, and the values of stock out in i's previous k timestamps are regarded as the features. We then utilize various regression algorithms, such as Neural Network, Linear Regression, SVM [2], Gaussian Process [7], regression tree [1], and gradient descent regression tree [3], to build regression models with optimized parameters for each item. These models are updated in a daily basis. An ensemble method [8] is employed to aggregate the predictions of these models.

The obtained result from the ensemble is purely originated from the perspective of the data itself, without considering the characteristics of inventory forecasting. To enhance the interpretability of forecasting, we treat the ensemble result as the forecasting basis, and further propose a dynamic model that takes into account various factors of inventory data, including seasonality, trend, and special events. Seasonality refers to the portion of item demand fluctuation accounted for by a reoccurring pattern [6]. In inventory management, such patterns often repeat over time. Comparatively, trend is the portion of item demand without reoccurrence. For instance, a trend may show a period of growth followed by a leveling off. Special events, such as holidays and sales promotion, may have great impact on the demand of items. These factors are integrated into an interactive interface shown in Figure 2 to provide dynamic prediction for demand forecasting.

Figure 2: Dynamic forecasting of item demand.

3.2 Inventory Anomaly Detection

Monitoring inventory index for anomaly detection is a very important task in inventory management. This problem becomes further difficult in the Big Data era as the data scale increases dramatically and the type of anomalies gets more complicated.

In our system, in addition to providing traditional statistical methods (e.g., parametric and non-parametric methods) and proximity-based methods [5], we also design and develop a context-aware anomaly detection method to identify abnormal items in inventory data. The data in inventory management includes both transaction data (i.e., time series) and item-related data (i.e., item catalog and description). We combine transaction data and product-related data and identify context clusters as items having similar transaction behaviors with similar item attributes. An instance (i.e., an item in a time interval) is anomalous if it is far away from any context clusters. To identify context clusters, we make use of spectral clustering where the similarity between transaction data (measured by their principal components) and the similarity between the item-related data (measured by their textual attributes) are combined with a learned kernel [4].

Our system builds the unsupervised model of context clusters based on a training set and then applies the model for new test instances. New test instances arriving every day can be cross-checked with the learned model and the model can also be updated with the new data. Figure 3 shows an example of the anomaly detection interface.

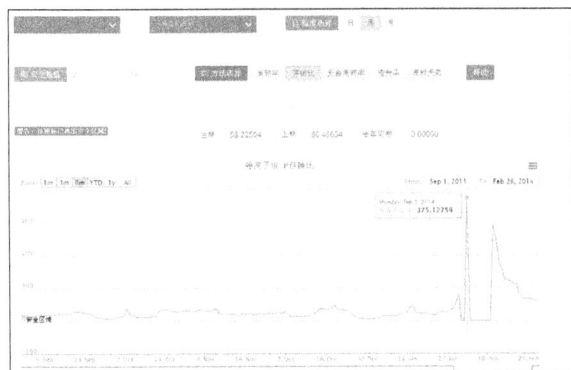

Figure 3: An example of anomaly detection.

3.3 Inventory Aging Analysis

The main purpose to monitor and analyze inventory aging is to prevent items from overstocking and reduce the overstocked items. In our system, an overstocked item at the time t is an item with the amount more than $x\%$ (e.g., 30%) over y (e.g., 6 months) old, where x and y can be set by users. We provide in the system both basic tools and advanced tools to analyze the inventory aging.

The basic tools allow users to visualize inventory aging distributions of a given item and compare current and historical inventory aging changes among different items. The advanced tools are able to help users find attributes of items correlated with overstocking. This further allows users to monitor the related attributes, and especially pay attention to those items of which the value of the related attribute is above or below a predefined threshold.

To indicate how related the item attributes are with overstocking, we model it as a feature selection problem. For each item and each timestamp when the item exists in stock, we generate a data sample, (x_i, y_i), where x_i are the attributes of the item and y_i is the label with value 1 indicating the item at that time is overstocked, and value 0 otherwise. The label information can divide the entire item collection $\mathcal{X}$ to overstocked items $\mathcal{X}_1$ and non-overstocked items $\mathcal{X}_0$. The system integrates several feature selections methods including Information Gain, mRMR and ReliefF to rank the

attributes, and allows users to configure which one will be used at running time. For each attribute, users can further compare its histograms on $\mathcal{X}_1$ and $\mathcal{X}_0$ to obtain a more intuitive sense of the relationship between the attribute and overstocking.

Using the related attributes, users can impose queries to retrieve the items that are likely to overstock and put them into the monitoring list. Figure 4 shows the interface of querying items using multiple attributes. A query is a logical conjunction of a set of literals, each of which corresponds to an attribute. For a continuous attribute a, its literal is in the form of $L_a \leq a \leq H_a$, where L_a and H_a are the lower and upper threshold of the attribute a, respectively. For a discrete attribute, the condition is in the form of $a = V_a$, where V_a is the given value of a. Given a literal for an attribute a, we can retrieve a subset of the items $\mathcal{X}^a \subset \mathcal{X}$. To help users compose the query, for attribute a, the system recommends a literal as $[L_a^*, +\infty]$ or $[-\infty, H_a^*]$ for continuous attributes and V_a^* for discrete attributes, with the goal of maximizing the probability of overstocking in the corresponding subset $p(y_i = 1|\mathcal{X}_a)$.

Figure 4: Attributes in inventory aging analysis.

ACKNOWLEDGMENT

The work was supported in part by the National Science Foundation under grants DBI-0850203, CNS-1126619, and IIS-1213026, the Army Research Office under grants W911NF-10-1-0366 and W911NF-12-1-0431, and an FIU Dissertation Year Fellowship.

4. REFERENCES

[1] L. Breiman, J. Friedman, C. J. Stone, and R. A. Olshen. *Classification and regression trees*. 1984.

[2] C.-C. Chang and C.-J. Lin. Libsvm: a library for support vector machines. *TIST*, 2(3):27, 2011.

[3] J. H. Friedman. Greedy function approximation: a gradient boosting machine. *Annals of Statistics*, pages 1189–1232, 2001.

[4] G. R. Lanckriet, N. Cristianini, P. Bartlett, L. E. Ghaoui, and M. I. Jordan. Learning the kernel matrix with semidefinite programming. *JMLR*, 5:27–72, 2004.

[5] T. Pang-Ning, M. Steinbach, V. Kumar, et al. *Introduction to data mining*. 2006.

[6] R. S. Pindyck and D. L. Rubinfeld. *Econometric models and economic forecasts*, volume 4. 1998.

[7] C. E. Rasmussen. Gaussian processes for machine learning. 2006.

[8] D. A. Unger, H. van den Dool, E. O'Lenic, and D. Collins. Ensemble regression. *Monthly Weather Review*, 137(7):2365–2379, 2009.

[9] C. Zeng et al. Fiu-miner: a fast, integrated, and user-friendly system for data mining in distributed environment. In *SIGKDD*, pages 1506–1509. ACM, 2013.

[10] P. H. Zipkin. *Foundations of inventory management*, volume 2. 2000.

RApID: A System for Real-time Analysis of Information Diffusion in Twitter

Io Taxidou, Peter M. Fischer
University of Freiburg, Germany
{taxidou,peter.fischer} @informatik.uni-freiburg.de

ABSTRACT

The advent of social media has facilitated the study of information diffusion, expressing information spreading and influence among users on social graphs. In this demo paper, we present a system for real-time analysis of information diffusion on Twitter; it constructs the so-called *information cascades* that capture how information is being propagated from user to user. We face the challenge of managing and presenting large and fast-evolving graph data. For this purpose, we have developed methods for computing and visualizing information flow dynamically, offering rich structural and temporal information. The interface offers the possibility to interact with the dynamic, evolving cascades and gives valuable insights in terms of how information propagates on real-time and how users are influenced from each other.

Categories and Subject Descriptors

H.3 [**Information Storage and Retrieval**]: General; H.5.2 [**Information Interfaces and Representation**]: User Interfaces

Keywords

Information diffusion; Information cascades; Visualizations

1. INTRODUCTION

Social media provides rich means of interactions among people in which they create, share, and exchange information. The advent of social platforms and the constant engagement of users on them provides a treasure of information for analysis. A crucial area that has recently gained attention in the data management community is the study of information diffusion, i.e. tracing, understanding and predicting how a piece of information is spreading in social networks [3]. Studying information flow yields valuable insights in the interaction patterns of users and provides opportunities to identify user roles like e.g., opinion leaders or spammers. These interactions are represented as *information cascades* which are temporal sub-graphs of the underlying social graph. They provide a model of information diffusion, where the nodes correspond to users and edges reveal "who was influenced by whom". Real-time

analysis of information diffusion is of particular interest for many, currently not well-supported use cases: Online journalists need to understand timely how to evaluate the sources of their information, while celebrities and politicians need to react quickly to public opinion, rumor spreading and the "echo" on their own publications.

A valuable source for studying information diffusion is Twitter which maintains a social graph of *friends* and *followers*. The act of *retweeting*, which is forwarding another user's tweet by giving credit to it, facilitates explicit information diffusion from user to user. In many countries, Twitter provides a relevant and representative coverage of the population, making it a *social sensor*. Finally, the fact that messages and the social graph is open to some extent makes such analysis viable in practice.

In this demo, we present a system that reconstructs and visualizes information cascades in Twitter with the following contributions: (1) We provide an infrastructure for our algorithm [4] that reconstructs information cascades on real-time. (2) We develop methods to visualize large cascades with collapsing techniques in order to understand their structure and properties. (3) We visualize temporal and geographical distribution of the cascades, as they grow in time.

There is only limited work on this kind of problem: reconstructing large information cascades on real-time is not a trivial task under data limitations and lack of observable diffusion paths [4]. Additionally, visualizing cascades of thousands of nodes in a dynamic way, that is assigning edges of user interactions while they are happening, is an equally challenging problem. Closest to our work is an online application called "Whisper" [2] which expresses the diffusion process in a coarse-grained manner. It contains temporal and spatial characteristics with lightweight sentiment analysis, but does not provide the accuary and level of detail that we aim for.

In Section 2 we provide an overview of the cascade reconstruction algorithm, followed by the techniques for visualizing large cascades in Section 3. We describe the components of the system infrastructure in Section 4 and provide a short demo tour in Section 5. Lastly, Section 6 concludes and gives future directions.

2. ALGORITHM AND MODELS

In order to facilitate the understanding of challenges for computing information cascades, we briefly discuss the algorithm presented in [4]. Since diffusion paths are almost never explicitly available, the algorithm takes the occurrence of specific information propagated in messages as well as the social graph connections into account. Based on this information, it derives possible likely influencers and thus the diffusion paths. For the specific case of Twitter retweets, only a reference to the initiator of the retweet cascade is provided, but no information on intermediate influencers.

The core part of this algorithm is the influence assignment mechanism, expressing the models proposed in [1]: In the naive case,

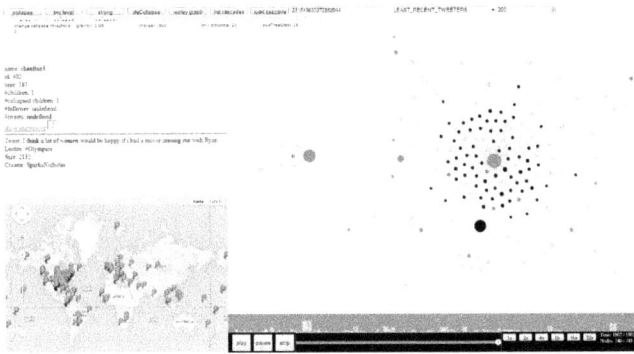

Figure 1: Visualized Information Cascade

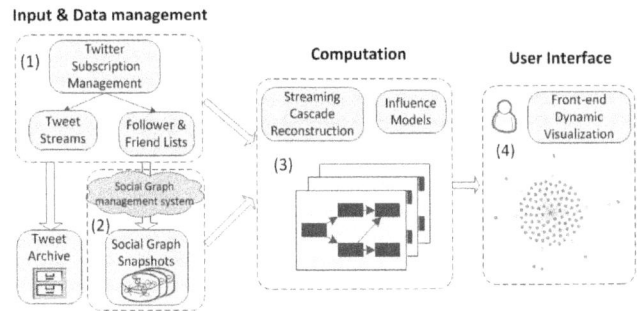

Figure 3: Architecture

when a user retweets a message, we assume that was influenced by all of his friends who (re)tweeted the same message in the past. For that, we need to access all follower data of these predecessor users, which leads to a quadratic complexity with regard to the cascade size. However, identifying all possible edges (influencers) is not needed. The algorithm currently supports four different influence models in order to trim influence edges. We can assume that every user who retweets is influenced by only one of his friends: (1) the one with the most followers or (2) most retweets or (3) the most recent influencer or (4) the least recent influencer. According to the influence model the semantics of influence change which has an impact on the structure of the cascade.

3. VIZUALIZATIONS

The cascade visualization interface is depicted in Figure 1. Our goal is to show the high level structure of the cascades as they grow dynamically on time. The visualization includes nodes and edges only, since any other additional information on the cascades would be obscured for large sized ones. The interface provides four complementary aspects: (1) dynamic representation of the structure of large, evolving information cascades, (2) real-time distributions, like temporal activity and geographical spread (3) relevant information for users participating in the cascade, when the corresponding node is pointed with the mouse, like user name, number of followers and location and (4) information for the original tweet, like text and number of retweets.

While there are many solutions to visualize static graphs, very few solutions exist for dynamic, large-scale graphs. Large cascades can grow up to hundred of thousands of interactions, which obscure the overall structure and dynamic behavior when visualized. The dynamic behavior of cascade graphs demands that updates are integrated instantaneously and properties are recalculated at the same time. To address these issues, we developed our own web-based visualization techniques for dynamic, large-scale cascade graphs which perform adaptive collapsing of node groups. The key idea of collapsing is based on the following observation: There is a skewed distribution in the number of social media users who influence their friends to react further to their messages; the majority of users fail to influence their friends, while very few users trigger many reactions. This creates many "leaf" nodes that stop the information flow, e.g., retweeters that trigger no additional reactions. Combining/collapsing these leaf nodes with their "parent" into a "supernode" provides a first step to significantly reduce the number of visible nodes while not losing relevant graph structure.

Given the complex structure of information cascades, we developed two more aggressive collapsing strategies that gradually shed

the structure, but retain most relevant information in the nodes: *Two level collapsing* aggregates the leave nodes of the cascade in their direct parent node iteratively, while the depth of the collapsed sub-tree should not exceed two levels. This method takes as a parameter the maximum number of nodes that can be collapsed in every parent node. The multilevel collapsing works iteratively as the two-level collapsing, without any sub-tree depth restriction. It is parametrized only by the number of possible collapsed nodes.

The size and the color of the nodes carries additional information as illustrated in Figure 2: The size of each node is proportional to the number of the collapsed nodes it carries. The number in the core of nodes shows the depth of the sub-tree that is collapsed. The red node in the middle is the root, while the green outlined nodes are leaves and yellow ones are bridges that connect two sub-graphs. Grey nodes have one child collapsed while blue nodes have more than one child collapsed. Since real-time reconstruction works on possibly incomplete data, nodes with no observable parent are assigned to the root and highlighted in black. Figure 2 shows a cascade of 34.221 nodes without any collapsing, with two level collapsing (1.095 visible nodes) and multilevel collapsing (212 visible nodes). For the last case, the parameter of sub-tree size is set to 5. More aggressive collapsing can be achieved if we increase this parameter. We observe that the high level structure, e.g. the two big components connected by a bridge, is not being lost.

These strategies were implemented on top of the D3 Javascript graph visualization library[1], supporting all major browsers. We can successfully represent cascades with up to 60K nodes. The selected cascade for dynamic reconstruction is streamed using Web Sockets in the form of edges, containing the incoming node and the parent node. The influence model is selected and used accordingly during reconstruction. The nodes that are going to be collapsed according to the collapsing strategy are integrated directly into their parent nodes. Newly visible nodes take dynamically their place and the cascade graph is being reorganized. While the nodes are arriving, their geographic location is pinpointed into a map. At any time during the dynamic reconstruction, the user can decollapse and collapse again nodes by clicking at them or change the collapsing strategy dynamically. Selecting a collapsed node will show the location of all collapsed leafs in addition to the parent, so that possible locality of influence can be seen. When the reconstruction is finished, the cascade can be replayed back and forth, stopped and paused while the temporal distribution is depicted.

4. SYSTEM

The system we present in this demo is based on the architecture shown in Figure 3. The nature of visualization and reconstruction

---

[1] http://d3js.org

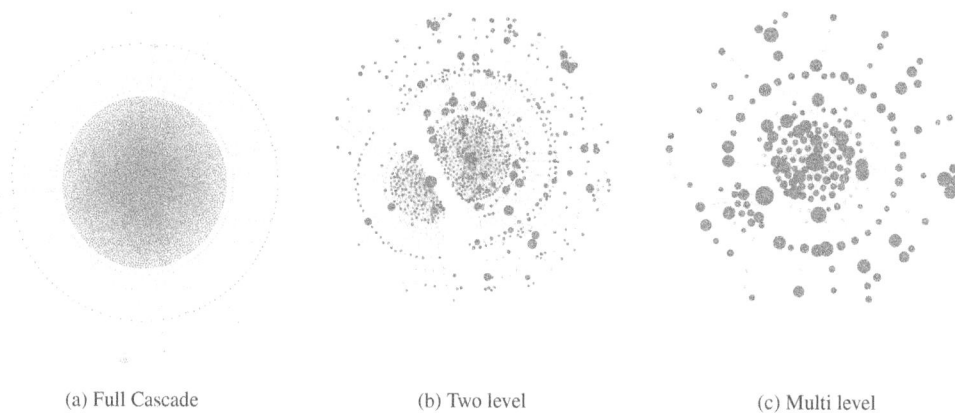

(a) Full Cascade   (b) Two level   (c) Multi level

Figure 2: Collapsing Techniques

requires matching dynamic data for messages and the social graph. We therefore need to perform (1) data collection and filtering and (2) historic data storage and retrieval. Based on this data, we can perform (3) computations for streaming cascade reconstruction using the algorithm presented in Section 2. This algorithm is implemented on top of Storm[2], a scalable, distributed data stream processing platform suitable for real-time computations. The results are then streamed to the (4) front-end visualization, which was described in Section 3. We therefore briefly present components (1) and (2) in this Section.

(1) Input Subscription Stream and Social Graph Manager: We used Twitter as a source for messages and social graph information. The input subscription stream manager serves as an interface to the different streams provided by Twitter, like the sample stream that is 1% of the public stream or filter subscriptions for terms/hashtags and users. Specific cascades can be addressed by a combination of these means. The subscription management delivers the (filtered) tweet steams to the downstream processing components and stores it into an archive for offline evaluation.

The input subscription social graph manager retrieves the social graph data in the form of followers or friend lists needed for reconstruction. We implemented a crawling facility and we maintain a cache of crawled social graph parts. An updating facility is also used in order to keep the social graph updated and in synchronization with the current cascades. Given its sheer size (100s of millions of users with their connections), we have to judiciously perform retrieval to have access to relevant and up-to-date information based on observed relevant activity.

(2) Social Graph management and maintenance: In order to reconstruct with with low latency, the algorithm presented in Section 2 needs efficient access to the huge social graph. To provide these means, we are working on distributing of the graph which exploits the locality of social interactions. For the purpose of the demo, in which we have a limited amount of users, we pre-load the relevant part of the social graph for reconstruction into main memory and load the remainder on demand.

5. DEMO TOUR

For the demo, we plan to show our cascade reconstruction infrastructure on a single machine, with *offline*-pre-recorded and *online*-live social media streams.

In the offline scenario, we will provide the ability to select pre-recorded cascades, load the corresponding social graph fragment

and perform the reconstruction. In the online scenario, we will choose among the currently most active running cascades and trace messages while they are arriving. Since we cannot pre-determine the part of the social graph needed for reconstruction, it will be loaded on demand and access will be slower in this case. We are currently working on distributing computation and social graph storage in such a way that real-time reconstruction is achieved for a full social graph by exploiting interaction locality.

In both cases, we will visualize the reconstructed cascades with different collapsing strategies as described in Section 3. These visualizations will provide a static and a dynamic mode. Static visualizations show the complete cascade in order to provide an overview on the complete structure. Dynamic visualizations show how the cascades evolve over time with the option of dynamic collapsing. In addition to the structure, the temporal and geographical distribution are visualized on a map.

For both demonstration scenarios, cascades are going to be reconstructed using different influence assignment models as described in Section 2. Thus we observe how the topology of the cascade changes by selecting a different influence model.

6. CONCLUSION AND FUTURE WORK

We present an innovative system for real-time analysis and visualization of information cascades on Twitter, providing immediate insights on how information is spreading in social media. The front end provides rich structural, temporal and user-oriented information while cascades are unfolding dynamically. We devise visualization techniques in order to present big cascades by preserving relevant information and the underlying structure. Information cascades are reconstructed with different influence models while the demo tour supports both offline and online modes. Currently, we are working on the distribution of the social graph for faster access on the online scenario, where data is not known in advance.

7. REFERENCES

[1] E. Bakshy et al. Everyone's an influencer: Quantifying influence on Twitter. In *WSDM*, pages 65–74, 2011.

[2] N. Cao et al. Whisper: Tracing the spatiotemporal process of information diffusion in real time. *Visualization and Computer Graphics, IEEE Transactions on*, 18(12):2649–2658, 2012.

[3] A. Guille et al. Information diffusion in online social networks: A survey. *SIGMOD Record*, 42(2):17, 2013.

[4] I. Taxidou and P. M. Fischer. Online analysis of information diffusion in twitter. In *WWW (Companion Volume)*, pages 1313–1318, 2014.

---

[2]http://storm.incubator.apache.org/

RecLand: A Recommender System for Social Networks

Ryadh Dahimene
CNAM
2 rue Conté
F75141 Paris, France
ryadh.dahimene@cnam.fr

Camelia Constantin
Univ. Pierre et Marie Curie
4 Place Jussieu
F75005 Paris, France
camelia.constantin@lip6.fr

Cédric du Mouza
CNAM
2 rue Conté
F75141 Paris, France
dumouza@cnam.fr

ABSTRACT

Social networks have become an important information source. Due to their unprecedented success, these systems have to face an exponentially increasing amount of user generated content. As a consequence, finding relevant users or data matching specific interests is a challenging. We present RECLAND, a recommender system that takes advantage of the social graph topology and of the existing contextual information to recommend users. The graphical interface of RECLAND shows recommendations that match the topical interests of users and allows to tune the parameters to adapt the recommendations to their needs.

Categories and Subject Descriptors

H.3.3 [**Information Storage and Retrieval**]: Information Search and Retrieval – Information filtering; H.2.8 [**Database Management**]: Database Applications – Data mining

Keywords

Recommendation, Social Networks, Link Prediction

1. INTRODUCTION

Social networks have become an important communication vector and are currently facing a spectacular increase in the number of users and their generated content. More than 550 million of Twitter accounts exchange over 500 million of tweets every day, whereas each of the 1.26 billion Facebook users publish on average 36 posts a month. Other similar systems like Google+, Instagram, Youtube or Sina Weibo, to quote the largest, also exhibit dramatic growth [1].

Recommender systems alleviate this information overhead and help the users to find relevant data/users that match their interests. Recommendation scores generally consider

[1] http://expandedramblings.com

CIKM'14, November 3–7, 2014, Shanghai, China.
ACM 978-1-4503-2598-1/14/11.
http://dx.doi.org/10.1145/2661829.2661850 .

user behavior as well as other information, such as user profiles or the social graph topology. For instance, collaborative filtering can be used to recommend Google news that were read by similar users [2]. The WTF service at Twitter [3] recommends users by using the SALSA algorithm on a bipartite social graph, where hubs are in the user's circle of trust computed by Personalized PageRank. Recommendation relevance is improved when the profile-based similarity is combined with explicit friendship links [7]. TwitterRank [7] for instance finds topic-level influential users by adding topical characterization extracted by LDA to the users of the Twitter graph. Graph links are weighted by the topic similarity between the corresponding users and user scores are computed by the Topic Sensitive PageRank. Similarly, [4] use Random Walk with Restarts on the social friendship network increased with user-provided annotations to improve music recommendation on last.fm.

In this demonstration we propose RECLAND, a recommender system that produces personalized user recommendations. Building on the idea that measures based on the graph topology are good indicators of user similarity, we extend the topological score of Katz used for link prediction [5] by integrating semantic information on users and their relationships and user authority. Unlike existing methods, a user has high authority only if he is highly followed (published content that is not followed is not considered). Also, an user is relevant if many other relevant users are encountered on the exploration paths. Furthermore, we propose approximate recommendation scores by adapting landmark-based approaches currently used for shortest-path approximations [6] to reduce computation cost at query time. The RECLAND interface allows to compare the recommendations produced by our algorithm with the ones produced by TwitterRank [7] and Katz [5]. It also allows the user to choose his own parameters and to verify the relevance of the resulting recommendations by exploring the underlying social graph. We illustrate the features of RECLAND in the context of the Twitter microblogging system, but our model is general and may be used for any microblogging sites where users publish content and receive posts from the accounts they follow.

2. MODEL AND DEFINITIONS

We model the Twitter social network as a directed labeled graph whose nodes u are users (accounts) and there is and edge $e = (u, v)$ from u to v if u follows v (*i.e* u receives v's updates). Each user is labeled with a set of n topics $\{t_i\}_{i=1}^n$ that characterize his posts. Edges $e = (u, v)$ are also labeled with a set of topics describing the interests of u for the posts published by v. Labels can be explicitly defined by users or automatically inferred from the posts, as described in Section 3.

Recommendation. RECLAND recommends to a user u relevant accounts (users) v on a query composed of several topics $\{t_1, \ldots, t_n\}$ and relies on the following assumptions: (i) *the topological proximity* is important, *i.e* u trusts his friends, the friends of his friends, etc., but this confidence decreases with distance [5]; (ii) *the number of paths* from u and v is also important, since user v is likely to be more important for u if there are many other relevant users for u that recommend v; (iii) the *topical relevance* of the paths between u and v must be considered for recommendations.

The recommendation scores proposed in RECLAND extend the Katz score which has been shown to perform well in the context of link prediction [5] by integrating the topical relevance of the paths. More precisely, we express the recommendation score $\sigma^k(u, v, t)$ of the user v for user u on a query topic t on paths $p = u \rightsquigarrow v$ of length less than k as :

$$\sigma^k(u, v, t) = \sum_{|p| \leq k} \beta^{|p|} \omega_p(t)$$

The total recommendation score of v on all query topics $\{t_1, \ldots, t_n\}$ is obtained by a weighted linear combination [1] where scores for each individual topic t_i are weighted by the relevance of t_i for the posts of u. $\beta^{|p|}$ is the Katz score that decreases as the length of the path $|p|$ grows, $\omega_p(t)$ is the topical score for the path from u to v of length $\leq k$. The topical score of a path $\omega_p(t)$ considers the relevance of the nodes (authority) and the one of the edges (topical similarity) on this path *w.r.t.* to the topic t.

Node authority: depends on the number of users that follow u on topic t:

$$auth(u, t) = \underbrace{\frac{|\Gamma^u[t]|}{|\Gamma^u|}}_{local} \times \underbrace{\frac{log(1 + \Gamma^u[t])}{log(1 + max_u(\Gamma^u[t]))}}_{global}$$

where $|\Gamma^u[t]|$ is the number of followers of u on t, and $|\Gamma^u|$ is the total number of followers of u. The *local authority* is higher for users u specialized on t (1 if u is followed exclusively on t) than for users that publish on a broad range of other topics. The *global popularity* is higher for users which are most followed on t (1 if u is the most followed user on t). We used the logarithm function to smooth the difference between popular accounts with huge number of followers and accounts with very few followers.

Edge relevance: we consider a path $p = u \rightsquigarrow v$ to be more relevant when the topics on the edges on p are semantically close to t. The relevance of each edge e at distance i ($i \leq k$) from u on path p is defined as:

$$\varepsilon_e(t) = \alpha^i \times max_{t' \in topics(e)}(sim(t', t))$$

the decay factor $\alpha \in [0, 1]$ decreases the influence of e when its distance i from u is higher, $sim : \Theta^2 \rightarrow \mathbb{R}$ is the semantic similarity between two topics t and t' given by the Wu and Palmer measure used in WORDNET [2] [3]. For edges labeled with several topics $topics(e)$, we only keep the maximum similarity among all topics of e to avoid high scores for edges labeled with many topics that have small similarity to t.

Finally, we consider that the weight of a path p is high when both the relevance of the nodes and the one of the edges of this path are high:

$$\omega_p(t) = \sum_{e \in p} \varepsilon_e(t) \times auth(end(e), t)$$

where $end(e)$ returns the end node of the edge e.

Approximate recommendation. For a graph with N vertices, computing exact recommendation scores for all nodes reachable in K hops supposes to handle node sets of size out_{avg}^K on average (with out_{avg} the average number of followed accounts), and of size N^K in the worst case (complete graph). We can compute instead approximate scores by using a landmark-based approach [6] that divides the graph around L selected landmarks to reduce the cost of handling a large graph and the computation overhead at query time.

During the preprocessing phase, we choose a set of nodes as landmarks according to one of the strategies proposed in Table 1 and precompute recommendation scores $\sigma^{k_2}(l, v, t)$ for all topics $t \in \Theta$, from each landmark l to all nodes v reachable in $k_2 < K$ hops. The number of explored node is N^{k_2} in the worst case.

At query time, we explore the graph at distance $k_1 = K - k_2$ from the query node u to search for landmarks, visiting N^{k_1} accounts in the worst case. We collect recommendations from any encountered landmark l at distance k_l and weight them based on recommendation score $\sigma^{k_l}(u, l, t)$ computed during this exploration. A linear combination of the collected results provides the final recommendations for u on topic t. The cost of this approach is consequently in $O(N^{k_1} + N^{k_2}) \ll N^K$. Observe that this approach estimates a lower-bound of the scores.

3. DEMONSTRATION

A video illustration of our demonstration scenario is available at *http://cedric.cnam.fr/~dahime_m/recland*. The recommendation engine is implemented in Java. The interface uses a force directed layout display powered by d3js [4] and shows in its main frame an excerpt of the labeled Social Graph (LSG) (see Figure 1). The left panel allows graph exploration while the right one is used to interact with the recommender system as well as to tune the display options. Recommendation scores are computed on a Twitter dataset with 400,000 users, 2.4 millions edges and nearly 4 million tweets, with a mean path length of 3.74 and an average local clustering coefficient of 0.144 (small world network). User profiles were generated by using OpenCalais[5] combined to a trained Naive-Bayses classifier (WEKA [6], with a precision of 0.83) to tag accounts with 18 topics extracted from their tweets. Edge labels are chosen from the intersection of the topics of the corresponding publishers and followers. RECLAND offers the following functionalities:

Labeled graph visualization: when selecting an account, the interface displays its posts on the right window and the corresponding user profile extracted from those posts. Graph can be explored by clicking on a following link from the current account, display link's labels and see the profile of the corresponding publisher.

---

[2] http://wordnet.princeton.edu/
[3] other semantic distances, e.g. RESNIK, could be used

[4] http://www.d3js.org
[5] http://www.opencalais.com
[6] http://www.cs.waikato.ac.nz/ml/weka

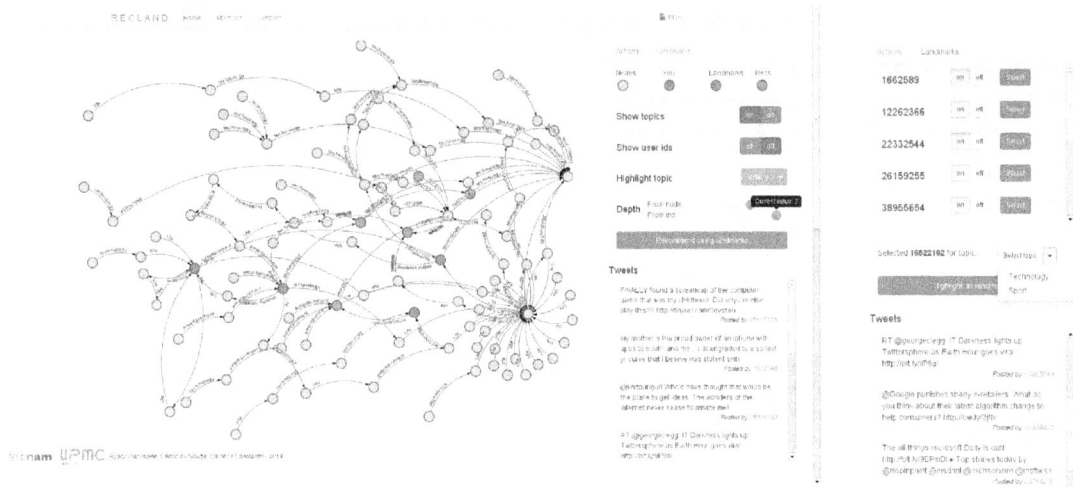

Figure 1: The RECLAND interface

Recommendation relevance comparison: the interface allows to compare RECLAND recommendations with the ones produced by Katz or TwitterRank [7]. Recommended accounts are displayed on the graph as a set of green-enlightened nodes with their scores and ranked by relevance. Recommendation relevance can be checked by selecting accounts from the ranked list and comparing their user profile and topic authority with the query topics.

Recommendation parameters tuning: by testing different exploration distances, we can compare local recommendations at small distance with the ones at greater distance that possibly involve all the social network. Tuning α and β allows to test the trade off between the influence of the topological and the semantic scores on the recommendations. For a fixed α, a higher β may lead to recommend distant nodes if their semantic score is high. When β is small, distant nodes are more unlikely to be recommended, even if they are semantically relevant. For a fixed β and a higher α, the position of the relevant arcs and nodes on the recommendation paths is less important. For a small α, a path is more important for recommendation if the semantically relevant nodes and edges are closer to the query account on this path.

Exact and approximate recommendations comparison: RECLAND allows to test the 10 landmark selection strategies in Table 1 and compare the resulting recommendations. The user specifies an exploration depth to search for landmarks. Found landmarks are displayed in the interface's right window, ranked by their relevance to the query node. When a landmark is selected, the users recommended by the landmark for the query topics are also highlighted. We can then choose a set of landmarks to use for recommendation and see the final list of recommended users, whose approximate scores were computed based on the chosen landmarks. This list can be compared with the the exact recommendations.

User validation. we conducted an user validation by asking 41 users, from which 44% were regular Twitter users to rate the recommendations for 5 topics on a scale from 1 (low relevance) to 10 (high relevance). We computed recommendations by graph exploration at distances K ranging from 2 to 5 (at distances ≥ 4 we possibly reach all graph nodes for a graph with mean path length of 3.74). For each K we shuffled the top 3 users recommended by RECLAND,

Algorithm	Description
RANDOM	Draw landmarks with an uniform distribution
FOLLOW	Draw landmarks with probability depending on their # of followers
PUBLISH	Draw landmarks with probability depending on their # of publishers
IN-DEG	Landmarks are nodes with highest in-degree
BTW-FOL	Draw landmarks among nodes with # of followers in [min_follow,max_follow]
OUT-DEG	Landmarks are nodes with highest out-degree
BTW-PUB	Draw landmarks among nodes with # of publishers in [min_publis,max_publish]
CENTRAL	Select landmarks reachable at a given distance from most of chosen seed nodes
OUT-CEN	Select the landmarks that cover the most different output seeds
COMBINE	Weighted combination between the 9 and 10

Table 1: Landmarks selection algorithms

TwitterRank and Katz before presenting them to the users. The mean average relevance scores for all distances (4.06 for RECLAND, 3.21 for Katz and 3.67 for TwitterRank) show that our proposal outperforms the others. The relevance of RECLAND shows an increasing tendency for greater exploration distances (3.98 for $K = 2$, 3.94 for $K = 3$, 4.10 for $K = 4$ and 4.24 for $K = 5$).

4. REFERENCES

[1] J. A. Aslam and M. Montague. Models for metasearch. In *SIGIR*, pages 276–284, 2001.

[2] A. S. Das, M. Datar, A. Garg, and S. Rajaram. Google news personalization: Scalable online collaborative filtering. In *WWW*, pages 271–280, 2007.

[3] P. Gupta, A. Goel, J. Lin, A. Sharma, D. Wang, and R. Zadeh. WTF: the Who to Follow Service at Twitter. In *WWW*, pages 505–514, 2013.

[4] I. Konstas, V. Stathopoulos, and J. M. Jose. On social networks and collaborative recommendation. In *SIGIR*, pages 195–202, 2009.

[5] D. Liben-Nowell and J. Kleinberg. The Link Prediction Problem for Social Networks. In *CIKM*, pages 556–559, 2003.

[6] K. Tretyakov, A. Armas-Cervantes, L. García-Bañuelos, J. Vilo, and M. Dumas. Fast fully dynamic landmark-based estimation of shortest path distances in very large graphs. In *CIKM*, pages 1785–1794, 2011.

[7] J. Weng, E.-P. Lim, J. Jiang, and Q. He. TwitterRank: Finding Topic-sensitive Influential Twitterers. In *WSDM*, pages 261–270, 2010.

MeowsReader: Real-Time Ranking and Filtering of News with Generalized Continuous Top-k Queries

Nelly Vouzoukidou
Pierre et Marie Curie
University
Paris, France
nelly.vouzoukidou@lip6.fr

Bernd Amann
Pierre et Marie Curie
University
Paris, France
bernd.amann@lip6.fr

Vassilis Christophides
R&I Center, Technicolor
Paris, France
vassilis.christophides@
technicolor.com

ABSTRACT

This demonstration presents *MeowsReader*, a real-time news ranking and filtering prototype. *MeowsReader* illustrates how a general class of *continuous top-k queries* offers a suitable abstraction for modeling and implementing *real-time search* services over highly dynamic information streams combining keyword search and real-time web signals about information items. Users express their interest by simple text queries and continuously receive the best matching results in an alert-like environment. The main innovative feature are dynamic item scores which take account of information decay, real-time web attention and other online user feedback. Additionally, a trends detection mechanism automatically generates trending entities from the input streams, which can smoothly be added to user profiles in form of keyword queries.

Categories and Subject Descriptors

H.3.3 [**Information Storage and Retrieval**]: Information Search and Retrieval—*Information filtering, Selection process*

Keywords

real-time ranking; social media attention; continuous top-k query processing; text streams

1. INTRODUCTION

Web 2.0 technologies permeate more and more all facets of human activity and users are striving for effective and efficient monitoring and filtering tools for a continuously growing number of information streams. News media like *nytimes.com*, *lemonde.fr*, and *www.huffingtonpost.com*, to name a few, daily produce many thousands of news articles for millions of users. To automatically receive the latest articles, users can *subscribe* to the RSS feeds produced by these sites, follow associated social media channels, *filter* information according to their interests and, in turn, *comment* and *share* the received information in their preferred social network. For example, Twitter enables millions of users to publish short text messages (*tweets*) referencing news articles through links, thus expressing a kind of indirect interest in its contents. This interest

CIKM'14, November 3–7, 2014, Shanghai, China.
ACM 978-1-4503-2598-1/14/11.
http://dx.doi.org/10.1145/2661829.2661851.

can be reinforced by other users through simple "retweet" and "favorite" feedback signals. Such kinds of social media attention [6] have been rapidly recognized as a valuable information for filtering and ranking news and social media contents [3, 1, 2].

Within this context, the implementation of real-time search services combining highly dynamic information with user feedback for millions of users has become a major challenge of modern Web 2.0 services and news recommendation websites. The main difference between real-time search services and standard web search services, is to be able not only to efficiently compute ranked (partial) query results, but also to *refresh* these results for reflecting the arrival of new information items (item stream) and the influence of new events (feedback, recommendation, etc.) on the score of existing items (event stream). Most of the existent real-time search solutions follow a standard information retrieval approach which consists in building efficient index structures for processing (periodic) snapshot queries combining temporal, similarity and social ranking features. For instance in Twitter, the top-k result of a user query (Twitter page) is periodically updated every few seconds with new tweets that are ranked higher than previous ones. The main challenge is to enable low-latency, high-throughput query evaluation with high ingestion rate and immediate data availability. This is achieved in the real-time search engine EarlyBird [1] by implementing a new parallel and highly concurrent read/write index structure exploiting the dominance of the temporal signal for ranking. In order to deal with high tweet arrival rates, TI-index [2] applies a different indexing approach which separates incoming tweets into distinguished tweets (which are indexed in real-time) and noisy tweets (which are processed by a batch indexing scheme). Both solutions are based on a pull-based client-server protocol where each user subscription generates a certain number of periodic snapshot queries. The alert functionality implemented in Google News for the ranked continuous filtering of news articles applies a similar periodic refresh strategy.

Our prototype *MeowsReader* demonstrates that such real-time search scenarios can be formally defined and efficiently implemented using an expressive framework supporting *continuous top-k queries* [4, 5] with *generalized scoring functions*. The key component that differentiates *MeowsReader* from the previous systems based on periodic query evaluation over efficient index structures, is a *top-k filtering* module which *continuously* processes the incoming stream of items and feedback signals for immediately identifying for each new item or signal the relevant top-k query results that have to be updated. Our goal is to practically demonstrate on a collection of more than $1,200$ RSS item streams and feedback signals obtained through publicly available Twitter streams that continuous top-k queries represent an elegant unified paradigm for modeling Web 2.0 real-time filtering services combining static (content

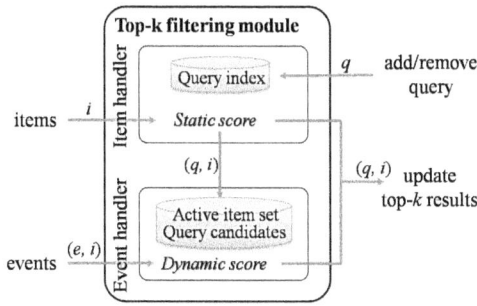

Figure 1: Real-time search with user feedback

relevance, source importance) and dynamic (user feedback, media attention) ranking scores.

2. FRAMEWORK

MeowsReader implements a *continuous top-k query* framework for real-time search over multiple Web 2.0 textual streams [4, 5]. The core component is illustrated in Figure 1 and we will describe in Section 3 how this component is implemented and integrated in the more general real-time news filtering and aggregation framework. The continuous *Top-k filtering module* takes as input a modifiable set of queries (*Query index*), a stream of *Items* to be ranked and a stream of *Events* on these items. This dynamic information is assembled through a continuous scoring function that takes into account the item contents, as well as static and dynamic signals for deciding if an item is relevant to some query in the *Query index*. More formally, the *total score* $\mathcal{S}_{tot}(q, i)$ of an item i over a query q linearly combines (1) a *static* query-dependent similarity score $\mathcal{S}_{qu}(q, i)$ (cosine similarity), (2) a *static* query-independent item score $\mathcal{S}_{sta}(i)$ (item's source authority) and (3) a *dynamic* query-independent item score aggregating all event scores $\mathcal{S}_{ev}(i, e)$:

$$\mathcal{S}_{tot}(q, i) = \alpha \cdot \mathcal{S}_{qu}(q, i) + \beta \cdot \mathcal{S}_{sta}(i) + \gamma \cdot \sum_{e \in E(i)} \mathcal{S}_{ev}(i, e) \quad (1)$$

where $0 \leq \alpha, \beta, \gamma \leq 1$ are weighting parameters. The final scoring function (which is not shown here) also takes account of information freshness by applying a *order-preserving decay function* to the total scores. A more detailed discussion about other approaches using count or time based sliding windows and about the advantages of using order-preserving forward/backward decay can be found in [5].

The main goal of the *Top-k filtering module* is to detect for each new incoming item or event the *top-k query results* to be updated. Figure 1 illustrates the general idea of the overall query processing model. The *Item handler* processes all incoming items i and immediately detects all queries q which have to be updated according to the static similarity and static item score (the dynamic item score is by definition equal to 0 at item arrival). The *Event handler* processes incoming event/item pairs (e, i) and continuously decides if a query result has to be updated because of the correspond item score change. The online decision algorithm is based on a set of *active items* (*Active item set*) that are likely to receive events, and for each such item, a set of candidate queries (*Query candidates*) that will be probably be updated by these events. The definition and maintenance of these two sets is an interesting optimization issue and *MeowsReader* currently implements a heuristics-based solution that will be described in Section 3.

3. THE *MeowsReader* PROTOTYPE

In this section we describe the architecture and implementation of *MeowsReader*, a complete Web 2.0 news aggregation prototype featuring non-homogeneous scoring functions which can take account of social media focus and user feedback streams for item filtering and ranking. We also illustrate how continuous top-k semantics open well-known opportunities for optimizing the filtering process [5].

Architecture: The overall system architecture of *MeowsReader* relies on a publish/subscribe interaction scheme as presented in Figure 2. On the back-end, the system collects *information items* and *feedback signals* as described in Section 2. The *Stream aggregation* module crawls an extensible collection of RSS/Atom feeds published in online media sources and generates a unique stream of information items i. Feedback signals are collected by the *Feed-*

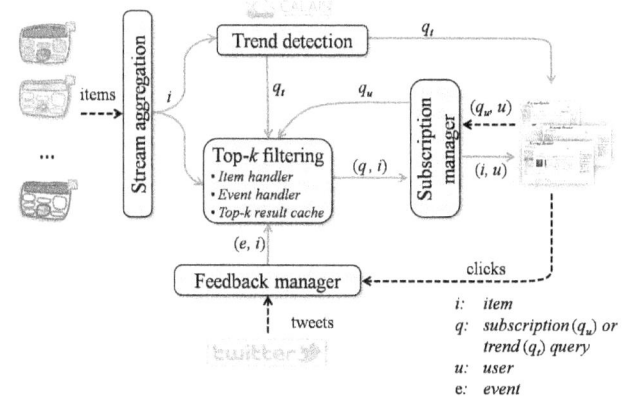

Figure 2: *MeowsReader* Architecture

back manager module from the real-time web (Twitter) and by capturing user clicks on *MeowsReader* interface. Among the collected tweets, we consider in particular those containing a link towards news items that are already registered in the system. These tweets represent feedback signals on these items and cause the dynamic item score to increase. The score change is a linear combination of the tweet related information (retweets, favorites) and author information (number of followers) similar to [2]. The front-end is composed of a *Web user interface* and the *Subscription manager*. The Web user interface[1] enables users to express and register their interest on incoming information items through *keyword queries*. It also collects user click behavior for the *Feedback manager*. The Subscription manager module takes care of the interaction between the *Top-k filtering* module and the user interface.

New items are simultaneously processed by the *Top-k filtering* and the *Trend detection* module which extracts entities with bursty behavior from the contents of recent items. A certain number of such "popular" entities are transformed into *trend queries* q_t, automatically registered in the *Query index* (Figure 1) and proposed to users through the Web user interface (see below for more details).

Top-k filtering: A major feature of our framework is the tight and efficient integration of a continuous *top-k filtering* technique with a real-time web based ranking approach (see Section 2). The implementation of this core component is an extension of the solution presented in [5] and available online[2]. Its main role is to match new items against queries which can be trends, user subscriptions

---

[1]http://gateway.lip6.fr:8080/meows
[2]http://code.google.com/p/continuous-top-k

or both. The generated result is a stream of query-item pairs (q, i) where i is added to the top-k result of q. *All* subscriptions to a given query simultaneously generate the same stream which is pushed to the Subscription Manager module for user notification. All detected query-item pairs are maintained in a *Top-k result cache* for immediately generating a result for new subscriptions to existing user-defined or system generated trend queries. This architecture simplifies the whole process and in particular the query processing task which becomes independent of the number of user subscriptions.

In [5] we have proposed a number of algorithms and data structures for the efficient evaluation of continuous top-k queries using score functions as defined in Equation 1. These algorithms only considered static scores which are not updated after the publication of an item and are implemented in the *Item handler* module (Figure 1). *MeowsReader* extends this solution by an additional *Event handler* processing dynamic item scores generated by feedback signals from the real-time web (Twitter). It is easy to see that these dynamic (real-time web) item scores can change very frequently. These score changes can affect any item and consequently any query result, which makes the detection of queries to be updated a highly cost-sensitive task. As described in Section 2 we try to solve this problem by maintaining a set of *active* items which receive events together with a set of *query candidates* for each item. The basic idea for generating these two sets consists in adding to the actual static item score of an item i an additional threshold score θ_i which reflects an estimated upper bound for the aggregated event score produced by future events. This extended score then allows the item handler not only to detect the queries that have to be updated, but also to compute all query candidates for i at some time instant. In the case when the total feedback score added to the item exceeds the θ_i constant, the item is re-evaluated through the original query index.

Trend detection is an important feature of online Web 2.0 media applications. The goal of this module is to automatically generate potential future subscriptions reflecting the contents of recently published information. The usage of trends is twofold. Trends indicate to users important news that might interest them and that they could potentially miss if they only observe a static set of subscriptions. What is more, once detected, trends are handled by the system as if they were user subscriptions and as such, matched item results are maintained in the top-k cache. Thus, trend queries always generate non-empty results and simulate ad-hoc query behavior (observe that any other *new* user-defined query starts from an initially empty stream of results). In *MeowsReader* we apply a straightforward trend detection mechanism based on named entity frequency statistics. *MeowsReader* uses the OpenCalais [3] service for extracting semantic entity phrases from incoming item contents. *MeowsReader* presents as trend queries those named entity phrases, that show the most *bursty behavior*. Bursty behavior is detected by comparing the relative difference between the *total* frequency observed so far and the *recent* frequency observed in a sliding window over the input item stream.

4. DEMONSTRATION SCENARIO

The demonstration includes two scenarios. The first scenario is based on a large collection of more than a thousand general and specialized U.S. news media RSS feeds and from related feedback continuously collected using Twitter Search and Stream APIs. Conference participants will be able to interact with the online *MeowsReader* application using the *MeowsReader Web user interface* on

any Javascript enabled web browser client. They can immediately access and explore a representative collection of trends related to events taking place at the same time as the conference. In addition, users can subscribe to queries defined in an ad-hoc manner or by refining existing trend queries. User interaction with the platform will also be registered by the system to influence the dynamic item score values.

The second demonstration scenario aims at providing a deeper insight of the capabilities and potential applications of *MeowsReader*. Users can directly interact with a sandbox version of the *MeowsReader* application for exploring different system configurations. In particular they can observe and compare the effects of changing the importance of registered sources for estimating the static item scores (for example, diversify the sources present in query results by promoting sources publishing less items), the decay function (linear/exponential, decay factor) and the linear combination constants α (high values reward content similarity), β (high values favor source importance) and γ (high value promote social media attention). These different configuration scenarios are applied on an archive of more than 10 million news articles and over 40 million tweets, collected over a five month period in a "fast forward" setting. By observing trend queries over past important events (e.g. "Football World Cup") or any other subscription query, users will be able to compare through a *charts dashboard* the system performance (memory usage, processing time, filter selectivity) under high item and event rates.

The demonstration is also publicly accessible http://gateway.lip6.fr:8080/meows.

5. REFERENCES

[1] M. Busch, K. Gade, B. Larson, P. Lok, S. Luckenbill, and J. Lin. Earlybird: Real-time search at twitter. In A. Kementsietsidis and M. A. V. Salles, editors, *IEEE 28th International Conference on Data Engineering (ICDE 2012)*, pages 1360–1369. IEEE Computer Society, 2012.

[2] C. Chen, F. Li, B. C. Ooi, and S. Wu. Ti: An efficient indexing mechanism for real-time search on tweets. In *Proceedings of the 2011 ACM SIGMOD International Conference on Management of Data*, SIGMOD '11, pages 649–660, New York, NY, USA, 2011. ACM.

[3] G. De Francisci Morales, A. Gionis, and C. Lucchese. From chatter to headlines: Harnessing the real-time web for personalized news recommendation. In *Proceedings of the Fifth ACM International Conference on Web Search and Data Mining*, WSDM '12, pages 153–162, New York, NY, USA, 2012. ACM.

[4] P. Haghani, S. Michel, and K. Aberer. The gist of everything new: personalized top-k processing over web 2.0 streams. In *Proceedings of the 19th ACM International Conference on Information and Knowledge Management (CIKM'10)*, pages 489–498, 2010.

[5] N. Vouzoukidou, B. Amann, and V. Christophides. Processing continuous text queries featuring non-homogeneous scoring functions. In *ACM Conference on Information and Knowledge Mangament (CIKM)*, pages 1065–1074, 2012.

[6] C. Wang, M. Zhang, L. Ru, and S. Ma. Automatic online news topic ranking using media focus and user attention based on aging theory. In *Proceeding of the 17th ACM Conference on Information and Knowledge Management (CIKM'08)*, pages 1033–1042, 2008.

---

[3] http://www.opencalais.com/

AMiner-mini: A People Search Engine for University

Jingyuan Liu*, Debing Liu*, Xingyu Yan*, Li Dong[#], Ting Zeng[#], Yutao Zhang*, and Jie Tang*

*Department of Computer Science and Technology, Tsinghua University
[#]Tsinghua University Library, Tsinghua University

{toothacher17, zhangyutao1106}@gmail.com, {jietang, debingliu}@tsinghua.edu.cn,
{dongli, zengting}@lib.tsinghua.edu.cn

ABSTRACT

We present a distributed academic search and mining system—AMiner-mini. The system offers intra- and inter- university level academic search and mining services. It integrates academic data from multiple sources and performs disambiguation for people names, which is a fundamental issue for searching people. We employ a two-phases approach that formalizes the disambiguation problem into a HMRF framework, which significantly improves the disambiguation performance. Based on the disambiguation results, AMiner-mini offers a people search function, which returns experts (or related researchers) for a given query by the user. The user can also choose different metrics to rank the search results and explore the results from different dimensions. The system is designed in a distributed structure. It can be deployed in a university as a stand-alone system for finding the right people who are working on a research topic. Multiple distributed systems can be also connected via Web services and perform search or mining in an asynchronous way and return the combination results. We have deployed the system in Tsinghua University and feedback from university academic users shows that the system worked well and achieved its primary objective.

Categories and Subject Descriptors

H.3.3 [**Information System**]: Information Search and Retrieval;
H.2.8 [**Database Management**]: Database Applications

General Terms

Algorithms, Experimentation

Keywords

Name Disambiguation; Academic Search; Distributed System

1. INTRODUCTION

With the rapid proliferation of digital academic information, it is becoming more and more challenging for mining the heterogeneous academic knowledge in order to satisfy different usage scenarios like expert finding [2,3] and academic search [5]. For example, in a university, students may want to find the best advisors to work with; faculties are trying to look for the best collaborators from different research fields. Traditional keyword based document search is clearly far from sufficient to meet these requirements.

CIKM'14, Nov 03–07 2014, Shanghai, China.
ACM 978-1-4503-2598-1/14/11.
http://dx.doi.org/10.1145/2661829.2661852

Traditional digital library system [4] is mainly designed to manage the *digital data*, e.g., to to collect digital information, build index and offer retrieval services for users. However, the trend of Web turns to be more *people-centric* rather than *data-centric*. Vivo System is a university-oriented system led by Cornell and shares motivations as mentioned before. However, it is also not in particular designed for searching people.

In this work, we present AMiner-mini system, a people search engine for university. The system is derived from ArnetMiner [5], but with more people-centric feature and with a distributed structure. The system has two *distinct advantages*: First of all, it can easily incorporate data inside a university (e.g., the library data and the faculty information), which not only offers a way to seamlessly integrate with existing systems, but also be able to use those data to improve the performance of name disambiguation; Second, we design and implement AMiner-mini as distributed system so that it can easily deploy to and connect other universities, which enables the system to conduct inter-university distributed search [4]. System's major contributions can be concluded as follows:

- *Name Disambiguation*: System employs a two-phases name disambiguation approach via integrating department and faculty staff information into a HMRF framework;

- *Academic Search:* We consider three factors, including relevance, importance, and popularity, when designing ranking algorithms for intra-university academic search;

- *Distributed Structure:* We propose distributed structure and mainly study re-ranking algorithms considering importance and serendipity for inter-university distributed search.

In the following sections, we first introduce the system architecture and then explain the core technologies used in the system. Finally, we give the demonstration plan.

2. TECHNOLOGY SPECIFICATION

2.1 System Architecture

AMiner-mini is a people search engine for universities and it is designed on a distributed platform. Figure 1 shows system architecture, with each node representing a single university.

The system mainly consists of the following components:

- *Data Preparation:* In this component, we preprocess data for the following search and mining. We extracted data from university library, complete missing data by extracting information from the public Web by automatic information extraction [5]. We also provide an interface for users to edit the potential incorrect extraction. Finally, all data has been stored in a MySQL database.

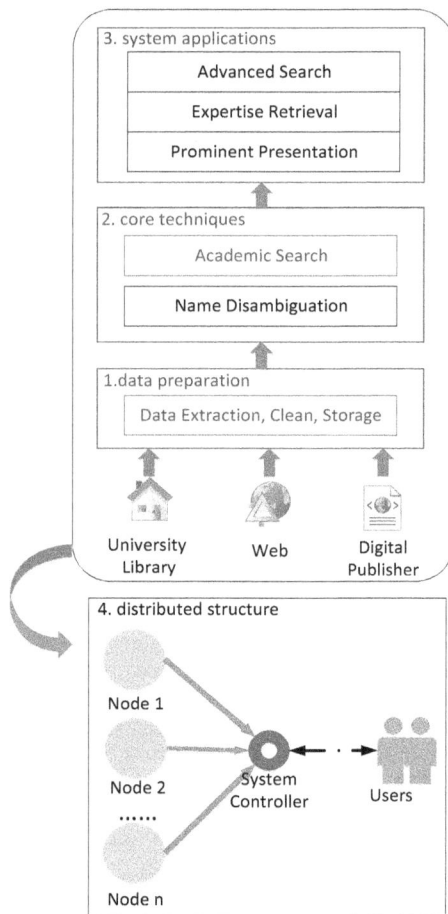

Figure 1: Architecture of AMiner-mini

- *Core Techniques:* This component is our major technical contribution. After data preparation, we design and test our algorithms including two-phases Name Disambiguation and intra-university Academic Search [3]. The former one solves name ambiguity problem when assigning papers and courses to faculties. The latter one is used to measure ranking scores for entities given a user query.

- *System Applications:* We implement system applications based on core techniques in this component. *Prominent Presentation* is used to present the prominent faculties with specific honorable titles, which is attractive to users like administrative officials. Expertise Retrieval [2] is to find expertise entities including faculties, courses, and papers in system database given a search query. Advanced Search is to search with several specific filtering requirements.

- *Distributed Structure:* AMiner-mini is designed with a distributed structure with each node representing a university [4]. On the top of the distributed structure, we studied re-ranking algorithms for Inter-university Distributed Search.

2.2 Name Disambiguation

Different faculties may share identical names. This results in the name ambiguity problem. Name ambiguity will greatly hurt the quality of most academic search and mining services. Thus we tackle name ambiguity as the first step. Name disambiguation generally includes two challenging subtasks: (a) how to cluster information of one person together; and (b) how to determine the number of persons who have the same name [1]. In AMiner-mini,

we use a two-phases approach to solve these challenges. In the approach, we leverage human labeled data as supervised constraints to help improve clustering performances.

More specifically, we cooperated with university library and accessed official human-labeled entities of different departments, which is a strong constraint that helps clustering and assignment. Disambiguation scale is set in a department range and we assigned entities (different kinds of information) to faculties within the department. Official labeled data is limited, but it can greatly improve algorithm performances via working as primarily assigned information.

Further, we integrate the above result into a probabilistic HMRF framework [1][5]. We first enrich academic knowledge from extern digital publisher, which does not have department information as constrains. We heuristically define paper attributes, paper relations and author attributes from first phase result as features for HMRF objective function [5]. During assignment iterations [1], we cluster primarily assigned papers together with the unassigned. The primarily assigned information is helpful considering it can "propagate" during iteration. Besides, the primarily assigned information could work as "cluster atom" to improve clustering performances [1]. We employ supervised learning methods such as Naïve Bayes, and SVM to train a classification model for improving the clustering performance [6].

2.3 Academic Search

Academic Search is to find expertise entities (people and other entities like courses) given a query and the key is to measure ranking scores [3]. In AMiner-mini, we studied intra-university academic search. The ranking score is:

$$Score_{intra} = \omega_R * Relevance + \omega_I * Importance_{intra} + \omega_p * Popularity_{intra} \quad (1)$$

where *Relevance*, *Importance_{intra}*, and *Popularity_{intra}* are the three factors, ω are their weights and set as 0.6, 0.2, 0.2 separately.

Relevance. *Relevance* is used to measure relevance between queries and entities. Given a query, for example "data mining", users not only want to find entities containing those words, but also intend to search for entities on "data mining" topics [5]. Blei et al. introduces LDA, an effective topic model for text and has been applied to academic search [3].

However, LDA alone is usually considered as "general" but "not specific", so "coarse" for search [3]. To balance between "generality" and "specificity", we combined LDA with LM.

Importance_{intra}. *Importance_{intra}* is used to measure intra-university entity importance. We define "prominent importance" to distinguish the prominent in a university. We heuristically assign higher grades to an entity if it enjoys some titles defined as important such as "fellow of Chinese Academy of Science".

We also consider the "network importance". We build social network from co-authorship of faculties and use random walk with restart to rank entities [3].

Popularity_{intra}. *Popularity_{intra}* is used to measure intra-university entity popularity. System logs user behaviors and calculate "feedback popularity" to better understand and measure their preferences [7]. For example, if most users click on the third entity in search result, we would treat the third one as more popular than the former two.

Current system collects 10,000+ faculties, 40,000+ courses, and 90,000+ papers in *Tsinghua University*. System has been put into operation since early 2014. At the beginning, *Popularity_{intra}* is initialized with the same weight for all entities. We test different weights of LDA and LM. Regarding baselines, we use the TFIDF method implemented in Lucene, popular free software for indexing and search full-text. We test 90 queries and asked 5 computer science majors (2 undergraduates, 1 PhD students and 2 engineers) to label the search result.

Table 1. LDA + LM combination weights experiments

Search Methods	P@5	P@10	MAP
0.3 LDA + 0.7 LM	**0.876**	0.8	**0.912**
0.2 LDA + 0.8 LM	0.864	**0.81**	0.89
0.0 LDA + 1.0 LM	0.872	0.77	0.79
Lucene (TFIDF)	0.773	0.726	0.73

As shown in the table, we can see the combination model obviously outperforms Lucene in terms of P@5, P@10 (Precision at top 5 and 10), and also MAP. Regarding the weight configuration for combining LDA and LM, 0.3 for LDA and 0.7 for LM achieves the best performance.

2.4 Distributed Structure

AMiner-mini is designed with a distributed architecture. It can deploy to multiple different universities and the search function can be connected each other. For Cohesion, every single university is considered as a node can works alone. For Concurrency, every node could concurrently react to the system and fasten the responding speed [8].

With the distributed structure, the system is able to offer inter-university distributed search [4]. Users search a query and the master server sends it to all other server nodes. All nodes concurrently conduct academic search and report back the result. The controller collects all search results then re-ranks it. The re-ranking score is:

$$Score_{inter} = \omega_R * Relevance + \omega_I * Importance_{inter} + \omega_p * Popularity_{inter} \quad (2)$$

where $Importance_{inter}$ denotes the inter-university importance and $Popularity_{inter}$ denotes the inter-university popularity, which are modified based on intra-university academic search.

Importance_{inter} $Importance_{inter}$ is used to measure inter-university entity importance. Entity importance from different universities varies. For example, users may view faculties from *Tsinghua* and *BUPT* differently. The challenge is how to quantitatively measure the "University importance". We can employ public school ranking list and user log statistic to initially calculate the score.

Popularity_{inter} $Popularity_{inter}$ is used to measure inter-university entity popularity. With the distributed structure, search results are largely enriched and simply use "feedback popularity" may cause search dilemma. For example, A is ranked before B and they are both very accurate for a search query. However, users may seldom notice B due to search page settings and increase A's popularity score unfairly, which somehow just violates the real meaning of popularity: to let the users define the most popular entities.

We define "serendipity popularity". Serendipity concern with the novelty of inter-university search result [9] and the challenge is how to assign "serendipity popularity" score fairly and

effectively. Heuristically, we randomly set "serendipity popularity" scores. The overall $Popularity_{inter}$ is as follows:

$$Popularity_{inter} = \theta_p * Popularity_{intra} + \theta_S * Serendipity \quad (3)$$

where $Popularity_{intra}$ is the intra-university popularity score and $Serendipity$ is the random serendipity score in a reasonable range, θ is used to normalize scores to the same scale.

3. DEMONSTRATION PLAN
We will present AMiner-mini in the following aspects:

- First, we will use a poster to give an overview of system architecture and briefly show system applications.
- Next, we will describe system's core techniques including name disambiguation and academic search in details.
- After that, we will introduce proposed distributed structure and inter-university search under it. The audience will gain more deep understanding on re-ranking algorithm.
- Finally, we will share our thoughts on the strengths and weakness of system. We will further discuss future work.

4. ACKNOWLEDGEMENTS
The work is supported by the National High-tech R&D Program (No. 2014AA015103), National Basic Research Program of China (No. 2014CB340500), Natural Science Foundation of China (No. 61222212), and Beijing key lab of networked multimedia. We also would like to thank Tsinghua University Library for official data and open test platform.

5. REFERENCES
[1] J. Tang, A.C.M. Fong, B, Wang, and J. Zhang. A Unified Probabilistic Framework for Name Disambiguation in digital library. In *TKDE*, Volume 24, Issue 6, Pages 975-987, 2012

[2] K. Balog, Y. Fang, M. de Rijke, P. Serdyukov and L. Si. Expertise Retrieval. In *FTIR*, Volume 6, 2012

[3] J. Tang, J. Zhang, R. Jin, Z. Yang, K. Cai, L. Zhang, and Z. Su. Topic Level Expertise Search over Heterogeneous Networks. In *Machine Learning Journal*, Volume 82, Issue 2, Pages 211-237, 2011

[4] R. Baeza-Yates and B. Ribeiro-Neto. *Modern Information Retrieval (2nd Edition)*. China Machine Press, 2010

[5] J. Tang, J. Zhang, L. Yao, J. Li, L. Zhang and Z. Su. ArnetMiner: Extraction and Mining of Academic Social Network. In *KDD'08*, pages 990-998, 2008.

[6] A. Ferrreira, M. Gnocalves, and A. Laender. A Brief Survey of Automatic Methods for Author Name Disambiguation. In *SIGMOD'12*, 2012

[7] T. Joachims, L. Granka, H. Hembrooke, F. Radlinski, and G. Gay. Evaluating the Accuracy of Implicit Feedback from Clicks and Query Reformulations in Web Search. In *TIS*, Volume 25, 2007

[8] G. Coulouris, J. Dollimore, and T. Kindberg. *Distributed systems: Concepts and Design (5th Edition)*. China Machine Press, 2011.

[9] M. Ge, C. Delgado-Battenfeld, and D. Jannach. Beyond accuracy: Evaluating recommender systems by coverage and serendipity. In *RecSys'10*, 2010

DEESSE: entity-Driven Exploratory and sErendipitous Search SystEm

Olivier Van Laere[1] Ilaria Bordino[2] Yelena Mejova[3] Mounia Lalmas[4]

[1,2,4]Yahoo Labs, Barcelona & London   [3]Qatar Computing Research Institute, Doha, Qatar
{[1]vanlaere, [2]bordino [4]mounia}@yahoo-inc.com   [3]mejova@qf.org.qa

ABSTRACT

We present DEESSE [1], a tool that enables an exploratory and serendipitous exploration – at entity level, of the content of two different social media: Wikipedia, a user-curated online encyclopedia, and Yahoo Answers, a more unconstrained question/answering forum. DEESSE represents the content of each source as an entity network, which is further enriched with metadata about sentiment, writing quality, and topical category. Given a query entity, entity results are retrieved from the network by employing an algorithm based on a random walk with restart to the query. Following the emerging paradigm of *composite retrieval*, we organize the results into topically coherent bundles instead of showing them in a simple ranked list.

Categories and Subject Descriptors

H.4.1 [**Information Systems Applications**]: World Wide Web—*Web searching and information discovery*

Keywords

Entity Search; Entity Networks; Composite Retrieval

1. BACKGROUND

To provide web users with an engaging search experience, modern search engines need to go beyond the pure relevance of search results and to consider more subjective qualitative factors, such as *serendipity* and *interestingness*. Serendipitous search systems [15] attempt to entertain users with information items that are surprising and interesting, albeit sometimes not fully related to their search intent.

In a recent work [6], we have proposed how to define, operationalize, and evaluate serendipitous search over user-generated content. We have introduced an entity search framework that supports a serendipitous exploration of two of the most popular social media: Wikipedia and Yahoo Answers. The former is a highly curated, collaboratively edited online encyclopedia, whereas the latter is the largest community question/answering system, representing a faithful mirror of people's interests and opinions.

In this paper we demonstrate the tool introduced in our previous work [6]. Our system, dubbed DEESSE (entity-Driven Exploratory and serendipitous Search SystEm), is based on the paradigm of *entity search* [2, 12, 13], which is nowadays a prominent alternative to document search to answer complex information needs by building semantically rich answers in the form of entities and their relations. DEESSE is available online [1].

DEESSE represents the content of each data source as a network of entities, which are connected based on the similarity of the documents in which they appear. Given a query entity, entity recommendations are retrieved from the network using an algorithm based on a random walk with restart to the query. Entity networks are enriched with further metadata, still derived from the documents, and regarding the intensity of the emotion, the quality of the writing, and the topical category of the text surrounding each entity.

In our previous work [6], we have used the above metadata to constrain the result sets, and measure the extent to which each dimension contributes to the perceived serendipity, proposing two different approaches for assessing the serendipity of search results. We showed that both Wikipedia and Yahoo Answers offer results that are relevant, and dissimilar to those found through a web search. However, Yahoo Answers showed to be better at favoring the most interesting entities. The usage of topical metadata was found to be helpful for discovering more interesting results.

The tool described in this paper implements our original framework, and presents some extensions that we introduce to provide users with an improved exploratory search experience: *multi-linguality* and *bundled retrieval*.

For the first aspect, we have enriched DEESSE, which could originally only support queries in the English language, with Spanish. A separate entity network is built and queried for each language.

The second extension concerns the retrieval module. We adopt the paradigm of *composite* retrieval [11], which recently emerged as a powerful way to assist the users with complex information seeking activities. The idea is to organize results into item *bundles* designed to satisfy a number of properties, based on the users's preferences or needs. After evaluating different methods based on the various metadata available in DEESSE, we implemented a topical-bundling algorithm that organizes search results into topically coherent bundles, based on the categories of the query entity.

2. SYSTEM DESIGN

The tool presented in this paper demonstrates our previous research [6], and improves it by adding support for multi-lingual and composite retrieval. DEESSE builds a separate module for each data-source/language combination. The architecture of such module consists in a back-end and a front-end part. The back-end works offline, extracting an enriched entity network from the considered dataset, and precomputing bundled result sets for every entity.

The front-end receives the query submitted by the user and sends a request to the back-end to retrieve the corresponding results. The technologies used for the front-end consist of a combination of a MySQL database, PHP, CSS, HTML and Javascript. D3.js[1] is being used to retrieve JSON formatted data and manipulate it for display, while the Bootstrap[2] framework is used to style the web interface.

We next describe the main components of the back-end.

Data and Languages. DEESSE exploits two main data sources, Yahoo Answers and Wikipedia, which are both available in different languages. While our original framework only considered English-language documents, the current, improved version of DEESSE also supports Spanish. From Yahoo Answers, we collected English and Spanish questions from 2010-2012, and the answers to these questions. For Wikipedia, we extracted the English and the Spanish dumps from December 2011. We use WikiExtractor[3] to strip the meta-content from each Wikipedia page.

Entity extractor. For entity extraction, we follow the common approach that for an extracted entity to exist, it must appear as a Wikipedia page [7, 10, 12, 13]. Our entity-extraction methodology, described in full details in the original paper[6], was chosen due to its suitability for large-scale data processing. It uses a machine-learning approach proposed by Zhou et al. [17] for resolving surface forms extracted from the text to the correct Wikipedia entity, and Paranjpe's *aboutness* ranking model [13] to rank the obtained entities according to their relevance for the text.

Network Extractor. Given the set of entities extracted from each language-specific dataset, we construct a network using a content-based similarity measure to create arcs between entities. Adopting the vector-space model [14], we represent each entity by a TF/IDF vector, extracted by the (order-insensitive) concatenation of all the documents where the entity appears. We then measure the similarity between any two entities in terms of the cosine similarity of the corresponding TF/IDF vectors. Because the TF/IDF weights cannot be negative, the similarity values will range from 0 to 1. We create an undirected network by computing all the pairwise similarities between the entities. However, the final network is not a complete graph. To avoid considering poorly significant relations, we restrict to the pairs of entities that co-occur in at least one document, and we prune all the arcs with similarity lower than a minimum threshold $\sigma = 0.5$[4]. The all-pairs similarity computation required to build the network was performed efficiently by using a distributed algorithm [3] that works on Hadoop.[5]

Entity feature extraction. The entity network was originally enriched with metadata regarding topic, quality and sentiment. Given that DEESSE currently displays only topical and sentiment features, we provide a brief description of these. The interested reader is deferred to the original paper [6] for a full description of the metadata extraction.

To build topical features, we exploit a proprietary taxonomy to assign topical categories to the documents in each dataset (full details in [6]). We derive category features for each entity in a graph, by aggregating over all the documents where the entity appears, and retaining the top 3 categories that are most frequently associated with such documents.

To assign a sentiment score to every entity, we classify the originating documents with SentiStrength,[6] obtaining a positive and a negative score that we combine into a *polarity* score [9], measuring the inclination towards positive or negative sentiment. By default, the tool computes document-level sentiment scores. However, a document is likely to mention many different entities, and the sentiment expressed around them may vary considerably. To handle this, we compute entity-level scores by considering small windows (20 words) of text around each mention of an entity, and then averaging across all mentions.

Entity Ranker. The entity ranker module extracts from a network, the top n entities that are most related to a query entity. Our core method [6] is inspired by random-walk based algorithms [8, 16], which have been successfully applied in many recommendation problems [4, 5].

The algorithm performs a *lazy* random walk with restart to the input entity. At each step, it either remains in the same node with high probability β, or follows one of the out-links with probability $1 - \beta$. In this case, the links are followed with probability proportional to the weights of the arcs. We rank all nodes based on the stationary distribution of this random walk, and select the top n with highest rank. Details concerning parameter settings, stopping criteria and corrections applied to reduce the bias towards popular entities, are provided in the original paper [6]. We use a `giraph`[7] implementation to perform the random walks efficiently.

Bundling algorithm. Our previous work [6] showed that the topic metadata contributed most to improve interestingness and relevance of the search results. Based on this, and on the fact that a topical organization of the results is a natural choice to facilitate the exploration of a large-scale knowledge base, we enrich our retrieval module with an algorithm that organizes search results into topically coherent bundles. We mentioned before that each entity has 3 categories. Our bundling algorithm produces a bundle for each of the categories associated with the query entity.

The bundle corresponding to one category is populated by taking from the ranking returned by the basic entity ranker, the top n entities among those belonging to the considered category. This approach may produce overlapping bundles. We choose not to force the algorithm to create disjoint bundles, not only because going further down in the rank would naturally hurt the relevance of the results, but also because this choice is more adherent with the natural scenario that happens for many queries, where the categories overlap. The current version of DEESSE extracts 3 topical bundles for each entity, with a maximum of 5 entities each.

---

[1]http://d3js.org/
[2]http://getbootstrap.com/
[3]medialab.di.unipi.it/wiki/Wikipedia_Extractor
[4]The value of the threshold was chosen heuristically
[5]hadoop.apache.org

[6]http://wwww.sentistrength.wlv.ac.uk
[7]http://giraph.apache.org

Indexing. Despite the fact that we use a distribute parallel implementation to perform random-walk computations on large-scale data efficiently, our retrieval algorithm requires a temporal computational cost of minutes to obtain results for a query entity. This cost makes running the ranking module at query time prohibitive. To make our solution viable, we perform the computation offline. To avoid storing the full stationary distribution of every node, we also run the bundling algorithm offline, and only store the resulting topical bundles obtained for each entity. Given the current settings, DEESSE stores a maximum of 15 (bundled) results per query, which requires on average $3KB$ per entity.

When a query comes from the front-end, the resulting (pre-computed) bundles are retrieved from the index. Complimentary metadata is provided by the entity feature extractor (e.g., sentiment) or fetched from external sources (abstract or image urls of Wikipedia page and top-rated Yahoo Answers question/answer pair).

3. SYSTEM INTERACTION

Regarding how the user can interact with DEESSE, the search results for the query entity are presented in the central panel of the web user interface. The results are grouped into 3 bundles, based on the categories of the query entity. For example, in the case of the query "NASA", the categories are *Astronomy & Space*, *Politics* and *Religion & Spirituality*.

For each of the entities in a bundle, an illustration of sentiment polarity is provided (if available), along with a link to the Wikipedia page of that entity. A click on an entity result will initiate a search with this entity as query.

Hovering an entity in the result list will trigger the retrieval of any available metadata from Wikipedia (thumbnail picture and Wikipedia abstract) and Yahoo Answers (top rated question and answer mentioning the entity).

Multiple searches can be carried out, and buttons will appear under the search bar to keep track of them. Clicking one of the previous searches will again show the results for that specific search, while clicking the close button in the top-right corner will remove the results for that query entity.

4. SYSTEM MAINTENANCE AND UPDATE

When it comes to updates of the data available in DEESSE, two constraints should be taken into account. First, the computation of the results for each query entity, as described in Section 2, is quite expensive due to the use of random walks. For this reason, results are precomputed and stored in an index. Next, when the number of query entities grows, the computation becomes even more expensive. Both these constraints make that a daily update of the data is not worth the minor improvement in query behaviour for the end user. Of course, having a slower process implies that we will not be able to serve extremely recent time-sensitive queries. However, we believe that this limitation is acceptable, given that DEESSE is a tool built to support the exploration of Yahoo! Answers data, and extremely time-sensitive queries are not a critical use case in this context.

5. CONCLUSIONS

We have presented DEESSE, a tool that enables an exploratory and serendipitous exploration of the content of different social media. It combines the exploration of data from both Wikipedia and Yahoo Answers, two platforms that allow contributions from their users, but are different in the nature of their moderation. We are currently investigating a number of natural extensions to this work.

First, we are working to include support for additional languages. Directly related to this is the question on how to link the results from different language domains. A first, naive, approach would be to aggregate the results from different languages, while a more advanced approach would be to enable cross-lingual entity linking. Second, we would like to explore better exploitation of the current metadata by devising new bundling algorithms, while we are considering to include new sources of metadata (e.g. temporal features) to enable adaptive filtering of results based on freshness (e.g., exclude the less recent Yahoo Answers discussions). Finally, to evaluate our tool at scale, DEESSE should be released to a fully open user base, which is not the case at this moment.

6. ACKNOWLEDGEMENT

This work was partially funded by the Linguistically Motivated Semantic Aggregation Engines (LiMoSINe[8]) EU project.

References

[1] URL http://deesse.limosine-project.eu.
[2] K. Balog, E. Meij, and M. de Rijke. Entity search: building bridges between two worlds. In *SEMSEARCH*, 2010.
[3] R. Baraglia, G. De Francisci Morales, and C. Lucchese. Document similarity self-join with mapreduce. In *ICDM*, 2010.
[4] F. Bonchi, R. Perego, F. Silvestri, H. Vahabi, and R. Venturini. Efficient query recommendations in the long tail via center-piece subgraphs. In *SIGIR*, 2012.
[5] I. Bordino, G. De Francisci Morales, I. Weber, and F. Bonchi. From machu picchu to rafting the urubamba river: Anticipating information needs via the entity-query graph. In *WSDM*, 2013.
[6] I. Bordino, Y. Mejova, and M. Lalmas. Penguins in sweaters, or serendipitous entity search on user-generated content. In *CIKM*. ACM, 2013.
[7] J. Hoffart, M. A. Yosef, I. Bordino, H. Fürstenau, M. Pinkal, M. Spaniol, B. Taneva, S. Thater, and G. Weikum. Robust disambiguation of named entities in text. In *EMNLP, 2011*, 2011.
[8] G. Jeh and J. Widom. Scaling personalized web search. In *WWW*, 2003.
[9] O. Kucuktunc, B. Cambazoglu, I. Weber, and H. Ferhatosmanoglu. A large-scale sentiment analysis for yahoo! answers. In *WSDM*, 2012.
[10] S. Kulkarni, A. Singh, G. Ramakrishnan, and S. Chakrabarti. Collective annotation of wikipedia entities in web text. In *SIGKDD*, pages 457–466, 2009.
[11] I. Mendez-Diaz, P. Zabala, F. Bonchi, C. Castillo, E. Feuerstein, and S. Amer-Yahia. Composite retrieval of diverse and complementary bundles. *IEEE TKDE*, 99 (PrePrints):1, 2014.
[12] D. Milne and I. H. Witten. Learning to link with Wikipedia. In *CIKM*, 2008.
[13] D. Paranjpe. Learning document aboutness from implicit user feedback and document structure. In *CIKM*, 2009.
[14] G. Salton, A. Wong, and C. S. Yang. A vector space model for automatic indexing. *Commun. ACM*, 18(11), 1975.
[15] E. Toms. Serendipitous information retrieval. In *DELOS Workshop*, pages 11–15, 2000.
[16] H. Tong and C. Faloutsos. Center-piece subgraphs: problem definition and fast solutions. In *KDD*, 2006.
[17] Y. Zhou, L. Nie, O. Rouhani-Kalleh, F. Vasile, and S. Gaffney. Resolving surface forms to Wikipedia topics. In *COLING*, 2010.

---

[8]www.limosine-project.eu

Manual Annotation of Semi-Structured Documents for Entity-Linking

Salvatore Trani[1,2], Diego Ceccarelli[1,3], Claudio Lucchese[1], Salvatore Orlando[1,4],
Raffaele Perego[1],

[1] National Research Council of Italy [2] University of Pisa
[3] IMT Lucca [4] Ca' Foscari University of Venice

{firstname.lastname}@isti.cnr.it

ABSTRACT

The *Entity Linking (EL)* problem consists in automatically linking short fragments of text within a document to entities in a given Knowledge Base like Wikipedia. Due to its impact in several text-understanding related tasks, EL is an hot research topic. The correlated problem of devising the most relevant entities mentioned in the document, a.k.a. *salient entities (SE)*, is also attracting increasing interest. Unfortunately, publicly available evaluation datasets that contain accurate and supervised knowledge about mentioned entities and their relevance ranking are currently very poor both in number and quality. This lack makes very difficult to compare different EL and SE solutions on a fair basis, as well as to devise innovative techniques that relies on these datasets to train machine learning models, in turn used to automatically link and rank entities.

In this demo paper we propose a Web-deployed tool that allows to crowdsource the creation of these datasets, by supporting the collaborative human annotation of semi-structured documents. The tool, called ELIANTO, is actually an open source framework, which provides a user friendly and reactive Web interface to support both EL and SE labelling tasks, through a guided two-step process.

Categories and Subject Descriptors

H.3.3 [**Information Storage and Retrieval**]: Information Search and Retrieval; H.5.2 [**Information Interfaces and Presentation**]: User Interfaces

1. INTRODUCTION

In the latest years many research efforts have been spent in the Entity Linking (EL) task applied to text documents. The task, also known as *Wikification*, has been introduced by Mihalcea and Csomai [8], and consists in finding small fragments of text (hereinafter named interchangeably *spots* or *mentions*) referring to an entity (identified by a URI) that is listed in a Knowledge Base like Wikipedia. Each

CIKM'14, November 3–7, 2014, Shanghai, China.
ACM 978-1-4503-2598-1/14/11.
http://dx.doi.org/10.1145/2661829.2661854.

Wikipedia article is considered as an *entity*, and the the title of an article (or the anchor text of the links that point to the article) are possible mentions of the same entity. As an example, consider a short text document containing the sentence: *"Maradona played his first World Cup tournament in 1982 when Argentina played Belgium in the opening game of the 1982 Cup in Barcelona".*

The goal of an EL system is to: *i)* spot the fragments of text referring to entities, e.g., **Maradona**, **Argentina**, or **Belgium**, and *ii)* link each spot to the referred entity, e.g., link the spot **Maradona** to the corresponding Wikipedia page http://en.wikipedia.org/wiki/Diego_Maradona. It is worth remarking that the second step is not trivial due to mentions' ambiguity: in our example the mention **Belgium** does not refer to its most common sense, i.e., the country, but rather to its national football team, i.e, http://en.wikipedia.org/wiki/Belgium_national_football_team. Figure 1 illustrates the result of a correct EL process applied to our running example.

The Salient Entity (SE) [2, 4, 10] discovery task can be thought as a subsequent step to EL. Given the entities mentioned in the document, only the most relevant ones should be returned. In our example, the most relevant entities are surely the ones linked to mentions **Maradona** and **1982 Cup**.

The SE discovery task may have a strong impact in the evaluation of EL algorithms. Let us consider two EL algorithms applied to the text of Figure 1, where the former produces the annotations for **Maradona** and **1982 Cup**, while the latter produces the annotations for **Belgium** and **Barcelona**. In terms of precision, the two algorithms appear to be equivalent, since both can correctly detect two correct entities. However, the former should be considered better than the latter, since it detected two entities that are more salient for the document. Indeed, this is a well-known issue in EL evaluation: although some algorithms are not able to discover SEs, they still score high just because they can match correctly trivial mentions, like the city referred to in the dateline of a news.

Unfortunately, publicly available benchmark datasets that contain accurate supervised knowledge about mentioned entities and their saliency ranking are currently very poor, both in number and quality. The importance of such data is two-fold. On the one hand, as discussed above they are necessary for a sound comparison of different EL techniques. On the other hand, these datasets can also be used to train

> **Maradona,** [http://en.wikipedia.org/wiki/Diego_Maradona] played his first **World Cup tournament**
> [http://en.wikipedia.org/wiki/FIFA_World_Cup] in 1982 when **Argentina** [http://en.wikipedia.org/wiki/Argentina_national_football_team] played
> **Belgium** [http://en.wikipedia.org/wiki/Belgium_national_football_team] in the opening game of the **1982 Cup**
> [http://en.wikipedia.org/wiki/1982_FIFA_World_Cup] in **Barcelona** [http://en.wikipedia.org/wiki/Barcelona].

Figure 1: Example of annotated document

machine learning models, in turn used to automatically link and rank entities.

This demo paper just focuses on the generation of human annotated datasets for the EL/SE tasks. Specifically, we present ELIANTO[1], an open-source Web-deployed framework that crowdsources the production of publicly available rank-enriched datasets for EL and SE tasks with the goal of involving the research community in producing publicly available rank-enriched datasets for EL and SE tasks. It supports human labelling of semi-structured documents through a guided two-step process. In the first step, entities mentioned in a given document are annotated by users. In a second step, such entities are ranked on the basis of the perceived relevance/saliency. Note that, such two-step process implicitly forces the user to evaluate twice the entities she annotated, and correct them if needed.

It is worth mentioning that ELIANTO is back-ended by the spotting module of Dexter [3], a framework that provides all the tools needed to develop any EL technique. ELIANTO thus exploits Dexter to identify a set of spots in the text documents to annotate, along with a list of candidate entities for each spot. This makes easier for the users the heavy job of identifying spots and associated entities in text document. In addition, ELIANTO allows users to provide new spots (not suggested by the tool) as well as new entities to associate with them.

2. ELIANTO

ELIANTO (Entity Linking Annotation Tool) allows to annotate collections of documents and provides tools for driving multiple users annotations (e.g., minimum number of annotator per document), for inspecting user annotations and for analyzing collection status.

The back-end of ELIANTO allows the ingestion of documents collection trough a command line program. It allows to process semistructured documents and to specify an HTML template describing how documents must be displayed.

In order to simplify the linking task, candidate spots and entities for each document are pre-computed. In the demo we used our open source system Dexter[2], but it could be replaced with another system if needed. We are investigating the merging of annotations from different tools, so as to avoid any bias.

ELIANTO offers a Web interface for annotator users. When annotator logs in to the system, an introduction to the Entity Linking task and a guideline explaining how to annotate documents are presented to him. Thanks to the login mechanism, we can monitor users activity. The annotation of

a document is organized in two steps as described in the following.

Step 1: Mention detection and linking

In the first step, the document is presented to the annotator on the left side of the page: if the system has candidate mentions for the document, these are displayed in red. If the annotator clicks on a mention the list of the candidates entities is displayed on the right side of the page. The annotator can decide to: i) select one entity from the list ii) add an other candidate entity inserting its Wikipedia url in a form iii) delete the mention if it is wrong or not relevant.

The annotator can also decide to create a new mention just highlighting a piece of text and selecting the option *Create Spot* from the contextual menu. If the annotator generates a new mention the system can automatically provide a list of candidates entities: this is performed calling a REST service that given a mention returns a list of candidate entities. In the demo we used Dexter which provides such service.

The mentions that the annotator links to entities are highlighted in green, while the currently selected mention is highlighted in yellow. In the contextual menu we provide an option that allows the annotator to extend an annotation to all the occurrences of the same mention in the document. The interface requires to the annotator to annotate (or delete) all the mentions before moving to the step 2.

It is worth to note that we also added the possibility to skip a document if the user thinks that is not a good to annotate *e.g.*, a web document containing only noisy text, or a tweet with no linkable entities. This was indeed useful in the annotation of the CoNLL dataset in which several documents contain table of sport competition results, i.e., a long list of person names.

Step 2: Rank entities by aboutness

In the second step, the system still presents the document on the left, and on the right the list of the distinct entities associated to the mentions in the previous step. The annotator is asked to rate the entities that she selected in the previous step, according to how much they are central to the document story. We defined 4 different ratings:

Top Relevant (3 Stars) if the entity tells you what a document is about, i.e., the main topics or the leading characters. We suggested the user to annotate about 3 entities per document in this category;

Highly Relevant (2 Stars) we named them *satellite entities*: they are not essential for understanding the document but provide important facets;

Partially Relevant (1 Star) entities that provide background information about the content of the document;

---

[1] For the source code, details on the framework, or a demo please visit the project webpage at http://dexter.isti.cnr.it/elianto

[2] dexter.isti.cnr.it

Not Relevant mentions that the annotator linked to an entity but they are not saying anything about the document.

3. SYSTEM ARCHITECTURE

The system architecture is composed of three layers:

The Data Access Object: allows to store and retrieve the collections and the user annotations, and provides all the object abstractions;

The Core: implements the logic of the application;

The Interfaces: a REST api that allows external applications to retrieve the documents and to submit the user annotations. Some command line programs to perform the indexing and dump the annotations.

We implemented a web interface using the Angular [3] and Bootstrap [4] frameworks, all the actions are performed calling the REST api provided by the server. We also provide a dashboard interface for the user that allows to see the previously annotated documents and to edit them if needed. It is possible to define admin users that can visualize analytics over all the dataset and the user annotations.

4. DEMONSTRATION SCENARIOS

The demonstration will present the main functionalities provided by our system. We will illustrate the two tasks on some documents, showing the annotation facilities provided by the interface. During the demo we will present two case studies: the annotation over the AIDA-CoNLL dataset, where we ask the users to perform both the EL and the ES tasks, and the annotation of a dataset extracted from Wikinews[5], a Wikipedia's project that collects news annotated by the Wikipedia's editors. We will show that is possible to perform just the ES task on this kind of dataset.

Finally we will discuss about how to merge different scores by different users on the same document, in order to create a golden truth: ELIANTO provides scripts for collecting the user annotations and computing different agreement measures, but there could be different ways to create a golden truth from these data. The project will be released open source.

5. RELATED WORK

Datasets and impact of entity saliency. One dataset frequently used for the evaluation of EL methods is the **IITB** dataset[6] by Kulkarni et al. [7]. The dataset contains 103 documents, annotated by 10 distinct human annotators. The majority of the documents are annotated by only one user, sometimes by two. The dataset contains $19,751$ distinct annotations, 54 annotations per document on average. Annotations such as Year, Month, Week, Day, Monday, Tuesday …occur very often even if they are not very informative. Milne and Witten [9] annotated a subset of the **AQUAINT** corpus, consisting of English news. The corpus is annotated in the *Wikipedia style*: only the first mention of each entity, and only the most important are linked.

Several works adopted the **AIDA-CoNLL** dataset, introduced by Hoffart *et al.* [6]. It consists of 1393 documents belonging to the CoNLL-2003 dataset, a subset of news from the Reuters Corpus V1, annotated with entities URI. The authors annotated the mentions referring to named entities, but not the common names. Entities are annotated at each occurrence of a mention.

Gamon *et al.* [4] proposed a dataset for SE: the dataset consists of 99 webpages annotated with named entities (on average 24 entities per page). For each named entity they asked 3 judges to give a salient score among Most Salient, Less Salient, or Not Salient, and they kept the score with the majority of votes. The difference with our approach is that authors used named entities (i.e., just text, no links to a knowledge base), so the EL task cannot be evaluated.

Manual Annotation Frameworks. We are not aware of any other open source framework for generating human assessments for entity linking, and for ranking the entities with respect to their saliency. We examined the Semantic Annotation Platforms reviewed by Reeve and Han [11] but we did not find a tool suitable for generating entity linking annotations. Bayerl *et al.* [1] propose a methodology for creating annotations, and different measures for evaluating agreement among assessors. Our interface was inspired by the *loomp On Click Annotator* proposed by Hinze *et al.* [5].

Acknowledgements This work was partially supported by the EU project E-CLOUD (no. 325091), the Regional (Tuscany) project SECURE! (POR CReO FESR 2007-2011), and the Regional (Tuscany) project MAPaC (POR CReO FESR 2007/2013).

6. REFERENCES

[1] P. S. Bayerl, H. Lüngen, U. Gut, and K. I. Paul. Methodology for reliable schema development and evaluation of manual annotations. In *Workshop on Knowledge Markup and Semantic Annotation*, 2003.

[2] P. Bruza and T. W. Huibers. A study of aboutness in information retrieval. *Artificial Intelligence Review*, 1996.

[3] D. Ceccarelli, C. Lucchese, S. Orlando, R. Perego, and S. Trani. Dexter: an open source framework for entity linking. In *Proceedings of ESAIR*. ACM, 2013.

[4] M. Gamon, T. Yano, X. Song, J. Apacible, and P. Pantel. Identifying salient entities in web pages. In *Proceedings of CIKM*. ACM, 2013.

[5] A. Hinze, R. Heese, M. Luczak-Rösch, and A. Paschke. Semantic enrichment by non-experts: usability of manual annotation tools. In *ISWC*. Springer, 2012.

[6] J. Hoffart, M. Yosef, I. Bordino, H. Fürstenau, M. Pinkal, M. Spaniol, B. Taneva, S. Thater, and G. Weikum. Robust disambiguation of named entities in text. In *EMNLP*, 2011.

[7] S. Kulkarni, A. Singh, G. Ramakrishnan, and S. Chakrabarti. Collective annotation of wikipedia entities in web text. In *SIGKDD*. ACM, 2009.

[8] R. Mihalcea and A. Csomai. Wikify!: linking documents to encyclopedic knowledge. In *Proceedings of the CIKM*, pages 233–242. ACM, 2007.

[9] D. Milne and I. H. Witten. Learning to link with wikipedia. In *Proceedings of the CIKM*, pages 509–518. ACM, 2008.

[10] D. Paranjpe. Learning document aboutness from implicit user feedback and document structure. In *Proceedings of CIKM*. ACM, 2009.

[11] L. Reeve and H. Han. Survey of semantic annotation platforms. In *Proceedings of SAC*, 2005.

---

[3] https://angularjs.org

[4] http://getbootstrap.com

[5] http://en.wikinews.org/wiki/Main_Page

[6] Annotations are available here http://www.cse.iitb.ac.in/soumen/doc/CSAW/Annot/CSAW_Annotations.xml

SmartVenues: Recommending Popular and Personalised Venues in a City

Romain Deveaud   M-Dyaa Albakour   Jarana Manotumruksa
Craig Macdonald   Iadh Ounis

University of Glasgow, UK
firstame.lastname@glasgow.ac.uk

ABSTRACT

We present SmartVenues, a system that recommends nearby venues to a user who visits or lives in a city. SmartVenues models the variation over time of each venue's level of attendance, and uses state-of-the-art time series forecasting algorithms to predict the future attendance of these venues. We use the predicted levels of attendance to infer the popularity of a venue at future points in time, and to provide the user with recommendations at different times of the day. If the users log in with their Facebook account, the recommendations are personalised using the pages they *like*. In this demonstrator, we detail the architecture of the system and the data that we collect in real-time to be able to perform the predictions. We also present two different interfaces that build upon our system to display the recommendations: a web-based application and a mobile application.

Categories and Subject Descriptors: H.3.3 [Information Storage & Retrieval]: Information Search & Retrieval

Keywords: venue recommendation; location-based social network; attendance prediction; time series forecasting; Foursquare; Facebook

1. INTRODUCTION

Mobile technologies are changing the way we look for and consume information. Search is becoming increasingly local, and is now mostly performed using mobile devices[1]. Looking for venues while on the move is a new task that is receiving growing interest, demonstrated by the popularity of Location-Based Social Networks (LBSNs) [11] such as Foursquare[2], Yelp[3], or Google Places[4]. In these LBSNs, users can broadcast their location to their friends (or to other users), and can rate or comment the venues they visited. The preferences of users are derived from this implicit

---

[1] http://marketingland.com/nielsen-time-accessing-internet-smartphones-pcs-73683

[2] http://foursquare.com

[3] http://yelp.com

[4] http://maps.google.com/

feedback, allowing the applications of the LBSNs to provide users with personalised venue recommendations [9, 10].

There are two main drawbacks in the current venue recommendation applications proposed by the leading LBSNs [3]. Firstly, they do not take the time of the day or the date into account. Indeed, the popularity of venues varies throughout the day, and can also depend on the day of the week or the season of the year. For example, bars are more likely to be crowded on week end nights, while parks are significantly more attractive during spring or summer time. Secondly, they require the users to rate large amounts of venues to perform accurate personalised recommendations. This drawback is also known as the cold start problem of recommender systems [8].

In this demonstrator, we present SmartVenues, a venue recommendation system for discovering popular and personalised venues in a city at different times of the day, without requiring the users to enter their preferences. SmartVenues aims at 1) modelling the popularity of individual venues over time by predicting their levels of attendance, 2) recommending personalised venues to the users by using the pages they *like* on Facebook, and 3) providing appropriate interfaces that are suitable for exploration (web-based) or discovery (mobile-based) scenarios. SmartVenues relies on a backend system that computes the predictions and recommendations (described in Section 2), on the top of which we have implemented the two different interfaces (Section 3). The web interface of SmartVenues can be accessed at http://demos.terrier.org/SMART/venuesuggestion, and the mobile application can be downloaded from the Google Play store at https://play.google.com/store/apps/details?id=gla.ac.uk.entertainme.ui.

2. DATA & ARCHITECTURE

The SmartVenues system is composed of two parts. The first one models the popularity of venues over time by querying Foursquare to obtain the levels of attendance for each venue in real-time, and by computing predictions of these levels of attendance. The second one is interactive and ranks the venues for a given Facebook user, at a given location and a given time. SmartVenues currently proposes recommendations for four cities: London, Amsterdam, San Francisco, and Glasgow.

2.1 Modelling and predicting the popularity of venues

We take a simple yet realistic definition of the popularity of a venue by considering its level of attendance: a venue that attracts a lot of people is more likely to be popular [5].

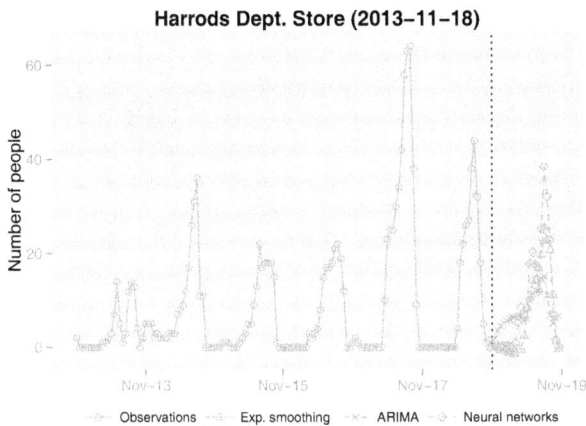

Figure 1: Predicting the attendance of the Harrods department store (London) on the 18th November 2013, using three state-of-the-art time series forecasting models. Models were trained from the 12nd to the 17th.

We use the API of Foursquare[5], which allows to obtain the number of people currently visiting the venue. By querying the API every hour for each venue, we build comprehensive time series of venue attendance. An example of such time series can be seen in Figure 1, where the green line represents the observations made over a six days period for the Harrods department store in London.

We predict the future levels of attendance of venues using time series forecasting algorithms, such as ARIMA (Autoregressive integrated moving average), Exponential Smoothing, or Neural Networks [7]. These algorithms use past observations to learn trends, seasonal variations, and recurring patterns in the data. It suits perfectly our use case, for which we have large amounts of very precise (i.e. hourly) data. Moreover, they offer the advantage to predict not only the value of the next point of the time series, but the values of the next N points. In our case, we predict the levels of attendance of each venue for the next 24 hours. An example of these predictions is displayed in Figure 1, where we see the output values of three forecasting models for the seventh day, after having trained the models on the first six days. All of the time series forecasting models were built using the well-known `forecast` package of `R` [4]. The ARIMA algorithm was found to be the most accurate according to our preliminary experiments, and we logically use it as our default forecasting model.

2.2 Recommending venues

The other part of SmartVenues focuses on the actual retrieval and recommendation of venues. However, this process does not rely on traditional collaborative filtering approaches, and hence does not require the users to enter a list of preferences nor does it ask them to rate venues. We personalise the recommendations by asking the users to log in with their Facebook account, thereby using the pages they *like* on the social network as a surrogate for their personal interests. We used the authentication software development kit provided by Facebook[6] in order to obtain the pages that users like without storing any personal information.

---

[5] http://developer.foursquare.com/docs/venues/herenow
[6] http://developers.facebook.com/docs/facebook-login

We employ a simple and straightforward approach for personalising the recommendations. First, we indexed the homepages of the venues using the Terrier IR platform [6]. Then, when the users – logged in with their Facebook account – request recommendations, we use the category (e.g. "music", "author", "museum", ...) of each of the Facebook pages they like as a query to retrieve a ranked list of venues. In other words, the score of a venue v is computed as follows:

$$score(v) = \frac{1}{|\text{likes}(u)|} \sum_{p \in \text{likes}(u)} RSV(\text{cat}(p), v) \qquad (1)$$

where $\text{likes}(u)$ denotes the set of Facebook pages liked by the user u, and $\text{cat}(p)$ is the category of the page p. In this demonstrator, we use the DPH weighting model [1] as the RSV function. Finally, we only keep the venues that are close to the location that the user entered as an input parameter, in order to recommend nearby venues. More specifically, we do not recommend venues that are more than 500 meters away from their location.

3. INTERFACES

The web-based application allows the users to set custom locations and to explore the recommendations, as well as the venue popularity predictions. Conversely, the mobile application focuses on a real-time scenario, where the users are in the city and want to obtain entertaining suggestions. We detail their components in the following sections.

3.1 Web-based application

First, users need to log in with their Facebook account to receive personalised recommendations. We set a predefined list of locations, represented as links that the user can click on, in order to help users in their exploration. They can easily change their location by double-clicking on a specific point of the map, thus triggering a change in the recommendations. The interface, depicted in Figure 2, is composed of three main parts.

The first one is the map (A), on which the venues are displayed as red balloons. The location of the user is represented by a green arrow. The second part is the recommendation list (B). When users click on a venue in this list, the map is centered around this venue and an information window – containing venue information such as its categories, its URL in Foursquare, and a randomly selected image – is displayed. The last part (C) is a graph showing the forecasted attendance of a selected venue for the past and coming hours, and is the main originality of this interface. The users can then look at the current popularity of the venues, and see when the system predict their popularity to be at its maximum. Moreover, they can drag the slider of this graph further into the "future", which will automatically recompute the recommendations and re-rank the venues by taking their future popularity into account. This feature can be used to explore the popularity of different venues (or an entire area of the city) at different times of the day, and can hence help the users to take decisions and plan their day.

3.2 Mobile application

While the web-based application focuses on exploration and allows the users to see how the rankings change depending on the hour, the mobile application is centered on an "on-the-move" scenario. In this scenario, the user does not have to specify his location, it is automatically inferred from

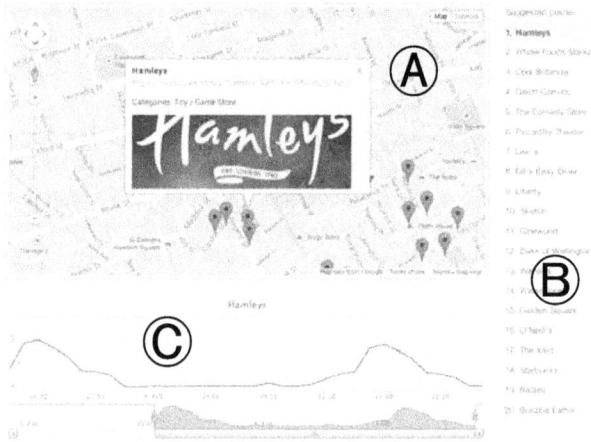

Figure 2: The web-based application is composed of three parts: (A) an interactive map, (B) a recommendation list, and (C) a graph showing the forecasted attendance of the selected venue.

the GPS or the mobile access data. Then, recommendations are provided using the approach detailed in Section 2.

Again, the users have to log in with their Facebook account to be able to see the personalised recommendations, as shown on the left-hand picture of Figure 3. The recommended venues are displayed on a map and are represented by icons associated to their categories (e.g. Food, Arts & Entertainment). A ranked list of recommendations is also presented to the user, showing information such as the total number of check-ins, the distance between the location of the user and the venue, or the rating. When clicking on a venue, the mobile application provides more detailed information, as shown on the right-hand picture of Figure 3. It includes a detailed map, along with pictures of the venue that have been taken by Foursquare users, some social information (number of likes, check-ins, and unique users), as well as the comments that have been provided by other users. The users can then choose to check in the venue, bookmark it, or ask the application to show them the directions towards the venue. Finally, when the users move to a new location (distant enough from the initial one), the application automatically sends them a notification and pushes new recommendation of nearby popular venues.

4. CONCLUDING DISCUSSION

We have described SmartVenues, a system that aims at providing popular and personalised venue recommendations to users, and we have presented two interfaces that we built on the top of this system. While the web-based interface is suitable for exploratory scenarios (e.g. "What will be the most interesting and popular venue in three hours around this location?"), the mobile application can be used whilst on the move and thereby can help to address increasing local and mobile information needs.

The context-aware suggestion of venues is still a challenge within the Information Retrieval community [2], especially in relation to the evaluation of such a complex task. Therefore, we envision several uses of the mobile application for evaluation purposes. Firstly, we could use the GPS function of the smartphones to actually see if a user visited a venue that was recommended, and derive several indicators such as the time spent in a venue. Secondly, we could use these information to perform A/B testing or interleaving evaluations

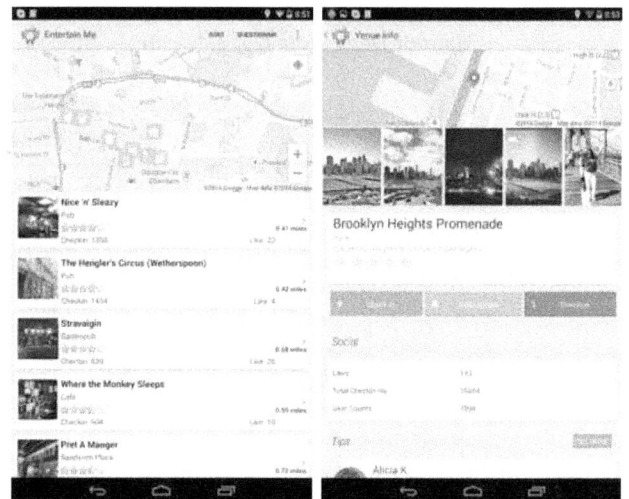

Figure 3: Two views of the mobile application. On the left-hand side, the recommended venues are displayed on the map and as a ranked list. Details about venues are provided when clicking on them, as shown on the right-hand side picture.

in order to compare the effectiveness of various recommendation or ranking algorithms. The interaction data could also be used to deploy algorithms that can learn over time if users prefer popular or personalised recommendations, and to re-rank venues accordingly. Finally, we could obtain city-wide data that would help us answer questions such as: why do people visit these venues? Are there areas of the city that need to be improved to attract more people?

Acknowledgments

This work has been carried out in the scope of the EC co-funded project SMART (FP7-287583).

5. REFERENCES

[1] G. Amati, E. Ambrosi, M. Bianchi, C. Gaibisso, and G. Gambosi. FUB, IASI-CNR and Univ. of Tor Vergata at TREC 2007 Blog Track. In *Proc. of TREC*, 2007.

[2] A. Dean-Hall, C. L. Clarke, J. Kamps, P. Thomas, N. Simone, and E. M. Voorhees. Overview of the TREC 2013 Contextual Suggestion track. In *Proc. of TREC*, 2013.

[3] R. Deveaud, M.-D. Albakour, C. Macdonald, and I. Ounis. Challenges in Recommending Venues within Smart Cities. In *Proc. of i-ASC at ECIR*, 2014.

[4] R. J. Hyndman and Y. Khandakar. Automatic Time Series Forecasting: The forecast Package for R. *Journal of Statistical Software*, 27(3), 2008.

[5] Y. Li, M. Steiner, L. Wang, Z.-L. Zhang, and J. Bao. Exploring venue popularity in Foursquare. In *Proc. of INFOCOM*, 2013.

[6] C. Macdonald, R. McCreadie, R. Santos, and I. Ounis. From Puppy to Maturity: Experiences in Developing Terrier. In *Proc. of OSIR at SIGIR*, 2012.

[7] S. G. Makridakis, S. Wheelwright, and R. Hyndman. *Forecasting: Methods and Applications*. Wiley, 1998.

[8] A. I. Schein, A. Popescul, L. H. Ungar, and D. M. Pennock. Methods and Metrics for Cold-start Recommendations. In *Proc. of SIGIR*, 2002.

[9] M. Ye, P. Yin, W.-C. Lee, and D.-L. Lee. Exploiting Geographical Influence for Collaborative Point-of-interest Recommendation. In *Proc. of SIGIR*, 2011.

[10] Q. Yuan, G. Cong, Z. Ma, A. Sun, and N. Magnenat-Thalmann. Time-aware Point-of-interest Recommendation. In *Proc. of SIGIR*, 2013.

[11] Y. Zheng. Location-Based Social Networks: Users. In *Computing with Spatial Trajectories*. Springer, 2011.

GTE-Rank: Searching for Implicit Temporal Query Results

Ricardo Campos [1,2,6], Gaël Dias [4], Alípio Mário Jorge [2,3], Célia Nunes [5,6]

[1] Polytechnic Institute of Tomar, Portugal; [2] LIAAD – INESC TEC; [3] DCC – FCUP, University of Porto, Portugal; [4] HULTECH/GREYC, University of Caen Basse-Normandie, France; [5] Department of Mathematics, University of Beira Interior, Covilhã, Portugal; [6] Center of Mathematics, University of Beira Interior, Covilhã, Portugal

ricardo.campos@inesctec.pt, gael.dias@unicaen.fr, amjorge@fc.up.pt, celian@ubi.pt

ABSTRACT

Temporal information retrieval has been a topic of great interest in recent years. Despite the efforts that have been conducted so far, most popular search engines remain underdeveloped when it comes to explicitly considering the use of temporal information in their search process. In this paper we present GTE-Rank, an online searching tool that takes time into account when ranking time-sensitive query web search results. GTE-Rank is defined as a linear combination of topical and temporal scores to reflect the relevance of any web page both in topical and temporal dimensions. The resulting system can be explored graphically through a search interface made available for research purposes.

Categories and Subject Descriptors

H.3.3 [**Information Storage and Retrieval**]: Information Search and Retrieval – *Query Formulation*

Keywords

Temporal Information Retrieval; Implicit Temporal Queries; Temporal Re-Ranking; Temporal Query Understanding

1. INTRODUCTION

Despite the emergence of a large spectrum of time-aware search and retrieval applications, most popular search engines still do not take advantage of the temporal information contained in web pages. Current search engines either give users the possibility to specify a point-in-time of their interest or apply freshness metrics to push to the top list the most recent web search results. While this may be a suitable solution for the news domain for which a huge quality of time-stamped web pages are available and for recent events which require evidence spike phenomena, it may prove to be inefficient if the user is more interested in wide coverage temporally diversified information. This is particular evident for implicit temporal queries (e.g., "*Haiti earthquake*", "*BP oil spill*" or "*Madagascar*"), which beyond not being explicitly tagged with a temporal feature, span over a broad timeline. In this paper, we present GTE-Rank an online search interface, which allows searching for topics through time. GTE-Rank is designed to enhance user's experience through a balanced approach that takes into account both the conceptual and the temporal dimensions of the topic. The rationale is that offering the user a comprehensive temporal contextualization of the topic is intuitively more informative than simply retrieving only the most recent results or just its contextual perspective. For instance, when querying for the well-known American actor "*Philip Seymour Hoffman*", who has passed away recently, it would be interesting

CIKM '14 , Nov 3-7, 2014, Shanghai, China.
ACM 978-1-4503-2598-1/14/11.
http://dx.doi.org/10.1145/2661829.2661856

to know who he was or when did he die, but also to be provided with other important topics and time information, such as, when did he begin acting in television, where he was born or which movie gave him the award for the best actor performance. Such a new presentation of the results would enable users to gain not only a broad insight of the topic but also to understand its multiple temporal dimensions, thus contributing to improve user's satisfaction [1].

Aware of the above, researchers have started to address the problem of returning documents that are not only topically relevant but that are also from the most important time periods and not just the latest. Different studies have been proposed to solve this problem. The research that are most related to our approach are [2,7,8]. Berberich *et al.* [2] for example, ranks documents according to the estimated probability of generating the query through a language model framework that requires documents and queries to be explicitly time stamped. The methods put forward by Metzler *et al.* [7] and Kanhabua & Nørvåg [8] suggest an alternative solution. They propose a time-dependent ranking model to explicitly adjust the score of a document in favor of those matching the determined time(s) of an implicit temporal query. None of these works however, consider extracting temporal features from the documents contents in order to determine the possible time(s) of the query. Metzler *et al.* [7] uses query logs and Kanhabua & Nørvåg [8] takes advantage of the creation date of the document, which may be significantly different from the actual content. We differ from previous studies on this subject in several other aspects. First, our methodology is unsupervised as no specific training process is needed to determine the time(s) of the query. Second, it is mostly language-independent as it implements a rule-based model supported by simple regular expressions to extract relevant dates. Finally, besides estimating the degree of relevance of a temporal expression, we propose to determine whether or not a date is query relevant, thus using this information to improve the re-ranking of web search results. The remainder of this paper is organized as follows. Section 2 describes the architecture behind the GTE-Rank system. Section 3 presents the proposed demonstration. Finally, Section 4 concludes this paper with some final remarks.

2. SYSTEM ARCHITECTURE

In this section, we describe the main components of the GTE-Rank system. GTE-Rank proceeds in two steps. First, the system evaluates the correlation between a given query and the candidate dates extracted within web snippets leading to the identification of top relevant dates. Second, a linear combination of topical and temporal scores is defined to reflect the relevance of any web snippet both in the topical and in the temporal dimensions. The overall structure of GTE-Rank architecture is represented in Figure 1 and consists of five different modules: (1) Web search; (2) Web snippet representation; (3) Temporal similarity; (4) Date filtering and (5) Temporal ranking.

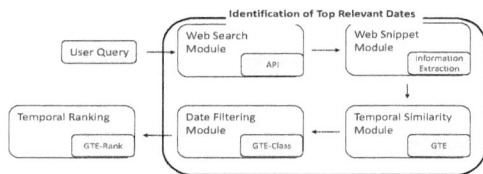

Figure 1: GTE-Rank Architecture.

The GTE-Rank interface receives a query from the user, fetches related web snippets from a given search engine and applies text processing to all web snippets. This processing task involves selecting the most relevant words and collecting the candidate years in each web snippet. Each candidate year is then given a temporal similarity value to the query computed in the temporal similarity module. We then apply a classification strategy in the date filtering module, to determine whether the candidate years are actually relevant or not to the query. Non-relevant ones will be simply discarded by the system. Each snippet is then reordered according to its contents and how they relate to the query both in the temporal and in the topical dimensions. A brief description of each component is provided below.

(1) Web Search. We apply a web search API, which, given an implicit temporal query, accesses an up-to-date index search engine to obtain a collection of web results. Since results are produced "on-the-fly", we simply return the set of n-top web snippets retrieved in response to the user's query, thus keeping the system computationally efficient.

(2) Web Snippet Representation. Each snippet is represented by a bag-of-relevant-words and a set of candidate temporal expressions extracted from the title of the snippet and from the text itself. As shown by Alonso *et al.* [1], web snippets offer an interesting alternative for the representation of web documents, where years often appear, thus avoiding the cost of parsing full web pages. We rely on a segmentation process and a numerical selection heuristic to extract relevant words[1] and a simple rule-based model supported on regular expressions to extract explicit temporal patterns. We focus on the extraction of temporal patterns of the year granularity level to keep the system mostly language-independent. The obtained result is a set of distinct candidate years extracted from the set of all web snippets.

(3) Temporal Similarity. Each candidate year d_j is then given a temporal similarity value representing its degree of relevance to the query q. To model this relevance, we apply our temporal similarity measure GTE [3], which retrieves a value ranging from 0 to 1. A web service of GTE is provided[2] so that it can be tested by the research community. The web service returns in XML format, the temporal similarity value calculated between the query and all the candidate dates, together with the corresponding contents where the candidate dates appear.

(4) Date Filtering. Next, the system determines whether or not the candidate temporal expressions are relevant to the query by applying GTE-Class [3], a classical threshold-based strategy, which considers a candidate date to be relevant, if and only if $GTE(q, d_j) \geq \lambda$ and non-relevant otherwise. Based on this, each snippet is no longer represented by a set of candidate temporal expressions but by a set of relevant dates. One consequence of this, is a direct impact on the quality of the retrieved results, as non-relevant or wrong dates are simply discarded. A description of the GTE-Class demo[3] can be found in our recent work [5].

(5) Temporal Ranking. The final step of the GTE-Rank architecture is our temporal re-ranking model. GTE-Rank relies on a linear combination approach that considers topical and temporal scores. The underlying idea is that a document should be ranked higher if its contents are topically and temporally related to the query. GTE-Rank is defined below. $\alpha \in [0,1]$ and $\beta = 1 - \alpha$ are the tuning parameters setting the importance of each of the two dimensions, q is the query, $d_{j,i}^{Rel} \in D_{S_i}^{Rel}, j = 1,..,u$ is one of the u relevant dates of the snippet S_i, $w_{h,i} \in W_{S_i}, h = 1,..,k$ is one of the k most relevant terms of the snippet S_i and IS [6] a second-order similarity measure that calculates the correlation between all pairs of two context vectors X and Y, where X is the context vector representation of q and Y of $w_{h,i}$. Both context vectors are formed by a combination of the best relevant terms and best relevant dates determined by the DICE coefficient measure.

$$GTE\text{-}Rank(q, S_i) = \alpha \sum_{j=1}^{u} GTE\left(q, d_{j,i}^{Rel}\right) + \beta \sum_{h=1}^{k} IS(q, w_{h,i})$$

Central to this ranking function is the computation of two similarities. GTE gives the similarity between the query and each of the relevant dates found in the snippet. IS gives the similarity between the query and each of the relevant words found in the snippet. Note that one of the advantages of our approach relies precisely on the use of GTE as it enables GTE-Class to filter out from the ranking module the set of all non-relevant dates. Experiments with a publicly available dataset[4] consisting of 1900 web snippets and 38 implicit text queries show that GTE-Rank is able to achieve better results under several evaluation metrics compared to three different baselines. A fully detailed description of the underlying scientific approach and the evaluation methodology can be found in [4].

3. DEMONSTRATION OVERVIEW
As a result of our research, we publicly provide an online demo (http://wia.info.unicaen.fr/GTERankAspNet_Server).GTE-Rank was implemented using .Net technology (C#) and asp.net on the server side. The implemented version is designed to demonstrate the current state of the demo, thus concerns of design nature where not taken into account. Although the main motivation of our work is focused on queries with temporal nature, GTE-Rank allows the execution of any query including non-temporal ones. Since our system does not pose any constraint in terms of language or domain, users can issue queries in any language, ranging from business (e.g. "*iPad*"), cinema (e.g. "*true grit*"), politics (e.g. "*Margaret Thatcher*"), natural disasters (e.g. "*Haiti earthquake*"), musical topics (e.g. "*Radiohead*"), to cite just a few. To retrieve the results, we use a prospective search where the query is first issued before results are gathered and indexed. For this purpose we rely on Bing Search API[5] with the *en-US* language parameter defined to retrieve 50 results per query. The proposed solution is computationally efficient and can easily be tested online (limited to 5000 queries per month). In response to a query submitted in a search box, GTE-Rank displays a set of ranked web snippets on the fly. We offer two types of retrieval: one that returns only web snippets having dates and one that returns the set of all the 50 web snippets, whether or not they have dates. In addition, we give users the chance to adjust the temporal and conceptual parts of the system. Through an interactive browsing tuning parameter, the user is thus able to define the importance of the two dimensions. α is currently preset to 0.8 as

---

[1] http://wia.info.unicaen.fr/TokenExtractor/api/Token?query= [May 29th, 2014]

[2] http://wia.info.unicaen.fr/GTEAspNetFlatTempCluster_Server/api/GTE?FilterDates=false&query=

[3] http://wia.info.unicaen.fr/GTEAspNetFlatTempCluster_Server [May 29th, 2014]

[4] http://www.ccc.ipt.pt/~ricardo/datasets/WCRank_DS.html [May 29th, 2014]

[5] https://datamarket.azure.com/dataset/5BA839F1-12CE-4CCE-BF57-A49D98D29A44 [May 29th, 2014]

GTE-Rank has achieved the best performance with this value in the experiments carried out. Each web snippet is also assigned a relevance ranking value reflecting its topical and temporal similarity with the user's query. This value is positioned in front of the number in red color, which defines the ranking position initially obtained by Bing search engine. In this demo, we show the ability of the ranking system not only in how it pulls up to the top the relevant documents, but also in how it pushes down to the tail the non-relevant ones, thus ensuring that they will not occupy top positions of the ranking results. An illustration of the interface is provided in Figure 2 for the query "*true grit*" (top 10 results). It is interesting to note that our algorithm retrieves in the second, third, sixth, seventh and tenth position, five relevant results that were initially retrieved by the Bing search engine in the thirty-fifth, thirty-first, twenty-first, thirty-ninth and twenty-fifth positions, respectively. Furthermore, we show that our algorithm is also able to promote to the top, relevant documents which do not include any temporal expression.

Figure 2: GTE-Rank interface for the query "true grit". Top 10.

Finally, Figure 3 shows the tail 5 ranking results for the same query. It is interesting to note that our algorithm is able to position well down in the list of the results, temporally non-relevant documents that were initially positioned at top positions by Bing search engine, of which IDs 5, 13 and 17 are elucidative examples. A video outlining the demo proceeding is available at http://www.ccc.ipt.pt/~ricardo/software.html.

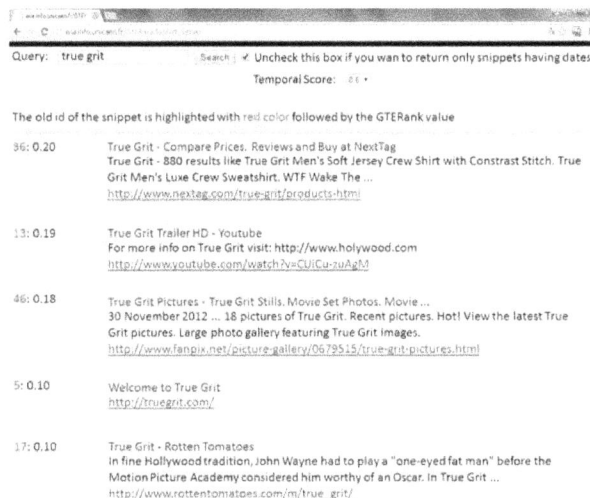

Figure 3: GTE-Rank interface for the "true grit". Tail 5.

4. CONCLUSION

In this article we present GTE-Rank - an online searching system that aims to retrieve in the top list of the results, documents that are not only topically relevant but that are also from the most important time periods. GTE-Rank relies on a similarity measure that is capable of identifying top relevant dates for queries where no temporal information is provided and a re-ranking model that combines both conceptual and temporal relevancies in a single score, thus offering a balanced approach of the results. We adopt a methodology that can be applied to real-world search scenarios and a content-based approach, which enables to return documents about a given period, as opposed to the retrieval of documents written or published at a given date. As a practical demonstration of our research, we provide a demo service so that GTE-Rank can be tested by the research community. Although we focus on web snippets, our approach is similarly applicable to small texts collections embodying temporal information, such as Twitter posts.

5. ACKNOWLEDGMENTS

This work is financed by the ERDF – European Regional Development Fund through the COMPETE Programme (operational programme for competitiveness), by National Funds through the FCT – Fundação para a Ciência e a Tecnologia (Portuguese Foundation for Science and Technology) within project «FCOMP-01-0124-FEDER-037281» and by the Center of Mathematics, University of Beira Interior, within project «PEst-OE/MAT/UI0212/2014».

6. REFERENCES

[1] Alonso, O., Baeza-Yates, R., and Gertz, M. (2009). Effectiveness of Temporal Snippets. In WSSP'09-WWW'09. Madrid, Spain.
[2] Berberich, K., Bedathur, S., Alonso, O., and Weikum, G. (2010). A Language Modeling Approach for Temporal Information Needs.
[3] Campos, R., Dias, G., Jorge, A. M., and Nunes, C. (2012). GTE: A Distributional Second-Order Co-Occurrence Approach to Improve the Identification of Top Relevant Dates. In CIKM'12.
[4] Campos, R. (2013). Disambiguating Implicit Temporal Queries for Temporal Information Retrieval Applications. PhD Thesis. UP, Portugal.
[5] Campos, R., Dias, G., Jorge, A. M., and Nunes, C. (2014). GTE-Cluster: A Temporal Search Interface for Implicit Temporal Queries. In ECIR'14.
[6] Dias, G., Alves, E., and Lopes, J. (2007). Topic Segmentation Algorithms for Text Summarization and Passage Retrieval: An Exhaustive Evaluation. In AAAI'07. Canada.
[7] Metzler, D., Jones, R., Peng, F., and Zhang, R. (2009). Improving Search Relevance for Implicitly Temporal Queries. In SIGIR'09.
[8] Kanhabua, N., and Nørvåg, K. (2010). Determining Time of Queries for Re-Ranking Search Results. In ECDL'10. Scotland.

Exploring Document Collections with Topic Frames

Alexander Hinneburg, Frank Rosner
Institute for Computer Science
Martin-Luther-University Halle-Wittenberg
Germany

Stefan Pessler, Christian Oberländer
Institute for Japanese Studies
Martin-Luther-University Halle-Wittenberg
Germany

ABSTRACT

Topics automatically derived by topic models are not always easy and clearly interpretable by humans. The most probable top words of a topic may leave room for ambiguous interpretations, especially when the top words are exclusively nouns. We demonstrate how part-of-speech (POS) tagging and co-location analysis of terms can be used to derive linguistic frames that yield more interpretable topic representations. The so-called topic frames are demonstrated as feature of the TopicExplorer system that allows to explore document collections using topic models, visualizations and key word search. Demo versions of TopicExplorer are available at http://topicexplorer.informatik.uni-halle.de/.

Categories and Subject Descriptors

H.4 [**Information Systems Applications**]: Miscellaneous

Keywords

topic model; visualization; topic frame

1. INTRODUCTION

Topic models offer a way to explore large document collections by presenting topics that show typical contents. As topic models are constructed by unsupervised learning, they can be applied without the need to manually annotate documents. During learning, a topic model assigns all word tokens in the documents to topics pursuing two conflicting goals: (i) topics should be assigned to as few different words as possible and (ii) a document should exhibit as few topics as possible [2]. Learning algorithms find trade-off solutions in this scenario that correspond to local optima of a free energy function in case of variational methods or to some probable global states in case of Gibbs samplers. However, all known algorithms cannot provide a guarantee on how well the derived topics are interpretable by humans.

State-of-the-art is to represent topics—which mathematically are distributions over words—as list of most probable top words. Interpreting such word lists may pose a difficult task for humans. Success depends on both background knowledge and familiarity with vocabulary. There are two possible problems that hinder an interpretation. First, the word list may mostly be composed of nouns whose interrelation may be ambiguous. Imagine a list of country names, even if these countries are only from a particular region, there are many different possible interpretations that would fit to such a list of names. Thus, such a list of topic words is not well interpretable. Second, the list of top words appears to be incoherent. That might be due to words that are unfamiliar to the analyst.

An open question is how to represent a topic in a way that is more clear and digestible to humans. Recent research on topic coherence shows: topics are more interpretable by humans when pairs of top words often appear together in documents [8]. Thus, representing topics as pairs of top words that are frequently co-located in documents could ease human understanding. However, that approach does not solve the list-of-nouns problem. A key observation is that verbs are often less prominent in topic distributions because they are more flexible used in different contexts. Thus, they appear less often in top word lists of topics.

Combinations of a noun and a verb could be seen as basic units for transmitting semantic content. Minski called such units frames in the early days of artificial intelligence [1, 10]. Thus, detecting a noun with a verb in close proximity in a document is a necessary condition for detecting a frame. A topic frame may be present when a topic model assigns both the noun and the verb to the same topic. Thus, a more interpretable representation of a topic is to show a list of frequent topic frames. We demonstrate that topic frames are a step towards interpretable representations of topics.

We implemented topic frames in our TopicExplorer system. The demo includes corpora in different languages. A suitable corpus for demonstration is one that is widely known. Thus, the user can verify the validity of topics and topic frames based on common background knowledge. Therefore, we demonstrate the system on a subset of articles of the English Wikipedia, and a collection of well known German fairy tales. Furthermore, we show a real application use case of TopicExplorer: supporting research in social sciences to access a collection of Japanese blogs discussing the Fukushima disaster of 2011 and social responsibility.

2. ANATOMY OF TOPICEXPLORER

The detection of topic frames requires additional data preprocessing steps that are not part of typical analysis

CIKM'14, November 3–7, 2014, Shanghai, China.
ACM 978-1-4503-2598-1/14/11.
http://dx.doi.org/10.1145/2661829.2661857.

pipelines for topic modeling. We describe the necessary steps and how they fit into the overall architecture of Topic-Explorer. We used three corpora covering English, German and Japanese to demonstrate the flexibility of TopicExplorer to handle different languages. The English corpus is a subset of the longest 10.000 Wikipedia articles. The German corpus covers German fairy tales collected by the Grimm brothers. The Japanese corpus originates from a pilot study of a project to analyze blog about the Fukushima disaster. Due to space restrictions, only results on English Wikipedia are presented in this articles. Demo versions with the other corpora are available at the TopicExplorer web site.

2.1 Linguistic data preparation

This kind of data preparation includes tokenization of documents, part-of-speech (POS) tagging, tag aggregation, token filtering and lemmatization. Tokenization breaks a document given as character string into a sequence of strings called tokens. For text data with Latin alphabets, white spaces indicate word boundaries. We used this kind of tokenizer for German and English language. For languages like Chinese and Japanese, more sophisticated tools are needed that predict word boundaries based on training data. We used MeCab (`http://mecab.googlecode.com`) that tokenizes, POS tags and lemmatizes Japanese text. We store the exact start position of each token with respect to the current document. This is viable to determine whether two tokens assigned to the same topic are close within a document.

POS tagging annotates tokens as noun, verb or other grammatical word classes. Currently available POS taggers assign more detailed word classes to tokens than necessary for our analysis. Therefore, word classes have to be aggregated to the broad and crude classes noun and verb. Tree-Tagger [11] for example, which is used for German and English, distinguishes between 5 different labels for verbs (VV, VVD, VVG, VVN, VVP, VVZ)[1] that we all treat as verbs. Beside using POS tags for detecting topic frames after topic modeling they can be used for filtering tokens that code less important content. In our demonstration, we filtered out all non-nouns and non-verbs including auxiliary verbs like forms of be, do and have.

Topic models compare words as strings. Therefore, reducing tokens to word lemmas helps to match words of same meaning. In summary, the output of linguistic preprocessing is a token sequence of nouns and verbs for each document, where each tokens is annotated with the aggregated POS tag, the lemmatized word as word type and exact start position of the original token in the respective document.

2.2 Topic modeling, post-processing and user interface

We build LDA topic models [4] of different sizes for all three corpora using MALLET [9]. It is important to obtain the topic assignments of all tokens in all documents. MALLET has an option to output this kind of information. For efficient processing, it is nice to have the output of the topic assignments in the same order as the input sequence of the word tokens. This allows to efficiently match word tokens with topic assignments using a kind of merge join algorithm. Thus, the result after merging the output of topic modeling with the data from linguistic preprocesing

---

[1]Description of labels: `http://www.cis.uni-muenchen.de/~schmid/tools/TreeTagger/data/stts_guide.pdf`

is a large table with columns `DocumentId`, `Token`, `Start-Position`, `WordType`, `POS` and `TopicId`. From this table, we compute the probabilities $P(\text{word type}|\text{topic})$, $P(\text{topic}|\text{word type})$, $P(\text{document}|\text{topic})$ and $P(\text{topic}|\text{document})$.

These probabilities are used for different rankings in the web-based TopicExplorer user interface. The probabilities $P(\text{word type}|\text{topic})$ are used to compute top words for each topic. Further, those probabilities are used to form a vector for each topic. We compute the full cosine similarity matrix between all topic vectors and use that matrix as input for hierarchical clustering. The hierarchical clustering in R outputs along with the clustering a serial ordering of the topics that are leaves in the clustering dendrogram. We use this ordering to assign colors to topics and arrange them horizontally at the bottom of the TopicExplorer user interface. Thus, similar topics are represented by similar color and closely located in horizontal ordering. Therefore, slowly moving the horizontal slider and reading the top word lists of the topics gives an uninterrupted impression of the contents in the document collection.

When clicking on the link above such a top word list a new tab is opened that shows a ranked list of documents. Documents are ranked according to $P(\text{document}|\text{topic})$. In the screenshot, the most right list of top word with red background indicates a topic about sports. This can be confirmed by looking at the titles of the top ranking documents for that topics, which are shown above. For each document, a title and the first few lines are shown. Further, the four most important topics for that documents according to $P(\text{topic}|\text{document})$ are indicated as colored circles. When typing words into the keyword search field, autocompletion kicks in and suggests words together with respective important topic ranked according to $P(\text{topic}|\text{word type})$. An earlier version of TopicExplorer having this features had been demonstrated elsewhere [7].

3. DEMONSTRATION OF TOPIC FRAMES

The merged data after topic modeling—containing token positions, POS tags and topic assignments of tokens—allow to compute topic frames. A list of k top nouns and k top verb is computed for each topic with respect to the probabilities $P(\text{word type}|\text{topic})$. A co-location of two tokens that (i) are closer than a given threshold t in a document, (ii) have matching word types with a top noun and a top verb respectively, (iii) and are both assigned to the respective topic constitute the occurrence of a topic frame. All occurrences of all possible topic frames are computed for each topic. For each topic frame, the number of occurrences and the number of documents containing such an occurrence are counted. For a topic, a list of topic frames in decreasing order of number of documents with the respective frame is an alternative representation of a topic.

Consider topics as shown in Figure 1. The topics are not clearly interpretable, especially the right topic starting with India shows just a list of country names. The topic could represent tourism or geography. The same is true for the middle topic that is something about America. Switching the topic representation to topic frames by clicking on the small icon in the upper left corner of the topic view in the bottom panel, the true meaning of the topics become more clear, Figure 2. The right topic starting with India is about foreign politics and the middle topic is about history of the United States. This demonstrates that topic frames consist-

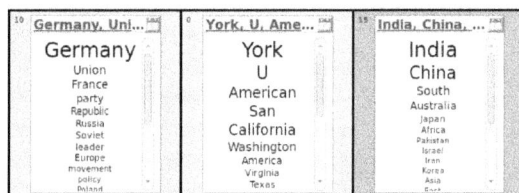

Figure 1: Topics with top word list that are not clearly interpretable.

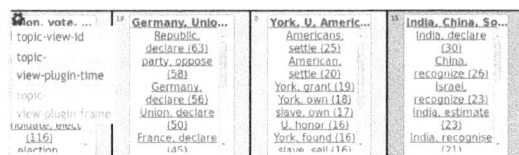

Figure 2: Topics represented by topic frames become more clearly interpretable.

(a) topic frame

(b) words with topic assignments

Figure 3: Topic frame (American, settle) in Wikipedia article Oregon trail.

ing of noun verb combinations are effective to more clearly represent the content of a topic.

The meaning of a topic can be confirmed by looking at the title of top ranking documents for a topic. For the America topic, the following Wikipedia articles are highly ranked: History of Missouri, African-American history, Abraham Lincoln, Ulysses S. Grant, Seminole Wars. It is also possible to click on a particular topic frame, e.g. (American, settle). That frame appears in 20 documents that are listed in a new tab. Choosing one of the listed documents, e.g. Oregon trail opens another tab that display the particular document. Topic frames as well as key word assignments could be marked in the text, Figure 3.

4. RELATED WORK

Related software projects include the Topic Model Visualization Engine[5] (http://code.google.com/p/tmve/) that transforms a topic model into a precomputed set of web pages. It shows important words for each topic as well as related documents and related topics. The Topical Guide[6] (https://facwiki.cs.byu.edu/nlp/index.php/Topical_Guide) shows similar information for each topic. Additionally, the top words for each topic could be presented with context information. It also allows to filter by topics, different metrics, words and documents and can produce parallel coordinates plots that relate topics with other meta-data. Also similar to our frame approach, n-grams related to a topic have been used to enhance the common top word visualization [3]. Another related project is the topic-based search interface Search-In-a-Box by Buntine (http://cosco.hiit.fi/search/sib.html). It allows to search documents by keywords and filters optionally afterwards by topical text. The result list shows the important topics of the documents. Additionally to the search engine functionality, it offers a topic browser that shows important words and documents for each topic.

Ackknowledgements

We thank Mattes Angelus, Benjamin Schandera and Gert Böhmer for their programming contributions to the code base of TopicExplorer. Further, we thank the Klaus Tschira Foundation for the support of the project.

5. REFERENCES

[1] K. Allan. Natural language semantics. 2001.

[2] D. Blei. Topic modeling and digital humanities. *Journal of Digital Humanities*, 2(1), 2012.

[3] D. M. Blei and J. D. Lafferty. Visualizing topics with multi-word expressions. *arXiv preprint arXiv:0907.1013*, 2009.

[4] D. M. Blei, A. Y. Ng, and M. I. Jordan. Latent dirichlet allocation. *J. Mach. Learn. Res.*, 3:993–1022, March 2003.

[5] A. Chaney and D. Blei. Visualizing topic models. In *Proc. of Int. AAAI Conf. on Weblogs and Social Media*, 2012.

[6] M. J Gardner, J. Lutes, J. Lund, J. Hansen, D. Walker, E. Ringger, and K. Seppi. The topic browser: An interactive tool for browsing topic models. In *NIPS Workshop on Challenges of Data Visualization*, 2010.

[7] A. Hinneburg, R. Preiss, and R. Schröder. Topicexplorer: Exploring document collections with topic models. In *Machine Learning and Knowledge Discovery in Databases*, pages 838–841, 2012.

[8] J. H. Lau, D. Newman, and T. Baldwin. Machine reading tea leaves: Automatically evaluating topic coherence and topic model quality. In *Proc. of the Europ. Chap. of the Assoc. for Computational Linguistics*, 2014.

[9] A. K. McCallum. Mallet: A machine learning for language toolkit. http://mallet.cs.umass.edu, 2002.

[10] M. Minsky. Frame-system theory. In P. N. Johnson-Laird and P. C. Wason, editors, *Thinking*, pages 355–377. Cambridge University Press, 1977.

[11] H. Schmid. Improvements in part-of-speech tagging with an application to german. In *In Proc. of the ACL SIGDAT-Workshop*, pages 47–50, 1995.

CONDOR: A System for CONstraint DiscOvery and Repair

Joshua Segeren, Dhruv Gairola, Fei Chiang
Department of Computing and Software
McMaster University
{segerej, gairold, fchiang}@mcmaster.ca

ABSTRACT

We present CONDOR, a tool for managing constraints towards improved data quality. As increasing amounts of heterogeneous data are being generated, integrity constraints are the primary tool for enforcing data integrity. It is essential that an accurate and up-to-date set of constraints exist to validate that the correct application semantics are being enforced. We consider the widely used constraint, functional dependencies (FDs). CONDOR is an integrated system that identifies inconsistent data values (along with suggestions for clean values), and generates repairs to both the data and/or FDs to resolve inconsistencies. We extend the set of FD repair operations proposed in past work, by (1) adding a set of attributes to an FD; (2) transforming an FD to a conditional functional dependency (CFD); and (3) identifying redundant attributes in an FD. Our demonstration will showcase the visualization and interactive features of CONDOR to help users determine the best repairs that resolve the underlying inconsistencies to improve data quality.

1. INTRODUCTION

As increasing amounts of heterogeneous data is generated, it has become increasingly difficult for organizations to derive value from raw data. Poor data quality has become a pervasive problem across all industries as real data often contains missing, erroneous, duplicated, and incomplete information. Integrity constraints are the primary tool for preserving data integrity as they represent specific application relationships that are enforced in the data. If all the constraints are enforced in the database, then as the data evolves, it will continue to conform to the constraints. However, in practice, not all the constraints will be strictly enforced, often for performance reasons. This occurs in data environments where there may be hundreds or thousands of constraints defined across dependent applications, and verifying each constraint can negatively affect performance. This weak enforcement policy allows the data to deviate from the constraints. Current declarative data cleaning approaches have proposed making minimal cost changes to the data to make it consistent with the constraints [2, 8, 9].

However, modern applications are increasingly operating in dynamic data environments where both the data and the constraints

CIKM'14, November 3–7, 2014, Shanghai, China.
ACM 978-1-4503-2598-1/14/11.
http://dx.doi.org/10.1145/2661829.2661858.

Table 1: University Courses.

id	Department	Course	Room	Faculty
t_1	Computer Science	CS 240	JHE 110	Engineering
t_2	Classical Studies	CS 240	KTH 222	Humanities
t_3	Communication Studies	CS 240	KTH 225	Arts
t_4	Computer Science	CS 100	ITB 137	Engineering
t_5	Materials Science	MAT 165	JHE 242	Engineering
t_6	Math	MAT 165	MCH 210	Science
t_7	Math	MAT 144	MCH 135	Science
t_8	Math	MAT 364	MCH 120	Science
t_9	Math	MAT 475	MCH 330	Arts

are evolving. Data does not remain static, but evolves as it is updated, and the usage and requirements of the data change. Similarly, the constraints may also change as the underlying business policies (that the constraints model) change, or in data integration tasks where the integrated data instance does not satisfy the constraints at each data source. In these cases, the constraints and the data become misaligned. In such settings, it may be preferable to modify the constraints, rather than the data, because the semantics of the data or application has evolved [1, 6, 10], and the data may be more consistent under a new, modified set of constraints that represent the application domain. For example, consider Table 1 listing information about University courses, and two functional dependencies (FDs), F_1: *Department $\rightarrow$ Faculty* and F_2: *Course $\rightarrow$ Room*. These FDs may have originally been defined such that they hold locally within each University department's database (within each Faculty). However, if the data from departments across the University are integrated into a consolidated table such as Table 1, then the original FDs may no longer hold. We observe that tuples $t_6 - t_9$ violate F_1. Based on support in the data, it appears that the data value in $t_9[Faculty]$ should be updated from 'Arts' to 'Science'. Tuples $t_1 - t_3$ and t_5, t_6 do not satisfy F_2. We can consider updating the room numbers to be the same, but there is insufficient evidence to determine which room number is the correct one. Furthermore, we would be updating values all with the same error. Recent work has shown that in such cases, it may be preferable to modify the FDs [1, 6]. In this case, if we add attribute *Department* to the left side attributes of F_2, then the modified F_2': *[Department, Course] $\rightarrow$ Room* is now satisfied. The tuples that were in violation are now distinguished by adding the *Department* attribute. In addition to adding attributes to an FD F, we can consider finding a subset of tuples from the relation where F is satisfied. This would require identifying a common characteristic (i.e., a condition) among the selected tuples. The FD F would then be modified to include this condition. As FDs are modified, the set of all FDs may, over time, contain redundant attributes. Having a set of non-minimal FDs with redundant attributes can negatively affect

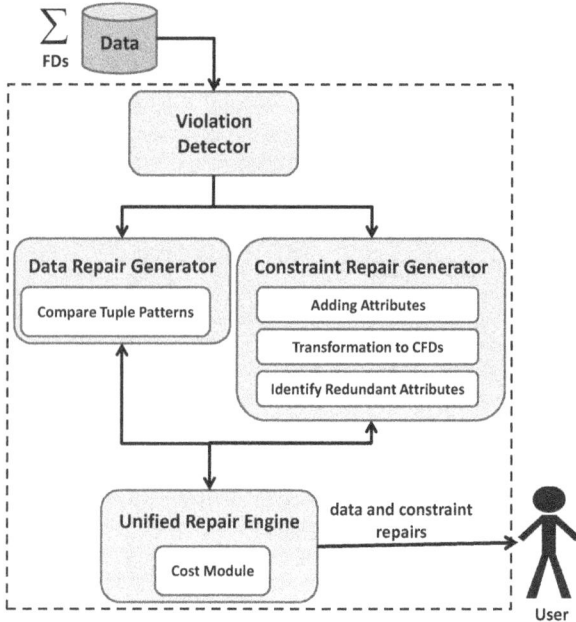

Figure 1: CONDOR System Architecture.

performance. In this case, we may want to identify such attributes and recommend they be removed. Hence, different types of inconsistencies will require different types of repair operations. While past work has considered subsets of these repair operations [6, 5], this work aims to provide a full suite of data and constraint repair operations, along with interactive visualizations of repairs.

We have shown an example that highlights the need for techniques that consider both data and constraint modifications. This is crucial in environments where new data is integrated with target databases, where business policies and regulations are regularly updated, and where the semantics and usage of the data evolves. In this demonstration, we present *CONDOR*, a system for CONstraint DiscOvery and Repair. Given a data instance and a set of constraints, CONDOR identifies the data inconsistencies and recommends to a user how best to resolve these inconsistencies by proposing modifications to the data and/or to the constraints. We focus on functional dependencies (FDs), as such constraints are a primary tool used to enforce data consistency in practice. CONDOR automates the repair process, and provides high accuracy repairs to re-align the data and the constraints.

2. SYSTEM ARCHITECTURE

CONDOR has been implemented as a working prototype using C++ and Python, and offers an interactive web interface implemented using the web2py framework and JavaScript libraries. These include jQuery for simplified client-side HTML scripting, jQuery UI and Twitter Bootstrap for modular user interface components, and D3/NVD3 for data visualizations. CONDOR was deployed on an Intel Xeon CPU E5-2670 processor (8 cores, 20 MB cache) and 16 GB of memory, running nginx as the web server, and interfacing with the web2py application via the uWSGI protocol.

Figure 1 illustrates the architecture of CONDOR, consisting of the following components: *violation detector, data repair generator, constraint repair generator* and *unified repair engine*. CONDOR works as follows. Given a data instance I and a set of FDs Σ, they are passed to the violation detector. The violation detector identifies all tuples that do not satisfy some FD $F \in \Sigma$. For

$F : X \rightarrow Y$, we define a tuple pattern p as a single tuple over XY that exists in $\Pi_{XY}(I)$. These tuple patterns are passed to the data repair generator and constraint repair generator for analysis. In the data repair generator, tuple patterns are compared against each other, and a set of candidate data repairs is considered. This candidate set of data repairs is passed to the unified repair engine which calculates the cost of the repairs. Alternatively, inconsistencies may have been caused by stale constraints, and CONDOR proposes modifications to the FDs. CONDOR considers three types of FD repair operations for F: adding a set of attributes to X, transforming F to a conditional functional dependency (CFD) [3], and identifying redundant attributes. Each of these FD modifications is considered, and passed to the repair engine, where the cost of the constraint repair is calculated. The unified repair engine compares the cost values across the different repair operations, and selects the repair with lowest cost. Candidate repairs that are not selected are returned to the repair generators. The unified repair engine considers all types of repairs equally, and uses a cost model that allows data repairs and constraint repairs to be compared on an equal footing. The lowest cost repair is selected and recommended to the user. In the following, we discuss each of these components in detail.

Violation Detector. This component takes the data and the set of defined FDs Σ, and computes the set of tuples that violate a $F \in \Sigma$. For example, in Table 1, tuples $t_6 - t_9$ violate F_1, and tuples $t_1 - t_3$, t_5, t_6 violate F_2.

Data Repair Generator. Given the set of violating tuples, we want to generate a set of candidate data repairs, i.e., modifications to the data that will resolve the inconsistencies. Let R be the set of relational attributes, I be an instance of a relation, and let $N = |I|$. A *tuple pattern* p is a single tuple over XY that exists in $\Pi_{XY}(I)$. We consider data repairs that can modify either values in the X or Y attributes. To compare potential data repairs, we assume for each $A \in XY$ a distance function, $0 \leq dist_A(v_1, v_2) \leq 1$ over the domain values of A, indicating how similar the values v_1 and v_2 are. We assume $dist_A(v, v) = 0$. Various distance functions tailored for the domain may be used. We use the Jaro-Winkler measure for strings. For tuple patterns, we assume the existence of a similarity measure between tuple patterns $0 \leq sim(p_1, p_2) \leq 1$ where $sim(p, p) = 1$. For our work, we define sim as the fraction of equal attributes in the patterns. We use a support threshold θ and a pattern similarity threshold β. Intuitively, tuple patterns with a frequency over $\theta * N$ will not be considered as candidates for a data repair (we call these *core patterns*). Furthermore, a candidate for a data repair (we call these *deviant patterns*) must be at least as similar to some other (core) pattern as our threshold β. The data repair generator proposes a candidate set of data repairs that update the data values in deviant tuples to its corresponding core tuple's data values.

Example: In Table 1, assume $\theta = 0.3, \beta = 0.4$. We have the following core and deviant patterns, labelled p and d, respectively. For F_1, p: (Math, Science) (with frequency = $3/9 > \theta$), d: (Math, Arts). We will consider a data repair to update the value *Arts* to the value *Science*. For F_2, all the violating tuples have frequency equal to 1, and do not qualify to be core patterns.

Constraint Repair Generator. This component proposes a set of constraint repairs and passes them to the repair engine for costing. In CONDOR, we consider three types of FD modifications described below:

(i) Adding Attributes. For $F : X \rightarrow Y$, we consider appending a set of attributes $W \in (R \setminus XY)$ to X. We use an algorithm based on reconstructability analysis that selects the set W based on the attribute value dependencies between W and XY. We evaluate attributes in W that have some correlation to attributes XY by

computing a measure called the variance of information [6]. This computation measures how well the attributes in W separate the conflicting tuples in F. The objective is to make F more selective by adding additional attributes W that cleanly separate the violating tuples from the clean tuples. Of course, we can consider making F a candidate key but this is the least desirable type of repair. In our continuing example, we consider adding attributes *Course, Room* to the antecedent of F_1, and *Dept, Faculty* to F_2.

(ii) Transformation to a CFD. To transform F towards a CFD, our objective is to repair F by finding a subset of the data where F' is satisfied. We use a similar approach to CFD discovery algorithms [4], where we identify the conditions (expressed by the attribute values in X) where F is satisfied.

(iii) Identify Redundant Attributes. Given the current set of FDs Σ, modifications to the FDs over time may result in a non-minimal set. This can be costly to enforce, particularly if redundant attributes exist in X. We apply the minimal cover algorithm to identify any redundant attributes in Σ. For $F : X \rightarrow Y$, we compute the closure of $(X \setminus B)^+$ for an attribute $B \in X$. If the closure contains B, this indicates that we can infer B from the remaining FDs in Σ. We do this for each $F \in \Sigma$. We refer the reader to the full paper for further details [7].

Unified Repair Engine. We take the proposed repairs and put them together in a unified repair engine that computes the cost to implement each of these repairs. Given a set of constraints Σ and a data instance I that is inconsistent with Σ, the repair engine selects a set of low cost data and constraint repairs that produce a Σ' and I' such that $I' \models \Sigma'$. The repair engine uses a cost model based on the Minimum Description Length (MDL) Principle. We define M to be a model containing a set of signatures where each signature $s \in \Pi_{XY}(I)$ is a tuple pattern. We want to find signatures that allow us to represent I via M as succinctly as possible. The MDL principle allows us to quantify this intuition via the description length function, $DL_F = L(M) + L(I|M)$ where $L(M)$ is the length of the model, and $L(I|M)$ is the length of the data instance I given M. We want to minimize DL_F. We define $L(M) = (S * |XY|) + r_T$, S is the number of signatures in the model M, and r_T is the total data repair cost for updated tuples in I. Then $L(I|M) = E * |XY|$ where E is the number of tuples not modeled by the S signatures in M. For constraint repair, we consider a new FD F' modified by any one of the repair operations discussed above. $|I \models F'| > |I \models F|$ (there are more tuples satisfying F' than F). We choose the constraint repair F' only if $DL_{F'} = (S' * (|XY| + |W|)) + (E' * (|XY| + |W|))$ is less than DL_F, where S' is the number of signatures in the model wrt F', W is the number of attributes added to F', and E' is the number of tuples not modeled by the S' signatures. At each step, the unified repair engine selects the repair that reduces DL the most.

Example: We show the cost evaluation for F_1 (F_2 can be computed in a similar manner). The model M is initially empty, and we have $L(M) = 0$ and $L(I|M) = 18$. For data repairs, we modify tuple $t_9[Faculty] = t_8[Faculty] = $ 'Science'. If we assume a unit cost to update each value, plus a unit cost to represent the (maximum) distance between the dirty and clean values, the cost of this update is $2 * 1$ tuple $= 2$. We get a signature *(Math, Science)*. We increase $L(M)$ by 2 to represent the new signature (a unit cost to represent a value), and decrease $L(I|M)$ by how frequent *(Math, Science)* occurs in I. The final description length is $DL'_{data} = L'(M) + r_T + L'(I|M) = 2 + 2 + (18 - 8) = 14$. In constraint repair, we consider adding attribute *Course* to F_1's antecedent. There are no signatures in M, and $DL'_{fd} = 27$ (3 attributes in the new FD times 9 tuples). Since $DL'_{data} < DL'_{fd}$, we select data repairs as the preferred fix.

3. DEMONSTRATION PLAN

We highlight CONDOR's features and visualizations by engaging the user towards the best set of data and/or constraint modifications to improve overall data quality. We use two real datasets: (1) *Yelp* data, from the Yelp dataset challenge, which provides information on local businesses; and (2) *movies* data scraped from the film review site *rottentomatoes.com*. We present two demo scenarios:

1) Continuous Repair: Using a sample from the Yelp dataset and the movies dataset, we will guide the user through an iterative repair process, where on each iteration, the data and the constraints will change. In reality, data and constraints do not remain static, and evolve over time. We simulate this behaviour, and on each iteration, the data will differ from the previous iteration (i.e, data values are updated, new tuples are inserted), and the set of constraints are modified to include new constraints, and antecedent attributes are added or removed. The user will be able to compare the different repair alternatives as CONDOR provides the visualizations showing how much of the data and the constraints are corrected, and at what cost. This scenario reflects the conditions that modern applications operate in dynamic data environments, and highlights the evolution of the data and of the constraints, and how the repairs are changing due to this evolution.

2) Scalability Analysis: We will show the performance and scalability of CONDOR as the schema complexity increases. Specifically, the user will be able to select from a set of data samples that have increasing attribute domains, and an increasing number of attributes. Similarly, the user will be able to evaluate the qualitative impact by selecting from a set of constraints that have an increasing number of antecedent attributes, constraints that have overlapping attributes, and an increasing number of constraints.

4. CONCLUSION

This demonstration highlights the features of CONDOR, an integrated and interactive data quality tool that focuses on data and a suite of constraint repair operations to resolve underlying data inconsistencies. Our working prototype allows users to interactively manage their data quality constraints, and provides data visualizations to facilitate a deeper understanding of the underlying attribute value and constraint relationships.

5. REFERENCES

[1] G. Beskales, I. Ilyas, L. Golab, and A. Galiullin. On the relative trust between inconsistent data and inaccurate constraints. In *ICDE*, pages 541–552, 2013.
[2] P. Bohannon, W. Fan, M. Flaster, and R. Rastogi. A cost-based model and effective heuristic for repairing constraints by value modification. In *SIGMOD*, pages 143–154, 2005.
[3] P. Bohannon, W. Fan, F. Geerts, X. Jia, and A. Kementsietsidis. Conditional functional dependencies for data cleaning. In *ICDE*, pages 746–755, 2007.
[4] F. Chiang and R. J. Miller. Discovering data quality rules. *Proc. VLDB Endow.*, 1(1):1166–1177, 2008.
[5] F. Chiang and R. J. Miller. Active repair of data quality rules. In *Intl. Conf. on Information Quality*, pages 174–188, 2011.
[6] F. Chiang and R. J. Miller. A unified model for data and constraint repair. In *ICDE*, pages 446–457, 2011.
[7] F. Chiang and Y. Wang. Repairing integrity rules for improved data quality. In *Intl. J. of Information Quality*, page 20 pages, 2014.
[8] M. Dallachiesa, A. Ebaid, A. Eldawy, A. Elmagarmid, I. F. Ilyas, M. Ouzzani, and N. Tang. NADEEF: A commodity data cleaning system. In *SIGMOD*, pages 541–552, 2013.
[9] F. Geerts, G. Mecca, P. Papotti, and D. Santoro. LLUNATIC data-cleaning framework. *PVLDB*, 6(9):625–636, 2013.
[10] M. Volkovs, F. Chiang, J. Szlichta, and R. J. Miller. Continuous data cleaning. In *ICDE*, pages 244–255, 2014.

DTMBIO 2014: International Workshop on Data and Text Mining in Biomedical Informatics

Luonan Chen
Shanghai Institutes for Biological Sciences, Chinese Academy of Sciences, China

lnchen @sibs.ac.cn

Doheon Lee
Department of Bio and
Brain Engineering
KAIST, Korea

dhlee@kaist.ac.kr

Hua Xu
School of Biomedical Informatics, University of Texas, USA

hua.xu @uth.tmc.edu

Min Song
Department of Lib. and Info. Science, Yonsei University, Korea

min.song@njit.edu

ABSTRACT

Held each year in conjunction with one of the largest data management conferences, CIKM, the Eighth ACM International Workshop on Data and Text Mining in Biomedical Informatics (DTMBIO 14) is organized to bring together researchers interested in development and application of cutting-edge biomedical and healthcare technology. The purpose of DTMBIO is to foster discussions regarding the state-of-the-art applications of data and text mining on biomedical research problems. DTMBIO 14 will help scientists navigate emerging trends and opportunities in the evolving area of informatics related techniques and problems in the context of biomedical research.

Categories and Subject Descriptors

J.3 [**Life and Medical Sciences**]: Medical information systems

General Terms

Algorithms, Management, Performance, Design, Experimentation, Security.

1. INTRODUCTION

With the advent of high-throughput technologies and electronic biomedical data collection, biomedical researchers need to effectively manipulate data to yield research answers. Biomedical data mining presents obstacles unseen in other fields that deal with large datasets. Biological data are more heterogeneous stemming from a wide range of experiments that generate many types of information, such as genetic sequences, interactions of proteins or findings in medical records. Acquiring the most useful information from this complex data and interpreting them in light of all the relevant prior knowledge remains a challenging task. The aim of the 2014 workshop has been to bring together researchers in the areas of data and text mining and computational biology, who are interested in integrating and analyzing heterogeneous, structured and unstructured data.

The call for papers attracted 22 submissions from all over the world. The selection process was highly competitive. Each paper went through a rigorous double-blinded peer review by at least 3 members of the Program Committee. Based on the referee reports, the papers were ranked according to their original contribution, and the program committee accepted 7 papers and 4 short papers (which will be invited to a supplement issue of BMC Decision Making and Medical Informatics) that cover a variety of topics, including novel information extraction techniques, ontologies, and application to large biomedical data. In addition, the program includes a keynote speech by Doheon Lee at KAIST. We hope that these proceedings will serve as a valuable reference for researchers and developers who are interested in applying Text Mining to Medical Informatics.

2. PAPER SUMMARY

Session 1 presents research pertinent to various data and text mining techniques in the biomedical domain. [1] uses brain pathway information from literature incorporated into pathway activity inference procedure to classify patients with Alzheimer's disease (AD) and amnestic mild cognitive impairment (aMCI). This study could impact interpretation of cognitive alterations and functional declines during AD progression. [2] analyzes loss and gain of function mutations to identify properties distinct to each of the two classes. By implementing classifications with the selected features, it is demonstrated that the selected features have good discriminative power. Empirical determination of whether a mutation confers loss or gain of function to the protein is desirable since it could conserve resources for bench scientists. To characterize molecular level commonality among brain diseases that share symptoms at the clinical level, [3] performed integrative gene expression analysis using a correlation-based biclustering approach. The results in this study provide valuable resources to show the common key molecular players affecting brain diseases in a transnosological manner as well as gene sets specific to each disease. Pathway analysis is a fundamental aspect for understanding the molecular mechanisms that underlie biological processes. [4] provides analysis of conflicting information as well as resolution in pathways as a means of maintaining robustness and integrity in biological databases. This pathway database cleaning in important for better secondary analyses such as gene/protein annotation, network dynamics and qualitative/quantitative simulation. [5] provides two methods to identify subtypes of cancer on the basis of somatic mutations found in them. Stratification of patients into distinct tumor types informs the prognosis as well as preferred treatments for the patient. Identification of virulence factors of pathogens can potentially help in appropriate treatment options during infections. [6] performs comparative genome analysis between virulent and non-virulent strains and determines that effects of genomic variations in the protein-coding regions are less significant than those on the regulatory regions. [7] proposes an approach to identify novel drug targets for E3 ligases by integrating networks of E3-substrates and neighboring known disease genes. The methodology is also generally applicable to mechanistic studies of the genes of interest.

Session 2 presents research in the area of text mining in the biomedical informatics field. Mapping of narrative text automatically to pre-defined codes would facilitate easy conversion for reporting purposes. [8] proposes use of a Non-Negative Matrix-Factorization model based method for the task in an emergency department setting and show that it outperforms other classifiers. [9] present a novel unsupervised collective inference approach to link entities from unstructured full texts of biomedical literature to 300 ontologies. Automatic Entity Linking (EL) problem in the life science domain is largely unexplored. The approach leverages the rich semantic information and structures in ontologies for similarity computation and entity ranking. [10] investigates the performance of three state-of-the-art parsers: the Stanford parser, the Bikel parser, and the Charniak parser, using two clinical datasets. The study demonstrates that re-training using clinical Treebanks is critical for improving general English parsers' performance on clinical text, and combining clinical and open domain corpora might achieve optimal performance for parsing clinical text. [11] proposes a robust hybrid approach for extracting relations on the basis of a rule-based approach feature set for PPI using public corpora. Automatic relation extraction from biomedical text is the focus of intense research in recent years.

3. CONCLUSION

This workshop continues the line of DTMBIO workshops organized in conjunction with CIKM in 2006, 2008, 2009, 2010, 2011, 2012, and 2013. We invite researchers and practitioners from a variety of backgrounds such as computer science, information system, information science, bioinformatics, medical informatics, and medical sciences. The main objective of the workshop will be to strengthen the cooperation within the growing community in medical data and text mining research, allowing lively exchange of ideas and foster new collaborations.

4. REFERENCES

[1] Lee, J., Kim, Y., Jeong, Y., Na, D.L., Kim, J-W., Lee, K-H and Lee, D. 2014. Discriminatory analysis of Alzheimer's disease through pathway activity inference in the resting-state brain. In *DTMBIO 14*.

[2] Jung, S., Lee, S., Kim, S. and Nam, H. 2014. Identification of Genomic Features in the Classification of Loss- and Gain-of-Function Mutation. In *DTMBIO 14*.

[3] Cha, K., Oh, K., Hwang, T. and Yi, G-S. 2014. Identification of coexpressed gene modules across multiple brain diseases by a biclustering analysis on integrated gene expression data. In *DTMBIO 14*.

[4] Yoon, S., Jung, J., Yu, H., Kwon, M., Choo, M., Park, K., Jang, D., Kim, S. and Lee, D. 2014. Systematic identification of context-dependent conflicting information in biological pathways. In *DTMBIO 14*.

[5] Kim, S., Sael, L. and Yu, H. 2014. Identifying cancer subtypes based on somatic mutation profile. In *DTMBIO 14*.

[6] Joe, S. and Nam, H. 2014. Identification of a Specific Base Sequence of Pathogenic E. coli through a Genomic Analysis. In *DTMBIO 14*.

[7] Min, B., and Yi, G-S. 2014. BSML: Inference of Disease E3s from Integrated Functional Relation Network. In *DTMBIO 14*.

[8] Chen, L. and Nayak, R. 2014. Injury Narrative Text Classification using the Factorization Model. In *DTMBIO 14*.

[9] Zheng, J.G., Howsmon, D., Zhang, B., Hahn, J., McGuinness, D., Hendler, J. and Ji, H. 2014. Entity Linking for Biomedical Literature. In *DTMBIO 14*.

[10] Jiang, M., Huang, Y., Fan, J-W., Tang, B., Denny, J. and Xu, H. 2014. Parsing clinical text: how good are the state-of-the-art parsers? In *DTMBIO 14*.

[11] Song, S.J., Heo, G.E., Kim, H.J., Jung, H.J., Kim, Y.H. and Song, M. 2014. Grounded Feature Selection for Biomedical Relation Extraction by the Combinative Approach. In *DTMBIO 14*.

DUBMOD'14 - International Workshop on Data-driven User Behavioral Modeling and Mining from Social Media

Jalal Mahmud, Jeffrey Nichols, Michelle Zhou
IBM Research – Almaden
650 Harry Rd, San Jose, CA 95120
{jumahmud, jwnichls, mzhou}@us.ibm.com

James Caverlee
Texas A&M University
College Station, TX
caverlee@cse.tamu.edu

Yi Zeng
Chinese Academy of Sciences
China
yi.zeng@ia.ac.cn

Liang Chen
Zhejiang University
China
cliang@zju.edu.cn

John O'Donovan
University of California, Santa Barbara
Santa Barbara, CA
jod@cs.ucsb.edu

ABSTRACT

Massive amounts of data are being generated on social media sites, such as Twitter and Facebook. These data can be used to better understand people (e.g., personality traits, perceptions, and preferences) and predict their behavior. As a result, a deeper understanding of users and their behavior can benefit a wide range of intelligent applications, such as advertising, social recommender systems, and personalized knowledge management. These applications will also benefit individual users themselves and optimize their experience across a wide variety of domains, such as retail, healthcare, and education. Since mining and understanding user behavior from social media often requires interdisciplinary effort, including machine learning, text mining, human-computer interaction, and social science, our workshop aims to bring together researchers and practitioners from multiple fields to discuss the creation of deeper models of individual users by mining the content that they publish and the social networking behavior that they exhibit.

Categories and Subject Descriptors

H.2.8 [**Database Management**]: Database Applications - Data Mining; J.4 [**Computer Application**]: Social and Behavioral Sciences

General Terms

Algorithms, Design, Experimentation.

Keywords

User Modeling; Social Media Analysis; Data-driven.

1. INTRODUCTION

People from all walks of life are using social media sites, such as Twitter and Facebook, to share data about social events, express opinions, discuss their interests, publicize businesses, recommend products, and, explicitly or implicitly, reveal personal information. Many research projects and commercial products have used this information to drive a variety of services, such as recommending local news stories [2], detecting events [3], determining group sentiment of products and brands [1], and smart crowd-sourcing [8]. The majority of this work, however, has focused on aggregating data across many users. In contrast, our focus is to create deep models of individual users from social media, including the content users publish and the behavior that they exhibit. This has been an active area of research recently and a number of papers on this topic have appeared in related conferences and workshops [4, 5, 6]. Various analytic techniques have been applied to infer users' home location [7], gender [4, 6], age [4], regional origin [4], ethnicity [5], political orientation [4, 5], and personality [9]. Although there is abundant work in this area, there are many technical challenges remaining to be addressed. Our workshop aims to bring together researchers and practitioners who are interested in this topic to share their experiences and discuss remaining challenges. While acquiring a deep understanding of users brings great benefits to businesses and individual users themselves, such an understanding may also reveal information that users would prefer to keep private. Such concerns are particularly important because individuals do not have complete control over the information they share about themselves; friends of a user may inadvertently divulge private information about that user in their own posts.

This workshop builds upon the success of our previously held workshops in conjunction with ACM IUI 2012, ACM CIKM 2012 and ACM CIKM 2013 and focuses more on data-centric analysis and mining aspects of user and user behavior understanding from social media. In particular, we plan to solicit work on topics in one or more of the following areas:

Analytics

- Interactive visual analytics for understanding derived user models
- Integrated content and social network mining and analysis to derive user insights
- Mining of heterogeneous data sources to derive user insights
- Discovery of trustworthy information and information sources

- Identification of significant user attributes (e.g., personality or preferences) for task-specific user behavior modeling and prediction (e.g., information collection or spreading tasks)
- Predictive analytics of user behavior
- User behavior modeling and mining at scale using Big Data approaches

Feasibility/challenges of understanding individual users from social media
- What aspects of an individual can be modeled from their public social media postings?
- What aspects cannot be modeled?
- What aspects should not be modeled?
- How accurate are the models that can be extracted?
- What are the best techniques to model user behavior?
- How might the creation of such models be thwarted? (e.g. to preserve privacy while still allowing participation on a social network)

Protecting user privacy
- What information about a user can be modeled while keeping the sensitive information private?
- How can users monitor what information has been revealed about themselves on social media and obfuscate any sensitive information that has been accidently revealed?

Domains and Applications
- Domain-specific user modeling using public social media including Twitter, Facebook, MySpace, social Q&A sites, and Amazon.com reviews for
  - Retail
  - Healthcare
  - Education
  - Sports
  - News
- Domain-independent user modeling using public social media such as twitter, Facebook, MySpace, and Foursquare to derive a wide variety of user traits including:
  - Locations
  - Behaviors/Personality
  - Demographics
  - Age
  - Gender
- Enterprise-focused user modeling using social media data on public social networks and communications (e.g., emails and blogs) within an enterprise
  - Employees' social and collaboration patterns in a workplace
  - Work-related personality traits such as innovativeness, flexibility, and adaptiveness
- Task-specific user modeling for
  - Information recommendation
  - Crowd-sourcing
  - Expert finding
  - Social Q&A

2. OBJECTIVE
This workshop aims to achieve three main objectives:

- Identify key research issues and challenges in designing and developing techniques for modeling and mining users and their behavior from social media; and

- Establish and grow a community that consists of researchers and practitioners from multiple disciplines to tackle the difficult problems of user behavior understanding from social media; and
- Initiate collaboration (e.g., creating and sharing public datasets) among different teams.

We hope to bring together researchers and practitioners from diverse areas, such as user modeling, social media analysis, natural language processing, data mining, machine learning, privacy and security, to discuss these issues and share results.

3. FORMAT
We will hold a half-day workshop program on Nov, 3, 2014. The program begins with a welcome note. After that there will be a madness session during which participants introduce themselves and their work in 5 minutes. Participants will be encouraged to make slides for the madness session, but this will not be required. Each paper session will conclude with a discussion led by a pre-chosen workshop participant. These discussions will tie together common themes of the presentations and hopefully lead to insightful discussions about further research directions. The program will end with a open discussion where participants will discuss the current state of the art, focus areas, and opportunities for future research.

4. ORGANIZERS
- Jalal Mahmud, IBM Research – Almaden, USA, jumahmud@us.ibm.com
- James Caverlee, Texas A&M University, USA, caverlee@cse.tamu.edu
- Jeffrey Nichols, IBM Research – Almaden, USA, jwnichls@us.ibm.com
- John O'Donovan, University of California, Santa Barbara, USA, jod@cs.ucsb.edu
- Michelle Zhou, IBM Research - Almaden, USA, mzhou@us.ibm.com
- Yi Zeng, Chinese Academy of Sciences, China. yi.zeng@ia.ac.cn
- Liang Chen, Zhejiang University, China, cliang@zju.edu.cn

5. REFERENCES
[1] http://twittersentiment.appspot.com
[2] Owen Phelan, Kevin McCarthy, and Barry Smyth. (2009). Using Twitter to Recommend Real-time Topical News. RecSys.
[3] T. Sakaki, M. Okazaki, and Y. Matsuo. Earthquake shakes twitter users: real-time event detection by social sensors. In WWW, 2010.
[4] Delip Rao, David Yarowsky, Abhishek Shreevats, Manaswi Gupta, Classifying Latent User Attributes in Twitter, In Proc. of SMUC '10.
[5] Marco Pennacchiotti and Ana-Maria Popescu, A Machine Learning Approach to Twitter User Classification, In Proc. of ICWSM'11.
[6] Popescu, A. and Grefenstette, G. Mining User Home Location and Gender from Flickr Tags. ICWSM '10.
[7] Brent Hecht, Lichan Hong, Bongwon Suh, Ed H. Chi, Tweets from Justin Bieber's Heart: The Dynamics of the "Location" Field in User Profiles, CHI 2011.
[8] Jeffrey Nichols and Jeon-Hyung Kang, Asking questions of targeted strangers on social networks, In Proc. of CSCW 2012.
[9] Thin Nguyen, Dinh Phung, Brett Adams, Svetha Venkatesh, Towards Discovery of Influence and personality traits through social link prediction, In Proc. of ICWSM 2011

Seventh Workshop on Exploiting Semantic Annotations in Information Retrieval (ESAIR'14)

CIKM 2014 Workshop

Omar Alonso
Microsoft
Mountain View, CA

Jaap Kamps
University of Amsterdam
The Netherlands

Jussi Karlgren
KTH & Gavagai
Stockholm, Sweden

ABSTRACT

There is an increasing amount of structure on the Web as a result of modern Web languages, user tagging and annotation, emerging robust NLP tools, and an ever growing volume of linked data. These meaningful, semantic, annotations hold the promise to significantly enhance information access, by enhancing the depth of analysis of today's systems. The goal of the ESAIR'14 workshop remains to advance the general research agenda on this core problem, with an explicit focus on one of the most challenging aspects to address in the coming years. The main remaining challenge is on the user's side—the potential of rich document annotations can only be realized if matched by more articulate queries exploiting these powerful retrieval cues—and a more dynamic approach is emerging by exploiting new forms of query autosuggest. How can the query suggestion paradigm be used to encourage searcher to articulate longer queries, with concepts and relations linking their statement of request to existing semantic models? How do entity results and social network data in "graph search" change the classic division between searchers and information and lead to extreme personalization—are you the query? How to leverage transaction logs and recommendation, and how adaptive should we make the system? What are the privacy ramifications and the UX aspects—how to not creep out users?

Categories and Subject Descriptors: H.3.3 [**Information Storage and Retrieval**]: Information Search and Retrieval

Keywords: Graph Search; Query Suggest; Semantic Annotation

1. THEME AND TOPICS

The goal of the seventh ESAIR workshop is to create a forum for researchers interested in the use of application of semantic annotations for information access tasks. By semantic annotations we refer to linguistic annotations (such as named entities, semantic classes or roles, etc.) as well as user annotations (such as microformats, RDF, tags, etc.).

There are many forms of annotations and a growing array of techniques that identify or extract information automatically from texts: geo-positional markers; named entities; temporal information; semantic roles; opinion, sentiment, and attitude; certainty and hedging to name a few directions of more abstract information found in text. Furthermore, the number of collections which explicitly identify entities is growing fast with Web 2.0 and Semantic Web initiatives. In some cases semantic technologies are being deployed in active tasks, but there is no common direction to research initiatives nor in general technologies for exploitation of non-immediate textual information, in spite of a clear family resemblance both with respect to theoretical starting points and methodology. We believe further research is needed before we can unleash the potential of annotations!

The previous ESAIR workshops made concrete progress in clarifying the exact role of semantic annotations in support complex search tasks: both as a means to construct more powerful queries that articulate far more than a typical Web-style, shallow, navigational information need, and in terms of *making sense* of the retrieved results on very various levels of abstraction, even non-textual data, providing narratives and paths through an intractable information space.

2. OBJECTIVES, GOALS, AND OUTCOME

The ESAIR'14 workshop will have far more focus than the earlier ESAIRs. While the goal remains to advance the general research agenda on this core problem, there is an explicit focus on the main remaining challenge of exploiting semantic annotations in the coming years.

One of the main outcomes of the previous ESAIRs has been not only an overview of various domains of application and experiments on real life data, but also a clearer "theoretical" view on the role of semantic annotations. The starting point, based on discussions at previous ESAIRs is a view of semantic annotation as a *linking procedure*, connecting a *content analysis* of information objects with a *semantic model* of some sort. All three are objects of study in their own right; the point of the ESAIR series is linking those three activities into a coherent and practical whole.

The obvious next step in the discussion is how to leverage known semantic resources (such as knowledge bases, ontologies, folksonomies, lexical resources, hand-annotated or not) to streaming realistic-scale data ("big data"), to be processed in real time, with incrementally evolving knowledge models. The challenge is to use an existing resource as a semantic model, provide an effective and practicable content analysis, and a scalable linking procedure which can handle the data flows we can expect in real life data.

Whilst the exact scope and reach of the emerging knowledge resources (such as DBpedia, Freebase) is not yet clear, there is a clear

CIKM'14, November 3–7, 2014, Shanghai, China.
ACM 978-1-4503-2598-1/14/11.
http://dx.doi.org/10.1145/2661829.2663539.

focus on enumerating factual content that can fruitfully be complemented by non-topical aspects. Over the last years there has been a massive interest in annotations on non-topical dimensions, such as opinions, sentiment or attitude, reading level, prerequisite level, authoritativeness, credibility, etc, both at the level of individual sentences or utterances as well as at more aggregative levels. It is clear that such annotations contain vital cues for matching information to the specific needs and profile of the searcher at hand, yet it is an open question how such annotations can be fruitfully exploited in information retrieval, either as additional criteria on the "relevance" of results in traditional search tasks, or in specific use cases where non-topical cues are key, or in contextual or personalized search that takes the searcher's state into account.

Both in terms of knowledge bases and in terms of non-topical annotation significant progress have been made in recent years. The main remaining challenge is on the user's side—the potential of rich document annotations can only be realized if matched by more articulate queries exploiting these powerful retrieval cues—and a more dynamic approach is emerging by exploiting new forms of query autosuggest. How can the query suggestion paradigm be used to encourage searcher to articulate longer queries, with concepts and relations linking their statement of request to existing semantic models? How do entity results and social network data in "graph search" change the classic division between searchers and information and lead to extreme personalization—are you the query? How to leverage transaction logs and recommendation, and how adaptive should we make the system? What are the privacy ramifications and the UX aspects—how to not creep out users?

3. ACCEPTED PAPERS

We requested the submission of short, 3 page papers to be presented as boaster and poster. We accepted a total of 11 papers out of 15 submissions after peer review (a 73% acceptance rate).

Cotelo et al. [2] investigate semantic cues to articulate more expressive queries by reviving various query operators and explore their value in a preliminary evaluation.

De Nies et al. [3] give a broad overview of the challenges in the context of entity tagged corpora, focusing on the annotation quality, appropriate similarity measures, data quality, and access problems.

Deolalikar [4] investigates within corpus text mining to cluster documents and combine cluster and document scores, demonstrating that coarse grained clusters are unable to capture specific intent of topically focused queries.

Ibrahim et al. [5] address the problem of entity linking in social streaming data, looking into the normalization of mentions due to cryptic abbreviations, the contextualization of short postings by shared hashtags, persons, and links, and the temporal trends of attention to time-sensitive entities.

Jan et al. [6] study the specific domain of searching IT service desk tickets, based on topic modeling, concept analysis, and clustering, leading to increased performance on a corpus of noisy statements of IT related problems.

Jiang et al. [7] investigate some heuristics to improve "explicit semantic annotation" by labeling documents with Wikipedia concepts.

Li et al. [8] revisit the answer type prediction problem of question answering systems, using dependency parsing and semantic role labeling rather than ad hoc heuristics.

Mao and Lu [9] focus medical literature search and return to the old problem of using controlled subject headings with a mixture language model and show that this promotes retrieval effectiveness.

Verma and Ceccarelli [10] study the problem of entity detection in non-head queries, observing similarities and differences in the types of entities occurring in slices of queries.

Yang [11] studies concept similarity measures comparing tree edit distance with textual similarity of subtrees or fragments over the open directory project's concept hierarchy.

Zuccon et al. [12] investigates reasoning with rigorous semantic concept hierarchies in medical literature search, and discusses the potential benefits of semantic-based retrieval as well as the risks of unconditionally embracing such inferences.

4. FORMAT

We start the day with a short introduction of the goals and schedule, and a "feature rally" in which each participant introduced her or himself, and stated her or his particular interest in this area. Next, we have keynote speakers that help frame the problem, and create a common understanding of the challenges. We continue with a boaster/poster session, where the papers from Section 3 are presented. The poster session continues over lunch. After lunch, we have break-out sessions in parallel that focused on specific aspects or problems related to the four themes. After the afternoon coffee, we have reports of the breakout sessions, followed by a final discussion on what we achieved during the day and how to take it forward. The workshop will continue with a more informal part, over drinks and dinner with all attendees of the workshop.

Acknowledgments

We thanks the CIKM workshop chairs (Huan Liu and Xiaofeng Meng) and the local organization team (Lanying Zhang, Xiaoyang Sean Wang) and Sheridan Printing (Lisa Tolles and Cindy Edwards) for their great support.

5. REFERENCES

[1] O. Alonso, J. Kamps, and J. Karlgren, editors. *ESAIR'14: Proceedings of the CIKM'14 Workshop on Exploiting Semantic Annotations in Information Retrieval*, 2014. ACM Press.

[2] S. Cotelo, A. Makowski, L. Chiruzzo, and D. Wonsever. Documents search using semantics criteria. In Alonso et al. [1], pages 1–3.

[3] T. De Nies, C. Beecks, W. De Neve, T. Seidl, E. Mannens, and R. Van de Walle. Towards named-entity-based similarity measures: Challenges and opportunities. In Alonso et al. [1], pages 4–6.

[4] V. Deolalikar. Can corpus similarity-based self-annotation assist information retrieval? In Alonso et al. [1], pages 7–9.

[5] Y. Ibrahim, M. A. Yosef, and G. Weikum. Aida-social: Entity linking on the social stream. In Alonso et al. [1], pages 10–12.

[6] E.-E. Jan, K.-Y. Chen, and T. Ide. A probabilistic concept annotation for it service desk tickets. In Alonso et al. [1], pages 13–15.

[7] Z. Jiang, M. Chen, and X. Liu. Semantic annotation with rescoredesa: Rescoring concept features generated from explicit semantic analysis. In Alonso et al. [1], pages 16–18.

[8] Z. Li, P. Exner, and P. Nugues. Using semantic role labeling to predict answer types. In Alonso et al. [1], pages 19–21.

[9] J. Mao and K. Lu. Leverage the associations between documents, subject headings and terms to enhance retrieval. In Alonso et al. [1], pages 22–24.

[10] M. Verma and D. Ceccarelli. Bringing the head closer to the tail with entity linking. In Alonso et al. [1], pages 25–27.

[11] H. Yang. A fragment-based similarity measure for concept hierarchies and ontologies. In Alonso et al. [1], pages 28–30.

[12] G. Zuccon, B. Koopman, and P. Bruza. Exploiting inference from semantic annotations for information retrieval: Reflections from medical ir. In Alonso et al. [1], pages 31–33.

LocWeb'14 – 4th International Workshop on Location and the Web

CIKM 2014 Workshop Summary

Dirk Ahlers
NTNU – Norwegian University
of Science and Technology
Trondheim, Norway
dirk.ahlers@idi.ntnu.no

Erik Wilde
EMC Corporation
USA
erik.wilde@emc.com

Bruno Martins
University of Lisbon, IST and
INESC-ID
Portugal
bruno.g.martins@ist.utl.pt

ABSTRACT

The LocWeb 2014 workshop continues a successful workshop series at the intersection of geospatial search, information management, and Web architecture with a focus towards *location-aware information access*. The workshop reflects a multitude of fields that demand and utilize location features, featuring presentations that look at the topic of location on the Web from an interdisciplinary perspective, including new approaches dealing with or utilizing geospatial information.

Categories and Subject Descriptors

H.3.3 [**Information Systems**]: Information Storage and Retrieval—*Information Search and Retrieval*; H.4 [**Information Systems Applications**]: Miscellaneous

General Terms

Documentation, Management

Keywords

Location-Aware Information Access; The Geospatial Web; Mobile Applications

1. INTRODUCTION

Location has quickly moved from the next hot thing into being accepted as an important aspect of the Web and, especially, the mobile Web. Its importance is growing even more, as mobile access is surpassing other forms of Web usage and many players adopt a mobile-first strategy. Location also plays a role in the form of the explicit or implicit location of resources, locations described in content, location of users, location APIs, or mobile apps, being also used in geospatial-aware data mining or large-scale analytics. It is thus a strong driver behind many recent innovations and research activities.

CIKM'14, November 3–7, 2014, Shanghai, China.
ACM 978-1-4503-2598-1/14/11.
http://dx.doi.org/10.1145/2661829.2663542 .

In the context of LocWeb 2014, the location topic is understood as a cross-cutting issue that not only concerns information retrieval, but databases, knowledge management, and systems as well. The workshop establishes an integrated venue where the location aspect can be discussed in depth within an interested community.

LocWeb follows the main theme of Location-Aware Information Access, with subtopics related to Search, Analytics, Mobility, Apps, Services, and Systems. It is designed to reflect the multitude of fields that demand and utilize location features from an interdisciplinary perspective.

The workshop reflects the organiser's previous work, e.g., in geospatial Web retrieval and geoparsing [13, 12], integration of location into the Web [15], geospatial retrieval on the Web [6], or focused address extraction and crawling [5].

2. WORKSHOP THEME AND TOPICS

LocWeb addresses the subject of location as a cross-cutting issue in Web research and technology, consequently examining location aspects in the domains of search, analytics, mobility, apps, services, and systems. We expect LocWeb to further the integration of the geospatial dimension into the Web, by promoting research on the topic.

The general aim is to establish a topic-specific venue where researchers from different fields and backgrounds, be it data mining, recommendation, search, systems, social media, applications, or standards, can discuss and develop the role of location. This can hopefully aid researchers in identifying common issues of geospatial information management across different fields and from different perspectives, and in learning about new approaches.

The main topics of interest, as announced in the call for papers, are: Location-Aware Information Access, Geospatial Web Search, Location-Based Services, Geospatial Web Analytics, Geospatial Visual Analytics, Location-Aware Data Mining, Location-Aware Text Processing, Location-Based Entity Retrieval, Conflation, Merging, Integration, Location-Based Recommendation, Place Semantics, Lifecycle of Location Data, Modeling Location, Geo-Social Media and Systems, Location-Based Social Networks, Geo-Crowdsourcing, Map-Based Interfaces and Geospatial HCIR, Geospatial Applications, Geospatial Awareness, Mobile Search and Recommendation, Mobile Apps and Mobile Context, Mobility Data, Location-Aware Web-Scale Systems, Large Ecosystems, and Location Standards.

2.1 Previous Workshops

LocWeb has previously been held at conferences from different topics, underlining its multi-disciplinary approach. The workshop series is indexed in the ACM Digital Library[1].

The first edition, *LocWeb2008*[2], was co-located with WWW 2008 in Beijing, China [1]. Its main topic was the extraction and exploitation of location information, towards more explicit spatial knowledge.

LocWeb2009[3] was held at CHI 2009 in Boston, USA [2]. It dealt with the HCI view towards Web-based geospatial services, including location sharing, location as context, and user interface design and testing.

LocWeb2010[4] was held at IoT – Internet of Things 2010 in Tokyo, Japan [3]. It addressed location aspects in multi-sensor devices and "things" with ubiquitous connectivity, focusing on Web technology and Web architecture.

Four years latter, *LocWeb2014*[5] is now being held at CIKM 2014 in Shanghai, China.

3. CONTRIBUTIONS IN LOCWEB 2014

The workshop accepted 6 papers for presentation and inclusion in the proceedings [4].

Liu, Vasardani, and Baldwin present a comparative analysis over various geoparsers in the task of identifying locative expressions, benchmarking their performance on informal language commonly found in social networks. They additionally work on corpus construction and error analysis [10].

Li, Kardes, Wang, and Sun report on the use of Hidden Markov Models to parse and segment addresses, aiming to use the results in a similarity function for record linkage [9].

Niu, Matsumoto, Saiki, and Nakamura worked towards the formal definition of data models for indoor positioning, abstracting from different implementations to allow for easier generation of location-based services [11].

Kufer and Henrich take on the issue of representing geo-tagged media collections in peer-to-peer networks, so as to make them searchable. Their hybrid approach optimizes selectivity and representation size to support the selection of those peers that potentially carry relevant results [8].

Tytyk and Baldwin consider the automatic selection of appropriate zoom levels in map interfaces, when presented with informal location descriptions. Their classification approach uses multiple features of geospatial descriptions and is evaluated on different levels of noisy data [14].

Chang, Fan, and Chen use a classification approach to understand human movement data, inferring place semantics of visited locations based on temporal patterns associated to the location tracking of participants in their study [7].

Acknowledgements

We would like to thank all authors of submitted papers and the members of the programme committee for their work in reviewing the contributions.

4. REFERENCES

[1] S. Boll, C. Jones, E. Kansa, P. Kishor, M. Naaman, R. Purves, A. Scharl, and E. Wilde, editors. *Location and the Web (LocWeb 2008)*, WWW '08. ACM, 2008.

[2] E. Wilde, S. Boll, K. Cheverst, P. Fröhlich, R. Purves, and J. Schöning, editors. *LocWeb '09: Proceedings of the 2nd International Workshop on Location and the Web*, CHI '09, 2009.

[3] S. Boll, E. Wilde, and J. Schöning, editors. *LocWeb 2010: Proceedings of the 3rd International Workshop on Location and the Web*, IoT '10. ACM, 2010.

[4] D. Ahlers, E. Wilde, and B. Martins, editors. *LocWeb'14 – Proceedings of the 4th International Workshop on Location and the Web*, CIKM 2014. ACM, 2014.

[5] D. Ahlers. *Geographically Focused Web Information Retrieval*, volume 18 of *Oldenburg Computer Science Series*. OlWIR, Oldenburg, Germany, 2011.

[6] S. Boll and D. Ahlers. A Web more Geospatial: Insights into the Location Inside. In D. De Roure and W. Hall, editors, *WebEvolve2008, Workshop on Understanding Web Evolution held at WWW08*. Web Science Research Initiative, 2008.

[7] C.-W. Chang, Y.-C. Fan, and A. Chen. On the semantic annotation of daily places: A machine-learning approach. In Ahlers et al. [4].

[8] S. Kufer and A. Henrich. Hybrid quantized resource descriptions for geospatial source selection. In Ahlers et al. [4].

[9] X. Li, H. Kardes, X. Wang, and A. Sun. Efficient and scalable HMM-based address parsing. In Ahlers et al. [4].

[10] F. Liu, M. Vasardani, and T. Baldwin. Automatic identification of locative expressions from social media text: A comparative analysis. In Ahlers et al. [4].

[11] L. Niu, S. Matsumoto, S. Saiki, and M. Nakamura. Considering common data model for indoor location-aware services. In Ahlers et al. [4].

[12] J. Santos, I. Anastácio, and B. Martins. Using machine learning methods for disambiguating place references in textual documents. *GeoJournal*, (accepted for publication), 2014.

[13] M. J. Silva, B. Martins, M. Chaves, A. P. Afonso, and N. Cardoso. Adding geographic scopes to web resources. *Computers, Environment and Urban Systems*, 30(4):378 – 399, 2006.

[14] I. Tytyk and T. Baldwin. Automatic zoom level prediction for informal location descriptions. In Ahlers et al. [4].

[15] E. Wilde and M. Kofahl. The Locative Web. In *Proceedings of the 1st International Workshop on Location and the Web*, LocWeb '08. ACM, 2008.

---

[1] http://dl.acm.org/event.cfm?id=RE412

[2] http://medien.informatik.uni-oldenburg.de/LocWeb2008/

[3] http://ifgi.uni-muenster.de/archives/locweb2009/

[4] http://medien.informatik.uni-oldenburg.de/LocWeb2010/

[5] http://dhere.de/locweb2014/

PIKM 2014: The 7th ACM Workshop for Ph.D. Students in Information and Knowledge Management

In conjunction with the 23th ACM Conference on Information and Knowledge Management ACM, CIKM, Shanghai, China, November 3rd, 2014

Gerard de Melo*
Tsinghua University
Beijing, China
gdm@demelo.org

Mouna Kacimi
Free University of
Bozen-Bolzano, Italy
Mouna.Kacimi@unibz.it

Aparna S. Varde †
Montclair State University
Montclair, New Jersey
vardea@montclair.edu

ABSTRACT
PIKM workshop offers to Ph.D. students the possibility to bring their work to an international and interdisciplinary research community, and create a network of young researchers to exchange and develop new and promising ideas. Similarly to the CIKM, PIKM workshop covers a wide range of topics in the areas of databases, information retrieval and knowledge management.

Categories and Subject Descriptors
H.2.0 [**Information Systems**]: Database Management; H.2.8 [**Information Systems**]: Database Management-Database Applications—*Data Mining*; H.3.3 [**Information Systems**]: Information Storage and Retrieval-Information Search and Retrieval

General Terms
Algorithms; Design; Experimentation; Performance; Theory

Keywords
CIKM; PIKM; doctoral consortium; Ph.D. forum; dissertations; database systems; information retrieval; knowledge management; interdisciplinary work; data mining

1. INTRODUCTION
PIKM is the Ph.D. workshop of the CIKM conference. PIKM aims at giving to Ph.D students the opportunity to present their work to a wide audience, stimulate feedback from reviewers, together with the general CIKM audience, and fa-

*Gerard de Melo's work is supported in part by the National Basic Research Program of China Grants 2011CBA00300, 2011CBA00301, and NSFC Grants 61033001, 61361136003.
†Aparna Varde's participation in PIKM workshops is supported by funds from the Dean of the College of Science and Mathematics at Montclair State University, NJ, USA.

cilite interactions among PhD students. This allows the students to describe their ideas into a scientific article, to practice scientific presentation, and to receive feedback from reviewers, fellow students, and the general CIKM audience. We believe that the research community, too, benefits from such a workshop: Ph.D. theses are the grassroots of research. They point out new research avenues and indicate current promising topics.

PIKM workshop covers topics in all areas of the general CIKM conference. This includes several subjects such as database query processing, semantic search, and data mining. PIKM is a well established workshop. This is the seventh time the workshop is being held, after successful workshops in 2007 [14, 15], 2008 [10, 13], 2010 [9, 8], 2011 [7], 2012 [16, 5], 2013 [11] at CIKM conferences. The workshop is one of the few Ph.D. workshops in conferences to target the three tracks of databases, information retrieval and knowledge management with some emphasis on interdisciplinary research across these tracks as well.

To offer students valuable feedback for their submissions, we form our program committee of experts from academia and industry, including both fresh doctorates and senior researchers, thereby allowing for different viewpoints on the proposed works. The program committee members are from various countries across the globe, including Australia, Belgium, Brazil, Canada, China, Egypt, Germany, Ireland, Israel, Italy, Korea, Qatar, Spain, Switzerland, the UK, and the United States. They have provided tough reviews yet constructive and detailed of papers submitted to the workshop, thus providing the students with useful feedback for their endeavors. We sincerely thank them for their efforts.

PIKM 2014 is organized as a full day workshop with four sessions including the keynote talk. This year, there were 10 submissions from 6 countries. We have selected 4 papers [6, 4, 1, 12, 3, 2] for full oral presentations and 2 papers [6, 4, 1, 12, 3, 2] for short oral presentations addressing the themes of information retrieval, databases, knowledge management, and data mining. This year, we have organized invited talks given by fresh doctorates to present their Ph.D work, share their experiences, and give some advices to early stage PhD students on how to proceed in their work.

2. HIGHLIGHTS OF PIKM2014

Keynote Speaker. Dr. Iadh Ounis from the School of Computing Science of the University of Glasgow. His talk is about creating and refining PhD thesis statements.

Invited Talks.
We have three invited talks with corresponding papers:

1. Facilitating Interactive Mining of Global and Local Association Rules, by Abhishek Mukherji, Samsung Research
2. Two-way Recommendation Methods for Social Networks, by Richi Nayak, Queensland University of Technology
3. Applications of Rule Mining in Knowledge Bases, by Luis Galárraga, Télécom ParisTech University

Best Paper Award. The best paper at PIKM workshop, as determined by the reviews of the program committee members, always receives a best paper award. This year's award will go to Arunav Mishra for his paper on Linking Today's Wikipedia and News from the Past [6]. The paper outlines interesting techniques for matching news and Wikipedia excerpts.

Best Reviewer Award. For his very thorough reviews, this year the best reviewer award goes to Fabian M. Suchanek, Télécom ParisTech, France.

We plan to write a review article that summarizes the proceedings of PIKM 2014. Such articles have been published in SIGIR Forum [15], SIGKDD Explorations [13], and SIGMOD Record [8, 5] for previous PIKM workshops.

3. ACKNOWLEDGMENTS

We would like to thank our program committee members for the tremendous effort in completing the reviews in a short period of time. The program committee members are:

Ram Akella: University of California Santa Cruz, USA
Leman Akoglu: Stony Brook University, USA
Linas Baltrunas: Telefonica Research, Spain
Rajkumar Buyya: University of Melbourne, Australia
Meeyoung Cha: KAIST, Korea
Maged El Sayed: Alexandria University, Egypt
Renata Guizzardi: Universidade Federal do Espirito Santo, Brazil
Georgiana Ifrim: University College Dublin, Ireland
Evgeny Kharlamov: University of Oxford, UK
Christina Lioma: University of Glasgow, UK
Claudio Lucchese: CNR, Italy
Yelena Mejova: Qatar Computing Research Institute, Qatar
Sebastian Michel: University of Saarland, Germany
Iris Miliaraki: Yahoo Labs Barcelona, Spain
Abhishek Mukherji: Samsung Research, USA
Anisoara Nica: SAP AG, Canada
Josiane Xavier Parreira: DERI/NUI Galway, Ireland
Filip Radlinski: Microsoft Research Cambridge, UK
Michal Shmueli-Scheuer: IBM Research, Israel
Fabian M. Suchanek: Télécom ParisTech, France
Martin Theobald: University of Antwerp, Belgium
Leong Hou U: University of Macau, China
Robert West: Stanford University, USA

We are also grateful to CIKM 2014 organizers for their support and help, especially to the CIKM workshops' chairs Huan Liu and Xiaofeng Meng.

4. REFERENCES

[1] K. Athukorala. Supporting exploratory search through interaction modeling. *In PIKM '14*, 2014.

[2] K. Bae and Y. Ko. An effective question expanding method for question classification in cqa services. *In PIKM '14*, 2014.

[3] Z. Bao and W. Kameyama. Two phases outlier detection in different subspaces. *In PIKM '14*, 2014.

[4] K. Hui. Towards robust and reusable evaluation for novelty and diversity. *In PIKM '14*, 2014.

[5] M. Kacimi, F. M. Suchanek, and A. S. Varde. Databases, information retrieval and knowledge management: exploring paths and crossing bridges. *SIGMOD Record*, 42(3):71–74, 2013.

[6] A. Mishra. Linking today's wikipedia and news from the past. *In PIKM '14*, 2014.

[7] A. Nica and F. M. Suchanek. PIKM 2011: the 4th ACM workshop for Ph.D. students in information and knowledge management. In *Proceedings of the CIKM 2011*, pages 2633–2634, 2011.

[8] A. Nica, F. M. Suchanek, and A. S. Varde. Emerging multidisciplinary research across database management systems. *SIGMOD Record*, 39(3), 2010.

[9] A. Nica and A. S. Varde, editors. *Proceedings of PIKM 2010, Toronto, Ontario, Canada, October 30, 2010*. ACM, 2010.

[10] P. Roy and A. S. Varde, editors. *Proceedings of the Second Ph.D. Workshop in CIKM, PIKM 2008, Napa Valley, California, USA, October 30, 2008*. ACM, 2008.

[11] F. M. Suchanek and A. Nica. PIKM 2013: The 6th ACM workshop for Ph.D. students in information and knowledge management. In *Proceedings of CIKM 2013*, pages 2561–2562, New York, NY, USA, 2013. ACM.

[12] M. S. Uysal, C. Beecks, and T. Seidl. On efficient query processing with the earth mover's distance. *In PIKM '14*, 2014.

[13] A. S. Varde. Challenging research issues in data mining, databases and information retrieval. *SIGKDD Explorations*, 11(1):49–52, 2009.

[14] A. S. Varde and J. Pei, editors. *Proceedings of the First Ph.D. Workshop in CIKM, PIKM 2007, Sixteenth ACM Conference on Information and Knowledge Management, CIKM 2007, Lisbon, Portugal, November 9, 2007*. ACM, 2007.

[15] A. S. Varde and J. Pei. Advances in information and knowledge management. *SIGIR Forum*, 42(1):29–35, 2008.

[16] A. S. Varde and F. M. Suchanek. PIKM 2012: 5th ACM workshop for phd students in information and knowledge management. In *21st ACM International Conference on Information and Knowledge Management, CIKM'12, Maui, HI, USA, October 29 - November 02, 2012*, pages 2776–2777, 2012.

PSBD 2014: Overview of the 1st International Workshop on Privacy and Security of Big Data

Alfredo Cuzzocrea
ICAR-CNR and University of Calabria
Rende, Cosenza, Italy

cuzzocrea@si.deis.unical.it

ABSTRACT

The *ACM 1st International Workshop on Privacy and Security of Big Data* (PSBD 2014), held in Shanghai, China on November 7, 2014, in conjunction with the *ACM 23rd International Conference on Information and Knowledge Management* (CIKM 2014), presents research on privacy and security of big data, an emerging challenge in actual database and data mining research. PSBD 2014 program has two interesting sessions on (*i*) *scalable privacy-preserving and security-control methods for big data processing*, and (*ii*) *user-oriented and data-oriented privacy methods for big data processing*, plus a panel discussing current challenges and future research perspectives of privacy and security of big data.

Categories and Subject Descriptors

H.2 [DATABASE MANAGEMENT]: H.2.7 Database Administration – *Security, integrity, and protection*

General Terms

Algorithms, Design, Management, Performance, Theory

Keywords

Privacy of Big Data, Security of Big Data

1. INTRODUCTION

The *ACM 1st International Workshop on Privacy and Security of Big Data* (PSBD 2014) focuses the attention on research issues and practical applications/systems pertinent to the problem of *preserving the privacy and guaranteeing the security of big data,* an emerging challenge in actual database and data mining research (e.g., [6,7]). The addressed problem is relevant for a wide range of research context, ranging from *social networks* to *smart grids*, from *OLAP methodologies* (e.g., [8,9]) to *spatial data*, and so forth. One of the most challenging scenario, however, is the one represented by *analytics over big data* (e.g., [10,11,12,13]), where analytics procedures run on large-scale amounts of distributed big data,

CIKM '14, Nov 03-07 2014, Shanghai, China
ACM 978-1-4503-2598-1/14/11.
http://dx.doi.org/10.1145/2661829.2663544

hence leading to critical privacy and security breaches in *Cloud-enabled outsourced databases*.

In line with these emerging trends, PSBD 2014 includes 5 full papers, accepted out of 12 submissions, grouped into two sessions: (*i*) *scalable privacy-preserving and security-control methods for big data processing*, and (*ii*) *user-oriented and data-oriented privacy methods for big data processing*. The topics are diverse, including methods for evaluating the impact of data anonymization approaches over large-scale interaction network data sets, privacy-preserving Apriori pattern discovery in *MapReduce* frameworks, systems for supporting the secure and big-data-adaptive cross-domain communication, probabilistic techniques for predicting privacy risks in user-search logs, skyline query processing over encrypted data. The program also includes a panel discussing current challenges and future research perspectives of privacy and security of big data.

2. SCALABLE PRIVACY-PRESERVING AND SECURITY-CONTROL METHODS FOR BIG DATA PROCESSING

This session focuses on the latest research results in the context of scalable privacy-preserving and security-control methods for big data processing. Mário J. Silva, Pedro Rijo and Alexandre Francisco [1] focus the attention on *the publication of a large academic information dataset addressing privacy issues*. They evaluate anonymization techniques achieving the intended protection goal, while retaining the utility of the anonymized data. The released data could help infer behaviors and subsequently find solutions for daily planning activities, such as cafeteria attendance, cleaning schedules or student performance, or study interaction patterns among an academic population. However, the nature of the academic data is such that many implicit social interaction networks can be derived from the anonymized datasets, raising the need for researching how anonymity can be assessed in this setting. Kangsoo Jung, Sehwa Park and Seog Park [2] consider *Hadoop*, a popular open-source distributed system that can process large scale data, and Data Mining as one of the techniques used to find *patterns* and gain knowledge from data sets, as well as improve massive data processing utility when combined with the Hadoop framework. However, Data Mining constitutes a possible threat to privacy, as widely understood. Although numerous studies have been conducted to address this problem, such studies were insufficient and had several drawbacks such as *privacy-data utility trade-off*. In order to fulfill this gap, authors *focus on privacy preserving data mining algorithm techniques*, particularly the *association rule mining algorithm Apriori*, and propose a novel *privacy-preserving association rule mining algorithm in Hadoop* that prevents privacy violation without the loss of data utility. Through the experimental results, the proposed technique is validated to prevent the exposure of sensitive data without degradation of data utilization. Avinash Srinivasan, Jie Wu and Wen Zhu [3] explore the context of *Cross Domain Communication* (CDC), and recognize that today's infrastructure primarily consists of *vendor-specific guard products* that have little inter-domain coordination at runtime. Unaware of the context and semantics of the CDC message being processed, these guards heavily rely on rudimentary filtering techniques making the information domains vulnerable to an *array of attacks*. This often necessitates time-consuming human intervention to adjudicate messages in order to meet the desired security and privacy requirements of the communicating domains, causing performance bottlenecks. By overcoming actual state-of-the-art research, authors present a set of key requirements and design principles for *a service oriented CDC Security Infrastructure in form of a CDC Reference Architecture*, featuring so-called *Domain Associated Guards* (DOGs) as active workflow participants. The proposed framework, called SAFE, is secure and adaptable. SAFE also provides the foundation for the development of protocols and Ontologies enabling runtime coordination among CDC elements. This enables more flexible, interoperable, and efficient CDC designs to serve mission needs, specifically among critical infrastructure domains as well as domains with significantly differing *security and privacy vocabulary*. Because of the DOG approach, SAFE also overcomes the scalability problems faced by exiting solutions.

3. USER-ORIENTED AND DATA-ORIENTED PRIVACY METHODS FOR BIG DATA PROCESSING

This session focuses on the latest research results in the context of user-oriented and data-oriented privacy methods for big data processing. Joanna Biega, Ida Mele and Gerhard Weikum [4] propose a new model of *user-centric, global, probabilistic privacy*, geared for today's challenges of helping users to manage their *privacy-sensitive information across a wide variety of social networks*, online communities, QA forums, and search histories. The approach anticipates an adversary that harnesses global background knowledge and rich statistics in order to make educated guesses, that is, *probabilistic inferences*, at sensitive data. The final goal is represented by a tool that simulates such a powerful adversary, predicts privacy risks, and guides the user. The devised framework is then specialized for the case of Internet search histories. Also, authors present preliminary experiments that demonstrate how estimators of global correlations among sensitive and non-sensitive key-value items can be fed into a probabilistic graphical model in order to compute *meaningful measures of privacy risk*. Suvarna Bothe, Alfredo Cuzzocrea, Panagiotis Karras and Akrivi Vlachou [5] address the problem of making co-existent and convergent the need for *efficiency of relational query processing* over Clouds and the *security of data* themselves, which is figuring-out how one of the most challenging research problems in the big data era. Indeed, in actual analytics-oriented engines, such as *Google Analytics* and *Amazon S3*, where *key-value* storage-representation and efficient-management models are employed as to cope with the simultaneous processing of billions of transactions, *querying encrypted data* is becoming one of the most annoying problem, which has also attracted a great deal of attention from the research community. While this issue has been applied to a large

variety of data formats, e.g. relational, RDF and multidimensional data, very few initiatives have pointed-out *skyline query processing over encrypted data*, which is, indeed, relevant for database analytics. In order to fulfill this methodological and technological gap, authors present *eSkyline*, a prototype system and query interface that enables the processing of skyline queries over encrypted data, even *without* preserving the order on each attribute as order-preserving encryption would do. The proposed system comprises of an encryption scheme that facilitates the evaluation of domination relationships, hence allows for state-of-the-art skyline processing algorithms to be used. In order to prove the effectiveness and the reliability of our system, we also provide the details of the underlying encryption scheme, plus a suitable GUI that allows a user to interact with a server, and showcases the efficiency of computing skyline queries and decrypting the results.

4. CONCLUSIONS

PSBD 2014 presents relevant research results and open discussion on next-generation research directions focusing the context of privacy and security of big data, that we hope will serve as a valuable and up-to-date reference for actual and future research efforts.

5. REFERENCES

[1] Silva, M.J., Rijo, P., and Francisco, A. Evaluating the Impact of Anonymization on Large Interaction Network Datasets. *Proc. of PSBD*, 2014.

[2] Jung, K., Park, S., and Park, S. Hiding a Needle in a Haystack: Privacy Preserving Apriori Algorithm in MapReduce Framework. *Proc. of PSBD*, 2014.

[3] Srinivasan, A., Wu, J., and Zhu, W. SAFE- Secure and Big Data Adaptive Framework for Efficient Cross-Domain Communication. *Proc. of PSBD*, 2014.

[4] Biega, J., Mele, I., and Weikum G. Probabilistic Prediction of Privacy Risks in User Search Histories. *Proc. of PSBD*, 2014.

[5] Bothe, S., Cuzzocrea, A., Karras, P., and Vlachou, A. Skyline Query Processing over Encrypted Data: An Attribute-Order-Preserving-Free Approach. *Proc. of PSBD*, 2014.

[6] Wu, C., and Guo, Y. Enhanced User Data Privacy with Pay-By-Data Model. *Proc. of BigData Conference*, 2013.

[7] Jensen, M. Challenges of Privacy Protection in Big Data Analytics. *Proc. of BigData Congress*, 2013.

[8] Cuzzocrea, A., Russo, V., and Saccà, D. A Robust Sampling-Based Framework for Privacy Preserving OLAP. *Proc. of DaWaK*, 2008.

[9] Cuzzocrea, A., Saccà, A. Balancing Accuracy and Privacy of OLAP Aggregations on Data Cubes. *Proc. of DOLAP*, 2010.

[10] Cuzzocrea, A: Analytics over Big Data: Exploring the Convergence of Data Warehousing, OLAP and Data-Intensive Cloud Infrastructures. *Proc. of COMPSAC*, 2013.

[11] Cuzzocrea, A., Song, I.-Y., and Davis, K.C. Analytics over Large-Scale Multidimensional Data: The Big Data Revolution!. *Proc. of DOLAP*, 2011.

[12] Cuzzocrea, A.. Analytics over Big Data: Exploring the Convergence of Data Warehousing, OLAP and Data-Intensive Cloud Infrastructures. *Proc. of COMPSAC*, 2013.

[13] Cuzzocrea, A., Bellatreche, L., and Song, I.-Y. Data Warehousing and OLAP over Big Data: Current Challenges and Future Research Directions. *Proc. of DOLAP*, 2013.

Web-KR 2014: The 5th International Workshop on Web-scale Knowledge Representation, Retrieval and Reasoning

Yi Zeng
Institute of Automation
Chinese Academy of Sciences
Beijing, P.R. China
yi.zeng@ia.ac.cn

Spyros Kotoulas
Smarter Cities Technology Center
IBM Research Ireland
Dublin, Ireland
spyros.kotoulas@ie.ibm.com

Zhisheng Huang
Department of Computer Science
Vrije Universiteit Amsterdam
Amsterdam, the Netherlands
huang@cs.vu.nl

ABSTRACT

We organize and present the 5th version of the International Workshop on Web-scale Knowledge Representation, Retrieval and Reasoning (Web-KR 2014) as a continuous effort to discuss and provide possible theories and techniques to deal with the barriers for knowledge processing at Web scale. This workshop was held in conjunction with the 2014 ACM International Conference on Information and Knowledge Management (CIKM 2014) on November 3rd, 2014 in Shanghai, China. Compared to previous workshops under the same title, accepted papers of this workshop cover even wider topics in the field. The contributions focus on semantic knowledge extraction, representation, knowledge clustering, inconsistency checking, entity relatedness and linking, query suggestions, etc. Many new approaches are proposed to investigate these topics in the context of Web-scale resources. This summary introduces the major contributions of accepted papers in the Web-KR 2014 workshop.

Categories and Subject Descriptors

I.2.4 [**ARTIFICIAL INTELLIGENCE**]: Knowledge Representation Formalisms and Methods; I.2.11 [**ARTIFICIAL INTELLIGENCE**]: Distributed Artificial Intelligence; H.3.3 [**INFORMATION STORAGE AND RETRIEVAL**]: Information Search and Retrieval

General Terms

Algorithms, Experimentation.

Keywords

Knowledge Representation, Knowledge Retrieval, Semantic Search, Web reasoning, Scalability.

1. INTRODUCTION

As a field of study, knowledge representation, retrieval and reasoning plays a key role since the beginning of Artificial Intelligence [1]. It raises many new challenges and opportunities when the Web becomes the largest knowledge source. In order to discuss current and future challenges and provide possible

*CIKM'*14, November 3-7, 2014, Shanghai, China
ACM 978-1-4503-2598-1/14/11.
http://dx.doi.org/10.1145/2661829.2663545

theories, methods, and techniques for Web-scale knowledge processing, the workshop series titled "Web-scale Knowledge Representation, Retrieval, and Reasoning (Web-KR)" was initiated in 2010, and four annual workshops under this title have been held (2010 in Toronto, Canada, 2011 in Lyon, France, 2012 in Hawaii, the United States, and 2013 in Burlingame, USA).

Following the previous workshops, the fifth version of the Web-KR workshop (Web-KR 2014) was held in conjunction with the 2014 ACM International Conference on Information and Knowledge Management (CIKM 2014) on November 3rd, 2014 in Shanghai, China. The workshop consisted of oral presentation sessions for accepted papers and a plenary session focusing on recent advances of constructing Web knowledge bases and Web-scale reasoning.

Introductions and proceedings of all the Web-KR workshops can be found through the link in [2]. We also keep a list of important topics related to Web-KR on this Web site.

2. RESEARCH PAPERS

Compared to previous workshops under the same title, contributions of the Web-KR 2014 workshop cover wider range of topics related to Web-scale knowledge representation, retrieval and reasoning. A clear trend is that this year, many authors try to combine several techniques together for processing Web knowledge sources, such as Semantic Web, Natural Language Processing and Machine Learning. In addition, several application domains were investigated to validate proposed theories and techniques.

Semantic relatedness is well investigated in ontology and semantic Web, while most efforts require explicit relationships among word terms. In [3], the author investigates this problem through learning word vectors. This effort brings ideas from Natural Language Processing to semantic knowledge processing. It gives hints on how these two fields can be related.

Machine Learning techniques are widely applied to process Web resources to obtain knowledge from them. In [4], the authors investigate on ontology matching based on learning using partially labeled data, while [5] presents a structure learning algorithm for uncertain knowledge representation and inference.

Emerging and hot topics have also been investigated in the papers of this workshop. Although query suggestion is not new in this field, while the investigation in [6] present an initial report on proactively suggesting queries which leads to novel information. The effort in [7] introduces their practical approaches for exploring sensor data with semantic techniques support at the backend. Conversion from one format to another for knowledge integration and utilization keeps a practically hot topic, and the effort in [8] presents a convertor from JSON to OWL. Recognizing that managing Web-scale knowledge resources remains an important and hard topic, the effort in [9] tries to utilize Wikipedia clusters to cluster and label Web documents. The effectiveness of this effort will continue to grow as Wikipedia clusters get better. Inconsistency checking is extremely necessary when the knowledge structure is built from various knowledge resources. One important problem is to deal with loops in taxonomies. In [10], the authors propose to solve this problem by MAP inference and rules of Thumb.

Several efforts were made from the application perspective. The effort in [11] investigates knowledge extraction techniques for organizing knowledge triples on natural disaster events obtained from Twitter. The effort in [12] can be considered as an application of entity recommendation considering both the relatedness factor and the time factor. The work in [13] investigates automatic learning of the mapping rules for user sentiment understanding based on Tweets. Social search remains attractive in many Web related conferences and workshops, and [14] provides a framework for social search considering both the graph structure and the temporal information.

ACKNOWLEDGMENTS

We thank all the Program Committee Members for their continuous support on the Web-KR workshops over the five years. For the Web-KR 2014 workshop, the PC members are Christophe Guéret (The Royal Netherlands Academy of Arts and Sciences, the Netherlands), Haofen Wang (East China University of Science and Technology, China), Guangyou Zhou (Huazhong Normal University, China), Ioan Toma (University of Innsbruck, Austria), Gong Cheng (Nanjing University, China), Jun Fang (Norwestern Polytechnical University, China), Edy Portmann (University of Bern, Switzerland), Wei Hu (Nanjing University, China), Zhichun Wang (Beijing Normal University, China), and Dongsheng Wang (Chinese Academy of Sciences, China). We would also like to thank the ACM CIKM 2014 conference organizers for providing an excellent venue, with researchers and practitioners from various backgrounds, ranging from Information Retrieval, Databases, and Machine Learning to Knowledge Management, to discuss research topics and efforts related to knowledge representation, retrieval and reasoning at Web scale.

REFERENCES

[1] John McCarthy. WHAT IS ARTIFICIAL INTELLIGENCE? Revised Version. November 12, 2007. http://www-formal.stanford.edu/jmc/whatisai/whatisai.html

[2] Web-KR workshop series. http://www.linked-neuron-data.org/workshops/Web-KR

[3] Qun Luo, Weiran Xu, and Jun Guo. A Study on the CBOW Model's Overfitting and Stability. In Proceedings of the 2014 International Workshop on Web-Scale Knowledge Representation, Retrieval, and Reasoning, 2014.

[4] Saravadee Sae Tan, Enya Kong Tang, Tek Yong Lim, and Lay Ki Soon. Learning to Match Heterogeneous Structures using Partially Labeled Data. In Proceedings of the 2014 International Workshop on Web-Scale Knowledge Representation, Retrieval, and Reasoning, 2014.

[5] Chao He, Kun Yue, Hao Wu, and Weiyi Liu. Structure Learning of Bayesian Network with Latent Variables by Weight-Induced Refinement. In Proceedings of the 2014 International Workshop on Web-Scale Knowledge Representation, Retrieval, and Reasoning, 2014.

[6] Ilona Nawrot, Oskar Gross, Antoine Doucet, and Hannu Toivonen. Novel Query Suggestions. In Proceedings of the 2014 International Workshop on Web-Scale Knowledge Representation, Retrieval, and Reasoning, 2014.

[7] Snehasis Banerjee, Abhishek Mishra and Ranjan Dasgupta. Semantic Exploration of Sensor Data. In Proceedings of the 2014 International Workshop on Web-Scale Knowledge Representation, Retrieval, and Reasoning, 2014.

[8] Yuangang Yao, Runpu Wu and Hui Liu. JTOWL: A JSON to OWL Convertor. In Proceedings of the 2014 International Workshop on Web-Scale Knowledge Representation, Retrieval, and Reasoning, 2014.

[9] Richi Nayak, Rachel Mills, Chris De-Vries, and Shlomo Geva. Clustering and Labeling the web scale document collection using Wikipedia clusters. In Proceedings of the 2014 International Workshop on Web-Scale Knowledge Representation, Retrieval, and Reasoning, 2014.

[10] Elie Merhej, Steven Schockaert, Martine De Cock, Marjon Blondeel, Daniele Alfarone, and Jesse Davis. Repairing Inconsistent Taxonomies using MAP Inference and Rules of Thumb. In Proceedings of the 2014 International Workshop on Web-Scale Knowledge Representation, Retrieval, and Reasoning, 2014.

[11] Sandeep Panem, Manish Gupta, and Vasudeva Varma. Structured Information Extraction From Natural Disaster Events on Twitter. In Proceedings of the 2014 International Workshop on Web-Scale Knowledge Representation, Retrieval, and Reasoning, 2014.

[12] Zhuoren Jiang, Xiaozhong Liu, and Liangcai Gao. Dynamic topic/citation influence modeling for Chronological Citation Recommendation. In Proceedings of the 2014 International Workshop on Web-Scale Knowledge Representation, Retrieval, and Reasoning, 2014.

[13] Saravadee Sae Tan, Lay Ki Soon, Enya Kong Tang, Tek Yong Lim, and Chu Kiong Loo. Understanding the Meaning in Tweets: Learning the Mapping Rules for Sentiment Analysis. In Proceedings of the 2014 International Workshop on Web-Scale Knowledge Representation, Retrieval, and Reasoning, 2014.

[14] Kostas Stefanidis and Georgia Koloniari. Enabling Social Search in Time through Graphs. In Proceedings of the 2014 International Workshop on Web-Scale Knowledge Representation, Retrieval, and Reasoning, 2014.

Author Index

CIKM2015

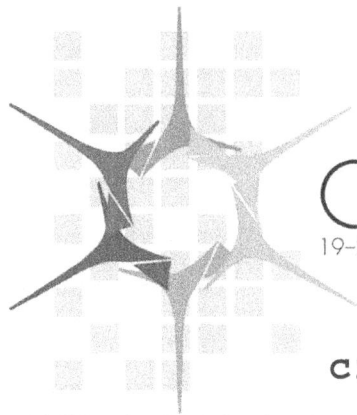

19–23 October 2015 Melbourne Australia

cikm-2015.org

Sponsored by

Association for Computing Machinery

SIGIR
Special Interest Group
on Information Retrieval

sig web

The 24ᵗʰ International Conference on Information and Knowledge Management

CIKM is a top-tier conference in the areas of Databases, Information Retrieval, and Knowledge Management. Sponsored by ACM, CIKM brings together leading researchers and practitioners from the three communities to identify challenging problems facing the development of advanced knowledge and information systems, and to shape future research directions through the publication of peer-reviewed, high-quality applied and theoretical research findings.

We encourage submission to CIKM 2015 of original papers on topics in the general areas of databases, information retrieval, and knowledge management. Refer to the conference website for a detailed list of areas of interest.

GENERAL CHAIRS
James Bailey (U. Melbourne)
Alistair Moffat (U. Melbourne)

PROGRAM CHAIRS
DB Track
Timos Sellis (RMIT U.)
Jeffrey Xu Yu (Chinese U. HK)
IR Track
Maarten de Rijke (U. Amsterdam)
Vanessa Murdock (Microsoft)
KM Track
Charu Aggarwal (IBM Watson)
Ravi Kumar (Google)

LOCAL ORGANIZATION
Anthony Wirth (U. Melbourne)
Rui Zhang (U. Melbourne)

Research and Industrial Papers

Abstracts due	May 1
Papers due	May 8
Acceptance notifications	July 3
Final versions due	July 31

Workshops and Tutorials

Proposals due	March 13
Proposal notifications	April 10
Workshop papers due	June 5
Paper notifications	July 17
Paper final versions due	July 31

All times PDT 23:59:59

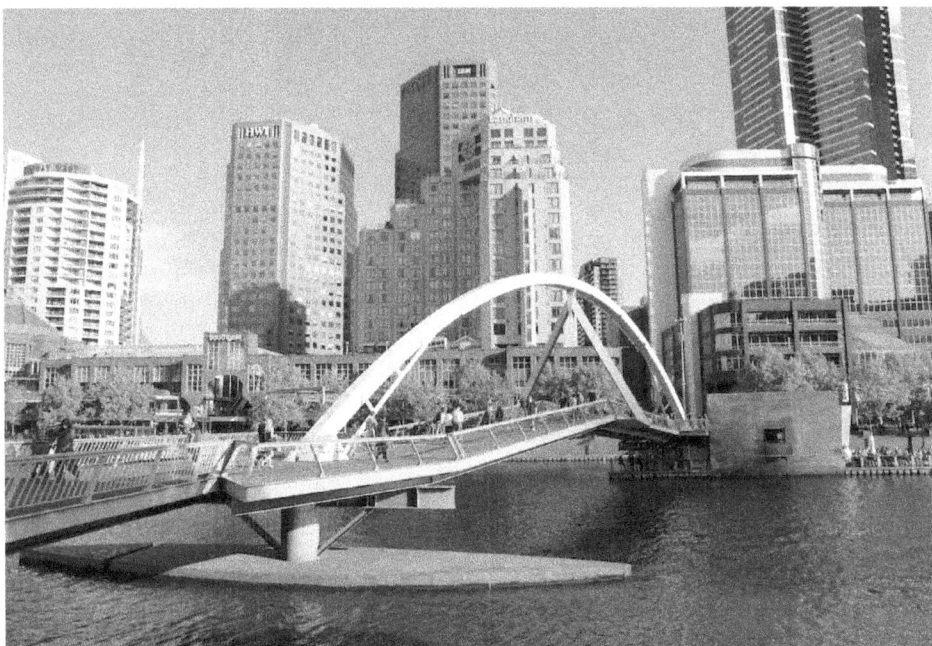

AUTHORS TAKE NOTE: The official publication date is the date the proceedings are made available in the ACM Digital Library. This date may be up to two weeks prior to the first day of your conference. The official publication date affects the deadline for any patent filings related to published work. (For those rare conferences whose proceedings are published in the ACM Digital Library after the conference is over, the official publication date remains the first day of the conference.)

www.ingramcontent.com/pod-product-compliance
Lightning Source LLC
Chambersburg PA
CBHW080710220326
41598CB00033B/5370